An Exposition of the Book of Proverbs

Charles Bridges

Alpha Editions

This edition published in 2020

ISBN: 9789354176463 (Hardback)

ISBN: 9789354179785 (Paperback)

Design and Setting By

Alpha Editions

www.alphaedis.com

email - alphaedis@gmail.com

PREFACE.

PROVERBIAL teaching is one of the most ancient forms of instruction. It was well adapted to the rudeness and simplicity of the first ages, when books were few, and philosophy little understood. The mind, unpractised to the slow process of reasoning, would be much more easily arrested by terse sentences, expressing a striking sentiment in the fewest words. The wise man himself has given the best definition of these sententious maxims. Their elegance he describes under the figure of "apples of gold in pictures (network) of silver."[1] Their force and permanent impression are "as goads and nails fastened by the Master of assemblies"[2]—driven closely home to the heart and conscience, and fastened in the memories by the appointed instructor of the people.

The antiquity of this teaching was recognized in the Church even before the age of Solomon.[3] Classic annals have recorded aphorisms similarly constructed from men of wisdom. All of these however were of a later date. Some possibly might be dim scintillations from this fountain light; so that he was, as an old expositor has remarked—'the disciple of none, but the instructor of them all.'[4] Indeed his mind largely dealt in this intellectual exercise. "He spake three thousand proverbs."[5] And from this valuable mass of thought he was directed under Divine inspiration, to "set in order" a collection for the instruction of the Church to the end of time.[6]

Possibly some would rather have desired the preservation of his discourses on Natural History[7] than on Practical Wisdom. But this Sovereign discrimination shows the real intent of the Scriptures—not to teach philosophy, but religion; not to make men of science, but men of sound godliness.

All competent judges will admit this Book to be eminently fitted for this great end. What the Roman Orator pronounced of Thucydides applies far more truly to this King of Jerusalem—'so full of matter, that he comprised as many sentences as words.'[8] This wonderful Book is in-

[1] Chap. xxv. 11.

[2] Eccles. xii. 11. LXX. write παροιμιαι (παρα οιμος—via—sayings spoken in the way. Comp. Dr. Johnson's definition) a word often used in New Testament for parables. John x. 6; xvi. 25, 29. Marg. Both were of the same popular character. A proverb is often given in the form of a parable.

[3] 1 Sam. xxiv. 13.

[4] Lavater. Comment. in Prov. Pref. Tigur. 1586.

[5] 1 Kings iv. 32.

[6] Ecclus. xii. 9. Grotius supposes the Book to be a compilation from preceding writers. This degradation of Solomon is a gratuitous conjecture, unsupported by a tittle of evidence. But such are the irreverent liberties, that proud learning dares to take with the Word of God!

[7] 1 Kings iv. 33.

[8] Cicero de Oratore, Lib. ii. 14. Elsewhere he gives nearly the same judgment of Euripides. Epist. Lib. xvi. 8.

deed a mine of Divine wisdom. The views of God are holy and reverential. The observation of human nature is minute and accurate. The rule of life and conduct is closely applied, to make "the man of God perfect, thoroughly furnished unto all good works;"[1] so that, as Mr. Scott well remarks—'we shall perceive the meaning and utility of the Proverbs, in proportion to our experience in true religion, our acquaintance with our own hearts, and with human nature, and the extent and accuracy of our observation on the character and affairs of men.'[2] Eusebius mentions the whole consent of the ancients, considering the Book of Proverbs to be 'Wisdom fraught with every kind of virtue.'[3] Bishop Hall draws out mainly from it a complete system of 'Divine Arts.'[4] And though the apostate Julian scornfully preferred to it the sayings of Heathen Philosophy;[5] yet the apostrophe of the son of Sirach was justly applied to its author—'How wise wast thou in thy youth, and as a flood filled with understanding! Thy soul covered the whole earth, and thou fillest it with dark parables.'[6]

As to its 'canonical authority'—Michaelis well observes 'that no Book of the Old Testament is so well ratified by the evidence of quotations.'[7] A few of the Jewish Talmudists appear to have expressed some doubt of its Divine stamp, but upon grounds so futile, that they were abandoned upon a more mature consideration.[8] Ecclesiastical History has recorded only one dissentient from the judgment of the universal Church; and that one condemned by her authoritative council.[9] Witsius has admirably refuted the neological cavils of his day.[10] Nothing has been said from any quarter to weaken the unhesitating decision of our judgment, that the pen is that of the King of Israel; but the words are the Wisdom of God.

Some difference exists among expositors as to the exact divisions of the Book. We have been led to divide it into three parts. In giving a more succinct account of these several parts, we shall avail ourselves largely, though necessarily in an abridged form, of the observation of a Biblical

[1] 2 Tim. iii. 16, 17. [2] Pref. to Comment. on Prov.

[3] Hist. Lib. iv. c. 25. πανάρετον σοφίαν. Jerome's direction to one of his friends for the education of his daughter is—'Let her have first of all the Book of Psalms for holiness of heart, and be instructed in the Proverbs of Solomon for her godly life.' Epist. vii. ad Lætam. Matthew Henry in his beautiful portrait of his mother describes her as one, 'that was very well versed in Solomon's Proverbs, and the rules of wisdom, which may be fetched from thence for the conduct of human life, and knew how to apply them, and to use knowledge aright.' Sermon on the Death of Mrs. Katharine Henry.

[4] 'Solomon's Divine Arts of Ethics, Politics, Economies—that is—the Government of Behavior, Commonwealth, Family—drawn into method out of his Proverbs and Ecclesiasties.' Works, viii. 427. Edited by Rev. P. Hall. Oxford, 1837.

[5] Apud Cyrill. Contra Julian, Lib. vii.

[6] Ecclus. xlvii. 14, 15. The whole passage (verses 12—22) is very beautiful. Eusebius remarks of Solomon, that while, inspired by Divine wisdom, he consecrated all his writings to the profit and salvation of souls; yet he used these 'dark parables' for the exercise of the mind. Contr. Marcell. Lib. i. c. iii. p. 17.

[7] Introd. to New Test. i. 207. Comp. especially in LXX. Chap. iii. 7, with Rom. xii. 16; 11, 12, with Heb. xii. 5, 6; 34, with James iv. 6. 1 Pet. v. 5; x. 12, with 1 Peter iv. 8; xi. 31, with 1 Pet. iv. 18; xxv. 6, 7, with Luke xiv. 8—10; 21, 22, with Rom. xii. 20; xxvi. 11, with 2 Pet. ii. 22; xxvii. 1, with James iv. 13, 14. It is a marked distinction drawn between this Book, and the Apocryphal Book of Wisdom so similar in character, that from the latter no quotation can be adduced in the New Testament.

[8] Hottenger. Thesaur. Philol. Lib. ii. c. 1. sect. 14. Comp. Carpzov. Introd. ad Lib. Canon. Part ii. c. iv. §. 7.

[9] Theodore Mopsuest condemned by 5th Council of Constantinople, A. D. 551.

[10] Miscell. Sacra. Lib. i. c. xviii. 30—34.

scholar, not more remarkable for his profound learning, than for his elegant taste.[1]

The First Part—all agree—extends from the opening of the Work to the close of the ninth chapter. It is—as Dr. Good observes—'chiefly confined to the conduct of early life. All the most formidable dangers to which this season is exposed, and "the sins which most easily beset it," are painted with the hand of a Master. And while the progress and issues of vice are exhibited under a variety of the most striking delineations and metaphors in their utmost deformity and horror; all the beauties of language, and all the force of eloquence are poured forth in the diversified form of earnest expostulation, insinuating tenderness, captivating argument and sublime allegory, to win the ingenuous youth to virtue and piety, and to fix him in a steady pursuit of his duties towards God and man. Virtue is pronounced in the very outset to be essential wisdom, and vice or wickedness essential folly. The only wise man therefore is declared to be the truly good and virtuous, or he that fears God, and reverences his law; while the man of vice and wickedness is a fool, a stubborn or perverse wretch, and an abomination to Jehovah.

'Wisdom is hence allegorized as a tree of life, yielding delicious shade, fruit and protection to those that approach her branches; throwing a garland of honor around their shoulders, and decorating their heads with a graceful chaplet, more precious than rubies. She is a sage and eloquent monitor, lifting up her warning voice at the gates and in the squares of the city; denouncing to the young the snares and dangers, to which they are exposed; and exhorting them to abandon "the way of the wicked, which is as darkness," for the path of the just, which is

——'As the brightening dawn,
Advancing and brightening to perfect day.'[2]

'*The Second Part* commences at the opening of the ninth chapter, as is obvious from the introductory clause. The style and manner of the second part are as different as possible from those of the first. It is evidently designed for the use of persons advanced from the state of youth to that of manhood. While in the preceding, addressed to the young, the richest ornaments of the fancy are made choice of to captivate their attention, and allure them to a right practice; in the present all is business and activity, brevity, continuity, and terseness. Every thought, though as highly polished, is at the same time as compressed as possible; and the Writer, thoroughly aware of the value of every moment of time at this important period, lays down a complete series of short rules of

[1] Extracts from an unpublished Translation of the Book of Proverbs, by the late Dr. Good, in his life by Dr. Gregory, pp. 286—306.

[2] We add two interesting testimonies, of a widely different character. 'The first part—including the first nine chapters—is a kind of exordium, and is varied, elegant, sublime, and truly poetical. The natural order is generally observed, and the parts are aptly connected together. It is embellished with very beautiful descriptions and prosopœas, and adorned with the most finished style, together with every kind of poetical ornament; so that it scarcely yields, in beauty, to any specimen of Sacred Poetry.' Bp. Lowth's Lectures on Heb. Poetry, xxiv. (Mr. Holden ventures to doubt whether this picture is not somewhat over-wrought. Pref. to Translation of Proverbs. xxxix.) 'The first nine chapters of the Book of Proverbs present us with a most interesting specimen of "acceptable words." There is in them an inimitable union of admonitory fidelity, and enticing and subduing kindness. Like Paul, he "exhorts, comforts, and charges, as a father doth his children." The whole soul of the writer is breathed out in the earnestness of benevolent desire.' Wardlaw on Ecclus. xii. 10.

life, and concentrates the most momentous precepts into the narrowest compass. The former appeals to the imagination; the latter to the judgment. The one exhibits all the genius of poetry; the latter all the art of composition; and hence the general matter is rendered as attractive in the one instance as in the other.

'The great object in each of the Proverbs of the present part is, to enforce a moral principle in words so few, that they may be easily learnt, and so curiously selected and arranged, that they may strike and fix the attention instantaneously; while, to prevent the mind from becoming fatigued by a long series of detached sentences, they are perpetually diversified by the changes of style and figure. Sometimes the style is rendered striking by its peculiar simplicity, or the familiarity of its illustration;[1] sometimes by the grandeur or loftiness or the simile employed on the occasion;[2] sometimes by an enigmatical obscurity,[3] which rouses the curiosity; very frequently by a strong and catching antithesis;[4] occasionally by a playful iteration of the same word;[5] and in numerous instances by the elegant pleonasms or the expansion of a single or common idea by a luxuriance of agreeable words.'[6]

The Third Part we conceive to comprise the last seven chapters. The first five were written by Solomon, and edited some centuries after by the royal scribes in the reign of Hezekiah. The two last were written by separate hands, but preserved by Divine care, and altogether worthy of the place they hold in the inspired Canon.

The time when this book was written is a matter of some uncertainty. We cannot doubt but its contents were a part of "the three thousand Proverbs,"[7] which "he spake" before his most lamentable fall. They were therefore the exercise of his vast and comprehensive mind, under the full influence of his Divine wisdom.[8] They might, however, as many judicious critics have thought, been "set in order"[9] in their present form at a period subsequent to that afflictive event. Both parts of this hypothesis read a most solemn practical lesson. Do we see "outlandish women causing him to sin"[10]—this "beloved of his God" falling himself into the snare which he so minutely described, and against which he so earnestly and repeatedly warned?[11] Christian Ministers! Does not Solomon no less than Paul[12] awfully teach us, that preaching to others will not save our own souls? The supposition of the posterior arrangement gives additional weight to his faithful admonitions. They come to us like the exhortations of the restored Apostle[13]—with all the force of painful experience—in the true spirit of his Master's command—"When thou art converted, strengthen thy brethren."[14]

The interpretation of this Book requires much care and sobriety. Believing the principles of the Old and New Testament to be essentially the same, it seems reasonable to expound the more obscure by the more clear. The primary duty is indeed to affix to each Proverb its own literal and precise meaning. This is undoubtedly its spiritual meaning—that is—the mind of the Spirit. In an extended application of this discovered

[1] Chap. x. 19; xvi. 3; xxii. ii.
[2] Chap. xii. 28; xv. 11; xxi. 16, 22.
[3] Chap. xvi. 24; xvii. 8; xviii. 20.
[4] Chap. xiv. 10; xvi. 16; xvii. 10; xviii. 4; xix. 12; xx. 14.
[5] Chap. xi. 15; xiii. 20; xvii. 13, 15.
[6] Chap. xvi. 32; xvii. 17, 27, 28; xix. 6
[7] 1 Kings iv. 32.
[8] Ibid. ver. 29.
[9] Eccl. xii. 9.
[10] Neh. xiii 26.
[11] Chap. v. vii. ix. xxii. 14; xxiii. 27, 28.
[12] 1 Cor. ix. 27.
[13] 1 Pet. i. 13, 17; iv. 7; v. 8, with Matt. xxvi. 35.
[14] Luke xxii. 32.

meaning, or in deducing inferences from it, judgment—not imagination—must be the interpreter. When no other than a literal meaning is plainly intended, the object must be—not to search out a new and mis-called spiritual meaning, but to draw practical instruction from its obvious sense.

There is however—we may remark—a line to be drawn between exposition and illustration. The figures used in this Book—*after their literal meaning has been wrought out*—may fairly be used as illustrative of other collateral truths, not specifically intended. The Sacred Writers appear to warrant this principle of accommodation,[1] though its use requires great delicacy and consideration; lest it should divest Scripture of its determinate meaning, and identify us with those artists, whom Dr. South memorializes—'who can draw any thing out of any thing.'[2]

But with all care to preserve a soundly-disciplined interpretation, we must not forget, that the Book of Proverbs is a part of the volume entitled—"The Word of Christ."[3] And so accurately does the title describe the Book, that the study of it brings the whole substance of the volume before us. It furnishes indeed the stimulating motive to search the Old Testament Scripture[4]—the true key that opens the Divine Treasure house; so that, as Mr. Cecil observes—'If we do not see the golden thread through all the Bible, marking out Christ, we read the Scripture without the Key.'[5] This remark however does not undervalue its large mass of historical and practical instruction. But unquestionably Christ is the Sun of the whole Scripture system; "and in his light we see the light,"[6] that reflects upon every point of practical obligation, and quickens life and energy throughout the whole Christian path. There is therefore, as Professor Franke reminds us—'much joy, comfort and delight to be found in the writings of the Old Testament (especially in reading those places, which before were wearisome and almost irksome) when we percieve Christ is so sweetly pictured there.'[7]

It has been recorded of Mary Jane Graham, 'that she was delighted in the course of her study of the Book of Proverbs to have Christ so much and so frequently before her mind'[8]—a recollection—her Biographer ventured to observe—of 'great moment for the spiritual discernment of the Divine Wisdom treasured up in this storehouse of practical instruction.'[9] Indeed—considering that these "Proverbs set in order—these words of the wise"—were originally "given from one Shepherd,"[10] whom we cannot surely fail to identify; we might naturally expect them to record a distinct testimony of himself.

We cannot but fear however, that this portion of the Sacred Volume is not generally estimated at its just value. Doubtless its pervading character is not either *explicit* statement of doctrinal truth, or lively exercises of Christian experience. Hence the superficial reader passes over to some (in his view) richer portion of the Scriptural field. Now we readily admit, that all parts of the Bible are not of equal importance. But to

[1] See the Apostle's application of Ps. xix. 4, at Rom. x. 18, and Doddridge's and Guyse's Paraphrase. Comp. Scott on Chap. xxv. 6, 7.
[2] Sermon on Matt. v. 44. [3] Col. iii. 16. [4] John v. 39.
[5] Mrs. Hawkes's Life, p. 171. So Augustine—'The Old Testament has no true relish, if Christ be not understood in it.' Ninth Tractat. on John.
[6] See. Ps. xxxvi. 9.
[7] 'Christ the sum and substance of Holy Scripture.' Sect. xxi.
[8] See Chap. i. viii. ix. &c. [9] Life, Chap. v. [10] Eccl. xii. 9—11.

value one part to the disparagement of another, is a slight to the Divine Testimony, that will be visited with a severe rebuke. Such a reader will only be possessed of mutilated fragments of truth, severed from their vital influence. He will never rise beyond a sickly sentimentalism. Seeking for novelty and excitement, rather than for the food of solid instruction; like Pharaoh's kine,[1] he devours much, but digests nothing. Never will he have light enough for the firm settlement of his faith. Neither can he receive the true moulding of the mind of the Spirit, or the impress of the Divine image.

But the question has been often asked—and that—not in a cavilling, but in an anxiously enquiring, spirit—'How can I read this Book profitably?' Not unfrequently the confession has been added—'My mind and soul do not get food from it. I think I am less interested in this, than in any other, part of Scripture. I acknowledge the wisdom of its sayings. I am fully persuaded, that—being the Word of God—it was not written in vain. The fault therefore must be in myself. Still the question returns—How am I to read it with profit?'

Now it might almost appear, as if the rules given at the opening of the Book[2] were intended to answer this question. Certain it is, that they do furnish the most satisfactory reply. The first and chief direction—that which gives life to every other—that which applies to every page and every verse of the Bible is—Begin with prayer—"Cry—lift up thy voice." Then combine a pondering mind with a praying heart. Actively apply thyself to "seek and search for the hid treasures." The riches lie not on the surface. Only those therefore, that dig into the bowels of the earth—not the readers, but "the *searchers—of the Scriptures*"[3]—are enriched. If the surface be barren, the mine beneath is inexhaustible. Indeed it is a wise discipline, that has made an active spirit of meditation necessary to give solid and fruitful interest to this study, and to possess ourselves of a blessing, which carelessness or indolence will never realize. The promise here held out to diligent investigation fixed that intelligent Christian just mentioned 'on one occasion in intense meditation for two hours. She appeared to be lost in astonishment and gratitude at the condescension and kindness of God in giving a promise, so free, so encouraging. She grasped it, as if determined not to let it go.'[4]

The habit of interested attention being fixed, how shall we best "apply the heart to the understanding" of the Book? Here the valuable exercise of Scripture reference will greatly expand our own thoughtful meditation. Gather contributions from all parts of the field. Many a doubtful or apparently uninteresting Proverb will thus be brightened in instructive application. We are persuaded, that an enlarged Scriptural study, with whatever collateral helps may be within our reach, will bring no regret in having rested awhile in this part of the field, instead of passing onwards to a more inviting surface. To advert once more to our Scriptural Student—'She frequently employed herself in the profitable exercise of "comparing spiritual things with spiritual"—Scripture with itself; thus making God his own interpreter. Much light and heavenly unction she conceived herself to have gained by this means.'[5] The fruit-

[1] Gen. xli. 20, 21. Comp. the picture drawn, 2 Tim. iii. 7.
[2] Chap. ii. 1—4. [3] John. v. 39. [4] Life of Mary Jane Graham, ut supra.
[5] Ibid.. Nichols's Exposition of this Book, and Scott's Marginal References, wil.

fulness of this exercise will be, when we "find God's words" as our treasure, "eat them" as our invigorating food, and "they" thus become "the joy and rejoicing of our hearts."[1] 'Set your affection'—saith the apocryphal writer—'upon my words. Desire them, and ye shall be instructed. Wisdom is glorious, and never fadeth away; yea, she is easily seen of those that love her, and found of such as seek her. She preventeth those that desire her, in making herself first known unto them. Whoso seeketh her early shall have no great travail; for he shall find her sitting at his doors. Whoso watcheth for her[2] shall quickly be without care. For she goeth about seeking such as are worthy of her, showeth herself favorably unto them in the ways, and meeteth them in every thought.'[3]

An accurate apprehension of the main end and scope of this Book will greatly facilitate the understanding of it. Different portions of Scripture may be seen to have different ends—all however subordinate to one end—primary and supreme. Without entering into detail foreign to our purpose, suffice it to remark, that the end of this Book appears to be—to set out a system of practical instruction, generally applicable. Nor let this be thought a low gradation in the Christian scheme. Unpalatable as it may be to the mere professor of godliness,[4] the true man of God will honor practical inculcation in its place, no less than doctrinal statement. "The truth as it is in Jesus"—that which flows from him, leads to him, and centres in him—that which "we are to be learned, and to be taught by him"—is practical truth.[5] While other parts of Scripture show us the glory of our high calling; this may instruct in all minuteness of detail how to "walk worthy of it." Elsewhere we learn our completeness in Christ;[6] and most justly we glory in our high exaltation, as "joint-heirs with Christ, made to sit together in heavenly places in Christ Jesus."[7] We look into this Book, and, as by the aid of the microscope, we see the minuteness of our Christian obligations; that there is not a temper, a look, a word, a movement, the most important action of the day, the smallest relative duty, in which we do not either deface or adorn the image of our Lord, and the profession of his name. Surely if the book conduced to no other end, it tends to humble even the most consistent servant of God, in the consciousness of countless failures. Not only therefore is the last chapter—as Matthew Henry would have it—'a looking-glass for ladies,' but the whole Book is a mirror for us all.

Nor is it only a mirror to show our defects. It is also a guide-book and directory for godly conduct. The details of the external life, in all

give much valuable assistance to this study. No foreign help however should damp the profitable interest of original research.

[1] See Jer. xv. 16. [2] 'Ο αγυπνήσας—whom wisdom scarcely affords to sleep.

[3] Wisd. vi. 11—16. The reader will find throughout this Exposition frequent reference to the Apocryphal Books of Wisdom—*but only as human authorities.* Mr. Horne has most demonstrably overthrown their claim to a place in the sacred canon. (Introd. to Script. Vol. i. Append. No. 1, last edit.) Never was it more important to mark the wide gulf between inspired and uninspired writings. Nevertheless there seems no necessity to lose much valuable and beautiful instruction, only because the writers were not inspired, or their writings were tainted with pernicious errors.

[4] We fear that Mr. Scott's hearers at the Lock as a sect have not died away. Their real objection—as his son admirably observed—'was not to Arminianism (of which they very probably scarcely knew the meaning) but to *half, or more than half, the word of God.* They had been accustomed to overlook it themselves, and could not bear to have it pressed upon their notice by another.' Scott's Life, pp. 232—235.

[5] See Eph iv. 20—24. [6] Col. ii. 10. [7] Rom. viii. 17. Eph. ii. 6.

the diversified spheres, are given or implied with perfect accuracy, and with a profound knowledge of the workings of the human heart. 'Beside a code of laws directly religious, a variety of admirable rules stream forth from the deep recesses of wisdom, and spread over the whole field.'[1] All ranks and classes have their word in season. The sovereign on the throne is instructed as from God.[2] The principles of national prosperity or decay are laid open.[3] The rich are warned of their besetting temptations.[4] The poor are cheered in their worldly humiliation.[5] Wise rules are given for self-government.[6] 'It bridles the injurious tongue,' corrects the wanton eye,[8] and ties the unjust hand in chains,'[9] It prevents sloth;[10] chastises all absurd desires;[11] teaches prudence;[12] raises man's courage;[13] and represents temperance and chastity after such a fashion, that we cannot but have them in veneration.'[14] To come to important matters so often mismanaged—the blessing or curse of the marriage ordinance is vividly portrayed.[15] Sound principles of family order and discipline are inculcated.[16] Domestic economy is displayed in its adorning consistency.[17] Nay—even the minute courtesies of daily life are regulated.[18] Self-denying consideration of others,[19] and liberal distribution[20] are enforced. All this diversified instruction is based upon the principles of true godliness.[21] Indeed the Writer may mention as one motive that led him to this work; that, having in a former Exposition[22] shown at large Christian experience to be built upon the doctrines of the gospel, he wished to exhibit Christian practice as resting upon the same foundation. That is not sound faith, that does not issue in practical godliness. Nor is there any true morality, apart from "the principles of Christ." This Book—if it be not—as the New Testament—the Rule of Faith—may surely be considered as a valuable Rule of conduct. And as Mr. Scott observes—'it would be very useful for those, who can command their time, at some stated season every day, to read and deliberately consider a few of these maxims, with reference to their own conduct, in the various affairs in which they are concerned.'[23] Doubtless if the world were governed by the whole wisdom of this single Book, it would be "a new earth, wherein dwelleth righteousness."

One other weighty consideration the Writer would advert to, as having directed his attention to this Book—*its distinctive character—as a Book for the Young.* The Wise man's father propounded a most anxious

[1] Lord Bacon's Advancement of Learning, Book viii. Chap. ii.
[2] Chap. viii. 15, 16; xvi. 10—13; xx. 8, 26; xxi. 1; xxv. 2—5; xxviii. 16; xxix. 14; xxxi. 1—9.
[3] Chap. xi. 14; xiv. 34; xxiv. 6; xxviii. 2.
[4] Chap. xviii. 11; xxiii. 4, 5; xxviii. 20, 22.
[5] Chap. xv. 16, 17; xvii. 1; xix. 1, 22; xxviii. 6.
[6] Chap. iv. 23—27; xvi. 32; xxiii. 1—3.
[7] Chap. iv. 24; x. 31; xvii. 20; xxv. 23; xxvi. 20—26.
[8] Chap. v. 20, 21; vi. 25—29; xxiii. 26, 27.
[9] Chap. xviii. 5; xxviii. 8.
[10] Chap. vi. 6—11; xii. 27; xiii. 4; xix. 24; xx. 4; xxiv. 30—34.
[11] Chap. xxi. 25, 26.
[12] Chap. vi. 1—5; xiv. 8, 15, 18; xxii. 3; xxv 6—10.
[13] Chap. iv. 14, 15; xxviii. 1.
[14] Chap. v. 15—19, with xxiii. 29—35. Basil quoted by Bp. Patrick.
[15] Chap. xviii. 22; xix. 14; xxxi. 10, with xii. 4; xix. 13; xxi. 9, 19.
[16] Chap. xiii. 24; xiv. 1; xix. 18; xxii. 6; xxiii. 14, 15; xxix. 15, 17, 19, 21.
[17] Chap. xxvii. 23—27; xxxi. 10—27.
[18] Chap. xxiii. 6—8; xxv. 17.
[19] Chap. iii. 27, 28.
[20] Chap. xi. 24; xxii. 9.
[21] Chap. xxxi. 10, 30.
[22] On Ps. cxix.
[23] Pref. to Comment. on Prov

question—"Wherewithal shall a young man cleanse his way?" His son in this Book has fully opened the answer—"By taking heed thereto according to thy word."[1] Nay he expressly states the Book to be written for the heeding of youth."[2] It takes them as it were by the hand, sets up way-marks to warn against coming danger and imminent temptations,[3] and allures them into the bright ways of God by the most engaging motives.[4] And never surely was the object so momentous, as at the present day. Our young are growing up at a period, when "the foundations of the earth are out of course;" and when subtle and restless efforts are making to poison their hearts, and pervert their ways. Nothing therefore can be more important, than to fortify them with sound principles; that, when withdrawn from the parental wing into a world or a Church (alas! that we should be constrained to use the term!) of temptation, they may be manifestly under a Divine cover—the children of a special Providence. What this invaluable Book impresses upon their minds is—the importance of deep-seated principles in the heart; the responsibility of conduct in every step of life; the danger of trifling deviations for expediency's sake; the value of self-discipline; the habit of bringing everything to the Word of God; the duty of weighing in just balances a worldly and a heavenly portion, and thus deciding the momentous choice of an everlasting good before the toys of earth.

[1] Ps. cxix. 9.
[2] Chap. i. 4; iv. 1, &c.
[3] Chap. i. 10—15· ii. 10—19; v. 1—13; vii.
[4] Chap. iii. 1—18; viii. 17, &c.

EXPOSITION

OF

THE BOOK OF PROVERBS.

CHAPTER I.

1. *The proverbs of Solomon, the Son of David, King of Israel;* 2. *To know wisdom and instruction; to perceive the words of understanding;* 3. *To receive the instruction of wisdom, justice, and judgment, and equity;* 4. *To give subtilty to the simple, to the young man knowledge and discretion.*

THE book naturally opens with a short account of its author. Solomon is recorded as the wisest of men—a man of wisdom, because a man of prayer.[1] His extraordinary wisdom was the admiration of the world.[2] Had he been the son of Jeroboam, he would have commanded respect. But he was *the son of David*—formed by his godly prayers[3] and counsels.[4] And if a King's sayings—even though without intrinsic merit—are preserved, much more should we listen with special interest to the wise teachings of this *King of Israel*.[5]

After all, however, valuable as were Solomon's maxims for their own wisdom (exceeding the sages of his own or any other time);[6] they claim our reverence upon infinitely higher ground. "Behold! a greater than Solomon is here."[7] Often does he speak in the person[8]—always under the inspiration[9]—of "the wisdom of God;" so that his sayings are in the highest sense "*Divine* sentences in the lips of the King."[10]

The great end of this inestimable book is to teach—not secular or political wisdom (though many excellent rules of each are interspersed)[11]—but that knowledge of God,[12] which, while it "maketh wise unto salvation, perfects and furnishes the man of God unto all good works."[13] This is set forth in all its glowing privileges.[14] It is pressed upon us with intense earnestness—as "the principal thing"—our very "life."[15] We are taught *instruction* as the means

[1] 1 Kings iii. 12. Comp. chap. ii. 1—6. [2] 1 Kings iii. 28; iv. 34. [3] Ps. lxxii. 1.
[4] Chap. iv. 1—4. 1 Kings ii. 1—4. 1 Chron. xxviii. 9. [5] Eccles. i. 1; xii. 9, 10.
[6] 1 Kings iv. 29—31. [7] Matt. xii. 42. [8] Verse 20; viii. ix.; xxiii. 26.
[9] 2 Tim. iii. 16. [10] Chap. xvi. 10.
[11] Chap. vi. 1—11; xxvii. 23—27, with xi. 14; xiv. 28, 34; xx. 18. [12] Verse 7.
[13] 2 Tim. iii. 15—17. Titus ii. 11, 12. [14] Chap. iii. 13—18. [15] Chap. iv. 5—9, 13.

of gaining it. We are directed *to perceive the words of understanding—to receive the instruction*, as a complete rule *of wisdom, justice, judgment, and equity*[1]—sound principles, and practical application. Here also *the simple*—so readily deluded[2]—learn that *subtilty*—so needful to dicriminate between truth and error;[3] to guard them from false teachers;[4] and to enable them to rebuke and convince gainsayers.[5] Specially is *the young man* directed to this book.[6] From want of discipline, his ardor runs to waste. Let him seek for that *knowledge and discretion*, here so richly treasured up for him. For the religion inculcated is not that of feeling, imagination, impulse, or sentiment: but it is the sound and healthful energy of godliness, flowing from the vital principles of Scriptural truth.

5. *A wise man will hear, and will increase learning; and a man of understanding shall attain unto wise counsels:* 6. *To understand a proverb, and the interpretation; the words of the wise, and their dark sayings.*

Not only *the simple and the young*—but even *the wise*—may here gather instruction. For a truly *wise man* is one—not who has attained—but who knows that he "has not attained," and is pressing onwards to perfection.[7] David, while conscious of comparative attainments, was ever seeking for higher light.[8] Indeed the richest stores would soon waste without constant additions. *Hearing* is a great medium of knowledge. Jethro instructed Moses[9]—our Lord his disciples.[10] Peter enlightened his fellow-Apostles.[11] Priscilla and Aquila "instructed Apollos in the way of God more perfectly."[12] And do not we feel ourselves to be learners, the longer we learn—more and more ready to *hear, that we may increase in learning?*[13] "Unto them that have, more shall be given."[14] And at such a crisis as this—a crisis both of the Church and of the world—how eagerly should we improve every medium of instruction, by which we might become "*men of understanding, and attain wise counsels*—to know what Israel ought to do!"[15] And just as the wise man himself expounded his *words and dark sayings* to the delight and instruction of his royal scholar;[16] so to a teachable *hearer* of the Divine Revelation many of its "deep things" will be *interpreted* in heavenly light. And hence the value of the minister of God—"an interpreter—one of a thousand"[17]—and of his office as the Divinely-appointed mean of coming

[1] Comp. chap. ii. 9. [2] Chap. xiv. 15; xxi. 11. Ezek. xlv. 20.
[3] Phil. i. 10; 1 Thess. v. 21. [4] Psalm xvii. 4. 1 John iv. 1. Comp. Acts xvii. 11.
[5] Titus i. 9; ii. 8. Comp. Matt. xxii. 15—46.
[6] Psalm cxix. 9. 'Over the gates of Plato's school, it was written—Μηδεις αγεωμετρητος εισιτω. (Literally- Let no one who is not a geometrician enter.) But very different is the inscription over these doors of Solomon—Let the ignorant, simple, foolish, young enter.'—Cartwright in loc.—Lavater in c. iv. 20—22.
[7] Phil. iii. 12. Comp. 1 Cor. iii. 18; viii. 2.
[8] Psalm cxix. 98—100, with 18, 33, 34. [9] Exod. xviii. 17—26
[10] Matt. xiii. 11—16. John xvi. 12. [11] Acts xi. 2—18. [12] Ibid. xviii. 24—26.
[13] Chap. ix. 9; xviii. 15. [14] Mark iv. 24. [15] 1 Chron. xii. 32.
[16] 1 Kings x. 1—5. [17] Job xxxiii. 23. Comp. Acts viii. 27—35.

to the perfection of knowledge.[1] How many disorders and heresies might have been spared to the Church, if—instead of indulging the perversity of an unsettled judgment—men had honored "the Priest as the messenger of the Lord of Hosts," and in humble simplicity had "sought the law at his mouth!"[2] Self-will may resist this suggestion as Romish domination. But a teachable subjection *to the faithful* "*steward of the mysteries of God*"—coming to learn, not to teach—to have, not the curiosity fed, but the conscience satisfied—this will issue in the "good thing of the heart established with grace"[3]—the rich fruit of reverencing the ordinance of God.

7. *The fear of the Lord is the beginning* (Marg.—principal part) *of knowledge: but fools despise wisdom and instruction.*

The preface has stated the object of this Book of Wisdom. The book itself now opens with a noble sentence of instruction. 'There is not'—as Bishop Patrick observes—'such a wise instruction to be found in all their books, (speaking of heathen ethics,) as the very first of all in Solomon's, which he lays as the ground of all wis dom.'[4] *The fear of the Lord is the beginning of knowledge.* So Job had pronounced before.[5] So had the wise man's father.[6] Such is the weight of this saying, that Solomon again repeats it.[7] Nay—after having gone around the whole circuit—after having weighed exactly all the sources of knowledge—his conclusion of the whole matter is this, that *the fear of God* in its practical exercise "is the whole of man"[8]—all his duty—all his happiness—his first lesson and his last. Thus when about to instruct us as from the mouth of God, he begins at *the beginning—the principal part.* All heathen wisdom is but folly. Of all knowledge—the knowledge of God is *the principal.* There is no true knowledge without godliness.[9]

But what is this *fear of the Lord?* It is that affectionate reverence, by which the child of God bends himself humbly and carefully to his Father's law. His wrath is so bitter, and his love so sweet; that hence springs an earnest desire to please him, and—because of the danger of coming short from his own weakness and temptations—a holy *fear*—anxious care and watchfulness "that he might not sin against him." This enters into every exercise of the mind every object of life.[10] The oldest proficient in the Divine school seeks a more complete moulding into its spirit. The godly parent trains up his familyunder its influence.[11] The Christian scholar honors it as *the beginning*—the head—

[1] Ephes. iv. 11—15. 1 Thess. iii. 10.
[2] Mal. ii. 7. Comp. Heb. xiii. 17, with 1 Cor. iv. 8; iii. 2—4.
[3] Heb. xiii. 9. [4] Preface to his Paraphrase [5] Job xxviii. 28. [6] Ps. cxi. 10.
[7] Chap. ix. 10. Compare the fine description by the son of Sirach. Ecclus. i. 14—20, 27.
[8] Eccles. xii. 13. Comp. Job xxviii. 12—14, with 28. [9] Comp. Deut. iv. 6, 7.
[10] Chap. xxiii. 17. [11] Gen. xviii. 19. Eph. vi. 4.

of all his knowledge; at once sanctifying its end, and preserving him from its most subtle temptations.

This is why the mass around us *despise wisdom and instruction.* Because *the beginning of wisdom*—"*the fear of God*—is not before their eyes."[1] They know not its value. They scorn its obligation. Wise they may be in their own sight. But surely God here gives them their right name. For *fools* they must be to *despise* such a blessing[2]—to rush into wilful ruin[3]—to treasure up work for despairing repentance.[4] 'From hardness of heart, and contempt of thy word and commandment, Good Lord deliver us.'[5] May thy reverential, affectionate, child-like *fear* be my *wisdom*—my security—my happiness!

8. *My son, hear the instructions of thy father, and forsake not the law of thy mother;* 9. *For they shall be an ornament of grace unto thy head, and chains about thy neck.*

Next to *the fear of the Lord*—and always connected with it—is reverence to parents. Let the young ponder this connection, and mark how the opening of this book puts honor upon "the first commandment with promise."[6] God here speaks in the character, and by the mouth, of a parent or teacher[7]—blending paternal tenderness with his Divine authority—*My son.* The command supposes the godly character of parents, and—unlike every other system—recognizes the responsiblity of *both* parents.[8] Their children are rational creatures. *Instruction*—not blind submission—must be inculcated. Yet they are wayward—*Instruction* must therefore be enforced with the authority of *law.* God himself puts his own stamp upon parental discipline. *Hear it—Forsake it not.* Reverence for *his mother's law* was the honorable mark of Timothy's profession.[9] Nor must this reverence be confined to the years of restraint. The disciple of the Bible will own himself to be a child in relative obligation, long after he has ceased to be a child in years.[10] Neither age nor rank give any just claim for exemption. Joseph—when ripe in years—the head of a family, and the first lord in Egypt—bowed before *his father's feet.*[11] Solomon, in the glory of his crown, forgot not the respect justly due to *his mother.*[12] And the crown *upon his*

[1] Psalm xxxvi. 1. [2] Jer. viii. 9.
[3] Verses 22, 24—32. Comp. 1 Sam. iv. 25. Jer. xxxvi. 22—32.
[4] Chap. v. 12, 13, xxix. 1. [5] Litany. [6] Ephes. vi. 2. Comp. 1 Tim. v. 4.
[7] Thus the prophets were called Fathers—2 Kings ii. 12; xiii. 14. Our blessed Lord used the same endearing address John xvi. 5. Compare Matt. ix. 2, 22. Thus the Apostles also acknowledged both their individual converts and collective Churches—1 Tim. i. 2. 2 Tim. i. 2. Titus i. 5. 1 Cor. iv. 15, with 1 John ii. 1; v. 21.
[8] See Judges xiii. 12. It is worthy of remark, that no ancient system but the Bible, recognizes the just and equal claims of the Mother. Compare chap. vi. 20; xv. 20; xx. 20; xxiii. 22; xxx. 17. Lev. xix. 3. Deut. xxi. 18—21. Also the description—Ecclus. iii. 1—16.
[9] 2 Tim. i. 5; iii. 14, 15. [10] Jer. xxxv. 8—10, 18. [11] Gen. xlvi. 29; xlviii. 12.
[12] 1 Kings ii. 19, 20. See also Queen Esther's respect for Mordecai, her reputed father—ii. 20.

head, and *the chain* of gold *about Joseph's neck*[1]—were not so *graceful*, as was this *ornament* of filial humility.[2] Wherever we see it, it is the "putting on of the Lord Jesus Christ" in his lovely example—"going down with his parents, and being subject to them"[3]—Yea, honoring his mother with his last dying command to his disciple—"Behold thy mother!"[4]

The same reciprocal obligation binds the spiritual father and his children. Authority softened by tenderness—*instruction* moulded in parental endearment—will always command its measure of reverential and affectionate attention. The Apostolical Ministry to the Churches of Philippi and Thessalonica, exhibits an exquisite pattern of this mutual love.[5] Humility, tenderness, mutual communion, cheerful subjection—this forms the harmony of Christian love and happiness.

10. *My son, if sinners entice thee, consent thou not.* 11. *If they say, Come with us, let us lay wait for blood, let us lurk privily for the innocent without cause;* 12. *Let us swallow them up alive as the grave; and whole, as those that go down into the pit;* 13. *We shall find all precious substance, we shall fill our houses with spoil:* 14. *Cast in thy lot among us; let us all have one purse:* 15. *My son, walk not thou in the way with them; refrain thy foot from their path.*

Here is *the instruction and law* of the godly parent and minister. Let the young *hearken* to it. Who that has the charge of youth does not mourn over the influence of evil companions—so eagerly, often so effectively, exerted? Would that the servants of the Lord were as energetic in His work, as sinners are in furthering the ends of their master! Almost as soon as Satan became an apostate, he became a tempter. And most successfully does he train his servants in this work![6] *If sinners entice thee*—This is no uncertain contingency. "My son"—said the wise son of Sirach—"if thou come to serve the Lord, prepare thy heart for temptation."[7] Yet against all multifold enticements,[8] the rule is one—*Consent thou not. Consent* constitutes the sin. Eve *consented*, before she plucked the fruit,[9]—David, before he committed the act of sin.[10] Joseph resisted, and was saved.[11] Job was sorely tried; "yet in all this, Job sinned not."[12] Remember—we need not yield. We cannot be forced to sin[13]—else we might throw the blame upon God. The habitual resistance of the will clears us of responsibility.[14] The consent of the will—even it be not carried out into action—lays the responsibility at our own door.

The *enticement* here was to deeds of robbery and blood—covetousness leading to murder. Most fiendish was the cruelty

1 Compare chap. iv. 9, with Gen. xli. 39, 42.
2 1 Peter v. 5.
3 Rom. xiii. 14, with Luke ii. 51.
4 John xix. 27.
5 Phil. iv. 9—19. 1 Thess. ii. 7—13.
6 Chap. xvi. 29. Gen. xi. 4. Isa. xli. 6; lvi. 12.
7 Ecclus. ii. 1.
8 Chap. vii. 5—23. Comp. Deut. xiii. 6—8. 1 Chron. xxi. 1. 1 Kings xiii. 15—19.
9 Gen. iii. 6.
10 2 Sam. xi. 2—4. Comp. Jos. vii. 21.
11 Gen. xxxix. 8, 9.
12 Job i. 22; ii. 10.
13 See James i. 14.
14 Comp Rom. vii. 14—17, 19, 20, 23.

of the plot. *The innocent* was to be murdered *without cause*[1]—*swallowed up alive and whole*—like Korah and his company; *going down into the pit* in their full strength.[2] The invitation was seemingly harmless—Only *come—come with us.* Soon the demand rises—*Cast in thy lot with us.* The *spoil* is sure. There is no one before to prevent, or afterwards to accuse.[3] *Precious substance will be found*, when our victim is destroyed.[4] *Precious substance!* say they—How can that be *substance* at all, which belongs only to a world of shadows?[5] Much more, how can the fruit of robbery be *precious* with the curse of God?[6]

Not that this horrible plot is usually propounded at first. But step by step—unless the Lord graciously restrains—it may come to this at last. Seldom indeed is the first temptation so broad. But the cover and varnish is here taken off, to show what sin is in its nature, character, and its certain end. What young man, but would shudder and start away from the wickedness, if presented to his imagination *alone?* But this is the history of many a deluded sinner, hurried on by the influence of company to lengths of sin that he had never contemplated.[7] Other *enticements* are prepared for the amiable and the uninitiated, just entering into life; less fearful and obvious, and therefore more really dangerous. For what "advantage does Satan get of us by our ignorance of his devices!"[8]

Is it safe then to trust in our good resolutions or principles? No—*Walk not in the way with them.* The invitation is—*Come with us.* The warning is—*Refrain thy foot from their path.*[9] Avoid parleying with them. No one becomes a profligate at once.[10] But "evil communications corrupt good manners."[11] The conscience—once tender—becomes less sensitive by every compliance. Who of us can stop ourselves in the down-hill road? One sin prepares for another—pleads for it—nay even makes it necessary for concealment. David committed murder to hide his adultery, and for its covering charged it upon the providence of God.[12]

Again then, we repeat with all earnestness—*Refrain. The path* may be strewed with flowers, but it is a path of *evil*—perhaps of *blood.*[13] Every step on Satan's ground, deprives us of the security of the promises of God. Often has ruin followed by not *refraining* from the first step.[14] The only safety is in flight.[15] Run then into "thy hiding-place, and behind thy shield," and

1 Gen. iv. 8. Ps. x. 8.
2 Num. xvi. 33.
3 But see Gen. iv. 10. 2 Kings ix. 26.
4 Comp. Matt. xxi. 38.
5 Psalm xxxix. 6.
6 Chap. xxi. 6. Ps. lxii. 9, 10.
7 Chartist Associations afford ample evidence of this awful delusion.
8 2 Cor. ii. 11.
9 Chap. iv. 14, 15. Compare Psalm i. 1.
10 'Nemo fuit repente turpissimus.'—Classical adage.
11 1 Cor. xv. 33.
12 2 Sam. xi. 4, 17, 25.
13 Verse 16. Isa. lix. 7. A very apt illustration of the total depravity of man in the perverted use of the members of his body.—Rom. iii. 15.
14 Comp. Mark xiv. 54, 71.
15 Gen. xxxix. 10, 12

boldly bid thy tempter "depart from thee."[1] Awful is the thought —that there is not a sin, that the highest saint of God may not commit, if trusting in himself. "Thou standest by faith. Be not high-minded, but fear."[2]

17. (*Surely in vain the net is spread in the sight of any bird*). 18. *And they lay wait for their own blood; they lurk privily for their own lives.* 19. *So are the ways of every one that is greedy of gain; which taketh away the life of the owners thereof.*

A striking picture of the infatuation of sin! Birds by their native instinct avoid *the net spread in their sight.* Man in his boasted wisdom rushes into it. These men thirsted for their neighbor's *blood.* But in the end *they laid wait for their own.* They *lurked privily for the innocent without cause.* But it proved to be *lurking privily for their own lives.*[3] Ahab and his guilty partner, in plotting the destruction of their *innocent* victim, worked out their own ruin.[4]—Little did Haman, when bent upon the murder of Mordecai;[5] or Judas when "seeking opportunity to betray his Master,"[6] see that they were digging a pit for themselves.[7] Yet the sinner, would he but use his own eyes, might see hell at the end of his path.[8] But sin is self-delusive—self-destructive. So are the ways—such the end—of *greedy,* often murderous *gain.*[9] *My son*—once more *hear thy Father's instruction*—"Flee these things."[10]

20. *Wisdom* (Marg. Wisdoms,) *crieth without; she uttereth her voice in the streets:* 21. *She crieth in the chief place of concourse, in the openings of the gates; in the city she uttereth her words, saying,* 22. *How long, ye simple ones, will ye love simplicity? and the scorners delight in their scorning, and fools hate knowledge?* 23. *Turn you at my reproof: behold, I will pour out my Spirit upon you, I will make known my words unto you.*

A Father's instruction has warned us against enticement. *Wisdom's* voice now invites us to her school. And if there be danger in listening to the counsel of Satan; not less is there in slighting the invitations of God. For it is God the Saviour here before us—the Personal Wisdom of God, in all the plentitude of his Divine power, authority, and grace.[11] And a glowing pic-

[1] Ps. cxix. 114, 115. Comp. Matt. iv. 10. [2] Rom. xi. 20.
[3] Verse 11 with 18. Comp. Job xviii. 8. Hab. ii. 10. [4] 1 Kings xxi. 4—24
[5] Esth. vii. 9. [6] Matt. xxvi. 14—16; xxvii. 3—5. [7] Ps. vii. 15, 16; ix, 15, 16
[8] Matt vii. 13.
[9] Comp. Job xxxi. 39, 40. Jer. xxii. 17—19. Mic. iii. 10—12. 'How great a cheat is wickedness! It ensnareth the ensnarers, and murders the murderers; holds a dark lantern in one hand, while with the other it discharges silently a pistol into our bosoms.'—Jermin. (Dr. M.) Comment on Prov. Folio 1638.
[10] Verse 8, with 1 Tim. vi. 9—11.
[11] *The cry—the chief place of concourse—the outpouring fountain of the Spirit* is identified—John vii. 37—39. This very remonstrance—accompanied, as here, with awakening and encouraging invitation—is also given in prophecy from the Saviour's own mouth. Isa. lv. 1—3. It seems impossible to give to the terms of the promise any other than a personal application. We can easily conceive a spirit to have wisdom. But that an attribute of wisdom may dispense his Spirit, or communicate his influence to others, is beyond conception. Moreover the Messiah when on earth assumed this personal title,

ture it is. Witness this great "Apostle"[1]—this heavenly preacher —full of yearning love to sinners—not only in the synagogue and in the temple—but *crying without in the streets—in the chief place of concourse—in the opening of the gates.*[2] *The simple and the scorner*—each *loving* his own way—the *fools*—ignorant only because they *hate knowledge*[3]—these are the objects of his compassionate remonstrance—*How long?*[4] A stimulating example for his servants to be "instant in season, out of season," with their Master's energy and earnestness in "plucking the brands out of the fire!" And who shall censure this standard of Divine devotedness?

But let us see how the sinner's case is dealt with—how all the suggestions of unbelief—all the heartless excuses of indolence—are swept away before him. God calls him to *turn at his reproof.* He cannot turn himself. But, *I will pour out my Spirit* as a living fountain *upon you.* He cannot see his way. But, *I will make known my words unto you.* 'I offer thee both my word outwardly to your ears, and a plentiful measure of my Spirit inwardly to your heart, to make that word effectual to you.'[5] Do you plead that God reckons with you for an inability, which you cannot help—innate without your consent? This is Satan's argument of delusion. He at once answers the charge, by offering to you present, suitable, and sufficient relief. He meets you on your way to condemnation with the promise of free and full forgiveness.[6] Your plea will be of force, when you have gone to him, and found him wanting, The power indeed is of Him. But he hath said—"Ask, and it shall be given you."[7] If then your helplessness is a real grievance, bring it to him with an honest desire to be rid of it. If you have never prayed, now is the time for prayer. If you cannot pray—at least make the effort. Stretch out the withered hand in the obedience of faith.[8] If your heart be hard—your convictions faint—your resolutions unsteady—all is provided in the promise —*I will pour out my Spirit upon you.* Move, then, and act in dependence upon the Almighty Mover and Agent.[9] Christian experience explains a mystery unfathomable to human reason. It

(Matt. xxiii. 34, with Luke xi. 49;) and his Apostle expressly gives it to him. (1 Cor. i. 24.) The plural noun joined with a singular verb, (Marg. Comp. chap. ix. 1.) seems to point him out as the author and whole substance of all wisdom,—'the very wisdom of the most wise God, "in whom are hid all the treasures of wisdom and knowledge," and by whom rivers of wisdom are poured into man by the word.' (Glass. Lib. iii. Tract i. Can. 24.) The future tense in the original may possibly give a prophetic character to the proclamation. Altogether, this interpretation, as Mr. Scott observes, 'gives to the exhortation of wisdom a peculiar majesty and emphasis,' setting forth 'the eternal uncreated wisdom of the Father, using all means to draw men to God; both by his works and by his word, inviting all men to know and love the truth.'—Bishop Hall. Compare notes on v. 24. viii. 1.

[1] Heb. iii. 1.
[2] Comp. c. viii. 1—5. Matt. xiii. 2. John vii 37—39; xviii. 20, 21. Psalm xl. 9, 10
[3] Verses 7, 29, 30. Job xxi. 14; xxiv. 13. John iii. 19, 20.
[4] Comp. Matt. xxiii. 37. Luke xix. 41. 42.
[5] Bishop Hall.
[6] Isa. i. 18; xliii. 23—26.
[7] Matt. vii. 7.
[8] Mark iii. 5
[9] Comp. Phil. ii. 12, 13.

harmonizes man's energy and God's grace. There is no straiten ing—no exclusion—with God. His promises with one mouth as sure a welcome to the willing heart. If it cannot move, cannot his Spirit compel—point—draw it to the Saviour? Yea, in the desire to turn, hath not the Saviour already touched it, and drawn it to himself?

24. *Because I have called, and ye refused; I have stretched out my hand, and no man regarded;* 25. *But ye have set at naught all my counsel, and would none of my reproof:* 26. *I also will laugh at your calamity; I will mock when your fear cometh;* 27. *When your fear cometh as desolation, and your destruction cometh as a whirlwind; when distress and anguish cometh upon you.* 28. *Then shall they call upon me, but I will not answer; they shall seek me early, but they shall not find me:* 29. *For that they hated knowledge, and did not choose the fear of the Lord:* 30. *They would none of my counsel; they despised all my reproof.* 31. *Therefore shall they eat of the fruit of their own way, and be filled with their own devices.*

The Saviour calls by his word—his providence—his ministers—conscience. But, *I called, and ye refused.* Not till his *calls* have been *refused*, does he thunder his warnings. But such grace, so rich and free, yet rejected—who can take the gauge of this guilt? All creatures beside are his servants.[1] Man alone resists his yoke. *He stretched out his hand*[2] to afford help: to confer a blessing: earnestly to beseech its acceptance—yea, even to command attention to his call.[3] *But no man regarded.* He gives the wisest *counsel*, and when this is unavailing—the most wholesome *reproof;* but all is *set at naught.* Thus does he "endure with much long-suffering the vessels of wrath fitted to destruction."[4] But, oh sinner! the day cometh, when he, who once yearned, and wept, and prayed, and died, will have no pity;[5] when he shall be as if he *laughed and mocked at your calamity;*[6] when he shall disdain your cry; when he shall delight in the exercise of his sovereign justice over you.[7] All will then be the *desolation* of realized *fear*[8]—sudden *as a whirlwind*[9]—the *distress and anguish* of utter despair.[10]

This is his solemn denunciation. But—as if he could bear these despisers no longer in his sight—he changes his address, and pictures the scene itself in its strongest colors. *They* would not hear when I called. *Then they shall call upon me, and I will not answer.* They would not listen to my warnings—I will not listen to their cries. *They shall call upon me*—yea, *they shall seek me early, but they shall not find me.*[11] Prayer, once omnipotent, will

[1] Psalm cxix. 91. [2] Isa. lxv. 2.
[3] See Acts xxi. 40. [4] Rom. ix. 22. [5] Ezek. v. 11; viii. 18, with xxxiii. 11.
[6] Comp. Judg. x. 14. Isa. i. 24. [7] Comp. Deut. xxviii. 63. Ezek. v. 13.
[8] Chap. x. 24.
[9] Chap. x. 25. Psalm lviii. 9. Isa. xvii. 13; xl. 24. Eastern travellers furnish abundant illustration of this striking figure. Paxton's Illustrations of Scripture Geography, pp. 412—416.—(Oliphant.)
[10] Job xv. 24. Dan. v. 5, 6, 30.
[11] Matt. xxv. 6—12. Luke xiii. 24—28. Dr. Owen admirably remarks upon this remonstrance as a proof of the Personality of Wisdom—"If these things express not a

then be powerless. 'The last judgment before the very last of all is come—the very outward court or portal of hell'[1]—the misery of deserted souls. To be forsaken of God at any time is awful woe;[2] how much more in the time of trouble?[3] But to have his countenance—not only turned from us, but turned against us—his frown instead of his smile—this will be hell instead of heaven.

Does this unmeasured wrath seem inconsistent with a God of love? But, is he not a just God—"a consuming fire?" And think of his *knowledge*—instead of being a delight—being *hated; his fear not chosen*—his gracious *counsel—none of it* regarded; all his *reproof despised.* Add to which—is it not just, that the sinner, obstinately bent upon the choice of *his own way;* should not only gather, but *eat the fruit of it?*[4] that it should enter into him, and become his substance; that he should be *filled with it,* even to satiety;[5] *and that*—not only during his road,[6] but at the end—throughout eternity.[7] The moral elements of sin constitute a hell of themselves, apart from the material fire. 'The fruit of sin in time, when arrived at full and finished maturity, is just the fruit of sin through eternity. It is merely the sinner reaping what he has sown. It makes no violent or desultary step, from sin in time to hell in eternity. The one emerges from the other, as does the fruit from the flower. It is simply, that the sinner *be filled with his own ways, and that he eat the fruit of his own devices.*"[8]

This picture might seem to be the foreboding of despair. Yet, such miracles of Divine grace have we seen—nay, such are we ourselves—that we despair of none. But we must not soften down God's own words by a misplaced presumptuous tenderness. Have we never seen them verified in the dying chamber of the hardened sinner, who has neglected and scoffed at the Gospel, and never sent up one cry for mercy on his soul? And is there no warning here of the danger of *a protracted* repentance; of the worthlessness of confessions extorted by terror—"howling on the bed—not weeping at the cross?"[9] And does it not solemnly tell us, that the day of grace has its limits;[10] that there is a knock, which will be the last knock; that a sinner may be lost on this side of hell; intreated—pleaded with—wept over—yet lost! lost even in the day of salvation! To "do despite to the Spirit *of grace*" (mark the endearing name)—the Spirit of all kindness—of alluring love—who speaks

person, and *that* a Divine person, the Scripture gives us no due apprehension of any thing whatever. Who is it that pours out the Holy Spirit? Who is it, that men sin against, in refusing to be obedient? Who is it, that in their distress they call upon, and seek early in their trouble? The whole Scriptures declare to whom, and to whom alone, these things belong, and may be ascribed.'—Prelim. Exercit. to Expos. Heb. xxvii. § 12.

[1] Bishop Reynolds's Works, p. 971. [2] Hos. ix. 12. [3] 1 Sam. xxviii. 15.

[4] Chap. xii. 12.

[5] Chap. xiv. 14. Comp. xxv. 16.—'Ad nauseam implebuntur, et comedent, ita ut consiliorum vehementer tandem, sed nimis serò, ipsos peniteant.'—Michaelis.

[6] Num. xi. 4, 20. Psalm cvi. 13—15. [7] Isa. iii. 11. Gal. vi. 7.

[8] Chalmers on Rom. vi. 21. [9] Hos. vii. 14, with Luke xviii. 13

[10] Gen. vi. 3. Heb. iv. 7.

so sweetly, and strives so tenderly with us—to wound him as it were to the soul—this is a provocation beyond words—beyond thought. What "remaineth," but that which might strike into the very centre of the man—"the fearful looking-for of judgment and fiery indignation, which shall devour the adversaries! It is a fearful thing to fall into the hands of the living God."[1]

32. *For the turning away of the simple shall slay them, and the prosperity of fools shall destroy them.* 33. *But whoso hearkeneth unto me shall dwell safely, and shall be quiet from fear of evil.*

Once again is the sinner's ruin laid at his own door. He *turns away* from Wisdom's voice—the voice of the pleading Saviour. He despises the only remedy. He dies a suicide. It matters nothing to what we turn. If we *turn away* from God, we turn from truth—from our true—our eternal—interests. And, oh! be it remembered, that every inattention—every wilful neglect—is a step towards this fearful apostasy. The word gradually becomes a burden, then a scorn. It may seem to be a prosperous way. But it is *the prosperity of fools*—the love of ease—indifference—ripening for destruction.[2] The lust of it is the embrace of our deadly enemy. Who that knows his own heart will not feel it a matter—not of congratulation—but of deep and anxious prayer? "In all time of our wealth—Good Lord, deliver us!"[3]

But to close with the sunshine of promise—Art thou, Reader—like God's own child—*hearkening unto him?* Then art thou under his cover. Thou hast already found thy place of safety, where no evil can reach thee—*dwelling* not only *safely*, but assured of safety—*quiet even from fear of evil;*[4] as Noah in the ark—in conscious security, while the world were perishing around him;[5] as David, fearless in imminent danger, because realizing a refuge in his God.[6] Yes!—even the *coming day of distress and anguish* brings with it no *fear of evil.*[7] "The day will burn like an oven." Thou shalt behold the world on fire and feel thou hast lost—thou canst lose—nothing. The "day of darkness and gloominess" will be to thee a day of unclouded sunshine—the entrance into everlasting joy?[8]

[1] Heb. x. 26—31.
[2] Job xxi. 11—13. Psalm lv. 19; lxxiii. 3—20. Jer. xii. 1—3. Luke vi. 24, 25; xii. 16—20; xvi. 19—24. James v. 1—5. Examples of Israel. Deut. xxxii. 15—25. Jer. xxii. 20—22. Hos. xiii. 6—9. Amos vi. 1—6. Babylon. Isa. xlvii. 7—9. Moab. Jer. xlviii. 11—15. Sodom. Ezek. xvi. 49. Tyre. Ib. xxvii. 2, 16, 17.
[3] Litany.
[4] Chap. iii. 21—26. Job v. 21. Psalm xci. 5; cxii. 6, 7. Isa. xxxii. 17—19.
[5] Gen. vii. 11—16. [6] Psalm iii. Compare 1 Sam. xxx. 6.
[7] Contrasting verses 26, 27. Luke xxi. 26. Rev. vi. 16—18.
[8] Mal. iv. 1, 2. Luke xxi. 28. 2 Peter iii. 10—13.

CHAPTER II.

1. *My son, if thou wilt receive my words, and hide my commandments with thee,* 2. *So that thou incline thine ear unto wisdom, and apply thine heart to understanding;* 3. *Yea, if thou criest after knowledge, and liftest up thy voice for understanding;* 4. *If thou seekest her as silver, and searchest for her as for hid treasures;* 5. *Then shalt thou understand the fear of the Lord, and find the knowledge of God.* 6. *For the Lord giveth wisdom: out of his mouth cometh knowledge and understanding.*

Wisdom having solemnly warned rebellious scorners, now instructs her dutiful children. If, as is supposed, these are the words of Solomon to his son, they are also the words of God to us. The dark question long before asked—"Where shall wisdom be found?"[1]—is now answered. Rules are given for its discovery. It is set before us—as *the fear and knowledge of God;*[2] a principle of practical godliness;[3] a preservation from besetting temptations:[4] and a guide into the right and safe path.[5] Hence follow the security of its scholars,[6] and the certain ruin of its ungodly despisers.[7]

The rules for its attainment are such as the simplest comprehension can apply. Most valuable are they to us. If carefully pondered and diligently improved, they will furnish a key for the understanding of the whole word of God. Let us examine them more distinctly.

Receive my words—Let them be "the seed cast into the good ground of an honest and good heart"[8]—a heart prepared of God.[9] Read the book of God—as one who "sat at the feet of Jesus, and heard his word."[10] Like the Bereans—"receive it with all readiness"[11]—like the Thessalonians—with reverential faith—acknowledging its supreme authority.[12] *Hide my commandments with thee.* Carry them about with thee as thy choicest treasure, for greater security;[13] as thy furniture always at hand for present use.[14] Let the heart be the hiding-place.[15] Here let the treasure be covered. Satan can never snatch it thence.

But there must be an active, practical, habit of attention.[16] *Ear and heart* must unite. Yet to *incline the ear and apply the*

[1] Job xxviii. 12, 20, 21. [2] Verse 5. [3] Verses 7—9. [4] Verses 10—19. [5] Verse 20. [6] Verse 21. [7] Verse 22. [8] Luke viii. 15. [9] Chap. xvi. 1. [10] Luke x. 39. [11] Acts xvii. 11. [12] 1 Thess. ii. 13. [13] Col. iii. 16. [14] Chap. iv. 20, 21; vii. 3. Job xxii. 22. Psalm cxix. 11. [15] Luke ii. 19, 51.

[16] Chap. xxii. 17; xxiii. 12. The Emperor Constantine stood whole hours to hear the word; and when he was requested to sit, he replied, 'that he thought it wicked to give negligent ears, when the truth handled was spoken of God.' (Euseb. de vita Constant. Lib. iv.) Foxe records of Edward VI. 'that never was he present at any sermon commonly, but would excerp them, or note them with his own hand.' Vol. v. 700, New Edition. Yet Bishop Hooper seems to have thought that his Royal Master's love for the preached word needed to be quickened. Sermon 7th on Jonas.

heart—"who is sufficient for these things?" Oh! my God! let it be thine own work on me—in me. Thou alone canst do it.[1] Let it be with me as with thy Beloved Son—"Waken my ear morning by morning to hear as the learned."[2] So let me under thy grace, "incline mine ear, and hear, that my soul may live."[3]

Without this spirit of prayer—there may be attention, earnestness, sincerity; yet without one spiritual impression upon the conscience—without one ray of Divine light in the soul. Earthly wisdom is gained by study; heavenly wisdom by prayer. Study may form a Biblical scholar; prayer puts the heart under a heavenly pupilage, and therefore forms the wise and spiritual Christian. The word first comes into the ears; then it enters into the heart; there it is safely hid; thence rises *the cry—the lifting up of the voice* in awakened prayer. Thus "the entrance of the word giveth life; it giveth understanding to the simple."[4] God keeps the key of the treasure-house in his own hand. "For this he will be enquired of"[5] to open it unto thee. No other inspiration can be looked for than Divine grace to make his word clear and impressive. Every verse read and meditated on furnishes material for prayer. Every text prayed over opens a mine of "unsearchable riches," with a light from above more clear and full than the most intelligent exposition. David[6] and his wise son[7] sought this learning upon their knees; and the most matured Christian will to the end continue to *lift up his voice* for a more enlarged *knowledge of God*.[8]

But prayer must not stand in the stead of diligence. Let it rather give life and energy to it.[9] Look at the miner—his indefatigable pains—his invincible resolution—his untiring perseverance —*seeking—yea—searching for hid treasures.* Such must be our standard in *searching* into the sacred store-house; leaving nothing untouched that lies before us.[10] To read—instead of "*searching* the Scriptures"—is only to skim the surface, and gather up a few superficial notions.[11] The rule of success is—Dig up and

[1] Chap. xx. 12. 'Thou giving me the ear, I have heard, as thou wouldest thy word to be heard.'—Jerome on Hab. iii. 2.

[2] Isa. l. 4. [3] Ibid. lv. 3. [4] Psalm. cxix. 130. [5] Ezek. xxxvi. 37.

[6] Psalm cxix. 18, &c. [7] 1 Kings iii. 9—12. [8] Eph. i. 17, 18.

[9] On one side is Luther's inestimable axiom—'Bene orasse est bene studuisse.' On the other side is the balance of the old proverb, 'Ora et labora.' Compare Matt. xi. 12. 'We are all,' says the heavenly Leighton, 'too little in the humble seeking and begging this Divine knowledge; and that is the cause, why we are so shallow and small proficients. "If thou cry and lift up thy voice for understanding, search for it as for hid treasures;" sit down upon thy knees, and dig for it. That is the best posture, to fall right upon the golden vein, and go deepest to know the mind of God, in searching the Scriptures, to be directed and regulated in his ways; to be made skilful in ways of honoring him, and doing him service. This neither man nor angels can teach him, but God alone.'—Sermon on Psalm cvii. 43.

[10] 'Viscera terræ extrahimus, ut digito gestiatur gemma, quam petimus. Quot manus afferuntur, ut unus niteat articulus! Simili studio, industriâ, constantiâ, Sapientiæ inquisitioni incumbendum erat.'—Plin. Lib. ii. c. 65.

[11] Comp. John v. 39. Gr.—a similar allusion to the miner's toil. 'I can speak it by experience'—said a wise man, 'that there is little good to be gotten by reading the Bible cursorily and carelessly. But do it daily and diligently, with attention and affection

down the field; and if the search be discouraging--dig again. The patient industry of perusal and re-perusal will open the embosomed treasure. "Surely there is a vein for the silver."[1] Yet what miner would be content with the first ore? Would he not *search* deeper and deeper, until he has possessed himself of the whole treasure; not satisfied with taking away much, but determined to leave nothing? Thus let it be our daily exercise to explore "the length, and the breadth, and the depth" of our boundless stores, until we be "filled with all the fulness of God."[2]

This habit of living in the element of Scripture is invaluable. To be filled from this Divine treasury—to have large portions of the word daily passing through the mind—gives us a firmer grasp, and a more suitable and diversified application of it. There can be no sound judgment without this feeding, enriching study. In the mere exercise of reading we often scarcely know where to begin, and we perform the routine without any definite object. Our knowledge therefore must be scanty and ineffective. Nor is the neglect of this habit less hurtful to the Church. All fundamental errors and heresies in the Church may be traced to this source—"Ye do err, not knowing the Scriptures."[3] They are mostly based on partial or disjointed statements of truth. Truth separated from truth becomes error. The mind, therefore, prayerfully occupied in the *search* of Divine truth,—*crying and lifting up the voice*—will never fail to discern the substance and preciousness of the two great principles of godliness—*The fear and knowledge of God.* There is no peradventure nor disappointment in this search—*Then shalt thou understand—The Lord giveth wisdom; it cometh out of his mouth.* None shall search in vain.[4]

7. *He layeth up sound wisdom for the righteous: he is a buckler to them that walk uprightly.* 8. *He keepeth the paths of judgment, and preserveth the way of his saints.* 9. *Then shalt thou understand righteousness and judgment, and equity; yea, every good path.*

Vanity[5] and foolishness[6] are the stamp on the wisdom of this world. Here is *sound wisdom.* It looks at things, not in their notions, but in their proper substance. It is *sound*, because it is practical. It is indeed a *hid treasure*[7]—so safe, that no spoiler can

and you shall find such an efficacy, as is to be found in no other book that can be named.'—Erasmus's Preface to Luke. Peter Martyr gives the same testimony, Epist. Dedic. to Comment on Rom. The following relic of our renowned Elizabeth, will be read both with interest and profit. It was written on a blank leaf of a black-letter Edition of St. Paul's epistles, which she used during her lonely imprisonment at Woodstock. The volume itself, curiously embroidered from her own hand, is preserved in the Bodleian.—'August. I walk many times into the pleasant fields of the Holy Scriptures, where I pluck up the goodlisome herbs of sentences by pruning, eat them by reading, chew them by musing, and lay them up at length in the high seat of memorie, by gathering them together, that so, having tasted their sweetness, I may the less perceive the bitterness of this miserable life.'—Miss Strickland's Queens of England, vi. 113.

[1] Job xxviii. 1. [2] Eph. iii. 18, 19. [3] Matt. xxii. 29.

[4] Job xxxii. 8. Isa. xlviii. 17; liv. 13. James i. 5, 17. Compare Gen. xli. 38, 39 Exod. iv. 12. Dan. i. 17.

[5] Eccles. i. 18. [6] 1 Cor. iii. 19. [7] Verse 4.

reach it; so free, that every sinner may have access to it. Yes; in the Son of God himself "are hid all the treasures of wisdom and knowledge." All these treasures in him are *laid up for the righteous*—made over to them.[1] Oh, let us draw upon this infinite treasure daily—hourly—according to present need. Here is our light to direct *an upright walk*. 'To those that are true and *upright* in heart, he will in his own good time reveal true and saving knowledge, and that *sound* spiritual *wisdom*, which shall make them eternally happy.'[2] Our faithful God *is a buckler to them that walk uprightly*[3]—covering us by the exercise of this wisdom from that subtle sophistry, which would spoil us of our treasure.[4] Our path indeed is fraught with danger; beset with temptation; yet is it safe[5]—*kept and preserved* by Almighty power; so that *the way of his saints*, even on the very edge of the enemy's ground,[6] is guarded from deadly ill.

We may observe also the completeness of this godly privilege. For not only does it enlarge our *knowledge of God*,[7] but it brings us to a full *understanding* of every practical obligation. That only is *sound wisdom*, that guides our feet into *every good path;* that "makes the man of God perfect, throughly furnished unto all good works."[8] The *wisdom* or grace that saves the soul, sanctifies the heart and life.[9]

10. *When wisdom entereth into thine heart, and knowledge is pleasant unto thy soul;* 11. *Discretion shall preserve thee, understanding shall keep thee.*

We have seen the good that *wisdom* brings to us.[10] Now see the evil, from which it *preserves* us. But observe its place—*in the heart*. Here only has it any life or power.[11] While it is only in the head, it is dry, speculative, and barren. *When it entereth into the heart*, all the affections are engaged, and how *pleasant is it to the soul!*[12] Religion *now* is no lifeless notion. It is handled, tasted, enjoyed. It gives a *discreet and understanding* direction to the whole conduct. It becomes not only an external rule, but a *preserving, keeping* principle;[13] like the military guard for the safety of the royal person.[14] Before, it was the object of our search.[15] Now, having found it, it is *our pleasure*. Until it is so, it can have no practical influence. It is "the man whose *delight is in the law of the Lord*," who is preserved from "walking in the counsel of the ungodly."[16] All other restraints—education, conviction, high moral principle—are, at best, only partially

[1] Col. ii. 3. 1 Cor. i. 30.
[2] Bishop Hall.
[3] Chap. xxx. 5. Psalm lxxxiv. 11.
[4] Chap. xxii. 12.
[5] Chap. iv. 11; viii. 20. Deut. xxxiii. 26—29. 1 Sam. ii. 9. Ps. xxxvii. 23, 24 lxvi. 9.
[6] 1 Sam. xxv. 39; xxvii. 1, with xxix. 2 Cor. xii. 7—9.
[7] Verse 5.
[8] 2 Tim. iii. 15—17.
[9] Titus ii. 11, 12.
[10] Verse 5.
[11] Chap. iv. 23.
[12] Chap. xxiv. 13, 14. Job xxiii. 12. Psalm cxix. 103. Jer. xv. 16.
[13] Chap. iv. 6; vi. 22—24. Psalm xvii. 4; cxix. 9—11, 104.
[14] 1 Sam. xxvi. 16. 2 Kings xi. 11.
[15] Verse 4.
[16] Psalm i. 1, 2. Comp. chap. vii. 4, 5.

operative. The reclaimed drunkard *may* be true to his Temperance pledge; but, if the "root of bitterness" be untouched, he may be a Socialist, or a Chartist, or revel in some other equally ruinous course. External wickedness may be exchanged for decent formality. Vagrant affections may be turned from some object of vanity; yet not fixed upon the Divine centre of attraction. The mind may be disciplined from utter unprofitableness, only to indulge in the idolatry of talent, or the fascinations of poisoned literature. The folly of the pride of life may be resisted, yet pride in other of its multiform fruits tenderly cherished. In all these cases, the principle is unsubdued. The forsaken sin only makes way for some more plausible, but not less baneful, passion. The heart, cast into the mould of the Gospel, is the only crucifixion of the flesh[1]—the only antidote to those snares from within and from without, which so imperceptibly, yet so fatally, estrange us from God. Never, till the vital principle is implanted, is their mischief discerned. Never, till then, does the heart find its proper object—its true resting-place.

12. *To deliver thee from the way of the evil man, from the man that speaketh froward things;* 13. *Who leave the paths of uprightness, to walk in the ways of darkness;* 14. *Who rejoice to do evil, and delight in the frowardness of the wicked;* 15. *Whose ways are crooked, and they froward in their paths.*

Some of the various snares for the young, are about to be detailed; a fearful picture of the temptations, to which our beloved children are exposed! Will it not awaken our earnest cries for their immediate and solid conversion to God; that *wisdom may indeed enter into their hearts,* and its *pleasures* be really enjoyed; that they may have a religious taste as well as a religious education; that they may know the Gospel—not only in the conviction of their conscience, or the excitement of their feelings—but in the entire renewal of their hearts before God? This—and nothing else—will preserve them from the snare of their cruel foe. Every town and village swarms with his emissaries: first, initiated themselves into the mysteries of his art; then going forth, laborious and practised teachers, well trained by their Master for his murderous work. Against one of these enticements we have been before warned.[2] Another is here given:—The tempter bears his character upon his lips; *the evil man, that speaketh proud things* against God—his law—his word; like a poisonous fountain sending up poisoned waters. Oh! how quickly does the contamination spread! He does not sin in ignorance. He and his companions[3] have probably been trained in *the paths of uprightness.* But they were ready for the first opportunity to *leave the paths* which they never loved, *to walk in the ways of darkness*—more suitable to their taste, and which their hearts do love.[4] And now, having left the hated paths, they

[1] Rom. vi. 17, 18. 2 Cor. iii. 18. Gal. v. 24.
[2] Chap. i. 10—16.
[3] The change to the plural number (*the man—who leave*) implies confederacy.
[4] Chap. iv. 16, 17. Job xxiv. 13—16. John iii. 19, 20.

become foremost in iniquity. They *rejoice*, like Satan himself, *to do evil*[1]—to draw their fellow sinners into the net; and they *delight in those*, who are most *froward* in their *wickedness.*[2] Thus they plunge deeper and deeper into sin, till all traces of the straight way are lost to their eyes, and all their *ways become crooked*, leading, with sure steps, to eternal ruin. Is not this the picture, drawn to the very life, of many a Sunday-scholar, or a child of godly parents, the subject of deep and tender care, "hardened through the deceitfulness of sin"[3]—the neglect of faithful warning—the stifling of solemn conviction? How do they deserve to be left of God, who have first left him with such fearful aggravation! Young man! especially shun companions, who are sinning against better knowledge and instruction. They are hardened in devotedness to their master's work. Oh! if misguided sinners could but see sin in its horrid deformity, and certain, eternal ruin, would not "their hearts meditate terror?" But, *the crookedness of their ways* hides the end from view. Satan presents the bait, palliates the sin, covers the enormity, closes the eyes, and conceals the certain end of all—Hell.[4] *The froward in their paths* cannot—will not—turn back.

16. *To deliver thee from the strange woman, from the stranger, which flattereth with her lips;* 17. *Which forsaketh the guide of her youth, and forgetteth the covenant of her God.* 18. *For her house inclineth unto death, and her paths unto the dead.* 19. *None that go unto her return again; neither take they hold of the paths of life.*

Another snare of the fowler is here, as often in the course of this Book, graphically portrayed.[5] *Wisdom hidden in the heart* is, as before, the most effectual *deliverance.* This *wisdom* will show itself in restraining even the eye from the hurtful object.[6] Ought not *the strange woman*—even if she be born and baptized in a Christian land—to be counted as *a stranger*,[7] and foreigner among us? A vile *flatterer with her lips!*[8] *forsaking* him, whom she willingly took as *the guide of her youth; forgetting* this solemn bond of *the covenant of her God.*[9] The slave of her lust—having

1 Comp. Isa. iii. 9. Jer. xi. 15. God's heavy judgment. 2 Thess. ii. 12.
2 The sin of the heathen. Rom. i. 32.
3 Heb. iii. 13.
4 Psalm cxxv. 5. Rom. vii. 21, with 2 Cor. iv. 3, 4.
5 Chap. v. 3—20; vi. 24; vii. 5—23; xxii. 14; xxiii. 27. Some commentators give an allegorical interpretation to these pictures—as descriptive of idolatry or false doctrine. 'But surely,' as Mr. Holden well observes, 'if there be any dependence to be placed upon the language of the sacred writer, any propriety in his expressions, it is to be understood in its literal sense, as a warning against the seduction of harlots. The spirit of allegorical interpretation may make the Scriptures speak whatever is prompted by the wildest fancy, or the deepest fanaticism.'—Improved translation of Proverbs. By Rev. George Holden, 8vo. 1819.—Comp. Scott in loco.
6 Comp. Job xxxi. 1, and our Lord's rule. Matt. v. 28.
7 *The strange woman—a stranger.* Two different words in the Hebrew—the latter appearing to mark a foreigner. Comp. Deut. xxiii. 17. Lev. xix. 29. It is however but too evident, that this abandoned class was not confined to foreigners. Comp. Gen. xxxviii. 12. Judges xi. 1. 1 Kings iii. 16.
8 Chap. v. 3; vii. 21.
9 Mal. ii. 14—16. Comp. Ez. xvi. 59, 60. Does not this sacred view of the marriage

no guide but herself; no will but her own; no pleasure but sensual gratification—quickly she becomes her own and her victim's murderer. Her house is the land of death.[1] Eternal death is her doom.[2] *Her paths incline to the dead*, with the awful monuments of Divine vengeance in olden time.[3] Some instances indeed of *deliverance* are given—not so much examples, as *special miracles*, of grace, to show how far the "arm of the Lord," and the Gospel of his grace can reach.[4] But so rare are they, that it is as if scarcely *none*[5] *that go unto her* were known to *return again*. And what madness is it to rush into the snare upon so faint and glimmering hope of escape! The spell of lust palsies the grasp, by which its victim might have *taken hold of the paths of life* for its *deliverance*. Those that are "saved—it is so as by fire"[6]—the wonder of heaven and earth?—"Is not this a brand plucked out of the fire?"[7]

20. *That thou mayest walk in the way of good men, and keep the path of the righteous;* 21. *For the upright shall dwell in the land, and the perfect shall remain in it;* 22. *But the wicked shall be cut off from the earth, and the transgressors shall be rooted out of it.*

Here is the consummating blessing of *engrafted wisdom*. Not only does it *deliver from evil men;* but it guides us *into the way of good men*. Thus endued with *wisdom*—thus clad with divine armor,—thou shalt have courage, like Joseph, to turn thy face from the enchantment of sin,[8] *and keep the paths of the righteous*—rugged indeed and difficult, yet the only paths of rest and security.[9] Thus shalt thou *dwell and remain in the land*, as its rightful inheritor;[10] having the best portion in earth, and an infinitely better portion in heaven; while *the wicked and transgressors*, though they may "enjoy the pleasures of sin for a season," shall be ultimately *cut off*, *rooted out*, and "driven away" into everlasting ruin.[11]

And now, what serious reader of this chapter can fail to estimate above all price, the privilege of being early enlisted under the banner of the cross; early taught in the ways, and disciplined in the school, of the Bible; and early led to hide that blessed book in the heart, as the rule of life, the principle of holiness, the guide to heaven?

Parents, Sponsors, Teachers of youth! ponder your deep responsibility with unceasing prayer for special grace and wisdom. Be

ordinance rebuke the sanction now given by our law, and accredited even by Christian professors, which has reduced it to the degradation of a mere civil contract?

1 Chap. v. 5.
2 Gal. v. 19—21. Eph. v. 5. Rev. xxi. 8; xxii. 15.
3 'The dead.'—Scott and Bishop Patrick in loco. Comp. chap. ix. 18. Heb. Mede's learned discourse, vii.
4 Solomon's own case. Comp. Luke vii. 37—50. 1 Cor. vi. 9—11.
5 None in comparison, very few. Comp. Isa. lix. 4; lxiv. 7.
6 1 Cor. iii. 15
7 Zech. iii. 2.
8 Gen. xxxix. 9, 10.
9 Cant. i. 7, 8. Jer. vi. 16.
10 Psalm xxxvii. 9, 11, 22, 29, 34. Matt. v. 5.
11 Chap. x. 30; xiv. 32; xv. 25. Psalm lii. 5—7; xcii. 7. Matt. iii. 10.

ware of glossing over sins with amiable or palliating terms. Let young people be always led to look upon vicious habits with horror, as the most appalling evil. Discipline their vehemence of feeling and ill-regulated excitement. Keep out of sight—*as far as may be*—books calculated to inflame the imagination. To give an impulse to the glowing passion, may stimulate the rising corruption to the most malignant fruitfulness. Oh! what wisdom is needed to guide, to repress, to bring forth, develop safely, and to improve fully, the mind, energies, and sensibilities of youth!

Young man! Beware! Do not flatter thyself for a moment, that God will ever wink at your sinful passions—that he will allow for them, as slips and foibles of youth. They are "the cords of your own sins," which, if the power of God's grace break them not in time, will "hold" you for eternity.[1] Shun then the society of sin, as the infection of the plague. Keep thy distance from it, as from the pit of destruction. Store thy mind with the preservative of heavenly wisdom. Cultivate the taste for purer pleasures. Listen to the fatherly, pleading remonstrance, inviting to thy hiding place, thy rest—"Wilt thou not from this time cry unto me; 'My Father! thou art the guide of my youth?'"[2]

CHAPTER III.

1. *My son, forget not my law; but let thine heart keep my commandments;*
2. *For long life, and peace shall they add to thee.*

THIS is not the stern language of command. We are listening to our Father's voice in all the endearing persuasiveness of promise—*My son.* He had before instructed us to *seek and search* after wisdom, and set out before us its invaluable blessings.[3] Now he calls us to bring it into practical exercise—*Forget not my law.* Not the infirmity of the memory, (for which a special, though we fear too much neglected, help, is provided,)[4] but the wilful forgetfulness of the heart,[5] is here implied. *Let thine heart*—like the ark of the testimony—be *the keeping place of my commandments.*[6] And is not this the child's desire—"O that my ways were directed to keep thy statutes?"[7] while his conscious helplessness takes hold of the covenant promise—"I will put my law in their inward parts, and write it in their hearts."[8]

Herein lies our interest, not less than our obligation. The reward of this lively obedience (need we add—a reward of grace?)

[1] Chap. v. 22. [2] Jer. iii. 4. [3] Chap. ii. [4] John xiv. 26.
[5] Chap. ii. 17. Psalm ix. 17; x. 4. Comp. chap. iv. 5. Deut. iv. 23. Psalm cxix. 93, 176.
[6] Chap. iv. 4. Deut. xi. 18. Isa. li. 7, with Exod. xl. 20. Heb. ix. 4.
[7] Psalm cxix. 6. Comp ver. 69, 129. [8] Jer. xxxi. 33.

is a long and happy life—the highest earthly good.[1] The wicked indeed live long, and the godly often "live out only half his days." The wicked die in outward comfort, the righteous in outward trouble.[2] But *length of days* is the promise to the righteous—whether for earth or for heaven, as their Father deems fittest for them. In itself the promise, as regards this life, has no charm. To the ungodly, it is a curse;[3] to the people of God, a trial of faith and patience;[4] to all a weariness.[5] But *peace added* forms the sunshine of the toilsome way[6]—"peace with God through the blood of sprinkling,"[7] eternal peace in his home and in his bosom[8]—where all the fightings of a rebellious flesh—all the counterstrivings of a perverse and ungovernable will, shall have ceased forever. "Blessed are they that do his commandments, that they may have right to the tree of life, and may enter in through the gate into the city."[9]

3. *Let not mercy and truth forsake thee; bind them about thy neck; write them upon the table of thine heart;* 4. *So shalt thou find favor and good understanding* (Marg. success), *in the sight of God and man.*

Mercy and truth are the glorious perfections of God—always in exercise—always in combination[10]—for his people's good. While we rest upon them for salvation, let us copy them in our profession. Are not his children new created in his image. Let then our Father's image be manifested in us, "as his dear children."[11] Let these graces be, as with God, in combination. 'The want of one buries the commendation of the other. Such a one is a *merciful* man to the poor; but there is no *truth* in him. Such a one is very just in his dealings, but as hard as flint.'[12] "Put on, as the elect of God, bowels of *mercy*. But lie not one to another. Speak every man *truth* with his neighbor."[13] Nor must these virtues be in temporary or occasional exercise. *Let them not forsake thee. Bind them* as jewels *about thy neck.*[14] Let them be "*written*—not in tables of stone, but in fleshly tables of the heart."[15] God indeed is not thy debtor—yet none shall serve him for naught. The man who shews *mercy* to his neighbor shall find it with him.[16] "They that deal truly are his delight."[17] So shalt *thou find favor and good understanding*[18]—(success)[19] both *in his sight, and in the*

[1] Psalm xxxiv. 12. Comp. ver. 16; iv. 10; ix. 11; x. 27. Job. x. 12.
[2] Eccles. ix. 2.
[3] Gen. iv. 11—15. Isa. lxv. 20.
[4] Gen. xxvii. 46; xlvii. 9. 1 Kings xix. 4. Phil. i. 23, 24. Rev. xxii. 20.
[5] Chap. xv. 15. Psalm xc. 10. Eccles. xii. 1.
[6] Psalm cxix. 165. Isa. xxxii. 17; xlviii. 17, 18.
[7] Rom. v. 1. Eph. ii. 13, 14. Col. i. 20.
[8] Psalm xxxvii. 37. Isa. lvii. 2.
[9] Rev. xxii. 14.
[10] Gen. xxxii. 10. Psalm xxv. 10; lxxxv. 10; lxxxix. 14; Ps. c. 5; cxvii. 2. Mic. vii. 18—20.
[11] Eph. iv. 24; v. 1, 2, 9.
[12] F. Taylor's exposition of Prov. I—IX. 4to. 1655–7.
[13] Col. iii. 12 with 9. Eph. iv. 25.
[14] Chap. vi. 21; vii. 3. Deut. vi. 8.
[15] Chap. vii. 3. 2 Cor. iii. 3.
[16] Psalm xviii. 25. Matt. v. 7.
[17] Chap. xii. 22.
[18] Psalm cxi. 10.
[19] Jos. i. 7, 8. (M. R.)

sight of man. Witness Joseph in Egypt[1]—David in the family of Saul[2]—the servants of God in the Eastern courts[3]—the early Christians with the people around them.[4] What is more lovely than thus to live down reproach by consistent godliness? What more acceptable to God, or more edifying to the Church?[5] Was not this the record of "the holy child, that he increased in wisdom and stature, *and in favor with God and man?*"[6] The highest crown of a youthful profession is conformity to the Divine pattern.[7]

5. *Trust in the Lord with all thine heart, and lean not to thine own understanding.* 6. *In all thy ways acknowledge him, and he shall direct thy paths.*

This is the polar-star of a child of God—faith in his Father's providence, promises, and grace. Let the eye look upward, and all will be light.[8] This is the privilege of adoption. The unmeaning expression of *trust* on the lips of the ignorant and ungodly is a fearful delusion. What ground of confidence can there be, when there is every thing to fear? Can the sinner's God—a just, avenging God—be an object of *trust?* What owe we to that precious atonement, which has opened up our way to a reconciled God,[9] and assured our confidence in him as our Friend and Counsellor! Nor is this the cold assent of the enlightened judgment. It is the *trust of the heart—of all the heart.* It is a child-like confidence without wavering,[10] in our Father's well-proved wisdom, faithfulness, and love. Any limit to this confidence is a heinous provocation.[11] He is truth itself. Therefore he loves, that we should take him at his word, and prove his word to the utmost extent of his power.

But our *trust* must not only be *entire,* it must be *exclusive.* No other confidence—no confidence in the flesh—can consist with it.[12] Man with all his pride feels that he wants something to *lean to.* As a fallen being, he naturally *leans to himself,*—to his own foolish notions and false fancies. Human power is his idol. He makes his *understanding* his god. Many would rather be convicted of want of principle than of want of talent. Many bring God's truth to their own bar, and cavil at it, as an excuse for rejecting it. In these and other ways, man "trusteth to himself, and his heart departeth from the Lord."[13] This is the history of the fall—the history of man from the fall—the dominant sin of every unhumbled heart—the lamented and resisted sin of every child of God. Need we advert to it as the sin of youth? How rare is the sight of the

[1] Gen. xxxix. 2—4, 21—23; xli. 37—43; xlv. 16. [2] 1 Sam. xviii. 5, 14—16.
[3] Dan. i. 8, 9; iv. 8, 9; v. 11; vi. 1—3, 27, 28.—His three companions, iii. 30. Ezra vii. 9—12.—Neh. ii. 1—6. Mordecai, Esth. x. 3.
[4] Acts ii. 44—47. [5] Chap. xvi. 7. Rom. xiv. 16—19. [6] Luke ii. 52.
[7] Comp. 1 Sam. ii. 26. [8] Matt. vi. 22. Comp. Psalm xxxii. 8; xxxiv. 5.
[9] Rom. v. 11.
[10] Comp. 1 Chron. xii. 33. 2 Chron. xiv. 11. Contrast Jam. i. 6—8.
[11] Psalm lxxviii. 18—21. [12] Comp. Phil. iii. 3. [13] Jer. xvii. 5.

"younger submitting unto the elder!"[1] If advice is asked, is it not with the hope of confirming a previously-formed purpose? In case of dissent, the young man's *own understanding* usually decides the course.

Great reason then is there for the warning—*Lean not to thine own understanding.* Once indeed it gave clear unclouded light, as man's high prerogative—created in the image of God.[2] But now—degraded by the fall,[3] and darkened by the corruption of the heart[4]—it must be a false guide. Even in a renewed man—a prophet of God—it proved a mistaken counsellor.[5] Yet throw it not away. Let it be diligently cultivated in all its faculties. In a world of such extended knowledge—ignorance is a reproach—the fruit of sloth, dissipation, or misguided delusion. Use it then actively. Religion strengthens—not destroys—its power. But—*lean not to it—lean—trust in the Lord.* Self-dependence is folly[6]—rebellion,[7] ruin.[8] 'The great folly of man in trials'—as Dr. Owen justly remarks—'is—their *leaning to or upon their own understanding* and counsels. What is the issue of it? "The steps of his strength shall be straightened, and his own counsel shall cast him down."[9] First he shall be entangled, and then cast down; and all by his own counsels, until he come to be ashamed of it.[10] Whenever in our trials we consult our own understandings, or hearken to self-reasonings, though they seem to be good, and tending to our preservation; yet the principle of living by faith is stifled, and we shall in the issue be cast down by our own counsels.'[11]

Next—let our confidence be uniform—In all thy ways acknowledge him. Take one step at a time—every step under plain warrant, and Divine direction.[12] Never venture to plan for yourself, except in simple dependence on God.[13] It is nothing less than self-idolatry to conceive, that we can carry on even the ordinary matters of the day without his counsel. He loves to be consulted. Therefore take all thy difficulties to be resolved by him. Be in the habit of going to him *in the first place* before self-will, self-pleasing,[14] self-wisdom, human friends, conveniences, expediency. Before any of these have been consulted, go to God at once. Consider no circumstance too clear to need his direction.[15] *In all thy ways*, small as well as great—in all thy concerns, personal or relative, temporal or eternal, let him be supreme. Who of us has not found the unspeakable "peace" of bringing to God matters too minute or individual to be entrusted to the most confidential

[1] 1 Pet. v. 5. [2] Gen. i. 26. Col. iii. 10. [3] Psalm xlix. 20.
[4] Eph. iv. 18. [5] 2 Sam. vii. 2—5. [6] Chap. xxviii. 26.
[7] Jer. ii. 13; ix. 23. [8] Gen. iii. 5, 6. Isa. xlvii. 10, 11. [9] Job xviii. 7.
[10] Hos. x. 6. [11] Treatise on Temptation, chap. viii.
[12] Comp. Ez. viii. 21—23. Neh. i. 11.
[13] Jam. iv. 14. *If the Lord will*—as Fuller remarks with his pithy quaintness—'a parenthesis, and yet the most important part of the sentence.'
[14] See the awful hypocrisy, and judgment of asking counsel of God under this deadly influence. Jer. xlii. 1—3, 19—22. Ezek. xiv. 1—6.
[15] See the evil consequence of this inconsiderate neglect. Jos. ix. 14.

ear?[1] Thus it was that Abraham *acknowledged God.* Wheresoever he pitched a tent for himself, there was always an altar for God.[2] In choosing a wife for his son there was a singular absence of worldliness. No mention of riches, honor, beauty, or of any thing, but what concerned the name and honor of his God.[3] Thus did the wise man's father *in all his ways acknowledge God*, asking counsel of him in all his difficulties, and never disappointed.[4] This is indeed to walk with God as a Father. This is true faith —not superseding, but invigorating exertion.[5]

Now if we be weaned from the idolatry of making our bosom our oracle, and our heart our counsellor; if in true poverty of spirit we go every morning to our Lord, as knowing not how to guide ourselves for this day—our eye constantly looking upward for *direction*,[6] the light will come down. *He shall direct thy paths.* We want no new revelations or visible tokens.[7] Study the word with prayer. Mark the Divine Spirit shedding light upon it. Compare it with the observation of the Providence of the day;[8] not judging by constitutional bias (a most doubtful interpreter), but pondering with sober, practical, reverential faith. Let the will be kept in a quiet, subdued, cheerful readiness, to move, stay, retreat, turn to the right hand or to the left, at the Lord's bidding; always remembering, *that* is best, which is least our own doing, and that a pliable spirit ever secures the needful guidance.[9] We may "be led," for the exercise of our faith, "in a way that we know not."[10]—perhaps a way of disappointment, or even *of mistake.* Yet no step well prayed over will bring ultimate regret. Though the promise will not render us infallible; our very error will be overruled for deeper humiliation and self-knowledge; and thus even this mysterious *direction* will in the end be greatly acknowledged—"He led me forth in the right way."[11]

7. *Be not wise in thine own eyes: fear the Lord, and depart from evil;* 8. *It shall be health to thy navel, and marrow to thy bones.*

Another warning against self-confidence![12] and who needs it not? So natural is it to idolize our own devices! Yet self-wisdom is self-delusion.[13] True wisdom is its opposite—*the fear of God and the fear of sin.*[14] God is loved and honored. Sin is hated, loathed,

[1] Phil iv. 6, 7. "*In every thing.*" [2] Gen. xii. 7; xiii. 18.
[3] Ib. xxiv. 1—8. Comp. also his servant, ver. 12—27.
[4] 1 Sam. xxiii. 9—11; xxx. 6—8. 2 Sam. ii. 1; v. 19. Compare the smarting rod from the neglect of this godly habit. 1 Sam. xxvii. 1, with xxix.
[5] Comp. Gen. xxxii. 9—20. Neh. ii. 4—20; iv. 9.
[6] Psalm v. 3; cxliii. 8—10; xxv. 4, 5. [7] Such as Ex. xiii. 21, 22.
[8] Psalm cvii. 43. [9] Comp. Psalm xxxii. 8, 9. Isa. xlviii. 17, 18, with xxx. 21.
[10] Isa. xlii. 16; l. 10. [11] Psalm cvii. 7.
[12] Verse 5. Comp. xxiii. 4. Rom. xii. 3, 16. See the mind of God expressed in that solemn woe, Isa. v. 21.
[13] Even a heathen could remark—'I suppose that many might have attained to wisdom, had they not thought they had already attained it.' Seneca de Irâ. Lib. iii. c. 36. Comp. 1 Cor. viii. 2. Gal. vi. 3.
[14] Chap. xiv. 27; xvi. 6. Gen. xxxix. 9, 10. Neh. v. 15. Job xxviii. 28.

resisted.[1] It lives indeed; but it is condemned to die.[2] It cleaves to the child of God; but his heart *departs from it*. Often is it the sickness of the body:[3] always of the soul.[4] *The departure from it*, in the exercise of self-denial and godly discipline, is *health* to the body.[5] The soul revives in fruitfulness.[6] The man that *feareth the Lord*, under "the healing beams of the Sun of Righteousness goeth forth,"[7] as from his sick chamber, full of life and Christian energy. "The joy of the Lord is his strength."[8]

9. *Honor the Lord with thy substance, and with the first-fruits of all thine increase;* 10. *So shall thy barns be filled with plenty, and thy presses shall burst out with new wine.*

This is the rule of sacrifice—a costly precept to the worldling and the formalist. But to the servant of God, is it not a privilege to lay aside a portion of *substance* with this sacred stamp, "This is for God?"[9] *The first fruits of the increase* were the acknowledgment of redemption from Egypt.[10] And shall we--redeemed from sin, Satan, death, and hell—deny the claim?[11] Nay, could we be happy in spending that *substance* on ourselves, which he has given us, wherewith *to honor* him?[12] What a value—what a dignity—does it give to the talent, that he should condescend to employ it for his grand eternal purposes! This sacred devotedness is moreover the true road to riches.[13] God challenges us to "prove him now herewith," if the abundant harvest, and the overflowing vintage shall not put unbelief and covetousness to shame.[14] A niggardly spirit, is therefore narrow policy, contracting the harvest, by sparing the seed corn.[15] There is no presumption or enthusiasm in looking for the literal fulfilment of the promise. If we doubt the temporal, should we not suspect our assumed confidence, in the spiritual engagements? If the Lord's word be insufficient security for *our substance;* much more must it be for the infinitely weightier deposite of our soul!

The rule and obligation, are therefore clear. Only let us carefully prove our motives, that we beware of bye-ends and selfish principles; that we *honor the Lord*, not ourselves. Let there be a self-renouncing spirit,[16] implicit faith,[17] constraining love,[18] special regard to his own people.[19] And doubt not, but he will affix his own seal—"Them that honor me, I will honor."[20]

11. *My son, despise not the chastening of the Lord; neither be weary of his cor-*

[1] Rom. vii. 18—24.
[2] Ibid. vi. 6.
[3] In sensual indulgence—chap. v. 8—11. Intemperance—xxiii. 29, 30. As a judicial infliction—Psalm xxxii. 3, 4; xxxviii. 1—8. 1 Cor. xi. 30.
[4] Hos. vii. 9.
[5] Verses 1, 2.
[6] Hos. xiv. 5—7.
[7] Mal. iv. 2
[8] Neh. viii. 10.
[9] 1 Cor. xvi. 2.
[10] Ex. xiii. 11—16. Deut. xxvi. 1—10.
[11] 1 Cor. vi. 19, 20.
[12] Matt. xxv. 14, 15. Luke xix. 13. Contrast xii. 16—21.
[13] Chap. xi. 24.
[14] Neh. iii. 10. 2 Chron. xxxi. 5—10.
[15] Chap. xi. 24. 2 Cor. ix. 6. Comp. Hag. i. 4—6.
[16] 1 Chron. xxix. 14—16. Matt. vi. 1—4; xxv. 37—39.
[17] 1 Kings xvii. 12—16.
[18] Rom. xii. 1. 2 Cor. v. 14, 15.
[19] Matt. x. 42; xxv. 40. Gal. vi. 10.
[20] 1 Sam. ii. 30. Comp. Chap. xi. 25; xxii. 9. Heb. vi. 10.

rection; 12. *For whom the Lord loveth, he correcteth; even as a father the son in whom he delighteth.*

Prosperity and adversity in their wise mixture and proportion form the present condition of man. Each is equally fruitful in opportunity of *honoring the Lord;* in prosperity—by the full consecration of *our substance;*[1] in adversity—by a humble and cheerful submission to his dispensations. In prosperity it is well to expect the rod; 'and suppose it be his pleasure let it not disatisfy thee, nor make thee either doubt of his gracious Providence, or out of impatience take any unlawful course to remove it from thee.'[2] His "exhortation"—the Apostle reminds us—"speaketh to us as unto children."[3] And indeed, under no character does he approach so near to us, and endear himself so closely to us, as that of a Father. Most precious at all times, especially under *correction*, is the privilege of adoption—*My son.*

This is a most important exhortation. Nowhere are our corruptions so manifest, or our grace so shining, as under the rod. We need it as much as our daily bread. If we be children of God, we are still children of Adam—with Adam's will, pride, independence, and waywardness. And nothing more distinctly requires Divine teaching and grace, than how to preserve in our behavior the just mean between hardness and despondency—*neither despising the chastening of the Lord, nor being weary of his correction.*[4] We are left to infer the rules from the evils mentioned, which will ever be the exercise of prayer, watchfulness, and conflict.

Too often, while we guard against an error on the right hand, we forget one not less hurtful on the left; like the man who feels he cannot go too far from the precipice on the one side, and rushes into some fearful hazard on the other. The middle path is the right path. *Doubtless the Lord means his chastening to be felt.*[5] A leviathian iron-heartedness[6] is the stubbornness of the flesh, not the triumph of the spirit; a frame most offensive to him, and most unseemly for the reception of his gracious discipline. To be as though no pain was felt or cared for; sullenly to "kick against the pricks,"[7] and to dare God to do his worst—this is indeed to *despise his chastening.*[8] But pride will lift up the head, stiff and unbending: many a stroke does it require to bring it down.

Yet alas! this is not the sin only of the ungodly. Do we not often see the child of God in an undutiful spirit?[9] He *then* cares

1 Verses 9, 10. 2 Bishop Patrick.

3 Heb. xii. 5. We must not overlook in the Apostle's application of this text, the testimony to the divine inspiration of the Book; and that the instruction of Wisdom throughout is the real instruction of our Heavenly Father to his beloved children.

4 The philosopher's definition is striking and accurate, but infinitely above his own practical standard—'Non sentiri mala tua, non est hominis; et non ferre, non est viri.'—(It is inhuman not to feel thine afflictions, and unmanly not to bear them.)—Seneca, Consol. ad Polyb. c. 36.

5 Comp. 2 Sam. xv. 30. Psalm xxxix. 10, 11.

6 Job xli. 24—29. Comp. Isa. xxvi. 11. Jer. v. 3. 7 Acts ix. 5.

8 Comp. Pharaoh—Ex. vii. 23. Jehoram—2 Kings vi. 31. Ahaz—2 Chron. xxviii. 22. Job xv. 25, 26. Isa. i. 5; ix. 9, 10, 13. 9 Comp. Job v. 17. Heb. xii. 9.

little whether his father smiles or frowns. The *chastening* is lightly passed over. He considers only second causes, or immediate instruments.[1] He is irritated by looking at the rod, rather than at the hand that inflicts it.[2] He shrinks from searching into the cause. He disregards his Father's loving voice and purpose. Hence there is no softening humiliation,[3] no "acceptance of the punishment of iniquity;"[4] no child-like submission; no exercise of faith in looking for support. Is not this to *despise the chastening of the Lord?*

But while some *despise* the hand of God as light, others "faint" under it as heavy.[5] They are *weary of his correction.* Beware of yielding to heartless despondency or fretful impatience.[6] Resist hard and dishonorable thoughts of God.[7] Their very admission spreads destruction. Very apt are we to judge amiss of our Father's dealings;[8] to neglect present duty;[9] to cherish a morbid brooding over our sorrows;[10] to forget our title and privilege of adoption;[11] or in obstinate grief to "refuse to be comforted" with the "hope of the end."[12] And is not this to be *weary of his correction?*

We must here remark, that the rules imply much more than their negative meaning. Instead of *despising*—reverence—*the chastening of the Lord.* Let it be a solemn remembrance to thee, that thou art under thy Father's *correction.*[13] Instead of being *weary* of it, hang upon his chastening hand, and pour thy very soul into his bosom.[14] Kiss the rod.[15] Acknowledge its humbling, but enriching, benefit.[16] Expect a richer blessing from sustaining grace, than from the removal of the deprecated affliction.[17]

After all we must add, that chastening is a trial to the flesh;[18] yet overruled by wonder-working wisdom and faithfulness to an end above and contrary to its nature. So that eyeing God in it, we see it to be love, not wrath; "receiving,"[19] not casting out. We are thus better with it than without it; nay—we could not be without it for our soul's salvation.[20] Faith understands the reasons of the discipline;[21] acknowledges it as a part of his gracious Providence,[22] and the provision of his everlasting covenant;[23] waits to see the end of the Lord;[24] and meanwhile draws its main support from the seal of adoption. He *corrects whom he loves,* and because he loves—*the son in whom he delighteth.*[25] He

[1] Comp. Amos iii. 6.
[2] 2 Chron. xvi. 10—12. [3] Psalm xxxii. 3, 4. [4] Lev. xxvi. 41, 43.
[5] Comp. Heb. xii. 5. Psalm xxxviii. 2, 3; xxxix. 10.
[6] Chap. xxiv. 10. Isa. xl. 27—31. Comp. 1 Sam. xxvii. 1. 1 Kings xix. 4. Job iii. 1—3. Jer. xx. 14—18.
[7] Psalm lxxiii. 14; lxxvii. 7—10. [8] Gen. xlii. 36. Judges vi. 13. Jonah iv.
[9] Jos. vii. 10—13. [10] Job vi. 1—16. [11] Heb. xii. 5.
[12] Psalm lxxvii. 2. Comp. Jer. xxix. 11; xxxi. 15—17.
[13] Lam. iii. 28, 29. Mic. vii. 9. [14] 1 Sam. i. 10—15.
[15] Job xxxiv. 31, 32. 1 Peter v. 6. [16] Psalm cxix. 67, 71. [17] 2 Cor. xii. 7—10
[18] Heb. xii. 11. [19] Heb. xii. 6. [20] Chap. i. 32. Comp. Psalm lv. 19. 1 Pet. i. 6.
[21] Deut viii. 2 15, 16. [22] Job v. 6, 7. [23] Psalm lxxxix. 30—32.
[24] Jam. v. 11. [25] Heb. xii. 7, 8. Rev. iii. 19.

'rejoiceth over his child to do him good,"[1] and as a wise and affectionate father, he would not suffer him to be ruined for want of *correction.*[2] It is correction—this is for our humbling. It is only correction—this is our consolation, the intolerable sting of penal infliction is removed. Here then the child has rest indeed![3] The rod is now meekly—yea—thankfully borne, because it is in the hand of One, supreme in wisdom as in love, who knows the time, the measure,[4] and the effectual working of his own discipline.[5] The child compares his affliction with his sin, and marvels not that it is so heavy, but that it is so light.[6] He knows that he more than deserves—that he needs it—all. 'O God, I have made an ill use of thy mercies, if I have not learnt to be content with thy *correction.*'[7]

Should then he, at any dark season ask—"If it be so, why am I thus?"[8]—you are thus, because this is your Father's school—his training discipline for heaven.[9] He loves thee so well, that he will bestow all pains upon thee. He will melt thee in his furnace, that he may stamp thee with his image.[10] He would make thee "partake of his holiness,"[11] that thou mightest partake of his happiness. But unless thou enter into his mind thou wilt—so far as thou canst—defeat his purpose and lose the benefit—a loss never to be told![12] Look then well into the dispensation.[13] Every rod is thy Father's messenger, and he will not bear to have his messenger *despised.* Be anxious to "hear the rod, and who hath appointed it;"[14] well "knowing that the Lord hath not done without cause all that he hath done."[15] Be more concerned to have it sanctified than removed; yea, above all things deprecate its removal, until it has fully wrought its appointed work.[16] We can but admire that considerate dispensation, which uses these "*light* afflictions" as the means of deliverance from the most deadly evil. And should flesh and blood rebel—should the earthly tabernacle shake with "the blow of his hand"[17]—yet shalt thou bless him throughout eternity, that even by this crushing discipline he should accomplish his most merciful purpose. Meanwhile, give him unlimited confidence, and if some steps of the way are hid, wait and "see the end."[18] Watch for the first whispers of his will—the first intimation of his Providence—the guidance of his eye.[19] Many a stroke will thus be saved to thy peace and quietness.

[1] Jer. xxxii. 41. [2] Chap. xiii. 24. Deut. viii. 5.
[3] 1 Sam. iii. 18. 2 Sam. xv. 25; xvi. 10, 11. Psalm xxxix. 9. Job. i. 21. Isa. xxxix. 5—8. Comp. John xviii. 11. The Heathen philosopher has accurately drawn the line—'Chastisement is on the sufferer's account. Vengeance is for the satisfaction of him that inflicts it.'—Arist. de Rhetor. b. i. c. x.
[4] Isa. xxvii. 7, 8. Lam. iii. 31—33. [5] Ibid. v. 9. [6] Lam. iii. 39.
[7] Bishop Hall. [8] Gen. xxv. 22.
[9] Job xxxiii. 14—29; xxxvi. 8—10. Heb. xii. 7, 8, ut supra.—The Greek term refers to the education of children.
[10] Isa. xlviii. 10. Zech. xiii. 9. Mal. iii. 3. [11] Heb. xii. 10. [12] Comp. Jer. vi. 8.
[13] Job x. 2. Psalm cxxxix. 23, 24. Eccles. vii. 14. Lam. iii. 40.
[14] Mic. vi. 9. [15] Ezek. xiv. 23. [16] Isa. iv. 4.
[17] Psalm xxxix. 10, ut supra. [18] Job xxiii. 8—10. James v. 11.
[19] Psalm xxxii. 8, 9.

Never forget that this is a golden opportunity, requiring for its due improvement much study, prayer, and retirement; tnat no communion is so close—so endearing—so fruitful—as with a chastening God; that we delight in a sense of his love in the midst, yea in the very form, of his chastening, that never have we such a full manifestation of his character[1] and perfections; that what we have before learnt in theory, we here learn experimentally; and what we have before imperfectly understood, is here more fully revealed.[2]

13. *Happy is the man that findeth wisdom, and the man that getteth* (Marg. draweth out,) *understanding;* 14. *For the merchandise of it is better than the merchandise of silver, and the gain thereof than fine gold;* 15. *She is more precious than rubies, and all the things thou canst desire are not to be compared to her.*

Who does not admire this glowing picture of happiness?[3] Yet cold and barren is admiration without an interest in the blessing. The *happy man has found* a treasure—possibly when he least expected it—under *the chastening of the Lord.* David[4] and Manasseh[5] found—as who hath not found?—'God's house of correction to be a school of instruction.'[6] Under all circumstances, however, prayerful diligence in the heart of *wisdom* ensures success.[7] The naturally wise man is a fool in heavenly *wisdom.* The man of prayer *getteth understanding, drawing it out* to light, as out of the hid treasure.[8] We wonder not at the merchantman's concentrated interest, at his untiring toil.[9] But here the wise man, though himself enriched with *the merchandise of fine gold*[10]—points out to us a *better merchandise.* It is the search for "the pearl of great price"—*more precious than rubies, yea, than all things that could be desired.*[11] So the apostle judged. So upon a trial he found it. All the world's shew—all his former

[1] Psalm cxix. 75.

[2] Job xlii. 5. Comp. the Apostle's most instructive and encouraging exposition, Heb. xii. There is some slight variation between Heb. xii. 6, and ver. 12. The one describes the mode and subject of *the chastening*—the other shews the Father's delight in his chastened child. Some by inverting the first clause, ver. 12, grossly pervert the meaning, and conclude themselves to be the Lord's beloved children, *because they are afflicted.* But though every child is corrected, not every one that is corrected is a child. The same hand—but not the same character—gives the stroke both to the ungodly and the godly. The scourge of the Judge is widely different from the rod of the Father.—Comp. 1 Sam. xxviii. 15—20, with 2 Sam. xii. 13, 14; chap. i. 26. Isa. i. 24, with Jer. xxxi. 18—20. Hos. xi. 7, 8; also Isa. xxvii. 7—9. Nor is it *chastening*, but the *endurance of chastening* according to the rules prescribed, that seals our adoption. Heb. xii. 7.

[3] *Happy man*—Heb. plural. Comp. Psalm i. 1; xxxii. 1. Blessedness—to mark supreme and perfect happiness. See the beautiful description of Wisdom. Eccles. xxiv. 1—19.

[4] Psalm cxix. 67, 71. Hence he commands it. Psalm xciv. 12.

[5] 2 Chron. xxxiii. 12, 13. [6] Trapp in loco. [7] Chap. ii. 1—6.

[8] M. R. Heb. Comp. chap. viii. 35. M. R. Chap. ii. 4. Matt. xiii. 44.

[9] Impiger extremos currit mereator ad Indos;
Per mare pauperiem fugiens, per saxa, per ignes. Hor. *Prob.* i. 1.

[10] 1 Kings ix. 26—28.

[11] Matt. xiii. 45, 46, with chap. xxiii. 23. Comp. Chap. viii. 11, 19. Job xxiii. 15—18. Most truly does the great Moralist define Wisdom to be 'The knowledge of the most honorable things—επιστημη των τιμιωτατων. Arist. Ethic. b. vi. chap. vii.

valuable "gain he counted as dung and dross" for "the true wisdom"—"the excellency of the knowledge of Christ Jesus his Lord."[1] Never will solid happiness be known without this singleness of judgment and purpose. This inestimable blessing must have the throne. The waverer—the half-seeker—falls short. Deter mined perseverance wins the prize.[2]

16. *Length of days is in her right hand, and in her left hand riches and honor;* 17. *Her ways are ways of pleasantness, and all her paths are peace;* 18. *She is a tree of life to them that lay hold upon her: and happy is every one that retaineth her.*

Behold this heavenly Queen dispensing her blessings on *the right hand and on the left! Her right hand* presents the promise of both worlds[3]—the rich enjoyment of this world's lawful comforts[4] and the yet higher joy of serving the Lord and his church—a privilege, for which the apostle was content for a while to be detained from heaven.[5] Add eternity to the balance—*length of days*, without end—and the amount sets at naught all computation. *Her left hand* offers *riches and honor*,[6] so far as may be for her children's good; yet, in their highest splendor, only a feeble picture of her more "durable *riches*," and of the *honor* of a heavenly crown.

But what say we of *her ways?* Often is she described 'as a sullen matron, who entertains her followers only on sighs and tears; so that to obtain the joys of the next life, we must bid eternal adieu to the contents of this life; that we must never more expect a cheerful hour, a clear day, a bright thought to shine upon us.'[7] This is the world's creed. And hence their wish—"Torment me not before the time." But this must be a slander of the great forger of lies to deter us from *wisdom's ways.* They must be *ways of pleasantness*, because—"Thus saith the Lord." And if we feel them not to be so, we know them not.

The man of pleasure utterly mistakes both his object and his pursuit. The only happiness worth seeking is found here; that which will live in all circumstances, and abide the ceaseless changes of this mortal life. *The ways* may be thorny, painful, dark and lonely. Yet how does the sunshine of reconciliation beam upon their entrance! Every step is lighted from above; strewed with promises; a step in happiness; a step to heaven. Wisdom's work is its own reward[8]—strictness without bondage.[9] God rules children, not slaves. They work neither from compulsion, nor for hire; but from an ingenuous principle of love and gratitude to their Benefactor; filial delight in their Father. *Pleasant* there-

[1] Phil. iii. 7, 8. [2] Ibid. ver. 12—14. [3] Ver. 2. Psalm xci. 16. 1 Tim. iv. 8
[4] 1 Tim. vi. 17. [5] Phil. i. 23, 24.
[6] See the treasures of *the right and left hand* promised to the wise man himself, Kings iii. 12—14.
[7] Bishop Hopkins' Works, iv. 354, 355. [8] Psalm xix. 11. Isa. xxxii. 17.
[9] Matt. xi. 29, 30.

fore must be the labor—yea—the sacrifices, of love; short the path, cheerful the way, when the heart goes freely in it.

It is saying far too little, that the trials of *these ways* are not inconsistent with their *pleasantness*. They are the very principles of the most elevated pleasure. 'The verdict of Christ,' says Dr. South, 'makes the discipline of self-denial and the cross—those terrible blows to flesh and blood—the indispensable requisite to the being his disciples.'[1] And yet, paradoxical as it may appear, in this deep gloom is the sunshine of joy. For if our natural will be "enmity to God,"[2] it must be the enemy to our own happiness. Our pleasure, therefore, must be to deny, not to indulge, it. Never are we more happy, than in the mortification of sinful appetites, that only "bring forth fruit unto death."[3] Even what may be called the austerities of godliness are more joyous than "the pleasures of sin." Far better to cross the will, than to wound the conscience. The very chains of Christ are glorious.[4] Moses endured not "his reproach" as a trial. He "esteemed it as a treasure—greater riches than the treasures of Egypt."[5] Never do we so enjoy the comfort of our principles as when we are making a sacrifice for them. Hannah yielded up her dearest earthly joy. But did she sink under the trial? Did she grudge the sacrifice? She took up her song, and prayed, and said—"*My heart rejoiceth in the Lord*;"[6] while—to shew that none serve him for naught—for one child that was resigned, five were added.[7] In fact, the world see only half the prospect. They see what religion takes away. But they see not what it gives. They cannot discern that, while it denies sinful, it abounds in spiritual, pleasure. We drudge in the ways of sin. But we "shall sing in the ways of the Lord."[8]

But *ways of pleasantness* are not always safe. Yet *all wisdom's paths are peace*. The deadly breach is healed. The cloud vanishes. Heaven smiles. And *peace*, the Saviour's last bequest, is realized even in the heat of "this world's tribulation."[9] "The feet are shod" for the rugged path "with the preparation of the Gospel of peace."[10] The subjugation of the will—the sorrow of contrition—the weariness of the cross—all end in peace.[11]

Yet nothing can make *wisdom's ways* palatable to a carnal mind. "They that are after the flesh do mind the things of the flesh;" so that—as "they cannot please God," God's ways cannot please them.[12] Nor again—though *wisdom's ways are ways of pleasantness*—are wisdom's children always happy. Sometimes a naturally morose temper gives a gloomy tinge to religion. Professors forget, that it is no matter of option, whether they should be happy or not; that it is their obligation, no less than their priv-

[1] Sermons, vol. i. 1. Matt. xvi. 24.
[2] Rom. viii. 7. [3] Ibid. vii 5. [4] Acts v. 41, 42; xvi. 24, 25.
[5] Heb. xi. 26. [6] 1 Sam. i. 26; ii. 1. [7] Ibid. ii. 20, 21.
[8] Isa. lvii. 10, with Psalm cxxxviii. 5. [9] John xvi. 33.
[10] Eph. vi. 15, with Deut. xxxiii. 25.
[11] Psalm xxxvii. 37. Isa. lvii. 2, with 20, 21. [12] Rom. viii. 5, 8.

ilege to be so; that the commands of God on this duty[1] carry weight, and demand obedience. The prophets in the burst of their rapture search heaven and earth, bring forth the most beautiful objects of nature; nay—call the inanimate creation into glowing sympathy with the joys of the Gospel.[2] The character of the servants of God[3]—especially in affliction[4]—sets a seal to this rejoicing spirit. Is then thy happiness clouded? Has there not been some deviation from *wisdom's paths?* Does not thy God call thee to search—to humble thyself—to return?[5]

Lastly—to the glory, beauty, and fruitfulness of wisdom, the Paradise of God alone can furnish the full counterpart.[6] '*The tree of life* was the means ordained of God for the preservation of lasting life and continual vigor and health, before man sinned. So true wisdom maintains man in the spiritual life of God's grace, and the communion of his Spirit.'[7] Once our way was barred up, and none could touch her.[8] Now our way is open to her in a better paradise.[9] We "sit down under her shadow with great delight." Her branches bend down upon this world of sin and misery. Her clusters hang within the reach of the youngest child, and "the fruit is sweet to the taste."[10] For what is so refreshing as near communion with God; access to him; boldness in his presence; admission to his most holy delight? And if the earthly shadow and fruit be so rich, what will be "on the other side of the river"—her monthly fruits—her healing leaves![11] And yet only the weeping, wrestling soul can *lay hold upon* the beloved object,[12] and embrace it in despite of all the enemy's struggle to loosen the grasp.[13] And even when Almighty power has enabled us to *lay hold;* the same continual miracle of grace—the same continually renewed effort of faith—is needed to *retain it.*[14] There must be "continuance in the ways"[15]—"settled—rooted and grounded."[16] "Keeping the works" holding the beginning of our confidence steadfast "unto the end."[17] *Happy is every one that retaineth her.* The promises are "to him that overcometh."[18] God honors perseverance in the weakest saint.

What think we of this lovely description of wisdom's blessings? It is no fancy picture, but Divine reality. Rest not, till thy heart is filled with its substance. Take it to the Lord in prayer, and ere long, thou shalt rejoice in thy portion.

19. *The Lord by wisdom hath founded the earth: by understanding hath he established* (Marg. prepared,) *the heavens.* 20. *By his knowledge the depths are broken up, and the clouds drop down the dew.*

[1] Such as Psalm xxxii. 11; xxxvii. 4. Phil. iv 4. 1 Thess. v. 16. Comp. the warning Deut. xxviii. 47.
[2] Psalm xcvi. 11—13; xcviii. Isa. xliv. 23; lv. 12, 13.
[3] Phil. iii. 3. Comp. Acts ii. 46, 47.
[4] 2 Cor. vi. 10; viii. 2. 1 Peter i. 6—8.
[5] Jer. ii. 17—19. Hos. v. 15; vi. 1.
[6] Rev. ii. 7.
[7] Diodati in loco.
[8] Gen. iii. 22—24.
[9] Heb. x. 19—22.
[10] Can. ii. 3.
[11] Rev. xxii. 2.
[12] Gen. xxxii. 26-28. Hos. xii. 3, 4.
[13] Matt. xi. 12.
[14] 1 Tim. vi. 12.
[15] Isa. lxiv. 5. John viii. 31.
[16] Col. i. 23; ii. 7.
[17] Rev. ii. 26. Heb. iii. 6, 14.
[18] Rev. ii. iii.

We have seen *wisdom*, as it is in man, with all its enriching blessings. Here we behold its majesty, as it is in the bosom of God and gloriously displayed in his works. 'Hereby he sheweth, that this wisdom, whereof he speaketh, was everlasting; because it was before all creatures, and that all things—even the whole world —were made by it.'[1] Behold it *founding the earth* "upon noth ing;" and yet "so sure, that it cannot be moved."[2] See how this great architect *hath established the heavens*, fixing all their bright luminaries in their respective orbits[3]—'such a glorious canopy set with such sparkling diamonds.'[4] Each of these departments declares his *knowledge*. In the earth—*breaking up the depths*—gathering them up into rivers and streams for the refreshment of man.[5] *In the heavens*—collecting the moisture into *dew*—dropping down fatness upon the parched ground;[6] each of these countless drops falling from this Fountain of life.[7] Thus does every particle of the universe glitter with infinite skill.[8] The earth—its pavement, and the *heavens*—its ceiling—"declare the glory of God."[9] How beautiful is the uniformity of the two great systems of God! Both are the work of the same architect. Both display the *wisdom and knowledge* of God.[10] The universe is a parable —a mirror of the gospel. Does not the manifestation of these Divine Perfections in the field of Creation open a rich provision for our happiness? And does not their more glorious exhibition in the great work of redemption, fill us with adoring praise? "O the depth of the riches both of *the wisdom and knowledge* of God."[11]

21. *My son, let them not depart from thine eyes: keep sound wisdom and discretion;* 22. *So shall they be life unto thy soul, and grace unto thy neck.*

Again we listen to wisdom's voice. Her repetitions are not "vain repetitions;" but well fitted to impress upon youth[12] the

[1] Notes to the Reformers' Bible.
[2] Job xxvi. 7. Psalm xciii. 1.
[3] Gen. i. 14—16. Psalm cxxxvi. 5. Jer. x. 12; li. 15.
[4] Leighton's beautiful fragment on Psalm viii. Works, Vol. ii.
[5] Chap. viii. 24—29. Gen. i. 9, 10. Job xxxviii. 8—12. Psalm civ. 8—13.
[6] Gen. xxvii. 28, 29. There is a philosophical difficulty in supposing "*the clouds* to drop down the dew," which is known to be the moisture rising from the lower region, sometimes a very few feet from the earth. Perhaps, however, the original may mean the air generally, thereby including the lower region.—See Geier in loco.
[7] Job xxxviii. 28.
[8] Psalm civ. 24.
[9] Psalm xix. 1.
[10] John i. 1—14. Eph. i. 8; iii. 9. Col. i. 13—17.
[11] Rom. xi. 33. Full of profound thought are the words of our admirable Hooker—'That which moveth God to work is goodness; that which ordereth his work is wisdom; that which perfecteth his work is power. All things, which God in these times and seasons hath brought forth, were eternally and before all time in God; as a work unbegun is in the artificer, which afterwards bringeth it into effect. Therefore whatsoever we do behold now in this present world, it was enwrapped within the bowels of Divine mercy, written in the book of eternal wisdom, and held in the hands of Omnipotent power; the first foundations of the earth being as yet unlaid. So that all things which God hath made are in that respect the Offspring of God. They are in him, as effects in their highest cause. He likewise is actually in them, the assistance and influence of Deity being their life.'—Book V. lvi.
[12] Isa. xxviii. 9, 10.

weight of her instructions.[1] As thy much loved treasure--as thy daily guide—*let them not depart from thine eyes.*[2] Worse than valueless are they, if received as notions; of inestimable price, if *kept* as principles. Man's instructions reach only "the form of knowledge." God's teaching is *sound wisdom*[3]—full of light and substance—transfiguring divine truth with heavenly glory. Therefore *keep* it close to thine heart. Exercise it in that practical *discretion,* which disciplines all our tempers and duties. Man's wisdom—how utterly devoid is it of all glow and energy! The soul, is "alienated from the life of God,"[4] is in a state of death, 'until the entrance of God's word giveth light and understanding,[5]—"the light of life."[6] The excellency of this knowledge is, that "with this light and understanding,"—"it giveth *life* to them that have it."[7] Every truth under its influence springs up into the new creature with heavenly glow, and with all *the grace* of "the beauty of the Lord,"[8] outshining, even in the most despised garb, the richest glory of an earthly crown.

23. *Then shalt thou walk in thy way safely, and thy foot shall not stumble.* 24. *When thou liest down, thou shalt not be afraid: yea, thou shalt lie down, and thy sleep shall be sweet.* 25. *Be not afraid of sudden fear, neither of the desolation of the wicked, when it cometh.* 26. *For the Lord shall be thy confidence, and shall keep thy foot from being taken.*

The habitual eyeing of the word keeps the feet in a slippery path.[9] David from inattention to wisdom's words "well nigh slipped."[10] Peter from the same neglect fearfully *stumbled.*[11] But our sleeping hours, no less than our waking steps, are divinely guarded. "So he giveth his beloved sleep."[12] "Underneath them are the everlasting arms."[13] They enjoy a childlike repose, sleeping in his bosom without fear. Thus did David 'sleep in God, and in a state of salvation,' amid the tumultuous warfare with his undutiful son.[14] Such was the sleep of Peter in prison—in chains—between two soldiers—on the eve of his probable execution—when "there seemed but a step between him and death." Yet in such a place—in such company—at such a moment—did *he lie down so fearless, and sleep so sweetly,* that an angel's stroke was needed to awaken him.[15] What would not many in troublous times—waking at every stir—give for one night of this *sweet sleep!* And yet how many such nights have we enjoyed; waking, as Jacob on his

[1] Comp. Phil. iii. 1. 2 Pet. i. 12.
[2] Comp. Chap. vii. 1–3. Deut. iv. 9; vi. 8. Jos. i. 7, 8.
[3] Chap. ii. 7. [4] Eph. iv. 18. [5] Psalm cxix. 130.
[6] John viii. 12. [7] Ecc. vii. 12. Comp. Chap. iv. 22; vi. 23.
[8] Psalm xc. 17; cxlix. 4. Com. Chap. i. 9. 'Grace to thy jaws,' is the Douay Version with the Marg. Explanation—'Merit for the words of thy mouth.'
[9] Chap. iv. 11, 12. Psalm xvii. 4; xxxvii. 23; cxix. 9, 11, 133. [10] Psalm lxxiii. 2—17.
[11] Matt. xxvi. 33—35, 69—75. [12] Psalm cxxvii. 2. Comp. cxxi. 3, 4.
[13] Deut. xxxiii. 27. Comp. Lev. xxvi. 6.
[14] 'Obdormit in Deo, et in statu salutis,' Lyra.—Psalm iii. iv. 8. Compare the beautiful picture, Ez. xxxiv. 25—28, in contrast with chap. iv. 16. Deut. xxviii. 66.
[15] Acts xii. 6, 7. Our Martyrologist records of John Rodgers, the Proto-Martyr in the Marian persecution, that 'on the morning of his execution, being found fast asleep, *scarce with much shogging could he be awaked.*'—Foxe, vi. 699.

stony—we might add—his downy pillow, in the conciousness of our Father's keeping! But where has been with us, as was with him, the renewed dedication to our God?[1]

But *sudden fear* may come. Yet *be not afraid.*[2] It is *the desolation of the wicked.* They must fear.[3] But child of God—run you to your *confidence*, and "be safe."[4] Surely *he shall keep thy foot from being taken.*[5] Noah found this security in the flood of the ungodly—Lot in the destruction of Sodom[6]—the Christians in Pella in *the desolation of the wicked* city. Luther sung his song of *confidence*:—"God is our refuge and strength."[7] In the consummating *desolation when it cometh*—what will then be the *sudden fear*—the undismayed *confidence?* "All the tribes of the earth will mourn" at the sight of their despised Saviour—then their Judge.[8] But, "when ye see these things, then look up, and lift up your heads, for your redemption draweth nigh."[9]

27. *Withhold not good from them to whom it is due,* (the owners thereof, Marg.) *when it is in the power of thine hand to do it.* 28. *Say not unto thy neighbor, Go, and come again, and to-morrow I will give; when thou hast it by thee.*

The wise man now comes to practical points. He strikes at the root of selfishness—*withholding dues.* Many are the forms of this dishonesty, borrowing without payment,[10] evading the taxes,[11] "keeping back the laborers hire."[12] But the rule probes deeper than this surface. If we have no legal debt to any, we have a Gospel debt to all.[13] Even the poor is bound by this universal law to his poorer neighbor.[14] Every one has a claim upon our love.[15] Every opportunity of doing good, is our call to do so. Our neighbors are the real *owners of our good.*[16] The Lord of all has transferred his right to them, with a special reference to "his own brethren."[17] Kindness is therefore a matter—not of option, but of obligation; an act of justice, no less than of mercy. To *withhold it* will be our eternal condemnation.[18]

Christian benevolence will also do good in the kindest manner. Delay is an offence against the law of love. Too often the cold repulse—*Go, and come again*—is a cover for selfishness. There is a secret hope, that the matter will be forgotten, dropped, or taken up by some other party. Often an application is put off from mere thoughtlessness. *We have it by us:*[19] but it does not just

1 Gen. xxviii. 11, 18—22.
2 Job v. 21—24. Comp. 2 Kings vi. 16, 17. Jer. xxxix. 15—18.
3 Isa. lvii. 20, 21.
4 Chap. xiv. 26; xviii. 10. Isa. xxvi. 1, 20.
5 Psalm xci. 1—3.
6 2 Peter ii. 5—9.
7 Psalm xlvi.
8 Chap. i. 27. Luke xxi. 26. Rev. i. 7; vi. 15—17.
9 Luke xxi. 28. Comp. 2 Thess. i. 7—10.
10 Psalm xxxvii. 21.
11 The example and admonition of Christ are evidently directed against this iniquity. Matt. xvii. 24—27; xxii. 15—21.
12 James v. 4. Jer. xxii. 13—17. Comp. Gen. xxxi. 7. Deut. xxiv. 14, 15.
13 Rom. xiii. 8.
14 Eph. iv. 28. Comp. 2 Cor. viii. 1—3.
15 Comp. Luke x. 29—37.
16 Marg.
17 Gal. vi. 10. Mark ix. 41. Matt. xxv. 35—40.
18 Matt. xxv. 41—45. Comp. Deut. xxiii. 3, 4.
19 See how Job rebutted his friend's accusation, xxii. 9, with xxxi. 16. Comp. James ii. 15, 16.

now suit our convenience. This is a serious injury to the applicant. A little given in time of need, is more, than a larger sum, when the time is gone by. We should cultivate a quick sensibility of others; putting ourselves as much as possible in their place; not only "doing good," but "*ready* to every good work."[1] If we are to "*do* justly"—which sometimes (as in the punishment of criminals) may be our sorrow; we are, after the example of our God,[2] to *love* mercy;[3] seizing the present, perhaps the only,[4] opportunity; rather anticipating the need, than wantonly or thoughtlessly delaying to relieve it. The[5] Gospel presents every neighbor before us, as a brother or sister needing our help, and to be loved and cared for "as ourselves."[6] Why do we not more readily acknowledge this standard? The Lord raise us from our selfishness, and mould us to his own image of mercy and love![7]

29. *Devise not evil against thy neighbor, seeing he dwelleth securely by thee.*
30. *Strive not with a man without cause, if he have done thee no harm.*

The command—*not to withhold good*—is naturally followed by the forbidding to *devise evil.* The treachery here rebuked was a scandal even to a heathen.[8] It is generally abhorred by the world, and should be doubly hated by a godly man. With him all should be clear and open as the day. *An evil device against a neighbor,* from whatever cause, is a cursed sin.[9] But to take occasion from confidence reposed, betrays "the wisdom that descendeth not from above—devilish."[10] Such was the craft of Jacob's sons against the unsuspecting Shechemites[11]—Saul's malice against David, when under his protection[12]—Joab's murder of Abner and Amasa[13]—Ishmael's of Gedaliah.[14] No trial cuts so keenly.[15] This was one of the bitters in the Saviour's cup of suffering.[16] And many a wounded spirit has been cheered by his sympathy with their poignant sorrow.[17]

Yet we must guard not only against secret malice, but against *causeless strivings.* A propensity to embroil ourselves in quarrels[18] kindles *strife,* instead of following the rule of peace.[19]

1 Tit. iii. 1. 1 Tim. vi. 18. 2 Mic. vii. 18.
3 Ibid. vi. 8. Comp. Rom. xii. 8. 2 Cor. ix. 7. 4 Chap. xxvii. 1. Gal. vi. 10.
5 2 Cor. viii. 10. 6 Lev. xix. 18.
7 Dr. South's caustic application may be wholesome probing—'Was ever the hungry fed, or the naked clothed, with good looks or fair speeches? These are but thin garments to keep out the cold; and but a slender repast to conjure down the rage of a craving appetite. My enemy perhaps is ready to starve; and I tell him; I am heartily glad to see him, and should be *very ready* to serve him. But still my hand is closed and my purse shut. I neither bring him to my table, nor lodge him under my roof. He asks for bread, and I give him a compliment—a thing indeed not so hard as a stone, but altogether as dry. I treat him with art and outside, and lastly, at parting, with all the ceremonial of dearness. I shake him by the hand, but put nothing into it. I play with his distress, and dally with that which will not be dallied with,—want of money, and a clamorous necessity.'—Sermon on Matt. v. 44.
8 'Fallere eum, qui læsus non esset, nisi credidisset.'—Cicero pro Roscio.
9 Chap. vi. 14—18. Deut. xxvii. 24. Psalm xxxv. 20; v. 20. Jer. xviii. 18—20.
10 James iii. 15. 11 Gen. xxxiv. 13—29; xlix. 5—7. 12 1 Sam. xviii. 22—26.
13 2 Sam. iii. 27; xx. 9, 10. 14 Jer. xli. 1, 2. 15 Psalm lv. 12—14.
16 John xviii. 13, with Psalm xli. 9. Comp. Matt. xxvi. 46, 58.
17 Heb. iv. 15. 18 Chap. xvii. 14; xviii. 6; xxv. 8, 9. 19 Rom. xii. 18.

This spirit is a just hindrance to holiness,[1] and inconsistent with a true servant of God.[2] Irritable persons strongly insist upon their rights, or what they conceive to be due to them from others—"Is there not"—say they—"a cause?" But impartial observers frequently judge it to be *striving without cause;* that no harm has been done—none at least to justify the breach of love; that more love on one hand, and more forbearance on the other, would have prevented the breach; that "there is utterly a fault—Why do ye not rather take wrong."[3] How valuable is a close application of the self-denying law of Christ![4] How earnestly should we seek from himself his meek and loving spirit![5] 'O Lord, pour into our hearts that most excellent gift of charity, the very bond of peace, and of all virtues; without which, whosoever liveth is counted dead before thee.'[6]

31. *Envy thou not the oppressor* (a man of violence, Marg.) *and choose none of his ways.* 32. *For the froward is an abomination to the Lord; but his secret is with the righteous.*

What is there—we might ask—to *envy in the oppressor?* The love of power is a ruling passion: and the slave of his own will enjoys a brutish pleasure in tyranny. Yet little reason have we to *envy him*—much less *to choose his ways.*[7] Can he be happy—going *froward* (*fromward*) the Lord, in perverse contradiction to his will? with the frown of heaven? For 'he who hateth nothing that he hath made, abhors those who have thus marred themselves. They are not only abominable, but "*an abomination*" in his sight.'[8] Really to be *envied*—or rather ardently to be desired—is the lot of *the righteous*—enriched with the *secret of the Lord*—'his covenant and fatherly affection, which is hid and secret from the world.'[9] Sinners he hates, but saints he loves. The one is *an abomination.* The other is his delight. 'They are God's friends, to whom he familiarly imparts, as men use to do to their friends, his mind and counsels, or his secret favor and comforts, to which other men are strangers.'[10] Communion with himself[11]—peace[12]—joy[13]—assurance[14]—teaching[15]—confidence[16]—an enlightened apprehension of Providence[17]—yea, all the blessings of his covenant,[18] this is *the secret* between God and the soul—an enclosed portion, hidden from the world—sealed to his beloved people. Here then—child of God—"dwell in the secret place of the Most

[1] Comp. Heb. xii. 14. Col. iii. 12—15. [2] 2 Tim. ii. 24. [3] 1 Cor. vi. 1—7.
[4] Such as Matt. v. 39—41. [5] 1 Peter ii. 21—23.
[6] Collect for Quinquagesima Sunday. 1 Cor. xiii. 4—7.
[7] Chap. xxiv. 1. Ecc. iv. 1.
[8] Henry in loco, chap. vi. 14—18; xi. 20; xv. 9. Mic. ii. 1, 2. See the Lord's open judgment, Ex. ix. 16; xiv. 28. Isa. xxxvii. 21—38. Acts xii. 1, 2, 23.
[9] Notes to Reformers' Bible.
[10] Pool's Annotations, 'He loves them dearly as his intimate friends, to whom he communicates the very secrets of his heart.'—Diodati.
[11] John xiv. 21—23. [12] Phil. iv. 6, 7. [13] Chap. xiv. 10. [14] Rev. ii. 17.
[15] Matt. xi. 25; xiii. 11—17; xvi. 17. John vii. 17. 1 Cor. ii. 12, 15.
[16] John xv. 15. [17] Gen. xviii. 17, 18. Psalm cvii. 43. [18] Psalm xxv. 14.

High."[1] If he hath given to thee the knowledge of himself, and of thine interest in Him—and to *the froward oppressor* only worldly advantage—is it not the seal of his love to thee, and rejection of him? Is it not infinitely more to dwell on high with thy God, than in the vain pomp of an ungodly world?[2]

33. *The curse of the Lord is in the house of the wicked; but he blesseth the habitation of the just.*

The contrast between the sinner and the saint affects us not only personally but relatively. *The curse or blessing of the Lord* follows us to our homes. Shall we then envy *the wicked*—with his cup of earthly joy filled to the brim? *The curse of the Lord is in his house*[3]—a "curse that never cometh causeless."[4] It is my Maker's curse—How awful, that my being and my curse should come from the same sacred source! It is not the impotent *wishing* of ill. Could we trace its deadly work, we should see the man wasting, withering, consuming under it. Observe "the roll in the house of the thief, and of the swearer—twenty cubits long"—a long catalogue of woes—"flying"—to mark its swiftness —"remaining in the midst of the house—consuming it, even with the timbers and stones thereof."[5] Is this an idle dream? Surely—but for the blindness of the heart—*the wicked* would see the naked sword hanging by a hair over his head, or the awful "handwriting upon the wall," solemnly proclaiming—"There is no peace—saith my God—unto the wicked."[6] Vainly will the proud worm resist. Ahab multiplied his house beyond all human average, as if to set at defiance *the curse* pronounced against it. Yet at one stroke all were swept away.[7] Similar instances[8] abundantly prove, whose words shall stand—man's or God's.[9] "Who hath hardened himself against him, and prospered. Who hath resisted his will?"[10]

But bright is the sunshine of *the just.* Not only *is the secret of the Lord with their souls*, but *his blessing on their habitation.* And when he blesseth, who can reverse it?[11] Many a homely cottage, tenanted by a child of Abraham, shines more splendidly, than the princely palace of the ungodly.[12] An heir of glory dwells here. A family altar of prayer and praise consecrates it as the temple of Jehovah.[13] Promises, like clouds of blessings, rest over it. God has been honored, and God will honor."[14] "They that dwell under his shadow shall return."[15] Is then my *house* under *the curse or*

[1] Psalm xci. 1. [2] Ibid. lxxxiv. 10. [3] Mal. ii. 2.
[4] Chap. xxvi. 2. [5] Zech. v. 1—4. [6] Dan. v. 5, 6. Isa. lvii. 21.
[7] 1 Kings xxi. 20—22. 2 Kings x. 1—11.
[8] Jeroboam and Baasha, 1 Kings xiv. 9—11; xvi. 1—4, 12, 13.—Jehu, 2 Kings xv 8—12. Hos. i. 4.—Hazael, Amos i. 4.—Jeroboam, vii. 9.—Jehoiakim, Jer. xxii. 13—19 —Coniah, 24—30.—Esau, Obad. 18. Comp. chap. xiv. 11; xv. 25.
[9] Jer. xliv. 28. [10] Job ix. 4. Rom. ix. 19. [11] Job xxxiv. 27.
[12] Job xxix. 4. Isa. iv. 5. Ενθα και οι Θεοι. 'The gods are within,' said the Heathen philosopher of his poor cottage.—F. Taylor in loco.
[13] Gen. xii. 8. [14] 2 Sam. vi. 11. Jer. xxxv. 18, 19. 2 Tim. i. 18.
[15] Hos. xiv. 7.

blessing of the Lord? Let my God be honored in his own gifts: that I and mine may be manifestly sealed with the full tokens of his love.

34. *Surely he scorneth the scorners: but he giveth grace unto the lowly.*

Two Apostles have combined with the wise man, to set out this rule of the Divine government.[1] On no point is the mind of God more fully declared, than against pride—the spirit of *scorning.* It displaces man, and would—if possible—displace God himself. Jealous therefore of his own glory, he sets himself in battle array, as against the usurper of his prerogative—the rebel against his dominion.[2] Witness the Babel-builders[3]—Pharaoh[4]—Sennacherib[5]—the proud opposers of his Gospel[6]—all the objects of *his scorn.* But most hateful to him is the sinner, that will not submit to his righteousness—that *scorns* the corner-stone of salvation. How fearfully does it then become "a rock of offence"—of eternal ruin![7] *Surely* without doubt—without way of escape from his frown—*he scorneth the scorners.*

A *lowly* spirit—a deep conviction of utter nothingness and guilt—is a most adorning grace. Nor is it an occasional or temporary feeling—the result of some unexpected hateful disclosure, but an habitual principle, "clothing" the man[8] "from the sole of the foot to the head." It combines the highest elevation of joy with the deepest abasement of spirit. And those who sink the lowest, stand nearest to the most exalted advancement. For "*he that scorneth the scorners, giveth grace to the lowly*"—"more grace,"[9] till his work is perfected in them. He pours it out plentifully upon humble hearts. His sweet dews and showers of grace slide off the mountains of pride, and fall on the low vallies of humble hearts, and make them pleasant and fertile."[10] The Centurion[11]—the Canaanite[12]—the penitent[13]—the publican[14]—such as these are the objects of his favor.[15] Their hearts are his dwelling-place.[16] Their inheritance is his kingdom.[17] The soul swelling with its proud fancies has no room for his humbling grace. Blessed exchange of the little idol of self-esteem for Him, who alone has the right!—when even his own graces are only desired as instruments to set out his glory.

[1] James iv. 6. 1 Peter v. 5.—The exact quotation of the LXX. save the substitution of Θεος for Κυριος. 'The Apostle's quotation of this passage, though somewhat different in the words, is the same in the sense with the original. For *scorners* in Scripture, are *proud, insolent, wicked men.* And to resist such persons, by rendering their schemes abortive, and by humbling them, is emphatically called *a scorning of them.*'—Macknight on James iv. 6.

[2] *αντιτασσεται*, LXX. [3] Gen. xi. 1—11. [4] Ex. xiv. 30.
[5] Isa. xxxvii. 33—38. [6] Psalm ii. 1—4.
[7] Rom. x. 3, with ix. 32—33. Matt. xxi. 41—44. [8] 1 Peter v. 5.
[9] James iv. 6. [10] Leighton on 1 Peter v. 5. Comp. also on chap. iii. 8.
[11] Matt. viii. 5—10. [12] Ibid. xv. 19—28. [13] Luke vii. 44—50.
[14] Ibid. xviii. 13, 14. [15] Isa. lxvi. 2. [16] Ibid. lvii. 15.
[17] Matt. v. 3.

35. *The wise shall inherit glory: but shame shall be the promotion of fools,* (exalteth the fools; Marg.)

This is the last contrast drawn to restrain *our envy* at the prosperity of the wicked.[1] It carries us forward to eternity. The difference between these two classes is not always shown to man's vision. But the day cometh, when all shall "discern" in the full light of eternity.[2] *The wise—the heirs of glory*—are identified with *the lowly*[3]—the heirs of grace. Our self-knowledge—the principle of lowliness—is the very substance of *wisdom*. Their inheritance also is one—*grace and glory*.[4] For what higher *glory* can there be, than the *grace*, which "hath redeemed" a vile worm of the earth, "and made him a king and priest unto God?"[5] Oh! let the redeemed cherish honorable thoughts of their present *glory*. Be careful to clear it from the defilement and degradation of the world's dust, and enjoy it in adoring praise to Him, who hath chosen thee to this so undeserved grace.[6]

But who can tell *the glory* of the after *inheritance*—not like this world's glory—the shadow of a name—but real—solid—'an infinite gain in the exchange of dross for down-weight of pure gold.'[7] All occasion of sin and temptation are shut out forever. 'The tree of knowledge shall be without enclosure. There shall be neither lust nor forbidden fruit; no withholding of desirable knowledge, nor affectation of undesirable. The glorified spirits touch nothing that can defile, and defile nothing they touch.'[8] But after all, the glory of this glory will be communion and likeness with our Lord—"to be with him—to behold his glory."[9] We need not pry too minutely. Thus much is clear. The value of our inheritance is beyond all price—its happiness unspeakable—its security unchangeable—its duration eternity. *The wise shall inherit glory.* "They that be *wise* shall shine as the brightness of the firmament forever and ever."[10]

Oh! will not the fools *then* discover the vanity of this world's glory—too late to make a wise choice? *Shame* is their present fruit.[11] Honor even now sits unseemly upon them.[12] But "what fruit will eternity bring" of those things, whereof they will "*then* be ashamed?"[13] Truly *shame will be their promotion.* Their fame will be infamous; their disgrace conspicuous, lifting them up, like Haman upon his elevated gallows,[14] 'a gazing-stock to the world.' How solemn and complete will be the great separation for eternity! "Many that sleep in the dust of the earth shall awake; *some to everlasting life, and some to shame and everlasting contempt.*"[15]

1 Verse 31. 2 Mal. iii. 18.
3 Ver. 34; xi. 2. 4 Psalm lxxxiv. 11. 5 Rev. v. 9, 10.
6 Ibid. i. 5, 6. 7 Leighton on 1 Peter v. 10.
8 Howe's Blessedness of the Righteous. Chap. v. xi.
9 John xvii. 24. 1 John iii. 2. 10 Dan. xii. 3. Comp. Matt. xiii. 43.
11 Chap. xiii. 18; x. 9. Comp. 2 Kings xiv. 24; xv. 9, 18, 24 36.
12 Chap. xxvi. 1. 13 Rom. vi. 21. 14 Esth. vii. 9. 15 Dan xii. 2

CHAPTER IV.

1. *Hear, ye children, the instruction of a father, and attend to know understanding.* 2. *For I give you good doctrine, forsake not my law.*

SURELY these frequent repetitions are as the angel's visit to the prophet; "waking him, as a man that is wakened out of his sleep."[1] A mind like Solomon's, "large even as the sand that is on the sea-shore,"[2] might readily have made every sentence a fresh discovery of knowledge. But more suitable to our sluggish and forgetful heart is "the word of the Lord, precept upon precept."[3] Often do we see children bereft or destitute of a parental instructor. Here these orphan *children* are taken up, and called to *hear the instruction of a father.* For truly does the wise man, like the Apostle in after-days, "exhort and charge *as a father doth his children.*"[4]

Solomon evidently speaks from the mouth of God, declaring his *doctrine*—his *law.* Therefore he claims *attention to know understanding,* for *I give you good doctrine.*[5] To many—exciting[6]—curious and speculative[7]—compromising[8]—self-righteous—self-exalting doctrine[9]—is more attractive. But—Young people—remember! that which humbles the soul before God; that which exhibits the free grace of the Gospel; which melts down the will, consecrates the heart, imbues with the spirit of the cross—however unpalatable to the flesh, is alone *good doctrine* for the soul. Therefore *forsake it not.*

3. *For I was my father's son, tender and only beloved in the sight of my mother.* 4. *He taught me also, and said unto me, 'Let thine heart retain my words: keep my commandments and live.* 5. *Get wisdom, get understanding; forget it not; neither decline from the words of my mouth.* 6. *Forsake her not, and she shall preserve thee: love her, and she shall keep thee.* 7. *Wisdom is the principal thing; therefore get wisdom; and with all thy getting get understanding.* 8. *Exalt her, and she shall promote thee: she shall bring thee to honor, when thou dost embrace her.* 9. *She shall give to thine head an ornament of grace: a crown of glory shall she deliver to thee.'*

Solomon here claims our *attention* as a teacher of youth, on account of his own godly education by such a father. He was *a tender* child[10]—*well-beloved,* as an *only* son.[11] The more dearly he was loved, the more carefully was he *taught.* Thus we are brought into the family of "the man after God's heart," to hear

[1] Zech. iv. 1.
[2] 1 Kings iv. 29. Comp. Eccl. xlvii, 14, 15.
[3] Isa. xxviii. 13.
[4] 1 Thess. ii. 11.
[5] Eccl. xii. 9—11.
[6] Ez. xxxiii. 31, 32.
[7] 2 Tim. iv. 3, 4.
[8] Isa. xxx. 10. Jer. v. 31.
[9] Gal. i. 6, 7.
[10] 1 Chron. xxii. 5; xxix. 1.
[11] Not *really* the *only* son. 2 Sam. v. 14. 1 Chron. iii. 5. Thus Isaac was called the only son, (i. e. most beloved,) when Ishmael was another son: Gen. xxii. 2, 12, 16, with xvii. 19. So the Church is called "the *only one—the choice*"—implying others out of which the choice was made. Can. vi. 9.

him "commanding his child" in the fear and service of the Lord![1] A special mercy is it to us, if we can tell of an Abraham or a David—of a Lois or an Eunice, having *taught* and bound us to the ways of God![2] Parents! remember—a child untaught will be a living shame.[3] Training discipline, not foolish indulgence, is the truest evidence of affection to our *tender and beloved.*[4]

But let us examine this beautiful specimen of parental instruction.[5] *Observe the anxiety for his son's heart-religion. Let thine heart retain my words.* Often (and this is a comfort to a weak memory) *words* may be lost to the memory, yet *retained in the heart* with a permanent sanctifying impression. This *heart-keeping* is the path of *life*, without which we "have only a name that we live, and are dead."[6] *Observe* again *the earnestness of the exhortation.* Many a parent, like Augustine's father,[7] insists—'Get wealth—worldly honor or wisdom.' This godly parent inculcates "line upon line"—*Get heavenly wisdom—get it with all thy getting*—at any cost and pains,[8] and when thou hast got it, *forget it not—decline not from it—forsake it not;*[9] and—as the cleaving principle of perseverance—*love*[10]*—embrace—exalt—her.* Such a *keeping* is she for thy soul![11] Such a treasure for thy happiness! Such a *promoting honor* even in this life! Such an *ornament of grace* in the Church! Such *a crown of glory* in heaven! Is not then *wisdom the principal thing*, not only important, but all-important? Shall it not then have our *first* choice[12]—infinitely above this world's glitter?[13] It can have no place, if it has not the first place. Earthly wisdom may be "a goodly pearl:" But this "wisdom from above" is "the pearl of great price;" worth *getting* indeed; but only to be *got*, by "selling all that we have to buy it."[14]

10. *Hear, O my son, and receive my sayings; and the years of thy life shall be many.* 11. *I have taught thee in the ways of wisdom; I have led thee in right paths.* 12. *When thou goest, thy steps shall not be straitened; and when thou run*

[1] Comp. also 1 Kings ii. 2-4. 1 Chron. xxii. 6—16; xxviii. 9, 10, 20. Comp. Gen. xviii. 19. Deut. vi. 8.

[2] 2 Tim. i. 5; iii. 14, 15. [3] Chap. xxix. 15. [4] 1 Kings i. 6. Comp. chap. xiii. 24

[5] Where David's instruction begins, is obvious. Where it ends is not so clear, whether it be ver. 6, 10, 12, or 13; or as F. Taylor asserts, at the close of the ninth chapter But as Geier observes—'Let the reader form his own judgment—provided that we pay due obedience to the instruction; it matters little, whether we have it in the words of David or Solomon."

[6] Ver. 13; vi. 23; viii. 34, 35. Isa. lv. 3. Zech. iii. 7, contrasted with Rev. iii. 1, 2.

[7] Of whom he records—'This Father of mine never troubled himself with any thought of—How I might improve myself towards thee, so that I proved eloquent, though I were withal left undrest by thy tillage.'—Confess. ii. 3.

[8] Chap. xxiii. 23. Comp. 1 Kings x. 1. Matt. xii. 42.

[9] See the great importance of this continuance. John vii. 30, 31. Col. i. 22, 23. Heb. iii. 6, 14, contrasted with Matt. xiii. 20, 21.

[10] Thus Jerome wrote to a friend—'Beg now for me, who am gray-headed of the Lord, that I may have wisdom for my companion, of which it is written—Love her, and she shall keep thee.'

[11] Chap. ii. 10—18. [12] Matt. vi. 33. [13] 1 Kings iii. 5—12. Phil. iii. 7, 8.

[14] Matt. xiii. 45, 46.

nest, thou shalt not stumble. 13. *Take fast hold of instruction: let her not go keep her; for she is thy life.*

It is instructive to see a king (whether David or Solomon) not forgetting in the midst of his royal cares his domestic responsibilities. 'Youth'—we are told—'will have its swing.' So—adds an old Commentator solemnly—'it may—to hell.'[1] For where else can a wayward will lead? Ponder the need of guidance of every step, both to take and to avoid. *The ways of wisdom* assure a happy life in the favor of God.[2] And what rest to the parent's conscience on the death-bed will be the recollection of children—not brought up for the world,—but *taught in these ways!* Yet this cannot be, if the rod, when needed, has been spared; if the will has been indulged; the love of the world cherished. *This will be*—if godly discipline has been exercised; if the Bible has been laid down as the rule of life; if habits of prayer,—love to the service of God,—fellowship with his people, have been encouraged. The path, though rough—sometimes lonely, is *a right path;*—and, though strait and narrow, a path of liberty.[3] The single eye and the humble heart, will preserve a steady, cheerful, and safe walk[4]—*Thou shalt run, and shalt not stumble.*[5]

And yet the animated exhortation to *take fast hold,* shews the struggle necessary to retain our principles. Feeble indeed is our *hold*—when connected *merely with* the excitement of novelty,[6] temporary convictions,[7] the restraint of education,[8] unestablished knowledge,[9] or the indulgence of sin.[10] The *fast hold of instruction* implies intensity of interest, determination of pursuit—"continuing in the things which we have heard and been assured of"—cleaving with purpose of heart unto the Lord.[11] "As Jacob detained the angel[12]—as the spouse *held fast hold* of her Beloved,"[13] —as the disciples "constrained the Saviour to abide with them"[14] —so—young Christian—*let not her go. Keep her* as the "man for joy" guarded his precious treasure.[15] So let thy heavenly treasure stand above every earthly blessing. Thus will it be *thy life.*[16] And while others "turn back, and walk no more" in the way, thine heart will turn to its only spring of happiness—"Lord! to whom shall I go? *Thou hast the words of eternal life.*"[17]

14. *Enter not into the path of the wicked, and go not in the way of evil men.* 15. *Avoid it, pass not by it, turn from it and pass away.* 16. *For they sleep not, except they have done mischief: and their sleep is taken away, unless they cause some to fall.* 17. *For they eat the bread of wickedness, and drink the wine of violence.*

1 Taylor in loco.
2 1 Tim. iv. 8, with chap. iii. 1, 2. Psalm xxxiv. 12—14. 1 Pet. iii. 10—12.
3 Psalm cxix. 32, 45.
4 Isa. xlviii. 17, 18. Matt. vi. 22.
5 Chap. iii 21—26. Comp. Hos. xiv. 9.
6 Matt. xiii. 20, 21.
7 Psalm lxxviii. 34—36; cvi. 12, 13.
8 2 Chron. xii. 1; xxiv. 2, 15—18.
9 Gal. iii. 1—4.
10 Mark vi. 18—26.
11 2 Tim. iii. 14. Acts xi. 23; ii. 42
12 Gen. xxxii. 26—29.
13 Can. iii. 4.
14 Luke xxiv. 28, 29.
15 Matt. xiii. 44.
16 Chap. iii. 18. Eccl. vii. 12.
17 John vi. 65—69

How often does fellowship with *the wicked* loosen the *fast hold of instruction!* *Their path* is so contrary to the way of *instruction*, that the very *entrance into it* is forsaking the way of God. The character of *the wicked* is here drawn in their Father's image—first sinners—then tempters. *Mischief* is their meat and drink.[1] 'To do evil is more proper and natural than to sleep, eat, or drink.'[2] With *sleepless* eagerness do they pursue their work,[3] caring little for any lengths of *violence*, so that *they do mischief, or cause some to fall.*[4] Judas with his midnight torches;[5] the early morning assemblage of the Jewish rulers;[6] the frenzied vow of the enemies of Paul;[7] and many a plot in after ages against the Church—all vividly portray this unwearied wickedness.

Yet if we be preserved from this undisguised malignity, what are all the allurements for every rank and circumstance of life, but the more subtle poison of the murderer? A light-minded young person pours into the ear of his companion—simple and inexperienced in the ways of sin—filthy conversation; or presents before him images of lasciviousness. What but a rooted principle of grace can save his unsuspecting victim? Or again—the venomous infidel, intent upon "spoiling"[8] his fellow creature of his most precious treasure, drops into his bosom the repetition of the first lie.[9] No principle appears to be given up; no fundamental doctrine denied; yet the foundation of an unwavering confidence is shaken to pieces. And are not these deeds of *mischief and violence*, malignant and destructive as the murderer's stab?

Is it not then mercy, that forbids needless intercourse with *the evil man?*[10] With a constitution prone to evil—when the alternative is—whether we shall shun or dare the danger—can we doubt our path? The whole Scripture is on the side of caution—to hazard nothing, except on a plain call of duty—tantamount to a call of Providence. Observe how the wise man heaps up his words—*Enter not into the path*—no—not so much as set thy foot into it. If some accident throws thee into it, *go not* on in it, *avoid it* with detestation.[11] *Pass not by it*, lest thou shouldest unwittingly turn in.[12] Not only *avoid it* when near; but avoid nearness to it.[13] It is like living in the atmosphere of contagion; taking up thy abode in a pest-house, in the midst of virulent and fatal disease. The earnest repetition of the warning shews at once the imminency of the danger, and the certainty of the injury. The world around us is the action of mind upon mind. We are continually, through the medium of intercourse, moulding ourselves

[1] Job xv. 16. Psalm xiv. 4. [2] Reformers' Notes.
[3] Job xxiv. 15, 16. Psalm xxxvi. 4. Mic. ii. 1.
[4] Chap. i. 10—14, 16; ii. 14; xxiv. 2. Psalm x. 8. Comp. 2 Peter ii. 14.
[5] John xviii. 3. [6] Ibid. v. 28. Luke xxii. 66.
[7] Acts xxiii. 12. Such a spirit is graphically described by the Classics—
Et si non aliqua nocuisses, mortuus esses.—Virgil, Ecl. iii. 15.
Ergo non aliter poterit dormiri; quibusdam
Somnum rixa facit.—Juvenal.
[8] Col. ii. 8. [9] Gen. iii. 3. [10] Eph. v. 11. [11] Leigh's Critica Sacra.
[12] Chap. v. 8. [13] See this danger in the case of Lot, Gen. xiii. 12; xiv. 12.

by other minds, and other minds by our own. Intercourse with the ungodly must therefore be fraught with fatal contamination.[1] The occasions, the company, the border, of temptation—all must be *avoided.*[2] It is far easier to shun the occasion of sin, than the sin, when the occasion presents it. There must be no tampering with it; no trial of strength, to see how far our resolutions will keep us. Let the examples of Lot[3]—Dinah[4]—Solomon[5]—Peter[6]—warn us—how far only the *entrance into the path of the wicked* may carry us; lengths, that we could never have contemplated in prospect without horror. Here and there some special miracle of preservation may be manifested. But no one comes out of *the path* without hurt or defilement;[7] and the general issue is an open door to ruin.[8] To pretend to dread sins without fearing temptation, is self-delusion. Satan has too nearly allied them for us to separate them. The evil company is loved—then the evil of the company.[9] To pray "not to be led into temptation;" yet not "watch that we enter not into it"[10]—is not this practically to contradict our prayers—to mock our God, by asking for what we do not heartily wish? "Come out then, and be separate"—is the voice of God. "Touch not the unclean thing."[11] "Watch and pray."[12] Walk with God and his people. Take care to *avoid* fellowship with them, who hinder thy fellowship with God.[13]

18. *The path of the just is as the shining light, that shineth more and more unto the perfect day.*

This is a fine picture of the Christian's *path* of light, in contrast with the dark and dangerous *path of the wicked.* It is not the feeble wasting light of a taper, nor the momentary blaze of the meteor; but the grand luminary of heaven, "coming out of his chamber, and rejoicing as a strong man to run his race,"[14] from earliest dawn to his noon-day glory. And a beautiful sight it is to see the soul thus rising out of darkness, beginning his course; rising higher and higher; taking in a wide circle; advancing onward with increasing brightness *unto the perfect day.* Knowledge—faith—love—holiness—irradiate every step. It is at first but a glimmering ray—the first dawn of day. But "following on"—the eye becomes more unveiled;[15] the heart more enlightened; the truth more vividly impressed upon the conscience; the "un-

[1] 1 Cor. xv. 33. Comp. Psalm cvi. 35. Chap. xxii. 24, 25.
[2] Chap. i. 10, 15. Gen. xxxix. 9, 10.
[3] Gen. xiii. 10—13.
[4] Ibid. xxxiv. 1, 2.
[5] 1 Kings xi. 1—5.
[6] Matt. xxvi. 58, 69—74.
[7] 2 Chron. xviii. 1—3; xix. 2; xx. 35—37.
[8] Chap. xiii. 20.
[9] Eusebius mentions a young man, whom St. John committed to the special charge of the Bishop of Ephesus; but who by evil company was drawn away to be a captain of robbers, until St. John went after him, and brought him back. B. iii. c. 23.—Augustine's recollection of his youthful theft was—'By myself alone I would not have gone. It was the company that I loved, who was with me in it.'—He adds,—'O nimis ir[illegible]ua amicitia.'—When they said—'Come, let us go, and do it, I was ashamed not to [illegible] as shameless as they.'—Confess. Lib. ii. 8, 9.
[10] Matt. xxvi. 41.
[11] 2 Cor. vi. 17. Comp. chap. ix. 6.
[12] Matt. xxv[illegible]
[13] Psalm cxix. 63, 114, 115, also xvii. 4; xxvi. 4, 5.
[14] Psalm xix. 5
[15] Hos. vi. 3. Comp. Mark viii. 22—25.

derstanding" more quick in "the fear of the Lord;" the taste more discerning between good and evil. Faith now becomes more strong in the Saviour's love, more simple in the promises of God. Subjection to the Redeemer's sceptre is more unreserved; love rises to a higher estimation, to a closer union with him—to a more intimate complacency in him. Experience may be confused. But light will clear away the mists. Practice in some points may be inconsistent. But, "beholding as in a glass the glory of the Lord, we are changed into his image from glory to glory, even as by the Spirit of the Lord."[1] Such is the godly man. Such is *his path.* The devout Nathanael was cheered with the promise of a brighter day.[2] The clouds upon the minds of the Apostles gradually melted away before a brighter sun.[3] The Eunuch and Cornelius sincerely seeking, rejoiced in the full sunshine of Gospel light.[4] The Thessalonian Church *shone more and more* with Christian graces.[5]

But is this *shining light* the picture of my *path?* There is no command given—"Sun—stand thou still."[6] Therefore it rebukes a stationary profession. It is a rising and advancing, not a declining, sun. Therefore it rebukes a backsliding state. It is not necessary that every thing should be perfect at once. There may be an occasional cloud, or even (as in the cases of David and Peter) a temporary eclipse. But when did the sun fail of carrying its early dawn *unto perfect day?* Be thankful then for "the day of small things. Despise it not."[7] But be not satisfied with it. Aim high, and you will reach nearer the mark. Religion must be *a shining* and progressive *light.* We must not mistake the beginning for the end of the course. We must not sit down at the entrance, and say to our soul—"Soul—take thine ease." Let us hasten on to *the perfect day*, when *the path of the just* shall be eternally consummated—when 'they shall come to full perfection—which is—when they shall be joined to their Head in the heavens.'[8] "Then shall they shine forth as the sun in the kingdom of their Father."[9] Their "sun shall no more go down; for the Lord shall be their everlasting light, and the days of their mourning shall be ended."[10]

19. *The way of the wicked is as darkness; they know not at what they stumble.*

The contrast is again repeated.[11] Each has his own way. *The*

[1] 2 Cor. iii. 18. Comp. Job xvii. 9. Psalm lxxxiv. 7.
[2] John i. 46—51.
[3] Mark vi. 52; x. 35; xvi. 14, with John xvi. 13. Acts. ii.
[4] Acts viii. 27—39, x.
[5] 1 Thess. i. 3. 2 Thess. i. 3.
[6] Jos. x. 12.
[7] Zech. iv. 10.
[8] Reformers' Notes. Comp. Diodati in loco.
[9] Matt. xiii. 43. Comp. Jud. v. 31.
[10] Isa. lx. 20. The LXX. version is very beautiful—'The ways of the righteous shine like the light; they grow and shine until the day be perfected.' Dr. Watts's Hymn on the Summer evening—written for the infant mind—but glowing to the finest taste—furnishes a most exquisite exposition of this verse,—

'How fine has the day been; how bright was the sun,' &c.

[11] See the same contrast drawn by our Lord, Matt. vi. 22, 23.—Schultens considers the original to express *increasing darkness*—thus answering to the *increasing light* of the opposite path. Comp. Job xv. 23.

path of the just is glowing light and joy. *The way of the wicked is darkness*—without direction, comfort, safety, or peace—till "his feet at last stumble on the dark mountains"—till he falls into "the blackness of darkness forever."[1] His *way* is not only dark—but *as darkness*—a compound of ignorance, error, sin, and misery. The love of sin "rebels against the light."[2] The *darkness* is wilful, and therefore accountable. There is no *stumbling in the path of the just.* So far as he is upright, the Lord keeps him.[3] *The wicked* go on "groping as if they had no eyes.;"[4] hurrying on blindly into misery, that they can neither foresee nor avoid.[5] *They know not at what they stumble.* Oh! if they did, would they not startle, and shrink back? For *they stumble* on the very foundation of the gospel; making the rock of salvation the rock of offence.[6] Would they but listen to the merciful warning of their Lord!—"Yet a little time the light is with you, walk while ye have the light, lest darkness come upon you: *for he that walketh in darkness knoweth not whither he goeth.*"[7]

20. *My son, attend to my words: incline thine ear unto my sayings.* 21. *Let them not depart from thine eyes; keep them in the midst of thine heart.* 22. *For they are life unto those that find them, and health to all their flesh.*

These repeated injunctions[8] are an admirable pattern to the Christian Parent or Minister. The desire of wisdom—the first step in the path—is encouraged. The means of obtaining it, and the privilege when obtained, are pointed out. Eye then the treasury of wisdom habitually. A neglected Bible is the melancholy proof of an heart "alienated from God." For how can we have a spark of love to him, if that Book, which is the full manifestation of his glory, be despised? And yet a superficial acquaintance with it is of no avail. If our ears were bored to the door of the sanctuary; *if the words never departed from our eyes;* yet, except they were *kept in the heart,* our religion would be a notion, not a principle; speculative, not practical: conviction, not love. Nor even here must they possess the mere threshold. Let *that* be for the world; let the word be *kept in the midst of the heart.* Here only can it be operative;[9] "for out of the heart are the issues of life."[10] Here it becomes lively and substantial truth. Here then let a home be made for it[11]— a consecrated sanctuary in the most honored chambers—*in the midst of the heart.* This inhabitation of the word is a covenant promise, the test of our interest in the Lord and in his people.[12]

This *keeping of the word* will be *life to those that find it.*[13] Vig

[1] Jer. xiii. 16. Jude 13. Comp. Job xviii. 5, 6, 18.
[2] Job xxiv. 13. John iii. 19. Comp. Isa. v. 20.
[3] Verse 12; iii. 23. Psalm xci. 11, 12.
[4] Isa. lix. 10.
[5] Job v. 14; xii. 25. Jer. xxiii. 12. Zeph. i. 17.
[6] Rom. ix. 32, 33. 1 Pet. ii. 8.
[7] John xii. 35, 36.
[8] Chap. iii. 1; v. 1; vi. 20, 21; xxii. 17.
[9] Chap. xxiii. 26. Psalm xl. 8; cxix. 11.
[10] Verse 23.
[11] Ενοικείτω εν υμῖν. Col. iii. 16.
[12] Jer. xxxi. 33.
[13] Verses 4, 10, 13; iii. 18

orous and *healthy* will be the soul,[1] that feeds upon this heavenly manna. We shall not then bear our religion as our cross, as a cumbrous appendage. We shall not drag on in Christian duties as our chain. Godliness will be to us an element of joy. The functions will be free and lively. The spirit will feel a vital glow. The mind will be enriched with Divine wisdom. The heart will be established with gospel grace.

23. *Keep thy heart with all diligence* (above all keeping, Marg.); *for out of it are the issues of life.* 24. *Put away from thee a froward mouth, and perverse lips put far from thee. Let thine eyes look right on, and let thine eyelids look straight before thee.* 26. *Ponder the path of thy feet, and let all thy ways be established,* (all thy ways shall be ordered aright, Marg.) 27. *Turn not to the right hand nor to the left: remove thy foot from evil.*

Invaluable are these rules as our safeguard. Assaulted as we are at every point, every inlet of sin must be strongly guarded—*the heart—the mouth—the eye—the feet.*

First—*the heart*—the citadel of man[2]—the seat of his dearest treasure. It is fearful to think of its many watchful and subtle assailants. Let it be closely garrisoned. Let the sentinel be never sleeping on his post. "Take heed to thy way, and *keep thy soul diligently.*"[3] Can then I *keep my own heart?* Certainly not. But, though it be God's work, it is man's agency. Our efforts are his instrumentality. He implants an active principle, and sustains the unceasing exercise.[4] The first act of conscious faith will be to "commit the *keeping of the heart* to our faithful Creator."[5] Then in his strength and guidance diligently improve all the means of preservation. Watch unto prayer. Cherish a humble dependent spirit. Live in the atmosphere of the word of God. Resist the admittance of an evil world, even in its most plausible forms.[6] Here lies the conflict to the end. 'The greatest difficulty in conversion is to win the heart to God, and after conversion to keep it with him.'[7] 'What is there'—asks Mede—'that will not entice and allure so fickle a thing as the heart from God?'[8]

Above all keeping—exhorts the wise man—*keep thine heart.* Here Satan keeps—here therefore must we keep—special watch. If the citadel be taken, the whole town must surrender. If the heart be seized, the whole man—the affections, desires, motives, pursuits—all will be yielded up. The heart is the vital part of the body; a wound here is instant death. Thus spiritually as well as naturally—*out of the heart are the issues of life.* It is the great vital spring of the soul—the fountain of actions—the centre and the seat of principle,[9] both of sin and of holiness.[10] The natural heart is a fountain of poison.[11] The purified heart is "a well of living water."[12] As is the fountain, so must be the streams. As

[1] Chap. iii. 8.
[2] Albert Schulten's Comment in Prov. 4to. 1748.
[3] Deut. iv. 9.
[4] Comp. Phil. ii. 12, 13. Jude 24 with 21.
[5] 1 Pet. iv. 19. Comp. Ps. xxv. 20.
[6] Jud. viii. 22, 23. 2 Kings v. 5, 16.
[7] Flavel's Saint Indeed,—a searching and valuable Treatise.
[8] See his valuable sermon on this text.
[9] Schultens in loco.
[10] Matt. xii. 34, 35.
[11] Matt. xv. 19.
[12] John iv. 14. Comp. chap. xiv. 14

is the heart, so must be *the mouth—the eyes—the feet.* Therefore *above all keeping—keep thine heart.* Guard the fountain—as they keep the precious wells of the east[1]—lest the waters be poisoned.

Not less necessary is it to keep the outlets of sin![2] What a world of evil does the heart pour out from *the froward mouth!*[3] Commit therefore both heart and mouth to Divine discipline.[4] Then let prayer and faith be the practical principles of Christian watchfulness. Not only shun—but *put away*—yea—*far from thee—the perverse lips.* Their evil—be it remembered—extends beyond ourselves; so that even should the peace-speaking blood speak peace to ourselves, still will remain the painful sense of injury to our fellow-creatures—perhaps without remedy.

Next to the heart and mouth—keep thine eyes—"the light of the body"[5]—the directive faculty of the soul, yet too often a most dangerous inlet to sin.[6] Therefore like Job—"make a covenant with them."[7] Place them under heavenly restraint.[8] *Let them look right on—straight before us.* Had Eve done so, she would have looked on the command of her God, not on the forbidden tree.[9] Had Lot's wife looked *straight before*, instead of "behind her," she would, like her husband, have been a monument of mercy.[10] Achan was ruined by neglecting this rule of wisdom.[11] David's example may warn the holiest men in the world to have a watchful jealousy.[12] In asking the way to Zion, be sure that your "*faces are thitherward.*"[13] Take the racer's motto, "This one thing I do"—Eye the mark, and press onward to it.[14]

Lastly, *keep your feet.* Oh! has not experience, no less than Scripture, shewn your need of a circumspect walk?[15] Snares are laid out for every path—yea for every step in your path; for your meat, your drink, your calling—perhaps more than all—for the service of God. What deep *pondering* should there be in a path so beset with danger! Every step should be carefully weighed.[16] Joseph *pondered*, and thereby *established his way.*[17] Peter, neglecting to *ponder*, was fearfully sifted.[18] David also, looking at the trial of the path, instead of *pondering* its direction, brought shame upon himself;[19] like the trouble, which Christian made for himself in the smooth exchange of Bye-path meadow for the rough and strait road.

Here then is the voice of wisdom. Beware of mistaking presumption for faith—temptations for Providential appointments. Never forsake a plain for a doubtful command.[20] Estimate every step by its conformity to the known will of God. Dare not to ad-

[1] Gen. xxvi. 18—21. [2] Chap. xiii. 3. [3] Jam. iii. 5, 6.
[4] Psalm xix. 13; cxli. 3, 4. [5] Matt. vi. 22.
[6] Gen. vi. 2; xxxiv. 1, 2; xxxix. 7. Matt. v. 28. 2 Pet. ii. 14. [7] Matt. xxxi. 1
[8] Psalm cxix. 37. [9] Gen. iii. 3—6. [10] Ibid. xix. 17, 26. [11] Jos. vii. 21.
[12] 2 Sam. xi. 2. Mede, ut supra. [13] Jer. l. 5. [14] Phil. iii. 12—14.
[15] Eph. v. 15. [16] Gen. xxiv. 5. Psalm xxxix. 1. Dan. i. 8; vi. 3, 4.
[17] Gen. xxxix. 9, 10. Comp. verses 14, 15. [18] Matt. xxvi. 58, 69—75.
[19] 1 Sam. xxvii—xxix. [20] 1 Kings xiii. 18—22.

vance one step without God. *In his path* you may fearlessly "tread upon the lion and adder."[1] But who shall venture into a path of his own choosing without a wound? See that "your feet are straight" like those of the Cherubim.[2] "The pleasures of sin" lie *on the right hand and on the left. The eyes* therefore, *looking right on*, escape the sight. *The pondering foot is established* in steady perseverance; and by marking small deviations,[3] and never turning out of the straight path to avoid a cross—*is removed from evil.*

May we all have grace and wisdom to ponder these sound practical rules! The man of God must only have one standard.[4] He must "know no man after the flesh."[5] He must often put aside the Church no less than the world, that he may listen more closely to the command—*walk before me.*[6] He must discern and crush the first motions of the scorpion's brood; guarding every avenue of sin—the senses—the memory—the imagination--the touch—the taste. He must walk by the straight rule of the gospel; else will he not only bring discomfort upon himself, but stumbling to the Church.[7] A single eye, steadily fixed upon the One Object, will make the path luminous.[8] *Straight-forward* progress will insure prosperity.[9] Keeping the middle path, and daily lifting up the voice for restraint and guidance.[10]

"Thine ears shall hear the word behind thee, saying—This is the way; walk ye in it—when ye turn to the right hand, and when ye turn to the left."[11]

CHAPTER V.

1. *My son, attend unto my wisdom, and bow thine ear to my understanding:* 2. *That thou mayest regard discretion, and that thy lips may keep knowledge.* 3. *For the lips of a strange woman drop as an honeycomb, and her mouth is smoother than oil:* 4. *But her end is bitter as wormwood, sharp as a two-edged sword.* 5. *Her feet go down to death; her steps take hold on hell.* 6. *Lest thou shouldest ponder the path of life, her ways are moveable, that thou canst not know them.* 7. *Hear me now, therefore, O ye children, and depart not from the words of my mouth.* 8. *Remove thy way from her, and come not near the door of her house:* 9. *Lest thou give thine honor unto others, and thy years unto the cruel:* 10. *Lest strangers be filled with thy wealth: and thy labors be in the house of a stranger;* 11. *And*

[1] Psalm xci. 11—13.
[2] Ezek. i. 7—9. Comp. Heb. xii. 13. Nearly the LXX. translation of the last clause of verse 26.
[3] See Ecclus. xix. 1. [4] Isa. viii. 20. [5] 2 Cor. v. 16.
[6] Gen. xvii. 1. [7] Gal. ii. 11—14. [8] Matt. vi. 22.
[9] Deut. xvii. 20. Jos. i. 7, 8. [10] Psalm cxix. 37; cxliii. 8—10.
[11] Isa. xxx. 21. The LXX. and Vulgate adds here—'For God knows the right path on the right hand. But those on the left are perverted. But he shall make thy ways, and advance thy steps in grace.' Geier remarks—'We have no ear for these words, as not belonging to the holy fountain. We leave them to the Papists.'

thou mourn at the last, when thy flesh and thy body are consumed, 12. *And say, How have I hated instruction, and my heart despised reproof;* 13. *And have not obeyed the voice of my teachers, nor inclined mine ear to them that instructed me!* 14. *I was almost in all evil in the midst of the congregation and assembly.*

PONDER this chapter—ye that know not the poison and corruption of fleshly lusts. Painful experience[1] had given the wise man *wisdom and understanding.* Therefore *attend to it* with fear and trembling. Man's own strength—the restraints of education or of self-discipline are powerless, as the green withes to bind the giant.[2] Engrafted wisdom is the only effectual safeguard. This heavenly influence teaches us to *regard discretion* for the covering of our souls, and *to keep knowledge* for the warning of our fellow-sinners.[3]

The extreme plausibility of the temptation is our call to *attention.* The deluded victim only sees the present gratification; only tastes, or expects to taste, *the honeycomb;* only hears the *wily smoothness* of the charmer's voice.[4] But never is the beginning so sweet, as the end is *bitter.* God shews *the wormwood; the two-edged sword;*[5] her path of death; every step *taking hold of hell,* as if invading it with a high hand, grasping it as her home.[6] One feature of the tempter's wiliness is most remarkable. She winds herself in a thousand *moveable ways,* to meet the varying humors and circumstances.[7] She works upon every weakness; seizes every unguarded moment—all this with one deeply hidden object —*lest thou should ponder the path of life.* The checks of conscience must be diverted. No time must be given for reflection. The intrusion of one serious thought might break the spell, and open the way of escape.[8]

Can we wonder then at the earnestness of parental anxiety, forcing back *the children* playing on the brink of a precipice. *Hear now—O ye children?* We mean no austere restraint upon youthful pleasures. Only avoid the tempter's touch—her word—even her look. *Remove thy way far from her.* Not only go not into her—but—such is the contagion—*come not near the door.*[9] To thrust ourselves into temptation, is to throw ourselves out of God's protection. The snare as one approaches becomes more enticing. The voice of wisdom therefore is—"*Flee youthful lusts.*"

The loss of *honor,*[10] taking the crown from the victim's head;[11] *years given to the cruel* mockers of his misery;[12] the waste of the family wealth;[13] servitude *in a stranger's house;*[14] *consumption—*

[1] 1 Kings xi. 1—8. Eccl. vii. 26. [2] Jud. xvi. 9.
[3] Chap. ii. 10, 11, 16; vi. 20, 24; vii. 1—5. Psalm xvii. 4; cxix. 9, 11.
[4] Chap. ii. 16; vi. 24; vii. 21. [5] Comp. Ps. lv. 21.
[6] Schultens in loco. Chap. ii. 18; vii. 27; ix. 18. 1 Cor. vi. 9, 18. Rev. xxi. 8.
[7] Chap. vi. 12, 13; vii. 12. [8] See Psalm cxix. 59. Ez. xviii. 28. Luke xv. 17.
[9] Comp. chap. iv. 14, 15; vi. 27, 28.
[10] Chap. vi. 32, 33. Gen. xxxviii. 23—26. [11] 2 Sam. xii. 14; xiii. 13. Neh. xiii. 26.
[12] Chap vi. 26; xxx. 3. Jud. xvi. 18—20.
[13] Chap. vi. 26, 35. Job xxxi. 12. Hos. vii. 9. Luke xv. 13, 30.
[14] Luke xv. 15, 16.

slowly bringing *the body* to the grave[1]—all is the bitter fruit of the neglected warning. Add to this the voice of conscience *at the last*, telling of slighted privileges, stifled convictions, abused knowledge. And will not this be the sting of thousands instructed in our schools, or the children of godly parents—now *despising the reproofs* of God, *and the voice of these teachers*, proclaiming their shame openly; perhaps making Christian *assemblies* the scenes *of almost all evil?*[2]

Such is the picture of sin—its "pleasure but for a season," "its wages death eternal."[3] Every sin unrepented here will bring its perpetual torment in eternity. Impenitence does not put away its sorrow. It only delays it to *mourn at the last*, when mercy shall have fled away forever,[4] and nothing will remain, but the piercing cry of the accusing conscience—"Son! remember."[5] There are no infidels in eternity, and but few on a death-bed. Sinner—*the path of life* is now open to thee. *Ponder* it anxiously—prayerfully. The light of the word, and the teaching of the Spirit guide thee to it.

15. *Drink waters out of thine own cistern, and running waters out of thine own well.* 16. *Let thy fountains be dispersed abroad, and rivers of waters in the streets.* 17. *Let them be only thine own, and not strangers, with thee.* 18. *Let thy fountain be blessed: and rejoice with the wife of thy youth.* 19. *Let her be as the loving hind and pleasant roe; let her breasts satisfy thee at all times; and be thou ravished always with* (err thou always in.[6] Marg.) *her love.*

A restless dissatisfaction with our present blessings cherishes the lust for forbidden pleasures. Where contentment is not found at home—*drinking out of our own cistern*, it will not be found abroad. Thus conjugal love—the greatest earthly blessing—is the Divine remedy against incontinence.[7] 'First—choose thy love; then love thy choice.'[8] Quench thy thirst *out of thine own*, and lust not after thy neighbor's, *well.*[9] 'Enjoy thou the lawful delights and contentments of thine own wife.'[10] Let the streams of a happy issue derived from thee, as little *fountains*, or springs from *the fountain*[11] —*be dispersed abroad*, fertilizing *the streets*[12] with their godly influence—children whom thou knowest to be *thine own*, and canst acknowledge without shame.[13] *Rejoice with the wife of thy youth.*[14]

[1] 1 Cor. vi. 18.
[2] Num. xxv. 6, 7. Ezek. viii. 5—16.
[3] Heb. xi. 25. Rom. vi. 23.
[4] Chap. i. 24—30.
[5] Luke xvi. 25.
[6] *Err.* The primary meaning of the Heb. is to expatiate—luxuriate—run wild. Hence 'to give a loose, indulge, or lose oneself in love.'—"*In errare*, tanquam sui oblitum, et amore quasi vagari."—Parkhurst.
[7] 1 Cor. vii. 2, 36. See the Marriage Service.
[8] Henry Smith's Sermons. 4to. 1611—1614.
[9] Ex. xx. 17. 2 Sam. xi. 2, 3. The beauty of the figure is illustrated from the circumstance, that the houses of the East appear each to have had their own cisterns. 2 Kings xviii. 31.
[10] Bishop Hall.
[11] Comp. Num. xxiv. 7. Deut. xxxiii. 28. Psalm lxviii. 29. Isa. xlviii. 1.
[12] Comp. Zech. viii. 5.
[13] Psalm cxxvii. 3—5; cxxviii. 13.
[14] Deut. xxiv. 5. Eccl. ix 9.

Receive her as the gracious gift of thy God.[1] Cherish her, not with a sensual, doting, passion, but, as *the loving hind and pleasant roe,*[2] with gentleness and familiarity.[3] Count thyself most happy, as *ravished with her love.* Never *err* in giving liberty to thy passion, save in her society. It is not the having, but *the loving* of, the wife, that covers the soul. A man chained to an uncongenial wife is in imminent temptation. It is when she is *as the hind and the roe,* that the pleasures of lawful love preserve from lust—pleasures without a sting—yes truly—shadowing out the great mystery; "loving and cherishing our own flesh, even as the Lord the church."[4]

20. *And why wilt thou, my son, be ravished with a strange woman, and embrace the bosom of a stranger?* 21. *For the ways of man are before the eyes of the Lord, and he pondereth all his goings.* 22. *His own iniquities shall take the wicked himself, and he shall be holden with the cords of his sins.* 23. *He shall die without instruction; and in the greatness of his folly he shall go astray.*

With such a view of the ruinous pleasures of lust,[5] and the holy delight of God's ordinances;[6] surely, if the sinner were not stupified, would he leave the pure *fountain* for the poisoned spring? Would he slight the "honorable" state of marriage,[7] to *embrace the bosom of a stranger*—'loveless—joyless—unendeared?' Would not the thought—that *the ways of man are before the Lord*—arrest him in his course?[8] But no. Practical atheism is the root of human depravity.[9] The eye of man—even of a child—is a check upon him.[10] But the thought of an all-seing God—even if it enters his mind[11]—inspires no alarm, conviction, or restraint. Oh! if men would but read—would but *believe*—their Bibles, how would this solemn truth—*he pondereth all his goings*—flash upon their consciences! Not only does he see and mark them as the Omniscient God;[12] but *he ponders them* as the just Judge.[13] Not one is hidden from his piercing eye.[14] "He will bring every secret thing to judgment."[15] He "will be a swift witness against the adulterers." No unclean person shall enter into his kingdom.[16]

But if no regard to reason, or to the All-seeing eye, will restrain the sinner, let him think of the trouble that he is bringing upon himself. He may go on awhile without trouble. God needs no chains or prison to bring him under his hand. Wherever he goes, *his sins*

[1] Chap. xix. 14. [2] Gen. xxiv. 67.

[3] Comp. 2 Sam. xii. 3. The *hind and the roe* were objects of special delight (Can. ii. 17; iii. 5.) and were treated with most tender endearment—a beautiful picture of the lively delight, which the wife naturally engages; relaxing in her society from severer duties, and taking the liveliest pleasure in her company. As Bishop Davenant beautifully observes—'Abroad he may consider himself as tossing in the waves, but at home with his wife, in repose, as in a desired haven.'—In Col. iii. 19.

[4] Eph. v. 25, 29. [5] Verses 9—11. [6] Verses 15—19. [7] Heb. xiii. 4.

[8] Job xxxiv. 21, 22. Psalm xciv. 6—9. Jer. xiii. 25—27; xvi. 17. Hos. vii. 2. See some striking thoughts in Mede's Sermon on iv. 23.

[9] Psalm xiv. 1—3. [10] Job xxiv. 15. Isa. xxix. 15.

[11] Psalm x. 4. [12] Ibid. cxxv. 3. Job xxxi. 4. Psalm cxxix. 1—4.

[13] Chap. xvi. 2. 1 Sam. ii. 3. Dan. v. 27. [14] Heb. iv. 13. [15] Ecc. xii. 14

[16] Mal. iii. 5. Eph. v. 5.

go with him, *as cords to hold him* for judgment.[1] Does he think that he can give them up when he pleases? Repetition forms the habit. The habit becomes a ruling principle. 'Every lust deals with him, as Delilah with Samson—not only robs him of his strength, but leaves him fast bound.'[2] Shutting his eyes against the light—*he dies without instruction*[3]—the victim of his own wil ful delusion—*the greatness of his folly leading him astray*—to perdition.[4]

But is there no remedy for this deadly curse? Thanks be to God, cleansing is provided for the impure;[5] "deliverance is proclaimed to the captive."[6] Blessed Saviour! cleanse the leper in thy precious fountain. Perform thy mighty commission. Set the captive free.

CHAPTER VI.

1. *My son, if thou be surety for thy friend, if thou hast stricken thy hand with a stranger,* 2. *Thou art snared with the words of thy mouth, thou art taken with the words of thy mouth.* 3. *Do this now, my son, and deliver thyself, when thou art come into the hand of thy friend; go, humble thyself, and make sure* (so shalt thou prevail with, Marg.) *thy friend.* 4. *Give not sleep to thine eyes, nor slumber to thine eyelids.* 5. *Deliver thyself as a roe from the hand of the hunter, and as a bird from the hand of the fowler.*

THE *son* has just been warned against the deadly wound of a stranger. He is now cautioned against a hurt from an imprudent friend. So graciously has our God made his book, not only our guide to heaven, but the directory of our common life. Yet we must often take its wise rules with some restriction. We are here earnestly warned against *suretyship*. But in some cases it is plainly allowed and approved.[7] "A man that hath friends must shew himself friendly."[8] And the passing of our word, or giving a bond, may be an act of prudent friendship, and of solid and permanent advantage. The caution is evidently directed against rash engagements,[9] to which the young and inexperienced are especially exposed; *striking hands* (the usual mode of plighting faith)[10] in an

[1] Chap. xi. 3, 5, 6; xxix. 6. 1 Sam. xxviii. 5, 20.

[2] Abp. Tillotson quoted in a valuable Commentary. By Rev. B. E. Nichols. 12mo. 1842. Jud. xvi. 19—21. 'Thus I,'—said Augustine—adverting to this hateful sin—'delighted with the disease of the flesh, and with the deadly sweetness of it, drew my shackles along with me, much afraid to have them knocked off; and as if my wound had been too hard rubbed by it, I put back my friend's good persuasions, as it were the hand of one that would unchain me.'—Confess. book vi. c. 12.

[3] Verse 12; Chap. i. 29; x. 21. Job iv. 21; xxxvi. 12. Hos. xv. 14, 17.

[4] 2 Peter ii. 14, 15.

[5] Zech. xiii. 1. 1 Cor. vi. 11.

[6] Isa. lxi. 1.

[7] Reuben and Judah for Benjamin. Gen. xlii. 37; xliii. 9; xliv. 32, 33. Paul for Onesimus. Philem. 18, 19.

[8] Chap. xviii. 24.

[9] Comp. also chap. xi. 15; xvii. 18; xx. 16; xxii. 26, 27.

[10] Chap. xvii. 18; xxii. 26. Job xvii. 3.

unguarded moment, and *snared* and *taken by the words of thy mouth*, by entering into virtual promises, without knowing how far they were pledged, or what might be the issue. Christian prudence will keep us clear from such engagements, which bring distress upon our families, dishonor upon our name, and reproach upon our religion.[1] While the "good man sheweth favor, and lendeth, he must guide his affairs with discretion;"[2] however grating it may be to incur the suspicion of unkindness. If, however, by any inconsiderate bond thou hast *come into the hand of thy friend;* the instant duty is, to *humble thyself, and make sure thy friend*—if *thou canst prevail with* him to answer for himself; and give thyself no rest, till, *as the roe and the hind*, thou be disentangled from the snare.

Our God, while he warns us against *suretyship*, has taken it upon himself. Praised be his name! He has given his word—his bond—yea—his blood—for sinners—a security, that no powers of hell can shake.

6. *Go to the ant, thou sluggard; consider her ways, and be wise:* 7. *Which having no guide, overseer, or ruler,* 8. *Provideth her meat in the summer, and gathereth her food in the harvest.* 9. *How long wilt thou sleep, O sluggard? when wilt thou arise out of thy sleep?* 10. *Yet a little more sleep, a little more slumber, a little folding of the hands to sleep:* 11. *So shall thy poverty come as one that travelleth, and thy want as an armed man.*

'It is a shame'—said the heathen philosopher—'not to learn morals from the small animals.'[3] Yet what a proof is it of the degradation of the fall, that "man, created in the image of God," and made wiser than the creation[4] should be sent—as here—to this insignificant school for instruction! *The ant, having no guide*, to direct her work, no *overseer* to inspect her, *or ruler* to call her to account;[5] yet *gathereth* with diligent foresight the *summer and harvest* store for her winter need.[6] Let *the sluggard consider her ways and be wise.* He sleeps over his work, and if for a moment, half-startled by some rousing call—still pleads for *a little more sleep, and folds his hands to sleep.* Present ease and freedom from trouble is all he calculates on—all he provides for. The future he carefully keeps out of sight, to be provided for, like the present, when it comes. Thus life runs to waste. *Poverty comes*

[1] Comp. Ecclus. viii. 13. [2] Psalm cxii. 5.
[3] Pudeat ab exiquis animalibus non trahere mores. Seneca De clementiâ. Lib. i.
[4] Gen. i. 26. Job xxxv. 11.
[5] Comp. Chap. xxx. 27, and contrast Ex. v. 13, 14. 1 Kings v. 16.
[6] Chap. x. 5; xxx. 25. The heathen moralist sends us to the same pattern of diligence—

'Exemplo tibi sit magni formica laboris,' &c.—Hor. Sat. i. 32.

See also Virgil's exquisite picture. Æn. iv. 302, &c. The hoarding spirit of the ants, though attested by numerous writers and naturalists, does not characterize these known to us; though the habits of the species in a warmer climate would probably widely differ from our own. Some however have thought, that Solomon only refers to her wisdom and prudence in preparing suitable food in summer and harvest, when it is most plentiful. See Kirby and Spence's Entomology, ii. 46.

step by step *as one that travelleth, and, like an armed man,* with irresistible violence.[1]

Perhaps he perverts his Master's word to excuse his sloth. But if we are to "take no *anxious* thought for the morrow," (his true meaning)[2] are we to take none at all? Care is a duty, a parental obligation,[3] and therefore a component part of Godliness.[4] Carefulness is a sin[5]—a needless burden to ourselves; an unworthy distrust of God.[6] Prudent care is distinct from covetousness. The stores of the ant were, not the hoarding for the distant indulgence, but the supply for immediate necessity. The diligent use of providential means is to the honor of God.[7]

But much more loudly would we call to the spiritual *sluggard.* Thou, that art sleeping away the opportunities of grace; not "striving to enter in at the strait gate;"[8] taking thy salvation for granted; hoping that thou shalt "reap that which thou hast not sown, and gather where thou hast not strawed,"[9]—*Go to the ant, thou sluggard; consider her ways and be wise.* Improve—after this pattern—*the summer and harvest* season—the time of youth—the present—perhaps the only—moment. *The ant hath no guide.* How many guides have you!—conscience—the Bible—ministers![10] *She has no overseer.* You are living before Him, whose "eyes are as a flame of fire."[11] *She has no ruler* calling her to account. "Every one of us must give account of himself unto God."[12] *How long then, wilt thou sleep, O sluggard,* on the brink of eternity? "Awake, thou that sleepest, and Christ shall give thee light."[13] Take heed of passing by conviction. The intended work of to-morrow is a delusion. A thousand such to-morrows there may be; and yet thou mayest be found at last perishing in thy *poverty,* and the king of terror will *come as an armed man* to summon thee to judgment.

Christian! Look at sloth—not as an infirmity, but as a sin, affecting the whole man; growing upon us with unperceived power; and therefore needing incessant watchfulness. Allow it no rest, no time to root itself. Resist it in all its forms—bodily, mental, spiritual: indulgence of sleep and appetite: self-pleasing, in all its subtle and plausible workings. Live by rule. Have your time strictly arranged. Be employed in early work for God. Store the mind with useful knowledge; ever reserving the first place for an industrious and prayerful study of the book of God.

[1] Chap. x. 4; xiii. 4; xix. 15, 24; xx. 4; xxi. 25; xxiv. 33, 34.

[2] Μεριμνάω. Matt. vi. 34.—'*Soliciti et anxie cogito;* at plus est solicitum esse, quam cogitare, as Erasmus notices, and that of Tully confirms. Solicitudo est ægritudo cum cogitatione. The root of the word expresses the dividing of the mind into divers thoughts.'—Leigh's Critica Sacra. Comp. Phil. iv. 6.

[3] 2 Cor. xii. 14. Comp. Gen. xxx. 30; xli. 33.

[4] 1 Tim. v. 8. Our Lord had a bag for the provision of his family. John xiii. 29.

[5] Luke x. 41. 1 Cor. vii. 32. [6] Matt. vi. 25—33. [7] Chap. x. 5; xxiv. 27.

[8] Luke xiii. 24. [9] Matt. xxv. 24.

[10] Job xxxii. 8. Psalm cxix. 105. Mal. ii. 7.

[11] Chap. xv. 3. Rev. i. 14; ii. 18. [12] Rom. xiv. 12.

[13] Eph. v. 14.

"Mortify" this baneful lust "through the Divine Spirit;"[1] drawing all your motives from the death,[2] the life,[3] the rules of Christ.[4] This will ensure victory, and how enriching will be the spoil!

12. *A naughty person, a wicked man, walketh with a froward mouth.* 13. *He winketh with his eyes, he speaketh with his feet, he teacheth with his fingers;* 14. *Frowardness is in his heart, he deviseth mischief continually; he seweth discord.* 15. *Therefore shall his calamity come suddenly; suddenly shall he be broken without remedy.*

What a contrast between the inactivity of the sluggard and the unwearied diligence of *the naughty person!* This man of Belial[5]—as if his *froward mouth*—itself "a world of iniquity"[6]—could not give sufficient scope for his malice, makes every member—*eyes—feet and fingers*—vocal and significant[7]—an active "instrument of unrighteousness."[8] These, however, are only the external manifestations. Deep within lies the laboratory of evil—"the chambers of imagery," teeming with "greater and yet greater abominations."[9] *Frowardness*[10] *is in the heart.* Here is the restless *devising of mischief,*[11] *sowing discord* instead of unity and love.[12] Such a pest to society brings on himself his own ruin—*suddenly and without remedy.*

The sight of this all-pervading power of sin is truly affecting. How utterly powerless is any remedy, save that, involved in the solemn declaration—"Ye must be born again!"[13]

16. *These six things doth the Lord hate; yea, seven are an abomination unto him:* (of his soul, Marg.) 17. *A proud look, a lying tongue, and hands that shed innocent blood,* 18. *An heart that deviseth wicked imaginations, feet that be swift in running to mischief,* 19. *A false witness that speaketh lies, and he that soweth discord among brethren.*

Man conceives of God in his heart as "such a one as himself,"[14] looking with indifference at sin. Here therefore Solomon names *six—yea—seven*[15] *abominations* (most of them mentioned in the preceding list) *which the Lord hateth,—a proud look,*[16] *a lying tongue,*[17] *a blood-stained hand.*[18] And, lest we should think, that he "looketh only on the outward appearance"—*the heart*—active in *devising wickedness*[19] is brought out, and its ready organ—*the*

[1] Rom. viii. 13. [2] Ibid. vi. 6. [3] Mark i. 32—35.
[4] Luke ix. 23. Rom. xiii. 11—14. [5] Heb. [6] Jam. iii. 6. [7] Isa. iii. 16.
[8] Chap. x. 10. Rom. vi. 13—19. [9] Ezek. viii. 8—15. Matt. xv. 19.
[10] 'Frowardnesses,' Heb. See Poole's Synopsis—not one but many—the heart so filled with them, that the vessel cannot hold more. Gen. vi. 5. Acts. xiii. 10.
[11] Psalm x. 7—9; xxxvi. 2—4. Comp. the striking figure, Hos. viii. 6. Chap. xvi. 28. Psalm lii. 3.
[12] Chap. x. 12. [13] John iii. 7. Comp. Titus iii. 3—5.
[14] Psalm l. 21. [15] Comp. chap. xxx. 15, 18.
[16] Chap. viii. 13; xxx. 13. Psalm xviii. 27. Isa. ii. 12. Jer. l. 31—the examples of Pharoah—Ex. ix. 16. Haman—Esth. vii. 10. Nebuchadnezzar—Dan. iv. 28—33. Herod—Acts xii. 21—23.
[17] Chap. xii. 22. Psalm v. 6. Rev. xxi. 8. Gehazi—2 Kings v. 25—27. Ananias and Sapphira—Acts v. 1—10.
[18] Gen. ix. 6. Can. iv. 8—12. Manasseh—2 Kings xxi. 15, 16. Specially the murderers of his dear Son—Matt. xxiii. 31—38.
[19] Ahithophel—2 Sam. xvi. 20—23; xvii. 23. Mic. ii. 1. 2 Pet. ii. 14.

feet swift in running to mischief.[1] How *hateful* also is *the false witness,*[2] surely reserved by him for judgment![3] Let the self-willed separatist remember the double stamp[4] upon him *that soweth discord among brethren.* If the heavenly "dew descends upon the brethren that dwell together in unity,"[5] a withering blast will fall on those, who, mistaking prejudice for principle, "cause divisions" for their own selfish ends.[6] Fearful is the Lord's mark upon them—"sensual, having not the Spirit."[7] If we cannot attain unity of opinion—"*perfectly* joined together in the same mind, and in the same judgment;"[8] at least let us cultivate unity of spirit—"Whereto we have already attained, let us walk by the same rule; let us mind the same thing."[9]

20. *My son, keep thy father's commandment, and forsake not the law of thy mother:* 21. *Bind them continually upon thine heart, and tie them about thy neck.* 22. *When thou goest, it shall lead thee; when thou sleepest, it shall keep thee; and when thou awakest, it shall talk with thee.* 23. *For the commandment is a lamp; and the law is light; and reproofs of instruction are the way of life:* 24. *To keep thee from the evil woman,*[10] *from the flattery of the tongue of a strange woman.*

The authority of parental instruction is again enforced[11]—God never intended young people to be independent of their parents. Instruction from every quarter is valuable. But from parents it is authoritative—the ordinance of God. Therefore let it not be a matter of occasional regard. *Bind it continually about thine heart,*[12] as thy rule; *about thy neck,*[13] as thine adorning. Let the law be the friend for all times and circumstances—a guide by day[14]—a solace by night[15]—yea—a friend for thy *waking* moments.[16] Take care that nothing hinders thy early converse with this faithful counsellor—before the world comes in, as the best means of keeping the world out. 'Happy is the mind, to which the word is an undivided companion.'[17] Such *a lamp*—so full of *light*—in this dark world[18] is an inestimable gift. Its *reproofs of instruction*—as the discipline of our wayward will—are to us as *the way of life.*[19]

Specially valuable is this *lamp and light* in sensual temptation.[20] Those who choose their own light and wisdom, are sure to fall into a *flattering* snare.[21] The neglect of parental warning will furnish in the end bitter matter for unavailing repentance.[22] Oh! let the

1 Chap. i. 16. Isa. lix. 7. Rom. iii. 15. 2 Zech. viii. 17.
3 Chap. xix. 5. Zech. v. 4. Mal. iii. 5. 4 Verses 14, 19. 5 Psalm cxxxiii.
6 Rom. xvi. 17, 18. 7 Jude 19. 1 Cor. iii. 3, 4.
8 1 Cor. i. 10—'a text'—says the godly Flavel—'to be commented upon rather by tears than by words.'—Sermon on text. 9 Phil. iii. 16.
10 Heb. 'Woman of wickedness'—the woman full of wickedness—wholly given to it. Comp. Zech. v. 7, 8.
11 Chap. i. 8, 9; iv. 1. 12 Chap. iii. 3; iv. 21; vii. 3.
13 Chap. iii. 3. Comp. Job xxxi. 36. 14 Chap. iii. 22, 23; iv. 12.
15 Chap. iii. 24. Psalm lxiii. 5. 16 Psalm cxxxix. 17, 18.
17 'Felix mens, cui verbum individuus comes.'—Bernard. Serm. xxxii. in Cant.
18 Psalm cxix. 105. See Bp. Patrick's note quoted in Scott.
19 Psalm xix. 11. 2 Tim. iii. 16, 17. Comp. Matt. vii. 13, 14.
20 Chap. ii. 10, 11, 16—19; v. 1—8; vii. 1—5. 21 Chap. ii. 16; vii. 21.
22 Chap. v. 11—13.

Father's instruction be heard betimes—"Wherewithal shall a young man cleanse his way? by taking heed thereto according to thy word."[1]

25. *Lust not after her beauty in thine heart; neither let her take thee with her eyelids.* 26. *For by means of a whorish woman a man is brought to a piece of bread: and the adulteress will hunt for the precious life.* 27. *Can a man take fire in his bosom, and his clothes not be burned?* 28. *Can one go upon hot coals, and his feet not be burned?* 29. *So is he that goeth in to his neighbor's wife; whosoever toucheth her shall not be innocent.*

Solomon here gives our Lord's own rule.[2] Resist *lust* in its first rising in the heart. By vain *beauty*,[3] and wanton *eyes*,[4] many a deluded victim has been *brought to a piece of bread.*[5] Nay—so insatiable is the seducer's malice, that—like the huntsman, who never loses sight of his prey, till he has pursued it to death—she never ceases to solicit, till she has *hunted for the precious life.*[6] Yet neither the present miseries of this wretched course, nor the certain horror of the end, can draw away the foot, that has dared to tread the forbidden path. Self-confidence sees and fears no danger. 'I can look to myself, I need not go too far, and I shall get no harm.' Did the infatuated sinner but open his eyes, he would as soon expect to take *fire into his bosom*, and *his clothes not be burned;* or to *go upon hot coals*, and *not be burned;* as to go wilfully into sin, and to escape the punishment.[7] Sin and punishment are linked together by a chain of adamant. 'The fire of lust kindles the fire of hell.'[8] He cannot afterwards plead the strength of the temptation. Why did he not avoid it? Who that knows how much tinder he carries about him, would wilfully light up the sparks? Heedlessly to rush into temptation, is to provoke the corruption, which is too ready to stir of itself. Beware of suspicious familiarities on the borders of sin.[9] The temptation to criminality in this atmosphere is fearful.[10] *Whosoever toucheth shall not be innocent.*[11]

30. *Men do not despise a thief, if he steal to satisfy his soul, when he is hungry;* 31. *But if he be found, he shall restore sevenfold; he shall give all the substance of his house.* 32. *But whoso committeth adultery with a woman lacketh understanding; he that doeth it destroyeth his own soul.* 33. *A wound and dishonor shall he get; and his reproach shall not be wiped away.* 34. *For jealousy is the rage of a*

[1] Psalm cxix. 9. Comp. v. 11; xvii. 4

[2] Matt. v. 28. Comp. Jam. i. 14, 15. Job xxxi. 1. Ps. cxix. 37.

[3] Chap. xxxi. 30. Gen. vi. 2; xxxix. 6. 2 Sam. xi. 2. Comp. Ecclus. xxv. 21.

[4] Gen. xxxix. 7. 2 Kings ix. 30. Marg. Isa. iii. 16. 2 Peter ii. 14. Comp. Paradise Lost, Book xi. l. 620.

[5] Chap. v. 10; xxix. 3. 1 Sam. ii. 26, 36. Job xxxi. 9, 12. Luke xv. 13, 30. Comp. the difference between Solomon's chaste and unholy age. 1 Kings x. 21, 27 with xii. 4.

[6] Gen. xxxix. 14. Jud. xvi. 18—21. Comp. Ez. xiii. 18, 20, 21.

[7] Ex. xx. 14, 17. Lev. xx. 10. 2 Sam. xii. 9. Mal. iii. 5. Even as a sin of ignorance it was liable to be visited. Gen. xii. 15—18; xx. 1—6; xxvi. 10. So strictly has the holy Lord fenced his own ordinance! See Mede's Sermon on Chap. iv. 23.

[8] Henry in loco. Comp. Job xxxi. 12. James i. 14, 15.

[9] Gen. xxxix. 10. Rom. xiii. 13. 1 Thess. v 22.

[10] 2 Sam. xi. 2—4.

[11] Gen. xx. 6; xxxix. 9. 1 Cor. vii. 1.

man: therefore he will not spare in the day of vengeance. 35. *He will not regard* (accept the face of, Marg.) *any ransom; neither will he rest content, though thou givest many gifts.*

Here is no excuse or impunity for *the thief.* The full *restitution* that he is compelled to make[1]—perhaps sweeping away *all his* little *substance*—proves that no extremity can excuse "the transgression of the law."[2] Let him earn his bread by honest industry. If the fruits of industry fail, let him, trusting in God, seek the help of his fellow-creatures. If he have faith to trust, he will never be forced to steal.[3] Yet his extreme temptation renders him an object rather of pity than of scorn—*Men do not despise him.*

But the sin of the adulterer claims no sympathy. His plea is not the cry of hunger, but of lust; not want, but wantonness; not *the lack* of bread, but *of understanding.*[4] He is wilfully given up to his sin. He *destroyeth his own soul.*[5] *He gets a rankling* wound upon his conscience,[6] *dishonor* and indelible *reproach* upon his name.[7] The tremendous passions of *jealousy and rage* shut out all forgiveness.[8] *The face* of no one who offered a *ransom* would be *accepted.* No compensation,[9] however costly, will *content.*

Such are the many sins[10]—the awfully destructive miseries[11]—flowing from the breach of God's holy commandment. 'Oh! how great iniquity'—exclaimed the godly Augustine—'is this adultery! How great a perverseness! The soul, redeemed by the precious blood of Christ, is thus for the pleasures of an hour given to the devil; a thing much to be lamented and bewailed: when that which delighteth is soon gone, that which tormenteth remaineth without end.'[12]

And shall not this fearful picture of sin and its consequences, (which Solomon, alas! was too well fitted to draw) teach us to dread the first approaches to danger; to close every avenue of sense to the entrance of this seductive poison; to shun all communications, that taint the purity of taste, that familiarize the

1 Ex. xxii. 1—4. *Seven-fold*—not literally. Four or five-fold was the extent of the Divine requirement. Comp. Luke xix. 8. It means full (ver. 3.) and satisfactory—an indefinite number. Comp. Gen. iv. 15, 24. Psalm lxxix. 12, and alia passim. Comp. Job xx. 18.

2 Comp. 1 Cor. vi. 10, with 1 John iii. 4.

3 See Matt. vi. 25—33.

4 Comp. Eccl. vii. 25, 26. Jer. v. 8, 21.

5 Lev. xx. 10. Chap. ii. 18, 19; v. 22, 23; vii. 22, 23. Eph. v. 5.

6 Psalm xxxii. 3, 4.

7 Chap. v. 9. Gen. xxxviii. 23; xlix. 4. 2 Sam. iii. 13; xiii. 13. 1 Kings xv. 5, with Matt. i. 6. Neh. xiii. 26. Comp. Deut. xxiii. 2.

8 Gen. xxxiv. 7; xlix. 5—7. Num. v. 14. Esth. vii. 7—10. Ez. xvi. 38. Schultens remarks that no version fully expresses the strength of the original. *Rage,* 'Ignito. In loco.

9 Gen. xxxix. 19, 20. Judges xix. 29, 30.

10 2 Sam. xi. 6—24.

11 The quaint lines of an old Chronicler give an awful picture—

'Corpus, opes, animum, famam, vim, lumina scortum,
Debilitat, perdit, necat, aufert, eripit, orbat.'

Quoted by Trapp. on ver. 26.

12 Lib. de honest. Mulier: quoted by Lavater on verse 26.

mind with impurity, that give a vivid interest to associations from which a chaste imagination recoils with disgust? Let us learn to seek divine strengthening to "watch and pray" continually; and while we "think we stand, to take heed lest we fall."[1]

CHAPTER VII.

1. *My son, keep my words, and lay up my commandments with thee.* 2. *Keep my commandments and live; and my law as the apple of thine eye.* 3. *Bind them upon thy fingers, write them upon the table of thine heart.* 4. *Say unto wisdom, thou art my sister, and call understanding thy kinswoman:* 5. *That they may keep thee from the strange woman, from the stranger that flattereth with her words.*

THE study of wisdom in the word of God is here commended to us with affectionate earnestness, and with a beautiful variety of imagery. Let us ponder these valuable rules for practical application.

Let the whole heart and mind be occupied with it. Keep it as the daily means of *life.*[2] Sir Matthew Hale told his children—'If I omit reading a portion of Scripture in the morning, it never goes well with me through the day.' *Lay it up*[3] carefully, not on our shelves, but in our hearts. Let *the whole* word of God be our precious treasure. Receive the promises from his grace with simple affiance, and *the commandments* from his holiness with ready obedience. Stand with your eye in the land of promise; but with your feet in "the land of uprightness."[4]

Maintain a jealous regard for the law. What care is necessary to *keep the apple of the eye*—that most tender part of the most tender member![5] With the same care preserve the integrity of *the law.* Let every part of it have its full weight. To explain it away, or to lower its requirements—breaks down the barrier, and gives an easy entrance to temptation. The sensual sinner is often a covert infidel.

Let it be at hand for constant use. Bind them upon thy fingers[6]—that, being always in sight, they may be always ready for the present moment. And for their practical influence—*write them upon the table of thine heart.* Oh! my God—this is thy Almighty work.[7] But thou hast engaged to do it for thy people.[8] I "take hold of thy covenant." Lord! seal thy promised grace.

Let it be the object of tender affection—as our sister—our kinswoman. It is her embrace, that throws the harlot's beauty into the shade. Man must have his object of delight. If wisdom is

[1] 1 Cor. x. 12.
[2] Chap. iii, 21, 22; iv. 4, 13; vi. 23. Comp. Isa. lv. 2, 3, Jer. xxii. 15.
[3] Chap. x. 14. Deut. xi. 18. Luke ii. 19, 51.
[4] Psalm cxliii. 10.
[5] Deut. xxxii. 10. Psalm xvii. 8. Zech. ii. 8.
[6] Chap. iii. 3. Deut. vi. 8; xi. 18.
[7] Isa. xxvi. 12. 2 Cor. iii. 3.
[8] Jer. xxxi. 33.

not loved, lust will be indulged. The Bible therefore—not merely read, but made the *cherished* object of familiar intercourse—proves a sacred exorcist to expel the power of evil.[1]

6. *For at the window of my house I looked through my casement,* 7. *And beheld among the simple ones, I discerned among the youths, a young man void of understanding,* 8. *Passing through the street near her corner: and he went the way to her house,* 9. *In the twilight, in the evening, in the black and dark night:* 10. *And, behold, there met him a woman with the attire of an harlot, and subtil of heart.* 11. (*She is loud and stubborn; her feet abide not in her house:* 12. *Now is she without, now in the streets, and lieth in wait at every corner.*) 13. *So she caught him, and kissed him, and with an impudent face said unto him,* 14. *I have peace-offerings with me: this day have I vowed my vows.* 15. *Therefore came I forth to meet thee, diligently to seek thy face, and I have found thee..* 16. *I have decked my bed with coverings of tapestry, with carved works, with fine linen of Egypt.* 17. *I have perfumed my bed with myrrh, aloes, and cinnamon.* 18. *Come, let us take our fill of love until the morning: let us solace ourselves with loves.* 19. *For the good man is not at home, he is gone a long journey:* 20. *He hath taken a bag of money with him, and will come home at the day appointed.* 21. *With her much fair speech she caused him to yield, with the flattering of her lips she forced him.* 22. *He goeth after her straightway, as an ox goeth to the slaughter, or as a fool to the correction of the stocks;* 23. *Till a dart strike through his liver; as a bird hasteth to the snare, and knoweth not that it is for his life.*

Solomon paints the deadly snare of *the strange woman* with a master's hand, with exquisite fidelity of coloring. *A young man without understanding,*[2] in company with *youths* as *simple* as himself, *taking in the dark of evening the way to the harlot's house.* She *meets* him—her *attire*;[3] her *subtilty*;[4] her *loud and stubborn voice*;[5] *her feet* at this late hour *not abiding in her house*;[6] *lying in wait at every corner of the street*;[7] *her impudent face* and conduct—all shew the harlot's forehead.[8] She allures her victim with the garb of sanctity. She had just been engaged in special religious duties. Now she was *come forth to seek diligently* her lover, that they might feast together upon her *peace-offerings,*[9] and *solace themselves with love,* with every indulgence. *The goodman* (perhaps the name of *husband* might have awakened conscience) *is gone a long journey till the time appointed.* Meanwhile therefore we may *take our fill of loves* without fear of interruption. Unarmed with principles, the weakness of resolution yields to the seduction of lust; and her unsuspecting prey rushes on to ruin.

Trace this sad end to its beginning. Was not idleness the

[1] Chap. ii. 10, 16; vi. 23, 24; xxiii. 26, 27.
[2] Chap. i. 4, 22; xiii. 16.
[3] Gen. xxxviii. 14, 15.
[4] Chap. xxiii. 27. Eccl. vii. 26. Jud. xvi. 4—20
[5] Chap. ix. 13.
[6] Comp. 1 Tim. v. 13. Titus ii. 5.
[7] Chap. ix. 14, 15; xxiii. 28. Dr. Richardson mentions seeing 'these wretched women in a large commercial town in Egypt, in the harlot's attire, sitting at the doors of their houses, and calling on the passengers as they went by, in the same manner as we read in the Book of Proverbs.'—Travels, Vol. i. p. 270.
[8] See Gen. xxxix. 7, 12. Jer. iii. 3.
[9] See Holden. Comp. Lev. vii. 16; xix. 6. Deut. xii. 6. Scott takes the same view—adding—'that it is no wonder, that these sacred ordinances should have given occasion to carnal indulgence, when our Christian festivals (Christmas especially) are abused for similar profanations.'

parent of this mischief?[1] The loitering evening walk—the unseasonable hour[2]—the vacant mind—all bringing the youth into contact with evil company[3]—was not this courting sin—tempting the tempter? "The house was empty," and therefore ready for his reception, and soon altogether in his possession.[4] How valuable are self-discipline, self-control, constant employment, active energy of pursuit, as preservatives under the Divine blessing from fearful danger!

See also the base varnish of religion. It is often a cover for sin.[5] 'She durst not play the harlot with man, till she had played the hypocrite with God, and stopped the mouth of her conscience with *her peace-offerings*.'[6] Nay—she seems to have emboldened herself in her wickedness, as if her meeting was a happy providence, the reward of her religious services.[7] Beware of any voice —from the most reverend quarter, that manifestly encourages forbidden indulgence.

Observe also the infatuation of the snare. 'Man cannot be ruined, till he has been made confident *to the contrary*. A man must get into his victim's heart with fair speeches and promises, before he can come at it with a dagger.'[8] Thus the harlot's *flattering speech* chained the youth blindfolded for destruction. As *the ox goeth to the slaughter*, unconscious of his fate—perhaps dreaming of rich pasture: *or as a fool goeth to the stocks*,[9] careless and unfeeling; so does this poor deluded victim rush on with pitiable mirth or indifference, *till the dart strikes through his liver.*[10] *He hasteth as a bird to the snare*,[11] thinking only of the bait, *and he knoweth not that it is for his life.*[12] What will recollection bring, but the fragrance of exciting perfume,[13] changed into the bitterness of wormwood and gall; the short night of pleasure succeeded by the eternal night of infernal torment!

Lastly—mark the danger of venturing into temptation. Could we expect any other results, when we *saw the youth going the way to the harlot's house?*[14] He intended merely his own idle gratification; and when he *yielded*, it was probably not without some struggle. But it is a just judgment, that those who fear not temptation, should fall into it. 'Who would avoid danger, must avoid temptation to sin. Who would avoid sin, must avoid temptation to sin.'[15] The force, to which the youth's own folly subjected him, he could not plead as an excuse. When the first bounds of modesty are broken through, the door of the fancy is open to the tempter for the kindling of lusts. Thus to rush into the very jaws of ruin, is to "enter into temptation," by our own will, instead of being led or falling into it, under the providential discipline and

[1] 2 Sam. xi. 2. [2] Judges xix. 25. Job xxiv. 15. Rom. xiii. 12, 13.
[3] Chap. xiii. 20. 1 Cor. xv. 33. [4] Matt. xii. 44, 45.
[5] 1 Sam. ii. 22. 2 Sam. xv. 8—11. John xviii. 28. [6] Gurnal.
[7] Verses 14, 15. 1 Sam. xxiii. 7. Zech. xi. 5. [8] South's Sermons, iii. 130.
[9] Ecc. vii. 26. Judges xvi. 15. [10] Hos. iv. 11, 14. [11] Ecc. ix. 12.
[12] Chap. ix. 18. [13] Verses 16, 17. [14] Chap. iv. 15; v. 8. Judges xvi. 15.
[15] Geier on ver. 9.

dispensation of God.[1] Self-confidence has ruined many a promising profession. Tenderness of confidence, sensibility of weakness, dependence on Divine strength and promise—this is the frame, in which "he that is begotten of God keepeth himself, and that wicked one toucheth him not."[2]

24. *Hearken unto me now, therefore, O ye children, and attend to the words of my mouth.* 25. *Let not thine heart decline to her ways, go not astray in her paths.* 26. *For she hath cast down many wounded: yea, many strong men have been slain by her.* 27. *Her house is the way to hell, going down to the chambers of death.*

In the hand of a licentious poet, or painter, a picture like this might serve to contaminate the unsanctified imagination. But as it stands on the page of inspiration, it is God's solemn warning to *children*—whether in years, understanding, or experience. *Now therefore*, that you have seen the end of sin,[3] *hearken unto me.* That you may *not go astray in her paths, let not thine heart decline.*[4] An impure thought, a polluted fancy, an idle book, filthy conversation, foolish company, theatres or places of vain resort—these are *her ways.* Dread the first steps, and dream not that you can stop yourself at pleasure in her course. Familiarity with sin weakens abhorrence. Soon will you begin to love the object of detestation, and what! should you find too late, that you have chosen as your home her house, which is *the way to hell, and to the chambers of death?*[5] *Many*, not of the meaner sort, but *strong men, has she cast down wounded and slain.* And a miracle is it of Almighty power and grace, that plucks the child of God from the brink of destruction!

Let not then the most established Christian dismiss this subject as of no personal concern to himself. Be it so—that "you are risen with Christ;" that you have "set your affections on things above;" that "your life is hid with Christ in God;" that you are looking for the glorious hope of his "appearing"—It is to you—in whom "fleshly lusts are yet warring against the soul,"[6]—that the exhortation is given—*mortify therefore your members that are upon the earth*—even the worst members of the old man—*fornication, uncleanness, evil concupiscence.*[7] And who—with the picture of *the wounded and slain* before him, will revolt?—"Is thy servant a dog, that he should do this thing?[8]—that he should need this warning? Look at the footsteps of the *strong men* who

[1] Matt. xxv. 41, with iv. 1. James i. 2.
[2] 1 John v. 18. [3] Verses 22, 23. [4] Chap. iv. 23· ". 8.
[5] Chap. ii. 18; ix. 18. The plural number (*the ways*, Heb.) seems to imply 'many other ways of guilt, branching out—many other paths of ruin coinciding.'—Hervey's Theron and Aspasio. Letter v. Schultens insists, that the present most wretched state—full of all horror and execration—is included, so that the man who hath entered the seducer's house may be said to have entered alive into hell, and gone down to the chamber of death.—Chap. v. 5.
[6] 1 Peter ii. 11.
[7] Col. iii. 1—5. A similar exhortation is given to another flourishing Christian Church. 1 Thess. iv. 3—5.
[8] 2 Kings viii. 13.

have gone in.[1] Whom do we see come out whole? 'Behold Kings stood not before her; how then shall we stand?"[2]

Nor let present steadfastness, or seclusion from temptation, blind our eyes to the liability of yielding to the vilest indulgence. The eye of God discerns a far deeper corruption than appears in the outer man—such a totality of depravation, that even the affections, designed to be the sources of our holiest delight, become the principle and occasion of the most awful departure from the ways of purity and peace.

The Gospel presents the only remedy. The love of Christ is the counteracting principle to the love of lust. 'If impure love solicits, remember the holy love of thy Saviour to thee, proved by his most shameful death. Think of him, as looking into thy heart boiling over with corruption, shewing thee his wounds and exciting thee to a reciprocal love of himself.'[3] The crucifixion of the flesh by a living union with Him "will keep us from our iniquity."[4] "How shall we, that are dead to sin, live any longer therein?"[5] "The flesh will still lust against the spirit."[6] But the man, who walks with God in Gospel liberty, and Christian discipline and watchfulness, is safe.[7]

But if sin be not mortified by these principles, sooner or later it will break out; if not, as here, to open disgrace,—yet so as to defile the conscience, to "quench the Spirit," and by a sure, though perhaps imperceptible course, to bring soul and body *to hell—to the chambers of eternal death.*[8]

CHAPTER VIII.

1. *Doth not wisdom cry? and understanding put forth her voice?* 2. *She standeth in the top of high places, by the way in the places of the paths.* 3. *She crieth at the gates, at the entry of the city, at the coming-in at the doors.* 4. *Unto you, O men, I call; and my voice is to the sons of man.*

LISTEN we now to the *calls of heavenly wisdom*—to the voice of the Son of God.[9] Careless soul! shall this Divine call be

[1] Samson—David—Solomon. Neh. xiii. 26. Vestigia terrent—Felix, quem faciunt aliena pericula cautum.

[2] 2 Kings x. 4. [3] Geier on ver. 18. Comp. 1 Cor. vi. 18, 20. 2 Cor. v. 14, 15.

[4] Gal. v. 24, with Psalm xviii. 23. [5] Rom. vi. 2, 3. [6] Gal. v. 17.

[7] Rom. vi. 14, with 1 Cor. ix. 27. [8] Rom. vi. 21. James i. 14, 15.

[9] We assume the speaker to be Personal—Essential wisdom. Apart from the general reasons before given, (Notes on chap. i. 20, 21, 24.) this description could not without unnatural force apply to an attribute. It sets out I. *Personal existence—brought forth—brought up*—in conjunction with Deity—*by Him*, (verses 24, 30.) II. *Personal properties*—(1.) *set up* (anointed, Heb.) *from everlasting*, for distinct office, (ver. 23.) (2.) *The efficient cause in the work of creation*, (verses 27—30.) (3.) Having *wisdom* (ver. 14.) which—as an attribute itself—could not be the property of an attribute—*and strength* (ver. 14.) an independent quality, not a property of wisdom. (4.) Personal authority, (verses 15, 16.) (5.) Leading into the ways of truth, (verses 19, 20.) (6.) Causing to

slighted, when the allurements of sin and vanity have had power to arrest thine ear?[1] Can ignorance be pleaded? *Doth not wisdom cry?* and that—not in the hour of darkness, and in the secret corners—but from place to place, in public concourse.[2] Loud and unfettered the call—not to devils, but *to men:* not to the righteous, but *to the sons of men*—children of guilty Adam. It is the proclamation of the Gospel "to every creature."[3] Wherever the word reaches, the offer is made. Wherever a lost sinner be found on this side of the grave, the free welcome of the Gospel meets him. If he be not saved, he is more lost than ever. His ruin lies at his own door.[4]

5. *O ye simple, understand wisdom; and, ye fools, be ye of an understanding heart.* 6. *Hear: for I will speak of excellent things; and the opening of my lips shall be right things.* 7. *For my mouth shall speak truth; and wickedness is an abomination to my lips.* 8. *All the words of my mouth are in righteousness; there is nothing froward or perverse in them.* 9. *They are all plain to him that understandeth, and right to them that find knowledge.* 10. *Receive my instruction, and not[5] silver; and knowledge rather than choice gold.* 11. *For wisdom is better than rubies; and all the things that may be desired are not to be compared to it.*

The great Teacher calls *the simple and fools to hear.*[6] And where else can they hear such *excellent things?* Worthy are they of the attention of princes![7]—his glorious person—his everlasting covenant—his rich and sovereign love to sinners.[8] Often does the truth of God, by the tradition of men,[9] or the subtilty of the father of lies,[10] become virtually a principle of error.[11] But here *all is* unchangeable *righteousness.* There is no *froward perversion.* *Every such wickedness is an abomination.*[12]

But are they within the reach of the multitude? They—who "lean to their own understanding;"[13] who care more to be learned than to be holy; who value the tree of knowledge more than the tree of life; who desire "meat for their lust," rather than manna for their souls—Such indeed make difficulties for themselves. The "voice out of the whirlwind" rebukes them, as "darkening counsel

inherit, (ver. 21.) III. Personal affections—hatred, (ver. 13.) love, (ver. 17.) joy, (verses 30, 31.) IV. Giving personal promises, (ver. 21.) V. Commanding obedience as a matter of life and death, (verses 32—36.) Whether Solomon fully understood his own words, may be a question. 1 Pet. i. 10. But receiving the words as from God; weighing their natural force; comparing them with Scripture parallels, we doubt not that they describe—not an attribute, but a Person—Eternal—Omnipotent—in the endearing relation to man—Creator—Mediator—Saviour. We may add, that this interpretation is generally accredited by the Christian Fathers.

[1] Chap. vii. [2] Chap. vii. 8, 9, with i. 20, 21; ix. 3. Psalm xlix. 1, 2.
[3] Mark xvi. 15. [4] Matt. xxiii. 37.
[5] Rather than silver. See next clause, and comp. Hosea vi. 6.
[6] Chap. i. 22; ix. 4, 5. [7] Heb. princely. [8] Verses 12—31.
[9] It was a keen reply of one of the Martyrs, when asking of Bonner's Chaplain—'Is not God's book sufficient for my salvation?'—the answer was—'Yes, it is sufficient for our salvation, but not for our instruction.' 'God send me the salvation, and you the instruction!'—Exam. of Thomas Hawkes, Foxe vii. 100.
[10] Comp. Matt. iv. 6, 7, with Psalm xci. 11. [11] Gal. i. 7-9
[12] Chap. xxx. 5. Psalm xix. 9; xxxiii. 4; cxix. 152, 160.
[13] Chap. iii. 5. 1 Cor. i. 20; iii. 18.

by words without knowledge."[1] But 'the word of God is easy to all that have a desire to it, and which are not blinded by the prince of this world.'[2] The "babes" are taught of God.[3] He not only unfolds the truth, but opens their hearts to receive it. There will indeed be great depths. But they will grasp important, saving, truths. Here 'the wisest Solomon may fetch jewels for ornament, and the poorest Lazarus bread for life.'[4]—Come then—sinner—"sit," with one of old, "at the feet" of thy Divine Teacher. *Receive his instruction*, more precious *than silver or fine gold.*[5] Enrich thyself with his satisfying and enduring treasures, *compared with which all the things that may be desired* are lighter than vanity.[6] And will not the children of God daily draw more abundantly from these treasures? Oh! let them not be—like the pomp of this world—the object of gaze, but of active desire and increasing enjoyment.

12. *I wisdom dwell with prudence, and find out knowledge of witty inventions.*

How adorable is the Being here before us! His glorious perfections, each *dwelling with* the other in such harmonious combination! All the *witty inventions* of science, are ultimately traceable to this heavenly source.[7] But his great mind was soaring far beyond. Now before his eyes was the vast discovery of man's salvation,[8] found out, not by laborious investigation, but by the intuition of the Infinite God-head. Here is his most splendid display of *wisdom*[9] *dwelling with prudence—wisdom* contriving for the highest end; *prudence* directing the most effective means. The same perfect combination controls all his arrangements, both as "the Head of the Church,"[10] and "the Head over all things to his Church,"[11] for her present good, and his eternal glory. And what owe we individually, to "the riches of his grace, wherein"—by the removal of insuperable difficulties, and the communication of suitable grace—"he hath abounded towards us in all *wisdom and prudence!*"[12]

Prudence is commonly thought to be only a moral quality. Here we see it to be an attribute of Deity. The humanity of our beloved Lord was filled with this perfection.[13] With what Divine acuteness of *wisdom* did he *find out the knowledge of the inventions* of his enemies, and put them to shame![14] And how did this combination of *prudence* restrain him from hasty confidence,[15]

[1] Job xxxviii. 1, 2.
[2] Reformers' Notes. Comp. chap. xiv. 6; xvii. 24. 'What wonder, if the unlettered and despised Christian know more of the mysteries of Heaven than the naturalist, though both wise and learned? Christ admits the believer into his bosom; and *He* is in the bosom of the Father.'—Leighton's Sermon on Heavenly Wisdom.
[3] Matt. xi. 25; xviii. 4.
[4] Bishop Reynolds on Hos. xiv. 9.
[5] Verse 19; xvi. 16. Job xxviii. 15—19. Psalm xix. 10; cxix. 127.
[6] Chap. iii. 15.
[7] Exod. xxxi. 3—6; xxxv. 30—35. 1 Chron. xxviii. 1, 2. Isa. xxviii. 24—29.
[8] Verses 22—31.
[9] Eph. iii. 10.
[10] Col. i. 18.
[11] Eph. i. 22.
[12] Verses 7, 8.
[13] Isa. xi. 2.
[14] Matt. ix. 4—8; xxii. 15—46.
[15] John ii. 23, 24.

remove him from premature danger,[1] and preserve him from giving needless offence![2] Praised be our God for such "treasures of *wisdom*," hid in "our glorious Head," ready for distribution for every emergency of his people's need![3]

13. *The fear of the Lord is to hate evil: pride, and arrogancy, and the evil way, and the froward mouth, do I hate.*

Such is the holiness of Divine *wisdom!* She *dwells with prudence.* But she cannot dwell with evil. Therefore *the fear of the Lord*, which is her very nature, is *to hate evil.*[4] Thus of *pride* in all its branches—*arrogancy* of spirit, *the evil way, and the froward mouth*—the wisdom of God declares without reserve—*I hate them.*[5] How clearly did he mark his *hatred* in the days of h' flesh by the full exhibition of the opposite grace! "The Son of man came not to be ministered unto, but *to minister.*"[6] A proud disciple of a lowly Saviour! how offensive is this contradiction to our Master! What a cause of stumbling to the world!

14. *Counsel is mine, and sound wisdom: I am understanding; I have strength.*

This *counsel*, as we have just hinted,[7] is not, as with man, the fruit of deliberation, but Divine intuition. It is not, that it flows from him; but that he is himself the essence—the Fountain-head.[8] It is not, that he *hath understanding* to order and govern the world. But *he is understanding.* All is in Him. All is derivable from Him.[9] "His understanding is infinite—His *strength* Almighty, everlasting."[10] Thus we adore Him, we rest in Him, as the great "Counsellor"[11]—One with his Father in the everlasting plan of salvation[12]—One with his Church; undertaking her cause;[13] guiding her in all her difficulties and perplexities;[14] His self-existent power ever ready to execute the purpose of his *counsel.*[15] Behold him then surrounded with the majesty of his mighty perfections—Christ the power of God, and the wisdom of "God."[16] In all thy doubts and anxieties—*counsel is mine and sound wisdom.*[17] In all thy conflicts and weariness—*I have strength.*[18] See him as Man, filled with these Divine perfections.[19] Remember his fulness is thy portion.[20]

15. *By me kings reign, and princes decree justice.* 16. *By me princes rule, and nobles, even all the judges of the earth.*

Another glorious contemplation of this Divine Person! He

1 Matt. xii. 14—16. John vi. 15.
2 Matt. xvii. 27.
3 Col. i. 19; ii. 3.
4 Chap. iii. 7; xvi. 6.
5 Chap. vi. 16—19; xvi. 5. Comp. Psalm xlv. 7. Zech. viii. 17.
6 Matt. xx. 28. Comp. xi. 29. Luke xxii. 27.
7 See on verse 12.
8 Isa. xl. 13, 14. Rom. xi. 34.
9 John i. 9.
10 Psalm cxlvii. 5. Isa. xl. 28; xxvi. 4.
11 Isa. ix. 6.
12 Zech. vi. 12, 13.
13 Ibid. iii. 1.
14 Isa. lxiii. 9—14.
15 Ibid. verses 1—6. Psalm lxxxix. 19. Comp. Job ix. 4; xii. 13, 16. Dan. ii. 20
16 1 Cor. i. 24.
17 Isa. xlviii. 17.
18 Ibid. xl. 28, 29.
19 Ibid. xi. 2.
20 1 Cor. i. 30. Col. ii. 10.

proclaims himself to be the source of power and authority, no less than of *counsel and wisdom*. "KING OF KINGS was the" mysterious "name written upon his vesture."[1] Yet his crown does not displace the regal diadem from the brow of earthly princes; nor is the sceptre to fall from their hands. These ensigns of power are to be held, but in subordination to his own. *By me kings reign*—not only by my permission, but by my appointment. They bear my name. They are stamped with my authority.[2] Proud anarchy disputes the prerogative, and traces the authority to the people; only that they may cast off the yoke of God, and "do that which is right in their own eyes."[3] Scripture politics lay down the offensive truth—"there is no power but of God; the powers that be are ordained of God. They are ministers of God," not servants of the people.[4] Government in all its administrations—kings, princes, nobles, judges—is a Divinely-consecrated ordinance.[5] Every kingdom is a province of the Universal empire of the "King of kings." Men may mix their own pride, folly, and self-will with this appointment. But God's providential counter-working preserves the substantial blessing. Yet if "the power be *exclusively* of God," then is *wisdom, by whom kings reign*, the very essence and person of God. And here is our rest, our anchor in this world's agitating storm. "The government of the world is on the shoulders" of "the Head of the Church."[6] All things—all power in heaven and in earth—is delivered unto him of his Father.[7] "The Lord reigneth; let the earth rejoice."[8]

17. *I love them that love me; and those that seek me early shall find me.*

Now behold the grace of this Divine Person to his *loving* children. None by nature are interested in it.[9] But such is the freeness of his grace, that he first implants *love* in their hearts, and then he cheers them with the assurance of his own *love*.[10] Thus the first kindling of the flame is of Him. We *love*, because we are drawn.[11] We *seek*—not by the impulse from within, but by the grace from above;[12] and *seeking we find*.[13] But it must be *early seeking—the first desire of the heart*[14]—the object of our

[1] Rev. xix. 12—26. Comp. i. 5; xvii. 14.
[2] Ex. xxii. 28. Psalm lxxxii. 6, with John x. 35.
[3] Judges xvii. 6; xix. 1; xxi. 25. Comp. Hos. viii. 4. 2 Peter ii. 10. Jude 8.
[4] Rom. xiii. 1—6.
[5] Psalm lxxv. 7. Jer. xxvii. 5—7. Dan. ii. 21, 37. 38; iv. 25, 32; v. 18. Comp. John xix. 11. It is interesting to trace this acknowledgment even in the darkness of Heathenism—Kings inheriting their sceptre from Jove; Magistracy consecrated by Augurs—the Assessors and Counsellors of Jove.
[6] Isa. ix. 6.
[7] Matt. xi. 27. xxviii. 18. Scott remarks the plural number in the original, as seeming to agree with the prediction of righteous kings and rulers in the latter times of the Church. Comp. Psalm lxxii. 1—3. Isa. xlix. 23; lx. 16, 17. See the national blessing of godly rulers—2 Chron. ix. 8. Isa. i. 26.
[8] Psalm xcvii. 1.
[9] Rom. viii. 7.
[10] 1 John iv. 19, with John xiv. 21.
[11] Jer. xxxi. 3.
[12] Chap. xvi. 1. Psalm cxix. 32.
[13] Isa. xlv. 19. Jer. xxix. 13. Matt. vii. 7, 8.
[14] Chap. i. 28. Psalm lxiii. 1. Hos. v. 15, with Matt. vi. 33.

dearest devotion and choice. It must be *early in the day*[1]—when our mind is most free;—the first-fruits of our time, consecrating the whole to him. Take care that we see his face *first*, before any other; else will our lamp be untrimmed, our soul estranged from his presence, our heart unready for his service. *Let it be the early breaking in of the day of grace*[2]—the improvement of the first—who knows that they be not the *only*, opportunities of salvation.[3] Never can it be too soon to *seek*. But how many have found it too late![4] And, oh! let it be *early*—the dawn of life[5]—giving to the Lord "the kindness of youth"—"the first love"—before it has been devoted to the world; before sin has hardened the heart; before habits of sin have been formed and fixed. Children! Here is a word and promise for you. Remember—the bud of life is specially acceptable to God[6]—specially honored by him.[7] Is it reasonable to offer the flower of youth to Satan, and reserve only the dregs of life for your Saviour?[8] Every day you lose a world of happiness, you bind a chain of sin, you take a step to hell. Come then, and answer the call that is drawing you to Him, who is worthy of all.[9] Never will you regret that you have come too soon. But many have been the sorrowing cries—Lord 'I have loved thee too late.' Come then by his help, and, in dependence on his grace, make him your first—your present choice. Lay claim by faith to this promise to *early seekers; and you shall find.*

18. *Riches and honor are with me; yea, durable riches and righteousness.* 19. *My fruit is better than gold, yea, than fine gold; and my revenue than choice silver.* 20. *I lead in the way of righteousness, in the midst of the paths of judgment:* 21. *That I may cause those that love me to inherit substance; and I will fill their treasures.*

What a treasure do *early seekers find!* This fading world is too poor a portion.[10] Theirs are *durable riches* of eternity[11]—the *honor* of "reigning" as kings "in life"[12]—a *righteousness*, in which they are accepted with God, and conformed to his image.[13] Is not this *fruit and revenue better than the choice silver?*[14] And then, when our way is shut up, how valuable is wisdom's counsel![15]—so carefully *leading in the midst of the paths*—'at a distance from the extreme'[16] on either side of the narrow way. Thus the sober-minded Christian is equally remote from formal service and enthusiastic delusion. His apprehensions of truth are alike distinguished from the dryness of system, and from loose unconnected

[1] Job. i. 5. Psalm v. 3; cxix. 147. Isa. xxvi. 8, 9. Mark i. 35.
[2] Job viii. 5—7. Isa. lv. 6. 2 Cor. vi. 2.
[3] Chap. xxvii. 1. Heb. iv. 7.
[4] Matt. xxv. 6—12. Luke xiii. 24, 25.
[5] 1 Kings xviii. 12. 2 Chron. xxxiv. 3.
[6] Hos. xi. 1—4.
[7] 1 Sam. ii. 18; iii. 19. Psalm xcii. 12, 15.
[8] Mal. i. 8.
[9] 1 Sam. iii. 9. Psalm xxvii. 8. Jer. iii. 4.
[10] Psalm xvii. 14, 15.
[11] Matt. vi. 19, 20. Luke x. 42. Rev. iii. 18.
[12] Rom. v. 17; viii. 17. Rev. i. 6
[13] Rom. iii. 22, with xiii. 14. Eph. iv. 24.
[14] Verses 10, 11; iii. 14, 15. Ecc. vii. 12.
[15] Chap. iii. 6; iv. 11, 12; vi. 22. Isa. xlviii. 17; xlix. 10.
[16] Scott. Chap. iv. 25—27.

principles. The intelligent and spiritually-minded Churchman is alike separate from exclusiveness or idolatry on the one side, and from indiscriminate Christianity on the other. He values highly his Scriptural ordinances; yet he neither mistakes them for the substance of the gospel, nor does he substitute self-willed effervescence in their room. This is the true *viâ media*—Christian unity, consistency, and fruitfulness. Here also is ***substance***—things that have a being, in contrast with "things that have not"[1]—solid realities[2]—"faith substantiating things that are hoped for."[3] Here is no yawning vacuum; but a grand object to give interest to life—to fill up every vacancy in the heart. All that we could add from the world would only make us poorer, by diminishing that enjoyment of God, for the loss of which there is no compensation. There is one point—only one—in the universe where we can look up, and cry with the saintly Martyn—'With thee there is no disappointment!'[4] Here all is sure possession, even while the earnest only is in hand.[5] Do we ask—Whence does this *substance* come? Man had no part in deserving it. Free grace, not free will—is the procuring cause. It is an *inheritance*[6]—endowed with such a royal—yea—Divine bounty, that the glorious Giver proclaims—*I will fill their treasures.*[7] And will not the countless throng of the redeemed unite in the testimony—*One Christ hath abundantly filled us all?*

22. *The Lord possessed me in the beginning of his way, before his works of old.* 23. *I was set up from everlasting, from the beginning, or ever the earth was.* 24. *When there were no depths, I was brought forth: when there were no fountains abounding with water.* 25. *Before the mountains were settled, before the hills was I brought forth:* 26. *While as yet he had not made the earth, nor the fields, nor the highest part of the dust of the world.* 27. *When he prepared the heavens, I was there: when he set a compass upon the face of the depth:* 28. *When he established the clouds above: when he strengthened the fountains of the deep:* 29. *When he gave to the sea his decree, that the waters should not pass his commandment: when he appointed the foundations of the earth:* 30. *Then I was by him, as one brought up with him: and I was daily his delight, rejoicing always before him:* 31. *Rejoicing in the habitable part of his earth; and my delights were with the sons of men.*

What strong figure of speech can suppose an attribute here? So glorious are the rays of eternal supreme Deity, distinct Personality, and essential Unity; that now undoubtedly stands before us that mysterious, ever-blessed Being—"the Word, who was in the beginning with God, and was God."[8] Curiously to pry into the mode of his subsistence, would be "intruding into those things which we have not seen."[9] To receive his own revelation of himself is our reverential privilege.

How clear is his essential unity with the Father! The Lord possessed me[10]—present with him in the bosom of Deity. *I was*

[1] Chap. xxiii. 5.
[2] Isa. xxix. 8, contrasted with Isa. lv. 2. [3] Heb. xi. 1. [4] Journals, Vol. ii. 130
[5] Heb. x. 34. [6] Matt. xxv. 34. Eph. i. 11. 1 Peter i. 4, 5. [7] Rev. xxi. 6
[8] John i. 1, 2. [9] Col. ii. 18. Comp. 1 Tim. vi. 16.
[10] LXX. and Syriac Translation—'*created*'—most unwarrantable—one of the main pillars of the Arian heresy.

by Him[1]—in the same essence and blessedness.[2] Such was "the glory, which he had with the Father before the world was."[3] Neither man nor angel could declare it. The mode of his existence in the Godhead is generation—*I was brought forth*—"the only-begotten Son"[4]—a term, which it is much safer to adore than to expound, expressing, as it does, what is unsearchable. 'Take care,' saith an old expositor, 'that in this generation we invent nothing temporal, carnal, or human. But rather let us worship this generation, beholding it by faith; and let us take heed from searching further than Scripture doth teach us thereof. Otherwise we should deserve to be blinded and punished for our great curiosity.'[5]

Not less clear is his eternal existence—in the beginning[6] *of the way of God*—coeval with his eternal counsels. *Before his works of old*[7]*—set up—anointed*[8]*—from everlasting* for his covenant offices[9]—'destined and advanced to be the Wisdom and Power of the Father, Light and Life, and All in All, both in the creation and the redemption of the world.'[10]

Connected with his eternity was his agency in the work of Creation. Before the works was he brought forth. But *when* they were in operation, *he was there*—and that not, like "the sons of God," interested spectators;[11] but an efficient cause.[12] The whole detail of the creative work is brought out, that uncreated Wisdom might be displayed in clear and undoubted glory. Most fully therefore is here set forth 'the Divinity and eternity of Wisdom; meaning thereby the eternal Son of God, Jesus Christ our Saviour.'[13]

[1] John i. 2. Geier remarks, that out of above sixty instances, where this preposition occurs, not one can be produced, where vicinity is not supposed, between two distinct persons or substances.

[2] Ibid. x. 30. [3] Ibid. xvii. 5.

[4] Ibid. i. 18; iii. 16. Col. i. 15,—'begotten before every creature.' Bishop Middleton on the Greek article in loco.

[5] Cope (Michael) Exposition of Proverbs. 4to. 1580.

[6] Holden strongly advocates the Translation—supported by many Ancient Versions, and some of the best Critics (See Poole's Synopsis)—'the beginning of the way'—and expounds it—'That Jehovah possessed by an eternal generation, Wisdom or the Son, who is the origin, or efficient cause, of all the works of God.'—Comp. Col. i. 18. Rev. iii. 14, also, i. 8; xxii. 13. Geier and other accredited authorities prefer the received version upon critical grounds. Holden's remark however holds good on either hypothesis.—'It is scarcely possible in the whole compass of the Hebrew language to select terms more expressive of the eternity of Wisdom, than those which Solomon employs from this verse to the thirtieth.'

[7] Contrast Job xxxviii. 4, 5. Comp. verses 23—25, with Psalm xc. 2—the sublime adoration of the eternity of God. Comp. also Ex. iii. 14, with John viii. 58. Mic. v. 2. Rev. i. 11.

[8] Heb. Anointing was the inaugurating ceremony in the consecration of prophets, priests, and kings—a figure of the eternal consecration of Messiah to those high offices. Comp. 1 Kings xix. 16, with Isa. xlii. 1; lxi. 1. Ex. xxix. 7, with Psalm cx. 4. 1 Sam. x. 1; xvi. 13. 2 Kings ix. 6, with Psalm ii. 6. Marg. xlv. 6, 7.

[9] 1 Peter i. 20. [10] Henry in loco. Comp. Eph. iii. 9.

[11] Job xxxviii. 6, 7. Heb. i. 2.

[12] John i. 3. Col. i. 16. Even in the creation of man—perhaps here alluded to as *the highest part of the dust of the world,*—he was a co-worker. Gen. ii. 7, with i. 26.

[13] Reformers' Notes.

Next he describes, the *unspeakable blessedness of his communion with his Father. I was by him as one brought up with him*—embosomed in him as the object of *daily delight*,[1] rejoicing before him as the Fountain and Centre of infinite joy. All this mutual intimate satisfaction and *delight* had respect to the *beginning of the way of God*—his eternal purpose, and "the counsel of peace which was between them both."[2] Here it was that the Father once and again proclaimed him to be *his delight*—"His elect, in whom his soul delighted—his beloved Son, in whom he was well pleased;"[3] 'willing that by the Son we should approach to him; in the Son we should honor and adore him; and honor the Son as himself.'[4]

Yet how deeply interesting is it to see him rejoicing, not only before his Father, but in the habitable part of the earth. Here indeed was to be the grand theatre of the work, that should fill the whole creation with wonder and joy.[5] Here "the Serpent's head was to be visibly bruised,"[6] the kingdom of Satan to be destroyed, precious "spoil to be divided with the strong."[7] Here was the Church to be framed as the manifestation of his glory—the mirror of all his Divine Perfections.[8]

But the wonder of wonders yet remains—that he, who was his Father's infinite delight, and infinitely delighting in him, should find *his delights* from all eternity *in the sons of men*—that he should, as it were, long to be with us—that he should solace his heart with the prospect—that he should anticipate the moment with joyous readiness;[9] that he should pass by the far nobler nature of angels "to take hold of man"[10]—to embrace man as one with his All-perfect self! But though he foresaw how they would despise, reject, and put him to shame; yet they were the objects of his everlasting love[11]—the purchase and satisfaction of the "travail of his soul"[12]—the eternal monuments to his praise.[13] Yes—thou adorable Redeemer, nothing but the strength of thine own love could have brought thee out from the bosom of ineffable delight to suffer such things for such sinners! But this was the joy set before thee, for which—unfathomable love! thou wast content to "endure the cross, despising the shame."[14]

32. *Now therefore hearken unto me, O ye children: for blessed are they that keep my ways.* 33. *Hear instruction and be wise, and refuse it not.*

[1] Comp. John i. 18—*the only-begotten Son, who is in the bosom of the Father*—'exhibiting at once'—as Dr. Jamieson admirably observes—'the ideas conveyed by both the terms—*brought forth and brought up.*' Vindication of Doctrine of Deity of Christ, i. 224. Holden with some others prefers the rendering—'Fabricator'—for *brought up.* But the scope appears to be—not the power of Messiah—but the mutual delight and communion between himself and his Father, as it were, never absent from each other.

[2] Zech. vi. 13. [3] Isa. xlii. 1. Matt. iii. 17; xvii. 5. Comp. Col. i. 13. Gr.
[4] Quoted by Scott. [5] Psalm xcviii. Isa. xliv. 23.
[6] Gen. iii. 15. Heb. ii. 14, 15. 1 John iii. 8.
[7] Isa. liii. 12. Luke xi. 21, 22. [8] Eph. iii. 20, 21.
[9] Psalm xl. 6—8. Heb. x. 7. [10] Heb. ii. 16. Mar. [11] Jer. xxxi. 3.
[12] Isa. liii. 10, 11. [13] Ibid. lv. 13.
[14] Heb. xii. 2. See Cowper's beautiful Paraphrase, Olney Hymns, B. i. 52.

Now therefore hearken. It is no mean and undeserving person that calls. It is none other than the Wisdom of God; the source of all light and knowledge;[1] the King of kings;[2] the loving rewarder of his children, specially of his young children;[3] the rich portion and unfailing guide of his people.[4] Look at him once again in his Divine glory, as "the only begotten Son of God;"[5] the Mediator in the everlasting Councils of Redemption;[6] the Almighty Creator of the world;[7] the adorable Friend of sinners.[8] It is he that calls *the children* of men to *hearken.* And how should his Divine Majesty and condescending love endear his *instruction* to us![9] Yet his promised *blessing* belongs only to practical hearing—to *those that keep his ways.*[10] For this obedience—that we may *hear, and be wise*—sovereign grace must open the heart, and give the ear.[11] The guilt of *refusing* is inexcusable—a resolved will against the most gracious call.[12]

Now therefore hearken, O ye children. Oh! happy moment, when the soul is made "willing in the day of his power:"[13] when "the bands of love are drawing"[14] us unto him! The cold, dead indifference is gone. The enmity is slain. And who will but now joyfully swear fealty—yea, count it his unspeakable delight to take such a yoke—to be bound to such a service? O my Prince! my Saviour! thou hast based thy dominion on thy blood. Thou hast purchased thy right by thy cross.[15] Thou rulest only that thou mightest save. Take to thyself the glory of thy victory. I am thine—not my own—for ever.

34. *Blessed is the man that heareth me, watching daily at my gates, waiting at the posts of my doors.* 35. *For whoso findeth me findeth life, and shall obtain favor of the Lord.* 36. *But he that sinneth against me wrongeth his own soul: all they that hate me love death.*

This is the *hearing* of faith—the voice of Christ to the inward ear—the impression of his word upon the heart.[16] The effect is unwearied diligence and patient expectation; like that of the *priest's* waiting *at the doors* of the tabernacle for the assured blessing;[17] or the people *watching at the temple gates* for his return from his holy ministrations.[18] This free and habitual attendance upon Sacred Ordinances forms an healthy appetite for Divine nutriment. The slight professor excuses himself from this "weariness"[19] by the fear of legality, or the danger of *overvaluing* the means. But is there not at least equal danger of *undervaluing* the means, to which our gracious Lord has annexed a promised blessing? If in gazing on the heavenly Jerusalem the Apostle "saw no temple

[1] Verses 12—14. [2] Verses 15, 16. [3] Verse 17. Comp. Heb. xi. 6. [4] Verses 15, 16. [5] Verses 22, 24. [6] Verse 23. [7] Verses 27—30. [8] Verse 31.
[9] See how the Father manifested the glory of his Divine Son to give constraining force to his instructions. Matt. xvii. 1—5.
[10] Isa. lv. 2, 3. Luke xi. 28. John xiv. 21—23. James i. 25.
[11] Chap. xx. 12, with Acts xvi. 14. [12] Acts iii. 22, 23. Heb. ii. 1—3; x. 25.
[13] Psalm cx. 3. [14] Hos. xi. 4. [15] 1 Cor. vi. 19, 20. Comp. Rom. xiv. 9.
[16] John v. 25. Rev. iii. 20. [17] Ex. xxix. 42. [18] Luke i. 10, 21. [19] Mal. i. 13.

therein,"[1] what right-hearted Christian will doubt, that the life-blood of his soul consists, while on earth, in "loving the habitation of God's house, and the place where his honor dwelleth?"[2] To be, like the servants of the temple, *watching daily at the gates—when not involving the neglect of other imperative obligations*—would doubtless bring an enriching *blessing.*[3] Under all circumstances Wisdom's child will be familiar with *Wisdom's gates.* The *Weekly* as well as the Sabbath assemblies will be his delight. The "way by the footsteps of the flock, *beside the Shepherd's tents,*" will be his constant resort.[4] All the ordinances of prayer—meditation—Scripture-reading—godly conference, will be his salutary provision. When it is not so—when the common routine satisfies—when the intervals between the Sabbath, pass without any appetite for food, or any effort to seek the bread of the sanctuary—Christian, is not thy pulse beating feebly? Hast thou not lost a message, many a precious message—from thy Lord?[5] Doth not he speak to thee—"Be watchful, and strengthen the things that remain, which are ready to die."[6]

Observe the *blessing* breathed down upon the Lord's waiting ones. They *find life.*[7] For he on whom they *wait* is the Author[8]—the Dispenser[9]—the Keeper—of life.[10] "He therefore that hath him, hath life,"[11] with all its present privileges of *favor of the Lord.*[12] 'The smiles of God make heaven; and they that *obtain favor of the Lord,* have a heaven upon earth.'[13] Set then this expectation before thine eyes in waiting on thy God—'I am seeking *life* for my soul—I will *wait at the posts of his doors;* missing no opportunity of a means of grace. I shall not wait in vain.'

Would that *the sinner*—the thoughtless sinner—not the daring and ungodly only—would ponder how his heartless neglect of wisdom *wrongeth his own soul!*[14] How cruel he is to himself, while he is despising his Saviour! Every bait of sin is the temptation to suicide—to soul-murder. The snatching at it is as if men were in love with damnation. '*They that hate me love death.*' They love that which will be their death, and put that from them which would be their life. Sinners die, because they will die; which leaves them inexcusable, makes their condemnation more intolerable, and will for ever justify God when he judges. "O Israel, thou hast destroyed thyself."[15]

[1] Rev. xxi. 22. [2] Psalm xxvi. 8. [3] Ibid. lxxxiv. 1, 4, 10. [4] Cant. i. 7, 8. [5] See John xx. 19, 24.
[6] Rev. iii. 2. Let Scott's excellent note be carefully pondered
[7] Isa. lv. 3. John v. 24. [8] John i. 4; xi. 25; xix. 6. [9] Ibid. x. 10.
[10] Col. iii. 3. 1 John v. 11. Jude 1. [11] 1 John v. 12. [12] Isa. lxiv. 5.
[13] Lawson (George) Exposition of Proverbs. 2 vols. 12mo. 1821.
[14] Chap. i. 17—19, 31; ix. 12. Jer. vii. 19. Acts xiii. 46. Comp. Num. xvi. 38.
[15] Hos. xiii. 9. Henry in loco.

CHAPTER IX.

1. *Wisdom*[1] *hath builded her house, she hath hewn out her seven pillars:* 2. *She hath killed her beasts;*[2] *she hath mingled her wine; she hath also furnished her table.* 3. *She hath sent forth her maidens: she crieth upon the highest places of the city,* 4. *Whoso is simple, let him turn in hither: as for him that wanteth understanding, she saith to him,* 5. *Come, eat of my bread, and drink of the wine which I have mingled.* 6. *Forsake the foolish, and live; and go in the way of understanding.*

We have delighted to contemplate the Divine Saviour in his glorious majesty, and specially in his wondrous love to *the sons of men.*[3] Here his love is poured out before us. The parable of the marriage-feast so clearly identifies the speaker, that we cannot mistake the voice. For who hath blessings so rich? Who gives an invitation so free—a welcome so encouraging? There the King made the feast, and sent his servants to invite the guests.[4] Here *Wisdom* is a Queen, attended, according to *Eastern* custom, by *her maidens,*[5] and *sending them forth* to bid to the feast. *She hath builded her house*—"the church of the living God,"—firm upon the *pillars* of eternal truth.[6] The great sacrifice supplies her feast.[7] And now that *she hath killed her beasts—mingled her wine* with the choicest spices,[8] and plentifully *furnished her table*, let *the simple* and *ignorant turn in hither—come, eat of the bread* of life—*drink of the wine* of gospel grace and joy.[9] Is there not besides a special invitation for her children—*a table* richly *furnished* for their refreshment; where they *eat of the bread, and drink of the wine*, such as "the world know not of?"[10]

But are not all comers welcome to the Gospel feast? The Master's heart flows along with every offer of his grace. His servants are ministers of reconciliation.[11] Their message is to tell of the bounty of Messiah's house, and bid sinners welcome to their Saviour. Here, sinner, is thy warrant—not thy worthiness, but thy need, and the invitation of thy Lord. All the blessings of his Gospel are set before thee—love without beginning, end, or change. Honor the freeness of his mercy. Let him have the full glory of his own grace.[12]

1 Wisdoms. Heb. Comp. note Chap. i. 20.
2 Comp. Gen. xliii. 16. Marg.
3 Chap. viii. 22.
4 Matt. xxii. 1—4, also Luke xiv. 16, 17.
5 Ex. ii. 5. Esth. iv. 4.
6 1 Tim. iii. 15. Comp. Eph. ii. 20—22. Heb. iii. 3, 4, also Matt. xvi. 18.
7 1 Cor. v. 7, with Psalm xxxvi. 7, 8. Isa. xxv. 6.
8 Bishop Lowth remarks the difference between the Classics and the Hebrews. The one by *mingled wine* understand wine diluted with water; the other intend wine made stronger by spices, or other exhilarating ingredients. Note on Isa. i. 22. Comp. chap xxiii. 29—31. Cant. viii. 2.
9 Matt. xxii. 4. Isa. lv. 1. Comp. Bishop Hall's note.
10 Ibid. xxvi. 26—28.
11 2 Cor. v. 18—20.
12 Calvin speaks of the pleading invitations of Christ, as 'his sweet and more than motherly allurement,' and beautifully adds—that 'the word of God is never opened to us but that he with a motherly sweetness opens his own bosom to us.'—On Matt. xxiii. 37

But this blessing can never be valued, till the path of *the foolish be forsaken.* Thou must *forsake* either them or Christ.[1] To abide with them, is to "remain in the congregation of the dead."[2] To *forsake them,* is the way *of life and understanding.*[3] "Save thyself then from this untoward generation." "Come out, and be separate, and touch not the unclean thing; and I will receive thee, saith the Lord Almighty."[4]

7. *He that reproveth a scorner getteth to himself shame: and he that rebuketh a wicked man getteth himself a blot.* 8. *Reprove not a scorner, lest he hate thee: rebuke a wise man, and he will love thee.* 9. *Give instruction to a wise man, and he will be yet wiser: teach a just man, and he will increase in learning.*

Wisdom's messengers must discriminate in the proclamation of their message. Only *the simple* will welcome it. *The scorner and wicked* will rebel. "Let them alone."[5] Yet we must distinguish between the ignorant and the wilful *scorner*—between one who rejects from the first rising enmity, and one, who deliberately refuses the blessing—self-excluded from the general ministerial commission.[6]

This is also the rule of Christian prudence. The Gospel is a thing too holy to be exposed to scoffing fools.[7] Why should we *reprove,* where more harm than good may be occasioned? Avoid irritations. Await a favorable opportunity. Sometimes a sad, serious, intelligible silence is the most effective reproof.[8] Whereas open *rebuke* might stir up a torrent of *hatred*[9] and abuse;[10] and, under provocation of spirit, the *reprover* might *get to himself a blot.*[11]

Yet this prudence must not degenerate into cowardice, and compromise the primary obligation boldly to rebuke sin,[12] and confess our Master.[13] Every sinner is not *a scorner.* And a 'word spoken in due season, how good is it!"[14] That false delicacy therefore, which recoils from an unflinching profession, is treachery to our Lord, and deep—perhaps eternal—injury to our fellow-sinners. Has not each of us a tongue to speak? To suffer any therefore to rush into perdition without opening our mouths to save them is a sin of omission, which will cause a bitter pang to the awakened conscience.

The *wise and just man* gladly encourages well-timed reproof.[15] Conscious of his own failings, he *loves his reprover* as a friend to

[1] James iv. 4.
[2] Chap. xxi. 16.
[3] Chap. xiii. 20. Psalm xxvi. 3—6; xxxiv. 12—14; cxix. 115. Amos v. 14.
[4] Acts ii. 40—46. 2 Cor. vi. 17, 18.
[5] Matt. xv. 14.
[6] Acts xiii. 45, 46, 50; xviii. 6. Comp. Matt. x. 14, 15.
[7] Matt. vii. 6.
[8] Amos v. 13; vi. 10.
[9] Chap. xv. 12; xxiii. 9. 1 Kings xxi. 10; xxii. 8. 2 Chron. xxv. 16.
[10] Gen. xix. 7—9. Amos vii. 10. Matt. vii. 6.
[11] Isa. xxix. 21. Comp. Ecclus. viii. 10.
[12] Eph. v. 10. 1 Thess. v. 14. 1 Tim. v. 20. Comp. Matt. xiv. 3, 4.
[13] Matt. x. 32, 33. Acts iv. 19, 20.
[14] Chap. xv. 23.
[15] Chap. xxviii. 23.

his best interest;[1] and would receive *instruction* from the lowest, as a means of becoming *yet wiser and increasing in learning.*[2]

After all—wisely to give, and humbly to receive, reproof, requires much prayer, self-denial, love, and sincerity. But where the mind of Christ is mutually exhibited, it cements a bond of the warmest affection.[3] "Faithful are the wounds of a friend."[4] Happy is that church, which receives the loving admonitions of the Christian pastor with humility and thankfulness![5]

10. *The fear of the Lord is the beginning of wisdom: and the knowledge of the holy is understanding.* 11. *For by me thy days shall be multiplied, and the years of thy life shall be increased.*

The repetition of this weighty sentence[6] deepens our estimate of its importance. *The fear of the Lord* was a lovely grace in the perfect humanity of Jesus.[7] Let it be the test of our "predestination to be conformed to his image."[8] It is the genuine spirit of adoption. The child of God has only one dread, to offend his Father; only one desire—to please and delight in him. *The fear* of God is therefore connected with his love. 'The heart that is touched with the loadstone of Divine love trembles still with godly fear.'[9] If this temper is *the beginning*, it is also (as the word imports) *the head—of wisdom*—not only its first rudiment, but its matured exercise. It is obviously combined with *the knowledge of the Holy One.*[10] For if men did but know *his holiness*—"who would not fear thee, O Lord?"[11] *Days multiplied* were the Old Testament reward.[12] And truly the value of life is only realized in the *knowledge* and service of God. Inconceivably joyous to us is the prospect of *years of life increased* into a boundless eternity—infinite desires, fully satisfied; yet excited unceasingly to more full and heavenly enjoyment.

[1] Lev. xix. 17. Psalm cxli. 5. Comp. 1 Sam. xxv. 33. 2 Sam. xii. 7—14, with 1 Kings i. 32—34.

[2] Chap. i. 5. Comp. Ex. xviii. 17—24. Acts xviii. 26.

[3] 1 Sam. xxv. 32—42.

[4] Chap. xxvii. 6.

[5] 2 Cor. ii. 1—9. Mr. Martyn—his Biographer observes—'felt reproof to be "a duty of unlimited extent and almost insuperable difficulty." But, said he, "the way to know when to address men, and when to abstain, is to love." And, as love is most genuine where the heart is most abased, he resolved not to reprove others, when he could conscientiously be silent, except he experienced at the same time a peculiar contrition of spirit.'—Life, chap. ii.

[6] Chap. i. 7. Comp. Job xxviii. 28. Psalm cxi. 10.

[7] Isa. xi. 2, 3.

[8] Rom. viii. 29.

[9] Leighton on 1 Peter ii. 17.

[10] The parallelism with the former clause seems to demand this meaning. The application of the plural number to the sacred name is elsewhere used by Solomon (ver. i. 1—20. Ecc. xii. 1.) as well as by others of the inspired Writers. Gen. i. 26. Job xxxv. 10. Isa. liv. 5. Bishop Horsley remarks—'God is the only being, to whom the same name in the singular and in the plural may be indiscriminately applied. And this change from the one number to the other, without any thing in the principles of language to account for it, is frequent in speaking of God in the Hebrew tongue, but unexampled in the case of any other being.' See his ingenious Sermon on the Watchers. The reason of this peculiar usage—we may add—is obvious to any one, who receives with implicit and reverential faith the Scriptural revelation of the Divine Essence.

[11] Rev. xv. 4.

[12] Chap. iii. 2, 16; iv. 10; x. 27.

12. *If thou be wise, thou shalt be wise for thyself: but if thou scornest, thou alone shalt bear it.*

The consequences of our conduct—good or bad—chiefly reflect on ourselves.[1] God cannot be profited by us;[2] and he is infinitely above our injury.[3] *The wise* man's light is a blessing to the church and to the world.[4] But he *is wise for himself*—for his own advantage.[5] *The scorner* is a grief to his minister, and a stumbling to his church. But he hurts no one so much as himself. *He alone shall bear it.*[6] A surety indeed there is. But *his scorning* rejects him. He sinks therefore into perdition under a millstone of guilt—without remedy.[7] This then is the ordinance of God. "Every man shall bear his own burden. Whatsoever a man soweth, that shall he also reap," life or death—a double harvest—for time and for eternity.[8]

13. *A foolish woman is clamorous: she is simple and knoweth nothing.* 14. *For she sitteth at the door of her house, on a seat in the high places of the city.* 15. *To call passengers who go right on their ways:* 16. *Whoso is simple, let him turn in hither: and as for him that wanteth understanding, she saith to him,* 17. *Stolen waters are sweet, and bread eaten in secret* (of secrecies, Marg.) *is pleasant.* 18. *But he knoweth not that the dead are there; and that her guests are in the depths of hell.*

Wisdom's free and gracious invitation has been before us. And we might almost ask—who could resist it? Now we have an allurement from the opposite quarter. For sin is no less earnest to destroy, than wisdom is to save. Fleshly lusts are directly opposed to Divine wisdom. 'The delight of the soul fixed on any thing but God and his grace is but spiritual adultery.'[9] *The woman of foolishness is clamorous,*[10] and, though "subtil in heart,"[11] in the devices of Satan, is *simplicity* itself in her utter ignorance of right. So fearfully do sensual pleasures darken the understanding, that the tempter, from the very habit of deceiving, becomes the victim of her own delusion![12] With a shameless front she dares to present herself *in the high places of the city,*[13] alluring, not only those who are "going the way to her house,"[14] but the inexperienced, *who are going right on their ways.* Thus even the high-way of God, though a path of safety,[15] is beset with temptation. Enticement or assaults wait on every step. *Stolen waters*[16] —*secret* indulgences[17]—forbidden pleasures—are the bait. This was the successful snare in paradise.[18] And who has not felt, that restraint provokes the dormant power of sin; as children will do that which is forbidden, *because* it is forbidden?[19] But let the vic-

1 Chap. xvi. 26.
2 Job xxii. 2, 3. Psalm xvi. 2. Luke xvii. 10.
3 Job xxxv 6, 7.
4 Matt. v. 14—16.
5 Chap. iii. 13—18; xxiv. 3. Ecc. viii. 1.
6 Chap. viii. 36. Ezek. xviii. 20. Luke vii. 30.
7 Chap. xxix. 1. Heb. x. 28, 29. Comp. Lev. xxiv. 15.
8 Gal. vi. 5, 7, 8.
9 Diodati.
10 Heb. Chap. vii. 10.
11 Ibid. ver. 11.
12 Hos. iv. 11. 2 Tim. iii. 13.
13 Chap. vii. 10—12. Gen. xxxviii. 14, 21. Jer. iii. 2, 3. Ezek. xvi. 24, 25, 31.
14 Chap. vii. 8.
15 Chap. x. 9.
16 Chap. v. 15—17. 2 Sam. xi. 2.
17 Chap. xx. 17. 2 Sam. xii. 12. Comp. Job xx. 12.
18 Gen. iii. 1—6.
19 Rom. vii. 8. 1 Cor. xv. 56. See Augustine's description of his robbing the pear-

tim—ere it be too late—contemplate the fearful close in eternity. It is as if we might almost see *that the dead are there ; and that her guests*—the wilful despisers of wisdom—are *in the very depths of hell.*[1] Ah ! if the blinded fool *know not this*, what but wilful inconsideration can have closed his eyes ?[2]

Reader—*the wisdom of God*, and the great deceiver of man—stand before you. Both are wooing thine heart—the one for life—the other for death. Both are intensely anxious for success. *Wisdom crieth. The foolish woman is clamorous.*[3] Both take their station *in the high places of the city.*[4] Both spread out this feast *for the simple* and ignorant.[5] But how opposite the purpose of each ! The one ready to make *the simple* wise unto eternal life. The other bearing away her willing captive into unutterable misery. Which is the voice that arrests thine ear—allures thine heart ? Which is the feast, that excites thine appetite ? Whose *guest* art thou ?—Oh ! remember that listening to the enticement cheats thee of thy present—no less than of thine eternal—happiness, and will banish thee forever from the paradise re-opened as thy home. The Lord preserve thee from the tempter's snares, by keeping thee closely walking with himself !

CHAPTER X.

1. *The proverbs of Solomon. A wise son maketh a glad father : but a foolish son is the heaviness of his mother.*

THE former chapters have beautifully set forth in continuous discourse, the nature and value of heavenly wisdom, contrasted with the fascinations of sinful folly. We now come to what are more properly (not of course excluding the foregoing)[6] *the Proverbs of Solomon.* They are for the most part unconnected sentences, remarkable for profound thought, and acute observation, ex

tree—not for the gain of the fruit (the greater part of which he threw away) but for the mere pleasure of sin *as sin—as breaking God's law.* Truly affecting also is it to see him, like the Psalmist (Psalm li. 5.), tracing the sin to its root—' Behold my heart, O Lord, behold my heart, which thou hadst pity upon in the very bottom of the bottomless pit.' Confess. iii 4, 6. How striking also is the confession of this rebellious propensity from the voice of a heathen conscience !

Quod licet, ingratum est ; quod non licet, acrius urit :
Ferreus est, si quis, quod sinit alter, amat.
Ovid. Lib. ii. Amor. Eleg. 19. v. 3.

Nitimur in vetitum semper, cupimusque negata :
Sic interdictis imminet æger aquis.
Quidquid servatur, cupimus magis, ipsaque furem
Cura vocat, pauci, quid sinet alter, amant.
Ibid. iii. Eleg. 4. v. 17.

[1] Chap. ii. 18 ; vii. 27.
[2] Chap. vii. 22. Isa. i. 3. 2 Pet. iii. 5.
[3] Verse 3 with 13.
[4] Verse 3 with 14.
[5] Verse 4 with 16.
[6] Chap. i. 1.

pressed in an antithetical or illustrative form; the whole comprising a Divine system of morals of universal application. The previous chapters form a striking introduction to the book. The glorious description of the Great Counsellor[1] commends to us his gracious instruction, as the principle of true happiness and practical godliness.

Perhaps this first sentence may have been placed in the front, to point to the value of a godly education in its personal, social, national influence, connected both with time and eternity. Do not we naturally look for rest in our children, as the choicest gift of God.[2] Faith indeed may be tried—perhaps severely tried.[3] But the child, watched, prayed over, instructed, and disciplined, shall in the Lord's best time, choose *wisdom's* paths,[4] and be *the gladness of his father's* heart.[5]

Many a *mother*, alas! is chastened with *the heaviness of a foolish son.*[6] In such cases—has not indulgence, instead of wholesome restraint—pleasure, instead of godliness—the world, instead of the Bible—educated the child? Want of early discipline; passing over trifles; yielding when we ought to command—how little do we think to what this may grow![7] God has laid down plain rules, plain duties, and plain consequences flowing from their observance[8] or neglect.[9] To forget a daily reference to them; to choose our own wisdom before God's;[10]—can we wonder that the result should be *heaviness?*[11]

2. *Treasures of wickedness profit nothing: but righteousness delivereth from death.*

The most substantial earthly *treasures profit nothing.*[12] Much more do *treasures of wickedness.*[13] What was the *profit* of Naboth's vineyard to Ahab, when in his "ivory palace" he was withering under the curse of God?[14] What was the *profit* of the thirty pieces of silver to Judas? Instead of *delivering from death*, their intolerable sting plunged him into death eternal.[15] What else will be the fruit of covetousness, but shame,[16] disappointment[17]—ruin?[18] "Thou, O man of God, flee these things, and follow af

[1] Chap. i. viii. [2] Gen. v. 28, 29; xxxiii. 5. Psalm cxxvii. 3.
[3] Ecc. xi. 1. [4] Chap. xxii. 6.
[5] Chap. xv. 20; xxiii. 15, 16, 24, 25; xxvii. 11; xxix. 3. Comp. Gen. xlv. 28 xlvi. 30.
[6] Gen. xxvi. 34. 35; xxvii. 46. [7] 1 Sam. ii. 24; iii. 13. 1 Kings i. 5, 6; ii. 2[illegible]
[8] Chap. xxii. 6; xxiii. 13, 14; xxix. [9] Chap. xxix. 15. [10] 1 Sam. ii. 29.
[11] Bishop Lowth supposes an antithesis between the relative terms, (Prelim. Dissert Isaiah,) which Bishop Jebb illustrates by the distinctive character of *the father's gladness*, whose affections are more disciplined, and *the mother's grief*, whose tenderness might blind her to the faults of her children, or lead her weakly to excuse them. Sacred Literature, Sect. ii. It may be doubted however whether this refinement of criticism is not beside the meaning of the inspired writer, who interchangeably ascribes these exercises of feeling to both parents. Chap. xvii. 24, 25; xix. 13; xxiii. 24, 25. Comp. Gen xxvi. 35. 2 Sam. xiii. 37—39. Comp. Glass. Phil. Sacr. Lib. iv. Tract. ii. Obs. 13 Schultens in loco.
[12] Chap. xxiii. 5. Matt. vi. 19. [13] Jer. xxii. 13. Amos iii. 10, 11. Hab. ii. 6—9
[14] 1 Kings xxi. 4—24, with xxii. 39. [15] Matt. xxvii. 3—5.
[16] 2 Kings v. 23—27. Rom. vi. 21. [17] Jer. xvii. 11. Comp. Wis. v. 8.
[18] Chap. xxi. 6, 7. Jos. vii. 20—26. Dan. v. 1—6.

ter *righteousness*."[1] This is "the breastplate,"[2] that covers the vitals in the fearful conflict. This is the pathway to eternal life.[3] This is the *deliverance* from the sting, the terror, the taste of death.[4] We must not flinch from this scriptural statement from fear of legality. Lay the foundation of acceptance deep and clear upon the righteousness of Christ. But upon this foundation, fear not to raise the superstructure of inherent righteousness. Take up the prayer and confidence of the man of God—"Let integrity and uprightness preserve me; for I trust on thee."[5]

3. *The Lord will not suffer the soul of the righteous to famish; but he casteth away the substance of the wicked.*

To spiritualize the temporal promises would be to lose great enlargement of faith. They are not restricted to the Old Dispensation. If David was preserved from *famishing*, and that too by those most unlikely to help him,[6] Paul could also in similar trial "set to his seal"—"I have all, and abound; I am full."[7] How does our gracious God double and redouble his engagements![8] He sends us to the fowls of the air for the confirmation of our "little faith."—"Are not ye much better than they?"[9] Yet 'the promises require faith, whereby we believe that God helpeth us.'[10] He may for the exercise of faith *suffer* us to hunger[11]—yet not to *famish*.[12] And does not his unfailing care for temporal provision convey the assurance, that *he will not suffer the soul to famish*. "The Good Shepherd knows his sheep." He "seeks them out in the cloudy and dark day," and brings them into his fold, where "they go in and out, and find pasture."[13] Awful indeed is the contrast of *the wicked—their substance cast out*[14]—themselves buried in the ruins of their own folly![15]

4. *He becometh poor that dealeth with a slack* (deceitful, Marg.) *hand: but the hand of the diligent maketh rich.*

Every day's observation confirms the fact, that *a slack hand* impoverishes,[16] and *the hand of the diligent enriches*,[17] the harvest. Justly is the slothful condemned as *deceitful*, because he pretends to serve his Master, when in truth he has been doing nothing.[18] *He becometh poor* by wasting away his trust.[19] His life, which

[1] 1 Tim. vi. 11. [2] Eph. vi. 14. 1 Thess. v. 8.
[3] Chap. xii. 28. Psalm xv; xxiv, 3—5. Isa. xxxv. 8. Matt. v. 8.
[4] Chap. xi. 4. John viii. 52. [5] Psalm xxv. 21.
[6] By Shobi the brother of his bitter enemy. 2 Sam. xvii. 27. with x. 4. Machir also of the house of Saul. Ibid. Comp. Psalm xxxvii. 25.
[7] Phil. iv. 18. [8] Heb. xiii. 5; five negatives in the original.
[9] Matt. vi. 25, 26. Comp. Psalm xxxiv. 13. [10] Cope in loco.
[11] 1 Cor. iv. 11. 2 Cor. xi. 27, with Deut. viii. 3. Matt. iv. 2—4.
[12] Psalm xxxvii. 3. Isa. xxxiii. 16. Matt. vi. 32.
[13] John x. 9, 14, with Ez. xxxiv. 12. [14] Job xx. 15.
[15] Psalm xlix. 6, &c. Luke xii. 19, 20; xvi. 23.
[16] Chap. xix. 15; xx. 4; xxiii. 21; xxiv. 30—34. Ecc. x. 18.
[17] Chap. xii. 4; xxi. 5.
[18] Matt. xxv. 26. Comp. xii. 24. Marg. Jer. xlviii. 10. Marg.
[19] Chap. xvii. 9. Comp. Matt. xxv. 28, 29.

might have been a continual feast, is a continual vexation. Industry was the law of Paradise:[1] and though now it bears the stamp of the fall,[2] it is overruled as a present blessing; and in the ordinary course of Providence *the hand of the diligent maketh rich.*[3] The Lord's visits of favor were never given to loiterers. Moses and the Shepherds of Bethlehem were keeping their flocks.[4] Gideon was at the threshing-floor.[5] 'Our idle days'—as Bishop Hall observes, 'are Satan's busy days.' Active employment gives us a ready answer to his present temptation—"I am doing a great work, and I cannot come down."[6]

Is then the man of God waxing low in his store? Has there not been *a slack hand* in drawing upon the sacred treasury? Has not he gazed upon the heavenly treasure, with "his hand in his bosom?"[7] Has he not *become poor* by slighting his rich consolations? The Lord gives His blessing, as he gives the fruits of the earth—not to those that wish,[8] but to those that "labor,"[9]—not to sentimental indolence, but to Christian energy and perseverance. And how enriching is this habit in the increase of our grace, and the enlargement of our confidence![10]

5. *He that gathereth in summer is a wise son: but he that sleepeth in harvest is a son that causeth shame.*

Indolence has just been contrasted with diligence. Forethought is here opposed to improvidence.[11] The importance of opportunity is practically admitted in temporal matters.[12] Joseph wisely *gathered in summer and harvest* for the coming need.[13] The woman of Canaan[14]—the blind men[15]—improved their present opportunities for their urgent need. And have not we our special season for attaining permanent good? *Such a season is youth,* when life is fresh—the time for discipline—storing the mind—stimulating the energies. How will the *wise gathering in this summer* give substance, vigor, high tone and power of usefulness in after-life! How often may we trace poverty of mind, enervation of character, unprofitable habits, to *sleeping in* this fruitful *harvest!*[16] 'He, who idles away the time of his youth, will bear the shame of it when he is old.' And specially when we look at this season, as the time of Christian instruction, and anxious promise; our Father's pleading time with the wayward heart,[17] ere yet it be hardened in habits of sin—is not the *sleeper in such an harvest a son that causeth shame?*[18] *Look, again, at the large harvest of opportunity* in laboring for God; the multitude of religious Societies; the great and diversified machinery of the work of God—all needing counsel and active devotedness; the mass of

[1] Gen. ii. 15. [2] Ibid. iii. 19.
[3] Chap. xii. 24, 27; xxii. 29. [4] Ex. iii. 1, 2. Luke ii. 8, 9. [5] Jud. vi. 11.
[6] Neh. vi. 3. [7] Chap. xix. 24. [8] Chap. xiii. 4; xx. 4.
[9] Ver. 3 with 4. John vi. 27. [10] Matt. xxv. 29. 2 Pet. i. 5—11.
[11] Chap. vi. 6—8. [12] Eccl. iii. 1; viii. 5. [13] Gen. xli. 46—56. Matt. xv. 22—30.
[14] Ibid. xx. 30. [15] Henry in loco. [16] Jer. iii. 4.
[17] Gal. vi. 10. [18] Matt. xii. 30.

fellow-sinners around us—all needing our sympathy and helpfulness—'While we have time, let us do good.' How high is the privilege of *gathering* with *Christ in such a harvest!*[1] How great the *shame* of doing nothing, where there was so much to be done! *Once more*, was ever an "accepted time" so encouraging? Mark the abundance of the means of grace—the living verdure of the gospel. The Bible opens the way. The Saviour invites. The Holy Spirit strives with the conscience. The Sabbath draws us aside from the world, and beams with the peace, joy and hope of heaven. What everlasting *shame* will cover the *sleeper* in this golden *harvest!*[2]

But am I the *wise son* gathering for my store? Or am I bringing *shame* to myself, by *sleeping* away the invaluable hours of "the day of salvation?" Can I bear the thought of that desponding cry of eternal remorse—"*The harvest* is passed; *the summer* is ended—and I am not saved?"[3]

6. *Blessings are upon the head of the just: but violence covereth the mouth of the wicked.* 7. *The memory of the just is blessed: but the name of the wicked shall rot.*

Is not affliction the lot of *the just?*[4] Yet how abundantly is it compensated by the *blessings that are upon his head*[5]—blessings temporal[6] and spiritual[7]—from man,[8] and from God![9] His very *memory is a blessing* to his family, and to the church.[10] Fragrant is the "good report of the elders" immortalized in the Apostolic Book of Martyrs.[11] Truly *blessed is the memory* of a godly parent[12]—of a faithful minister[13]—of a righteous king[14]—of a public benefactor[15]—of a self-denying Christian.[16] No such honor belongs to *the wicked.* Often some outward stroke of *violence covers their mouth*,[17] and marks them for condemnation,[18] as they will all be so marked at the day of retribution.[19] And even now *their memory rots* in corruption.[20] Contrast the memory of the "man after God's heart," with that of "Jeroboam the son of Nebat;"[21] or, in later times, Ridley and Latimer with *the name of their wicked* persecutors. Such is *the blessing* and curse of God, long after the men had passed into eternity! 'Thou mayest choose'—said godly Bishop Pilkington—'whether thou wilt be remembered to thy praise or to thy shame.'[22]

[1] 2 Cor. vi. 2.
[2] Matt. xxv. 8—10. Comp. Isa. lv. 6. Luke xiii. 28, 29. Chap. i. 24—28.
[3] Jer. viii. 20. Comp. chap. v. 11—13.
[4] John xvi. 33. Acts xiv. 22. 2 Tim. iii. 12.
[5] Chap. xxviii. 22. Comp. Gen. xlix. 26.
[6] Deut. xxviii. 1—6. 1 Tim. iv. 8.
[7] Isa. xxxii. 17.
[8] Chap. xvi. 7. Job xxix. 11—13.
[9] Psalm iii. 8; v. 12. Isa. lxiv. 4, 5. Matt. v. 3—12.
[10] Psalm cxii. 6.
[11] Heb. xi. 2.
[12] Ibid. xiii. 7.
[13] Chap. xxxi. 28.
[14] 2 Chron. xxxv. 24, 25. Zech. xii. 11.
[15] 2 Chron. xxiv. 6.
[16] Mark xiv. 9.
[17] Psalm cvii. 42.
[18] Esth. vii. 8.
[19] Rom. iii. 19.
[20] Job xviii. 17. Psalm xlix. 11, 12; cix. 13. Ecc. viii. 10. Isa. lxv. 16. Jer. xxii. 18, 19; xxix. 22, 23.
[21] 1 Kings xi. 26; xiv. 14—16, with xv. 3, 11. 2 Kings xiv. 3.
[22] Works, p. 366.

8. *The wise in heart will receive commandments; but a prating fool will fall,* (be beaten, Marg.)

The heart is the seat of true *wisdom,* and a teachable spirit is the best proof of its influence. For who that knows himself would not be thankful for further light? No sooner therefore, *do the commandments* come down from heaven, than the well-instructed Christian *receives them,* like his father Abraham,[1] with undisputed simplicity welcomes the voice of his heavenly teacher;[2] and when he knows that "it is the Lord, girds himself" with all the ardor of the disciple to be found at his feet.[3]

But look at the professor of religion destitute of this *heart-seated wisdom.* We find him a man of creeds and doctrines, not of prayer; asking curious questions, rather than listening to plain truths;[4] waiting to know events rather than duties; occupied with other men's business to the neglect of his own.[5] In this vagrant spirit, with all his thoughts outward-bound, he wanders from church to church, and from house to house, *a prating fool* upon religion; bold in his own conceit,[6] while his life and temper fearfully contradict his fluent tongue. Too blind to respect himself,[7] too proud to listen to counsel,[8] he will surely *fall* into disgrace, *beaten* with the rod of his own foolishness.[9] Let me look at this picture as a beacon against the folly of my own heart. Young Christian! Beware of a specious religion—without humility, consistency, love; because separated from close walking with God.

9. *He that walketh uprightly walketh surely; but he that perverteth his ways shall be known.*

An upright walk is Christian—not sinless—perfection;[10] "walking before God," not before men.[11] Impurity indeed defiles the holiest exercise. But if the will be right bent, the integrity will be maintained. 'Shew me an easier path'—is nature's cry. 'Shew me'—cries the child of God—'a *sure* path.' Such is *the upright walk,* under the shield of the Lord's protection[12] and Providence;[13] under the shadow of his promises;[14] in the assurance of his present favor,[15] and in its peaceful end.[16] There will be difficulties. But a deliverance will be wrought through them; as the Babylonish captives were delivered through the fire from the infinitely greater danger of apostacy.[17]

From the want of *this uprightness of walk,* Peter denied the foundation of the Gospel.[18] Learn then the value of this principle for an enlightened and full reception of the truth; that we may

[1] Heb. xi. 8. Gen. xxii. 1—3.
[2] 1 Sam. iii. 10. Acts x. 33. Comp. Psalm xxvii. 8; lxxxvi. 11; cxliii. 8—10.
[3] See John xxi. 7.
[4] Ibid. verses 21, 22.
[5] Luke xiii. 23, 24. Comp. 1 Tim. v. 13.
[6] 3 John 10.
[7] Chap. xviii. 2.
[8] Ver. 17, xv. 32.
[9] Chap. xviii. 6, 7. Eccles. x. 12. 2 Kings xiv. 8—14.
[10] Job i. 8.
[11] Gen. xvii. 1.
[12] Chap. ii. 7. Ps. lxxxiv. 11.
[13] Chap. i. 33. Eccl. viii. 5. Isa. xxxiii. 15, 16.
[14] Ps. xxiv. 3—6.
[15] John iii. 18—22.
[16] Ps. xxxvii. 37. Isa. lvii. 1, 2.
[17] Dan. iii. 21—29.
[18] Gal. ii. 14.

welcome "a Prince as well as a Saviour;"[1] combine his sceptre with his sacrifice, his holy precepts with his precious promises: and mark the influence of a vital faith in godly practice. We shall thus carry out the rule of the Gospel into every thing, making God the master of every thought, word, temper, motive, not less in our secular calling, than in our spiritual devotedness.[2] Such an *upright walk* will bring a happy confidence. But to bend our rule to our own humor; to *pervert our ways* to escape trouble, or for some interested end, will shake our confidence far more than the heaviest cross. The eye of God *knows* the deviation already,[3] and will bring it to shame.[4] Thus was Jacob chastened to the end of his days.[5] Peter was openly rebuked[6]—Judas[7] and Ananias[8] are *known* in the records of the church as a beacon to the end of time. "Let my heart be sound it thy statutes, that I may not be ashamed. I will walk in my integrity; redeem me, and be merciful unto me."[9]

10. *He that winketh with his eye causeth sorrow; but a prating fool shall fall.*

The contrast here intended seems to be between the man, who brings trouble on his fellow-creatures, and one who brings it upon himself.[10] Mischievous sport to *cause sorrow* for selfish gratification![11] to make the eye an instrument of wanton sin![12] Scarcely less affecting is it to see the tongue a world of *foolishness*. But not a trace is visible of the likeness, in which man was first created. Every member is perverted from its proper use and glorious end. Man is a plague to his neighbor, because he is an enemy to his God. And because "*the fool* despises wisdom,"[13] *he falls* the victim of his own folly.

11. *The mouth of a righteous man is a well of life: but violence covereth the mouth of the wicked.*

The Indwelling Spirit—"a well of living water"—is the glorious privilege of *the righteous*.[14] Hence *his mouth*, replenished from the heavenly source, is *a well of life*, sending forth refreshing waters.[15] The precious talent of speech is thus consecrated to His service, "who made man's mouth." "Grace is *in its measure* poured upon our lips;"[16] and our "tongues" become "our glory."[17] Wit, originality, imagination, may furnish 'the feast of reason, and the flow of soul.' But how impoverishing is this pleasure compared with the godly instruction—perhaps with little intellectual attraction—that pours forth from *a well of life!* Servant of God! honor your high privilege of thus ministering a blessing to the Church.[18] Enlarge its exercise by increasing your spiritual store, and walking in closer fellowship with your God. What owe you

[1] Acts v. 31. [2] 1 Cor. x. 31. Col. iii. 17. [3] John vi. 70, 71.
[4] Luke xii. 1, 2. 1 Tim. v. 24. [5] Gen. xxvii. with xlii. 36—38.
[6] Gal. ii. 11—14. [7] Matt. xxvii. 3—5. [8] Acts v. 1—10.
[9] Ps. cxix. 80; xxvi. 1—11. [10] See Bishop Hall. [11] Ver. 23; xxvi. 18, 19.
[12] Chap. vi. 13. Ps. xxxv. 19. Comp. Ecclus. xxvii. 22. [13] Chap. i. 7.
[14] John iv. 14; vii. 38. [15] Chap. xvi. 23. [16] Ps. xlv. 2.
[17] Psalm lvii. 8; cviii. 1. [18] Ver. 21; xv. 7. Eph. iv. 29.

to His grace, who hath made *your mouth a well of life*, while *the violence of the wicked* falls back upon themselves, and *covers their mouth* with confusion!

12. *Hatred stirreth up strifes: but love covereth all sins.*

A simple but forcible contrast? *Hatred*, however varnished by smooth pretence, is the selfish principle of man.[1] Like a subterraneous fire, it continually *stirs up* mischief, creates or keeps alive rankling enmity, disgusts, dislikes, "envyings and evil surmisings;" carps at the infirmities of others; aggravates the least slip;[2] or resents the most trifling, or even imaginary, provocations. These *strifes* are kindled[3] to the great dishonor of God, and the marring of the beauty and consistency of the gospel. Is not here abundant matter for prayer, watchfulness, and resistance? Let us study 1 Cor. xiii. in all its detail. Let it be the looking-glass for our hearts, and the standard of our profession. *Love covers*, overlooks, speedily forgives, and forgets.[4] Full of candor and inventiveness, it puts the best construction on doubtful matters, searches out any palliation; does not rigidly eye, or wantonly expose[5] a brother's faults; nor will it uncover them at all, except so far as may be needful for his ultimate good. To refrain from gross slander, while abundant scope is left for needless and unkind detraction, is not *covering sin.* Nor is the "seven-times forgiveness" the true standard of love,[6] which, like its Divine Author, *covers all sins.*[7] And who does not need the full extent of this *covering?* What is our brother's *all* against us, compared with our *all* against God? And how can we hesitate to blot out a few pence, who look for the *covering* of the debt of ten thousand talents?[8] Oh! let us "put on the Lord Jesus" in his spirit of forbearing, disinterested, sacrificing love—"Even as Christ forgave you, so also do ye."[9]

13. *In the lips of him that hath understanding wisdom is found; but a rod is for the back of him that is void of understanding.*

Solomon and his son admirably illustrate this contrast. Such *wisdom was found in his lips*—the fruit of an *understanding*[10] heart—that "all the world came to hear of it."[11] And "happy were they" justly pronounced, which stood continually before him, and "heard his *wisdom*."[12] Rehoboam was as *void*, as his father was

[1] Tit. iii. 3. [2] Isa. xxix. 21. [3] Chap. xv. 18; xvi. 27, 28; xxviii. 25; xxix. 22.
[4] Gen. xlv. 5, 8. [5] Ibid. ix. 23.
[6] Matt. xviii. 21. [7] Psalm lxxxv. 2. [8] Matt. xviii. 22—35.
[9] Col. iii. 13. Comp. 1 Pet. iv. 8. The first clause of the verse, compared with the Apostle's application of the second, clearly proves, that the subject is *the covering* of our brother's *sin* before men. Este—one of the most evangelical of the Romish interpreters—thus limits the application. No gloss therefore of man's covering sins before God is utterly groundless. Comp. Chap. xvii. 9. Calvin and Geier conceive James v. 20. to be only an allusion to the Proverb. The latter adds—'It is one thing to cover sin before men, another thing to cover it before God. The first is the act of love, (1 Cor. xiii. 4. Gal. vi. 2.) The last requires an infinite price, equal to the turning away of the eternal wrath of God.' Rom. iii. 25. 1 John i. 7. Ps. xxxii. 1, &c.
[10] 1 Kings iii. 12. [11] Ibid. iv. 29-34; x. 1. [12] Ibid. x. 8.

full, of *understanding*. His folly prepared a *rod for his back*.[1] Learn then to seek for *wisdom* at the lips of the wise.[2] The want of this wisdom—or rather the want of a heart to seek it—will surely bring us under *the rod*. In many a chastisement we shal feel its smart—in the loose education of our children;[3] in the neglect of family discipline;[4] in carnal indulgence.[5] And how different is this *rod* from our Father's loving chastisement! That —the seal of our adoption[6]—This, the mark of disgrace[7]—Will not the child of God cry—"Turn away the reproach that I fear, for thy judgments are good?"[8]

14. *Wise men lay up knowledge: but the mouth of the foolish is near destruction.*

Solomon well proved his title as *a wise man* by his diligence in *laying up knowledge!*[9] No wonder that *wisdom is found in the lips;* when "out of the abundance of the good treasure of the heart the mouth speaketh."[10] It is "the householder" storing his mind not for selfish gratification, but for liberal and useful distribution.[11] If the hoarding *wisdom* be cultivated in youth,[12] what a store of valuable treasure would be *laid up;* yet all little enough to meet the coming trial! Let every day add something to the stock. So inexhaustible is the treasure, that no doubt, difficulty, temptation, or duty, will be found unprovided for.

Wise men lay up knowledge, for their own use—*Fools lay* it out. For want of sound wisdom, they only open *their mouths* for their own mischief—in profane rebellion;[13] grovelling selfishness;[14] ungodly worldliness;[15] or hateful pride[16]—*near to destruction*,[17]—how *near*—who can say?—But if they be not "taken away with a stroke" without remedy;[18] they only stand out as monuments of the "much long-suffering of God, enduring the vessels of wrath fitted to *destruction*."[19]

15. *The rich man's wealth is his strong city; the destruction of the poor is their poverty.*

This is as it appears on the surface. *The rich man's wealth* fences him from many invading evils,[20] obtains for him influence and respect,[21] and serves to him as a talisman against all sorrows.[22] Thus "in his own conceit" it is *his strong city*.[23] So prone are

1 1 Kings xii. 13—24. Comp. Chap. xix. 29; xxvi. 3. The rod was the usual corporal punishment under the Mosaic law. Deut. xxii. 18; xxv. 2, 3.
2 Verses 11, 21; xiii. 20; xv. 7. 3 Chap. xxix. 21. 4 Ibid. Ver. 21.
5 2 Sam. xii. 9—11. Isa. xxxix. 1—7. 6 Chap. iii. 11, 12, with Heb. xii. 6, 7.
7 1 Pet. ii. 20. 8 Psalm cxix. 39. 9 Eccl. xii. 9, 10.
10 Matt. xii. 34. Jerome mentions of his friend Nepotian, that 'by daily reading and meditating in the sacred volume, he had made his soul a library of Christ.'—Letter to Nepotian.
11 Ibid. Ver. 52. 12 Comp. Chap. vi. 5; xviii. 1, 15.
13 Ex. v. 2. Ps. xii. 3—5; lii. 1—5. 14 1 Sam. xxv. 10, 11, 38.
15 Luke xii. 18—20. 16 Acts xii. 21—23.
17 Comp. Chap. xii. 13; xiii. 3; xviii. 7. Eccles. x. 12, 13. 18 Job xxxvi. 18
19 Rom. ix. 22 20 Eccl. vii. 12. 21 Chap. xviii. 4, 6. Gen. xxiii. 6. Esth. iii. 1—3
22 Eccl. x. 19. 23 Chap. xviii. 11.

we to rest on the creature as the stay and comfort of life.[1] All notions of God are blotted out, and man becomes a God to himself. *The poor*, having no such defence, dwell as "a city without walls," exposed to every assault.[2] "*Poverty* comes upon them as an armed man,"[3] and sinks the spirit in *consternation*.[4]

How secure—how happy then—we are ready to say—are the rich! How wretched the condition of the poor! But the glass of God's word discovers a more even balance. "Hath not God chosen *the poor* in this world, rich in faith, and heirs of his kingdom?"[5] Think of Jesus sanctifying the state of poverty by his own blessed example.[6] Think of the riches of his grace, raising the poor out of the dunghill, that he may set him with the princes of his people.[7]

Both states, however, have their besetting temptations, needing special grace.[8] The safety of both is, when *the rich are poor in spirit*"[9] and larger in heart: and *the poor* "rich in faith," and "contented with the gain of godliness."[10] "Let the brother of low degree rejoice, in that he is exalted: but *the rich*, in that he is made low."[11]

16. *The labor of the righteous tendeth to life: the fruit of the wicked to sin.*

Labor—not idleness—is the stamp of a servant of God: cheered by the glowing confidence, that it *tendeth to life*.[12] "Occupy till I come—Do all to the glory of God"[13]—this is the standard. Thus the duties even of our daily calling *tend to life*.[14] God works in us, by us, with us, through us.[15] We work in and through him. Our *labor* therefore is his work—wrought in dependence on him; not for life, but *to life*.[16] And this is *life* indeed—the only exercise deserving the name—the only object worth living for.[17] Lord! quicken us to "*life* more abundantly." "Sowing" thus "to the Spirit, of the Spirit we shall reap life everlasting."[18] With *the wicked*, self is both the object and the end. *His fruit* therefore *is sin*.[19] His master, so long as he serves him faithfully, cares little how or in what sphere. "He that soweth to the flesh, shall of the flesh reap corruption." Each *tendeth* to its own end. "Whatsoever a man soweth, that shall he also reap."[20]

17. *He is in the way of life that keepeth instruction: but he that refuseth reproof erreth.*

Mercy unspeakable is it, that *the way of life* is opened! *Instruc*

1 Ps. xlix. 6; lxii. 11. Jer. ix. 23. 1 Tim. vi. 17. Comp. Ecclus. xl. 26.
2 Chap. xiv. 20; xix. 7; xxii. 7; John vii. 48, 49.
3 Chap. vi. 11.
4 This is the accurate rendering.—See Schultens, Holden, Scott.
5 Jam. ii. 5. Comp. Zeph. iii. 12.
6 Luke ii. 7—12; iv. 22; viii. 3. Matt. viii. 20.
7 Ps. cxiii. 7, 8. Comp. 1 Sam. ii. 8.
8 Chap. xxx.
9 1 Chron. xxix. 14. 1 Tim. vi. 18.
10 Job i. 21. 1 Tim. vi. 18.
11 Jam. i. 10, 11
12 John vi. 27.
13 Luke xix. 13. 1 Cor. x. 31.
14 Chap. xi. 19. Jer. xxii. 15, 16.
15 Isa. xxvi. 12.
16 Rom. viii. 13. 1 Cor. xv. 10. Phil. ii. 12, 13.
17 Phil. i. 21.
18 Gal. vi. 8.
19 Chap. xxi. 4. Tit. i. 15. Comp. Matt. xii. 34; xv. 19
20 Gal. vi. 7, 8.

tion sets the way before us. *He that keepeth instruction* cannot fail of finding and enjoying it.[1] The more we value that most needful part of *instruction*—discipline;[2] the more shall we regard every practical lesson in the heavenly school. To *refuse the reproof*—to be deaf to the voice that would save us from ruin—is a most fearful *error*—the proof of a foolish and unhumbled heart;[3] the certain forerunner—if not corrected—of irremediable destruction.[4] Child of God! is it not matter of shame and sorrow, that you should be so slow to *keep* such inestimable *instruction;* so prone to *err from the way of life;* and, though having the full promise of Divine guidance, still so often acting as the slave of your own will?

18. *He that hideth hatred with lying lips, and he that uttereth a slander, is a fool.*

Scripture history from the first chapter of fallen man abundantly illustrates this proverb. Cain talking with his brother;[5] Saul plotting against David;[6] Joab's treachery to Abner and Amasa;[7] the enemies of the Church on the return from Babylon[8]—*all hid hatred with lying lips.* Such was also the smooth tongue of the Herodians,[9] and more than all— the deadly kiss of Judas.[10] So perfectly—yet with the most exquisite sensibility of pain—did our blessed Lord identify himself with the trials of his people! Closely allied with the hypocrite is *the slanderer*[11]—both stamped by God with the mark of *fools.* For of what avail is this mask? Is there not an eye that looks through, and a hand that will tear off, the flimsy cover?[12] And—if their *hatred* be vented against the godly, is not the day at hand, when their "rebuke and *slander* shall be taken away from the earth?"[13]

But is this "root of bitterness" thoroughly mortified in the Christian's heart? Is there no insincerity in our intercourse with those to whom we feel, if not *hatred*, at least strong repugnance? In the language of polite courtesy, is there not much that is hollow, if not false. Do we really mean what we say? Or rather is there not the profession of regard absolutely contrary to our real feelings? Do we never bring them under ridicule, set them out in an unfavorable light, assert things upon mere suspicion, or attempt to raise our own name upon the ruin of their reputation? This surely in the eyes of God is *slander*—an offence against the "new commandment of love"—the badge of all the disciples of Jesus.[14] These noxious humors are the bane of true godliness. They must not only be restrained, but "laid aside," if ever we would "as newborn babes, desire the sincere milk of the word, that we may grow

1 Chap. xiii. 34, 35. 2 Chap. vi. 23; xxii. 17—19.
3 Chap. xii. 1; xviii. 12. 2 Chron. xvi. 7—10; xxv. 15, 16.
4 Chap. i. 25, 26, 30; v. 12; xv. 10; xxix. 1. Comp. Jer. vi. 10. Zeph. ii. 2—7
5 Gen. iv. 8. 6 1 Sam. xviii. 21, 22, 29.
7 2 Sam. iii. 27; xx. 9, 10. Comp. xiii. 23—29. Ps. v. 9; lv. 21.
8 Ezra iv. 1—16. Neh. vi. 2. 9 Luke xx. 20, 21.
10 Ibid. xxii. 47, 48, with Ps. lv. 12—14; xli. 9. 11 Ps. l. 16—20.
12 Chap. xxvi. 23—28. Comp. Psalm l. 21. Luke xii. 1, 2. 13 Isa. xxv. 9.
14 John xiii. 34, 35.

thereby."[1] Lord, purge our hearts from these hateful, hidden cor ruptions—even though it be by "the Spirit of judgment and the Spirit of burning."[2]

19. *In the multitude of words there wanteth not sin: but he that refraineth his lips is wise.*

Hypocrisy and *slander* are not the only sins of the tongue. *In the multitude of words there is the sin of egotism.* "Our own mouth praises us, not another."[3] We love to hear ourselves talk; presenting our own judgment intrusively. *There is also the sin of vain babbling*, a canker to the vital principle.[4] The fool talks—not because he is full, but because he is empty—not for instruction, but from the pure love of talking. 'Conversation is,' as Bishop Butler truly remarks, 'merely the exercise of the tongue, no other human faculty has any place in it.'[5] The government of the tongue is therefore a searching test of the soundness of our religion.[6] Considering therefore the *sin* connected with the *multitude of words*, it is surely our *wisdom to refrain our lips*,[7] not indeed in silence, but in caution; that we may weigh our words before uttering them; never speaking, except when we have something to say; speaking only just enough; considering the time, circumstance, and person;[8] what is solid, suitable, and profitable.[9] This *wisdom* is especially valuable under provocation.[10] And even in the unbending of innocent recreation, the discipline of godly sobriety is of great moment. The sins of this "little member" are not trifles. They need the full application of the Gospel? What but "the blood of sprinkling" could enable us to meet the account "for every idle word at the day of judgment."[11] Woe to us, if the great Surety did not bear the sins of our vain words, no less than of our grosser wickedness! Never let us think of these sins as anything less than the "nails, that pierced his hands and his feet." And will not this sensibility of sin quicken our prayer for more of this *refraining wisdom?* "Set a watch, O Lord, before my mouth; keep the door of my lips."[12]

20. *The tongue of the just is as choice silver: the heart of the wicked is little worth.* 21. *The lips of the righteous feed many: but fools die for want of wisdom*, (of heart, Marg.)

The wisdom of refraining our lips must always be connected with diligence in improving our talent. If our tongue be our

[1] 1 Pet. ii. 1, 2. Comp. Jam. i. 21. [2] Isa. iv. 4.
[3] Chap. xxvii. 2. [4] 2 Tim. ii. 16, 17. Comp. Eccl. x. 13, 14. 1 Tim. v. 13.
[5] Sermon on the Government of the Tongue. 'One meets with people in the world, who never seem to have made the wise man's observation, "that there is a time to keep silence." These times one would think should be easily distinguished by everybody; namely, when a man has nothing to say, or nothing but what is better unsaid.' Ibid. Comp. Ecclus. xix. 6; xx. 5—7.
[6] James i. 26; iii. 2.
[7] Chap. xvii. 27, 28. Comp. Job xiii. 5. Eccl. v. 3. James i. 19.
[8] Job xxxii. 4—7. [9] Chap. xv. 23. Eph. iv. 29. Col. iv. 6.
[10] 1 Sam. x. 27. 2 Kings xviii. 36. [11] Matt. xii. 36. [12] Psalm cxli. 3.

shame in the overflowing of sin;[1] is it not also our glory?[2] When employed in "speaking of the things touching the king,"[3] or in sketching the features of his transcendent loveliness[4]—is it not then *as choice silver*, refined from this world's dross, and shining with heavenly brightness? Who would not eagerly gather up the *silver* scattered in the streets? And shall not we enrich our store from *the choice silver of the just man's tongue*, pouring out its precious instruction before us? If, as regards this world's wealth, the Lord's poor must say—"Silver and gold have I none;" at least they may scatter *choice silver* with a widely extended blessing—"As poor, yet making many rich."[5]

But we observe not only the excellency, but the usefulness of this member. *The lips of the righteous feed many* from the rich stores of the "indwelling word,"[6] ministering to them grace, the sole true and proper nourishment![7] 'Their breath is food to others as well as life to them.'[8] When "the priest's *lips* keep knowledge, and they seek the law at his mouth," he *feeds* the church of God.[9] And as our great Master broke the bread, and gave it to his disciples for their distribution;[10] so does he now dispense to his servants heavenly provision, suitable and abundantly sufficient for the need of their flock. And every Sabbath is the wondrous miracle displayed before our eyes. The imperishable bread multiplies in the breaking. The hungry, the mourners, the weary and fainting; yea, all that feel their need, are refreshed and invigorated.

The wicked—his coffers may be full. But *his heart* being empty of the *choice silver*, *is little worth*.[11] So far from *feeding* others, *the fool dies himself* for *want of wisdom;* or rather, *for want of heart* to seek it. He despises *the lips that would feed him*, and 'dies of famine in the midst of the rich pastures of the Gospel.'[12] Oh! how often are we reminded that sin is self-destruction. "In me is thy help."[13]

22. *The blessing of the Lord, it maketh rich, and he addeth no sorrow with it.*

We have been told,[14] that *the hand of the diligent*—here we see that *the blessing of the Lord—maketh rich.* Both are consistent. The one marks the primary—the other the instrumental and subordinate—cause. Neither will be effective without the other. The sluggard looks for prosperity without diligence—the practical atheist from diligence alone—the sound-hearted Christian from *the blessing of God* in the exercise of diligence. This wise combination keeps him in an active habit, humble, and dependent on God.[15]

[1] Verses 18, 19. [2] Psalm lvii. 8; cviii. 1. [3] Ibid. xlv. 1.
[4] Ibid. 2. Can. v. 10—16. [5] Acts iii. 6, with 2 Cor. vi. 10.
[6] Col. iii. 16. [7] Eph. iv. 29. Comp. Job iv. 3, 4; xxix. 22, 23.
[8] Flavel on Soul of Man. Works, 8vo. ii. 551.
[9] Mal. ii. 7, with Jer. iii. 15. John xxi. 15. Acts xx. 28. 1 Peter v. 2. Of Bishop Ridley our Martyrologist records in his own beautiful style, that 'to his Sermons the people resorted, swarming about him like bees, and coveting the sweet flowers and wholesome juice of his fruitful doctrine.'—Foxe, vii. 407.
[10] John vi. 11. [11] Jer. xxii. 28. [12] Schultens, Comp. Acts xiii. 41, 45, 46.
[13] Hosea xiii. 9. [14] Ver. 4. [15] 1 John vi. 27.

For "except the Lord build the house, they labor in vain, that build it. The race is not to the swift, nor the battle to the strong."[1] The rich then may receive their portion[2] *as the blessing of the Lord*;[3] carefully using it as a talent for his service,[4] and for the good of their fellow-creatures.[5] The poor may enjoy the same *enriching blessing* in the "gain of godly contentment."[6] Their cottage is a palace, as the habitation of the King of kings; and neither life nor death, neither time nor eternity, can separate them from their God.[7]

The blessing of the Lord moreover hath this prerogative. *He addeth no sorrow with it.* Accumulation of riches may be the accumulation of sorrows.[8] Lot's covetous choice was fraught with bitterness.[9] Ahab wore a crown, and "lay sick on his bed" in discontent.[10] Gehazi was laden with his bags; but the plague of leprosy was on him.[11] Haman's mortification was the canker in his boasted glory.[12] The rich youth's rejection of Christ, was the source of present—must we not fear?—everlasting *sorrow*?[13] The worldling's recompense for his daily toil, is "eating the bread of sorrow. So"—mark the striking contrast—"he giveth his beloved sleep."[14] Happy portion of the children of God! They "know both how to be abased, and they know how to abound."[15] "All things are theirs."[16] "*Thy blessing* is upon thy people."[17]

23. *It is as sport to a fool to do mischief: but a man of understanding hath wisdom.*

The wanton *sport* of putting others to pain, argues the perverseness of *a fool* both in judgment and heart.[18] Sometimes this cruel amusement may engage a man in the tempter's work.[19] For *fools who make sport for mischief* may heedlessly go on to "make a mock of sin."[20] But even without going so far, should not we guard against *mischievous* jokes, tending to wound a neighbor's character, or to give him uneasiness? Are we sufficiently careful against indulging our wit or humor at his expense? All this is not less unmanly, than it is inconsistent with the sobriety and gravity of a Christian profession. It is the pure native selfishness of the human heart. Should not also children's play be sometimes under restraint? Young people cannot be too strongly disciplined to thoughtfulness and consideration of others. Never let hilarity of spirits lead them to make *sport* of that, which ought to call forth sympathy and tenderness. *A man of understanding is too wise* to find a reckless delight in his neighbor's injury. The spirit of our Divine Master was according to his own law[21]—eminently con-

[1] Psalm cxxvii. 1. Eccl. ix. 11. [2] Eccl. ii. 24—26; iii. 13; v. 18—20.
[3] Gen. xxiv. 35; xxvi. 12. 1 Chron. xxix. 14. Comp. Deut. viii. 17, 18. Hos. ii. 8.
[4] Luke xix. 13. [5] 1 Tim. vi. 17, 18. [6] 1 Tim. vi. 6. [7] Rom. viii. 38, 39.
[8] Chap. xx. 21; xxviii. 22. 1 Tim. vi. 9, 10.
[9] Gen. xiii. 10, 11; xiv. 12; xix. 30; Comp. 2 Pet. ii. 8.
[10] 1 Kings xxi. 4. [11] 2 Kings v. 24—27. [12] Esth. v. 11—13. [13] Luke xviii. 23.
[14] Psalm cxxvii. 2, with Eccl. ii. 26; v. 12. [15] Phil. iv. 12. [16] 1 Cor. iii. 22.
[17] Psalm iii. 8. [18] Verse 10; xv. 21; xxvi. 17, 18. Comp. 2 Sam. ii. 14—16.
[19] Chap. i. 11—14. [20] Chap. xiv. 9. [21] Gal. vi. 2.

siderate and sympathising.[1] Let us who bear his name, cultivate his self-denying, loving mind.[2]

24. *The fear of the wicked, it shall come upon him: but the desire of the righteous shall be granted.*

The sport of the wicked—how soon it is gone![3] But *his fear*—the evil which he *feared, comes upon him.* The Babel-builders were punished with the evil which they had labored to prevent.[4] Ahab's device could not shelter him from his foreboded judgment.[5] The rebellious Jews rushed into the ruin from which they fled.[6] Belshazzar's trembling was realized in his speedy destruction.[8] Thus are "the wicked like a troubled sea"—full of tossing anxiety.[7] Do not "their hearts" in solitude "meditate terror?"[9] Do not their consciences turn pale at the question—"Where shall the ungodly and sinner appear?"[10] And will it not be the constrained confession at the great day of the Lord—"According to thy *fear* so is thy wrath?"[11]

But if *the fear of the wicked*—so also will *the desire of the righteous*—be fully realized. Let them only be bounded by the will,[12] and centered in the enjoyment of God;[13] and to their utmost extent *will they be granted.*[14] God did not raise them to be our torment, but our rest. True indeed—they are mixed with much infirmity, and their *unreserved gratification,* as with his favored servant,[15] would be our destruction. But he is no less wise than kind: he separates the evil, and fulfils the good.[16] He answers, not according to our wishes, but our wants; not as in our ignorance we may have asked, but as an enlightened regard to our best interests would have led us to ask.

But if our *desires be granted,* and even exceeded;[17] faith and patience will be tried in the very *grant.* Growth in grace will be given by deep and humbling views of our corruption. Longings for holiness shall be fulfilled by painful affliction. Prayer will be answered in crosses.[18] Yet the ground of our confidence is firm. All things needful will be given, and at the grand consummation every *desire* will be eternally fulfilled. "As for me, I shall behold thy face in righteousness; I shall be satisfied, when I awake, with thy likeness."[19]

25. *As the whirlwind passeth, so is the wicked no more: but the righteous is an everlasting foundation.*

Thus suddenly—*as the whirlwind*[20]—does *the fear of the wicked* often *come upon him.* All his hopes, pleasures, and dependences;

[1] Luke vii. 11—15. [2] Phil. ii. 4, 5. [3] Eccl. vii. 6. [4] Gen. xi. 4, 8, 9.
[5] 1 Kings xxii. 28—37. [6] Jer. xlii. xliii. [7] Dan. v. 6, 30. [8] Isa. lvii. 20, 21.
[9] Ibid. xxxiii. 18. Comp. Deut. xxviii. 65—67. Job iii. 25; xv. 20, 21.
[10] 1 Pet. iv. 18. [11] Psalm xc. 11, with Mal. iv. 1. [12] 1 John v. 14.
[13] Psalm iv. 6; xxxvii. 4. [14] Ps. lxxxi. 10. [15] Ex. xxxiii. 18, 20.
[16] Ibid. Ver. 19. [17] Gen. xlviii. 11. 1 Kings iii. 7—13. Comp. Eph. iii. 20.
[18] See a beautiful hymn in Olney Collection. Book iii. 36.
[19] Psalm xvii. 15, also xvi. 11.
[20] See n. 9, p. 9. Comp. Jer. xxiii. 19. Hos. xiii. 3, also Job xx. 8, 9; xxi. 13; xxvii. 13, 19—21; xxviii. 10, 35, 36. Psalm xiii. 19, 20.

all his opportunities of grace, and offers of mercy, are swept away in a moment forever. Such *a whirlwind* was the destruction of the old world:—of the cities of the plain:[2]—of Sennacherib's army.[1] And such *a whirlwind*, infinitely more terrible, will be the coming of the Lord.[1] "But he that doeth the will of God abideth ever,"[2] as *an everlasting foundation.* Faith hath fastened him to the Rock of Ages; hath built his house upon this Rock; and no storm can root him up.[5] But remember, this is the confidence of *the righteous.* Sin allowed and indulged will shake this foundation far more than all the outward assaults of earth and hell. "Hold fast then thy rejoicing" in a jealous godly fear. Thy portion is secure. Thy hopes, joys, and prospects are unchangeable. Thou canst look at trouble—yea, at death itself—without dismay—and feel 'I am safe.' But while "thou standest by faith, be not high-minded, but fear."[6]

26. *As vinegar to the teeth, and as smoke to the eyes, so is the sluggard to them that send him.*

A lively figure of the vexation of *the sluggard* to his employers.[7] Suppose a fire to be extinguished, medical assistance needed, a message of urgent haste to be conveyed—he is worse than unserviceable. Common prudence dictates the selection of active and industrious servants. And such, when influenced by godly principles, are "worthy of double honor."[8]

Does then *the sluggard* disappoint and provoke his earthly master? See that we be not such *sluggards* to our heavenly Master. Men born of the Laodicean church are specially hateful in his sight.[9] The slothful minister carries in a tremendous account *to him that sent him.* No more pitiable object is found, than the man who has time to spare; who has no object of commanding interest; and is going on to the end, as if he had spent his whole life in children's play, and have lived for no useful purpose. He may probably have parcelled out a portion of his time for some miscalled religious duty. But he might as well be asleep as on his knees, in dissipation as meditation—so little pain—so little heart—is connected with his duties! Why "standeth he idle in the market-place?" It cannot be that, "No man hath hired him." His Master's call sounds in his ears—"Go ye into the vineyard."[10] And at his peril he disobeys it.[1]

27. *The fear of the Lord prolongeth days: but the years of the wicked shall be shortened.*

The fear of the Lord is not a single grace. It includes the substance of all godly tempers. For all are radically one principle, from one source. It essentially differs from *the fear of the*

[1] Luke xvii. 26—29. [2] 2 Kings xix. 35. [3] Luke xvii. 30. 1 Thess. v. 2, 3.
[4] 1 John ii. 17. [5] Ver. 11. Comp. Matt. vii. 26. Psalm cxii. 6—8.
[6] Rom. xi. 20.
[7] Contrast Chap. xxvi. 6, with xiii. 17; xxv. 13. Comp. 1 Kings xi. 28.
[8] Chap. xxii. 29. Gen. xxiv. 1—14. Eph. vi. 6, 7. [9] Rev. iii. 15, 16.
[10] Matt. xx. 6, 7, [11] Ibid. xxv. 14, 24—30.

wicked. They fear whom they hate. The child of God—whom he loves. Whether his temporal life be shortened or *prolonged*, he lives long in a little time. He is an infinite gainer by the contraction of life—*his days prolonged* and swallowed up in one unclouded day, of which "the sun shall no more go down."[1] Justly is *the fear of the Lord* contrasted with *the wicked;* because the absence of his grace is their distinguishing mark,[2] the principle of all their ungodliness.[3] And often do we see the letter of this curse realized in *the shortening of their years.* Excessive worldliness wears out the spring of life.[4] Sin often brings to an untimely end.[5] Sometimes the God of vengeance breaks out, and "takes away the daring offender with his stroke."[6] Yet if he be "visited after the visitation of all men," awful indeed is the course of a long life wasted in folly and sin—living little in a long time—"The sinner, being an hundred years old, shall be accursed."[7]

28. *The hope of the righteous shall be gladness: but the expectation of the wicked shall perish.*

The fear of the Lord—so far from being opposed to, is often connected with *the hope of the righteous.*[8] And well may this *hope be gladness;* for 'it is accompanied with sweet patience, joyful hope, and crowned with a happy issue.'[9] It has its origin in eternity.[10] Its substance is Christ and Heaven.[11] The foundation is the work of Christ.[12] The security, the unchangeable engagements of God.[13] Who then can doubt its character—"a hope that maketh not ashamed—sure and steadfast?"[14] Instead of—as is commonly supposed—bidding farewell to *gladness*, it brings the only sunshine of the soul. Beaming from the precious cross, how does it dry up the penitent's tears![15] Or if the *gladness* be withheld for a time, yet it is sown; and the "sheaves of joy shall doubtless" follow the "weeping."[16] And then—carrying as it were heaven in and about us[17]—how refreshing is the hope in its clear insight into eternity: as Bunyan describes, in one of his beautiful touches, his feelings on witnessing Christian and Hopeful's welcome into the heavenly city—'which when I had seen, I wished myself among them.' Oh! there must be a reality in that hope, which bears us away from earth, and makes its meanest heir richer and happier, than if he were the sole possessor of this world's glory. Let me hasten towards it—longing, yet not impatient. For how can I but desire to change my traveller's lot for my home; my toil for rest; my sorrow for joy; my body of sin for the likeness to

[1] Chap. ix. 11. Psalm xci. 16, with Isa. lx. 19, 20. [2] Psalm xxxvi. 1.
[3] Rom. iii. 10—18. [4] Eccl. v. 10—12.
[5] Impurity, Chap. v. 9—11. Drunkenness, xxiii. 29—32. Malice, Psalm lv. 23. 1 Kings ii. 31—34. Wickedness, Psalm xxxvi. 9, 10. Eccl. vii. 17. Jer. xvii. 11. Comp. Job xv. 32, 33; xxii. 15, 16.
[6] Job xxxvi. 18. Acts v. 1—10. [7] Isa. lxv. 20. [8] Psalm lxxxiii. 18; cxlvii. 11.
[9] Diodati. [10] Tit. i. 2.
[11] Rom. v. 2. 1 Pet. i. 3, 4. 1 Tim. i. 1. Col. i. 27. [12] 1 Pet. i. 3, 21.
[13] Heb. vi. 17, 18. [14] Rom. v. 5. Heb. vi. 19. Comp. 2 Thess. ii. 16.
[15] Isa. xii. [16] Psalm xcvii. 11; cxxvi. 6. Comp. Isa. xxxv. 10. [17] Heb. x. 34.

my Lord; "the tents of Kedar" for "the innumerable company of angels, and the church of the first-born?"[1] Do I grasp this *hope?* Then—as a godly man exclaimed—'Let who will be miserable: I will not—I cannot.'

But *the wicked*—they too have *their expectation.* For none have a stronger hope, than those who have no ground for hope.[2] And this delusion too often reaches to the moment of eternity[3]—nay, even to the "day" of the Lord—to the very throne of God;[4] expecting the door to be "opened to them" after it has been "shut forever;"[5] as if dreaming of heaven, and waking in hell! *The expectation of the wicked shall perish.*[6]

Christian! make sure the ground of *your hope.*[7] Then set out its *gladness,* as becometh an heir of glory. Let not a drooping spirit tell the world the scantiness of *your hope.* But let it be seen, that you can live upon it with joy and *gladness,* until you enter into its perfect and everlasting fruition.[8]

29. *The way of the Lord is strength to the upright: but destruction shall be to the workers of iniquity.*

Observe how *the gladness of the righteous* is "their *strength.*"[9] In the roughness of *the way*—"Go in this thy might"—is the cheering voice. "Have not I sent thee?"[10] "He giveth power to the faint, and to them that have no might he increaseth *strength.*"[11] This promise however implies help for our work, not rest from our labor. We shall have *strength* for the conflict. But "there is no discharge from this war." There is supply for real—not for imaginary—wants; for present, not for future, need. The healthful energy of the man of God is also supposed. And who does not find the glow of health in an active rather than in a sedentary and indolent life? What makes *the way of God* practicable is—to be always in it—to have the heart always on it. What before was drudgery, will now be meat and drink. Our strength will be in creased, not spent or wasted.

Thus was *the way of the Lord strength to the upright* Nicodemus. His first step was feebleness and fear. Walking onwards, he waxed stronger;[12] standing up in the ungodly council, and ultimately the bold confessor of his Saviour, when his self-confident disciples shrunk back.[13] Innate sufficiency we have none. The strongest in their own strength shall "faint and be weary." The weakest in the Lord's strength shall "march on and shall not faint."[14] Thus—*thus alone*—"the righteous shall hold on their way; going from strength to strength; strengthened in the Lord, and walking up and down in his name."[15] When we look at our

[1] Psalm cxx. 5, with Heb. xii. 22, 23. [2] Deut. xxix. 19. [3] Matt. xxv. 10
[4] Ibid. vii. 22, 23. [5] Ibid. xxv. 11.
[6] See the hope of the worldling, Psalm xlix. 6—14. Luke xii. 19, 20. Of the wicked, Job xi. 20; xviii. 14. Of the hypocrite, Job viii. 13, 14; xxvii. 8.
[7] 2 Pet. i. 10. [8] Psalm xvi. 11. [9] Neh. viii. 10. [10] Judges vi. 14
[11] Isa. xl. 29. [12] Job xvii. 9. [13] John iii. 2; vii. 50, 51; xix. 39.
[14] Isa. xl. 31. Bishop Lowth's Version.
[15] Job xvii. 9. Psalm lxxxiv. 5—7. Zech. x. 12.

own resources, we might 'as well despair of moving sin from our hearts, as of casting down the mountains with our fingers.'[1] Yet who of us need to shrink from the confession—"I can do all things through Christ which strengtheneth me?[2]

No such resources support *the workers of iniquity.* Captives instead of soldiers, they know no conflicts, they realize no need of *strength.* Even now "*destruction* is in their ways,"[3] and the "voice of the Judge will fearfully seal their doom.—Depart from me, ye *workers of iniquity.*"[4]

30. *The righteous shall never be removed: but the wicked shall not inhabit the earth.*

The frailty of our present condition, common to all,[5] was not in the wise man's eye; but the state of the two classes, as in the purpose and mind of God. *His way is strength to the upright. The righteous,* walking steadily in the way, *shall never be removed.*[6] 'They enjoy in this life by faith and hope their everlasting life.'[7] No weapon that is formed against them shall prosper. "The mountains shall depart, and the little hills shall be *removed;* but my loving-kindness shall not depart from thee; neither shall the covenant of my *peace be removed;* saith the Lord that hath mercy on thee."[8] Is not this a confidence, that earth nor hell can never shake?[9]

The wicked—have they any such confidence? So far from being *never removed, they shall never inhabit.* They have no title, like *the righteous,*[10] as sons and heirs, to the blessings of *earth;* no hope or interest in the land, of which *the earth* is the type.[11] Often are they cut off from *inhabiting* the one.[12] Never will they be suffered to *inhabit* the other.[13] As our character is, so is our hope and prospect. We gain or lose both worlds.

31. *The mouth of the just bringeth forth wisdom: but the froward tongue shall be cut out.* 32. *The lips of the righteous know what is acceptable: but the mouth of the wicked speaketh frowardness.*

Another image[14] of the fruitfulness of a gracious tongue! It *bringeth forth wisdom*[15]—and that too in the practical exercise of *knowing what is acceptable.* This gift needs to be deeply pondered, and carefully cultivated,[16] to give it a free scope, while we jealously confine it to its own sphere of influence. There is evidently much diversity of application. The same statement of truth does not suit all.—And how—what—when—to whom—to speak—is a matter of great wisdom.[17] Yet this consideration of

[1] Bishop Reynolds' Works. [2] Phil. iv. 13. [3] Isa. lix. 7. Rom. iii. 16.
[4] Luke xiii. 27. Comp. Chap. xxi. 15. Job xxxi. 3. Psalm xxxvi. 12.
[5] Eccl. ix. 2, 11.
[6] Psalm xv; xxxvii. 22, 28, 29; cxii. 6; cxxv. 1. 2 Pet. i. 5—11.
[7] Reformers' Notes. [8] Isa. liv. 17, 10. [9] Rom. viii. 38, 39.
[10] Matt. v. 5. 1 Cor. iii. 22. [11] Psalm xxxvii. 29.
[12] Ver. 27; ii. 22. Psalm xxxvii. 22. Ezek. xxxiii. 24—26.
[13] 1 Cor. vi. 9. Rev. xxi. 27. [14] Comp. Verses 11, 20, 21.
[15] Psalm xxxvii. 30. [16] Chap. xv. 23; xxv. 11. Comp. Job vi. 25
[17] Eccl. viii. 5.

acceptableness must involve no compromise of principles. Let it be a considerate accommodation *of mode* to the diversity of tastes, a forbearance with lesser prejudices and constitutional infirmities avoiding—not *all* offences (which faithfulness to our Divine Master forbids) but all *needless* offences; all uncalled-for occasions of irritation. "The meekness of wisdom"[1] should be clearly manifested in Christian faithfulness. Thus Gideon melted the frowardness of the men of Ephraim.[2] Abigail restrained David's hands from blood.[3] Daniel stood fearless before the mighty monarch of Babylon.[4] *Their lips knew what was acceptable*, and their God honored them.

But most of all—let the Minister of God study to clothe his most unpalatable message in an *acceptable* garb. Let him mould it in all the sweetness of persuasion,[5] compassion,[6] and sympathy.[7] With what parental earnestness does the 'Preacher of Jerusalem,' in his introductory chapter, allure us to Wisdom's voice and instruction! Yet were his "*acceptable* words upright, even words of truth."[8] And thus must "the priest's lips keep knowledge," if he would have his people "seek the law at his mouth, as the messenger of the Lord of Hosts."[9] He must discriminate his statements, without diluting them. The "truth is to be proclaimed upon the housetop" to the multitude. But it is to be refrained from ungodly scorners.[10] Always must he gain his people's ears, that he may win their hearts.

The froward tongue, pouring forth its own *frowardness*, provokes its own ruin. It *shall be cut out*.[11] O my God, what do I owe thee for the bridle of discipline, that restrains me from self-destruction!

CHAPTER XI.

1. *A false balance is abomination to the Lord: but a just weight* (a perfect stone,[12] Marg.) *is his delight.*

How valuable is the Book of God in its minute detail of principles for every day's conduct! Commerce is a providential appointment for our social intercourse and mutual helpfulness. It is grounded with men upon human faith, as with God upon Divine

[1] James iii. 13. [2] Judges viii. 2, 3. [3] Sam. xxv. 23—33. [4] Dan. iv. 27.
[5] 2 Cor. v. 11, 20. [6] Rom. ix. 1—3. 2 Cor. ii. 1—6. Phil. iii. 18.
[7] Tit. iii. 2, 3. 2 Cor. xi. 28, 29. [8] Eccl. xii. 10. [9] Mal. ii. 7.
[10] Matt. x. 27, with vii. 6.
[11] Chap. viii. 13; xviii. 6, 7. Psalm xii. 3, 4; lii. 1—5; cxx. 3, 4. Comp. Num. xvi. 1—33.
[12] In many shops in Palestine now, the only weights in the balance are smooth stones. Narrative of Scottish Mission to the Jews.—Saphet, p. 274. Comp. Chap. xvi. 11, Marg.

faith. *Balances, weights*, money, are its necessary materials. Impositions; double-dealings; the hard bargain struck with self-complacent shrewdness[1]—this is the *false balance* forbidden alike by the law[2] and the Gospel.[3] Men may "commend its wisdom;"[4] God not only forbids, but he *abominates* it.[5] *The just weight* often passes unnoticed. But 'such a *perfect stone* is a perfect jewel, and a precious stone in the sight of God.'[6] It is *his delight*[7]—a testimony infinitely above all human praise!

We must not put away this proverb as a mere moral maxim. It was given as a warning to a flourishing Christian Church;[8] and the sin here reprobated has been a leprous spot upon many a highly-gifted professor.[9] Is it not a solemn thought, that the eye of God marks all our common dealings of life, either as an *abomination or a delight?* Have we never found when upon our knees, the frown of God upon some breach in our daily walk?[10] Look and see, whether the "conscience has been void of offence towards man."[11] "The righteous Lord loveth righteousness; his countenance doth behold the upright."[12] They—they only—"shall dwell in his presence."[13]

2. *When pride cometh, then cometh shame: but with the lowly is wisdom.*

Pride was the principle of the fall,[14] and therefore the native principle of fallen man.[15] When pride had stripped us of our honor, *then*—not till then—*cometh shame.*[16] This is the wise discipline of our God to scourge the one by the other. The Babel-builders,[17]—Miriam[18]—Uzziah[19]—Haman[20]—Nebuchadnezzar[21]—Herod[22]—all are instances of *shame*—treading upon the heels of *pride.* Even in common life—a man will never attempt to raise himself above his own level—but *then cometh shame*[23]—the most revolting recompense. And thus our God puts to shame the man, who refuses to stand on the low ground on which he has placed him. "Every one that exalteth himself shall be abased."[24]

Such is the folly of *pride. With the lowly is wisdom.* What a splendor of *wisdom* shone in the *lowly* child, "sitting at the doctors' feet, astonishing them at his understanding and his answers!"[25] And will not this spirit be to us the path of *wisdom?* For does not the Divine Teacher "reveal to the babes what is hidden from the wise and prudent?"[26] There is no greater proof of proud folly than believing only what we understand; thus grounding our faith on knowledge, not on testimony: as if the word of God

[1] Chap. xx. 14. [2] Lev. xix. 35, 36. [3] Matt. vii. 12. Phil. iv. 8.
[4] Luke xvi. 1—8.
[5] Chap. xx. 10, 23. Deut. xxv. 13—16. Amos viii. 5. Mic. vi. 10, 11.
[6] Jermin in loco. [7] Chap. xvi. 11; xii. 22. [8] 1 Thess. iv. 6.
[9] 1 Cor. vi. 8. [10] Psalm lxvi. 18. [11] Acts xxiv. 16.
[12] Psalm xi. 7. [13] Ibid. xv. 1, 2; xxiv. 3—5; cxl. 13. [14] Gen. iii. 5.
[15] Mark vii. 22. [16] Gen. iii. 7—10, with ii. 25. [17] Gen. xi. 4—9.
[18] Num. xii. 10. [19] 2 Chron. xxvi. 16—21. [20] Esth. iv. 11, 12; vii. 10.
[21] Dan. iv. 29—32. [22] Acts xii. 22, 23. Comp. Isa. xiv. 12. Zeph. ii. 9, 10, 15.
[23] Luke xiv. 8—11. Comp. Chap. xii. 9.
[24] Luke xviii. 14. Comp. Isa. ii. 11—17. Mal. iv. 2. [25] Luke ii. 46, 47.
[26] Ibid. x. 24. Comp. Psalm xxv. 9.

could not be implicitly received, except as corroborated by other witnesses. Happy is that *lowliness* of spirit, that comes to God's revelation as it were without any will or mind of our own; humbly receiving what he is pleased to give; but willing—yea—thankful—to be ignorant, when he forbids us to intrude![1]

3. *The integrity of the upright shall guide them: but the perverseness of transgressors shall destroy them.* 4. *Riches profit not in the day of wrath: but righteousness delivereth from death.* 5. *The righteousness of the perfect shall direct his way: but the wicked shall fall by his own wickedness.* 6. *The righteousness of the upright shall deliver them: but transgressors shall be taken in their own naughtiness.* 7. *When a wicked man dieth, his expectation shall perish: and the hope of unjust men perisheth.*

Integrity or righteousness is a most valuable *guide* in all perplexities.[2] The single desire to know the will of God, only that we may do it,[3] will always bring light upon our path. It is also a covert from many dreaded evils. "God is a buckler to them that walk uprightly. Who therefore is he that will harm you, if ye be followers of that which is good?"[4] Let the Christian "stand—having on the breastplate of *righteousness;* and that wicked one toucheth him not."[5] Often indeed does it deliver from temporal[6]—always from eternal *death.* "Whoso walketh uprightly shall be saved. In the pathway thereof there is no death. If a man keep my sayings, he shall never see—never taste of death."[7]

The *perverseness* that neglects this godly principle is the sinner's own snare and *destruction.*[8] And when *the day of wrath* cometh—as come it will—"a great ransom will not deliver."[9] *Riches will profit nothing;*[10] not even will they obtain "a drop of water to cool the tormented tongue."[11] In vain will "the rich men of the earth" seek a shelter from "the wrath of the Lamb."[12] They and their *hopes will perish* together.[13] 'They were not living, but lying hopes, and dying hopes.'[14] What a contrast to that "hope, which is as an anchor of the soul, both sure and steadfast, and which entereth into that within the veil!"[15]

8. *The righteous is delivered out of trouble, and the wicked cometh in his stead.*

Thus do these two classes change places in the dispensation of

[1] Col. ii. 18. [2] Matt. vi. 22. Comp. Chap. xiii. 6. [3] Psalm cxliii. 8—10.
[4] Chap. ii. 7. 1 Peter iii. 13. Comp. Gen. xxx. 33.
[5] Eph. vi. 13, 14. 1 John v. 18. [6] Gen. vii. 1; xx. 5, 6. 2 Kings xx. 3—6.
[7] Chap. xxviii. 18; xii. 28. John viii. 51, 52. Comp. Chap. x. 2. Ez. xiv. 20; xviii. 27.
[8] Chap. xxviii. 18. 2 Sam. xvii. 23. Ecc. vii. 17. Isa. i. 28. Ez. ix. 9, 10. Hos. xiv. 9.
[9] Job xxxvi. 18, 19. [10] Chap. x. 2. Ez. vii. 19. Zeph. i. 18.
[11] Luke xvi. 19—24. [12] Rev. vi. 15—17.
[13] Chap. x. 28. Job viii. 13, 14; xi. 20; xviii. 14—18. Ps. xlix. 17, 18; cxlvi. 4. One of Bunyan's graphical and accurate sketches represents Ignorance ferried over the river by one Vain Hope—ascending the hill alone without encouragement—and ultimately bound and carried away. 'Then I saw'—adds he with fearful solemnity—'that there was a way to Hell, even from the gates of Heaven!'
[14] Leighton on 1 Peter i. 3.
[15] Heb. vi. 19. Does not this verse prove the knowledge of a future state; since, as respects this life, the *expectation of the righteous*—alike with that of *the wicked—perisheth?* Comp. 1 Cor. xv. 19.

God. The same providence often marks Divine faithfulness and retributive justice. The Israelites *were delivered out of the trouble* of the Red Sea; the Egyptians *came in their stead.*[1] Mordecai was *delivered* from the gallows; Haman was hanged upon it.[2] The noble confessors in Babylon were saved from the fire; their executioners were "slain" by it;[3] Daniel was preserved from the lions; his accusers were devoured by them.[4] Peter was snatched from death; his jailors and persecutors were condemned.[5] Thus "precious in the sight of the Lord is" the life, no less than "the death, of his saints."[6] For the *deliverance* of one precious soul *out of trouble* he will bring a nation into distress.[7] Yea—for the ransom of his own chosen people, he gave not only "Egypt" of old, but in later times "Ethiopia and Seba"—men for them, and people for their life.[8] To what source but his own free and sovereign love can we trace this special estimation? "*Since thou wast precious in my* sight, thou hast been honorable, and I have loved thee."[9] We do not always mark the same outward manifestation. But the love is unchangeably the same. And how should it at once lay us in the dust, and build our confidence upon an unshaking foundation!

9. *An hypocrite with his mouth destroyeth his neighbor: but through knowledge shall the just be delivered.*

Haman under the pretence of loyalty would have *destroyed* a whole nation.[10] Ziba under the same false cover would have *destroyed his neighbor.*[11] The lying prophet from mere wilfulness ruined his brother.[12] Such is *the hypocrite's mouth!* "a little member;" but "a world of iniquity: set on fire of hell."[13]

Then look at him in the church—"a ravening wolf in sheep's clothing," devouring the flock;[14] "making merchandise with feigned words;"[15] an apostle of Satan, so diligent in his Master's work of *destruction.*[16] "These false Christs"—we are warned—"deceive many, *if it were possible,*—the very elect."[17] But they—*the just—are delivered through knowledge*—'by the light and direction of the Holy Ghost, and by the lively *knowledge* of God's word, which giveth unto the faithful man wisdom sufficient for his preservation.'[18] Learn the value of solid *knowledge.* Feeling, excitement, imagination, expose us to a "tossing" profession.[19] *Knowledge* supplies principle and steadfastness. "Add to your faith

1 Ex. xiv. 21—28. 2 Esth. v. 14; vii. 10. 3 Dan. iii. 22—26.
4 Ibid vi. 22—24. 5 Acts xii. 6, 19, 23. 6 Ps. cxvi. 15.
7 1 Sam. xxiii. 25—28.
8 Isa. xliii. 3, 4, with 2 Chron. xiv. 9—11. 2 Kings xix. 9. Comp. Chap. xxi. 18. How different their estimation in the eyes of man, when an Eastern autocrat was willing to cut them off at a single blow as a worthless thing! Est. iii. 8—14. Comp. 1 Cor iv. 13.
9 Isa. xliii. 4. ut supra. 10 Est. iii. 8—13. 11 2 Samuel xvi. 1—4.
12 1 Kings xviii. 22. 13 Jam. iii. 5, 6. 14 Matt. vii. 15.
15 2 Pet. ii. 1—3. 16 2 Cor. xi. 3, 13.
17 Matt. xxiv. 11, 24.
18 Diodati. Comp. Heb. v. 14. 1 John ii. 20, 27. 2 Peter iii. 17, 18.
19 Such as Eph. iv. 14.

knowledge."[1] Guard against plausible error, usually built upon some single truth separated from its connection, and pressed beyond its due proportion. Do not the many delusions of our day give force to the earnest exhortation.—"Take fast hold of instruction; let her not go; keep her, for she is thy life?"[2]

10. *When it goeth well with the righteous, the city rejoiceth;* **and** *when the wicked perish, there is shouting.* 11. *By the blessing of the upright the city is exalted: but it is overthrown by the mouth of the wicked.*

The world, in despite of the native enmity of the heart, bears its testimony to consistent godliness,[3] and *rejoices* in the prosperity of *the righteous.*[4] Their elevation to authority is a matter of general joy.[5] A godly king;[6] a premier, using his authority for the glory of God;[7] a man of God of high influence in the church[8]—these are justly regarded as a national *exaltation.*[9] Their prayers,[10] wisdom,[11] disinterestedness,[12] and example,[13] are a public blessing.

The wicked—they are only a curse to the community. Often has *it been overthrown,* or endangered *by their mouth.*[14] So that *their perishing* is a matter of present exultation.[15] Such was the joy at Rome on the death of Nero, and the public rejoicings in the French revolution at the death of Robespierre.[16] The people of God unite in *the shouting;* not from any selfish feeling of revenge; much less from unfeeling hardness towards their fellow-sinners. But when a hindrance to the good cause is removed;[17] when the justice of God against sin,[18] and his faithful preservation of his church[19] is displayed, ought not every feeling to be absorbed in a supreme interest in his glory? Ought they not to *shout?*[20] Is not the "Alleluia" of heaven an exulting testimony, that in the righteous judgments of the Lord our God is seen the hastening forward of his glorious kingdom?[21]

12. *He that is void of wisdom* (destitute of heart, Marg.) *despiseth his neighbor: but a man of understanding holdeth his peace.*

Pride and uncharitableness shew a man to be *void of wisdom*—ignorant alike of himself, his neighbor, and his God. For could he delight in magnifying "the mote in his neighbor's eye," had he *wisdom* to "consider the beam that is in his own eye?"[22] Could he *despise his neighbor,* did he really know him to be his own

[1] 2 Peter i. 5. [2] Chap. iv. 13. [3] Chap. xvi. 7. Mark vi. 20.
[4] Chap. xxviii. 12. [5] Chap. xxix. 2. Est. viii. 15, 16.
[6] 2 Chron. xxx. 25, 26. 'All things prosper in every respect, so long as thou rulest well,'—was the speech of the Senate to the emperor Severus. Comp. Isa. xxxii. 1, 2. 1 Tim. ii. 1, 2.
[7] 2 Chron. xxiv. 16. [8] 2 Kings ii. 12; xiii. 14. [9] 2 Chron. xxxvii. 20—23.
[10] Ex. xxxiii. 12, 17. Isa. xxxii. 14—36. Jer. xviii. 20. James v. 16—18.
[11] Gen. xli. 38—42. Ecc. ix. 15. [12] Est. x. 3. [13] Job xxii. 30.
[14] Chap. xxix. 8. Num. xvi. 3, 41. 2 Sam. xv. 1—14; xx. 1.
[15] Job xxvii. 23 [16] Comp. 2 Chron. xxi. 19, 20.
[17] Chap. xxi. 11; xxviii. 28. Ecc. ix. 18. [18] 1 Sam. xxv. 39. 2 Sam. xviii. 14—28
[19] Ex. xv. 21. Judges v. 31. 2 Kings xi. 13—20.
[20] Psalm lii. 6, 7; lviii. 10. Rev. xviii. 20. Comp. Isa. xxxv. 1, with xxxiv.
[21] Rev. xix. 1—7. [22] Matt. vii. 3—5.

flesh;[1] perhaps even "a member of the body, and of the flesh, and of the bones of his Lord?"[2] Could he look down upon him in the plenitude of pride, did he realize the consciousness, that—if he differs, it is God—not himself—"that hath made him to differ?"[3] Surely this blindness is to be *void of wisdom and destitute of heart.* 'It denotes the want of a right state of mind, judgment, and affections. Such a man is *without heart* to what is wise and good.'[4]

A man of understanding may see much in *his neighbor* to excite his pity, and stir up his prayers, but nothing to *despise.* He may be called openly to condemn him. But his general course will be loving forbearance; *holding his peace;* 'keeping himself from speaking or doing anything in scorn of another,'[5] "*considering thyself*, lest thou also be tempted."[6] Self-knowledge shews *the man of understanding*, and forms the man of love.

13. *A tale-bearer revealeth secrets: but he that is of a faithful spirit concealeth the matter.*

Another breach of love is here reproved.[7] *A tale-bearer*, having no business of his own, trafficks with his neighbor's name and honor, and vends his wares of scandal, as it may be, whether for gain or wantonness.[8] It is most unsafe to be within the breath of this cruel trifler with the happiness of his fellow-creatures.[9] For as readily as he *reveals our neighbor's secrets* to us, will he reveal ours to him.[10] All the bonds of confidence and friendship are broken in pieces. Let ears and lips be closed against him. If there be no vessel to receive his base matter, his words will fall to the ground, and die away. Children and servants—inmates in the house, and visitors in the family—should guard most carefully against *revealing secrets*, that have been spoken before them in the unreserved confidence of domestic life. This busy idleness has always been a sore in the church—a religion always abroad, occupied impertinently with foreign interference;[11] while at home it is "the field of the slothful, grown over with thorns."[12] Would we have our friend rest his anxieties on our bosom?[13] Let him not see the results of misplaced confidence dropping out of our mouth. It is of great moment to our peace—that those about us should be of *a faithful spirit*, fully worthy of our confidence; to whom it is not necessary on every occasion to *enjoin secrecy;* true to our interest as to their own; who would rather refuse a trust than betray it; whose bosom is a cover of *concealment*, except when the

[1] Isa. lviii. 7. Mal. ii. 10. Acts xvii. 26. [2] Eph. v. 30. [3] 1 Cor. iv. 7.
[4] Scott in loco—Comp. Chap. xiv. 21. John vii. 47—49.
[5] Diodati. [6] Gal. vi. 1. [7] Lev. xix. 16, 17.
[8] Neh. vi. 17—19. [9] Chap. xvi. 28; xviii. 8; xxvi. 22.
[10] Chap. xx. 19. Horace has given us this same warning:
Percontatorem fugito; nam garrulus idem est;
Nec retinent patulæ commissa fideliter aures.
Epist. I. 18. l. 69, 70.
[11] 1 Thess. iv. 11. 2 Thess. iii. 10—12. 1 Tim. v. 13. 1 Peter iv. 15.
[12] Chap. xxiv. 30, 31. [13] Chap. xvii. 17.

honor of God and the interests of society plainly forbids.[1] Invaluable is such a friend, but rare indeed in this deceitful world.[2] Yet let it never be forgotten, that Christian consistency includes the *faithful spirit;* and the habitual absence of it under a plausible religion makes it most doubtful, whether the spirit and mind of Christ is not altogether wanting.

14. *Where no counsel is, the people must fall: but in the multitude of counsellors there is safety.*

Even in private matters the value of wise counsellors is generally admitted. The agreement of *the multitude* gives *safety* to our decision. And their difference, by giving both sides of the question, enable us to ponder our path more safely. Much more is the nation without counsellors, like a ship in the midst of the rocks without a pilot—in imminent peril. God has given to some the gift for government—"wisdom that is profitable to direct."[3] *Where there is no counsel the people must fall.* In the dark time of the Judges, the want of a king led to anarchy, and the *people fell* into their enemies.[4] Ten parts of *the people fell*, when Rehoboam listened to evil *counsel.*[5] What *a fall* again was there of *the people*, when the counsel of godly Jehoiada was removed![6] The Good Lord deliver us from the deserved national judgment of weak and blinded counsellors![7]

Daniel and Solomon, though themselves specially endowed with wisdom, governed their kingdoms prosperously by wise counsellors.[8] The larger the multitude of such counsellors, the greater the safety. To one such, a heathen monarch owed the *safety* of his kingdom from desolating famine.[9]

Often has the church been preserved by this blessing.[10] Shall we not now plead for her *safety* in this day of her distress, that *her people* may not *fall* by the want of *counsel;*[11] that her ordained *counsellors* may be largely filled with the "spirit of power, and of love, and of a sound mind,"[12] to establish her people more firmly in the pure faith of the Gospel?[13]

15. *He that is surety for a stranger shall smart* (be sore broken. Marg.), *for it: and he that hateth suretyship is sure.*

This repeated warning against *suretyship*[14] is intended to inculcate considerateness; not to excuse selfishness, or to dry up the sources of helpful sympathy. It must not be *for a stranger*,[15] whose character and responsibilities are unknown to us. For such incautious kindness—too often done to the injury of our family—

[1] 1 Sam. iii. 17, 18; xix. 1, 2. Jer. xxxviii. 24—27. Contrast Judges xvi. 16—20.
[2] Chap. xx. 6. [3] Eccl. x. 10. [4] Judges ii. 8—23; xxi. 25.
[5] 1 Kings xii. 16—19. 'Fall like leaves.'—LXX.
[6] 2 Chron. xxiv. 17—21. [7] Eccl. x. 16. Isa. iii. 1—4; xix. 11—14.
[8] Psalm cxix. 98—100, with 2 Sam. xv. 12; xvii. 14, also 1 Kings xii. 6.
[9] Gen. xli. 38—57.
[10] Acts xv. 6—31. Comp. Chap. xv. 22; xx. 18; xxiv. 6. Psalm cxxii. 6—9.
[11] Ez. xxxiv. 4—6 Matt. xv. 14. Luke xi. 52. [12] 2 Tim. i. 7.
[13] Acts xvi. 4, 5. [14] Chap. vi. 1—5. [15] Chap. xxvii. 13.

we shall *smart*—if not be *sore broken.* To *hate* such engagements is therefore our prudent security.

But one exception we can never forget. The blessed Jesus, from his free grace—unsought—unasked[1]—became *surety*—not for a friend (in which case we should have had no interest) but *for a stranger.* He became One with us in nature, that he might be One with us in law. He took our place under the curse of the broken law.[2] He put his soul to the fullest extent in our soul's place; and then made our nature pay the debt, which all the angels of heaven could never have discharged. Oh! this was a *smart* indeed. Yea—*sore broken* was he under the stroke of his Father's hand.[3] The Upholder of the universe was prostrate in the dust;[4] his own creature strengthening his sinking frame.[5] Had he *hated suretyship, he would have been sure;* (for what could have disturbed his self-existent happiness?) but we should have perished. Glory to his name! Though from all eternity he knew the bitterness of *the smart,* instead of *hating*—he "rejoiced and delighted" in his work.[6] His was no rash engagement. For it was the arrangement of the everlasting covenant.[7] Every way it was lawful. There was an infinite treasure to discharge the liabilities. The claims of justice were fully satisfied.[8] Sin was as thoroughly punished, as it was thoroughly pardoned. There was no injury, but rather indirect benefit to the family of God.[9] What then remains for us, but to fall down before this grace, and spend our days, as we shall spend our eternity, in adoring this wondrous manifestation of Divine glory![10]

16. *A gracious woman retaineth honor: and strong men retain riches.*

Everywhere the excellency of godliness meets our eyes. What loveliness, dignity, and influence does it impart to the female character![11] *A gracious woman* is known, not by her outward beauty,[12] but by her "inner becoming ornaments;"[13] which remain in full lustre, when external accomplishments have faded away."[14] And though "the weaker vessel," she *retaineth honor,* as firmly as *strong men retain riches.* She preserves her character unblemished.[15] She wins her children,[16]—perhaps her ungodly husband[17]—into the ways of holiness. Thus Deborah *retained honor* as "a mother in Israel"—the Counsellor and the stay of a sinking people.[18] Esther *retained* her influence over her heathen husband for the good of her nation.[19] And still the *gracious woman retaineth honor* long after she has mingled with the dust. Sarah the obedient wife;[20] Hannah the consecrating mother;[21] Lois, Eunice,

1 John x. 15, 17, 18. Phil. ii. 6—8. 2 Gal. iii. 13.
3 Isa. liii. 5, 10—*bruised—sore broken.* 4 Mark xiv. 35, with Heb. i. 3.
5 Luke xxii. 43. 6 Chap. viii. 31. Heb. x. 5—8, with Psalm xl. 6—8.
7 Isa. liii. 10—12. 1 Pet. i. 20. 8 Isa. i. 27; xlii. 21. Rom. iii. 25, 26.
9 Eph. i. 10. Col. i. 20. 10 Rev. i. 5, 6; v. 12. 11 Chap. xxxi. 10—31.
12 Chap. xxxi. 30. 13 1 Tim. ii. 9, 10. 1 Pet. iii. 3, 4. 14 Chap. xxxi. 25, 26.
15 Ruth iii. 11. 16 Chap. xxxi. 28.
17 Ibid. verses 12, 28. 1 Cor. vii. 16. 1 Pet. iii. 1, 2. 18 Judg. iv. 4; v. 7.
19 Esth. ix. 12, 13, 25 20 1 Pet. iii. 5, 6. 21 1 Sam. i. 19—28.

and "the elect lady,"[1] in the family sphere; Phœbe and her companions in the annals of the Church;[2] the rich contributor to the temple;[3] the self-denying lover of her Lord;[4] Mary in contemplative retirement;[5] Dorcas in active usefulness:[6] are not these "good names" still had in *honorable* remembrance?[7]

17. *The merciful man doeth good to his own soul: but he that is cruel troubleth his own flesh.*

Mercifulness is not natural benevolence, without God or godliness. It is "the fruit of the Spirit;"[8] the image of our Father;[9] the constraint of the love of Christ;[10] the adorning of "the elect of God."[11] It is not pity in words and looks. It is when our neighbor's trouble descends into the depth of our hearts, and draws out thence bowels of kindness and practical sympathy.[12] *The merciful man* will ever find a merciful God.[13] The widow of Sarepta and the woman of Shunem, each for their kindness to the Lord's prophets, "will receive a prophet's reward."[14] The alms of Cornelius brought *good to his own soul.*[15] In watering others with our mercy, our own "souls will become a watered garden."[16] Even now "God is not unrighteous to forget our work and labor of love."[17] At the great day he will honor it before the assembled universe.[18]

But not less certainly will *cruelty* bring its own mischief.[19] Unsubdued passion is carrying about us the very element of hell, wanting nothing but immortality to perfect the misery. Cain found his brother's murder an intolerable *trouble to his flesh.*[20] Joseph's brethren severely smarted for their unfeeling wantonness.[21] Adoni-bezek was constrained to acknowledge the justice of his chastisement.[22] The doom of Ahab and Jezebel was the curse of their own *cruelty.*[23] "The treasures of selfishness will eat as doth a canker in *our own flesh.*"[24] O my God, save me from the tyranny of my own lust, and may thy perfect image of mercy be my standard and my pattern!

18. *The wicked worketh a deceitful work: but to him that soweth righteousness shall be a sure reward.* 19. *As righteousness tendeth to life: so he that pursueth evil pursueth it to his own death.*

Did Satan fulfil all his promises, truly his servants would be abundantly enriched.[25] But *the wicked worketh a deceitful work*—ending in disappointment. Abimelech doubtless expected peace as the result of his murderous work.[26] But *he pursued evil to his own death.* Ahab anticipated rest from the riddance of Naboth.

[1] 2 Tim. i. 5; iii. 15. 2 John 1—4. [2] Rom. xvi. 2—6. Phil. iv. 3.
[3] Mark xii. 42—44. [4] Ibid. xiv. 3—9. [5] Luke x. 39. [6] Acts ix. 36.
[7] Psalm cxii. 6. [8] Gal. v. 22. [9] Luke vi. 36. [10] 2 Cor. viii. 1—9.
[11] Col. iii. 12, 13. [12] Luke x. 30—37. [13] Psalm xli. 1—3. Matt. v. 7.
[14] 1 Kings xvii. 2 Kings iv. 8—37; viii. 1—6, with Matt. x. 41. [15] Acts x. 2—4.
[16] Ver. 25. Isa. lvii. 7—12. Comp. xxxii. 8. Psalm cxii. 4—9, with 2 Cor. ix. 6—11.
[17] Heb. vi. 10. Comp. Matt. x. 42. [18] Matt. xxv. 34—40. 2 Tim. i. 16—18.
[19] James ii. 13. Comp. Matt. xviii. 34, 35. [20] Gen. iv. 13, 14.
[21] Ibid. xlii. 7—21. [22] Judg. i. 6, 7.
[23] 1 Kings xxi. 23; xxii. 38. 2 Kings ix. 36, 37.
[24] James v. 1—3. Comp. Job xx. 19—23. [25] Gen. iii. 4, 5. Matt. iv. 8, 9
[26] Judg. ix. 22—51.

But the words of his troublesome reprover were to him as the "piercings of a sword."[1] How little did Gehazi contemplate the plague of the leprosy, as the issue of his well-contrived plan![2] Were the temptation presented in a naked form—'For this pleasure sell thy soul—thy God—thy heaven'—who would not fly with horror from the most enticing bait? But the tempter *worketh a deceitful work*, painting the present pleasure, and hiding the certain reality of ruin.[3] Oh! it is affecting to see his poor victim eagerly *pursuing evil*[4]—yet *to his own death.* Not only his open acts, but his thoughts, motions, pursuits, ends—all *tend to death.*[5] God has no place in his heart. And what else can be the end of a life without God? Thus the religious professor *deceives* others—perhaps himself. But his *deceitful work* will be the delusion of a moment—an eternity of confusion.

The sure reward of righteousness stands out in bright contrast. The "seed is precious;" and "the sheaves shall doubtless" follow.[6] Yet the reward is not of merit, but of consequence—mercifully, but surely linked with Christian perseverance.[7] But it must be *righteousness.* A routine of duties may skirt the borders of religion, at the utmost distance from the Spirit of God, and equally remote from the vital principle of the heart. But *righteousness* not only "delivereth from death,"[8] (a special mercy even with the loss of all;)[9] but it *tendeth to life*[10]—full of living enjoyment—of infinite—eternal pleasure. What importance then attaches to every godly principle! All have reference to eternity. If *righteousness* be our main end, God will make it our best friend; nor will he, like the world has done, reward us with ciphers instead of gold. Who will not love and serve thee, when "in keeping thy commandments there is a *sure reward!*"[11]

20. *They that are of a froward heart are abomination to the Lord: but such as are upright in their way are his delight.* 21. *Though hand join in hand, the wicked shall not be unpunished: but the seed of the righteous shall be delivered.*

The froward and the upright are often contrasted, as God looks at them.[12] *Frowardness is abomination to the Lord.*[13] All the contests between God and man, are—whose will shall stand?[14] Most thankful should we be for the school of discipline,[15] that makes us feel the privilege of "subjection to the obedience of Christ."[16] *Frowardness in the heart* is specially hateful[17]—most of all under the garb of external religion.[18] Sinners encourage one another in sin[19]—*hand joining in hand.* But all such "confederacies shall be broken in pieces."[20] For as "it is the same

[1] 1 Kings xxi. 4—24. [2] 2 Kings v. 20—27. [3] Chap. i. 15—18, xxii. 8.
[4] Chap. iv. 16, 17. [5] Chap. v. 1—5; vii. 22, 23; viii. 36; ix. 18.
[6] Psalm cxxvi. 6. [7] Ecc. xi. 6. Hosea x. 12. 1 Cor. xv. 58. Gal. vi. 8, 9.
[8] Verse 4; x. 2. [9] Gen. xix. 16.
[10] Chap. x. 16; xii. 28. Isa. iii. 10. Rom. ii. 7. Gal. vi. 8. [11] Psalm xix. 11.
[12] Ver. 3. Chap. iii. 32. Ps. xi. 5—7; xviii. 25, 26; cxli. 11—13.
[13] Chap. vi. 16, 17; viii. 13. [14] Ex. v. 2. Jer. xliv. 16, 28.
[15] 2 Chron. xvi. 7—10. [16] Psalm cxix. 67, 71. [17] Chap. xvi. 5.
[18] Isa. lxv. 2—5. Luke xvi. 14, 15. [19] Chap. i. 11—14. Isa. xli. 8.
[20] Isa. viii. 9. Gen. xi. 1—9. Num. xvi. 1—33. Josh. ix. 1, 2; x. 5.

with him to save by many or by few;"[1] so when he lifts his arm of vengeance, it is the same, "whether it be against a nation or a man only."[2] The flood; the judgment on Egypt; the chastenings of rebellious Israel in the wilderness; the destruction of Sennacherib's army—plainly prove, that *hand joining in hand* is a vain resistance to the hand of God.[3]

The upright in the way are contrasted with *the froward in heart;* because, as the heart is, so is the way. These are *Jehovah's delight.*[4] He singles them out from the ungodly world.[5] Nay, even he points to one of them as a challenge to Satan to do his worst.[6] Such is the condescension of his sovereign love—accepting his own work; stamping with open honor the graces of his people, sullied though they be with such base defilement!

Nor is their blessing confined to themselves. *The seed of the righteous shall be delivered.*[7] 'The best way for any man to do his children good, is to be godly himself.'[8] For have they not a place in their father's covenant?[9] And is not this an encouragement—not indeed to indolence and presumption—but to parental faith—in leaving our children in this naughty world unprotected and alone?[10] "The children of thy servants shall continue, and their seed shall be established before thee."[11]

22. *As a jewel of gold in a swine's snout, so is a fair woman which is without* (departeth from,[12] Marg.) *discretion.*

A most distasteful and yet an apt comparison! Let us see things as the Bible shews them to us. If *a fair*, light-minded young *woman* would see her own face in this mirror, she might well start aside with horror. Beauty indeed is to be honored as the gift of God.[13] Yet in itself it is a fading vanity;[14] and *without discretion*, it is as misplaced—as misbecoming, *as a jewel of gold in a swine's snout.*[15] Would the ornament beautify the filthy animal? Rather would not the unnatural combination make it more than ever an object of disgust? All the charms of beauty are lost upon a foolish woman. Instead of "retaining honor,"[16] she only brings upon herself disgrace. For just as *the jewel* is soon employed and besmeared in raking the mire; so too often does the *fair indiscreet woman* become subservient to the vilest passions.[17] No ornament can give comeliness to a fool;[18] while "wisdom maketh the face to shine."[19]

Learn then to value far beyond beauty of face, the inner "orna-

[1] 1 Sam. xiv. 6. 2 Chron. xiv. 11. [2] Job xxxiv. 29. [3] Chap. xvi. 5.
[4] Chap. xii. 22. Psalm lxxxiv. 11.
[5] Gen. vii. 1. Num. xiv. 24. John i. 47. [6] Job i. 8.
[7] Chap. xx. 7. Psalm xxxvii. 26; cxii. 1, 2. Comp. 1 Kings xv. 4. 2 Kings xix. 34.
[8] Exposition of Proverbs by John Dodd and Robert Cleaver, 4to. 1614.
[9] Gen. xvii. 7. Acts ii. 39. [10] Psalm ciii. 17. [11] Ibid. cii. 28.
[12] Chap. vii. 10; ix. 13.
[13] See Moses, Acts vii. 20. David, 1 Sam. xvi. 12. Est. ii. 7. Job's daughters, xlii. 15
[14] Chap. xxxi. 30. [15] Isa. iii. 21. See Bishop Lowth's interesting note. [16] Ver. 16
[17] Ezek. xvi. 16. Neh. iii. 4. Comp. 2 Sam. xi. 2; xiv. 25, 26; xv. 1—6.
[18] Chap. xxvi. 9. [19] Ecc. viii. 1. Chap. xxxi. 30.

ments" of grace, "which are in the sight of God of great price."[1] Many a lovely form enshrines a revolting mind. All external—even all intellectual—accomplishments *without discretion* issue in barrenness. So entirely do we depend upon God's grace, for a fruitful improvement of his own gifts!

23. *The desire of the righteous is only good: but the expectation of the wicked is wrath.*

'*Desire* is the wing of the soul, whereby it moveth, and is carried to the thing which it loveth, as the eagle to the carcase, in the Scripture Proverbs,[2] to feed itself upon it, and to be satisfied with it.'[3] *The desire of the righteous* must be *good*, because it is God's own work.[4] It must be *only good*, because it centres in himself.[5] God in Christ is *his portion:* and what earthly portion can compare with it?[6]—*his object;* and what object is worth living for—worth half a serious thought—besides?[7] Only let me subordinate my *desires* to his will;[8] and I shall be equally happy, whether they be granted or withheld.[9] As a physician, "he knoweth my frame"[10]—what is—what is not—expedient for me. "As a Father, he pitieth" my weakness.[11] As a God, he fully supplies my *real* need.[12] *The desire*, therefore, inwrought by him, fixed on him, submitted to his will—must be *good*. But might not an angel weep to see the corrupt mixture[13] of worldliness,[14] selfishness,[15] pride.[16] Yet is this against our better will.[17] The main strength of *the desire* is to God; even though the tossing tempest of sin and Satan may combine and drive it out of its course.[18] In despite of this mighty assault—"Lord, all my desire is before thee: thou knowest all things; thou knowest that I love thee."[19] 'Thou didst put into my mind good desires; and thou wilt bring the same to good effect!'[20]

But *the expectation of the wicked* is discontent and opposition to God. Often is it indulged, but with the fearful accompaniment of *wrath*.[21] And how shortly will the deluding dream end in inexpressible—eternal *wrath!*[22] Oh! let me daily test my *desires* by the true standard, and discipline them, that they may be fixed upon the true object; so that, "delighting myself in the Lord," I may find them "*granted*" "exceeding abundantly above" my largest expectations.[23]

24. *There is that scattereth, and yet increaseth, and there is that withholdeth*

[1] 1 Pet. iii. 4, 5. [2] Job xxxix. 30. Matt. xxiv. 28.
[3] Bishop Reynolds' Treatise on the Passions. Works, p. 666.
[4] Psalm x. 17. Rom. viii. 26. [5] Psalm lxxiii. 25. Isa. xxvi. 8, 9.
[6] Psalm iv. 6, 7. [7] Rom. xiv. 8, 9. 1 Cor. vi. 19, 20. Phil. i. 21.
[8] 1 John v. 14. [9] 1 Kings viii. 17, 18. [10] Psalm ciii. 14.
[11] Ibid. verse 13. [12] Phil. iv. 19. [13] Comp. Article ix.
[14] Mark x. 35—37. [15] 2 Sam. xxiii. 15. Jon. iv. 8—11.
[16] 1 Chron. xxi. 1, 2, 8. [17] Rom. vii. 15—17. [18] Ibid. v. 22.
[19] Psalm xxxviii. 9. John xxi. 17. [20] Collect for Easter-Day.
[21] Num. xi. 18—33. Psalm lxxviii. 29—31; cvi. 15. Comp. Hos. xiii. 11.
[22] Verse 7. Chap. x. 28. Luke xvi. 23. Rom. ii. 8, 9. Heb. x. 27.
[23] Chap. x. 24. Psalm xxxvii. 4; lxxxi. 10. Eph. iii. 20.

more than is meet, but it tendeth to poverty.[1] 25. *The liberal soul* (soul of blessing, Marg.) *shall be made fat: and he that watereth shall be watered also himself.*

God has put a mark of distinguishing favor upon the exercises of that mercy, which is his own attribute. He scatters his blessings richly around;[2] and those that partake of his spirit do the same. Men may *scatter* in improvidence and sin, *and it tendeth to poverty.*[3] But *there is that scattereth, and yet increaseth.* The husbandman, scattering his seed "plentifully" over his field, expects a proportionate increase. And shall not the man of God, "dispersing abroad" the seed of godliness[4]—consecrating his substance and influence—to the Lord,—"as he has opportunity, doing good unto all men"[5]—shall not he receive a plentiful increase?[6] The men of the world hazard all in uncertain, and often ruinous, speculations. But in this *scattering* there is no uncertainty—no speculation. Have faith in God; and laying out for him will be laying up for ourselves.[7] This will be abundantly manifest either in a visible enlargement of earthly blessings,[8] or in a satisfying enjoyment of a more limited portion.[9] The reward of grace will be given in the gracious acceptance of our God,[10] and in a blissful reception into everlasting habitations."[11]

But is the covetous worldling happier—nay—is he richer—in *withholding more than is meet?*[12] 'Seldom does he prosper much even in the world. For God metes to men in their own measure; and bad crops, bad debts, expensive sickness, and a variety of similar deductions, soon amount to far more than *liberal* alms would have done.'[13]

Still more clearly does the Lord mark his blessing and his blast in the spiritual dispensation. *The liberal soul is made fat* in the healthful vigor of practical godliness;[14] and while he is *the soul* of blessing to others, *he is watered himself* with the descending showers.[15] Is not the minister refreshed by his own message of salvation to his people? Does not the Sunday School Teacher learn many valuable lessons in the work of instruction? Does not the soul of the District Visitor or the Christian friend glow, in carrying the precious name of Jesus to a fellow-sinner? Is not every holy temper, every spiritual gift, every active grace, increased by exercise; while its efficiency withers by neglect?[16]

26. *He that withholdeth corn, the people shall curse him: but blessing shall be upon the head of him that selleth it.*

Let us never forget, that we are the stewards of the gifts of God.[17] To use them therefore for our own interests, without a due

[1] 'There are those, who, sowing their own, make it more; and those who gather and are impoverished.'—LXX.
[2] Psalm xxxiii. 5; xxxvi. 5—7; cxix. 64. [3] Chap. xxi. 17. Luke xv. 13, 14.
[4] Psalm cxii. 9. [5] Gal. vi. 10. [6] 2 Cor. ix. 6, 11.
[7] Chap. iii. 9, 10; xiv. 22; xix. 17; xxviii. 27.
[8] Luke vi. 38, *into thy bosom*—the sensible experience of the blessing.
[9] Deut. xv. 10. Luke xi. 41. [10] Heb. xiii. 16.
[11] Luke xvi. 9. Comp. 1 Tim. vi. 11—19. [12] Hag. i. 4—10. Comp. Chap. iii. 27.
[13] Scott in loco. [14] Isaiah xxxii. 8.
[15] Isa. lviii. 10, 11. [16] Matt. xxv. 29. [17] 2 Cor. ix. 11.

regard to our neighbor, is unfaithfulness to God.[1] Is it not therefore a flagrant sin to withhold the very "staff of life;"[2] thus holding back the hand of God stretched out in bounty over our land? This may indeed be a prudential restraint in a time of scarcity.[3] Private interest may also claim a measure of consideration. But a grasping and grinding spirit—a spirit of selfish monopoly—raising the price for gain with manifest suffering to the poor—will bring a piercing curse. And here *the curse of the people* may be the curse of God.[4] For if the cry of oppressed individuals[5]—much more that of an oppressed people—will "enter into the ears of the Lord of Sabaoth."[6]

The point of the antithesis apparently fails, only to give stronger security to the blessing. *The curse* comes directly from *the people—the blessing* from above. To him that subordinates his own interest to the public good—*blessing shall be upon his head*,[7] descending immediately from the fountain of all grace.

Would that the cry for the bread of life were as earnest and universal as for the bread that perisheth! But if he be justly *cursed that withholds* the one; much more he that unfaithfully and cruelly *withholds* the other. And if *blessing be upon the head of him that selleth the corn* of this life; what is his privilege, who *sells* not indeed the bread of life, but dispenses it to his fellow-sinners "without money, and without price!"[8] Will not "the blessing of him that was ready to perish come upon him?"[9] The supply is abundant. Let the invitation be welcomed.

27. *He that diligently seeketh good, procureth favor: but he that seeketh mischief, it shall come unto him.*

There is no negative existence. All of us are living for *good* or for *mischief*. True happiness—solid usefulness—consists in centering the interest on one valuable object—*seeking good*. Nor must this be done cursorily. We must not wait to have it brought to us. We must look out for it, *seek it diligently*, rise up early, and spring with joy to the work. Let us awake to the conscious responsibility of having the means of blessing our fellow-sinners in our own hands. Every talent finds its suitable sphere, and may be "put out to usury" with large returns. There is the practical exercise of "pure and undefiled religion—visiting the fatherless and afflicted;"[10] the teaching of the ignorant; the instruction of the young—the rising hope of our Church—a work of deepening interest and anxiety. Let each of us try what we can do; and, whether it be little or much, do it prayerfully, faithfully, heartily: not damped by trifling hindrances;[11] nor making the power of doing little an excuse for doing nothing. In living for others, we

[1] Matt. xxv. 26, 27. [2] Isa. iii. 1. [3] Gen. xli. 46—49.

[4] The original implies he piercing of a sword, or dagger, as if the selfish spoiler, as it were, pierced through and stabbed to death by the *curses of the people*.—Cartwrigh in loco.

[5] Ex. xxii. 22—24. James v. 4. [6] Amos viii. 4—8.

[7] Chap. x. 6. See Gen. xlix. 26. [8] Isa. lv. 1. [9] Job xxix. 13.

[10] Jam. i 27. Comp. Matt. xxv. 35, 36. 2 Tim. i. 16, 17. [11] Eccl. xi. 4.

live for our true happiness. In *seeking diligently their good, we procure favor;* often from man;[1] always from God.[2] He honors a little strength laid out for him.[3] He accepts the single talent.[4] And 'filling up every hour with some profitable labor, either of heart, head, or hands (as Brainerd justly observed) is an excellent means of spiritual peace and boldness before God.'[5]

But Satan finds employment for his servants in *seeking mischief.*[6] And how does their ceaseless energy put to shame our indifference! Yet *their own mischief often comes to them.*[7] So Satan himself found it. The *mischief* that he brought upon man *came upon his own head.*[8] His servants often become the victims of their own delusions,[9] with the fearful aggravation of having dragged multitudes with them into the pit of ruin. What then will be the fruit of my diligence? Will it be a blessing or a curse to my fellow-sinners? O my God! may it be from thee, and for thee!

28. *He that trusteth in his riches shall fall: but the righteous shall flourish as a branch.*

Here is the cause and misery of the fall. Man seeks his rest in God's blessings, in opposition to himself.[10] *Riches* are one of his grounds of trust.[11] He depends on them, as the saint upon his God.[12] And is not this the "denial of the God that is above?"[13] A revolting truth indeed![14] such as only the heart crucified to the world by the cross of Christ can receive. Not that the possession of riches is a sin,[15] but the *trusting in them.*[16] Nor may it be always wrong to improve an opportunity of increasing them. But no one that cares for his own soul, and believes the testimony of the Word of God,[17] will *seek* such an opportunity; or even avail himself of it without a plain call, and clear advantage for the glory of God.[18] Let God be our satisfying portion. Let him be supremely loved and honored, and he will determine for us, whether the worldly advantage be a Providence, or a temptation in our path.

Disappointment will be the certain end of this trust.[19] When we need a staff, we shall find a piercing spear.[20] Or we *shall fall,* like the withered leaf or blossom before the blast.[21] And how many a lovely blossom has thus *fallen!*[22] Thus does "the rich man fade away in his ways!"[23]

1 Chap. xvi. 7. Gen. xlvii. 25. Esth. x. 3.
2 Chap. xii. 2; xiv. 22. Neh. v. 16—19. 3 Rev. iii. 8. 4 2 Cor. viii. 12.
5 Life of Brainerd—Edwards's Works, 8vo. Vol. iii. 148. 6 Ps. xxxvi. 3, 4.
7 Ver. 3, 15, 16. Esth. vii. 10. Ps. x. 2; lvii. 6. 8 Gen. iii. 1—6, 14, 15.
9 2 Thes. ii. 10, 11. 2 Tim. iii. 13. 10 Comp. Jer. ix. 23, 24.
11 Chap. x. 15. Luke xii. 16—21. 12 Chap. xviii. 10, 11.
13 Job xxxi. 24, 25, 28. 14 Luke xvi. 9—14.
15 See the gift of God to Abraham, Gen. xxiv. 35; to David, 1 Chron. xxix. 12—16; to Solomon, 2 Chron. i. 10—12; to Job, xlii. 11, 12.
16 Mark x. 24. 17 Comp. Mark x. 25—27. 1 Tim. vi. 9, 10.
18 Luke xvi. 9; xix. 13. 1 Tim. vi. 18, 19.
19 Chap. xxiii. 5. Ps. xlix. 6—12. Ecc. v. 10, 11; vi. 2. Jer. xlix. 4, 5.
20 1 Tim. vi. 10. 21 Deut. viii. 17—19. 1 Tim. vi. 10, 11. 22 Mark x. 21, 22
23 Jam. i. 10, 11.

But *the righteous* is *the branch*—not like the leaf or blossom, easily shaken and withered;[1] but abiding in the true and living vine: full of life and fruit.[2] There may be, as in nature's winter, times of apparent darkness. But the spring returns, and with it *the branch flourishes;* never ceasing from yielding fruit; yea—filled with the fruit of righteousness;"[3] the branch of "the Lord's planting; the work of his hands, that he may be glorified;" to be transplanted in his own best time to the other side of the river, where "the leaf shall not fade, neither shall the fruit thereof be consumed."[4] Shall not this prospect fill us with lively joy and praise?

29. *He that troubleth his own house shall inherit the wind: and the fool shall be servant to the wise of heart.*

A house at unity with itself, flourishes under the special favor of God.[5] But *a house troubled* with division, "cometh to desolation."[6] Often also the irreligion or ungoverned passions of the Head blights the comfort of the family.[7] Indeed he cannot neglect his own soul without injury to *his house.* He deprives them of the blessing of holy prayers and godly example; while he *troubles* them with the positive mischief of his ungodliness, and himself *inherits the wind* in utter disappointment.[8] Thus did the rebellion of Korah[9]—the sin of Achan[10]—the neglect of Eli[11]—the wickedness of Jeroboam and Ahab[12]—the perverseness of the rebuilder of Jericho[13]—*trouble their house* to its ruin. Prayerless, careless Parents! ponder the responsibility of bringing a curse instead of a blessing upon your families. What! if your "root should be as rottenness, and your blossom go up as dust?"[14]

What if a man—instead of building up his house, should be '*so foolish* as to misspend himself, and come to be *a servant* at the last to him that is *wise* to get and keep his own?'[15] Such retributions have been known.[16] The abuse of the gifts of God, and the neglect of Christian responsibility, will not be forgotten.

30. *The fruit of the righteous is a tree of life; and he that winneth* (taketh, Marg.) *souls is wise.*

Here is *the fruit* of the *flourishing branch.*[17] The whole course of *the righteous*—his influence, his prayers, his instruction, his example—*is a tree of life.* What the tree of life was in paradise—what it will be in heaven—that he is in this wilderness—fruitful,[18] nourishing,[19] healing.[20] *Wisdom to win souls* is the precious *fruit.* For though only he, who purchased souls by his

1 See the same contrast, Ps. lii. 7, 8.
2 John xv. 4, 5. 3 Jer. xvii. 8. Phil. i. 11. 4 Isa. lx. 21. Ez. xlvii. 12.
5 Psalm cxxxiii. 6 Matt. xii. 25. 7 1 Sam. xxv. 17.
8 Hos. viii. 7. Psalm xlix. 11, 12. 9 Num. xvi. 32, 33.
10 Josh. vii. 24, 25 Comp. Chap. xv. 27. 11 1 Sam. ii. 30—33.
12 1 Kings xiv. 9—11; xxi. 20—22. 13 Ibid. xvi. 34.
14 Isa. v. 24. 15 Bishop Hall. 16 Luke xv. 13—15. 17 Ver. 28.
18 Rev. xxii. 2, with Chap. x. 11, 31, 32. Can. iv. 12—16.
19 Rev. ii. 7, with Chap. x. 21. 20 Rev. xxii. 2, with Chap. xii. 18; xv. 4.

blood, can *win* them to himself (and who that knows the work but will give him all the praise?); yet has he set apart men given to the work; 'drawing souls to God, and to the love of him; sweetly gaining and making a holy conquest of them to God.'[1] This was the *wisdom* of our Divine Master. He "taught the people as they were able to bear it,"[2] accommodating himself to their convenience,[3] and their prejudices,[4] if that he might *win their souls.* And truly were these opportunities "his meat and drink." For when "wearied with his journey, he sat down on the well," thirsting for water; far more intensely did he thirst for the soul of the poor sinner before him; and, having *won* her to himself, he forgot his own want in the joy of her salvation.[5] In close walking after this pattern of *wisdom,* did the great Apostle "become all things to all men, that he might by all means gain some."[6] God grant that no Minister of Christ may spend a day, without laboring to *win* at least *one soul* for heaven!

But—blessed be God!—this *fruit—this wisdom*—is not confined to the Ministers of the Gospel. Do we love our Lord? Arise! let us follow him in this happy work, and he will honor us. *The righteous* wife *wins her husband's soul* by the *wisdom* of meekness and sobriety.[7] The godly neighbor *wins* his fellow-sinner to the ways of God, by the patient energy of faith and love.[8] The Christian, who neglects his brother's salvation, fearfully hazards his own. He is gone back to his native selfishness, if his profession does not exhibit some image of that "love and kindness of God, which hath appeared unto men." What is the wisdom of the philosopher, the scholar, or the statesman—compared with this *wisdom to win souls?* If any one *soul be taken,* the honor passeth thought. No ambition so great—no results so glorious. "They that be *wise* shall shine as the brightness of the firmament; and they that turn many to righteousness as the stars forever and ever."[9] Every soul *won by this wisdom,* will be a fresh jewel in the Saviour's crown—a polished stone in that temple, in which he will be honored throughout eternity.

31. *Behold! the righteous shall be recompensed in the earth; much more the wicked and the sinner.*

The inspired application of this proverb infallibly expounds the mind of God.[10] It is introduced to us with a special call to attention—*Behold!* Let *the righteous* expect from their relation to God—not immunity—but strict *recompence.*[11] They are under the discipline, though not under the curse, of the rod. Such is our too high estimation of the world, conformity to its ways and spirit, and forgetfulness of our inheritance and home; that but for the

[1] Diodati. [2] Mark iv. 33. [3] Ibid. vi. 31—34.
[4] Matt. xi. 16—19; xvii. 24—27. [5] John. iv. 6, 32—34.
[6] 1 Cor. ix. 20—22; x. 33. [7] 1 Cor. vii. 16. 1 Pet. iii. 1, 2.
[8] Jam. v. 19, 20. [9] Dan. xii. 3.
[10] 1 Peter iv. 18, is verbatim, LXX. translation of this version—'Si justus vix vivit impius et peccator—ubi reperietur?'—Syr.
[11] Amos iii. 2. 1 Pet. iv. 17. Comp. Jer. xxv. 29.

rod, we should soon backslide to our stubborn wantonness. *The righteous* therefore *are recompensed in the earth.*[1] Every perfection of God is glorified in his dispensation towards them. As a wise Father, he will not indulge them in sin. As a holy God, he must show in them his abhorrence of it. As a faithful God, he will make the chastisements of his rod the means of their restoration.[2] But—blessed be God—all the penal curse is subtracted. We *are recompensed in the earth;* not, as we deserve to be, in hell. Nay—"we are chastened of the Lord, that we might not be condemned with the world;"[3] punished here, that we might be spared forever; *recompensed in the earth,* to be made meet for heaven.[4]

Much more then will the wicked and the sinner be recompensed. If the children be scourged, much more the rebels. If the fatherly corrections be so terrible, even when the child be accepted; what must be the unmingled wrath for the wilful sinner! "If the righteous scarcely be saved; where shall the ungodly and the sinner appear?"[5] "If they do these things in the green tree, what shall be done in the dry?"[6] "Behold, the day of the Lord cometh, that shall burn as an oven; and all that do wickedly shall be as stubble."[7] Let the *wicked* tremble. Let the child of God be humbled in the dust—"My flesh trembleth for fear of thee, and I am afraid of thy judgments."[8]

CHAPTER XII.

1. *Whoso loveth instruction loveth knowledge: but he that hateth reproof is brutish.*

Instruction—as we gather from the contrast, chiefly implies discipline[9]—that most needful course for acquiring spiritual *knowledge.*[10] For so contrary is it to our proud hearts, that the submission of the will is our only road to Christian attainment.[11] Yet the value of this attainment abundantly covers the cost.[12] A faithful ministry, therefore, is a most valuable blessing; and indeed, all *instructive* discipline "may well be *loved* as the way of life."[13]

To hate reproof—as if it were an affront to be told of our faults

[1] Jacob, Gen. xxvii, with xxxvii. Moses and Aaron, Num. xx. 12, with Deut. iii. 23—26; xxxii. 48—52. Ps. xcix. 6—8. Eli, 1 Sam. ii. 27—36. David, 2 Sam. xii. 9—12. Ps. xxxii. 3, 4; xxxviii. 1—5. Solomon, 1 Kings xi. 9—13. The disobedient prophet, Ibid. xiii. 21—24. Hezekiah, Isa. xxxix. 1—7.
[2] Ps. lxxxix. 30—32. [3] 1 Cor. xi. 32. [4] Heb. xii. 10.
[5] 1 Pet. iv. 18. [6] Luke xxiii. 31. [7] Mal. iv. 1.
[8] Ps. cxix. 120. [9] Comp. Judg. viii. 16. Jer. vi. 8.
[10] Ps. cxix. 67, 71. [11] Matt. xviii. 3, 4. [12] Phil. iii. 8.
[13] Chap. ix. 8. Ps. cxli. 5, with Chap. vi. 23. Comp. Ps. xvi. 7; xcii. 12. Jer. xxxi. 18.

—argues not only want of grace,[1] but want of understanding—*brutish* folly:[2] 'like the horse, which bites and kicks at the man, who performs a painful operation upon him; though absolutely necessary for removing a dangerous distemper. He is surely *a brute*, and not a rational creature, who has swallowed poison, and will rather suffer it to take its course, than admit the necessary relief of medicine, lest he should be obliged to confess his folly in exposing himself to the need of it.'[3] O for a teachable spirit, to "sit at the feet of our Divine Master," and "learn of Him!"

2. *A good man obtaineth favor of the Lord: but a man of wicked devices will he condemn.*

Goodness is "the fruit of the Spirit."[4] *The good man* therefore is a man filled with the Spirit. He reflects the munificent goodness of God.[5] He is not only the subject, but the almoner, of grace; not only "enriched" with all blessings for himself, but "unto all bountifulness"[6] for the service of his fellow-creatures.[7] As a benefactor to mankind, he commands our devoted gratitude. but as a far richer reward (of grace indeed—not of debt[8]) he *obtaineth favor of the Lord.*[9] What are all this world's treasures compared with it?[10] Is it not the joy of our salvation;[11] our soothing mercy;[12] our covering shield,[13] in the near prospect of eternity—our absorbing interest?[14] And if here, in a world of sin, it be "life, yea, better than life;"[15] what will be the unclouded sunshine—'the path of life"—"the fulness of joy in his heavenly presence—the pleasures at his right hand for evermore!"[16]

The contrast to *the good man* is—not the man—(which alas! may be a child of God[17]) in whom *wicked devices* are found, but *the man of these devices.* He lives in them as his element; his mind is set upon them. He contrives them. He follows them as his course and delight.[18] Instead of *favor*, here is *condemnation* justly merited. He is "*condemned already.*"[19] Nay—his sting of conscience and the curse of God is present *condemnation.*[20] But what will it be, when the All-seeing Judge "shall be a swift witness against him!"[21]

3. *A man shall not be established by wickedness: but the root of the righteous shall not be moved.*

The man of evil devices may prosper for a time, but *he shall not be established by wickedness;* except so far as God may permit it, in the sovereignty of his purposes, and the judicial chasten-

[1] Chap. x. 17; xv. 10. [2] Isa. i. 2, 3. Jer. viii. 7.
[3] Lawson in loco—Comp. Ps. xxxii. 9. [4] Gal. v. 22.
[5] Matt. v. 44, 45. [6] 2 Cor. ix. 11. [7] See Rom. v. 7. [8] Luke xvii. 10.
[9] Isa. lviii. 8—11. Comp. Neh. xiii. 14, 22, 31. 1 Pet. i.i. 11, 12.
[10] Psalm iv. 6, 7. [11] Ibid. lxxx. 19; lxxxv. 6, 7.
[12] Ibid. cxix. 76. [13] Ibid. v. 12. Rom. viii. 31. [14] 2 Cor. v. 9, 10.
[15] Psalm xxx. 5; lxiii. 3. [16] Ibid. xvi. 11.
[17] 1 Sam. xxv. 21, 22. 2 Sam. xi. 12—15.
[18] Chap. i. 10—12; vi. 18; xiv. 17. Isa. xxxii. 6, 7. [19] John iii. 18, 19.
[20] Isa. xlvii. 10, 11. Zech. v. 3, 4. 1 Kings xii. 25—30; xiv. 10.
[21] Mal. iii. 5. Ps. l. 16—21.

ing of his wrath. But how soon was the successful treason of Abimelech,[1] and the Israelitish kings[2] brought to an end! Ahab strove to *establish* himself in despite of the threatened curse of God. He increased his family, trained them with care under the tutelage of his choicest nobility. And surely one at least out of seventy might remain to inherit his throne. But this was the vain "striving" of the worm "with his Maker." One hour swept them all away; and not a word of the threatening fell to the ground.[3] The *evil device* of Caiaphas also, to *establish his nation by wickedness* was the means of its overthrow.[4] Such is the infatuation of sin!

Firm and unshaken is the condition of *the righteous*. Their leaves may wither in the blast. Their branches may tremble in the fury of the tempest. But *their root*—the true principle of life *shall not be moved*. They "are scarcely saved"[5]—not without many tossings. But they are surely saved—beyond the powers of hell to destroy. Does not thy faith—Christian—sometimes *faint* in the wearisome assaults of thy implacable enemy? Rejoice in the assurance, that it cannot *fail*.[6] Thou art "rooted and grounded" in a sure foundation.[7] "The Lord, who is thy strength"—let him be "thy song"—'He only is my Rock and my salvation, I shall not be greatly moved—I shall *not be moved* at all.'[8]

And how bright is this prospect for the Church! *It shall not be moved*.[9] Triumphant is her confidence in the day of conflict. "The gates of hell shall not prevail. No weapon that is formed against her shall prosper."[10]

4. *A virtuous woman is a crown to her husband: but she that maketh ashamed is as rottenness in his bones.*

Faithful,[11] chaste,[12] reverentially obedient,[13] immoveable in affection,[14] delighting to see her husband honored, respected, and loved; covering as far as may be his failings; prudent in the management of her family,[15] conscientious in the charge of her domestic duties;[16] kind and considerate to all around her;[17] and—as the root of all "fearing the Lord."[18]—Such is *the virtuous woman*—"the weaker vessel" indeed, but *a woman of strength*,[19] with all her graces in

[1] Judg. ix. 54—57.
[2] 1 Kings xvi. 9, 10, 16. 2 Kings xv. 10—14. Comp. 2 Chron. xxi. 4, 13—15.
[3] 1 Kings xxi. 21, with 2 Kings x. 1—7. Compare the striking figure in the book of Job xv. 29; xx. 5—9; xxvii. 13—17.
[4] John xi. 49, 50, with Matt. xxi. 39—44; xxiii. 32—39.
[5] 1 Pet. iv. 18.
[6] Luke xxii. 31, 32.
[7] Eph. iii. 7. Col. ii. 7. Isa. xxviii. 16.
[8] Isa. xii. 2. Ps. lxii. 2, 6. Comp. Micah vii. 8. Rom. viii. 31—39.
[9] Ps. cxxv. 1, 2. Isa. xxvi. 1.
[10] Matt. xvi. 18. Isa. liv. 17. Comp. Zech. xii. 3.
[11] Chap. xxxi. 11, 12. Ruth iii. 11. 1 Tim. iii. 11.
[12] Tit. ii. 5. 1 Pet. iii. 2.
[13] Eph. v. 22, 23. Tit. ii. 5. 1 Pet. iii. 1, 4—6. Comp. 1 Cor. xiv. 34, 35. 1 Tim. ii. 11, 12.
[14] Tit. ii. 4.
[15] Chap. xiv. 1; xix. 14. Tit. ii. 4.
[16] Chap. xxxi. 27, 28.
[17] Ibid. verses 20, 26.
[18] Ibid. verse 30.
[19] Heb. Chap. xxxi. 10. Ruth iii. 11. γυνη ανδρεια.—LXX. Strenua, Schultens, Fortis, Geier. The etymolog of αρετη in Greek, and virtus in Latin gives the meaning

godly energy. Not only is she the ring on her husband's finger or the chain of gold around his neck. That were far too low She is his *crown*—his brightest ornament[1]—drawing the eyes of all upon him, as eminently honored and blessed.[2]

Truly affecting is the contrast of "a contentious,"[3] imperious, extravagant, perhaps unfaithful wife; in the levity of her conduct forgetting her proper place and subjection: seeking the admiration of others, instead of being satisfied with her husband's regard. This is indeed a living disease—*rottenness in his bones*;[4] marring his usefulness; undermining his happiness; perhaps driving him into temptation, and "a snare of the devil." Let a young woman, in contemplating this holy union, ponder well and in deep prayer its weighty responsibility. Will she be *a crown to her husband*, or one *that maketh ashamed?* Will she be what God made the woman—"an help meet,"[5] or—what Satan made her—a tempter *to her husband?*[6] If she be not *a crown* to him, she will be a shame to herself. If she be *rottenness to his bones*, she will be a plague to her own. For what is the woman's happiness, but to be the helper of her husband's joy? Oh! let their mutual comfort be sought, where alone it can be solidly found—in "dwelling together as heirs of the grace of life."[7] Better never to have seen each other, than to live together forgetful of this great end of their eternal happiness.

5. *The thoughts of the righteous are right: but the counsels of the wicked are deceit.* 6. *The words of the wicked are to lie in wait for blood: but the mouth of the upright shall deliver them.* 7. *The wicked are overthrown, and are not: but the house of the righteous shall stand.*

The workings of good and evil are here traced to the fountain-head.[8] *The thoughts of the righteous*—"renewed in the spirit of their mind"[9]—*are right.*[10] He learns to measure every thing by the unerring rule, and to lean upon his God in the careful distrust of himself. Many indeed are his deviations. But there is an overcoming law within that, in despite of all oppositions, fixes *his thoughts* with delight on God and his law,[11] and gives to them a single bias for his service.[12] Widely different are the thoughts of *the wicked*, ripening into *counsels* fraught with *deceit.* Such were *the counsels* of Joseph's brethren to deceive their father;[13] of Daniel's enemies, under pretence of honoring the king;[14] of Sanballat, under the guise of friendship;[15] of Haman, under the cover

of manly courage. In the first ages of barbarism this was the primary virtue, and therefore naturally became the generic term of virtue.

[1] Perhaps there may be some allusion to *the crown* on the nuptial day.—Comp. 1 Cor. xi. 7.

[2] Chap. xxxi. 23. Comp. Ruth iii. 11.

[3] Chap. xix. 13; xxi. 9, 19.

[4] Jerome aptly compares it to the worm eating into the heart of the tree, and destroying it. Trapp in loco.

[5] Gen. ii. 18.

[6] Ibid. iii. 6. Comp. 1 Kings xxi. 25. Job ii. 9, 10.

[7] 1 Pet. iii. 7.

[8] See Chap. xxiv. 9. Gen. vi. 5.

[9] Eph. iv. 23.

[10] Chap. xi. 23.

[11] Psalm cxxxix. 17, 18. Rom vii. 15—23.

[12] Psalm cxxxii. 3—5. Dan. i. 8.

[13] Gen. xxxvii. 18—20.

[14] Dan. vi. 4—7.

[15] Neh. vi. 2.

of patriotism;[1] of Herod, under the profession of worshipping the infant Saviour.[2] Indeed, from such "a corrupt fountain" as man's heart, what else can be expected but "bitter waters?"[3]

Then look at *words*—the natural organ of *the thoughts*. How murderous were *the words* of Ahithophel,[4] the trap laid for our beloved Lord;[5] the conspiracy against the great Apostle[6]—*lying in wait for blood!*[7] The fiercer ebullitions of humanity may indeed be softened down and restrained.[8] But the principles remain the same. The fiery elements only lie in slumbering cover, and often break out, wasting the very face of society. Yet even in this bursting storm *the mouth of the upright preserves them.*[9] The wisdom of our Divine Master was an unfailing *preservative.*[10] The same *mouth* was a cover to his *upright* disciples, with little of man's help, and much of man's opposition; "None could gainsay or resist."[11]

But do we not wonder at the long suffering, that suffers *the wicked* thus to load the earth with such a mass of guilt and misery? Yet their triumphing is but for a moment.[12] Look at Haman—*his deceitful counsels, his bloody words. He is overthrown, and is not.*[13] For "shall not God avenge his own elect?"[14] *Their house*, feeble as it often is, and brought low,[15] *shall stand.* They shall "have a place in the Lord's house," immoveable here,[16] and in eternity.[17] Yes—those whose *thoughts and words are upright* they *shall stand*, when all is sinking around—"They shall be mine, saith the Lord, in that day when I shall make up my jewels."[18]

8. *A man shall be commended according to his wisdom: but he that is of a perverse heart shall be despised.*

The ordinary judgment of this world is to "put darkness for light,"[19] and therefore to *commend* according to folly, rather than *according to wisdom*. And yet even hated *wisdom* often carries its voice of conviction both to conscience and judgment, and *a man is commended according to it.* Hence the elevation of Joseph[20] and Daniel;[21] the honor paid to David in private life;[22] and the universal respect shown to his wise son.[23] Our Lord's *wisdom* was also *commended*—not only by the popular voice,[24] but even from the testimony of his enemies.[25] The wisdom of Stephen, literally

1 Esth. iii. 8—10. 2 Matt. ii. 7, 8.
3 Jer. xvii. 9. Matt. xv. 19. 4 2 Sam. xvii. 1—4.
5 Luke xx. 19—21. Comp. Matt. xxvi. 59—66.
6 Acts xxiii. 14, 15; xxv. 3. Comp. Chap. i. 11—16; vi. 18. Micah vii. 1, 2.
7 Chap. xxix. 10. Ps. xxxvii. 12, 14, 22.
8 See Rom. iii. 15, as the proof of universal and total depravity, verses 9, 10.
9 Chap. xi. 9. Dan. i. 11—13. 10 Matt. xxii. 34, 35, 46.
11 Luke xxi. 14, 15. Acts iv. 13, 14.
12 Job xx. 5; xxvii. 18, 19. Psalm xxxvii. 35, 36. Comp. Chap. x. 25, 30.
13 Esth. iii. 6—9; vii. 10; ix. 10. 14 Luke xviii. 7.
15 1 Kings xv. 4. 2 Kings viii. 19. Psalm cxxxii. 17. Verse 3.
16 Isa. lvi. 4, 5. Comp. Chap. x. 25, 30. 17 Rev. iii. 12. 18 Mal. iii. 16—18.
19 Isa. v. 20. 20 Gen. xli. 39.
21 Dan. i. 17—21; ii. 46—48; v. 11, 12, 29; vi. 3. 22 1 Sam. xvi. 18; xviii. 30.
23 1 Kings iii. 28; iv. 29—34; x. 1. 24 Matt. vii. 28, 29. 25 John vii. 46.

"making his face to shine," overpowered his beholders with solemn awe.[1] How thrilling will be *the commendation of wisdom* before the assembled universe![2] Who will not then acknowledge the *wise* choice of an earthly cross with an heavenly crown?[3] This then brings honor—Not dignity, riches, or talent, but *wisdom.*[4] This is the Lord's *commendation.* It must be right.[5] It will stand for eternity.

What then makes a man *despised?* Not his poverty, obscure circumstances, or misfortune. But *perverseness of spirit,*[6] too proud to be taught, following a mad course to ruin. *Perverse* Nabal was *despised* by his own family.[7] And of all such, shame will be their present promotion[8]—their eternal doom.[9]

9. *He that is despised, and hath a servant, is better than he that honoreth himself, and lacketh bread.*

A man, who has only a competency, sufficient to *have a servant,*[10] and making no appearance, may be *despised* by his richer neighbors.[11] But his state *is better* than the proud show of rank, without the means of sustaining it, or of one humbled by Providence, yet unhumbled in heart.[12] Nothing is so despicable as to be proud, where there is nothing to be proud of; when a man sometimes, from the foolish vanity of keeping up appearances, debars himself from the common comforts of life—*honoring himself, and lacking bread.* Such slaves are men to the opinion of the world! Principle is sacrificed to pride; and men rebel against Him, who makes no mistake in his allotments, and often appoints a descent from wordly elevation as a profitable discipline.[13] Yet it is hard, even for the Christian, as Bunyan reminds us, 'to go down the valley of Humiliation, and catch no slip by the way.' We need our Master's unworldly elevated spirit[14] to make a safe descent. Remember—"the pride of life is not of the Father, but is of the world."[15] "Let our moderation be known unto all men," under the constraining recollection—"the Lord is at hand."[16] How will the dazzling glare of man's esteem fade away before the glory of his appearing!

10. *A righteous man regardeth the life of his beast: but the tender mercies* (bowels, Marg.) *of the wicked are cruel.*

The minuteness of Scripture is one of its most valuable properties. It shows the mind of God on many points apparently trivial. Here it tests our profession by our treatment of the brutes. They were given to man as the lord of the creation, for his use, comfort, and food;[17] not for his wantonness. *A righteous man regardeth the life of his beast,* duly attends to its comfort,[18] and never presses

1 Acts vi. 10, 15. Eccl. viii. 1. 2 Luke xii. 42—44. 3 Matt. v. 11, 12.
4 2 Sam. xx. 18—22. 5 2 Cor. x. 18.
6 1 Kings xii. 16. Jer. iv. 30. Mal. ii. 8, 9. 7 1 Sam. xxv. 17, 25.
8 Chap. iii. 35; xi. 2; xviii. 3. 9 Dan. xii. 2. 10 Chap. xxx. 8, 9.
11 1 Sam. xviii. 23. 12 Chap. xiii. 7; xxv. 14. Luke xiv. 11.
13 James i. 10, 11. Comp. Dan. iv. 32—37. 14 John vi. 15. 15 1 John ii. 16.
16 Phil. iv. 5. Comp. Mark xiii. 1, 2. 17 Gen. i. 28; ix. 1, 2. 18 Ibid. xxiv. 32.

it beyond its strength.[1] The brutal habits therefore, the coarse words, inhuman blows,[2] and hard tyranny on the public roads is disgraceful to our nature. The delight of children in putting animals to pain for amusement, if not early restrained, will mature them in cruelty, demoralize their whole character, and harden them against all the sympathies of social life. For as Mr. Locke wisely observed, 'they who delight in the sufferings and destruction of inferior creatures, will not be apt to be very compassionate and benign to those of their own kind.'[3] Thus *the tender mercies of the wicked are cruel*—having no right feeling;[4] only a milder exercise of barbarity;[5] and usually meted out for some selfish end.[6]

But why is this humanity marked as the feature of *a righteous man?* Because it is the image of our heavenly Father, who spreads his cherishing wings over his whole creation.[7] As though the field of man was too small for his goodness, *he regardeth the life of the beast.*[8] Witness the sanctions of his law,[9] and the dispensations of his judgments.[10] Nay, even did he by miraculous interference put into the mouth of the stupid ass to plead as it were the cause of the dumb creation.[11] Must not then his children reflect his whole image of love?[12] And is not the want of any feature of this image a mark of doubtful relationship to him?

11. *He that tilleth his land shall be satisfied with bread: but he that followeth vain persons is void of understanding.*

Special honor is given to the work of *tilling the land.* God assigned it to Adam in Paradise.[13] He chose it as the employment of his eldest son.[14] Its origin appears to have been under immediate Divine Teaching.[15] In ancient times it was the business or relaxation of Kings.[16] A blessing is ensured to diligence; sometimes abundant;[17] always such as we should be *satisfied with.*[18]

The principle applies alike to every lawful calling. Industry is an ornamental grace,[19] and a Christian obligation.[20] Most amply is its reward in the work of God. How rich is the harvest for the diligent student of the Scriptures! Truly he shall be *satisfied*

1 Ibid. xxxiii. 13, 14. 2 Num. xxii. 27.
3 Thoughts concerning Education. 4 Gen. xxxvii. 26—28.
5 1 Sam. xi. 1, 2. Luke xxii. 13—16. John xix. 1—4. Acts v. 41.
6 Acts xxiv. 26, 27.—'We have been used to hear much of the benevolence of infidels, and the philanthrophy of deists. It is all a pretence. Self is the idol, and self-indulgence their object, in the accomplishment of which they are little scrupulous about the means. Where self is the idol, the heart is cruel. While they talk universal charity, they regard not the cruelty of robbing millions of the consolations of religion. While they clamor about reform, they would with unfeeling barbarity exult in the demolition of venerable establishments. While they speak of harmless gaiety and pleasure, they would treacherously corrupt piety, and pollute unsuspecting innocence.'—Holden in loco.
7 Ps. xxxiii. 5; cxlv. 9, 16; cxlvii. 9. 8 Ibid. xxxvi. 6, 7.
9 Exod. xxii. 30. Deut. v. 14; xxii. 6, 7; xxv. 4.
10 Exod. ix. 19. Jonah iv. 11. 11 Num. xxii. 28—30. 12 Matt. v. 44, 45.
13 Gen. ii. 15. 14 Ibid. iv. 2. 15 Isa. xxviii. 23—26.
16 2 Chron. xxvi. 10. Comp. 2 Kings iii. 4. 'Omnium rerum ex quibus aliquid acquiritur, nihil est agricultura melius, nihil uberius, nihil dulcius, nihil homine libero dignius.' Such was the judgment of the Roman Moralist.—Cicero De Offic. I. xlii.
17 Gen. xxvi. 12. 18 Chap. xiii. 23; xiv. 4; xxvii. 23, 27; xxviii 19.
19 Chap. xxxi. 13—22. 20 Rom. xii. 11. 1 Thess. iv. 11.

with bread. But idleness is a spot upon our royal name.[1] 'The proud person,' as an old writer observes—'is Satan's *throne*, and the *idle* man his *pillow*. He sitteth in the former, and sleepeth quietly on the latter.'[2] The man therefore that *followeth vain persons*, instead of honest labor, proves himself to be *void of understanding*, and will reap the fruits of his folly.[3] "If he has not been faithful in the unrighteous Mammon, who will commit to his trust the true riches?"[4]

12. *The wicked desireth the net of evil men: but the root of the righteous yieldeth fruit.*

Man is always restless to press onwards to something not yet enjoyed. The Christian reaches forth to higher privileges and increasing holiness.[5] *The wicked* emulate each other in wickedness; and if they see *evil men* more successful than themselves, they *desire their net*[6]—to discover their plans, in order to imitate them. Not satisfied with the honest "gain of godliness," they *desire a net*, in which they may grasp richer treasures of this world's vanity.[7] The history of the church strongly illustrates this energy of sin—Infidelity and Popery—one *net* following another with more crafty device. Such is the root of evil—fraught with destruction. *But the root of the righteous yieldeth fruit*—true, solid, abundant fruit; not always visible, but always acceptable.[8] Dependence on Christ is the source of this blessing; necessary *in order to fruit*,[9] and never failing to produce it.[10] The spiritual branches 'are nourished and increased by the living root of God's grace and blessing.'[11]

13. *The wicked is snared by the transgression of his lips: but the just shall come out of trouble.*

We have seen the intense *desire* of the *wicked* to snare others in the *net*.[12] Here he is *snared* himself: *The transgression of his lips* becomes the *snare* of his life.[13] 'Many have felt the lash upon their backs for the want of a bridle on their tongues.'[14] Such a snare were *the lips* of the Amalekite bringing the tidings of Saul's death. Expecting a reward, he found his death.[15] Such also was Adonijah's deceitful petition;[16] the hypocritical loyalty of Daniel's enemies;[17] the fearful imprecation of the devoted nation.[18] *The lips*

[1] 2 Thess. iii. 10—12. [2] Swinnock's Christian Man's Calling, Part I. 346
[3] Chap. xiii. 20. Jud. ix. 4. 2 Sam. xv. 11; xviii. 7. Acts v. 36, 37.
[4] Luke xvi. 9. [5] Phil. iii. 12—14.
[6] Ps. x 8—10. Jer. v. 26—28. Hab. i. 15, 16. [7] 1 Tim. vi. 8—10.
[8] Ps. vi. 8; xxxviii. 9; lvi. 8. Mal. iii. 16, 17.
[9] John xv. 4. Rom. vii. 4. It was the remark of a venerable relative of the writer's, who was never suspected of enthusiasm—'As surely as the vine-branch can have no powers, independent of the root; so surely cannot the Christian *think, act, or live, as such*, but only so far as he derives his abilities from the stock, on which he is engrafted.' The Rev. William Jones' (Nayland) Enquiry upon the Spring, p. 36.
[10] John xv. 5. [11] Diodati. [12] Verse 12. [13] Chap. xviii. 7. Ps. lxiv. 8.
[14] Henry in loco. [15] 2 Sam. i. 2—16, also iv. 5—12.
[16] 1 Kings i. 51—53; ii. 13—25. [17] Dan. vi. 7, 8, 24.
[18] Matt. xxvii. 25.

of the wicked miss their mark, and become the instruments of his ruin.[1]

On the other hand the godly exercise of the lips often delivers *out of the trouble*, into which the wicked rush headlong.[2] The noble confession of Caleb and Joshua brought them safe *out of the trouble*, which was frowning upon their rebellious brethren.[3] And even when *the just* "are overtaken with" a *transgression of the lips*, still their faithful God makes a difference. He will not indeed wink at sin in his own children.[4] But while his covenant provides stripes for *their transgressions*, it ensures deliverance in the end.[5] Thus a presumptuous confidence is restrained, and a humbling, self-abasing, tender confidence is established.

14. *A man shall be satisfied with good by the fruit of his mouth: and the recompence of a man's hands shall be rendered unto him.*

We have seen the snare of the tongue. Here is its blessing, not to others[6] only, but to ourselves. Have we the mark of "the saints of God, to speak of the glory of his kingdom?"[7] What a dignity will this grand subject give to our conversation! What a preservative from that frivolous "talk of the lips, which tendeth only to penury!"[8] What a tone of elevation to our whole character![9] How shall we be *satisfied with good by the fruit of our consecrated lips!*[10] When our God becomes not our visitor, but our inmate; *the fruit of our mouth* is no artificial effort, but "out of the abundance of the heart."

From the devotedness of the lips flows the ready exercise of *the hands*. For is not every member of the body his purchased possession?[11] And here also is a sure *recompence*. For who ever "served God for naught?"[12] "He is not unrighteous to forget our work and labor of love. A cup of cold water given to a disciple in his name shall in no wise lose its reward."[13] The meanest exercise of love will be abundantly and eternally *recompensed*.

15. *The way of a fool is right in his own eyes: but he that hearkeneth unto counsel is wise.*

The fool's conceit hinders his wisdom.[14] A discouraging case![15] *His way is right in his own eyes.*[16] He needs no direction, asks no *counsel*, is stubborn in his own way, because it is his own,[17] and follows it to his own ruin. His chief danger is his security.[18] There may be no flagrant sin—nothing that degrades him below the level of his respectable neighbor. He has no doubt of heaven. Instead of the way being so narrow, that few find it;[19] in his view it is so easy of access, that few miss it. Thus all his religion is

1 Ps. xxxv. 8.
2 Jer. xxvi. 12—16.
3 Num. xiv. 6—10, 22—24.
4 Amos iii. 2.
5 Psalm lxxxix. 32, 33. Comp. Gen. xii. 11—20; xx. 12—16; xxvi. 7—11.
6 Chap. x. 20, 21.
7 Psalm cxlv. 10, 11.
8 Chap. xiv. 23.
9 Mal. iii. 16, 17.
10 Chap. xiii. 2; xiv. 14; xv. 23; xviii. 20, 21.
11 1 Cor. vi. 19, 20.
12 Job i. 9, 10. Mal. i. 10.
13 Heb. vi. 10. Matt. x. 42.
14 Job xi. 12.
15 Chap. xxvi. 12. Eccles. iv. 13.
16 Chap. xvi. 2.
17 Jud ii. 19.
18 Deut. xxix. 19. John ix. 43.
19 Matt. vii. 14.

self-delusion.[1] O my God, save me from myself—from my own self-deceitfulness.

What a proof of wisdom is a teachable spirit! What an excellent means of increasing it![2] Was not Moses wiser for *hearkening to Jethro's counsel;*[3] and David for listening to the restraining advice of Abigail?[4] How precious then to the child of God is the office of the Divine "Counsellor!"[5] How wise the reverential faith, that *hearkens to his counsel!* Whom does he ever disappoint? Whom does he upbraid?[6]

16. *A fool's wrath is presently* (in that day, Marg.) *known: but a prudent man covereth shame.*

Let the tongue be ever under discipline. An unbridled tongue is the proof of an unrenewed heart.[7] But specially never let it be loose in a moment of *wrath.* How readily is *the fool known by his wrath!* He has no command of himself. On the first rising, he bursts out with an ungovernable impulse.[8] Truly is *wrath* called *shame.* For is it not a *shame,* that unruly passions should as it were trample reason under foot, disfigure even the countenance, and subjugate the whole man to a temporary madness?[9] What else were Saul's unseemly sallies against David and Jonathan;[10] Jezebel's boiling rage against Elijah;[11] Nebuchadnezzar's unreasonable decree to kill his wise men, because they could not interpret his vision?[12]

Yet far more painful is the sight of *the fool's wrath* in the children of God; in Moses, the meekest of men;[13] in David, "the man after God's own heart;"[14] in "Asa, whose heart was perfect with God all his days."[15] Nothing more excites the scoff of the ungodly, than the sight of these gross ebullitions, which Divine grace ought to restrain. But what is "man in his best estate," if left to himself! animated with the spirit of a wild beast! *in that day* he becomes an object of *shame.*[16]

Self-control, that *covers the shame,* and represses the rising fermentation, is true Christian *prudence.*[17] Even as a matter of policy, it is most commendable.[18] But as a gracious principle, it is indeed a victory more honorable than the martial triumph;[19] not only subduing our own spirit, but melting the hardness of our adversary.[20]

Do we feel our temper at any time ready to rise? Cry instantly to Him who quiets the storm.[21] Keep before our eyes his blessed example, "who, being reviled, reviled not again;"[22] and be what we behold.[23]

[1] Chap. xiv. 12. [2] Chap. i. 5; ix. 9. [3] Ex. xviii. 14—24.
[4] 1 Sam. xxv. 23—32. [5] Isa. ix. 6. [6] James i. 5.
[7] Ibid. verse 26; iii. 2. [8] Chap. xiii. 16; xiv. 17, 29; xxv. 28; xxix. 11.
[9] Dan. iii. 19. [10] 1 Sam. xviii. 10, 11; xix. 9—11; xx. 30—34.
[11] 1 Kings xix. 1, 2. [12] Dan. ii. 12, 13. Comp. 2 Kings vi. 31. Esth. i. 12.
[13] Num. xii. 3; xx. 10, 11. [14] 1 Sam. xxv. 33. [15] 2 Chron. xv. 17; xvi. 10.
[16] Chap. xvii. 12. [17] Chap. xxix. 11. Comp. Jude 2, 3. 1 Sam. xvii. 29, 30.
[18] 1 Sam. x. 27. [19] Chap. xvi. 32. Comp. xix. 11; xx. 3. [20] Rom. xii. 18—21
[21] Matt. viii. 26. Psalm lxv. 7. [22] 1 Pet. ii. 23. [23] 2 Cor. iii. 18.

17. *He that speaketh truth sheweth forth righteousness: but a false witness deceit.*

This proverb may appear almost too obvious to need remark. But the Scripture not only sets out what is deep and searching, but stamps the every-day truths with the seal of God for our more reverential obedience. Yet there is here more than lies on the surface. It might seem enough for a faithful witness to *speak truth.* But no—he must *show forth righteousness*; what is just, as well as what is true. The best-intentioned purpose must not lead us to conceal what is necessary to bring the cause to a righteous issue; "rejoicing not in iniquity, but rejoicing in the truth."[1]

A false witness does not always deal with open lying, but with *deceit*—truth misrepresented, concealed, and thus turned into falsehood. Thus was Doeg *a false witness* against the priests. He states the fact, but with his own perverse interpretation.[2] *The false witness* condemned our Lord by a similar perverse misconstruction of his words.[3] Oh, cherish a deep abhorrence of *deceit* in all its forms and beginnings.[4] Christian obligation and privilege alike forbid it.[5] *Truth and deceit* are not mere moral qualities, but the distinctive mark of the two classes of the world. Look to it, that the broad stamp of *truth and righteousness* brings out the testimony—"Behold! an Israelite indeed, in whom is no guile."[6]

18. *There is that speaketh like the piercings of a sword: but the tongue of the wise is health.*

Who has not felt the piercing of false, unkind, inconsiderate *speeches?* How keenly have the servants of God suffered from this *sword!*[7] Many will speak daggers without compunction, who would be afraid to use them. Surely it was not without reason, that our Lord charges an angry word or tongue with the guilt of murder.[8] The source of this mischief demonstrably shows its malignity. "The tongue is a fire, a world of iniquity, *and it is set on fire of hell.*"[9] Indeed, 'a great and almost incredible calamity is it, that man, who was created for humanity, should be so corrupted, that no animal in the world is more ferocious and malignant.'[10]

Yet is the little member no less powerful to heal than to wound. It gives instant healing to *the piercings of the sword,*[11] even to the very wound, which it may have been constrained to inflict.[12] But it is *the tongue of the wise that is health.* Its unrestrained and unregulated vent might be hurtful. *Wisdom* is the guiding

[1] 1 Cor. xiii. 6.
[2] 1 Sam. xxi. 1—7, with xxii. 9, 10.
[3] Matt. xxvi. 60, 61, with John ii. 19—21.
[4] Chap. xiii. 5. Ps. cxix. 163.
[5] Eph. iv. 22, 25.
[6] John. i 47.
[7] Job xii. 1—3; xiii. 4; xvi. David, Psalm xlii. 10; lii. 2; lv. 21; lvii. 4; lix. 7; lxiv. 3; cxl. 1—3. Jeremiah xviii. 18—23. Lam. iii. 14. Paul, 2 Cor. x 1—11; xi. 11, 12.
[8] Matt. v. 21, 22.
[9] James iii. 6.
[10] Daillè on Col. iii. 8.
[11] Jud. viii. 1—3. 1 Sam. xix. 1—7; xxv. 22—33.
[12] Psalm cxli. 5. Comp. the *healing* counsel, 2 Cor. ii. 6—11.

principle;—not a loose loquacity; but a delicate discriminating tact, directing us how, when, what, to whom to speak; sometimes repressing; sometimes quickening: "the tongue of the learned, to speak a word in season to him that is weary."[1] This is no negative responsibility. It is not enough, that there is no poison in the tongue. It must be *healing:* not only purified from "corrupt communication," but "ministering grace unto the hearers."[2] What need have we of the "indwelling of the word in all wisdom," that in "teaching and admonishing one another, our speech may be always with grace," wholesome and edifying, to the glory of our common Lord![3]

19. *The lip of truth shall be established forever; but a lying tongue is but for a moment.*

How important is it to eye eternity in all our words! *Truth* would then be seen in its permanent value and results. The profession may bring us into present trouble.[4] But *its lips shall be established forever.* Who will gainsay the Martyr's testimony—'Be of good comfort, Master Ridley; play the man. We shall this day light such a candle by God's grace in England, as I trust, *shall never be put out?*'[5] *The lip* also of the faithful Minister of God is *established forever.* For "whatsoever he binds and loosens on earth, shall be bound and loosened in heaven."[6]

Truth then is eternal. *Lying*, even if it suits our purpose as an easy escape from difficulty (a miserable—short-lived policy!) *is but for a moment.*[7] Nay—should it escape detection for a whole life; yet with eternity before us, what a moment it is. And what will be the relief of this short moment under the tremendous wrath of God?[8] We observe in God's own people their momentary escape from trouble followed by shame and confusion.[9] In the ungodly, the fruit of Gehazi's lie was the pleasure for a moment. The shame endured unto the end.[10] Under the same withering curse will *the lying tongue* of false teachers pass away;[11] while truth remains constant. 'None are so visibly blasted, as those who make no conscience of a lie.'[12] Children! ponder it well—eternity is at once the gain of truth, and the cost of a lie.[13] But oh! the infinite difference between this eternity—in heaven or in hell!

20. *Deceit is in the heart of them that imagine evil: but to the counsellors of peace is joy.* 21. *There shall no evil happen to the just: but the wicked shall be filled with mischief.* 22. *Lying lips are abomination to the Lord: but they that deal truly are his delight.*

The principle of *deceit* is here traced to its fountain—*the heart.* How early it is found there, the first lispings of infancy too plainly

[1] Isa. l. 4. [2] Eph. iv. 29. [3] Col. iii. 16; iv. 6.
[4] Matt. x. 32—39. [5] Foxe, vii. 550. [6] Matt. xvi. 19. John xx. 23.
[7] Psalm lii. 4, 5. [8] Rev. xxi. 8; xxii. 15.
[9] Abraham, Gen. xx. 1—16. Isaac, xxvi. 1—10. Peter, Matt. xxvi. 69—75.
[10] 2 Kings v. 25—27. The *momentary* advantage of the Gibeonite's lie unfollowed by shame. Jos. ix.
[11] 2 Tim. iii. 6—9. [12] See Matthew Henry's Life, Chap. xiii.
[13] Psalm xv. 1, 2, with Rev. xxi. 8, ut supra.

prove. A lie is ready upon the lips of a child, when the temptation is presented to it; when nothing is to be gained by it but the hateful pleasures of sin. Yet though *deceit* is the native fruit of *the heart*, all are not equally ready in *imagining evil*—"inventors of evil things."[1] The principle is not equally active, or equally developed in all. But when it does operate, *the wicked are filled with mischief*, and reap the full harvest in disappointment and ruin.[2]

How frightful also is it to remark the outward expression of *deceit* in *lying lips!* Diversified indeed are its forms—falsehood, exaggeration, coloring, wilful perversion, wrong impressions produced or encouraged.[3] But all these forms have the deep mark—*abomination to the Lord.*[4] With this sin were Ananias and Sapphira hurried into eternity.[5] And fearfully does a righteous God, even in "forgiving his offending child, take vengeance on his inventions."[6] The wilful liar proves his parentage,[7] and will be classed in eternity with all that is hateful.[8] So, truly (and it is a sentence worthy of not only children, but of all men to ponder[9]) *are lying lips an abomination to the Lord.*

Here however is *peace*—the contrast of evil inventions: and to them "that seek" and pursue it *there is joy.*[10] Interested themselves in "the counsel of peace,"[11] they are *counsellors of peace*, breathing their Master's spirit of peace and love.[12] A blessed office indeed is it, to pour in the balm of peaceful counsel upon irritated feelings. They will meditate; explain and cover with considerate prudence all the little causes of excitement. They will bring out the strong and unchangeable obligations of brotherly love. They will seize the happy moment of softening, to rekindle confidence—Happy indeed are they in *the joy* of their own conscience—in their dignity as "the children of God,"[13] in the rich harvest of their Christian exertions.[14] Instead of being *filled with mischief*, *no evil shall happen to them. Evil*, whenever permitted, will become their good.[15] They shall be supported in it,[16] delivered out of it,[17] sanctified by it.[18] Its sharpness will pierce their corruptions. Its bitterness will wean them from the creature. Its furnace will

[1] Chap. xiv. 22. Micah ii. 1. Rom. i. 30.

[2] Esther vii. 10. Job v. 12, 13. Jer. ix. 6—9; xiii. 12—14.

[3] 'One common but most responsible instance of this,' (observes Mr. Goode in his valuable Sermon on this text,) 'is instructing servants to say—'*Not at home.*' Great is their guilt, who thus tempt a fellow-creature to utter a palpable untruth for the palpable convenience of a Master. No Christian servant will consent to defile his conscience by acquiescing in any such iniquity. 'It is a matter of common consent, and every one understands it.' Be it so—it is untruth still, and *lying lips are abomination to the Lord* Moreover, *if it be* so generally understood, and admitted without offence, then how much more honorable and Christian to say at once—'We are engaged. We wish to be alone.' Who that accepts one excuse, will not readily accept the other.

[4] Chap. vi. 16, 17. Psalm v. 6.

[5] Acts v. 1—10.

[6] Ps. xcix. 8. Comp. the example of Jacob. Gen. xxvii., with xxxvii. 31--35 David's lie punished with such dreadful results. 1 Sam. xxi. 2; xxii. 18, 19.

[7] John viii. 44.

[8] Rev. xx. 8.

[9] Lavater in loc.

[10] 1 Peter iii. 10, 11.

[11] Zech. vi. 13. Isa. liv. 10.

[12] Col. iii. 14, 15.

[13] Matt. v. 9.

[14] James iii. 17, 18.

[15] Rom. viii. 28.

[16] 1 Cor. x. 13.

[17] Ver. 13, with Psalm xxxiv 19.

[18] Psalm cxix. 67, 71

mould them into the image of their Lord. Thus, what to the ungodly would be a mass of sorrow, *to the just* becomes a world of blessing.

Freedom from *deceit* is their broad mark in the promiscuous crowd. They not only speak, but *they deal, truly;* uniform in light and life.[1] They bear the image of a God of truth, and he *delights in them.*[2] "They are children that cannot lie. So he is their Saviour."[3]

23. *A prudent man concealeth knowledge: but the heart of fools proclaimeth foolishness.*

Knowledge is a talent to be wisely—not promiscuously—communicated.[4] In Scriptural *knowledge* indeed there must be no *concealment* of fundamental truths;[5] or in declaring on suitable occasions the gracious dealings of God with our own souls.[6] Yet every truth is not fitting for every person, or for every time.[7] Our blessed Lord charged upon his disciples the *prudent concealment of knowledge,* after his example, till a more favorable season.[8] The Apostle *concealed his knowledge* for fourteen years, and even then mentioned it reluctantly, to vindicate his own rightful claims of Apostleship.[9] Elihu, though "full of matter," and longing to give vent, yet *concealed his knowledge,* till his elders had opened his way.[10] Here was genuine humility—godly prudence.

Circumstances also may sometimes *prudently* dictate *concealment.* Abraham spared the feelings of his family, and cleared his own path, by hiding the dreadful message of his God.[11] Joseph *concealed* his kindred for the discipline of his brethren.[12] Esther, from a *prudent* regard to consequences to herself.[13] Nothing can justify speaking contrary to the truth. But we are not always obliged to tell the whole truth. Jeremiah answered all that he was bound to speak; not all that he might have spoken.[14] In all these cases "the wise man's heart will discern both time and judgment;"[15] yet always in the exercise of a tender conscience and an ardent love for truth.

The fool however everywhere *proclaims his foolishness.*[16] He imprudently opens his heart.[17] He is dogmatical in dispute, when wiser men are cautious. He will be teaching, when he ought to take the learner's place; his self-confidence *proclaiming* his emptiness.[18] Self-distrust and humility are most important to enable us to improve the gifts of God for his glory.

1 John iii. 21. 2 Chap. xi. 1.
3 Isa. lxiii. 8. Comp. xxxiii. 15, 16. Psalm xv. 1, 2.
4 Chap. ix. 8. Matt. vii. 6. 5 Psalm xl. 9, 10. 1 Cor. ii. 2; xv. 3.
6 Psalm lxvi. 16. 7 Eccles. iii. 7. Amos v. 13.
8 Matt. xvi. 20; xvii. 9, with John xvi. 12. 9 2 Cor. xii. 1—6.
10 Job xxxii. 18, 19, with 4—7.
11 Gen. xxii. 1—5. Comp. Moses' conduct, Ex. iv. 18. 12 Gen. xlii. 7, 21.
13 Esther ii. 10, 20. 14 Jer. xxxviii. 15—27, with xxxvii. 18—20.
15 Eccles. viii. 5. Chap. xv. 2; xxix. 11.
16 Chap. xv. 2; xxix. 11. Ecc. x. 3, 12—14. Comp. Ecclus. xx. 7.
17 Judg. xvi. 17. 18 1 Tim. vi. 3, 4.

24. *The hand of the diligent shall bear rule: but the slothful shall be under tribute.*

Diligence is the ordinary path to advancement. Pharaoh required men of activity for the charge of his cattle.[1] Solomon for the administration of his kingdom.[2] This was Joseph's road to *bearing rule.*[3] But if it does not raise in the world, diligence will always command influence in its own sphere. In the Gospel "the faithful steward is made *ruler* over his Lord's household."[4] The active trader *bears rule* over many cities.[5] Diligence, therefore, is not a moral virtue separate from religion, but rather a component part of it.[6]

From the love of ease, the people of God—instead of *bearing rule*—were continually *under tribute.*[7] The same *slothful* spirit still brings man under bondage. 'He is perpetually needing counsel of others, and hanging upon it.'[8] In the grand concern, he is the slave of his own lust; in the worst service, under the most degrading tyranny; "wicked" because "*slothful*," and "cast out, and condemned as an unprofitable servant."[9] Christian Professor! tremble at this responsibility of doing nothing; of living for thine own ease; neglecting the great object of life—the only object that tells upon eternity.

25. *Heaviness in the heart of man maketh it stoop; but a good word maketh it glad.*

'This maxim points out an easy and cheap way of being useful'[10]—the cheering efficacy of a *good word* to a stooping heart. And how full is the Gospel of these *good words!* Is it distress for sin? "Come unto me, all ye that labor and are heavy laden; and I will give you rest."[11] Is it the pressure of affliction? How *good is the word*, "that speaketh unto us, as unto children;" warning us neither to "despair nor to faint under, the chastening of the Lord!"[12] Is it despondency?—Oft is the *good word* repeated—"Fear not."[13] Know we not the voice—"It is I; be not afraid?"[14] Human sympathy may give temporary relief. But 'that was the grace, softer than oil, sweeter than roses, which flows from the Saviour's lips into the sinner's wounds; and, being poured into the contrite heart, not only heals, but blesses it, yea, and marks it out for eternal blessedness. Oh! how sweet is the voice of pardon to a soul groaning under the burden of sin!'[15] David, but for these *good words*, "would have perished in his affliction."[16] What beside *made glad the jailor's drooping heart?*[17] Precious indeed is the privilege, when a Christian strengthens the weak hands "with *a good word* of God;"[18] when he takes his

[1] Gen. xlvii. 6. [2] 1 Kings xi. 28.
[3] Gen. xxxix. 3—6; xli. 38—44. Comp. Chap. xxii. 29.
[4] Matt. xxiv. 45—47. [5] Ibid. xxv. 21—23.
[6] Rom. xii. 11. [7] Jud. iii. 8, 12; iv. 2.
[8] Dathè in loco. 'The slothful shall become subservient to others.' French and Skinner's translation of Proverbs with notes, 1831. Comp. Chap. x. 4; xi. 29.
[9] Matt. xxv. 26—30. [10] Scott. [11] Matt. xi. 28.
[12] Heb. xii. 5, with Chap. iii. 11. [13] Isa. xli. 10, 14; xliii. 1.
[14] Matt. xiv. 27, 31. [15] Leighton's Meditations on Ps. cxxx. 4.
[16] Psalm cxix. 92. [17] Acts xvi. 28—34, also ii. 37—47. [18] Isa. xxxv. 3, 4.

chair by the mourner's side, and "comforts him with the same comfort, wherewith he himself is comforted of God."[1] Precious is the ministry of the gospel, commissioned with *the gladdening word to the heavy* of heart.[2] Yet more precious the office of the beloved Saviour, "gifted with the tongue of the learned," and filled with the unction of the Spirit, for the express purpose of "comforting them that mourn."[3] How tenderly did he perform this office, let his last sermon testify.[4] See then the provision for joy--so rich, so free, so ready. Beware—"lest Satan should get advantage" by a brooding spirit.[5] Ponder thy obligation and thy privilege to "rejoice in the Lord."[6]

26. *The righteous is more excellent* (abundant, Marg.) *than his neighbor: but the way of the wicked seduceth him.*

God and the world are at issue in their estimate of his own people. *The righteous* is low indeed in man's scale. Yet is he *more excellent* in character—*more abundant* in privilege—not only than the wicked, but *than his neighbor*, be his external advantage and endowments ever so great. Look at his birth, a child of God;[7] his dignity, a King;[8] his connections, a member of the family of heaven;[9] his inheritance, a title to both worlds;[10] his food, the bread of everlasting life;[11] his clothing, the righteousness of the Saviour;[12] his prospects, infinite and everlasting joy.[13] *Mark the honor which his God puts upon him.* He is the fulness of Christ;[14] "the temple of the Holy Ghost,"[15] throwing the splendor of Solomon's temple into the shade.[16] Angels, while "beholding the face of their Father which is in heaven," count it an honor to "minister to him as an heir of salvation."[17] How can *his neighbor's* most exalted privileges compare with his? *Contrast his high walk with God* in "the holiest;"[18] his heavenly profession before men;[19] his Christian victory over himself[20]—with his grovelling neighbor. For 'what an unprofitable drudgery is the service of the greatest prince in the world, in comparison with the work of a poor Christian, that liveth in communion with God!'[21] *And then—passing to the last contemplation*—see him in the full enjoyment of his present prospects—"carried by the angels into Abraham's bosom;"[22] "entering into the joy of his Lord;"[23] welcomed before the assembled world;[24] then fixed on the throne of his Lord[25]—to be with him[26]—near him[27]—like him[28]—for ever—what are *his neighbor's* prospects, but as hell compared with heaven?[29] Can

[1] 2 Cor. i. 4. [2] Job xxxiii. 19—25. Isa. xl. 1, 2. [3] Isa. l. 4; lxi. 1, 2.
[4] John xiv—xvi. [5] 2 Cor. ii. 7—11. Comp. Chap. xv. 13; xvii. 22.
[6] Phil. iii. 3; iv. 4 1 Thess. v. 16. [7] John i. 12, 13. 1 John iii. 1.
[8] Rev. i. 6. [9] Heb. xii. 22, 23. [10] Matt. v. 5. 1 Cor. iii. 22, 23.
[11] John vi. 35—58. [12] Isa. lxi. 10. [13] Ibid. xxxv. 10.
[14] Eph. i. 23. [15] 1 Cor. vi. 19. [16] Isa. lxvi. 1, 2.
[17] Matt. xviii. 10. Heb. i. 14. [18] Heb. x. 19, 20. [19] Phil. ii. 15, 16; iii. 20
[20] Chap. xvi. 32. Matt. xvi. 24. [21] Manton on Psalm cxix. 45.
[22] Luke xvi. 22. [23] Matt. xxv. 21, 23. [24] Ibid. v. 34.
[25] Rev. iii. 21. [26] John xii. 26; xiv. 2, 3. [27] Rev. vii. 15.
[28] 1 John iii. 2. [29] Chap. xiv. 32. Matt. xxv. 34, 41.

we doubt this testimony—*The righteous is more excellent than his neighbor?*—'A Christian is the highest style of man.'[1]

The way of the wicked, is more pleasant to flesh and blood—more generally approved. Hence it easily *seduces* him with the appearance of the right way,[2] and blinds him to his own ruin.[3] Let me weigh my path most carefully—With whom am I walking? In what way?

27. *The slothful man roasteth not that which he took in hunting: but the substance of a diligent man is precious.*

How miserable and ruinous is the habit of sloth! It is a dead palsy, under God only to be checked by early discipline and constant resistance. Sometimes however the man makes a vigorous and successful effort. He rouses himself even to the toil of *hunting.* But his fit of exertion is soon over. He cannot be at the pains of preparing his prey for his repast.[4] He leaves it to others—perhaps even to his dogs; and quickly relapses into his beloved habit.

Is not this a graphical picture of the *slothful* professor? He will take up religion under a strong excitement. He begins a new course, and perhaps makes some advances in it. But, "having no root in himself," his good frames and resolutions wither away.[5]—The continued exertion required;[6] the violence that must be done to his deep-rooted habits; the difficulties in his new path; the invitations to present ease; the delusive hope of better success at a future day—all these hang as a weight upon his efforts. So that—not knowing the only secret of resistance to his powerful enemy—earnest and persevering prayer—he grows slack, and with just life enough to feel himself dying, he sits down upon his little attainments—thus virtually throwing them away—content to lose heaven itself, if it is to be gained at such a cost.[7] What use—Professor! is it to make an effort if you do not seek the grace of perseverance? No present blessing can be enjoyed without grasping something beyond.[8] Godliness without energy loses *its full reward.*"[9]

Such is the reward of the *diligent*—real *substance,*[10] *precious,* as the fruit of his toil; preserving what he has gained, and therefore increasing his *substance.*[11] Unwearied exercise has doubled his talents, and conquered his difficulties. Here—Christian—is success indeed. Live more in thy work—"Spend and be spent" in it. Thy privileges will be enlarged. Thy *substance* will be enriched. Thy God will be honored.[12] Thy crown will be secured.[13]

28. *In the way of righteousness is life: and in the pathway thereof there is no death.*

Much is said in this chapter in praise of *righteousness.* Here it

[1] Young. [2] Chap. xiv. 12. [3] Isa. xliv. 20.
[4] Contrast Gen. xxvii. 30, 31. [5] Matt. xiii. 20, 21. [6] Ibid. xi. 12.
[7] Chap. xiii. 4; xxi. 25; xxvi. 15. [8] Phil. iii. 12—14. [9] 2 John 8
[10] Chap. viii. 21; xv. 6, 16. [11] Matt. xxv. 16, 28, 29.
[12] John xv. 8. Phil. i. 11. [13] 2 Peter i. 5—11.

is crowned with "*life* and immortality."[1] So clearly did the wise man see beyond this dying world; and catch the sunbeams of glory "brought to light by the Gospel."[2] *The way of righteousness* is the way of God's salvation,[3] in which his children come to him; the way of his commandments, in which they love to walk with him.[4] Not only is there *life* in the end—but a present life[5]—a passage from death unto life eternal.[6] 'Those who seek after *righteousness* preserve and increase in themselves the spiritual life of God's grace, and of the presence of his Spirit, and so attain to life everlasting.'[7] Thus the life of grace is possessed, and the life of glory is secured. It is "hid with Christ in God;"[8] so that—"Because I live, ye shall live also."[9]

In this pathway there is no death.[10] The curse of the first death hath passed away.[11] The power of "the second death cannot hurt."[12] "The body is dead because of sin."[13] Yet it "sleeps" rather than dies under the care of Jesus.[14] "Surely the bitterness of death is past."[15] Now, "O death! where is thy sting!"[16] Sheathed in the body of Jesus.

And is not this cheering privilege—this glorious hope—an infinite recompence for all the crosses of *the way*? Contrast the ways of sin—full of death[17]—ending in death eternal.[18] Then wonder at the multitudes "loving death."[19] Pity—pray for them—"pull them out of the fire."[20] Adore the riches and power of Sovereign grace, which has saved you from ruin, and brought you to *righteousness*—*to life*—to salvation.

CHAPTER XIII.

1. *A wise son heareth his father's instruction: but a scorner heareth not rebuke*

Such *a wise son* in filial reverence was Solomon himself.[21] The connection however of *instruction with rebuke* mainly points us to that instruction, which is obtained by discipline.[22] Here then we turn to our great Exemplar. Was not he *a wise son*, when his ears were opened to his Father's discipline?[23] How did he condescend to this painful school to "learn obedience!"[24] How good is it in

[1] 'In the path of righteousness is life—yea—the highway is immortality.' MS. Translation of Proverbs by the late Dr. Good. See also Schultens.
[2] 2 Tim. i. 10. [3] John xiv. 6. [4] Isa. xxxv. 8.
[5] Chap. viii. 35; x. 16; xi. 19. [6] John v. 24. Rom. vi. 23. [7] Diodati.
[8] Col. iii. 3. [9] John xiv. 19. [10] John viii. 51; xi. 25.
[11] Rom. v. 21. [12] Rev. ii. 11; xx. 6. [13] Rom. viii. 10; v. 12. Gen. iii. 19.
[14] Acts vii. 60. 1 Thess. iv. 14. [15] 1 Sam. xv. 32. [16] 1 Cor. xv. 55.
[17] Chap. xxi. 16. Rom. viii. 6. Eph. ii. 1. 1 Tim. v. 6.
[18] Chap. ii. 16—18; v. 3—5; vii. 26, 27; ix, 18. Matt. vii. 13. Rom. vi. 21, 23.
[19] Chap. viii. 36. [20] Jude 23. [21] Chap. iv. 1—4.
[22] Chap. xii. 1. Schultens. [23] Isa. l. 4, 5. [24] Heb. v. 8.

our daily practical walk to keep our eyes steadily fixed on him. Is it not the pathway to heaven to follow Him closely in this child-like habit?

But the proud spirit does not easily bend. The son, who never *heard his father's instruction* with deference, will soon take "the *scorner's* seat."[1] When *rebuke* becomes necessary, he *hears it not*;[2] turns from it to his own course—at the extreme point from wisdom;[3] on the brink of ruin;[4] carrying about him a fearful mark of reprobation![5] Let me remember if I am reluctant to *hear the* faithful *rebuke* of men, I am prepared to resist the rebuke of God. And how soon may this stubborn revolt bring his long-suffering to an end,[6] and my soul to destruction![7] 'From hardness of heart, and contempt of thy word and commandment, Good Lord, deliver me.'[8]

2. *A man shall eat good by the fruit of his mouth: but the soul of the transgressors shall eat violence.*

The first clause has been lately put before us.[9] But let it ever be fresh upon our minds, that if the Christian is walking with God, his tongue will pour out godly communication. Whatever be the effect on others, at least his own soul will be warmed, refreshed, and edified. *He shall eat good by the fruit of his mouth.* Never shall we carry upon our lips that Beloved Name to our fellow-sinners in simplicity, but its "savour" to our own souls will be "as ointment poured forth."[10] We shall feed ourselves in the Christian distribution of the heavenly manna.

The transgressor also *eats the fruit of his mouth*—yet not *good. His soul* sets his tongue on a flame. He loves *violence*—and therefore *eats it* to his own ruin.[11] "Death as well as life are in the power of the tongue."[12] Let us look, that it be under the influence of Divine grace, restrained from evil, disciplined for usefulness, the fruitful instrument of our own happiness.

3. *He that keepeth his mouth keepeth his life: but he that openeth wide his lips shall have destruction.*

The last Proverb contrasted a fruitful and mischievous—this a cautious and ungoverned tongue. "Keep thine heart."[13] This guards the citadel. *Keep thy mouth.* This sets a watch at the gates. If they be well guarded, the city is safe. Leave them unprotected—Thus was Babylon taken. 'He that looketh carefully to his tongue takes a safe course for preserving *his life*, which is oft in danger by much and wild talking.'[14] Think before we speak—ponder our words—their substance, manner, time, place, audience. The unruly member needs a strong bridle, and a strong hand to hold it.[15]—Though it be necessary to open our lips, yet to *open them*

1 Ps. i. 1. 2 Chap. xv. 12. 3 Chap. i. 7, 8; xii. 1; xv. 5.
4 Chap. xv. 10; xxix. 1. 5 1 Sam. ii. 25. 6 2 Chron. xxxvi. 15, 16.
7 Jer. v. 3. Zeph. iii. 2. 8 Litany. 9 Chap. xii. 14. 10 Can. i. 3.
11 Psalm lxiv. 8. 12 Chap. xviii. 21. 13 Chap. iv. 23.
14 Bishop Hall, Chap. xxi. 23. Psalm xxxiv. 12, 13. 15 James iii. 2 3.

wide—to let all come out—is a fearful hazard.[1] For if "in the multitude of words there wanteth not sin,"[2] sin must bring us within the jaws of *destruction*.

"Set a watch, O Lord, before my mouth; and keep the door of my lips"[3]—was the prayer of one, who knew the danger of an ungoverned tongue, and the only way to tame it. Shall we not call in God's help, in the recollection that the great tempter is always at hand? How often has our unguarded tongue "given place to the devil,"[4] and "grieved the Holy Comforter?"[5] How much more matter do we make for repentance by our speaking than by our silence! Apply the practical power of faith to this besetting evil; quickening watchfulness and prayer, self-abasement and self-discipline, godly fear and energy of conflict.

4. *The soul of the sluggard desireth, and hath nothing: but the soul of the diligent shall be made fat.*

Another vivid contrast of the *sluggard with the diligent!*[6]—*The sluggard desires* the gain of diligence without the diligence that gains. He would be wise without study, and rich without labor. His religion is of the same heartless character. *He desires* to overcome his bad habits,—to enjoy the happiness of God's people. So far well. *Desires* are a part of religion. There can be no attainment without them. Many have not even *the desire*. They ridicule it as enthusiasm. Yet *the sluggard hath nothing*, because it is *desire* without effort. 'He ever desireth; but he taketh no pains to get any thing.'[7] He would fain go to heaven, if a morning dream would carry him there. And *many a wish* (alas!—*of prayer* he knows nothing) he sighs for "the death of the righteous."[8] He would gladly be a Christian, if it cost him no trouble. His duties are a force upon him—and, when they are over, he feels as if relieved from a heavy weight. This is no rare case. Often do we hear the cry—and that year after year—'I desire to be a child of God.' And yet the soul continues at the same point, or rather settles down more resolutely in a lifeless profession. 'Hell'—says an old writer—'is paved with such *desires*.'

Oh! be industrious—if anywhere—in religion. Eternity is at stake. Hours—days are lost. Soon they come to years—and for want of energy all is lost. Heartless wishes will not give life.—The halting step will not bring us to God. A few minutes' cold prayer will not seize the prize. To expect the blessing without diligence is delusion.

Diligence brings its own reward in the world[9]—much more in religion. It will not be content with *desiring*, but possessing. Here is reality—rich privilege—The "exercise of godliness" tends to health and profit.[10] Useful habits are formed—dormant energy is

[1] Chap. x. 14; xii. 13; xviii. 7. Comp. 1 Sam. xxv. 10, 11, 33. [2] Chap. x. 19.
[3] Psalm cxli. 3. [4] Eph. iv. 26, 27. [5] Ibid. verses 29, 30.
[6] Chap. x. 4; xii. 24, 27. [7] Reformers' Notes. [8] Num. xxiii. 10.
[9] Chap. x. 4; xii. 24; xxii. 29. [10] 1 Tim. iv. 7, 8.

excited. The conflict of faith, the violence of prayer, become sources of enjoyment.[1] God honors the trading of talents, where he has the full revenue of his gifts.[2]

Shake off, then, the dust of sloth—child of God! Take care that the bed of ease *doth not* pall thine appetite, and hinder thee from seeking food for thy soul. Let thy graces be vigorous and radiant. Let thy profession be always progressing—deepening—expanding. If thou be in Christ, seek to be "rooted and grounded in him."[3] Let there be "life more abundantly."[4] "Be strong in the grace that is in Christ Jesus."[5] Let "the joy of the Lord be thy strength."[6] *Then thy soul shall be made fat*—healthful—vigorous—in all fruit and grace.[7]

5. *A righteous man hateth lying: but a wicked man is loathsome, and cometh to shame.*

Observe the accuracy of Scripture. It is not that *a righteous man never lies.* David lied.[8] Peter lied.[9] Yet David could say—"*I hate and abhor lying.*"[10] He prayed to have it "removed from him."[11] He would not suffer the "liar in his sight."[12] Peter in the painful remembrance of his sin earnestly shewed the happiness of departure from it.[13] The child of god—though always a sinner—maintains an holy antipathy against sin,—"What *I hate*, that do I."[14]

Nor is it a proof of *a righteous man, that he avoids lying.* Selfish motives—regard for character—may dictate restraint—without any *hatred of the sin as sin.* But true religion brings in the new taste—conformity to the mind of God. Therefore "lying lips"—however common, profitable, convenient, or pardonable, they may be counted—as they "are abomination to the Lord," the *righteous man hateth them.*[15] He would rather suffer by truth, than sin by lying.[16]

And yet is not strict truth—even in the Church—often sacrificed to courtesy? Is not *lying* sometimes acted, insinuated, or implied, where we should be ashamed of plainly speaking it? Is not the simple truth often colored with exaggeration? "Abstain from all appearance of evil"[17]—is the rule for the man of God. If "the appearance" be not cautiously shunned, the reality will soon be loved. Our tongue is only safe, when it is ordered under the restraint and guidance of the God of Truth.[18]

A wicked man indeed takes pleasure in deceit. Scripture gives him his right name—loathsome. His base means often bring him to *shame* on this side of the grave.[19] But however this be—*shame* will be his "everlasting recompence."[20]

[1] Matt. xi. 12. [2] Ibid. xxv. 14—29. [3] Col. ii. 7. [4] John x. 10.
[5] 2 Tim. ii. 1. [6] Neh. viii. 10. [7] Psalm xcii. 12—14. Mal. iv. 2.
[8] 1 Sam. xxi. 2; xxvii. 9, 10. [9] Matt. xxvi. 70—74. [10] Psalm cxix. 163.
[11] Ibid. ver. 29. Comp. Chap. xxx. 8. [12] Psalm ci. 7.
[13] 1 Pet. iii. 10, 11, also ii. 1. [14] Rom. vii. 15, 19.
[15] Chap. xii. 22. Comp. Rom. xii. 9. [16] 1 Kings xxii. 12—23. Dan. iii. 14—22.
[17] 1 Thess. v. 22. [18] Psalm xix. 14; li. 15; cxli. 3. [19] 2 Kings v. 27.
[20] Dan. xii. 2. Rev. xxi. 8.

6. *Righteousness keepeth him that is upright in the way: but wickedness overthroweth the sinner.*

Would that the repetition of this aphorism[1] might deepen its impression! It is indeed a straight way to heaven. "Lead me in it, O my God,"[2] and keep me there. The many deviations even of the children of God prove our need of Divine keeping. The fear of man;[3] the flinching of the flesh from positive duty;[4] the grasp of some desired object;[5] the subtle allurements of sin[6]—all these have turned him out of the path; embracing his Father's will in many things; in others preferring his own. *Righteousness*—steady conformity to the mind of God—keeps the soul *upright*, and so *keeps it in the way.*[7] Not that we exalt it to any meritorious efficiency; or put it in the place of simply "looking unto Jesus"[8] for life and salvation. The Christian, while "walking in his integrity,"[9] never loses his sense of sin, or forgets his need of mercy. Yet—his "*righteousness* is a breast-plate"[10] *keeping* him from many assaults of sin,[11] and covering him from threatening wrath.[12] But this is *righteousness*—not perfection—mixed with much cleaving infirmity. Yet—blessed be God—the uprightness is accepted, and the frailty is covered.[11]

But while 'saints are secured *from* ruin, sinners are secured *for* ruin.'[14] *The sinner's own wickedness overthroweth him.*[15] He is bent upon his own way— the sure road to destruction. 'Let him not blame the Lord, or any mortal man besides himself, inasmuch as he is the Author of ruin to himself.[16]

7. *There is that maketh himself rich, yet hath nothing; there is that maketh himself poor, yet hath great riches.*

What a bubble are the world's riches! Yet such a jewel are they counted, that some will affect their shew, in order to gain the respect usually connected with them[17]—*making themselves rich, yet having nothing.* Others will hide the real possession, lest they should be robbed of it[18]—*making themselves poor, yet having great riches.* Both practice a deceit upon God; the one by pretending to have received—the other by virtually denying—his gracious gifts. Both dishonor his wisdom and goodness; the one by discontent with his dispensations; the other by neglecting the communication of his blessings.[19]

The Church presents the counterpart of both these classes.—The boasting Pharisee,[20] the gifted Corinthian;[21] the proud beggarly Laodicean[22]—all admire their nothing, as if it were *great riches.* Others again *make themselves poor* in "voluntary humility."

[1] Chap. xi. 3, 5, 6. [2] Ps. v. 8; xxvi. 11.
[3] Gen. xii. 11—13; xx. 2. [4] John i. 1—3. [5] Gen. xxvii. 19—24.
[6] 2 Sam. xi. 2. 1 Kings xi. 1—8. [7] Psalm xxv. 21. [8] Heb. xii. 2.
[9] Psalm xxvi. 11. [10] Eph. vi. 14. [11] Gen. xxxix. 9. Neh. v. 15.
[12] Gen. vii. 1. 2 Peter ii. 7—9. Isa. xxxiii. 15, 16. Ezek. xiv. 14, 20.
[13] 2 Chron. xv. 17. [14] Henry in loco. [15] 2 Chron. xxviii. 23.
[16] Muffet's, (Peter) Commentary on Proverbs, 12mo., 1596.
[17] Chap. xii. 9. [18] Eccl. vi. 1, 2. [19] Comp. 1 Tim. vi. 18.
[20] Luke xviii. 11, 12. [21] 1 Cor. iv. 8, 10. [22] Rev. iii. 17, 18.

Describing their whole course as unmingled sin, they deny the Almighty work of grace. They give excuse for lying under the power of their corruptions, instead of quickening the energy of a successful conflict. Thus they promote the very evil which they deprecate, and sink the soul into a hopeless despondency, alike prejudicial to their happiness and usefulness. It is the ruin of the self-deceiver to think himself better, it is not less the sin and the folly of the upright to think himself worse, than he is.

The true path of simplicity is to renounce all dependence of the flesh, and gladly to welcome the gospel of grace.[1] Such disciples —rich in their holy poverty—are honored of the Lord.[2] 'O Blessed Lord, who resistest the proud, and givest grace to the humble, give me more humility—that I may receive more grace from thee. And thou, whose gracious rain shelves down from the steep mountains, and sweetly drenches the humble vallies, depress thou my heart more and more with true lowliness of spirit, that the showers of thy heavenly grace, may sink into it, and make it more fruitful in all good affection and all holy obedience.'[3]

8. *The ransom of a man's life are his riches: but the poor heareth not rebuke.*

The last Proverb rebuked discontent with our lot—whether of riches or poverty. The wise man here strikes the balance between these two conditions. *A man's riches may be the ransom of his life.* They may be the price of deliverance from his enemies.[4] They may save him from the punishment of the law,[5] or from imminent danger of his life.[6] Yet if "money is a defence,"[7] so also is often want of money. If "the rich man's wealth is his strong city,"[8] *the poor* man's poverty is often his safeguard. He is beneath notice. *He hears not many a rebuke*, he escapes many a danger, which is destruction to his richer neighbor.[9] Had Isaac's flocks been less numerous,[10] or Jacob less prosperous,[11] they would not *have heard so much rebuke* from their selfish enemies. *The poor* with his empty pocket travels with security. His cottage offers little temptation to the nightly robber. "A man's life" therefore—his true happiness—"consisteth not in the abundance of the things which he possesseth."[12]

His riches may be the ransom of his life. But "what shall he give in exchange for his soul?"[13] Too "precious" is it to be "redeemed with corruptible silver and gold."[14] So far as he is concerned, "it ceaseth forever."[15] Praised be the Lord! when all the treasures of earth would have been beggared in *the ransom*, the riches of heaven were freely poured out.[16] The blood of the Son

[1] Phil. iii. 3—9. [2] Isa. lxvi. 1, 2. Luke xviii. 13, 14. Rev. ii. 9.
[3] Bishop Hall's Devotional Works, Vol. viii. 276. [4] 2 Kings xviii. 13, 16.
[5] Ex. xxi. 29, 30. Comp. Chap. vi. 35.
[6] Jer. xli. 8. Comp. Gen. xxxii. 6, 7, 20, with xxvii. 41. Also Job ii. 4. 'The primitive Christians quoted this proverb in defence of their occasional habit of giving money to restrain the fury of their persecutors.'—Geier in loco.
[7] Ecc. vii. 12. [8] Chap. x. 15.
[9] 2 Kings xxiv. 14; xxv. 12. Jer. xxxix. 9, 10. [10] Gen. xxvi. 13—25.
[11] Ibid. xxxi. 1, 2. [12] Luke xii. 15. [13] Matt. xvi. 26.
[14] 1 Pet. i. 18. [15] Psalm xlix. 6—9. [16] 1 Pet. i. 19. Heb. x. 5—8.

of God was the acceptable price. The voice was heard from heaven—"Deliver him from going down to the pit; I have found *a ransom*."[1]

9. *The light of the righteous rejoiceth: but the lamp of the wicked shall be put out.*

Who can estimate the worth of a Christian's bright shining *light*?[2] Happy in his own soul, like his counterpart in the heavens, he sheds a *joyous* light around him.[3] But how glowing then, is the light of the Church in the combined shining of all her members! Many of them have no remarkable individual splendor. Yet the whole—like the lesser stars forming the milky way—present a bright path of holiness in the spiritual firmament. This happy, heavenly *light* "shineth into perfect day;"[4] and that day will never set.[5] Sometimes it may be obscured, but only that it may break out more gloriously;[6] and soon will it be a day without a cloud.[7]

But it is *the light of the righteous that rejoiceth.* Sin therefore will bring the cloud. Do we hope to shine in the heavenly firmament? Then must we shine with present glory in the firmament of the Church. So delicate is the Divine principle, that every breath of this world dims its lustre.

The wicked have their *lamp*, a cold profession of the name of religion. But, being without oil, it will soon *be put out*.[8] Even while it lasts, it *rejoiceth not.* It sheds no light upon the soul. It guides no fellow-pilgrim with its light. Fearful will be the end. He takes his leave of the light of this world, only to enter into eternal darkness, without even a flickering ray to cheer "the blackness of darkness forever."[9]

10. *Only by pride cometh contention: but with the well advised is wisdom.*

Most accurately is *contention* here traced to its proper source.[10] All the crudities of the day—all the novelties of doctrine producing contention[11]—originate in the *proud* swelling of the fleshly mind."[12] Men scorn the beaten track. They must strike out a new path. Singularity and extravagance are primary charms. They are ready to quarrel with every one, who does not value their notions as highly as they do. The desire of pre-eminence;[13] the revolt from authority[14] or sound doctrine;[15] party spirit, with the *pride* of knowledge and gifts[16]—all produce the same results. Is it too much to say, that vain-glory hath lighted up all the sinful *contentions*, that have ever kindled in the Church? We must indeed "*contend* for the faith,"[17] though it be with our own compromising brethren.[18] But

[1] Job xxxiii. 24.
[2] Matt. v. 14—16. Phil. ii. 14—16.
[3] Chap. iv. 18, with Psalm xix. 5.
[4] Chap. iv. 18, ut supra.
[5] Isa. lx. 19, 20.
[6] Micah vii. 8.
[7] Isa. xxxv. 10. Rev. xxi. 23, 24.
[8] Job xviii. 5, 6; xxi. 17. Chap. xx. 20; xxiv. 17. Matt. xxv. 3, 8.
[9] Ps. xlix. 17—19. Matt. xxii. 13. Jude 13.
[10] Chap. xxviii. 25.
[11] 1 Tim. i. 4. 2 Tim. ii. 23.
[12] Col. ii. 18. 1 Tim. vi. 3, 4.
[13] Matt. xviii. 1—4; xx. 20—24. 3 John 9, 10.
[14] Num. xii. 1—3.
[15] 2 Tim. iv. 3, 4
[16] 1 Cor. i. 11, 12; iii. 3, 4, with iv. 8.
[17] Gal. ii. 5. 1 Thess. ii. 2. Jude 3.
[18] Gal. ii. 11—14

even here how quickly—yet imperceptibly, may *pride* insinuate itself under the cover of glorifying God ![1]

This mischievous principle spreads in families, or among friends. 'Some point of honor must be maintained; some affront must be resented; some rival must be crushed or eclipsed; some renowned character emulated; or some superior equalled and supported.'[2] Even in trifling disputes between relatives or neighbors—perhaps between Christians—each party *contends* vehemently for his rights, instead of satisfying himself with the testimony of his conscience, and submitting rather to be misunderstood and misjudged, than to break the bond of the Divine brotherhood.[3] In the wide field of the world we may well ask—"From whence come wars and fightings among you? Come they not from this lust?"[4] Often has wounded pride[5]—even without any proved injury[6]—brought destructive *contention* upon a land.

The proud man conceives himself wise enough. He asks no counsel, and thus proves his want of wisdom. But *with the* modest—*well-advised—there is* the *wisdom* that is from above, "which is first pure, then peaceable."[7] Many a rising *contention* has it quelled.[8] "Let nothing be done through strife or vain-glory; but in lowliness of mind let each esteem other better than themselves."[9] Christian *wisdom* will keep us within our own line; knowing our own measure and bounds;[10] and—whatever be our place, parts or gifts—humble, active, loving, constant, thankful, in the improvement of them.

11. *Wealth gotten by vanity shall be diminished: but he that gathereth by labor shall increase.*

This Proverb does not imply the means, by which *wealth has been gotten*;[11] but the impoverishing use to which it is applied. However large, *by vanity* it will soon *be diminished.* Frivolous and expensive pursuits, empty amusements, and the vain pomp and show of dress, will soon prove that "riches certainly make themselves wings;"[12] that the treasure is "put into a bag with holes;"[13] and that nothing remains but the awful account of unfaithfulness to a solemn trust.

On the other hand—God's blessing is upon Christian industry, and, so far as is good, *he that gathereth with his labor shall increase.* Only let him remember, that the security for his *increasing wealth* is the dedication of himself and his substance to the Lord; the ready acknowledgment, that he is not his own, but God's property for God's glory.[14] 'All that man can have, we have it on this condition; to use it, to have it, to lay it out, to lay it

[1] Acts xv. 37—39. [2] Scott in loco. [3] 1 Cor. vi. 7. [4] Jam. iv. 1.
[5] Judges xii. 1—6. [6] 2 Kings xiv. 10. [7] James iii. 17, with 14—16.
[8] Gen. xiii. 7—11. Judges viii. 1—3. 1 Kings xii. 22—24. Acts vi. 1—6.
[9] Phil. ii. 3. [10] 2 Cor. x. 13—16.
[11] The interpolation of our translators is uncalled for, and misleads the reader. The word '*vain*' is of very frequent occurrence, and always implies, not what is sinful, but what is empty and unsubstantial. See Parkhurst.
[12] Chap. xiii. 5. [13] Hag. i. 6. [14] 1 Cor. vi. 19, 20.

down unto the honor of our Master, from whose bounty we received it.'[1] The Lord deliver us from the guilt of wasting on *vanity* what is due to Himself!

12. *Hope deferred maketh the heart sick: but when the desire cometh, it is a tree of life.*

The first springing of *hope* is a pleasurable sensation, yet not unmixed with pain. It is the hunger, that makes our food acceptable. But *hope deferred*, like hunger prolonged, brings a kind of torture. It *maketh the heart sick.*[2] Yet *when the desire*—the fulfilment of the *hope—cometh*, what *a tree of life it is*—so reviving—so invigorating![3]

We must however limit this application to the spiritual world. Elsewhere the fulfilment of the desire would be—instead of *a tree of life*—disappointment and vanity.[4] Here however the child of God is often tried in his faith, but never disappointed of his hope. "The patience of hope" issues in "the full assurance of hope." What was it to Abraham, when, after long *deferred hope—the desire came*, and he called the child of promise—Laughter![5] What was it, "when the Lord turned again the captivity of Zion, and they were like unto them that dream!"[6] What was it to old Simeon and the waiting remnant, when *the desire* of all nations *came!*[7] What to the disciples, when at the manifestation of their risen Lord, their *sickening hearts* "believed not for joy, and wondered!"[8] What to the little flock met together in the faintness of *deferred hope* to plead for Peter's deliverance, when *the desire came*—the answer to prayer—so marvellously vouchsafed![9]

To come to more personal experience. Such was the trial of faith, appointed for our beloved Lord. Such was the joyful issue.[10] Many a waiting, *sickening heart* has been thus refreshed from *a tree of life.*[11] But what will be the joy of the grand consummation of *hope!*[12] "The earnest expectation of the creation waiteth for the manifestation of the sons of God."[13] Time seems long—trials heavy—hearts failing. But—"yet a little while, and he that shall come, will come, and will not tarry."[14] The first moment of the glorious manifestation will blot out the remembrance of all toils, weariness, and trial. Yes—*the desire cometh*—come it will—in God's best time—"quickly." One moment sick; the next—"the inhabitant of that land" where sickness is no more.[15] One moment clad in the rags of the flesh; "in the twinkling of an eye" arrayed in the glory of the Saviour's image.[16] "Come, Lord Jesus! Come quickly."[17]

1 Swinnock's True Christian, 4to. 1663. p. 169. 2 Ps. cxix. 82, 123; cxliii. 6, 7.
3 Verse 19. 4 Eccl. ii. 1—11. 5 Gen. xv. 2, 3; xxi. 3—6.
6 Ps. cxxxvii. with cxxvi. 7 Luke ii. 25—30, with Hag. ii. 7.
8 Ibid. xxiv. 17, 21, 41. 9 Acts xii. 5, 12—16.
10 Psalm xxii. 1—3, with 22—25; lxix. 1—3, with 30—35.
11 Ibid. xiii. 12 Rom. viii. 23—25. 2 Cor. v. 1—4.
13 Rom. viii. 19. 14 Heb. x. 37, 38. Hab. ii. 3. Rev. xxii. 7, 12, 20.
15 Isa. xxxiii. 24. Rev. xxi. 1. 16 1 Cor. xv. 51—54. 17 Rev. xxii. 20.

13. *Whoso despiseth the word shall be destroyed: but he that feareth the commandment shall be rewarded.*

God as a God of holiness will not be trifled with. As a God of grace—none serve him for naught. The presumptuous *despiser of his word* cannot escape. The world before the flood was the object of his long-suffering. "A preacher of righteousness" warned them of their danger. But the *despisers* provoked their own ruin.[1] Pharaoh, often provoked—sometimes half-resolved—yet at length *despising the word, was destroyed.*[2] Jehoiakim's daring rebellion met its righteous recompence.[3] The warnings of Sinai are as *a voice* of thunder. "If every transgression of the word spoken by angels received its just recompence of reward; how shall we escape, if we neglect so great salvation, spoken by the Lord? If they escaped not, that refused him that spake on earth; much more shall not we escape, if we turn away from him that speaketh from heaven. See that ye refuse not him that speaketh."[4]

Let God and his word be our *fear*, not our terror. The heart can never be right, till *it fears the commandment* above every earthly consideration. The slave *fears* the penalty; the child *the commandment.* And this he fears more than if an angel from heaven were standing in his way with a flaming sword. Here is no bondage—no legality. It brings its own reward. The "heart that stands in awe of God's word," rejoices in it, "and is largely enriched with its spoil."[5] Here too is sunshine in the special favor of God—"To this man will I look, even to him that is poor, and of a contrite heart, and that *trembleth at my word.*"[6]

14. *The law of the wise is a fountain of life, to depart from the snares of death.*

Reverence to *God's commandment* has just been enforced. The blessing of *the law* or instruction[7] *of the wise* is here shown. It is as a fountain of life,[8] to a teachable and thirsting heart. It is as a grand conservative principle in a world full of *snares*, not of danger only, but of *death.* There is no safe treading but in the ways of God. The word of God gives the necessary warning.[9] *The law of the wise*—his instruction with all the authority of *a law*—applies it. This was David's seasonable instruction to Solomon[10]—Solomon's to us.[11] Hear this warning *law of the wise* from an Apostle's mouth. The love of money was fearfully destroying souls. "Thou, O man of God, flee these things."[12] This is the grand end of the Ministry of the Gospel—to "deliver them from the snares of the devil: who taketh men captive at his will."[13] Let the young take heed to their feet, where every step is a *snare of death.* Let the instruction of thy God and his Ministers be *the*

[1] 1 Peter iii. 20. 2 Peter ii. 5. Luke xvii. 26, 27.
[2] Ex. v. 2; x. 16, 17, 28; xiv. 28.
[3] Jer. xxxvi. 23—32.
[4] Heb. ii. 2, 3; xii. 25.
[5] Psalm cxix. 161, 162.
[6] Isa. lxvi. 2. Comp. Ezra x. 2.
[7] Chap. iii. 1; iv. 2.
[8] Chap. x. 11.
[9] Psalm xvii. 4; cxix. 9, 11.
[10] Chap. iv. 4—12.
[11] Chap. v. 1—13; vii. 21—27.
[12] 1 Tim. vi. 9—11.
[13] 2 Tim. ii. 24—26.

law of the wise to keep thy path in safety. "Ponder the path of thy feet, and let all thy ways be established."[1]

15. *Good understanding giveth favor: but the way of transgressors is hard.*

Good understanding in the wise man's meaning is the true knowledge of religion—not a cold and dry apprehension—but practical godliness.[2] Natural conviction is often constrained to do homage to it, as the image of God stamped upon his servants.[3] The histories of Joseph,[4] Samuel,[5] David,[6] Daniel[7]—testify, that it *giveth favor.* Our blessed Lord, as "he increased in wisdom, increased also in *favor* both with God and man."[8] Thus the way of wisdom with all its crosses, is cheered with sunshine.

Can we say this *of the way of transgressors?* They dream of a flowery path; but they make to themselves *a hard way.* 'Wicked men live under a hard taskmaster.'[9] His work is drudgery indeed.[10] Men fight their way to hell, as they do to heaven[11]—"through much tribulation." Sinful affections must be a source of pain. The continual warfare with conscience,[12] the absence of peace,[13] the sting of sin,[14] the certainty of destruction[15]—all prove the loss of "the promise of the life that now is, no less than of that which is to come."

Which then is the way of my choice? Lord, do thou choose for me. Help me under thy guidance, to choose the safe and pleasant path of wisdom,[16] the rich portion of godliness for both worlds.[17] *The way of transgressors is hard.* The end of that way is death.[18] The taskmaster will have his full "tale" of work. The paymaster will pay down the well-earned wages to the uttermost farthing —Death eternal.[19]

16. *Every prudent man dealeth with knowledge; but a fool layeth open* (spreadeth, Marg.), *his folly.*

How often is even valuable *knowledge* frittered away from the want of *prudent* application! We must ponder the time, measure, helps and means of *dealing with it,* so as to put it out to its full advantage.[20] And how wide is the sphere for trading with this responsible talent? *In daily life* it provides against foreseen dangers,[21] as it makes a way to escape in appointed difficulties.[22] Not less useful is it in the *family economy*—in the training of children;[23] in the "guidance of affairs;"[24] in looking well to household occupations.[25]

[1] Chap. iv. 26. [2] Psalm cxi. 10.
[3] Chap. iii. 3, 4; xiv. 35; xvi. 7. Deut. iv. 6. [4] Gen. xli. 38—40. Acts vii. 10.
[5] 1 Sam. ii. 26. [6] Ibid. xviii. 5, 14—16.
[7] Dan. i. 9, 19, 20; vi. 1—3. See also Abraham, Gen. xxiii. 10, 11. Paul, Acts xxvii. 43; xxviii. 2. Comp. Rom. xiv. 18.
[8] Luke ii. 52. [9] Caryl on Job xv. 20.
[10] Isa. v. 18; xlvii. 13; lvii. 10. Jer. ix. 5. [11] Acts xiv. 22.
[12] Ibid. ix. 4. [13] Isa. lvii. 20, 21; lix. 8.
[14] Chap. xxiii. 29—32. Gen. iv. 11—15. Jer. ii. 17—19. [15] Isa. ix. 7.
[16] Chap. iii. 17. [17] 1 Tim. iv. 8. [18] Matt. vii. 13. Rom. vi. 21.
[19] Rom. vi. 23. [20] Chap. xv. 2. [21] Chap. xxii. 3. Gen. xxxii. 4, 5.
[22] Acts xvi. 37, 38; xxii. 25; xxiii. 7. [23] Judg. xiii. 8, 12.
[24] Chap. xiv. 1. Ps. cxii. 5. [25] Chap. xxxi. 27.

Must we not also *deal with it in the Church*—in a wise accommodation to circumstances,[1] in the conviction of gainsayers;[2] in forbearing with the prejudices of the weak;[3] in the exercise of Christian admonition?[4] The want of it is the source of an unstable profession. In understanding we are children, not men."[5] Most precious therefore is "the word of knowledge," as "the manifestation of the Spirit given to us to profit withal."[6] Greatly also do we need this gift *in our intercourse with the world*, to avoid occasions of stumbling;[7] to mark seasonable times of reproof;[8] and to refrain from needless offence.[9] Nay—even *in the political world* what need have we of "understanding of the times, to know what Israel ought to do!"[10] Thus to *deal with knowledge* in the diversified application, is the responsibility of *a prudent man* of God.[11]

In the want of this *prudence—the fool layeth open his folly.* He pours out his wrath.[12] He vaunts out his vanity.[13] He exposes his thoughtlessness.[14] He exercises no judgment,[15] and fills his sphere of influence with mischief.

Let us study the minute details of our Master's well-filled life. *He shall deal prudently*[16]—This was his distinctive character. The Spirit of *prudence* was the furniture for his work.[17] How gloriously did it shine forth in the confounding of his enemies,[18] and in tender sympathy with his afflicted people![19] How good is it to have our *knowledge* disciplined by his teaching, and consecrated to his service!

17. *A wicked messenger falleth into mischief: but a faithful ambassador is health.*

A messenger proves his character by his neglect or discharge of his trust. *A wicked messenger* betrays his trust,[20] damages his master,[21] and—as a just recompence—*falls into mischief. Faithfulness* is the servant's glory, and his master's gain. He brings and receives a blessing. Gehazi's unfaithfulness brought him *into mischief.*[22] Eliezer, "shewing all good fidelity," was blessed in himself, *and health* to his master.[23]

But to speak of the *messenger and ambassador of the Lord.*[24] What words can tell the awful *mischief* of *the wicked messenger*—ignorant of the worth of his commission, and utterly careless in the discharge of it! Yet *the mischief* returns upon his own head;

[1] Gal. ii. 2. [2] Tit. i. 9. 1 Pet. iii. 15. [3] Acts xv. 22—29.
[4] Rom. xv. 14. [5] 1 Cor. xiv. 20, with Eph. iv. 14. [6] 1 Cor. xii. 7, 8.
[7] Ezra viii. 22. Neh. vi. 11.
[8] Chap. ix. 7, 8; xv. 23. 1 Sam. xxv. 36. Amos v. 13. Matt. v. 6.
[9] Neh. ii. 5. Speaking of his land before a heathen King, in reference, not to the God of Israel, but to the sepulchre of his fathers.
[10] 1 Chron. xii. 32. Comp. Esth. i. 13. [11] Chap. xiv. 8, 15.
[12] Chap. xii. 16. 1 Sam. xxv. 10, 11, 17, 25. [13] 1 Sam. xvii. 44.
[14] Luke xiv. 28—32. [15] Chap. xviii. 13. [16] Isa. lii. 14.
[17] Ibid. xi. 3. [18] Matt. xxi. 24; xxii. 42—46. [19] Isa. l. 4.
[20] Luke xvi. 1. [21] Chap. x. 26; xxvi. 6. Matt. xxv. 26, 27.
[22] 2 Kings v. 20—27. [23] Gen. xxiv. 33—56. Tit. ii. 10. Comp. Chap. xxv. 13.
[24] Mal. ii. 7. 2 Cor. v. 20.

laden as he is with the guilt of the blood of souls; overwhelmed himself in the eternal damnation of those, who have perished through his neglect.[1]

Faithfulness marks the true *ambassador.*[2] He "shuns not to declare the whole counsel of God;"[3] not obtruding offensive truths in unnatural prominence; but not withholding them in their just scriptural proportion. He condescends to the capacities of his people; but he will not humor their prejudices or antipathies. He "handles not the word of God deceitfully; but by manifestation of the truth he commends himself to every man's conscience in the sight of God."[4] "The tongue of such *an ambassador*" *is health*[5]—both to himself and to his people.[6] "The wilderness rejoices" under his fertilizing blessing;[7] and the burst of joy and peace is heard on every side—"How beautiful upon the mountains are the feet of him, that bringeth good things, that publisheth peace!"[8]

18. *Poverty and shame shall be to him that refuseth instruction; but he that regardeth reproof shall be honored.*

The *instruction* of discipline is God's ordinance. Little do those who *refuse* it know, what a blessing they cast away![9] *Poverty and shame* are often the Lord's rod for his wayward children[10]—two dreaded evils—the one bringing them to want—the other hiding their heads; both disappointing the "lust of the flesh, the lust of the eye, and the pride of life."[11] Young persons! Learn to dread the liberty of being left to your own choice. Dread the first step in the downward course—*refusing instruction*—Remember your birth—"as the wild ass's colt."[12] Know your besetting temptation—"as the horse and the mule"[13]—impatient of restraint. If the remonstrance of parents, friend, ministers be slighted. all may end in *poverty and shame*—embittered with the poignant sting of death-bed remorse.[14]

But here is *honor* contrasted with *shame.* For reverently to *regard reproof* will ensure honor from man.[15] Honor from God will be abundant. "If ye endure chastisement, God dealeth with you as with sons."[16] Humbled under his reproof—raised to his throne.[17] To have our ears opened to receive discipline is to walk in the path of life and happiness,[18]—the honor of conformity to our Divine Saviour.[19] Man's pride deems it a degradation to receive reproof. God counts it "brutish to hate it."[20] Which judgment is according to truth and right?

19. *The desire accomplished is sweet to the soul: but it is abomination to fools to depart from evil.*

[1] Ezra iii. 17, 18; xxxiii. 7, 8. 1 Cor. ix. 16.
[2] 1 Cor. iv. 1, 2: vii. 25. 1 Thess. ii. 3—6. 1 Tim. i. 12.
[3] Acts xx. 27. [4] 2 Cor. iv. 2; ii. 17. [5] Chap. xii. 18.
[6] Job xxxiii. 23—26. [7] Isa. xxxv. 1. [8] Ibid. lii. 7. [9] Heb. xii. 10, 11.
[10] Chap. vi. 9, 11. Isa. lxv. 11, 12. Luke xv. 12—16.
[11] 1 John ii. 16. [12] Job xi. 12. [13] Psalm xxxii. 9.
[14] Chap. v. 9—14. [15] Chap. xxv. 12. [16] Heb. xii. 7.
[17] James iv. 10. 1 Peter v. 6. [18] Chap. vi. 23. Job xxxvi. 8—10.
[19] Isa. l. 4, 5. Heb. v. 8. [20] Chap. xii. 1. Comp. Jer. v. 3, 4.

This must be limited to "*the desire* of the righteous"[1].—As that is "only good," it "will be granted,"[2] and the *accomplishment is sweet to the soul*—Infinitely *sweeter* will be the full—the eternal *accomplishment*—"I shall be satisfied, when I awake, with thy likeness."[3]

May not all enjoy this *sweetness?* All might—but all will not—be happy. The object is so revolting to the "enmity of the carnal mind." Perhaps those who have been early trained in the ways of God, cannot experimentally estimate the bitterness of this enmity. But what can give a more awful view of this principle than the truth—that which is abomination in God to see, *is abomination to the fool to depart from.*[4] A striking figure of heaven and hell—in full contrast—with the great gulf, that is fixed between them. Holiness makes heaven—sin makes hell. See then for which place the ungodly are fitting. Hatred of holiness is meetness for hell. Oh—what a mighty change must that be, that can slay the enmity—and make it to the soul an abomination to commit *evil*, as it now *is to depart from it!*

20. *He that walketh with wise men shall be wise: but a companion of fools shall be destroyed.*

Every one desires to engrave his own image upon his *companions.* We naturally therefore take our mould from their society. It is not left to us to determine whether there shall be any influence—only, what that influence shall be. Walking *with the wise*—under their instruction, encouragement and example, *we shall be wise.* Our principles and habits will be fixed, our interest excited, and the resolution formed—"We will go with you, for we see that God is with you."[5] See here the blessing of living in a godly family—hearkening daily to "the wise man's learning,"[6] or in membership with a Church, where each imparts from his store for the increase and edifying of the body.[7] Mark—young people—the responsibility of the choice of friends. How much hangs upon the determination to be "a companion of all them that fear God, and keep his precepts!"[8] The world may allure, the ungodly may mock, the evil heart may consent to their voice. But seek you your strength from God, and resolve to *walk with the wise*—"As the Lord liveth, and as my soul liveth, I will not leave thee."[9]

Joash, while he *walked with his wise* guardian, *was wise. But* when after his guardian's death, he became *a companion of fools, he was destroyed.*[10] And how often does the scaffold warn us of the corruption from evil communications![11] Many a promising professor has been brought step by step to *destruction.* The horror of sin—the instinctive recoil from it—gradually abates. The fear

[1] See on verse 12. [2] Chap. xi. 23; x. 24. [3] Ps. xvii. 15. [4] Chap. xv. 21.
[5] Zech. viii. 23. [6] Chap. xvi. 23. 1 Kings x. 8.
[7] Eph. iv. 15, 16. Acts ii. 42. Heb. x. 24.
[8] Psalm cxix. 63. Comp. xxvi. 4, 5. Chap. ii. 20.
[9] 2 Kings ii. 4. Comp. Psalm cxix. 115. [10] 2 Chron. xxiv.
[11] 1 Cor. xv. 33. Comp. 2 Kings xvii. 15. Ps. l. 18—21; cvi. 28, 29, 35, 36. Jer. ii. 5.

of God—the cover from sin[1]—is weakened. The hold on the great hopes of the gospel is relaxed. Other objects gain the ascendency, and the ruin is complete. And when—we might ask—have the godly *companied with fools*, without injury to their profession, and hazard to their souls?[2] If we can live in a worldly element, without feeling out of our own element; if we can breathe a tainted atmosphere without sensibility of infection; if we can familiarize ourselves with the absence of religion in the ordinary intercourse of life, is there no ground of alarm, lest unsubdued worldliness should be regaining dominion?

The first warning to sinners just plucked out of the fire, was—"Save yourselves from this untoward generation."[3] And to the end of the path the rule will be—"Have no fellowship with the unfruitful works of darkness, but rather reprove them."[4] *Connection* we must often have with them.[5] But let our *delight* be with the saints of God.[6] God may soon decide for an halting professor. His patience may be exhausted. His justice may take its course; and those, who are now his *companions in folly*, will be his tormentors in hopeless misery.

21. *Evil pursueth sinners; but to the righteous good shall be repaid.*

'Sinners are sure to find *evil* at last—*righteous, good*.'[7] The histories of sin from the beginning—Cain,[8] Achan,[9] Abimelech,[10] Ahab,[11] and his wicked wife,[12] with many others, are solemn demonstrations, that *evil pursueth sinners*, even when they seem to have found a refuge.[13] The delay even of centuries does not weaken the certainty.[14] As sure as the shadow follows the substance,[15] as the avenger of blood *pursued* the manslayer—"evil shall hunt the violent man to overthrow him."[16] Yet often the sinner goes on in his blind infatuation. 'No one has been witness to his sin. Or no one will make account of it. Or his accusers, being as guilty as himself, will hold their peace; or, should he be discovered, prudence or pleading will secure him from punishment.'[17] And then, though "the iniquity of his heels compasseth him about,"[18] he thinks only of present gratification, never looks back, and therefore sees not the *evil pursuing him.* His blindness thus makes his ruin more certain.[19] And how dearly are his momentary pleasures purchased at the cost of eternity![20]

Yet not more certain is the *evil that pursueth sinners*, than *the good which shall be repaid to the righteous.*[21] The one follows

[1] Gen. xxxix. 9. Neh. v. 15. [2] 2 Chron. xviii. 3, 31; xix. 2.
[3] Acts ii. 40. [4] Eph. v. 11. Comp. Chap. xiv. 7. 2 Cor. vi. 14—16.
[5] 1 Cor. v. 10 [6] Psalm xvi. 3. [7] Jermin in loco.
[8] Gen. iv. 10—13. [9] Josh. vii. 20—26. [10] Judges ix. 24, 56, 57.
[11] 1 Kings xxi. 19; xxii. 38. 2 Kings ix. 26.
[12] 1 Kings xxi. 23. 2 Kings ix. 30—36. [13] 1 Kings ii. 28—31.
[14] Ex. xvii. 14. 1 Sam. xv. 3—7. [15] Num. xxxv. 19.
[16] Psalm cxl. 11. Comp. Chap. xi. 19, 21. Acts xxviii. 4.
[17] Lavater in loco. [18] Psalm xlix. 5.
[19] Deut. xxix. 19, 20. Job xi. 18, 20. 1 Thess. v. 3.
[20] Ecc. xi. 9. [21] Isa. iii. 10, 11. Rom. ii 6—10.

in just retribution. The other is the reward of grace. Not the smallest *good*—even "a cup of cold water to a disciple,"[1] or honor shown to his servants[2]—shall be without its payment.[3] And if a single act is thus remembered, much more "a course—a fight"—held out to the end.[4] How manifestly is this the constitution of grace; that, when perfect obedience can claim no recompence,[5] such unworthy defiled work, should be so honored with an infinite, overwhelming acceptance!

22. *A good man leaveth an inheritance to his children's children: and the wealth of the sinner is laid up for the just.*

The good to be repaid to the righteous has just been mentioned. Here we have a particular instance of it; It cannot however be meant as an universal statement. Many *good men* have no inheritance to leave; or they have no *children;* or none that survive them, or no *children's children;* or this generation may be in poverty. *The wealth of the sinner also*—instead of being *laid up for the just*—descends to his posterity for successive generations.[6] Yet Scripture gives many examples of this dispensation of Providence, showing the blessing of personal godliness to unborn posterity. Abraham left his covenanted *inheritance to his children's children.*[7] Caleb's children inherited their father's possession.[8] "Although David's house was not so with God" as he could have desired; yet his lamp continued to burn for upwards of seventeen generations.[9] Often also has the Divine blessing upon the discreet guidance of his affairs,[10] and the special promise to Christian liberality,[11] preserved *the good man's inheritance.* And if there is no earthly substance to leave, yet a church in the house—a family altar—the record of holy example and instruction; and above all—a store of believing prayer laid up for accomplishment, when we shall be silent in the grave—will be *an inheritance* to our children of inestimable value. For though no trust can be placed in hereditary religion;[12] yet the recollection of the path in which their fathers' walked, and in which they themselves were trained, may under God's grace, continue the entail of religion in our families, so that "instead of the fathers may be the children."[13]

But *the good man's inheritance* is also increased from *the wealth of the sinner.* Laban's *wealth was laid up for* Jacob;[14] the spoils of Egypt[15] and Canaan[16] for Israel; Haman's *wealth for* Esther and Mordecai.[17] Indeed this appears to have been a prominent feature of the Old Dispensation;[18] and it will be openly renewed in the latter-day glory of the Church.[19] Probably therefore the fulfilment

[1] Matt. x. 42. [2] Ibid. v. 41. 1 Kings xvii. 16—23. 2 Kings iv. 17—37.
[3] Heb. vi. 10. [4] 2 Tim. iv. 7, 8. [5] Luke xvii. 10.
[6] Psalm xvii. 14. [7] Gen. xvii. 7, 8. Comp. Psalm xxv. 12, 13; cxii. 2
[8] Jos. xiv. 14. 1 Chron. iv. 15.
[9] 2 Sam. xxiii. 5, with 1 Kings xv. 4. 2 Chron. xxi. 7; xxiii. 3.
[10] Psalm cxii. 5. [11] Chap. iii. 9, 10; xi. 24. [12] John i. 13.
[13] Ps. lxxviii. 5, 6; xlv. 16. [14] Gen. xxxi. 1, 9, 16. [15] Ex. xii. 35, 36.
[16] Jos. viii. 27; xi. 14. Psalm cv. 44. [17] Esth. viii. 1, 2.
[18] Chap. xxviii. 8. Job xxvii. 13, 16, 17. [19] Isa. lxi. 6.

is far more frequent than meets the eye. Often also *the wealth of the sinner, laid up for* the aggrandizement of his own name in his posterity, becomes the portion of *the just* in his own holy seed, consecrating it to the service of their Lord and his church.[1]

23. *Much food is in the tillage of the poor: but there is that is destroyed for want of judgment.*

The produce of the soil is the fruit of industry.[2] *Much good is in* the *tillage of the poor;* because, being wholly dependent on their own exertions, they spare no pains or labor. So that by careful husbandry they may gain support from a small plot; while a large and fertile estate may be *destroyed for want of judgment.*[3] Indeed, for want of prudent management the richest tillage may come to waste. Egypt with her abundant crops would have been *destroyed*, but for Joseph's *judgment* in preserving the *much food for the tillage.*[4] Solomon's prudent administration of his household restrained waste and extravagance.[5] Even our Divine Master, in the distribution of the food, directed that "the fragments should be gathered up, that nothing be lost,"[6] or *destroyed for want of care and judgment.*

But what is the practical and extended application? If talents lie inactive, or if their activity is not wisely directed, a rich harvest is *destroyed for want of judgment.* The same ruin flows from the neglect of religious advantages. The harvest of grace withers into a famine. Slothful professor! rouse thyself to *till the* ground; else wilt thou starve for want of *food.* Then let thy roused energy be directed by a *sound judgment;* for want of which, the fruits of industry, temporal, intellectual, and spiritual, will run to waste.

24. *He that spareth his rod hateth his son: but he that loveth him, chasteneth him betimes.*

Among the many modern theories of education, how often is God's system overlooked! Yet should not this be our pattern and standard? *The rod* of discipline is its main character—not harsh severity, but a wise, considerate, faithful exercise; always aiming at the subjugation of the will, and the humbling and purifying of the heart. But here God and man are at issue. Man often *spares the rod*, because he loves the child. This at least he calls love. But is not our Father's love to his children inconceivably more yearning than that of an earthly parent? Yet does he not *spare the rod*—"What son is he, whom the father chasteneth not?"[7] Is *the rod* the proof of his *hatred?* "Whom the Lord *loveth*, he chasteneth."[8] Nay—he gives us his Divine judgment—*He that spareth the rod, hateth the child.* Does he not act at least as if *he hated him;* omitting a duty so necessary for his welfare; winking at the indulgence of vicious habits and a wayward will—so

[1] Eccl. ii. 26. [2] Chap. xii. 11; xiv. 4. Gen. iii. 19.
[3] Chap. xxiv. 30, 34. [4] Gen. xli. 33—36, 46—49.
[5] 1 Kings iv. 27, 28. [6] John vi. 14. [7] Heb. xii. 7.
[8] Ibid. v. 6. Deut. viii. 5. Rev. iii. 19.

surely issuing in bitter sorrow?[1] Is not this delivering him up to his worst enemy. Better that the child had been trained in the house of strangers, than that he should thus be the unhappy victim of the cruelty of parental love.

The discipline of our children must therefore commence with self-discipline. Nature teaches to love them *much*. But we want a controlling principle, to teach us to love them *wisely*. The indulgence of our children has its root *in self-indulgence*. We do not like putting ourselves to pain. The difficulties indeed can only be known by experience. And even in this school one parent cannot measure the trials of another. But all our children are children of Adam—"Foolishness is bound up in their hearts."[2] All choose, from the first dawn of reason, the broad road of destruction.[3] And can we bear the thought, that they should walk in that road? We pray for their conversion. But prayer without teaching is mockery, and Scripture teaching implies *chastening*.[4] Discipline therefore must be. All need the rod, some again and again. Yet it must be the father's rod, yearning over his *chastened* child,[5] even while he dares "not spare him for his crying."[6] The rod without affection is revolting tyranny.

But often do we hear mourning over failure. And is not this the grand reason? We do not *chastise betimes*.[7] Satan begins with the infant in arms![8] The cry of passion is his first stir of the native corruption. Do we begin as early? Every vice commences in the nursery. The great secret is—to establish authority in the dawn of life; to bend the tender twig, before the knotty oak is beyond our power.[9] A child, early trained by parental discipline, will probably preserve the wholesome influence to the end of life.

But fearful indeed is the difficulty, when the child has been the *early* master, to begin *chastening*, when the habit of disobedience has been formed and hardened; to have the first work to do, when the child is growing out of childhood, and when the unreserved confidence needs to be established. Rarely indeed does this late experiment succeed: while the severity necessary to enforce it is not less dangerous than painful. "It is good for a man that he bear the yoke in his youth."[10]

25. *The righteous eateth to the satisfying of his soul: but the belly of the wicked shall want.*

This is one of the many proofs, that "*the righteous* is more excellent than his neighbor."[11] Temporal blessings are assured—so far as they are really good for him; whether little or much—

[1] Chap. xxix. 15. 1 Sam. iii. 13. 1 Kings i. 6; ii. 25. Comp. 2 Sam. xiii. 39.
[2] Chap. xxii. 15. Gen. viii. 21. [3] Isa. liii. 6.
[4] The Scripture term combines chastening with instruction.—LXX. Verse 18. Eph vi. 4. Heb. xii. 6. Comp. Psalm xciv. 12; cxix. 67, 71.
[5] Ps. ciii. 13. [6] Chap. xix. 18. Ecclus. xxx. 1. [7] Ibid.
[8] Psalm lviii. 3. Isa. xlviii. 8. [9] Ecclus. xxx. 11, 12.
Principiis obsta; sero medicina paratur,
Cum mala per longas convaluere moras.—OVID.
[10] Lam. iii. 27. [11] Chap. xii. 26.

enough to satisfy his wants, not to "fulfil his lusts."[1] Indeed 'he can never want a sufficiency, because his desires are moderate, and he makes a temperate use of God's blessings.'[2] He therefore shall *eat to his satisfying*, while *the wicked* shall want. Jacob was fed with the best of the land, while the Egyptians were destitute[3] Elijah was fed—first by ravens, afterwards by a widow, when *the wicked* nation were in extremity.[4] The fare of *the righteous* may be coarse, and that of *the wicked* "sumptuous." But did not Daniel and his friends *eat* their pulse with more *satisfaction*, than their fellow-captives did their richer dainties?[5] And—as to higher food and heavenly *satisfaction*—Christ is a substitute for every thing—nothing for him.—'If then,' as the noble Luther declares, 'we live here by begging our bread, is not this well-recompenced, that we are nourished with the food of angels—with eternal life and Christ himself?'[6]

Such a chaos of desires is the soul of *the wicked*, that no abundance can satisfy *his want.* Ahab's crown could give him no rest, without Naboth's vineyard.[7] So full is the ungodly heart of insatiable cravings![8] But how intolerable will be this conscious want throughout eternity, when a drop of water to cool the tormented tongue shall be denied![9]

CHAPTER XIV.

1. *Every wise woman buildeth her house; but the foolish plucketh it down with her hands.*

We have seen the wife to be a blessing or curse to her husband.[10] Such is she to his *house.* Her *wisdom* may supply many of his defects; while all the results of his care and prudence may be wasted by her folly. The godly matron instructs her children by her example, no less than by her teaching. She educates them for God and for eternity; not to shine in the vain shew of the world, but in the Church of God. Her household order combines economy with liberality;[11] strict integrity in the fear of God.[12] Thus, as godly servants bring a blessing to the house,[13] so *does the wise woman build her house*[14] under the blessing of God, 'establishing it in a firm and durable state.'[15] Who can estimate the worth of a Christian mother—a Hannah[16]—an Eunice?[17]

1 Chap. x. 3. Ps. xxxiv. 10; xxxvii. 3, 18. 2 Bishop Patrick.
3 Gen. xlvii. 11—13. 4 1 Kings xvii. 1—11; xviii. 5. 5 Dan. i. 12—16.
6 Luther on Psalm cxxxii. 16. Comp. Psalm xxxvi. 8. John vi. 35, 55.
7 1 Kings xxi. 1—4. Job xx. 20—22.
8 Psalm xvii. 14. Isa. lxv. 13, 14. Hos. iv. 10. Mic. vi. 14.
9 Luke xvi. 24. 10 Chap. xii. 4. 11 Chap. xxxi. 13, 18, 27.
12 Ibid. ver. 30. 13 Gen. xxx. 27; xxxix. 5. 14 Chap. xxiv. 3—5.
15 Diodati. Chap. xxxi. 28—31. 16 1 Sam. i. 27, 28. 17 2 Tim. i. 5; iii. 15.

But mark *the foolish woman*—her idleness, waste, love of pleasure, want of all forethought and care—her children's wills allowed—their souls neglected—their happiness ruined! We see her *house plucked down* in confusion. A sad issue, if an enemy had done this. But it is the doing—or rather the undoing—of *her own hands*. In proportion to her power and influence is her capability of family mischief. Such was Jezebel—the destroyer of her house.[1]

What responsibility then belongs to the marriage choice, linked with the highest interests of unborn generations! If ever there was a matter for special prayer and consideration, this is it. Here to err once, may be an undoing of ourselves and of our house. Of how little account are birth, fortune, external accomplishments, compared with godly *wisdom!*[2]

2. *He that walketh in his uprightness feareth the Lord: but he that is perverse in his ways, despiseth him.*

There can be no stream without the fountain. Grace in the heart is the spring of *the upright walk.*[3] The proof that we believe the reality of religion, is that we walk in the power of it. The proof of the influence of *the fear of God* is, that we "are in it all the day long,"[4] not saints in our prayers, and worldlings in our conduct; not substituting active zeal for personal devotedness; not teaching our families half of religion—to read and pray; but "whatsoever things are true, honest, just, pure, lovely, and of good report—to think on these things."[5] Man may boast of his moral *uprightness*—that he would scorn a mean action. But the heart-searching Saviour lays open the root of worldly selfishness, and shews *his way to be perverse* before him.[6] Does he remember—or does he know—while he slumbers in the delusion of external decency, that the allowed supremacy of any earthly object,[7] or the indulgence of a secret lust[8]—brings him under the fearful guilt of the *despising God?*

3. *In the mouth of the foolish is a rod of pride: but the lips of the wise shall preserve him.*

How many figures does the wise man employ to shew the destructive evils of the tongue![9] Here it is a rod[10]—*a rod of pride. The rod in the mouth* is often sharper than the rod in the hand. Sometimes it strikes against God[11]—sometimes it is "the rod of his anger"[12] against his people permitted,[13] yet restrained.[14] Always in the end is it *the rod* for the *fool* himself.[15] Yet when the heart is humbled, and filled with *wisdom, the tongue* becomes the *pre-*

[1] 1 Kings xvi. 31—33; xxi. 24, 25. Comp. 2 Kings. xi. 1.
[2] Mr. Scott here aptly quotes the proverb—that 'a fortune in a wife is better than a fortune with a wife.'
[3] Chap. iv. 23. Matt. xii. 33. [4] Chap. xxiii. 17. [5] Phil. iv. 8.
[6] Luke xvi. 14, 15. [7] 1 Sam. ii. 29, 30. [8] 2 Sam. xii. 9, 10.
[9] Jer. xviii. 18. [10] Ezek. vii. 10, 11.
[11] Ex. v. 2. Psalm xii. 3, 4. 2 Kings xix. 10—13. [12] Isa. x. 5—14.
[13] Rev. xiii. 5, 6. [14] Ps. cxxv. 3. [15] Psalm lxiv. 8. Jer. xxv. 8—14

servative from imminent dangers[1]—even from the threatened scourge of *the rod of pride*.[2]

Were this iron *rod* to rule the earth, who could tolerate the abodes of men?[3] But adored be the grace, which converts this unruly boasting member of unrighteousness, to be "an instrument of righteousness unto God!"[4]

4. *Where no oxen are, the crib is clean: but much increase is by the strength of the ox.*

Oxen are the Eastern instruments of husbandry.[5] *Where*, therefore, *no oxen are*, to till the ground, *the crib is clean*.[6] Because, where is no labor, there can be no food wherewith to supply it. God works by means, not by miracles. There must be good husbandry, in order to an abundant harvest. Let the *ox* be put to his work, and *much increase will be by his strength*.[7] In the spiritual husbandry, where there are no laborers, all is barrenness and desolation. But see the *much increase*—the harvest of precious souls—the fruit of *their strength* and effectiveness.[8] "In all labor"—both in the natural and spiritual husbandry—"there is profit."[9] But God will never acknowledge a slothful servant.

5. *A faithful witness will not lie; but a false witness will utter lies.*

This might seem to be a truism—unworthy of inspiration. But a closer inspection brings out a valuable maxim of practical wisdom. *A faithful witness* is moved neither by entreaties nor bribes, neither by promises nor threats, to swerve from truth. He is the man to trust. *He will not lie. But a false witness* has lost all principle of truth. *He will utter lies*—without any inducement but his own interest or pleasure. *Flee from his very breath*.[10]

The faithful witness answers God's requirements.[11] He is therefore his delight.[12] He is the citizen of the heavenly Zion,[13] and the ornament of Godliness.[14] In the Sacred office *he will not lie*. His spirit is firm and independent.[15] His message is full and transparent truth.[16] But *the false witness* is a true child of "the father of lies."[17] Awful indeed is his *utterance* in common life;[18] more awful in the profession of the gospel;[19] awful beyond conception in the Sanctuary.[20] A minister of God in his commission—a Minister of Satan in his work,[21] delivering a *lying* message; "subverting the gospel of Christ,"[22] to the destruction of his people, to the double destruction of his own soul.

1 Chap. xii. 6. 2 Job v. 21. Psalm xxxi. 19, 20. 3 Psalm lvii. 4; cxx. 5—7.
4 Rom. vi. 13. 5 Deut. xxii. 10; xxv. 4. 1 Kings xix. 19. Job i. 3, 14.
6 See Amos iv. 6. 7 Psalm cxliv. 13, 14.
8 1 Cor. iii. 9; ix. 9, 10. 1 Tim. v. 18, and the image of the minister, Rev. iv. 7, seem to warrant this application of the proverb.
9 Verse 23. 10 Chap. xxv. 19. 11 Psalm li. 6.
12 John i. 47. 13 Psalm xv. 2; xxiv. 3, 4. Isa. xxxiii. 15—17.
14 Phil. iv. 8. 15 Acts xxvi. 16 1 Thess. ii. 3, 4.
17 John viii. 44. 1 Kings xxi. 13. Comp. verse 25. 18 Chap. vi. 19; xxv. 18.
19 Acts v. 1—4. 20 Jer. v. 31. Ezra xiii. 4—16. 21 2 Cor. xi. 13—15.
22 Gal. i. 7.

Thus "the good and the corrupt tree"—each brings forth its own fruit[1]. Let us remember, that our principles—good and evil—are exemplified in the most trivial transactions, and gather strength from the slightest, as well as from the most important exercise.[2]

6. *A scorner seeketh wisdom, and findeth it not: but knowledge is easy unto him that understandeth.*

What then? Is the promise belied—"He that seeketh findeth?"[3] The failure lies at *the scorner's* own door. He *seeks* indeed, but without seriousness;[4] without honesty of purpose;[5] without delight;[6] for his own interest.[7] He 'finds therefore matter enough for his humor, but none for his instruction!'[8] He charges the darkness upon the Scripture—not upon his own heart. He feels himself able to comprehend the subject, and therefore free to reject what is beyond his conception, or contrary to his prejudices. He *scorns* the humbling submission of faith, so that the glory even of the wisdom of God is foolishness with him.[9] No wonder that while he makes an effort to seek, he *findeth not.*[10] He seeks his object, but neglects the means, and perishes in the *scornfulness* of his own unbelief.[11]

To another class of *seekers knowledge is easy.*[12] The Ethiopian Eunuch gathered his knowledge from simplicity.[13] God gave him a ready will, a right taste; and in "doing his will he knew his doctrine."[14] Obedience is the path of *understanding.* "Whosoever shall humble himself as a little child, the same is the greatest in the kingdom of heaven."[15]

Shall not we thus unite with our Divine Master in adoring the gracious Sovereignty of this dispensation? "Thou hast hid these things from the wise and prudent, and hast revealed them unto babes."[16] Shall not we seek for deeper humility, as the pathway to higher instruction? While we "are in our Father's hands" as the object of his love, think of the privilege of "sitting down at his feet, every one to receive of his words."[17]

7. *Go from the presence of a foolish man, when thou perceivest not in him the lips of knowledge.*

Fellowship with the ungodly is absolutely forbidden. And it is never safe to contradict a plain command.[18] Let us labor to win their souls to Christ. But the rule of prudence directs—"Cast not your pearls before swine." 'Avoid'—says the holy Leighton—'the mixture of an irreverent commonness of speaking of holy things

[1] Matt. vii. 17, 18; xii. 33. Comp. Chap. xii. 17.
[2] Luke xvi. 10.
[3] Matt. vii. 7, 8. Isa. xlv. 19.
[4] John xviii. 38.
[5] Jer. xlii. 1—3; xliii. 1—4. Ezra xiv. 1—4; xx. 1—3. Matt. xxii. 15, 16.
[6] Chap. xvii. 16; xviii. 2.
[7] Acts viii. 18—23.
[8] Lord Bacon quoted by Bishop Patrick.
[9] Rom. ix. 31, 32; x. 3.
[10] Chap. xxiv. 7. 2 Tim. iii. 7.
[11] 1 Cor. iii. 19.
[12] Chap. viii. 9; xvii. 24.
[13] Acts viii. 27—39. Comp. Psalm xix. 7; cxix. 130.
[14] John vii. 17. Matt. vi. 22.
[15] Matt. xviii. 4. Comp. Ecc. xxxix. 24.
[16] Matt. xi. 25, 26.
[17] Deut. xxxiii. 3.
[18] Chap. ix. 6. 2 Cor. vi. 14—17.

indifferently in all companies.'[1] Therefore—*when we perceive not in the foolish man the lips of knowledge—go from his presence.* Some may be called to dispute with him. But take care that the call is clear. It is at least the safest path to despatch your business with him as in a shower of rain, and not to loiter in his society.

Sweet indeed is the glow of the Saviour's name upon the young Christian's lips. Its warmth may put elder Christians to shame. But we must warn him—Harm may be got in an imprudent endeavor to do good. Confess your Master, wherever he may open your door and your mouth. But better retreat from cavillers.[2] You may be foiled by specious reasonings. Beware of tampering with your simplicity by the hazardous experiment how much poison your constitution may bear.[3] If our Lord exposed himself to moral danger—yet think of the impenetrable cover of his sanctity—his perfect self-government—his rules of godly prudence. Do we feel secure in the strength of our Christian habits? None are so confirmed as to be safe in relaxation of watchfulness, and wanton rushing into danger. There is a perpetual warfare with the old principles of corruption. No dependence can be placed upon any habits, that do not produce right conduct, and right apprehension of present duty. The path of sin is much more easily avoided than relinquished. We can far more readily keep out of the course of the stream, than stem the torrent. Walk closely with God; and under his cover and shield bear a protest against the ungodly.[4] Commune much with his people. The very sight of a man of God is refreshing.[5]

8. *The wisdom of the prudent is to understand his way: but the folly of fools is deceit.*

This is not *the wisdom* of the learned, but *of the prudent;* not abstract and speculative, but sound and practical. It is self-knowledge and self-control looking upward for Divine guidance. And how much is this *wisdom* needed to *understand our way!* The restless professor eagerly follows his own impulse. His constitutional bias interprets Providences, and makes openings for himself. Every thing is out of place. He is so "fervent in spirit," that he becomes "slothful in business." He conceives himself to be doing good; the more so because it is different from his brethren. He pleads the constraint of zeal as an excuse for indiscretion; as if religion was meant to destroy, and not rather to rectify, his judgment.

But "God hath made every thing beautiful in his time."[6] Religion is an orderly thing, as wise as it is warm. Whatever be the excitement to an irregular course, more good is done in steady consistency. To break the ranks in disorder; to "busy ourselves in

[1] Matt. vii. 6. Leighton in loco. Vol. iii. [2] Chap. xxvi. 4. 1 Tim. vi. 4, 5.
[3] 1 Cor. xv. 33. [4] Psalm cxix. 114, 115. [5] Chap. xxvii. 9, 17.
[6] Eccl. iii. 11.

other men's matters;"[1] to be eager to *understand* our neighbor's way,[2] obscures the light upon our own. The true *wisdom is to understand* what belongs to us personally and relatively.[3] "As God hath distributed to every man, so let him walk, and abide with God."[4] Let the eye do the work of the eye, and the hand of the hand. If Moses prayed on the Mount, and Joshua fought in the valley,[5] it was not, because the one was deficient in courage, or the other in prayer; but because each had his appointed work, and *understood his own way.* Many steps of *our way* are different from our neighbors, and may often be difficult to discern; being rather involved in the principles, than expressed in the detail, of Scripture. But *the wisdom of the prudent* will enable us *to understand* what the will of the Lord is.[6] "A single eye" and a sound heart will make our way plain.[7] True greatness does not consist in doing extraordinary things, but in doing common things from a right motive.

But while the attention of a truly wise man is occupied in ascertaining the conduct which his duty calls him to pursue, the arts of *deceit* engross the polluted minds of the wicked.[8] Their wisdom of *deceit* is really *folly.* Gehazi's overreaching wisdom proved *folly* in the end.[9] Daniel's accusers "were taken in their own *craftiness.*"[10] Ananias and Sapphira vainly endeavored to hide their covetousness under the cover of liberality.[11] Who can deceive a heart-searching God? The attempt to do so is fearful provocation—certain confusion.

9. *Fools make a mock at sin: but with the righteous there is favor.*

What! Are there such as will count sin a sport? They have never seen the sight—never felt the weight. Look into eternity. Is hell a matter of sport? Look deeper still. How does God feel it?[12] How did Christ sink under the load? Shall we make a *mock* at that, which was a crushing burden to the Son of God? Go to Gethsemane. Go to Calvary. Learn there what sin is.[13] Ask converted souls—awakened consciences—dying sinners—do they speak lightly of sin? How will the wretched *mocker* call himself in eternity what God calls him now—*a fool!* The *mocking* cannot be beyond the grave; except it be the sport of the cruel enemy at the unchangeably hopeless torments of his deluded victim. The damnation of souls is sport in hell. Is not then the poor *mocker*, rushing into the woe—the object of our pity and prayer? We warn—we weep—we would yearn over him.

The righteous—they cannot *mock*, like this hardened *fool.* While 'he makes himself merry with his sin, and scoffs at the re-

[1] 1 Pet. iv. 15. Comp. 1 Thess. iv. 11. 2 Thess. iii. 11, 12.
[2] John xxi. 21, 22.
[3] 1 Kings iii. 6—9. Eccl. viii. 5
[4] 1 Cor. vii. 17, 20, 24.
[5] Ex. xvii. 9—13.
[6] Eph. v. 17. Col. i. 9, 10; iv. 12.
[7] Matt. vi. 22.
[8] French and Skinner's Translation of Proverbs.
[9] 2 Kings v. 20—27.
[10] Dan. vi. 24. 1 Cor. iii. 19.
[11] Acts v. 1—10.
[12] Isa. xliii. 24. Jer. xliv. 4. Ezek. vi. 9. Amos ii. 13.
[13] Matt. xxvi. 36, 38; xxvii. 46.

proof and judgment which pertains thereunto;"[1] "they have the mark of those that sigh and cry for the abominations of the land"—the sure seal of the Lord's *favor*.[2] Soon does the sport of the fool come to an end. But here is *favor* unchangeable—abundant. Our God looks over, pities, bears with, guides, loves, saves, eternally. What are crowns and kingdoms compared with such a portion!

10. *The heart knoweth its own bitterness: and a stranger doth not intermeddle with his joy.*

A graphical illustration of man's proper individuality! "What man knoweth the things of a man, save the spirit of a man that is in him?"[3] The history of the soul is unseen by human eyes; but it is fully known and felt by the conscious subject. Each *knoweth his own bitterness*—deep—interior.[4] The most poignant sufferings often arise from causes, which cannot be told to our dearest friend.[5] No two of us are framed alike; and this diversity of mind and character precludes a *perfect* reciprocity, even in the warmest glow of human sympathy. Each only knows where the heart is wrung. Each therefore must in a measure tread a solitary path, and in that path often submit to be misunderstood. Hannah—*knowing her own bitterness*—was rashly rebuked by him, who ought to have been her Comforter.[6] Gehazi harshly repelled the Shunamite, through ignorance of her bitter sorrow.[7] Job's friends, from misconception, proved to be "miserable comforters—physicians of no value."[8]

But think of Him—who made himself "a man of sorrows," that he might be "touched with the feeling of our infirmities."[9] Here is perfect sympathy. *The heart's bitterness* is experimentally *known*, and effectually relieved.[10] Alive as he is to all our sorrows,[11] none of his members are too low for his highest and most endearing thought. Into this bosom we may pour the tale of woe, which no ear beside can receive. My Saviour! Has *my heart a bitterness*, that thou dost not *know*, that thou dost not feel with me, and for which thou dost not provide a present cordial and support?

No less individual is the *heart's joy*. It lies deep within itself. *A stranger doth not intermeddle with it.* Michal could understand David's bravery—not *his joy*. She knew him as a man of

[1] Bishop Hall.
[2] Ezek. ix. 4—6. 2 Kings xxii. 19, 20. Dan. ix. 4—21. See the contrast by God himself. Isa. lxvi. 2—5.
[3] 1 Cor. ii. 11.
[4] 1 Kings viii. 38, 39. 'Every one is inwardly the only true and faithful judge of his own joys and sorrows, and none else can truly perceive them.'—Diodati in loco. 'Each mind has an interior apartment of his own, into which none but itself and the Divinity can enter.'—Foster on a Man writing memoirs of himself, Letter vii.
[5] Thus the Saviour separated himself even from his chosen disciples. Mark xiv. 32—35.
[6] 1 Sam. i. 10—13.
[7] 2 Kings iv. 27.
[8] Job xiii. 4; xvi. 2.
[9] Isa. liii. 3. Heb. iv. 15.
[10] Isa. l. 4, 5.
[11] Ibid. lxiii. 9.

war—not as a man of God.[1] Indeed, joy is a plant in "a garden enclosed"—a stream from "a fountain sealed."[2] It is "the secret of the Lord, which is with the righteous."[3] It is the indwelling "Comforter, whom the world cannot receive."[4] Yes! truly—that is the highest joy, that lies covered from observation—that the man hides in his own bosom. There is no noise or froth on the surface. But the waters flow deep from a Divine spring. Christ takes the believer apart from the crowd, feeds him on hidden manna,[5] and makes him partaker of his own joy. Whatever cause there may be for mourning, there is infinitely more ground for joy; and mourning will soon be ended forever.[6]

11. *The house of the wicked shall be overthrown: but the tabernacle of the upright shall flourish.*

The feeblest state of *the upright* is more stable than the prosperity of *the wicked.* They build *a house.* The earth is their home, where they would settle, and take their rest. *The upright* —knowing the uncertainty of earth, and seeking a better house—only set up *a tabernacle*[7]—weak and trembling. Yet *the house is overthrown,* and the *tabernacle flourishes.*[8] The strongest support of man totters.[9] The support of God to the weakest is Omnipotence.[10] The eye of sense seems however to see the contrary—the flourishing of the wicked, and the overthrow of the upright. And a sore trial is it to the servant of God.[11] But "we must walk by faith, not by sight."[12] "The sanctuary"—the word of God—will explain.[13] Wait awhile. The great day will set all in order before us, and show that "the Judge of all the earth doeth right."[14] Meanwhile let us leave him to do his own work, and to fulfil his own word in his own time.

12. *There is a way which seemeth right unto a man: but the end thereof are the ways of death.*

The way of open ungodliness is manifestly wrong.[15] And who can doubt the end?[16] But other paths in the broad road—*seemingly right*—are not less certainly in their *end, the ways of death.* Thus does "the fool—right in his own eyes,"[17] mistake death for life. Indeed it is the fearful property of sin to hide its own character and tendency. The blindness increases in proportion to our familiarity with it. Its victim "feedeth on ashes; a deceived heart hath turned him aside, so that he cannot deliver his soul, nor say, Is there not a lie in my right hand?"[18]

'Take care then'—as the saintly Leighton warns us—'of sleeping unto death in carnal ease.'[19] Look well to the foundation and

[1] 1 Sam. xviii. 13, 20, with 2 Sam. vi. 12—16.
[2] Can. iv. 12. [3] Chap. iii. 32. Ps. xxv. 14. [4] John xiv. 16, 17.
[5] Rev. ii. 17. [6] Isa. lx. 20. [7] Heb. xi. 9, 10.
[8] Chap. iii. 33; x. 25; xii. 7. [9] Job viii. 15. Psalm xlix. 12.
[10] Isa. xl. 29; xli. 10, 14—16. [11] Psalm lxxiii. Jer. xii. 1. [12] 2 Cor. v. 7.
[13] Psalm lxxiii. 16, 17. Comp. Job xviii. 14—17, 21.
[14] Gen. xviii. 25. Psalm lviii. 11. [15] 1 Tim. v. 24. [16] 1 Cor. vi. 9, 10.
[17] Chap. xii. 15; xvi. 2. [18] Isa. xliv. 20. [19] On 1 Pet. iii. 21.

soundness of thy faith.[1] Search carefully both thy Bible and thine heart. Go to the Lord in prayer, and to his Ministers, to show you the true way.[2] "Prove thine own work."[3] If not a bold rebel against thy God—hast thou yielded freely thine heart to him? If thou be free from open wickedness, art thou not equally free from vital godliness? The most moral unrenewed professor is the slave of sin. Terrible indeed will it be to meet the bridegroom with a bright, but unfurnished lamp—to fall from high expectations of heaven into the depths of hell![4] The Lord keep our eye steadily on the *end of our way*, and make that end sure for heaven!

13. *Even in laughter the heart is sorrowful: and the end of that mirth is heaviness.*

Many a sigh is heaved amid the loud *laughter* of folly.[5] As soon might true joy be found in hell, as in the carnal heart. As soon might we "gather grapes of thorns, or figs of thistles," as this "fruit of the Spirit"[6] from 'nature's barren soil.' As soon might the tempest-tossed ocean be at rest, as the sinner's conscience.[7] He may feast in his prison, or dance in his chains. He may drink away his trouble. But it is a vain show of happiness. Ask him what is in his bosom. Is not his smile a counterfeit to hide a reality of woe? The voice of conscience and experience will make itself heard—"It is mad—what doeth it?"[8] If he has found a diversion from present trouble, has he found a cure from everlasting misery? It is far easier to drown conviction than to escape damnation. And to be merry for a day, and to be in torment for eternity—who would envy—who would not flee from—such a portion?

Nor do we speak only of the coarse *mirth* of the vulgar. Take the fullest cup of earth's best joys. What is this to satisfy desire, to allay trouble, to meet eternity? Even the present *end of this* short-lived *mirth is heaviness*[9]—sometimes so intolerable, that death is fled to—as the cure of the anguish; and to avoid the fear of hell, the wretched sinner leaps into it.[10] And at best eternity will change the face of *this mirth*, when that will remain, which would be the most desirable riddance—the sting of conscience, as enduring, as the pleasures of sin were momentary.[11]

But the end of *that mirth* seems to imply another *mirth* with a different end. Contrast the prodigal's *mirth* in the far country, with his return to his father's house—"*They began to be merry.*"[12] The fruit of carnal *mirth ends in heaviness.* Penitential sorrow begets a *mirth*, that ends in everlasting joy.[13] Lord! choose mine inheritance for me among thy weeping people.

14. *The backslider in heart shall be filled with his own ways: and a good man shall be satisfied from himself.*

[1] 2 Cor. xiii. 5. [2] 1 Sam. xii. 23. Mal. ii. 7.
[3] Gal. vi. 4. Ps. cxxxix. 23, 24. [4] Matt. xxv. 1—12. [5] Esth. v. 9—13
[6] Matt. vii. 16. [7] Isa. lvii. 20, 21. [8] Eccl. ii. 2.
[9] 1 Kings i. 9, 41, 49. Dan. v. 3—6. Amos v. 3—7.
[10] 2 Sam. xvii. 23. Matt. xxvii. 3—5. [11] Luke vi. 24; xvi. 21—24. Rom. vi. 21
[12] Luke xv. 13—24. [13] Psalm cxxvi. 5, 6. Isa. xxxv. 10.

Every spot is not the leprosy. Every mark of sin does not prove *a backslider.* "A man may be overtaken in a fault;"[1] or it may be the sin of ignorance;[2] or sin abhorred, resisted, yet still cleaving.[3] *Backsliding* implies a wilful step; not always open; but the more dangerous, because hidden. Here was no open apostacy, perhaps no tangible inconsistency. Nay—the man may be looked up to as an eminent saint. But he is *a backslider in heart.* A secret canker of unwatchfulness, neglect, or indulgence, has insensibly "devoured his strength."[4] The first step—instead of alarming, and bringing him to secret weeping[5]—hurried him onwards from one liberty to another, till he lost all power of resistance. His unsoundness was known to God long before it was manifested to the Church. Before the matter of Uriah, indolence and security had probably unhinged the man of God, and laid him open to the tempter.[6] *The backslider* needs no other rod than *his own ways. To be filled with them*—thus to become the fountain of his own misery—is the most fearful of all Divine judgments.[7]

The good man is also filled *from himself;*[8] yet not—as *the backslider*—with misery, but with solid *satisfaction.* God has given him a fountain fed from a higher fountain; a living spring within himself;[9] the witness of the Spirit;[10] the life and joy of the Heavenly Comforter;[11] the rejoicing testimony of his conscience;[12] the assured hope of glory.[13] This is not independent of God—the one source of self-sufficiency. But it is Himself dwelling in the heart, and filling it with his fulness. Let the sinner compare the satisfaction of sin and godliness—the curse and the blessing—and lift up his heart for the direction of a right choice.

15. *The simple believeth every word: but the prudent man looketh well to his going.*

To *believe every word* of God is faith. To *believe every word* of man is credulity. Faith is a principle of infinite moment. Eternal life and death hang upon it.[14] But it must be grounded upon evidence, and it can only be exercised according to the character and measure of the evidence. An indiscriminate faith is therefore fraught with mischief. Was not the world ruined by this *simplicity?*[15] Often since has it been the occasion of sin,[16] and even of downfall.[17]

Look at the fruit of this folly in the Church, when "our faith stands in the wisdom of men, not in the power of God."[18] Men become loose in fundamental principles. They are "carried about with divers and strange doctrines," and never know "the good

[1] Gal. vi. 1. [2] Lev. iv. 2. Num. xv. 22—29. Heb. v. 2; ix. 7.
[3] Rom. vii. 15—24. [4] Hosea vii. 9. Comp. Judg. xvi. 20. [5] Matt. xxvi. 75.
[6] 2 Sam. xi. 1, 2. [7] Psalm xxxii. 3—5. Jer. ii. 19; iv. 18.
[8] αυταρχης Phil. iv. 11, self-sufficiency. Comp. 2 Cor. ix. 8.—Gr.
[9] John iv. 14. [10] Rom. viii. 16. 1 John v. 10. [11] John xiv. 16, 17.
[12] 2 Cor. i. 12. Comp. Gal. vi. 4. [13] Col i. 27. Heb. x. 34.
[14] Mark xvi. 16. John iii. 36. [15] Gen. iii. 1—6.
[16] Ibid. xxxix. 19. 2 Sam. xvi. 1—4. Esth. iii. 8—11. [17] 1 Kings xiii. 11—19
[18] 1 Cor. ii. 5.

thing of a heart established with grace."[1] The novelties of fancy, accredited by some favorite name, readily pass for the revelation of God. We do not thus sit down to our food blindfolded; not knowing whether we take food or poison. But how ready men are to drink of any cup that is presented to them, like children, who think every thing good that is sweet. Thus are "unstable souls beguiled" and corrupted from their simplicity.[2] Errors—never solitary—are built upon some partial, insulated, or perverted truth. Excitement of feeling comes in the place of solid practical principle.

But the prudent looketh well to his going. Cautious consideration should mark our general conduct; trying before we trust; never trusting an uncertain profession.[3] Specially in the Church—carefully ponder whom we follow. Sift the most plausible pretensions.[4] Never set up great names against the Divine testimony.[5] Admit only the one standard; like the noble Bereans, who would not believe even an apostle's word, except it was confirmed by the written testimony.[6] Ask wisdom of God. Carefully regulate the energy of religion by the Divine rule. Enlist feelings on the side and under the direction of sound judgment. This *prudent carefulness* will exhibit a well-ordered Christian profession.

16. *A wise man feareth, and departeth from evil: but the fool rageth, and is confident.*

Fear is sometimes thought to be an unmanly principle. But look at the terrible extent of *the evil* dreaded. Without—it is vanity and disappointment.[7] Within—it is the sting of guilt.[8] Upward—we see the frown of God.[9] Downward—everlasting burnings.[10] Surely then, *to depart from this evil*[11]—yea—to *fear it* worse than death[12]—is true *wisdom.*

The fool however—stout and stubborn in his mind—never *fears* till he falls. The voice of God is unheard amid the uproar of passion, like a raving tempest. Bravely independent, he sits amid the threatenings of God, as unalarmed, as Solomon amid his brazen lions; 'carried by his rash will, and blind passion, without apprehending the end and issue of things.'[13] His character is here drawn to life. *He rageth and is confident.* Such *a fool* was Rehoboam, when his self-willed confidence rejected the counsel of wisdom and experience.[14] Such *a fool was the raging* Assyrian, blindly *confident* in his own might, till the God whom he despised, turned him back to his destruction. And will not the child of God bless his Father's painful discipline, so needful to curb his *raging* will, and bring down his high *confidence*?[15] "Thou hast chastised me, and

[1] Heb. xiii. 9. Comp. Eph. iv. 14. 2 Tim. iii. 7.
[2] 2 Pet. ii. 14. 2 Cor. xi. 3.
[3] 1 Sam. xxii. 22. Neh. vi. 2—4. John ii. 24.
[4] 1 Thess. v. 21. 1 John iv. 1.
[5] Isa. viii. 20.
[6] Acts xvii. 11.
[7] Rom. vi. 21.
[8] Chap. xiii. 15. 1 Cor. xv. 56.
[9] John iii. 36.
[10] Psalm ix. 17. Mark ix. 44.
[11] Gen. xxxix. 9, 10.
[12] Dan. iii. 16—18; vi. 10. Comp. Luke xii. 4, 5
[13] Diodati, 2 Chron. xxv. 15—22.
[14] 1 Kings xii. 13—15.
[15] 2 Kings xix. 28—3[illegible]

I was chastised, as a bullock unaccustomed to the yoke: turn thou me, and I shall be turned; for thou art the Lord my God."[1]

17. *He that is soon angry dealeth foolishly: and a man of wicked devises is hated.*

Different gradations of sin are here opposed to each other—the sudden passion, and the deliberate purpose—the gust, and the continuance of the storm. An hasty temper convicts us of *foolishness* before our fellow-men.[2] What frightful mischief may be the consequence of an *angry* word![3] How fearful did the "man after God's own heart" suffer the fire to burst out.[4] Who then—with this example before us—will dare to let down the watch? But are these sins of temper matters of sorrow and humiliation? Does the remembrance of their cost to our crucified Friend exercise our constant watchfulness and prayerful resistance? Is not the rod of our loving Father sometimes needful to bring conviction of their guilty *foolishness*?[5] Oh! for a rich vouchsafement of that "charity, that is not easily provoked!"[6] 'Let us give our hearts no rest, until we have purged their gall, and tempered and seasoned them with the sweetness and gentleness of our Lord and Saviour.'[7]

But sin grows from weakness to wilfulness. 'The first makes a man contemptible—the second—abominable.'[8] *Wicked devices:*[9] cherished malice;[10] one act preparing for another; always aiming at the uttermost[11]—all this shows the true picture of man—"*hateful*, and hating one another."[12] Such a man is *hated* of God, as "an abomination."[13] Man holds him up to his righteous scorn.[14] Absalom's pillar—the monument of his name—is to this day the object of universal contempt.[15] The *hatred* of Haman's *wicked devices* is perpetuated from generation to generation.[16] Why are these warnings, if we regard them not? Our dignity is our likeness to God! What shame and degradation must there be in this contrariety to him!

18. *The simple inherit folly: but the prudent are crowned with knowledge.*

The simple and prudent are again[17] contrasted. The child of Adam is born to *folly*.[18] That is his *inheritance*. He "received it by tradition from his fathers"[19]—yea—from his first father.[20] So long as he remains *simple*, he confirms his title. Unlike an earthly *inheritance*, he cannot relinquish it. He holds it in life, and when he "returns naked to the earth, from whence he came,"[21] he still holds it firm in death, and reaps its bitter fruits throughout eterni-

[1] Jer. xxxi. 18. [2] 2 Kings v. 11—13.
[3] Judg. xii. 1—6 Jam. iii. 5. [4] 1 Sam. xxv. 21. [5] Num. xx. 10—12.
[6] 1 Cor. xiii. 5. [7] Daille on Col. iii. 8. Comp. Col. iii. 13. [8] Diodati.
[9] Psalm xxxvi. 2—4; lxiv 2—9. Isa. xxxii. 7. Jer. v. 26—29.
[10] Gen. iv. 8; xxvii. 41. 2 Sam xiii. 22—29. [11] 2 Sam. xv. 2—12.
[12] Titus iii. 3. [13] Chap. vi 16—18. [14] Psalm lii. 2—7.
[15] Calmet mentions the habit of passing travellers throwing stones at Absalom's pillar, to show their hatred of a son's rebellion against his father; and that now the accumulation of stones hides the lower part of the monument. This tradition is confirmed by recent travellers.
[16] Esth. iii. 6; ix. 23—28. [17] Verse 15; xii. 16. [18] Job xi. 12.
[19] 1 Pet. i. 18. [20] Gen. v. 3. Psalm li. 5. [21] Job i. 21. 1 Tim. vi. 7.

ty. Here is no injustice—no just cause of complaint. Sinner! is not wisdom freely offered to thee in asking for it?[1] Dost not thou therefore continue *simple* only by thy wilful neglect? If knowledge is at hand, to be satisfied with ignorance, is to throw away a talent of inestimable price. 'I confess'—says Doctor South—'God has no need of any man's learning; but certainly then he has much less need of his ignorance.'[2] *The prudent*—instructed in heavenly *knowledge*—are enabled to behold Divine objects in a Divine light. Is not this *knowledge* therefore their *crown*—not of laurel—not of perishing gold—but beautifying the man with all the light, holiness, joy, and glory of life eternal? This is not a religion of eccentric singularities—obscuring the glory of the Divine image. Steady consistency is stamped upon it, such as enthrones its possessor in the conviction and regard even of those, who are unfriendly to his principles.[3] Thus "the wise" in this life, "inherit glory."[4] What shall be their glory in eternity—sitting on the throne of God —crowned with the hand of God himself!

19. *The evil bow before the good; and the wicked at the gates of the righteous.*

This is not the general rule of the present dispensation. *Righteous* Lazarus *bowed at the wicked man's gate.*[5] Thus faith is tried,[6] and the foundation of our heavenly hopes more deeply grounded.[7] And yet often has the very letter of the proverb been verified. The Egyptians and Joseph's brethren *bowed before Joseph;*[8] the proud Pharaoh and his people before Moses;[9] Saul to David;[10] Jehoram and Naaman before Elisha;[11] Haman before Esther;[12] the magistrates before the Apostles.[13] More often still is the spirit of this proverb illustrated in the constrained testimony of *the wicked* to the pre-eminence of *the righteous.*[14] The millennial era will exhibit a more glorious fulfilment.[15] The grand consummation will set all things right, and shed a Divine splendor over this profound aphorism. "The upright shall have dominion over the wicked in the morning.[16] "The saints shall judge the world."[17] They shall then appear in their suitable rank, exalted with their glorious Head over the whole creation.[18] Oh! let the sunshine of this glory irradiate every clouded morn. If this be not enough to counterbalance the scorn of the ungodly, where is our faith? Had we a clear apprehension of this glory, should we have an eye for any thing else? Would not all besides—except as it had a reference to this day—be an utter impertinence?

20. *The poor is hated even of his own neighbor: but the rich hath many friends.*

1 James i. 5.
2 Sermon on 1 Kings xiii. 33, 34. Vol. 1.
3 1 Pet. ii. 12; iii. 16.
4 Chap. iii. 35.
5 Luke xvi. 19—21.
6 Psalm lxxiii. 12—17.
7 2 Cor. iv. 17, 18. Heb. x. 32—34; xiii. 13, 14.
8 Gen. xli. 43; xlii. 6.
9 Ex. viii. 8; ix. 27, 28; xi. 8.
10 1 Sam. xxiv. 7—21; xxvi. 21.
11 2 Kings iii. 12; v. 9.
12 Esth. vii. 7.
13 Acts xvi. 37—39.
14 Chap. xvi. 7. Rev. iii. 8, 9.
15 Isa. xlv. 14; xlix. 23; lx. 14. Dan. vii. 22. Rev. xx. 4.
16 Psalm xlix. 14. Comp. Mal. iv. 1—3, also Wisd. v. 1—5.
17 1 Cor. vi. 2.
18 Rev. ii. 26—28; iii. 21.

An humbling—but how common an illustration of native selfishness! Sometimes however we hear of cheering exceptions. "Ruth clave to Naomi" in her poverty;[1] Jonathan to David, when stripped of royal favor.[2] But too generally *the poor*—instead of being pitied and comforted[3]—is *hated* or neglected[4] *of his own neighbor.*[5] Yet *the rich* is not in a more enviable condition. He has *many friends* indeed to his money and favor, but few to his interest. Many would be the deserters, should a change of circumstance cut off the supplies for their appetites, pleasures, or covetousness.[6] But Jesus—how endearing is his love! He was emphatically the Friend of the poor.[7] He sought *his many friends*, among the wretched and forlorn;[8] and still does his powerful compassion plead for those *hated* ones among their fellow-sinners![9] Shall not we then, like the tried saint of old, look off from earthly destitution in a cleaving confidence in Him as the Rock of our salvation?[10] The practical exercise of this confidence will be a vigorous and successful conflict against our selfish propensity; cultivating that tenderness, which—instead of shrinking from the sight of misery—hastens, though at the expense of personal sacrifice, to its sympathizing relief.[11]

21. *He that despiseth his neighbor sinneth: but he that hath mercy on the poor, happy is he.*

The last proverb shewed the general standard of selfishness. Here we see its positive sinfulness.[12] Some men are so high, that they cannot see their lower brother. Yet infinitely precious and honored may be this *despised* one, in the Saviour's eyes, as the purchase of his blood. And what a span is the distance between him and his most elevated fellow-creature, compared with the infinite space between him and his God! Yet doth he "that dwelleth on high"—instead of *despising*—write his name upon him, "raise him from the dust, and lift him out of the dunghill, that he may set him with the princes of his people."[13] The plain command is—"Honor all men"[14]—not all with equal measure. But in all, honor our own nature—the remains—however defaced—of the image of God. To look therefore upon the meanest, as if he were made to be *despised*—to neglect to *have mercy on him*[15]—this is reflecting on God's own Providence;[16] overlooking his example; setting up our own judgment against his; *sinning* against his law of love.[17] And most fearfully will this sin be visited at the day of recompence.[18]

1 Ruth i. 14, 21, 22.
2 1 Sam. xix. 1—7; xxiii. 16
3 Job vi. 14. Isa. lviii. 7
4 Comp. Gen. xxix. 31.
5 Chap. x. 15; xix. 4, 7. Luke xvi. 20, 21.
Nil habet infelix paupertas durius in se,
Quàm quod ridiculos homines facit.—Juvenal.
6 Chap. xix. 4, 6. Job xxx. 1—14.
7 Psalm lxxi. 12, 14.
8 Matt. iv. 18—22; ix. 10, 11.
9 Psalm cix. 31.
10 Job xix. 13—27.
11 Luke x. 33—35.
12 Chap. xi. 12.
13 Ps. cxiii. 7, 8.
14 1 Pet. ii. 17.
15 Chap. xxi. 13. Jam. ii. 13—16. Luke x. 31, 32.
16 Verse 31; xvii. 5.
17 James ii. 1—9.
18 Job xxxi. 13—15. Matt. xxv. 42—45.

But oh! the felicities of him *that hath mercy on the* poor;[1] "hoping for nothing again,'[2] constrained by love to Christ and his fellow-sinners! 'He shall be happy beyond expression.'[3] Does not every exercise of love enlarge our own happiness?[4] Do we not ourselves richly feed on the bread with which we "feed the hungry?"[5] And will not the great day declare and honor every act of love for our Divine Master?[6]

22. *Do they not err that devise evil? but mercy and truth shall be to them that devise good.*

Scripture traces actions to principles. Wicked as it is to *do evil*, it is far more hateful to *devise it*.[7] *Devising* is the incipient working of the principle. *Devising evil* therefore—if it comes not to the act—shows the purpose.[8] They may be men of consummate wisdom in other matters; but here at least *do they not err?* They miss either their object, or their anticipated happiness from it. Witness the shame of the Babel-builders;[9] the confusion of Haman's *device*;[10] the overruling of the wicked plot against our beloved Lord.[11] How did the *devisers* thwart their own purpose to their fearful cost! How little did Judas estimate the result of his *devising of evil*—"a little matter kindling an unquenchable fire!"[12]

Children of God! Do you exhibit the same diligence and determination in *devising good?* Even if your fruit be frustrated, your work will be accepted.[13] *Mercy and truth* are the reward of grace—often set out as the cheering encouragement to practical godliness. What can be more glowing than the glorious perfections of Jehovah pouring into the soul the quickening energy of Divine blessing—*mercy* the fountain-head—*truth* the pledge and fulfilment of unchangeable mercy![14]

23. *In all labor there is profit; but the talk of the lips tendeth only to penury.*

This is not universally true. What *profit is in the labor of sin*,[15] or of ill-timed work? Fruitful also *is the talk of* teaching *lips*.[16] But the contrast is intended between what is solid on the one hand and what is shadowy on the other—between lawful—well-directed *labor*, and empty *talk*. "Bread eaten in the sweat of the face" is the *profit of* bodily *labor*.[17] But the idler is con-

[1] 'Ut qui miseretur inopum, O beatitudines illius!'—Schultens. Scott and Holden also mark the peculiar emphasis of this claim in the repetition of the pronoun. Comp. Psalm xli. 1—3; cxii. 9. Jer. xxii. 16. Dan. iv. 27. Matt. v. 7.
[2] Luke vi. 35. [3] Scott. [4] Chap. xi. 17. [5] Isa. lviii. 7, 8.
[6] Matt. x. 42; xxv. 35—40. Heb. vi. 10. [7] See ver. 17.
[8] Chap. xxiv. 9. [9] Gen. xi. 4—9. [10] Esth. vii. 10.
[11] Psalm ii. 1—4. Matt. xxi. 41—44. Comp. Job v. 12. Psalm ix. 15, 16.
[12] Matt. xxvi. 14—16; xxvii. 3—5, with Jam. i. 14, 15; iii. 5.
[13] 1 Kings viii. 18. Comp. Isa. xxxii. 8.
[14] Gen. xxiv. 27. 2 Sam. xv. 20. Psalm xxv. 10; lxi. 7; cxxvii. 2. Micah vii. 20. 'Note'—says an old expositor—'that Solomon here is no lawgiver, but an evangelist, leading us unto Jesus Christ. For we can obtain no mercy but in him only. For "the promises of God are yea and amen in him."—Cope in loco.
[15] Rom. vi. 21, [16] Chap. x. 20, 21; xv. 2—7. [17] Gen. iii. 19.

demned *to penury* upon *the talk of his lips.*[1] Enlargement of mind is also *the profit of mental labor.*[2] But "the prating fool"[3] 'cuts himself off from all advantage, except that of being entertained by his own talk; his business in coming into company not being at all to be informed, to hear, to listen, but to display himself, and to talk without any design at all.'[4] Clearly therefore, *the talk of his lips tendeth only to penury.* Rich beyond conception is *the profit of spiritual labor.*[5] The Son of man gives to *the laborer* enduring meat. The violent take the kingdom of heaven by force. "The *labor* of love God is not unrighteous to forget."[6] *But the talk of the lips* gives husks, not bread. It is 'all running out in noise.'[7] There is no instruction, because there is no "good treasure" within.[8] "What manner of communications are these that ye have one to another?"[9]—is a searching question. Ministers, doctrines, the externals, circumstantials, disputations of religion—all may be the mere skirts and borders of the great subject,[10] utterly remote from the heart and vitals. And indeed, the discussion of the substance of religion, without reverence, without a sense of the Divine presence, and a single eye to edification, will but alienate the precious truths from their true purpose. It will only be the deluding indulgence of a refined lust, *tending only to penury.* Mere religious talk is a waste of time, and an injury to the soul. Take care that religious conversation deserves the name. Let the stamp of the profession of the saints of God be visible.[10] Let the burning theme of the Saviour's love flow from the heart.[11] Let the beloved "name" be upon our lips "as ointment poured forth," so that "the whole house"—all that are living with us—"may be filled with the odor of the ointment."[12]

24. *The crown of the wise is their riches: but the foolishness of fools is folly.*

The godly first are made *wise* and honorable by being "crowned with knowledge."[13] Then *the crown of the wise are their riches.* For though as a fearful temptation,[14] no *wise* man would desire them; yet as the gift of God[15] (an inferior gift indeed—the gift of his left hand)[16] they may become his *crown.* They enhance his reputation, and enlarge his usefulness as a consecrated talent for God. What *a crown* were they to David and his wise Son, as the materials for building the temple;[17] and to Job, as employed for the good of his fellow-creatures![18] So that though wisdom "under all circumstances is a blessing, it is especially pronounced to be "good *with an inheritance.*"[19]

But if *riches are the crown of the wise,* they cannot disguise

[1] Chap. xx. 3; xxi. 25. 2 Thess. iii. 10—12. [2] Ecc. xii. 9, 10.
[3] Chap. x. 8, 10. [4] Bishop Butler's Sermon on the Government of the Tongue
[5] Chap. x. 16. [6] John vi. 27. Matt. vi. 12. Heb. vi. 10.
[7] Henry. 1 Tim. v. 13. See Bunyan's graphical portrait of Talkative.
[8] Matt. xii. 34. [9] Luke xxiv. 17. [10] Psalm cxlv. 10—12.
[11] Luke xxiv. 14—32. [12] Can. i. 3, with John xii. 3. [13] Verse 18.
[14] Matt. xiii. 22; xix. 22—24. 1 Tim. vi. 9, 10. [15] 1 Kings iii. 13. Psalm cxii. 3.
[16] Chap. iii. 16. [17] 1 Chron. xxix. 1—5. 2 Chron. v. 1.
[18] Job xxix. 6—17. Comp. Psalm cxii. 9. [19] Ecc. vii. 11, 12.

fools. They only serve to make their *folly* more conspicuous. Wasted on their selfish gratifications, they become—not their *crown* —but their *foolishness*.[1] The *foolish* son of this wise father with all his riches, only exposed his folly more egregiously, and lost ten precious jewels from his royal crown.[2] Whatever be our talents, let them be traded with for eternity, and they will be our everlasting *crown*.[3]

25. *A true witness delivereth souls: but a deceitful witness speaketh lies.*

How weighty is the responsibility of testimony.[4] Every Christian has in him a principle of conscientious faithfulness. As *a true witness he would deliver* the innocent from oppression or ruin. But an ungodly man would prove *a deceitful witness*, the agent of Satan,[5] *speaking lies* for his neighbor's destruction.[6] What need have we to "walk before God" in our words, ready to hazard all for the interests of truth;[7] considering our obligations to one another;[8] realizing our solemn appearing before the God of truth, when "by our words we shall be justified and condemned!"[9] If the responsibility be so great to the *witness* in court, how much more to the *witness* in the pulpit![10] Oh! Is the Minister of God *a true witness*, by the declaration of his message, assured, that no other truth—no adulteration of his truth—will *deliver souls!*[11] Or is *he speaking lies*—holding back or denying truth, to the ruin of *the souls*, whom he was charged to *deliver?*[12] 'As they are the most profitable *witnesses*, which preach to us Jesus Christ; even so, the most exquisite deceivers are they, who under the shadow of religion do set forth men's traditions.'[13]

26. *In the fear of the Lord is strong confidence: and his children shall have a place of refuge.*

"Fear hath torment."[14] It is the trembling of the slave[15]—the dread of wrath, not of sin. There is no *confidence* here. It is pure selfishness. It ends in self. There is no homage to God. But the true *fear of God* is a holy, happy,[16] reverential, principle; not that which "love casts out,"[17] but which love brings in. It is reverence tempered with love. We fear, because we love. We "fear his goodness"[18] no less than his justice; not because we doubt his love, but because we are assured of it.[19] We fear, yet we are not afraid.[20] The holiest and humblest is the most fixed and trusting heart. The fear of man produces faintness.[21] Here is the

[1] 1 Sam. xxv. 36—38. Psalm xlix. 10—13. Luke xii. 19, 20.
[2] 1 Kings xii. 1—20.
[3] Luke xix. 13, with xvi. 9. 1 Tim. vi. 18, 19.
[4] Chap. xxiv. 11, 12.
[5] 1 Kings xxi. 13.
[6] Matt. xxvi. 60. Acts vi. 13. Comp. Chap. xii. 6, 17.
[7] Psalm xv. 2, 4, 5; xxiv. 3—5.
[8] Eph. iv. 25.
[9] Matt. xii. 37.
[10] Lavater and Scott in loco.
[11] 1 Tim. iv. 16.
[12] Jer. v. 31. Ez. xiii. 17—19. Comp. ver. 5.
[13] Cope in loco.
[14] 1 John iv. 18. Acts xxiv. 25.
[15] Rom. viii. 15.
[16] See Psalm cxii. 1. Comp. xxxiii. 18; cxlvii. 11. Isa. lx. 5.
[17] 1 John iv. 18.
[18] Hos. iii. 5. Comp. Psalm cxxx. 4.
[19] Heb. xii. 28. 1 Pet. i. 17, 18.
[20] Psalm cxii. 1, 7.
[21] Chap. xxix. 25. Jon. i. 3. Gal. ii. 12.

Christian paradox—*confidence—strong confidence*—issuing out of *fear*. Abraham sacrificed his son in *the fear of God:* yet fully *confident* "that God was able to raise him up from the dead."[1] *The fear of God* led the Babylonish captives with unshaken *confidence* into the fiery furnace.[2] And thus does the child of God, while walking in godly *fear* rejoice in *confidence*, even in the most frowning dispensation.[3] His covenant privilege covers him,[4] "and that wicked one toucheth him not."[5]

And how happy is the change wrought on our profession! Before—we fled *from God;* now—as *his children*—we "*flee to* him—to hide us."[6] The atonement, which has "made an end of sin;" the righteousness, which has brought in the sunshine of favor; the intercession, which maintains our standing of acceptance—this is our ground of *confidence*—strong as death, stronger than hell.[7] Yes—if heaven and earth shake, God hath ordained and secured, that *his children shall have a place of refuge*, such as they need, and when they need;[8] when the enemy is most strongly assaulting;[9] at the last extremity, when every other *refuge* shall have been swept away.[10] Oh! does not every act of faith strengthen our *confidence*, and realize more sensibly the peaceful security of our *refuge?*[11] But remember—nothing short of a *full* application of the atonement can establish our *confidence*, and deliver us from slavish *fear* and uncertainty.

27. *The fear of the Lord is a fountain of life, to depart from the snares of death.*

How glowing is this Divine principle! refreshing like the springs of Canaan;[12] full of life[13]—temporal[14]—spiritual[15]—eternal.[16] It is the influence of the heavenly Comforter, as a *fountain* "springing up into everlasting life."[17] Its preserving tendency is invaluable. It is always connected with the fear of sin,[18] as grieving our most beloved friend, and separating from our only happiness; though *it keeps us from the snares of death*[19]—"the end and wages of sin."[20] How complete then is its application! Not only is it *a refuge* from danger, but *a fountain of life.* Not only does Christain *confidence* open a cover from the guilt, but its holy influence roots out the power, of sin. For among the countless throng of the redeemed, not one finds a cover from condemnation, who is not renovated unto spiritual life. Thus does this invaluable grace flow with the full streams of gospel blessing. How much of that worldliness that soils our profession, and of the restraint that contracts our spiritual joy—may be traced to the sparing or defective application of this Christian principle!

[1] Gen. xxii. 12, with Heb. xi. 17—19. [2] Dan. iii. 16—18.
[3] Job i. 1, with xiii. 15. Mic. vii. 7—9. Hab. iii. 16—19. [4] Jer. xxxii. 40.
[5] 1 John v. 18. Chap. xix. 23. [6] Gen. iii. 8, with Psalm cxliii. 9.
[7] Rom. viii. 31—39. [8] Psalm xlvi. 1; xlviii. 3. Isa. xxxii. 2.
[9] Psalm lvi. 1—4. Isa. xxv. 4. [10] Isa. xxviii. 16, 17.
[11] Chap. i. 33; xviii. 10. Isa. xxxii. 18, 19. [12] Deut. viii. 7. Jos. xv. 19.
[13] Chap. xxii. 4. [14] Chap. x. 27. [15] Chap. xix. 23. Mal. iv. 2.
[16] Psalm ciii. 17. [17] John iv. 14. [18] Chap. iii. 7; xvi. 6.
[19] Ecc. vii. 18, 26. [20] Rom. vi. 21, 23.

28. *In the multitude of people is the king's honor; but in the want of people is the destruction of the prince.*

The Bible is a book for all. Even *the King* is interested in it, and was commanded to treasure it.[1] It describes him as a curse or a blessing to his people, as he is led by his own caprice,[2] or directed by Divine wisdom.[3] 'He is not appointed for luxury or for pleasure; but that as a Head he may preside over his members; as a Shepherd, he may care for his flock; as a tree, he may nourish those who dwell under his shadow.'[4] *In the multitude of people are his honor.* They are the stay and strength of his kingdom.[5] *In the want of people is his destruction.* His revenue fails. His strength is enfeebled. His enemies take advantage of his weakness.[6] His interests and his people's are one. In promoting their happiness, *the prince* secures his own *honor.*[7] If he be the father of his numerous family, he will always have "a quiver full of arrows to meet his enemies in the gate."[8] How great then is *the honor of* our heavenly *King in the countless multitude of his people!* How overwhelmingly glorious will it appear, when the completed number shall stand before his throne;[9] each the medium of reflecting his glory;[10] each with a crown to cast at his feet,[11] and a song of everlasting joy to tune to his praise![12]

29. *He that is slow to wrath is of great understanding: but he that is hasty* (short, Marg.) *of spirit exalteth folly.*

The world judge very lightly of *a hasty spirit*, except when it touches themselves. 'It is a fit of passion, soon over and forgotten.' But does God judge thus? See how his word stamps the native rooted principle. It is "giving place to the devil;[13] grieving the Holy Spirit;"[14] contrary to the mind and example of Christ;[15] inconsistent with the profession of the Gospel;[16] degrading human nature;[17] a work of the flesh, that shuts out from heaven,[18] and condemns to hell.[19] Surely thus to be *slow to wrath*—such a fruitful source of sin and misery—is a proof of *great understanding.*[20] It is as if we felt our just dignity, and high obligations. *A hasty spirit* is the tinder, which lights into a flame the most trifling matters, such as in cooler moments we should be ashamed of having contended for. This is indeed *exalting folly,* placing it on an eminence, to be seen by all.[21] Yet too often passion serves instead of law and reason, and this *folly* is deemed high-mindedness and proper passion. Oh! it is a mercy to be delivered from

[1] Deut. xvii. 18—20. [2] 1 Kings xii. 13—19. 2 Kings xiii. 1—3.
[3] 2 Chron. ii. 11; ix. 8. [4] Geier in loco.
[5] 1 Kings iv. 20. 2 Chron. xvii. 14—19. Yet this *honor* had well nigh proved *the destruction of the prince* in the chastisement of his pride. 2 Sam. xxiv.
[6] 2 Kings xiii. 4—7. Comp. Jer. xiii. 18—20. [7] Psalm lxxii. 1—10.
[8] Ibid. cxxvii. 4, 5. [9] Rev. vii. 9, 10. [10] 2 Thess. i. 10.
[11] Rev. iv. 10, 11. [12] Ibid. v. 9—13. [13] Eph. iv. 26, 27.
[14] Ibid. verse 30, 31. [15] Matt. xi. 29. Phil. ii. 3—5. 1 Pet. ii. 23.
[16] Col. iii. 8, 12, 13. [17] Chap. xvii. 12; xxv. 28; xxix. 20.
[18] Gal. v. 19—21. [19] Matt. v. 22.
[20] Chap. xix. 11; xx. 3. Jam. iii. 17. [21] Ver. 17; iii. 35.

the standard of this world, and to live, act, and judge by the standard of God and his word.

But let the children of God remember, that an *hasty spirit* condemned the meekest of men.[1] Never was *folly more exalted* than by the selfish fretfulness of a prophet of the Lord.[2] The gentlest spirit needs to be cast into a deep mould of lowliness and love for communion with God.[3] Who can plead inability to resist? Has not God given understanding to show the temper; reason to govern it; his Word and Spirit to crucify it? Realize our obligations to sovereign grace, as the effective discipline for this baneful propensity.[4]

30. *A sound heart is the life of the flesh: but envy is the rottenness of the bones.*

Many will admit religion to be good for the soul. But they conceive its fancied gloom to be injurious to the body. The wise man however teaches, that it is *the life of the flesh;*[5] and surely *a sound heart*, freed from corroding passions, and imbued with Christian habits—though it will not bring immortality—must be eminently conducive to health.[6] The contrast, however, here distinguishes *a sound heart* by the absence of selfishness,[7] and rejoicing in another's happiness or honor.[8] *Envy* is wounded at the prosperity of another, like him who could not see the happiness of Paradise without destroying it.[9] It is indeed the deadliest fruit of selfishness. Nothing flourishes under its shade.[10] Often is it a fretting sickness[11]—a pining despondency;[12] a true figure of the moral disease—one entire mass of corruption, like the destruction of the bodily system by *the rottenness of the bones.* 'Truly'—as Bishop Hall observes—'this vice is executioner enough to itself!'[13] Such a hell does the man carry in his own bosom! Alas! that this plant should be the growth of our own soil.[14] So contrary is it to the mind of Christ,[15] and to the spirit of his gospel.[16] So surely will it exclude from heaven![17]

31. *He that oppresseth the poor reproacheth his Maker: but he that honoreth him hath mercy on the poor.*

Are not *the poor*, no less than the rich, "made in the image of God?"[18] Both "meet together" before their Maker, without respect of persons.[19] Both carry the same undying principle in their bosom. Both sink to the same humiliating level of death. Both rise to the same eminence of immortality. Besides—have not *the poor* a spe-

1 Num. xii. 3; xx. 12. Psalm cvi. 32, 33. 2 Jon. iv.
3 Isa. lvii. 15. 1 John iv. 16. 4 Jam. i. 18, 19.
5 Chap. iii. 7, 8; xv. 13; xvii. 22.
6 'The soul disburdened of passions and perturbations, helpeth strength and liveliness of body very much.'—Diodati.
7 Cor sanator, Schultens—a benevolent heart. 8 Num. xi. 27—29.
9 Gen. iv. 5; xxvi. 13, 14; xxx. 4. 1 Sam. xviii. 9, 12, 29. Acts vii. 9, with Gen. iii. 1.
10 Jam. iii. 16. 11 1 Kings xxi. 4. Esth. vi. 6, 12. 12 Ps. cxii. 9, 10.
13 Sermon on Rom. xii. 2. Works v. 251. 14 Mark vii. 22, 'evil eye.' Jam. iv. 5.
15 Rom. xiii. 13, 14. 16 1 Cor. xiii. 4. 17 Gal. v. 21. Comp. Rom. i. 29.
18 Gen. ix. 6. 19 Chap. xxii. 2. Job xxxi. 13—15; xxxiv. 19. Eph. vi. 9.

22

cial interest in the Gospel?[1] Was not the Gospel first spread by the poor?[2] Has not the voluntary poverty of the Son of God for us put high honor upon the lowly condition?[3] Then what ground is there to *oppress the poor*, as if they were of a lower grade than ourselves? This involves the guilt of *reproaching our Maker.*[4] It is despising his own ordinance,[5] and charging him with injustice, as if he had formed *the poor* to be the footstool of *their oppressors.*[6] Would we *honor God?* We must not only refrain from *oppressing;* but we must *have mercy on the poor.* Sure and large is the interest of this *mercy*[7] in the case of the Lord's poor; high indeed is the privilege, and everlasting the recompence, of *honoring* the Saviour in *his* own person.[8]

32. *The wicked is driven away in his wickedness: but the righteous hath hope in his death.*

Eternity is here realized before us—*the wicked and the righteous* each "going to his own place."[9] Let us ponder the sight with deep-toned solemnity—O my soul! "make thy calling sure!" *The wicked is driven away.* He is dragged out of life, like a criminal to execution; torn away from his only heaven here, with no joyous heaven beyond.[10] Dreadful beyond imagination to be thus forced out of the body, to die a violent death. Fain would he stay. But he cannot. He cannot live. He dares not die. Sometimes he departs with a horror that no words can paint. Hell is manifestly begun on this side eternity.[11] But even where he has "no bands in his death, but his strength is firm,"[12]—when do we hear of "a desire to depart?"[13] Though he may fall asleep as softly as a lamb, he will wake to live forever "with the devil and his angels." His few moments of peace are only the respite from hopeless, never-ending torments. *His wickedness* was his element in life. It will cleave to him still—the sting of the undying worm —the fuel of unquenchable fire.

But *the righteous*—is he *driven away?*—He dies by his own consent. It is a glad surrender—not a forcible separation.[14] The tabernacle is not rent or torn away, but "put off."[15] He can take death by his cold hand, and bid him welcome. 'I can smile on death'—said a dying saint—'because my Saviour smiles on me.' There is courage to face the "king of terrors," and delight in looking homeward to his God.[16] There is loveliness and sunshine in his death—such as flashes conviction upon the most hardened conscience.[17] *The righteous hath hope in his death.* His death

[1] Matt. xi. 5. Jam. ii. 1—5. Comp. Ps. lxviii. 10; lxxiv. 19.
[2] Matt. xxviii. 19, 20, with Acts iv. 13.
[3] Luke ii. 7. Phil. ii. 6, 7. 2 Cor. viii. 9. Matt. viii. 20.
[4] Ver. 31. Chap. xvii. 5. [5] Deut. xv. 11. Matt. xxvi. 11.
[6] 1 Sam. ii. 7. [7] Chap. xix. 17. Ps. xli. 1—3. [8] Matt. xxv. 35—40.
[9] Acts i. 25. [10] Job xviii. 18; xxvii. 20, 21. Luke xii. 19, 20.
[11] 1 Sam. xxviii. 15—20. Matt. xxvii. 3—5. [12] Ps. lxxiii. 4.
[13] Contrast Phil. i. 23. [14] Psalm xxxi. 5. Acts vii. 59. [15] 2 Peter i. 14.
[16] 2 Cor. v. 8. *Θαρρουμεν*—undaunted boldness. *Ευδοκουμεν*—we are well pleased Comp. Matt. iii. 17. [17] Num. xxiii. 10.

is full of *hope*. Job pierced his dark cloud of sorrow with this joyous *hope*.[1] David rested his way-worn spirit upon the Rock of salvation.[2] Stephen anchored within the veil, undisturbed by the volley of stones without.[3] Paul triumphed in the crown, as if it was already on his head.[4] And hear we not daily "the voice from heaven," assuring to us the "blessedness of them that die in the Lord?"[5] Praise to our Immanuel! 'When thou didst overcome the sharpness of death, thou didst open the kingdom of heaven unto all believers.'[6] By thee as the way to the Kingdom we go freely, gladly, out of life. We go to what we love—to our native home—to our Saviour's bosom—to our rest—our crown—our home—our everlasting joy. "Now, Lord, what wait I for!—I have waited for thy Salvation, O Lord."[7]

33. *Wisdom resteth in the heart of him that hath understanding: but that which is in the midst of fools is made known.*

Often does the wise man show the blessing of *wisdom* on the lips.[8] Here we trace it to its home. It flows from the head, and *rests in the heart*. Thus did *it rest* without measure in the humanity of Jesus,[9] and most glorious was its manifestation;[10] and when it *rests in our hearts*, incalculable is its value, as a fixed principle. It preserves us from the tossing of "divers and strange doctrines," and gives us "the good thing of a heart established with grace"[11]—We see now the vital difference between speculation and experience; between the convictions of the judgment and the movement of the will.

Widely does it differ from mere worldly disputation. This—as Bishop Taylor observes—'covers no vices, but kindles a great many. Though men esteem it learning, it is the most useless learning in the world.'[12] True *wisdom*, while it fixes its *rest*, sets up its throne, *in the heart*. All is therefore Christian order and holiness.

But there is another fountain always bubbling up.[13] *The fool's*

1 Job xix. 25—27. 2 2 Sam. xxiii. 5.
3 Acts vii. 55—60, with Heb. vi. 19, 20. 4 2 Thess. iv. 6—8. 2 Cor. v. 1.
5 Rev. xiv. 13. 6 Te Deum.
7 Psalm xxxix. 7. Gen. xlix. 18. Does not this text clearly prove that, while "life and immortality were *brought to light* by the gospel," (2 Tim. i. 10,) the dawn of the day beamed upon the Old Testament saints. What could *this hope of the righteous* be, but the consummating prospect of the Gospel? Bishop Warburton (Div. Leg. B. vi. §. 3.) expounds, 'that they shall be delivered *from* the most imminent danger.' That sagacious mind could never have confounded two things so essentially distinct—as hope in death, and hope of escape from death, had it not been necessary to subserve a favorite hypothesis. Equally satisfactory and beautiful is the note of a learned German critic—'A splendid testimony of the knowledge of the Old Testament believers in a future life! The wicked in this calamity is agitated with the greatest terror. He knows not where to turn. But the godly in this last evil has no fear. He knows to whom to flee, and where he is going.'—Dathe in loco. Again—'He (the righteous) dieth in God's grace, and in an assured confidence of the salvation of his soul, and of the glorious resurrection of his body.'—Diodati.
8 Chap. x. 11, 20, 21; xv. 2, 7; xvi. 21, 23. 9 Isa. xi. 2. John iii. 34.
10 Luke ii. 46, 47, 52; iv. 22. Matt. xxii. 15—46. John vii. 46. 11 Heb. xiii. 9
12 Via Intelligentiæ—preached before the University of Dublin.
13 Chap. xv. 2, 28; xxix. 11.

multitude of words,[1] selfish indulgence,[2] uncontrolled passions, *make manifest what is in the midst of him.*[4] Let him stand out as a warning beacon against display. Self-conceit is self-ignorance —Never—never let our prayers cease, until He, who is "The wisdom of God,"[5] takes his *rest in our hearts.*—Have we received the precious gift? Then, let us realize our need of more; and seek the increase by a close union with him and an entire dependence upon him.[6]

34. *Righteousness exalteth a nation: but sin is a reproach to any people.*

If it be not beneath statesmen to take lessons from the Bible, let this sound political maxim—the rule of God's national dispensation —be deeply pondered. The annals of the chosen people—as they were a *righteous or sinful nation*—are marked by corresponding *exaltation*[7] *or reproach.*[8] Not the wisdom of policy, extent of empire, splendid conquests, flourishing trade, abundant resources—but *righteousness—exalteth a nation.*[9] Greece in her proud science —Rome in the zenith of her glory—both were sunk in the lowest depths of moral degradation.[10] Their true greatness existed only in the visions of poesy, or the dreams of philosophy. Contrast the influence of *righteousness*, bringing out of the most debased barbarism a community impregnated with all the high principles that form a nation's well-being.[11] Thus to Christianize, is to regenerate, the community—to elevate it to a more dignified position—to *exalt the nation.*[12] *But sin is a reproach to any people.* No nation is so low as not to sink lower under it; while, to the mightiest people, it is a blot in their escutcheon, that no worldly glory can efface. What an enemy is an ungodly man to his country!—Loudly as he may talk of his patriotism, and even though God should make him an instrument of advancing her temporal interest: yet he contributes—so far as in him lies—to her deepest *reproach.*

Beloved Britain! nation highest in the profession of *righteousness!* For thee we "rejoice with trembling." The combined effort of a little band, to promote the honor of the Sabbath;[13] to resist the encroachments of Popery; to enlarge the usefulness and efficiency of thy Church; to circulate the word and preaching of

[1] Eccl. v. 3; x. 14. [2] 1 Sam. xxv. 10, 11, 17.
[3] Ibid. xx. 30—34. 1 Kings xix. 1, 2. Comp. ver. 16; xii. 16.
[4] Chap. x. 9; xii. 23; xiii. 16; xviii. 2. Eccl. x. 3. [5] 1 Cor. i. 24.
[6] Ibid. ver. 30.
[7] Deut. xxviii. 13. Jos. x. 42. 1 Kings iv. 20—24. 2 Chron. xvii. 11, 12; xxxii. 22, 23.
[8] Deut. xxviii. 43, 44. Judg. ii. 7—15. 2 Kings x. 31, 32; xviii. 11, 12. 2 Chron. xv. 26; xxxvi. 11—17. Jer. vii. 29. See the names of *reproach* given by God himself. Isa. i. 10; lvii. 3. Hos. i. 6—9. Zeph. ii. 1.
[9] A Heathen sage admitted this truth—speaking of moral righteousness—*ερμα πολεως* —the pillar and support of the city.—Plato De Legibus, Book vi.
[10] Rom. i. 29—32, was a picture of the Heathen world in the best ages of refinement.
[11] The Missionary Records of New Zealand and the South Sea furnish ample proof of this statement.
[12] Comp. Deut. xxvi. 16—19.
[13] See how heavily the honor of the Sabbath weighs in the scale of national dispensation. Neh. xiii. 15—18. Isa. lviii. 13, 14. Jer. xvii. 24—28. Ez. xx. 15—24.

the gospel to the ends of the earth—this is thy *national exaltation.* But the evil example among the Heathen,[1] the accredited influence of Romish heresy;[2] the flood of infidelity, lawlessness, and ungodliness; the want of a full recognition of God in thy public acts—this is thy *reproach.* Let the little remnant in the midst of thee remember their high responsibility.[3] Let them take care that their personal and relative profession, add to the *righteousness*—not to the *sin* of the *nation.* Let them plead for their country's true prosperity with humiliation, faith, and constancy.[4] Let them labor for her *exaltation* with more entire union of heart.

35. *The king's favor is towards a wise servant; but his wrath is against him that causeth shame.*

The administration of *the wise servant* is often the working cause of *national exaltation.*[5] *The king's favor towards him*[6] is therefore the rule of sound policy. Not less so *is his wrath against him that causeth shame*[7] to the office which he beareth, and to the Prince's choice.'[8]

Thus is it with the great King. All of us are his *servants,* bound to him by the highest obligations;[9] animated by the most glowing encouragements.[10] All of us have our responsibilities, our talents, our work, our account. Towards "the faithful and *wise servant,*" who has traded with his talents, who has been diligent in his work, and who is ready for his account—*his favor* will be infinitely condescending and honorable.[11] *But against him that causeth shame*—reflecting upon his Master, neglectful of his work, and unprepared for his account—*his wrath* will be tremendous and eternal.[12] What will the solemn day of reckoning bring to me? May I—may we all—be found *wise servants* to the best of *Kings!* looking with confidence for his welcome!

CHAPTER XV.

1. *A soft answer turneth away wrath: but grievous words stir up anger.*

WHAT a mine of practical wisdom is this Book of God! Let

[1] Ez. xxxvi. 20—23. Rom. ii. 23. 'What a God must he be'—said a poor Indian of the Spaniards—'who has such bloody men for his servants and children!'

[2] What must be the national guilt connected with the annual dedication of upwards of £100,000 of our Revenue (including the ungodly grant to Maynooth) to the support of Popery! Who that receives implicitly the Scripture testimony, Rev. xviii. 4, must not tremble at the consequence of our nation madly *going into Babylon,* instead of *coming out of her?* The admission of Jews to legislate for a Christian land has added another reproach on our national profession.

[3] Isa. i. 9. Matt. v. 13.

[4] What a pattern does Dan. ix. furnish for this exercise of Christian Patriotism!

[5] 2 Chron. xxiv. 1—16.

[6] Gen. xli. 38—40. Dan. vi. 1—3. Comp. Chap. xvi. 13; xxii. 29.

[7] Esth. vii. 6—10.

[8] Diodati.

[9] Psalm cxvi. 16. 1 Cor. vi. 19, 20; vii. 23.

[10] Matt. xxv. 21, 23; xxiv. 41—46.

[11] Luke vii. 36, 37. John xii. 26.

[12] Matt. xxiv. 48—51; xxv. 24—30.

us ponder this valuable rule for self-discipline, family peace, and Church unity. Scripture often illustrates the different effects of the tongue. *The soft answer* is the water to quench[1]—*Grievous words* are the oil to *stir up*, the fire.[2] And this is, alas! man's natural propensity—to feed rather than to quench the *angry* flame. We yield to irritation; retort upon our neighbor; have recourse to self-justification; insist upon the last word; say all that we could say; and think we "do well to be angry."[3] Neither party gives up an atom of the will. Pride and passion on both sides strike together like two flints; and "behold! how great a matter a little fire kindleth!"[4] Thus there is the self-pleasing sarcasm; as if we had rather lose a friend, than miss a clever stroke. All this the world excuses as a sensitive and lively temper. But the gospel sets before us our Saviour's example;[5] imbues with his spirit;[6] and imparts that blessed "charity, that is not easily provoked;"[7] and therefore is careful not to provoke a chafed or wounded spirit. If others begin, let us forbear from continuing, the strife.[8] *Soft* and healing words[9] gain a double victory—over ourselves,[10] and over our brother.[11]

2. *The tongue of the wise useth knowledge aright: but the mouth of fools poureth forth foolishness.*

Before we had the tongue of *love.* Here is *the tongue of wisdom.* The tongue shews the man. *The wise* commands *his tongue. The fool*—his tongue commands him. He may have a mass of *knowledge* in possession. But from the want of the *right use* it runs to waste. Wisdom is proved, not by the quantum of *knowledge*, but by its *right* application. Observe our Divine Master with "the spirit of *knowledge* resting upon him."[12] In condescending to the ignorance of the people;[13] in commanding their respect;[14] in silencing the gainsayers;[15] in alluring sinners to himself[16]—how did this *wise tongue use knowledge aright!* Thus did his great Apostle give to all the same *knowledge*, but wisely—not the same form or gradation.[17] Instead of exasperating his Heathen congregation by an open protest, he supplied their acknowledged defect, by bringing before them the true God, "whom they were ignorantly worshipping."[18] He pointed an arrow to Agrippa's conscience, by the kindly admission of his candor and

[1] See Jacob with Esau, Gen. xxxii. xxxiii: Aaron with Moses, Lev. x. 16—20: the Reubenites with their brethren, Jos. xxii. 15—34: Gideon with the men of Ephraim, Judg. viii. 1—3: David with Saul, 1 Sam. xxiv. 9—21: xxvi. 21, Abigail with David, xxv. 23—32.

[2] See the instances of Jepthah, Judg. xii. 1—6: Saul, 1 Sam. xx. 30—34: Nabal, xxv. 10—13: Rehoboam, 1 Kings xii. 12—15: the Apostles, Acts xv. 39.

[3] Jon. iv. 9. [4] Jam. iii. 5. [5] 1 Pet. ii. 23.

[6] 2 Cor. iii. 18. Phil. ii. 3—5. [7] 1 Cor. xiii. 5.

[8] Chap. xvii. 14. Even a Heathen could give this excellent advice—'Let dissension begin from others, but reconciliation from thee.'—Seneca.

[9] Chap. xxv. 15. Comp. James iii. 17, 18. [10] Chap. xvi. 32.

[11] Rom. xii. 19—21. [12] Isa. xi. 2. [13] Mark iv. 33.

[14] Matt. vii. 29. John vii. 46. [15] Matt. xxii. 15—46.

[16] Ibid. xi. 28—30, with Isa. l. 4. [17] 1 Cor. ii. 2; iii. 2. [18] Acts xvii. 22, 23,

intelligence.[1] This *right use of knowledge* distinguishes the "workman approved of God, and that needeth not to be ashamed."[2] The want of it often gives out truth so loosely and unsuitably, as to open rather than to shut the mouth of the gainsayer; rather to bring discredit upon the truth, than conviction to the adversary. Specially will *the tongue of the wise* direct a *right* application of *knowledge* to those, who have newly entered the path of God. May we not sometimes, in our present stature, forget our own feeble infancy; and that, if now we "strike our roots as Lebanon,"[3] time was, when it was with us only, "the least of all seeds?" Let our considerate instruction pluck the thorn out of their tender feet, "lest that which is lamed be turned out of the way; but rather let it be healed."[4]

But judge what must be the waters flowing from such a *fool's* fountain.[5] Listen to Baal's worshippers;[6] Rabshakeh's proud boasting:[7] the fretting murmurings of the people of God[8]—all *pouring out foolishness.* Oh! for a large infusion of sound *knowledge* in the treasure-house within, that the tongue may be at once disciplined and consecrated!

3. *The eyes of the Lord are in every place, beholding the evil and the good.*

Adored be this All-seeing God![9] His inspection of the universe, so minute, exact, unwearied![10] The first mark of the apostacy was a dread of his presence.[11] The ungodly try to forget it,[12] and often succeed in banishing him out of their thoughts.[13] Yet in despite of all their efforts to hide, he does see them. *His eyes are in every place.* Heaven, hell—the secret places of the earth—are all open before him.[14] He *beholds the evil*—whether the King on his throne,[15] or in his palace;[16] or the servant indulging his secret sin.[17] Yes—he may shut out the sun from his retreat, but he cannot shut out the eye of God, "from whom the darkness hideth not."[18] Reckless indeed is he to do or think what he would hide from God; and then—such is the secret root of atheism![19]—thinking he can do so.[20]

But *his eyes also behold the good.* He sees them in outward destitution,[21] in secret retirement,[22] in deep affliction.[23] He pierces the prison walls.[24] He "covers their heads in the day of battle."[25] He is with them in the furnace,[26] and in the tempest.[27] *His eye*

[1] Ibid. xxvi. 27—29. [2] 2 Tim. ii. 15. [3] Hos. xiv. 5. Matt. xiii. 32.
[4] Heb. xii. 13. [5] Matt. xv. 19. [6] 1 Kings xviii. 26.
[7] 2 Kings xviii. 26—29. [8] Num. xiv. 2—10; xvi. 13.
[9] Psalm cxxxix. 1—6. [10] Jer. xxiii. 23, 24. Ps. xi. 4, 5. [11] Gen. iii. 8; iv. 16
[12] Ps. x. 11; lxxiii. 11; xciv. 5—7. Ez. viii. 12. Hos. vii. 2. [13] Ps. x. 4.
[14] Ver. 11. Ps. cxxxix. 7—10. Amos ix. 2, 3. [15] Acts xii. 21—23.
[16] Dan. iv. 29; v. 5. [17] Chap. v. 20, 21. 2 Kings v. 20.
[18] Job xxiv. 15, 16; xxxiv. 21, 22. Psalm cxxxix. 11, 12. Jer. xvi. 17.
[19] Ps. xiv. 1. [20] Isa. xxix. 15.
[21] Gen. xvi. 7, 13. Ps. xxvii. 10. [22] John i. 48. Acts x. 9—13.
[23] Ex. iii. 7. Psalm xci. 15.
[24] Gen. xxxix. 21. 2 Chron. xxxiii. 12, 13. Acts xii. 7; xvi. 25.
[25] Ps. cxl. 7. [26] Dan. iii. 25 Isa. xliii. 2.
[27] Matt. viii. 23—27. Acts xxvii. 23, 24.

guides them as their journeying God,[1] and will guide them safe home;[2] full of blessing,[3] protection,[4] and support.[5] 'He fills hell with his severity, heaven with his glory, his people with his grace.'[6]

But how shall I meet these *eyes!* As a rebel or as a child? Do they inspire me with terror, or with love? Do I walk carefully under their lively impression?[7] Conscious corruption leads me to shrink from the eyes of man. But Oh! my God! I would lay myself naked and open to thee. Search me; try me; shew me to myself. Bring out my hidden iniquities, and slay them before me.[8] How is the overwhelming thought of this piercing eye more than counterbalanced by the view of the great High Priest, who covers and cleanses all infirmities and defilements, and pleads and maintains my acceptance notwithstanding all discouragement![9]

4. *A wholesome tongue* (the healing of the tongue, Marg.) *is a tree of life: but perverseness therein is a breach in the spirit.*

Wisdom is finely portrayed as *a tree of life:*[10] So is also the genial influence of the righteous[11]—here the fruitfulness of his little member. A high image of what it ought to be—not negative—not harmless, but *wholesome.* As the salt cast into the spring cleansed the bitter waters;[12] so, when there is grace in the heart, there will be *healing in the tongue.*[13] "The speech will be with grace, seasoned with salt."[14] Large indeed is the sphere, and abundant the blessing. When employed in soothing the afflicted, calming the troubled waters with words of peace, it creates a paradise around. It is not like 'the thorny bush, pricking and hurting those that are about us, but a fruitful tree—*a tree of life.*'[15]

But if the gracious *tongue be healing,* the evil tongue is wounding. The meekest of men felt its *perverseness* a *breach in the spirit.*[16] The tongue of Job's friends broke "the bruised reed," which needed to be bound up.[17] Even our beloved Lord, who never shrunk from external evil, keenly felt the piercing edge of this sword in his inmost soul.[18] May it be with me, as with my Divine Master, that "grace may be poured upon my lips,"[19] so that it may be *a wholesome tongue,* full of blessing and of good fruits!

5. *A fool despiseth his father's instruction, but he that regardeth reproof is prudent.*

Alas! We cannot wonder at this *folly.* Remember the birth of the fool—"as a wild ass's colt,"[20] *despising* discipline and restraint. Yet subjection to parents is the law of nature, recognized by the most uncivilized nations. Much more is it the law of God.[21]

[1] Psalm xxxii. 8. Gen. xxviii. 15.
[2] Psalm xxiii. 4; xlviii. 14. Isa. xlii. 16. [3] Gen. xxvi. 3.
[4] 2 Chron. xvi. 9. Ps. xxxiii. 18, 19; xxxiv. 15. 1 Pet. iii. 12.
[5] Isa. xli. 10, 14. [6] Charnock. [7] Gen. xvii. 1.
[8] Psalm cxxxix. 23, 24. [9] Heb. iv. 13, 14. [10] Chap. iii. 18.
[11] Chap. xi. 30. [12] 2 Kings ii. 21, 22. [13] Chap. xii. 18.
[14] Col. iv. 6. [15] Leighton's Exposition of the Sixth Commandment. Vol. iv.
[16] Num. xvi. 1—14, with xii. 5. [17] Job xiii. 1—5. [18] Psalm lxix. 9, 19, 20.
[19] Ibid. xlv. 2. [20] Job xi. 12.
[21] Ex. xx. 12. Eph. vi. 1, 2. Comp. Deut. xxi. 18—21.

The authority of parents is the authority of God.[1] The wayward resistance of the ungodly will be fearfully scourged.[2] And even the Christian penitent has felt the smart of the rod to the end of life.[3] If example would put this *folly* to shame, do we not read of One child able to teach—yea to command—his parents, who yet exhibited the lovely pattern of filial subjection?[4] But pride must be broken down, and the "clothing of humility worn,"[5] before the child will see that his parents know better than himself; and that to count their word law—to "bear the yoke in the youth,"[6] and to *regard* counsel, and even *reproof*—as it is the path of honor[7]—so it is the path of *prudence*.[8] Solomon's wisdom, though the special gift of God, was doubtless connected with this filial *regard* to his wise *father's instruction*.[9] Will those, who *despise their* earthly *father's instruction*, be ready to listen to their heavenly father? How surely therefore will this untractable spirit exclude from the *Kingdom* of God![10]

6. *In the house of the righteous is much treasure: but in the revenues of the wicked is trouble.*

The comparison between *the righteous and the wicked* always turns in favor of *the righteous*.[11] Even in *treasure*[12]—the world's idol, he exceeds. For though *his house* may be destitute of money, yet is there *much treasure;* often unseen,[13] yet such that *the revenues of the wicked*, compared with it, sink into nothing. 'Drop millions of gold, boundless *revenues*, ample territories, crowns and sceptres; and a poor contemptible worm lays his One God against all of them.'[14] The treasures of the wicked are too much for their good, and too little for their lust. They cannot satisfy their senses—much less their souls.[15] They may "take wings"[16] at any moment; and while they continue,—unlike *the treasures of the righteous*[17]—they are burdened with *trouble*.[18] But is it not the crown of the Christian's crown, and the glory of his glory, that his portion is so full, that he cannot desire more? All the excellences of the creation are only dark shadows of its more substantial excellence. What a mercy to be delivered from the idolatrous bait—so ruinous alike to our present peace and eternal welfare![19] But a greater mercy still, to be enriched with that *treasure*—beyond the reach of harm, that raises to heaven, a portion in God—his favor—his image—his everlasting joy.

[1] This was even Aristotle's standard—'Τιμην καθαπερ Θεοις.' Eth. ix. 2. Comp. viii. c. 14. Plato de Leg. Lib. iv.
[2] 1 Sam. ii. 22—25.
[3] See Memoirs of Mrs. Hawkes, p. 524.—A most instructive Biography.
[4] Luke ii. 49—51. 'Quis Quibus? Deus hominibus. Who was subject? And to whom? God to men.' Bernard, Homil. i.
[5] 1 Pet. v. 5. [6] Lam. iii. 27. [7] Chap. xiii. 18.
[8] Verses 31, 32; xix. 20. [9] 1 Chron. xxii. 11—13; xxix. 9, 20.
[10] Matt. xviii. 3, 4. [11] Chap. iii. 33; xiv. 11, 32. [12] Verses 16, 17; viii. 21.
[13] 2 Cor. vi. 10.
[14] Bishop Hopkins' Works, i 43. Treatise on Vanity of the World.
[15] Ecc. v. 10, 11. [16] Chap. xxiii. 5. [17] Chap. x. 22.
[18] Ecc. iv. 6; v. 12—14. Jam. v. 1—4. [19] 1 Tim. vi. 9, 10.

7. *The lips of the wise disperse knowledge: but the heart of the foolish doeth not so.*

The "right use of knowledge" is—first to "lay it up" in a store-house;[1] then out of the store-house to *disperse it.* The sower scatters the seed in the furrow, and calculates upon a proportionate harvest.[2] Thus *the lips of the wise disperse* the precious seed, "giving a portion to seven, and also to eight," not discouraged by trifling difficulties, but "sowing morning and evening," and committing the result to God.[3] The Ministry of our Lord thus *dispersed* the heavenly *knowledge* of his gospel.[4] He commanded his Apostles to scatter the seed through the vast field of the world.[5] The persecution of the Church was overruled for this great end.[6] The Reformers widely *dispersed* their treasures both by preaching and writing; and rich indeed was the fruit. Do we remember—that our gifts and talents are the riches of the Church,[7] that we are blessed—like our father Abraham—not for our own sakes—but to "be a blessing."[8] And does not conscience speak of the waste of many—of important—opportunities, when Christians meet, and not an atom of *knowledge* is *dispersed?* We contend for no eccentric irregularity. We wish for no passing of our proper boundary—no intrenchment upon paramount obligations. But be careful, lest in quenching unnatural fire, we inadvertently damp some genuine spark of holy flame. Be mindful of small opportunities. The careful cultivation of the smallest field ensures an abundant harvest. The acceptance is not to the number, but to the improvement of the talents; not necessarily "where much have been given," but where we "have been faithful in a few things."[9]

The sin of *the wicked* is, not always that they "pour out foolishness;"[10] but that they *do not so.* They neglect to *disperse.* They do not abuse their talent, but they omit to improve it. If not blots, they are blanks in the Church. They do no harm, but they do nothing.[11] Indeed, they can *disperse* nothing from their empty store-house. They can only trade with the trash of the world, not with the commerce of substantial *knowledge.* The end of both is according to their works—"Unto every one that hath (actively improves) shall be given, and he shall have abundance; but from him that hath not (uses not) shall be taken away even that which he hath."[12]

8. *The sacrifice of the wicked is an abomination to the Lord: but the prayer of the upright is his delight.* 9. *The way of the wicked is an abomination unto the Lord: but he loveth him that followeth after righteousness.*

Let the reader ponder this awful question. What am I—what is my service—when upon my knees before God? *an abomination, or a delight?* Man judges by acts; God by principles. *The*

[1] Chap. x. 14, with verse 2. [2] 2 Cor. ix. 6. [3] Eccl. xi. 2, 4, 6.
[4] Matt. iv. 23; ix. 35. Ps. xl. 9, 10. [5] Matt. xxviii. 19, 20.
[6] Acts viii. 1—4. [7] 1 Cor. xii. 7. 1 Pet. iv. 10. [8] Gen. xii. 2.
[9] Matt. xxv. 21. Comp. Luke xvi. 10. [10] Ver. 2. [11] Matt. xxv. 25—28.
[12] Matt. v. 29

sacrifice of the wicked—though it be part of God's own service, yet 'will be found in his register in the catalogue of sins to be accounted for.'[1] Instead of an acceptable offering, it is an insulting provocation.[2] It is not only vain,[3] but abominable—yea *abomination* itself.[4] That is wanting, "without which it is impossible to please God;" the lack of which stamped *the sacrifice* of Cain as an *abomination.*[5] It is a 'work, that doth not flow from a lively faith, and therefore hath in it the nature of sin.'[6] Not that prayer itself is a sin. 'It is'—as Archbishop Usher expounds—'a good duty, but spoiled in the carriage.'[7] And far indeed would we be from discouraging *the wicked* from prayer.[8] We would only press the awaking conviction, that it must be done in God's order and way; else never can it find his acceptance.

But not only *the sacrifice*—but *the way of the wicked;* not only his religion, but his common course—natural as well as moral—*is abomination.*[9] All is the course of a rebel against God. All his doings are the corrupt stream from a corrupt fountain. Awful indeed is the thought of every step of life as being hateful to God!

Is he then finally rejected? Far from it. His desire to seek the Lord would be the beginning of *the prayer*, that ensures acceptance. *The prayer of the upright* from its first feeblest utterance, is not only acceptable to the Lord, but *his delight.*[10] The golden censer above,[11] and the gracious intercession within,[12] combine with fragrant odor before our God. Never could we faint in prayer, did we realize more habitually this pure ground of acceptance. Not less pleasing to him is the course of the upright. He has given him a measure of *righteousness*, and an effort for more. And though he fulfils it not, he *follows after it*, cheered with the smile of his father's gracious *love.*[13]

10. *Correction is grievous unto him that forsaketh the way: and he that hateth reproof shall die.*

But is it not also "*grievous*, for the present" to the child of God? He knows his need of it, kisses the rod, bows his will, and reaps a fruitful blessing.[14] But *grievous* indeed *is it to him that forsaketh the way.* He is humbled by force—not in spirit. He kicks at it, and, like an untractable child under the rod, only increases his own chastisement. There is no surer step to ruin, than this *hatred of reproof.*[15] How do "the spots of God's children"[16] here warn us—"Cease ye from man!"[17]

1 Bishop Hopkins' Works, ii. 481. Comp. Isa. lxvi. 3. Hag. ii. 12—14.
2 Isa. i. 11—15; lxi. 8. Jer. vi. 20. Ezra. xiv. 4. Amos v. 22. Mal. i. 7, 8.
3 Matt. xv. 7—9. 4 Chap. xxi. 27. 5 Gen. iv. 3—5, with Heb. xi. 4, 6.
6 Art. xiii. 7 Eighteen Sermons on Eph. ii. 1. 8 Acts viii. 22.
9 Chap. xxi. 4. Tit. i. 15. 10 Can. ii. 14; iv. 11. 11 Heb. x. 19—22.
12 Rom. viii. 26, 27. 13 Chap. xxi. 21. Isa. lxiv. 5. Phil. iii. 12—14.
14 Heb. xii. 11.
15 Chap. i. 30; v. 11, 12, 23; xxix. 1: Pharaoh, Ex. x. 24—29: Ahab, 1 Kings xviii. 17; xxi. 20; xxii. 8, 37: Amaziah, 2 Chron. xxv. 15, 16, 27: Ahaz, xxviii. 22, 33: the Jews, xxxvi. 15—17. Jer. vi. 16—19.
16 2 Chron. xvi. 10, with 1 Kings xv. 14. 17 Isa. ii. 22.

But *correction* turns back him who had *forsaken the way.* Then it is *grievous* no more. Had not Manasseh more cause to bless God for his fetters than for his crown—for his dungeon than for his palace ?[1] "This man was born there." We would always look hopefully at a sinner under *correction.* For surely so long as the physician administers the medicine, there is no ground for despondency.

Child of God ! Dost not thou still need the *correction* ? Oh ! when the thorn is in the flesh, pray for grace in the heart.[2] Seek thy Father's favor, more than thine own ease. Desire the sanctifying, rather than the removal, of his rod. Mock him not by the empty ceremonial of repentance. But in true penitence look up to thy smiter to be thy healer[3]—yet not till his *correction* has fully accomplished his gracious work. Lord ! let me know the smart of thy rod, rather than the eclipse of thy love. Shew me thy love—then do with me what thou wilt.

11. *Hell and destruction are before the Lord: how much more then the hearts of the children of men?*

Once more[4] behold we the Omniscient—Omnipresent God. *Hell and destruction*—every recess of the vast Hades—the state of the dead and the place of the damned—*are before the Lord*[5]—before his eye; open to his cognizance. *How much more then the hearts of the children of men*[6]—unsearchable though they be ![7] No depth is there within, that he cannot fathom; no manner of deceit so complicated, that he cannot track them ; and yet what a mass of practical unbelief is there in this plain demonstrative truth ! For would men dare to indulge their vain thoughts, their light notions, their trifles, their impurities, did they really believe that the Lord searched their hearts ? Would they attempt a forced concealment from his eye;[8] as if outward service, lip-worship, would avail, while the heart was cherishing its unrepented sin ? It is an awful moment in privacy to stand the test of this searching eye. Awful is the thought of the idolatrous[9] sinner ; to the lover of pleasure, distinction, or low ambition. Thine heart is open before thy God. Never will he condescend to occupy the second place there. Thy covering of deceit is swept away. The refuges of lies are pierced and laid bare.

The conscious sinner shrinks from this appalling view. The believer walks undismayed in the sight of this "consuming fire." His godly fear is the exercise of filial confidence.[10] The sins that are opened to his Father's knowledge are covered from his justice.[11] When he "cannot do the things that he would ;" when he finds the law "that when he would do good, evil is present with him,"

[1] 2 Chron. xxxiii. 11—13. Comp. David, Psalm cxix. 67, 71 ; Ephraim, Jer. xxxi. 18—20 ; the Prodigal, Luke xv. 12—20.
[2] 2 Cor. xii. 7—9.
[3] Hos. vi. 1.
[4] Ver. 3.
[5] Job xxvi. 6. Psalm cxxxix. 7, 8. *Destruction.* Heb. Abaddon. Comp. Rev. ix. 11
[6] 1 John iii. 20.
[7] Jer. xvii. 9, 10.
[8] Isa. xxix. 15.
[9] See Col. iii. 5.
[10] Heb. xii. 28, 29.
[11] Ibid. iv. 13. Psalm xxxii. 1.

he can look up—"All my desire is before thee."[1] Thus does the Gospel clothe the Divine attributes with light and love.

And see we not here a testimony to the Divine Glory of Immanuel?—For *are not hell and destruction before him*,[2] as his vast empire? May not we appeal to his omniscient eye, in despite of all accusing from the enemy—"Lord—thou knowest all things—thou knowest that I love thee?"[3]

12. *A scorner loveth not one that reproveth him: neither will he go unto the wise.*

How different from David's spirit—thankful for the "kind smiting of the righteous,"[4] and from the lovely humility of an Apostle, who shewed before the Church his honor and *love to his reprover!*[5] Yet we had need to be wise with "the wisdom that is from above" to give reproof aright. So cleaving is the mixture of our own spirit to every Christian exercise! Not less grace and wisdom does it require to receive reproof, and, instead of revolting from our reprover—to *go unto him*, and ask the continuance of his faithful offices. *The scorner* has been his own flatterer so long, that he cannot bear to be brought down to his proper level. *He loveth not* therefore—yea—he hateth—*one that reproveth him*,[6] though before he might have reverenced him.[7] "The Pharisees derided our beloved Lord with marks of external *scorn*, when he struck at their right eye, and reproved their hypocritical service.[8] "Every one that doeth evil hateth the light; neither cometh he to the light, lest his deeds should be reproved."[9]

13. *A merry heart maketh a cheerful countenance: but by sorrow of the heart the spirit is broken.*

How close is the sympathy between the body and soul, though framed of such opposite elements! A man's countenance is the index of his spirit. In the sensation of joy '*the heart* sits smiling in the face, and looks *merrily* out of the windows of the eyes.'[10] Yet who has a right to *a merry heart*, but he that is walking in acceptance with God?[11] It was this spring of joy, that lighted up Hannah's sorrowful countenance into godly cheerfulness.[12] Stephen stood before his judge, with his heavenly prospects beaming in his "angel's face."[13] Everywhere does the hearty reception of the gospel "give beauty for ashes"—sunshine for gloom.[14]

[1] Gal. v. 17. Rom. vii. 21. Ps. xxxviii. 9.
[2] Rev. i. 18.
[3] John xxi. 17. Comp. Rev. ii. 23.
[4] Ps. cxli. 5.
[5] Gal. ii. 11—13, with 2 Peter iii. 15.
[6] Chap. ix. 8. 1 Kings xviii. 10; xxi. 20; xxii 8. Comp. Amos v. 10; vii. 10—13.
[7] Mark vi. 17—20.
[8] Luke xvi. 13, 14. εξεμυκτηριζον· from μυκτηρ, nostril—contempt shown by the nostrils—μυσσω, to blow—'They blowed their nose at him.' See Leigh's Critica Sacra, and Parkhurst on μυκτηριζω.
[9] John iii. 20.
[10] Trapp in loco. This merriment, however, widely differs from the noisy mirth of the ungodly (Chap. xiv. 13.) The word is of frequent use among our old writers. It is Foxe's favorite description of the holy joys of the martyrs. Comp. Ecc. ix. 7.
[11] Ps. xxxii. 1, 2, 11.
[12] 1 Sam. i. 7—18.
[13] Acts vi. 15; vii. 55.
[14] Isa. lxi. 2, 3.

Sad indeed, is the contrast of *a heart broken* by worldly *sorrow.*[1] Too often does a mischievous gloom worm itself into the vitals of the child of God.[2] The melancholy victim drags on a weary—heavy-laden existence, clouding a distinct feature of his character;[3] despoiled of one of the most attractive ornaments of his profession.[4] His hands slacken; his whole energies are paralyzed for the work of God;[5] and he sinks into desponding apathy and indolence.[6]

In times of depression, let sense and feeling be kept within their bounds; and the Saviour's voice, encouraging confidence, will be practically regarded.[7] Even our very "sighing and crying for the abominations of the land"[8] must not issue in heartless complaints, but rather stimulate to the diligent improvement of present opportunities. Did we realize, as we ought, our present privileges, and grasp our eternal prospects; *no sorrow of the heart would break our spirit.* The gleam of sunshine would be to us the earnest of what it will be, when—as Rutherford beautifully observes—'we shall be on the sunny side of the Brae.'[9] Meanwhile—the first step in religion is not only beginning to be serious, but to be happy. To maintain our Christian balance, even "godly sorrow" must be disciplined; lest it *break the heart,* which it was intended only to humble; lest it give advantage to the enemy, and bring hindrance to the Church.[10]

14. *The heart of him that hath understanding seeketh knowledge: but the mouth of fools feedeth on foolishness.*

Observe the man of natural *understanding.* Every apprehension quickens the appetite to *seek knowledge.* He is ready to learn from any quarter, even from a child. He is all eye—all ear—all heart—for his object. Much more will spiritual *understanding* stimulate the desire.[11] Beware of the lust to be "wise above what is written." But let every vigorous effort be made to be wise, up to what is written. David, with his high attainments, was ever crying for Divine teaching.[12] His wise son *sought knowledge* upon his knees,[13] and not less in the diligent habit of application.[14] The Queen of Sheba, "coming from the utmost parts of the earth;"[15] Nicodemus and Mary, sitting at the feet of Jesus;[16] the Eunuch, journeying to Jerusalem;[17] Cornelius and his company, drinking in the precious message of salvation;[18] the Bereans, carefully "searching the Scriptures"[19]—do not all these shew *the understanding heart, seeking* a larger interest in the blessing?

Invaluable indeed is the gift. Warm affections need the discipline of *knowledge* to form principle and consistency, Christian

[1] 1 Sam. xxviii. 16. 2 Cor. vii. 10. [2] Chap. xii. 25; xviii. 14.
[3] Phil. iii. 3. [4] Psalm xxxiii. 1.
[5] Comp. Neh. viii. 10. Phil. iv. 4. [6] Chap. xvii. 22. [7] Isa. l. 10.
[8] Ez. ix. 4. [9] Rutherford's Letters. [10] 2 Cor. ii. 7—11.
[11] Chap. i. 5; ix. 9 [12] Ps. cxix. 98—100, with 33, 34, &c.
[13] 1 Kings iii. 5—10. [14] Eccl. xii. 9, 10. [15] 1 Kings x. 1. Matt. xii. 42
[16] John iii. 1, 2. Luke x. 39. [17] Acts viii. 28. [18] Ibid. x. 33.
[19] Ibid. xvii. 11.

completeness and proportion:[1] seeking for wholesome food, not intoxicating draughts; not deeming novelty the most desirable thing; but rather with the wise Sir M. Hale—'to be impressed and affected, and to have old and known truths reduced to experience and practice.'

But while the *man of understanding* is never satisfied with *knowledge, the fool* is fully satisfied with folly. So brutish is his taste, that *his mouth feeds upon foolishness.* It is his meat and his drink. His spirit "is of earth, earthy." Many such fools we find in religion, who prefer empty speculations and disputings on matters indifferent to the rich pasture of the children of God.[2] Let us ponder the responsibility of "going on to perfection; that, being of full age, we may have our senses exercised to discern both good and evil."[3]

15. *All the days of the afflicted are evil: but he that is of a merry heart hath a continual feast.*

The abounding consolation of Christian affliction, does not blot out its penal character. As the fruit and chastening of sin, it is an evil; and therefore *all the days of the afflicted are evil.*[4] Yet the child of God in affliction is not so miserable as he seems to be.[5] The darkest of these *evil days* can never make "the consolations of God small with him."[6] He can sing in the prison as in a palace.[7] He can "take joyfully the spoiling of his goods."[8] He can praise his God, when he hath stripped him naked.[9] He can rejoice in him, as his portion in earthly destitution.[10] 'Who is it'—said the heavenly Martyn in a moment of faintness—'that maketh my comforts to be a source of enjoyment? Cannot the same hand make cold, and hunger, and nakedness, and peril, to be a train of ministering angels conducting me to glory?'[11] What real *evil* then can affliction bring? Or rather, what does it bring but many *feast-days?* A few days' feasting would soon weary the epicure. But here *the merry heart hath a continual feast.*—And 'all his trouble is but the rattling hail upon the tiles of his house,'[12] not disturbing his enjoyment. Fed with this heavenly portion, shall I not thank my God, that he hath rooted me up from present satisfactions? "Let me not eat of this world's dainties. Thou hast put gladness into my heart, more than in the time that their corn and their wine increased."[13]

16. *Better is little with the fear of the Lord, than great treasure and trouble therewith.* 17. *Better is a dinner of herbs where love is, than a stalled ox and hatred therewith.*

Here are the sources of *the merry heart—the fear of the Lord* and *love* to man. And here also is the *continual feast,* so satisfy

[1] Phil. i. 9. Comp. Psalm cxix. 66.
[2] Verse 21; x. 20. Hos. xii. 1. Acts xvii. 21.
[3] Heb. vi. 1; v. 14.
[4] Gen. xlvii. 9. Ps. xc. 7—9.
[5] 2 Cor. vi. 10.
[6] Job xv. 11.
[7] Acts xvi. 25.
[8] Heb. x. 34.
[9] Job i. 21.
[10] Hab. iii. 17, 18.
[11] Life, Chap. ii.
[12] Leighton on 1 Pet. i. 2; iii. 1[illegible].
[13] Ps. cxli. 4; iv. 6, 7.

ing, that the saint's *little* is better than the worldling's all.[1] It is his Father's gift;[2] the fruit of his Saviour's love;[3] enjoyed by special promise,[4] and sweetened with the "great gain of godly contentment."[5] If it be only *little*, it is not from lack of his Father's care and love; but because his wisdom knows what he really needs,[6] and that all beyond would be a temptation and snare. Truly "a man's life consisteth not in the abundance of the things which he possesseth."[7] The universe will not fill a worldly,[8] while a *little* will suffice for an heavenly,[9] heart. There must be *trouble with great treasure*, without *the fear of the Lord.*[10] And far more destitute is its possessor in his unsubstantial happiness, than the man of God, who is eating his bread in the sweat of his brow. 'Jacob's ladder, which conveys to heaven, may have its foot in the smoking cottage.'[11] And as to this world's comforts—the *dinner of herbs*—the homely meal *of love*, is better than *the stalled ox*, prepared for a sumptuous,[12] but unbrotherly, feast.[13] *Love* sweetens the meanest food. *Hatred* embitters the richest feast.[14] How did the presence and converse of the Lord of angels dignify the humble fare![15] How much more refreshing were the social meals of the Pentecostal Christians, than the well-furnished tables of their enemies![16] When the Lord's ordinance is marred by man's selfishness—When wealth, rank, or adventitious accomplishments, govern the choice of life's companion, rather than the *fear of the Lord;* what wonder, if *the stalled ox, and hatred therewith*, be the order of the house? Mutual disappointment is too often the source of criminal indulgence abroad; always the bane of peace and unity at home. Few alas! practically believe this divine testimony. Parents!—Do you seek the solid happiness of your children? Then lead them to expect little from the world; every thing from God.

18. *A wrathful man*[17] *stirreth up strife: but he that is slow to anger appeaseth strife.*

This Proverb requires no explanation. But observe the principles of *hatred and love*, contrasted in active exercise. Some persons make it their occupation to sit by the fire, to feed and fan the flame, lest it be extinguished—An useful and friendly employment, were it a fire to warm. But when it is an injurious, consuming, and destructive element, it would seem difficult to discover the motive of these incendiaries,[18] did we not read, that "out of the

[1] Chap. xvi. 8. Psalm xxxvii. 16. [2] Matt. vi. 11.
[3] 2 Pet. i. 3. [4] Ps. xxxiv. 10; xxxvii. 3, 19. Isa. xxxiii. 15, 16.
[5] 1 Tim. vi. 6. Phil. iv. 11, 12. [6] Matt. vi. 32. [7] Luke xii. 15
[8] Ecc. i. 8. [9] Gen. xxviii. 20. [10] Eccl. v. 6; v. 12.
[11] Bishop Reynolds's Sermon on 1 Tim. vi. 17—19.
[12] Matt. xxii. 4. Luke xv. 23. [13] Chap. xvii. 1; xxi. 19; xxiii. 6—8.
[14] 1 Sam. xx. 24—34. 2 Sam. xiii. 23—29. Est. i. 10—12. [15] John xxi. 9—22
[16] Acts ii. 46. Comp. Ps. cxxxiii.
[17] A man of wrath, Heb. constantly indulging it; unwilling to put it away; a firebrand, 'Vir flagrantiæ.'—Schultens. Comp. xxix. 22.
[18] Chap. x. 12; xvi. 27, 28; xxvi. 20, 21.

heart proceed evil thoughts, murders, wickedness, an evil eye, pride, foolishness."[1]

What then is the Christian's experience? Instead of *stirring up—to appease strife;* to bring water—not fuel—to the fire; by "a soft answer to turn away wrath;"[2] by a yielding spirit to melt, subdue, and bring peace.[3] Let me remember that I owe my very salvation to this attribute—*slow to anger.*[4] And shall I not endeavor to imbue my profession with this lovely adorning, and to "be a follower of God, as his dear child, walking in love?"[5] Will not this temper of the gospel secure my earthly enjoyment of godliness?[6] Will it not also seal my title as a child of God?[7]

19. *The way of the slothful man is as an hedge of thorns; but the way of the righteous is made plain,* (raised up as a causey, Marg.[8])

Another picture of *the slothful man* drawn to life! He plants his own *hedge,* and then complains of its hindrance. Every effort to break through his difficulty, like a *fresh thorn-bush* in *his way,* tears his flesh. He is brought to a stand. Indecision, delay, reluctance, sluggishness, paralyze his exertions.[9] He not only exaggerates his real,[10] but pictures to his mind imaginary,[11] difficulties; so that, after a feeble struggle of conscience, with much to do, but no heart to do any thing, he gives himself up to idleness or pleasure.[12]

This sloth is a ruinous evil in temporals. Young men! remember, that one or two hills of difficulty, vigorously climbed in youth, will *make the way plain* for future and successful progress. But to put half the soul to the work; to drag to it as an unavoidable task; to avoid present difficulties in order to find a smoother path, will make *a hedge of thorns,* harassing to the end of the journey.

Much more ruinous is this evil in the Christian life. The sluggard in religion is miserable—never at ease. He knows his need of a change. He makes an effort to pray. But all withers for want of purpose of heart. *His way is a hedge of thorns.* Exertion is absolutely impossible. He sees no hope of overcoming, and lies down in despair.[13] Child of God! Beware of yielding to a sluggish spirit. Soon will nothing remain but the dead form of religion; the bare walls of the house, instead of the temple filled with the glory; the heartless externals of godliness, while the spirit that breathed life into them is gone.

After all—the difficulties are more in the mind than in the path. For while the *slothful* sits down by the side of his *hedge* in despondency; *the righteous,* in the habit of diligence, finds his *way made plain.*[14] An honest desire and effort make the way easy.

[1] Mark vii. 21, 22. [2] Verse 1. References. [3] Gen. xiii. 7—9. Eccl. x. 4.
[4] Ps. ciii. 8. 2 Pet. iii. 15. [5] Eph. v. 1, 2.
[6] Matt. v. 5. [7] Ibid. ver. 9.
[8] '*A highway*—a path so formed as to be easy to the foot of the traveller.'—French and Skinner. Comp. Isa. xxxv. 8. Also 2 Chron. ix. 11. Marg.
[9] Comp. Lev. xxvi. 7, 8, with Jud. i. 3, 4. [10] Num. xiii. 27—33.
[11] Chap. xxvi. 13. [12] Ibid. verses 14, 15. [13] Chap. xii. 27.
[14] Num. xiii. 30; xiv. 2—9.

Faith brings him to the strong for strength. Hope, love, and joy are conquering principles. "The mountains are threshed"[1] by the energy of faith. Religion, with all its crosses, is found to be a practicable thing.[2] The victory over sloth opens a happy and prosperous way to heaven.[3]

20. *A wise son maketh a glad father: but a foolish man despiseth his mother.*

Do not the brightest joys,[4] and the bitterest tears[5] in this world of tears, flow from parents' hearts? Whatever be the delight to see a son prospering in life, the Christian father finds no rest, until *a wise son maketh him glad.* And here we need not any development of talent or superior attainment, but the true *wisdom;* humble and docile, marked (as the contrast suggests) by filial reverence, specially by the cleaving choice of that fear of the Lord which "is the beginning of wisdom."[6] Such a son does indeed rejoice his father, as he watches with equal pleasure and thankfulness the daily growth and healthiness of his choice vine.

But what if *folly,* instead *of gladdening, despise, a mother?*[7] She—whose tender love,[8] and yearning faithfulness,[9] is a faint picture of the heart of God—She is *despised* by "the son of her womb!"[10] The law of God commands honor[10] and reverence;[11] and the transgression of the law will not be forgotten.[12] But is not this neglect a chastening rebuke for capricious indulgence? What grace and wisdom is needed, so that parents may be a valuable blessing to their children for their highest interests!

21. *Folly is joy to him that is destitute of wisdom: but a man of understanding walketh uprightly.*

Let this Book of instruction probe our profession. What think we of *folly?* Not only does the ungodly practise it. But *it is joy* to him. He sins without temptation or motive. He cannot sleep without it.[13] It is "the sweet morsel under his tongue."[14] He "obeys it in the lusts thereof."[15] He "works it with greediness."[16] He hates the gospel, because it proposes to "save him from it."[17] But hear the humbling confessions of a child of God—"I am carnal, sold under sin. O wretched man that I am! who shall deliver me?" Verily would he sink under his hated burden, but for the confidence "I thank God—There is no condemnation."[18]

What greater proof can there be of being *destitute of wisdom,* than this appetite of sin? That which hath turned this fair and blooming world into a sepulchre—nay—that which hath kindled "everlasting burnings"—is *his joy.* And thus he goes on, intent

[1] Isa. xli. 10—14. [2] Phil. iv. 13.
[3] Chap. iv. 18. Job xvii. 9. Matt. xi. 12.
[4] Chap. x. 1; xxiii. 15, 24, 25. 1 Kings i. 48.
[5] Chap. xvii. 25. 2 Sam. xvii. 33; xviii. 1—4.
[6] Verse 33; i. 7. [7] Chap. xix. 26; xxiii. 22. [8] Isa. lxvi. 13.
[9] Ibid. xlix. 15. [10] Ex. xx. 12. [11] Lev. xix. 3, 30.
[12] Chap. xx. 20; xxx. 17. Ez. xxii. 2, 7. [13] Chap. iv. 16, 17.
[14] Ver. 14; ix. 17. Job xx. 12. [15] Rom. vi. 12. [16] Eph. iv. 19.
[17] Matt. i. 21. Acts iii. 26; with John iii. 19. [18] Rom. vii. 14, 24, 25; viii. 1

upon the trifles of the day; and trifling with eternal concerns; preferring shadowy vanities to everlasting glory. Will he not open his eyes to the discovery; that "they that observe lying vanities, forsake their own mercy?"[1] The Lord save him—ere it be too late—from reaping the bitter fruits of his foolish choice!

But how know we the man of understanding? He gives his heart and mind to the word of God. He has *joy* in wisdom,[2]—as the sinner in *folly*. Even his painful discoveries of indwelling corruption, ground him deeper in solid religion, than those who know only the surface. He is taught of God, and *his upright walk* is a bright "shining path."[3] Give me, O my God, *understanding*, that my *joy* may be in thy wisdom—not in my own *folly*.

22. *Without counsel purposes are disappointed: but in the multitude of counsellors they are established.*

Consider how weak and ignorant we are. Were our judgment perfect, the first impressions would be infallibly right. But feeble and shaken as it is by the fall, every dictate needs pondering. How much evil has been done by acting upon impulse in a few hasty moments, or by a few warm words or lines without consideration![4] Our wisdom lies in self-distrust, at least leaning to the suspicion that we may be wrong. Yet, guard also, on the other side, against that indecision of judgment, which is carried about by every person's opinion. Upon the whole, Christian prudence suggests the expediency—especially in important matters—of experienced *counsel*. By the neglect of this advantage, many good *purposes have been disappointed*.[5] God has ordained the commerce of wisdom for mutual benefit, and *by the multitude of counsellors* many valuable *purposes have been established*.[6] But as the wisest of these are fallible, and often in error, is it not our only safe path, in the use of human means, to look up to the great "Counsellor"[7] of his Church for guidance, and in reverential thankfulness, to take "his testimonies as the men of our *counsel*?"[8] Blessed be God for this special privilege of *counsel* always at hand! In humility and confidence, we shall not materially err.[9]

23. *A man hath joy by the answer of his mouth: and a word spoken in due season, how good is it!*

A word for our Divine Master to our fellow-sinners he will condescend to bless. The remembrance—"Who made man's mouth?"[10]—puts away pride. But have we not *joy by the answer of our mouth?*[11] The pain that every right-minded Christian feels in giving "open rebuke," is abundantly compensated by *the joy* of the happy issue.[12] Even an unsuccessful effort brings *the joy* in

[1] Jon. ii. 8. [2] Chap. xxi. 15. [3] Chap. iv. 18.
[4] Chap. xix. 2.
[5] Rehoboam, 1 Kings xii. 13—19. Ahab, xxii. 18—30; even David, 2 Sam. xxiv 1—4, 15.
[6] Chap. xi. 14; xx. 18; xxiv. 6. Acts xv. 6, 31. [7] Isa. ix. 6.
[8] Ps. cxix. 24. M. R. [9] Chap. iii. 5, 6. [10] Ex. iv. 11.
[11] Chap. xii. 14; xiii. 2. [12] Chap. xxvii. 5. 2 Sam. xii. 1—13.

"the testimony of our conscience." It must however be *a word spoken in due season.*[1] "How forcible are right words;"[2] well-timed, though from feeble lips![3] 'There are some happy seasons, when the most rugged natures are accessible.'[4] Yet many a good word is lost by being given out of season. Would we bring true conviction? Then pass by the moment of irritation, and wait for the return of calmness and reason.[5] Give reproof privately,[6] not exasperating, except when the occasion calls for it,[7] by public exposure. Never commence with an attack—an enemy's position, that naturally provokes resistance. Study a pointed application. A word spoken for every one, like a coat made for every one, has no individual fitness. When "the wise man's heart discerneth both time and judgment,"[8] the word is doubly effective. Manoah's wife upheld her husband's faith.[9] Abigail restrained David's murderous intent.[10] Naaman's servants brought their Master to sober reason.[11] Paul withheld the jailor's hand from self-destruction, and opened salvation to his soul.[12] Sweet indeed also is the Minister's *joy from the answer of his mouth*, when his gifted tongue "speaks a *word in season* to him that is weary."[13] And will it not be an element of his consummating joy "at that day," when he shall welcome those, instrumentally saved *by the answer of his mouth*, as his "glory and joy?"[14]

24. *The way of life is above to the wise, that he may depart from hell beneath.*

The way of life—the way in which alone life is found—the way to God—the way to glory—is but one. That way is Christ.[15] If therefore I come to him—renouncing all other hope, casting all my hope on Him, and every step of my way "looking unto Him"[16] —am not I in this way? And if I follow Him in "the obedience of faith," am not I advancing in that way?[17] *This way is above* —of heavenly origin. Fools rise not high enough to discern it, much less to devise and walk in it. Their highest elevation is grovelling. God does not allow them even the name of life.[18] Cleaving to the dust of earth, they sink into *the hell beneath.* But this is *the way of the wise*—born from *above*—taught from above —therefore walking above, while they are living upon earth—A most transcendent life! "partaker of the Divine nature!"[19] the life

[1] Chap. xxv. 11.
[2] Job vi. 27.
[3] Chap. xxiv. 26. Thus Luther, after the pattern of the great Apostle, gladly acknowledged his obligation.—'The word of a brother, pronounced from Holy Scripture in a time of need, carries an inconceivable weight with it. The Holy Spirit accompanies it, and by it moves and animates the hearts of his people, as their circumstances require. Thus Timothy, and Titus, and Epaphroditus, and the brethren who met St Paul from Rome, cheered his spirit, however much they might be inferior to him in learning and skill in the word of God. The greatest saints have their times of faintness, when others are stronger than they.'—Scott's Contin. of Milner, i. 332.
[4] Bishop Hopkins's Works, iv. 485. 'Mollia tempora fandi.'
[5] 1 Sam. xxv. 37.
[6] Matt. xviii. 15.
[7] 1 Tim. v. 20. Acts xiii. 6—11.
[8] Ecc. viii. 5. Comp. iii. 1, 7.
[9] Judg. xiii. 23.
[10] 1 Sam. xxv. 32, 33
[11] 2 Kings v. 13, 14.
[12] Acts xvi. 28—31.
[13] Isa. l. 4.
[14] 1 Thess. ii. 19, 20.
[15] John xiv. 6.
[16] Heb. xii. 2.
[17] John viii. 12.
[18] 1 Tim. v. 6
[19] 2 Pet. i. 4.

of God himself[1]—in humble sublimity, ascending above things under the sun—above the sun itself—The further we walk in *this way above*, the further we *depart from hell beneath*. Heaven and Hell are here before us—Soon will our state be fixed for eternity. What am I? Where am I? Those "who mind earthly things, their end is" the *hell beneath*. Those who walk in *the way above*—"their conversation is in heaven;" their hope is fixed on the Lord's coming from thence; their everlasting joy will be this complete transformation into his own image.[2]

Children of God! walk like yourselves; with "your hearts lifted up in the ways of the Lord;"[3] with a holy loftiness above the debasing pleasures of earth; "looking at the things that are unseen;"[4] "having respect unto the recompence of the reward;"[5] walking in *the way above* where your hope is[6]—where your treasure[7]—where your home[8]—above all—where your ascended Saviour is;[9] and where one golden ray of his favor, one reflected beam of his glory—will outshine all the glare of a shadowy world. Grant, we beseech thee, that like as we do believe thy only-begotten Son, our Lord Jesus Christ, to have ascended into the heavens; so we may also in heart and mind thither ascend, and with him continually dwell.'[10]

25. *The Lord will destroy the house of the proud: but he will establish the border of the widow.*

The administration of the Divine Government is to humble *the proud*, and to exalt the humble.[11] The contrast seems to mark *the proud* oppressor—an usurper of God's rights. He deals with him therefore as a traitor, and *destroys* not only his person, but *his house*.[12] And who can but acknowledge the retributive vengeance of the Judge of the earth![13]

But *the widow*, whom many care not for, many are ready to trample on—what a Friend and Protector has she![14]—"Let thy widows trust in me."[15] God condescends to link himself with them in a special relation, concentrating all his care and tenderness on their bereaved condition.[16] Did not he provide for sorrowing Naomi, a staff in her faithful daughter; and ultimately *establish her border* in Israel?[17] Did he not supply the pressing need of the Minister's widow[18] (a cheering warrant of faith in similar affliction), and take up the Shunamite's oppression, and again *establish her border*?[19] And shall we forget, how he teaches the returning penitent to plead the gracious manifestation—"In thee the fatherless findeth mercy?"[20]

[1] Eph. iv. 18. [2] Phil. iii. 19—21. Comp. Psalm xvii. 14, 15.
[3] 2 Chron. xvii. 6. Comp. Isa. xxxiii. 16; xl. 31; lviii. 14. [4] 2 Cor. iv. 18.
[5] Heb. xi. 24—26. [6] 2 Cor. v. 1—5. Col. i. 27. Heb. vi. 19.
[7] Matt. vi. 20. [8] 2 Cor. v. 6—8. Heb. xi. 16; xiii. 14. [9] Col. iii. 1.
[10] Collect for Ascension Day. [11] Luke i. 51, 52.
[12] Esth. vii. 10; ix. 10. Jer. xxii. 13—30. [13] Ps. x. 14, 18; xii. 5; lviii. 11.
[14] Chap. xxiii. 10, 11. [15] Jer. xlix. 11. Comp. 1 Tim. v. 5.
[16] Ps. lxviii. 5; cxlvi. 9. Deut. x. 17, 18. [17] Ruth i. 7—18; iv. 14—17.
[18] 2 Kings iv. 1—7. [19] Ibid. viii. 1—6. [20] Hos. xiv. 2, 3.

26. *The thoughts of the wicked are an abomination to the Lord: but the words of the pure are pleasant words,* (words of pleasantness, Marg.)

How lightly do the mass of men think of the responsibility of their thoughts! as if they were their own, and they might indulge them without restraint or evil. But they are the seminal principles of sin.[1] And as the cause virtually includes its effects; so do they contain, like the seed in its little body, all the after fruit. They are also the index of character. Watch their infinite variety—not so much those that are under the control of circumstances, or thrown up by the occasion, as the voluntary flow, following the habitual train of our associations. "For as a man thinketh in his heart, so is he."[2] Let the Christian yield himself up to the clear radiance of "the word, as a discerner of *the thoughts* and intents of the heart;"[3] and what a mass of vanity does only one day—one hour—bring to account! What then is the result with *the wicked!* "Evil thoughts" are the first bubbling of the corrupt fountain.[4] The tide of evil rolls on unceasingly. Thoughts of iniquity"[5]—"vain thoughts lodging within"[6]—all are *an abomination.*

Very different is his mind towards his own people. The *words of the pure*—the expressions of *their thoughts*[7]—*are pleasant words.* How *pleasant*—is manifest from his inviting call to their intercourse with him;[8] yet more from the open reward prepared for them before the assembled world—"They that *spake* often one to another—and *thought* upon his name—they shall be mine, saith the Lord, in that day, when I make up my jewels."[9]

27. *He that is greedy of gain troubleth his own house: but he that hateth gifts shall live.*

What an awful stamp has God fixed upon covetousness! Idolatry;[10] abomination,[11] an evil eye, and the cause of poverty;[12] "the root of all evil!"[13] Not only is it a curse to the sinner, but often *a trouble to his house.* So did Lot,[14] Achan,[15] Saul,[16] Ahab,[17] Gehazi,[18] Jehoiakim,[19] and the Jews,[20] find it. And often in our own day has *greediness of gain* plunged whole families into misery in ruinous speculations![21] For where the enriching blessing of God is not desired or sought, we cannot wonder that it be withheld!

Can the man of God do so? Not only would he refuse, but *he*

[1] Chap. xxiv. 9. Gen. vi. 5. Even an Heathen accurately described them. Αυτοχθονας πηγας της κακιας. 'The indigenous fountain of evil.'—Plutarch. Moral. Again—'If thou wouldest unlock the door of thine heart, thou wilt find a storehouse and treasury of evils diversified and full of numberless passions.' Ibid.

[2] Chap. xxiii. 7.

[3] Heb. iv. 13. κριτικὸς—a critic, censuring the errata with the most minute accuracy.

[4] Matt. xv. 19. [5] Isa. lix. 7. [6] Jer. iv. 14.

[7] Matt. xii. 34. Comp. Ps. xxxvii. 30, 31. [8] Ver. 8. Cant. ii. 14.

[9] Mal. iii. 16, 17. [10] Eph. v. 5. Col. iii. 5. Comp. Job xxxi. 24.

[11] Psalm x. 3. [12] Chap. xxviii. 22. [13] 1 Tim. vi. 9, 10.

[14] Gen. xiii. 10, 11; xiv. 12; xix. 14, 30. [15] Jos. vii. 1, 15, 24, with Deut. vii. 28.

[16] 1 Sam. xv. 19—26. [17] 1 Kings xxi. 1—14, 19—22. 2 Kings ix. 24—26.

[18] 2 Kings v. 20—27. [19] Jer. xxii. 13, 18—30. [20] Ibid. vi 12, 13; viii. 10

[21] Hab. ii. 9, 10.

hateth gifts, not only in the corrupting influence of bribes,[1] but in any case, that would bring dishonor upon his God. For this reason Abraham refused the gifts of the king of Sodom,[2] and Peter the enticement of Simon.[3] The man who thus walks in integrity, does not he *live* on high in the special favor of his God?[4] Does not he, who *hateth* this world's *gifts* for the affliction of the cross, 'receive an hundred-fold recompence in this life, and, in the world to come, everlasting life?"[5] 'Let their money perish with them' (was the noble confession of the Marquis of Vico, nephew to Paul V.) 'that prefer all the world's wealth before one day's communion with Jesus Christ and his despised people.'[6]

28. *The heart of the righteous studieth to answer: but the mouth of the wicked poureth out evil things.*

Consideration is an important part of the Christian character; nowhere more important than in the discipline of the tongue. Think twice before we speak once. "The wise man's *heart* is in his right hand,"[7] that he may weigh his words, and *study how to answer,*[8] and be ready "always to give an answer to him that asketh a reason of the hope that is in him."[9] Though there may be "good treasure" within, yet we must carefully ponder to draw from it "a word in due season."[10] Often may we reflect upon ourselves, for speaking hastily.[11] And indeed, when that comes out which is uppermost, nothing but the dross of evil can be looked for? Many stumblings have been made by speaking from the hasty feeling of the moment, rather than from a well-balanced and considerate judgment. In this haste, Joshua was beguiled by the Gibeonites;[12] David indulged a burst of murderous revenge;[13] Peter would fain have dissuaded his master from the work,[14] which he came down from heaven to do, and without which we should have been a world eternally lost. Cultivate a pondering mind. If ever asked to open an important subject, throw it not off hastily; nor give an answer, till it has been obtained from God. For *the heart's study to answer,* necessarily implies prayer—the only medium of receiving the "wisdom that is profitable to direct."[15] Nehemiah darted up his prayer for the *answer* for the moment, and how graciously was it vouchsafed![16] This is more especially a Ministerial responsibility for the many cases of conscience, that require "the tongue of the learned"—a word of wisdom, conviction, or consolation. How can "the priest's lips keep knowledge,"[17] unless *the heart,* under his Master's teaching, *studieth to answer?*

The *wicked* have no such restraint. He cares not what he says

1 Ex. xviii. 21; xxiii. 8. Deut. xvi. 19.
2 Gen. xiv. 22, 23.
3 Acts viii. 18—20.
4 Ps. xv. 5. Isa. xxxiii. 15, 16. Jer. xxii. 15, 16. Ez. xviii. 5—9.
5 Heb. xi. 24—26. Matt. xix. 29, 30.
6 See his interesting history in Dr. M'Crie's Reformation in Spain.
7 Eccles. x. 2.
8 Chap. x. 31, 32; xiii. 16; xvi. 23.
9 1 Pet. iii. 15.
10 Ver. 23. Matt. xii. 34.
11 Ps. xxxi. 22; cxvi. 11.
12 Jos. ix. 14, 15.
13 1 Sam. xxv. 13—21.
14 Matt. xvi. 22.
15 Chap. ii. 1—6. Eccl. x. 10.
16 Neh. ii. 1—6.
17 Mal. ii. 7.

It is of little consequence to him, whether it be true, or well-timed, or whom it wounds. His poisoned fountain *poureth out* poisonous waters.[1] Yet fearful is it to think, how every light word brings its account,[2] and will be found a 'hot coal to make the fire of hell burn more fiercely.'[3] Such a plague often infests the Church.[4] "From such withdraw thyself."[5] Separation is the keeping of the soul.

29. *The Lord is far from the wicked: but he heareth the prayer of the righteous.*

Such is the Lord's difference between these two classes. He is equally near to them both in his essence.[6] But in his favor *he is far from the wicked*,[7] and rejects their prayer.[8] He is near to *the righteous, and heareth* them.[9] His distance from the *wicked* is to their hearts' desire.[10] Yet does he sometimes make them groan,[11] as they will sink hereafter, under its final and everlasting curse.[12] But who can estimate the grace that calls these "stout-hearted, that are afar off, to hearken, and brings near righteousness and salvation to them?"[13] Inexpressible must be the guilt of despising such free, abounding, mercy![14]

But to *the righteous*, he is most graciously near.[15] *He heareth* their breath, when there is no voice;[16] their desire and weeping, when there are no words;[17] their stammering, when there is no gift.[18] Wonderful indeed is it, that he should *hear such prayers*, polluted as they are in their very breath. Yet does our compassionate High Priest wait for these vile offerings at the door of the oracle; and in his golden censer they appear spotless before the throne.[19] For his sake we are not only borne with, but accepted. Add to which—our prayers his own Spirit has dictated.[20] How then can he turn away from them?

Yet the enemy will suggest the doubt. *Does he hear?* Well he knows, what a shelter prayer is from his assault; and gladly would he drive us from it. 'Am I *righteous?*' Be it so, that thou art not. But is not thine advocate so?[21] Then put thy prayers in his hands. Thou canst not doubt his access to God; or that the ear, that may be shut to thee, is open to him. "Wouldst thou be spoken for to the king?"[22] Stammer out the prayer to thy Friend—"O Lord, I am oppressed; undertake for me."[23]

'But I see no answer.' Correct the errors of sense by faith in his word, which declares—whatever appearances may be—*He heareth.* Judge not by thy feelings or conceptions, but by his own

[1] Ver. 2; xiii. 16. Ecc. x. 3, 12—14. [2] Matt. xii. 36.
[3] Cartwright in loco. [4] Tit. i. 10, 11. 2 Pet. ii. 18. [5] 1 Tim. vi. 3—5
[6] Ver. 3. Jer. xxiii. 23, 24. Acts xvii. 27, 28.
[7] Psalm xxxiv. 16. Jer. xviii. 17. Amos ix. 4.
[8] Isa. i. 11. Jer. xiv. 12. Ez. viii. 18. [9] Ps. xxxiv. 15. 1 Pet. iii. 12.
[10] Job xxi. 14. [11] Ex. xxxiii. 1—7. 1 Sam. xxviii. 6. Hos. v. 15. Mic. iii. 4
[12] Ps. lxxiii. 27. Matt. xxv. 41. 2 Thess. i. 9. [13] Isa. xlvi. 12, 13.
[14] Acts xiii. 38—46. [15] Ps. xxxiv. 18; cxlv. 18, 19.
[16] Neh. ii. 4. Lam. iii. 56. [17] Ps. xxxviii. 9; vi. 8. [18] Is. xxxviii. 14.
[19] Rev. viii 3, 4. [20] Rom. viii. 26, 27. [21] 1 John ii. 1.
[22] 2 Kings iv. 13. [23] Isa. xxxviii. 14.

unchangeable word—by the manifestation of his name;[1] that he will refuse thee nothing that is really good; that thou dost obtain, if not what thou desirest, yet what upon the whole is best and fittest for thee. Have patience with God. Dictate nothing. Commit thy will to him. Say not—"I will that thou give me by and by."[2] Leave time and all to him. If he does not answer in thy time, he will in his own far better season.[3]

Study the character of God. It is not the Judge on his seat; or the King on his throne of state; but the Father in the full flowing of his love. Is not this attraction? In the sharpest trial—not all the world—not all the power of hell—can bar thine access to him. No child runs to his Father with such a confidence as thine. Never will he chill the heart, that throws itself upon his love.

Then honor him in this confidence. Shew that you really mean what you say. Bring to him no general petitions (the signs of an heartless frame) but definite objects. Tell him what you want, and all that you want. Prize his presence supremely—the pleasures of the closet above all privileges. No creature—not even the company of Apostles—can compensate for the loss of Him. Wrestle in prayer, but sit still in faith. He has bound himself by his own promises. And the fulfilment of them in answer to prayer will quicken confidenee and praise.

30. *The light of the eyes rejoiceth the heart; and a good report maketh the bones fat.*

The eye is the medium of the most rational enjoyment. Most elevating is the sight of the wonders of the creation! The Psalmist's Hymns of praise finely portray his delight.[4] Glowing was the joy, which burst from the wise man's heart in the sight of the morning glory—"Truly light is sweet, and a pleasant thing it is for the eyes to behold the sun."[5] Look also at gracious and unexpected providences—How did *the light of* the aged Patriarch's eyes *rejoice his heart*, when he embraced his long-lost son![6] A sunbeam truly was it in the cloud of despondency! And when the eye fastens upon the one object of attraction, does not one look clothed with light, cast a glory on the soul, and fill it with life and joy?[7] "They looked unto him and were lightened."[8] And what will it be, when the whole soul, animated with Divine Power, shall centre in the eye, when *the light of the eyes* shall present him to unclouded view, whom all heaven adores with everlasting praise!

But let us look at the joy of hearing. See how the Patriarch's heart bounded at *the good report* of his beloved Joseph.[9] The absent Minister seems to live again in the *good tidings* of his thriving people.[10] 'How delightful must it be to the humbled sinner to hear *the good report* of salvation, and to have his eyes enlightened to behold the glory of God in the face of Jesus

[1] Ps. lxv. 2. [2] See Mark vi. 25. [3] Isa. xxx. 18.
[4] Ps. xix. 1; cxi. 2. [5] Ibid. viii. civ. [6] Ecc. xi. 7.
[7] Gen. xlvi. 29, 30. Comp. Chap. xxv. 25. [8] Psalm xxxiv. 5.
[9] Gen. xlv. 27, 28. Comp. Chap. xiii. 12. [10] 1 Thess. iii. 5—9.

Christ!"[1] The animating delight with which the Shepherds saw the *good report* realized before their eyes, can scarcely be conceived.[2] So joyful is it still to the humbled sinner, that the very "feet of its messengers are beautiful" in his eyes.[3] "Blessed are the people, that know the joyful sound."[4]

31. *The ear that heareth the reproof of life abideth among the wise.* 32. *He that refuseth instruction despiseth his own soul: but he that heareth reproof getteth understanding*—(possesseth an heart, Marg.)

What a contrast to the "scorner," lately described, who "goeth not unto the *wise*."[5] The circumcised *ear heareth the reproof* that tends *to life*,[6] and welcomes it as a probing medicine, needful for the soul's health.[7] It is indeed the absolute law of social life, a component part of the love of our neighbor,[8] the bounden obligation to be "our brother's keeper" to the utmost of our power.[9] And yet for its discharge there should be a special office or relation, or concurrent providential circumstances. So wisely has God fenced its exercise from needless or wilful provocations. No wise man would incur the reproach of a tale-bearer,[10] by thrusting himself into this ungracious work. But beautiful indeed is the sight of "a wise reprover upon an obedient ear."[11] The man of God *abode with the wise.* He took his meek reprover to his wife.[12] He honored the faithful messenger of his Father's rod with his highest confidence.[13] The Apostle's affectionate testimony to his reproving brother showed, that he had *heard the reproof of life.*[14] This considerate and humble temper always *gets understanding.*[15] Nothing teaches like experience, and no experience is more useful, because none so abasing, as rebuke.[16]

But he that refuseth instruction, despiseth his own soul.[17] He will not indeed own the charge. But does he not underrate its high value and imminent danger, when he despises God's warning and provision for its salvation?[18] "Be thou instructed, O Jerusalem, lest my soul depart from thee."[19]

33. *The fear of the Lord is the instruction of wisdom: and before honor is humility.*

The fear of the Lord is described as the substance[20]—the beginning or principal part[21]—here *the instruction—of wisdom.* For is it not the medium of the deepest—most heavenly—*wisdom?* Though given under the law, it is linked with the full privileges of the Gospel.[22] The fear of terror melts away. The fear of rev-

[1] Scott in loco. [2] Luke ii. 15—17. [3] Isa. lii. 7.
[4] Ps. lxxxix. 15. [5] Ver. 12. [6] Chap. vi. 23.
[7] Ver. 5; xii. 18. Comp. Ps. cxli. 5. [8] Lev. xix. 17, 18.
[9] This obligation was repudiated by the first transgressor. Gen. iv. 9.
[10] Lev. xix. 16. [11] Chap. xxv. 12. [12] 1 Sam. xxv. 39—42.
[13] 2 Sam. xii. 7—12. 1 Kings i. 32. Comp. chap. xxviii. 23.
[14] Gal. ii. 11, with 2 Pet. iii. 15. [15] Chap. i. 5; ix. 9; xii. 1.
[16] Chap. xxix. 15. Rev. iii. 19. [17] Ver. 10.
[18] Matt. xvi. 26, with Chap. viii. 35, 36. [19] Jer. vi. 18. Comp. Zeph. iii. 2.
[20] Job xxviii. 28. [21] Chap. iv. 7; ix. 10. Ps. cxi. 10
[22] Acts ix. 31. Heb. xii. 28.

erence fills the soul. God rejoices in his mercy—the child of God in his confidence. But as it realizes the presence of a holy God, it must always be connected with *humility*. Indeed what Christian grace of the Gospel can exist without this conservating principle? Every dispensation of God strikes at the root of self exaltation, and tends to that real absence of self-esteem and self-sufficiency, which most of us rather long after than attain.

Most wise therefore is our Father's discipline. *Before honor, humility.* Indeed, without *humility, honor* would be our temptation, rather than our glory. Had not the Apostle been kept down by a most humbling trial, his *honor* would have been his ruin.[1] The exaltation of the Lord's people in providence, is therefore often conducted through the valley of *Humiliation.* Joseph was raised from the prison to the throne. Moses and David were taken from the Shepherd's fold to feed the Lord's inheritance.[2] Gideon acknowledged himself to be of "the least of the families of Israel."[3] Ruth was humbled by adversity, ere she was raised to the high *honor* of a Mother in Israel, and progenitor of the Saviour.[4] Abigail confessed herself unworthy to wash the feet of her Lord's servants, before she was honored to be his wife.[5] And in the daily walk of life, the lowest place is the pathway to *honor.*[6]

The same principle obtains in the dispensations of grace. "He that humbleth himself shall be exalted in due time."[7] Not that in the forgetfulness of our high privileges and confidence, we are to be weighed down in a sense of degradation. The true humility, which realizes our vileness, casts us most simply upon the full resources of the gospel, so that the most humble is the most triumphant believer. 'The lower, then, any descend in humiliation, the higher they shall ascend in exaltation. The lower this foundation of *humility* is laid, the higher shall the roof of *honor* be overlaid.'[8]

And was not this the track of our beloved Lord—*before honor, humility*—the cross before the crown? How deep was that descent, by which he, who was infinitely more than man—became "a worm and no man!"[9] And yet *the honor* which rewarded this humility, what tongue can tell![10] 'We must not disdain to follow Jesus Christ.'[11] Is it a light privilege to follow in the pathway consecrated by his steps—irradiated by his smile?[12]

[1] 2 Cor. xii. 7—9. [2] Ex. iii 1—12. Ps. lxxviii. 70—72. [3] Judg. vi. 15, 16.
[4] Ruth ii. iv 13—22. Matt. i 5. [5] 1 Sam. xxv. 41, 42. [6] Luke xiv. 7—11.
[7] Ibid. xviii. 14. 1 Pet. v. 6. [8] Trapp in loco. [9] Ps. xxii. 6.
[10] Phil. ii. 5—11. [11] Cope in loco.
[12] Matt. xi. 29, 30; xx. 26—28. John xiii. 14, 15.

CHAPTER XVI.

1. *The preparations* (disposings, Marg.) *of the heart in man, and the answer of the tongue, is from the Lord.*

The grand question is here decided—Who is the first mover in the work of conversion? Can man prepare his own heart for the grace of God? *The preparations of the heart in man are from the Lord.*[1] He takes the stone out of the heart, that it may feel;[2] draws it, that it may follow; quickens it, that it may live. He opens the heart, that he may imprint his own law, and mould it into his image.[3] He works, not merely by moral suasion, or by the bare proposal of means of uncertain power; but by invisible Almighty agency. The work then begins with God. It is not, that we first come, and then are taught. But first we learn; then we come.[4] His grace both prevents and co-operates.[5]

Shall we then indolently wait, until he works? Far from it. We must work, but in dependence upon him. He works not without us, but with us, through us, in us, by us; and we work in him.[6] Ours is the duty; his is the strength. Ours the agency; his the quickening life. His commands do not imply our power to obey, but our dependence upon him for the grace of obedience. He gives what he commands, and 'his promises are the ground of our performances.'[7] Our works are not the cause, but the effect of his grace; and never could they come out of us, until God had first put them in us.

The fruit also as well as the root—*the answer of the tongue,* no less than *the preparation of the heart—is from the Lord.* The tongue of the ungodly is under Divine restraint.[8] And when the Christian's thoughts are marshalled in due order, does not he depend upon the Lord for utterance?[9] Often in prayer, the more we speak, the more we leave unspoken, till *the answer of the tongue* is fully given, "crying, Abba, Father."[10] But the fluency of the tongue without the preparation of the heart—when prayer is without special business, when we read the precious promises, and carry not a word to plead before the throne—this is man's dead formality —not *from the Lord*—an abomination in his sight.

This habit of dependence must continue to the end. We can no more prepare ourselves after grace received, than before it.[11] He who "is the author," must be "the Finisher, of faith."[12] He is

[1] Ps. x. 17. 'From him all holy desires, all good counsels, and all just works, do proceed.'—Liturgy.
[2] Ez. xxxvi. 26.
[3] Acts xvi. 14. Jer. xxxi. 33. 2 Cor. iii. 3, 18.
[4] John vi. 44, 45.
[5] Art. x.
[6] Phil. ii. 12, 13, with Job xi. 13.
[7] Bishop Reynolds's Works, p. 129.
[8] Num. xxii. 18—20. John xi. 49—52.
[9] Eph. vi. 19.
[10] Gal. iv. 6.
[11] Isa. xxvi. 12. 2 Cor. iii. 5. 'I beg'—said Jerome—'that I may receive; and when I have received, I beg again.'
[12] Heb. xii. 2.

"Alpha and Omega, the beginning and the end,"[1] in this Almighty work. Our happiness and prosperity is in the humbling praising acknowledgment—"By the grace of God I am what I am:"[2] Dependence is not the excuse for indolence, but the spring of active energy.[3]

And if man's reason disputes—'If God does not give me grace, how can I come?'—we ask—Did you ever desire—did you ever ask for grace?—If not—how can you complain that you have never received it? If helplessness is really felt—if it brings conviction, grace is ready to be vouchsafed. Ask, and have.

2. *All the ways of a man are clear in his own eyes: but the Lord weigheth the spirits.*

If man were his own judge, who would be condemned? But man judges by acts; God by principles. His eye therefore beholds a mass of corruption; while *all the ways of a man are clean in his own eyes.*[4] He confesses himself indeed to be a sinner. But what his sins are he knows not; probably only venial, and abundantly compensated by his fancied virtues. "Ye are they,"—said our Lord to men of this stamp—"that justify yourselves before men: but God knoweth your hearts, for that which is highly esteemed among men is abomination in the sight of God."[5] Sometimes we see this delusion under the most shadowy cover. Pilate washed his hands, and was *clean in his own eyes*, from the blood of his condemned victim.[6] The murderers of Christ were *clean*, by refraining from the defilement of the judgment-hall, and by eating the passover.[7] The persecution of the Church blinded their consciences in the sincerity of unbelief.[8] Often has the self-deceiver passed into eternity under a credible profession. But how does he stand before God? He never acted from principle: He had the form and shape of a Christian, so drawn to life as to pass for a living man. But the eyes that are as a flame of fire bare witness—"Thou hast a name that thou livest, but thou art dead."[9] External forms without a sanctified heart is a baseless religion. *The Lord* "weighs" not "the actions"[10] only but *the spirit.* His eye discerns if 'but one' grain too light, and pronounces the sentence. Saul was thus "weighed in the balances, and found wanting."[11] And "if thou, Lord, shouldst mark iniquities"—the shortcomings of thy full and righteous demands, "O Lord, who shall stand?"[12]—Must we not fly from Omniscience to satisfied justice, and

[1] Rev. xxii. 13. [2] 1 Cor. xv. 10.

[3] 'Quamvis enim, nisi adjuvante illo, sine quo nihil possumus facere, os non possumus aperire; tamen nos aperimus illius adjumento et opere nostro.' Aug. contra duas epist. Pelag. ad Bonif. Commentators appear to be much perplexed on the translation of this verse. Many give it, as if the preparations or disposings (Marg.) of the heart were in man, but the answer of the tongue from the Lord. But Holden, as the result of a minute and critical examination, has substantially vindicated the received translation.

[4] Gen. vi. 5. Ps. xiv. 2, 3, with chap. xxi. 2. [5] Luke xvi. 15.

[6] Matt. xxvii. 24. [7] John xviii. 28. [8] Ibid. xvi. 2. Acts xxvi. 9.

[9] Rev. iii. 1. [10] 1 Sam. ii. 3; xvi. 7.

[11] Ibid. xv. 7—24. Dan. v. 27. [12] Ps. cxxx. 3. Comp. cxliii. 2.

there find, that "there is forgiveness with God?"[1] Joyous indeed is it to mark the even balances of our Judge;—in one scale his own perfect law; in the other—his Son's perfect obedience. Here, O my God, is my peace, my security. "Thou, most upright, dost *weigh* the path of the just."[2] But oh! place the blood of thy beloved Son ever in the scale of thy justice, and we will render to thee the glory of thy wondrous work of grace.

3. *Commit thy works unto the Lord, and thy thoughts shall be established.*

No moral rules can effectively discipline an unsettled mind—that canker to Christian peace. Faith is the only principle of solid *establishment.*[3] Here was our original happiness and security. Independence was the destruction of our well-being.[4] The return to this humble simplicity was the blessing of the gospel. "In all thy ways acknowledge him"[5]—is the rule of peace. Eliezer found his way prospered, and *his thoughts established, in committing his work to the Lord.*[6] This confidence was the stay of our beloved Lord in his great work.[7] Prayer was the exercise of his faith. *Establishment* was the issue.[8] Has the fretting spirit ever tried this true remedy? Actively were the two hands of faith and prayer engaged in making over our burdens to our Father. To have a sanctuary to flee to—a God, on whom to roll our cares;[9] to lean to his wisdom, and rest on his faithfulness—Here is a chamber of quietness in the most distracting anxieties—"So he giveth his beloved sleep."[10] *Commit then all thy works to him.* Seek to him for strength and guidance in all—Look to him for success in all. Roll on him the great *work* of thy soul's salvation. Be satisfied with his management of thy concerns. The active energy of faith at the throne of grace will *establish thy thoughts* in the peace of God, and keep thy soul in fortified security.[11] Thy burden is now cast upon one, who is better able to bear it.[12] The mind is now easy; the thoughts composed; quietly waiting the issue of things; knowing that all, that is for thy good, and the glory of thy God, shall be brought to pass.[13] Thus "we which have believed do enter into rest."[14] "But if ye will not believe,"—so speaks the solemn warning—"surely ye shall not be established."[15]

4. *The Lord hath made all things for himself: yea, even the wicked for the day of evil.*

Every workman has some end for his work. God has the highest end. It is his exclusive prerogative to be his own end in all his works.[16] *The Lord hath made all things*—all the events of

1 Gal. iii. 10, 13, with Ps. cxxx. 4. 2 Isa. xxvi. 7.
3 Ps. cxii. 7. Isa. xxvi. 3. 4 Gen. iii. 5. 5 Chap. iii. 6.
6 Gen. xxiv. 7 Isa. xlix. 4; l. 7—9. 8 John xvii. xviii. 1, 2.
9 M. R. 'Volve in Dominum quæ tibi facienda sunt.'—Michaelis. Ps. xxxvii. 5. M. R.
10 Ps. cxxvii. 2. 11 Phil. iv. 6, 7, φρουρησει. 12 Ps. lv. 22. 1 Pet. v. 7.
13 Ps. cxii. 7. Rom. viii. 28. 14 Heb. iv. 3. 15 Isa. vii. 7—9. 2 Chron. xx. 20.
16 Isa. xliii. 7: xlviii. 11, 12. Rom. xi. 36. Rev. iv. 10, 11. See President Edwards's thoughtful and interesting discussion.—'God's chief end in creation.' Chap. i

nations—all the dispensations of Providence—*for himself;* not to fill up a vacuum (for what vacuum could there be to the fountain of sufficiency?)—but for the manifestation of his glory to the intelligent creation.[1] Even *the wicked*—though their existence might seem scarcely reconcileable to the divine perfections—are included in this grand purpose. 'It is the greatest praise of his wisdom, that he can turn the evil of men to his own glory!'[2] *He hath made even the wicked for the day of evil.*—*Wicked* they are of themselves. He made them not so.[3] He compels them not to be so.[4] He abhors their wickedness. But he foresaw their evil. He permitted it, and though "he hath no pleasure in their death,"[5] he will be glorified in them *in the day of evil*,[6] as the monuments of his power, his justice, and his long-suffering.[7]

Clearly therefore God is not the Author of sin. He cannot impart what he has not—what is contrary to his nature. Infinite perfection cannot impart imperfection. Absolute holiness cannot be the cause of sin, though (like the law)[8] it may be the innocent occasion or excitement of it. If he foreknows—'infinite foreknowledge'—as Edwards profoundly observes—'proves the necessity of the event foreknown; yet it may not be the thing which causes the necessity.'[9] He can decree nothing but good. If he permits evil, so far as not to hinder it, he hates it as evil, and permits it only for the greater good—the greatest of all good—the more full manifestation of his own glory in it, and out of it. He will be glorified in, or on all his creatures. "All thy works shall praise thee; O Lord."[10] His retributive justice, no less than the riches of his glory.[11] The flames of hell exalt the reverential praises of heaven.—"And again they said—Alleluia. And her smoke rose up for ever and ever."[12]

5. *Every one that is proud in heart is an abomination to the Lord: though hand join in hand, he shall not be unpunished*—(held innocent, Marg.)

The hatefulness of a proud look has been mentioned.[13] But the Searcher of hearts marks *pride in heart* under a humble look.[14] Men see no *abomination* in this secret spirit. It brings no disgrace. Nay, it is often thought to be high-minded. But it keeps back the heart from God. It lifts up the heart against him. It speaks, as

Works i. Could there be a clearer demonstration of the divinity of Christ, than the representation of him, as the great end of creation? Col. i. 16.

[1] Isa. xliii. 21; lx. 21; lxi. 3. Eph. i. 5; iii. 10. [2] Bishop Hall.
[3] Gen. i. 26, 27. Eccl. vii. 29. [4] John iii. 19. [5] Ez. xxxiii. 11.
[6] Job xxi. 30. 2 Pet. ii. 9. [7] Rom. ix. 17, 22.
[8] Ibid. vii. 5, 8, 11—13. 1 Cor. xv. 56.
[9] Treatise on Will, Part ii. Sect. 12. See also Doddridge's valuable note on Luke xxii. 22.
[10] Ps. cxlv. 10.
[11] Rom. ix. 22, 23. Bishop Sanderson's Sermon on Rom. xv. 6.
[12] Rev. xix. 3. 'God made man neither to save nor damn him, but for his own glory. And it is secured, whether in his salvation or damnation. (See 2 Cor. ii. 15.) Nor did, nor does, God make man wicked. He made man upright. Man makes himself wicked; and being so, God may justly appoint him to damnation for his wickedness; in doing which he glorifies his justice.' Gill in loco. See also Scott.
[13] Chap. vi. 17. [14] Zech. vii. 5. Matt. vi. 16. Luke xvi 15.

if contending the supremacy with him.[1] When it thus strikes at God, what wonder that God strikes at it[2]—that he stamps it as *an abomination to him?*

How unseemly moreover is this sin! Such a creature—so utterly dependent—so fearfully guilty—yet *proud in heart!* This is indeed a true child of a fallen parent, who, in dreaming himself to be as God, made himself like the devil.[3] Many are the forms of this hateful spirit. Some are *proud* of their beauty; some of their talents; some of their rank; some of their goodness—all forgetting, that they "have nothing which they have not received;"[4] all unconscious, that they are *an abomination to the Lord.*

Perhaps, however, this declaration applies more distinctly to *proud* combinations against God—*hand joining in hand.*[5] What is all this force, but the worm "striving with his Maker?[6] "Who is the Lord?"—was the boast of haughty Pharaoh.—Let him and his people go to the Red Sea, and learn.[7] *Hand joining in hand* shall not be *held innocent*—shall not be *unpunished.* The Babel combination was blasted with confusion.[8] The "associations" against the holy child Jesus were "broken in pieces."[9] The infidel conspiracies of Voltaire and his school have been overthrown. And thus in our own day, will all Social and Chartist banding together for wickedness, only manifest more gloriously—"There is no wisdom, nor understanding, nor counsel against the Lord."[10]

6. *By mercy and truth iniquity is purged: and by the fear of the Lord men depart from evil.*

The purging of iniquity directs us at once to expiation.[11] Therefore, to connect it with man's *mercy and truth,* is to overturn the foundation of the Gospel. These are duties to be performed; not atonement for sin. And often are they performed by men destitute of the grace of God, whose *iniquities therefore are not purged.* It is then God's *mercy and truth*—shadowed forth in the daily sacrifices—that here irradiates the system of practical godliness. Man would *purge iniquity* by repentance; God by sacrifice—not by a simple deed of *mercy,* nullifying the sanction of the law; but by the combined manifestation of *truth,* fulfilling these sanctions upon the Surety, which *mercy* provided.[12] So gloriously do these two attributes harmonize! We enquire not to which we owe most. Both, like the two pillars of the temple[13]—combine to support the Christian confidence;[14] so that, though there may be, and is, material for condemnation, even in the holiest saint; actual condemnation there is not—there cannot be.[15]

Yet *iniquity is not purged,* that we should wallow again in the

[1] Ez. xxviii. 2. Zeph. ii. 15. [2] 1 Pet. v. 5. [3] Gen. iii. 4.
[4] 1 Cor. iv. 7. [5] Chap. xi. 21. Ps. lix. 3, 12, 13. [6] Isa. xlv. 9.
[7] Ex. v. 2; xiv. 26—30. [8] Gen. xi. 1—9. [9] Isa. viii. 9. Ps. ii. 1—5.
[10] Chap. xxi. 20.
[11] Junius and Tremellius, Schultens, Geier, Michaelis, &c. Comp. Heb. i. 3; ix 14; x. 2.
[12] Isa. liii. 6. 2 Cor. v. 21. [13] 1 Kings vii. 21. [14] Ps. lxxxv. 9, 10.
[15] Rom. vii. 14—25, with viii. 1.

mire. God shows the deepest abhorrence of sin in the very act of its expiation. And do not you, Christian, know his "forgiveness, that he may be feared?"[1] Do you not learn to *depart from evil*,[2] "perfecting holiness *in the fear of God*?"[3] Not that we are held to our duty by a legal fear. The slave is changed into a child. Filial confidence, like a sevenfold shield, covers him from sin. Its very touch is hateful, and all its ways are abhorred and forsaken.

7. *When a man's ways please the Lord, he maketh even his enemies to be at peace with him.*

Often is the favor of God and man combined to the man of God.[4] He will always have *his enemies*—if from no other source—from "his own household."[5] To seek *peace with them* by compromise of principle, would be to forfeit his character at a dreadful cost. Let him hold fast his principles in the face of *his enemies*. 'Though they mean him no good, they shall do him no harm.'[6]

How then do we explain the persecution of the saints[7]—of him especially, whose *ways always pleased the Lord*?[8] Each statement limits the other. The one shows the native enmity of the heart: the other its Divine control. It shall be let loose, so far as is for the glory of God. Beyond this, it shall be restrained.[9] His Church shall have her season of rest.[10] He hath all tongues, all hands, all hearts, under his power. Who needs to fear man, that walks in the fear of God?[11] 'The best way for *our enemies* to be reconciled to us, is for us to be reconciled to God.'[12] All our danger lies in his wrath, not in their anger. No creature can touch us without his permission.[13] Laban followed Jacob as *an enemy*, but was constrained to be *at peace with him*.[14] Esau, when about to execute his long-brooded threat, was melted down to brotherly endearment.[15] Israel's lands were preserved from invasion, while they were engaged in the service of God.[16] The enemies of the godly kings were manacled, and bowed before them.[17] Often have the Lord's people exhibited a majesty of the brow of holiness, that commanded the reverence, and bound up the hands of the ungodly.[18] And such will be the ultimate victory of the Church over all opposition.[19]

But even if *the enemies* be let loose; yet if their harm be overruled to larger good, is not the promise substantially fulfilled?

[1] Ps. cxxx. 4.
[2] Chap. iii. 7; viii. 13; xiv. 16, 17.
[3] 2 Cor. vii. 1. Comp. Luke i. 74, 75. Rom. vi. 1.
[4] Chap. iii. 3, 4. Luke ii. 52. Rom. xiv. 18.
[5] Matt. x. 36.
[6] Bishop Sanderson's Sermon on text.
[7] 2 Tim. iii. 13.
[8] John viii. 29, 37; xv. 18—20.
[9] Ps. lxxvi. 10. Isa. xxvii. 8; xxxvii. 33, 34.
[10] Ps. cxxv. 3. Acts ix. 31.
[11] Rom. viii 31. 1 Peter iii. 13.
[12] Bishop Patrick.
[13] See Job i. 9—12. Ps. cv. 13—15.
[14] Gen. xxxi. 24, 29, 44—55.
[15] Ibid. xxvii. 41; xxxiii. 1—4.
[16] Ex. xxxiv. 23, 24.
[17] 1 Kings iv. 21—25; x. 23—29. 2 Chron. xvii. 10.
[18] vi. 24—28. David, 1 Sam. xxiv. 17. Daniel and his fellow-captives, i. 6—21 iii. 26—30; vi. 24—28. John the Baptist, Mark vi. 20. Paul, Acts xxvii. 43.
[19] Rev. iii. 9.

'No wise man will tax him with breach of promise, who, having promised a *pound of silver*, giveth *a talent of gold*. Or who can truly say, that that man is not so good as his word, that is apparently much better than his word?'[1] Student of holiness! Thy God will take care of thee. Peace or war shall turn to thy everlasting good.[2]

8. *Better is a little with righteousness, than great revenues without right.*

We have before had this proverb in substance.[3] It seems almost too plain to need illustration. Yet so blind is the love of gain, that it looks only at its own selfish end, and the present moment; and fancies—what never can be—enjoyment[4] and security.[5] Retributive justice is at hand.[6] Far *better is the little with righteousness.* Was not the widow of Zarephath richer with her scanty fare, than Jezebel in her royal attire;[7] the poor prophet, sharing her pittance, than the King, with his *revenues without right*;[8] Zaccheus, when reduced to his comparative *little with righteousness*, than with his former abundance of the unrighteous Mammon.[9] This is the present manifestation. Much more clearly will the day declare it. The *little righteously* employed will then open the door of heaven.[10] The treasures of wickedness will be found treasures of wrath eternal.[11]

Few however of us amass *great revenues*. But the most trifling acquisitions *without right* will canker a large possession. Beware of the hair-breadth deviation from the straight principle. "Mortify that member of the earth," which "is idolatry"[12] against God, and "the root of all evil" to ourselves.[13] Godliness is great riches[14] in this life; what will it be in eternity!

9. *A man's heart deviseth his way: but the Lord directeth his steps.*

A fine description of the Sovereign government of God! Inscrutable indeed is the mystery, how he accomplishes his fixed purpose by free-willed agents. Man without his free will is a machine. God without his unchangeable purpose ceases to be God.[15] As rational agents we think, consult, act, freely. As dependent agents, the Lord exercises his own power in permitting, overruling, or furthering our acts.[16] Thus man proposes; God disposes. *Man devises; the Lord directeth.* He orders our will without infringing our liberty.

We observe this supremacy, in *directing*—not only an important end—but every step towards it; not only the great events, but

1 Bishop Sanderson ut supra.
2 Rom. viii. 28. Comp. Phil. i. 12—19.
3 Chap. xv. 16.
4 Ps. cxxvii. 2. Eccl. v. 12.
5 Chap. x. 3; xxi. 6, 7. Jer. xvii. 11.
6 Jam. v. 4.
7 1 Kings xvii. 13. 2 Kings ix. 32—37.
8 1 Kings xxi. 19, with xvii. 15.
9 Luke xix. 2, 8.
10 Matt. xxv. 34—40. Luke xvi. 9.
11 Hab. ii. 6, 9. Jam. v. 1—3.
12 Col. iii. 5.
13 1 Tim. vi. 10.
14 Ibid. ver. 6; iv. 8.
15 Ibid. Mal. iii. 6.
16 Chap. xix. 21; xxi. 30. Ps. xxxiii. 11. Isa. xlvi. 10. Lam. iii. 37.

every turn;[1] not only in his own people,[2] but in every child of man.[3] How little did Joseph's brethren contemplate the overruling *direction* to their evil *devisings!*[4] When Saul's *heart was devising* "slaughter against the disciples of the Lord;"[5] when the renegade slave was running in his own path[6]—little did they think of that gracious *direction of their steps*, to the salvation of their souls. Often also has the path of the Lord's people been encouraged by the counteracting of their enemies' *devising*, and the backward *direction of their steps*, at the moment when they were ready to grasp their prey![7]

Most interesting also is it to mark the minutiæ of circumstances, as parts and pieces of Divine Providence. A matter of common business;[8] the indulgence of curiosity;[9] the supply of necessary want;[10] a journey from home[11]—all are connected with infinitely important consequences. And often has *the way of our own devising* been blocked up, and an opposite way marked out, with the ultimate acknowledgment—"He led me forth in the right way."[12] The Divine control of the Apostles' movements—apparently thwarting their present usefulness—turned out to the greater furtherance of the gospel in the planting of flourishing churches.[13] After all however we need much discipline to wean us from our own devices, that we may seek the Lord's direction *in the first place.* The fruit of this discipline will be a dread of being left to our own devices, as before we were eager to follow them.[14] So truly do we find our happiness and security in yielding up our will to heavenly guidance!

10. *A divine sentence* (Divination.[15] Marg.) *is in the lips of the king; his mouth transgresseth not in judgment.* 11. *A just weight and balance are the Lord's; all the weights of the bag are his work.* 12. *It is an abomination to kings to commit wickedness; for the throne is established by righteousness.* 13. *Righteous lips are the delight of kings; and they love him that speaketh right.*

Here is a manual for kings; shewing, not what they are, but what God requires them to be, that they may be a blessing to their people, and benefactors to the world.[16] If this standard be neglected, the wisely-arranged ordinance fails of its end. "One man ruleth over another to his own hurt;"[17] and ruler and people—may each become a curse to the other.[18]

The king is not indeed wiser by birth than his subjects; but he is under stronger obligations to seek wisdom.[19] And when God's law is his law, *a divine sentence is in his lips.* Such was the

1 What vast results hang upon the sleepless night of the Eastern autocrat! Esth. vi. 1.
2 Psalm xxxvii. 23. 3 Chap. xx. 24. Jer. x. 23.
4 Gen. xxxvii. 26—28; xlv. 5. 5 Acts ix. 1—6. 6 Epistle to Philemon.
7 1 Sam. xxiii. 27. Is. xxxvii. 7, 8. 8 1 Sam. ix. 3, 15, 16.
9 Luke xix. 4, 6, 19. 10 John iv. 7. 11 Acts xvi. 14.
12 Ps. cvii. 7. Comp. Isa. xlii. 16.
13 Acts xvi. 6—12, with Phil. i. 1. 1 Thess. i. 1. 14 Ps. cxliii. 8—10.
15 Not Divination—strictly so called, which was absolutely forbidden; (Deut. xviii 0;) but penetration in discovering truth. See Parkhurst.
16 2 Sam. xxiii. 3, 4. 17 Eccl. viii. 9. 18 Judg. ix. 20.
19 1 Kings iii. 9. Comp. 2 Sam. xiv. 1

wisdom of Solomon, when in a delicate and difficult cause *his mouth transgressed not in judgment.*[1]

Such a King (and this is the glory of royalty) will have no interest of his own, apart from the public good. The remembrance, that the *balances and weights are the Lord's—his work*—made by his appointment—dictates an even-handed justice.[2] Not only will he refrain from *wickedness;* but it will be *abomination to him to commit it.* Not only will he be careful to remove evil from his person;[3] but he will surround himself with faithful counsellors. *Righteous lips will be his delight.*[4] Admirable was Eli's regard to Samuel's *lips,* even when they spoke daggers to his heart.[5]

Nothing is wanting to such a reign but stability. And thus speaks the word—unnoticed indeed by worldly statesmen, but well-warranted by experience—*The throne is established by righteousness.*[6] Godliness is the foundation of national prosperity.[7] The *righteous* are the pillars of the earth[8]—"the lions around the King's throne—his glory and defence.[9]

And shall not we make intercession for our beloved Queen, that she may embody this royal standard in her personal character and high responsibilities?[10] And may we not see here some faint delineation of the glorious King of Zion? What *divine sentences* of discriminating *judgment* dropped from his lips![11] How even are *the balances* of his perfect standard![12] How fully is his *throne established by righteousness!*[13]—himself "loving righteousness, and hating iniquity!"[14] And what and who are *his delight?—righteous lips—He that speaketh right.*[15]

14. *The wrath of a king is as messengers of death; but a wise man will pacify it.* 15. *In the light of the king's countenance is life; and his favor is as a cloud of the latter rain.*

The King's vast power is now developed in a graphic picture of Eastern despotism. Life and death are in his hands. His will is

[1] 1 Kings iii. 26—28. 'Who would have expected to have found in this proverb a proof of the Pope's infallibility? 'If Kings are infallible much more Popes.' Arguments must be extremely scarce, when such are alleged.' Scott.

[2] Deut. xxv. 15, 16. Ez. xlv. 10. The Jews used to keep their weights in *bags.* Amos vi. 11.

[3] Chap. xx. 8, 26. Contrast xxix. 12.

[4] Chap. xxii. 11. Ps. ci. 6, 7. Dan. iii. 28—30; vi. 24—28. Constantius, the father of Constantine, tested the character of his Christian servants by the imperative command to offer sacrifices to his gods. Some sunk under the trial. Those, who had *really* "bought the truth," would sell it for no price, (Chap. xxiii. 23.) they were inflexible. He banished the base compliants from his service. The true confessors he entrusted with the care of his own person. 'These men'—said he—'I can trust. I value them more than all my treasures.' This was sound judgment. For who are likely to be faithful to their king, as those, that have proved themselves faithful to their God?

[5] 1 Sam. iii. 15—18. Contrast 1 Kings xxii. 8. 2 Chron. xvi. 7—10; xxv. 15, 16. Mark vi. 17, 18.

[6] 1 Kings ii. 3, 4. 2 Chron. xxxii. 22, 23. Jer. xxii. 13—20.

[7] Chap. xiv. 34. [8] Ps. lxxv. 3. [9] 2 Kings xiii. 14.

[10] 1 Tim. ii. 1, 2. Ps. lxxii. 1. [11] Matt. xxii. 15—46.

[12] Ps. xlv. 6. Is. xi. 3, 4; xxxii. 1. [13] Isa. ix. 7. Jer. xxiii. 5.

[14] Ps. xlv. 7. [15] Chap. xi. 1; xii. 22. Ps. xv. 1, 2; xxiv. 3—5.

his law.[1] Every sign of *his wrath*—even the frown on his face, or the word out of his *mouth, is a messenger of death.*[2] The despot issues his order, and the executioner performs his warrant without delay or resistance.[3] No common *wisdom* was needed to *pacify this wrath.* Jonathan appeased his father's *wrath.*[4] Daniel *pacified* the outrageous autocrat of Babylon.[5] What a blessing —in contrast with this tyranny—is our own constitution! Such an admirable counterpoise between the power of the people and the caprice of the Sovereign! The just authority of the crown is preserved, without invading the due liberty of the subject.

The King's favor marks the same absolute power. The restoration of Pharaoh's butler to his place was as life from the dead.[6] The captive monarch found renewed *life in the light of his Master's countenance.*[7] Nehemiah's depression was cheered by his Sovereign's kind manners, and still kinder indulgence.[8] And was not the golden sceptre held out to Esther;[9] as the *reviving cloud of the latter rain*—the security of "the joy of harvest?"[10]

But think of the King of kings, before whom the mightiest Monarch is as dust.[11] How much more is his *wrath to be dreaded as messengers of death!*[12] The Kings themselves will fly to the rocks in vain for a shelter from its fury.[13] *Wise* indeed is *the man who pacifies it.* What owe we to that blood, which speaks our peace?[14] Sinner—ere it be too late—listen to the pleading call— "Be ye reconciled unto God."[15]

And if *in the light of the earthly King's countenance*—much more "in *His favor is life*"[16]—"gladness" infinitely more than all the treasures of earth;[17] refreshing *as the latter rain.*[18] 'Christ liveth,' said the noble Luther—'else I would not desire to live one moment.' Yea—Christian!—bitter and deep as thy sorrow may be, dread above all thy troubles the clouding of thy Lord's *countenance.* Watch every interval to obtain a glimpse of it. Seize every leisure to exchange a word or a look. Count every moment of separation irksome to thee. Above all—look and hasten to that time, when thou shalt walk up and down in the unclouded *light.* Oh my Lord! 'let the splendor of that day irradiate my soul, even at this distance from it, and leave no space void of its light and comfort. Yea—let it eclipse all other joys, and by its glistening

[1] Eccl. viii. 3, 4.
[2] Esth. vii. 7—10. Comp. Chap. xix. 12. 1 Kings i. 46—49.
[3] 1 Sam. xxii. 16—18. 1 Kings ii. 24, 25, 46. 2 Kings vi. 31—33. Matt. xiv. 10. Comp. Paxton's Sacr. Geogr. 405.
[4] 1 Sam. xix. 4—6.
[5] Dan. ii. 5—15, 16. Comp. Acts xii. 20—22.
[6] Gen. xl. 20, 21.
[7] 2 Kings xxv. 27—30.
[8] Neh. ii. 1—8.
[9] Esth. v. 2, 3, with iv. 16.
[10] Deut. xi. 14. Job xxix. 23. Joel ii. 23. Zech. x. 1. Jam. v. 7. As the Jews began their civil year after the Autumnal Equinox, the latter rain fell in the spring, 'and the more wet the spring'—says Dr. Russel—'the later the harvest, and the more abundant the crop.' Harmer's Observ. i. 71.
[11] Isa. xl. 22.
[12] Matt. xxii. 11—13. Luke xii. 4, 5.
[13] Rev. vi. 15—17.
[14] Col. i. 20. Heb. xii. 24.
[15] 2 Cor. v. 20; vi. 2.
[16] Ps. xxx. 5; lxiii. 3.
[17] Ibid. iv. 6, 7; xxi. 6. Acts ii. 28.
[18] Ibid. lxxii. 6. Hos. vi. 3.

beauty cause the small contentments of this world to be as so many glow-worms, which shine only in the night. Impress on my heart such a lively sense of thee, and of thy glory, that I may sooner forget myself, than thee and thine appearing.'[1]

16. *How much better is it to get wisdom than gold! and to get understanding rather to be chosen than silver!*

This—apart from inspiration—must be considered to be a competent judgment. It was formed by one, who had the largest portion of both blessings, that ever fell to the lot of man.[2] Calculate in the balances of the sanctuary, the overwhelming interests of heaven above earth, of the soul above the body, of eternity above time; and who will dispute this verdict? One, who had made the *choice*, counted all things but loss and dung in the comparison.[3] It is more valuable,[4] more abiding,[5] more fruitful,[6] more satisfying.[7] It is inexpressibly *better*. It is a question of admiration and delight. *How much better to get wisdom than gold! understanding than silver!*

The security of the possession heightens its value. Multitudes labor night and day for *gold*; yet miss the treasure. But who was ever disappointed in the effort to *get wisdom?*[8] When has earnestness and prayer failed of success?[9] "Wisdom is the principal thing; therefore get wisdom; and with all thy getting, *get understanding*."[10] Nothing less than "salvation" is the great end.[11] How rich must be that blessing, of which the Son of God is the store-house! "In him are hid all the treasures of wisdom and knowledge."[12] And none shall spoil us of our portion.

17. *The highway of the upright is to depart from evil: he that keepeth his way preserveth his soul.*

The highway is the plain beaten path. *The highway of the upright*—his ordinary course of profession—is the way of holiness"[13]—*departing from evil.*[14] Here let him be seen, peculiar in his practice, as in his principles. Each of us have our own world of *evil*—an inner circle, where the conflict is far more sharp—where the need of divine discipline is far more sensibly felt, than in the grosser forms of sin. Show great forbearance to others, but none to ourselves. Admit no foibles or infirmities. Count nothing small, that hinders the completeness or consistency of profession. The real injury is not from our living in the world, but from the world living in us. So delicate is the vital principle, that it never can emit its glowing influence, except in the atmosphere of heaven.

To *keep therefore this way, is to preserve our soul.*[15] Thus Joseph was saved;[16] while David, forsaking the path, fell into

[1] Bishop Patrick's Glorious Epiphany, pp. 110, 114. [2] 1 Kings iii. 12, 13.
[3] Phil. iii. 7, 8. [4] Chap. iii. 13—15; viii. 10, 11, 19.
[5] Chap. xxiii. 5, with viii. 19. [6] Ecc. vii. 12. [7] Ibid. v. 10, with Chap. viii. 21.
[8] Matt. xi. 12. [9] Chap. ii. 3—5. Jam. i. 5. [10] Chap. iv. 5—7.
[11] 2 Tim. iii. 15. [12] Col. ii. 3. [13] Isa. xxxv. 8.
[14] Ps. xviii. 23; cxix. 1—3. [15] Chap. iv. 23—27; xix. 16.
[16] Gen. xxxix. 9. 10.

grievous sin.[1] The quick perception of evil—the sensibility of danger from lawful things—at once tests our heavenly birth, and covers us from many subtle devices.[2] The unclean shall not pass over this highway; "but the redeemed shall walk there."[3]

18. *Pride goeth before destruction, and a haughty spirit before a fall.* 19. *Better is it to be of an humble spirit with the lowly, than to divide the spoil with the proud.*

What more vivid exposition of these Proverbs is needed, than our own ruined condition? Our father's *pride*—desiring to "be as God"—hurried his whole race to *destruction.*[4] 'O Adam'—was the exclamation of a man of God,—'what hast thou done?'[5] The most awful strength of Divine eloquence seems to be concentrated to delineate the character and ruin of pride.[6] Example abounds throughout the Scripture[7]—each sounding this solemn admonition —"Be not high-minded, but fear"[8] Fearful indeed is our danger, if the caution be not welcomed, if the need for it be not deeply felt!

The haughty spirit[9] carries the head high. The man looks upward, instead of to his steps. What wonder therefore, if, not seeing what is before him, he *falls?* He loves to climb. The enemy is always at hand to assist him;[10] and the greater the height, the more dreadful the fall. Yet is the state of heart, that prepared him for the fall, the worst part of his condition. Have we been preserved from open disgrace? Examine secret faults. Trace them to their source—a subtle confidence in gifts, attainments, or privileges. And then praise thy God for his painful discipline—the preserving mercy from ruinous self-exaltation.[11] Truly the way down to the valley of humiliation is deep and rugged. Humility therefore is the grand preserving grace. The contrite publican was safe when the boasting Pharisee was confounded.[12] *Better* then—more happy, more honorable, more acceptable to God and man—is *a humble spirit* companying *with the lowly, than the spoil* of the haughty conqueror, ministering only to his *destruction.*[13] May my Lord's example keep me low! 'When majesty'—said pious Bernard—'humbled himself, shall the worm swell with pride?'

20. *He that handleth a matter wisely shall find good: and whoso trusteth in the Lord, happy is he.*

Two things are needed for the success of *a matter*—wisdom and faith. One teaches us what to do for ourselves; the other what

[1] 2 Sam. xi. 2. [2] 1 John v. 18.
[3] Isa. xxxv. 8, 9. [4] Gen. iii. 5. [5] Adams's Private Thoughts.
[6] Isa. xiv. 4—19. Ez. xxviii. xxix. Comp. Job xl. 11, 12.
[7] Pharaoh, Ex. ix. 16, 17; Amaziah, 2 Chron. xxv. 15—20; Haman, Esth. v. 11; vii. 10; Nebuchadnezzar, Dan. iv. 29—33; Herod, Acts xii. 21—23; *In the* Church, David, 2 Sam. xxiv. 1; Uzziah, 2 Chron. xxvi. 4, 16; Hezekiah, xxxii. 25; Peter, Matt. xxvi. 33, 69—74.
[8] Rom. xi. 20. Comp. 1 Cor. x. 12. 1 Tim. iii. 6.
[9] Altifrons elatio spiritus.—Schultens. [10] Matt. iv. 5, 6.
[11] 2 Cor. xii. 7—9 [12] Luke xviii. 14. [13] Jam. i. 9.

to expect from God. "Wisdom is profitable to direct"[1]—specially in important *matters*. Joseph's *wise* management in a great emergency *found good*.[2] The Apostles *wisely handled the matter* of the ministration of the widows; relieving themselves from the secular work, and, for the greater satisfaction, choosing the officers (as seems probable from the original of the names[3]) from the complaining party. And great *good did they find* from the arrangement.[4] Let the young Christian earnestly study this *wisdom*. His first glowing impulse would cast away every relic of his former course, and stamp his religion with needless singularity. But he may learn, that true self-denial is more an internal exercise than an external badge of difference;—that there may be a martyred singularity without the genuine love; that the distinction between enthusiasm and zeal, is not the energy, but the direction, of the principle. This *wisdom* will be profitable for Christian humility and consistency.

After all, however, the most profound human wisdom may be outwitted.[5] Prudence without faith will come to naught.[6] True *wisdom handles the matter* in self-distrusting dependence.[7] Eliezer's discreet *handling* was in the spirit of faith.[8] In the same spirit did Jacob conduct his prudential defence against his brother.[9] Esther *wisely handled her* delicate *matter;* using 'a fast to call upon God, and a feast to obtain favor with the King.'[10] This is in all cases true wisdom—to make man the exercise of diligence; God the object of trust.

And where—as in this practical *trust*—shall we find so Divine—so simple—a recipe of *happiness?* Never did God intend to create our happiness out of our own resources. To feel that we know nothing—that we can do nothing—contrive nothing; then to look up to him as our supreme good, and to trust him as our only friend—when was such reliance and expectation ever disappointed?[11] We feel that we are in his hands. We have nothing more to do with ourselves. A thousand perplexing thoughts are scattered to the winds. God now takes the place once filled by most unquiet agitations. We can fearlessly look an extremity in the face. The soul is fixed on God. He reigns over all with an all-seeing eye and an all-moving hand. All the world cannot rob us of one word of God. Providence may seem to oppose his promises. But there is more reality in the least promise of God, than

1 Ecc. x. 10.

2 Gen. xli. 25—44. Hence the removal of wise men is a national judgment. Isa. iii. 1. Comp. also Chap. xiii. 15; xvii. 2; xix. 8.

3 Scott in loco.

4 Acts vi. 1—7. Similar *good* result was shown in their *wise handling of* the difficult *matter* of circumcision. Ibid. xv.

5 2 Sam. xvii. 14.

6 Isa. xxii. 5—11. Comp. 2 Kings xviii. 13—17. Man *at his best estate* vanity Verses 5, 6.

7 Chap. iii. 5, 6. Ps. xxxvii. 5.

8 Gen. xxiv. 3, 34—53, with 10—14.

9 Ibid. xxxii. xxxiii.

10 Esth. iv. 16; v. 5; vii. 1—7. Bishop Reynolds on Hos. xiv. 3.

11 Ps. ii. 12; xxxiv. 8. Jer. xvii. 7, 8.

in the greatest performance of man. 'I will therefore ever trust him on his bare word; with hope, besides hope, above hope, against hope; for small matters of this life. For how shall I hope to trust him in impossibilities, if I may not in likelihoods?'[1]

21. *The wise in heart shall be called prudent: and the sweetness of the lips increaseth learning.*

The heart is the proper seat of *wisdom.*[2] There "it dwells with prudence."[3] Their combined exercise is essential to the completeness of a Christian profession. Intellectual *wisdom* without a *prudential* application tends to no practical end. The pervading want of prudence gives needless offence to the gospel, and destroys influential weight of character. Often also do spiritual affections run to waste for want of *prudent* direction or discipline. Moral habits from this defect become either morbid or hardened. There is either a superstitious scrupulousness, or a reckless indifference; sometimes a conscience about every thing, sometimes about nothing. *Prudent wisdom* gives establishment to the whole system. The eye directs the foot, and we walk safely upon firm ground.

These internal qualities gain increasing acceptance from external gifts. "When we are enriched with all utterance, as well as with all knowledge;"[4] when we are enabled to clothe our thoughts in a flowing style, and clear expression—this doubtless gives a great advantage in communicating knowledge.[5] *The sweetness of the lips increaseth learning.* Ambrose's mellifluous eloquence arrested and gradually brought conviction to Augustine's mind.[6] Yet we would not confine this advantage to natural eloquence. *Wisdom is in the heart* as in a treasury, and "of the abundance of the heart, the mouth speaketh."[7] When therefore "the heart is inditing a good matter, speaking of the things touching the King; the tongue"—like the Apostle's[8]—without any adventitious attractiveness, "is the pen of a ready writer."[9] And when without measure "grace was poured upon the lips"[10] of the King himself, what wonder, that he should have constrained the admiration,[11] and fixed the attention,[12] of his hearers! How inestimable the privilege of his true disciples to sit at his feet, *increasing learning from the sweetness of his lips!*

22. *Understanding is a well-spring of life unto him that hath it: but the instruction of fools is folly.*

A religion of notions—what is it? All is death. There is no pulse in the affections—no motion in the heart. But when the *understanding* is enlightened, to apprehend spiritual things in their spiritual glory, notions become principles; feelings flow from

[1] Bishop Hall's Works, viii. 8. [2] Chap. ii. 10; x. 8.
[3] Chap. viii. 12. Hos. xiv. 9. [4] 1 Cor. i. 5.
[5] Eccl. xii. 10, 11. [6] Confess. lib. v. c. 13, 14.
[7] Matt. xii. 34. Comp. ver. 23. [8] 1 Cor. ii. 1—4. [9] Ps. xlv. 1.
[10] Ibid. ver. 2. [11] Matt. vii. 28. Luke iv. 22. John vii. 46. [12] Luke xix. 48.

light, and are filled with *life*. This is indeed *a well-spring of life to him that hath it*, refreshing to himself, and a blessing to all around him.[1] *The well-spring* shews that the work is not on the surface—not a mere forced impulse. It is not the summer stream, but a deep, overflowing fountain.[2] If it be not always bubbling,[3] there is always a supply at the bottom spring.

But the stream must be as the fountain. What therefore but *folly* can be the *instruction of fools*?[4] Justly did our Lord stamp with this rebuke the senseless *instruction* of the Scribes and Pharisees.[5] What else could their teaching be, but "the blind leading the blind, both falling into the ditch?"[6]

Christian professor! ponder—unless thy *understanding* be filled with heavenly light, it will be a poisoned fountain—not *a well-spring of life*. What if thy *understanding* be clear, and thy heart be dark; if thou be learned in the truth of Christ, *yet not* "*taught by him, as the truth is in Jesus*;"[7] if like Balaam, thou be sound in theology, yet damned in sin![8] 'Let us not think much of ourselves,' says the excellent Bishop Reynolds—'though God should have adorned us with the most splendid natural gifts—with quickness of *understanding*, almost like that of angels; unless at the same time he adds to all, the gift of his spiritual grace, by which we may attain to a knowledge and delight in the heavenly mystery.'[9]

23. *The heart of the wise teacheth his mouth, and addeth learning to his lips.*

The well-spring of life, however silently it may flow, cannot be concealed. The weighty instruction, pouring out from a Divinely-instructed heart, shews the heavenly source, from whence *the well-spring* is supplied. While the "talk of the lips impoverishes,"[10] *the teaching of the heart addeth learning*. Who does not know the difference between one who speaks of what he has read or heard, and one who speaks of what he has felt and tasted? The one has the knowledge of the gospel—dry and spiritless. The other has "*the savour* of this knowledge"[11]—fragrant and invigorating. The theorist may exceed in the quantum (for Satan, as an angel of light, is a fearful proof, how much knowledge may be consistent with ungodliness;) but the real difference applies—not to the extent, but to the character, of knowledge; not to the matter known, but to the mode of knowing it. 'Unbelievers'—as Dr. Owen admirably observers—'may know more of God, than many believers; but they know nothing as they ought; nothing in a right manner; nothing with an holy and heavenly light. The excellency of a believer is, not that he hath a large apprehension of things; but that what he doth apprehend (which perhaps may be very little)

[1] John iv. 14; vii. 38. [2] Chap. xviii. 4. [3] Chap. xvii. 27, 28.
[4] Chap. xiii. 16; xv. 2. [5] Matt. xxiii. 15—22. [6] Ibid. xv. 14.
[7] Eph. iv. 20, 21. [8] Num. xxiii. 19—23, with xxxi. 8. 2 Pet. ii. 15, 16.
[9] Animalis Homo—an admirable Sermon preached before the University of Oxford. Works, p. 822.
[10] Chap. xiv. 23. [11] 2 Cor. ii. 14.

he sees it in the light of the Spirit of God, in a saving, soul-transforming light. And this is that which gives us communion with God.'[1] These apprehensions therefore are manifestly of God. The object has a real existence. The unlearned Christian, without any theological aid, comes to the enjoyment of "all the riches of the full assurance of understanding;"[2] to a clearer certainty of the truth, than by the most demonstrable theorems.[3] And this experimental theology gives a rich unction to his communications. Divinity is not said by rote. *The heart teacheth the mouth.*

Take as an illustration the doctrine of the Trinity—that mystery, of which every letter is mysterious. The disputant of the school, in attempting to expound it, only "darkens counsel by words without knowledge."[4] *The heart of the wise*—heaven-taught—realizes the indwelling of the three sacred persons in undivided essence; and every act of prayer is through God—by God—to God.[5] Conscious weakness needs Divine breath. Conscious guilt trusts in Divine advocacy. *The heart*, thus taught in the school of experience, expounds the doctrine in simplicity, and super-*addeth learning to the lips.* How much better is faith understood in the practical exercise, than in the accurate definition! He who lives most simply "a life of faith on the Son of God"[6] will explain most clearly its office and influence. Contrast also proud reasoning man replying to the Sovereignty of God, with the humbled heart, *teaching the mouth* the adoration of wonder and praise.[7]

This *heart-teaching* gives the Minister the tongue of the *learned* for the refreshment of the weary soul, when he "declares" not only "what he has seen and heard,"[8] but "what his hands have handled of the Word of life."[9] He then speaks, not only the message of God, but from the mouth of God; and his "gospel comes not in word only, but in power, and in the Holy Ghost, and in much assurance."[10]

In fine—man's religion begins with the head; God's with the heart. "Out of the heart are the issues of life."[11] Let my heart be Divinely taught. Then let it *teach my mouth, and add learning to my lips*, for the praise of my God, and the edifying of his Church.

24. *Pleasant words are as honeycomb: sweet to the soul, and health to the bones.*

The sweets of pleasure are not always *health*.[12] *The honeycomb* combines both. Description may give a fancied notion of it. But the taste affords the only true apprehension. The professor may enjoy a passing sweetness in *the words* of God.[13] But it is only "the drinking in of them" that realizes their solid *pleasure*[14]

[1] On the Mortification of Sin in Believers. Chap. xii. [2] Col. ii. 2.
[3] 1 John ii. 20, 27; v. 20 [4] Job xxxviii. 2. [5] Eph. ii. 18.
[6] Gal. ii. 20. 1 John v. 10. [7] Rom. ix. 19, 20; xi. 33.
[8] Isa. l. 4, with 2 Cor. i. 4. Comp. Job v. 23. [9] 1 John i. 1—3.
[10] 1 Thess. i. 5. [11] Chap. iv. 23. [12] Chap. v. 3—5; ix. 17, 18.
[13] Ez. xxxiii. 32. Matt. xiii. 20. Heb. vi. 4, 5.
[14] Heb. vi. 7. Comp. Chap. ii. 10.

"*sweeter than honey* or *the honeycomb*."[1] We go on our way like Samson—eating our *honeycomb*;[2] like Jonathan, revived.[3] We take the Lord's words to the throne of grace; and, pleading them humbly and thankfully—most *pleasant* are they to our taste. Yea, so overwhelming often is their richness, that we can only ask, as concerning the manna—"What is it?"[4] Not less *healthful* are they than *pleasant*; invigorating to our inner principles,—those *bones*—so to speak—the strength of our spiritual system.[5]

The like *pleasure and health* flow from the words of man in the things of God.[6] How did "David and Jonathan in the wood, strengthen each other's hands in God!"[7] How was the Eunuch cheered by Philip's exposition of the precious Scripture![8] What *health* did Paul's most *pleasant words* pour into the heart of the desponding jailer![9] And how was his own spirit revived by the meeting at Appii Forum;[10] as the diciples had been refreshed by the converse of their Divine Master on the walk to Emmaus![11] When he is the subject and his spirit the teacher, *pleasant indeed will be the words* of Christian communion beyond any earthly enjoyment.

25. *There is a way that seemeth right unto man: but the end thereof are the ways of death.*

Again[12] we have this solemn, searching, caution. For so fearful is the danger of self-delusion, that we are only safe by warning upon warning.[13] Not defect of understanding, but love of sin, is the cause.[14] The judgment is perverted, because the heart is blinded.[15] It is no proof that *a way is right*, because it *seemeth right*.[16] "All the ways of a man are right in his own eyes;"[17] yet *the end thereof are the ways of death*. *The way of disobedience seems* to be necessary; or it is only a small deviation; yet was it punished as "witchcraft and idolatry."[18] *The way of deceit* seems *to be right*—an easy way of escaping difficulty;[19] or obtaining some present advantage.[20] "But a lying tongue is but for a moment;"[21] and the unrepenting liar finds his "part in the lake, that burneth with fire and brimstone."[22] *The Pharisee* is dazzled with his own goodness.[23] All his religion is in externals. He has compounded for the internal work, to add to the pomp of the heartless ceremonial. He brings to God the formal duty, which he abhors,[24] and he refuses the spiritual service, which he demands.[25] *Yet this way seems to be right.* But his countenance

[1] Ps. xix. 10. Comp. cxix. 103. [2] Judg. xiv. 8, 9.
[3] 1 Sam. xiv. 27. [4] Ex. xvi. 15. Marg.
[5] Chap. iii. 8; iv. 22. [6] Verses 21, 23; xv. 23, 26; xxvii. 9.
[7] 1 Sam. xxiii. 16. [8] Acts viii. 35—39. [9] Ibid. xvi. 27, 34.
[10] Ibid. xxviii. 15. [11] Luke xxiv. 32. [12] Chap. xiv. 12.
[13] Phil. iii. 1. [14] John iii. 19. Comp. Rom. i. 20—22, 28.
[15] Isa. v. 20; xliv. 20. Eph. iv. 18. [16] Chap. xii. 26. John xvi. 2. Acts xxvi. 9.
[17] Ver. 2; xii. 15; xxi. 2. [18] 1 Sam. xv. 20—23. [19] Ibid. xxi. 2.
[20] 2 Kings v. 22. [21] Chap. xii. 19. [22] Rev. xxi. 8.
[23] Chap. xxx. 12. Luke xviii. 11, 12. [24] Isa. i. 10—14. [25] Matt. xv. 7—9.

is hated,[1] his prayer is cast out;[2] his goodness is an abomination.[3] *The orthodox professor* takes up his opinion, and puts on appearances—only to keep the Spirit out of the heart, and to quiet his conscience without coming to the true point. *Yet his way*—with so much doing in religion—*seemeth right unto him.* Onward he goes to the grave; yea—even to the presence of his God, when heaven shut, and hell opened, shews him the truth too late.[4] Madness indeed is it to dream of heaven, when every step is the way of hell. *The end* tests the safety of the path. Hence it is the enemy's grand design to shut it out of view, that he may make his *way seem to be right. The ways of death* are many. The way of life is but One—"I am the way; no man cometh to the Father, but by me."[5] Oh! the transcendent mercy of the eyes opened to see the awful danger of our own way, and our ears opened to hear the voice behind us, saying—"This is the way; walk ye in it!"[6]

26. *He that laboreth, laboreth for himself; for his mouth craveth it of him.*

A state of labor is the penal appointment of God.[7] It is the law of God in his Church, so that those who are no workers, are counted "disorderly walkers."[8] Yet is mercy mingled with this curse. What if there were no obligation to labor? Every imagination of the heart"[9]—unmingled, unceasing "evil"—would, for want of other occupation, be left to its own undisturbed energy. Wise, then, and gracious is the decree—Rest in heaven—*labor* on earth. This is the necessary condition of the great mass of mankind. *Their mouth craveth it of them*,[10] bowing as a suppliant to receive the needful food. This is *laboring for ourselves.* The harvest is our rich recompence. Only take care that we labor not for vanity,[11] or for "evil covetousness."[12] This is working our own ruin.[13] Ponder the satisfying object of *labor*—"not the meat which perisheth, but that which endureth unto everlasting life.[14] Ponder the certain harvest—"The Son of man will give it." Look over the field of *labor*—the gospel of his grace—where every promise is there to meet thee, to wait on thee, to "perform all things for thee;"[15] and yet of what avail, if thou dost not ponder, and take it to thyself? Happy indeed for us, when the spiritual appetite is created; *and our mouth craveth this labor of us* for satisfaction. All other objects find their place, when the primary object is rightly determined. Our hands and our time are given to the world; our hearts to God. Our activity is in our calling; our affections above it. This is in the highest sense *laboring for ourselves*—for our best—most enduring good—when all is cen-

[1] Ver. 5; chap. vi. 16, 17. [2] Luke xviii. 14. [3] Isa. lxv. 5. Luke xvi. 15.
[4] Matt. vii. 22, 23; xxii. 11—13; xxv. 10—12. [5] John xiv. 6.
[6] Isa. xxx. 21. Comp. Jer. vi. 16. [7] Gen. iii. 19.
[8] 1 Thess. iv. 11. 2 Thess. iii. 10—12. [9] Gen. vi. 5. [10] Eccl. vi. 7.
[11] Chap. xxiii. 4, 5. Isa. xlvii. 12, 13. Hab. ii. 13. [12] Hab. ii. 9.
[13] Chap. xxviii. 22. 1 Tim. vi. 9, 10. [14] John vi. 27. [15] Ps. lvii. 2.

tered in God. And our heart responds to Augustine's confession; 'All other plenty besides my God is mere beggary to me.'[1]

27. *An ungodly man* (a man of Belial, Marg.) *diggeth up evil: and in his lips there is as a burning fire.* 28. *A froward man soweth strife; and a whisperer separateth chief friends.* 29. *A violent man enticeth his neighbor, and leadeth him into the way that is not good.* 30. *He shutteth his eyes to devise froward things: moving his lips, he bringeth evil to pass.*

A vivid picture indeed of the energy of sin! *The man of Belial* has broken away every yoke of restraint. Every member of his body—every power of his mind—is "a servant of iniquity unto iniquity."[2] May we not learn in humiliation the true standard of concentration of mind—singleness of object, diligence, delight, perseverance? Instead of "covering all sins," his pleasure is to *dig up evil*;[3] as if he was "searching for hid treasure;" to revive what had been long buried and forgotten, and lay it open with exaggerating circumstances. The tongue is usually the chief instrument of mischief. In what black color has the Divine pen set out this vile criminal—*a burning fire*—"a world of iniquity, set on fire of hell!"[4] And as he *diggeth* so he *soweth, evil*—seed that comes up only with a blast. *Strife he soweth* in every furrow;[5] jealousies among nations,[6] war between the Sovereign and his people,[7] divisions among Churches,[8] coldness between Ministers and their flocks[9]—ill will among friends[10]—a spirit eminently hateful to God.[11] Where open contentions might not work, *whisperings*,[12] —"evil surmisings"—idle and slanderous reports, are employed to *separate even chief friends.*[13] Again we find him in his father's native work—a tempter—*a violent man* indeed; but combining with loud and overbearing speech *enticements for his neighbor, to lead* the unwary *into the way that is not good.*[14] His whole soul is filled with this Satanic object. Observe him sometimes *shutting his eyes* from outward distractions; *moving his lips*, as if engaged in deep thought to *bring evil to pass*;[15] all 'expressing the profound study, with which he contrives his neighbor's ruin!'[16]

Such is the heavy service of the most cruel Master! He wears out both the minds and bodies of his slaves, and gives them at the end only the fearful wages of eternal death.[17] If the way to hea-

[1] Confess. Lib. xiii. c. 8. [2] Rom. vi. 19. [3] Chap. x. 12, with Ps. vii. 14, 15.
[4] Jam. iii. 6—8. Ps. lii. 1—4; lvii. 4. 'His tongue is a burning firebrand to set all the world in combustion.' Bishop Hall. The LXX. Version is very strong—'The perverse man carrieth perdition in his own mouth. The foolish man diggeth up evil to himself; he treasureth up fire on his own lips.'
[5] Chap. xv. 18. [6] 2 Sam. x. 3. [7] Ibid. xx. 1.
[8] 1 Cor. i. 11, 12; iii. 3. [9] Ibid. iv. 8. 2 Cor. xii. 15. Gal. iv. 16.
[10] 2 Sam. xvi. 3. [11] Chap. vi. 16, 19.
[12] 1 Sam. xxiv. 9. Ps. xxxv. 15. 2 Cor. xii. 20. This sin is numbered in the black catalogue of Heathen abominations. Rom. i. 29.
[13] Chap. vi. 14; xviii. 8.
[14] Chap. i. 11—14; iv. 16, 17. Acts xx. 30. 2 Pet. ii. 1, 2.
[15] Chap. vi. 12—14; x. 10.
[16] Bishop Patrick—'A furnace of mischief'—is the addition of LXX. Comp. Isa. xxxii. 6, 7. [17] Rom. vi. 23.

ven be narrow, is not "the way of transgressors hard?"[1] Is there not more toil in the way to hell—and that—without one beaming hope of the cheering home—one staff of the heavenly promise, that upholds the servants of God in all their weariness and trial? "Gather not my soul with sinners, in whose hands are mischief," and where "destruction and misery are in their paths."[2]

31. *The hoary head is a crown of glory, if it be found in the way of righteousness.*

The hoary head is the old man's glory,[3] and claim for reverence.[4] God solemnly links the honor of it with his own fear.[5] "The ancient" are numbered with "the honorable."[6] The sin of despising them is marked,[7] and, when shown towards his own prophet, awfully punished.[8]—Wisdom and experience may justly be supposed to belong to them,[9] and the contempt of this wisdom was the destruction of a kingdom.[10]

But the diamond in *the crown* is, when *it is found in the way of righteousness.* Even an Heathen monarch did homage to it;[11] and an ungodly nation and king paid to it the deepest respect.[12] The Fathers of the Old and New Testament reflected *its glory;* the one dying in waiting faith for the Lord's salvation—the other ready to "depart in peace" in the joyous sight of it.[13] "Zacharias and Elizabeth, walking in all the ordinances of the Lord blameless;"[14] Anna—"a widow indeed" in the faith and hope of the Gospel;[15] Polycarp with his eighty and six years in his Master's service.[16]—*Crowns of glory were their hoary heads* shining with all the splendor of royalty. Earnestly does the holy Psalmist plead this *crown* for the usefulness to the Church[17]—the Apostle, for the cause of his converted slave.[18] And who more honorable than those, who, having been "planted" in youth within the courts of the Lord, grow up to "bring forth fruit in old age," manifesting the glory of the Lord's faithfulness and love?[19] Truly is an old man's 'diadem that, which, not the art of man—but the finger of God—hath fashioned and set on his head.[20] And is not the earthly *glory* brightened by its nearness to the unfading, everlasting crown?

But separate the heavenly virtues from *the hoary head.* "*The crown is fallen.*" It lays dishonored in the dust. For what is a more lamentable spectacle, than a graceless old man, only gaining by his score of years a proportionate score of guilt? Time is no

[1] Matt. vii. 14, with Chap. xiii. 15. [2] Ps. xxvi. 9, 10. Rom. iii. 16.
[3] Chap. xx. 29. [4] Chap. xxiii. 22. 2 Sam. xix. 32, 39.
[5] Lev. xix. 32. The Roman satirist intimates, that the neglect of "rising up before the hoary head" was punishable with death. Juven. Satir. 13. The reverence paid by the Lacedæmonians to the hoary head is well known. Comp. Ovid Fasti. v. See a serious and instructive paper in the Rambler, No. 50.
[6] Isa. ix. 15. [7] Ibid. iii. 5. [8] 2 Kings ii. 23, 24.
[9] Job xii. 12; xxxiii. 4—7. [10] 1 Kings xii. 13—20. [11] Gen. xlvii. 7—10.
[12] Samuel, 1 Sam. xxv. 1. Elisha, 2 Kings xiii. 14. Jehoiada, 2 Chron. xxiv. 15, 16.
[13] Gen. xlix. 18. Luke ii. 28, 29. [14] Luke i. 6. [15] Ibid. ii. 36, 37.
[16] Euseb. lib. iv. c. 15. Milner's Church History, i. pp. 209—222.
[17] Ps. lxxi. 16, 17. [18] Philemon 9. [19] Ps. xcii. 13—15.
[20] Muffet in loco.

empty duration. It is fitted up with talents for eternity, a field for their exercise, helps for their improvement, and account for their neglect or abuse. The white hairs therefore of ungodliness bespeak ripeness for wrath—"wrath treasured up" with every day's uninterrupted increase "against the day of wrath."[1] "The sinner being an hundred years old shall be accursed."[2]

32. *He that is slow to anger is better than the mighty: and he that ruleth his spirit, than he that taketh a city.*

A great conflict and a glorious victory are here set out—a conflict not in notion, but in action: hidden from *the mighty* ones of the earth: known only to those, who, having enlisted under the baptismal banner, are 'manfully fighting,'[3] against their spiritual enemies. The heart is the field of battle. All its evil and powerful passions are deadly foes. They must be met and triumphed over in the strength of God. Those who are ignorant of God and of themselves make light of them. They scarcely acknowledge them as such. Instead of being *slow to anger*, under provocation, they think, that they "do well to be angry."[4] It is a disgrace to put up with wrong. An hasty temper is an infirmity. They are hardly responsible for it, nay—the indulgence is a relief, and they hope to cool down in time, utterly unconscious of any sin against God. Thus—instead of *having rule over their spirit*—they are captives—not conquerors.

But can a Christian do so?—he who hath "yielded himself unto God, as one that is alive from the dead?"[5] "How shall we that are dead to sin live any longer therein?"[6] Must we not vigorously "keep under the body and bring it into subjection"[7]—specially that "little member," which is such a mighty instrument of evil? To bridle the tongue, so as to check the expression of passion, or "speaking unadvisedly with our lips"—is a victory,[8] that can only be achieved by Almighty strength.

The glory of this victory is far above *the mighty*. *The taking of a city* is child's play, compared with this "wrestling with flesh and blood." That is only the battle of a day. This, the weary unceasing conflict of a life. There, the enemy may be mastered by a single blow. Here, he is to be chained up, and kept down with unremitting perseverance. The magnifying of the conflict exalts the glory of the triumph. Gideon's *rule over his spirit* was *better* than his victory over the Midianites.[9] David's similar conquest was *better*, than could have been Nabal's spoils.[10] The renowned conqueror of the East lived and died a miserable slave. He lost more honor at home, than he gained by his conquests abroad; the Lord of nations, but the vassal to his own lust; famous in war, but degraded by a brutish foe.[11] Though valor is

[1] Rom. ii. 5. [2] Isa. lxv. 20. [3] Baptismal Service.
[4] Jon. iv. 9. [5] Rom. vi. 13. [6] Rom. vi. 2.
[7] 1 Cor. ix. 27. [8] See Jam. iii. 2. [9] Judg. viii. 1—3.
[10] 1 Sam. xxv. 13, 32—34.
[11] 'So old and no older'—wrote Philip Henry in his Diary, when he had completed

commendable, as a natural gift of God;[1] yet 'to be our own masters, is far more glorious for us, than if we were the masters of the world.'[2] 'Among all my conquests'—said the dying emperor Valentinian—'there is but one, that now comforts me—I have overcome my worst enemy—my own haughty heart.'—This then is to subdue an enemy, that has vanquished conquerors. This surely is to be "more than conquerors." Christian! Never forget the source of victory—"Through him that loved us."[3]

This recollection brings us to the true point. Keep close to this glorious standard of an almighty, most loving, Saviour: Never is victory severed from it. Trials may be appointed, yet only to discipline for triumph—to draw us from our fancied, to his real, strength.

Often does the Christian soldier win the day, even when he has been wounded in the fight. Yet think not the war is ended, because a battle is won. The enemy may have been stabbed at the heart; yet will he get up, and renew the fight. Thou must walk—yea—sleep in thine armor. It must be worn—not laid up. There is no discharge from this work, till thy body of sin and death is laid in the grave. Meanwhile victory is declared, before the conflict begins. Let every day then be a day of triumph. The promises are to *present* victory.[4] With such stirring stimulating hopes, thou shalt surely *have rule*, if thou wilt but dare to have it. And if thou hast not courage enough to be a Christian, thou must be a slave for life to the hardest of task-masters.

This bloodless victory—so contrary to the turmoil of war[5]—is the crown of Christian grace.[6] No other grace of the gospel can be exercised without its influence. Yet does not the daily conquest anticipate the final victory, the spoils of which will be reaped throughout eternity?"[7]

his thirtieth year—'Alexander was, when he conquered the great world: but I have not yet subdued the little world—myself.' 'Thou art a slave of slaves'—said the proud philosopher (Diogenes) to this mighty conqueror,—'for thou art a slave to those appetites, over which I rule.'

1 Judg. vi. 12. 2 Lawson in loco. 3 Rom. viii. 37.

4 Rev. ii. iii. Him that *overcometh*. 5 Isa. ix. 5. 6 Rom. xii. 19—21.

7 Many striking sentiments from Heathen Ethics might illustrate this aphorism. Cato the elder (in Plutarch) declared him to be the best and most praiseworthy general, who had rule over his own passions. Livy brings in Scipio speaking to his friend—'The danger of our age—believe me—is not so much from armed men, as from the pleasures scattered all around us. He that has disciplined them by his own temperance, has obtained to himself much honor and a greater victory, than we had in the conquest of Syphax.' Lib. xxx. c. xv. 'In all ages fewer men are found, who conquer their own lusts, than that conquer an army of enemies.' Cicer. Ep. Lib. xv. Ep. 4. Thus Seneca writes to a friend—'If you wish to subject all things to yourself, subject yourself to reason. You will rule many, if reason ruleth you.'

Latius regnes, avidum domando
Spiritum, quam si Libyam remotis
Gadibus jungas, et uterque Pœnus
Serviat uni. Hor. Carm. Lib. ii. Ode. 2.

Alas! that this shou l be all final barren sentiment, not—as in the Christian principle!

Video meliora, *proboque;*
Deteriora sequor. (Medea in Ovid.)

33. *The lot is cast into the lap: but the whole disposing thereof is of the Lord.*

The lot cast into the lap, or into the bottom of an urn,[1] often determined important matters. Officers were thus chosen[2]—work determined[3]—dwellings fixed[4]—discoveries made[5]—"contentions caused to cease."[6] Yet ***the Lord's disposal*** was manifestly shown. Canaan was thus divided, so as to accord fully with Jacob's prophecies.[7] The offender was brought to justice. What could be more beyond human direction? Yet what more entirely under the Divine *disposal?*[8] Man could not govern beyond his knowledge. It must have been therefore the hand of God—as steady, as his eye is clear. Even when the lot was cast profanely or superstitiously—the same Sovereignty overruled. Haman's lot was so *disposed*, as wholly to overthrow his exterminating project; giving full time for the deliverance of his victims.[9] The soldier's lot was the direct fulfilment of a prophecy, that could not otherwise have been accomplished.[10] The heathen sailors *cast* it in ignorance; yet was it the Divine discovery of the guilty criminal.[11] Heathen divinations were controlled by the same absolute power.[12]

The lot is however a solemn matter, not to be lightly *cast.*[13] It is an acknowledgment of absolute Sovereignty—giving up our personal responsibility, and virtually appealing to an Omniscient, Omnipresent, Omnipotent God. It teaches us that things that we conceive to be accident are really under Providence. 'What is chance to man, is the appointment of God.'[14] ***The lot cast*** 'at peradventure—carrying a show of casualty'[15]—is under a certain *disposal.* Yet admitting it to be a Scriptural ordinance, its expediency under our more full light is more than doubtful. We have at least a more sure word of prophecy—"a lamp to our feet, and a light to our path."[16] The rule is more clear in itself, and linked with a most encouraging promise—"In all thy ways acknowledge him, and he shall direct thy paths."[17] It is far better to exercise faith, than indolently to tamper with personal responsibility.

The instructive lesson to learn, is, that there is no blank in the most minute circumstances. Every thing is a wheel of Providence. Who directed the Ishmaelites on their journey to Egypt, at the very moment that Joseph was cast into the pit?[18] Who guided Pharaoh's daughter to the stream, just when the ark, with its pre-

[1] Parkhurst translates the word to mean the bottom or midst of an urn or vessel, into which the lots were cast.
[2] 1 Chron. xiv. 5. [3] Luke i. 9. [4] Neh. xi. 1.
[5] 1 Sam. xiv. 41. [6] Chap. xviii. 18.
[7] Num. xxvi. 55, &c., with Gen. xlix. Comp. Jos. xviii. 5—10. [8] Jos. vii. 16.
[9] Esth. iii. 7; ix. 1, 2. [10] John xix. 24, with Ps. xxii. 18. [11] Jon. i. 7.
[12] Ez. xxi. 21, 22. [13] Acts i. 24—26. [14] Scott in loco.
[15] Bishop Hall. [16] 2 Peter i. 19. Ps. cxix. 105. [17] Chap. iii. 6.
[18] Gen. xxxvii. 25. 'The unparalleled story of Joseph'—as Dr. South remarks in his striking Sermon on this text—'seems to be made up of nothing else but chances and little contingencies, all tending to mighty ends.'

cious deposit, was committed to the water?[1] What gave Ahasuerus a sleepless night, that he might be amused with the records of his kingdom?[2] Who prepared the fish, at the very time and place that Jonah's lot was cast?[3] Who can fail to see the hand of God—most wonderful in the most apparently casual contingencies? 'When kingdoms are tossed up and down like a Tennis-ball;[4] not one event can fly out of the bounds of his Providence. The smallest are not below it. Not a sparrow falls to the ground without it. Not a hair, but it is numbered by it.'[5]

CHAPTER XVII.

1. *Better is a dry morsel and quietness therewith, than a house full of sacrifices with strife.*

THE allusion is to the Jewish ordinance of feasting at home upon the remains of the *sacrifices.*[6] *A house full of sacrifices* was therefore a house of plentiful provision. Yet, when the spirit of love does not rule, self predominates—the fruitful source of *strife* and confusion. Well may the Christian be content with his *dry and quiet morsel,* to be delivered from such jarrings. 'Holy love found in a cottage,'[7] *is better* than the most luxurious feast in the palaces of *strife.*[8] True happiness is not adding to our condition, but straitening our desires, and proportioning them to our condition. The secret dew of the Lord's blessing brings the rich gain of godly *quietness*[9] and contentment, and provides a sanctified meal, and a well-furnished house in the poorest dwelling.

Was not the marriage feast—comparatively *a dry morsel*—yet a feast of love, *better than* the Pharisee's house, *full of sacrifices with strife?*[10] Would we then enjoy our temporal mercies? Welcome the Saviour to them. Cherish his spirit—eye his glory in their enjoyment. The scanty fare or the more abundant store will be alike blessed with the token of his presence, and the seal of his everlasting love.

2. *A wise servant shall have rule over a son that causeth shame: and shall have part of the inheritance among the brethren.*

Folly naturally tends to *shame;* wisdom to honor.[11] *The son*—the heir of the family—may degrade himself by misconduct, and instead of being the glory of the house, *cause shame. A wise ser-*

[1] Ex. ii. 3—5. [2] Esth. vi. 1. [3] Jon. i. 7, 17.
[4] Isa. xxii. 18. [5] Polhill on the Divine Will, p. 159.
[6] Lev. vii. 16; xix 6. Deut. xii. 4—7. 1 Sam. ix. 13. Comp. Chap vii. 14.
[7] Henry. [8] Chap. xv. 17. [9] 1 Tim. vi. 6.
[10] John ii. 1—3, with Luke vii. 36—39; xi. 37, 38, 45, 53. [11] Chap. iii. 35.

vant—though having only a temporary interest in the house, may be promoted to *rule over him.* The Scripture hath recorded no *literal* instances of this interchange of place. But retributive providence has ordained, that "the foolish shall be servant to *the wise* in heart."[2] The prodigal in conscious *shame* was ready to take his place among the "hired servants."[3] *The wise servant* has however sometimes shared the *inheritance among the brethren.* Jacob, by marrying Laban's daughter, was portioned with the *inheritance.*[4] Solomon's own *servant* probably thus verified this proverb.[5] Abraham also would have made his *wise servant* his heir, but for the interposing mercy of God.[6]

Yet this promotion is a dangerous eminence. No one can bear elevation safely without special grace and painful discipline.[7] Great wisdom—much prayer—continued watchfulness—is needed to promote humility and Christian consistency; as well as to silence the envy and jealousy, which unexpected prosperity naturally excites.[8] Honor from man calls for abasement before God, and careful holiness in adorning our profession.

3. *The fining-pot is for silver, and the furnace for gold: but the Lord trieth the hearts.*

The refiner's *fining-pot and furnace try* his metals. But Jehovah claims to himself the prerogative of *trying the hearts.*[9] "His eyes are as a flame of fire."[10] Nothing deceives—nothing escapes his probing search. The gold must be put into *the furnace.* So mixed is it with dross, that the workman's eye can scarcely discover it. No burnishing is of any avail. Till it has undergone the fire, it is unfit for use. And must there not be a furnace for the child of God?[11] None of us know ourselves, until "the fire has tried every man's work, of what sort it is."[12] The hidden evil is thus brought out for humiliation;[13] the hidden good for honor.[14] Deep personal or relative affliction; "the knowledge of the plague of our own hearts;"[15] the discovery of secret sins; circumstances of daily trial in trifles, known perhaps only to the heart that feels them[16]—all or any of these are a searching, piercing *furnace.* Painful indeed is the purifying process. The flesh trembles at the fire. Yet shall we not let the refiner do his work, though it be by Nebuchadnezzar's furnace?[17] Shall we not commit ourselves with well grounded confidence to his wisdom, tenderness and love.—"O Lord, correct me; but with judgment?"[18] Is not any furnace, that "purges away our dross"[19] of earthliness, that brings us to know ourselves, our God, and his dispensations with

[1] John viii. 35. [2] Chap. xi. 29. [3] Luke xv. 19.
[4] Gen. xxx. 27—34; xxxi. 1. [5] 1 Kings iv. 7, 11. Comp. 1 Chron. ii. 34, 35.
[6] Gen. xv. 3, 4. [7] 2 Cor. xii. 1—7. [8] Dan. vi. 3 5.
[9] 1 Kings viii. 39. Jer. xvii. 9, 10. [10] Rev. i. 14. Comp. xv. 11; xvi. 2.
[11] Isa. xxxi. 9. [12] 1 Cor. iii. 13. Comp. Matt. xix. 16 22.
[13] Deut. viii. 2. 2 Chron. xxxii. 31. [14] Gen. xxii. 1, 2, 12. Matt. xv. 23—28.
[15] 1 Kings viii. 38. [16] Chap. xiv. 10. [17] Dan. iii. 19.
[18] Jer. x. 24. [19] Isa. i. 25.

us—a mighty blessing? If the process be slow, its results are sure. Nothing but dross will perish. The vilest earth will be turned into the finest gold. No refiner ever watched the furnace with such exactness and care. Strange as it may seem to see the gold left in the fire, 'he that put it there would be loth to lose it. Not one grain—not one drachm shall be lost.'[1] He "sits" in patient watchfulness,[2] moderating the heat, and carefully marking the moment, when it "shall be brought *through the fire*,"[3] and set out in all the shining of the purifying trial. Here then in the furnace—Child of God—see the seal of thine election;[4] the ground and establishment of thy confidence;[5] thy joyous anticipation, that thy 'faith, that is here in the furnace, shall, when thy Lord shall appear, be then made up into a crown 'of pure gold—be found unto praise, and honor, and glory.'[6]

4. *A wicked doer giveth heed to false lips; and a liar giveth ear to a naughty tongue.*

Here is a black, but true picture of human nature. *The wicked doer*, not content with the stirring impulse of his native lust, seeks foreign stimulants to give it increasing activity.[7] Amnon thus stimulated his own lust, by *giving heed to the false lips* of his friend.[8] Ahab, to secure his desired object, eagerly listened to the counsels of his murderous wife.[9] The Jews *gave* delighted ears to the flattering prophets[10] in their wickedness. Active and intense was the malice of the ungodly, in suborning false witness for our Lord's condemnation.[11] Yet 'there would not be so many open mouths, if there were not as many willing ears to entertain them.'[12] But be it remembered, that the listening *ears* share the responsibility of the *naughty tongue;* as all are involved in the treason, that are directly or indirectly acquainted with the plot.

Gladly does *the liar give ear* to that, which countenances his own wickedness.[13] If he did not "love a lie," he would not listen to it. But thus he shrinks from the condemning light of truth, into his own atmosphere of darkness.[14] How unlike is this spirit to the true "charity" of the Gospel, which "rejoiceth not in iniquity, but rejoiceth in the truth!"[15] 'If then'—said good Bishop Hall[16]—'I cannot stop other men's mouths from speaking ill, I will either open my mouth to reprove it, or else I will stop mine ears from hearing it, and let him see in my face, that he hath no room in my heart.' Let the guilty talker ponder how certainly will this "reproach taken up against his neighbor" exclude from the heaven of light and love![17] Oh! my God, fill my heart and tongue with thine own gracious spirit!

1 Leighton on 1 Pet. i. 7. 2 Mal. iii. 2, 3. 3 Zech. xiii. 9.
4 Isa. xlviii. 10. 5 Job xxiii. 10. Zech. xiii. 9.
6 1 Pet. i. 7. Leighton ut supra. 7 Chap. iv. 16, 17. Ps. lxiv. 5, 6.
8 2 Sam. xiii. 1—6. 9 1 Kings xxi. 4—7.
10 Isa. xxx. 9—11. Jer. v. 30, 31. Mic. ii. 11. Comp. 1 John iv. 5.
11 Matt. xxvi. 59, 60. Comp. Acts vi. 11—13. 12 Bishop Hall's Works, viii. 7.
13 Chap. xxviii. 4. Comp. 1 Sam. xxiii. 19—21. 14 John iii. 20.
15 1 Cor. xiii. 6. 16 Works, ut supra. 17 Ps. xv. 3.

5. *Whoso mocketh the poor reproacheth his Maker: and he that is glad at calamities shall not be unpunished,* (held innocent, Marg.)

The sin against our Maker of "oppressing the poor," has before been noticed.[1] In this *mocking* probably there might be no power to oppress. The *poor* is so, not by fortune, but by Providence. The *reproach* therefore falls—not on the *poor*, but on *His Maker*—on Him who made him, and made him *poor*. "Woe unto him that" thus "striveth with his Maker!"[2]

Specially when poverty is brought on by *calamity*—when the hand of God is therefore more manifest—then to be glad *at calamities* is a fearful provocation. This was the sin of Shimei, scorning his fallen Sovereign.[3] This sin brought the enemies of God's people under his severest *punishment*.[4] Very different is the spirit of the Bible: teaching us, even where *calamity* is the fruit of misconduct—instead of being *glad*—to sympathize; instead of crushing, to raise, a fallen brother, or even a fallen enemy.[5]

All slight of *the poor*, is evidently here rebuked. And who, that knows himself, and his obligations, could ever disdain? 'Why should I'—asks Bishop Reynolds—'for a little difference in this one particular—of worldly wealth, despise my poor brother? When so many and great things unite us, shall wealth only disunite us? One sun shines on both; one blood bought us both; one heaven will receive us both; only he hath not so much of earth as I, and possibly much more of Christ. And why should I disdain him on earth, whom happily the Lord will advance above me in heaven?[6]

6. *Children's children are the crown of old men; and the glory of children are their fathers.*

This Proverb has its limit. What a *crown* of thorns to each other are an ungodly progeny and graceless parents! Little *glory* indeed did Rehoboam and his son add to *their fathers*.[7] As little was the godly Hezekiah dignified by his reprobate parent.[8] But in the ordinary course gracious children and parents reflect honor upon each other. Such parents rejoice in the number and growth of their *children*. Such children regard *their father's* name as *their glory*. Joseph was indeed *a crown* to his aged father;[9] as was Jacob himself *the glory of his child*, even in a Heathen nation.[10] 'A good root maketh the branches to flourish, by virtue of

[1] Chap. xiv. 31.
[2] Isa. xlv. 9. Comp. Job xl. 2. See Bishop Sanderson's Sermon on 1 Peter ii. 17. § 13.
[3] 2 Sam. xvi. 5—8. 1 Kings ii. 8, 9.
[4] Babylon, Lam. i. 21, 22. Ammon, Ez. xxv. 6, 7. Tyre, xxvi. 2, 3. Edom, Obad. 10—15. Contrast this barbarous delight with the godly tenderness of the Lord's prophets in foretelling *calamities*, Is. xvi. 9—11. Jer. ix. 1; xvii. 16. Mic. i. 8. The *gladness*, elsewhere expressed *in the calamities* of the enemies of the Church, were obviously the admiring discovery of the Lord's faithful keeping of his Church, and of his glory in the deserved punishment of his irreconcilable rebels. Ex. xv. Psalm xxxv. 8—10, 19—26. Rev. xviii. 20.
[5] Chap. xxiv. 17, 18. Job xxxi. 29. Ps. xxxv. 13, 14. Rom. xii. 20, 21.
[6] Works, p. 908.
[7] 1 Kings xii. xv. 1—3.
[8] 2 Chron. xxviii. xxix.
[9] Gen. xlvi. 29; xlvii. 11, 12.
[10] Ibid. xlvii. 7—10.

the lively sap that it sendeth up. And flourishing branches win praise to the root, for the pleasant fruit which they bring forth.'[1]

The Old Testament promise—"length of days"[2]—was enhanced, when accompanied with the blessing of children;[3] yet more—when crowned with the increase of *children's children.*[4] The true blessing however could only be known, when children, early brought up into God's covenant, were trained in his ways, and "declared them to their children, that they might set their hope in God."[5] "Happy was the man, who had his quiver full of such children!"[6] Happy the children, thus crowned with the example of such fathers! Abraham was the honorable, though delusive, boast of of his seed.[7] David was *the glory of his children,* preserving to them the throne of Judah for seventeen generations.[8] And may not godly parents, under a larger dispensation of grace, educating their children by example, no less than by precept—may they not look for "a godly seed"—the children of the covenant[9]—who shall acknowledge infinite, eternal obligations to parental faith and godliness?[10]

7. *Excellent speech* (a lip of excellency, Marg.) *becometh not a fool; much less do lying lips a prince.*

Men naturally speak as they are. The *lip* is the organ of the heart. *The lip of excellency*—to speak suitably of high and lofty things—evidently *becometh not a fool.*[11] A grave discourse on godliness *becometh* not an ungodly man.[12] It carries no weight, and, so far from doing good, it often brings contempt.[13] Christ would not accept even a sound confession from the lips of Satan, lest it should bring an occasion of stumbling.[14] So unseemly was *excellent speech* from so corrupt a source!

Much less do lying lips become a Prince—the Minister and Guardian of truth.[15] Yet in a world, where self reigns supreme, such inconsistencies are but too prevalent.[16] The pure doctrine of our Divine Master alone secures Christian consistency in heart, lip and life. Never let us forget, that, if *excellent speech becometh not a fool,* it does *become* the gospel of Christ—the "saints of God."[17] And Oh! let it be fully manifested in all its gracious unction and power, for "the edifying" of the Church,[18] and for the conviction of gainsayers."[19]

[1] Clever on Chap. i. 1. [2] Chap. iii. 2, 16. [3] Gen. xv. 3; xxx. 1.
[4] Gen. xlviii. 11; l. 23. Job xlii. 16. Ps. cxxviii. 6. [5] Ps. lxxviii. 5—7.
[6] Ibid. cxxvii. 5. [7] Matt. iii. 9. John viii. 33.
[8] 1 Kings xi. 12, 13; xv. 4. 2 Chron. xxi. 7. [9] Gen. xvii. 7. Ps. cxxvii. 3.
[10] 2 Tim. i. 5; iii. 15. [11] Chap. xxvi. 7, 9. [12] Ps. l. 16, 17.
[13] Matt vii. 3—5. Rom. ii. 21—24. [14] Mark i. 34. Comp. Acts xvi. 16—18.
[15] Chap. xvi. 10—13.
[16] Heathen morality from the lips of one of her wisest teachers allowed *the lying lips of princes,* because they governed for the public good. 'All others'—he adds—'must abstain.' Plato De Repub. iii. 'Qui nescit dissimulare, nescit regnare'—has been too often a royal maxim. Far more *becoming a prince* was the saying of Louis IX. of France—'If truth be banished from all the rest of the world, it ought to be found in the breast of *princes.*' Alphonsus of Arragon declared, (Lavater in loco) that 'one word of a prince should be a greater security than a private man's oath.'
[17] Phil. i. 27. Eph. v. 3, 4. [18] Eph. iv. 29. [19] Col. iv. 6. Tit. ii. 8.

8. *A gift is as a precious stone in the eyes of him that hath it; whithersoever it turneth it prospereth.*

'A gift is so tempting, that it can no more be refused than a lovely jewel, by him to whom it is presented; and such is its power, it commonly prevails over all men, dispatches all business, carries all causes, and—in a word—effects whatever a man desires.'[1] Such is the sympathy between a lusting eye and a glittering gift. The covetous prophet[2]—nay even an Apostle[3]—was wilfully beguiled by its fascination. The heathen soldiers sold themselves to its slavery.[4] A King's Minister was won over by its allurement.[5] Even a King—and such as the man after God's own heart—was sinfully perverted in the snare.[6] Seldom does it fail to *prosper whithersoever it turneth.* But who would envy a *prosperity* for evil? All Ministers of law were wisely directed (like fabled Justice) to give their decisions blindfolded; not looking at this *precious stone*, lest they should be dazzled by its sparkling attraction.[7] Unfaithfulness was always visited with the heavy displeasure of the Great Judge.[8]

And is not the child of God often pressed with this temptation? Does the influence of a gift—the sense of obligation, never repress the bold consistency of godliness? Does no bias of friendship—no plausible advantage entice into a crooked path? Oh! be resolute in a better strength than thine own in the resistance of the sin. The conflict is not with violent temptation, or with open sin, but with subtle, and apparently harmless, deviations from the strait path. Exercise thy "integrity and uprightness," in the spirit of faith, and doubt not that they will "keep thee."[9] The man of God, thus walking with God will look down upon this corruption with indignant abhorrence—"Let thy gifts be to thyself—Thy money perish with thee."[10]

9. *He that covereth a transgression seeketh love: but he that repeateth a matter separateth very friends.*

Seeketh love! A beautiful expression—much to be kept in

[1] Bishop Patrick—'What a description'—adds Mr. Scott—'of the mercenary selfishness of mankind!' Comp. also verse 23; xviii. 16. Even the Heathen conscience seems to have had a just perception of this evil. The saying of Philip of Macedon is well known, that 'there was no fortress so strong, but it might be stormed, if an ass laden with gold was brought to the gate.' The poet finely illustrates this remark, referring also to the current report of its author, that—'not Philip—but Philip's gold—conquered Greece.' Hor. Od. Lib. iii. 16. Comp. also Ovid. de Arte. iii. 'Auro loquente, iners omnis Oratio.' Greg. Nazian. 'Gold and silver pervert many things, especially motives of right. Money hath a great power with those that are in power. A golden key will open any prison door, and cast the watchman into a deep sleep. Gold will break open gates of iron, as well as silence the orator's voice, and blind the judge's eyes. It will bind the strong man's hands, and blunt the edge of the sword. It makes war, and it makes peace. What almost can it not do with corrupt minds?'—Caryl on Job xxxi. 21.

[2] Num. xxii. 7, 8, 21. 2 Peter ii. 15. [3] Matt. xxvi. 14—16.

[4] Ibid. xxviii. 12—15. [5] Acts xii. 20. [6] 2 Sam. xvi. 1—4.

[7] Ex. xxiii. 8. Deut. xvi. 19.

[8] Deut. xxvii. 25. Isa. v. 22, 23. Mic. iii. 11, 12; vii. 3, 4. [9] Ps. xxv. 21.

[10] Dan. v. 17. Acts viii. 18—20.

mind! It shows a delight in the atmosphere of *love*—man's highest elevation in communion with his God.[1] It implies not the mere exercise of *love*, where it is presented, but the searching—making opportunity for it. A forbearing spirit is a fine manifestation of it. Our motives are often misconstrued. We meet in a world of selfishness cold reserve, instead of glowing confidence. Prejudice builds a wall against Christian intercourse. Wounded pride would return unkindness with contempt. Resentment stirs up recrimination. Disappointment kindles morbid suspicion. Here is the noble field for Christian victory; instead of resenting, to *cover the transgression* with a mantle of love[2]—with that act of amnesty, by which we are saved—the most aggravated *transgression*—the most unprovoked injuries—*covered* in eternal forgetfulness.[3]

The repeating a matter has often *separated friends* by uncovering a forgotten quarrel.[4] Mischief might not be intended. But to amuse ourselves with the follies or weakness of our brethren, is sinful trifling, fraught with injury. Justly are "tattlers and busybodies" described, as "speaking things which they ought not."[5] A disciplined tongue is a restraining mercy to the Church.

10. *A reproof entereth more into a wise man, than an hundred stripes into a fool.*

If we should *cover transgression*, we should not forbear *reproof*. *Reproof* distinguishes the wise man from the *fool*.[6] A word is enough for the wise. The discipline of *stripes* is needful for *the fool*. Parents and tutors should specially study the character of children, that they may temper *reproof* wisely. Many a fine spirit has been spoiled by unsuitable treatment.

If this be true of man's *reproof*, much more of God's. A word was enough for David.[7] A look[8] *entered more into* Peter's heart *than an hundred stripes into* Pharaoh[9]—Ahaz[10]—Israel.[11] *Stripes* only scourge the fool's back. They never reach his heart. He is therefore a fool still. "Though thou shouldest bray him in a mortar among wheat with a pestle, yet shall not his foolishness depart from him."[12]

What then makes the difference as the effect of *reproof*? "The stony heart is taken away, and an heart of flesh is given?"[13] A needle pierces deeper into flesh, than a sword into stone. A wakeful ear, a tender conscience, a softened heart, a teachable spirit—these are the practical exercises, by which a wise and loving father disciplines his children for his service—for his cross—for his crown.

11. *An evil man seeketh only rebellion: therefore a cruel messenger shall be sent against him.* 12. *Let a bear robbed of her whelps meet a man, rather than a fool*

[1] 1 John iv. 16. [2] Chap. x. 12. 1 Cor. xiii. 7. [3] Heb. viii. 12.
[4] Chap. xvi. 28. [5] 1 Tim. v. 13. [6] Chap. xiii. 1.
[7] 2 Sam. xii. 1—7; xxiv. 13, 14. [8] Luke xxii. 61, 62. [9] Ex. ix. 34, 35.
[10] 2 Chron. xxviii. 22. [11] Isa. i. 5; ix. 13. Jer. v. 3. [12] Chap. xxvii. 22.
[13] Ez. xxxvi. 26.

in his folly. 13. *Whoso rewardeth evil for good, evil shall not depart from his house.*

Some awful pictures of man are here set out. *Look at his way wardness—seeking only rebellion*—resisting all authority of God and man. This is no light sin.[1] *Therefore a cruel messenger*—one that will not be turned from his work—*shall be sent against him.* The disobedient son in the family;[2] Korah in the Church;[3] Absalom,[4] Shebna,[5] and Pekah,[6] in the kingdom—all stand out as monuments of retributive justice. Not that *rebellion* is the only sin, but that it is the grand outbreaking of the stubborn will. It may be hidden under a peaceful and amiable cover. But it "is not dead, but sleepeth."[7] Let God remove the restraint; let Satan bring the occasion of temptation; and when before all appeared love and unity; "hateful, and hating one another"[8]—will be the broad features.

Look again at man in his folly. The graphical accuracy of the figure can scarcely be surpassed. The savage beast under the strongest excitement[9]—*a bear robbed of her whelps*—is less dangerous to meet. Witness Jacob's sons putting a whole city to fire and sword for the folly of one man;[10] Saul slaying a large company of innocent priests;[11] Nebuchadnezzar aggravating the heat of the furnace;[12] Herod murdering the children in Rama;[13] "Saul breathing out threatenings and slaughter against the disciples of the Lord"[14]—was not all this the rage of a beast, not the reason of a man? Humbling indeed is this picture of man, once "created in the image of God."[15] More humbling is it to see this *folly* in a child of God—to see David binding himself with an oath to massacre a whole family, some of whom had taken up his cause against the sottish offender. Yet the melting away of his fury under wise remonstrance showed the man of God covered with the shame of his *folly*, not *the fool* living *in it*, as his nature, habit, and delight.[16]

But to turn nearer home—are there no households, where uncontrolled anger governs all at pleasure? Does the self-willed victim remember, that 'nothing is said or done in a passion, but may be better said or done afterwards?'[17] Do we never see the Christian, whom his Master's discipline and example ought to have transformed to a lamb, still like *the bear robbed of her whelps?* Man—the holiest—left of God to try him, that he might know *all* that was in his heart[18]—"man"—so left to himself—"verily at his best estate is altogether vanity."[19]

[1] 1 Sam. xv. 23. [2] Deut. xxi. 18—23.
[3] Num. xvi. [4] 2 Sam. xv. 12; xviii. 15, 16. [5] Ibid. xx. 1, 22.
[6] 2 Kings xv. 27—30.
[7] The philosophical remark of Burke—'Those who do not love religion, hate it'—is the spirit of our Divine Master's saying, Matt. xii. 30.
[8] Tit. iii. 3. [9] Comp. 2 Sam. xvii. 8. Hos. xiii. 8.
[10] Gen. xxxiv. xlix. 5—7. [11] 1 Sam. xxii. 11—18. [12] Dan. iii. 13, 19.
[13] Matt. ii. 16. [14] Acts ix. 1. [15] Gen. i. 26.
[16] 1 Sam. xxv. 21—32. [17] Matthew Henry's Sermon on Meekness.
[18] 2 Chron. xxxii. 31. [19] Ps. xxxix. 5.

Look again at man in his ingratitude. God forbids to *reward* evil for evil; much more *evil for good.* This sin even the Heathen deemed to include every other.[1] And so hateful is it to God, that he visits the *evil,* not only on the sinner himself, but on *his house.* Israel was punished for the ill return to Gideon.[2] The traitor's *house* was doomed to a curse.[3] And how fearful *the evil* to the ungrateful nation,—who does not know?[4]

And surely *evil rewarded for good* was the stamp of our father's sin.[5] And ever since has the curse been fearfully verified—*Evil shall not depart from his house.* Nor is this unjust severity. What say we to a child, nourished with the tenderest care, yet casting off all filial regard, and *rewarding evil for good?* Could any other appearances of virtue atone for this unnatural abomination—this awful deformity? And yet is not this sin—the astonishment of heaven and earth—the mark of every child of fallen Adam? "I have nourished and brought up children, and they have rebelled against me."[6] But for the transfer of this mighty mass of guilt upon the great sacrifice, how could we stand before God?—And who of us still in the consciousness of this guilt, will not seek for a deeper interest in that no less perfect work, by which the rebel spirit is tamed, and humbled into the meekness and love of the Gospel?

14. *The beginning of strife is as when one letteth out water: therefore leave off contention, before it be meddled with.*

Both the destructive elements—fire and water—illustrate the danger of *the beginning of strife.*[7] To neither element can we say—"Hitherto shalt thou come, and no further!"[8] As well might we command the raging storm, as the uncontrolled passion—"Peace! be still."[9] The dam may restrain a large body of waters. But cut the sluices, and *the letting out of water* may be a sweeping inundation.[10] Thus fearfully has *the beginning of strife* issued in the murder of thousands;[11] in the desolation of kingdoms.[12]

No less destructive is it in ordinary life. One provoking word brings on another. Every retort widens the breach. Seldom, when we have heard the first word, do we hear the last. An inundation of evil is poured in, that lays desolate peace, comfort, and conscience. Does not grace teach us the rule over our own spirit; to keep down the expression of resentment; and rather to bear provocation than to break the bond of unity?

Truly is it wise to stop the evil at *the beginning.*[13] The bank

[1] Ingratum si dixeris, omnia dixeris. Yet was it the aggravation of their own sin Rom. i. 21.
[2] Judg. viii. 35; ix. 56, 57. Comp. Jon. xviii. 20—23.
[3] Ps. lv. 12—15; cix. 9—13.
[4] Matt. xxvii. 25, with xxiii. 32—39.
[5] Gen. iii. 5, 6, with ii. 8—18.
[6] Isa. i. 2.
[7] Chap. xxvi. 21. Judg. ix. 19, 20. Jam. iii. 5.
[8] Job xxxviii. 11.
[9] Mark iv. 39.
[10] See Virgil's elegant picture, Æn. ii. 496—499.
[11] Judg. xii. 1—6. 2 Sam. ii. 14—27.
[12] 2 Chron. x. 14—16; xiii. 17; xxv. 17—24.
[13] Chap. xx. 3.

is much more easily preserved than repaired. The breach once made, if it only *let out* a drop of *water*, is *the beginning* of an evil, the fruit of which cannot be calculated. As one strongly observed—'Man knows the beginning of sin; but who bounds the issues thereof?' Abraham nobly yielded in the *contention* with Lot, and the evil was stayed.[1] Paul and Barnabas—neither would yield; "and the *contention* was so sharp between them—that—'sad record!'—they departed asunder one from the other."[2] Moses restrained himself in the rising provocation with his wife.[3] Israel prudently refrained from contention with Edom in the churlish refusal of water.[4] David answered gently to his brother's irritating suspicion[5]—He was as a deaf man to his enemies, who were seeking contention with him.[6] The time to *leave off contention* is not, when we see its worst, but its *beginning*—yea—*before it be meddled with;* restraining the first rising in ourselves; mortifying our own proud tempers, and cultivating our Master's meek and self-denying spirit.

15. *He that justifieth the wicked, and he that condemneth the just, even they both are an abomination to the Lord.*

Judicial iniquity is an awful abuse of God's authority.[7] The judge or magistrate "is a minister of God for good."[8] The appeal is to him for justice, as the Representative of God.[9] If the great Judge "loveth righteousness, and hateth iniquity,"[10] this unrighteous *justifying of the wicked must be abomination to him.*[11] This guilt of Samuel's sons—so contrary to his own integrity—was the immediate cause of the abolition of the Theocracy.[12] The judges in David's time seem to have been guilty of both these branches of injustice.[13] Ahab's house was ruined by *his condemnation of the just.*[14] "Not this man, but Barabbas"[15]—combined the double sin—the perfection of injustice—the most aggravated abomination.

Not however to confine the application to official iniquity—Do we not all need great watchfulness, that we may "judge righteous judgment;"[16] that no corrupt bias may prejudice the exercise of our private judgment, either in favor of *the wicked*, or in the *condemnation of the just?*

But let us place ourselves before the "Judge of all" accused by Satan—conscience—law—and convicted of every charge—yet justified. Does God then in thus "justifying the ungodly"[17] contravene this rule?—Far from it. If he *justifies the wicked*, it is on account of righteousness.[18] If he *condemn the just*, it is on the imputation of unrighteousness. Nowhere throughout the universe

[1] Gen. xiii. 8, 9. [2] Acts xv. 39. [3] Ex. iv. 25, 26.
[4] Num. xx. 14—21 [5] 1 Sam. xvii. 28, 29. [6] Ps. xxxviii 12—14.
[7] Ex. xxiii. 7. [8] Rom. xiii. 2, 3. [9] Deut. xxv. 1.
[10] Ps. xlv. 7. Comp. Deut. xxxii. 4.
[11] Isa. v. 23. Comp. Sophocles Œdip. Tyr. verses 622, 623, also Chap. xxiv. 23, 24.
[12] 1 Sam. viii. 3—9, with xii. 3. [13] Ps. lxxxii. 2; xciv. 20, 21.
[14] 1 Kings xxi. 13—19. [15] John xix. 40. [16] John vii. 23, 24.
[17] Rom. iv. 5. [18] Ibid. iii. 25, 26.

do the moral perfections of the Governor of the world shine so gloriously, as at the cross of Calvary.[1] The satisfaction of the holy law, and the manifestation of righteous mercy, harmonize with the iustification of the condemned sinner.[2] And this combined glory tunes the song of everlasting praise.'[3]

16. *Wherefore is there a price in the hand of a fool to get wisdom, seeing he hath no heart to it?*

A question of wonder and indignation! Why *a fool* so blessed, if he have *no heart* to improve his blessing? Birth, religious privileges, talents, time, influence, opportunity—all are *a price to get wisdom.* If the *fool* throws it away, the account of unprofitableness seals his sentence.[4] The grand *price is in our hand*[5]—of inestimable value. Yet how many thousand *fools have no heart* to buy, would rather lose it, than labor for it; rather go sleeping to hell, than toiling to heaven! The Gadarenes threw away the pearl.[6] Herod eyed it with curiosity;[7] Pilate with indifference;[8] the Jews with scorn.[9] The rich man preferred his own "goodly pearls" to it.[10] Felix hoped to turn it to his own selfish purpose.[6] Agrippa dared not purchase it.[12] Were not all these, pictures of the every-day *fool*, that meets our eye?—'That which "is more precious than rubies"[13] is to him more worthless than a pebble. That which is more sweet than honey is tasteless as the white of an egg.'[14] As if the world could be a God to us—could fill up God's vacant place in our heart! Yet thus the realities of eternity—the mighty things of the Gospel—things that should drink up our spirits, are like "a tale that is told." Enough that they should have a place in our creed, though never in our hearts. The world is preferred to heaven, time to eternity; and the immortal soul—for which such a cost has been paid, and such prospects prepared—perishes in folly. But will it not be a sword in the awakened conscience—'I might have been enriched, had I not wasted the golden opportunities of salvation, and fooled away the glorious days of the Son of man?' Yea—will not this be the sting of the never-dying worm—'Had I come to Christ when I might, I should not have been in this place of torment. I would not come then.[15] I cannot come now.'[16] 'Lord save me'—cries the pious Howe—'from trifling with the things of eternity.'[17]

[1] Isa. liii. 5—10. 2 Cor. v. 21. [2] Ps. lxxxv. 10. Isa. xlv. 21.

[3] Bishop Davenant justly quotes this text, as an example of the forensic use of the term justification—'not the infusion of a quality, but the pronouncing a sentence.' (Discourse on Inherent Righteousness, Chap. xxii. Allport's Translation.)—The true sense, in which it is used in reference to our justification before God—pronounced just in God's own court of judgment.

[4] Matt. xxv. 24—30.

[5] Chap. viii. 4, 5; ix. 4—6. Isa. lv. 1—3. Rom. x. 8. Rev. iii. 20.

[6] Matt. viii. 34. [7] Luke xxiii. 8. Comp. Acts xvii. 21, 32.

[8] John xviii. 38. [9] Acts xiii. 46. [10] Mark x. 22.

[11] Acts xxiv. 25—27. [12] Ibid. xxvi. 28. [13] Chap. iii. 15; viii. 11.

[14] Lawson. [15] Matt. xxiii. 37. John v. 40.

[16] Matt. xxv. 10. Luke xiii. 25—28; xvi. 26. [17] Works, iii. 130

17. *A friend loveth at all times, and a brother is born for adversity.*

This beautiful picture of friendship has been drawn by moral ists, sentimentalists, and poets. But the reality is only found, where Divine grace has melted away natural selfishness into disin·terested love. If virtue is the best ground of friendship, then is this most heavenly virtue the firmest ground of all. What passes under the name is too often, as Bishop Hall[1] describes it, 'brittle stuff.' This fickle excitement cools by distance, or by the coldness of our friend. Worldly degradation of circumstances, converts it into indifference;[2] or even hatred.[3] The friend, who had left the right path, is forsaken, instead of being followed, watched over, and every opportunity improved for reclaiming him. "But the true *friend loveth at all times*, through evil, as well as good, report." He is not ashamed of poverty[4] or of a prison.[5] In any jarrings of the flesh, *adversity* cements love.[6] The *loving friend* becomes now *a brother born for adversity.*[7] Such was the love of Joseph to his brethren; unshaken by vicissitudes—unabated by ingratitude.[8] Such was the firm cleaving of Ruth to her desolate mother;[9] the identity of heart between David and Jonathan;[10] the affectionate sympathy of the beloved disciple to the mother of his Lord.[11]

We must not indeed look for perfection. Can we doubt the sincerity of the disciples, while we are humbled, instructed, and warned by their frailty?[12] For frailty it was; not wilfulness—nor hypocrisy. "Ye are they, that have continued with me in my temptations"—was their Master's kindly acknowledgment at the very moment of infirmity, when "they all forsook him and fled."[13]

But—Ah! it is to him that we must look as the perfect exemplar—To see the Son of God in our nature, that he might be our *friend and brother;*[14] to hear him "not ashamed to call us brethren"—this is a mystery of *friendship*—unsearchable. Truly is this Friend[15]—he alone—worthy of our unlimited confidence. Such is the constancy of his *love—at all times*[16]—even unto death;[17] unaltered by the most undutiful returns; "turning and looking upon" the disciple (such a look of tenderness and power![18]) whom we should have excommunicated. Such the sympathy of his love

[1] Works, viii. 38. Meditations and Vows. [2] Job vi. 14, 15.
[3] Chap. xix. 7. 1 Sam. xvi. 21, 22, with xviii. 5—9. Job xix. 17—20. Comp. Ovid's elegant lines, Lib. de Ponto.
[4] 2 Sam. xv. 19—22; xvii. 27—29. [5] Phil. ii. 25. 2 Tim. i. 16—18; iv. 11.
[6] See the melancholy dispute between Bishops Hooper and Ridley upon ceremonials, and the cementing love of the prison, with Foxe's beautiful remarks, vi. 640, 641.
[7] Bishop Patrick. Comp. Job ii. 11—13. Ecclus. vi. 7, 8, 10, 16.
[8] Gen. xlv. 5—8; l. 19—21. [9] Ruth i. 16, 17.
[10] 1 Sam. xviii. 3; xix. 2; xx. 33; xxiii. 16. 2 Sam. i. 16; ix. 1.
[11] John xix. 27. [12] Matt. xxvi. 40, 41. [13] Luke xxii. 28, with Matt. xxvi. 56.
[14] Heb. ii. 14. [15] Ibid. verses 11—13. [16] John xiii. 1.
[17] Ibid. xv. 13. 'Mine is an unchanging love;
Higher than the heights above;
Deeper than the depths beneath;
Firm and faithful, strong as death.—Cowper.
[18] Luke xxii. 61.

—*born for adversity*; So united to us—*the friend and the brother* we need; never nearer to us than when in our lowest depths of trouble; and, though now our glorified *Brother* in heaven, yet still "touched with the feeling of our infirmities;"[1] still "afflicted in all our afflictions."[2] 'Here is sympathy—here is indeed *a Brother born to adversity.* Trust him, O ye trembling believers, at all times, and in all places. You will then be possessed of the happy art of living beyond the reach of all disappointment.'[3]

18. *A man void of understanding* (heart,[4] Marg.) *striketh hands, and becometh surety in the presence of his friend.*

Though we are to feel ourselves *born for adversity,* ever ready to "bear one another's burdens:"[5] yet we must not befriend our *brother* at the risk or expence of injustice to our family. We have therefore another warning against imprudent suretyship.[6] Beware of *striking hands* in agreement, without ascertaining, whether we can fulfil our engagement, or whether *our friend* is not equally able to fulfil it himself. This shews *a man void of understanding*; specially to do this *in the presence of his friend.* For why is not his word taken, but from the suspicion of insolvency or dishonesty? A prodigal, thoughtless kindness may gain us a popular name. But the principle, closely examined, will be found to be another form of selfishness. There is no true benevolence in rash engagements, which may involve our name and family in disgrace or ruin. True indeed—had not those *hands* that were nailed to the cross, *been stricken* in suretyship, the hand writing that was against us could never have been cancelled.[7] Yet the eternal counsel is no pattern for our simple folly. Nor is infinite love, combined with perfect wisdom, a plea for our rash generosity. Religion, though it warns its professors against imprudences, yet too often unjustly bears the blame of them. To adorn the Christian profession, and to avoid occasion of stumbling to the ungodly—"provide for honest things, not only in the sight of the Lord, but also in the sight of man."[8]

19. *He loveth transgression that loveth strife; and he that exalteth his gate seeketh destruction.*

[1] Heb. iv. 15.
[2] Isa. lxiii. 9.
[3] Howels' Sermons, ii. 252. 'Though solitary and unsupported, and oppressed by sorrows unknown and undivided, I am not without joyful expectations. There is one *Friend who loveth at all times; a Brother born for adversity*—the help of the helpless; the hope of the hopeless; the strength of the weak; the riches of the poor; the peace of the disquieted; the companion of the desolate; the friend of the friendless. To him alone will I call, and he will raise me above my fears.' Memoir of Mrs. Hawkes, pp. 127, 128. The ancient Jews applied this Proverb to Christ, adducing it as a testimony, that the Divine Messiah would by his incarnation become the brother of man. Gill in loco.
[4] Chap. vii. 7; x. 13; xi. 12; xv. 21; xxiv. 30. 'It denotes the want of a right state of mind, judgment, and affection, or in general, of all the faculties of the soul, through ignorance, carelessness, and the prevalence of evil propensities of various kinds.' Scott on xi. 12.
[5] Gal. vi. 2.
[6] Chap. vi. 1—5; xi. 15.
[7] Col ii. 14.
[8] 2 Cor. viii. 20, 21.

We may indeed fall into *strife*, without *loving* it.[1] But let us always look at it as a branch from the root of sin[2]—the prolific source of sin.[3] The *love* of it is therefore *the love of transgression.* Yet who will own the charge? The man engaged in *strife* protests, that he loves peace; only his neighbor's perverseness drives him into *strife*. And yet if we are frequently in it; if we take no pains, make no sacrifice of self-will or interest, to avoid the occasion of *strife*—does not conscience bring home the charge? Ah! the *love of transgression* lies deeper than we often see. It shows itself in forms, that the world may overlook, but which prove its nature to be "carnal."[4]

Very generally it proceeds from the root of pride.[5] The man *exalts his gate*[6] above his neighbor, and affects a style beyond his rank. Or his ambition would tread his neighbor under his feet. Nay he will sometimes rise against his Sovereign,[7] or even stand in defiance of his God.[8] The sluggard sees his ruin before him, and indolently waits for it, without making any effort to avert it.[9] But the proud man *seeketh destruction.* He puts himself in the road, and sooner or later his day comes; and his name, glory, and honor are swept away.[10] Watch over me, O my God, to preserve me from the first rising of my proud heart. Or if my frailty yield to it, O keep me from the prevalence of this presumptuous sin, that hurries me as a rival against thy throne into the pit of *destruction.*

20. *He that hath a froward heart findeth no good; and he that hath a perverse tongue falleth into mischief.*

Such is the history of God's ancient people—a picture of *frowardness* with all its barren results. Let their long-suffering God do what he would to them and for them, they *found no* satisfying good.[11] Self-will—even in its fullest indulgence—instead of bringing the desired *good*, always ends in disappointment—and when *the perverse tongue* breaks out—in frightful *mischief.*[12] The best of us are too often governed by this waywardness. Even when we seek to walk with God, how does the *froward heart* struggle to walk by its own inclination! The good Lord give us a mortified spirit, to restrain us from the guidance of our corrupt fancies! Many an erratic course in the Church we trace to some unhappy bias, not disciplined by the Divine Spirit, not moulded to reveren-

[1] Gen. xiii. 7, 8. [2] Gal. v. 19—21. [3] 2 Cor. xii. 20, 21. James iii. 14—16.

[4] 1 Cor. iii. 3, 4. 'I never loved those Salamanders, that are never well, but when they are in the fire of contention. I will rather suffer a thousand wrongs, than offer one. I will rather suffer an hundred than inflict one. I will suffer many, ere I will complain of one, and endeavor to right it by contending. I have ever found, that to strive with my superior is furious; with my equal doubtful; with my inferior sordid and base; with any, full of unquietness.' Bishop Hall, Meditations and Vows, Works, viii. 18.

[5] Chap. xiii. 10.

[6] An allusion to *the gates* of splendid palaces in the East, generally elevated according to the vanity of their owner. Morier quoted in Burder's Oriental Customs.

[7] 2 Sam. xv. 1; xx. 1. 1 Kings i. 5; xvi. 9—18. [8] Rom. xiii. 1, 2.

[9] Chap. vi. 11. [10] Chap. xvi. 18. Isa. xxii. 15—19. Jer. xxii. 13—19.

[11] Ps. lxxviii. Acts xiii. 18. [12] Chap. xi. 20; xviii. 6, 7.

tial faith. Most graciously therefore does our God assert his own right to supremacy; promising us—not freedom from restraint, but a yoke,[1] a binding law, a strict obligation, and—above all—the heart to love and obey.[2] Here is now self-control—stability; not impulse and feeling, but fixed and steady principle. Shall not we then cry with filial simplicity—'Not my will—O Lord—let me have any thing but my own way. Leave me not to my perverse heart?' In proportion as *the froward heart* is thus subdued, *the perverse tongue* is bridled; and we have the "perfect man" in Christian consistency, humility and love.

21. *He that begetteth a fool doeth it to his sorrow: and the father of a fool hath no joy.*

Among the "vanities, to which the creature is made subject," Solomon elsewhere enumerates one, of which he probably had a feeling experience—leaving the labor of his hand—he knoweth not to whom—whether he shall be a wise man or *a fool.*[3] The latter prospect is here realized. The weeping parent not only finds *no joy* in the fondly-cherished object of his expectation; but a cankering grief embitters all his joys, and often brings him "down with *sorrow* to the grave."[4] And how is this sorrow aggravated, should there be an unhappy humbling consciousness, that undue indulgence or severity, injudicious treatment, and more than all—neglect of prayer for the child, and of the diligent improvement of God's appointed means, virtually suffered the evil propensities to grow to a direful harvest of ruin!

Yet let the godly parent expect every thing from prayer—*provided it be not palsied by despondency.*[5] In the deepest distress never lose hold of the covenant of grace.[6] Let the determined faith of a praying mother encourage perseverance.[7] God exercises faith; but he never fails to honor it. He delays to answer prayer; but every word—every sigh—is registered for acceptance in his best time. Let Solomon's word be a quickening—not a fainting—word—"*profitable*" indeed "for reproof, and for correction;" but not less so "for instruction in righteousness."[8]

22. *A merry heart doeth good like a medicine; but a broken spirit drieth the bones.*

This is not true of all *merriment.* The wise man justly describes the loud and noisy mirth of fools—to be—not *medicine*—but "madness."[9] Our Lord made *a merry heart* by his message of Divine forgiveness; and this doubtless was a more healing *medicine* to the paralytic than the restoration of his limbs.[10] If I be a pardoned sinner—an accepted child of God, what earthly trouble can sink me? "Paul and Silas sang praises to God in the inner

[1] Matt. xi. 29. Lam. iii. 27.
[2] Jer. xxxi. 33. Ez. xxxvi. 26, 27.
[3] Eccl. ii. 18, 19.
[4] Gen. xlii. 38.
[5] See Gal. vi. 9. Comp. John xi 40
[6] Gen. xvii. 7.
[7] Matt. xv. 22—28.
[8] 2 Tim. iii. 16.
[9] Eccl. ii. 2. Comp. 1 Sam. xxv. 36, 37.
[10] Matt. ix. 2—7.

prison with their feet made fast in the stocks."[1] The martyrs "glorified God in the fire."[2] They were "tortured, not accepting deliverance, that they might obtain a better resurrection."[3] All earthly enjoyments are now doubly blest with heavenly sunshine.[4]

There is also the Christian flow of natural spirits. For when consecrated to the Lord, they become a means of enjoyment—not only to ourselves,[5] but to those around us. Often has the mourning saint been encouraged—often also has the worldling been convicted—by a brother's cheerful words or looks.[6] To the former it has been a *medicine.* To the latter a lesson.

Most watchful therefore should we be against the withering influence of *a broken spirit.* Allow not the imagination to dwell needlessly in gloom. Constitutional temperament will have its influence. External things act upon the body, and, through the body, upon the mind. We are some of us—creatures even of weather; not the same on a misty as on a bright day. There is much in our physical economy rather within the province of the physician than the Minister; much perhaps that we may be inclined too hastily to censure in a brother, when a better knowledge would open our sympathy. When outward and inward troubles unite, what wonder if the vessel, like Paul's ship "where two seas met,"[7] give way?[8] Yet—let it be remembered, that every indulgence increases the evil. Allowed prevalence will produce a fixed melancholy. Where spiritual causes operate, it is a spurious humility and *brokenness,* centering in self. The gospel encourages humiliation—not despondency. It deals in the realities—not of woe and despair, but of hope, peace, and joy. Its life and glory is he, that "bindeth up the broken *bones,*"[9] who "will not break the bruised reed,"[10] or crush under his feet "the prisoners of hope."[11]

Christian! Show that you really find God's ways to be "ways of pleasantness and peace;"[12] that you believe their joys, not because you have read and heard of them, but because you have tasted them. If they are happy, be happy in them. Joy is a forbidden fruit to the ungodly.[13] But let it be the adorning of thy profession.[14] It is a sin against thy God to be without it.[15] It is disparaging his heavenly comfort to lay too much to heart his counterbalancing afflictions. "Let the Lord be magnified, which hath pleasure"—not in the misery—but "in *the prosperity of his servants.*"[16] He giveth liberty to be cheerful—ground to be cheerful—and he will give thee an heart to be cheerful.

After all however—let each be careful to cultivate a just and

[1] Acts xvi. 25. [2] Isa. xxiv. 15. [3] Heb. xi. 35.
[4] Eccles. ix. 7—9. [5] Chap. xv. 13. Comp. Eccles. xxx. 22.
[6] Chap. xii. 25. Eccles. viii. 1. [7] Acts xxvii. 41.
[8] Chap. xii. 25; xv. 13. Job xxx. 30. Ps. xxxii. 3, 4; cii. 3—5; cxix. 83. Comp Eccles. xxx. 23; xxxviii. 18. Ovid's beautiful lines. Lib. i. de Ponto. This mixture of bodily and mental anguish forms the completeness of our Lord's sufferings. Ps. xxii. 15; lxix. 3.
[9] Isa. lxi. 1, 2. [10] Ibid. xlii. 3. [11] Zech. ix. 12.
[12] Chap. iii. 17. [13] Hosea ix. 1. [14] Isa. lii. 1, 2; lx. 1.
[15] Deut. xxviii. 47. [16] Ps. xxxv. 27.

even balance. Liveliness needs a guard, lest it should degenerate into levity; a grave temperament—lest it should sink into morbid depression. Christian discipline *on both sides* is the principle of enlarged happiness, and steady consistency.

23. *A wicked man taketh a gift out of the bosom, to pervert the ways of judgment.*

Again we are warned of the corruption of gifts.[1] No sin has a deeper stamp of wickedness, none a more awful mark of Divine visitation.[2] The temptation is the test of principle. Sir M. Hale (as his Biographer writes) 'had learned from Solomon, that *a gift perverteth the ways of judgment.*'[3] He always therefore rejected it with courteous integrity. Not even a good cause will justify the evil practice. The Apostle, though restrained in bondage from his great and blessed work, would not gratify his covetous judge by purchasing his release.[4] The rules of the gospel are clear and decisive. Let us not "do evil, that good may come. Let not your good be evil spoken of. Abstain from all appearance of evil."[5]

Even a corrupt world is ashamed of this sin. *The gift is in the bosom,*[6] concealed from the eye of man. But how fearfully unveiled is it to the eye of God, who will not wink at the endeavor *to pervert his ways of judgment.* How will he one day 'vindicate his Omniscience from all the insults put upon it in the world by those foolish men, who were not ashamed to do those things in the face of God himself, in which they would not have wished the meanest of his creatures to detect them."[7]

Let every child of Abraham hear the command given to his Father—"Walk before me, and be thou perfect."[8] "He that walketh righteously, and speaketh uprightly—he that shaketh his hands from holding of bribes—he shall dwell on high."[9]

24. *Wisdom is before him that hath understanding; but the eyes of a fool are in the ends of the earth.*

Let us trace our interest in *wisdom* from the beginning. It first "enters into the heart."[10] There it "rests in *him that hath understanding,*"[11] as his principle of conduct. Now it *is before his eyes* in the Book of *Wisdom* as his rule of faith and life.[12] It is the centre, to which all his thoughts, motives, and pursuits tend. All is now order. Every faculty, desire, and affection, finds its proper place. '*He that hath understanding* fixeth his eyes upon *wisdom,* and contenteth himself with that object; whereas *the eyes of a fool* are constantly wandering everywhere; and his thoughts settle upon nothing that may avail to his good.'[13] *His eyes are in the ends of the earth,* rolling and wandering from one object to

[1] Verse 8.
[2] See p. 224, note 8, also Job xv. 33. Ez. xxii. 12, 14. Am. ii. 6, 7. Comp. Chap. xviii. 5.
[3] Bishop Burnet's Life.
[4] Acts xxiv. 26.
[5] Rom. iii. 8; xiv. 16. 1 Thess. v. 22.
[6] Chap. xxi. 14.
[7] Lawson in loco
[8] Gen. xvii. 1.
[9] Isa. xxxiii. 15, 16. Ps. xv. 1, 5.
[10] Chap. ii. 10.
[11] Chap. xiv. 33.
[12] Ibid. verse 8.
[13] Bishop Hall.

another. His thoughts are scattered. He has no definite object no settled principle, no certain rule. Talent, cultivation of mind, improvement of opportunity—all are frittered away.

This diversion is a great engine of the enemy. His great object is to turn the mind aside from what is immediate to what is indefinite, from plain and important matters to what is unsearchable;[1] from what is personal to what is irrelevant.[2] Many trifles take the place of the "One thing needful." And is not this waste and loss of time often a temptation to the Christian? Where are *his eyes*—his thoughts—at prayer? Alas! too often—instead of "looking unto Jesus"[3]—his great object—the life of prayer—the only way to God—are they not *in the ends of the earth*, as if there was no nearer, no better object of attraction? Oh! do not we want simplicity of spiritual *understanding* to keep Him—the great uncreated *wisdom*—constantly *before our eyes?* Lord! I am ashamed of my base inconstancy. But it is thou alone canst heal it. "Turn away mine eyes from beholding vanity."[4] Fix them—O fix them—on Him, on whom all heaven—all the redeemed—delight to gaze forever.

25. *A foolish son is a grief to his father, and bitterness to her that bare him.*

Surely the Divine Spirit did not repeat the Proverb[5] for naught. Was it not to deepen our sense of parental responsibility and filial obligation? Can parents be insensible to the prospect of this *grief?* Can children be hardened into the unnatural selfishness of piercing a parent's heart with such *bitterness?*[6] The mother's anguish is here added to the *father's grief.*[7] "As a sword in her bones," is the apprehension of having "brought forth children to the murderer."[8] How uncertain are the dearest comforts of earth! Our fallen mother anticipated the joy of "having gotten a man"—perhaps the promised seed—"from the Lord."[9] Yet to the *bitterness* of her soul "he was of that wicked one, and slew his brother."[10] Her daughter naturally "remembereth no more the anguish, for joy that a man is born into the world."[11] Already she grasps the delightful vision of infant training, and ripening maturity. And yet too often he proves in the end *a foolish son—the bitterness of her that bare him.*

Absalom was named 'His Father's peace.' Yet was he the source of his most poignant *grief.* This is not the "weeping of a night," succeeded by a "joyous morning,"[12] but the "heaviness that maketh the heart stoop"[13]—perhaps for years—perhaps to the end of days. Its connection with eternity gives to the trial the keenest edge. To see *a foolish son* hurried irrevocably into his fixed destiny—Oh! this to the godly parent is an awful conflict.[14] Strong indeed must be that faith (*yet such faith has been vouch-*

[1] Deut. xxix. 29. Col. ii. 18. [2] Luke xiii. 23, 24. John xxi. 21, 22.
[3] Heb. xii. 2. [4] Ps. cxix. 37. [5] Verse 21.
[6] Chap. xix. 13. [7] Gen. xxvii. 34, 35. [8] Hos. ix. 13.
[9] Gen. iv. 1. [10] 1 John iii. 12. [11] John xvi. 21.
[12] Ps. xxx. 5. [13] Chap. xii. 25. [14] 2 Sam. xviii. 33.

safed,)[1] which bows reverentially to the Divine Sovereignty, and maintains the serenity of peaceful submission.

But parental anxieties and sorrows must stimulate the enquiry —How may this piercing thorn be spared—this bitter *grief*—the bitterest that ever a parent's heart can know—averted? The primary root of this sorrow is the indulgence of the will.[2] The vast power of parental influence must be used wisely—at once—at any cost. We must not instruct—or entreat only—but command:[3] We must allow no appeal from our authority, no reversal of our decision. This discipline, in the spirit of love, and enforced by example, is God's honored ordinance. Would we look for rest in our beloved children?[4] Hold them loose for ourselves—fast for God. Connect them early with his Church. Train their first years in his yoke. Plead with them and for them before our God. Instead of a sinking *grief* to us, they will be "the restorers of our life, and the nourishers of our age."[5] Instead of being our *bitterness*, as rebels against God, He will own and seal them as "a seed to serve him—to declare his righteousness," to set forth his praise.[6]

26. *Also to punish the just is not good: nor to strike princes for equity.*

Often is the wise man's meaning much beyond his words. *To punish the just* not only *is not good*,[7] but it is a gross "abomination"[8]—an evident token of perdition.[9] If rulers are "a terror to good works," they are ministers of God in authority, but ministers of Satan in administration.[10] And how will such injustice "abide the day of his coming," when he shall "lay judgment to the line, and righteousness to the plummet!"[11]

Not less wicked is the sin of the people. *To strike princes* is high treason against God.[12] The Apostle confessed the unwitting sin of his smiting words.[13] Much more guilty is it *to strike them for equity.* A godly king—ruling in *equity*, "scattering away all evil with his eyes,"[14]—will raise to himself many and powerful enemies. The evil-minded will undermine his influence,[15] or resist his authority.[16] If they dare not *strike* him openly, they will "curse him in their thoughts."[17] To *strike*—even in word—is our sin.[18] To pray is our duty.—And who knoweth, but a prayer-hearing God would send a righteous administration—a covert and blessing to the land?[19]

27. *He that hath knowledge spareth his words: and a man of understanding is of an excellent* (cool, Marg.) *spirit. Even a fool, when he holdeth his peace, is counted wise; and he that shutteth his lips is esteemed a man of understanding.*

1 Lev. x. 1—3. 1 Sam. iii. 18.
2 Chap. xxix. 15.
3 Gen. xviii. 19, with 1 Sam. ii. 23—25.
4 Gen. v. 29. Marg.
5 Ruth iv. 15.
6 Ps. xxii. 30, 31; xcii. 13—15.
7 See this same meiosis. Chap. xvi. 29; xviii. 5; xx. 23. Ez. xxxvi. 31.
8 Verse 15.
9 Phil. i. 28.
10 1 Kings xxi. 11—13. Matt. xxvi. 3, 4. Acts iv. 1—3.
11 Isa. xxviii. 17, with Mal. iii. 2, 5.
12 Ex. xxii. 20. Job xxxiv. 18.
13 Acts xxiii. 5. Comp 1 Sam. xxiv. 5, 6. 2 Sam. xvi. 5—7.
14 Chap. xx. 8.
15 2 Sam. xv. 1—6.
16 Ibid. xx. 1.
17 Eccl. x. 20.
18 2 Peter ii. 10. Jude 8.
19 1 Tim. ii. 1—3. 2 Sam. xxiii. 4. Isa. xxxii. 1, 2.

The wisdom of these Proverbs will be acknowledged by those, who know the sins of the tongue, and the immense difficulty of restraining the unruly member. *A man of knowledge will spare his words*, when the probable prospect is harm rather than good.[1] The good treasure is far too valuable to be unprofitably spent. Silence is often the best proof of wisdom.[2] Our Lord in his Divine *knowledge*, careful as he was to improve every opportunity for instruction—sometimes *spared his words.*[3]

This restraint is most important under provocation.[4] Passion demands immediate judgment. *A cool* well-tempered *understanding* asks further time for consideration. The fiery ebullition of the Apostles, their master judged to be the want of *an excellent understanding.*[5] Nehemiah, by repressing the first vent of his righteous anger, gave a reasonable and convincing answer for the occasion.[6] The prophet wisely refrained even a message from God to a king in the moment of passion.[7] 'A little spark blows up one of a sulphureous temper, and many coals, greater injuries, and reproaches are quenched, and lose their force, being thrown at another of a *cool spirit.*'[8] Indeed *a fool* may purchase to himself the reputation of *wisdom*—let him only *shut his mouth*, instead of exposing his folly to common observation.[9] 'He cannot be known for a fool, that says nothing. He is a fool—not who hath unwise thoughts—but who utters them. Even concealed folly is wisdom.'[10]

How infinitely momentous is the account, which God takes of the tongue! "Death and life are in the power of it."[11] Our eternal acceptance or condemnation will hang on it.[12] How could we endure the judgment for "every idle," no less than for every wicked, "word,"[13] if there were not for the self-abased penitent, a covering from this condemnation—a cleansing from this guilt—a seal of acceptance![14]

[1] Ps. xxxix. 1, 2. Matt. vii. 6.

[2] Chap. x. 19. Job xiii. 5. Dr. Good in his note on this verse in Job, gives a translation of an Arabic poetical proverb—

> Keep silence then; nor speak, but when besought;
> Who listens long, grows tired of what is told;
> With tones of silver though thy tongue be fraught,
> Know this—that silence of itself is gold.

[3] Matt. xvi. 4. [4] Num. xii. 1, 2. Ps. xxxviii. 12—14. Comp. Isa. liii. 7.

[5] Luke ix. 54, 55.

[6] Neh. v. 6—11. Cicero advises his brother Quintus (a proconsul in Asia) most diligently to restrain his tongue under anger, which—he adds—is no less a virtue, than freedom from anger itself. Epist. ad Q. Fratrem. Lib. i. 1.

[7] 2 Chron. xxv. 16. [8] Leighton on 1 Pet. iii. 9.

[9] Contrast Chap. xv. 2; xxix. 11. [10] Bishop Hall. Works viii. 83

[11] Chap. xviii. 21. [12] Matt. xii. 37. [13] Ibid. verse 36.

[14] See Isa. vi. 5—7.

CHAPTER XVIII.

1. *Through desire a man, having separated himself, seeketh and intermeddleth with all wisdom.* 2. *A fool hath no delight in understanding, but that his heart may discover itself.*

DESIRE is the chariot-wheel of the soul, the spring of energy and delight. The man of business or science is filled with his great object, and *through desire he separates himself* from all lets and hindrances, that he may *intermeddle with* its whole range. "This one thing"—saith the man of God—"I do."[1] This one thing is every thing with him. *Through desire he separates himself* from the entanglements of vain company, trifling amusements or studies, needless engagements, that he may *seek and intermeddle with all wisdom.* John *separated himself* in the wilderness;[2] Paul in Arabia,[3] our blessed Lord in frequent abstraction,[4] in order to greater concentration in their momentous work. Deeply does the Christian Minister feel the responsibility of this holy *separation*, that he may "give himself wholly to" his office.[5] And without it —Christian—thy soul can never prosper. How canst thou *intermeddle with the great wisdom* of knowing thyself, if thy whole mind be full of this world's chaff and vanity? There must be a withdrawal, to "commune with thine own heart"—to ask the question—"Where art thou? What doest thou here?" Much is there to be enquired into and pondered. Every thing here calls for our deepest, closest thoughts. We must walk with God in secret, or the enemy will walk with us, and our souls will die. "Arise, go forth into the plain, and I will there talk with thee."[6] "When thou wast under the fig tree, I saw thee."[7] Deal much in secrecy, if thou wouldst know "the secret of the Lord." Like thy Divine Master—thou wilt never be less alone than when alone.[8] There is much to be wrought, gained, and enjoyed. Thy most spiritual knowledge, thy richest experience, will be found here. Look around thee—what a world of heavenly *wisdom to intermeddle with!* The sight overwhelmed the Apostle with adoring astonishment.[9] Even "the angels desire to look into it."[10] The redeemed will be employed throughout eternity in this delighted searching, exploring "the breadth, and length, and depth, and height," until they "be filled with all the fulness of God."[11]

Yet *the fool hath no delight in this understanding.* All his desire is to pour out his own frivolity, to come abroad for public observation—*that his heart may discover itself*—an humiliating discovery indeed—at once of the scantiness of his knowledge, and the vanity of his mind.

[1] Phil. iii. 13. [2] Luke i. 80. [3] Gal. i. 17, 18.
[4] Mark i. 35; vi. 31. Luke vi. 12. [5] 2 Tim. ii. 4. 1 Tim. iv. 15.
[6] Ez. iii. 22. [7] John i. 48. [8] Ibid xvi. 32.
[9] Rom. xi. 33. [10] Eph. iii. 10. 1 Peter i. 12. [11] Eph. iii. 18, 19.

3. *When the wicked cometh, then cometh also contempt, and with ignominy reproach.*

Selfishness is the character of *the wicked*—'Wheresoever he cometh, he is apt to cast *contempt and reproach* upon every man's face.'[1] His neighbor's circumstances or infirmities furnish materials to hold him up to scorn. The word of God has no favor in his eyes. His people are the objects of his *reproach*. Their seriousness he calls gloom, their cheerfulness levity.[2] If "none occasion or fault can be found,"[3] invention forges it with unwearied ingenuity. "As saith the proverb of the ancients, wickedness proceedeth from the wicked."[4] We must calculate upon this furnace, though the fires of martyrdom are extinguished.—Our blessed Lord bore all the evils of the world without flinching. But *contempt and reproach* pierced his soul more keenly, than the "nails his hands and his feet." "*Reproach*," saith he—"hath broken my heart."[5] And must not the servant expect to be as his Master?[6] Often however does retributive justice overwhelm *the wicked* themselves with *ignominy and reproach*.[7] A scornful spirit against the godly is never forgotten. Every bitter word is registered against the great day.[8] And what a sight will it then be, when the reviled shall stand forth, clothed with all the glory of "the King of saints," and the faces of their persecutors shall be covered with "everlasting shame and *contempt*!"[9] The sight of that day will never be blotted out. "The rebuke of his people shall be taken away from off all the earth, for the Lord hath spoken it."[10]

4. *The words of a man's mouth are as deep waters, and the well-spring of wisdom as a flowing brook.*

The first clause is limited by the second to *the words of a wise man*. When "a man has intermeddled with all wisdom," his *words* are in themselves *deep waters*, and in their communication fruitful *as a flowing brook*.[11] His wisdom is *a well-spring*, 'which sends up full brooks, that are ready to overflow their banks. So plentiful is he in good discourse and wholesome counsel!'[12] So *deep were the waters* from the wise man's spring, that *his words* nearly overwhelmed the capacity of his royal hearer.[13] One "greater than Solomon" "astonished the people" by the clearness, no less than by the *depth, of the waters*.[14] No blessing is more valuable than a "rich indwelling of the word," ready to be brought out on all suitable occasions of instruction.[15] If the wise man sometimes "spares his words,"[16] it is not for want of matter, but for greater edification. The stream is ready to flow, and sometimes can

[1] Bishop Hall. Comp. Chap. xxix. 16. [2] Matt. xi. 18, 19.
[3] Dan. vi. 3—5. [4] 1 Sam. xxiv. 13. [5] Ps. lxix. 9, 20. Matt. xxvii. 39—44.
[6] Matt. x. 24, 25. John xv. 20. [7] 2 Sam. vii. 20—27. Esth. vii. 9, 10.
[8] 1 Pet. iv. 4, 5. Jude 14, 15. [9] Isa. lxvi. 5. Dan. xii. 2.
[10] Isa. xxv. 8. [11] 1 Kings x. 8
[12] Bishop Hall. Comp. Chap. x. 11; xvi. 22; xx. 5. [13] 1 Kings x. 4—7.
[14] Matt. vii. 28, 29 [15] Col. iii. 16; iv. 6. [16] Chap. xvii. 27.

scarcely be restrained.[1] The cold-hearted speculative professor has his *flow*—sometimes a torrent of words, yet without a drop of profitable matter; chilling, even when doctrinally correct; without life, unction, or love. Good Lord! deliver us from this barren "talk of the lips!"[2] May our *waters be deep*, flowing from thine own inner sanctuary, refreshing, fertilizing the church of God!

This *well-spring* is specially invigorating, when, as in Chrysostom, it gives an heavenly glow to outward eloquence. Consecrated mind and talent are the gifts of God. Oh! let them be improved in simplicity, not for the creature's honor, but for the glory of the Great Giver.

5. *It is not good to accept the person of the wicked, to overthrow the righteous in judgment.*

Were not "the foundations of the earth out of course," should we hear of so gross a violation of the rule of right?[3] But in a world, of which Satan is the God and the Prince, injustice is a natural principle of administration. The godly king of Judah pointed his Judges to the Divine example. Look—and be like Him.[4] Every thing revolting is connected with *wickedness.* There is no one so noble, that it does not degrade; so lovely, that it does not deform; so learned, that it does not befool. *To accept therefore his person, is indeed not good.*[5] "Abomination" is its true name—the stamp of God.[6] 'Whatever excuses man may make for this course, it is an offence to God, an affront to justice, a wrong to mankind, and a real service done to the kingdom of sin and Satan.'[7] *In judgment* let the cause be heard, not the person. Let the person be punished for his wickedness, not the wickedness be covered for the person's sake. When this is done *to overthrow the righteous in judgment;* it overthrows the throne of judgment in the land. The Shechemites were sharply punished for their sin—*accepting* Abimelech to the overthrow of the righteous claims of Gideon's house.[8] No wonder. The rights of God are despised; the claims of his justice are cast off. "He that ruleth over men must be just, ruling in the fear of God."[9] Such was our Divine pattern in the flesh; "of quick understanding in the fear of the Lord," and therefore "judging in righteousness."[10] Such will be his judgment, when "he shall judge the world in righteousness."[11] His decision will be exact—his sentence unchangeable.

6. *A fool's lips enter into contention, and his mouth calleth for strokes.* 7. *A fool's mouth is his destruction, and his lips are the snare of his soul.*

It is not a little remarkable, that the Apostle, when giving the anatomy of man's depravity, should dwell chiefly upon "the little

[1] Job xxxii. 19. Jer. xx. 9. Acts xvii. 16. [2] Chap. xiv. 23.
[3] Ps. lxxxii. 2—5. [4] 2 Chron. xvii. 7—9.
[5] Chap. xvii. 26; xxiv. 23; xxviii. 21.
[6] Chap. xvii. 15. Comp. Lev. xix. 15. Deut. i. 16, 17. [7] Henry.
[8] Judg. ix. 2—5, 45—49. [9] 2 Sam. xxiii. 4. [10] Isa. xi. 3, 4.
[11] Acts xvii. 31.

member" with all its accompaniments—the throat—the tongue—the lips—the mouth.[1] Such "a world of iniquity is it, defiling the whole body![2] We often see its mischief to others; here its mischief to itself. *The fool's lips enter into contention.* This is folly indeed. The wise man may be drawn into it by infirmity of temper,[3] or the force of circumstances.[4] But "as much as in him lies, he will live peaceably with all men,"[5] quenching even the first rising of *contention.*[6] *The fool enters into it,* by intermeddling needlessly with strife,[7] or wilfully stirring it up,[8] 'like the alarum of war, and drums beating up to the battle.'[9] And thus he makes a rod for himself.[10] He puts a weapon into the hands of Satan, with which to beat his own head. His "burning coals" are the forge, where he hammers him with fearful *strokes.*[11] The wilful *contention* of the men of Succoth and Penuel with Gideon *called for strokes.*[12] The scoffing mouth of the little children was their merited *destruction.*[13] The slanderous *lips* of Daniel's persecutors were *the snare of their soul.*[14] There is no need to dig a pit for the *fool.* He digs it for himself.[15] The mouths of wild beasts devour each other. *The fool's mouth is his own destruction.*[16] The fowler's snare is not wanted; for "he is snared by the transgression of his lips."[17] He is not only the cause, but the agent, of his own *destruction.*

And shall not the child of God watch in godly fear, lest his *folly should call for* his Father's *stroke?* Sharply may he "hew" by the sword,[18] as if he would seem to kill, in order to make alive. Yet always is it wise and gracious love; as one of the Fathers says —'threatening that he may not strike: and striking, that he may not destroy.' If shewing the rod will effect the purpose, gladly will he forbear to strike. But if our folly—as Leighton speaks—'pulls punishment out of his hands,'[19] whom but ourselves have we to thank for the smart?

8. *The words of a talebearer are as wounds, and they go down into the innermost parts of the belly.*

Do men deny, question, or soften down, the depravity of our nature? Mark again how the virulent poison of only one member destroys practical godliness, social orders and mutual friendship. *The talebearer* was expressly forbidden by the law,[20] and not less is he opposed to the spirit of the gospel.[21] No character indeed is more despicable; no influence more detestable. It is right indeed to "bring an evil report"[22] for the prevention of sin. Eli was thus enabled, though without effect, to remonstrate with his sons.[23] The

[1] Rom. iii. 13, 14. [2] James iii. 6. [3] Acts xv. 39. [4] Gen. xiii. 5—9
[5] Rom. xii. 18. Comp. xiv. 19. [6] Chap. xvii. 14. [7] Chap. xx. 3; xxvi. 17.
[8] Chap. xvi. 27, 28. [9] Cartwright in loco. [10] Chap. xiv. 3; xix. 19, 29.
[11] Chap. xxvi. 21. [12] Judg. viii. 4—17. [13] 2 Kings ii. 23, 24.
[14] Dan. vi. 12, 13, 24. Comp. Ps. lii. 1—5. [15] Ps. vii. 14, 15; lxiv. 8.
[16] Chap. x. 8, 14; xiii. 3. Eccl. x. 12, 13. [17] Chap. xii. 13.
[18] Hos. vi. 5. [19] Works, v. 114. [20] Lev. xix. 16.
[21] 1 Cor. xiii. 6. [22] Chap. xxiv. 11, 12. Gen. xxxvii. 2. Lev. v. 1
[23] 1 Sam. ii. 23, 24.

life of an Apostle was preserved.[1] Serious evils in the church were restrained or corrected.[2] But this can never be done rightly by *the talebearer*, because he does it with levity and pleasure.[3] With him it is pure selfishness, without a principle beyond the love of sin for its own sake. He lives upon the scandal of the place, and makes it his hateful business to carry about tales, or slanders of his neighbor's faults.[4] Such reports are eagerly devoured, and the mischief-maker feeds with greedy appetite upon the fruit of his cruel indulgence. To him this may appear harmless play. But, if it draws no blood, and no outward hurt is shown, an internal, and often incurable, *wound* is inflicted.[5] We may seem to make light of *the tale* brought to our ears, and wholly to despise it. But the subtle poison has worked. 'Suppose it should be true. Perhaps, though it may be exaggerated, there may be some ground for it.' The thought, indulged only for a moment, brings suspicion, distrust, coldness; and often it ends in the separation of chief friends.[6] So dangerous a member in the frame is the tongue without stern determined control! *The tale* of an unguarded moment may be a tremendous irreparable injury. We may find the evil humor in good society. It may meet with a welcome audience. *But no favor* can alter its real character, as an abomination both with God and man. Ah! what but the power of holy love, opening freely the channels of kindness and forbearance, can overcome this mischievous propensity? And what will bring this spirit of love, but a true interest in Christian privileges, and a corresponding sense of Christian obligations?[7]

9. *He also that is slothful in his work is brother to him that is a great waster.*

Observe the affinity of the different principles and workings of corruption. The sluggard and the prodigal belong to the same family. The man who "hid the Lord's talent," was equally unfaithful with him who "wasted his goods."[8] *The slothful* has no heart for *his work*. Important opportunities slip by. His stock, instead of increasing by trade, gradually dwindles into penury. 'God hath a bountiful "hand, and filleth all things living with plenteousness."[9] But unless we have a diligent hand, wherewith to receive it, we may starve. He that by the *sloth* of his hand disfurnisheth himself of the means of getting, he is as near of kin to a *waster* as may be.'[10] *He is the brother of a great waster*—the lord of a large estate, who—instead of husbanding, improving and enjoying it,

[1] Acts xxiii. 15—22. Contrast Jer. xl. 13—16; xli. 1, 2.
[2] 1 Cor. i. 11; xi. 18. [3] Jer. xx. 10.
[4] 'The word properly signifies a pedlar, who buys goods (stolen ones it may be) at one place, and sells them at another, taking care to make his own market of them. So a talebearer makes his own visits, to pick up at one place, and utter at another, that which he thinks will lessen his neighbor's reputation, that he may build his own upon it.' M. Henry's Sermon on Friendly Visits. Comp. Chap. xi. 13; xx. 19.
[5] Chap. xxvi. 22. 1 Sam. xxii. 9.
[6] Chap. xvi. 28; xvii. 9. 1 Sam. xxiv. 8; xxvi. 19. 2 Sam. xvi. 1—4.
[7] Col. iii. 12—14. [8] Matt. xxv. 25, with Luke xvi. 1. [9] Ps. cxlv. 18
[10] Bishop Sanderson's Sermon on 1 Cor. vii. 24.

wastes it away in extravagance and folly. It is the same in religion. The one is content with heartless orthodoxy. His secret prayer brings no after-remembrance. His family worship is a routine of formality, not the influential ordinance of the day. "Communing with his heart" is mere barren generality, bringing no accurate humbling knowledge of himself. And wherein does he differ from the careless *waster* of his privileges? Where is the important distinction between him, who prays—reads—works formally, and him, who utterly casts these high privileges away? Both take the same course, though by a somewhat different track. The one folds his arms in sloth. The other opens his hands in wastefulness. The one gets nothing. The other spends what he gets. The one sits still, and waits the arrival of beggary.[1] The other rushes into it. The one dies by a slow, subtle, sure consumption. The other by a rapid and violent disease. Yet fearful is the guilt, solemn is the account, certain is the ruin—of both. God gives talents, not only to enrich, but to employ. And whether they be selfishly neglected, or carelessly thrown away—"Thou wicked servant"—will be the condemnation. "Outer darkness" will be the just and eternal doom.[2] Servant of Christ! let thy Master's life be thy pattern and thy standard. Not a moment with him was *slothfully* neglected—not a moment unprofitably *wasted*. Equally fervent was he in daily work, as in nightly prayer. Follow him in his work, and thou wilt be honored with his reward.[3]

10. *The name of the Lord is a strong tower: the righteous runneth into it, and is safe* (set aloft, Marg.) 11. *The rich man's wealth is his strong city, and as an high wall in his own conceit.*

Consciousness of danger induces even the animal creation to seek for refuge.[4] To man, *a strong tower* offers such a covert.[5] But man as a sinner—does he realize his imminent peril—his threatening ruin? Oh! let him believe and embrace the testimony of the gospel. This glorious manifestation of *the name of the Lord* shews to him *a strong tower*. The full "declaration of *this name*" sets out most powerfully the extent and completeness of the refuge. Every letter adds confirmation to our faith.[6] Every renewed manifestation brings a fresh sunbeam of light and blessing.[7] Sense of danger—knowledge of the way—confidence in the *strength of the tower*—all give a spring of life and earnestness to *run into it*.[8] We fear not here the sharpest or swiftest dart that may be shot against us. We realize our security from external trouble,[9] and in trying exercises of faith![10] We are *safe* from his avenging justice, from the curse of his law, from sin,

[1] Chap. vi. 11; xxiv. 34. [2] Matt. xxv. 26—30.
[3] John xii. 26. [4] Chap. xxx. 26. Ps. civ. 18.
[5] Judg. ix. 50. 2 Chron. xiv. 7; xxvi. 9; xxvii. 4. [6] Ex. xxxiv. 5—7.
[7] See the New Testament names of God. Rom. xv. 5, 13. 2 Cor. i. 3; v. 19. 1 Peter v. 10. Comp. Ps. ix. 10.
[8] See the examples of Jacob, Gen. xxxii. 11, 28, 29. David, 1 Sam. xxx. 6. Ps lvi. 3. Asa, 2 Chron. xiv. 11. Jehoshaphat, xx. 12. Hezekiah, 2 Kings xix. 14—19.
[9] Deut. xxxiii. 27—29. Ps. lxi. 3; xci. 2. Isa. liv. 14. [10] Isa. l. 10.

from condemnation, from the second death. We joy in our *safety*[1] —yea—in our *exaltation.*[2] Our best interests are beyond the reach of harm;[3] and *the righteous* nation takes up the song of triumph—"We have a strong city: Salvation will God appoint for walls and bulwarks."[4] But only *the righteous* are found here. What know the ungodly of this refuge? 'Our God's mercy is holy mercy. He knows how to pardon sin, not to protect it. He is a sanctuary to the penitent, not to the presumptuous."[5] What joy is it, that the gates of this city are always open. No time is unseasonable. No distance, no feebleness, hinders the entrance. The cripple may *run,* like "Asahel, swift of foot."[6] All that enter are garrisoned to salvation. 'Satan is raising batteries against the fort, using all means to take it, by strength or stratagem, unwearied in his assaults, and very skilful to know his advantages."[7] But notwithstanding all his disturbing power, "the peace of God" daily fortifies our hearts from fear of evil.[8] Such is our *strong tower!* What owe we to our gracious Saviour, who has made our way to it so free, so bright?[9] We repose in the bosom of God, and are at peace.

But the rich man has his strong city—yea—*and his high walls?*[10] Well does the wise man add—*in his own conceit.* Little does he think, that in a moment they may crumble to the dust, and leave him in the fearful ruin of an unsheltered state. 'Trouble will find an entrance into his castle. Death will storm and take it. And judgment will sweep both him and it into perdition.'[11]

An affecting contrast truly between a real and an imaginary refuge.[12] Every man is as his trust. A trust in God communicates a Divine and lofty spirit. We feel that we are surrounded with God, and dwelling on high with him. O the sweet calm of a soul thus shut up in an impregnable fortress! A vain trust brings a vain and proud heart—the immediate forerunner of ruin.

12. *Before destruction the heart of man is haughty, and before honor is humility.*

We have had both these Proverbs separately.[13] Surely this repetition, like our Lord's often repeated parallel,[14] was intended to deepen our sense of their importance. It is hard to persuade a man that he is proud. Every one protests against this sin. Yet who does not cherish the viper in his own bosom? Man so little understands, that dependence upon his God constitutes the creature's happiness, and that the principle of independence is madness, and its end—destruction.[15] The *haughty* walk on the brink of a fear-

[1] Ps. xviii. 1—3. Isa. xxv. 4. [2] M. R. Isa. xxxiii. 16. [3] Col. iii. 3.
[4] Isa. xxvi. 1—4. [5] Bishop Reynolds on Hos. xiv. 1, 2. [6] 2 Sam. ii. 18.
[7] 1 Pet. i. 5. Gr. Leighton on passage.
[8] Phil. iv. 7. Gr. Comp. Chap. i. 33; xiv. 26.
[9] Matt. xi. 27. John i. 18; xiv. 6. [10] Chap. x. 15.
[11] Scott. Comp. Ez. xxviii. 1—10. Luke xii. 18—20. See also a fine passage in the Rambler, in Dr. Johnson's best style of solemn instructiveness. No. 65.
[12] Comp. Isa. l. 10, 11. Matt. vii. 24—27. [13] Chap. xvi. 18; xv. 33.
[14] Matt. xxiii. 12. Luke xiv. 11; xviii. 14. See Hor. Od. i. 34.
[15] Gen. iii. 5, 6.

ful precipice, only a miracle preserves them from instant ruin. The security of the child of God is, when he lies prostrate in the dust. If he soar high, the danger is imminent, though he be on the verge of heaven.[1]

The danger to a young Christian lies in an over-forward profes sion. The glow of the first love; the awakened sensibility to the condition of his perishing fellow-sinners; ignorance of the subtle working of inbred vanity; the mistaken zeal of injudicious friends—all tends to foster self-pleasing. Oh! let him know, that *before honor is humility*. In the low valley of humiliation special manifestations are realized.[2] Enlarged gifts, and apparently extending usefulness, without growing more deeply into the humility of Christ, will be the decline, not the advancing, of grace. That undoubtedly is the most humbled spirit, that has most the spirit of Christ. The rule of entry into his school—the first step of admission to his kingdom is—"Learn of me, for I am meek and lowly in heart."[3] Yet this *humility* is not in words, meltings, or tears. Its fruit is lowliness of mind, meekness of temper, thankfulness in receiving reproof, forgetfulness of injury, readiness to be lightly regarded. This is *the humility*, "which the King delighteth to honor." "Blessed are the poor in spirit; for theirs is the kingdom of heaven. He raiseth up the poor out of the dust, that he may set him with princes, even with the princes of his people."[4]

13. *He that answereth a matter* (returneth a word, Marg.) *before he heareth it, it is folly and shame unto him.*

Too often is this Proverb verified in common life. Men will scarcely hear out what is unacceptable to them. They will break in upon a speaker, before they have fully heard him; and therefore *answer a matter*, which they have little weighed, and but imperfectly understood. The eager disputant prides himself on his acute judgment. He interrupts his opponent, and confutes arguments, or contradicts statements, *before he has fairly heard them*.[5] Job's friends seem to have erred here.[6] Elihu, on the other hand, considerately restrained himself, till he had thoroughly *heard the matter*.[7] Job himself prudently "searched out the cause that he knew not."[8] This impatient spirit tells little for candor or humility, and only stamps a man's character with *folly and shame*. It is fraught with injustice in the court of law.[9] Here at least the judge must carefully hear and weigh both sides for a satisfactory verdict. The wise man thoroughly heard his difficult case, before he gave judgment.[10] Job was scrupulously exact in thus "contending with his servant."[11] Potiphar, from the want of this upright considerateness, was guilty of the most fla-

[1] 2 Cor. xii. 1—7.
[2] Job xlii. 5, 6. Isa. vi. 5—7. Dan. ix. 20—23. [3] Matt. xi. 29.
[4] Ibid. v. 3. Ps. cxiii. 7, 8. [5] See the wise rules, Ecclus. xi. 7, 8.
[6] Job xx. 1—3; xxi. 1—6. [7] Ibid. xxxii. 4, 10, 11. [8] Ibid. xxix. 16.
[9] John vii. 45—52. [10] 1 Kings iii. 16—28. Comp. Chap. xxv. 2.
[11] Job xxxi. 13.

grant wrong.[1] The Eastern autocrats seldom cared to sift accusations. Even "the man after God's heart," grievously sinned in this matter. But their hasty decisions brought *shame* upon them, being either covered over, or virtually retracted.[2] Our Lord's *matter was answered, before it was heard.*[3] The Apostle met with similar treatment,[4] though at other times he found a more impartial judgment.[5]

This *folly* was directly forbidden by God's law.[6] It was no less contrary to his own procedure. He examined Adam, before he pronounced judgment.[7] He came down to see Babel and Sodom, previous to their destruction, for the clear demonstration of his justice.[8] While on earth, patient investigation marked his decisions.[9] "All his ways are judgment; a God of truth, and without iniquity; just and right is he."[10]

14. *The spirit of a man will sustain his infirmity: but a wounded spirit who can bear?*

Man is born in a world of trouble, with considerable power of endurance. Natural courage and vivacity of spirits will bear us up even under the pressure of ponderous evils, poverty, pain, sickness, want. Instances of Heathen fortitude abound in the records of history.[11] Christian principle strengthens the natural strength. David, in the most fearful extremity, "encouraged himself in the Lord his God."[12] The Apostle "took pleasure in *infirmities.*"[13] The martyrs "were more than conquerors" under the most cruel tortures.[14] Outward troubles are tolerable—yea—more than tolerable, if there be peace within. *The spirit of a man may sustain his infirmity.* But if *the spirit be wounded*—if the prop itself be broken—all sinks. *The wound of the spirit* is so much the more piercing, as the spirit itself is more vital than the body. When he who made it, *wounds*, or permits Satan to *wound*, we might challenge the whole creation—*Who can bear it?* The suffering of the soul is the soul of suffering. Spiritual wounds, like the balm that heals them, can never be known, till they are felt. It is sometimes, as if the arrows of the Almighty were dipped in the lake of fire, and shot flaming into the very midst of the soul, more sensitive than the apple of the eye.[15] The best joys of earth can never soothe the envenomed sting. Mirth is madness[16] and vexation.[17]

There is a hell for the wicked on this side eternity. Cain's

[1] Gen. xxxix. 17—20.
[2] Esth. iii. 8—11; viii. 5—13. Dan. vi. 9, 14, 24. 2 Sam. xvi. 1—4; xix. 26—30.
[3] Luke xxii. 66—71.
[4] Acts xxii. 21, 22; xxiii. 2.
[5] Ibid. xxiii. 30—35; xxiv. 1—22; xxv. 1—5, 24—27; xxvi. 30—32.
[6] Deut. xiii. 12—14. John vii. 24.
[7] Gen. iii. 9—19.
[8] Ibid. xi. 5; xviii. 20, 21.
[9] Matt. xxii. 15—33, with Isa. xi. 3.
[10] Deut. xxxii. 4. Comp. 1 Sam. ii. 3.
[11] See Virgil's fine picture of Æneas. Æn. i. 208, 209
[12] 1 Sam. xxx. 3—6.
[13] 2 Cor. xii. 10.
[14] Rom. viii. 35—37.
[15] Job vi. 4; xix. 11. Ps. lxxxviii. 15.
[16] Eccl. ii. 2.
[17] Chap. xxv. 20

"punishment was greater than he could bear."[1] Saul was given up to the blackness of despair.[2] Zimri in rebellious madness threw himself into the flames.[3] Pashur was made a terror to himself.[4] Ahithophel and Judas "chose strangling rather than life."[5] Such is the foretaste of hell—only a few drops of wrath—for a few moments! What will be the reality—the substance—for eternity!

Observe the poignancy of the *wounded spirit* in the children of God. Job, delivered "for a small moment" into the enemy's power, "cursed the day of his birth."[6] David "roared for the disquietness of his heart. The arrows of the Almighty stuck in him, and his hand pressed him sore."[7] The martyrs,[8] in a moment of temporary apostacy, could not endure the anguish of *the wounded spirit*, and chose the flames, as the less bitter alternative. Such is the sharpness of the Lord's sword, and the weight of his hand, that every stroke is deadly. Conscience is the seat of guilt, and its vivid power turns—so to speak—"the sun into darkness, and the moon into blood,"[9]—the precious promises of free forgiveness into arguments of hopeless despondency. And but for the gracious restraint of the Lord's power and love, hardened despair would be the successful "advantage of Satan's devices."[10]

But look at Gethsemane—*the wounded spirit there*—the fainting humanity of the Son of God—"his strong crying and tears"—his prostrating sorrow—his "exceeding great and bitter cry," under the darkness of desertion.[11] If all the support of the indwelling Godhead was demanded for his upholding—with trembling astonishment we cry—*A wounded spirit who can bear?*

Yet is not this *wounded spirit* the Christian's first seal of mercy—the preparation for all future and eternal mercy?[12] Bitter indeed is the anguish, when the mass of sin is raised from the grave of oblivion, and "set in order before our eyes."[13] But is not this the sight that makes Jesus and his free salvation inexpressibly precious?[14] And does not this spirit place us within the sphere of his healing commission?[15] We ask now—not—*who can bear*,—but who can heal—it? Well did Luther say—and there is no better judge on such matters—'it is as easy to make a world as to quiet a troubled conscience.' Both are Creation-work—the Almightiness of God.[16] To him that "wounded must we return for healing."[17] His remedy is the sight of Himself wounded for us.[18] And that sight—so healing—so reviving—how does it tune the heart to everlasting praise!

15. *The heart of the prudent getteth knowledge; and the ear of the wise seeketh knowledge.*

[1] Gen. iv. 13. [2] 1 Sam. xxviii. 6, 15. [3] 1 Kings xvi. 18.
[4] Jer. xx. 4. [5] 2 Sam. xvii. 23. Matt. xxvii. 3—5. Job vii. 15.
[6] Job ii. 6; iii. 1; x. 17. [7] Ps. xxxii. 3, 4; xxxviii. 1—8.
[8] Bainham—Bilney—Cranmer. See Foxe's Records. [9] Joel ii. 31.
[10] 2 Cor. ii. 7—11. [11] Matt. xxvi. 37—39; xxvii. 46.
[12] Acts ii. 37; xvi. 27—30. [13] Psalm l. 21.
[14] Acts ii. 41—47; xvi. 31—34. Comp. Matt. ix. 12. [15] Isa. lxi. 1, 2.
[16] Gen. i. 1. Isa. lvii. 19. [17] Hos. vi. 1. [18] Isa. liii. 5.

Knowledge is gathering its rays on every side But all that is intrinsically valuable centres in Divine *knowledge*. 'All arts'—as Bishop Hall teaches—'are maids to Divinity. Therefore they both vail to her, and do her service.'[1] Yet the value of *knowledge* in the Divine sphere is estimated according to its character. When it is speculative, not experimental; general, without practical influence, it is worse than valueless. It is power for fearful evil. Lamentable is it to think of the mass of triflers in Divine *knowledge;* hearing without retaining; retaining withont intelligence, or without personal application. So often "is the price in the hands of a fool, who hath no heart for it."[2] But here is *the prudent.* He has pondered, and formed a just estimate of the blessing. *His heart* has fastened upon it,[3] and, as the means are free, and the success sure,[4] he has *gotten it.* As the proof of his possession, he *seeks* for more. For who that has a treasure, will be satisfied with his store, content with a lesser measure, while a larger is within his reach?—*His ear* is now wakened to seek the ministry of the word, and the conversation of experienced Christians. Every avenue of instruction is diligently improved.[5]

A word to the young—Think how much important *knowledge* is to be *gotten.* Be up early in its pursuit. Let it have your most —your first—your best time. Begin, before your minds are corrupted with false principles; before you have learned too much that must be unlearned as disciples of Christ. What is the tone of your prayers? Does it show the concentration of the soul, filled with one desire, and carrying it where it will be accepted and satisfied? The only saving *knowledge* cometh down from heaven, and is fetched thence upon our knees. What is the pulse of your exertion? Does it prove the heart to be delighted in the object? Or is it only a start for a moment, and then a sinking back to the slumber of the sluggard? *Knowledge* from heaven leads thitherward. Clearer knowledge sweeps away many clouds. We see our work better, and it is more easy to us. We see our road, and walk more pleasantly. We can not only guide ourselves; but we are "able also to admonish one another."[6] Hasten onwards then, "grow in knowledge."[7] Happiness and usefulness, light and glory, are before us.

16. *A man's gift maketh room for him, and bringeth him before great men.*

We have before spoken of the corrupting influence of *gifts.*[8] But we may justly apply this proverb to their legitimate use. Eliezer's *gifts made room for him* in Rebekah's family.[9] Jacob's *gifts made room for him* in his brother's heart.[10] Nor was it inconsistent with his integrity, by sending his present to the governor of Egypt, to *bring* his sons with acceptance *before the great man.*[11]

[1] Works, viii. 107. [2] Chap. xvii. 16. [3] Chap. xv. 14.
[4] Chap. ii. 3—6. Hcs. vi. 3. Jam. i. 5. [5] Chap. i. 3; ix. 9.
[6] Rom. xv. 14. [7] 2 Peter iii. 18. [8] Chap. xvii. 8, 23. Comp. xix. 6.
[9] Gen. xxiv. 30—33. [10] Ibid. xxxiii. 1—11. [11] Ibid. xliii. 11.

Ehud's gifts *made room* for his errand;[1] Abigail's, for the preservation of her house.[2] Often indeed were they presented simply as a tribute of respect,[3] as now in some parts of the East; so that without them an inferior would scarcely feel, that he had any claim upon his superior for favor or protection.[4] The minister of the Gospel recognizes their value, *making room for him*—perhaps also for his message. Sympathy gives weight to his instruction, when after the example of his Divine master, he combines kindness to the body with love for the soul. Great wisdom and discrimination is however obviously required, to prevent the serious evil of a well-intentioned charity. A wise consideration may also *make room* for us with *great men* for the advancement of the Christian cause. But in this most delicate exercise, let our own principles be fully acknowledged; else even in the service of God, we shall be "carnal, and walk as men"[5]—not as the dignified servants of a heavenly Master.

Blessed be God! We want no *gifts to bring us before him.* Our welcome is free—our door of access ever open. Our treasure of grace in his unchanging favor, unsearchable.

17. *He that is first in his own cause seemeth just; but his neighbor cometh and searcheth him.*

We have lately had a rule against judging others.[6] Here we are warned against justifying ourselves. Self flattery is our cherished nature,—highly valuing our fancied excellences, very blind to our real imperfections. So ready are we to place *our own cause* in a strong light; and sometimes, almost unconsciously, to cast a shade over, or even omit, what might seem to balance on the opposite side. It is so difficult to state facts and circumstances with perfect accuracy, where our own name or credit is concerned. Hence, *our cause* coming *first, seemeth just.* But our *neighbor*, acquainted with the real case, cometh and *searcheth* us, exposes our fallacy, and puts us to shame. Saul made himself appear *just in his own cause.* The necessity of the case seemed to warrant the deviation from the command. But Samuel *searched him*, and laid open his rebellion.[7] Ziba's cause *seemed just* in David's eyes, until Mephibosheth's explanation *searched him* to his confession.[8] Job's incautious self-defence was laid open by Elihu's probing application.[9] An eloquent advocate may easily make a bad *cause coming first seem just.* But, according to the Proverb, 'the first tale is good, till the second is heard.' The plaintiff is always right, till the defendant's case has been opened. Yet the true rule of justice would be, to judge neither to be right, till both sides have been heard. Let the whole evidence be sifted; and often the

1 Judg. iii. 17, 18. 2 1 Sam. xxv. 11—27. 3 Ibid. ix. 7.
4 See Paxton's Illustrations, ii. 29. 5 1 Cor. iii. 3. 6 Verse 13.
7 1 Sam. xv. 13—26.
8 2 Sam. xvi. 1—4; xix. 26. Comp. Chap. xxviii. 11. See Bishop Sanderson's Sermons. Job xxix. 14—17. 9 Job xxxii. 10—14; xxxiii. 8—12.

plausible cover is swept away by a more *searching* investigation. Judges are therefore bound to "consider, take advice, and speak;"[2] carefully guarding against prejudging the cause, till the whole has been fully before them; else he that is last *in the cause* may come with disadvantage, though it may be the cause of right. In our *own cause*, always be alive to conviction. Watch against a self-justifying spirit. Cultivate the spirit of self-distrust. Balance our enemy's statement against our own prejudices. Judge as under the eye of God, and with the sincere anxious prayer to lay ourselves open to his searching disclosure of hidden evil. Deceit in any form never answers its end. "A conscience void of offence both towards God and man" must be our great exercise.[3]

18. *The lot causeth contentions to cease, and parteth between the mighty.*

The general use of the lot has been before explained.[4] It is here adverted to, as an ordinance of peaceful settlement. Whether from the evenness of the balance, or from want of confidence in the judgment a legal appeal might be of doubtful authority. Contending parties therefore agree to abide by the decision of the lot. Important matters of order under the Divine Theocracy were thus determined.[5] How many *contentions* would there have been *between the mighty*, in settling the respective boundaries of the tribes, had not this means been adopted to *make them cease!*[6] When Saul was thus chosen to the kingdom,[7] and Matthias "numbered among the Apostles,"[8] the election was acquiesced in, as the voice of God. There seems, therefore, no scriptural prohibition to the use of this ordinance, provided it be exercised in a reverential dependence upon God,[9] and not profaned for common purposes or worldly ends.

At the same time—as we have before observed—the word of God appears to be more fully recognized as the arbiter of the Divine will. All *contentions cease* in a simple, child-like, unreserved readiness to be guided by this "more sure rule." The extent of forgiveness, is here clearly defined,[10] and the principle and motive for its exercise effectively supplied.[11] Perhaps it was more easy to abide by the decision of the lot than of the word. The last requires more self-denial, humility and patience, and therefore is more practically useful.

19. *A brother offended is harder to be won than a strong city: and their contentions are like the bars of a castle.*

Adverting to *the ceasing of contentions*, how affecting is this case of special difficulty! *A brother*—not an enemy—*is harder to be won than a strong city;* as if the nearer the relation, the wider the breach.[12] The thread once snapped, is not easily joined.

[1] Acts xxiv. 1—5, 12, 13.
[2] Jud. xix. 30.
[3] Acts xxiv. 16.
[4] Chap. xvi. 33.
[5] 1 Chron. vi. 63; xxiv. 31. Neh. xi. 1.
[6] Num. xxxiii. 54.
[7] 1 Sam. x. 20—24.
[8] Acts i. 26.
[9] Ibid. verses 24, 25.
[10] Matt. xviii. 21, 22.
[11] Col. iii. 12—14.
[12] 'Acerrima firma proximorum odia sunt.'—Tacitus.

'What a view does it give us of our corruption, that the natural love implanted in us should degenerate into Satanic hatred.'[1] Such was the *contention* of Cain with Abel;[2] of Joseph's brethren with himself;[3] of Absalom and Amnon;[4] the civil wars between Benjamin and his brethren;[5] in later times between Judah and Israel;[6] in our own country, the long continued and ruinous *contentions* between the Houses of York and Lancaster. Cities in olden times were strongly fortified with *bars* of iron against a siege.[7] What a long siege did Esau's *strong* city stand, before it was *won* by the power of love, and *the bars of his castle* opened their avenues for conciliation![8]

No where is concord so important as in the Church. Never can she prosper—except she maintain the form of Jerusalem—"a city compact together."[9] Begotten as we are by the same word, living on the same food, animated by the same life, ought we not, with all our lesser differences—to hold "the unity of the Spirit?"[10] If ties so close cannot unite us, at least let our common welfare, and common danger, quench this unholy fire; just as the fear of the enemy without, might allay mutual misunderstanding within. But how painfully did *the contentions* between Luther and Calvin (not to mention others of more recent date in the Church) show the fearful difficulty of *winning a brother offended!*[11]

Yet the extreme difficulty does not diminish the obligation. Let it not therefore paralyze the effort. Nothing can be more plain and decisive than the gospel rule. Yet so repugnant is it to flesh and blood, to all nature's pride, feelings, and high notions, that we cry with the disciples of old—"Lord, increase our faith!" Call in this only principle, that can constrain the heart, and the Christian victory is ensured. Grace reigns triumphant.

20. *A man's belly shall be satisfied with the fruit of his mouth: and with the increase of his lips shall he be filled.* 21. *Death and life are in the power of the tongue: and they that love it shall eat the fruit thereof.*

Who would not be careful what seed he puts into a fruitful field, when he knows that his harvest will be according to his seed?[12] Here is not a field—but "a world"[13] to be cultivated, so that we may be *satisfied with the fruit, and filled with the increase.* What this *fruit and increase* may be, is a fearful alternative. *The fruit of our lips—the power of our tongue*—will be poisonous

[1] Geier in loco. [2] Gen. iv. 5—8. [3] Gen. xxxvii. 3—5, 18—27.
[4] 2 Sam. xiii. 22—32. [5] Judg. xx.
[6] 2 Chron. xiii. 16, 17. [7] See Isa. xlv. 2.
[8] Gen. xxvii. 41—45; xxxiii. 5—11. The rooted enmity of the nation seems to render doubtful the cordiality of the reconciliation. See Num. xx. 14—21. Ez. xxxv. 5 Obad. 10—14. [9] Psalm cxxii. 3.
[10] Two reasons made a godly and learned man (Strigelius) long to leave the world. '1. That I might enjoy the sweet sight of the Son of God and the Church of God. 2. That I may be delivered from the cruel and implacable hatred of Theologians.' Melchior Adam. in vitâ. Chrysostom gives this rule. 'Have but one enemy—the devil. With him never be reconciled; with thy brother never fall out.'
[11] Luke xvii. 3—5. [12] Gal. vi. 7, 8. [13] James iii. 6.

or wholesome—*death or life.*[1] Evil words tend to death, good words to life.[2]

This is clearly manifested in public responsibilities. The testimony of witnesses; the legal decision of the judge; the doctrine of false or true teachers; all show that *death or life is in the power of the tongue.* In the common intercourse of life, it is "the fountain both of bitter waters and sweet;" as powerful to destroy as to edify; the poison or the antidote, as it may be used. 'A man by using his tongue aright, in talking, exhorting, witnessing, counselling, may save; and, by abusing it in any of these ways, or any other, may destroy.'[3] Either way he will be *filled with the fruit.* The curse of destroying others will return upon himself.[4] In administering a blessing to his neighbor, his whole soul will be fed.[5] *They that love it shall eat the fruit of it.* It is however, the habitual, not the occasional, use of this formidable little member, that determines its fruit. A saint may "speak unadvisedly"—a sinner acceptably—"with his lips." Neither would thus determine his true character.

Are not then the sins of the tongue an overwhelming manifestation of the long-suffering of God? "Woe is me! for I am a man of unclean lips."[6] When I think of its *power* even for eternal *death*[7] *or life,* shall I not—as Chrysostom warns—'guard it more than the pupil of the eye?'[8] Shall I not cry to my God, that he would restrain it;[9] yea—cry more earnestly, that he would consecrate it;[10] that it might be my glory, not my shame; my organ of praise; my exercise of joy?[11] In the inner man the heart is the main thing to be kept[12]—in the outer man the tongue.[13] O my God, take them both into thine own keeping, under thine own discipline, as instruments for thy service and glory.

22. *Whoso findeth a wife findeth a good thing, and obtaineth favor of the Lord.*[14]

This is obviously to be taken with limitation. Manoah *found a good thing in his wife.*[15] So did not Job.[16] Some find "a crown to their head;" others "rottenness to their bones."[17] That which alone deserves the name is indeed *a good thing.* If in a state of innocence "it was not good for man to be alone;"[18] much more in a world of care and trouble "two are better than one," for mutual

[1] Verse 7. Ps. l. 20, 21. Matt. v. 22; xii. 36. Jude 14, 15.
[2] Chap. xii. 14; xiii. 2. Ps. xxxiv. 11, 12.
[3] Muffet in loco.
[4] Chap. xiii. 2.
[5] Chap. xi. 25.
[6] Isa. vi. 5.
[7] Matt. xii. 37.
[8] Homily 62 on Matt.
[9] Ps. cxli. 3.
[10] Ibid. li. 15.
[11] Ibid. lvii. 7, 8.
[12] Chap. iv. 23.
[13] Chap. xxi. 23. Jam. iii. 2.
[14] Dr. Kennicott elaborately insists upon supplying the distinctive limitation from the reading of the LXX. Vulgate, and some old Chaldee paraphrase, (Second Dissertation on the Hebrew Text, pp. 189—192.) But, the general term, frequently used by the wise man for the obvious limitation, is sufficient to explain his meaning, Chap. xv. 10; xvi. 10; xxii. 1; xxix. 4. Eccl. vii. 28. The LXX. adds—'He that casteth out a wife—casteth out good things: but he that retaineth a strange woman is foolish and ungodly.'
[15] Judg. xiii. 22, 23.
[16] Job ii. 9, 10; xix. 17.
[17] Chap. xii. 4.
[18] Gen. ii. 18.

support, helpfulness and sympathy.[1] *The good thing* implies godliness, and suitable fitness. Godliness is found, when the man marries "only in the Lord,"[2] and only one who is the Lord's. The "unequal yoke with unbelievers"[3]—the union for life of a child of God with a child of Satan—is a most awful anomaly. 'I wish'—said pious Bishop Hall,—'that Manoah could speak so loud, that all our Israelites might hear him. Is there never a woman among the daughters of thy brethren, or among all God's people, that thou goest to take a wife of the uncircumcised Philistines? If religion be any other than a cipher, how dare we not regard it in our most important choice? Is she a fair Philistine? Why is not the deformity of the soul more powerful to dissuade us, than the beauty of the face to allure us?'[4] The destruction of the world grew out of this self-pleasing delusion.[5] And many a flood of iniquity has come into a godly man's family from the same source.[6]

There may however be godliness on both sides, without that mutual fitness, which makes the wife "a help-meet for the man."[7] *The good thing* is, when he honors her—not as the wisest or the holiest, but as the person, whom God saw to be the best and fittest for himself in the whole world—a comfort for life—an help for heaven.[8] Such a communion spiritualizes his affections, and elevates him from earth to heaven.

But how is this *good thing found?* Isaac *found it*, where every Christian looks for his blessing—as an answer to prayer.[9] A man's choice for his own indulgence will bring a curse upon himself and his family.[10] "Choose thou mine inheritance for me"[11]—is the cry and confidence of the child of God. Then truly will he *obtain* the gift, not as the result of fortune, or as the proof of his own good discernment—but—as Adam received his wife—"from the Lord"[12]—a token of his special *favor*.

23. *The poor useth entreaties: but the rich answereth roughly.*[13]

It is natural to *the poor*—sensible of their dependence—to *use entreaties.* And very natural is this humiliation, as the discipline for that poverty of spirit, which the Lord seals with his first blessing.[14] Yet shame is it to *the rich*, that he should often *answer these entreaties* roughly. Instead of the kindly feelings flowing out, he seems to be bound against them with iron chains. He hears with indifference the tale of woe, and, having never himself tasted the bitter bread, he has no heart of sympathy and helpfulness. Often we find the well-bred man of the world, who is all courtesy and refinement in his own circle, to those under his feet insufferably rude and unfeeling. His good breeding indeed is only

1 Ecc. iv. 9, 10. See the Marriage Service.
2 1 Cor. vii. 39. 3 2 Cor. vi. 14. 4 Contemplations, x. 3.
5 Gen. vi. 1—6. 6 2 Chron. xviii. 1; xxi. 5, 6. 7 Gen. ii. 18.
8 Luke i. 6. See the beautiful picture, Chap. xxxi. 10—31. Comp. also Ecclus xxvi.
9 Gen. xxiv. 12—63. 10 2 Chron. xviii. 1, 2; xxi. 1—6. 11 Ps. xlvii. 4.
12 Chap. xix. 14. Gen. ii. 21—23.
13 This and the succeeding verse are omitted in LXX. 14 Matt. v. 3.

the polish of selfishness. So little does he make the true use of his power, that the exercise of it only transforms him into a tyrant. Instead of scattering his blessings around, he only makes himself feared and hated by his misused responsibility.[1] Would he but study the character of his Divine Master, he would see the exercise of power combine with true greatness. Was he not as considerate to blind Bartimeus, as to the nobleman of Capernaum?[2] All ranks alike shared in his tenderest sympathy.

And yet as the rich in their conscious superiority may be overbearing, so *the poor, in using their entreaties*, may show a servile, crouching spirit,[3] shrinking from that bold integrity of character, which gives dignity alike to the lowest as to the highest of men. To all of us our Providential circumstances bring their besetting temptations. Close walking with God is our only safeguard.

But surely *the rich in their rough answering of the poor* would do well to consider, how much more dependent is he upon his God, than his meanest brother is upon himself! And when he comes before his God, must he not then wear the garb of *poverty*—though he be a king[4]—*using entreaties*—not advancing claims? Yes—all of us alike are *poor* before the throne of grace. All of us must *use entreaties* there. Yet when does our gracious Father *answer his poor* suppliant child *roughly*, except as he wisely disciplines his faith, while his own heart is full of yearning, parental love, towards him?[5]

24. *A man that hath friends must shew himself friendly: and there is a friend, that sticketh closer than a brother.*

A true friend is no common acquisition.[6] There are many pretensions—many professions—of friendship. But the jewel itself is as rare, as it is precious. Yet what is life without this cheering, enriching blessing? Kings have left awhile their royalties for its enjoyment.[7] To Alexander the conquered world without his Hephæstion would have been a wilderness. But if *a man hath friends*, and would keep them, he must *show himself friendly*. To throw them away by neglect, caprice, unreasonable disgust, or needless offence, is to show himself utterly unworthy of the blessing. Observe Ruth and Naomi—each with warm reciprocity of interest laying herself out for the other;[8] David acknowledging the kindness of his friends in distress;[9] the Apostle's delicate dealing with his friend's wounded sensibility;[10] and his considerate care for the comforts of his companions.[11] It is by such kind offices that the bond is mutually cemented. *A man having friends shows himself friendly.* Love begets love, and is accompanied with love.

But let us take care to base our friendships upon the true founda-

[1] 1 Sam. xxv. 11, 12, 17.
[2] Mark x. 46—52. John iv. 46—50.
[3] 1 Sam. ii. 36.
[4] Psalm xl. 17; lxxxvi. 1.
[5] Matt. xv. 26. Comp. Gen. xlii. 6, 7.
[6] Chap. xvii. 17.
[7] Ps. lv. 13, 14.
[8] Ruth i. 16; ii. 11, 18, with iii. 1—14, 16; iv. 16.
[9] 1 Sam. xxx. 26—31.
[10] Philem. 8—20.
[11] Tit. iii 13.

tion. Otherwise they may be snapped asunder by the veriest trifle, or they may become idolatrous love, usurping God's place in the heart. Sanguine and affectionate dispositions are much exposed to sudden fancies and mistaken impressions. But the charm is broken by the cold return, or empty professions, of the misplaced love; and the illusion is swept away in humbling disappointment.

The bond of real friendship is often closer than the natural tie. "The friend is as one's own soul."[1] Such was Jonathan unto David—*a friend that sticketh closer than a brother*[2]—tender and sympathizing, while his *brother* was fraught with unkind suspicion.[3] He dared the deadly displeasure of his father by open adherence, while his wife showed her love at the expense of his name.[4] Job's friends, notwithstanding their harsh misconceptions, abode fast with the afflicted sufferer, when his wife and family were "strange to him."[5] And do we not remember, that, when *the brethren* of Jesus shrunk from the near position to his cross "*there stood by the cross* the disciple, whom Jesus loved," gladly receiving from his lips the sacred deposit of his bereaved mother?[6] Even natural minds, of a high tone of feeling, may exhibit this strength of friendship. But its surest bond is, that which unites the whole family of God. The identity of sanctified taste; sympathy of experience; holy consecration for mutual helpfulness; above all—union as Members of one body to one Head—hence flows magnetic attraction—heavenly—Divine friendship.

But where shall we find the complete filling-up of this exqusite picture, except in Him, who became our Brother, that he might cleave to us *closer than a brother* in tenderness and help?[7] Truly he "loveth at all times"[8]—a present Friend; in temptation opening, when needed, "a way of escape;"[9] in affliction cheering with the Divine Comforter;[10] "in sickness making our bed;"[11] in death sustaining us by "his rod and staff;[12] in eternity "receiving us to himself."[13] What *brother sticketh* so close as he?

And then, when we think of the objects of his love[14]—its freeness[15]—its costliness[16]—its perseverance notwithstanding all the discouragements of our perverseness and folly[17]—"loving us to the end"[18] as parts and members of himself—how can we duly honor this our faithful, tender, unchanging unchangeable friend? Are there none, who boast of their faithfulness to the creature, who yet have no

[1] Deut. xiii. 6.

[2] Bishop Coverdale's version is beautifully simple—'A friend that delighteth in love, doth a man more friendship, and sticketh faster unto him than a brother.'

[3] 1 Sam. xvii. 28, with xviii. 3; xix. 2—4. 2 Sam. i. 26. It is interesting to observe the reciprocity with one exception (2 Sam. xvi. 1—4.) on David's part to the end of life, 2 Sam. ix. 1; xxi. 7.

[4] 1 Sam. xviii. 20, 28; xix. 12—17, with xx. 24—33. Comp. Ecclus. xxii. 25.

[5] Job iii. 11—13, with xix. 13—17.

[6] John xix. 25—27.

[7] Heb. ii. 11, 14—18.

[8] Chap. xvii. 17.

[9] 1 Cor. x. 13.

[10] John xiv. 17, 18.

[11] Ps. xli. 3.

[12] Ibid. xxiii. 4.

[13] John xiv. 3; xvii. 24.

[14] Rom. v. 8.

[15] John vi. 37.

[16] John xv. 13; 1 John iii. 16.

[17] Isa. xlii. 4. Hos. xi. 7, 8. Mal. iii. 6.

[18] John xiii. 1. See the beautiful Hymn in Olney Collection, B. i. 53.

heart for this Divine friendship—no reciprocal affection to this surpassing friend? Will not our very sensibilities condemn our indifference? For what stronger proof can there be of their depravity and disorder, than that they should flow so fully to the creature-object, yet be cold and dead to the Divine Friend? Oh! let Him be the first choice of youth—the tried and chosen Friend of maturing age—the Friend for eternity!

CHAPTER XIX.

1. *Better is the poor that walketh in his integrity, than he that is perverse in his lips, and is a fool.*

POVERTY is never a disgrace, except when it is the fruit of ill-conduct. But when adorned with godly *integrity*, it is most honorable. *Better is the poor man than* he, whom riches lift up in his own eyes; and he is given up to his *perverseness and folly.*[2] Often man puts under his feet those, whom God lays in his bosom; honors the *perverse* for their riches, and despises the *poor* for their poverty. 'But what hath the rich, if he hath not God? And what is a poor man, if he hath God? Better be in a wilderness with God, than in Canaan without him.'[3] Was not Job on the dunghill, *walking in his integrity, better* than ungodly Ahab on the throne?[4] Was not Lazarus in his rags, *better* than Dives with his "fine linen and sumptuous fare?"[5] Calculate wisdom by God's standard, who judges not by station, but by character. Estimate things in the light of eternity. How soon will all accidental distinctions pass away, and personal distinctions alone avail! Death will strip the poor of his rags, and the rich of his purple, and bring them both "naked to the earth from whence they came."[6] Meanwhile let us learn from our Lord's voice to his despised people.—"I know *thy poverty;* but thou art rich."[7] How glorious the stamp upon the outcast professors *walking in their integrity*—"Of whom the world was not worthy[8]—For such is prepared the honor that cometh from God only—his seal—his smiles—his everlasting crown.

2. *Also, that the soul be without knowledge, it is not good; and he that hasteth with his feet sinneth.*

Also—seems to trace the *fool's perverse ways* to their source. His *soul is without knowledge*. Ignorance gives perpetuity to *folly. Knowledge* is valuable even to the mind. It expands its powers, and, when rightly directed, preserves from many besetting tempta-

[1] This and the following verse is omitted in LXX.
[2] Chap. xxviii. 6.
[3] Bishop Reynolds's Works, p. 9, 10.
[4] Job ii. 7, 8.
[5] Luke xvi. 19—21.
[6] Job i. 21. Ecc. xii. 7.
[7] Rev. ii. 9.
[8] Heb. xi. 37, 38.

tions. 'Be assured,'—says an eloquent Preacher, 'it is not, because the people know much, that they ever become the willing subjects of any factious or unprincipled demagogue. It is just because they know too little. It is just because ignorance is the field, on which the quackery of a political impostor ever reaps its most abundant harvest.'[1] *Knowledge* also opens much wholesome enjoyment. The intelligent poor are preserved in their home-comforts from the temptations of the ale-house. The most educated are raised above the frivolities of dissipation. Thus both classes are restrained from the sensualities of ungodliness.

But—much more for *the soul*—made for God—*to be without his knowledge is not good.* Here it is not merely expansion or restraint, but light and life. Without it—what know we of present forgiveness and peace,[2] or of life eternal ?[3] The careless worldling, immersed in pleasure, and playing with trifles—what is he, but a "man without understanding," justly compared to "the beasts that perish ?"[4] Is ignorance then the mother of devotion ? Is it not the worst of evil—the centre of all evil[5]—the parent of irreligion, and the precursor of ruin.[6] Awful indeed are its aggravations—to be ignorant in a time of knowledge—blind in a land of light—unenlightened in "the valley of vision !"

But let us mark the practical evil of this want of *knowledge.* 'Where no discretion is, there the soul is not well.'[7] The uninstructed child or savage acts rashly. Thus the man *without knowledge*, instead of "pondering his path,"[8] *hasteth with his feet*—misseth his aim—*sinneth. Haste*, as opposed to sloth, is the energy of Divine grace.[9] 'As opposed to consideration, acting *hastily is sin.* Not taking time to enquire, he is *without knowledge.* This impatience is a ruling evil—the genuine exercise of self-will—"not waiting for the counsel of the Lord." Godly Joshua offended here.[10] Saul's impatience cost him his kingdom.[11] David's *haste* was the occasion of gross injustice.[12] Jehoshaphat's precipitancy—asking counsel after, instead of before, his course—was sharply rebuked.[13] Rash experiments—the result of *haste*—often threaten serious evils in the state. The same spirit rends the Church with schism. The *heady* professor wanders from Church to Church, and from sect to sect, without pondering. In common life how much *sin* has been the fruit of a few rash words or hasty lines ! A sudden impulse has taken the place of considerate principle. Let us ever remember, that without self-discipline, there can be no Christian consistency or stability ; that in a thousand cases *haste* may plunge *our feet into sin,*[14] if not into ruin ; and that our strength is to stand or sit still, and see how God will appear on

[1] Chalmers' Commercial Discourses, p. 375. [2] Luke i. 77—79.
[3] John xvii. 3. [4] Psalm xlix. 20.
[5] Isa. i. 3, 4. Acts iii. 17. 1 Cor. ii. 8. 1 Tim. i. 13.
[6] Chap. x. 21. Hos. iv. 6. Luke xix. 41, 42. [7] Bishop Coverdale's translation.
[8] Chap. iv. 26. [9] Ps. cxix. 60. Luke xix. 6. [10] Jos. ix. 14, 15.
[11] 1 Sam. xiii. 12—14. [12] 2 Sam. xvi. 1—4. [13] 2 Chron. xviii. 1—4; xix. 2.
[14] Chap. xxviii. 20, 22.

our side, to make a way for us through many a deep water of perplexity.[1] "He that believeth shall not make haste."[2]

3. *The foolishness of man perverteth his way; and his heart fretteth against the Lord.*

Such was *the foolishness* of Adam! First he *perverted his way,* then he charged upon God its bitter fruit. "God—making him upright"—made him happy. Had he been ruled by his will, he would have continued so. But—"seeking out his own inventions"[3]—he made himself miserable. As the author of his own misery,—it was reasonable, that he should fret against himself. But such was his pride and baseness, that *his heart fretted against the Lord,* as if He—not himself—was responsible.[4] Thus his first-born, when his own sin had brought punishment on him, *fretted,* as if it "were greater than he could bear."[5] This has been *the foolishness* of Adam's children ever since. God has linked together moral and penal evil—sin and sorrow. The fool rushes into the sin, and most unreasonably *frets* for the sorrow;[6] as if he could "gather grapes from thorns, or figs from thistles."[7] He charges his crosses—not on his own perverseness, but on the injustice of God. But God is clear from all the blame;[8] He had shown the better. Man chooses the worse.[9] He had warned by his word—by conscience. Man, deaf to the warning, plunged into the misery; and while "eating the fruit of his own ways," *his heart frets against the Lord.* 'It is hard to have passions, and to be punished for indulging them. I could not help it. Why did he not give grace to avoid it.'[10] Such is the pride and blasphemy of an unhumbled spirit! The malefactor blames the judge for his righteous sentence.[11]

But let us look a little at this bold impeachment of God's righteousness. 'Why did he not give me grace?' Is then God bound to give his grace? Have we any claim upon God? Is not God's grace his own?[12] Is not the fool following his own will, and therefore responsible for his doing? Why cannot he turn to God? He will not listen or obey. The means are free before him. No force of natural impossibility hinders. It is only his stubbornness,—that is his impotency. He cannot, because he will not; and therefore, if he perish, it is not in his weakness, but in his wilfulness.[13] The worst part of his wickedness is the wicked will. It is not that his nature is wicked, but that he is willing that it should be so. Did he but feel his moral inability; would he but look to him, who is "eyes to the blind," "ears to the deaf," "feet to the lame;" his healing would be sure.

This perverseness shows itself in every rising of corruption. The

[1] Ex. xiv. 13. Isa. xxx. 7. [2] Isa. xxviii. 16. [3] Ecc. vii. 29. [4] Gen. iii. 6—12. [5] Ibid. iv. 8—13. [6] See 1 Kings iii. 7—14. [7] Matt. vii. 16. [8] Ez. xviii. 25. [9] Jam. i. 13, 14. [10] See Jer. vii. 10. [11] Isa. viii. 21, 22. Rev. xvi. 9—11, 21. [12] Matt. xx. 15. Rom. ix. 15—24. [13] Matt. xxiii. 37. John v. 40.

Pharisee mocks God by his hypocritical service, and then *frets*, because no good comes out of it.[1] The proud worm cherishes a discontented humor with Providence. Either the desired comfort is withheld, or the will has been crossed. If his tongue is quiet, *his heart frets.* Had he been placed differently, he would have succeeded better. God therefore has the blame of his failure. Whereas it is obvious, that if he is not ready now to serve God, he needs a change of heart, not a change of place. The disease is within, and therefore would follow him through altered circumstances with the same result; leaving him as far as ever from happiness. The constant struggle of the will is to be any where, but where God has placed us for our best welfare.

Humbling it is to see this *foolishness* in the Lord's people. Our carelessness or waywardness provokes the rod; yet *the heart fretteth* under the rebuke.[2] While we shun what is positively sinful, too often we allow occasions of sin—circumstances, society, which experience has taught us, hinders prayer, damps the spiritual taste, and wounds the conscience. Why then indulge it? At least, charge on yourselves, not on God, the bitter consequence. Often also we are found quarrelling with what we cannot alter, and only doubling the burden, by adding guilt to our trouble. If "a fool's contention" with his brother "calleth for strokes,"[3] much more when we have a murmurer and complainer against God;[4] "the man striving with his Maker;"[5] or rather the child kicking against his Father's rod, instead of "humbling himself under his mighty hand."[6] Did he but know himself—could he but trust his God—he would look, not at the rod, but at the hand that holds it.[7] Could *the heart fret* to see it in his Father's hands? Should he not kiss it, even while it smites him; peacefully—yea, thankfully—"accepting the punishment of his iniquity?"[8]

This turbulent insurrection against Divine sovereignty brings its own torment. It sets all the powers of the soul out of course. There is no peace or tranquillity, but in complacency with the will of God, being fully reconciled to his disposals and dispensations. While "Ephraim was as a bullock unaccustomed to the yoke," it was only the more *fretting*. After that he "was turned, and instructed," and "quieted himself as a weaned child," he found ease.[9]

Always let us be ready with the cry—"Show me wherefore thou contendest with me. That which I see not, teach thou me. If I have done iniquity, I will do so no more."[10] Instead of "complaining for the punishment of our sins, let us search and try our ways, and turn again unto the Lord." "I will bear the indignation of the Lord, because I have sinned against him."[11] The discipline that schools the will into subjection, is an invaluable blessing.

[1] Isa. lviii. 3. Mal. iii. 14. [2] 2 Sam. vi. 4—8. Jon. iv. 9.
[3] Chap. xviii. 6. [4] Jude 16. [5] Isa. xlv. 9.
[6] 1 Pet. v. 6. [7] 1 Sam. iii. 18. 2 Sam. xvi. 11. Ps. xxxix. 9.
[8] Lev. xxvi. 41. [9] Jer. xxxi. 18, 19. [10] Job x. 2; xxxiv. 32.
[11] Lam. iii. 39. Mic. vii. 9.

Well satisfied are we, that all that God does will appear, when the mystery is finished; that every leaf of his Providence will be expounded with the full manifestation of his glory; that the cross of disappointed wishes was the gracious means of saving us from ruining ourselves, and of exercising us for endurance,[1] and ultimately for enjoyment. Joy and delight indeed will it be to look back upon every step of "the right way, by which our Father has led us to the city of habitation,"[2] and to mark, how needful was the discipline at every point, how suited to every exigency; and what abundant matter of praise does it furnish for that unwearied patience, with which our loving Father "suffered our manners in the wilderness."[3]

4. *Wealth maketh many friends; but the poor is separated from his neighbor.*

We have had the substance of this proverb before.[4] It is nominally true, that *wealth maketh many friends.* But generally they are little worth. 'Riches have them'—says Bishop Hall—'not the man.'[5] The principle is selfishness—no earnest for true and permanent friendship. Few among them will be found "loving us at all times, brethren born for adversity."[6] God has made poverty a gradation of rank; and as such we are bound to regard it. Man makes it a wall of separation. It tries our own faith and patience, and not less the love and sincerity of our friend.[7] But what, if the Lord's *poor be separated from* his selfish *neighbor?*[8] There is one that "knoweth his soul in adversity,"[9] and that hath pledged his word—"I will never leave thee, nor forsake thee."[10] Yes! this is the joy, the stay of his confidence—"I am poor and needy; but the Lord thinketh on me."[11] Poverty may *separate him from his neighbor.* But who or what shall separate him from his God?[12] "Joint-heir as he is with him, whom God hath appointed heir of all things," what can he want?[13] 'If it were possible for him to stand absolutely in need of the use and service of the whole creation, all the creatures in the world would surely wait on him, and be appropriated to him.'[14]

5. *A false witness shall not be unpunished, and he that speaketh lies shall not escape.*

If "a true witness delivereth souls,"[15] *a false witness* destroyeth them. Fearful guilt and responsibility[16]—reaching—without the atoning sacrifice—throughout eternity! Can we wonder, that the detection should bring him under certain condemnation?[17] It is an offence against both tables of the law. The perjurer "takes God's

[1] 'Quos Deus amat, indurat et exercet.' Seneca De Otio. Sape. c. 4.
[2] Psalm cvii. 7.
[3] Acts xiii. 18.
[4] Chap. xiv. 20. Comp. verse 6.
[5] Works, viii. 77.
[6] Chap. xvii. 17.
[7] 'Amicus certus in re incertâ cernitur.'—Cicero.
[8] Verse 7.
[9] Ps. xxxi. 7.
[10] Heb. xiii. 5.
[11] Ps. xl. 17.
[12] Rom. viii. 38, 39.
[13] Ibid. verse 17. Heb. i. 3, with 1 Cor. iii. 21—23.
[14] Bishop Reynolds' Works, p. 11.
[15] Chap. xiv. 25.
[16] Verse 28.
[17] Verse 9; xxi. 28. Deut. xix. 16—21.

name in vain." The *false witness* is a direct transgressor against the law of our neighbor. This wickedness does not however come to this height at once. But the habit of *speaking lies*, the allowance of untruth in sport, or perhaps under the pretence of good,[1] grows to this aggravation.[2] The indulgence of a lie soon banishes all fear of an oath. It may escape detection from man. But it lies open and unveiled before the eye of God. It shall *not be unpunished—it shall not escape*, there. The liar may perhaps have thought or intended no harm. But no palliation is admitted at the bar of God. "*All* liars shall have their part in the lake, that burneth with fire and brimstone."[3]

6. *Many will entreat the favor of the prince; and every man is a friend to him that giveth gifts.* 7. *All the brethren of the poor do hate him: how much more do his friends go far from him! he pursueth them with words, yet they are wanting to him.*

The fourth verse is here further opened with too accurate a description of man's native selfishness. 'A prince never wants suitors for his favor.'[4] Every one loves, or professes to love, those from whom they expect a benefit; "having men's persons in admiration, because of advantage;"[5] valuing them for their possessions, not for their virtues. Yet if "riches make to themselves wings, and flee away,"[6] will not they take their flight with them? If the same person, now fawned on for his gifts, were by Providence brought to poverty, the same *friends would hate* or neglect him. 'Which of them'—asks Bishop Hall—'would dare acknowledge him, when he is going to prison?'[7] *The friends of the poor go from him*, deserting him in his calamity, and, if *he pursueth them with words, yet* they are deaf to his entreaties for help and sympathy. Job found these "summer" friends a great aggravation to his affliction.[8] Jerusalem in its days of prosperity was "the joy of the whole earth." In the time of after-destitution "they called thee"—said the mournful prophet—"an outcast, saying—this is Zion, whom no man seeketh after."[9]

But how ought we to *entreat the favor of our Prince!* What *gifts does he give* to his beloved people! And shall not they exhibit his rule of mercy to their poorer brethren,[10] specially to his poor—the princes and heirs of his kingdom?[11] As a spiritual writer pleads[12]—'Lord! in my greatest plenty, help me to mind and feel others' poverty; and in my most prosperous condition keep me from forgetting the afflictions of thy Joseph.'

[1] Rom. iii. 8. [2] Jer. ix. 3—5. [3] Rev. xxi. 8. [4] Bishop Patrick.
[5] Jude 16. [6] Chap. xxiii. 5. [7] Works, viii. p. 77.
[8] Job vi. 15—22; xix. 13—19; xxix xxx.

Donec eris felix, multos numerabis amicos,
Tempora si fuerint nubila, solus eris.
Ovid De Trist. Lib. i.

[9] Ps. xlviii. 2, with Jer. xxx. 17. [10] Gal. vi. 10. Heb. vi. 10.
[11] Ps. cxiii. 7, 8. Jam. ii. 5.
[12] Swinnock's Christian Man's Calling, Part ii. 338.

8. *He that getteth wisdom loveth his own soul: he that keepeth understanding shall find good.*

It would seem that self-interest might win us to religion. Careless sinner! little do you know your loss of solid happiness. If any thing is worth *getting*, and when got—worth *keeping*—"Wisdom is the thing: therefore *get wisdom*, and with all thy getting *get understanding*."[1] How this blessing is to be obtained, Solomon had before explained. Apply thine heart diligently to the search; then bring thine heart to God for his light and teaching; and the treasure is thine own.[2] Yet it requires as much care to *keep* the blessing, as to *get* it. Soon may it slip away from a negligent hand. "Keep thy soul diligently;"[3] and thou wilt keep thy treasure; as the man, who, having found the hidden treasure in the field, buys the field to secure it.[4] It is no carnal *good*, however, that is *found* here. This is the Christian's sacrifice, not his portion.[5] Yet it is real, infinite, heavenly; "whoso findeth me, findeth life"[6]—all in me—all with me. Is not this the chief good. above every earthly good[7]—the eternal good, when every earthly good shall have passed away?[8] Whether Christ or the world shall have our highest love, our supreme trust, our first time, and our choicest talent—one should be ashamed to admit the question. Is not the very mention of it a sufficient answer? It is like comparing pebbles with pearls, dust with diamonds, dross with gold. To follow our own way is then to destroy—not to *love—our own souls*. "Whoso sinneth against me wrongeth his own soul; all they that hate me love death."[9]

9. *A false witness shall not be unpunished, and he that speaketh lies, shall perish.*

"A God of truth, and without iniquity; just and right is he—A God that cannot lie—Faithful and True."[10] Such is the revealed character of Jehovah! We cannot wonder at the repeated denunciations against deceit. So gross a dishonor is it to his unchangeable attribute! One addition is here made to the former sentence.[11] The punishment shall not only be certain—"*he that speaketh lies* shall not escape,"—"but it shall be utter ruin:—*He shall perish*.[12] "Lies and desolation" are linked together.[13] "I will be a swift witness against false swearers—and them that fear not me—saith the Lord of Hosts."[14]

10. *Delight is not seemly for a fool: much less for a servant to have rule over princes.*

What has *a fool* to do with *delight?* This world's prosperity—so far as he knows it—can only be a curse to him.[15] *Delight* "is

[1] Chap. iv. 5—7. [2] Chap. ii. 1—6. [3] Deut. iv. 9.
[4] Matt. xiii. 44. [5] Luke xiv. 33. [6] Chap. viii. 35.
[7] Psalm iv. 6, 7. [8] Ibid. lxxiii. 25, 26; ciii. 15—17.
[9] Chap. viii. 36. Comp. ver. 16; xxix. 24.
[10] Deut. xxxii. 4. Tit. i. 2. Rev. xix. 11. [11] Verse 5.
[12] Jer. xxviii. 15—17; xxix. 31, 32. 2 Pet. ii. 1—3. Rev. xxii. 15.
[13] Hos. xii. 1. [14] Mal. iii. 5. [15] Chap. i. 32.

comely to the righteous,"[1] suitable to his character. He has a right and title to it.[2] But it *is not seemly for the fool.*[3] He has indeed his merriment and folly.[4] But solid joy he knows not. Far more suitable to him a chastening rod.[5] And should the Lord graciously sanctify this dispensation—as in how many instances he has done so!—then indeed will it introduce him to that "*delight,* which will then *be seemly to him.*"[6]

Much less seemly is the exhibition of *a servant having rule over princes.* Such an elevation is dangerous to the individual.[7] To the kingdom it is one of the "things which the earth cannot bear."[8] *The servant* has indeed the same rational power with his sovereign. But contracted habits of mind unfit him to rule. Exceptions there are, as in the case of Joseph.[9] But seldom is God's order reversed without anarchy and confusion.[10] Such was the reign of our second Edward, when worthless minions *had rule over the prince;* chosen either for their external accomplishments, or for their subserviency to his folly. Peace and happiness belong to godly contentment.[11] "Let every man, wherein he is called, therein abide with God."[12] To those whom he has placed in a subordinate station our Father's voice is full of instruction—"Seekest thou great things for thyself? Seek them not."[13]

11. *The discretion of a man deferreth his anger; and it is his glory to pass over a transgression.*

What is *anger*, but temporary madness? To yield therefore to its paroxysm—to act without deliberation under its impulse, is to do we know not what, and what will surely bring work for repentance.[14] An interval between the inward rising and the outward manifestation of the *anger* is most important. *The discretion of a man deferreth his anger.* Mindful of his own infirmity, he will guard against indecent sallies of temper, taking time to weigh, and careful not to overcharge the offence.[15] An affront therefore is the test, whether he has *discretion*, or whether he is the slave of his own passion. The standard of common usage is—'To be *even*, and return one insult by another.' The Christian standard is to be *above;* "not rendering railing for railing, but contrariwise blessing."[16]

[1] Psalm xxxiii. 1. [2] Ibid. xxxii. 11. [3] Chap. xxvi. 1.
[4] 1 Sam. xxv. 25, 36. Ecc. vii. 5, 6. Isa. v. 11, 12; xxii. 12—14. Hos. vii. 3—5. Amos v. 3—6.
[5] Chap. x. 13, 14; xxvi. 3. [6] 2 Chron. xxxiii. 11—43. Luke xv. 14—24.
[7] Esth. iii. 1, 2; vii. 10. 'Ex insolentiâ, quibus nova bona fortuna det, impotentes lætitiæ insanire.' Liv. Lib. xxx. c. 42. Comp. Lib. xxiii. c. 18.
[8] Chap. xxx. 22. Comp. Eccl. x. 5—9. [9] Gen. xli. 39—45.
[10] 2 Sam. iii. 24, 25, 39. Isa. iii. 5. [11] 1 Tim. vi. 6. [12] 1 Cor. vii. 24.
[13] Jer. xlv. 5. [14] Chap. xiv. 17, 29.
[15] Chap. xvi. 32. Ecc. vii. 9. Jam. i. 19. Comp. 1 Sam. x. 27. Even Heathen moralists acknowledge the value of this *discretion*—'I would have beaten thee, if I was not angry,' said the philosopher to his offending servant. Augustus under the impulse of anger was requested to repeat the alphabet, to give him time to cool. 'It is easier—as Seneca wisely observed—'not to admit the passion, than, when admitted, to govern it.' Justin Martyr, when asked what was Christ's greatest miracle—named his so great patience in such great trials.
[16] 1 Peter iii. 9. The example of Joseph, Gen. xlv. 4—15; l. 21. David. 1 Sam

Again—*To pass over a transgression*—such is the proud folly of man's judgment—is disgrace—want of courage and proper spirit. But Solomon—a wise man—a King—declares it to be weakness, not strength or greatness, to be able to bear nothing.[1] *It is glory to pass over a transgression.* So it must be, because it is likeness to God. What a motive! What a pattern is his long-suffering with such wilful—daily—hourly provocations![2] If he create us anew, it must be, as before, in his own image. Forbearance and forgiveness will therefore take the place of resentment and malice. Moral strength may in some men curb the outward expression. But the poison lurks within. Forbearance from a pure motive—*passing over transgression* in free love—is a noble triumph of grace—most honorable to God—fraught with the richest spoils to our own souls.

12. *The king's wrath is as the roaring of a lion: but his favor is as dew upon the grass.*

The monarch of the forest is a just comparison to the monarch of the land.[3] "The lion hath roared; who will not fear?"[4] The rocks and hills echo the terrific cry. The whole race of the animals of the forest are driven to flight, or petrified to the spot. Such is *the king's wrath* in a land of despotism[5]—reigning without law—above law—his will his only law—an awful picture of cruelty,[6] tyranny,[7] or caprice![8] Unlimited power is too much for proud human nature to bear, except with special grace from above. Just so is *the king's power* a reviving blessing, *as dew upon the grass*—the nourishment of vegetative life in the East, where the more powerful influence is only partially or periodically known.[9]

But if *the wrath of a king* be so terrible—Oh, my soul, what must be the wrath of God![10] If it be so terrible in this world, where every drop is mixed with mercy; what will it be in eternity, where it is "poured out without mixture"—without cessation[11]—where his power is so fearfully manifested—not only in tormenting, but in preserving—"establishing for correction."[12] Oh! let this wrath be the grand object of my reverential fear. Let me flee from it by the only way of escape, while escape is open to me; and seek his *favor*, as the enriching "dew" unto Israel—invigorating and fertilizing my barren soil.[13]

xxiv. 7—19. Ps. xxxv. 7—14; xxxviii. 12—14. The prophet, 1 Kings xiii. 4—6. Mr. Scott justly remarks upon the identity of the Old Testament standard, with Christ and his apostles. Comp. Matt. v. 38—42; xviii. 21, 22. Rom. xii. 17—21, with Chap. xxv. 21, 22.

[1] The Roman moralist could say:—
Infirmi est animi exiguique voluptas.
Ultio. Juven. Sat. 13.

[2] Eph. iv. 31, 32. Col. iii. 13.
[3] Comp. Jer. iv. 17; l. 17. 2 Tim. iv. 17.
[4] Amos iii. 8. Rev. x. 1—3. See Homer's fine picture, Iliad xx. 166—171.
[5] Chap. xvi. 14; xx. 2; xxviii. 15.
[6] Matt. ii. 16—18.
[7] Ex. v. 4—9. Dan. iii. 1—19.
[8] Dan. ii. 5—12.
[9] Chap. xvi. 15. 2 Sam. xxiii. 3, 4.
[10] Luke xii. 4, 5.
[11] Mark ix. 44. Rev. xiv. 10, 11.
[12] Hab. i. 12.
[13] Hos. xiv. 5—7. Comp. Ps. lxxii. 6.

13. *A foolish son is the calamity of his father: and the contentions of a wife are a continual dropping.*

'Many,' observes an old commentator—'are the miseries of a man's life; but none like that, which cometh from him, who should be the stay of his life.'[1] As "a wise son maketh a glad father,[2] so *a foolish son is the father's calamity*[3]—a multitude of calamities meeting in one, such as no earthly portion—no riches, honor or station—can alleviate or balance. The denunciation—"Write this man childless"[4]—would be to his heart a comparative boon. The throne of grace to the Christian *father* will be the only refuge for his grief. There will he pour out the bitterness of his soul in humiliation for himself, and supplication for his child; and find rest.[5] Oh! can we be too earnest for the prevention of this *calamity?* Shall we not seek early grace for our children, and—*combined with this*—special grace for ourselves,[6] to preserve us from unwittingly sowing the seed in their young hearts, that will afterwards spring up with such deadly fruit?

Another domestic *calamity* is mentioned, not less poignant. *The contentions of a wife* are as *a continual dropping*[7] of rain through the roof of an old house. Such a *dropping* utterly destroys his household comfort, and "wears away" a heart as firm as a "stone."[8] This trial is the more fretting, because there is no lawful escape. The *foolish son* may be cast out.[9] The *contentious wife* must be endured.[10] Yet would this cross have been, were the plain Scriptural rule of subjection duly honored?[11] Or is it not the just chastening for the neglect of the Divine injunction, so essential to secure happiness in the yoke?[12] Or may it not be the "thorn in the flesh"—the needful restraint from some imminent—subtle—fearful danger?[13] Self-will and impatience would flee from the cross. Faith will seek strength to bear it meekly to the honor of God, extracting a solid blessing out of a heavy trial.[14] And who knoweth but *the contentious wife* may be given to persevering prayer and patient forbearance, as an helpmeet to her husband, and both shall ultimately "dwell as heirs together of the grace of life?"[15]

But surely our God teaches us a valuable lesson of this world's vanity, by fixing disappointment on its most substantial comforts. Let his children beware of building their rest on an earthly portion, of being ensnared by their best blessings, else will their jealous Father embitter their sweetest sources of enjoyment, and

1 Jermin in loco. 2 Chap. x. 1; xv. 20; xxix. 3.
3 Heb. Plur. Chap. xvii. 21, 25.
4 Jer. xxii. 30. Augustus in a burst of grief in his domestic trials, is said to have applied to himself Hector's exclamation against his cowardly brother—'Would that thou hadst never been born, or never married.' Iliad iii. 40.
5 2 Sam. xxiii. 5. 6 Judg. xiii. 12. 7 Chap. xxvii. 15, also xxi. 9, 19; xxv. 24.
8 Job xiv. 19. 9 Deut. xxi. 18. 10 Matt. v. 32; xix. 3—9. 1 Cor. vii. 11.
11 Gen. iii. 16. 1 Cor. xiv. 34. Eph. v. 22—24. Col. iii. 18. Tit. ii. 5.
12 1 Cor. vii. 39. 2 Cor. vi. 14. 13 2 Cor. xii. 7. 14 Ibid. verses 8, 9.
15 1 Peter iii. 7. Gen. ii. 18. Comp. 1 Cor. vii. 16.

teach them by painful discipline to look to enter in o no rest but his.

14. *House and riches are the inheritance of fathers: and a prudent wife is from the Lord.*

"Every good gift is *from the Lord*;"[1] only some in the ordinary course; others more directly from him. *Houses and riches*—though his gifts—come by descent. *They are the inheritance of fathers.*[2] The heir is known, and in the course of events he takes possession of his estate. But *the prudent wife* is wholly unconnected with the man. There has been no previous bond of relation.[3] She is often brought from a distance.[4] "The Lord brought her to the man"[5] by his special Providence, and therefore as his special gift. The history of Ruth beautifully illustrates the train of matrimonial Providence. The Moabitess married, contrary to all human probability, a man of Israel, that she might be brought into Naomi's family, return with her to her own land, and in course of filial duty be brought under the eye, and drawn to the heart of Boaz, her appointed husband.[6] Often do the wheels of the Lord's working in this interesting matter constrain the admiration of men not well exercised in spiritual observation.[7] And how much more endearing and secure is a special gift of God! The bread coming down from heaven was more valued than if it had been the fruit of labor. Thus is *the prudent wife* honored—as 'a special blessing of God's immediate choosing, and therefore to be obtained by our prayers at the hand of the giver.'[8] The *prudence* however, here described, implies not only her wise governing of her household,[9] but that godly consideration connected with Divine wisdom,[10] by which she becomes the joy and confidence of her husband,[11] as *the contentious wife* is his trouble and disgrace.

But is not the husband, no less than *the wife, from the Lord?* Let each prospectively seek the blessing of God's ordinance from *himself*; never trusting to our own judgment and affections, without primary reference to his guidance.[12] Let us realize the responsibility, as well as the indulgent comfort, of the union; ever counting it a talent for God, for his service and glory: and not doubting for ourselves, that 'all things shall turn to our commodity and comfort, if we draw the yoke in one concord of heart and mind.'[13]

15. *Slothfulness casteth into a deep sleep; and an idle soul shall suffer hunger.*

All experience and observation attest the fact, that *slothful* habits destroy mental energy, and *idleness* is the road to want. What could we expect from a sluggard lying in his bed all the day? As

[1] Jam. i. 17.
[2] Chap. xiii. 22. Num. xxvii. 7. Deut. xxi. 16. 1 Kings xxi. 3, 4. 2 Cor. xii. 14.
[3] 1 Sam. xxv. 39—42.
[4] Gen. xxiv. 4, 5.
[5] Ibid. ii. 22.
[6] Ruth i. 1—4; iv. 13.
[7] Gen. xxiv. 50.
[8] Bishop Hall.
[9] Chap. xxxi. 27.
[10] Chap. viii. 12.
[11] Chap. xxxi. 11, 23, 28; xviii. 22.
[12] Chap. iii. 6.
[13] Homily on Matrimony.

little from the *slothful*, who goes about his work, as if he was *cast into a deep sleep.*[1]

Thoughtless sinner! Think how this applies to the work of God. You persuade yourself that all is well, because you will not trouble yourself to open your eyes to the truth; and you are content to let things run their course. You do not rebel against the Gospel. But has not our Divine Master said—"He that is not with me is against me?"[2] You conceive that you have done no harm. But is it no harm to have hitherto wasted every opportunity for eternity? to have wandered about in vanity from your cradle, instead of living to God? You are determined to sleep at any rate. And though the two grand treasures—the favor of God, and your own soul—are in imminent peril; yet still you "say to your soul—Soul, take thine ease."[3] Instead of weeping love, wrestling prayer, and working dilligence—you are *cast into a deep sleep.* "Awake, thou that sleepest;"[4] else wilt thou sleep the sleep of eternal death.

Professor! do you expect the grace of God to work as a charm, without, or independent of, means? This were a deadly delusion, *casting you into the deep sleep* of presumption. Such an *idle soul shall suffer hunger!*[5] The enduring meat is the gift of God; but, like every other blessing of the Gospel, it is given only to labor.[6] *The idle mouth*—full only of heartless complaints, perhaps sending up a dull prayer for the present quiet of his conscience—*shall suffer hunger.* The soul can never flourish, if it be not in earnest with God. It may be roused for a while; but only to be *cast into a deeper sleep* than ever. Now look at the child of God awakened out of *a deep sleep;* set out in good earnest for the kingdom; enabled to fight—yea—to conquer. But sleep has followed; and, instead of improving the advantage, a sudden assault of the enemy has laid him low.[7] Mind thy work and thy conflict more than thine ease and comfort; else wilt thou be—not a conqueror, but a captive. In time of ease, how naturally, as Bunyan's pilgrim found it, does the air of the plain make us drowsy! And then the soul, instead of being "satisfied as with marrow and fatness,"[8] *suffers hunger*, and becomes faint for want of its proper nourishment. Nothing but the unceasing prayer and exercise of a mortified spirit can shake off this "baneful disease that cleaveth to us." Be thou, Lord, our Helper, our Strength, our Physician!

16. *He that keepeth the commandment, keepeth his own soul; but he that despiseth his ways shall die.*

The fearing of *the commandment* is the path of honor.[9] *The keeping* of it is our security. *Keep the word*, and the word will keep us securely. Our duties are thus identified with our privi-

[1] Chap. vi. 9—11. [2] Matt. xii. 30.
[3] Luke xii. 19. [4] Eph. v. 14. [5] Chap. x. 4, 5; xx. 4.
[6] John vi. 27, with Heb. vi. 11, 12. 2 Peter i. 5, 11.
[7] Invadunt urbem somno, vinoque sepultam. Virg. Æn. ii. 265.
[8] Psalm lxiii. 5. [9] Chap. xiii. 13.

leges.[1] This is the first successful effort to shake ourselves from *the deep sleep of slothfulness;* when we "stir up ourselves to take hold of God, "choosing the things that please him, and joining ourselves to him, to serve him, and to love his name."[2] Yet the power to *keep the commandment* is not in a man's self.[3] Is it not God working in us—through—by—with—us?[4] Thus "all our deeds are wrought in him;"[5] and nothing is left but the thankful humbling acknowledgment—"Yet not I, but the grace of God that is in me."[6] Let then the world know, that we do not exercise obedience in a covenant of works, nor reject it as a system of bondage and despondency; but that *keeping the commandment* evangelically is *keeping our own souls*[7]—the way of present happiness[8]—the seal of everlasting mercy[9]—the pathway to heaven.[10]

But alas! the multitude, instead of *keeping the commandment,* "go at all adventures,"[11] careless of *their ways,* reckless of their end. It is with them scarcely worth looking into—whether God is displeased or not; whether they be walking in the narrow or broad path;—and what the end of that path may be. Sometimes they come into the world fresh from the influence of a religious education. For a while they yield alternately to their conscience and their corruptions. They are touched a moment under the convictions of the word, or the corrections of the rod. Yet the want of steadiness and consistency soon sweeps all away into "worse" hardness than before.[12] They are "carried away unto their idols, even as they were led;"[13] and—slaves of their wills, their lusts, their fancies—they know not;—they care not to know—"that for all these things God will call them to judgment."[14] They *despise their ways, and die.*

Young people—'Ponder the path of your feet.' Look to it well at every step, that "your ways be established"[15] in converting grace—the only security for Christian steadfastness.[16] Keep the conscience tender—the Divine rule before your eyes—the promise in the heart. Cherish a pliable spirit for your Father's guidance. How solemn the warning—*He that despiseth his ways shall die.* Sinner! would that thou wouldst ponder this death! It is no creation of a distempered fancy. It is the death, which sin bringeth forth to perfection.[17] It is the harvest from that seed.[18] It is the death such as a soul can die—an eternal reality of infinite—unchangeable misery; the extinction—not of thy being, (that were a boon indeed!) but of thy happiness. What must it be to be immoveably linked with the wrath of God? Yea—to have the wrath of an immortal God filling the conscience of thine immortal soul,

[1] Ps. xix. 11; cxix. 165. Isa. xxxii. 17. [2] Isa. lxiv. 7; lvi. 4—6.
[3] Jer. x. 23. [4] Isa. xxvi. 12. Phil. ii. 12, 13. [5] John iii. 21.
[6] 1 Cor. xv. 10. [7] Chap. x. 17; xvi. 17; xxii. 5.
[8] Isa. lxiv. 5. John xiv. 21—23. 1 John ii. 5; iii. 24. [9] Ps. ciii. 17, 18.
[10] Isa. xxxv. 8—10. Rev. xxii. 14. [11] Lev. xxvi. 21. Marg.
[12] 2 Peter ii. 20—22. [13] 1 Cor. xii. 2.
[14] Ecc. xi. 9, with 2 Kings x. 31. Jer. xliv. 17. [15] Chap. iv. 26.
[16] 2 Pet. iii. 17, 18. [17] Jam. i. 14, 15. [18] Gal. vi. 7, 8.

with all its power eternally enlarging to receive the full and eterna impression. And whilst thou art "going on frowardly in the way of thine heart,"[1] remember "there is but a step"—who knows how short a step—how soon taken?—"between thee and this death."[2] "Why wilt thou die"—when the oath of thy God testifies—"he hath no pleasure in thy death"—when his gracious voice to thee is—"Turn and live.[3] Consider thy ways."[4] Oh! listen—ere thou learn the wisdom of fools—to be wise too late.

17. *He that hath pity upon the poor lendeth unto the Lord; and that which he hath given will he pay him again.*

The ordinance of God is, that "the poor shall never cease out of the land."[5] Hence the universal obligation is to *have pity upon the poor*. This is according to the New Testament standard, which inculcates the spirit no less than the act.[6] We must open our heart as much as our hands,[7] "draw out our soul" as well as our bread, "to the hungry,"[8] thus doubling the alms, by giving a part of ourselves. It is possible to "give all our goods to feed the poor," without one atom of the true charity of the heart.[9] But whatever we give, "if we shut up the bowels of compassion from our brother, how dwelleth the love of God in us?"[10] The good Samaritan showed true practical *pity*. Never let us forget our Lord's application—"Go, and do thou likewise."[11]

The appointment of the Deacons in the Primitive Church;[12] the anxiety of the Apostles when delegating a commission to their brethren;[13] the high commendation of the Macedonian Churches;[14] the weekly rule of charity laid down (not enforcing a fixed standard, but "*as God hath prospered*")[15]—all this shows the acceptableness of this Christian service.

The worldly philanthropist however has no conception of the Divine honor of this principle. If our brother is the object of *pity*, in truth the majesty of Heaven is concerned. It is *lending to the Lord*. Selfishness would evade the obligation under the cover of prudence. But *what we give* is only a loan, to be paid *again*, and *that* with such security, as can never fail. The Lord of heaven condescends to be the Surety for *the poor*. He takes the debt upon himself, and gives us the bond of his word in promise of payment. Though he has a right to all, and is beholden to none,[16] he becomes a debtor to his own. Many acts of kindness have been buried and forgotten. The witness of our conscience is the only fruit. But here is a safe deposit in the very heart of God. It can never be lost or forgotten.[17] 'If then'—as Bishop Hall writes—'we will needs lay up, where should we rather repose it, than in the Christian's treasury? The poor man's hand is the treasury of

[1] Isa. lvii. 17. [2] 1 Sam. xx. 3. [3] Ez. xxxiii. 11; xviii. 32.
[4] Hag. i. 5, 7. [5] Deut. xv. 11.
[6] Luke vi. 30—36. Col. iii. 12. Comp. Chap. xiv. 21. [7] Deut. xv. 7, 10.
[8] Isa. lviii. 10. [9] 1 Cor. xiii. 3. [10] 1 John iii. 17.
[11] Luke x. 33—37. [12] Acts vi. 2—6. [13] Gal. ii. 9, 10.
[14] 2 Cor. viii. ix. [15] 1 Cor. xvi. 2. [16] Ps. xvi. 2. Rom. xi. 36.
[17] Matt. x. 42; xxv. 40. Heb. vi. 10.

Christ. All my superfluity shall there be hoarded up, where I know it will be safely kept, and surely returned me.'[1]

It is indeed an act of faith—often of naked faith, when there seems no hope of return.[2] But this is the principle, which "the King delighteth to honor." Franke's Orphan Institution stands out before us. Doubtless the experience of the Lord's people—were it fully brought out—would declare many similar manifestations of His faithfulness to his word. The resurrection day will bring all to light.[3] Meanwhile let us admire this his wondrous grace. He puts the desire into the heart—disposes the heart, opens the opportunity, 'and after all accepts the act,' as if it had been the Creator's work, without spot or pollution!

18. *Chasten thy son while there is hope, and let not thy soul spare for his crying.*

Christian Parents! carefully study the word of God. See here our Father's wise and loving discipline with his children. "Like as a Father, he pitieth his children." "As one whom his mother comforteth, so will I comfort you."[4] Yet when his children need *chastening*; though the flesh cries—*spare*; though every groan enters into his heart[5]—he loves so well, that *his soul spares them not for their crying.*[6] He uses the rod—yea—if need be—heavily.[7] He will wither their brightest comforts—children—property, if they turn them to idols; and this—"not for his pleasure, but for their profit."[8] And what child has not blessed him, that he did not refrain his discipline, till it had done "its perfect work?"

Is not this then our pattern—our standard; setting out the sound principles of Christian education? "Fathers, provoke not your children to wrath; lest they be discouraged."[9] But let not the rule—*chasten—spare not*—be "a hard saying." Is not tenderness for the child a cover for the indulgence of weak and foolish affections? There is much more mercy in what seems to be harshness, than in false tenderness.[10] Let the child see, that we are resolved; that we are not to be diverted from our duty by the *cry* of weakness or passion. Far better that the child should *cry* under healthful correction, than that the parents should afterwards *cry* under the bitter fruit to themselves and children, of neglected discipline. 'Eli could not have devised which way to have plagued himself and his house so much, as by his kindness to his children's sin. Parents need no other means to make themselves miserable than sparing the rod.'[11] Yet much less of it would be needed, did they govern, as they ought to do, by the steady decision of a word—a frown—a look.

But the great force of the rule is its timely application—*while there is hope.* For hopeless the case may be, if the remedy be de

[1] Works, viii. 32. [2] Luke vi. 38. Comp. Chap. xxviii. 27.
[3] Matt. xxv. 34—40. Luke xiv. 12—14.
[4] Ps. ciii. 13. Isa. lxvi. 13. [5] Ex. ii. 23, 24. Judg. x. 16.
[6] Psa. lxxxix. 30—32. [7] Ps. xxxix. 10. 1 Pet. v. 6.
[8] Heb. xii. 10. Comp. Lam. iii. 33. [9] Col. iii. 23. [10] Chap. xxiii. 13, 14.
[11] Bishop Hall's Contemplations, Book xi. vii.

layed. "Betimes"[1]—is the season, when the good can be effected with the most ease, and the fewest strokes. *Sharp chastening* may fail later to accomplish, what a slight rebuke in the early course might have wrought. But is there not too often a voluntary blindness, that does not choose to see what it is painful to correct? The false notion—'Children will be children'—leads us often to pass over real faults, and consider their tempers and waywardness too trifling to require prompt correction. And thus sin, winked at in its beginning, hardens in all the strength of deep-rooted corruptions. Whereas—who would neglect the most trifling bodily ailment in children, which might grow into serious results? If they cannot be argued with, they must be controlled. How often have we found in after life the evil of fixed habits, which early discipline might have subdued with far less cost of suffering.[2] Oh! what grace and wisdom is needed to discipline our minds, judgment, and affections to that tone of self-government, which will enable us to train our children practically for the service of God, and for their own happiness.

19. *A man of great wrath shall suffer punishment: for if thou deliver him, yet thou must do it again.*

How often does the unchastened child grow up to *a man of great wrath*, bringing himself into trouble by his boisterous and ungoverned passions! Adonijah, whom "his father had not displeased at any time," rebels against his brother, and *suffers punishment*.[3] The wretched victim gained nothing by experience. *Delivered* from one broil, he plunges into another. Indeed who knows what will be the end of undisciplined passion? Cain—*a man of great wrath*—the murderer of his brother—*the punishment that he suffered* was "greater than he could bear."[4] The friendly efforts to restrain this wrath must be repeated again and again[5]—too often ineffectually. Meanwhile the man *suffers his own punishment*—the miseries of a fierce intestine war—driven about by the fury of his raging lust. Truly "it is a man's discretion to defer his anger,"[6] as the first, often the successful, effort to restrain an indulgence, which leaves him degraded and defenceless.[7]

After all that man boasts of his self-government, there is a fermentation within, which restraint may bind, but cannot subdue. Wounded pride and unquelled resentment leave the wretched criminal in his brooding chamber within—*suffering* an intolerable burden of self-inflicted *punishment*—What then is the radical cure? "Learn of me, for I am meek and lowly in heart."[8] The glory and encouragement of the gospel is that religion with all its difficulties is a practicable thing.[9] "My grace is sufficient for thee"—is the cheering word of Him, who sealed the faithfulness of the promise with his blood. Doubt not then, that "he will perfect

[1] Chap. xiii. 24; xxii. 15. [2] 1 Kings i. 6; ii. 24, 35.
[3] Ibid. i. 50—53; ii. 13—21. Comp. also 2 Sam. xvi. 7. 1 Kings ii. 46.
[4] Gen. iv. 5—8, 13. [5] 1 Sam. xix. 1—11; xx. 32, 33. [6] Verse 11.
[7] Chap. xxv. 28 [8] Matt. xi. 29. [9] 2 Cor. xii. 9.

that which concerneth us"[1]—even to the moulding of the *man of great wrath* into his own image of meekness, gentleness, and love.

20. *Hear counsel, and receive instruction, that thou mayest be wise in thy latter end.*

We have just had a word for parents directing their Christian discipline. Here the children are exhorted to humility. Again are they awakened to *hear counsel and instruction.*[2] And constantly do they need the word. "Childhood and youth are vanity."[3] Present gratification is the main object. Oh! remember that the seed, now sown in the season of youth, will produce either blessed or bitter fruit *in the latter end.* Rich indeed was the harvest from Timothy's early attention to *instruction.*[4] Fearful indeed was the judgment upon the scoffers;[5] the awful death of the profligate,[6] the ruin of the holy nation[7]—all the fruit of despising timely wisdom and instruction. Rehoboam[8]—and Amaziah[9]—might they not have escaped the ruin of their kingdom, had they *heard counsel*, and thus obtained *wisdom in their latter end?* 'I am going to die,' said a thoughtless King on his death-bed; 'and yet I have not begun to live.' How does the wisdom of mature age depend upon diligence in *hearing counsel* and instruction—upon "bearing the yoke in the youth"—a "good" thing indeed, fraught with profit.[10] Who can refrain, in the sight of the mass of ungodliness, from the weeping lamentation of the man of God: "Oh! that they were wise! that they understood this! that they would consider their latter end!"[11]

21. *There are many devices in a man's heart; nevertheless the counsel of the Lord, that shall stand.*

When God and man were as one, it was "as the days of heaven upon earth." But ever since the fall, *man's devices and God's counsel* are at opposite. Which will triumph, who can doubt? "There is no wisdom, nor understanding, nor counsel against the Lord. I will work and who shall let it? My counsel shall stand, and I will do all my pleasure."[12] We mark this conflict in every-day life. Man looks for advancement. God in mercy restrains him from it. *Man's devices* are to be rich. God's wise *counsel* keeps him poor. Man sets his heart upon enjoying his stores. God in a moment "requires his soul.[13] Thus man proposes—God disposes. *The devices* in the heart of godly Isaac resisted—though in vain, the declared *counsel of the Lord.*[14] And what is the page of history, but the overruling of *man's devices*

[1] Ps. cxxxviii. 8. [2] Chap. iv. 1, 2; v. 1, 2; vii. 1, 2.
[3] Eccl. xi. 10. [4] 2 Tim. iii. 14, 15. [5] Chap. i. 25; xxix. 1.
[6] Chap. v. 9—14. [7] Matt. xxiii. 37—39. Luke xix. 41, 42.
[8] 1 Kings xii. 12—19. [9] 2 Chron. xxv. 15—20. [10] Lam. iii. 27.
[11] Deut. xxxii. 29. [12] Chap. xxi. 30. Isa. xliii. 13; xlvi. 10.
[13] Luke xii. 19, 20. [14] Gen. xxvii. 1—7, with xxv. 23.

for the accomplishment of *the Lord's counsel*.[1] The malice of Joseph's brethren was the means of fulfilling the Divine *counsel* in the salvation of his Church.[2] The plot laid for the destruction of Israel furthered their prosperity.[3] The vain attempts at opposition to Christ were subservient to the great end of "the determinate *counsel* and foreknowlege of God."[4] The *device of man* to prevent the Apostle's journey to Rome was signally defeated.[5] How vain the impious attempt to "fight against God!"[6] "Woe unto him that striveth with his Maker!"[7] All is clear above, however cloudy it be below. All is calm in heaven, however stormy it may be on earth. There is no confusion there. One will alone reigns. Every purpose reaches its appointed end—"He is of one mind, and who can turn him? And what his soul desireth, even that he doeth."[8]

22. *The desire of a man is kindness, and a poor man is better then a liar.*

The privilege of doing good is within the reach of all. For when the poor fails, *the desire of a man is his kindness*, as acceptable as the most expensive proof of love. "If there be a willing mind, it is accepted, according to that a man hath, not according to that he hath not."[9] The dealings of God to his people are grounded on this principle. David's *desire* to build the temple was accepted and honored, as the act itself appointed for his son.[10] Such also was our Saviour's estimate of the value of the widow's mite,[11] of the box of ointment poured upon himself,[12] of the "cup of cold water given to a disciple."[13] *The desire was the kindness*, more rich and fruitful than the offerings of self-pleasing abundance.[14]

Yet *the desire* must be active—not indolent excitement but "the communication of faith effectual" according to the power given to us.[15] Such a *desire* is far *better* in the sight of God, in the heart of one of his *poor* people, than a man with large opportunities and hollow professions, who proves himself to be *a liar*.[16] *The poor* gives readily. The rich cannot afford. He denies that he has the ability. He promises, and does nothing. *The poor man is better than the liar*. Only take heed to the motive. Men know not the heart. "The Lord weigheth the spirits;"[17] and "the fire will try every man's work of what sort it is."[18]

23. *The fear of the Lord, tendeth to life: and he that hath it shall be satisfied: he shall not be visited with evil.*

The fear of the Lord as a legal principle, is a privilege to be exempt from.[19] As a grace of the gospel, cultivate it to the utter-

[1] Ps. xxxiii. 10, 11. [2] Gen. xxxvii. 19; xlv. 5, 6. [3] Ex. i. 8—12, 17.
[4] Ps. ii. 1—6, with Acts iv. 26—28; ii. 23. [5] Acts xxiii. 12—15, with 11.
[6] Ibid. verse 39. [7] Isa. xlv. 9. [8] Job xxiii. 13.
[9] 2 Cor. viii. 12. [10] 2 Chron. vi. 8; vii. 12—17. [11] Mark xiii. 41—44.
[12] Ibid. xiv. 8, 9. [13] Matt. x. 42. [14] Luke xxi. 4.
[15] Philemon 6. 2 Cor. viii. 11. [16] Ver. 1. Ps. lxii 9. [17] Chap. xvi. 2.
[18] 1 Cor. iii. 13. [19] Luke i. 74. Rom. viii. 15. 2 Tim. i. 7.

most.[1] Threefold fruit is here set before us—*life—satisfaction—security. It tendeth to life*—not the mere natural life, common to the ungodly—(though this blessing, so far as is good, is included[2]) but a heavenly—yea an eternal—life, in the favor and enjoyment of God.[3] So far as we are under its influence, we speak, pray, think, and deal with man, as if God was standing by. The genial beams of "the Sun of righteousness" nourish this holy principle;[4] and soon will it be perfected in the service above.[5]

Meanwhile the *satisfaction* which it imparts is a precious privilege. The worldling's heart is torn with 'an aching void.' He travels from one source of his happiness—crying—"who will shew me any good?" "Lord! lift thou up the light of thy countenance upon me"—is the cry and solid *satisfaction* of a child of God above the best portion of earth.[6] Whoever wants, "they that *fear the Lord* want no good thing. Their souls dwell at ease."[7] *He that hath it shall abide satisfied.* Is not this the very soul of happiness?

Still an object of *fear* usually brings dread. 'But add, whom. *He that feareth the Lord*—That touch turns it into gold. He that so fears, fears not.'[8] He has his "confidence and place of refuge."[9] We do not begin to enquire the way. "God *is known* in the palaces of Zion as a sure refuge."[10] We go to him as a God with whom we are acquainted, and who is engaged in covenant to us. And now taking our sanctuary in God, we sit and sing under his shadow. In this hiding-place how can any *evil*—properly so called—*visit us?*[11] What is *evil* in itself will turn to good.[12] It cannot separate from God. It will tend only to bind us closer to him. We can tread upon scorpions unhurt, when our conscience is kept tender, and our heart fixed in his ways. We fear not his uplifted arm. But his frown of rebuke "enters into our soul." His mercy sweeps away the fear of terror. His holiness maintains the fear of reverence. Conscious security only tends more than ever to make us dread departure and separation from his love.

24. *A slothful man hideth his hand in his bosom, and will not so much as bring it to his mouth again.*

Another forcible figure of the palsy of sloth![13] It so grows on its victim, that he has no heart to do even necessary things for himself; as if he could not take *his hand out of his bosom;* and would rather suffer the cravings of hunger, than make the exertion of putting his food into his mouth. A melancholy picture it is of many fair intentions and promises, and apparently good beginnings in religion—all stopped for want of the effort to overcome the least hindrance. Every religious duty is a burden. The

[1] Heb. xii. 28. 1 Pet. i. 17. [2] Chap. ix. 11; x. 27.
[3] Ps. xxxiii. 18, 19; xxxiv. 11, 12. [4] Mal. iv. 2. [5] Rev. xv. 3, 4.
[6] Ps. iv. 6, 7. [7] Ibid. xxxiv. 9, 10; xxv. 12, 13.
[8] Leighton's Sermon on Psalm cxii. 7. [9] Chap. xiv. 26. [10] Ps. xlviii. 3.
[11] Chap. xii. 21. [12] Rom. viii. 28. Heb. xii. 11.
[13] See similar figures Chap. xii. 27; xxvi. 15. Eccl. iv. 5.

struggle necessary for prayer—the only means of receiving our spiritual food—is too hard. And the soul that seemed to have been awakened, sinks into its former lethargy; and the effort to rouse it becomes each time fainter and more hopeless.

Some indeed seem to feel little or no exertion to be necessary, a plain proof that they have never been really in earnest about this momentous concern. The conflict is not imaginary. "Woe unto those," who reposing on the lap of indulgence, "are at ease in Zion."[1] A religion without sacrifice, without diligence, will never open a way to heaven. It is treasuring up unavailing repentance against the latter days. If the work of the day—much more the work of eternity, calls for all diligence,—if the Emperor Titus could mourn, that he 'had lost a day,' what will be the stinging remorse of having lost a life! To think, that by a right beginning, followed up by "a patient continuance in well doing,"[2] we might have effectively "served the will of God in our generation,"[3] so as to have been missed in the world, after we had "fallen asleep;" to think that we might have sown seed for eternity, so that our "memory" instead of "rotting," would have been "blessed"[4]—that all this was wished, contemplated—nay—even resolved—yet not an atom of it accomplished: will not this be a thorn for a dying pillow—perhaps the tormenting worm for eternity?

How then shall we resist this deadly disease? Thomson's excuse for reposing in his own 'Castle of Indolence' was—that he had nothing to do. The want of an object makes an idler of a man of talent. Oh! then have this grand object ever in sight. "To me to live is Christ."[5] Be employed for God and for his Church. Form habits of early energy. Beware of a dreaming sentimentalism. Cultivate bodily activity. Regard the incursions of sloth as the effects of those poisons, which, while they cause sleep—unless counteracted by constant resistance—must prove fatal. Yet with all these means, never forget the one only principle, that makes them effectual—prayer, unceasing, believing—"looking unto Jesus"—who not only gives life, but liveliness.[6]

But are we then struggling in the conflict? Forget not to thank God for every victory—yea—for the continued strength, enabling us to persevere in the fight; for the wise dispensation also that appoints this holy conflict, as the means of invigorating our faith, our hope, our meetness for the crown, and our joyful expectation of it. If peace with God is our life, "the joy of the Lord is our strength,"[7] our health, our happiness, yet not to be found in a listless enervated habit.

25. *Smite a scorner, and the simple will beware: and reprove one that hath understanding, and he will understand knowledge.*

There is a difference of opinion upon the profit of punishments.

[1] Amos vi. 1. [2] Rom. ii. 7. [3] Acts xiii. 36.
[4] Chap. x. 7. [5] Phil. i. 21. [6] Heb. xii. 1, 2. John x. 10.
[7] Neh. viii. 10.

Some will have it, that, if the will does not give way to reason, forced obedience is of little use. But God's word and ordinance is our standard, though great wisdom is regarded in the measure and adaptation. Two kinds are here mentioned; each measured out according to the character of the offender; but both wholesome in their results. *The scorner* is a bold sinner. *Smite him, that the simple may beware.*[1] It may be a timely warning to those that are led by him. The taking the ring-leader of a mischievous party may put an end to the combination. This is the benefit of laws. Often an example made, though the sinner himself continues hardened, is for the good of the whole body. Thus 'God strikes some, that he may warn all.'[2]

But *a man of understanding reprove.* There is no occasion to *smite.* "A *reproof* entereth more into a wise man, than an hundred stripes into a fool."[3] In *the scorner's* case, the profit is to others. In the wise man's, it is to himself. *He will understand knowledge.*[4] His wisdom enables him to profit, and to be thankful for the seasonable check.[5] Never let us forget the mercy of being kept from sin, or being restored from it, though it be by our Master's sharp and gracious rebuke—"As many as I love, I rebuke and chasten; be zealous therefore, and repent."[6]

26. *He that wasteth his father, and chaseth away his mother, is a son that causeth shame, and bringeth reproach.*

This is alas! not an ideal picture of recklessness. "Without natural affection"[7]—is an awful mark of unrestrained depravity. Man is the debased slave of his selfish lust. The profligate may *waste his father's* substance by extravagance, and his spirits and health by his ill-conduct. Absalom *wasted his father* by his undutiful rebellion.[8] And often has a mother's tenderness been repaid with crushing unkindness—the insolence of an ungrateful son virtually *chasing* her from her home—her idol becoming her curse! Such monsters in human shape—outraging every principle of humanity—have been found in every generation. Yet seldom do they escape without some mark of retributive justice even in this life.[9] And though they may be callous to public opinion, while *causing shame and bringing reproach* on their names; yet conscience will speak;[10] and sooner or later the stroke will fearfully fall. Children! A parent's sorrows carry a heavy account before the bar of God. If "the commandment be with promise,"[11] will not the breach of the commandment cut off the entail of the promise, with an awful and aggravated weight of condemnation?

27. *Cease, my son, to hear the instruction that causeth to err from the words of knowledge.*

[1] Chap. xxi. 11. Acts xiii. 6—12.
[2] Bishop Hall. Comp. Ex. xviii. 10, 11. Deut. xiii. 11; xix. 20; xxi. 21. Acts v. 1—11. Rev. xi. 13.
[3] Chap. xvii. 10; xv. 5.
[4] Chap. ix. 8, 9.
[5] Psalm cxli. 5.
[6] Rev iii. 19.
[7] Rom. i. 30, 31.
[8] 2 Sam. xv. 1—14.
[9] Chap. xxx. 11, 17.
[10] Is. lvii. 20.
[11] Eph. vi. 2, 3.

Hear the same caution from the lips of our Divine Master—"Beware of false prophets. Take heed what you hear."[1] All *instruction* is not to life. Teachers of evil—"Ministers of Satan"[2]—abound—their *instruction, causing to err from the words of knowledge,* is more palatable to the perverseness of the heart; more alluring to the inexperience of the young, than solid Scriptural teaching.[3] The Apostle reproves the Galatian Church for listening to teachers, *causing them to err* fatally *from the words of knowledge.*[4] And would he not have warned us against the same teaching, so fearfully prevalent: placing ordinances in the stead of Christ, or conjoined with him; man's proud work of voluntary humility and external service in the room of pure simplicity of reliance on the Redeemer's work? When the soul has thus "fallen from grace,"[5] what ground of confidence can we bring before God? What is his service, but the bondage of outward ceremonies, leading to cheerless despondency?

This *instruction* is not generally a bold and direct departure from truth. Bnt, as in the first temptation,[6] it *causeth to err* so gradually, that the deviation from the straight line is scarcely perceptible, till the mischief has been accomplished. Had Eve at once *ceased to hear*, she would not have *erred from the words of knowledge.* But the success of the first attempt has emboldened the seducer to deal out his deadly poison to her enfeebled children. And what faithful Pastor does not feel a "godly jealousy" for his flock, lest by the same beguilement "they should be corrupted from the simplicity that is in Christ?"[7]

Often does the warning voice cry—*Cease from hearing.*[8] Needlessly to tamper with error, is "entering into temptation." Nay it is most hazardous to deal with it at all, ere our minds are thoroughly grounded in the truth, and we have obtained "the good thing of the heart established with grace."[9] Yet we have senses given for discernment. Use increaseth this discernment.[10] Increasing clearness should be the matter of daily supplication.[11] We are bound therefore to exercise our senses by the plainest commands.[12] Our Divine Master distinctly rebukes indolence.[13] When the words came with the stamp of an apostle, the appeal to the unerring standard was highly commended.[14] Should we give up our judgment to the Church, be it remembered, that "every one of us shall bear his own burden—shall give an account of himself to God."[15] Be the son—not the slave—of the Church. Reverence her just authority. But maintain that right of private judgment, which constitutes our personal responsibility.

This Christian independence however must be held with humility

[1] Matt. vii. 15. Mark iv. 24. [2] 2 Cor. xi. 13—15.
[3] Isa. xxx. 10. Jer. v. 31. [4] Gal. i. 6, 7; iii. 1—4; v. 7, 8.
[5] Ibid. v. 4. [6] Gen. iii. 1—6. [7] 2 Cor. xi. 2, 3.
[8] Rom. xvi. 17, 18. 1 Tim. vi. 3—5. 2 Tim. ii. 16, 17. [9] Heb. xiii. 9.
[10] Ibid. v. 14. [11] Phil. i. 9, 10. M. R. [12] 1 Thess. v. 21. 1 John. iv. 1.
[13] Luke xii. 57. [14] Acts xvii. 11. Comp. Isa. viii. 20.
[15] Rom. xiv. 12. Gal. vi. 5.

and simplicity. Self-will and self-conceit must be carefully restrained. We must not attend the ordinances to try the Minister. We must hear as learners, not as judges; seeking wholesome food, not intoxicating excitement: watchful that a sound appetite does not give place to a spiritual lust.[1] While the right of judgment is our great privilege, the licentiousness of it is a cankering evil.

But what—if our lot be manifestly cast, and our sphere of Christian obligation opened, where *words of knowledge* are not found? Let not the ungodliness of the Minister be an excuse for the neglect of Christian ordinances. Activity in the Church will be a quickening means of grace. The constant application of the touchstone will be a preservation from error. The food of the word will be more precious. And who knows but an unenlightened Minister may be given to the power of believing prayer, and to the living influence of godly meekness, patience, and consistency.[2]

28. *An ungodly witness* (witness of Belial, Marg.) *scorneth judgment, and the mouth of the wicked devoureth iniquity.* 29. *Judgments are prepared for scorners, and stripes for the back of fools.*

Justly is this man called *a witness of Belial.* Satan himself hath suborned him for his own malicious purposes.[3] *Scorning*—instead of regarding—*judgment,* his testimony is worthless. He has "cast the law behind his back." He *devours iniquity* with greediness, feeds upon it as his proper food, and, sinning without remorse, he is always ready to trade in his deceit, either for gain or revenge.

But in this greedy *devouring* he has swallowed the hook with the bait. *For such scorners judgments are prepared.* For such *fools* as thus "make a mock of sin"[4]—*stripes* are ready *for their backs*—often inflicted by men,—the instruments of God. *Scorners* are warned "lest their bands be made strong"[5] for *judgment,* which, however they may despise, they cannot resist—"Can thine heart endure, or can thine hands be strong, in the day that I shall deal with thee? Who shall dwell with the devouring fire? Who shall dwell with everlasting burnings? It is a fearful thing to fall into the hands of the living God."[6] Oh! that thoughtless, light-minded young persons would lay such words to heart! When they join in the laugh of their more hardened companions, and learn from them to *scorn judgment,* in spite of the accusing of a conscience not yet silenced; let them tremble, lest from "standing in the way of sinners;" they may go on to "sit in the seat of the *scornful,*"[7] and may even exceed their companions in despising the threatenings of God.

And when under these slighted *judgments,* who is to blame for them? 'Our sin'—saith Bishop Hall—'is our own, and the wages

[1] See 2 Tim. iv. 3.
[2] See a remarkable instance in the Life of Mr. Walker of Truro.
[3] 1 Kings xxi. 13. Such was the keen description of the Roman Satyrist—
Tam facile et pronum est superos contemnere testes, &c. Juven. Sat. 13.
[4] Chap. xiv. 9. [5] Isa. xxviii. [6] Ez. xxi. 14. Isa. xxxiii. 15. Heb. x. 31.
[7] Psalm i. 1.

of sin is death." He that doth the work, earns the wages. So then the righteous God is cleared both of our sin and our death. Only his justice pays us what our will needs deserve. What a wretched thing is a wilful sinner, that will needs be guilty of his own death!"[1] Blessed—blessed day!—should it ever see him bemoaning himself thus—"Thou hast chastised me, and I was chastised, as a bullock unaccustomed to the yoke; turn thou me, and I shall be turned; for thou art the Lord my God."[2]

[1] Works viii. 31. [2] Jer. xxxi. 18.

CHAPTER XX.

1. *Wine is a mocker, strong drink is raging: and whosoever is deceived thereby is not wise.*

THE history of the world from the days of Noah[1] proves that the love of *wine and strong drink* is a most insidious vice. The wretched victims are convinced too late, that they have been *mocked* and grievously *deceived.* Not only does it overcome them before they are aware, but it promises pleasure which it can never give. And yet so mighty is the spell, that the besotted slave consents to be *mocked* again and again, till "at last it biteth like a serpent, and stingeth like an adder."[2]

Its *raging* power degrades below the level of the beast. The government of reason is surrendered to lust, appetite, or passion.[3] Ahasuerus, with his "merry heart" showed himself most irrational.[4] The conqueror of the East murdered his friend. All is tumult and recklessness. The understanding is gradually impaired.[5] "The heart uttereth perverse things."[6] Other sins of the same black dye follow in its train,[7] often hurrying into the very jaws of destruction.[8] Surely then *whosoever is deceived thereby is not wise.*

Humbling indeed is it to human nature, to see, not only the mass of the ignorant, but splendid talents, brutalized 'by this lust,'—that which was once "created in the image of God," now sunk into the dregs of shame! Yet more humbling is the sight even of God's own people "wallowing in this mire." The example of Noah and Lot are recorded,[9] not as a laughing-stock to the ungodly, but as a beacon to the saint. "Let him that thinketh he standeth, take heed lest he fall."[10] Even an Apostle had practically learnt, that his security lay not in the innate strength of his principles, but in the unceasing exercise of Christian watchfulness.[11] "Take heed to yourselves,"—is the needful warning of our Divine Master,—"lest your hearts be overcharged with surfeiting and drunkenness, and so that day come upon you unawares. Be not drunk with wine"—said the great Apostle—"wherein is excess; but be filled with the Spirit."[12]

2. *The fear of a king is as the roaring of a lion: whoso provoketh him to anger sinneth against his own soul.*

[1] Gen. ix. 21. [2] Chap. xxiii. 31, 32, 35.
[3] Ibid. verses 29, 30. 1 Sam. xxv. 36. Isa. lvi. 12. Hos. vii. 5.
[4] Esth. i. 10—12.
[5] Isa. xxviii. 7. Hos. iv. 11. Plato determines, that not only old men, but drunkards, come to childhood. De Legibus I.
[6] Chap. xxiii. 33.
[7] Gen. xix. 33. Isa. v. 11, 12, 22, 23. See the fine description, 1 Esdras iii. 13—24.
[8] 2 Sam. xiii. 28. 1 Kings xvi. 8—10; xx. 16. Jer. li. 39, 51. Dan. v. 1—4. Nah. i. 10.
[9] Gen. ix. 21; xix. 33, et supra. [10] 1 Cor. x. 12. [11] Ibid. ix. 27.
[12] Luke xxi. 34. Eph. v. 18.

The wrath of the king has been before mentioned under this figure.[1] Here *his fear* is described—the effect for the cause. Even Joab with all his valor trembled at this *roaring of the lion*, and fled for refuge to the horns of the altar.[2] Jonathan felt the strong necessity for appeasing it.[3] Such was the power *of the King* (unknown in our happy land)—the sole—uncontrolled arbiter of life and death;[4] that *whosoever provoked him to anger—sinned*—as Adonijah found to his cost[5]—*against his own soul.* What must then be *the fear of* the Great King! 'Armies of terrors and doubts are nothing to a look of his angry countenance. "O Lord," says that holy man, (considering the frailty of poor man, and the power of God) "who knoweth the power of thine anger! according to thy fear, so is thy wrath."'[6] Even "a little kindling" is ruin past conception, without remedy.[7] Nay—his very "enduring long-suffering" kindles the fire more fiercely for "the vessels of wrath," whose aggravated provocations of it have "fitted them for destruction."[8] 'Miserable sinner! deprecate his wrath. Seek a Mediator. Beware of continuing to sin.'[9]

3. *It is an honor for a man to cease from strife: but every fool will be meddling*

The opposition of this precept to the maxims of the world proves it to be from God. A world of sin must always be a world of *strife*, because governed by "the wisdom that descendeth not from above," the parent of "*strife*, confusion, and every evil work."[10] And yet an evil world is a fine theatre for the display of the grace of God, in the fruits of "the wisdom that is from above"—meekness—gentleness.[11] We have been before reminded, that "it is the glory of a man to pass over a transgression"[12]—here to *cease from strife.* Many, from the love of quiet, if not from a better motive, would overlook an injury. Yet if they were embroiled in *strife*, they would feel their *honor* at stake—not in *ceasing from it*, but in following it up—striking the last blow. Far more difficult is it to gather back the waters once let out, than to restrain them within their proper bounds. To "leave off contention,"[13] especially when we see that we are in the wrong—or *if* in the right—that no good will come from it—this "is an high *honor for a man*—a noble triumph over the flesh."[14] Abraham thus *ceased from strife* by disinterested concession.[15] Isaac showed himself a man of peace under the vexatious annoyance of the Philistines.[16] The prophet "went his way," to prevent a further kindling of anger.[17] But how much more commonly is *strife* fed by the folly of man's pride, than ex-

[1] Chap. xix. 12.
[2] 1 Kings ii. 28—34.
[3] 1 Sam. xix. 4—6. Comp. Eccl. x. 4.
[4] Chap. xvi. 14. Esth. vii. 8.
[5] 1 Kings ii. 23.
[6] Leighton's Sermon on Jer. x. 23, 24. Ps. xc. 11.
[7] Ibid. ii. 12.
[8] Rom. ix. 22.
[9] Geier in loco.
[10] Jam. iii. 14—16.
[11] Ibid. 17, 18.
[12] Chap. xix. 11.
[13] Chap. xvii. 14. Indeed—as Schultens remarks—Solomon is here giving full significance to this former proverb, which however—he adds—'considered by itself, strongly sets out the disgraceful and most dishonorable lust of quarrelling.'
[14] Chap. xvi. 32. Rom. xii. 21.
[15] Gen. xiii. 8, 9.
[16] Ib. xxvi. 17—31.
[17] Jer. xxviii. 11.

tinguished by a peaceful and loving spirit![1] *The meddling fool* rushes into strife as his element[2]—a torment to himself, and a plague to those around him. To return "a soft answer" to "grievous words"[3]—to keep out of the way of an angry person,[4] is the path of wisdom. "Put on meekness, long-suffering—let the peace of God rule in our hearts"—are the marks of "the elect of God"—the example of our Divine Master.[5]

4. *The sluggard will not plow by reason of the cold: therefore shall he beg in harvest, and have nothing.*

Again[6] are we instructed by a vivid picture of a most baneful vice. *The sluggard* always has his excuses ready, to shift off any work that requires exertion. *He will not plow by reason of the cold;* although the season (our autumn) offered no hindrance, where the heart was in the work. And does not the most trifling difficulty hinder, where the heart is *cold* in the service of God? Let the professor ask himself—Have his prayers during his whole life cost him exercise answering to one hour's *plowing?* What has he given to God but the shadow of duties, when the world has had his full glow and energy? The flesh flinches from suffering; and even under the wakefulness of temporary conviction, the heart is "sorrowful" at the requisitions of Christianity, which it cannot admit.[7] Farewell heaven forever, if it must be obtained at such a cost! How affecting is the contrast between our work for Christ, and his work for us—We grudging exercise for him; He so filled with the absorbing interest of his work for us—"How am I straitened until it be accomplished!"[8]

But *the sluggard* must reap the fruit of his sin. *If he will not plow* in the seed-time, he cannot reap *in harvest.* At that happy season—the recompense of the laborer's toil—*he shall beg, and have nothing.* 'Men's hearts are justly hardened against that man, who by his own sloth and wilfulness hath brought himself to want.'[9] And what else can the spiritual *sluggard* look for? *The cold* keeps him heartlessly from the house of God. His soul is therefore perishing for lack of food. If wishing would secure heaven, who would miss it? But heartless wishes, without the crucifixion of the flesh, will stop short of the prize. Millions have perished in serious religion from want of diligence and self-sacrificing devotedness. And what will it be to *beg in the* great *harvest,* and beg in vain;[10] then to have all wicked excuses silenced,—and the fearful doom pronounced upon the unprofitable servant![11]

Christian professor! Is it time to stand idle, when we stand at the door of eternity? to be slack, when so near our great salvation?[12] 'Blessed are those, who have sown much for God in their life-time. Oh! the glorious harvest that those shall have! The very

[1] Judg. viii. 1; xii. 1.
[2] Chap. xviii. 6; 2 Sam. x. 1—14; 2 Kings xiv. 8.
[3] Chap. xv. 1.
[4] Chap. xxii. 24; xxv. 8.
[5] Col. iii. 12—15.
[6] Chap. xix. 15, 24.
[7] Matt. xix. 21, 22.
[8] Luke xii. 50.
[9] Poole's Annotations.
[10] Matt. xxv. 3—9. Luke xvi. 24.
[11] Matt. xxv. 26—30.
[12] Rom. xiii. 11.

angels shall help them to take in their harvest at the great day. And Oh! the joy that there shall be in that harvest! The angels will help to sing the harvest-song, that they shall sing, who have been sowers of righteousness!'[1]

5. *Counsel in the heart of man is like deep water; but a man of understanding will draw it out.*

The depths in the heart of man are not easily fathomed. Often is it the subtilty of evil.[2] David was duped by the smooth promises of Saul,[3] and afterwards by the religious hypocrisy of his ungodly son.[4] The counsel of Daniel's enemies was too *deep* for Darius to see the bottom of it.'[5] The *counsel* of Herod probably blinded the wise men as to his real intentions.[6] And yet *a man of understanding* will often *draw out* the subtle *counsel*, and set it in its true light. David described the *deep counsels* of his enemies, as one who had penetrated the bottom.[7] Job accurately discovered the true, but indirect *counsel* of his mistaken friends.[8] Paul *drew out* the secret counsel of selfishness in the schismatical preachers of the gospel.[9]

But let us look at the bright side. Observe the man of God—instructed by God. Natural sagacity of intellect is deepened and enlarged by spiritual light. His mind is enriched with the fruits of scriptural study and meditation—here *are the deep waters of heavenly counsel.*[10] The talkative professor in his superficial judgment sees nothing. *But a man of understanding* will discern and *draw out* valuable instruction. The Queen of Sheba thus *drew out* from the wise man's capacious well, *deep* and wholesome *water.*[11] Often, however, men of a comprehensive mind have little sympathy with general intercourse. We may be in contact with them, without consciousness of their worth. *The waters are deep.* But there is no bubbling up. Yet a well directed excitement will *draw out* flowing water from the well-spring of wisdom. And often the intercourse—hitherto lost—with a godly and experienced minister, or a soundly instructed Christian, becomes most precious,—"He that walketh with wise men shall be wise.[12] But above all is to be prized familiarity with *the deep waters of the counsel* of God. Say not—"I have nothing to draw with, and the well is deep."[13] A thinking habit in a prayerful spirit will enable you "with joy to draw water from the wells of salvation."[14] Nay—will it not bring into your own soul "a well of water, springing up unto everlasting life?[15]

6. *Most men will proclaim every one his own goodness; but a faithful man who can find?*

The last Proverb showed *the depth* of the heart—this is deceit-

[1] Burroughs on Hosea x. 12. [2] Jer. xvii. 9. [3] 1 Sam. xviii. 17—26. [4] 2 Sam. xv. 7—9. [5] Dan. vi. 4—9. [6] Matt. ii. 8. [7] Ps. lxiv. 5, 6; cxix. 98. [8] Job xxii. 27, 28. [9] Phil. i. 15. [10] Chap. xviii. 4. Contrast xxvi. 7, 9. [11] 1 Kings x. 1—7. [12] Chap. xiii. 20. [13] John iv. 11. [14] Isa. xii. 3. [15] John iv. 14.

fulness and pride. Judge a man by his own estimate of himself; and we need no further proof of his want of self-knowledge.[1] Even the ungodly *proclaims his own goodness*. "Jehu took no heed to walk in the way of the Lord." Still—said he—"come, see my zeal for the Lord."[2] Absalom, while treason was at work within, "stole the hearts" of the people by his loud pretensions to *goodness*.[3] The whole nation, while given up to all manner of iniquity, boasted of its integrity.[4] The Pharisee *proclaimed his goodness* at the corner of the streets[5]—yea—even in the presence of his God.[6] Such is the blindness of a self-deceiving heart! Lord! teach me to remember—"That which is highly esteemed among men is abomination in the sight of God."[7]

After all, however, does not this glass—honestly used—exhibit more resemblance to our own features, than we would readily admit? We all condemn the Pharisaic broad open boasting. But too often we eagerly catch at the good opinion of the world. Contrivance is made to gain the shadowy prize! A *seeming* backwardness and retiredness is only, in order that others may bring us forward. Care is taken that it be known that *we* were the authors, or at least had a considerable part, in some work that might raise our name in the Church. Sometimes we are too ready to take a degree of credit to ourselves, which we do not honestly deserve;[8] while we shrink from real reproach and obloquy for the gospel's sake.

In opposition to this self-complacent goodness, Solomon—an accurate observer of human nature—exclaims almost in despondency —*A faithful man*[9]—as a parent—a reprover—an adviser—one "without guile"—*who can find?* Canst thou find him in thine own sphere? Look closer—view thyself in the glass of the word. Does thy neighbor—thy friend—find thee *faithful* to him?[10] What does our daily intercourse witness? Is not the attempt to speak what is agreeable often made at the expence of truth? Are not professions of regard sometimes utterly inconsistent with our real feelings? In common life, where gross violations are restrained, a thousand petty offences are allowed, that break down the wall between sin and duty, and on the first step of forbidden ground bring the charge of guilt. Never let it be forgotten, that the sound influence of the virtues of society can only be maintained by the graces of the gospel. Never let the Christian professor deem moral integrity to be a low attainment. The man of God bursts forth into fervent praise for the upholding grace of God.[11] And what can bring greater honor to God, than the proof manifested in

[1] Chap. xvi. 2. [2] 2 Kings x. 16, 19—31. [3] 2 Sam. xv. 1—6.
[4] Jer. ii. 23, 35; v. 1. Comp. Rom. ii. 17—23.
[5] Matt. vi. 1, 2, 5, 16; xxiii. 5. Comp. chap. xxvii. 2. [6] Luke xviii. 11, 12.
[7] Ibid. xvi. 15.
[8] Chap. xxv. 14. Thus Lysias the chief captain represented to the governor, that he had interposed for Paul from his zeal for a Roman citizen; when the simple truth was, that he was ignorant of the fact at the time, and was about to scourge him as a rebel. Acts xxiii. 27, with xxi. 38, xxii. 24.
[9] Ps. xii. 1. Comp. Mic. vii. 1, 2. [10] Ibid. ci. 6. [11] Ibid. xli. 11, 12.

the conduct of his people, that their daily transactions are animated with the soul of integrity—that their word is unchangeable? Never does godliness show more bright than in "showing all good fidelity in all things."[1]

7. *The just man walketh in his integrity: his children are blessed after him.*

The faithful man is here fully drawn—rich in the blessing of his God. Take the history of the father of the faithful—Abraham was *the just man*—accepted with God, and "*walking* before him" *in his integrity.* And did not the covenant of his God engage an everlasting *blessing for his children after him?*[2] And thus does every child of Abraham, *walking in the same integrity,* secure "an inheritance for his children's children."[3] It is 'not however for the merits of the parents, that they deserve it; but such is the mercy of God to the root and the branches, that, because the fathers are loved, their children also are embraced.'[4] But we must show our *integrity,* as did our father Abraham, in the practical habit of faith; not only "taking hold of the covenant" on our children's behalf, but bringing them under the yoke of the covenant.[5]

Christian parents!—let *integrity* as before God, be the standard of our family responsibility. Walk not according to the maxims of the world yourselves, nor allow them in your children. Make God's word—his whole word—our universal rule; his ways—however despised—our daily portion. "Seek *first,*" for our children as for ourselves, "the kingdom of God and his righteousness."[6] Thus *walking in our integrity*—look for the honored blessing of being the parents of a godly race. *Our children are blessed after us.*

8. *A king that sitteth in the throne of judgment scattereth away all evil with his eyes.*

This is the picture of a godly king, such as the wise man's father described and exemplified—"just, ruling in the fear of God;"[7] making it his great care and business to execute judgment. In those days he *sat himself on the throne of judgment,* and decided the law.[8] And such might be conceived to be his influ-

[1] Tit. ii. 10. [2] Gen. xvii. 1, 2, 7.

[3] Chap. xiii. 22. Comp. Ex. xx. 5, 6. Ps. xxv. 12, 13; xxxvii. 26; cxii. 2.

[4] Muffet in loco. 'The branches fare better for the sap of grace in the root.' Swinnock's Christian Man's Calling, i. 383, 'Where God saith—He will be a God to the godly man and to his children, I believe he intended more in that promise for the comfort of godly parents, than most of them think of.' Acts. ii. 39. Gen. xviii. 7. 'The children of believers are heirs apparent to the covenant of grace in their parent's right.' Ibid. The True Christian, p. 193.

[5] Chap. xxii. 6, with Gen. xviii. 19.

[6] Matt. vi. 33. This was Mr. Scott's grand rule of education, and the manifest honor which his Master vouchsafed to his singleness and integrity in acting it out, is well known. 1 Sam. ii. 30. See Life, pp. 611—614.

[7] 2 Sam. xxiii. 4, with viii. 15. 1 Kings xv. 5.

[8] 1 Kings iii. 16—28, with x. 9. A Romish commentator (Corn. a Lapidè) mentions the custom of St. Louis of France to sit twice a week *in the throne of judgment,* and his

ence, that the wicked dared not come and sin in his presence. "Will he force the queen also *before me?*"[1]—was the indignant exclamation of a sovereign, on feeling not only his own rights, but the reverence for royalty, grossly outraged. David, as a man of God, and a sovereign of his people, could not endure the wicked in his presence.[2] And always in proportion as the ruler realizes his responsibility, *evil* will be made to flee, and be *scattered away* from him.[3]

But what is it to be ever standing before the Great *King, who scattereth away all evil with his eyes?* "Thou art of purer eyes than to behold *evil*, and canst not look on iniquity. The foolish shall not stand in thy sight. All things are naked and opened unto the eyes of Him, with whom we have to do."[4] May the High Priest ever stand between the sinner and the Holy God, that while we walk in reverence, we "may not be afraid with any amazement!"

9. *Who can say, I have made my heart clean, I am pure from my sin?*

Behold the great *King sitting on the throne of judgment*, and challenging every child of Adam—"Gird up now thy loins like a man, for I will demand of thee? and answer thou me."[5] The questions are confounding. The answers humble us in the dust—*Who can say*—truly say—*I have made my heart clean?* A sinner in his self-delusion may conceive himself to be a saint. But that a saint should ever believe that he *made himself so*—is impossible. *Who can say—I am pure from sin?* What! no vain thoughts—no sinful imaginations—lodging within! No ignorance, pride, wandering, coldness, worldliness, unbelief indulged! The more we search the heart, the more will its impurity open upon us. "Turn thou yet again, and thou shalt see greater abominations"[6]—evils hitherto unsuspected. Vain boasters there are, who proclaim their good hearts. But the boast proves—not their goodness, but their blindness—that man is so depraved, that he cannot understand his own depravity.[7] What say they, who have entered into the presence of the King, whose holiness *scattereth all evils away?* "Behold! I am vile!"—said one. "Now mine eye seeth thee. Wherefore I abhor myself." Woe is me, said another—"for I am a man of unclean lips, for mine eyes have seen the King—the Lord of hosts."[8] The clean heart is the heart cleansed. If none can *say—I have made my heart clean*, myriads can bear witness to the blood of the Son of God cleansing it from guilt,[9] and to the mightiness of the Creator to renew it unto holiness.[10]

dying charge to his successor, not only to appoint the most upright judges, but to overlook them in the discharge of their office. Does not the Court of *the Queen's Bench* suppose the Sovereign to be sitting there in determination of judgment?

[1] Est. vii. 8. [2] Ps. ci. 3—8.

[3] V. 26; xxv. 4, 5. Comp. 2 Chron. xv. 16. Plutarch relates of Cato, that such was the reverence of his character, that the bad women of Rome could not bear his look.

[4] Hab. i. 13. Ps. v. 5. Heb. iv. 13. [5] Job xxxviii. 3. [6] Ezek. viii. 13.

[7] 1 John i. 8. Comp. 1 Kings viii. 46. Ecc. vii. 20. Jer. ii. 35. Hos. xii. 8.

[8] Job. xl. 4; xlii. 5, 6. Isa. vi. 5. [9] 1 John i. 7. [10] Ps. li. 10.

But are there not many, who in the house of God will confess themselves miserable sinners, and at the holy table will acknowledge 'the burden of their sin to be intolerable,' who yet will go back to the world, and boast or comfort themselves in the confidence of their goodness? confessing indeed, that they are sinners, but stoutly warding off every charge of sin? Ah! such are not the "heavy-laden," to whom Christ hath promised "rest;"[1] not "the lost,—whom the Son of Man is come to seek and to save."[2] They will lie beside the cleansing fountain, but never care to "wash and be clean." But observe in this proverb the fundamentals of the gospel—man's total corruption; his inability to make his heart clean; and his grievous tendency to self-deception. Hence his need—hence—when that need is felt—the value of the cleansing remedy. "If I wash thee not, thou hast no part in me." If this be so—then—Lord—"not my feet only, but my hands and my head."[3] "Wash me thoroughly from my transgression, that I may be whiter than snow." "Create in me a clean heart, O God, and renew a right spirit within me."[4]

10. *Divers weights* (a stone and a stone, Marg.) *and divers measures*, (an ephah and an ephah, Marg.) *both of them are alike abomination to the Lord.*

This probably refers to the iniquitous custom of having *different weights and measures* for buying, and for selling—one *stone* too light—the other too heavy. Such practices seem to have been among the crying sins of the nation, that brought down the judgment of God upon it.[5] So opposite are they to the character of "a God of truth and without iniquity,"[6] that the very *stone and ephah were abomination to him.*[7] The disuse of barter, and th more accurate system of inspection, have in some measure restrained this gross form of fraud. But the cheats of trickery and close dealing, the evasion of legal duties, taking advantage of the ignorance of the unwary—all those deviations from the rule are *alike abomination to the Lord.* What a fearful disclosure will the great day make, to the "shame and everlasting contempt" of the ungodly trafficker! Every man of moral integrity will scorn the flagrant breach of the golden rule. But—Christian—let it be a wholesome warning to remember, that Churches fruitful in the graces of the gospel, needed to be reminded, "that no man go beyond or defraud his brother in any manner,"[8] and that the most aggravated forms of deceit were detected in connection with a high profession of godliness. Let this, as every other temptation—be a matter of prayerful watchfulness.[9] And be not satisfied with the restraint from this hateful vice. But blot out its darkness by the bright steady shining of an upright profession, full of simplicity,

[1] Matt. xi. 28. [2] Luke xix. 10. [3] John xiii. 8, 9.
[4] Ps. li. 2, 7, 10. [5] Hos. xii. 7. Amos viii. 4, 5. Mic. vi. 10, 11.
[6] Deut. xxxii. 40. [7] V. 23; xi. 1. Mic. vi. 10. Comp. Ps. v. 6
[8] Eph. iv. 25, with i. 16. Col. iii. 9, with i. 3, 4. 1 Thess. iv. 6, with i. 3.
[9] 1 Cor. vi. 8, with i. 5.

love, self-forgetfulness, and active sympathy with our neighbor's wants.

11. *Even a child is known by his doings*[1] *whether his work be pure, and whether it be right.*

Let parents watch their children's early habits, tempers, *doings.* Generally the discerning eye will mark something in the budding of the young tree, by which the tree in maturity *may be known.* The child will tell what the man will be. No wise parent will pass over little faults, as if it was only a child doing childish things. Every thing should be looked at as the index of the secret principle, and the work or word judged by the principle. If a child be deceitful, quarrelsome, obstinate, rebellious, selfish, how can we help trembling for his growth? A docile, truth-loving, obedient, generous child—how joyous is the prospect of the blossom and fruit from this hopeful budding! From the childhood of Samuel,[2] Timothy,[3] much more of the Saviour,[4] we could not but anticipate what the manhood could be. The early *purity* and *right* principles promised abundant and most blessed fruit.

But do we mourn over the evil of our child, specially when tracing it to its original source? Oh! let it be our stimulus to earnest and persevering prayer—to the diligent use of the appointed means for that entire change of heart and nature, which we so intensely desire. Take the child to the covenant of grace. Put the finger on the parental promise,[5] and plead—"Remember the word unto thy servant, whereon thou hast caused me to hope."[6] The answer may be delayed. But "though it tarry, wait for it. For at the end it shall come; it shall not tarry." Meanwhile "live by faith"[7]—work in faith. Despair not of the grace of God. Doubt not his faithfulness. Hold on in active energy and patient hope. The prodigal shall yet return. "The end of the Lord" will put unbelief to shame.[8]

12. *The hearing ear, and the seeing eye, the Lord hath made both of them.*

Seeing and hearing are the two senses, by which instruction is conveyed to the mind. They are component parts of that Divine structure, so "fearfully and wonderfully made."[9] The natural senses are gifts common to all. The spiritual senses are the special gifts of sovereign power and grace.[10] It was left for man to make the ear that cannot hear, and the eye that cannot see; and then to degrade himself to the senseless level, by worshipping the work of his own hand.[11] But *the hearing ear, and the seeing eye, the Lord hath made both of them.*

1 'A child is known by his conversation.' Bp. Coverdale.
2 1 Sam. i. 28; ii. 26; iii. 19, 20.
3 2 Tim. iii. 14, 15, with i. 5. Phil. ii. 20, 21.
4 Luke ii. 50—52.
5 Gen. xvii. 7.
6 Ps. cxix. 49.
7 Hab. ii. 3, 4.
8 Jam. v. 11.
9 Ps. cxxxix. 14. Comp. Ps. xciv. 9. Ex. iv. 11. The celebrated Galen is said to have been converted from Atheism by an attentive observation of the perfect structure of the eye.
10 Matt. xiii. 16, with Deut. xxix. 2—4.
11 Ps. cxv. 4—8.

Man is deaf and blind in the things of God—"Having ears, he hears not; having eyes, he sees not."[1] The voice of mercy is disregarded. To his need, and to his remedy, he is alike insensible. His ear is open to sound advice, to moral doctrine, to the dictates of external decency. But as to the gospel—he is a perfect statuary, without life. All his senses are blinded, deadened, chained.[2] His moral disabilities can only be removed by that almighty power, which on earth gave ears to the deaf, and sight to the blind.[3] As soon could we create our natural, as new-create our spiritual, self. '*The hearing ear*, which Solomon intends is that, which believeth and obeyeth what it heareth. The *seeing eye* is that, which so seeth, as that it followeth the good which it seeth.'[4] But who of us, whose *ears* are wakened, and whose *eyes* are opened, but will rejoice in the adoring acknowledgment—*The Lord hath made both of them.* Would Lydia have ascribed "the opening of her heart" with a new power of attention and interest, to her own natural effort?[5] O my God—may the *ears and eyes which thou hast made* be for thyself alone! to hear thy voice[6]—to "behold thy beauty!"[7]

13. *Love not sleep, lest thou come to poverty; open thine eyes, and thou shalt be satisfied with bread.*

Use 'sleep, as tired nature's sweet restorer.'[8] So man requires it. So God graciously gives it.[9] Without it "man" could not "go forth to his work and to his labor."[10] Thus recruited for the active diligence of the day, *he opens his eyes;* "in the sweat of his brow *he eats his bread,*[11] *and is satisfied with it.*" But *love not sleep* for its own sake. The indulgence is a baneful and ruinous habit, by which the man of talent, who has much responsibility upon his hand, and no heart to act up to it—*cometh to poverty.* Valuable opportunities for improvement are let slip, and "the strong man armed" readily takes possession of his prey.[12] Strange inconsistency and delusion! Man wishes for a long life, and yet wilfully shortens the life given him, by dozing it away in sleep![13] The time given for eternity is wasted. The talent entrusted for trading is hid in a napkin. Nothing is done for God—for the soul—for his fellow-creatures—for heaven. Justly is he cast out as a wicked, because a slothful, servant.[14]

Should not those of us, who are of a drowsy habit of body, listen to the call—*Love not sleep?* Here perhaps may be the Christian conflict. Could ye not "in the house of God" watch one hour? "Watch and pray, that ye enter not into temptation."[15] When

[1] Matt. xiii. 13, 14. [2] 2 Cor. iv. 3, 4.
[3] Mark vii. 34; viii. 22—25, with Isa. xxxv. 5. [4] Caryl on Job xxxiv. 3.
[5] Acts xvi. 14. Comp. Isa. l. 4. [6] 1 Sam. iii. 9. Ps. lxxxv. 8.
[7] Ps. xxvii. 4; lxiii. 2. [8] Young. [9] Ps. iii. 5; iv. 8; cxxvii. 2.
[10] Ibid. civ. 23. [11] Gen. iii. 19. [12] Chap. vi. 9—11.
[13] Chap. xix. 15. Dr. Doddridge's life, though far from reaching the age of man (Ps. xc. 10,) was yet, by the resistance of this besetting temptation, virtually extended to the ordinary bounds. By this successful energy of redeeming time from sleep, he accomplished his invaluable work in the midst of multiplied engagements. See Family Expositor on Rom. xiii. 13. [14] Matt. xxv. 14—30. [15] Ibid. xxvi. 40, 41.

resisted, it is an infirmity; when allowed, or only feebly opposed, it is sin. At all events, in the service of God it is safer to consider it—not as a weariness to be encouraged, but as an indulgence to be mortified, and *that* with vigorous energy of conflict. Else whilst the self-denying Christian will *open his eyes and be filled with bread*, the power of the flesh may impoverish the spirit by the indulgence of a lifeless habit of prayer, hearing, and meditation.

14. *It is naught, it is naught, saith the buyer; but when he is gone his way, then he boasteth.*

The Bible gives abundant proof, that man has always been the same in every generation since the fall. Where is the market, where the counterpart to this disclosure of fraud and selfishness centuries ago is not found? Commerce—the Lord's providential dispensation to bind man to man—is marred by man's depravity. Solomon had before detected the iniquity of the seller.[2] Here he lays bare *the buyer*—and to bring it home more closely—he gives even the market-language—*It is naught—it is naught*—'The article is of an inferior quality. I can get it cheaper elsewhere. If it is worth so much—yet not to me—I have no present want of it—no particular care about it.' And when, having struck a shrewd bargain by these convenient falsehoods, *he is gone his way; he boasteth*, laughing at the simplicity of the seller, and is probably highly commended for his cleverness.[3]

The same principle of fraud applies to the seller. If the one says—*It is naught—it is naught*—the other no less eagerly cries —'It is good—it is good'—'when neither of both speaketh, either as he thinketh, or as the truth of the thing is.'[4] The one is bent on buying cheap; the other on selling dear. The one decries unjustly; the other praises untruly. He asks one price, when he means to take another, and takes advantage of the confidence of his customer to impose on him a worthless article.[5] In fact—'no man's experience would serve him to comprehend, no man's breath to declare, the infinite variety of those more secret and subtle falsehoods, that are daily invented and exercised everywhere under the sun.'[6]

All of us are engaged in pecuniary transactions. With many, it is the main business of life. Yet such are the temptations from our own interest or self-defence, the selfishness of others, and the general example of the world, to deviate from the straight line; that we should be most thankful for this probing analysis of deceit.

[1] Ver. 14—19 are omitted in LXX. [2] Ver. 10. Comp. Eccl. xxvii. 2.
[3] James iv. 16. [4] Bp. Sanderson's Sermon on 1 Sam. xii. 3.
[5] Am. viii. 6. See the contrast of the disinterested transaction, Gen. xxiii. 3—18. Augustine mentions a somewhat ludicrous, but significant, story. A mountebank published in the full theatre, that the next entertainment he would show to every man present what was in his heart. An immense concourse attended, and the man redeemed his pledge to the vast assembly by a single sentence—'Vili vultis emere, et caro vendere'—'You all wish to buy cheap and to sell dear,' a sentence generally applauded; every one, even the most trifling—as Augustine observes—finding the confirming witness in their own conscience. De Trin. Lib. xiii. c. 3. [6] Bp. Sanderson, ut supra.

The man of God stands on the frontier of the line of demarcation, and warns against a single step of encroachment. Passing over the line is bidding defiance to the Great King. The gain may be trifling. But the sin is vast. Enough of guilt was included within the dimensions of a single apple to 'bring death into the world and all its woe' to successive generations. And here the law of God is deliberately broken;[1] conscience is violated; deceit is practised; "evil is called good, and good evil;"[2] our duty to our neighbor transgressed—and all this perhaps without a moment of remorse—only to feed man's covetousness.

But do Christian professors always "prove themselves clear in this matter?" Yet how can we be Christians *really*, if not relatively and universally; if not in the week, as well as on the Sabbath; if not in our dealings with men, as well as in our communion with God? What is our title to the name of disciples of Christ, unless we yield to his authority, and in heart, hand, and tongue, are governed by his laws? Let us each ask—Have we trembled before the solemn warnings of the great Lawgiver?[3] Are we ready to be tried by his rules of guileless simplicity[4] and reciprocal justice?[5] Have we always acted as under the eye of God? Are there no money transactions, that we should be ashamed to have "proclaimed upon the house-tops?" Are we prepared to go to the bar of a heart-searching God with "a conscience void of offence both towards God and towards man?"[6]—Let us never forget the gospel as the only expulsive principle of selfishness—in its active exercise of grateful devoted love—in its holy spirit of "doing all to the glory of God."

15. *There is gold, and a multitude of rubies; but the lips of knowledge are a precious jewel.*

This is not the standard of the world. There *gold and rubies* are far above *the lips of knowledge.* So the young man made his choice, and preferred his "great possessions" to those gracious words, that arrested the admiration of the multitude.[7] But when "gold is our hope and confidence," it will surely be our ruin.[8] Solomon's estimate was that of one, to whom "the Lord had given a wise and understanding heart."[9] *Gold* and precious *rubies* were abundant in his days.[10] Yet all these earthly treasures were as nothing in his eyes in comparison of heavenly teaching. *The lips of knowledge were a more precious jewel.*[11] It is Divine *knowledge* only, however, that stands out in this high preeminence. Human wisdom may captivate the imagination, and furnish its measure of useful information. But the words for the most part

[1] Comp. Lev. xix. 18; xxv. 14. [2] Isa. v. 20.
[3] Col. iii. 25. 1 Thess. iv. 6. [4] Matt. v. 37. [5] Ibid. vii. 12.
[6] Acts xxiv. 16. [7] Matt. xix. 22, with Luke iv. 22.
[8] Job xxxi. 24, with 1 Tim. vi. 9, 10. [9] 1 Kings iii. 9. [10] Ibid. x. 27.
[11] Chap. iii. 15; viii. 10, 11, 19; xvi. 16. Job gave the same verdict, chap. xxviii. 12—19.

die away upon the ear. They do not feed the heart. They furnish no comfort to the afflicted, no hope to the desponding, no teaching to the ignorant in "those things that belong to their" everlasting "peace."[1] If therefore they be "goodly pearls," at least they are not "the pearl of great price"—that *precious jewel*, which dims the lustre of earth's most splendid vanities.[2]

How *precious a jewel are the lips of knowledge*, when the messenger of the gospel "bring his glad tidings of great joy" to the burdened conscience—to him "that is ready to perish!" Truly the very sound of his feet is welcome for the sake of his message.[3] *Precious* also will be the communications of Christian fellowship. Though falling infinitely short of the grace that dwelt in our Divine Master; yet, in proportion as we are taught of him, will our "tongues be as choice silver,"[4] and our "*lips* will disperse *knowledge*"[5] *as a precious jewel*, enriching, adorning with the glory of our heavenly Lord.

16. *Take his garment, that is surety for a stranger; and take a pledge of him for a strange woman.*[6]

Again and again are we warned against such *suretiship for a stranger*[7]—any new acquaintance, whose company may entice; much more *for a strange woman*, whose character has lost all credit. This is the sure road to beggary and ruin. If a man is so weak as to plunge into this folly, he is not fit to be trusted. Lend nothing to him without good security. Nay—if needful—*take his garment* as his pledge. The letter of the Mosaic law forbad this extremity.[8] But the spirit and intent of the law pointed at the protection of the poor and unfortunate: who were forced to borrow for their own necessity, and therefore claimed pity. The command here touches the inconsiderate, who deserve to suffer for their folly, in wilfully plunging themselves into ruin. Nor does it in any degree incur the just suspicion of covetousness or close dealing. The love of our neighbor does not involve the forgetfulness of ourselves. The path of godly prudence is the safest for all parties. It never can be wise to assist, where kindness only gives advantage to hurry on to ruin. The refusal may be an exercise of self-denial. It is well that it should be so. Let it be clearly seen to be the sacrifice—not the indulgence of self: prudence, not selfishness. This grace is one of the combined perfections of Immanuel.[9] Let it not be wanting in the profession of his people. It is necessary to the completeness of the Christian profession, and to avoid many occasions of offence to the Gospel.

[1] Luke xix. 42. [2] Matt. xiii. 45, 46.
[3] Is. lii. 7. Rom. x. 14, 15. Such was the delight of hanging upon the lips of the golden-mouthed Chrysostom, that the common proverb was—Rather let the sun not shine, than Chrysostom not preach.
[4] Chap. x. 21. [5] Chap. xv. 7. [6] Chap. xxvii. 13.
[7] Chap. vi. 1—5; xi. 15; xvii. 18.
[8] Ex. xxii. 26, 27. Deut. xxiv. 12, 13. Comp. Job xxii. 6. Am. ii. 8.
[9] Chap. viii. 12.

17. *Bread of deceit is sweet to a man; but afterwards his mouth shall be filled with gravel.*

'Holiness is sweet in the way and end too. Wickedness is sometimes sweet in the way, but always bitter in the end.'[1] It is with *deceit*, as with every other sin, Satan always holds out a bait; always promises gain or pleasure as the wages of his service, and as surely disappoints the victims of his delusion.[2] If corn be threshed upon *a gravelly* floor, the grating soil would spoil the *sweetness of the bread.* Oh! how many has this arch-deceiver allured by the *sweetness of his bread*, whose *mouths have been afterwards filled with gravel!* '*The bread*, which *a man* hath got by fraud and cozenage, seems *sweet* and pleasant at the first taste of it; but by that time he hath chewed it a little, he shall find it to be but harsh *gravel*, that crasheth between his teeth, galls his jaws, and wounds his tongue, and offends his palate.'[3] 'Every thing gotten wrongfully is here implied.'[4] Look at Gehazi. What profit had he from his talents of silver, and changes of garments? Bitter indeed was *the bread of deceit* to him.[5] Look even at Jacob—a true servant of God—and yet chastened heavily almost to the end of his days with the bitter fruit of *deceit.*[6] To the mass of such blinded sinners, it is eternal ruin. Whatever be the tempter's proffered advantage, his price is the soul—to be paid in the dying hour. Oh! the undoing bargain! an eternal treasure bartered for the trifle of a moment! Charmed we may be with the present *sweetness*—but bitter indeed will be the after-fruits, when the poor deluded sinner shall cry—"I tasted but a little honey, and I must die."[7] So surely is the bitterness that springs out of sin the bitterness of death!

Not a single step can be trodden in the way of godliness, without an entire renunciation of every accursed practice. Not even the smallest violation of the law admits of palliation. To venture on what we fancy the lesser shades of sin is a most dangerous experiment. The smallest sin breaks down the fence; and, this once overstepped, the impulse is beyond our restraint. Universal uprightness is the mark of the child of God. Let the man of doctrine exhibit the holiness of doctrine. Never let our religion be one thing, and our business another. But let the image and glory of the Lord give the pervading expression to our whole history. Every turning aside from the straight path "grieves the Holy Spirit of God," darkens the sunshine of our soul, blasts the consistency of our profession, and wounds the church of God.

18. *Every purpose is established by counsel: and with good advice make war.*

This is true wisdom—to deliberate before we act, and to *establish our purpose by* sound and experienced *counsel.* Even the wisest

[1] Caryl on Job xx. 14. [2] Chap. ix. 17, 18; xxviii. 31, 32. Job xx. 12—16.
[3] Bishop Hall. Comp. Lam. iii. 16. [4] Bishop Patrick. [5] 2 Kings v. 20—27.
[6] Gen. xxvii; xlii. 36–38. [7] 1 Sam. xiv. 31.

of men valued this strengthening resource.[1] God has placed us in society more or less dependent upon each other. And therefore while it is most important to possess a calm and decided judgment, it is not less so to guard against an obstinate and exclusive adherence to our own opinions.[2] Especially in the national counsels the rule is most weighty. *With good advice make war.*[3] Wars for the purpose of ambition or aggrandizement can never be wisely made. Fearful may be the result of inconsiderate, self-willed measures. David took counsel of the Lord;[4] Nehemiah, while supporting his courage by faith,[5] *established his purpose by counsel*, and called his counsel to deliberate in all emergencies.[6] Ahab, asking counsel of his false prophets;[7] Amaziah, despising the sound counsel given to him[8]—both with bad *advice made war* to their own ruin. Even godly Josiah—neglected to *establish his purpose by the counsel* of the Lord's prophets then living among his people—was chastened with temporal destruction.[9]

Now ponder Bishop Hall's description of the spiritual *war*. 'It admits of no intermission. It knows no night, no winter. It abides no peace, no truce. It calls us not into garrison, where we may have ease and respite, but into pitched fields continually. We see our enemies in the face always, and are always seen and assaulted; ever resisting, ever defending, receiving and returning blows. If either we be negligent or weary, we die. What other hope is there, while one fights and the other stands still? We can never have safety and peace but in victory. Then must our resistance be courageous and constant, when both yielding is death, and all treaties of peace mortal.'[10] Does not this war bring the greatest need of deliberate *counsel*, carefully counting the cost;[11] cleaving to our All-wise Counsellor[12] and Almighty Helper? Yet fear not—under the conscious direction of his *counsel*, and support of his grace—to take up the song of praise—"Blessed be the Lord, my strength, which teacheth my hands to war, and my fingers to fight!"[13]

19. *He that goeth about as a talebearer revealeth secrets: therefore meddle not with him that flattereth with his lips.*

Never let us forget, that all intercourse of social life must be based on love. Any breach of this is highly displeasing to God. Witness *the talebearer*. His name describes his work—indulging an impertinent curiosity, making *a tale* of every thing he sees or hears. It is the business of his life, for which all other business is sacrificed—as if the whole man were one tongue; in its restless babbling discovering the grand secret of perpetual motion. Such a one—*meddle not with him*. We would not wish him to look over our wall; much less to enter into our houses; least of all to as-

1 1 Kings xii. 6. 2 Chap. xv. 22.
3 Chap. xi. 14; xxiv. 6; xxv. 8. 4 2 Sam. v. 17—23.
5 Neh. ii. 17—20; iii.; iv. 1. 6 Ib. iv. 19, 20. 7 1 Kings xxii. 6.
8 2 Kings xiv. 8—12. 9 Ibid. xxiii. 29. 10 Holy Observations, xxv
11 Luke xiv. 31—33. 12 Isa. ix. 6. 13 Psalm cxliv. 1.

sociate with our family circle, where his whole employment would be either to draw out, or to put in, what "was not convenient."[1]

The flagrant blot, however, in this contemptible, yet dangerous, character is his unfaithfulness—*going about—revealing secrets.*[2] This is peculiarly offensive to a God of truth. Even when matters have been given to him under a seal, his restless irritation breaks through the feeble bond. There he 'dismantles and rends the robe from the privacies of human intercourse. Who entrusts a secret to his friend, goes thither as to a sanctuary; and to violate the rites of that is sacrilege and profanation of friendship.'[3] Never let us think this to be a trifle. Never let us undertake a trust without the most resolute determination of Christian faithfulness.

Observe his other name—*flattering with his lips.* Thus he insinuates himself into *the secrets* of the unwary, and gains his materials for *talebearing; flattering* the present at the expense of the absent. Watch and pray earnestly against this deadly evil. Keep thine own vineyard carefully.[4] Else if thine eye be abroad, when it ought to be at home, it will be like "the vineyard of the slothful, full of thorns and nettles;"[5] like the 'curious people,' whom Augustine rebuked, who 'pry into another's heart and life, but are slothful to amend their own.'[6] Be diligent in our own calling, serving the Lord and his church. Study the obligation of Christian character, according to the standard of the Divine Example, where every word was fraught with the flowing of love. Oh! how many in self-indulgence, and forgetfulness of their own obligation, having no employment for their hands, set their tongues to work;[7] bringing as it were the plague of flies with them;[8] buzzing from house to house, from one neighbor to another, all the report of evil heard or done! A sharp reproof is their just desert, and an effectual means of driving them away.[9]

20. *Whoso curseth his father or his mother, his lamp shall be put out in obscure darkness.*

If *darkness* be the punishment—is it not also the cause—of this atrocious sin? For surely even the light of nature must be extinguished, ere the child should *curse* those, who under God have taught it to speak—the authors and preservers of its existence—its greatest earthly benefactors. Even an undutiful look—much more a word—is an offence against the commandment. What then must be the weight of guilt involved in the *cursing* of them! The deepest reverence is due to them when they are dead.[10] What then must be the provocation of sinning against them, while they are living for their children, in all the active, self-denying energy of

[1] 'Hic niger est: hunc tu, Romane, caveto'—is the indignant warning of the Roman Satyrist. Hor. Sat. lib. i. 4, 81—85.
[2] Chap. xi. 13. [3] Bishop Taylor's 'Sermon on the Good and Evil Tongue.'
[4] Mark the complaint, Chap. i. 6. Compare our Lord's probing advice, Matt. vii. 3—5
[5] Chap. xxiv. 30, 31. [6] Confess. book x. c. 3. [7] 1 Tim. v. 13.
[8] Ex. viii. 24. [9] Chap. xxv. 23. [10] Jer. xxxv. 1—10.

love and service! This *cursing*, according to our Lord's standard, includes "setting light by father and mother"[1]—wilful disobedience—a fearful, palpable mark of the last days.[2] How God regards it—let his own curse on mount Ebal[3]—his judgment of temporal death[4]—testify. The present degradation of Africa is a witness, on the confirming page of history, of the frown upon an undutiful son[5]—*his lamp put out in darkness.*[6] And if the temporal sentence of death is repealed, the more awful judgment still remains unchangeably upon the Divine statute-book—*obscure darkness*—"the blackness of darkness"—darkness eternal without a ray of light—of which "blackness" is only the shadow, to show what the substance must be.

21. *An inheritance may be gotten hastily at the beginning; but the end thereof shall not be blessed.*

The wise man obviously limits his observation to *an inheritance gotten* dishonestly. The advancement of Joseph in the glory of Egypt,[7] of Mordecai in the Persian courts,[8] of Daniel in Babylon[9]—was *gotten hastily*—in a moment; yet under the special Providence of God. The evil eye, *hasting* to be rich[10] or great, may *get an inheritance at the beginning; but the end thereof shall be* blasted,[11] not *blessed.* Absalom[12] and Adonijah[13] reached after a kingdom to their own ruin. One king of Israel succeeded another, treading on each other *hastily;* and each hurrying on to destruction.[14] In our own history, Richard the Third ended his *hastily gotten* crown in shame. In our own day—Napoleon rose with inconceivable rapidity to a magnificent *inheritance.* Yet he finished his course in disgraceful banishment. Less splendid possessions end in the same disappointment. What a curse was that *hastily gotten inheritance* of Naboth's vineyard to the reckless oppressor![15] Let not the warning be in vain—"They that will be rich"—what is the fruit?—"Many foolish and hurtful lusts—many piercing sorrows."—What is the end? "Destruction and perdition."[16] Place the cross and crown of Jesus in view. The world fades—selfishness dies—at every sight. One object only attracts and satisfies. "O my soul! thou hast said unto the Lord, Thou art my Lord—the portion of mine *inheritance.*"[17] Here is *blessing* beyond conception—without end.

[1] Matt. xv. 3—6. [2] 2 Tim. iii. 2. See also the black mark, Rom. i. 30, 31.
[3] Deut. xxvii. 16.
[4] Ex. xxi. 15, 17. Lev. xx. 9. Deut. xxi. 18—23. Comp. chap. xxx. 17. The Roman punishment for a parricide was to be sewed up in a sack, and cast into the sea. Cicer. pro Sext. Rosc. Amorino. xi.
[5] Gen. ix. 22—25.
[6] Chap. xiii. 9. Job xviii. 5, 6, 18. Judg. 13. 'The pupils of his eyes shall behold darkness.' LXX.
[7] Gen. xli. 14—45. [8] Est. vi. 11; viii. 15; x. 3. [9] Dan. ii. 46, 48.
[10] Chap. xxviii. 20, 22. [11] Chap. x. 2, 3, xxi. 5; xxviii. 8.
[12] 2 Sam. xv. 10; xviii. 9—17. [13] 1 Kings i. 5—9; ii. 25. [14] Ibid. xvi. 8—22.
[15] Ibid. xxi. 1—15, 19. Comp. Job xv. 29; xx. 18. Am. viii. 4—8.
[16] 1 Tim. vi. 9, 10. [17] Ps. xvi. 2, 5.

22. *Say not thou, I will recompense evil; but wait on the Lord, and he shall save thee.*

"Vengeance belongeth unto me"—is the awful proclamation of God.[1] Most reverently do his people adore this high prerogative.[2] Who besides is fitted to wield it? He is Omniscient. We know but imperfectly. He is without passions. We are blinded by our selfish lusts. He is just—"without partiality." We are prejudiced on our own side. What presumption, therefore, not to say—impiety,—for the angry worm to entrench upon his prerogative! Revenge is indeed a cherished lust of the flesh.[3] And but for the Divine restraint upon it, this world would be an "Aceldama—a field of blood." But never did the Lord allow it in his people.[4] Not even an Edomite—their most bitter enemy; not even the Egyptian—their most cruel oppressor—was to be "abhorred."[5] The folly and sin of this passion are alike manifest. 'He that studieth revenge, keepeth his own wounds open.'[6] His enemy could not do him a greater injury. The tongue is the great instrument—"speaking like the piercings of a sword."[7] Yet often, when the open purpose is restrained, the passion broods only the more fiercely within.[8] Or at least it is only a reluctant obedience; not the glorious victory exhibited in the history of the men of God—"overcoming evil with good."[9]

What then is the remedy? In humility and faith lay our matters before the Lord. Put them in his hands—*wait on him, and he shall save us.* Revenge rises, only because we have no faith. For did we believe that God would take up our cause, should we not leave ourselves implicitly in his hands? How did he plead the cause of "the meekest man upon earth."[10] With what confidence did David rest himself in the midst of reproach;[11] thus warranting his rule of faith by his own experience![12] And thus did David's Lord "commit himself unto him that judgeth righteously."[13] After this blessed example therefore "let those, that suffer according to the will of God, commit the keeping of their souls to him in well-doing, as unto a faithful Creator."[14] Be satisfied with his management. Suffice his word, that "he shall deliver and save, because we put our trust in him."[15] Let us, as

[1] Deut. xxxii. 35. Rom. xii. 19. Heb. x. 30.
[2] Ps. xciv. 1. Rev. vi. 10.
[3] So even the Heathen acknowledged it—
'Est vindicta bonum, et vitâ jucundius ipsâ.'
Juven. Sat. 13.
[4] Chap. xxiv. 29. Lev. xix. 18. Observe the identity of this standard with that of the New Testament—the teaching of our Lord—Matt. v. 38, 39; and his apostles, Rom. xii. 17, 19—21. 1 Thess. v. 15. 1 Pet. iii. 9. Comp. Ecclus. xxviii. 1—8.
[5] Deut. xxiii. 7. [6] Lord Bacon. [7] Chap. xii. 18; xxv. 18.
[8] Gen. xxvii. 34. 2 Sam. xiii. 22—29.
[9] Rom. xii. 21. Comp. Joseph, Gen. xlv. 5; l. 20. David, 1 Sam. xxiv. 18—21.
[10] Num. xii. 1—10. [11] 2 Sam. xvi. 12. Ps. xxxviii. 12—15.
[12] Psalm xxxvii. 5, 6. [13] 1 Pet. ii. 23. [14] Ibid. iv. 19.
[15] Ps. xxxvi. 39 40.

his praying people, stay our souls on the great consummation—"Shall not God avenge his own elect, which cry day and night unto him, though he bear long with them? I tell you, that he will avenge them speedily."[1]

23. *Divers weights are an abomination unto the Lord; and a false balance is not good.*

Here let us search into the mind of God. Thrice does he bring home one point of practical detail.[2] Yet doubtless this is not a "vain repetition."[3] There is a "needs be" for it. Instead of "precept upon precept, and line upon line,"[4] the infinite "treasures of wisdom and knowledge" might have poured forth endless variety of instruction. We wonder not to see the apostolic ministry once and again upon the same argument of a sinner's justification before God.[5] And we gather from this repetition the primary importance, and the revolting character of the doctrine.[6] Does not then this continuous inculcation similarly teach the great weight of the principle involved, and the innate resistance to its full operation? If we feel, that we cannot be too often gladdened with the manifestation of the grace of God; and yet shrink from a frequent and probing application of practical obligation; if we love to be told, what we owe to God on the Sabbath, but revolt from the minute detail of the week—the market and the shop; we do not receive the whole revelation of God, and therefore do not savingly receive any part of it. Ours is not "the wisdom that is from above—without partiality, and without hypocrisy."[7]

Most palpable is the need for this repeated word. The evil runs throughout our commercial sphere. *The divers weights*—though once and again declared to be abominable—yea, *an abomination*[8] to God—yet how often are they palliated, as of daily occurrence—perhaps even of necessity! But 'the scant measure will fill up a full measure of guilt, and the light weights bring upon the soul an heavy weight of judgment.'[9] If Job was fearful, lest his "land and furrows should cry against him,"[10] let the trader beware, lest his weights and measures bear witness against him. Cause indeed have we for watchfulness! What means this cumbrous and expensive machinery of administration, with all its checks and counter-checks—its fearful multiplication of oaths; but the humiliating declaration—than man cannot trust his fellow-man? Oh! let me not forget, that of all this deceit my heart is the native soil; that nothing but the culture of Divine principle keeps down these poisonous weeds, and nourishes in their room "the fruits of righteousness to the praise and glory of my God."[11] 'The love of God

[1] Luke xviii. 7, 8. [2] Verses 10, 14, 23.
[3] Matt. vi. 7. [4] Isa. xxviii. 10.
[5] See Epistles to the Romans and the Galatians. [6] Rom. x. 2, 3
[7] James iii. 17. [8] Chap. xi. 1. Mic. vi. 10, 11.
[9] Bp. Reynolds' Sermon on Mic. vi. 6—8. [10] Job xxxi. 28. [11] Phil. i. 11.

constrains his servant. God is true to him; and he will not be false to others. God is merciful to him; and he will not be unjust to others."[1] This is the practical influence of the Gospel.

24. *Man's goings are of the Lord; how can a man then understand his own way?*

God's uncontrollable power and sovereignty; man's absolute dependence and helplessness—let these be foundation principles. Here is no infringement of liberty on the one side; no excuse for passive indolence on the other. Man often acts, as if he were the master of his own purposes; as if *his goings* were of himself. Or else, in the crude notion of the predetermination of every event,—instead of diligently working out the Lord's purposes, he finds "his strength is to sit still."[2] But the humble heaven-taught Christian acts free agency in the spirit of dependence. The consciousness that *his goings are of the Lord* gives energy to his faith. It is written—"The way of a man is not in himself."[3] It is written again—"This is the way—walk ye in it."[4] Thus does Scripture guard Scripture. Here is dependence without passivity; diligence without presumption or self-confidence. Antagonal principles thus work together in harmonious combination.

The true liberty of the will is the power of acting according to choice, without external restraint. Divine agency, so far from hindering its freedom, removes the obstacle of a corrupt and tyrannizing bias. This let removed, it acts more freely, more powerfully. The man is not moved as a machine, unconscious of its operations and results, but acted upon by intelligent principles. He is not carried along the way, but enabled to walk. He is "drawn," not driven; "with the cords of a man," not of a beast; and those cords so wisely applied, that they are felt to be "bands of love."[5] He is enlightened, so that he sees; softened, so that he turns; "drawn, so that he runs."[6] He is moved effectually, but willingly; invincibly, but without constraint. Nothing is distorted. There is no unnatural violence. It is "the day of the Lord's power," who "worketh in him to will and to do of his good pleasure."[7] *His goings are of the Lord.*

The world of Providence shows the same over-ruling agency Man determines and acts freely in the minute circumstances of life. Yet the active pervading influence, disposing every step at the right time and place, makes it plain, that *man's goings are of the Lord.* Rebekah came to the well just at the moment, that Abraham's servant was ready to meet her. "He being in the way, the Lord led him."[8] Pharaoh's daughter goes out to bathe just at the crisis, when the infant Moses was committed to the water.[9] Was

[1] Polhill's Speculum Theologiæ, p. 438. [2] Isa. xxx. 7. [3] Jer. x. 23.
[4] Isa. xxx. 21. [5] Hos. xi. 4. [6] Can. i. 4. Comp. Ps. cxix. 32.
[7] Ps. cx. 3. Phil. ii. 13. Comp. Daillè in loco, and Disputation between Eck and Carlstadt. D'Aubigne's History of Reformation, book v. ch. 4.
[8] Gen. xxiv. 15, 27. [9] Ex. ii. 1—5.

this the working of chance, or some fortunate coincidence? Who can doubt the finger, or the leading, of God? A curse of extermination was pronounced against Eli's house. The word was fulfilled by a combination of apparently casual incidents. David flees to Abimelech for relief. *That very day* Doeg was there—not in the ordinary course, but "*detained* before the Lord." He gives information to his cruel master, and in the moment of anger the curse was accomplished.[1] Who can doubt but *the goings* of Doeg and of David meeting together *were of the Lord?* All parties acted freely. What was false in Doeg was righteous in God, whom we adore as a sin-hating God, even while, as in the crucifixion of Christ,[2] he makes use of sin for the fulfilment of his own purposes.

Man's goings therefore, being *of the Lord*, must often be enveloped in mystery. *How then can he understand his own way?* Often does it run counter to his design. The Babel-builders raised their proud tower to prevent their dispersion: and it was the very means of their dispersion.[3] Pharaoh's "wise dealing" for the aggrandizement of his kingdom, issued in its destruction.[4] Haman's project for his own glory was the first step of his ruin.[5] Often also is the way, when not counter, far beyond our own ken. Little did Israel *understand* the reason of their circuitous *way* to Canaan. Yet did it prove in the end to be "the right way."[6] As little did Ahasuerus *understand* the profound reason, why "on that night could not the king sleep"—a minute incident seeming scarcely worth recording, yet a necessary link in the chain of the Lord's everlasting purposes of grace to his Church.[7] Little did Paul *understand his own way*, or suppose that his "*prosperous* journey" to see his beloved flock in Rome, would be a narrow escape from shipwreck, and to be conducted a prisoner in chains.[8] Little do we know what we pray for. "By terrible things wilt thou answer us in righteousness, O God of our salvation."[9] We go out in the morning, *not understanding our way*—"not knowing what an hour may bring forth."[10] Some turn connected with our happiness or misery for life, meets us before night. Joseph, in taking his walk to search for his brethren, never anticipated a more than twenty years separation from his father. And what ought those cross ways or dark ways to teach?—Not constant trembling anxiety, but daily dependence. "I will bring the blind by a way that they know not: I will lead them in paths that they have not known."[11] But shall they be left in the dark perplexity? "I will make darkness light before them, and crooked things strait. These things will I do unto them, and not forsake them."[12] Often do I look back, amazed at the strangeness of my course—so different—so contrary to my way. But it is enough for me, that all is in thine

[1] 1 Sam. ii. 30—32, with xxi. 6, 7; xxii. 9—18. [2] Acts ii. 23.
[3] Gen. xi. 4—9. [4] Ex. i. 8—10, with xiv. 30. [5] Esth. vi. 6—13.
[6] Ex. xiii. 17, 18, with Ps. cvii. 7. [7] Esth. vi. 1.
[8] Acts xxvii.; xxviii. 20 30 with Rom. i. 10. [9] Ps. lxv. 5.
[10] Chap. xxvii. 1. [11] Gen. xxxvii. 11—14. [12] Isa. xlii. 16.

hands; that "my steps are ordered of thee."[1] I dare trust thy wisdom, thy goodness, thy tenderness, thy faithful care. Lead me—uphold me—forsake me not. "Thou shalt guide me with thy counsel, and afterward receive me to glory."[2]

25. *It is a snare to the man who devoureth that which is holy, and after vows to make inquiry.*

In every path has the great fowler laid his snares. Perhaps, however, the most subtle are reserved for the service of God. Offerings made *holy* to the Lord often were *devoured* by the hypocritical worshippers, and sacrilegiously appropriated to their own use. Thus Achan—robbing the treasury of the Lord—found *a snare* to his ruin.[3] This was the sin of "the whole nation"—and fearful indeed was the judgment—"Ye are cursed with a curse."[4] Voluntary vows were commonly practised,[5] yet sometimes *inquiry made after*, which ought to have been made before. They were at full liberty not to vow, but having vowed, they were bound to pay.[6]

As the counterpart to this hollow half-hearted profession—'a man vows in distress to give something to God: but, having obtained his desires,' *devoureth that which is holy, and after vows makes inquiry*, 'how he may be loosed from this obligation.'[7] Often too in a moment of excitement—perhaps under the glow of a religious meeting—has a sacrifice been pledged to God; and—the impulse having subsided—*after the vow inquiry is made* how the bond might be retracted. Such evasions—what a revolting exhibition do they present of man's deceitfulness! 'He entangleth his soul in the *snares* of death, who resumeth unto a profane use that which is once consecrated unto God; and who, after he hath vowed aught unto the Lord, argues within himself, how to alter that holy purpose, and to defeat God of his due.'[8] Alienation of the gift proves the prior alienation of the heart. Let Ananias and Sapphira testify, that God is a jealous God.[9] Take care of rash—be faithful to upright—engagements. *Before* entering into the service of God, *make inquiry* into its full requisitions. Beware of a religion of temporary excitement; far different from deep, solid, permanent principle. And whatever be the cost, be true to the consecration of thyself as "a living sacrifice"[10] on the altar of thy God.

26. *A wise king scattereth the wicked, and bringeth the wheel over them.*

Solomon, *a wise king*, was constantly eyeing his own responsibilities. His standard was—not to commit wickedness himself,[11] nor to allow it in his people; to *scatter*, not to encourage, *the wicked.* As the husbandman's *wheel, brought over* the grain, cut

[1] Ps. xxxvii. 23. Comp. chap. xvi. 9. [2] Ibid. lxxiii. 24.
[3] Jos. vi. 19; vii. 1. [4] Mal. iii. 8—10. [5] Lev. xxvii. 9, 10, 28—33.
[6] Deut. xxiii. 21, 22. Eccl. v. 4—6. [7] Bishop Patrick.
[8] Bishop Hall. [9] Acts v. 1—10, with Deut. iv. 24. [10] Rom. xii. 1.
[11] Verse 8. Chap. xvi. 12. Comp. the contrast, 1 Kings xiv. 16.

the straw, and separated the chaff;[1] his sifting administration of justice brought the wheel of vengeance on *the wicked*, and *scattered* them as worthless chaff,[2] or crushed them in ruin.[3] In the same spirit did his father David destroy them, when they boldly claimed his countenance.[4] Godly Asa removed wickedness from the high place nearest his own throne and heart.[5] Amaziah justly punished it with death.[6] Nehemiah—that true reformer—rebuked it even in the family of the high priest.[7] Our own Alfred appeared to maintain this standard, as a witness for God in an age of darkness. But it is the King of kings alone, that can make this separation complete. Often does he sift his church by trial, for her greater purity and complete preservation.[8] But what will it be, when he shall come "with his fan in his hand, and shall thoroughly purge his floor!"[9] What *a scattering* of chaff will there be! Not an atom will go into the garner. Not a grain of wheat will be cast away. O my soul! what wilt thou be found at this great sifting day! "Who may abide the day of his coming? And who shall stand when he appeareth?"[10]

27. *The spirit of man is the candle of the Lord, searching all the inward parts of the belly.*

God has not left himself without witness in his own benighted world.[11] At the first creation bright indeed was *the candle of the Lord*, shining in the little world—man.[12] But every faculty partook of the fall. Still enough is left in the inner mind and conscience, to show, even in the thick darkness of heathenism, the Divine perfection[13]—the just desert of sin,[14] and even some faint glimpses of the standard of right and wrong.[15] But dim indeed is *this candle*, except it be lighted at God's lamp.[16] When the Word and Spirit of God give light to it, it will effectually perform its important offices—(as Bishop Reynolds defines them)—'direction, conviction, and consolation;'[17] not only exhibiting the outward acts, but *searching the innermost parts of the belly*—all the hidden acts and conduct of the inner man.[18] The man of ungodliness would be glad to extinguish this *candle*. He is too great a coward to venture into his secret chamber in the dark; yet he hates the light, which, in spite of all his opposition, drags forth into day many secret lurking evils; never allowing the plea—"Is it not

[1] Isa. xxviii. 28, 29. This is an obvious allusion to the way of threshing in the East. One mode was by a wain, which had *wheels* with iron teeth like a saw. The axle was armed with serrated *wheels* throughout. It moved upon three rollers armed with iron teeth or wheels, to cut the straw. See Bishop Lowth's note on Isa. xxviii. 27. Comp. Amos. i. 3.
[2] Psalm i. 4.
[3] 1 Kings ii. 25—46.
[4] 2 Sam. i. 2, 16; iv. 5–12. Comp. Ps. ci. 7, 3.
[5] 2 Chron. xv. 16.
[6] Ibid. xxiv. 25; xxv. 3, 4.
[7] Neh. xiii. 28, 29.
[8] Amos ix. 9.
[9] Matt. iii. 12.
[10] Mal. iii. 2.
[11] Acts xiv. 16, 17.
[12] Gen. i. 26.
[13] Rom. i. 19, 20.
[14] Ibid. Verses 20, 21, 32.
[15] Rom. ii. 14, 15.
[16] Chap. vi 23. Ps. cxix. 105.
[17] Treatise on the Passions, ch. xli.
[18] 1 Cor. ii. 11. Comp. Job xxxii. 8.

a little one?"[1] Most valuable is *this candle*, throwing the light of God upon the narrow path; so that we 'are not scrupulous and nice in small matters, negligent in the main; we are still curious in substantial points, and not careless in things of an inferior nature; accounting no duty so small as to be neglected, and no care great enough for principal duties; not so tything mint and cummin, that we should forget justice and judgment; nor yet regarding judgment and justice, that we should contemn mint and cummin.'[2]

Now let me ask—when God causes *his candle* to shed a clearer light, can I abide it? Do I welcome the hateful discoveries which it brings out? Do I value its light, as opening the secret business of communion between a sinner and a jealous holy God? Do I exercise myself to preserve the light from being dimmed in the atmosphere of sin; to guard its purity, as the means of establishing my confidence with God?[3] Oh! let there be *no inward part* of my soul, where I am not most willing—most earnest—to bring *the candle of the Lord*, that all secret indulgences may be searched out and mortified. "He that doeth good cometh unto the light, that his deeds may be made manifest, that they are wrought in God."[4]

28. *Mercy and truth preserve the king: and his throne is upholden by mercy.*

Punishment is indeed a necessary security against the infringement of the law.[5] Yet a wise *King* will follow the example of the Great Sovereign, and "make judgment his strange work," and *mercy* his "delight."[6] And so long as *truth* inviolably is his guiding principle, the abuse of *mercy* need be little feared. Nay, *mercy is the upholding* pillar *of his throne.*[7] For who does not know, that, while *truth* commands reverence, it is *mercy* that wins the heart? Solomon himself had a strong body-guard around him, for the safety of his person.[8] Yet were *the mercy and truth* of his government not only the most splendid jewels of his crown, but the 'best guard of his body, and supporters of *his throne*.'[9]

How lovely is this combination in the administration of the Great *King!* "Justice and judgment are the habitation of thy throne; *mercy and truth* shall go before thy face."[10] Much more bright is the manifestation of these glorious perfections in that great work, by which he sacrificed even his beloved Son, that man might be saved without the tarnish of one spot upon his infinitely adorable name.[11]

29. *The glory of young men is their strength: and the beauty of old men is the gray head.*

Every stage of life has its peculiar honor and privilege. 'Youth is the glory of nature, and *strength is the glory of youth.* Old age

[1] John iii. 20. [2] Bishop Hall's Works, viii. 112.
[3] Acts xxiv. 16. 1 John iii. 20, 21. [4] John iii. 21. [5] Verse 26.
[6] Comp. Isa. xxviii. 21. Mic. vii. 18. [7] Isa. xvi. 5. [8] Cant. iii. 7
[9] Trapp in loco. [10] Ps. lxxxix. 14. [11] Ps. lxxxv. 10.

is the majestic beauty of nature, and *the grey head* is the majestic *beauty* which nature hath given to old age.'[1] Yet these pictures describe the use—not the abuse. It is the youth usefully exercised, especially consecrated to God, and employed for his glory. Otherwise, as an occasion of wantonness[2] or vain glorious boast[3] —*its strength* is its shame, and will end in vanity.[4] The silver crown brings honor, and reverence, and authority—only "in the way of righteousness."[5]

Yet *the beauty of the grey head* is most likely to be found, where *the strength and glory of youth* have been dedicated to God. The young plant, stunted and deformed in its youth, will generally carry its crookedness into advancing growth. But who can calculate upon the extent of fruitfulness, where "the beginning of our strength"—"the dew of our youth"—has been given to the Lord?[6] Let youth and age however each beware of defacing their glory. Each takes the precedence in some things, and gives place in others. Let them not therefore envy or despise each other's prerogatives. The world—the state—the church needs them both —*the strength of youth* for energy, and the maturity of *age* for wisdom.

30. *The blueness of a wound cleanseth away evil: so do stripes the inward parts of the belly.*

Chastisement is the Lord's ordinance—the pain of the flesh for the subjugation of the spirit; sometimes even "the destruction of the flesh, that the spirit may be saved in the day of the Lord Jesus."[7] It describes not the gentle stroke, but the severity of parental discipline; not in pleasure or caprice—much less in anger—but for profit.[8] The diseased body needs medicine no less than food, and indeed to give nourishment. The diseased will needs chastening no less than consolation, and as the main preparation for consolation. But if *the blueness of the wound*—the mark of severe chastisement—*cleanseth away evil*, is it not the lesser evil, as the means of subduing the greater? Do not the Lord's *stripes cleanse the inward parts?* Misery beyond measure miserable is the untamed stubbornness of self-will. A gentle stroke is first tried. When this remedy is ineffectual, *the blueness of the wound* is needful. Manasseh's Babylonish chains doubtless prevented the "everlasting chains of darkness."[9] Similar discipline was effectual with the holy nation,[10] the prodigal son,[11] and the incestuous Corinthian.[12] Multitudes have borne witness to the love, wisdom, and power of their Father's discipline—"chastened of the Lord that they might not be condemned with the world."[13] *The evil was cleared away*, and those, who groaned under *the stripes*, to all eternity will tune their harps to the song—"I know, O Lord,

[1] Jermin in loco. [2] 2 Sam. ii. 14—16. [3] Jer. ix. 23.
[4] Isa. xl. 30. [5] Chap. xvi. 3, and references. Comp. Ecclus. xxv. 6, 7.
[6] Ps. xcii. 13—15. [7] 1 Cor. v. 5. [8] Heb. xii. 10.
[9] 2 Chron. xxxiii. 12, 13, with Jude 6. [10] Ibid. xxxvi. 14—16, with Ez. ix. 4.
[11] Luke xv. 16—20. [12] 2 Cor. ii. 6—8. [13] 1 Cor. xi 32.

that thy judgments are right, and that thou in faithfulness hast afflicted me."[1]

Child of God! Think of your Father's character. "He knoweth your frame. He doth not afflict willingly."[2] Nothing will be given in weight or measure beyond the necessity of the case.[3] But truly blessed are *the stripes*, that humble and break the proud will.[4] Rich indeed are "the fruits of righteousness" from the conflict and suffering of the flesh.[5]

CHAPTER XXI.

1. *The king's heart is in the hand of the Lord, as the rivers of water: he turneth it whithersoever he will.*

THE general truth here implied has been before stated—man's entire dependence on God.[6] It is taught here by the strongest illustration—his uncontrollable sway over *the king's heart*—the most absolute and unsubjected will. He turns all his most despotic rule—all his political projects—to his own purposes, with the same ease, that *the rivers of water* are turned by every inflexion of the channel.[7] While their course is directed, *the waters* flow naturally and unforced on their own level. *The king's heart* he directs as a responsible agent, without interfering with the moral liberty of his will.

Nehemiah fully acknowledged this prerogative when, having a favor to ask of the king, he "prayed unto the God of heaven."[8] And indeed Scripture witness is abundant. Abimelech's *heart was in the hand of the Lord* for good.[9] Pharaoh's heart was turned towards Joseph.[10] The Babylonish monarchs shewed kindness to Daniel and his captive brethren.[11] The Persian monarchs countenanced and assisted in the building of the temple.[12] The hearts of wicked kings are alike in *the hand of the Lord*;[13] yet he hath no part in their wickedness.[14] The hatred of Pharaoh; the ambition of Sennacherib and Nebuchadnezzar,[15] were his instruments for his own purposes. Ahab's murderous heart was restrained, and even made to accomplish the downfall of Baal.[16] The counsels of

[1] Ps. cxix. 75. [2] Ibid. ciii. 14. Lam. iii. 33. [3] Isa. xxvii. 8. Jer. x. 24.
[4] Jer. xxxi. 18—20.
[5] Job xxxiv. 31, 32; xxxvi. 9, 10. Isa. xxvii. 9. Heb. xii. 11.
[6] Chap. xvi. 1; xx. 24.
[7] The allusion evidently is to channels made for the distribution of waters according to will, for gardens or irrigation of fields. See Paxton's Illustrations, i. 173. Bishop Lowth's note on Isa. i. 30. Comp. the beautiful figure, Ecclus. xxiv. 30, 31.
[8] Neh. ii. 4, 5. [9] Gen. xx. 6. Ps. cv. 14, 15. [10] Gen. xli. 37—45.
[11] Dan. i. 19—21; ii. 47—49; iii. 30; v. 29; vi. 1—3, 28. Ps. cvi. 46.
[12] Ezra i. 1; vi. 22; vii. 27; ix. 9. Neh. i. 14; ii. 4—9. [13] Rev. xvii. 16, 17.
[14] Ex. i. 8—22. Ps. cv. 25. [15] Isa. x. 7. Jer. xxv. 9. [16] 1 Kings xviii. 40, 46

the kings of the earth against Christ were under Divine control.[1] Thus does "the wrath of man praise him; and the remainder he restrains."[2] The same Almighty agency is visible by its effects in the minutest affairs. Ahasuerus's sleepless night;[3] Nebuchadnezzar's divination;[4] the appointment of the year of general taxation[5]—these seemingly unimportant events were turning points in the dispensations of God, fraught with immensely momentous results.

The history of our blessed, though now calumniated, Reformation shows the same sovereign control of the royal heart. Henry VIII. was employed as an unintentional instrument, and his godly son as a willing agent, in furthering this great work. The recollection encourages us to refer all anxious care for the Church to her great Head; to rejoice that, not kings, but the King of kings reigneth.[6] And shall not we be quickened to earnest prayer for our beloved sovereign;[7] that her *heart, being in the Lord's hand, as rivers of water*, may be disposed to rule for his glory, as a nursing-mother to his Church[8]—a blessing to her people?

2. *Every way of a man is right in his own eyes: but the Lord pondereth the hearts.*

Let me be thankful for the repetition[9] of this weighty proverb; most valuable for the close probing of my heart, and the testing of the vital spirituality of my profession. So "deceitful is the heart above all things"[10] that it deceives—not others only, but—what even Satan never does—itself. Every intelligent Christian bears painful witness to this self-deception. How differently we judge of the same action in others, and in ourselves! Often do we palliate, if not justify, in ourselves the very habits, which we condemn in others. Never therefore is the prayer out of season—"Search me, O God; know me, try me; show me to myself."[11]

Hid as the self-deluded professor is from himself—*his way is right in his own eyes.* But is it right in God's eyes? *The Lord pondereth the heart.* Solemn and awakening recollection! He thoroughly reads every heart. And what defilement does he see in those *ways* that are most *right in our own eyes!* Saul thought that he was serving God acceptably. But the all-searching eye discovered pride, covetousness, disobedient rejection of his God.[12] What more self-satisfying than Israel's strict fast and humiliation? But the defective motive marred the sacrifice. "Did ye at all fast *to me, even to me?*"[13] Little did the self-complacent ruler suspect the spiritual pride, false confidence, and worldliness, which his heart-searching God brought to view.[14] And how much base alloy is hidden even in a sound-hearted profession! The disciples covered their own spirit under the pretence of vehement zeal for their Master.[15] *The Lord pondereth the heart*—

[1] Acts iv. 25—28. Comp. John xix. 10. [2] Ps. lxxvi. 10.
[3] Esth. vi. 1, 2. [4] Ezek. xxi. 21. [5] Luke ii. 1—7.
[6] Isa. ix. 6. [7] 1 Tim. ii. 1—3. [8] Isa. xlix. 23.
[9] Chap. xvi. 2. [10] Jer. xvii. 9. [11] Ps. cxxxix. 23, 24.
[12] 1 Sam. xv. 13—26. [13] Zech. vii. 1—6. Comp. Isa. lviii 3—5. Jer. ii. 35.
[14] Matt. xix. 16—22. [15] Luke ix. 54—56.

He "weigheth the spirits"[1]—proving exactly what is of himself, and what is of a baser kind—what—how much—there is of God—what—how much—of man. The principles of the heart lie deep. The work may be good in itself. But what are the ends? The same work—according to its end—may be accepted—or be cast away. Jehonadab and Jehu both were engaged in the same exterminating work. With the one it was right service—with the other, vile hypocrisy.[2] Self-distrust is therefore the wisdom of true godliness,[3] daily—hourly trembling in ourselves; yet readily grounding our confidence in God! But for the covering of the High Priest, how could we stand for one moment under the piercing eye of our Judge? Did our dearest earthly friend know what was passing in our thoughts at any one hour, could he ever deem us worthy of confidence? Must not his heart revolt from contact with such vileness? Yet does our gracious *Lord*—while *pondering our hearts*, and privy to all their hidden corruptions—forgive—accept—yea—rejoice in us as his people.

3. *To do justice and judgment is more acceptable to the Lord than sacrifice.*

Did Solomon mean to undervalue *sacrifice?* Never did man more highly honor it.[4] Perhaps the splendor of his sacrificial service may have given rise to the national perverted trust in external forms. *Sacrifice* was appointed as a type of the Great Sacrifice for sin.[5] But never was it intended to take the place of that universal moral obedience, which the law of God had from the beginning indispensably required. Yet how soon did man mistake the intention of the ordinance! How easily did he substitute the offering of bulls and goats for the more self-denying service of the heart![6] Israel abounded in the observance of their outward ceremonials, while, indulging the sin of Sodom and Gomorrah.[7] The Corban *sacrifice* stood in the room of filial obligation.[8] The lesser services of "anise and cummin" were scrupulously observed, to the neglect of "the weightier matters of the law—*judgment*, mercy, and faith."[9] Justly therefore did our Lord commend the "discretion" of the scribe, who gave the due place and proportion to the ceremonial and moral service.[10] Both are his requirements. And a soundly instructed conscience will aim at both. Yet plainly has he in some instances dispensed with the former;[11] never with the latter.[12] He has accepted the moral without the ceremonial; but never the ceremonial without the moral, observance. What would the world be without that *justice and judgment*, which at once "establish the throne,"[13] "exalt the nation,"[14] and realize to their disciples a true interest in that richest of all possessions—the love of God![15]

[1] Chap. xvi. 2. [2] 2 Kings x. 15, 23, 31. [3] Chap. xxviii. 26.
[4] 1 Kings iii. 4; viii. 64—66. [5] Heb. x. 1. [6] 1 Sam. xv. 22. Ps. l. 13, 14.
[7] Isa. i. 11—17. Comp. Jer. vii. 22, 23. Hos. vi. 6. Amos v. 21—26, with Acts vii. 42, 43. Mic. vi. 6—8.
[8] Mark vii. 9—15. [9] Matt. xxiii. 23. [10] Mark xii. 32-34.
[11] Matt. xii. 1—7. Acts x. 34, 35. [12] Matt. xxii. 37-39. [13] Chap. xvi. 12.
[14] Chap. xiv. 34. [15] Chap. xv. 9. Comp. Isa. lxiv. 5.

We indeed have no *sacrifices* to place in the stead of these invaluable principles. But the same preference and indeed exaltation of external service prevails among us. Whether under the grosser form of Popery, or the more plausible cover of Tractarian delusion, it is the true religion of man's heart—something to recommend us to the favor of God—something easier and less humbling, than the "living sacrifice"[1] for his service. Christian professor! art thou resting in the shell and surface; or art thou worshipping in the spirituality of service? Dost thou hear the voice calling thee from the dead forms, to seek the living power of godliness? Those externals, that stand in the place of a consecrated heart, are the delusion of the great deceiver. Let thine heart be with God, walking with him in the sound exercise of Christian obligation.

4. *An high look, and a proud heart, and the plowing* (the light, Marg.) *of the wicked, is sin.*

Another stamp of abomination upon pride![2] We cannot mistake the mind of God so continually declared. Yet so many shapes does this sin assume, that until the Spirit of God shows a man to himself, he rejects the idea of any concern in it. Nay—he will be proud of his very pride—proud of a high spirit; counting a Christian mean and cowardly, who in the true spirit of the Gospel, yields up his rights to a stronger hand.[3]

But not only the haughtiness, but even the natural actions—*the plowing—of the wicked—is sin.* "This is an hard saying—who can hear it?"[4] How can *the plowing* of the soil—in itself a duty[5]—become *a sin?* The motive determines the act. The most natural actions are inculcated for Christian ends.[6] They become therefore moral actions—good or bad—according to their motives. The man, who *plows* the soil, acknowledging God in his work, and seeking his strength and blessing—"does it" acceptably "to the glory of God." It is essentially a religious action. But *the wicked*, who does the same work without any regard to God—for want of a godly end—*his plowing is sin.*[7] His idleness is sin against a plain command.[8] His industry is the sin of ungodliness—putting God out of his own world. The substance of his act is good. But the corrupt principle defiles the very best action.[9] "Every thought, every imagination, of the natural heart" is unmixed "evil."[10] If the fountain-head be bitter, how can the waters be pure? Sin indeed defiles every motive in the Christian's heart.

1 Rom. xii. 1. 2 Chap. iii. 34; viii. 17; xvi. 5.
3 Matt. v. 39—41. 1 Cor. vi. 7. 4 John vi. 60.
5 Gen. iii. 19. 6 1 Cor. x. 31. Col. iii. 17.
7 'Holy intention is to the actions of a man that, which the soul is to the body, or form to its matter, or the root to the tree, or the sun to the world, or the fountain to the river, or the base to a pillar. Without these, the body is a dead trunk, the matter is sluggish, the tree is a block, the world is darkness, the river is quickly dry, the pillar rushes into flatness and ruin, and the action is sinful, or unprofitable and vain.' Bishop Taylor's Holy Living, chap. i. sec. iii.
8 2 Thess. iii. 10. 9 Tit. i. 15. 10 Gen. vi. 5.

But here it is the substance of sin. In the one case it is infirmity of walk in the straight path. In the other, it is an habitual walk in a crooked path. With *the wicked*—'his eating as well as his gluttony; his drinking as well as his drunkenness; his commerce, negociation, and trafficking, as well as his covetousness, and inordinate love of the world; are all set down and reckoned by God for sins, and such sins as he must reckon for with God.'[1] Fearful indeed is his condition. Would that he could see it! Whether he prays[2] or neglects to pray[3]—it is abomination. He cannot but sin; and yet he is fully accountable for his sin. To die—is to plunge into ruin.[4] To live in unregeneracy is even worse; it is daily "heaping up wrath against the day of wrath."[5] Ought he then to leave his duties undone? 'The impotency of man must not prejudice God's authority, nor diminish his duty.'[6] What then ought he to do? Let him learn the absolute necessity of the vital change —'Ye must be born again."[7] The leper taints every thing that that he touches. But let him seek to the Great Physician, whose word is sovereign healing;[8] whose divine blood cleanses from every spot.[9] His nature once cleansed, his works will be clean. His thoughts and principles, all will be for the glory of God; all acceptable to God.[10]

5. *The thoughts of the diligent tend only to plenteousness; but of every one that is hasty, only to want.*

The diligent is usually contrasted with the slothful:[11] here with the *hasty*. *The thoughts* of each work their own fruit—*for plenteousness, or for want.* The patient plodding man of industry perseveres in spite of all difficulties; content to increase his substance by degrees, never relaxing, never yielding to discouragement. This care of *diligence* is profitable under the blessing of God.[12] 'Thou mayest as well expect' (says an old writer) 'riches to rain down from heaven in silver showers, as to provide for thy family without industry in thy calling.'[13] *Haste* has much of *diligence* in its temperament. But as indolence is its defect, this is its excess—its undisciplined impulse. The hand too often goes

[1] Bishop Hopkins's Works, ii. 481. [2] Ver. 27. Chap. xv. 8. Isa. i. 13.
[3] Psalm x. 4. [4] Psalm ix. 17. Matt. xxv. 41—46. [5] Rom. ii. 5.
[6] Bishop Reynolds's Works, p. 94. [7] John iii. 7. [8] Matt. viii. 1—3.
[9] 1 John i. 7.

[10] Tit. i. 15, first clause. Many good commentators, following the old versions, adopt the marginal reading. (Comp. xiii. 9; xxiv. 20. Job xxi. 17.) But as the word is used in a similar sense (chap. xiii. 23,) and as our version is well supported, and gives a most important meaning, we have been content to adhere to it. Bishop Patrick explains the plowing in the figurative sense of devising. But as the two first illustrations in the verse are literal, it seems more consonant to unity to take the third on the same ground—'What can they (the wicked) think, say, or do; even when they eat, play, fast, or pray, they are always under the guilt of sin, because all flows from an impure heart, and the bad tree cannot bring forth good fruit?' Matt. vii. 18. Cartwright in loco. 'The wicked man hath a haughty look and a proud heart. Neither are his dispositions only sinful. But those—his very actions and endeavors—which in another man would be harmless, are in him no other than sin.' Bishop Hall. See also Scott in loco.

[11] Chap. x. 4; xii. 24, 27; xiii. 4. [12] Chap. x. 22.

[13] Swinnock's Christian Man's Calling, Part. i. 345.

before, and acts without, the judgment. The *hasty* man is driven under a worldly impulse into rash projects; and high-raised delu sive expectations he finds to be the short and sure road to *want.*[1] Need we remark—how rich the harvest of Christian *diligence*—of patient perseverance in well-doing—"eternal life?"[2] The hea venly race is not to be run by so many heats, but by a steady course. "Run"—not with *haste* or speed—but "with patience, the race set before us."[3] The seed springing up *in haste* withered.[4] Excitement is delusion, and ends in disappointment. What so important as to cultivate a deep work of grace, pervading the whole man, and abounding with fruit to the glory of God?

6. *The getting of treasures by a lying tongue is a vanity tossed to and fro of them that seek death.* 7. *The robbery of the wicked shall destroy* (saw, Marg.) *them, because they refuse to do judgment.*

A graphical picture of *the hasty spirit*—its own crooked ways *tending to want. Treasures may be gotten by lying.* But they become *vanity.* They are "put into a bag with holes,"[5] and sink away. They are like a ball *tossed to and fro* by a withering blast, or dust and chaff before the wind.[6] Unrighteous gain is a dear bargain. The wrath of God mingles gall and bitterness with the wages of iniquity.[7] Eagerly did Judas desire to get rid of his ill-gotten treasure as an intolerable curse. Yet he could not fly from his torturing conscience. He *sought death,* and he found it.[8]

Indeed it is with the ungodly, as if they *sought death* as their reward. So fondly do they love the way of eternal *death!* Their own sin is the seed of destruction. *Their robbery* virtually *destroys them.*[9] And who can they blame but themselves? It is not ignorance, or inconsideration, but wilfulness, that *destroys*—*because they refuse to do judgment.* "Know ye not, that the unrighteous shall not inherit the kingdom of God?"[10]—that "the wages of sin" invariably—inevitably—"is *death*"?[11] What else did *the robbery* of Achan and Gehazi bring to them?[12] Short indeed was the enjoyment of Ananias and Sapphira in "the part of the price kept back" at the expence *of a lying tongue*—Sudden and everlasting *destruction* was their doom—a beacon to worldly professors—half-hearted—self-deceiving![13]

[1] Chap. xix. 2; xxiii. 5. [2] Rom. ii. 7. Comp. Heb vi. 11, 12.
[3] Heb. xii. 1. [4] Matt. xiii. 5, 6, 20, 21.
[5] Hag. i. 6. [6] Chap. x. 2; xxii. 8. Jer. xvii. 11.
[7] Zech. v. 3, 4. Comp. Isa. i. 23, 24. Jer. vii. 9—11, 15. Ezek. xxii. 13, 14. Hab. ii. 6—8.
[8] Matt. xxvii. 3—5. [9] Chap. i. 11, 18, 19; xxii. 22, 23. Hab. ii. 10—13.
[10] 1 Cor. vi. 9. [11] Rom. vi. 23. [12] Jos. vii. 21—26. 2 Kings v. 20—27.
[13] Chap. xii. 19. Acts v. 1—10. The marginal reading seems to imply aggravated destruction—probably with shame. Comp. 2 Sam. xii. 31. Heb. xi. 37. Also Luke xii. 46. 'Search your chests; search your hearts, all ye that hear me this day; and if any of you find any of this adulterated gold among your heaps, away with it. As you love yourselves, away with it. Else know, that, as Chrysostom wittily says—'You have locked up a thief in your counting-house, who shall carry away all: and—if ye look not to it the sooner—your soul with it.' Bishop Hall's Sermon on the Righteous Mammon. Works, v. 109, 110.

8. *The way of man is froward and strange: but as for the pure, his work is right.*

Observe the striking contrast—man by nature; man by grace Who will say that man is now, as he first came from his Maker's hands?[1] How is he born? *Froward*, "as a wild ass's colt."[2] How soon does he develope his nature! "Foolishness is bound up in the heart of a child—childhood and youth are vanity."[3] Need we add that this is *a strange way?* How *strange* from God who made and loved him! Turned from God—"turned to his own way;"[4] with no law but his lust, no rule but his will;[5] loving his own liberty, but despising true liberty; made by his own self-delusion "the servant of corruption"[6]—ignorant—licentious—wanton; lusting only to be the fountain of his own happiness—the maker of his own sufficiency.

Take him in his noblest path—the pursuit of wisdom. Here too *his way is froward and strange.* Is not forbidden wisdom his delight, wisdom—not as wisdom—but as forbidden—"intruding" into the counsels—prying into the ark—of God?[7] Such was the first lusting of *frowardness*—not desiring to know God, which "is life eternal;"[8] but to know *as God,*[9] which was pride in its principle, and death in its issue.

But man—by grace made *pure*—new "created in the image of his God"[10]—mark him well—his will now conformed to God; his actions regulated by his perfect standard. Therefore his rule and aim being right, *his work is right.*[11] He lives now—as does his divine Saviour—"to God."[12] Such is the dignity of his great object! Such his fellowship with his glorious Head! Such his earnest of heaven, and growing meetness for it! Oh! the mercy of being turned from our own *froward and strange way* to the *pure* service of our God! Yet such remains of *the frowardness* still—such intricacies of self-deceitfulness—such twisted workings of depravity—that—O my God—show me to myself, so far as I can bear the sight, that I may be kept humbled—self-abased—always near my Saviour—always applying his precious blood—always covering myself in his *pure* and perfect work of righteousness!

9. *It is better to dwell in a corner of the house-top, than with a brawling woman in a wide house* (a woman of contention in a house of society, Marg.)

In the spacious houses in the East several families lived together in *society. A brawling woman* would be a grievous disturbance to the little community; and a peaceable man would prefer the *corner of the housetop,*[13] exposed to all the inconveniences of wind and weather; to the ample accommodation of *a wide house* in the atmosphere of *contention.*[14] A solitary life without would be better

[1] Eccl. vii. 29. [2] Job xi. 12. [3] Chap. xxii. 15. Eccl. xi. 10.
[4] Isa. liii. 6. [5] Eph. ii. 3. Tit. iii. 3. [6] 2 Peter ii. 19.
[7] Col. ii. 18. [8] John xvii. 3. [9] Gen. iii. 5.
[10] Ephes. iv. 24. [11] Tit. i. 15. [12] Rom. vi. 10, 11.
[13] Comp. Deut. xxii. 8. Jos. ii. 6—8. 2 Sam. xi. 2. Acts x. 9.
[14] Verse 19; xxv. 24.

than a quarrelsome life within. Some intervals of comfort might be abroad; none at home. Infinitely greater is this trial, when it comes from a man's own flesh; when she, who ought to be "a crown to her husband," becomes "rottenness to his bones;"[1] when she that is bound to be his choicest treasure, becomes his piercing scourge. 'It cannot but be a miserable thing to behold, that yet they are of necessity compelled to live together, which yet cannot be in quiet together.'[2] The intent of the Divine ordinance is here contravened. For it would seem "good for the man to be alone," rather than his "help-meet"[3] should turn to be his hindrance and his curse. But how many bring this bitter trouble upon themselves! They plunge into the important connexion on adventure; with no thought of the duties to be done, the temptations to be avoided, the crosses to be borne. They never sought direction in the momentous choice. The wife, not being sought from the Lord, came not from him, and brought no "favor of him."[4] Lust, avarice, or waywardness, brought a calamity, that no external accomplishments, no advantages of riches or rank, could for a moment counterbalance.

The only safe entrance into this 'honorable estate' is when each party—as Chrysostom instructs—commit themselves to God—'Bestow me as thou wilt, and on whom thou wilt.'[5] The only security for happiness is when, with due regard of mutual fitness, mutual love is grounded reverentially upon the ordinance, which makes of "twain one flesh."[6] *Contentions* will be restrained by the preventive habit of Christian discipline. Each will consider, that passion improves nothing, and patience much, and that it is far better to "give place" to each other, than "to the devil."[7] The husband in his claim for submission will remember, that he has found—not a servant, but a wife. She on her side, will not forget the beauty and order of graceful sacrifice and ready concession; and that her glory is departed from her, should she lose "the ornament of a meek and quiet spirit"—lovely in the sight of man—and "in the sight of God of great price."[8] 'Each severally performing their faithful duties, every thing around them acquires firmness and stability.,'[9]

10. *The soul of the wicked desireth evil: his neighbor findeth no favor in his eyes.*

A lively portraiture of Satan himself! not only doing, but *desiring evil! Evil* is the very nature of *the wicked*. What wonder then if his very *soul desireth it?* His "heart is fully set to do it."[10] He craves it as his appetite, his main delight.[11] What "fitting for destruction" must there be in vessels thus full of sin, and therefore full "of wrath!"[12] And here lies the difference between the godly and *the wicked;* not that the one is pure from evil, and the other

1 Chap. xii. 4.
2 Homily on Matrimony.
3 Gen. ii. 18.
4 Chap. xix. 14; xviii. 22.
5 Homil. in Coloss.
6 Gen. ii. 24, with xxiv. 67.
7 Eph. iv. 27.
8 1 Pet. iii. 4.
9 Chrysost. in Coloss. Hom. x.
10 Eccl. viii. 11.
11 Chap. iv. 16; xii. 12; xiii. 19.
12 Rom. ix. 22.

commits it; but that the one does it from constraint--the other from delight. The one testifies—"What I hate"—the other—What *my soul desireth*—"that do I."[1] As the essence of this native cherished principle—self to *the wicked* is both his god and his object. Intent upon his own will—not only his enemy, or a stranger—but even *his neighbor*, who might have a claim upon him, *findeth no favor in his eyes.* His charity does not extend beyond his own door.[2] No one is regarded, who stands in the way of his own interest. Friend and brother must give place to selfish gratification.

Such is sin in its hateful character and baneful fruits. "Men are lovers of their own selves—hateful, and hating one another!"[3] Look at the man of God—his heart enlarged and softened with the pervading influence of the gospel. Where is *the neighbor* in distress, that does not *find favor in his eyes*?[4] "Charity seeketh not her own"[5]—is his spirit. "Bear ye one another's burdens"[6]—is his rule. "The members of the body have the same care one for another."[7] Oh! for a larger measure of this gracious spirit—"as the dew of Hermon descending upon the mountains of Israel,"[8] upon the church of God!

11. *When the scorner is punished, the simple is made wise: and when the wise is instructed, he receiveth knowledge.*

This proverb in substance has been given before,[9] as an instructive illustration of the Lord's providential discipline. No stroke of his rod is without its effect. The blow that strikes one, reaches two—*the scorner for punishment; the simple* for improvement. If *the punishment* be without fruit to *the scorner*,[10] it reads a lesson of *wisdom to the simple*, who had been, or were in danger of being, misled by his evil example.[11] Nay—even the man of God learns a lesson of love mingled with wholesome trembling, from this awful dispensation. "Thou puttest away all the wicked of the earth like dross; therefore I love thy testimonies. My flesh trembleth for fear of thee; and I am afraid of thy judgments."[12]

The wise—though already taught of God—through his daily teaching thankfully *receives* increasing *knowledge*.[13] Among his most fruitful lessons are the *instructions* of the rod—*instructions* (mark the difference of the terms)—not *punishment*. Often does the teaching rod seal the teaching law. And the well-disciplined child is ready with his acknowledgments—"Blessed is the man, whom thou *chastenest*, O Lord, and *teachest* him out of thy law. I will bless the Lord, who hath given me counsel; my reins also chasten me in the night season. It is good for me that I have been afflicted, that I might learn thy statutes."[14]

[1] Rom. vii. 15—21, with vi. 12, 16, 17.
[2] 1 Sam. xxv. 4—11.
[3] 2 Tim. iii. 2. Tit. iii. 3.
[4] Luke x. 31—35.
[5] 1 Cor. xiii. 5.
[6] Gal. vi. 2.
[7] 1 Cor. xii. 25, 26.
[8] Ps. cxxxiii. 3.
[9] Chap. xix. 25.
[10] Isa. i. 5. Jer. v. 3
[11] Ps. lxiv. 7—9.
[12] Ps. cxix. 119, 120. Comp. Heb. x. 26—31.
[13] Chap. i. 5.
[14] Ps. xcii. 12; xvi. 7; cxix. 71

12. *The righteous man wisely considereth the house of the wicked: but God overthroweth the wicked for their wickedness.*

The punishment of *the wicked* reads a lesson not only of love and trembling, but of *wise consideration.* Yet many are the perplexing mysteries of Providence. *The righteous man* does not always see with his right eyes. The prosperity of the wicked staggers his faith, excites his envy, and induces hard thoughts of God.[1] But when he looks with the eye of faith, he sees far beyond the dazzling glory of the present moment. He *wisely considereth their house*—not its external splendor and appurtenances—but how it will end. He justifies God, and puts himself to shame.[2] "Shall not the Judge of all the earth do right?"[3] Here we rest, until he shall "arise and plead his own cause," and "with the breath of his mouth, and the brightness of his coming, destroy"[4] the very existence of evil. Meanwhile—when the superficial eye sees nothing but confusion, let *the righteous man wisely consider* lessons of deep and practical profit. The shortness of the prosperity,[5] and the certainty of *the overthrow of the wicked*;[6] the assurance of a day of recompense;[7] the contrast of the substance of the godly for time and for eternity[8]—these are the apprehensions of faith. Do they not marvellously set out the perfections of God, and call to each of his children—"My son, give glory to God?"

13. *Whoso stoppeth his ears at the cry of the poor, he shall also cry himself, but shall not be heard.*

If there were no poor, much of the word of God, applying to their comfort, and directing our obligations—would have been written in vain. The obligation implies not only an helping hand, but a feeling heart; *hearing the cry of the poor* with sympathy,[9] cheerfulness,[10] self-sacrifice.[11] The *stopping the ears* implies cruelty[12] or insensibility;[13] turning away from real and known distress;[14] any kind of oppression; beating down "the hire of the laborer"[15] beyond the power of earning the necessaries of life; and neglecting, so far as is in our power, to defend them against oppression.[16]

Sometimes indeed it might be our duty to *stop our ears.* The law of God discountenances the trade of begging, with all its pathetic cries and appeals.[17] To retain therefore the poor in idleness, however compassionate or self-pleasing the motive, is to encourage

[1] Ps. lxxiii. 2—14.
[2] Ib. verses 16—22.
[3] Gen. xviii. 25.
[4] Psalm lxxiv. 22; lxxxii. 8. 2 Thess. ii. 8.
[5] Job xx. 4, 5. Ps. xxxvii. 35, 36.
[6] Chap. xii. 7; xiii. 3—6; xiv. 4; xv. 25. 2 Pet. ii. 4—9.
[7] Job xxi. 28—30. Ps. lviii. 10, 11.
[8] Job xxii. 15—20. Ps. lxxiii. 23—26
[9] Deut. xv. 7—11. Isa. lviii. 6—9.
[10] Rom. xii. 8. 2 Cor. ix. 7.
[11] 2 Cor. viii. 1—4. Howard's rule—so nobly expounded by his own self-denying devotedness—is a fine comment on this example—'That our superfluities give way to other men's convenience; that our conveniences give way to other men's necessaries and that even our necessaries sometimes give way to other men's extremities.' See his Life.
[12] Comp. Acts vii. 37.
[13] Chap. xxix. 7. Comp Neh. v. 1—8.
[14] Luke x. 30—32
[15] Jam. v. 4.
[16] Luke xviii. 2—4.
[17] 2 Thess. iii. 10.

—if not to participate in—sin. Considerate discretion—not feeling—should direct our charity.[1] Honest distress taxes most of us to the utmost of our power; considering our responsibility to put out all that we have—little or much—to the most profitable use. Yet ever let the withholding of charity be a constraint upon our feeling, not the indulgence of our selfishness. Count it a privilege, no less than an obligation, to minister to the poor. Ponder it as conformity to our Divine Master's spirit and work.[2] Consider niggardliness in giving; the useless expenses that abridge our power of helping; luxuries, while our brethren are starving around us; restraining the full extent of what we ought and might give—all this as virtually *stopping our ears against their cry.* Covetousness and sensuality harden the heart; and when the heart is hard, the ear is deaf.[3] This sin was wrongfully charged upon Job.[4] But wherever it be found, the stamp of Divine displeasure is fearfully marked;[5] and the great day will openly stamp it as the ground of condemnation.[6]

And even now—as the selfist's hardness shows no love to God,[7] he will find no love from God. "With the same measure that he meted withal, it shall be measured to him again."[8] Did he *stop his ears at the cry of the poor?* God will stop his ears against his cry.[9] He that would not give a crumb on earth, was denied a drop of water in hell.[10] "He shall have judgment without mercy, that hath showed no mercy."[11] Christian professor! study the character of thy God—"pitiful, and of tender mercy;"[12] and be like him. Remember—"bowels of mercies—kindness" are the mark and ornament of the elect of God.[13]

14. *A gift in secret pacifieth anger: and a reward in the bosom strong wrath*

We have before noticed[14] cases of resentment, where a legitimate and prudent distribution of *gifts* may quell the storm, and restore the calm. But *a gift in secret* implies a perversion;[15] else why should the light be dreaded?[16] Both parties are involved in the guilt. The giver acts as a tempter. The receiver wilfully breaks the law of God.[17] The passions of men are easily charmed. Rarely will a covetous man be so angry with his friends, as not to be *pacified with his gift*, especially when, *given in secret*, it tells no tales. *A reward in the bosom* to such a man is stronger far than *strong wrath;* and when it has shown its errand, the melting process is rapidly accomplished.[18] Thus is the wounded pride expelled by another ruling passion—avarice! Who then can excuse himself in the indolent cry—'I cannot help my passion or gain any

1 Chap. xxix. 7. 2 Matt. xiv. 14—21. 3 1 Sam. xxv. 10, 11, 36, 37.
4 Job xxii. 5—7, with xxix. 16; xxxi. 6, 17—20.
5 Chap. xi. 24, 26; xxviii. 27. Jer. xxxiv. 10—22. Matt. xviii 30—34.
6 Matt. xxv. 41—45. 7 1 John iii. 17.
8 Luke vi. 38. Comp. Jud. i. 6, 7. 1 Sam. xv. 33.
9 Job xxxiv. 24—28. Zech. vii. 9—13. See Ecclus. iv. 4—6.
10 Luke xvi. 21, 24, 25. 11 Jam. ii. 13. 12 Ibid. v. 11.
13 Col. iii. 12. 14 Page 249. 15 Chap. xvii. 23.
16 John iii. 20. 17 Ex. xxiii. 8. Deut. xvi. 19. 18 Eccl. x. 19.

power over it?' Secret covetousness cankers many a plausible exercise of forbearance. How do we need a close watch and keeping of our own hearts, in order to a Christian walk with God!

15. *It is joy to the just to do judgment: but destruction shall be to the workers of iniquity.*

It is not that *the just does judgment.* Conscience may dictate this—at least externally—while the bias of the heart is on the side of sin. But *it is joy to the just to do it.* His rest, purpose, affections—all centre in it. He has as much delight *in doing judgment,* as "the soul of the wicked desireth evil"[1]—as his own soul ever desired it.[2] *It is joy,* but only *to the just.*[3] To the mere professor of religion it is conviction—fear; the service of a slave. He knows God only as a Master, and conceives of him as a task-master. He has never known him as a Father, and therefore never served him as a child. It is this service—is it not—Christian? that identifies holiness and happiness, and brings its own rewards with it, as naturally as heat accompanies fire, and beams flow from the sun.—Such is its refreshing, its smiles, its income of happiness, that "the way of the Lord is strength to the upright."[4] Was it not thus with our beloved Lord? He could say—"I delight to do thy will, O my God. My meat, that the world knows not of, is to do my Father's will, and to finish his work."[5] Oh! that the servant might be in spirit like his Lord!

What then is the gloom and sadness charged upon religion? Truly the children of this world have never tasted the clusters of Canaan. How then can they know their sweetness? Christian! look up, and be cheerful, for the honor of your God and his gospel. Live not as if some affliction had happened to you; but as one snatched from destruction—as a child of God—an heir of heaven. Let the world see in you, that the "work of righteousness is peace," and "the yoke of Christ is easy;"[6]—nay—that the sharpest sacrifices for him are sweet; that there is more pleasure in "plucking out the right eye" for him, than in using it for sin or for Satan. And then think further, if this be the happiness amidst all the clogging hindrances of sin, what will it be, when these hindrances shall be removed, and we shall serve him without sin forever![7] If such be the wilderness, what will the Canaan be!

But what know the ungodly of this reality? Sin is to them a mockery[8]—a sport[9]—even a joy.[10] But never can it be their *solid joy.* It is their weariness—never their rest.[11] *To the workers of iniquity* belong only vanity and disappointment, ending in *destruction.*[12] Hear the testimony of God—"*Destruction* and misery are in their ways, and the way of peace have they not known. There is no peace, saith my God, to the wicked."[13]

[1] Verse 10. [2] Eph. ii. 2, 3. Tit. iii. 3. [3] Ps. xxxii. 11; xcvii. 11, 12.
[4] Chap. x. 29. [5] Ps. xl. 8. John iv. 32—34. [6] Isa. xxxii. 17. Matt. xi. 30.
[7] Rev. vii. 15; xxii. 3. [8] Chap. xiv. 9. [9] Chap. x. 23; xxvi. 18, 19.
[10] Chap. xv. 21. [11] Isa. xlvii. 13; lvii. 10, 20. Jer. ix. 5.
[12] Chap. v. 22. Matt. vii. 23. [13] Rom. iii. 16, 17. Isa. lix. 7, 8; lvii. 21.

16. *The man that wandereth out of the way of understanding, shall remain in the congregation of the dead.*

This seems to describe the fearful and irretrievable ruin of apostates.[1] God has opened *the way of understanding*. The *wandering out of it* implies, that *the man* was once in it; at least that he was instructed, and professed to walk in it. The end of wilful wandering is eternal death. Such was the character and end of the wicked son of Jehoshaphat;[2] and the rebellious children of godly Josiah,[3] apostates from the religion "received by tradition from their fathers."

But—not to go to olden times. It is no rare sight to see the children of godly parents cast off the privileges of their birthright, as despised in their eyes. Early instructed in "the Holy Scriptures;" instead of "continuing in the things which they have learned, and been assured of,"[4] they have "loved to *wander*."[5] They have never proved a real apprehension of the substance of truth—never a just appreciation of its value. *The way* has been too strait—too humbling. Novelties have been preferred: self-confidence indulged; self-pleasing delusions cherished; the want of godly sincerity has darkened the path;[6] conscientious error, varnished with external holiness, is readily admitted; and *the man*, destitute of a solid scriptural standard, *wanders out of the way of understanding*.

Wandering indeed is man's fallen nature.[7] But light, conviction, advantages of instruction, awfully aggravate the responsibility.[8] Take care of the first *wandering* step—whether it may be in doctrine or in practice. It may fix in a state of apostacy; like Bunyan's blinded *wanderers* out of the straight path, who were found among the tombs—*remaining in the congregation of the dead*. A special mercy will it be, if the wayward *wanderer* does not find his last and final *remaining* among 'the mighty dead,' "to whom is reserved the blackness of darkness forever."[9] "It had been better for him not to have known the way of righteousness, than, after he has known it, to turn from the holy commandment delivered unto him."[10] Let such as be remember, that *remaining among the congregation of the dead* shows their character, their state, and their home; and that, though they be by birth Abraham's children, born of godly parents; yet, *wandering out of the way of understanding*, they are out of the way of life.

One can only wish to view such sad apostates, as Faithful and Hopeful did, with tears gushing out of our eyes, silently pondering.

[1] Psalm cxxv. 5. [2] 2 Chron. xxi. 1, 4—6, 18, 19.
[3] Ib. xxxvi. 1—17. Jer. xxii. 17—19, 28—30.
[4] 2 Tim. iii. 14, 15. [5] Jer. xiv. 10. [6] Matt. vi. 23.
[7] Isa. liii. 6. [8] Ib. xxviii. 12, 13. Comp. Zeph. i. 4—6.
[9] Jud. 12, 13. 'Mighty dead.' See Dr. Good's note on Job xxvi. 5. Parkhurst and most critics consider intensity to be implied. Comp. Isa. xiv. 9. See on chap. ii. 18, page 18, n. 4. Dr. Graves quotes this text with several others in this Book (iv. 18, 19; viii. 35, 36; xii. 28; xiv. 32) in evidence of the knowledge of the future state under the old dispensation. Lectures on Pentateuch, Part iii. Lect. iv.
[10] 2 Pet. ii. 2.

Do they not stand as warnings to us, that we should tremble—yea —"rejoice with trembling?"[1] While we "stand by faith," must we not remember the needful caution—"Be not highminded, but fear?"[2] Ever let us combine self-distrust with our Christian confidence; "fearing lest a promise being left us of entering into rest, any of us should seem to come short of it;"[3] thankful alike for the warnings to make us fear, and for the encouragements to preserve us from despondency.

But the great mass are also here described. They never profess; they never have professed. They know that "wisdom crieth without," yet they "refuse to hear the voice of the charmer."[4] Many will occasionally hear, yet "they go their way, and straightway forget what manner of men they were."[5] Noah's mighty congregations were of this character; and they *remained in the congregation of the dead.*[6] And will not every one, who, with the opportunities to attain wisdom, refuses, departs, turns away—be found here—"dead in their trespasses and sins"[7]—dead eternally?

17. *He that loveth pleasure shall be a poor man; and he that loveth wine and oil shall not be rich.*

What then? are we to have no *pleasure?* This were indeed to drive men from religion. Why—*pleasure* is the very character of the ways of God;[8] *pleasure* infinitely more satisfying "than in the time that corn and wine increased."[9] Are we not—again—to rejoice in our earthly comforts? "The living God giveth us richly all things to enjoy."[10] This large flow of happiness is more than doubled by the rule of "thanksgiving."[11] Yet, strange as it may seem—the way to enjoy *pleasure* is not to *love it;* to live above it;[12] to "rejoice as though we rejoiced not; to use the world, as not abusing it."[13] The man bent upon *pleasure*—giving his whole heart and time to *the love of it*—sacrificing to it all his prudence and foresight—is surely on the high road to *poverty.*[14] On the same road is *he that loveth wine*—under the power of a "mocking delusion."[15] *He that loveth oil*—one of the most precious fruits of Canaan[16]—may find, that "those who could not live without dainties come to want necessaries."[17] But the most melancholy sight in the universe is the man who sacrifices to *the love of pleasure* the interest of his immortal soul. Salvation is thrown away as a

[1] Psalm ii. 11. [2] Rom. xi. 20.
[3] Heb. iv. 1. [4] Chap. i. 18. Ps. lviii. 5. [5] Jam. i. 24.
[6] 1 Pet. iii 19, 20. 2 Pet. ii. 5. [7] Eph. ii. 1. [8] Chap. iii. 17.
[9] Ps. iv. 6, 7. [10] 1 Tim. vi. 17. Comp. Eccl. ii. 26; iii. 22; ix. 7—9
[11] 1 Tim. iv. 4, 5.
[12] It is a fine remark of Cyprian's—'The greatest pleasure is to have conquered pleasure; nor is there any greater victory, than that which is gained over our own appetites.' De bono Pudicitiæ.
[13] 1 Cor. vii. 30, 31.
[14] Verse 20. The instance of the profligate, v. 10, 11; of Sampson, Judg. xvi 1—21; of the Prodigal, Luke xv. 13—16.
[15] Chap. xx. 1; xxiii. 21.
[16] Deut. viii. 8; xi. 14. Judg. ix. 9. Ps. xxiii. 5. Mic. vi. 15. Hab. iii. 17.
[17] Henry in loco. Comp. Isa. xxxii. 9—12; xlvii. 8, 9. Zeph. ii. 15. Rev. xviii. 7

thing of naught.[1] Fearful indeed is *the poverty*—the utter—eternal ruin of this wilful infatuation. "Woe unto you that are rich; for ye have received your consolation! Son! remember! that thou in thy life-time receivedst thy good things, and likewise Lazarus evil things; but now he is comforted, and thou art tormented."[2]

Christian! you wonder not, that those who know not heaven, should take their portion on earth. But should not the heirs of heaven live above the love of earth, having no more sympathy with the sensual devotee, than with the pleasure of "the sow wallowing in the mire?" Mark well the danger and temptation—the need of unceasing watchfulness, that in the necessary use you keep within its due measure—the heart loosened here and fixed above.[3] For should you be growing in the *love of* earthly *pleasure, you shall be a poor man* indeed—growing indifferent to prayer; heartless and dead to God; fancying shadows to be substance, and despising the true substance as a shadow. Heavenly pleasures will lose their sweetness, as earthly *pleasures* are relished. Keep then ever before you the witness of your better experience—the emptiness[4] and bitterness[5] of the world's *pleasures*; the all-sufficiency of your real portion.[6] And shall a man's appetite and poisoned taste blot out these records—this solemn judgment of experience? God forbid!

18. *The wicked shall be a ransom for the righteous, and the transgressor for the upright.*

The *ransom* is here spoken of only in a popular sense, as equivalent to a substitute.[7] God sometimes, for wise reasons, involves *the righteous* in the same judgment with *the wicked*. Sometimes the punishment of *the wicked* is the ordained means of averting calamity from *a righteous* nation.[8] Often, in the Lord's retributive justice, *the wicked* are brought into the very trouble which they design for *the righteous*.[9] Thus, suffering in their stead, they are as it were *a ransom for them*. God may seem in trouble to "sell his people for naught;"[10] yet "so precious are they in his sight," that a whole nation shall—if needful for their preservation—be given to ruin. Egypt and Ethiopia were thus *a ransom* for Jerusalem, when God turned Sennacherib's fury against them, and warded off the threatened stroke from the sacred city;[11] just as a bait, thrown to a beast of prey, would give opportunity to the devoted victim to escape. Often does God blind the enemies of the church to fight among themselves, so that the destined scourge for his church is turned to another quarter, as if the crushed

[1] Eccl. xi. 9. 1 Tim. v. 6. 2 Tim. iii. 4. 1 Pet. iv. 3—5.
[2] Luke vi. 24; xvi. 25. Comp. Ps. xvii. 14. [3] Luke xxi. 34. [4] Eccl. ii. 11.
[5] Chap. xiv. 13. [6] Ps. xvi. 5, 6; xvii. 15; lxxiii. 25, 26.
[7] Ps. xlix 7, 8. [8] Jos. vii. 24—26.
[9] Chap. xi. 8, and references. See also the first-born of Egypt given for the deliverance of Israel. Ex. xi. 4—8; xii. 29—36.
[10] Ps. xliv. 12; Comp. Jud. i. 14; ii. 8; iii. 2, &c.
[11] Isa. xliii. 3, 4. Ransom, the same word in the original. Comp 2 Kings xix. 7—9

nation was *a ransom*—a victim in the stead of the innocent. However lowering the prospects of the church may be, yet there is no ground for faintness or trembling for the ark of God. His promises to his church are not empty sounds, but "the munitions of rocks." "No weapon that is formed against thee shall prosper. He that toucheth you, toucheth the apple of mine eye."[1] The night may be dark; but the morn will look forth gloriously.

19. *It is better to dwell in the wilderness, than with a contentious and an angry woman.*

Another,[2] perhaps even a stronger, picture of the misery of domestic dissension. *It is better* to be destitute altogether of the communion of social life, if it must be purchased at so dear a rate, as the companionship of one, whose *contentions* will turn every comfort into bitterness. *It is better to dwell*, not only "upon the house-top," where there might be alleviation, but even *in the wilderness;* giving up all social indulgences for desolation, solitude, and even dangers.[3] Oh! it is the poison in 'the sweetest cup of earth's best joy,' where "two are joined to each other, and made one flesh;"[4] yet not "joined to the Lord," and so "made one spirit."[5] *The woman* only is mentioned. Yet the disruption is as frequent, and at least as guilty, from an imperious husband, as from a scolding wife. Surely our gracious God here teaches his children a lesson too often neglected to their cost—to put their necks into this sacred yoke, 'reverently, discreetly, advisedly, soberly, and in the fear of God.'[6] Let them carefully ponder the fact, that a choice influenced by the fascinations of manners or disposition, by intellect or accomplishments, if made without reference to godliness, can give no promise of the Divine blessing, or of individual happiness. Often indeed it issues in a state of degradation, too painful to dwell upon, into which one or both parties are content to plunge, making themselves odious for the sake of indulging their *angry* passions. Nor does this apply only to the matrimonial yoke. All members of the family circle, bound together by natural ties, and living together by providential arrangements, may do not a little towards embittering each other's happiness. The subjects of these uncontrolled tempers must, however, reap the natural harvest of their seed sown, and suffer under the mortifying consciousness, that others recoil from their society, and would readily embrace—if need be—the alternative of *the wilderness*, as a welcome change from perpetual irritation.

'The family,' as Mr. Cecil justly observes, 'is sometimes a fierce fire. Our family comprehends the greatest portion of our world. It is to us the most interesting, and therefore is capable of becoming the most trying, portion.'[7] The child of God is bound in-

1 Isa. liv. 17. Zech. ii. 8. 2 Ver. 9.
3 See Mark i. 13. "I had rather"—said the wise son of Sirach—"dwell with a lion and a dragon, than keep house with a wicked woman." Ecclus. xxv. 16. Comp. xxvi. 7, 27. 4 Matt. xix. 5.
5 1 Cor. vi. 17. 6 Marriage Service. 7 See his Sermon on Hannah.

deed to recognize effectual and fatherly discipline in his trials from the tempers of those around him. Yet not less strange the fact, that even among Canaan's pilgrims, words are often uttered, that must produce pain; and thus thorns, which our heavenly Father hath not planted, are strewn in our brother's or sister's path. Effects still more lamentable are to be traced in impressions made upon the young, or on others watching the exhibition of such inconsistencies, where better things might have been expected.

The matrimonial "thorn in the flesh" may be a needful chastening, overruled as a preventive against self-confidence,[1] and for the exercise of adorning Christian graces.[2] Yet much prayer and forbearance are required to avoid needless occasion and subjects of irritation, to keep aloof from the immediate bursting of ungoverned passion; to realize present support under this heavy cross, in the assured prosperity and intense longing for the home of everlasting peace.[3]

20. *There is treasure to be desired and oil in the dwelling of the wise: but a foolish man spendeth it up.*

[1] 2 Cor. xii. 7.

[2] Hooker's meek endurance of the "continual dropping" (chap. xix. 13) must have read to George Cranmer and others who witnessed it, a striking lesson on the influence of practical religion. Buxtorf quoted a Jewish saying—'How will a man prove his spirit? By enduring a bad wife.' When Socrates was asked—'Why he endured his wife? By this means'—he replied—'I have a schoolmaster at home, and an example how I should behave myself abroad. For I shall'—said he—'be the more quiet with others, being thus daily exercised and taught in the forbearing of her.' Homily on Matrimony. Chrysostom gives the story, like the Homilists, with a striking application. Homily on 1 Cor. xi. 16.

[3] Is it not a grave question—whether divorces or conventional separations—such as we hear of in the Church of God—are not rather the flinching from, than the enduring and honoring, the cross? The supposition that *it is better to dwell in the wilderness* implies, that the worse alternative of *the contentious and angry woman* may be appointed. This was Job's lot. 'The Devil' (as M. Henry observed) 'spared his wife to him, not only to be his tempter, but his tormentor.' Yet did not he put away his matrimonial cross. The endurance of it was doubtless a component part of that patience, which is commended to our imitation, and which was honored with a double increase of family blessing. (James v. 11; Job xlii. 12, 13.) Our Lord, in restoring this ordinance to its original strictness of obligation, admits but one exception, thereby excluding every other. (Matt. v. 32; xix. 1—9.) According to this rule, an unfaithful wife must be put away as a sin; but a *contentious* wife restrained, and endured as a cross. The Apostle, in discussing the question of casuistry submitted to him (1 Cor. vii. 2—5), lays down the general law, and admits no revulsion of taste or feeling—much less pretence of religion—to put asunder (save *for a time*, by mutual consent, and for a spiritual purpose, 5) what God hath joined together. If in an extremity the unbeliever was suffered to depart (15), no analogy can be applied from an heathen marriage, where the light of Revelation had never shown the obligation, to that of Christian professors, where its full force was intelligently understood, and voluntarily recognized. Constrained providential separations, where the hearts are in unity, maintain the principle of the bond. But wilful settled separation rejects the distinct ground, on which the ordinance stands. The woman (save where the primary law of nature—self-preservation—dictates) is obviously bound by the same indissoluble tie. (1 Cor. vii. 10.) If on either side it be defended, as avoiding the open scandal of continual contention; let the duty of humiliation and mortification of the sins, which have produced this painful extremity, be instantly and habitually applied. Let the high offence of the infraction of God's ordinance be deeply pondered; as shaking the foundation of an appointment, expressly framed to "make of twain one flesh" (Gen. ii. 24; Matt. xix. 5); ordained as a type of the unchangeable relation betwixt Christ and his church (Eph. v. 32); and of which "the Lord, the God of Israel saith, that He hateth putting away." (Mal. ii. 16.)

To love an earthly *treasure* is the way to poverty.[1] Yet we may thankfully enjoy the prudent gathering, as the fruit of the Lord's blessing,[2] like *the oil* of Canaan,[3] for refreshment. This is not the forbidden "laying up for ourselves treasures upon earth"[4] —a hoard for selfishness and distrust of God.[5] This *treasure is in the house of the wise.* For prudence is not worldliness;[6] an indifference to coming trial is not faith, but foolish simplicity.[7]

Even the cottage of the godly poor[8] often contains this *desirable treasure*—the reward of Christian diligence. Yet poor indeed is the palace, where this is the primary treasure. The Bible with its stores of unsearchable riches is the grand treasure of man. *The oil* of gladness, which it poureth out richly, is his choicest comfort. Wherever this treasure is pre-eminently prized—this is *the house of the wise*—whether it be the prince or the pauper.

Whatever the earthly treasures of *the foolish man* may have been, or however obtained, his improvidence is a wide gulf to *spend it up.* All goes one way. Drunkenness, wasteful expenditure, idleness, gambling, devours it all. He serves a master, who will leave him nothing at the year's end; and, as the only reward of his drudgery, will bring him to utter destitution. Such was the prodigal's course; yet in the gracious mercy of his Father the means of changing him from his folly into a better mind, and bringing him to *the house of the wise*—a possessor of *a treasure more desirable*, than his earthly appetite had ever longed for.[9]

But there are other *foolish men* besides the drunkard and the spendthrift; and other *treasure* infinitely more *desirable, that is spent up.* Admission to *the house of the wise*—the opportunity of thus growing rich in knowledge and holiness[10]—what a "price would it be, in the hands of a fool," had he but "an heart for it." But the golden moment is lost; *the treasure is spent up.* Time is wasted in reckless frivolity of pursuit in innumerable ways. The entire absence of an holy aim in his daily employments deadens all sense of responsibility. He lives only as the creature of the present moment, with no object worthy of an immortal being—with no object connected with eternity. Oh my God! leave me not to my own folly, lest I *spend up my treasure*, instead of trading with it, and thus enlarging it for my best welfare.

21. *He that followeth after righteousness and mercy, findeth life, righteousness, and honor.*

Here the *desirable treasure* is not *spent up* but *followed after* with a distinctness of purpose that shows a perception of its value. This is the Christian standard—"Not as though I had already

[1] Ver. 17. [2] Chap. x. 22. [3] See note on ver. 17.
[4] Matt. vi. 19. [5] Luke xii. 16—22.
[6] Chap. vi. 6—8; x. 5. See Gen. xli. 48. [7] Chap. xxii, 3.
[8] The original implies a small dwelling (domicilium—not domus, chap. iii. 33). *Treasure and oil* are mentioned—first the general term—then one of its valuable items. A similar idiom may be found, chap. xxii. 7; Mark xvi. 7.
[9] Luke xv. 13—24. [10] Chap xiii. 20.

attained, either were already perfect. But I *follow after.*[1] Heaven—"the prize of our high calling"—is the bright consummating object. But *righteousness and mercy*—all our obligations to God and man—are the pathway to it—the meetness for it.[2] Holiness must be our daily habit, as well as our religious service—"in all manner of conversation."[3] There must be nothing at home or abroad, where the man of God is not seen.[4] The true evidence of Divine Grace on the heart is the practical influence upon the temper and conduct.[5]

But this *following after* is not the toiling at a daily task; not a compulsory law, chaining the conscience against the inclinations of the will. It is delight, freedom, enlargement;[6] the flow of the heart filled with fearless love.[7]

Nor is this *following* for the sake of the reward. Yet it finds the reward in its exercise[8]—a reward of grace indeed it must be. For how infinitely is it above our faint and sinful efforts! *He that followeth, findeth life*[9]—that which is the life of life—the treasure of the best happiness; fellowship with God; the sunshine of his face; the enjoyment of his love.[10] *He findeth righteousness*—a retributive blessing from a God of grace.[11] *He findeth honor.* For "if any man serve me"—saith our Divine Master—"him will my Father honor." "To them, that by patient continuance in well-doing, seek for glory, and *honor* and immortality, he will render eternal life."[12] Then—to depart in the joy of conscious acceptance—"I have finished my course. Henceforth there is laid up for me a crown of righteousness."[13]

Such is godliness, with its faithful and precious promises for both worlds![14] Are they not worth *following after*? Yet where—Christian professor—do we see this strenuous sustained effort—this plying to the real work of the daily cross—this making a business of religion? We look for the picture of men on the stretch;—all energy—all pursuit; nothing diverting from the object; pressing all their might with constant urgency in the momentous service. This high standard of perseverance will only just bring us to the goal.[15] The half-hearted—temporary professor—the creature of

[1] Phil. iii. 12—14. [2] Ps. xv. Isa. xxxiii. 15—17; xxxv. 8.
[3] 1 Pet. i. 15. [4] 1 Cor. x. 31. Col. iii. 17. Comp. Zech. xiv. 20.
[5] Tit. ii. 11, 12. [6] See Psalm lxiii. 8.
[7] 'The will is in love with those chains, which draw us to God. And as no man will complain, that his temples are restrained, and his head is prisoner, when it is encircled with a crown; so, when "the Son of God hath made us free," and hath only subjected us to the service and dominion of the Spirit, we are free as princes within the circle of their diadem; and our chains are bracelets, and the law is a law of liberty, and "God's service is perfect freedom;" and the more we are subjects the more we "reign as kings;" and the further we run the easier is our burden; and Christ's yoke is like feathers to a bird, not loads, but helps to motion; without them the body falls.' Bp. Taylor.
[8] Ps. xix. 11. Isa. xxxii. 17. [9] Chap. viii. 35; xii. 28; xxii. 4.
[10] Chap. xv. 9. Isa. lx.v. 5. John xiv. 21—23.
[11] Matt. x. 41, 42. Luke vi. 38. Heb. vi. 10. [12] John xii. 26. Rom. ii. 7—10.
[13] 2 Tim. iv. 7, 8. [14] 1 Tim. iv. 8. Comp. Ecclus. iv. 11—14; xxxiv. 16, 17.
[15] 1 Peter iv. 18.

impulse—instead of the child of faith—though for a while he may "run well," will utterly fall short.

22. *A wise man scaleth the city of the mighty, and casteth down the strength of the confidence thereof.*

The art of war has always shown the pre-eminence of wisdom above strength.[1] Prudent tactics, or a wise application of courage, triumphs above mere personal prowess. Joshua's stratagem in taking of Ai was a proof of military *wisdom.*[2] Solomon seems to have known of a *wise man* singly delivering his city from the power of a mighty king; a proof of *wisdom* quite tantamount to the strength of an aggressor *scaling the walls*, and thus *casting down its confidence.*[3] Much more therefore will spiritual *wisdom*—the immediate gift of God, overcome difficulties as formidable, as *the scaling of the city of the mighty. A wise* calculation of the cost is eminently serviceable in achieving most important triumph.[4] For does not conscious weakness lead to a single dependence upon God? And what difficulties are too great for an Almighty arm? "By thee"—said a valiant soldier in the army—"I have run through a troop; and by my God have I leaped over a wall."[5] "Weapons of a spiritual, not of a carnal," temper, "are mighty through God to the pulling down of strongholds,"[6] impregnable to the power of man. All the promises are "to him that overcometh."[7] Let the soldier go to the conflict "strong in the Lord," and "putting on his whole armour"[8]—the triumph is sure. The heavenly *city will be scaled.* "The kingdom of heaven suffereth violence, and the violent take it by force."[9]

23. *Whoso keepeth his mouth and his tongue keepeth his soul from troubles.*

How frequently does the wise man remind us of the responsibility connected with the use "of the little member!"[10] Yet as the test of a sound or unsound religion, can we have it too often before our eyes?[11] How large a portion of this world's ceaseless *troubles* may be traced to this prolific source! It is the unbridled horse, that brings his rider into fearful jeopardy.[12] *The mouth* has been opened rashly. *The tongue* has flowed unguardedly; and "behold how great a matter a little fire kindleth!"[13] Our neighbor

[1] Chap. xxiv. 5, 6. Eccl. vii. 19. [2] Jos. viii. 3—22.
[3] Eccl. ix. 13—18. [4] Luke xiv. 31, 32.
[5] Ps. xviii. 29. Comp. Ps. cxliv. 1. [6] 2 Cor. x. 4.
[7] Rev. ii. 7, and to all the Apocalyptic churches. [8] Eph. vi. 10—12.
[9] Matt. xi. 12.
[10] Chap. x. 14; xii. 13; xiii. 3; xiv. 3; xvii. 20; xviii. 6, 7, 21.
[11] James i. 26. [12] Ib. iii. 2, 3, 5.
[13] Ib. ver. 5. 'The tongue'—says Bp. Taylor, in his bold imagery—'is a fountain both of bitter water and of sweet. It sends forth blessing and cursing. It is sometimes "set on fire," and then it puts whole cities into combustion. It is unruly, and no more to be restrained than the breath of a tempest. It is volatile and fugitive. Reason should go before it; and when it does not, repentance comes after it. It was intended for an organ of Divine praises. But the Devil often plays on it, and then it sounds like the screech-owl, or the groans of death. Sorrow and shame, folly and repentance, are the notes and forcible accents of this discord.' Sermon on the Good and Evil Tongue.

has been injured; God has been dishonored; and bitter *trouble of soul* has been the fruit.

What then is our preventive from this imminent temptation? Cultivate a deep and watchful sensibility. Walk closely with God. Cherish the tender spirit of his constraining obligations. Keep *the tongue* for his service; asking for his grace at once to restrain and employ it.[1] Thus consecrated to God, it becomes "the glory of man;"[2] not only *keeping him from trouble*, but elevating him to fellowship in the ceaseless praises of the heavenly world.

24. *Proud and haughty scorner is his name, who dealeth in proud wrath.*

And who gave him this *name?* Even he, who "will destroy the tongue that speaketh proud things; who have said, "With our tongue will we prevail; our lips are our own: who is Lord over us?"[3] See how God loads him with disgrace. Man's rebukes may be "the curse causeless, that will not come."[4] But God's stamp is indelible. *Proud and haughty scorner!* Such is *his name.* He may pride himself upon his *scorning.* But contrast him with the man, to whom God looks—him that "is poor, and of a contrite spirit, and that trembleth at my word."[5]

Look at this vivid picture in Pharaoh—that *haughty scorner* bursting out in his *proud wrath*—"Who is the Lord, that I should obey his voice?"[6]—in Sennacherib—"reproaching and blaspheming the Holy One of Israel."[7] Haman meets with an affront. His *proud wrath* kindles. He cares neither for God, nor man. The ruin of his single enemy will not suffice. He must glut himself with the blood of a whole unoffending nation.[8]

Scorner is his name. Not an empty *name.* Never let us separate *the name* which God hath given, from the doom which he hath denounced. "The day of the Lord of Hosts shall be upon every one that is *proud* and lofty, and upon every one that is lifted up; and he shall be brought low. Behold! the day cometh, that shall burn as an oven; and *all the proud* shall be as stubble; and the day that cometh shall burn them up, saith the Lord of Hosts, that it shall leave them neither root nor branch."[9] Now we call *the proud* happy. "But how shall they abide the day of his coming?"[10] Oh! with such a manifestation of the mind of God—never think lightly of *a proud* thought, or a *scornful* feeling or expression.

It may be, that this hateful abomination[11] is indulged in God's own children. Yet he will not wink at this sin, nor spare his rod. The glory of their name shall be darkened. His frown shall be made visible. If "Asa's heart was" in the main "perfect with God all his days," yet for the sin of *haughtiness and proud wrath*, his

[1] Ps. cxli. 3; li. 15. [2] Ib. lvii. 8. [3] Ib. xii. 3, 4. [4] Chap. xxvi. 2. [5] Isa. lxvi. 2. [6] Ex. v. 2.
[7] 2 Kings xviii. 35; xix. 21, 22, 28. Comp. Chap. iii. 34. [8] Est. iii. 5, 6; v. 9.
[9] Isa. ii. 12. Mal. iv. 1. [10] Mal. iii. 15, with 2.
[11] Chap. vi. 16, 17; viii. 13; xvi. 5. Comp. Ecclus. x. 12, 13.

sun went down in a cloud.[1] "Even our God is a consuming fire."[2]

25. *The desire of the slothful killeth him: for his hands refuse to labor.* 26. *He coveteth greedily all the day long: but the righteous giveth and spareth not.*

Often have the shame and wretchedness of *sloth* been before us. Here is the finishing stroke. *The desire of the slothful killeth him.* It leads to no effort, therefore to no fruit. "Hope deferred maketh the heart sick;"[3] and perpetual vexation frets him to death.[4] 'What he longs for, he does not set his hand to purchase. But he would rather sit still and starve.'[5] He thinks to live by wishing, not by working.[6] Some faint *desires* he may have to work. But the effort to "take his hand out of his bosom"[7] is too great. *His hands* therefore—as if they were given him only to be folded—*refuse to labor.* There is no want of physical power and activity. He could spend his whole time in 'busy idleness.'[8] But for useful *labor* he has no heart. Meanwhile, with all his inactivity, he is a prey *all day long* to a *greedy covetousness;* tantalized with insatiable desires; while the hope of enjoyment, though not out of sight, yet, from want of exertion, is out of reach. Thus he dies with his desires in his mouth; envying those, whose industrious diligence enables them to *give, and spare not.*[9]

Such is the temporal evil of sloth; one of the many forms of moral selfishness, that paralyze alike our energy and our comfort. But far more ruinous is it in the higher and deeper concern. The stamp of death is broad and palpable upon the heartless professor.[10] We ask—What is his religion? He hopes he has *a desire;* and he has often heard, that 'the desire of grace is grace.' Now this is true—*if the desire be predominant.* Faith as it may be in its first dawn, it "is the day of small things, not to be despised."[11] It is "the smoking flax," which the Saviour "will not quench,"[12] but kindle into a flame. But if it is always a *desire*, and no more, habitually overcome by a contrary inclination; instead of grace, it is a delusion—a mere sentimental excitement, to lull the conscience asleep. 'How can an object, which standeth in a fixed distance from the nature which it should perfect, be procured by idle and standing affections? Those affections must have life in them, which would bring life after them. Dead desires are deadly desires.'[13] Take care then of the sluggard's prayer. His *desires*, instead of carrying life in them, are cold things, that strike death into the soul. Earnest seeking is the test of godly desire.[14] No quarter will be left unexplored, where we might find our God;[15] no means of grace unimproved, where we might enjoy his presence.[16]

[1] 1 Kings xv. 14., 2 Chron. xvi. 10—13. [2] Heb. xii. 28, 29. [3] Chap. xiii. 12.
[4] Virtutem exoptant, contabescuntque relictâ. Persius. [5] Bp. Hall.
[6] Chap. xii. 27; xiii. 4; xx. 4. Jam. iv. 2. [7] Chap. xix. 24.
[8] 1 Tim. v. 13. [9] Ps. xxxvii. 26; cxii. 9. Eph. iv. 28. [10] Rev. iii. 1.
[11] Zech. iv. 10. [12] Matt. xii. 20.
[13] Bp. Reynolds's Treatise on the Passions, chap. xviii.
[14] Ps. xxvii. 4. Isa. xxvi. 8, 9. Comp. Ps. xxiv. 6. [15] Job xxiii. 3, 8, 9.
[16] Isa. lxiv. 5.

Some will call this active energy legal. But our Lord's command to "labor"[1] proves that it is scriptural. Whoever does not strive to come near to the standard, has never really apprehended it. Whoever *desires* only, and *refuses to labor* to be a growing Christian daily, gives doubtful evidence, whether he be a Christian at all. Not that the power is in ourselves. But when did God ever fail to help the sinner's endeavor? "That thou givest, we gather."[2] Prayer and diligence, dependence and energy, harmonize in the Bible; however they may be discordant in the crude systems of man's devising. Divine agency is given, not to excuse the neglect of human means, but to encourage their improvement.[3]

What then want we for active service, but the continued exercise of faith? This gave power at first; this alone sustains the power. There is no moment, when the Lord is not giving; when he has not bound himself to give by infinite, most loving obligations. Deliberately devote yourselves. Put the resolution into practical form, habit, and place. Make all sacrifices for it. Seize all opportunities for making it good. Our work will be our recompense; our labor our wages. And while the slothful man only *covets* for himself, *the righteous*, in the flowing of the willing heart lives for the Church. He has to *give, and he spares not*—"a blessing in the midst of the land."[4]

27. *The sacrifice of the wicked is abomination; how much more, when he bringeth it with a wicked mind?* (in wickedness, Marg.)

This is the repetition of a former proverb[5] with additional intensity. At no time—under no circumstances—can *the sacrifice of the wicked* be acceptable. All the true requisites of holy worship are wanting. *There is no heart.* The service is therefore only formality or hypocrisy.[6] *There is no way of access*[7]—no "altar to sanctify the gift."[8] Therefore it is presumption, self-righteousness, will-worship.[9] *There is no "faith,* without which is is impossible to please God."[10] The material act—considered in itself—may be good; but the corrupt principle makes *the sacrifice an abomination.*[11]

How much more—the sin is double—*when he bringeth it with*

[1] John vi. 27. Comp. Luke xiii. 24. [2] Ps. civ. 28. [3] Phil. ii. 12, 13.

[4] The following exhortations are well worth our pondering—'Our heart being naturally at a distance from God, it is not a *single* step, that will bring us near to him. Neither will a few minutes of cold prayer suffice to support our souls.—Let us beware of indolence. Many are the hours and days we lose on our road to heaven. These days will soon amount to years; and we shall be too late at last for the marriage supper. We should willingly exert ourselves to climb a mountain for the sake of a fine view, or a pure air. Let us then use all our strength to climb the mountain of Zion, where we shall breathe a truly vivifying atmosphere, and from whose heights we shall behold the true Eden, the valley of peace, through which flow living waters, and where the tree of life flourishes. May the Lord bestow upon us all the necessary will and energy!' Letters and Biography of Felix Neff—a most interesting supplement to Dr. Gilly's 'Memorial' of a short Life filled up with usefulness, and crowned with glory.

[5] Chap. xv. 8. [6] Matt. xv. 7—9. [7] John xiv. 6. [8] Heb. xiii. 10. Matt. xxiii. 19. [9] Gen. iv. 3—5. [10] Heb. xi. 6. [11] Comp. Mal. i. 7, 8.

a wicked mind!—as when Balaam *brought his sacrifice*, that he might curse Israel;[1] Saul, in wayward disobedience.[2] Absalom and Jezebel, to cover their treachery;[3] the adultress, as a lulling to her unwary prey;[4] the Pharisees, as a handle to their covetousness;[5] Antinomian professors, for the indulgence of their lusts![6] What *an abomination* must this service be before him, who is "of purer eyes than to behold evil, and cannot look on iniquity!"[7]

And yet *apparent* acceptance is sometimes granted to *the sacrifice of the wicked.* God, as the moral governor of the world, externally rewards actions externally good.[8] But never does he fail to punish the evil principle in those very actions, which are the subjects of his reward. Our Lord's love of the amiable victim of self delusion, was the compassion of his humanity, not Divine complacency; and fully consistent with holy abhorrence of his proud rejection of the gospel.[9]

What then are *the wicked* to do, rejected as they are under the most favorable circumstances? Shall they lie down in despondency, or harden themselves in rebellion?[10] Or shall they wait for better dispositions, and prepare themselves for the gospel? The door of prayer is their only refuge.[11] *That* door opens the gospel to them with a free warrant of faith, abundant encouragement, and sure acceptance.[12]

28. *A false witness* (witness of lies, Marg.) *shall perish: but the man that heareth speaketh constantly.*

The last clause of the proverb seems to fix and restrict the first. *A false witness* often becomes so by the culpable habit of thoughtlessly repeating, without examination or certain knowledge. A man may thus do very serious injury to his neighbor's character or property. It proves a very loose conscience, and an utter want of that "charity, which covers," instead of exposing, faults.[13] It is rejoicing in iniquity, rather than "rejoicing in truth."[14] This *false witness* will certainly be punished by God;[15] and even 'by man he will be confounded and silenced. No one for the future will regard or credit his testimony.'[16] *But the man that heareth*—the true witness—that speaketh only what *he heareth*, and is fully acquainted with—*he speaketh constantly*—to conviction. He holds to his testimony—never contradicts himself. His word, even if it had been slighted at first, gains more and more credit and authority when *the false witness shall have perished.*[17]

Thus "the faithful and true witness" declared for himself and his servants—"We speak that we do know, and testify that we have seen."[18] The apostles, to give this solid weight to their testi-

[1] Num. xxiii. 1—3, 13. [2] 1 Sam. xiii. 8—15; xv. 21—23. [3] 2 Sam. xv. 7—13. 1 Kings xxi. 9—12. Comp. Isa. i. 13—16. [4] Chap. vii. 14, 15. [5] Matt. xxiii. 14. [6] Jam. iv. 3. [7] Hab. i. 13. [8] 1 Kings xxi. 27—29. 2 Kings x. 29—31. [9] Mark x. 17—21. [10] Jer. ii. 25; vii. 10. [11] Acts viii. 22. [12] Isa. i. 16—18; lv. 6, 7. [13] Chap. x. 12. [14] Contrast 1 Cor. xiii. 6, 7. [15] Chap. xix. 5, 9. [16] Poole in loco. [17] Chap. xii. 19. [18] Rev. iii. 14. John iii. 11.

mony, would fill up the vacancy in their body only from among those, "who had companied with them all the time that the Lord Jesus went in and out among them;"[1] as if those only, who *had heard, would speak constantly.* They claimed authority to their commission, as having *heard* from the mouth of God, and therefore being assured of its Divine warrant.[2] And indeed this constitutes the main power of testimony. A feeble and hesitating tone is spiritless and ineffective.[3] A decided accredited presentment of truth—*speaking constantly*—commands conviction. "We believe and therefore we speak."[4]

29. *A wicked man hardeneth his face: but as for the upright, he directeth his way.*

A hardened face—without shame or blush for sin—is a fearful manifestation of a hardened heart. Cain standing bold in the presence of his God, with his hands reeking with his brother's blood;[5] Gehazi with his fearless lie;[6] the Traitor, bearing to be pointed out by his Master, without visible emotion,[7] then afterwards with unblushing effrontery kissing his sacred cheeks[8]—how *hardened* must have been *their faces* in determined *wickedness*! The adulteress also, clothing her seductive witcheries with an impudent face, stands out before us.[9] Sometimes *the wicked man*, bent upon his way, *hardens his face* against the most distinct warnings and intimations of the will of God. Nothing would hinder Balaam from his own "perverse way." He even anticipated the conditional permission of his God, lest it should ultimately stand in his way.[10] Ahab determinately *hardened his face* against the clear forbidding will of God.[11] Jehoiakim, before his whole council, set his God at defiance.[12] His people "ran" with the bravery of madmen "upon the thick bosses of his buckler."[13] And does not sin stand out before us with a brazen face?[14] The drunkard reels at noon-day. The swearer pours out his wickedness in the open crowd. The sensualist "glories in his shame."[15] Truly this is the spirit of Satan. How near to hell! How awful is the plain stamp of the seal of wrath![16]

Cheering is it to contrast the tender spirit of the child of God. This is rest indeed—to put ourselves under the Lord's hands, fearful of taking one step alone; carefully ordering our steps, lest by inadvertence, much more by wilfulness, they should bring shame upon *his face.*[17] Godly simplicity greatly clears the eye of the soul. Where the heart is set in the duty, there will be seldom any great difficulty in discovering the path.[18] Secret heavenly direction is engaged.[19] An unfixed, unresolved mind gives great

[1] Acts i. 21, 22.
[2] 1 Cor. xi. 23; xv. 3, 4. 2 Pet. i. 16—18. 1 John i. 1—3.
[3] Comp. 2 Cor. i. 17. [4] Ib. iv. 13. [5] Gen. iv. 8, 9.
[6] 2 Kings v. 25. [7] John xiii. 21—30. [8] Matt. xxvi. 47—49.
[9] Chap. vii. 10—13. [10] Num. xxii. 20—22, 32.
[11] 1 Kings xxii. 3—6, 18—29. [12] Jer. xxxvi. 23, 24.
[13] Ib. xliv. 16, 17, with Job xv. 25, 26. [14] Isa. iii. 9. Jer. iii. 3; vi. 15.
[15] Phil. iii. 19. [16] Rom. ii. 5. [17] Ps. cxix. 5, 6, 80. [18] Matt. vi. 22. [19] Chap. iii. 6.

advantage to the enemy's assault. Here lies the contrast—*the wicked man hardens his face* against God's ordinances. The godly *directs his way* by it; not waiting in indolent passivity for miraculous leading, but improving ordinary means for the light upon every step. Temporals as well as spirituals; trifles as well as important matters, are brought under the eye of our gracious God. Child-like confidence brings sunshine and acceptance.

30. *There is no wisdom, nor understanding, nor counsel against the Lord.* 31. *The horse is prepared against the day of battle: but safety* (victory, Marg.) *is of the Lord.*

This proverb is not true in the strict letter. All the *wisdom* and policy of earth and hell are in active operation. But all is in vain *against the Lord.* The history of the Church abundantly proves this. 'The decrees and counsels of God are firm as adamant—immoveable, notwithstanding all human machinations; no more to be stayed than the course of the sun.'[1] *Wisdom and understanding*—the best-contrived *counsel*—when *against the Lord*—come to foolishness.[2] "He taketh the wise"—not in their ignorance, but "in their craftiness;"[3] not when their *wisdom* was fading, but when it was at the utmost zenith. Ahithophel's *counsel* was befooled at the time, when "it was as if a man had inquired at the oracle of God."[4] Pharaoh's *counsel* to depress the chosen nation issued in their increase.[5] His murderous decree, as a link in the chain of Providence, nurtured the Leader and Lawgiver of the people.[6] Balak's desire to curse Israel was overruled for blessing.[7] The wise man vainly set up in his darker days his own *wisdom* against the declared purpose of God.[8] Ahab's project to ward off the threatened stroke against his life;[9] his determination to avert the extinction of his family;[10] Athaliah's deep-laid plot to exterminate the family of David,[11] and so to frustrate the Divine promise; the enmity against the builders of the temple[12]—all this diversified mass of *wisdom, and counsel, and understanding against the Lord*—what was it?—a thing of nought.[13] 'They all signify nothing, if they oppose the counsels and decrees of heaven.'[14]

Mark the history of our Lord. It would seem, as if nothing could have hindered the success of Herod's *wisdom and counsel* against his infancy.[15] What a combination of *wisdom* from all quarters vainly strove to "entangle him in his talk!"[16] How near to failure were the prophecies connected with his death, burial, and resurrection! Stoning was the sentence for the charge laid

[1] Lavater in loco. [2] Ps. xxxiii. 10, 11.
[3] Job v. 13. 1 Cor. iii. 19. [4] 2 Sam. xvi. 23; xvii. 7, 14, 23, with xv. 31.
[5] Ex. i. 8—12. [6] Ib. verses 15—22, with ii. 1—10. [7] Num. xxiv. 10.
[8] 1 Kings xi. 11, 40. [9] Ib. xxii. 30—34.
[10] Ib. xxi. 21. 2 Kings x. 1—7. [11] 2 Kings xi. 2. [12] Neh. vi.
[13] Isa. viii. 11; xiv. 27; xlvi. 10. [14] Bishop Patrick. [15] Matt. ii. 8, 16.
[16] Matt. xxii. 15—46

against him.[1] His burial was appointed among the wicked.[2] His resurrection—so far as man could do—was effectually prevented.[3] But God had ordained crucifixion for his death,[4] his burial among the rich,[5] his resurrection as the confusion of all their counsel.[6] The event proved, that there *was no wisdom, nor understanding, nor counsel against the Lord.* 'God's desire is fulfilled by those, who have the least mind to it. All man's wisdom, while it strives for masteries, is overmatched.'[7]

Let us look at that kingdom of Providence—so finely represented by "the wheels full of eyes round about them."[8] To deny an absolute superintending control, is to 'place an idle sceptre in the hands of Him, who governs the universe.'[9] How many movements baffle alike previous calculation and subsequent inquiry! effects for which no adequate cause is producible; anomalies manifestly intended to remove our eyes from second causes to the First Great Spring of agency, moving above all, and in despite of all opposition. The raging Dioclesian struck his medal—'Christianity is extinguished.' The Great Author brings out from the very fire the palpable proof, that 'the blood of the martyrs is the seed of the church.' 'Oh! the folly and blindness of men, that think to carry all to their minds, and walk as masters of their own designs, and never have any serious thought of him, in whose hands both they, and all their business, and all the affairs of states and kingdoms of this world, are as a piece of wax, to frame them to what he pleases!'[10] And do not some of us remember with shame our "striving with our Maker"[11]—how long we endeavored to defeat his purposes of love—until at length we were brought to cast our weapons at his feet, and to acknowledge that *there is no wisdom, nor understanding, nor counsel against the Lord?*

But—putting away rebellion—beware of vain confidence, scarcely less displeasing to the Lord. *The horse* was a forbidden confidence in *the day of battle.*[12] The most glorious days of victory were, when that veto was regarded.[13] Declension commenced from the transgression of the law; defeat from the very quarter of confidence.[14] The after-renunciation of this confidence was a time of gracious acceptance.[15] *The horse* indeed may be legitimately employed as a means of defence. But never let the material of war fare be our confidence. Use the means, but idolize them not. They that "trust in them fall." Those—that remember that *safety is of the Lord*—"are risen, and stand upright."[16] "*The*

[1] Lev. xxiv. 16 [2] Isa. liii. 9. [3] Matt. xxvii. 62—66. [4] Gal. iii. 13. [5] Isa. liii. 9. Bp. Lowth. Comp. Matt. xxvii. 57—60. [6] Matt. xxviii. 1—15. [7] Trapp. Comp. Acts ii. 23, 24; iv. 27, 28. [8] Ez. i. 18.

[9] Abp. Magee's interesting Sermon on this text. Works, ii. 354. Comp. Job. xii. 21 22. Isa. xliv. 25.

[10] Leighton's Sermon on Jer. x. 23, 24. [11] Isa. xlv. 9. [12] Deut. xvii. 16. [13] Jos. xi. 6, 9. Jud. iv. 3—15. 2 Sam. viii. 4. [14] 1 Kings x. 26—28. 2 Chron xii. 8, 9. Comp. Isa. xxxi. 1—3. [15] Hos. xiv. 3, 4. [16] Ps. xx. 7, 8.

horse is a vain thing for *safety*."[1] "The remembrance of the name of the Lord" was mightier to the young warrior than the strength of the giant.[2] Much more—in the spiritual warfare—let us have the *active* exercise of dependence. "Salvation is of the Lord"[3]—free—complete—everlasting—triumphant victory over all the powers of hell.

CHAPTER XXII.

1. *A good name*[4] *is rather to be chosen than great riches, and loving favor rather than silver and gold.*

But what is this *good name*, here commended as a precious jewel? Not the *name*, which the Babel-builders would "make to themselves."[4] Not as Absalom, who reared a pillar to "keep his *name* in remembrance," or rather to commemorate his shame.[5] It is not the popular voice. So different is God's standard from man's, that to have "all men speak well of us," would be *a bad name!*[6] So apt are men to "put darkness for light; and light for darkness,"[5] that the reputation too often serves in the place of the reality, the false glare for the genuine principle, the shadow for the substance, the tinsel for the gold. The *good name* is gained by godly consistency.[8] The possessor is either unconscious of the gift, or humbled with the conviction, that it is wholly undeserved. The *loving favor* connected with it is often seen in early childhood.[10] It was the heavenly seal upon the Pentecostal Christians.[11] And every servant of God values it as a trust and talent for his Master's service and glory.[12]

Such is its value, that it *is rather to be chosen than great riches,—than silver and gold.*[13] A bye-word may be attached to *riches*.[14] Add to which—"They fly away upon eagles' wings."[15] But *the good name* "will be in everlasting remembrance."[16] And even now it brings confidence and respect.[17] It largely adds to useful-

[1] Ib. xxxiii. 17. Job xxxix. 19.
[2] 1 Sam. xvii. 45.
[3] Ps. iii. 8; xxxvii. 39, 40; lxviii. 20. Jon. ii. 9.
[4] A name—meaning a good name. See page 253, note 14.
[5] Gen. xi. 14.
[6] 2 Sam. xviii. 18.
[7] Luke vi. 26; xvi. 15.
[8] Isa. v. 20.
[9] Heathen intelligence seemed to have some glimpse of this medium. Agesilaus—being asked how a good name was to be obtained—replied—'By speaking the best, and doing the most upright, things.' Socrates to the same question answered—'By studying really to be what you wish to be accounted.'
[10] 1 Sam. ii. 26. Luke ii. 52.
[11] Acts ii. 47.
[12] Neh. vi. 10, 11. Phil. ii. 15, 16; iv. 8, 9.
[13] Comp. Ecclus. xli. 12.
[14] 1 Sam. xxv. 3, 17, 25.
[15] Chap. xxiii. 5, with Ps. cxii. 6. Comp. Ecclus. xli. 13; xliv. 13, 14; xlix. 1.
[16] Luke vii. 4, 5. Acts ix. 36—39.
[17] Gen. xxxix. 4—21; xli. 37. Est. ii. 9, 15, 17. Dan. ii. 48, 49; vi. 1—3.

ness; gives authority to reproof, counsel, and example; so that—if the world cannot love, neither can they despise. Hence the Christian obligation to be "blameless, as well as harmless, to shine as lights in the world."[1] Hence the honor of "having a good report of all men, and of the truth itself."[2] Hence the qualification for efficiency in the sacred office—"blameless—having a good report of them which are without."[3] But how often do the "dead flies" spoil "the precious ointment!"[4] Satan, when he cannot hinder the instruments, will blemish them, to give currency to error, to stumble the ungodly and unstable.[5]

This ornament is too often indiscreetly underrated. 'So long as my conscience is clear, I care not what the world think or say of me. Other consciences are not my judges.' Now in resisting the efforts of the world to turn us aside from the path of duty, 'we may seasonably comfort ourselves in our own innocency, fly for refuge against the injuries of tongues into our own consciences, as into a castle, there repose ourselves in security, disregarding the reproaches of evil men.'[6] But it should be our great care to stop the mouths of gainsayers; and while we count it "a very small matter to be judged of man's judgment," most anxiously to "provide things honest, not only in the sight of the Lord, but also in the sight of men."[7]

Yet precious as this blessing is, take care it be not purchased at the expence of conscience. Far better that others should blot our name, than that we should wound our consciences. 'Two things there are, saith St. Augustine, whereof every man should be specially chary and tender—his conscience and his credit. But that of his conscience must be his first care; this of his name and credit must be content to come in the second place. Let him first be sure to guard his conscience well; and then may he have a due regard of his name also. Let it be his first care to secure all within, by making his peace with God and in his own breast. That done—but not before—let him look abroad, if he will, and cast about as well as he can, to strengthen his reputation with and before the world.'[8]

But that God should register *a good name* in the annals of the church[9]—"in the book of remembrance[10]— in the book of life"[11]—Oh! is not this infinitely above all this world's glory?[12] And how gladly will he own these jewels at the day of his appearing![13] How sure and glorious is his promise to his faithful servant—"I will not blot out his name out of the book of life; but I will confess his name before my Father and before his angels!"[14]

[1] Phil. ii. 15. [2] 3 John 12. Comp. Acts xvi. 2. 2 Cor viii. 18.
[3] 1 Tim. iii. 2, 7; iv. 16. [4] Eccl. vii. 1; x. 1. [5] 2 Sam xii. 14.
[6] Bp. Sanderson's Sermon on Eccl. vii. 1, § 30.
[7] 1 Cor. iv. 3, with 2 Cor. viii. 21. Comp. 1 Cor. ix. 15. 2 Cor. xi. 12. 1 Pet. ii. 12.
[8] Bp. Sanderson, ut supra, § 23. [9] Matt. xxvi. 6—13. [10] Mal. iii. 16.
[11] Phil. iv. 3. [12] Luke x. 20. [13] Mal. iii. 17.
[14] Rev. iii. 5.

2. *The rich and the poor meet together: the Lord is the maker of them all.*

There is great diversity in the several stations and circumstances of mankind. Yet the difference is mainly superficial; the equality in all important matters manifest. *The rich and the poor*—apparently so remote from each other—*meet together*. All have the same birth.[1] All enter the world naked,[2] helpless, unconscious beings; all stand in the same natural relation to their God; dependent on him for their birth;[3] the children of his Providence;[4] the creatures of his moral government.[5] All are subject to the same sorrows, sicknesses, infirmities, and temptations.[6] "All go to one place."[7] All—"small as well as great—shall stand before God."[8]

We *meet together* on the same level as sinners. All are tainted with the same original corruption.[9] "All, like sheep, have" personally "gone astray."[10] All need alike the same new-birth to give them life, the same precious blood to cleanse them, the same robe of righteousness to cover them.[11] It is in fact a common need,[12] a common salvation.[13] In all these matters *the rich and the poor* are as one—"God is no respecter of persons."[14] The difference appears only as the outward garment.[15] Yet what a distance it makes! The one scarcely hears or knows the other!

And when redeemed into the family of God, is not every member of the family our brother?[16] Here then—*rich and poor*—we meet on equal standing at the same throne of grace—in the same soul and body—at the same holy table.[17] We communicate to each other the same blessed hopes, feel the same sympathies, anticipate the same home.

Nor is this a constitution of accident, or of mechanical arrangement. *The Lord is the maker of them all.* Not only does he make us as men; but he *makes us rich and poor*.[18] Adored be that infinite wisdom, that has knit *the rich and the poor* together so closely in mutual dependence, that neither can live without the other;[19] neither can say to the other, "I have no need of thee."[20]

Yet this Christian equality before God does not annihilate the gradation of rank before men. "The servants under the yoke must not despise their believing masters, because they are brethren; but rather do them service, because they are faithful and beloved."[21]

[1] Job xxxi. 15. Mal. ii. 10. Acts xvii. 26. [2] Job i. 21. Ecc. v. 15.
[3] Job. xii. 10. Acts xvii. 25, 28. [4] Psalm cxlv. 9, 15, 16.
[5] Dan. iv. 35. [6] Heb. xiii. 3.
[7] Job iii. 19. Ps. lxxxix. 48. Eccl. ii. 16; iii. 20; vi. 6; ix. 11. Heb. ix. 27.
[8] Rev. xx. 12. [9] Gen. v. 3. Job xxv. 4. Ps. li. 5. [10] Isa. liii. 6.
[11] Rom. iii. 21, 22.
[12] In the ordinance of redemption all were to give alike, as an acknowledgment of equal need. Ex. xxx. 15.
[13] Jude 3. [14] Acts x. 34. Job xxxiv. 19. [15] Luke xvi. 19, 20.
[16] Gal. iii. 28. Col. iii. 11. This is implied in the rebuke, Jam. ii. 2—5.
[17] 1 Cor. x. 17; xii. 13. [18] 1 Sam. ii. 7. [19] Eccl. v. 9.
[20] 1 Cor. xii. 21. [21] 1 Tim. vi. 1, 2.

Could men continue in equality of rank, for a single day? Difference of mind and talents, industry, self-denial, providences, would shake the balance before the morning was gone. God never meant to level the world, any more than the surface of the earth. The distinction of *rich and poor* still remains in his appointment, and all attempts to sink it must end in confusion. To each of us are committed our several talents, duties, and responsibilities both to God and man. Let each of us therefore be given to our own work, and "abide in our calling with God."[1] "Let the brother of low degree rejoice, in that he is exalted; but the rich, in that he is made low."[2] Soon shall we all be one family in our Father's house—to "go out no more."[3]

3. *A prudent man foreseeth the evil, and hideth himself: but the simple pass on, and are punished.*[4]

God has not given to us the knowledge of futurity. This would only have encouraged presumption. But he has given us *prudence*, naturally *foreseeing evil*, and forecasting the most effectual means of deliverance. David was thus directed to *hide himself* from Saul;[5] Elijah from Jezebel.[6] The disciples were taught to *flee* from impending *evil.*[7] Paul repeatedly *hid himself* from threatened destruction.[8] Even our Divine Master acted on this rule of *prudence,*[9] till his hour was come.[10]

But to apply this rule to spiritual *evils foreseen*—"Noah, moved with fear, prepared an ark for the saving of his house."[11] Josiah endeavored to ward off the threatened judgment by humiliation before God.[12] Paul "labored" for the covering of present acceptance; *foreseeing* the tremendous *evil* of "appearing" unsheltered "before the judgment-seat of Christ."[13]

Not that *the prudent man* is gifted with supernatural knowledge. He only uses the discernment which God hath given him. He regards the signs of the times. He studies the word of God in reference to coming judgment; and he acts accordingly. To walk carelessly in the midst of evil is reckless folly. We cannot "stand by faith" only, but "by faith" balanced with fear;[14] yet not the fear of bondage and scrupulosity, but of care, watchfulness, and diligence.[15] In such a path as ours—guilty, wandering, tempted, afflicted, dying, does not common—at least does not Christian—*prudence,* show us our need of an *hiding-place?* Except we seek one in time, we are lost for eternity. Did we but realize the huge mass of guilt lying upon us, and the infinite wrath that for that guilt hangs over us, could we rest in an unsheltered state? Should not we tread upon all that lies in our way to run to shelter?

[1] 1 Cor. vii. 24.
[2] James i. 9, 10. [3] Rev. iii. 12. [4] Chap. xxvii. 12.
[5] 1 Sam. xx. 19; xxiii. 19—21; xxvi. 1. [6] 1 Kings xvii. 3; xix. 3.
[7] Matt. x. 23; xxiv. 15—18. [8] Acts ix. 23—25; xvii. 14; xxiii. 17.
[9] Mark iii. 6, 7. Luke iv. 29, 30. John viii. 59; x. 39. [10] Matt. xxvi. 47—57.
[11] Heb. xi. 7. [12] 2 Chron. xxxiv. 21, 26—28. [13] 2 Cor. v. 9, 10.
[14] Rom. xi. 20. [15] Heb. iv. 1, 11.

Coming judgments there may be. But set our face towards our hiding-place. God will undertake for our dangers. Nay—does not his most loving voice, point to a shelter in himself—in his own perfections?—"Come, my people; enter thou into thy chamber, and shut thy door about thee; hide thyself, as it were for a little moment, until the indignation be overpast."[1]

Very different is the course of *the simple.*[2] Devoid of all *prudence; foreseeing no evil;* fearing none; given up to their own ways, and reckless of all consequences, *they pass on and are punished,* by their own folly.[3] Oh! many such are there, who, "when the Lord's hand is lifted up, will not see;"[4] who will not hear the distant thunder, betokening the approaching storm; who in their fancied security laugh at those, who are preparing for an evil day; laugh even on the brink of that destruction, which—unless Sovereign grace interpose—will make them wise too late.

4. *By* (the reward of, Marg.) *humility and the fear of the Lord are riches, honor, and life,* (lives, Marg.)

Who then will say—"It is vain to serve God?"[5] *Riches, honor, and life* to enjoy them—such an accumulation and completeness of happiness!—all belong to his service. But observe the two marks of his ways, *humility and the fear of the Lord. Humility* is not the mere meekness of modesty.[6] This, though a lovely temper is not a Christian grace. Nor is it the servility of the hypocrite for his own selfish ends;[7] or the temporary conviction of external humiliation.[8] We may easily distinguish the genuine principle by its accompaniment—*the fear of the Lord*—that blessed holy reverence, which none but his children feel, and which, while it represses presumption, establishes *humility.* A just apprehension of God will always lay us in the lowest dust before him. The contrasted sight of his majesty with our meanness, of his holiness with our defilement, constrains the cry from one—"Behold! I am vile; I abhor myself"[9]—from another—"Woe is me, for I am undone."[10] *Humility* is thus the truest glory. The most humble is the most triumphant Christian. Depressed indeed he may be; yet is he highly exalted. *Riches* are his—both of grace and of glory. None can deprive him of them.[11] *Honor* is his—the true fruit[12]—the gracious reward[13]—of *humility*—high and glorious; the title and present privilege of a child of God—"an heir of God, and joint-heir with Christ."[14] *Life* is his[15]—*lives*—every kind of life—not natural only, but spiritual and eternal; life with the Father and the Son, now "hid with Christ in God; and when Christ, who is

1 Isa. xxvi. 20.
2 Chap. xiv. 15, 16.
3 Chap. vii. 7, 22, 23; ix. 17, 18.
4 Isaiah xxvi. 11.
5 Mal. iii. 14.
6 1 Sam. x. 22.
7 2 Sam. xv. 5.
8 1 Kings xxi. 27.
9 Job xl. 4; xlii. 5, 6.
10 Isa. vi. 5.
11 Chap. viii. 18.
11 Chap. xv. 33; xviii. 12.
13 Luke xviii. 13 14.
14 Rom. viii. 16, 17.
15 Chap. xix. 23. Ps. xxii. 27. Comp. Ecclus. i. 11, 12, 18; ii. 8, 9; xl. 26, 27.

our life, shall appear"—then to be manifested in all its fulness of everlasting joy.[1] Shall we look then beyond the narrow limit of time, and search what is the character of the heirs of glory? "He will beautify the meek with salvation. Blessed are the poor in spirit; for theirs is the kingdom of God."[2] Thus glorious is the end of this lowly path of *humility and godly fear!*

5. *Thorns and snares are in the way of the froward: he that doth keep his soul shall be far from them.*

A forcible image to show, that nothing stands so much in a man's way, as the indulgence of his own unbridled will. The man who is most perversely bent on his purposes, is most likely to be thwarted in them. He thinks to carry all before him; whereas his *frowardness* makes *thorns and snares* for *his way*.[3] 'He is as a man on all sides encompassed with *thorns and snares*. His stubbornness brings him into infinite perplexities, out of which he can find no issue.'[4] Sarah,[5] Jacob,[6] Balaam,[7] found *the way of the froward* full of hindrance and entanglement. A special mercy is it, when *the thorns* embitter the way, and bring the *froward* sinner as an humbled child, asking and seeking the road to his father's house.[8] If there be difficulties in the ways of God, are there none in the ways of sin? A fair balance would prove, which yoke—which burden—is the more "easy and light." The stings of conscience; the rebukes of Providence; the disappointment of the cherished desires, the tyrannical power of lust—all tend to make "the way of transgressors to be hard."[9] Nay—not the world only—but even the holy Gospel, is made *a snare in the way of the froward*. Such are "the depths of Satan"[10] and his devices, that he "turns the grace of God into lasciviousness," and the occasion or excuse of sin!

Here then lies the security of a close walk with God. An humble submission to the Lord; desiring nothing so much as conformity to his will; dreading nothing so much as being left to our own waywardness—thus *keeping our soul*, we shall be *far from the thorn and snares of the froward*.[11] We shall "make straight" and safe—if not smooth—"paths for our feet," and "all our ways shall be established."[12] "He that is begotten of God *keepeth himself*, and that wicked one toucheth him not."[13]

6. *Train up*[14] *a child in the way he should go: and when he is old, he will not depart from it.*

[1] Col. iii. 3, 4. [2] Ps. cxlix. 4. Matt. v. 3.
[3] Jer. xxiii. 12, 13. Jud. ii. 2, 3. [4] Bishop Hall.
[5] Gen. xii. 10—20; xvi. 1—6; xx. 2—14. [6] Ibid. xxvii.
[7] Num. xxii. 22—32. [8] Luke xv. 12—20.
[9] Chap. xiii. 15. [10] Rev. ii. 24. 2 Cor. xi. 14.
[11] Rom. iii. 8; vi. 1. Jude 4. [12] Heb. xii. 12. Chap. iv. 26. [13] 1 John v. 18.
[14] There is a considerable difference in the translation of the original word; but all coming to the same point. All commentators stamp it as a most significant term—*Imbue*. Schultens. Geier—'gives it the first dip, dye, seasoning.' *Initia*—'Begin the first in-

The hopes of at least two generations hang upon this most important rule. How can we look on a child without thoughtful anxiety? An existence is commenced for eternity. No power of earth or hell can crush it. The whole universe does not afford an object of deeper interest. It is an "arrow in the hand of a mighty man"—a most powerful instrument of good or evil, according to the direction that is given to it.[1]

Every thing depends on his *training*. Two ways lie before him—the way in which he *would* go—headlong to ruin, and *the way in which he should go*—the pathway to heaven. The rule for *training* implies obliquity; else he would not need it. A young and healthy tree shoots straight upwards, and instead of putting forth crooked and deformed branches, gives promise of a fine and fruitful maturity.

Begin the *training of the child*, as Hannah did, with his dedication to God.[2] This done—train him as God's child—entrusted to your care, asking guidance from day to day—"How shall we order the child, and how shall we do unto him?"[3] Train him as a baptized child, in the principles of his baptismal engagements. Pray for him. Teach him to pray. Instruct him "from a child in the Holy Scriptures" as the sole rule of faith, and directory of conduct."[4] Never was this *training* so momentous. From a defect here many young persons are tossed to and fro in every vacillation of error; and the anxious attempt to set them right we find to be—'building, where there is no foundation, or rather, where there is not so much as ground to build upon.'[5] In fact, the mind —abhorring a vacuum—must have some notions. And the alternative is not between sound principles and none; but between wholesome truth and those crude or poisonous errors, which the subtle enemy is ever ready to inject, and the corrupt heart equally prepared to receive. Nor let the formation of sound practical habits, diligence, industry, and self-government be forgotten. Let *the child be trained*, as the soldier under arms, to endurance, order, and subjection.

Wisely does Solomon direct us to begin *at the mouth* or entrance *of his way*[6]—at the first opening intelligence. The more early the *training*, the more easy the work, and the more encouraging the results. It is a matter of experience, that what is early learnt,

struction—lay the groundwork—the first stone.' *Instruc.* This is substantially the margin;—catechise—like Abraham's servants—instructed (catechised, marg.) alike in the art of war and in the fear of God. Gen. xiv. 14; xviii. 19. The word elsewhere conveys the idea of dedication to the service of God. (Comp. Deut. xx. 5. 1 Kings viii. 6. 2 Chron. vii. 5; title to Ps. xxx.) In this view a judicious expositor conceives the illustration may be thus—'As a house, altar, or temple, newly built, and not yet profaned, is fitted by certain rites and sacrifices for its future use; so *a child*, as a newly-formed edifice, is fitted by a certain course for the service and the church, and his heart is made meet as an habitation of God, and the temple of the Holy Ghost.' Geier in loco.

[1] Psalm cxxvii. 4. [2] 1 Sam. i. 28. [3] Jud. xiii. 12.

[4] 2 Tim. iii. 15. Comp. the Wise Man's own Training, chap. iv. 3, 4.

[5] South's Sermon on the text, vol. v. 1.

[6] Heb. See Schultens, and the general voice of critics.

is most tenaciously retained. It stands the friction of time with the least injury. Far better, instead of waiting for the maturity of reason, to work upon the pliability of childhood.[1] The gardener begins to graft in the first rising of the sap. If the crooked shoots of self-will and disobedience are not cut off, their rapid growth and rapidly growing strength will greatly increase the future difficulty of bending them. Present neglect occasions after risk and perplexity. We may begin our work too late, but we can scarcely begin it too soon.[2] If the child be too young to teach to read, he cannot be too young to teach to obey. Never let the watchfulness to check the buddings of evil, and to cherish the first tenderness of right feeling, be relaxed. The ceaseless activity of the great enemy teaches the value of early *training.* Be beforehand with him. Pre-occupy the ground with good seed, as the most effectual exclusion of his evil tares.[3] Be *at the mouth of the way* with wholesome food, ere he has the opportunity of pouring in his "bread of deceit;" ere nature is hardened by the habits of sin—brutalized by familiarity with vice.

But this training must be practical. The mere talk to *a child* about religion, without bringing it to bear upon his loose habits, and self-willed tempers, is utterly ineffective. Here also lies the momentous weight of Christian consistency. If *the child* hears of godliness, and sees but wickedness, this is bringing him bread with one hand and poison with the other; 'beckoning him with the hand to heaven, and at the same time taking him by the hand, and leading him in the way to destruction.'[4] Who would receive even the choicest food from a leprous hand! Neglect is far better than inconsistency; forgetfulness, than contempt of principle. *A child* is influenced by the eye more than by the ear. He is ready to look out for apologies for his own faults; and their discovery in parental example will harden him in infidelity or ungodliness.

This is indeed a work of watchful anxiety, attended with painful, and often long-protracted exercise, of faith and patience. Who could hold on in it, but for the Divine support of the parental promise—*When he is old, he shall not depart from it.* The man will be, as the child is trained. Education is utterly distinct from grace. But—*when conducted in the spirit, and on the principles of the Word of God*—it is a means of imparting it. Sometimes

[1] The Heathen moralists seem well to have understood the subject. Horace—after alluding to the early discipline of the colt and the hound—applies it—

———'Nunc adbibe puro
Pectore verba, puer: nunc tu melioribus offer.
Quo semel est imbuta recens, servabit odorem
Testa diu.' Epis. I. i. ii. 64—69.

———'Adeo in teneris consuescere multum est.'
Virg. Geor. ii. 272.

'Udum et molle lutum es; nunc, nunc properandus, et acri
Fingendus sine fine rotâ.' Persius. Sat. iii. 23.

[2] See Eccl. xi. 6. Isa. xxviii. 9, 10. Lam. iii. 27.

[3] Matt. xiii. 25—28.

[4] Abp. Tillotson's Sermons on Education.

the fruit is immediate, uniform, and permanent to the end.[1] But often "the bread cast upon the waters of the covenant is found" not till "after many days"[2]—perhaps not till the godly parent has been laid in the grave.[3] Yet the fruit, though late, will not be the less sure.[4] *The child may depart* when he is young. *But when he is old*—in after years—smothered convictions will bring back the power of early impressions. The seeds of instruction will burst forth into life.[5] He will find it "hard," in a course of sin, "to kick against the pricks."[6] The scriptures early fastened on his memory, will force themselves upon him with many a sharp and painful struggle. Conscience will disturb his pleasures, and embitter the sweetness, which he had found, or fancied that he had found, in his sins. The remembrance of his father's house brings the prodigal "to himself," and he comes home with shame in his face, tears in his eyes, and godly sorrow in his heart.[7]

Cultivate, then, the exercise of parental faith; trusting—not to what we see, but to what God has promised; like our father Abraham—"against hope, believing in hope."[8] Expect the fulfilment of the parental promise, as confidently as any other free promise of the gospel.[9] Exercise faith in the full energy of Christian diligence,

[1] 1 Sam. i. 28; ii. 2; xii. 2, 3. Comp. Ps. xcii. 13—15. [2] Eccl. xi. 1.

[3] 2 Chron. xxxiii. 11—13. 'It is no small mercy,' said Mr. Flavel, alluding to this case, 'to have thousands of fervent prayers lying before the Lord, filed up in heaven for us.' Fountain of Life, Sermon xx.

[4] Hab. ii. 3.

[5] Timothy was instructed as a child, but not converted till adult age. Comp. 2 Tim iii. 15, with 1 Tim. i. 2.

[6] Acts ix. 5. [7] Luke xv. 17—20. [8] Rom. iv. 18—20.

[9] Such as John vi. 37—couched in the same grammatical terms—a promise connected with a duty, as the encouragement to the duty—"*Him that cometh—he that traineth; in no wise cast out—will not depart.*" Yet the latter is often considered a general promise, admitting of various and indefinite exceptions. The other is "Yea and Amen." But we might ask—How can we loosen the ground of one promise, without shaking the foundation of all? And do not admitted exceptions in the educational promise give occasion to many an exercised Christian to find his own exception in the Gospel promise? We fully concede that here the ground is more clear to the exercise of faith. We have the demonstrable certainty of the work of the Son, the faithfulness of the Father, and the agency of the Spirit, drawing the "given to come" (vv. 37, 44, 65)—the compact of the Eternal Three unchangeably fulfilled. In this parental promise the manifestly imperfect training of the parent, and the wanton rebellion of the child, obscures the ground of faith to our vision. But this touches only the apprehension of the ground, not the ground itself. If the performance of the parent's duty in the one promise were as certain, as the work of God in the other, would not the assurance of the promise in both cases be equally firm? We cannot indeed anticipate an universal fulfilment of the promise. Yet, as believers in the inspiration of Scripture, we are bound implicitly to receive it. Is it not far safer and more satisfactory to take all the promises of the Bible upon the same ground? The cases that appear to contravene the educational promise may be fairly explained. Not that the promise is falsified, but that the Lord's time of fulfilment is not yet come. Or—has not some important element of education been omitted? Has not some disproportion of one or other part of the system hindered the efficiency of the whole? Has instruction and discipline been always accompanied with prayer and faith? Or has prayer been always confirmed by consistent practice? Does not man's indolence, self-indulgence, unbelief, unfaithfulness to the conditions implied, wither the blessing? While Abraham—training up his family for God—shall find him "faithful that hath promised" (Gen. xviii. 19, with Heb. x. 23) the Elis and the Davids—good men but bad parents—(1 Sam. iii. 13; 1 Kings i. 6) shall know "God's breach of promise."

and in the patience of Christian hope. Leave God to accomplish his own gracious will. If his Sovereignty reserves the time and means to himself, his faithfulness secures the promise to us, which is, and ever must be, "Yea, and Amen"—"I will be a God to thee, and to thy seed after thee. I will pour out my Spirit upon thy seed, and my blessing upon thine offspring."[1]

This is faith—the reward of faith—of those who make the salvation of the soul the primary object of education. The mass of mankind deal with their children as if they were born only for the world—'Must they not be like others, to make their way in the world?' Thus they fearlessly bring them into contact with the evil around them, set their feet in the "broad road of destruction," and bid them go on with the rest. In all important matters they educate them consistently for time, not for eternity. They concentrate their grand interest on matters in which the soul has no concern; accomplishments or scholarship, not godliness; refinement of taste and manners, not soundness of faith. Need we say that this is an education without God—without his promise—without rest? The parents of such children, and the children of such parents, are alike objects of compassion. Eternity will bring a solemn account to both.

7. *The rich ruleth over the poor, and the borrower is servant to the lender.*

"The rich and the poor meet together,"[2] for mutual sympathy and helpfulness; yet God has appointed one to *rule* and the other to submit. And this gradation of rank in all its forms, involves distinct obligations to be carefully sought out and followed. Subjection, on the one hand, is cheerfully acknowledged as God's own ordinance; while the sense of responsibility is enlarged on the other. *The rule* applies to all the domestic relations between dependants and superiors. Yet let it be *the rule* of order, not of pride, caprice, or selfishness. And especially, when exercised over young persons of refined minds and education, let dependence be soothed by "the hand of kindness," elevating them to an high rank far above the menials of the house. The golden rule of love will diffuse Christian happiness without disorder or compromise of obligation.

Too often, however, it is *a rule* of harshness.[3] And, indeed, without a practical submission to God's rule over us, we can scarcely be trusted with power over our fellow-men. Obligations—such as that of the *borrower to the lender*—often forces the dependent to a *servile* bondage. Man becomes an alien to his brother; the victim of his gratification, not the object of his sympathy.[4]

(Num. xiv. 34.) It is too deep for man to reconcile the absolute election of God with weak, imperfect, unfaithful fulfilment of duty. Nevertheless in all cases—"Let God be true, and every man a liar." (Rom. iii. 4.)

[1] 2 Cor. i. 20. Gen. xvii. 7. Isa. xliv. 3—5.

[2] Verse 2.

[3] Chap. xviii. 23. Amos ii. 6; iv. 1; v. 11, 12; viii. 4—6. James ii. 6; v. 4. Comp. Ecclus xiii. 19.

[4] 2 Kings iv. 1. Neh v. 3—5. Matt. xviii. 25, 29. Compare the blessing, Deut. xv. 6; xxviii. 12.

Very important is it to maintain an independence of mind, quite distinct from pride, which elevates far above doing or conniving at evil, for the sake of pleasing a patron. Many have been forced to great entanglement of conscience—perhaps to vote contrary to their conscience—rather than lose the great man's smile. This is a tyrannizing *rule of the rich over the poor*—thus to make them the creatures of their own will. Shun, therefore, that proud independence, which scorns the kindly offer of needful help. But avoid all needless obligations. 'Sell not your liberty to gratify your luxury.'[1] If possible "owe no man anything but love." 'Guard against that poverty, which is the result of carelessness or extravagance. Pray earnestly—labor diligently. Should you come to poverty by the misfortune of the times, submit to your lot humbly; bear it patiently; cast yourself in childlike dependence upon your God.'[2]

8. *He that soweth iniquity shall reap vanity: and the rod of his anger shall fail,* (with the rod of his anger he shall be consumed, Marg.)

The seed-time and harvest furnish a striking scriptural image, full of practical use.[3] They are linked together in the spiritual, not less than in the natural, world. The harvest is according to the seed.[4] Such is the transcendant dignity and worth of the soul, that eternity is stamped upon all its actions. Every thought—every principle (is not this a solemn recollection ?)—is a seed for eternity, issuing in an harvest of eternal joy or "desperate sorrow." The wise man only adverts to the latter harvest. All experience and observation testify to the fact, that the diligent perseverance of the ungodly *sower* can only end in *vanity*—in utter and eternal disappointment.[5]

The connexion, however, of the two clauses of the Proverb may intimate, that the iron *rod of the rich ruling over the poor*—following the dictates of selfishness—will insure disappointment. Their abused power will shortly *fail*, and they will reap only the harvest of their injustice. Often may oppressors prosper for a time. God may use them as his chastening rod. But the *seed-time of iniquity* will end in the harvest *of vanity*, and when they have done their work, *the rod of their anger shall fail*. Such was Sennacherib in olden time.[6] Such was Napoleon in our own day. Never has the world seen so extensive *a sower of iniquity*—never a more abundant harvest of *vanity*. A fearful *rod of anger* was he to the nations of the earth. But how utterly was *the rod* suffered *to fail*, when the purpose was accomplished! Despoiled of empire—shorn of greatness—an exiled captive—such is not the harvest from God's seed! "A sure reward"[7]—not of *vanity*, but of substantial everlasting joy.[8] Here may we "sow bountifully, that we may reap also bountifully!"[9]

[1] Henry in loco. [2] Geier in loco.
[3] Ps. cxxvi. 5, 6. Hos. x. 12. Matt. xiii. 3, 24—30. [4] Gal. vi. 7, 8.
[5] Job iv. 8. Rom. vi. 21. [6] Isa. x. 5—12, 24, 25; xxx. 31. Comp. Zech. x. 11.
[7] Chap. xi. 18. [8] Ps. cxxvi. 5, 6. [9] 2 Cor. ix. 6, 9.

9. *He that hath a bountiful* (is good of, Marg) *eye shall be blessed: for he giveth of his bread to the poor.*

The heart often looks out at the eye.[1] *The bountiful or good eye* is contrasted with "the evil eye."[2] This man can look with indifference on distress,[3] satisfy himself with the heartless expression of good-will,[4] and find many reasons for withholding his charity. But the man *of a good eye* delighteth in contriving acts of kindness.[5] He not only relieves what is brought before him, but he looks out for objects, and looks pleasantly on them. Nehemiah was a bright example of this *bountifulness.* Instead of using his ample power for his own aggrandizement, he spent his substance in feeding the people at his own table—*giving of his bread to the poor.*[6] His great work required a large heart. And such a heart God had given him. Ever remember—Christian—that sacrifice—not convenience—is God's acceptable service. *Giving of our bread*—letting *the poor* share with ourselves.[7] Nor must it be wrung from us by importunity. "God loveth a cheerful giver."[8] His "charge is, that we be *ready* to distribute, willing to communicate."[9] This is his own pattern of *bountifulness.* "He openeth his hand, and satisfieth the desire of every living thing. He giveth to all liberally, and upbraideth not."[10] We are only the stewards of his bounty. Of our property—whether it be little or much—we must be *ready* to say—"We are not our own."[11] But mind that the motive be higher than the mere gratification of kindly feelings. Cherish carefully godly simplicity. "Let your light shine before men for your Father's glory."[12] But "take care that you give not your alms before men *to be seen of them,* otherwise you have no reward of your Father which is in heaven."[13]

This *bountifulness* is a privilege which earth possesses above heaven. Many a rich *blessing* is sealed to it;[14] and the man that shows it "hath a continual feast," because his objects are always before him. Man will *bless* it according to his ability;[15] and when "they cannot recompense thee, thou shalt be recompensed at the resurrection of the just;"[16] when 'one good work done for God will be seen'—as Luther says—'to show more glory than the whole frame of heaven and earth.' It is the power of his grace, the following of his pattern, the reflection of his image, the "shewing forth of his virtues."[17]

[1] Luke x. 33—35. [2] Chap. xxiii. 6. Deut. xv. 9; xxviii. 54, 56. Matt. xx. 15
[3] 1 Sam. xxv. 3, 10, 11. Luke x. 31, 32; xvi. 19—21. [4] James ii. 15, 16.
[5] Isa. xxxii. 8. [6] Neh. v. 16—18. [7] Comp. Job xxxi. 17.
[8] 2 Cor. ix. 6, with Deut. xv. 10. [9] 1 Tim. vi. 17, 18.
[10] Ps. cxlv. 16. James i. 5. [11] 1 Cor. vi. 19, 20. [12] Matt. v. 16.
[13] Ibid. vi. 1—3; xxv. 34—40.
[14] Deut. xv. 10. Isa. lviii. 10, 11. Matt. v. 7. Comp. Ecclus. xxxi. 23, 24.
[15] Job xxix. 11—13; xxxi. 16—20.
[16] Ps. xli. 1, 2. Luke xiv. 14. 1 Tim. vi. 19.
[17] 1 Pet. ii. 9, marg.

10. *Cast out the scorner, and contention shall go out; yea, strife and reproach shall cease.*

This is a word to rulers. *The scorner* is a firebrand of *contention* in the church.[1] He must be restrained.[2] If restraint be ineffectual, he must be—if possible—*cast out.*[3] If "his seat" be allowed in the family,[4] *strife and reproach* must be the issue. A jeer or biting taunt is more provoking than a blow. If therefore "peace is to the house," and "the love of peace is to abide there,"[5] —*cast out the scorner and the contention will cease.*[6] He must not be argued with.[7] We must keep no terms with him. We must meet him with bold and open rebuke, lest his influence should overthrow the faith of the simple.[8] If God "scorneth the scorners,"[9] what less can we do, than banish them from our society? "Depart from me, ye wicked; I will keep the commandments of my God."[10] Yet if we *cast him out,* cast him not off. Pray for him. Remember, "such were some of you."[11] While we abhor the sin, let us pity the sinner.

But what if we should not be able to *cast him out?* He may be a husband—a child. At least give a protest. Show that you stand not on the same ground. Turn away from his scorning. this will mortify if not silence. Turn from him to your God.[12] This will bring peace. Dwell with him sighing, as David in Mesech.[13] One greater than David teaches by his example. Honor your Divine Master by "enduring," as he did, year after year, "the contradiction of sinners."[14] And who knoweth, but this meek and silent endurance, with a loving bleeding heart, may have power to *cast out* the scorning, and to mould *the scorner* into the lowliness of the cross? Then who would be a more welcome member of the church or of the family? *Strife and reproach* would cease in both, should the persecutor of the faith become a monument of grace[15]—a shining witness to the truth.[16]

11. *He that loveth pureness of heart, for the grace of his lips the king shall be his friend.*

Pureness of heart describes not the natural, but the renewed, man. It is no external varnish—no affectation of holiness; but sincerity, humility, shrinking from sin, conformity to the image of God. He who hath fully attained this *pureness* is before the throne of God. *He who loveth it* is the child of God on earth. His perfection is desire, constant progress, pressing towards the mark.[17] When the fountain is cleansed, it sendeth forth sweet

[1] 3 John 10. [2] 2 Tim. iii. 8, 9.
[3] 1 Tim. i. 20. Tit. iii. 10, 11. [4] Psalm i. 1. [5] Luke xx. 5, 6.
[6] Gen. xxi. 9, 10. Comp. chap. xv. 18; xvi. 28.
[7] Chap. xxvi. 4. 2 Kings xviii. 36. [8] 2 Tim. iii. 1—7. [9] Chap. iii. 34.
[10] Psalm cxix. 115. Comp. Neh. xiii. 28. [11] 1 Cor. vi. 11.
[12] Psalm xxxv. 16—24; lxix. 11—13. [13] Ibid. cxx. 5—7. [14] Heb. xii. 3.
[15] 1 Tim. i. 13—16. [16] Gal. i. 23, 24. [17] Phil. iii. 12—15.

waters. When "the tree is made good, the fruit will be good." "Of the abundance of the heart the mouth speaketh."[1] *Pureness of heart* sheds such refinement over the whole character, and pours such *grace upon the lips*, as attracts the admiration of those who do not understand its source, and cannot appreciate its principle.[2] Such was the *grace upon the lips* of the holy Saviour, that "the multitude hung upon them, wondering at the gracious words which proceeded out of his mouth."[3] The moral influence also of this *purity* of character is to put impurity to shame.

Solomon doubtless spoke his own determination—that *the king should be the friend* of the gracious servant. This had been his father's resolution.[4] This character smoothed the way to royal favor for Joseph,[5] for Ezra,[6] and Daniel.[7] Nay—we find godly Obadiah in the confidence of wicked Ahab.[8] So powerful is the voice of conscience, even when God and holiness are hated. Yet this choice of the gracious lips is too often rather what ought to be, than what is.[9] Well is it for the kingdom, when the Sovereign's choice is according to this rule.[10] Such—such alone—the great *King* marks as *his friends.* Such he embraces with his fatherly love.[11] Such he welcomes into his heavenly kingdom.[12] "Blessed are the pure in heart; for they shall see God."[13]

12. *The eyes of the Lord preserve knowledge, and he overthroweth the words of the transgressor.*

The eyes of the Lord often describe his searching Omnipotence[14]—here his fatherly care.[15] So many inlets to false principles—such specious appearances to warp the judgment—does the subtle enemy pour in; so strong is the natural tendency in the same direction—that, but for his gracious covering to *preserve knowledge* in our hearts, *the words of the transgressor* might "overthrow our faith."[16] Oh! let us seek our Christian establishment in close communion with Him, for continued *preservation* from a cloud upon our intellectual faculties and spiritual apprehensions.

But the proverb illustrates upon a wider scale His faithful keeping of the truth in the world. Indeed it may be regarded as a prophecy in the course of fulfilment to the very end of time?[17] For how wonderfully has the *knowledge* of God been *preserved* from age to age; and all the plausible or malignant schemes to blot it out been *overthrown!* The Scriptures, as the words of *knowledge*, have *been preserved* in a far more accurate state than any other book of corresponding antiquity; though man's wisdom has never been wanting in ingenuity to corrupt it. When *knowledge* seemed

[1] Matt. xii. 33, 34. [2] Chap. xxxi. 10, 26. [3] Ps. xlv. 2, 7. Luke xix. Gr. iv. 22.
[4] Ps. ci. 6; cxix. 63. [5] Gen. xli. 37—45. [6] Ezra vii. 6, 21—25.
[7] Dan. vi. 1—3, 28. See i. 8, 9. [8] 1 Kings xviii. 3, 12. Comp. 2 Kings xiii. 14
[9] Chap. xvi. 12, 13. [10] Chap. xxviii. 2; xxv. 5. [11] Chap. xv. 9.
[12] Ps. xv. 1, 2; xxiv. 3, 4. [13] Matt. v. 8. [14] Chap. v. 21; xv. 3. Ps. xi. 4.
[15] 2 Chron. xvi. 9. Ps. xxxiv. 15. Zech. iv. 10. [16] 2 Tim. ii. 17—19.
[17] Scott in loco.

on the eve of perishing, a single copy of the Scriptures, found as it were accidentally, *preserved* it from utter extinction.[1] For successive generations the Book was in the custody of faithful librarians, handed down in substantial integrity.[2] When the Church herself was on the side of the Arian heresy, the same watchful *eyes* raised up a champion,[3] to *preserve* the testimony. In the succeeding dark ages witnesses prophesied, as from the earliest eras of Revelation[4]—some indeed for a long time in sackcloth,[5] until the dawn of a brighter day. Nor was this in peace and quietness. Often has the infidel *transgressor* labored with all might of man for its destruction.[6] Often has Rome partially suppressed it, or committed it to the flames, or circulated perverted copies and false interpretations. Yet all these *words* and deeds of *the transgressors have been overthrown.* And notwithstanding all heretical corruptions, *the eyes of the Lord have preserved knowledge.* Still is his word continued among us with its Divine credentials unimpaired, and its unsearchable store undiminished—a standing miracle of the faithfulness of its Almighty Keeper. Full of joy and confidence is the believer's acknowledgment—"Concerning thy testimonies, I have known of old, that thou hast founded them forever."[7]

13. *The slothful man saith, There is a lion without, I shall be slain in the streets.*[8]

Real difficulties in the way of heaven exercise faith. And such there are, far too great for those who have never "counted the cost," or who "go to the warfare at any time at their own charges."[9] But imaginary difficulties are the indulgence of sloth. *The slothful man* is a coward. He has no love for his work, and therefore he is always ready to put a cheat upon his soul, 'inventing some vain excuse, because he will not do his duty.'[10] He shrinks from every work likely to involve trouble.[11] Fancied dangers frighten him from real and present duties. *There is a lion without; I shall be slain in the streets*—an absurd excuse![12]—as if public *streets*—except in special cases—were the haunts of wild beasts.[13] He is afraid of being *slain without*, when he willingly gives himself up to be slain within.[14] Thus the unbelieving spies—when holding up to view the exuberant fruit of Canaan, added—"*But we be not able to go up against the people.* The cities are walled up to heaven—and the giants are there."[15] As if the promise of God was not a stronger ground of faith than the giants of fear![16] But much more sad is it to see Moses shrinking[17]—nay—Jonah

[1] 2 Chron. xxxiv. 14—18. [2] Rom. iii. 2.
[3] Athanasius. [4] Enoch, Jude 14, 15. Noah, 2 Pet. ii. 5.
[5] Rev. xi. 3—11; xii. 14—17.
[6] Jer. xxxvi. 23. Company of Voltaire and his associates. [7] Ps. cxix. 152.
[8] Chap. xxvi. 13. [9] Matt. viii. 19, 20, with xi. 12. Luke xiv. 28—30.
[10] Reformer's Notes. [11] Chap. xv. 19; xix. 24.
[12] 1 Kings xiii. 24; xx. 36. 2 Kings ii. 24. [13] Psalm civ. 20—22.
[14] Chap. xxi. 25. [15] Num. xiii. 27—33. [16] Num. xiv. 6—8, with Gen. xi. 7.
[17] Ex. iv. 10—14.

running away—from the Lord's work.[1] All excuses against doing it partake of this cowardly spirit. And who has not felt the temptation, when called to a plain but self-denying duty; to encounter painful opposition to the gospel, or to a faithful rebuke of sin? *There is a lion without.* True. But hast thou forgotten the promise in the ways of God? "Thou shalt tread upon *the lion* and adder; *the young lion* and the dragon shalt thou trample under feet?"[2] Does not our Master's word, "Follow me?"[3]—call us to tread in his steps—to follow him in a life of self-devoted conflict and energy? Ponder the terms of discipleship. "If any man will come after me, let him deny himself, and take up his cross *daily, and follow me.*"[4] Godly courage, "endurance of hardness," "standing in the *whole* armor of God"[5]—all this is needed—all this must be daily and hourly sought for—not only by those who stand in the forefront of the battle, but by the meanest soldier of the cross; else, though "armed, and carrying the bow, he will turn back" disgracefully "in the day of battle."[6]

14. *The mouth of strange women is a deep pit: he that is abhorred of the Lord shall fall therein.*

This fearful temptation has been already frequently opened.[7] But in a book specially for the young, who that knows the power of "youthful lusts,"[8] and the seductive witcheries of sin,[9] will deem a fresh warning needless? Is it not the voice of mercy? For what but unbounded compassion could stand as it were at the edge of *the pit*, and unfold to the unwary its awful peril? *A deep pit* indeed it is[10]—easy to fall into; hard—next to impossible—to get out of.[11] So besotting is this sin to the flesh—to the mind—to the conscience![12] It is *the mouth of a pit far deeper.* "For her feet go down to death; her steps take hold of hell."[13] What more humbling proof can there be of the total depravity of the nature, than the fact, that those affections, originally given as the purest enjoyments of life, should become the corrupt spring of such a defilement. The sin and snare would seem to be a judicial infliction for those, whose wilful rejection of God have made them *abhorred of him.*[14] They have turned away from instruction, hated reproof, resisted conviction, and, given up to their abomination, they give too plain proof, that they are abandoned by God[15]—*abhorred of the Lord!* Is the embrace of *the strange woman* a compensation for such a judgment? Every curse—eternal frown and banishment—

[1] Jonah i. 1—3. [2] Ps. xci. 11—13.
[3] Matt. iv. 19; viii. 22; ix. 9. [4] Luke ix. 23.
[5] 2 Tim. ii. 3. Eph. vi. 12, 13. 'Invictus ad labores; fortis ad periculum; durus adversus illecebras.' Ambrose—a fine exhibition of Christian energy.
[6] Psalm lxxviii. 9.
[7] Chap. ii. 16—19; v. 3; vi. 24—29; vii. 5, &c.; ix. 16—18.
[8] 2 Tim. ii. 22. [9] Chap. v. 3; vii. 21. [10] Chap. xxiii. 27.
[11] Chap. ii. 19. Comp. Eccl. vii. 26.
[12] Judg. xvi. 20, 21. Neh. xiii. 26. Hos. iv. 11.
[13] Chap. v. 5; ii. 18; vii. 27; ix. 18. 2 Pet. ii. 10—12. Rev. xxi. 8.
[14] Rom. i. 28. Comp. Ps. lxxxi. 11, 12. [15] Chap. v. 7—13.

the weight of infinite unmingled wrath—is involved in this awful name. Not that he willeth the death of the vilest sinner.[1] But must not his justice and his holiness be in array against those, who of their own will choose evil, and reject alike the warnings of his wrath, and the invitations of his love?

15. *Foolishness is bound in the heart of a child; but the rod of correction shall drive it far from him.*

What parent—what instructor of children will not bear sad, but decisive, testimony to the *foolishness of the child*? 'A little innocent'—is the miscalled name of fondness and fancy. One only of Adam's race, and he—adored be his name! preserved by his holy conception[2]—lays claim to it. *Foolishness* is the birthright of all besides. The early development of waywardness and passion—even before the power of speech[3]—before the child is capable of observing and imitating those around him—is a touching but undeniable evidence of the innate principle.

Observe—it is *foolishness*—not childishness. *That* might belong to an unfallen child. No moral guilt attaches to the recollection—"When I was a child, I spake as a child, I understood as a child, I thought as a child."[4] 'A child is to be punished'—as Mr. Scott wisely observed—'not for being a *child*, but for being *a wicked* child.'[5] Comparative ignorance, the imperfect and gradual opening of the faculties, constitute the nature, not the sinfulness, of the child. The holy "child increased in wisdom."[6] But *foolishness* is the mighty propensity to evil—imbibing wrong principles, forming bad habits, entering into an ungodly course. It includes all the sins of which a child is capable—lying, deceit,[7] wilfulness, perverseness, want of submission to authority[8]—all seeds of future evil, multiplying to a fruitful harvest.

We delight in our children's harmless play. We would make ourselves one with them in their sportiveness. But *this foolishness*—visible every hour before our eyes—never let it be a subject of sport, but of deep and constant sadness. Nor let childhood plead as an excuse for it. Children's sins—though not chargeable with the guilt of adult responsibility, yet God has awfully shown, that they are sins against Himself. The judgment on the "*little children*" of Bethel is enough to make "both the ears of" thoughtless parents "tingle."[9]

But whence the origin of this *foolishness*? "Look unto the rock whence we are hewn. Look unto" Adam, "our father, and unto" Eve "that bare us."[10] As is the root, so are the branches. As is the fountain, so are the waters. Our nature was poisoned at

[1] Ezek. xviii. 32; xxxiii. 11. [2] Luke i. 35.

[3] Augustine mentions his being struck with the sight of an infant before it could speak—showing an evident look of envy and passion towards another infant about to share its nourishment. He adds—in reference to himself—'When, I beseech thee, O my God, in what places—when or where—was I *innocent*?' Confess. lib. i. c. 7.

[4] 1 Cor. xiii. 11. [5] Life, p. 622. [6] Luke ii. 52.

[7] Psalm lviii. 3. [8] Job xi. 12. [9] 2 Kings ii. 23, 24, with 1 Sam. iii. 11.

[10] Isa. li. 1, 2.

the spring. Our sinful parent, having lost God's image, could only "beget a son after his image"[1]—a sinner begetting a sinner. "That which is born of the flesh is flesh,"[2] and could be nothing else. For "who can bring a clean thing out of an unclean?"[3] The creature therefore is produced into being with a radical enmity against God," and "by nature" therefore "a child of wrath."[4] The entail is held from "our first father," and can never be cut off. There is no division of this sad inheritance. Each of his children has the whole. His Maker testifies concerning him, as "a transgressor from the womb—that his heart is evil from his youth."[5] In shame he acknowledges the testimony—"Behold! I was shapen in iniquity, and in sin did my mother conceive me." If the joy of a child's birth blots out the remembrance of its pain and sorrow,[7] yet must not this joy be chastened in the humbling recollection of what the man-child brings into the world—*foolishness?*

Observe also the rooted character of this evil. It lies not on the surface, like some of the childish habits, easily corrected. *It is bound in his heart*—held firmly there by chains invincible to human power.[8] It is woven and incorporated into his very nature. And so various are its forms, so subtle its workings, that the wisest parent is often at a loss how to detect and treat the evil.

The general rule however—the prescribed remedy—is clear. It is vain to bid the *foolishness* depart. It is no less vain to persuade the child himself to *drive it far away. The rod of correction* is distinctly named, and repeatedly inculcated, as God's own means for this important end.[9] And surely the thought of having been an instrument of producing an envenomed nature against a God of love must constrain the parent to use the means thus divinely appointed for destroying the deadly poison.

Only let the child see that, as with our heavenly Father, love is the ruling principle;[10] that we follow the example of the wisest and best of parents; that we use his rod for *driving foolishness away;*[11] that, like him, we "chasten, not for our pleasure, but for our child's profit;"[12] not from caprice or passion, but from tenderness to his soul. Use the Lord's means, and we can then—what *otherwise* we cannot do—wait in faith for the promised blessing. Many a stirring movement of the flesh may be restrained. Shame of sin will ripen into abhorrence; and in sorrow and humiliation the path of wisdom will be chosen, loved, and followed.[13]

16. *He that oppresseth the poor to increase his riches, and he that giveth to the rich, shall surely come to want.*

These two men seem to be at opposite. Yet they meet at the same centre. Both are equally destitute of the love of God and of

[1] Gen. v. 3. [2] John iii. 6.
[3] Job xiv. 4; xxv. 4. [4] Eph. ii. 3. [5] Isa. xlviii. 8. Gen. viii. 21.
[6] Ps. li. 5. [7] John xvi. 21.
[8] Cartwright in loco. Comp. Gen. xliv. 30. 1 Sam. xviii. 1.
[9] Chap. xix. 18; xxiii. 13, 14; xxix. 17. [10] Chap. xiii. 24, with iii. 11, 12.
[11] See 2 Chron. xxxiii. 12, 13. [12] Heb. xii. 6, 10. [13] Chap xxix. 15.

their brother. Both alike are seeking their own aggrandizement. The one *oppresseth the poor* to increase his riches. The other *giveth to the rich*, "hoping for something again." Both courses—paradoxical as it may appear—are the road to want. "*For the oppression of the poor*—now will I arise—saith the Lord. Him that loveth violence his soul hateth."[1] 'Sin pays its servants very bad wages; for it gives the very reverse of what it promised. While the sin of oppression promises mountains of gold, it brings them poverty and ruin.[2] Injuries done to the poor are sorely resented by the God of mercy, who is the poor man's friend, and will break in pieces his oppressor.'[3] But if *oppression* is the road to poverty, is not liberality the way to riches? Doubtless it is, if it be for God.[4] But here the man was putting forth a false show of munificence to ensure gifts in tenfold return; while he could at the same time indulge his selfishness in grinding the poor with impunity. Our Lord, therefore, forbids his host to "make a feast for the rich, looking for a recompence."[5] "If ye do good to them"—said he to his disciples—"that do good to you—if ye lend to them, of whom ye hope to receive—what thank have ye?"[6] *To give to the rich* is perverting our stewardship for the service of the poor. But retributive justice will blast the ill-gotten gains of selfishness;[7] and hypocrisy will meet its just reward of shame and disappointment.[8] Oh! let the Christian ever hear his Father's voice—"I am the Almighty God; walk before me, and be thou perfect."[9]

17. *Bow down thine ear, and hear the words of the wise, and apply thine heart unto my knowledge.* 18. *For it is a pleasant thing, if thou keep them within thee; they shall withal be fitted in thy lips.* 19. *That thy trust may be in the Lord, I have made known to thee this day, even to thee.* 20. *Have not I written to thee excellent things in counsels and knowledge.* 21. *That I might make thee know the certainty of the words of truth: that thou mightest answer the words of truth to them that send unto thee?*

Solomon here seems to change his mode of address. From the tenth chapter he had chiefly given detached, sententious aphorisms in an antithetical form; contrasting right and wrong principles with their respective results. His observations are now more connected and personal; like a wise minister preaching to his people, not *before* them; and preaching to them, not only in the mass, but in contact with their individual consciences.

He begins with an earnest call to attention. He was speaking no ordinary matters, but *the words of the wise—Bow the ear—apply the heart unto knowledge*[10]—as to a message from God. Lord! "waken mine ear to hear as the learned."[11]

Observe the attractiveness of wisdom. It is a pleasant, no less than a profitable, *thing*. And who is not alive to the call of plea-

[1] Ps. xii. v; xi. 5. [2] Jer. xxii. 13—15.
[3] Lawson in loco. Comp. verses 22, 23. [4] Chap. iii. 9, 10.
[5] Luke xiv. 12. [6] Luke vi. 33—35.
[7] Job xx. 19—22. Isa. v. 8, 9. Mic. ii. 2—5. Zech. vii. 9—14. James ii. 6, 13; v. 1—4.
[8] Luke xii. 1, 2. [9] Gen. xvii. 1. [10] Chap. ii. 2; xxiii. 12. [11] Isa. l. 4.

sure! Yet incomprehensible is it to the world to connect religion with pleasure. It spoils all their pleasure. And what amends can it make? It includes in their view much to be done, but nothing to be enjoyed; somewhat very serious, perhaps important in its place, but grave and gloomy: a duty, not a privilege. Yet how little has our profession wrought for us, if it has not realized it as *a pleasant thing*, adorned with somewhat of an angel's smile. Often alas! it fails to comfort and invigorate us—a body indeed of truth, but "a body without the spirit;" cold and lifeless. *It is a pleasant thing* only, if *we keep it within us.*[1] Heart-religion conveys vital happiness. The fruit is of "the tree of life;"[2] its taste "sweeter than honey or the honey-comb."[3] "Thy words were found, and I did eat them, and thy word was unto me as the joy and rejoicing of my heart."[4]

Mark also the connection between the religion of the heart and of the lips. Keep it within thee. "Let this word dwell in your heart;" and how graceful will be the furniture of *the lips*; *fitting* them to speak with natural simplicity and suitable application![5] When "the heart is inditing a good matter, the tongue is the pen of a ready writer."[6] It becomes as "choice silver." The words are *fitted* 'like a string of rich and precious pearls.'[7] "The lips of the righteous feed many."[8] Yet *the words* will be but little *fitted in the lips,*[9] where there is no treasure in the heart. Never let the mouth attempt to "speak of wisdom," until "the meditation of the heart has been of understanding."[10]

But how powerless are even the words of wisdom without personal application! Let each for a while isolate himself from his fellow-men, and be alone with God, under the clear searching light of his word. If prayer be cold, graces be languid, privileges be clouded, and profession unfruitful, is it not, because religion has been taken up *in the gross*, without immediate personal contact with the truth of God? O, my soul, the message of God is *to thee—even to thee*[11]—*this day*—"To-day while it is called to-day"[12]—welcome his voice with reverential joy. "Take fast hold of his instruction, for it is thy life."[13] *That thy trust may be in the Lord*—that thou mayest claim thine interest in him—that thou mightest seal his truth upon thine heart—*he hath made it known to thee—even to thee.* Believe—love—obey—be happy here and for eternity. *And who can doubt the excellency of the things that are written, so rich in counsels and knowledge*—'words fit for a prince to speak, and the best man in the world to hear?'[14] Such free—such pleading invitations![15] Such deep manifestations of the

1 Chap. vi. 21; vii. 1, with ii. 10.
2 Chap. iii. 18.
3 Chap. xxiv. 13, 14. Ps. xix. 10; cxix. 103.
4 Jer. xv. 16.
5 Ps. cxix. 171; Matt. xii. 34. Col. iii. 16.
6 Ps. xlv. 1.
7 Chap. x. 20. Diodat. i.
8 Ib. ver. 21. Comp. xv. 23; xvi. 21; xxv. 11.
9 Chap. xxvi. 7, 9.
10 Ps. xlix. 3.
11 See the same emphatic reduplication, chap. xxiii. 15.
12 Heb. iii. 13; iv. 7, with Ps. xcv. 7.
13 Chap. iv. 13.
14 Chap. viii. 6. Scott in loco.
15 Chap i. viii. ix.

Divine counsels![1] Such wise, earnest, parental warnings against sin![2] Such encouraging exhibitions of the service of God.[3] Such a minute and practical standard for relative life and social obligation![4]

But let us not forget the great end of this Revelation—*that we may know the certainty of the things*—that *we may give an answer* concerning our confidence. The Gospel itself was written with a special reference to this important end.[5] Yet this confidence is not a natural, but a Divine, attainment. "The word must come with power, and with the Holy Ghost," in order to come "with much assurance."[6] That cannot be a sound faith, which does not extend to the whole of the testimony. And even a general admission of the authority of the whole, without an individual application, would—if carefully analyzed—prove to be a want of cordial reception of any part of the Revelation. A lodgment in the heart can alone bring that full conviction—"Now we believe, no because of thy saying; for we have heard him ourselves."[7]

Doubts may arise as to the integrity of the foundation. But a candid and intelligent survey of the external evidence would satisfy all reasonable minds.[8] And a fair trial for ourselves would confirm the mass of proof with all the weight of internal evidence. Far better to make the trial at once, than to paralyze the modicum of remaining strength by unreasonable doubtings. The Bible exhibits a Divinely-appointed remedy commensurate with man's infinite distress, and accepted of God in its power and prevalence. Let this at least encourage the effort to fit our case to the remedy, and to apply the remedy to our case. If there be any shaking, it will be in the exercise, not in the foundation, of our confidence.

No further proof can be expected. None, in fact, could be given, save a voice from heaven, which the busy enemy, working upon the imagination, would readily convert into a vehicle of doubt. Actual demonstration would leave no room for faith, which is clearly man's discipline in the present dispensation; humbling him in the consciousness alike of his ignorance and his dependence upon God. We have only therefore thankfully to receive, and diligently to improve, the sufficient evidence vouchsafed to us. Paley has given us a golden maxim of Christian philosophy—defining 'true fortitude of understanding to consist, in not suffering what we do know to be disturbed and shaken by what we do not know.'[9] To delay, therefore, "the obedience of faith,"[10] until we shall have solved all the ten thousand objections of a proud infidelity, is to waste the urgent responsibilities of the present moment in an unwarranted expectation of light, which was never promised, and never intended to be given.

Yet the importance of a soundly-assured confidence cannot be

[1] Chap. viii. [2] Chap. v. vii. [3] Chap. iii. [4] Chap. x—xxii.
[5] Luke i. 1—4. 2 Pet. i. 15, 16. [6] 1 Thess. i. 5. [7] John iv. 42.
[8] See Dr. Alexander's Canon of the Old and New Testament Scriptures ascertained—a valuable volume from America—reprinted in London.
[9] See his Natnral Theology, chap. v. [10] Rom. xvi. 26.

over estimated. It constitutes the weight and effectiveness of the sacred office. "The priest's lips keep knowledge, and they shall seek the law at his mouth, as the messenger of the Lord of Hosts."[1] But except *he know himself the certainty of the words of truth*, how can he *answer the words of truth to them that send unto him?* Scarcely less necessary, and on the same ground, is it for the Christian, that he may "be ready always to give an answer to every one, that asketh him a reason of the hope that is in him."[2] Temporary scepticism may be a chastisement of a disputatious spirit. But prayer, and humility, with all its attendant graces, will ultimately lead to Christian establishment. Thus shall we be preserved from the fearful, but alas! too prevalent danger, of receiving the traditions of men in the stead, and with the authority, of the testimony of God. Ours will not be a blind Romish faith in the priest or in the Church; but *alone* "in the law and the testimony;"[3] standing not in the wisdom of men, but in the power of God;[4] stamped by the impress of the Spirit, as "the witness in ourselves."[5] No power of Satan or his emissaries will drive us permanently from this stronghold. We "know whom" and what "we have believed,"[6] and confidently "testify," for the support of our weaker brethren, "that this is the true grace of God wherein we stand."[7]

22, 23. *Rob not the poor, because he is poor; neither oppress the afflicted in the gate: for the Lord will plead their cause, and spoil the soul of those that spoil them.*

Perhaps after so solemn an exhortation, we might have expected something more important. Yet what can be more important than the law of love, and to rebuke the breaches of that law? *Robbery and oppression*, under any circumstances, are a breach of the commandment.[8] But to *rob the poor because he is poor*, and has no means of protection, is a cowardly aggravation of the sin.[9] Much more base is it to *oppress the afflicted at the gate*—the place of judgment:[10] to make his only refuge a market for bribery,[11] and to pervert the sacred authority of God given for his protection.[12] 'The threatenings of God against the *robbers of the poor* are sometimes laughed at by the rich and great. But they will find them in due time to be awful realities.'[13] 'Weak though they be, they have a strong one to take their part.'[14] He *will plead their cause.* And woe to the man, against whom he pleads. "What mean ye"—demands the poor man's pleader—"that ye beat my people to pieces, and grind the face of the poor?"[15]

The accumulation of Divine vengeance is heaped upon this sin.[16] Ahab's judgment testified to the fearful *spoiling of those, who*

[1] Mal. ii. 7. [2] 1 Pet. iii. xv. [3] Isa. viii. xx. Comp. Acts xvii. 11.
[4] 1 Cor. ii. 5. [5] 1 John v. 10; ii. 20, 27. [6] 2 Tim. i. 12.
[7] 1 Pet. v. 12. [8] Ex. xx. 15. [9] 2 Sam. xii. 1—6.
[10] Ruth iv. 1. 2 Sam. xv. 2; xix. 8. Job. v. 4. Amos v. 15.
[11] Ex. xxiii. 6. Amos v. 12. [12] Ps. lxxxii. 4. Comp. lxxii. 1—4.
[13] Lawson on verse 16. [14] Bp. Sanderson's Sermon on 1 Sam. xii. 3.
[15] Isa. iii. 15. Comp. Chap. xxiii. 10, 11. Jer. l. 33, 34. [16] Ps. cix. 6, 16.

spoil the poor.[1] The captivity in Babylon was the scourge for this wickedness.[2] and when the deeds of secrecy shall be brought to light, how black will be the catalogue of sins of *oppression!* How tremendous the judgment of *the oppressor!*[3] Meanwhile let the poor commit himself to his God;[4] yea, take up the song of praise,[5] in the confidence, that the Divine *pleader* will "maintain his cause,"[6] and triumphantly carry it through, to the eternal confusion of his sinful *spoilers*.

24, 25. *Make no friendship with an angry man; and with a furious man thou shalt not go: lest thou learn his ways, and get a snare to thy soul.*

Sin is contagion. Alas! our corrupt constitution predisposes us to receive it in any form, in which it may be presented to us. The unlovely passions of *a furious man* rather repel than attract.[7] But sin never loses its infectious character. *Friendship* blinds the eye; and where there is no light in the mind, no true tenderness in the conscience, we can see hateful things done by those we love with blunted sensibilities. Common intercourse *with a furious man* is fraught with danger. His unreasonable conduct stirs our own tempers. One fire kindles another. Occasional bursts of passion soon form the habit. The habit becomes the nature. Thus we *learn his ways, and get a snare to our soul.*[8] How soon does a young person, living with a proud man, get the mould of his society, and become imperious and overbearing![9] Evil ways, especially when they fall in with our natural temperament, are much sooner learnt than good, and are much more powerful to "corrupt good manners,"[10] than good manners to amend the evil. We learn anger easier than meekness. We convey disease, not health. Hence it is the rule of self-preservation, no less than the rule of God —*Make no friendship with an angry man.*

26. *Be not thou one of them that strike hands, or of them that are sureties for debts.* 27. *If thou hast nothing to pay, why should he take away thy bed from under thee?*

Avoid contention, not only *with angry*, but with imprudent, perhaps unprincipled, associates. *Strike not your hands*[11] *as a surety* without forethought, sometimes without upright principle. Repeated warnings have been given of this danger.[12] The putting your hand to a bill may be almost signing a warrant for your own execution. At all events it is a fraud, to give security for more than you are worth; promising what you are unable to perform. The creditor may fairly in this case proceed to extremities[13]—not with the debtor (whom he knows to be worth nothing, and whom indeed the law of God protected[14])—but with the surety. And *why*—the wise man

1 1 Kings xxi. 18—24. Comp. Isa. xxxiii. 1. Hab. ii. 8.
2 Ez. xxii. 29—31.
3 Mal. iii. 5.
4 Ps. x. 14.
5 Ib. cix. 30, 31
6 Ib. cxl. 12.
7 Chap. xxi. 25; xxv. 28; xxvii. 4.
8 Ps. cvi. 35, 36.
9 Ecclus. xiii. 1.
10 1 Cor. xv. 33.
11 Chap. vi. 1.
12 Ib. verses 1, 2; xi. 15; xvii. 18.
13 Chap. 20.
14 Ex. xxii. 26, 27. Deut. xxiv. 12, 13.

asks—shouldst thou rashly incur beggary and ruin, so as to *have the bed taken from under thee?*

There is, however, so much danger of erring in over caution, and of indulging selfishness under the cover of prudence, that these wholesome cautions must be considerately applied. Yet, in "devising liberal things,"[1] we must combine scrupulous regard to justice and truth.[2] Else our very charity will prove the scandal, instead of the glory, of our profession.[3] 'We may "take *joyfully* the spoiling of our goods," for the testimony of a good conscience. But as the fruit of our own rashness and folly, we cannot but *take it heavily*.'[4] Oh! let our Divine Master be honored in our profession by well doing "putting to silence the ignorance of foolish men."[5]

28. *Remove not the ancient landmark, which thy fathers have set.*

Every one has an undoubted right to his own. He must therefore have the means of knowing and securing his right. Even the heathen admitted the sacredness of *the landmark*. The stone or the staple was honored as the god, without whose kindly influence every field would be the subject of contention.[6] *The landmark* was protected by the wise laws of Israel. God himself set the bounds to the respective parts of his own world, restricting each part within its proper limits.[7] Thus also he distributed the different nations,[8] and appointed the same security for the several allotments of his own people.[9] *The ancient landmark* stood as a witness and memorial of each man's rights, *which his father had set*. Its *removal* therefore was forbidden, as a selfish and unjust invasion of property,[10] included in the curses of Ebal,[11] and noted, in subsequent ages, as the head and forefront of national provocation.[12]

All sound expositors[13] warn us, from this Proverb, to reverence long-tried and well-established principles, and not rashly to innovate upon them. Some scorn *the ancient landmarks*, as relics of byegone days of darkness. Impatient of restraint, they want a wider range of wandering, to indulge either their own prurient appetite for novelties, or the morbid cravings of others for this unwholesome excitement.[14] Endless divisions and dissensions have been the fruit of this deadly evil. The right of individual judgment oversteps its legitimate bounds; and in its licentious exercise "every man" feels justified to "do" and think "that which is right in his own eyes."[15]

Rome, on the other hand, charges us with *removing the ancient landmark* of unwritten Tradition, *which our fathers have set*. We ask—What right had they to *set it up?* We do reverence to

[1] Isa. xxxii. 8. [2] Phil. iv. 8.
[3] Rom. xiv. 16. 1 Tim. v. 22. Heb. xii. 13. [4] Heb. x. 34. Henry in loco.
[5] 1 Pet. ii. 12; iii. 16. [6] See Ovid. Fast. ii. 639—648. Also i. 50.
[7] Gen. i. 6—10. Job xxxviii. 10, 11. [8] Deut. xxxii. 8. [9] Num. xxxiv.
[10] Deut. xix. 14. Comp. chap. xxiii. 10. Job xxiv. 2. [11] Deut. xxvii. 17.
[12] Hos. v. 10.
[13] Bp. Patrick, Scott, Geier, &c. Romish expositors naturally apply it to their own traditions. Estè quotes the venerable Bede. See also Corn. in Lapidè.
[14] 2 Tim. iii. 7; iv. 3, 4. [15] Jud. xxi. 25.

no unwritten traditions upon the footing of "the law and the testimony."[1] We rebut the charge against Rome, and contend, upon the broad ground of historic testimony, that *she has removed the ancient landmarks*, and substituted her own in their place; that Protestantism (not in name, but in principle) is the old religion, and Popery a comparative novelty.[2]

If we turn to our own beloved and venerated Church—The last age witnessed a rude, but by Divine mercy an unsuccessful, effort, to root up her *landmarks*.[3] We have seen a subtle and insidious attempt to *remove* them from the place, where *our* well-instructed *fathers have set* them, and fix them nearer Rome; leaving but a narrow boundary of division between Christ and Anti-christ. This is indeed the rooting up of the foundations of the grace of God, which ought—if need be—to "be resisted unto blood."[4] The Lord make us "valiant for the truth," and consistent witnesses of its power!

29. *Seest thou a man diligent in his business? he shall stand before kings; he shall not stand before mean men.*

Seest thou a man? He is marked out for our special notice.[5] And who is it? *A man diligent in his business*—quick, ready, actively improving his time, his talents, his opportunity for his work—like Henry Martyn—who was known in his college, as 'the man who had not lost an hour.'[6] *A mean* sphere is too low for such a man. *He shall stand*—as Joseph,[7] Nehemiah,[8] Daniel,[9] —all *diligent in their business*—did—*before kings*. If the letter of the promise is not always fulfilled, "*the diligent man* will bear rule" in his own sphere.[10] Such was the honor put upon Eliezer's care, forethought, and activity for his master's interest.[11] 'Nobleness of condition is not essential as a school for nobleness of character. It is delightful to think, that humble life may be just as rich in moral grace and moral grandeur, as the loftier places in society; that as true a dignity of principle may be earned by him, who in homeliest drudgery plies his conscientious task, as by him, who stands entrusted with the fortunes of an empire.'[12]

Diligence, even without godliness, is often the way to worldly advancement. Pharaoh chose Joseph's brethren, as "men of activity," to be rulers of his cattle.[13] Jeroboam owed his elevation in

[1] Isa. viii. 20.

[2] The historical dates of the distinctive principles of Popery, accredited as articles of faith, are many centuries subsequent to the primitive era. See a valuable tract by Rev. Thomas Lathbury—'Protestantism the Old Religion, Popery the New.' Also 'Our Protestant Forefathers,' by the Rev. Dr. Gilly.—As regards our own church—Mr. Soames's interesting and elaborate work on the Anglo-Saxon Church.

[3] The Socinian Association, at Feathers Tavern, supported by men of influence and dignity, with the avowed object of sweeping away all Creeds, Articles, and Subscriptions.

[4] Heb. xii. 4.
[5] Chap. xxvi. 12; xxix. 20.
[6] Life, chap. ii.
[7] Gen. xxxix. 3–6; xli. 42.
[8] Neh. i. 11; ii. 1. Dan. vi. 1—3; vii. 27.
[9] Dan. vi. 1—3; viii. 27.
[10] Chap. xii. 24. Comp. Ecclus. x. 25.
[11] Gen. xxiv.
[12] Chalmers's Commercial Discourses, p. 107.
[13] Gen. xlvii. 6.

Solomon's house to his "industrious" habits.[1] But when a man "serves the Lord in fervency of spirit,"[2] faithfully occupying his own talent for the day of reckoning[3]—*the mean man* of the world will be too low for him. *He shall stand before the King* of Kings with unspeakable honor, with unclouded acceptance—"Well done! good and faithful servant; enter thou into the joy of thy Lord."[4]

And if "the servants of the wise king were" happy, *which stood continually before him*, and heard his wisdom, what must be the joy of *standing before the* great *King*, seeing his face, and serving him forever![5] "This honor have all his saints."[6] "If a man serve me," saith our gracious Master, "where I am, there shall also my servant be; if any man serve me, him will my Father honor."[7]

CHAPTER XXIII.

1. *When thou sittest to eat with a ruler, consider diligently what is before thee:* 2. *and put a knife to thy throat, if thou be a man given to appetite.* 3. *Be not desirous of his dainties: for they are deceitful meat.*

THE book of God is our rule of practice, not less than of faith. It enforces religion not only in our religious, but in our natural, actions.[8] It directs in the daily details of common life. Suppose we are invited, in the way of Providence, to the table of a man of rank—how wise the caution—*Consider diligently what is before thee!* Think where you are—what is the besetting temptation—what impression your conduct is likely to make. Wantonness of appetite, or levity of manner, gives a plausible ground of prejudice to the ungodly, or "stumbling to the weak."[9]

But after all—ourselves are mainly concerned. May not the luxuries of the table spread before us stir up disproportionate indulgence? The rule is plain and urgent. *If thou* art conscious of being *given to appetite*—making it thy first object and delight—bridle it as by force and violence.[10] Act as if *a knife was at thy throat.* Be stern and resolute with thyself.[11] Give no quarter to the lust. Resist every renewed indulgence. The *dainties are deceitful meat*—sometimes from the insincerity of the host;[12] always from the disappointment of the anticipated pleasure.[13] To use them may be lawful. To *be desirous of them* is fearfully dangerous.

[1] 1 Kings xi. 28. [2] Rom. xii. 11.
[3] Luke xix. 13. [4] Matt. xxv. 21—23.
[5] 1 Kings x. 8, with Rev. vii. 15; xxii. 3, 4. [6] Ps. cxlix. 9.
[7] John xii. 26. [8] 1 Cor. x. 31.
[9] 1 Cor. viii. 9. Rom. xiv. 21. [10] Matt. xviii. 8, 9.
[11] Ver. 31. Ps. cxli. 4. [12] Ver. 6—8. [13] Eccl. ii. 10, 11.

Who that knows his own weakness will deem this caution needless? Alas! was not "the lust of the flesh" the first inlet to that sin, which has overwhelmed us all?[1] How has sensual pleasure tarnished may a Christian profession,[2] and damped the liveliness of spiritual apprehensions and enjoyment![3] If Christ's disciples—conversant only *with mean and homely fare*—needed a caution to "take heed;"[4] much more must it apply to *a ruler's table*, where every thing ministers to the temptation.

It is man's high prerogative to "have dominion over the creature."[5] It is his shame, therefore, that the creature in any form should have dominion over him. God gives us a body to feed, not to pamper; to be the servant, not the master, of the soul. He gives bread for our necessities[6]—man craves "meat for his lust."[7] We are to "make provision" for the wants, not "for the lust, of the flesh."[8] And surely a soul, that "puts on the Lord Jesus Christ," can never degrade itself to be a purveyor of the flesh. If an heathen could say, 'I am greater, and born to greater things, than to be the servant of my body'[9]—is it not a shame for a Christian—born as he is—the heir of an everlasting crown—to be the slave of his carnal indulgences?

To go as near as we can to the bounds of intemperance is to be in imminent danger of exceeding. 'He that takes his *full* liberty in what he may, shall repent him.'[10] Temptation presses hard. Then put the strongest guard at this weak point. 'Curb thy desires, though they be somewhat importunate; and thou shalt find in time incredible benefit by it.'[11] Take the prayer of our Church—'Grant unto us such abstinence, that, our flesh being subdued unto the spirit, we may ever obey thy godly motions.'[12] Connect with it the resolution of one apostle—"I keep under my body, and bring it into subjection"[13]—and the rule of another—"Add to your faith temperance."[14] This practical warfare will break the power of many a strong temptation, and triumph over the flesh gloriously.[15]

4. *Labor not to be rich; cease from thine own wisdom.* 5. *Wilt thou set thine eyes* (cause thine eyes to fly, Marg.) *upon that which is not? for riches certainly make themselves wings; they fly away as an eagle toward heaven.*

We have now a warning against covetousness. If riches come from the blessing of God, receive them thankfully,[16] and consecrate them wisely and freely for him. But to *labor to be rich*—is the dictate of *our own wisdom*—not of that "which is from above." 'Let them be gotten if they can, and how they can,' without needless scrupulosity.[17] Solomon, however, describes by a beautiful

[1] 1 John ii. xvi. Gen. iii. 6. [2] 1 Cor. 11, 21. Phil. iii. 18, 19. Jude 12, 13. [3] Gen. xxv. 28; xxvii. 4, with 26—29. [4] Luke xxi. 34. [5] Gen. i. 26, 28; ix. 2. [6] Matt. vi. 11, 25—33. [7] Ps. lxxviii. 18. [8] Rom. xiii. 14. [9] Seneca. [10] Bp. Hall's Works, viii. 101. [11] Bp. Sanderson's Sermon on Ps. xix. 13. [12] Collect for first Sunday in Lent. [13] 1 Cor. ix. 27. [14] 2 Peter i. 5, 6. [15] Dan. i. 8. Compare Augustine's ingenuous and instructive Confessions, book x. c. 31. [16] Chap. x. 22. Gen. xxxi. 9. [17] Chap. xxviii. 20, 22. Ez. xxviii. 4, 5. Luke xvi. 4—8.

figure their true nature—a mere non-entity—an illusion—*that which is not.* Folly indeed then must it be to *set the eyes* (to *cause them to fly*, like a ravenous bird upon its prey[1]) upon this nullity, continually eluding the grasp. At one moment it seems to be within reach. The next it has *flown away as an eagle towards heaven.*

And yet practically to acknowledge the stamp of vanity upon this idolized treasure is a lesson not learnt in a day—learnt only in the school of discipline. The eagerness for the earthly, and the neglect of the heavenly, object, show, either that eternity is a delusion, or that the world is mad. For were the things of eternity *really* believed, would not the thoughts be fixed, and the heart be filled with them, with but little time or room for the engrossing vanities of life? As to intrinsic value, Luther not less truly than boldly declared—that 'the whole Turkish empire in all its vastness was only a crust, which the great Father of the family cast to the dogs.' And then—as to the abiding—there is no need to invent *wings. Riches make them to themselves.* The man who concentrates all his wisdom, talents, and energy, who sacrifices all his peace; "rising up early, and late taking rest,"[2] in the *labor after riches*, may be, and often has been, at one stroke deprived of all, just as he supposed himself to be secure of all. Divine chastisement,[3] indolence,[4] extravagance,[5] injustice,[6] robbery, may bring to the lowest poverty.[7] The longest stay is but a moment. Eternity is at the door;[8] and naked shall we go out of the world, as we came into it.[9] Yet even this palpable consciousness fails to teach men the important lessons, to *cease from their own wisdom,* to seek true substance on earth,[10] and in God's wisdom to lay up enduring "treasures in heaven."[11]

Here then lies the contrast. The world apprehends realities only in the objects before them; the Christian only in invisible things. Therefore if our judgment looks upon the one as a shadow, and the other as substance—mind that we proportion our affections accordingly; giving the shadow of love to the things of earth, the marrow and substance of the heart to the things of eternity. Thank our God for the present possession of "a better and enduring substance."[12] But are there not moments of rest and indulgence, when "uncertain riches" become our confidence,[13] and we need a sharp lesson to remind us, how *certainly they make to themselves wings, and flee away?* Oh! think—Christian—of thy heavenly birth—thine eternal expectations; what manner of man thou wilt be in a short moment, when the false pageant shall have given way to the real manifestation of the Son of God, and thou shalt be on the throne with him for ever.[14] With this glory in

[1] Comp. Jer. xxii. 17. Hos. ix. 11.
[2] Ps. cxxvii. 2.
[3] Gen. xiii. 5—11; xiv. 14.
[4] Chap. vi. 9—11.
[5] Luke xv. 12—16.
[6] Chap. xx. 21; xxi. 6. Jam. v. 2, 3,
[7] Job i. 14—17. Ps. cxix. 61.
[8] Luke xii. 20.
[9] Job i. 21. Ps. xlix. 17. 1 Tim. vi. 7.
[10] Chap. viii. 18—21.
[11] Matt. vi. 20.
[12] Heb. x. 34.
[13] 1 Tim. vi. 17.
[14] Phil. iv. 5. Col. iii. 1—4.

prospect, what a degradation is it to *set thine eyes* upon a "fashion that passeth away!"[1]

6, 7. *Eat thou not the bread of him that hath an evil eye, neither desire thou his dainty meats: for as he thinketh in his heart, so is he: 'Eat and drink,' saith he to thee; but his heart is not with thee.* 8. *The morsel which thou hast eaten shalt thou vomit up, and lose thy sweet words*

Kindly intercourse with our neighbors is a part of the courtesies of life.[2] Yet we ought not to entertain the invitation of a niggardly man, who grudges the very food we eat, or of a deceitful man, whose friendship is a cloke for selfish purposes. *The evil eye* will peep through the covers of his *dainty meats*, and betray him, in spite of his effort for concealment. We judge him not by his words; *for as he thinketh in his heart, so is he.* And while *he saith, Eat and drink*, it is but too plain, that *his heart is not with us.*[3] "Better is a dinner of herbs where love is," than his *dainty meats.* "A poor man is far better than such a liar."[4] Every *morsel* at his table is loathsome; and gladly would we retract, and *lose the sweet words*, with which we had unworthily complimented[5] our host.

No such danger attaches to the invitations of the Gospel. There is no *evil eye*[6]—no grudging—"Ho, every one that thirsteth, come ye to the waters."[7] And *while he saith*—"*Eat*, O friends; yea *drink* abundantly, O beloved,"[8] his whole *heart is with us.* There are no repentings—no disappointments here. Every taste increases the appetite for more. And the prospect is near at hand, when we "shall be abundantly" and eternally "satisfied with the fatness of his house."[9]

9. *Speak not in the ears of a fool: for he will despise the wisdom of thy words.*

Our Lord's rule is to the same purport—"Give not that which is holy unto the dogs; neither cast ye your pearls before swine, lest they trample them under foot, and turn again and rend you."[10] Cast not away your good counsels upon incorrigible sinners. So long as there is any hope of reclaiming *the fool*, make every effort for his precious soul. In the true Spirit of our Master, bring the Gospel to the worst and the most unwilling; and never make the rule of prudence the excuse for indolence. Yet "there is a time to keep silence, as well as a time to speak."[11] Such a time we shall

[1] 1 Cor. vii. 29—31. It is a fine remark of a Heathen philosopher—'Nothing can be called great, which to despise is great. Thus riches, honors, dignities, authorities, and whatever beside may have the outward pomp of this world's theatre, cannot be to a wise man pre-eminent blessings, since the contempt of them is a blessing of no mean order. Indeed those who enjoy them are not so much entitled to admiration, as those who can look down upon them with a noble superiority of mind.' Longin. de Sublimit. sect. vii. The Roman Satyrist adverts to Solon's warning to Crœsus, when he refused to admire his immense riches (a warning despised at the time, but afterwards remembered when he was bound to the stake).

———'Crœsum, quem vox justi facunda Solonis
Respicere ad longæ jussit spatia ultima vitæ.'—Juv. x. 274.

[2] 1 Cor. v. 10, 11; x. 27. [3] Luke xi. 37. [4] Chap. xv. 17; xix. 22.
[5] 2 Sam. xi. 13; xiii. 26—28. [6] Matt. xx. 15. [7] Isa. lv. 1.
[8] Can. v. 1. [9] Ps. xxxvi. 8; xvi. 11. [10] Matt. vii. 6.
[11] Eccl. iii 7. Chap. xxvi. 4, 5.

understand by the trial to our own spirit. We long to speak in compassion. But self-denial—not self-indulgence—restrains.[1] We have before been warned against untimely rebuke.[2] This caution extends further—*Speak not in the ears of a fool.* Such was our Master's silence before Herod.[3] If he would hear, there would be hope. But, instead of being thankful for instruction, *he will despise the wisdom of thy words,*[4] and take occasion from them only to scoff and blaspheme the more. Many doubtful cases however require much wisdom. And the safe rule will be, never to speak without prayer for Divine guidance, and simplicity, and love.

10, 11. *Remove not the old landmark; and enter not into the fields of the fatherless; for their Redeemer is mighty; he shall plead their cause with thee.*

The general prohibition to *remove the old landmark* has been before given.[5] A special warning, and a powerful reason is here added. Many would not dare to touch the rich, while they oppress the poor at their will. But *the field of the fatherless* is under the Almighty protection. Beware of arming against yourself the Divine vengeance by *entering into it.* Helpless they may seem to be. But have they no counsel to plead their cause? *Their Redeemer is mighty; he shall plead their cause with thee.*[6] Was the nearest of kin bound to be the Goel—*the Redeemer* of his kinsman's wrongs?[7] Adored be the unsearchable pity, grace, and condescension of Emanuel! When he could not redeem as God, he became our kinsman, that he might be our Redeemer![8] And he now bears the endearing title of "the Father of the fatherless."[9] His moral government shows, that "in him they find" not "mercy"[10] only, but justice also.[11] Is not here their strong confidence, when human help is gone? "The poor committeth himself unto thee; thou art the helper of *the fatherless.*[12] "Pure and undefiled religion is" therefore to follow his heavenly pattern—"to visit *the fatherless* and widows in their affliction."[13] Hence the special provision made for the apostolical ministration for these friendless objects of Christian help.[14] The Gospel reflects the image of Christ when native selfishness thus melts away under the influence of sympathizing love.

12. *Apply thine heart unto instruction, and thine ears to the words of knowledge.*

The frequent repetition of these counsels[15] implies an humbling truth—familiar to every day's experience—man's natural revulsion from Divine *instruction,* and his inattention *to the words of knowledge.* It is well to have these injunctions renewed from time to time. We all need "precept upon precept, line upon line;"[16] and *that* to the very end of our course. The best taught and most ad-

[1] Ps. xxxix. 1, 2. [2] Chap. ix. 8. [3] Luke xxiii. 9.
[4] Chap. i. 7. [5] Chap. xxii. 28.
[6] Ib. Verses 22, 23. Jer. l. 33, 34. Comp. Ez. xxii. 22—24. Job xxii. 9, 10; xxxi. 21—23; xxxiv. 28. Isa. x. 1—3.
[7] Lev. xxv. 25. Num. xxxv. 12. Ruth iii. 12. [8] Heb. ii. 14—16.
[9] Ps. lxviii. 6, with 18. [10] Hos. xiv. 3. Ps. cxlvi. 9. [11] Ps. ciii. 6.
[12] Ib. x. 14 17, 18. [13] James i. 27. [14] Acts vi. 1. 1 Tim. v. 3—5, 9, 10
[15] Chap. ii. iii. iv. vii. xix. 20 [16] Isa. xxviii. 13.

vanced Christian will be most earnest in seeking more *instruction*, and will most gladly sit at the feet of the Lord's ministers, to hear *the words of knowledge*. Here lies the value of the Bible, as the one source of *instruction*, and the alone treasure-house of *the words of knowledge*. The simple reference to this standard is the keeping of the soul from Romish errors, whether on Romish or Protestant ground.

Observe the connexion between *the application of the heart and of the ears.*[1] *The heart*, open to sound advice or moral precept, is yet shut to Christ and his doctrine. It is closed up in unbelief, prejudice, indifference, and the love of pleasure. A listless *heart* therefore produces a careless ear. But when the heart is graciously opened, softened, and enlightened, the attention of the ear is instantly fixed.[2] This indeed is the Lord's Sovereign creation work;[3] yet wrought by a God of order in the use of his own means. Awakened desire brings to prayer.[4] Prayer brings the favor and the blessing.[5] And how precious then is *every word of knowledge*—more "than thousands of gold and silver."[6]

13. *Withhold not correction from the child: for if thou beatest him with the rod, he shall not die.* 14. *Thou shalt beat him with the rod, and shalt deliver his soul from hell.*

Christian parents do not always recognize the scriptural standard of discipline. "Foolishness is bound in the heart" of the parent, no less than "of the child." Does "the wild ass's colt"[7] tame itself? Surely it must always need its measure of *correction*. The rule therefore is—notwithstanding all the pleas of pity and fondness—*withhold it not*. Do the work wisely, firmly, lovingly. Persevere notwithstanding apparently unsuccessful results. Connect it with prayer, faith, careful instruction. Use it as God's means, linked with his blessing.

But are not gentle means more likely to be effectual? Had this been God's judgment, he would not as a God of mercy have provided a different regimen. Eli tried them, and the sad issue is written for our instruction.[8] 'Must I then be cruel to a child?' Nay—God charges thee with cruelty, if thou *withhold correction from him*. He "goes on in his own foolishness."[9] Except he be restrained, he will die in his sin. God has ordained the rod to purge his sins, and so *deliver his soul from hell*. What parent then, that trembles for the child's eternal destiny, can *withhold correction*? Is it not cruel love, that turns away from the painful duty? To suffer sin upon a child, no less than upon a brother, is tantamount to "hating him in our heart."[10] Is it not better that the flesh should smart, than that *the soul should die*? Is it no sin to omit a means of grace, as Divinely appointed as the word and the sacraments? Is there no danger of fomenting the

[1] Chap. ii. 2. [2] Acts xvi. 14. [3] Chap. xx. 12. Rev. iii. 7.
[4] Ps. cxix. 18; xix. 10. [5] Chap. ii. 3—6.
[6] Ps. cxix. 14, 72, 127. [7] Job xi. 12.
[8] 1 Sam. ii. 23—25; iii. 13. [9] Chap. xxii. 15. Eccl. xi. 10.
[10] Lev. xix 18, with Chap. xiii. 24.

native wickedness, and thus becoming accessory to the child's eternal destruction? What if he should reproach thee throughout eternity, for the neglect of that timely *correction*, which might have *delivered his soul from hell*? Or even if he be "scarcely saved," may he not charge upon thee much of that difficulty in the ways of God—the influence of deep-rooted habits of evil, which early discipline might have restrained or subjugated?

Yet let it not be used at all times. Let remonstrance be first tried; like our Heavenly Father, who will never stir the rod with his children, if his "still small voice" of instruction prevail. Magnifying trifles into grave offences; chiding every slip of childishness or troublesome forgetfulness, casts a baneful gloom upon home. It is "a continual dropping in a very rainy day."[1] This indiscriminate *correction* soon brings a callous deadness to all sense of shame. Let it be reserved, at least in its more serious forms, for wilfulness. It is medicine, not food. It is the remedy for constitutional diseases, not the daily regimen for life and nourishment. And to convert medicine into food, gradually destroys its remedial qualities.

Some parents, indeed, use nothing but *correction*. They indulge their own passions at the expense of their less guilty children. Unlike our Heavenly Father, they "afflict and grieve their children *willingly*;"[2] to vent their own anger, not to subdue their children's sins. This intemperate use of a scriptural ordinance brings discredit upon its efficacy, sows the seed of much bitter fruit; engendering in their children a spirit of bondage and concealment, sometimes of disgust, and even of hatred, towards their unreasonable parents. 'If parents'—said a wise and godly father—'would not correct their children, except in a praying frame, when they can "lift up their hands without wrath," it would neither provoke God nor them.'[3]

Other parents freely threaten *the rod*, yet *withhold* it. It was only meant to frighten. It soon becomes an empty sound, powerless and hardening. This again contravenes our Great Exemplar. *His* threatenings are not vain words. If his children will not turn, they will find them faithful and true to their cost. This threatening play is solemn trifling with truth; teaching children by example, what they had learnt from the womb,[4] to "speak lies." Let our words be considerate, but certain. Let our children know, that they must not trifle either with them or with us. Truthful discipline alone can convey a beneficial influence.

After all, parents have much to learn. We must not expect too much from our children; nor be unduly depressed by their naughtiness. Yet we must not wink at their sinful follies. We must love them not less, but better. And because we love them, we must *not withhold—when needed—correction from them.* More painful is the work to ourselves than to them. Most humbling is

[1] Chap. xxvii. 15. [2] Contrast Lam. iii. 33. Heb. xii. 10.
[3] Matthew Henry's Life, chap. xiii. [4] Psalm lviii. 3.

it. For since the corrupt root produces the poisoned sap in the bud, what else is it, but the *correction* of our own sin? Yet though "no chastening for the present be joyous, but rather grievous;"[1] when given in prayer, in wisdom, and in faith, it is ordained for the pain of the flesh, that *the soul may be delivered from hell.*[2] 'Lord, do thou be pleased to strike in with every stroke, that the rod of correction may be a rod of instruction.'[3] 'It is a rare soul' —said good Bishop Hall—'that can be kept in constant order without smarting remedies. I confess mine cannot. How wild had I run, if the rod had not been over me? Every man can say, he thanks God for his ease. For me, I bless God for my trouble.'[4]

15. *My son, if thine heart be wise, my heart shall rejoice, even mine,* (I will rejoice, Marg.) 16. *Yea, my reins shall rejoice, when thy lips speak right things.*

The wise man now turns from parents, and addresses himself most tenderly to children[5]—perhaps to his own child. What Christian parent but responds? Could we be happy to see our child honored in the world, admired, talented, prosperous, without godliness? *If thine heart be wise*—this is the spring of parental joy—*my heart shall rejoice, even mine.* His health, his comfort, his welfare, are inexpressibly dear to us. But while we watch over the casket, it is the jewel that we mainly value. The love of our child's soul is the life and soul of parental love.[6] None but a parent knows the heart of a parent. None but a Christian parent knows the yearning anxiety, the many tears, prayers, and "travailing in birth again" for the soul of a beloved child; or the fervor of joy and praise, when the first budding of heavenly *wisdom* bursts to view.[7] The sight brings joy into the innermost depths of the bosom.[8] Parents, who have not sympathy with these sensations, and with whom Solomon's language is unfelt and uninteresting, realize but little either of their responsibilities or their privileges.

Greatly is the parent's joy heightened to hear *his son's lips speaking right things;* to see him in a day of apostacy and unstable profession openly standing forth on the Lord's side; "asking for the old paths of rest," now that the "highways are" too often "unoccupied, and the travellers walking through bye-ways."[9]

[1] Heb. xii. 11.
[2] Comp. 1 Cor. v. 5; xi. 32. The Heathen philosopher adverts to the subject of punishments as an instrument of healing produced by means apparently contrary. Arist. Eth. ii. 3.
[3] Swinnock's Christian Man's Calling, ii. 35.
[4] Silent thoughts, xxi.
[5] Chap. i. 8, 10, 15, &c.
[6] See Solomon's own education, chap. iv. 3, 4.
[7] Verses 24, 25; x. 1; xv. 20; xxix. 3. 'Lord, let thy blessing so accompany my endeavor (was the pleading of a godly parent) that all my sons may be Benaiahs (the Lord's building); and then they will be all Abners (their Father's light); and that all my daughters may be Bethiahs (the Lord's daughters); and then they will be all Abigails (their Father's joy).' Swinnock's Christian Man's Calling, ii. 29, 30.
[8] *The reins*, as deeply seated in the body, are a frequent scriptural illustration of the inner thoughts and affections. Ps. xvi. 7; xxvi. 2. Jer. xii. 2. Lam. iii. 13.
[9] Jud. v. 6. Jer. vi. 16.

But surely this child—now such a joy to his father—is one, *from whom correction has not been withheld.*[1] The "foolishness bound in his heart has thus been driven from him,"[2] and its place graciously supplied by a *wise heart*—a witness to the rule and promise subsequently given—"Correct thy son, and he shall give thee rest."[3]

And are not ministers also partakers of this parental joy? "Paul the aged" was filled with prayerful delight in his "beloved son in the faith."[4] The thriving churches were "his glory and joy."[5] Another apostle "had no greater joy, than to hear that his children walked in truth."[6] And may we not rise higher, and adore the manifestation of this joy in heaven[7]—yea! the rejoicing in the bosom of God himself over the return of his *corrected child* to a *wise heart*—"This my son was dead, and is alive again; he was lost, and is found?"[8]

17. *Let not thine heart envy sinners; but be thou in the fear of the Lord all the day long.* 18. *For surely there is an end; and thine expectation shall not be cut off.*

Exactly similar is David's counsel. He sets out *the end*, and shows how little reason we have to *envy sinners*, and what is the true path of duty and quietness.[9] He was, however, himself, for a while perplexed and shaken by this temptation. And though he did not *envy sinners*, so as to covet their worldly prosperity, yet comparing their condition with his own 'chastening,' "it was too painful for him, until he went into the sanctuary of God. Then understood he their *end*,"[10] and learnt to rest in the assurance—*Thine expectation shall not be cut off.*

What then is the safeguard proposed against this temptation? Just what the Psalmist had found so effectual—a close walk with God—"being continually with him"[11]—the very spirit of the rule—*Be in the fear of God all the day long.* Here he gathered confidence for both worlds—"Thou shalt guide me with thy counsel, and afterward receive me to glory."[12] With such a portion both for time and for eternity, could his heart then *envy sinners?* "I have set the Lord alway before me. Thou wilt show me the path of life, the fulness of everlasting joy."[13] What more could he desire? *His heart*—instead of *envying sinners*—would be drawn out in compassionate pleading for them, who have no portion, but a dying world,[14] no *expectation*, but that which shall quickly be *cut off.*[15]

But this habitual *fear of the Lord* is nothing separate from common life. It gives to it an holy character. It makes all its

[1] Verses 13, 14. [2] Chap. xxii. 15. Comp. xxix. 15.
[3] Chap. xxix. 17. [4] 2 Tim. i. 2—5. [5] 1 Thess. ii. 19, 20; iii. 8, 9.
[6] 2 John 4. 3 John 4. [7] Luke xv. 7, 10. [8] Ibid. verses 13—24.
[9] Ps. xxxvii. 1—9, 35, 36. Comp. chap. xxiv. 1, 2, 19, 20.
[10] Ibid. lxxiii. 3—17. Even a Heathen discovered the power of this temptation. Socrates, being asked what was most troublesome to good men? answered—'The prosperity of the wicked.'
[11] Ibid. verse 23. [12] Ps. lxxiii. 24. [13] Ib. xvi. 8—11.
[14] Ib. xvii. 14. Luke xvi. 25. [15] Chap. xxiv. 20. Comp. Ecclus. ix. 11.

minute details not only consistent with, but component parts of godliness. Acts of kindliness are "done after a godly sort."[1] Instead of one duty thrusting out another, all are "done heartily, as to the Lord, and not unto man."[2] Some confessors confine their religion to extraordinary occasions. But Elijah seems to have been content to await his translation in his ordinary course of work;[3] an example that may teach us to lay the great stress upon the daily and habitual, not the extraordinory, service. Others are satisfied with a periodical religion; as if it was rather a rapture or an occasional impulse, than a habit. But if we are to engage in morning and evening devotions, we are also to "wait upon the Lord *all the day*."[4] If we are to enjoy our Sabbath privileges, we are also to "abide in our weekly" "calling with God."[5] Thus the character of a servant of God is maintained—"devoted to his fear."[6]

In this Christian walk with God, all is safe for eternity. The hope of the ungodly,[7] the hypocrite,[8] the worldling,[9] shall perish. But *thine expectation shall not be cut off*.[10] It is "a hope that maketh not ashamed.[11] It is grounded upon "the immutability of God's counsel," and "entereth into that within the vail."[12] *Surely there is an end* for this. If the cross be heavy, thou hast but a little time to bear it. If the way be wearisome to the flesh, *the end* drawing nearer will abundantly compensate.[13] If the light be not visible, "it is sown" for thee. And in waiting for the glorious harvest—"here is the patience and faith of the saints."[14] Meanwhile judge not the Lord hastily, by sense and feeling. Hold fast by God's word. Give time to his providence to explain itself. Pronounce nothing upon an unfinished work. Wait, and "see *the end* of the Lord." "I know the thoughts that I think towards you, saith the Lord; thoughts of peace, and not of evil, to give you an expected end. What I do thou knowest not now; but thou shalt know"—and not only know, but approve—"hereafter."[15]

19. *Hear thou, my son, and be wise, and guide thine heart in the way.* 20. *Be not among winebibbers; among riotous eaters of flesh:* 21. *For the drunkard and the glutton shall come to poverty: and drowsiness shall clothe a man with rags.*

These repeated exhortations to *hear*, remind us of our Lord's earnest and affectionate calls—"Who hath ears to hear, let him hear."[16] They show the great importance of *hearing*, as the first step to *being wise*. For wisdom, no less than "faith, cometh by hearing."[17] "*Guide thine heart in the way.*" The promise to make this call effectual, is—"I lead in the way of righteousness, in the midst of the paths of judgment."[18]

[1] 3 John 5, 6. [2] Eph. vi. 6 Col. iii. 23. [3] 2 Kings ii. 1—12.
[4] Psalm xxv. 5, with Num. xxviii. 4 [5] Ps. lxxxiv. with 1 Cor. vii. 20, 24.
[6] Ps. cxix. 28. [7] Chap. xi. 7. [8] Job viii. 13, 14.
[9] Luke xii. 19, 20. [10] Chap. xxiv. 14. Ps. ix. 18. Eccl. viii. 12. Phil. i. 20
[11] Rom. v. 5. [12] Heb. vi. 17—19.
[13] 'O passi graviora, dabit Deus his quoque finem!'—Virg. Æn. i. 199.
[14] Rev. xiii. 10. [15] James v. 11. Jer. xxix. 11. John xiii. 7.
[16] Matt. xi. 15; xiii. 7. [17] Rom. x. 16, with chap. i. 5. [18] Chap. viii. 20.

But the call especially warns against a besetting temptation. God's creature abuses his gifts.[1] *Wine* becomes the occasion of excess. *Riotous eaters of flesh* degrade the soul as the slave of the body. Not only be not one of them, but *be not amongst them.*[2] Can we be among the leprous without infection? May we not get a stain, that will not easily be wiped out? Do we not insensibly receive the world in our society?[3] Did not Lot probably learn his dreadful wickedness by contact with the ungodly?[4] The right love is not to sit down with them, but to labor for their conversion; and—this being ineffectual—to avoid them. Young people! remember—'Tinder is not apter to take fire, wax the impression of the seal, paper the ink, than youth to receive the impression of wickedness.'[5] Fancy not that the enemy in this snare intends even your present happiness. His malice holds out a poisened bait. *Poverty and shame* are the temporal fruits.[6] But the eternal ruin of his deluded victims is his far more deadly design.

Noah *as a winebibber*,[7] and the Corinthian converts—profaning the sacred feast by *drunkenness and gluttony*[8]—warn the man of God—"Watch and pray that ye enter not into emptation."[9] Always however evangelize these parental warnings, on the moving principles of the Gospel. "Walk *not in rioting and drunkenness; but put ye on the Lord Jesus Christ*,"—the only effectual covering from the wantonness of the flesh—"*Having these promises*, dearly beloved, let us cleanse ourselves from all filthiness of the flesh and spirit."[10]

22. *Hearken unto thy father that begat thee, and despise not thy mother when she is old.*

"We have had fathers of our flesh, and we gave them reverence."[11] Such is the rule of nature. Such is the law of God.[12] The wise man here enforces its special application to aged parents —*thy mother when she is old.* Then surely, love and reverence are doubly due. 'A thing comely and pleasant to see,' says Bishop Hall—'and worthy of honor from the beholder, is a child understanding the eye of his parent.'[13] More lovely still is this filial exercise, when the age of the child has naturally loosened the restraints of authority. Respect is then the effect of principle and gratitude. The child no more feels at liberty to *despise* his parents' wishes, than if he were subject to their early discipline. The Scripture examples are beautiful patterns for our imitation. Isaac with Abraham;[14] Jacob with both his parents;[15] Joseph's deference to his aged father, and desiring his blessing on his own

[1] Isa. v. 11, 12, 22; xxii. 13. Hab. ii. 5, with Ps. civ. 14, 15. 1 Tim. iv. 3—5.
[2] Chap. xxviii. 7.
[3] Ps. cvi. 35. Comp. Matt. xxiv 49.
[4] Gen. xix. 30—32, with Ez. xvi. 49, 50.
[5] Greenhill on Ezek. xix. 4.
[6] Chap. vi. 11; xx. 13; xxi. 17. Isaiah xxviii. 1—3. Joel i. 5. Luke xv. 13—16.
[7] Gen. ix. 20, 21.
[8] 1 Cor. xi. 21.
[9] Matt. xxv. 41.
[10] Rom. xiii. 13, 14. 2 Cor. vii. 1.
[11] Heb. xii. 9
[12] Ex. xx. 12. Lev. xix. 3. Eph. vi. 1, 2. Comp. chap. i. 8; vi. 20.
[13] Holy Observations, v.
[14] Gen. xxii. 9.
[15] Ibid. xxviii. 1 5

children;[1] Moses with his father-in-law;[2] Ruth with her mother-in-law;[3] Solomon in the grandeur of royalty paying respect to his mother;[4] the Rechabites hearkening to their deceased father's command;[5] and above all the rest—the Saviour's tender care for his mother in his own dying agonies.[6]

The contrary conduct is marked with the most awful reprobation.[7] It forms a part of the dark mass of Heathen depravity,[8] and one of the signs of "the perilous times" threatened "in the last days."[9] The spectacle will ever bring a blot upon the child's name and character.[10]

But is not this trial of neglect the Lord's chastening of foolish fondness of our children when young, of unwise treatment, or inconsistent conduct? Sinful indulgence will always in the end make us *despised* in their eyes, and lay our authority in the dust for them to trample under foot. Christian dignity and consistency, on the other hand, commands the impressive influence of respect, even where they fail of producing the full practical results.[11] Oh! what need have we of divine grace and wisdom, honorably to maintain parental responsibility?

23. *Buy the truth, and sell it not: also wisdom and instruction, and understanding.* 24. *The father of the righteous shall greatly rejoice: and he that begetteth a wise child shall have joy of him.* 25. *Thy father and thy mother shall be glad, and she that bare thee shall rejoice.*

This is the merchantman, who purchased the "pearl of great price at the cost of all that he had."[12] The blessing can indeed only be "*bought* without *price*."[13] It is as free as it is precious. But the figure sets out the importance of gaining it at any cost. First, however, let us satisfy ourselves, that the seller is no deceiver—that he is perfectly upright in his dealings. "*Buy of me*"[14]—saith the Saviour. This sets the matter at rest. If we do not really want the article, we shall not pay much heed to the injunction—"Buy those things that ye *have need of*"[15]—is the rule. Ponder also its inestimable value. It is *the truth*—the only means of salvation[16]—the only deliverance from sin[17]—the only principle of holiness[18]—the "One thing needful."[19] Place the blessing fully in view—"The excellency of the knowledge of Christ Jesus our Lord. That I may win Christ, and be found in him. That I might attain unto the resurrection of the dead."[20] We cannot be de-

[1] Gen. xlviii. 9—14. [2] Ex. xviii. 13—24. [3] Ruth ii. 22, 23.
[4] 1 Kings ii. 19. [5] Jer. xxxv. 6.
[6] John xix. 26, 27. Dr. Taylor's 'godly exhortation to his son,' as Foxe remarks in his exquisite Biography, 'is worthy of all youth to be marked'—'When thy mother is waxen old, forsake her not; but provide for her to thy power, and see that she lack nothing; for so will God bless thee, give thee long life upon earth, and prosperity, which I pray God to grant thee.' Vol. vi. 692. Comp. Ecclus. iii. 8—14; vii. 27, 28.
[7] Chap. xx. 20; xxx. 11, 17. Deut. xxi. 18—21; xxvii. 16. Isa. iii. 5.
[8] Rom. i. 30. [9] 2 Tim. iii. 1, 2. [10] Chap. xix. 26.
[11] Chap. xxxi. 28. [12] Matt. xiii. 45, 46. [13] Isa. lv. 1.
[14] Rev. iii. 18. [15] John xiii. 29. [16] 1 Tim. ii. 4.
[17] John viii. 32 2 Tim. ii. 25, 26. [18] John xvii. 17. [19] Luke x. 42.
[20] Phil. iii. 8—11.

frauded in the purchase. It is a cheap purchase at any price.[1] No cost was too great for the baubles of Vanity Fair. But Bunyan beautifully describes his pilgrims, answering the sneering reproach—'What will you buy?' They lifted up their eyes above, saying—'We will *buy the truth.*'

But like the well-practised merchant, we must secure the genuine article. Much counterfeit coin is current.[2] Bring every thing "to God's standard."[3] That which brings *wisdom, instruction, and understanding*, is *the truth* of God.

Then—having ascertained its riches and its purity—not only wish for it—gaze at it—commend it—but *buy the truth.* Not only bid—make an offer; but strike the agreement. Make it thine. The man did not *wish* for the field with the "hidden treasure;" but he "sold all that he had, and *bought*[4] it." And let thy purchase be the whole truth. Every particle—the very filings of the gold—are invaluable—"Set thine heart *upon all* that I shall show thee."[5] Many are content to be at some pains, but they stop short of the prize.[6] Herod shrunk from the full price.[7] So did the young ruler;[8] and Agrippa;[9] and therefore they *bought* it not. Moses gave up for it "the treasures of Egypt;"[10] Paul his Jewish privileges and high reputation.[11] The Hebrews "took joyfully the spoiling of their goods."[12] The martyrs "loved not their lives unto the death."[13] And who of these repented of the costly purchase?

Having thus made the purchase, shall we part with it? Should we not find it all we expected; or should we after all discover that we did not want it, we should doubtless be glad to be rid of it. Many an estate has been bought and sold again from disappointed expectations. But though usually what we have *bought*, we are at liberty to *sell;* here is a command to *buy*, but a prohibition to *sell.* And a merciful prohibition it is! For those who *sell the truth*, sell their own souls with it. And "what shall it profit a man, if he shall gain the whole world, and lose his own soul!"[14] Can we look at Esau,[15] Judas,[16] Demas,[17] *selling* their treasures for a thing of naught, without sorrowful trembling? Yet their apostacy clearly proved, that they had never "received the truth in the love of it;"[18] that it was some shining shadow, merely notional and speculative; never engrafted in their hearts. Having therefore never felt the power, or known its price, they could *sell it* for this world's lust or pleasure, or for the more flattering delusions of their own hearts. Reader: have you ever known that apprehension of Divine Truth, that has made it, in your eyes, worth every

[1] Chap. iii. 15. [2] 2 Cor. xi. 3, 14. Gal. i. 6, 7.
[3] 1 Thess. v. 24. 1 John iv. 1. Isa. viii. 20. [4] Matt. xiii. 44.
[5] Ez. xl. 4. [6] 2 Tim. iii. 7. [7] Mark vi. 17—20.
[8] Luke xviii. 23. [9] Acts xxvi. 28. [10] Heb. xi. 24—26.
[11] Phil. iii. 4—8. [12] Heb. x. 34. [13] Rev. xii. 11. Acts xx. 23, 24.
[14] Matt. xvi. 26. [15] Heb. xii. 16, 17. [16] Matt. xxvii. 3—5.
[17] 2 Tim. iv. 10. [18] 2 Thess. ii. 10. Comp. 1 John ii. 19.

sacrifice to *buy it?* No one—be assured—who has really *bought* it, will ever be willing to *sell it.*

A joyous sight it is to see children realizing their parent's fondest hopes; proving "a wise heart"[1] by a diligent enquiry about this only gainful purchase: not content with receiving it by education, but making the contract for themselves; discovering that religion must be a personal concern, an individual transaction between God and their own souls. Cause is it indeed for *greatly rejoicing*, to see their righteous children thus enriched for eternity, in possession of a treasure which they can never spend, and which no troubles, no changes, no malice of hell can touch. If the godly parents have had a seed-time of tears, their precious sheaves of joy are an abundant recompense.[2] The stern exclusive system, which recognizes little, save the Divine purpose and Sovereignty, annuls, or at least, enervates, the responsibility of means, and thus loses the privilege both of trusting the promise, and witnessing its accomplishment. Will not the child feel the constraining obligation to fulfil his parent's *rejoicing* thus vividly portrayed? Most unnatural must he be, if his heart does not glow with the desire thus to repay *his father's* anxious love, and the yearning tenderness of *her that bare him.* They ask no other requital than the *joy and gladness* of seeing *a righteous and a wise son.* Selfishness itself might supply a motive; since parental *gladness* is the child's own joy, walking in "*wisdom's* ways of pleasantness and peace."

26. *My son, give me thine heart, and let thine eyes observe my ways.* 27. *For a whore is a deep ditch; and a strange woman is a narrow pit.* 28. *She also lieth in wait as for a prey, and increaseth the transgressors among men.*

Solomon here manifestly rises above himself, and speaks in the name and Person of Divine Wisdom.[3] For who else could claim *the gift of the heart*—the work of his own hands—the purchase of his own blood? *My Son.* Such is the relationship which God acknowledges; including every blessing which he can give, and all the obedience that he can claim. No obedience can be without the believing and practical acknowledgment of this relation—*My Son*—not a stranger—not an enemy—not a slave—but *a son;* invited to return. An amnesty of the past—a perpetual jubilee of joy—awaits thee at thy Father's house.

Many are the claimants for *the heart.* Heaven and hell contend for it. The world with its riches, honors, and pleasures—and science with its more plausible charms—cries—*Give me thine heart.* Nay, even Satan dares to put in a loud and urgent plea—"If thou wilt worship me, all shall be thine."[4] The loving Father calls—*My Son, give me thine heart.* The answer too often is—'I have no heart for God. It is engaged to the world. I cannot make up my mind to be religious—at least not yet.' And so the

1 Verses 15, 16
2 Ps. cxxvi. 6. Comp. chap. x. 1; xv. 20. Contrast xvii. 25.
3 Chap. i. 20; viii. 1.
4 Luke iv. 7.

"darling is given to the lion"—*the heart* to the murderer. And to him, who alone deserves it—few hearken—and many even of those, only when they have proved to their cost the falsehood and disappointment of all other claimants.

An honor indeed he puts upon his creatures, in condescending to receive as *a gift* what is his most rightful debt, and what he might at any moment command for himself. But his call wakens his child to recollection and conscious dependence. It is the Father's striving with his child's will. It is the test of his child's obedience. It is a pointed arrow of conviction to his conscience for wilful resistance to his call—the only hindrance to his *giving his heart* being, that he has already given it to claimants, infinitely unworthy of it. 'My guilt is damnable'—exclaimed an humbled saint—'in withholding my heart; because I know and believe his love, and what Christ has done to gain my consent—to what?—my own happiness.'[1]

Indeed happiness is bound up in this gracious command. For what else can 'fill the aching void' within, but "the love of God shed abroad in the heart by the Holy Ghost."[2] Created objects only seem to widen the chasm. If our appetite is satisfied, it is but for a moment; while every irritation increases the general dissatisfaction. The heart, wilfully remaining at a moral distance from God, can find its home only in a land of shadows. It grasps nothing solidly; while its incessant conflict with conscience, is "the troubled sea, which cannot rest."[3] God will never abate one atom of his full requisitions. He asks not for magnificent temples, costly sacrifices, pompous ceremonials, but for the spiritual worship of the heart.[4] He demands—not the hands, the feet, the tongue, the ears, but that which is the moving principle of all the members —*the heart.*[5] Give that. It is all he desires. Withhold it,—Nothing is given. What the heart does not do, in a great measure is not done at all. The cold conformity of a lifeless faith is a dead— not "a living"—not therefore an acceptable "sacrifice"[6]—not "a reasonable service." "How canst thou say, I love thee, when *thine heart* is not with me?"[7]

Never will he dispense with this claim of the love of *all our heart.*[8] We must not deal with Him as Lot's wife, moving slowly forward, while the heart is behind;[9] or like Orpah, stopping at the very moment that the cross is to borne.[10] Dream not of dividing the heart with the world.[11] He loves a broken heart. He spurns a divided throne. Satan will seem to be content with a part; because he knows that, as God will accept nothing less than all, the whole will thus fall to him. It is far beneath the Majesty of heaven

[1] Adams's Private Thoughts. [2] Rom. v. 5.
[3] Isa. lvii. 20, 21. [4] Ibid. lxvi. 1, 2, with John iv. 23, 24.
[5] 'Non caput, non manum, non pedem, non cætera membra; sed omnium membrorum principium, radicem, et vitæ humanæ fontem, qui cor est, dari sibi Deus postulat.' Glass. Philolog. Sacr. Lib. ii. Pars i. Tract ii. sect. iii.
[6] Rom. xii. 1. [7] Judg. xvi. 15. [8] Matt. xxii. 37.
[9] Gen. xix. 26. [10] Ruth i. 14. [11] Matt. vi. 24.

to possess any thing less than the throne[1]—a mean throne at best for the Almighty Sovereign of the universe. But his claims are paramount. And never are we truly our own, till we unreservedly acknowledge ourselves to be his. Indeed all false religions in the world are but vain substitutes for this plain and most happy duty. However plausible the show, if it does not lead the heart to God, it is fearful delusion. Whatever principles, practices, or society, turn our hearts from God—it is the high road of ruin.

And doth he ask his child for *his heart?* and will he refuse to *give* it? Does it open immediately to Satan and the world—yea—even before they knock? And is the beseeching Father to be excluded? Are there no "bands of love to draw?"[2] Out of what rock was it hewn, that it can be proof against the pleadings of Divine parental love? Canst thou not give it him? Surely hadst thou the will, thou wouldst have the power too. If thou hast the faintest will, at least show though but the feeblest effort. Offer it, though but with a trembling hand. His hand will meet thine, and take it of thee. The happiest day of life is now arrived—a day, the recollection of which will never be tinged with one shade of regret.

If thou hast not done it—do it now. If thou hast—do it daily. Thou canst not do it too soon or too often. The command does not hale us (as Saul haled his victims[3]) to the service of God. The citadel is not stormed, but it opens its gates. A principle of immortal energy constrains the heart; yet only by "making it willing."[4] The reluctancy is melted away, and by the power of love the heart is "compelled to come."[5] What so free as a gift? And never is the will so free, as when it moves towards God. Weak as he is, yet the child can testify, that to *give his heart*, is his first desire; that he never designs or intends any thing less; that he longs for the consuming of every corruption, which hinders the full surrender. Oh— my God—thy grace alone can enable me—I am ashamed of the gift. Nothing can be more unworthy. But because thou callest for it, it is thine own. Take it as it is. Make it what it is not. Keep it with thyself. Bind it so close to thee with the cords of love, that it may never cast a wishful look away from thee. Had I a thousand hearts, all should be thine. This one thou alone canst fill. Thou alone art worthy of it. Exalt thine own throne in it forever.

And now when the first command is duly regarded, the second will soon follow. *The heart once given to God, the eyes will observe his ways.*[6] '*Our heart* given, gives all the rest. This makes eyes, ears, tongue and hands, and all to be holy, as God's peculiar people."[7] His word will be our rule;[8] His Providence our interpreter.[9] The *heart*—no longer divided, is now at full liberty for the service of God. *The* eyes, no longer wandering, like "the

[1] Matt. x. 37. [2] Hos. xi. 4. [3] Acts viii. 3.
[4] Psalm cx. 3. [5] 2 Cor. v. 14. Luke xiv. 23.
[6] Chap. iv. 23—25. [7] Leighton on 1 Pet. ii. 4, 5.
[8] Chap. vi. 23. Ps. cxix. 9—11, 105. [9] Psalm cvii. 43.

eyes of a fool, in the ends of the earth"[1]—are now fixed upon an object supremely worthy, and abundantly satisfying.

Here also is our power of resistance to the gross seductions of the enemy[2]—"I have opened my mouth unto the Lord, and I cannot"—I will not—"go back."[3] He hath *my heart*, and he shall have it. True indeed—so long as we carry about us a body of sin and death, we need a continual supply of "the Spirit to mortify the deeds of the body."[4] But in our new atmosphere of heavenly light, the mask falls off from the allurements of sin. *The strange woman* appears frightful as *a deep ditch*—or what is even more—*a narrow pit*—with no room to escape from the ruin.[5] Mighty and strong men have fallen into it.[6] The tempter hides the danger, while *she lays wait for the prey;* and thus she successfully *increases the transgressors among men.*[7] Blessed be God—if, while fleshly lusts "have destroyed their thousands and tens of thousands,"[8] we have, *by giving our heart* to its Divine Lord, been enabled to abhor the temptation, and to ascribe to our faithful God the glory of our deliverance.

29. *Who hath woe? who hath sorrow? who hath contentions? who hath babbling? who hath wounds without cause? who hath redness of eyes?* 30. *They that tarry long at the wine: they that go to seek mixed wine.* 31. *Look not thou upon the wine when it is red, when it giveth his color in the cup, when it moveth itself aright.* 32. *At the last it biteth like a serpent, and stingeth like an adder.* 33. *Thine eyes shall behold strange women, and thine heart shall utter perverse things.* 34. *Yea, thou shalt be, as he that lieth down in the midst of the sea, or as he that lieth upon the top of a mast.* 35. *They have stricken me, shalt thou say, and I was not sick; they have beaten me, and I felt it not: when shall I awake? I will seek it yet again.*

A warning was lately given against keeping company with sensualists.[9] Here it is enforced by the most graphical delineation of the sin in all its misery, shame, and ruin. It is the drunkard's looking-glass. Let him see his own face. Let it be hung up in his cottage—in the alehouse. Could he go there? The picture is drawn with such a vividness of coloring. 'No translation or paraphrase can do justice to the concise, abrupt, and energetic manner of the original.'[10] Drunkenness is a time of merriment. But what must be the stupifying insensibility, that can find a moment's joy, with such an accumulation of *woe.*[11] Every sin brings its own mischief. But such woe—such *sorrow*—in all its multiform misery—*who hath it?* The brawls and *contentions* over the cup;[12] the *bab-*

[1] Chap. xvii. 24.
[2] Chap. ii. 10, 11, 16.
[3] Jud. xi. 35. Comp. Gen. xxxix. 9.
[4] Rom. viii. 13. Gal. v. 16.
[5] Chap. xxii. 14; ii. 19.
[6] 1 Kings xi. 1—8, with Neh. xiii. 26. Jud. xvi. 4—20. 'He (Samson) broke the bonds of his enemies; but he could not break the bonds of his own lusts. He choked the lion; but he could not choke his own wanton love.' Ambrose; quoted by Jermin in loco.
[7] Chap. vii. 4, &c.; ix. 13—18.
[8] Chap. vii. 26.
[9] Verses 20, 21.
[10] Scott in loco. Comp. Bp. Hall.
[11] 'Agmen malorum colligit, quæ ebrietas secum trahit.' Lavater. 'Nemini certius ingentia imminere pericula, tam quoad facultates ac famam, quam ipsam quoque valetudinem, vitam, ac animæ salutem, quam hominem temulentum.' Geier.
[12] Chap. xx. 1. 1 Tim. iii. 2. Comp. Hor. Od. iii. 21.

bling words of pollution;[1] *the wounds*—often to murder[2]—*without cause;* the *redness of eyes*, showing the effect of liquor on the countenance; the impure appetites that are kindled; the infatuation almost incredible—this is sensuality in all its wretchedness.

Whence this world of *woe and sorrow?* It is the curse of indulged will. Not satisfied with healthful refreshment, many will "add drunkenness to thirst."[3] *They continue long*, "morning to night, till wine inflame them."[4] *They go to seek the mixed wine*—the strongest and most inebriating drink.[5]

Wisdom's voice therefore is—Avoid the allurements of sin. Often has a *look*—harmless in itself—proved a fearful temptation.[6] *Look not therefore at the wine when it is red.* Its very color; its sparkling transparency *in the cup;* the relish with which it *moves itself aright*, 'or goes down pleasant,"[7] all tends to excite the irregular appetite. Crush it in its beginnings, and prove that you have learnt the first lesson in the Christian school—"Deny yourself."[8] Whatever be its present zest, *at the last it biteth like a serpent, and stingeth like an adder.*[9] Did it *bite* first, who would touch it? Did Satan present the cup in his own naked form, who would dare to take it? Yet it comes from his hand as truly, as if he were visible to the eyes. If poison was seen in the cup, who would venture upon it? Yet is the poison less dangerous, because it is unseen? *The adder's sting* is concealed, yet most fatal. The cup of sparkling wine becomes "a cup of fearful trembling in the hands of the Lord."[10]

Seldom does any sensual indulgence come alone. One lust prepares the way for others; the first step is sure to lead onwards. The poor deluded victim cannot stop when he pleases. Drunkenness opens the door for impurity.[11] The inflamed eye soon catches fire with *the strange woman;* and who knoweth what the end may be? Loathsome indeed is *the heart* of the ungodly laid bare. Drink opens it, as far as words can do; and through the organ of the tongue it does indeed *utter perverse things.*[12] 'Blasphemy is wit, and ribaldry eloquence, to a man that is turned into a brute.'[13]

But the delirium is the most awful feature of the case. The unhappy victim, having lost all will and power to escape, sleeps quietly amid dangers as imminent, as *lying down in the midst of*

[1] Dan. v. 4. [2] 2 Sam. xiii. 28. 1 Kings xvi. 9, 10; xx. 16—20.
[3] Deut. xxix. 19. [4] Isa. v. 11.
[5] Chap. ix. 2, note. Homer describes his celebrated Helen as mixing exhilarating ingredients in the bowl, to revive the spirits. Odyss. Δ. 219—229.
[6] Gen. iii. 6; xxxix. 7. Jos. vii. 21. 2 Sam. xi. 2.
[7] Holden. Comp. Can. vii. 9.
[8] Matt. xvi. 24. Augustine gives an instructive example of his mother's nurse. Confess. ix. 8. See also George Herbert's excellent advice in his well-known poem—'The Temple.'
[9] Comp. chap. xx. 17. [10] Comp. Joel i. 5.
[11] Gen. xix. 32. Comp. Jer. v. 8. Ez. xvi. 49, 50. Hos. iv. 18. Rom. xiii. 13. 1 Pet. iv. 3.
[12] Ps. lxix. 12. Hos. vii. 5. The libertine poet praises the inspiring excitement of wine to the genius of poesy.—Hor. Ep. i. 19.
[13] Lawson in loco.

the sea, or upon the top of the mast.[1] Nay—even the senses seem to be stupified. *Stricken and beaten* he may be. But "his heart is as a stone,"[2] and he thanks his drunkenness, that *he felt it not.* Therefore "as the dog to his vomit, the fool returns to his folly,"[3] craving fresh indulgence—*When shall I awake? I will seek it yet again.* More senseless than the brute who satisfies nature, not lust; so lost to shame; his reason so tyrannized over by his appetite, that he longs to be bound again, and only seeks relief from his temporary *awakening* to a sense of his misery, by yielding himself up again to his ruinous sin.[4]

Oh! how affecting is the thought of the multitude of victims to this deadly vice in every age and clime, and among all ranks of society! Perhaps there is no sin which has not linked itself with it, while the unconsciousness in the act of sin only serves, not to palliate the guilt, but to increase the responsibility.

While we see the whole nature so depraved in taste—so steeped in pollution—we ask—"Is any thing too hard for the Lord?" Praised be his name for a full deliverance from the captivity of sin—of all and every sin—even from the chains of this giant sin![5] The mighty, though despised, instrument is "Christ crucified—the power of God, and the wisdom of God."[6] It is this, which, when vows, pledges, and resolutions—all have failed; works secretly, yet most effectually imparting new principles, affections, and appetites. The drunkard becomes sober; the unclean holy; the glutton temperate. The love of Christ overpowers the love of sin. Pleasures are now enjoyed without *a sting*, (for no *serpent*, nor adder is here) and the newly-implanted principle transforms the whole man into the original likeness to God—"Whatsoever is born of God doth not commit sin, for his seed remaineth in him; and he cannot sin, because he is born of God. He that is begotten of God keepeth himself and that wicked one toucheth him not."[7]

CHAPTER XXIV.

1. *Be not thou envious against evil men, neither desire to be with them:* 2. *For their heart studieth destruction, and their lips talk of mischief.*

THIS counsel has been lately given.[8] But it is very difficult in the false glare of this world's glory to "walk by faith," as the evidence of things not seen.[9] In the confined atmosphere of impa-

[1] Isa. xxviii. 7, 8. Hos. iv. 11. Comp. chap. xxxi. 4, 5.
[2] 1 Sam. xxv. 36, 37. [3] Chap. xxvi. 11. Isa. lvi. 12. [4] Jer. ii. 25.
[5] John viii. 34—36. 1 Cor. vi. 10, 11. [6] 1 Cor. i. 23—25.
[7] 1 John iii. 9; v. 18. See an affecting evangelical pleading with this case in that valuable manual—'Jowett's Christian Visitor.'
[8] Chap. xxiii. 17. [9] 2 Cor. v. 7. Heb. xi. 1.

tience and unbelief, "the spirit that is within lusteth to *envy*."[1] This evil spirit, if it does not bring the scandal of open sin, curses our blessings, withers our graces, cankers our peace, clouds our confidence, and stains a Christian profession. The full cup in the house of evil men stirs up the *desire to be with them*.[2] But if their fearful end did not restrain, their awful character is warning enough.[3] It is the malignity of Satan himself—*studying destruction in their heart; mischief in their lips*.[4] Take away then the delusive veil; and who would envy them? When Haman was *studying the destruction* of the holy nation, the barbed arrow of discontent was corroding his vitals.[5] Who would *envy* Judas, *studying his master's destruction?* In the agony of remorse, his "soul chose strangling rather than his life."[6] "Gather not my soul with sinners"—is the prayer of the child of God—"nor my life with bloody men, in whose hands is *mischief*."[7] Let me, instead of *studying the destruction*—study the salvation of my fellow-sinners—what can I do to win them to Christ? Let me *desire to be with* the man of God, employed in this God-like work. The Christian is the only *enviable* person in the world. 'The seeming blessings of *evil men* are God's heavy curses; and the smart of the stripes is a favor too good for them to enjoy. To judge wisely of our condition, it is to be considered, not so much how we fare, as upon what terms. If we stand right with heaven, every cross is a blessing; and every blessing a pledge of future happiness. If we be in God's disfavor, every one of his benefits is a judgment; and every judgment makes way for perdition.'[8] Instead *of envying sinners* in their successful wickedness, is therefore their character and influence to be dreaded—no less than their end!

3. *Through wisdom is an house builded: and by understanding it is established:* 4. *And by knowledge shall the chambers be filled with all precious and pleasant riches.* 5. *A wise man is strong; yea, a man of knowledge increaseth strength.* 6. *For by wise counsel thou shalt make thy war; and in multitude of counsellors there is safety.*

Why should we envy the prosperity of the wicked? Even if their *house be built*,[9] it cannot be *established*,[10] by iniquity. 'It is only the snow-palace, built in the winter, and melting away under the power of the summer's sun.'[11] "The wise woman *buildeth her house*"[12] upon piety and prudence—a far more solid *establishment*. Let every *chamber* of the mind *be enriched with these precious and pleasant* endowments. Without them the man is feeble in the springs of action; without strength of character; the creature

[1] James iv. 5.
[2] Ps. lxxiii. 10—14.
[3] Chap. xxiii. 18. Comp. verses 19, 20, infra.
[4] Chap. i. 11—14; iv. 16; vi. 18. 1 Sam. xxiii. 9. Job xv. 35. Ps. vii. 14; lxiv. 2—6. Mic. vii. 3.
[5] Est. iii. 8, 9; v. 13.
[6] Matt. xxvi. 16; xxvii. 3—5. Job vii. 15.
[7] Psalm xxvi. 9; xxviii. 3.
[8] Bishop Hall's Works, viii. 206.
[9] Mic. iii. 10.
[10] Chap. xii. 3. Jer. xxii. 13—18. Am. v. 11.
[11] Geier in loco.
[12] Chap. xiv. 1.

of accident, circumstances, or society, thinking and living upon the opinion of others. A general irresolution marks his insignificant course. If the soul is *a house* consecrated as God's dwelling,[1] it will be *built on* an enlightened *understanding* of Divine Truth: and every *chamber will be filled with the precious and pleasant riches* of godly fruits. Heresy is restrained by conceding supreme authority to the Bible. The crude professor acts under feverish impulse,—a sickly sentimentalist in religion. Instead of retaining a firm hold of truth, he imbibes with ease the most monstrous opinions. He is "carried about with divers and strange doctrines," instead of exhibiting "the good thing of an heart established with grace."[2] A "growth in" spiritual, as distinct from speculative, "knowledge," will always be accompanied with "growth in grace."[3]

In extending this view to the *building* of the spiritual *house*, may we not observe, how God has laid its foundations, shaped and framed the materials by his own Divine *wisdom*, and *filled all the chambers with his precious and pleasant riches*? Delightful is the contemplation of the building, as it is rising, and as it will be when it is finished. 'O the transcendent glory'—exclaimed the heavenly Martyn—'of this temple of souls; lively stones, perfect in all its parts, the purchase and work of God!'[4]

But *a wise man is strong*.[5] Every view confirms Lord Bacon's far-famed aphorism—'Knowledge is power.' The discovery of the mechanical forces, and of the power of steam, *has increased strength* in an hundred fold proportion to physical force. Intellectual knowledge wisely applied has immense moral ascendency. It restrains the King from unadvised *wars*;[6] and if forced into the field—instead of treading his perilous path alone, he ensures the *safety* of his kingdom by *multitude of counsellors*.[7] *The man of* spiritual *knowledge* is a giant in strength. He combines the power to draw the bow, with a steady hand and eye to guide to the mark. Conscious ignorance is the first principle of his knowledge. "I am but a little child"—said the wisest of men; and the moral power of this humility of wisdom, was *the establishment* of his kingdom.[8] The Christian, who is "filled with all *wisdom and spiritual understanding*," is also "*strengthened*" in his warfare "with all might according to the glorious power of his God."[9] For the people that do know their God shall be strong, and do exploits.[10]

7. *Wisdom*[11] *is too high for a fool: he openeth not his mouth in the gate.*

The commendation of wisdom is here continued. The man richly endowed with it comes forth with authority, and *speaks at the gate* among the wise. *The fool*, destitute of wisdom, is debarred from this honor. The humble[12] and diligent[13] prove, that the

[1] 2 Cor. vi. 16. [2] Heb. xiii. 9. [3] 2 Pet. iii. 18; i. 5. [4] Life, chap. iii.
[5] Chap. xxi. 22. Eccl. vii. 19; ix. 16. [6] Chap. xx. 18.
[7] Chap. xi. 14; xv. 22. [8] 1 Kings iii. 7; v. 12; x. 23—29. Comp. 2 Chron. xxvii. 6.
[9] Col. i. 9, 11. [10] Dan. xi. 32.
[11] "Wisdoms." Heb. all kinds of Wisdoms. Comp. Ps. xlix. 4. Schultens—Geier.
[12] Chap. viii. 9; xiv. 6. Matt. xi. 25. [13] Chap. ii. 1—6. John vii. 17.

treasure is not really out of reach. But *it is too high for the fool.* His grovelling mind can never rise to so lofty a matter. He has no apprehension of it;[1] no heart to desire it;[2] no energy to lay hold of it.[3] And therefore, though in the Gospel it "is nigh him, even in his mouth, and in his heart,"[4] it is inaccessible. Its holy spirituality is *too high* for his reach. He commands therefore no respect in his own station of society.[5] His counsel is not sought. His opinion, if given, is of no account. Though he may have a babbling tongue in the street, yet *he openeth not his mouth in the gate;* utterly unfit to give judgment in the presence of wise and judicious men. Nor is this from natural defect, but from wilful perverseness. His Lord had committed at least one talent to his trust. But he had frittered it away—not traded with it.[6] Oh! let *wisdom* be sought, while it is within reach; while it is so freely promised.[7] When found, let it be diligently improved for the great ends of life. What! if we should die without it, under the fearful responsibility of having done nothing for God or our fellow-creatures; of having neglected the way of life: and "in the greatness of our folly gone astray to everlasting ruin!"[8]

8. *He that deviseth to do evil shall be called a mischievous person.* 9. *The thought of foolishness is sin: and the scorner is an abomination to men.*

What a picture is here of human depravity, in its active working, its corrupt fountain, and its fearful end! To see talent, imagination, active mind, so debased, as to be all concentrated upon Satan's own work—*devising to do evil.*[9] He was the first *deviser,*[10] and he practises his children, till he makes them, like himself, masters of mischief; contriving new modes of sinning, ways of trickery and deceit; like the degraded Heathen, "inventors of evil things."[11] To do evil is the principle; *devising to do evil* is the energy, of his service. For this craft of evil, Balaam might justly be stamped as *a mischievous person.*[12] Abimelech has earned for himself the same reputation.[13] Jeroboam's subtle *mischief* has stamped his name with the black mark of reprobation —"who made Israel to sin."[14] Jezebel,[15] and others of less note, though equally industrious in evil, will appear in the same ranks at the great day.

Even when it is not wrought out into action, *the thought of foolishness*—giving it lodgment,[16] instead of casting it out as loathsome—*is sin.* But what guilt—it is asked—can there be in *a thought?* 'It is but an airy notion; next to nothing. It can make no impression. A malicious thought cannot hurt. A covetous thought cannot rob. What guilt or danger can belong to so

1 Ps. x. 5; xcii. 5, 6. 1 Cor. ii. 14.
2 Chap. xvii. 16, 24.
3 Chap. xiii. 4; xxi. 25.
4 Rom. x. 6—8.
5 Contrast Job xxix. 7—10.
6 Matt. xxv. 24—30.
7 Jam. i. 5.
8 Chap. v. 23.
9 Verse 2. Ps. xxxvi. 3, 4.
10 Gen. iii. 1.
11 Rom. i. 30.
12 Num. xxxi. 26. Rev. ii. 14.
13 Jud. ix.
14 1 Kings xii. 26—33; xv. 30.
15 Ib. xxi. 27. Rev. ii. 20.
16 See Jer. iv. 14.

minute a being?' Perhaps did we deal with man, these might be trifling evils. But as *the thought* is the fountain of the act, God counts it as the act, and holds us responsible for it.[1] The smallest sin involves us in the breach of the whole law.[2] This is his decision, and who can answer against it?

The awakened sinner admits his total depravity upon the same demonstration as his own existence—*consciousness.* One sin gives birth to another. Countless multitudes follow its rapid and continuous succession. "*Every* imagination of *the thoughts of the heart* is only evil continually."[3] Did we fully realize this apprehension, the flitting moments of the day—each bringing with it an increase of guilt—could not slide away so pleasantly from us; not at least without shame and humiliation; without habitual application of the Divine remedy. Job's sensitive conscience carried his sons continually to the atoning sacrifice.[4] Bunyan (unlike many loose professors, who are never troubled about their thoughts,) was deeply afflicted in the remembrance of one sinful thought. Nor was this a morbid temperament, or weakness of faith; but the tender sensibility of a heart humbled in the sight of the great sin offering before his eyes. To have sympathy with this mourning is a clear mark of Divine teaching and grace.

But let us follow out this *thought of foolishness* unrestrained. It gathers strength in every action, till its full influence is developed in the "scorner's seat,"[5] *an abomination*, not only to God, but *to man.*[6] For however misused wit and talent may gain the fool bad preëminence; he secures no respect, and is generally avoided or dreaded,[7] and ultimately brought to shame.[8]

10. *If thou faint in the day of adversity, thy strength is small,* (narrow, Marg.)

Let this be a word of strengthening encouragement. The marvel is, that those who know not where to look for a refuge, when the storm is breaking over their heads, do not *always faint.* But natural courage and buoyancy, or a deeper plunge into the world, as a diversion from sorrow, raises them above their troubles for a while; estranging them yet further from God.

But why should the child of God, contrary to his Father's injunction,[9] *faint? Thy privilege* is—"The eternal God is thy refuge, and underneath are the everlasting arms;"[10] *thy duty*—"Call upon me in the time of trouble: I will deliver thee, and thou shalt glorify me;"[11]—*thy security*—"I will never leave thee, nor forsake thee. For a small moment have I forsaken thee; but with great mercies will I gather thee."[12] Trial can indeed sweep

[1] Comp. chap. xv. 26. Ps. xciv. 11. Matt. ix. 3, 4; xv. 19. Acts viii. 22. Rom i. 15. Even an Heathen moralist could write—

'Nam scelus intra se tacitum qui cogitat ullum,
Facti crimen habet.'—Juv. xii. 209, 210.

[2] Jam. ii. 10, 11. [3] Gen. vi. 5. [4] Job i. 5.
[5] Ps. i. 1. [6] Chap. xxi. 24. Mal. ii. 8, 9.
[7] 2 Kings xviii. 37. [8] Jer. xxxvi. 23, with xxii. 19. [9] Chap. iii. 11
[10] Deut. xxxiii. 27. [11] Ps. l. 15; xci. 15. [12] Heb. xiii. 5. Isa. liv. 7.

away our earthly comforts. But it cannot "separate us from the love of Christ."[1]

Yet we "speak not parables." Every Christian's heart responds to the confession—that he is apt to *faint.* 'The strongest and holiest saint on earth is subject to some qualms of fear,'[2] not from the greatness of the danger, but from the weakness of his faith.[3] When he seeks his strength from his own resources;[4] when faith gives way to distrust;[5] praise to murmuring;[6] hope to despondency;[7] when relinquished pleasures vividly come to mind,[8] and protracted toils press heavily[9]—then he *faints in the day of adversity.*

For this *day* we must prepare. "Man is born to trouble,"[10] as his portion inherited from his first father. He may be called to drink a deep draught of the bitter cup, requiring much *strength,* that "patience may have its perfect work."[11] *The day* is needful for the trial of our principles. What seemed more promising than the confidence of the stony-ground hearers, or than the longer endurance of the Apostle's companions? But the *day of adversity* exposed their hollow profession.[12] Often also, even when "the root of the matter is found," a painful exhibition of *faintness,*[13] unable to weather out a bad day, proves the *smallness*—not the vigor—*of strength.*

But why—again we ask—should the child of God *faint?* If "affliction came from the dust, and sprung out of the ground,"[14] he might be discouraged by his ill fortune. But where every minute circumstance has been the fruit of eternal counsel, where "the hairs of his head are all numbered,"[15] well may he "stay himself upon his God." If his soul—like Israel of old—"be much discouraged because of the way,"[16] it leadeth to his Father's house. If he be wearied with his burden, soon will he rest eternally in his Saviour's bosom. Never will he be called to a martyr's trial, without a martyr's faith.[17] The chastening rod is the seal of everlasting love.[18] The temporal cross comes from the same hand as his everlasting crown. If *thy strength*—Christian—*be small,* go to the strong for strength. "He giveth power *to the faint,* and to them that have no might *he increaseth strength.*"[19] Commit thyself to him for "grace sufficient for thee." So go onward, meeting thy real trials with real faith; weak and strong at once; weak in order to be strong; strong in thy weakness, "his strength being made perfect in it;" and thou at length "glorying in thy" depress-

1 Rom. viii. 35—39.
2 Bp. Hall's Contemplations, B. xviii. Cont. 8.
3 Matt. xiv. 30.
4 Isa. xl. 30.
5 Ps. lxxviii. 19, 20.
6 Ex. xv. 1, 23; xvii. 3.
7 Num. xiv. 3.
8 Ex. xvi. 3. Num. xi. 4—6.
9 Job vii. 1—4.
10 Ib. v. 7.
11 Jam. i. 4.
12 Matt. xiii. 20, 21. 2 Tim. iv. 16; i. 15.
13 Moses, Ex. iv. 10—13; Num. xi. 11; Joshua vii. 6—10; David, 1 Sam. xxvii. 1; Ps. xxxi. 22; cxvi. 11; Elijah, 1 Kings xix. 3, 4; Jeremiah xx. 7—18; Jonah, iv. 8, 9; Peter, Matt. xxvi. 35, 69—74: the disciples, ib. verses 35, 36.
14 Job v. 6.
15 Matt. x. 30.
16 Num. xxi. 4, 5.
17 'Be of good heart'—said Ridley to his brother Latimer, with a wondrous cheerful look running to him, and embracing and kissing him—'for God will either assuage the fury of the flame, or else strengthen us to abide it.' Foxe, vii. 548.
18 Chap. iii. 12. Isa. xlviii. 10.
19 Isa. xl. 29.

ing "infirmity, that the power of Christ may rest upon thee;"[1] not only sustained, but "strengthened unto joyfulness."[2]

Oh!—hasten the time, when the dark and cloudy day shall be changed for unclouded sunshine; the crown of thorns for the crown of glory; "the spirit of heaviness" for the garment of "everlasting praise."[3]

11. *If thou forbear to deliver them that are drawn unto death, and those that are ready to be slain;*[4] 12. *If thou sayest, Behold, we knew it; doth not he that pondereth the heart consider it? and he that keepeth thy soul, doth not he know it? and shall not he render to every man according to his works?*

Suppose a fellow-creature in imminent danger—as it were *drawn unto death, and ready to be slain,* unjustly,[5] or from wickedness.[6] If the magistrate—standing in the place, and invested with the power, of God[7]—*forbear to deliver*—on the false pretence that *he knew it not*—the Lord will require it. This obligation, with all the responsibility of its neglect, is the universal law of the gospel.[8] Whoever knows his brother's danger, and *forbears to deliver—doth not he that pondereth the heart consider it? Will he not render?* The Hebrew midwives,[9] and Esther in after ages,[10] thus delivered their own *people drawn unto death.* Reuben *delivered* Joseph from the pit.[11] Job was the *deliverer* of the poor in the moment of extremity.[12] Jonathan saved his friend's life at imminent risk to himself.[13] Obadiah hid the Lord's prophets.[14] Ahikam and Ebed-melech saved Jeremiah.[15] Johanan attempted to *deliver* the unsuspecting Gedaliah.[16] Daniel preserved the wise men of Babylon.[17] The Samaritan rescued his neighbor from death.[18] Paul's nephew *delivered* the great Apostle, by informing of the murderous plot.[19] The rule includes every kind of oppression, which has more or less the character of murder.[20]

Excuses are always at hand. 'We want charity, but abound in self-love. Our defect in that appeareth by our backwardness to perform our duties to our brethren; and our excess in this by our readiness to frame excuses for ourselves.'[21] But *he that pondereth the heart* will thoroughly sift; his Omniscience will perfectly *know;* his retributive justice will *render.* Disinterested kindness will be *considered.*[22] But to *forbear deliverance*—whether from cruelty,[23]

1 2 Cor. xii. 7—9. 2 Col. i. 11. 3 Isa. lx. 18—20.

4 'To deliver them that are ready to be slain—if thou forbear!' First—he lays down the duty. Then he adds the warning, armed with a thunderbolt of retributive judgment upon the *forbearance.* Schultens.

5 1 Sam. xxiv. 11; xxvi. 18—20. 1 Kings xxi. 8—13. 6 Luke x. 30.

7 Ps. lxxxii. 3—6. Comp. Baruch vi. 35—38—where the idols are proved to be no gods, because they cannot do the work of God, here delegated to the magistrates as his representatives.

8 Luke x. 29—36. 9 Ex. i. 13—17. 10 Est. iii. 6—13; iv. 13, 14; viii. 4—6.

11 Gen. xxxvii. 22—24. 12 Job xxix. 12, 13, 16, 17.

13 1 Sam. xix. 4; xx. 26—33. 14 1 Kings xviii. 4.

15 Jer. xxvi. 24; xxxviii. 11—13. 16 Ibid. xl. 13—16.

17 Dan. ii. 12—15. 18 Luke x. 33—37. 19 Acts xxiii. 12—22.

20 Comp. Ecclus. xxxiv. 21, 22. 21 Bp. Sanderson's Assize Sermon on this text.

22 Ex. i. 18. Jer. xxxviii. 7—13; xxxix. 16—18. 23 1 Sam. xxii. 9—18.

selfishness,[1] or fear of personal consequences[2]—involves an awful account before the great Judge.

But how much more guilty to *forbear* the *deliverance* of immortal souls!—in ignorance, ungodliness, or unbelief, *drawn unto death, and ready to be slain!* Ought they not to be the objects of our deepest, most yearning anxiety? What shall we then say to that frozen apathy, which *forbears to deliver?* 'We have no right to judge—*We knew it not*—"Am I my brother's keeper?"[3] It is no concern of mine.' But might not many a soul have started back from the brink of ruin, if only the discovery of his danger had been made, ere it was too late? Yet the one word, that might have saved him, was *forborne.* Is there no brother, child, or neighbor, who may pierce the conscience to eternity with the rebuke—'Hadst thou dealt faithfully with my soul, I had not been in this place of torment.'[4] If others may charge us with the bodies of our fellow-creatures, God commits their souls to our care. The Lord preserve us from an indictment in the court of heaven for the murder of our brother's soul, by *forbearing to deliver!*

And does not this ring a solemn peal of warning to those, whose special office it is to *deliver them that are drawn unto death?* How little will this plea avail—*We knew it not!* Ought we not to have been "watching for souls, as those that must give account?"[5] And what will be the tremendous reckoning for souls, perishing by the neglect of their pledged and Divinely appointed guardians! "While thy servant was busy here and there"—upon his own pleasure—the soul "was gone!" "But his blood will be required at the watchman's hand."[6]

13. *My son, eat thou honey, because it is good; and the honeycomb, which is sweet to thy taste:* 14. *So shall the knowledge of wisdom be unto thy soul: when thou hast found it, then there shall be a reward, and thy expectation shall not be cut off.*

Honey was the choice produce of Canaan;[7] the food of its inhabitants,[8] even of children,[9]—*good and sweet to the taste.* So—when "the spiritual senses are exercised"[10]—will the *knowledge* of wisdom be 'unspeakably delectable,[11] *to thy soul*—that knowledge of Christ, without which we are undone, and in which we are supremely happy.[12] Eating only can convey—what the most accurate description fails to give—a just perception of the *sweetness of*

[1] Ibid. xxv. 10, 11. Luke x. 30–32. [2] John xix. 4—13.
[3] Gen. iv. 9. [4] Jam. v. 19, 20. [5] Heb. xiii. 17.
[6] 1 Kings xx. 39, 40. Ez. xxxiii. 8. See Doddridge's striking sermon on this text given from his works in Williams's Christian Preacher.
[7] Ex. iii. 6. Ez. xx. 6.
[8] Jud. xiv. 9. 1 Sam. xiv. 27. Matt. iii. 4. Luke xxiv. 41, 42. Comp. Ecclus. xxxix. 26.
[9] Isa. vii. 15. [10] Heb. v. 14.
[11] Bishop Hall. Chap. xvi. 24. Psalm xix. 10; cxix. 103.
[12] Phil. iii. 8. 'Lo! this'—says good Bishop Hall—'is the honey that I desire to eat. Give me of this honey, and I shall receive (like Jonathan of old—1 Sam. xiv. 29) both clearness to mine eyes and vigor of my spirits, to the foiling of all my spiritual enemies.' Soliloquies, liv.

the honey-comb.[1] Experimental *knowledge* alone gives spiritual discernment, and proves the gospel to be, not a golden dream, but a Divine reality. And who ever mistakes *honey* for any other substance? Who would not instantly detect a counterfeit? And what intelligent Christian would mistake the semblance of heavenly *wisdom* for its substance? The soul hungering for bread, and feeding upon an experimental apprehension of Christian doctrine, realizes solidly what no formalist ever knows. He possesses only a plausible shadow—emotion, impulse, conviction, external reformation.[2] But the living faith carries its own witness with it. 'It is all true—"I believed, and therefore have I spoken."'[3] The treasure is *found* with the transport of Archimedes—bringing its own reward.[4]

Thy expectation—so far from being *cut off*—shall be infinitely exceeded. "The love" that is manifested "passeth knowledge."[5] "The peace" that is sealed "passeth all understanding."[6] "The joy" that is felt is "unspeakable, and full of glory."[7] Shall we then timidly exhibit these privileges, as if they would lower the obligations of holiness, or paralyze exertion? They are not opiates, but cordials. They invigorate, while they refresh. Depression unnerves; fear unchains; but "the joy of the Lord is strength."[8] It inspires energy, elevates hope, and makes our 'service perfect freedom.'

15. *Lay not wait, O wicked man, against the dwelling of the righteous; spoil not his resting-place:* 16. *For a just man falleth seven times, and riseth up again: but the wicked shall fall into mischief.*

The wise man breaks off from affectionate counsel to the children of God, with a solemn warning to *the wicked man.* Should we exclude him from the circle of instruction? If he be left unconverted, it is his own guilt. But if he be unwarned, uninstructed, beware lest "blood-guiltiness" be charged.

Hatred to *the righteous* is deeply rooted in *the wicked man's* heart.[9] He imagines—especially if he be in power,[10] that he can tyrannize over them with impunity. But it is venturing upon an hazardous course—"He that toucheth you, toucheth the apple of mine eye.[11] I am Jesus, whom thou persecutest"—was a voice, that struck the most relentless of persecutors "trembling"[12] to the earth. The plots against their *dwelling—the spoiling of their resting-place*—may prosper for a while.[13] But if *the just man falleth seven times,* overwhelmed with the assault, *he riseth again.*[14] Courage then—poor afflicted soul! Look thy foe in the face, and sing triumphant—"Rejoice not against me, O mine enemy, *though I fall, I shall rise again.*[15] He shall deliver thee in six troubles;

[1] Jud. xiv. 18. [2] Heb. vi. 4, 5. [3] 2 Cor. iv. 13.
[4] Ευρηκα; ευρηκα. Comp. Jer. xv. 16. [5] Eph. iii. 19.
[6] Phil. iv. 7. [7] 1 Pet. i. 8. [8] Neh. viii. 10.
[9] Chap. xxix. 27. Gen. iii. 15. Ps. xxxvii. 22. 1 John iii. 12.
[10] 1 Sam. xix. 11. Acts xii. 1—3. [11] Zech. ii. 8. [12] Acts ix. 5, 6.
[13] 1 Sam. xix. 11. Ps. lix. Title. Acts viii. 3, 4. [14] Ps. xxxvii. 24.
[15] Mic. vii. 8.

yea in seven shall no evil touch thee. Who delivered us from so great a death, and doth deliver; in whom we trust, that he will yet deliver." "Cast down, but not destroyed."[1] Here is our conflict, and our security. The life is untouched, yea—it is strengthened and "made manifest" by the successive supplies of upholding mercy.[2] Many trials cannot overwhelm the righteous.[3] But one is sufficient to sweep away the wicked. *He falleth into mischief;*[4] and there is no *rising again*[5] —no recovery—no remedy. He lies where he falls, and he perishes where he lies. Sinner! whatever be thy wickednes; the Lord save thee from the millstone of condemnation—the persecuting of the saints of God!"[6]

17. *Rejoice not, when thine enemy falleth, and let not thine heart be glad, when he stumbleth:* 18. *Lest the Lord see it, and it displease him, and he turn away his wrath from him.*

Yet did the chosen people of God *rejoice* with Divine exultation *in the fall of their enemies.*[7] Nay—is not this joy the triumph of the righteous?[8] Is it not the adoration of heaven, as the manifest glory of God?[9] But how different is this sublime sympathy in the triumph of the Church, from the malignant joy of private revenge! A secret, if not an avowed, pleasure *in the fall of an enemy,* is nature's impulse.[10] But what has grace done for us, if it has not overcome nature by an holier and happier principle? David "wept and chastened his soul" in his enemies' affliction.[11] David's Lord wept in the prospective ruin of the infatuated race fraught with malignity against himself. *To rejoice in the fall of an enemy,* would be to fall deeper than himself; to fall not into trouble, but into sin; to break the commandment, which enjoins us to "love our enemies,"[12] and to repay cursing with blessing and prayers.[13] This selfish cruelty is most hateful to God.[14] It has often *turned away his wrath from* the criminal to the mocker at his calamity.[15]

[1] Job v. 19. 2 Cor. i. 10; iv. 9. [2] 2 Cor. iv. 11.
[3] Ps. xxxiv. 19; xxxvii. 39, 40. 1 Cor. x. 13. [4] Ps. vii. 13—16; ix. 16.
[5] Job xv. 30. Amos viii. 14.
[6] The *just man rising* from his fall is most unwarrantably applied to the perseverance of the saints. The word *fall* frequently occurs in this work—always in reference to trouble, not sin. (Chap. xi. 5, 14; xiii. 17; xvii. 20; xxvi. 27; xxviii. 10, 14, 18.) The antithesis obviously fixes this meaning. 'There are plain texts enough to prove every scriptural doctrine. But pressing texts into any particular service, contrary to their plain meaning, not only serves to deceive the inconsiderate, but to rivet the prejudices, and confirm the suspicions, of opposers; just as bringing forward a few witnesses of suspicious character would cause all those, however deserving of credit, who should be examined in the same cause, to be suspected also, and create a prejudice against it in the minds of the court and of all present.' Scott. Comp. Bp. Patrick.
[7] Ex. xv. 1. Jud. v. 31. [8] Chap. xi. 10. Job xxii. 19. Ps. lviii. 10.
[9] Rev. xv. 5—7; xviii. 20; xix. 1—6.
[10] Ps. xxxv. 15, 16; xlii. 10. 2 Sam. xvi. 5—7.
[11] Ps. xxxv. 13, 14. 2 Sam. i. 11, 12. Comp. Job xxxi. 29.
[12] Luke xix. 41—44. [13] Matt. v. 44. [14] Chap. xvii. 5. Zech. i. 15.
[15] This ellipsis is not unfrequent in this book—chap. xix. 1, 22. 'Lest the Lord be angry, and turn his wrath from him to thee.' Bishop Coverdale. Comp. Jud. xvi. 25—30. Micah vii. 10. Edom, Ezek. xxxv. 15; xxxvi. 5—7; Obad. 10—14. Tyre, Ez. xxvi 2. Babylon, Ps. cxxxvii. 7—9; Isa. li. 22, 23; Lam. i. 21; iv. 21, 22. Moab, Jer. xlviii. 26, 27. Ammon, Ez. xxv. 1—7.

Does the glass of the word show our character in the sin that is rebuked, or in the contrast of our compassionate Lord?

19. *Fret not thyself because of evil men, neither be thou envious at the wicked;* 20. *For there shall be no reward to the evil man; the candle of the wicked shall be put out.*

This *fretting* temper must be a deep-rooted disease to need such repeated discipline.[1] One moment's recollection of our mercies might show, how little reason there is for it. Mercies infinitely more than we discover ought to be sufficient to sweep the clouds from our sky, and to make us ashamed of our despondency. Before—*the envy of the wicked* was checked by the remembrance, that there *was an end*—surely an happy end—to the righteous.[2] Let them wait for it. It will not disappoint them. Here we are further reminded—there is *no end*[3]—*no reward to the evil man.* Leave him to his judge. *His candle*—notwithstanding all his efforts to keep it burning[4]—*shall be put out.*[5] Sometimes he puts out his own candle in daring presumption. 'I give'—said the infidel Hobbes—'my body to the dust, and my soul to the Great Perhaps. I am going to take a leap *in the dark.*' Alas!—was it not a leap—a fearful leap—*into the dark*—into "the blackness of darkness forever?"

Take then the balance of eternity. Learn neither to overvalue the fancied sunshine of *the wicked*, or to undervalue our own real happiness. *Envy not* his lot. Repine not at our own. Ours is far beyond his reach. His is far below our *envy.* 'His candle burneth; his prosperity flourisheth, until it hath kindled hell-fire, and then it is extinguished; whereas the lamp of the godly is put out here, to shine as a star in heaven.'[6]

21. *My son, fear thou the Lord and the king: and meddle not with them that are given to change:* 22. *For their calamity shall rise suddenly; and who knoweth the ruin of them both?*

We have another affectionate exhortation to *the fear of God.*[7] And what wonder? Is it not the substance of our holiness and our happiness? Oh! reverence his majesty. Acknowledge thy dependence upon him. Be as careful in "walking before him" in thy secret thoughts, as in thy outward conduct. No more allow the indulgence of a sinful motive than a gross sin. If there be no rod of outward shame, will not the thought keenly pierce thy heart—how unkindly does this defilement requite such unspeakable love?

The connexion between *the fear of God and the King* is not local or accidental.[8] The one is the spring of the other. Dis-

[1] Verse 1; xxiii. 17.
[2] Chap. xxiii. 18.
[3] Same word in Heb. as xxiii. 18. 'There shall be none end *of plagues* to the evil man.' Old Version.
[4] 1 Kings xxi. 21, with 2 Kings x. 1—7.
[5] Chap. xiii. 9; xx. 20. Job xviii. 5, 6; xxi. 17.
[6] Jermin in loco.
[7] Chap. xxiii. 17.
[8] Our Lord and his apostles have similarly linked these two commands. Matt. xxii. 21. 1 Pet. ii. 17.

loyalty has often been a libel upon godliness. But the Christian is loyal, because he is godly.[1] "Subjection to the powers that be" is repeatedly inculcated,[2] and the neglect is visited with the most heavy condemnation.[3] Yet there is no interference with the primary obligation. Solomon 'puts God before the king, because God is to be served in the first place, and our obedience is to be given to the king, only in subordination to God; and not in those things, which are contrary to the will of God.'[4]

Man's independence however naturally kicks against submission. The popular cry is for the voice and sovereignty of the people; a plain proof that "there is no new thing under the sun;"[5] as the picture of those demagogues has been drawn to life nearly two thousand years ago—"walking after the flesh—despising government—presumptuous, self-willed—not afraid to speak evil of dignities."[6] Such men love change for the sake of change. To become leaders of a party, they disturb the public peace, by proposing changes, without any promise of solid advantage.[7] "O my soul, come not thou into their secret!"[8] It is dangerous to *meddle with* them. To oppose all change indeed, is to set up a plea of perfection. Every improvement (and where is there not room for improvement?) is a change. But public evils are not to be mended by railing. To be *given to change;* to be weary of the old, and captivated with the new, however untried; to make experiments upon modes of government—is a fearful hazard. It is losing the substance of real good in the dream of imaginary improvements; as if we must undo every thing, rather than be idle. This waywardness we see in Korah's sin;[9] in Absalom's rebellion;[10] in the continual struggle for royalty in the Israelitish Kings.[11] How *suddenly did their calamity rise*, even when they seemed to be in the grasp of their object![12] *Who knoweth the ruin—which both* the Lord and the king[13] may inflict on the despisers of their authority[14]—often fearful beyond precedent—without remedy?[15]

23. *These things also belong to the wise. It is not good to have respect of persons in judgment.* 24. *He that saith unto the wicked, Thou art righteous; him*

[1] See 1 Sam. xxiv. 6.
[2] Matt. xvii. 24—27. Rom. xiii. 1—7. Tit. iii. 1. 1 Pet. ii. 13—17.
[3] Rom. xiii. 2.
[4] Poole in loco. Comp. 1 Sam. xxii. 17, 18. Dan. iii. 16—18. Acts iv. 18, 19; v. 27—29.
[5] Eccl. i. 9. [6] 2 Pet. ii. 10. Jude 8. Comp. 1 Sam. x. 27.
[7] 'He that goeth about,' saith our judicious Hooker, 'to persuade men, that they are not so well governed as they ought to be, shall never want attentive and favourable hearers'—That which is wanted in the aptness of their speech is supplied by the aptness of men's minds to accept and believe it.' See the whole paragraph opening his great work, Eccl. Polit. Book i.
[8] Gen. xlix. 6. [9] Num. xvi. 1—13. [10] 2 Sam. xv. 10—13.
[11] 1 Kings xvi. 8—22. [12] 2 Sam. xv. 13; xviii. 9—16.
[13] French and Skinner. This is the view of the best critics (Geier, Dathe, Lavater, &c.) It seems most natural to apply the distinctive term (*them both*) to the separate persons. The ruin foreboded is thus connected with the persons, who had been described separately as the object of fear.
[14] 2 Sam. xviii. 7, 8; xx. 1, 2, 22. 2 Kings xvii. 21 23. Eccl. viii. 2—5. Acts v. 36, 37. [15] Num. xvi. 29—33.

shall the people curse, nations shall abhor him: 25. But to them that rebuke him shall be delight, and a good blessing shall come upon them. 26. Every man shall kiss his lips that giveth a right answer.

We have had a solemn exhortation to the people. We have now a word *to the wise*, specially to those in authority. God has given many warnings against *respect of persons in judgment.*[1] *It is not good.*[2] Nay—rather he rebukes it as an abomination, with most pungent remonstrance.[3] Let truth be considered, not favor. This is an evil in church as much as in state. No responsibility is more momentous in our sacred high-places, than "Doing nothing by partiality."[4] Man, corrupt as he is—often *abhors* unrighteous judgment.[5] A bad magistrate deprives us of the blessing of good laws.

On the other hand there is no greater national blessing than a government *rebuking the wicked.*[6] This was a part of Job's God-fearing character.[7] *The good blessing that came* upon Nehemiah's upright administration is abundantly manifest.[8] Indeed for the most part *every one will kiss*—pay the homage of love and respect[9] to—*him who giveth a right answer* in judgment. He is a public treasure; "a blessing in the midst of the land."

Is the responsibility of rulers, and the welfare of thousands depending on them, a quickening impulse to prayer? And may not our want of "godly quietness" be traced to this neglect?[10]

But we are not rulers. Yet are not many of us in authority—Parents—Heads of Families—Teachers and Guardians of the young? Uprightness and consistency alone can maintain that influence so essential to usefulness. For a spiritual ruler to *say to the wicked—Thou art righteous*, is indeed perfidious dealing with his Divine Master; cruel deceit to immortal souls; hiding the ruin which he is bound to reveal; acting the part of a minister of Satan, under the cover of a minister of Christ. *His people* will live to *curse and abhor him*, perhaps throughout eternity. Whereas even the very people that hate both his Master and his message will *kiss his lips, that giveth a right answer*—a reluctant but honorable witness to his faithfulness.

27. *Prepare thy work without, and make it fit for thyself in the field; and afterwards build thine house.*

This rule of prudence applies to all worldly matters, Religion, so far from forbidding, inculcates care and forethought. Much of our domestic comfort hangs upon it. Much inconvenience and suffering flow from its neglect. Acting upon this useful direction, the wise builder first *prepares his work without.* He collects his materials, calculates upon the quantity required; then *he makes*

[1] Ex. xxiii. 6—8. Lev. xix. 15. Deut. i. 17; xvi. 19.
[2] Chap. xviii. 5; xxviii. 21. [3] Ps. lxxxii. 2—4. [4] 1 Tim. v. 21.
[5] 1 Sam. viii. 1—5. [6] 2 Sam. xxiii. 3, 4. [7] Job i. 1, 8; xxix. 7, 11—17.
[8] Neh. v. 7—9; xiii. 8—11 25, 28, with 31.
[9] Comp. 1 Kings xix. 18. Job xxxi. 26, 27. Ps. ii. 12. Hos. xiii. 2.
[10] 1 Tim. ii. 1, 2.

his work fit by shaping and bringing them into their place; *and afterwards*—having all things in readiness—*he builds his house.* *The work was thus prepared* for Solomon's magnificent temple, before *the house was built.*[1] The spiritual house is similarly raised of materials *prepared and fitted*, and thus it "groweth unto an holy temple of the Lord."[2]

But ponder well the care, with which the great *work should be prepared.* Count the cost anxiously. Consider whether the profession will stand the storm.[3] Lay the foundation deep upon the Rock.[4] Be much in prayer for Divine strength. Avoid that outward display, which so often shames the inconsiderate builder, who had begun to *build his house*, without having thoroughly *prepared his work.*

Need we suggest to the minister of the Gospel the special need of *preparing his work?* An unfurnished minister cannot be "a wise master-builder." Even when the foundation is laid, "let every man take heed how he buildeth thereupon." Let him look well to the day of trial.[5] And let all the Lord's servants weigh deeply their responsibility. Indigested haste, and crude judgment have blasted many a Christian project. Let us be guided by the well-considered wisdom of experienced men,[6] and collect our materials from their prudence, forethought, and sound-judging energy. *A house will thus be built* to the honor of our God, and for the service of his Church.

28. *Be not a witness against thy neighbor without cause; and deceive not with thy lips.* 29. *Say not, I will do so to him, as he hath done to me: I will render to the man according to his work.*

The welfare of society may sometimes constrain to *be witness against a neighbor.* But never let it be *without cause.* Yet when compelled to this revolting duty—whatever be the temptation or consequence—*deceive not with thy lips.* Speak plainly, truthfully, the whole truth. Doeg's *witness against his neighbor was without cause*—not from conscience, but from malice. The main fact also was concealed of David's imposition upon Abimelech, which would have cleared him from the suspicion of treason, and saved his life.[7] This garbled *witness* therefore *deceived with his lips* and bears the black stamp of "a deceitful tongue."[8]

Profit is the bait to the thief, lust to the adulterer, revenge to the murderer. But it is difficult to say, what advantage redounds to this evil *witness*, or what allurement belongs to the sin, save that which Satan himself feels—the love of sin for its own sake, or for the satisfaction that is vainly anticipated from the commission. Should we however be clear from the grosser forms of this sin; yet do we resist the unkind *witness against our neighbor*, in magnify-

[1] 1 Kings v. 18; vi. 7. [2] Eph. ii. 21, 22.
[3] Luke xiv. 28—30. [4] Ibid. vi. 48. [5] 1 Cor. iii. 10—15.
[6] Matt. xviii. 17, 18. [7] 1 Sam. xxii. 9, 10; xxi. 1, 2.
[8] Ps. lii. 3, 4; cxx. 2—4.

ing his failings, and measuring them with a far stricter line than our own; rashly censuring his indifferent or doubtful actions; and censuring even his sins with an unchristian intention?

And then—as to indulging personal resentment—it is natural to *say*, though only in the heart—***I will do as he hath done to me.*** But shall we dare thus to take the sword out of God's hands, and place ourselves upon his tribunal? "Vengeance belongeth unto me; I will repay—saith the Lord."[1] 'Let wisdom and grace be set to work to extinguish the fire from hell, before it gets head.'[2] Far sweeter will be the recollection of injuries forgotten than revenged. But grace alone can enable us to "*forgive from the heart.*"[3] And yet too often its exercise is so feebly cherished, that natural feelings gain the ascendancy; and, if there be not an actual recompence of evil, there is merely a negative obedience to the rule —a refraining from the ebullition, rather than an active exercise of the opposite principle. The wise man sets out in this book the true rule,[4] according to the mind and image of God; more lovely, more constraining, as enforced by the Divine example.[5] Humility and tenderness mark the self-knowing Christian, forgiving himself little, his neighbor much.

30. *I went by the field of the slothful, and by the vineyard of the man void of understanding;* 31. *And, lo, it was all grown over with thorns, and nettles had covered the face thereof, and the stone wall thereof was broken down.* 32. *Then I saw, and considered it well: I looked upon it, and received instruction.* 33. *Yet a little sleep, a little slumber, a little folding of the hands to sleep;* 34. *So shall thy poverty come as one that travelleth; and thy want as an armed man.*

Every thing around us reads an useful lesson to an observant eye. Every particle of creation may be taxed to furnish its quota to our store of knowledge. We can extract good even from evil, and "gather grapes of thorns, and figs of thistles." Solomon describes with his usual vigor of thought and strength of coloring, an affecting sight, that had passed before his eyes—***the field and vineyard of the slothful—grown over with thorns and nettles, and the wall utterly broken down.*** Instead of turning away, ***he considered it well and received instruction. The slothful*** by strange delusion conceives himself to be wise.[6] Yet how manifestly is he ***void of understanding; without heart*** to improve his many advantages! He might enrich himself by ***his field and vineyard.*** But he has never cultivated or weeded it. ***The broken wall*** leaves it a prey to any invader; while he lives as a mere animal in sensual indulgences, bringing himself gradually,

[1] Rom. xii. 19. Comp. Gen. l. 16—19. [2] Matthew Henry's Works, p. 459.

[3] Matt. xviii. 35, with Luke xvii. 3—5. 'The excellency of the duty is sufficiently proclaimed by the difficulty of the practice. For how hard is it, when the passions are high, and the sense of an injury quick, and the power ready, for a man to deny himself in that luscious morsel of revenge! To do violence to himself, instead of doing it to his enemy!' South's Sermon on Matt. v. 44.

[4] Chap. xx. 22; xxv. 21, 22.

[5] Matt. v. 44, with Luke xxiii. 34. 1 Pet. ii. 21—23. [6] Chap. xxvi. 16.

but irresistibly *to poverty.*[1] Not that he means to come to beggary. He only wants *yet a little sleep, a little slumber more*—and then he will bestir himself. But this *little* insensibly increases. Every hour's indulgence strengthens the habit, and chains the victim in hopeless bondage. His efforts for exertion are only the struggles of the paralytic, without energy or effectiveness. If his dependence is upon his own industry—manual or mental, sloth must hasten on his ruin. In a higher station it deprives him of the means of using his influence aright, or of employing his talents to any valuable purpose. This is *poverty* to himself, impoverishing the springs of solid happiness, and frittering away the true ends of life.

But let us look at the spiritual sluggard. If a neglected field is a melancholy sight, what is a neglected soul! a soul—instead of being cultivated with the seeds of grace, left to its own barrenness; *overgrown with* the native produce of *thorns and nettles.*[2] Time, talents, opportunities have been vouchsafed; perhaps the blessing of a godly education added—every encouragement for hopeful promise. But if diligence is needed; if the man must "labor and strive,"[3] then his field must be left—at least for the present. He must have a *little more sleep* first.[4] And thus he sleeps on, and shuts both eyes and ears against every disturbance of his fatal slumber. Nothing is done or attempted for God, for his own soul, or for his fellow creatures. His *vineyard* is left open. All his good purposes are *the stone wall broken down.* Satan "goes out and returns at his will."[5] All is devastation and ruin.

Christian! is there no danger of this evil creeping into our religion? No habit is so ruinous. It enervates, and at length stops, the voice of prayer. It hinders the active energy of meditation. It weakens the influence of watchfulness. It checks every step of progress in the Divine life; so that "the soul," instead of being "a well-watered garden,"[6] sending forth refreshing fragrance and grateful fruits—relapses into its former wilderness state; laid open to every temptation; and too often ultimately a prey to sensual appetites.[7]

Let our Father's voice be instantly heard—"Son, go work *to-day in thy vineyard.*"[8] Dost thou not see that it is *overgrown with thorns?* Look forward—not backward. Not complain, but decide. Not pray only—but strive. Always connect privilege with practice. Prove the principles of moral character as well as spiritual experience. Aim at every active exercise, that may strengthen re-

[1] Chap. vi. 10, 11. The Roman Satirist gives a lively description of the stirring of the slothful man's excitement of lust—

'Mane, piger, stertis? Surge, inquit avaritia: eja
Surge: negas? Instat, surge, inquit; non queo; surge,' &c.
Persius, Sat. 5.

[2] Gen. iii. 18. [3] John vi. 27. Luke xiii. 24.
[4] See Augustine's instructive reference to his own case. Confess. Lib. viii. c. 5.
[5] Matt. xii. 45. 2 Tim. ii. 26. [6] Jer. xxxi. 12.
[7] Chap. xxiii. 21. 2 Sam. xi. 2. Ezek. xvi. 49. Comp. Ovid. Rem. Amor. 161.
[8] Matt. xxi. 28.

ligious habits. 'Surely if we look to stand in the faith of the sons of God, we must hourly, continually, be providing and setting ourselves to strive. It was not the meaning of our Lord and Saviour in saying—"Father, keep them in thy name"—that we should be careless to keep ourselves. To our own safety our sedulity is required.'[1]

CHAPTER XXV.

1. *These are the proverbs of Solomon, which the men of Hezekiah king of Judah copied out.*

THIS seems to be a third division of this sacred book.[2] The selection was probably made (with several repetitions from the former part [3]) from "the three thousand Proverbs which Solomon spoke;"[4] and which, having been carefully preserved, *the men of Hezekiah copied out*, nearly three hundred years after. Thus the word of God, brought out of obscurity for the instruction of the people, stamped the reformation of the godly king.[5] The New Testament fully authenticates this section of the book as a part of the inspired canon.[6] We are not reading therefore the maxims of the wisest of men. But the voice from heaven proclaims—"These are the true sayings of God."

The Holy Spirit mentions not only the author, but the copyists of these Proverbs. And often has good service been done to the Church, not only by original writers, but oftentimes by those, who have *copied* and brought out their writings into wider circulation. The world usually honors only the grand instruments; while the more humble agency is cast into the shade.[7] But God honors not only the primary, but the subordinate, instruments; not only the five—but the one talent—faithfully laid out for him. The blessing is not promised to their number, but to their improvement.[8]

[1] Hooker 'On the certainty and perpetuity of Faith in God's Elect.'
[2] See Chap. i. and x.—xxiv.
[3] Verse 24, with xxi. 9; xxvi. 13, with xxii. 13; 15, with xix. 24; 22, with xviii. 8; xxvii. 12, with xxii. 3; 13, with xx. 16; 15, with xix. 13; xxviii. 6, with xix. 1; 18, with x. 9; 19, with xii. 11; 21, with xviii. 5; xxiv. 23.
[4] 1 Kings iv. 32. Comp. Eccl. xii. 9. Does not the Divine discrimination, which has withheld the whole of Solomon's writings from us, reprove the indiscriminate publication *of all* that eminent men may have left in manuscript. Crudities and even gross errors have been thus accredited by the authority of great names, not less unjust to their memory than injurious to the Church.
[5] 2 Chron. xxxii. 21. Comp. the subsequent Reformation under Josiah, chap. xxxiv. 14—30. We mark the same Divine stamp of mercy upon our own precious, though reviled, Reformation.
[6] Verses 6, 7, with Luke xiv. 7—10; 21, 22, with Rom. xii. 20: xxvi. 11, with 2 Pet. ii. 22; xxvii. 1, with Jam. iv. 14.
[7] Ecc. ix. 15, 16. [8] Matt. xxv. 21—23.

2 *It is the glory of God to conceal a thing: but the honor of kings is to search out a matter.* 3. *The heaven for height, and the earth for depth, and the heart of kings is unsearchable* (there is no searching, Marg.)

The great King of heaven and the puny kings of earth are here finely contrasted. *The glory* of each is opposite—*of God to conceal; of kings to search out.* Whether "he dwelleth in his pavilion of thick darkness,"[1] or whether "clothed in his garment of light, and dwelling in unapproachable light"[2]—*it is the glory of God to conceal a thing.* What glory indeed could belong to a God, whose name, and ways, and works were open to the view, and within the comprehension of worms of the earth? What he has brought to light only shows how much is *concealed.* We look at his works—"Lo! these are parts of his ways; but how little a portion is heard of him!"[3] We study the dispensations of his Providence—"Thy way is in the sea, and thy path in the great waters; and thy footsteps are not known!"[4] We ponder the great purposes of his grace; and our hearts only find vent in reverential adoration—crying—"Oh! the depth!"[5]—'rather standing on the shore, and silently admiring it, than entering into it.'[6] To be wading in those depths is the sure way to be overwhelmed in them.

Thus does he educate his children in mystery, that he may exercise them in the life of faith,[7] coming to his revelation without any mind or will of their own. And is not this shade of mystery our highest joy, as the dwelling-place of our adorable God and Saviour? Are not the clouds of his *concealment* the effulgence of his glory,[8] as the most simple—yet the most incomprehensible Being, whom the mightiest intellect can never "by searching find out to perfection?"[9] 'As there is,' says Bishop Hall, 'a foolish wisdom, so there is a wise ignorance. I would fain know all that I need, and all that I may. I leave God's secrets to himself. It is happy for me, that God makes me of his court, though not of his council. O Lord! let me be blessed with the knowledge of what thou hast revealed. Let me content myself to adore thy Divine wisdom in what thou hast not revealed.'[10]

[1] 1 Kings viii. 12. Ps. xviii. 11; xcvii. 2. [2] Ps. civ. 2. 1 Tim. vi. 16.
[3] Job xxvi. 14. 'Lo! these are the outlines (marginal or boundary lines) of his ways; and the mere whisper (opposed to the crashing "thunder" of the next clause) we can hear of him.' Dr. Good.
[4] Ps. lxxvii. 19. Comp. xxxvi. 6. [5] Rom. xi. 33.
[6] Leighton on 1 Pet. ii. 8. [7] John xiii. 7. [8] Hab. iii.4.
[9] Job xi. 7—9. Ps. cxlv. 2.
[10] Bp. Hall, viii. 5; xi. 84. This *glorious concealment* is however no precedent for the Tractarian principle of Reserve, which at once eclipses the freeness and fulness of the Gospel, and paralyzes the energy of Christian life and hope. Blessed be God! "The things that belong to our peace are brought to light by the Gospel." (2 Tim. i. 10.) The doctrine of the atoning cross is "delivered *first of all*, (εν πρωτοις, 1 Cor. xv. 3)—the primary truth in the forefront of the Gospel. With self-abasing humility we acknowledge, that "Secret things belong to the Lord our God." But guilty indeed is the presumption of casting a cloud of *concealment* on "the things that are revealed, and which belong to us, and to our children for ever"—not only as the foundation of our hope, but as the principle of our obedience. Deut. xxix. 29. Yet do not some of us need

The highest glory of earth is at an infinite remove—*God conceals.* For who could bear his full irradiation?[1] *But the honor of kings is to search out a matter.*[2] They must not affect to be like God. By themselves they know nothing beyond their people. Yet as all depends upon them, they must, by *searching out,* avail themselves of all stores of wisdom. Hence the Divine command, that they should write out a copy of the law, for their daily study and direction.[3] This wise king had himself attained singular discernment in *searching out a matter,* even without external evidence, and with all the perplexity of conflicting testimony.[4] The lawgiver must however often frame his councils with much caution and reserve. Many of his purposes are far beyond the comprehension of the great mass of his people, so that to their minds *the heart of kings is unsearchable,* and they might as soon think of measuring *the heaven for height,* or fathoming *the earth for depth.* Ought not this to teach forbearance in pronouncing judgment? Are not the "presumptuous and self-willed, who are not afraid of speaking evil of dignities," convicted of the guilt of "speaking evil of the things that they understand not?"[5] Is not "prayer for kings and for those in authority," a far more fruitful and "acceptable" exercise?[6]

4. *Take away the dross from the silver, and there shall come forth a vessel for the finer.* 5. *Take away the wicked from before the king, and his throne shall be established in righteousness.*

The finer produces "the vessel unto honor," by *taking away the dross from the silver;*[7] which mars its beauty and purity. Such is the influence of *the wicked* in the royal councils, tending to destruction.[8] *Take them then away from before the king.* Let him purify his court and government from this *dross.* Let him exclude it from high places. Let him discountenance it in authority at any cost.[9] David thus *established his throne in righteousness,*[10] and commended this resolution by his dying counsel to his wise son.[11] This is political wisdom on scriptural principles. If "righteousness exalteth a nation,"[12] the open acknowledgment of it is the sure path to national prosperity.[13] And will not *the throne* of our great King *be established* by the entire and eternal removal of the wicked?[14] O my soul! In the great day of trial and decision shall I be found reprobate or purified silver? Lord! let me, under the refiner's hand, be purified as an offering of righteousness in that day!

6. *Put not forth thyself* (set not out thy glory, Marg.) *in the presence of the king, and stand not in the place of great men:* 7. *For better it is that it be said*

to be drawn further from the "secret things," and nearer to the "things that are revealed?"

1 Ex. xxxiii. 20. Dan. x. 5—8, 17. Rev. i. 12—17.
2 Ezra iv. 15, 19; v. 17; vi. 1. Comp. Job xxix. 16.
3 Deut. xvii. 18, 19.
4 1 Kings iii. 16—28.
5 2 Pet. ii. 10, 12. Jude 8, 10.
6 1 Tim. ii. 1—3.
7 Mal. iii. 2, 3.
8 1 Kings xii. 10—16. 2 Chron. xxiv. 17—24.
9 Chap. xx. 8, 26.
10 Ps. ci. 4—8.
11 1 Kings ii. 5, 6, 32, 33, 44, 45.
12 Chap. xiv. 34.
13 1 Kings xv. 13. 2 Chron. xiv. 1—7.
14 Mal. iii. 17, 18. Matt. xiii. 41—43; xxv. 31—46.

unto thee, Come up hither; than that thou shouldest be put lower in the presence of the prince whom thine eyes have seen.

Our Lord applies this proverb more generally.[1] Who needs not this caution against ambition? Even godly Baruch seems to have "sought great things for himself."[2] Not even the fellowship of the Saviour, his heavenly instruction, his Divine pattern of holiness[3] could restrain the "strife among the disciples—Who should be the greatest;"[4] repeated even after the most wondrous exhibition of humility[5]—nay—after they had just partaken with him of the holy feast.[6] "Loving to have the pre-eminence," is the bane of godliness in the Church.[7]

Wolsey's fall is an instructive beacon to ambitious men, not to *put forth themselves, or to set out their glory in the presence of the king.*[8] The usurpation also of *the place of great men* usually subjects a man to be *put lower*, to his own mortification. "Before honor is humility;"[9] shown in a backwardness to obtrude either our presence or our opinion upon those in higher stations; shrinking from external respect, rather than courting the "vain show." Gideon[10]—Saul in his early and better days[11]—David—were thus advanced to honor.[12]

Let each of us lay himself to the work of casting down our high tower of conceit; cultivating a deep sense of our utter worthlessness, and carefully pondering that example, which is at once our pattern and our principle. Oh! think of him, who was "fairer than man," being the most humble of men—nay—of him, who was infinitely more than man, making himself "a worm and no man."[13] 'What!' cries Bernard, 'shall the Majesty of Heaven become a worm, and man—the proud worm—exalt himself!' Think of that day, which will set us all on our own true base; when each of us shall stand before the Great *Prince*,[14] just that—and that only—which he counts us to be! What will it be to be *put lower*—to be utterly cast out in *his presence*, whom *our eyes shall then see* to our eternal confusion![15]

8. *Go not forth hastily to strive, lest thou know not what to do in the end thereof, when thy neighbor hath put thee to shame.* 9. *Debate thy cause with thy neighbor himself; and discover not a secret to another;* (of another, Marg.) 10. *Lest he that heareth it put thee to shame, and thine infamy turn not away.*

Dissension under any circumstances is a serious evil. The considerate Christian will rather concede rights, than insist upon them to the hazard of his own soul, and to the injury of the Church.[16]

[1] Luke xiv. 8—11.
[2] Jer. xlv. 5. Comp. Rom. xii. 16. [3] Matt. xi. 29. [4] Ib. xviii. 1—4.
[5] John xiii. 1—15. [6] Luke xxii. 19—27. [7] 3 John 9, 10.
[8] Comp. Ecclus. vii. 4. The Poet elegantly contrasts Dædalus and Icarus—father and son, both provided with wings. The father—contenting himself with skimming the ground—was safe. The son soaring aloft—perished. Hence a lesson of humility. Ovid. Trist. Lib. iii. El. ii. 21.
[9] Chap. xviii. 12. [10] Jud. vi. 15—17. [11] 1 Sam. ix. 21, 22; xv. 17.
[12] Ib. xviii. 18—20. Comp. Ps. cxxxi. 1. [13] Ps. xlv. 2, with xxii. 6.
[14] Rev. i. 5. [15] Ib. verse 7. [16] See 1 Cor. vi. 1—7.

Hasty strife must always be wrong. Think well beforehand whether the case be right—or even if it be—whether it be worth the contention. Duly calculate the uncertainty or consequence of *the end.* See the fruits in Gaal's quarrel with Abimelech[1]—Amaziah's *strife* with his brother king of Israel[2]—godly Josiah's unadvised contention with Pharaoh.[3] So little do we *know what to do in the end thereof.* Often has a man brought himself to ruin by a *hasty strife* at law. Instead of triumphing, *his neighbor has put him to shame.* So long as 'meum and tuum' are in the world, sin and Satan will stir up contention. Yet never forget, that not "hatred and wrath" only, but "variance and *strife*" are "works of the flesh," excluding from heaven.[4] Hence the constraining obligation to "seek peace, and pursue it;"[5] after the noble example of our father Abraham, who quenched "the beginning of the strife," by yielding to his nephew his natural terms of superiority, and his just rights.[6]

Yet—if after all, *strife* be inevitable, then let us ponder, how much wisdom, and rule over our own spirit, is needful to conduct it honorably to our profession. *Debate thy cause with thy neighbor himself.* Show him that the great object is not to make good *thy cause,* but to put a speedy end to the strife. Abraham, instead of complaining to others, carried his wrongs straight to the king, who was answerable for them.[7] Jephthah thus *debated his cause* with the king of Ammon himself, as the best means of bringing it to an amicable settlement.[8] But to *discover secrets to others,* even though we enjoin them to secrecy, is a breach of integrity.[9] And if—as often is the case—confidence is betrayed, the just consequence must be to ourselves[10]—*infamy,* that may *not turn away from us.* Backbiter will be the stamp on our name. And many privacies hitherto unknown may be published in retaliation, to our shame.

How many unholy heats would be restrained by the practice of these rules of wisdom and love! A generous self-forgetting warmth of kindness puts down the first evil; denying ourselves the pleasure of testifying our cause, or triumphing over our opponent; instead of standing upon punctilious reforms, or waiting for an acknowledgment from the offender. And as to the other evil—if it be more easy to talk of our neighbor's faults to others, than wisely and prayerfully to tell him of them alone—ask for self-discipline, and the mind of Christ. "Let the peace of God rule in your hearts, to the which also ye are called in one body."[11]

11. *A word fitly spoken* (spoken upon his wheels, Marg.) *is like apples of gold*

[1] Jud. ix. 26—40. Comp. Ecclus. viii. 1.
[2] 2 Kings xii. 8—12.
[3] 2 Chron. xxxiv. 21, 22.
[4] Gal. v. 19—21.
[5] Ps. xxxiv. 14.
[6] Gen. xiii. 8. Comp. chap. xvii. 14.
[7] Gen. xxi. 25—32.
[8] Jud. xi. 12—27. Comp. the rule of the great Lawgiver, Matt. xviii, 15.
[9] Comp. Ecclus. viii. 17—19; xxvii. 16—21. Bp. Hall's Medit. and Vows. Cent. ii 38, 39. 'To tell our own secrets'—says our great moralist—'is generally folly; but the folly is without guilt. To communicate those with which we are entrusted is always treachery, and treachery for the most part combined with folly.' Rambler, No. 13.
[10] Jud. xvi. 6—21.
[11] Col. iii. 15.

in pictures of silver. 12. *As an earring of gold, and an ornament of fine gold, so is a wise reprover upon an obedient ear.*

The allusion is to the curiously wrought baskets of *silver* net-work, in which delicious fruits were served up. The beauty of the texture set off the fruit with additional charms. So does a lovely medium enhance the attractiveness of truth.[1] "The preacher should strive to find out acceptable words"[2]—*words fitly spoken*—giving to each their proper meat—and *that* "in due season,"[3] suited to their ages and difference of temperament. "How forcible are right words!"[4] Our Lord witnessed of himself, as "gifted with the tongue of the learned, that he might know how to speak the word in season"[5]—a *word upon his wheels*—not forced or dragged, but rolling smoothly along, like the chariot wheels. His discourses on the living water and the bread of life[6] arose naturally out of the conversation,[7] and therefore were full of arresting application. Paul powerfully charged superstition on the Athenians, by an inscription on their own altar; and strengthened his reasoning by quoting from one of their own poets.[8] To a corrupt and profligate judge he preached "righteousness, temperance, judgment to come."[9]

In general intercourse much depends upon *the word* given, the occasion, the spirit of giving it. Many who feel strongly the impulse of being "instant out of season," neglect the not less Christian obligation of being "instant in season."[10] We must consider the time and the person, no less than the truth. We may think to relieve our conscience by speaking our mind. But to do it rudely and harshly may put a stumbling-block in our brother's way. The *apples of gold* in their beautiful cover, evidently imply good sense, good taste, with good things. A well-meaning absurdity rather brings contempt than conviction.[11]

All of us are bound to rebuke broad and palpable sins;[12] yet on more doubtful individual nature the duty is far more restricted. Some Providence will direct into it. There must be intimate connection, full knowledge of the case, some right from age or station to warrant it. From the extreme difficulty of receiving it, no *words* require to be more *fitly spoken.* No duty calls for more delicacy of feeling, and more "meekness of wisdom." Yet reproof well-timed and well taken, *a wise reprover to an obedient ear is an earring of gold, and an ornament of gold* set out to the best advantage. Such was Eli's word to Samuel;[13] Abigail's and Nathan's to David;[14] Isaiah's to Hezekiah.[15] We see the good fruit in Jehoshaphat, whom, instead of producing revulsion, it stimulated to higher service of God.[16] The

[1] See Bishop Lowth's beautiful exposition. Prælect. xxiv.
[2] Eccl. xii. 10. Chap. xv. 23. [3] Luke xii. 42. Comp. 2 Tim. ii. 15.
[4] Job vi. 25. [5] Isa. l. 4. [6] John iv. vi.
[7] Comp. Luke xiv. 15, 16. [8] Acts xvii. 22—28. [9] Ib. xxiv. 25.
[10] 2 Tim. iv. 2.
[11] Comp. 1 Sam. xxv. 36, 37. Chap. xxxi. 26. 'Mollissima fandi tempora.' Virg Æn. iv. 493, 494. [12] Lev. xix. 17.
[13] 1 Sam. iii. 11—18. [14] Ib. xxv. 31—34. 2 Sam. xii. 1—13.
[15] 2 Kings xx. 14—19. [16] 2 Chron. xix. 2—4.

Apostle's probing reproof to the Corinthian Church worked so efficiently, that "in all things they approved themselves clear in the matter."[1] What a triumph of grace is it, when the kindness of *reproof* is acknowledged,[2] and the motive of love appreciated.'[3] Faithful indeed is the blessing, when the gift of *an obedient ear* prepares the Lord's children for a profitable hearing of his *reproof.*[4]

13. *As the cold of snow in the time of harvest, so is a faithful messenger to them that send him: for he refresheth the soul of his masters.*

Snow itself would be unseasonable *in the time of harvest.* But *the cold* of snow would be most refreshing to the parched and fainting reapers, "*So is a faithful messenger to them that send him.*"[5] How did Eliezer *refresh the soul of his master*, when 'he returned with a true account and speedy dispatch of the important affair committed to him!'[6] Judge of Isaac's feelings in his evening walk of meditation—his heart full of the great matter under suspense—when "he lifted up his eyes, and behold! the camels were coming," bearing the desired blessing.[7] How was Cornelius *refreshed*, when his *messenger* returned with the joy of his heart, and the answer to his prayers.'[8] Often does the Apostle acknowledge this *refreshment* to his anxious spirit, when burdened with "the care of all the churches."[9] And may we not ascend to the highest, and with reverence mark our Divine Master condescending to receive *refreshment* through the agency of his *faithful messengers?* "*We are unto God,*" saith the Apostle—"*a sweet savour of Christ.*" He appears to be overwhelmed with the contemplation, and in prostrate astonishment he cries out—"Who is sufficient for these things?"[10] Yet does the Great Master vouchsafe to acknowledge his *messengers* as "the glory of Christ."[11] And as his crown will he honor them at the great consummating day. "They that turn many to righteousness shall shine as the stars for ever and ever."[12]

14. *Whoso boasteth himself of a false gift,*[13] (in a gift of falsehood, Marg.) *is like clouds and wind without rain.*

The last Proverb described an invaluable blessing. This marks a destructive curse. Suppose a drought, as in the days of Elijah, threatening desolation to the land,[14] and a thick *cloud*, seemingly big with the fruitful blessing, yet passing over—*the wind without rain.* This is a true picture of *the boaster;* rich in promises, but performing nothing; exciting large expectations, then sinking them in disappointment. Whether it be a vain conceit of his own understanding, or an hypocritical desire to

[1] 1 Cor. v. 1. 2 Cor. ii. 1—3; vii. 11. [2] Ps. cxli. 5. Comp. chap. ix. 8.
[3] Chap. xxvii. 5, 6. Comp. Ecclus. xix. 13, 14.
[4] Hab. ii. 1—3. Chap. xx. 12. xv. 31. [5] Chap. xiii. 17. [6] Poule.
[7] Gen. xxiv. 63, 64. [8] Acts x. 4—6, 25.
[9] Comp. 1 Cor. xvi. 17, 18. Phil. ii. 25—30. 1 Thess. iii. 1—7.
[10] 2 Cor. ii. 15, 16. [11] Ib. viii. 23. [12] Dan. xii. 3.
[13] 'Whoso maketh greate boastes, and giveth nothing.' Bishop Coverdale.
[14] 1 Kings xviii 5.

maintain a profession, it is *a boasting in a gift of falsehood.* If it be bad to promise and deceive; it is far worse to promise with an intention to deceive. This was the very character of the Great Deceiver. Did he not put before our unhappy parent *a false gift*—a promise, which could never be realized—"Ye shall be as gods knowing good and evil?"[1] Nay—did he not with a presumption, that hell itself might almost be ashamed of, *boast himself of his false gift*, offering the world to its own Maker, as a temptation to the vilest blasphemy?[2]

How melancholy is it to find this character in those, who stand in the place of God! Yet the church has ever been chastened with *false* teachers; ministering delusion, instead of instruction.[3] And are there none among ourselves, feeding the flock with *false gifts;* seeking to maintain their hollow profession even in the sight of Him, whose frown at the great day will banish them for ever from his presence?[4] Oh! let those that bear the Lord's message, take heed, that if they be counted "as deceivers," they may be "yet true."[5] Not as those, which corrupt the word of God; but as of sincerity, as of God, in the "sight of God," let them "speak in Christ."[6]

15. *By long forbearing is a prince persuaded, and a soft tongue breaketh the bone.*

The wise man had before given a general rule for gentleness.[7] Here he takes an extreme case, and shows its power with the *prince*, whose anger—having no restraint upon him—may rise to immediate revenge.[8] Yet submission, *long-forbearing*, has mighty power to *persuade.* David thus wrought upon Saul's enraged temper.[9] Often by putting a case before an angry *prince* at a fitting opportunity, he may be *persuaded* by "the meekness of wisdom" against his present mind.

But the general principle is most instructive. The *soft* member *breaking the hard bone* may seem to be a paradox. But it is a fine illustration of the power of gentleness above hardness and irritation. Apply it to those who are set against the truth. Many a stout heart has been won by a *forbearing*, yet uncompromising, accommodation to prejudice.[10] In reproof Jehovah showed what he could do in "the strong wind and the earthquake." But his effective rebuke was in the "still small voice"—without upbraiding—sharp, yet tender.[11] So powerful is the energy of gentleness! As regards endurance—it is a manifest fruit of regeneration;[12] a clear exhibition of the mind of Christ,[13] and the practical resemblance of his own *long-forbearance* amidst our continued and

[1] Gen. iii. 3—5. [2] Matt. iv. 8—10.
[3] 1 Kings xxii. 11. Jer. v. 31, with 2 Cor. xi. 13—15. Gal. i. 7. Comp. 2 Pet. ii. 17—19. Jude 12, 16.
[4] Matt. vii. 22, 23. [5] 2 Cor. vi. 8. [6] Ib. ii. 17. Comp. iv. 2.
[7] Chap. xv. 1. [8] Eccl. viii. 3; x. 4. Comp. 1 Sam. xxii. 17, 18.
[9] 1 Sam. xxiv. 8—20; xxvi. 13—25. [10] 2 Tim. ii. 24—26. 1 Cor. ix. 20—22.
[11] 1 Kings xix. 11—13. [12] Jam. i. 18, 19. [13] Matt. xi. 29.

most aggravated provocations. For, when we have been indulged with the privilege of the beloved disciple—"leaning upon Jesus's breast,"[1] nothing have we felt to be there, but gentleness, tenderness, and love.

16. *Hast thou found honey? eat so much as is sufficient for thee, lest thou be filled therewith, and vomit it.*

Solomon lately had warmly invited us *to eat honey.*[2] Here, however, he imposes a restraint. *Eat so much as is sufficient.* So far it is sweet. Beyond this it is nauseating. The principle directs to a thankful, but temperate, enjoyment of our earthly blessings. "Every creature of God is good, and nothing to be refused, if it be received with thanksgiving."[3] But as a needful balance to this universal privilege—"Let your moderation be known unto all men."[4] Satisfy the wants, but mortify the lusts, of the flesh.[5] Then the gifts of God become blessings to us, and we glorify him in them, and by them. But the most elevated pleasures of earth become in the excess, distasteful, and injurious; fraught with disappointment, when separated from the great end.[6] Our affections can never safely flow out to any object, unless they are primarily fixed on God. 'Then we may be sure not to offend, either in the object or measure. No man can in God love whom he should not; nor immoderately love whom he would. This holy respect doth both direct and limit him, and shuts up his delights in the conscience of a lawful fruition.'[7] In earthly pleasure however, we can never forget how slight the boundary law is between the lawful and the forbidden path. Sin and danger begin on the extremity of virtue. For does not the legitimate indulgence of appetite to its utmost point bring us to the brink—and often hurry us to the allowance—of gluttony? Does not the undisciplined glow of earthly affections endanger idolatry? Nay, even spiritual luxury may need self-control; lest it be excitement without deep principle, which must eventually prove unsubstantial and delusive.

But in *eating* the *real honey* of the Gospel there is no danger of excess. Never shall we know satiety in this delight. The increasing desire will be fully satisfied only in eternity. 'O God, let me but taste and see, how sweet the Lord Jesus is in all his gracious promises; in all his merciful and real performances. I shall want no more to make me happy. This is not the honey, whereof I am bidden not to eat too much. No, Lord, I can never eat enough of this celestial honey. Here I cannot surfeit; or if I could, this surfeit would be my health.'[8]

[1] John xiii. 23; xxi. 20. [2] Chap. xxiv. 13. [3] 1 Tim. ii. 4.
[4] Phil. iv. 5. Comp. 1 Cor. vii. 29—31. Jud. 12.
[5] Rom. xiii. 14. Col. iii. 5. Comp. Luke xxi. 34.
[6] Eccl. ii. 10, 11. [7] Bp. Hall's Works—Select Thoughts, II.
[8] Bp. Hall's Soliloquies, LIV. Yet let *the Antinomian professor* remember—'There is no such dangerous surfeit, as upon the sweet and luscious truths of the gospel.' Bp. Hopkins on Isa. xliii. 25.

17. *Withdraw thy foot from thy neighbor's house; lest he be weary of thee, and so hate thee.*

No code of laws enters, as the Bible, into minute regulations for the courtesies of life. Yet surely we do not mar the sanctity of religion by spreading it over the face of human society. Daily life is evangelized by the pervading influence of its wholesome principles. This rule illustrates some of our own Proverbs, which have lost nothing of their significancy by traditional usage. 'Too much of a good thing. Familiarity breeds contempt.' Kindly intercourse with *our neighbor* cannot be maintained without a considerate feeling. An ordinary acquaintance would give just umbrage in claiming the free and unrestrained intercourse of intimate friendship. And the intruder would probably receive a plain intimation, that he was an unwelcome guest. To *withdraw the foot* is an useful rule to prevent so mortifying a result. "*Make thy foot precious*"[1] *to thy neighbor*, by not giving it too often. It is far safer to err on the side of reserve, than to incur contempt by the opposite mistake.[2]

Nay—even the closer bond of friendship requires its measure of prudent restraint. It is worth all our care to preserve this invaluable blessing from interruption. It is the sweet of life. And yet in this *honey* there may be a surfeit.[3] Without mutual respect it may nauseate. Unseasonable interruption to our friend's time; frequent visits without call or object; interference with his necessary engagements, or family comforts; inconvenient tax of expense—perseverance in this course might produce *weariness*, if not disgust, or even *hatred*.

Blessed be God! there is no need of this caution and reserve in our approach unto him. Once acquainted with the way of access, there is no wall of separation. Our earthly friend may be pressed too far. Kindness may be worn out by frequent use. But never can we come to our heavenly Friend unseasonably. Never is *he weary* of our importunity.[4] His gates are always open; and "blessed are they, that are watching and waiting there."[5] The more frequent the visits, the more welcome, and the more fruitful. What with man would be intrusion, with God is confidence. Earnestly does he invite to his closes and most endearing fellowship.[6] And does his child presume upon this most gracious privilege? Far from it. While he has the "boldness of access;"[7] he seeks for "grace whereby he may serve God acceptably with reverence and godly fear."[8]

18. *A man that beareth false witness against his neighbor is a maul, and a sword, and a sharp arrow.*

False witness is universally condemned. But where, save in

[1] Heb. See Holden. Comp. 1 Sam. iii. 1—"precious" in both cases, because rare.
[2] Comp. Ecclus. xxi. 22.
[3] Verse 16.
[4] Luke xi. 5—9; xviii. 1.
[5] Chap. viii. 34.
[6] Can. v. 1.
[7] Eph. iii. 12. Heb. iv. 16; x. 19, 20.
[8] Heb. xii. 28.

the word of God, is its true character and deep aggravation of guilt adequately set forth? What a picture is here of cruelty and malice—nay—even intentional murder! Three murderous instruments are before us, identifying the sixth and ninth commandments. The tongue—intended as "a tree of life"—becomes a weapon of death.[1] Who knows the sin involved in this fearful perversion? Often does the open perjury, as *a sword and sharp arrow,* pierce the fountain of life.[2] And little better are those calumnies and unkind insinuations—all breaches of charity—uttered so freely in common conversation. 'Consider—ye that deal in such conversation—whether you could think of treating the objects of your defamatory discourse as Jael did Sisera,[3] or as Joab did Abner.[4] Would you shrink with horror at the thought of beating out your neighbor's brains with an hammer, or of piercing his bowels with *a sword, or a sharp arrow?* Why then do you indulge in the like barbarity; destroying as far as you can that reputation, which is dear to men as their life, and wounding all their best interests, by mangling their character?'[5]

Truly affecting is it to think of the multitude of these *mauls, swords, and sharp arrows* even in the Church of God. It is not "setting the battle in array against the Philistines, army against army,"[6] but brother against brother. The Shibboleth of a party,[7] not the standard of the cross, is the watch-word for the destructive conflict. "How long, Lord! How long."

19. *Confidence in an unfaithful man in time of trouble is like a broken tooth, and a foot out of joint.*

The broken tooth and disjointed foot are not only useless for their respective offices, but sources of pain and uneasiness. So is *an unfaithful man in time of trouble.* "A friend loveth at all times, and a brother is born for adversity."[8] But many have the name only. Very friendly are they, when they are not needed, when we are dispensing, not receiving our gifts; when there is no cost to pay. But in *the time of trouble,* "a faithful man who can find?"[9] Keenly did Job feel this was a sinking *confidence in his time of trouble.*[10] David was sorely tried by this affliction,[11] even at the very last stage of life.[12] The brethren came out to meet the Apostle at Appii Forum. Yet of a time, when their support would have been especially cheering—he records—"At my first answer no man stood by me, but all men forsook me."[13] Need we wonder at this appointed cross? His Master had endured it before him; and "it is enough for the servant that he be as his Lord."[14]

The world abounds with instances of this disappointment.

[1] Chap. xv. 4, with xii. 18. Comp. Ps. lii. 2; lv. 21; lvii. 4; lix. 7; lxiv. 3, 4. Jer. ix. 3, 8.
[2] Gen. xxxix. 14—20. 1 Kings xxi. 10—13. Matt. xxvi. 60—66. Acts vi. 13, 14.
[3] Jud. iv. 21.
[4] 2 Sam. iii. 27.
[5] Lawson in loco.
[6] 1 Sam. xvii. 21.
[7] Jud. xii. 6.
[8] Chap. xvii. 17.
[9] Chap. xx. 6.
[10] Job vi. 14—17.
[11] Ps. lv. 12—14.
[12] 1 Kings i. 19, 25.
[13] Acts xxviii. 15, with 2 Tim. iv. 16.
[14] Matt. xxvi. 56, with x. 24, 25.

Micah's Levite ungratefully repaid the trust reposed in him.[1] Mephibosheth's trust in Ziba[2]—Israel's dependence upon an arm of flesh—showed the broken reed, not the staff of real support. Truly, when has the world ever answered its fair promises? When has it ever given *a faithful confidence in time of trouble?* When has it failed to make the soul "ashamed of its hope?" A merciful correction to the child of God, when in an evil hour he turns aside from his true *confidence* to vain dependences!

But whoever be *unfaithful*, God is true. Who ever trusted in him, and was confounded? Who has ever built upon his sure foundation, and not witnessed its unshaken security?[4] Though he has pledged himself never to forsake his servants,[5] yet specially —"I will be with him *in trouble*—a very pleasant help in time of trouble."[6]

20. *As he that taketh away a garment in cold weather, and as vinegar upon nitre, so is he that singeth songs to an heavy heart.*

What could be more inhuman than *taking away* a poor man's *garment*, or the coverlid of his bed, *in cold weather?* Such an act of cruelty was forbidden by the God of the poor.[7] Again—what could be more unfitting than pouring *vinegar upon nitre;* which, instead of being serviceable, would only dissolve it with violent effervescence?[8] Not less unseasonable would be the merriment of *singing songs to an heavy heart.*[9] "Give wine"—is the inspired rule—"unto them that be of *heavy hearts.*"[10] But however great be the charms of music,[11] they are ill-suited to sooth the pangs of sorrow.[12] A constrained song was a keen edge of the Babylonish affliction.[13] And where no unkindness is intended, inconsiderate levity, or even excessive cheerfulness, is as "a sword in the bones." The tenderness, that shows a brother's tears; that knows how to "weep with them that weep,"[14] as members of the same body;[15] and directs the mourner to the mourner's friend and God—this is Christian sympathy—a precious balm for the broken heart.

The outward expression of this sympathy may not be always needful. But Oh! let its spirit be deeply cherished, specially by Christians of a buoyant or frigid temperament; most of all by the minister of Christ, that he may take his chair by the mourner's side, and "comfort him with the same comfort, wherewith he him-

[1] Jud. xvii. 7—12; xviii. 20—24. [2] 2 Sam. xvi. 1—4; xix. 24—28.
[3] Assyria, 2 Chron. xxviii. 20, 21. Hos. v. 13. Egypt, Isa. xxx. 1—3; xxxi. 1—3 Jer. xxxvi. 5—7. Ez. xxix. 6, 7.
[4] Isa. xxviii. 16. [5] Heb. xiii. 5.
[6] Ps. xci. 15; xlvi. 1. Comp. Jer. xvii. 5—8.
[7] Deut. xxiv. 12, 17. Comp. Job. xxiv. 7—10. Isa. lviii. 7.
[8] The nitre of Scripture is not that salt that commonly goes by the name, but a soda or mineral alkali (the Roman natrum), which strongly ferments with all acids. Dr. Blayney remarks on Jer. ii. 22 (the only other example of the word)—'In many parts of Asia it is called soap earth, because it is dissolved in water, and used like soap in washing.
[9] Eccl. iii. 4. [10] Chap. xxxi. 6. Comp. Ps. civ. 15.
[11] 1 Sam. xvi. 23. 2 Kings iii. 15.
[12] Job. xxx. 31. Dan. vi. 18. Comp. Ecclus. xxii. 6. [13] Ps. cxxxvii. 1—4.
[14] Rom. xii. 15. Comp. Job ii. 11—13. [15] 1 Cor. xii. 26. Heb. xiii. 3.

self is comforted of God."[1] Much may be done to correct a constitutional deficiency. Redundancy of feeling, however, needs self-control. But never let us forget that our Divine Saviour for this end "took our infirmities, and bare our sicknesses," that "he might be touched with the feeling of them."[2] Yes—"he knoweth our frame;"[3] and his work is not to *take away the garment* from his child in *the cold weather*, but to cherish him with all the tenderness of his own bosom.[4] Instead of unsuitably *pouring vinegar upon nitre;* like the good Samaritan, he "pours in his oil and wine for the healing of the wound."[5]

21. *If thine enemy be hungry, give him bread to eat; and if he be thirsty, give him water to drink:* 22. *For thou shalt heap coals of fire upon his head, and the Lord shall reward thee.*

In what heathen code of morals shall we find this perfection of love? Every system concedes largely to man's selfishness. None reach beyond "loving those that love us," of which the true Lawgiver justly asks, "What reward have ye?"[6] Nay—even the corrupt teachers of Israel could not rise to this sublime standard. 'They did not, it seems, perceive anything to be disapproved in hatred more than in good-will. And, according to their system of morals, "our enemy" was the proper natural object of one of these passions, as "our neighbor" was of the other.'[7] They could not come up to the law; and therefore—perverting the rule of judicial, to authorize private, vengeance[8]—they brought the law down to their own level.

The agreement between the Old and New Testament codes[9] is most complete. Both were dictated by the same Spirit. Each stamps the other with Divine authority. 'The law of love is not expounded more spiritually in any single precept either of Christ or his Apostles, than in this exhortation.'[10] We need not therefore disparage one system, in order to exalt the other. "The new commandment is that, which we had from the beginning;" old in its authority; "new" only, as enforced by a new principle and example.[11] To suppose that the gospel stretches beyond the measure of the law, would imply, either that the law demanded too little or the Gospel too much. Neither supposition honors the law as the unchangeable transcript of the Divine perfections.

There may be no overt breach of the law, while yet the heart secretly revolts from its high standard. Circumstances may hinder open retaliation. Our enemy may be out of our reach, or too great to offend with impunity. But the grudge remains.[12] There would

[1] 2 Cor. i. 4—6. [2] Matt. viii. 17. Heb. iv. 15. [3] Ps. ciii. 14.
[4] Isa. xl. 11. [5] Ib. lxi. 2, 3, with Luke x. 34. [6] Matt. v. 46, 47.
[7] Bp. Butler's Sermons at the Rolls. Serm. VIII.
[8] Matt. v. 43, with Num. xxv. 16—28. Deut. vii. 1, 2; xxiii. 6; xxv. 17—19.
[9] Comp. Rom. xii. 20, 21, with text. Ex. xxiii. 4, 5, with Matt. v. 44. Our church has not neglected to imbue her worshippers with this blessed spirit. See the Litany, and Collect for St. Stephen's-day.
[10] Scott in loco. [11] John xiii. 34. 1 John ii. 7, 8. 2 John 5, with Lev xix. 18.
[12] Lev. xix. 18. Jam. v. 9.

be a pleasure at his misfortune.[1] We think of him only in reference to our injuries. The spark may be confined for years, and on some favorable opportunity burst out into a murderous flame.[2] And even when we seem to be in the way, how many haltings and shiftings are there, before we fully and practically embrace the obligation! How much of a retorting spirit, or measuring our conduct towards our enemy by his towards us! And if on any point we have constrained our selfish hearts to return good for evil, what ministering to self-complacency, or self-righteousness?

Too often also our love "to our enemies" is only ceasing to quarrel with him. If we put off revenge as inconsistent with our Christian name; yet do we "put on as the elect of God, bowels of mercies—forgiving one another, if any man have a quarrel against any?"[3] 'Love is of too substantial a nature to be made up of mere negatives; and withal too operative, to terminate in bare desires.'[4] We may profess our good-will towards *our enemy*—that we forgive and pray for him from our heart. But unless we are ready with the practical exercise of sympathy—*feeding him, when he is hungry, and giving him to drink, when thirsty*, we are only the victims of our own self-delusion. 'O noble revenge of Elisha' —exclaims pious Bishop Hall—'to feast his persecutors! To provide a table for those who had provided a grave for him! No revenge but this, is heroical, and fit for a Christian imitation.'[5] To *feed our hungry enemy* with the tenderness of a nurse, who breaks the portion into morsels for her infant's nourishment[6]—what a splendor does the opposition of nature give to this victory of grace!

No man ever conquered his enemy's heart by revenge; many by love. Was it not thus, that the Almighty Saviour dissolved the hardness of our unyielding hearts? Let the effort be tried. Surround the untractable metal beneath and above; not only putting it over the fire, but *heaping coals of fire upon it.* Few hearts are so obdurate, as not to melt under the mighty energy of patient, self-denying, burning love.[7] Or even should it be dross, that resists the vehement flame, all will not be lost. *If thine enemy* will not recompense thee for all the good done to him, concern not thyself with that. *The Lord shall reward thee.* The God of love will honor his own image on his own children.[8] David in this confidence restrained the rising vengeance in his zealous servants,[9] and in similar forbearance found his "prayer for his enemy's good returned into his own bosom."[10] We are directed to return "blessing

[1] Chap. xxiv. 17, 18.
[2] 2 Sam. xiii. 23, 28.
[3] Col. iii. 12, 13.
[4] South's Sermon on Matt. v. 44.
[5] Contemplations, Book xix. Cont. 9, on 2 Kings vi. 22, 23. See another equally noble example, 2 Chron. xxviii. 12—15, 'If by revenge thou destroyest one enemy, by forgiving thou shalt conquer three—thine own lust, the devil's temptation, thine enemy's heart.' Flavel's Keeping the Heart.
[6] Ψώμιζε. LXX. Rom. xii. 20. Comp. Schleusner.
[7] 1 Sam. xxiv. 16—20; xxvi. 25.
[8] Matt. v. 44, 45.
[9] 2 Sam. xvi. 9—12. Comp. Ps. vii. 4.
[10] Ps. xxxv. 13. Comp. Matt. x. 13.

for railing; knowing that thereunto are we called, that we should inherit a blessing."[1]

To dispute the reasonableness of the precept is to say—that 'man is the proper object of good-will, whatever his faults are, when they respect others; but not when they respect myself. I am sure,' (adds Bishop Butler—probing this principle to the bottom) 'there is nothing in it unreasonable. It is indeed no more, than we should not indulge a passion, which, if generally indulged, would propagate itself, so as almost to lay waste the world."[2]

But most reasonable as this precept is, it is infinitely removed from man's native power. The rules, no less than the doctrines, of God are "foolishness to him."[3] Let those, who look to "enter into life, by keeping the commandments," begin with this. They would see, that they might as soon turn the sun backward; that they could as readily "cut off a right hand," as to reach it out, to *feed an enemy* in distress. Such an exhibition of love would be in their eyes an ideal perfection; or at least, like an exquisite piece of workmanship, which every one admires, but no one attempts to imitate.

Yet is it really impracticable? So the world counts it. So my own corrupt heart finds it. But "I can do all things"—this then among the rest—"through Christ which strengtheneth me."[4] It shall then be done willingly—joyfully. My enemy has no claim upon my love; yet he that bids me love him, claims and deserves my full obedience.[5] 'We are the disciples of him, who died for his enemies.'[6] Did we but drink more largely into his spirit, this impracticable precept would be, not our task or our cross, but our delight and indulgence.

23. *The north wind driveth away rain: so doth an angry countenance a backbiting tongue.* (The north wind bringeth forth rain: so doth a backbiting tongue an angry countenance. Marg.[7])

The backbiter—who should tolerate him? He is a pest in society;[8] in the circle of friendship;[9] in the church of God.[10] Neither his plausible garb, nor the good company, who give him the hearing, can hide his real character. If the *north wind driveth away the rain,* let *an angry* countenance frown him from our presence. *If it brings the rain:* let the very sight of him bring a rebuke of holy indignation. This is to "be angry, and not sin."[11] Indeed, not to be angry here, would be to sin. Holy anger is a property in God.[12] It was manifested in the humanity of Jesus.[13] When

[1] 1 Pet. iii. 9. [2] Bp. Butler's Sermons at the Rolls, Serm. IX.
[3] 1 Cor. ii. 14. [4] Phil. iv. 13. [5] John xiv. 15.
[6] Bishop Wilson. Rom. v. 10. Comp. Luke xxiii. 34. Was not this his own obedience to his own law? Matt. v. 44.
[7] Many valuable critics, after the LXX., prefer the marginal to the received reading. The ordinary meaning of the Hebrew word is to produce, or bring forth, chap. viii. 24. And yet comp. Job xxxvii. 22. Homer also speaks of the north wind bringing fine weather. Il. O. 170. The meaning however is the same with either rendering.
[8] Chap. xxvi. 20. [9] Chap. xvi. 28. [10] 2 Cor. xii. 20.
[11] Eph. iv. 26. [12] Deut. ix. 8. Ps. vii. 11. Nah. i. 2. [13] Mark iii. 5; viii. 33.

God's name was dishonored, "the meekest man upon earth waxed hot"[1] in anger, while his heart was melting in love to the rebels.[2] And should not we feel this, when *the backbiting tongue* breaks his law of love—dear to him, as his own Godhead? And yet rare indeed is the exception—alas!—even in Christian circles when the faults of others—real or imagined—do not occupy conversation; or at least, when some lowering of the absent, or some ridicule of their infirmities, is not admitted!

This *tongue* wounds four at one stroke—*the backbiter* himself, the object of his attack, the hearer, and the name of God. All involves the Christian professor in the fearful guilt of "offending the little ones."[3] For how can the weak and inexperienced but be stumbled at so inconsistent an exhibition of the gospel of love?

But if he be rather welcomed than repelled, is not the willing listener thus partaker of his sin? Flee this deadly pest. Keep thine ears as well as thy mouth from the poison. Let thine *angry countenance drive away* either the slander from him, or the slanderer from thee. Where remonstrance cannot be given, a marked displeasure of *countenance* is often an effective rebuke to the shameless offender.[4]

24. *It is better to dwell in the corner of the housetop, than with a brawling woman in a wide house.*

This Proverb has been given before.[5] Scriptural repetitions show not want of matter, but the deep importance of the matter laid out. Such is the vexation connected with this evil, that the most uncomfortable dwelling, where the soul might retire for communion with God, would be a grateful alternative.

This Book presents a graphical picture of conjugal happiness, where "the wife is as the loving hind and the pleasant roe"—her husband's most satisfying delight.[6] Here is a vivid contrast of misery, from which *the wide house* provides no refuge—no rest.

The relative position of the parties in the Sacred ordinance is wisely appointed. Equality would only have provoked contention for superiority. The Divine appointment preserves peace without degradation.[7] If "man is the head of the woman," "the woman is the glory of the man"[8]—the diadem in his domestic circle,[9] and upon her slightly lowered level—still his support, solace, and "help-meet."[10] *The brawling woman*, revolting against her Maker's rule of subjection, is no less a tormentor to herself than to her husband.

[1] Ex. xxxii. 19, with Num. xii. 3. [2] Ibid. verses 30—32. [3] Matt. xviii. 6.

[4] Augustine's biographer mentions of him, that these two lines were written in his dining-room—

'Quisquis amat dictus absentum rodere vitam,
Hanc mensam vetitam noverit esse sibi.'

It is added—that a bishop, indulging this habit at his table—he said to him—'Either I will blot out these verses on the wall, or begone from my table.' See the fine description, Ecclus. xxviii. 13—20.

[5] Chap. xxi. 9. Comp. ib. v. 19; xix. 13; xxvii. 15, 16. [6] Chap. v. 18, 19.

[7] Gen. iii. 16. 1 Tim. ii. 11—14. [8] 1 Cor. xi. 3, 7. [9] Chap. xxxi. 28.

[10] Gen. ii. 18.

Let the Christian professor beware of trifling with the law of this ordinance—"Only in the Lord."[1] If he comes into the world, instead of "coming out;" if, instead of "being separate," he unites himself in the closest bond; if, when forbidden to "touch the unclean thing," he makes himself "one flesh" with it,[2] let him not wonder, if his God "curse his blessing,"[3] and leave him to choose for himself an house of contention, unvisited with one ray of heavenly sunshine. Young man! ponder the deep responsibility of the marriage-choice. Let it be manifestly the Lord's choice for thee, not thine for thyself. Yea—let him be thy first choice, and he will order the rest.[4] Watch and distrust thine own will. Consult the "lamp and light of thy path."[5] Mark the Providence of thy God;[6] and his blessing "that maketh rich, and addeth no sorrow with it," will sanctify his own gift.[7]

Christian women! Think not these Proverbs unworthy your attention. Be it so, that you answer not to the revolting picture. But surely the repeated exhibition strongly inculcates the cultivation of the opposite graces, the absence of which clouds the female character in painful deformity.[8]

25. *As cold waters to a thirsty soul, so is good news from a far country.*

What were the *cold waters* to Hagar and her child in the wilderness;[9] to Israel, at Rephidim;[10] to Samson at Lehi![11] Such is the cordial of *good news from a far country.* Solomon had before spoken of the "refreshment of the messenger;"[12] here of the message. This Proverb, like many others, was probably familiar to his own experience. The return of his fleets sent to *a far country* for precious merchandize (like our own merchant-ships) were doubtless welcomed with no common delight.[13] The exile from his country, or one that has interests in a foreign land—near and dear relatives, from whom the separation has been long—will fully realize this lively illustration. Had Joseph's brethren brought to their sorrowing father as many pieces of gold as grains of corn, it would have been nothing to the *good news from a far country*—"Joseph is yet alive."[14] Distant intelligence is naturally more cheering, than tidings in themselves equally interesting—nearer home. The long interval of these tidings; the lengthened separation from the beloved object; the anxiety necessarily excited by want of intercourse; the uncertainty of his welfare and prospects—all combine to make these *cold waters* specially refreshing *to the thirsty soul.* "Hope deferred maketh the heart sick; but when the desire cometh, it is a tree of life."[15]

1 1 Cor. vii. 39. 2 2 Cor. vi. 14—17, with Eph. v. 31.
3 Mal. ii. 2. 4 Matt. vi. 33. 5 Ps. cxix. 105.
6 Gen. xxiv. 12—60. Ruth iii. 18. 7 Chap. xix. 14; x. 22.
8 1 Tim. ii. 9, 10. 1 Pet. iii. 1—6. 9 Gen. xxi. 16—19.
10 Ex. xvii. 1—6. Comp. Num. xx. 11.
11 Judg. xv. 18, 19. See Virgil's beautiful image, Eclog. v. 46—48. 12 Verse 13.
13 1 Kings ix. 26—28. 14 Gen. xlv. 25—28. Comp. xliii. 27—30.
15 Chap. xiii. 12. Comp. xv. 30. Contrast Neh. i. 2—4.

Reader! if thy heart has ever leaped within thee at the news of some earthly advantage—hast thou heard and welcomed the *good news from the far country?* Dost thou know thy need—thy danger of perishing? Then what refreshment can compare with the "good tidings of great joy" brought to thee from heaven—"Unto you is born a Saviour?"[1] Mountains of gold could never have purchased the blessing now brought to thine ears—yea—to the door of thine heart—"without money and without price."[2] Does not thine heart spring in the song of praise—"How beautiful upon the mountains are the feet of him, that bringeth good tidings, that publisheth peace!"[3] Most grateful also are the messengers' tidings from *a far country*, of the welcome reception of their message.[4] The angelic harps strike up the song.[5] Even the bosom of God is filled with adorable joy![6]

25. *A righteous man falling down before the wicked is as a troubled fountain, and a corrupt spring.*

Eastern *fountains and springs* (where the rains are only periodical, and at long intervals) are of no common price.[7] The injury of *corrupting* them is proportionate.[8] The well is therefore a blessing or a curse, according to the purity or impurity of the waters. *A righteous man* in his proper character is "a well of life—a blessing in the midst of the land."[9] But if *he fall down before the wicked* by his inconstant profession,[10] the blessing becomes a curse, *the fountain is troubled, and the spring corrupt.* What a degradation was it to Abraham to *fall down* under the rebuke of an Heathen King;[11] to Peter, to yield to a servant-maid in denying his Lord![12] How did David's sin *trouble the fountain*, both to his family[13] and his people![14] How did the idolatry of his wise son *corrupt the spring* through successive generations![15]

When a Minister of Christ apostatizes from the faith[16] (and mournfully frequent have been such spectacles) or compromises his principles from the fear of man,[17] *the springs and fountains* of truth are fearfully corrupted. When a servant of God, of standing and influence, crouches and *falls down under the wicked*,[18] the transparency of his profession is grievously tarnished. Satan thus makes more effective use of God's people than of his own. The gross wickedness of the ungodly passes in silence. But he makes the neighborhood ring with the failings of Christian professors. Godly consistency so grates upon the consciences of the world, that at any breach of it they clap their hands with Satanic joy; to see the Lord "wounded in the house of his friends."[19] Principles and practices

[1] Luke ii. 10, 11. [2] Isa. lv. 1. [3] Ib. lii. 7. Rom. x. 15.
[4] Acts xv. 3. Comp. xi. 18, 23. [5] Luke xv. 7, 10.
[6] Ibid. verses 20—24. [7] Gen. xxvi. 18—22. Deut. viii. 7. Jos. xv. 18, 19.
[8] See Ez. xxxii. 2; xxxiv. 18. [9] Chap. x. 11. Gen. xii. 2.
[10] *Falling down* is to be taken in a moral sense (making a slip). Parkhurst.
[11] Gen. xii. 18—20. Comp. xx. [illegible]; xxvi. 10. [12] Matt. xxvi. 69—72.
[13] 2 Sam. xi. 2, with xiii. 11—14; xvi. 22. [14] Ibid. xii. 14.
[15] 1 Kings xi. [illegible] 2 Kings xxiii. 13. [16] Philem. 22, with 2 Tim. iv. 10.
[17] Gal. ii. [illegible] [18] 2 Kings xviii. 5, 6, with 13—16. [19] Luke xiii. 6.

are sanctioned, that wound our Divine Master. The consciences of the ungodly are lulled. "The lame," instead of being "healed," are "turned out of the way."[1] Thus 'the scandalous falls of good men are like a bag of poison cast by Satan into the *spring*, from whence the whole town is supplied with water.'[2]

Nor let this be considered as the responsibility only of eminent Christians. All are by profession "the salt of the earth, and the light of the world." Let all therefore see to it, that "the salt does not lose its savor," and that the candlestick gives its clear light.[3] None of us stand or act alone. "None of us"—be it well pondered —"liveth unto himself."[4] The conduct of each has its measure of influence on the body. Each is the centre of a circle more or less extended. Each is either a pure *spring*, or *a troubled fountain.* Lord! "cast the salt into the spring of the waters that they may be healed."[5]

27. *It is not good to eat much honey: so for men to search their own glory is not glory.*[6]

Honey is good; but in moderation.[7] *It is not good to eat much honey.*[8] A man's own name and reputation is *honey* to him. Let him carefully preserve it from "the dead fly that spoils it."[9] The honor of God is connected with the honorable profession of his people. But this carefulness is a virtue on the brink of vice; a duty on the borders of imminent danger. To be puffed up by our own endowments; to listen to our praise; to force ourselves upon public attention[10]—thus *to search out our own glory,*[11] *is not glory*, but shame. As unseemly is it to seek *our own glory*, as to ascribe to ourselves our own being.

Yet is there no danger of seeking the fame rather than the substance of godliness—a well-known name in the Church, rather than an unknown name in the book of life? Few ministers, but have been severely exercised here; identifying their usefulness with their honor; cherishing the desire for public approbation, rather than for unnoticed fruitfulness; dreading to be counted upon an ordinary level, as "vessels of wood and earth," rather than of "gold and silver."[12] Oh! it is a mighty victory over self, to trample man's judgment under foot, and eye only God's approval. Nothing is right, except it be wrought in the true spirit of the gospel—"doing nothing in vain glory, but in lowliness of mind each esteeming others better than himself."[13] The great apostle spoke of matters of glorying only by compulsion.[14] A vain-glorious spirit cankers many

[1] Heb. xii. 13. [2] Flavel's Method of Grace, Sermon XXXV.
[3] Matt. v. 13—16. [4] Rom. xiv. 7. [5] 2 Kings ii. 21, 22.
[6] Critics seem to be much perplexed on the translation of this last clause. The grammatical objection to supply a negative led Mr. Scott to suggest an interrogative version—"Is it glory for men to search out their own glory?"
[7] Chap. xxiv. 13. [8] Verse 16. [9] Phil. iv. 8, with Eccl. x. 1.
[10] Chap. xx. 6; xxvii. 2. [11] Gen. xi. 4; 2 Kings x. 16. Dan. iv. 30.
[12] 2 Tim. ii. 20. [13] Phil. ii. 3. Comp. Gal. v. 26.
[14] 2 Cor. xii. 1, 11. See Lyttleton on Conversion of St. Paul.

a plausible profession.[1] Did we turn from the flattering glass of self-love to the pure and faithful mirror of the law; the inconceivable deformities opening to view would constrain us to take the lowest place among the most unworthy. Most wholesome is the recollection—"That which is highly esteemed among men is abomination in the sight of God."[2]

28. *He that hath no rule over his own spirit is like a city that is broken down, and without walls.*

A former proverb declared "him that had rule over his spirit" to be a mighty conqueror.[3] And certainly the noblest conquests are gained or lost over ourselves. For *he that hath no rule over his own spirit* is an easy prey to the invading foe. Any one may irritate and torment him, and spoil him of his comfort.[4] He yields himself to the first assault of his ungoverned passion—offering no resistance—*like a city broken down and without walls*—the object of pity and contempt.[5] Thus having no discipline over himself—every temptation becomes the occasion of sin, and hurries him on to fearful lengths, that he had not contemplated. The first outbreaking of anger tends to murder.[6] Unwatchfulness over lust plunges into adultery.[7] The mightiest natural strength is utter feebleness in the great conflict.[8] How should such an object excite our tenderest compassion!

But there are many cases of this moral weakness—less shameful, and yet scarcely less injurious to the soul. Every out-breaking of irritation—every spark of pride—kindling in the heart, before it shows itself in the countenance, or on the tongue—must be attacked and determinately resisted. It is the beginning of a breach in *the walls of the city.* Without instant attention, it will widen to the ruin of the whole.[9] The natural man may talk of 'self-control,' as if the reins were in his own hand. But he who has been "born of the Spirit," and taught "to know the plague of his own heart"—is made to feel that effective 'self-control' is Divine grace, not his own native power. What then is to be done? On the first assault, fortify *the walls* by prayer. Never dare to trust to the strength of the citadel. Have not repeated defeats taught us the need of calling in better strength than our own? How could we enter into the conflict—much less hold on the fight—but for the promise—"Sin shall not have dominion over us?"[10] Oh! for simple—cleaving faith, to draw out from this mighty source—energy—continual watchfulness—perseverance—triumphant victory!

[1] John v. 44; xii. 43. [2] Luke xvi. 15.
[3] Chap. xvi. 32. [4] Esth. iii. 5, 6; v. 13. [5] Neh. i. 3; ii. 17.
[6] Gen. iv. 5—8. Comp. 1 Sam. xx. 30—33; xxv. 33. Dan. iii. 13, 19.
[7] 2 Sam. xi. 2—4. [8] Jud. xvi. 1—19. [9] Comp. chap. xvii. 14.
[10] Rom. vi. 14.

CHAPTER XXVI.

1. *As snow in summer, and as rain in harvest; so honor is not seemly for a fool.*

THE richest blessings lose their value, when unsuitably bestowed. *Snow* is the beauteous wintry covering of the earth;[1] preserving the seed from the killing cold.[2] But *in summer* it is out of season. *Rain* in its season is a fruitful blessing.[3] But *in harvest* it is an unsuitable interruption to the reaper's work—and often a public calamity.[4] Just so, *honor*, unsuitably bestowed on *a fool, is not seemly for him.* 'He neither deserves it, nor knows how to use it.'[5] *Honor* bestowed on Joseph and Daniel, suitably to their wisdom, was seemly to themselves, and a blessing to the land.[6] But when *a fool*—sometimes a scoffer at religion—is promoted to a station of public influence, how ungracefully does his *honor* sit upon him! In Haman it was only the display of his pride and vain glory—the occasion of his more public disgrace.[7]

Learn then to adorn our profession with consistency. Seek that heavenly wisdom, which will make us worthy of any honor that may be appointed for us. "He that is faithful in that which is least, is faithful also in much."[8]

2. *As the bird by wandering, as the swallow by flying, so the curse causeless shall not come.*

Groundless fears are real evils, and often press heavily upon enfeebled minds. A curse flies out of an angry mouth undeserved, unprovoked. 'What if it should come to pass?' But we need no more fear *the causeless curse*, than *the birds wandering* over our heads. *The swallow flying* up and down never lights upon us; *so the curse causeless shall not come* to hurt us. Powerless was the curse of Moab, though attempted to be strengthened with the divination of the wicked prophet.[9] Goliah's curse against David was scattered to the winds.[10] What was David the worse for the curse of Shimei;[11] or Jeremiah for the curse of his hateful persecutors?[12] Under this harmless shower of stones we turn from men to God, and are at peace. "Let them curse; but bless thou; when they arise, let them be ashamed; but let thy servant rejoice."[13]

But if the *curse* be not *causeless*, it *will come.* Jotham's righteous curse came upon Abimelech and the men of Shechem.[14] Eli-

[1] Job xxxvii. 6. [2] Isa. lv. 10.
[3] Ibid. Job xxxviii. 26, 27. Ps. lxv. 9—13; civ. 13, 14. Jam. v. 7.
[4] 1 Sam. xii. 17, 18.
[5] Poole. Chap. xix. 10; xxx. 21, 22. Eccl. x. 5—7. Comp. Ps. xii. 8.
[6] Gen. xli. 38—40. Dan. vi. 1—3. [7] Est. iii. 1—6; v. 11. [8] Luke xvi. 10.
[9] Num. xxii. 4—6; xxiii. 8. Deut. xxiii. 4, 5. Neh. xiii. 2.
[10] 1 Sam. xvii. 43. [11] 2 Sam. xvi. 12. [12] Jer. xv. 10.
[13] Ps. cix. 28. [14] Jud. ix. 56, 57.

sha's curse fearfully came on the young mockers of Bethel[1] The curse abides on Jericho from generation to generation.[2] And—reader—if thou be an unconverted, unbelieving sinner, without love to thy Saviour—there is *a curse* for thee—not *causeless*—justly deserved; and come it must—*come it will.*[3] Yea—has it not already come from thy Maker and thy God?[4]—thy blessing and thy curse—awful thought! coming from the same mouth! Nor is this an impotent wishing of ill, but the substance of God's everlasting wrath centering in thy heart. Oh! flee from it, while time is given; while the refuge is open to thee![5] If thou be under cover, *it shall not come.*[6] Thou shalt rejoice in "thy redemption from it,"[7] and find confidence in complete security.[8]

3. *A whip for the horse, a bridle for the ass, and a rod for the fool's back.*

This proverb inverts our ideas. We should have given *the bridle for the horse, and the whip for the ass.*[9] But the Eastern asses are a very superior race, both in beauty and spirit; valuable property to their owners.[10] The *bridle* is necessary to curb and to guide them; while *the horse*—perhaps badly broken in—may need *a whip*—if dull, to accelerate his speed; if fiery, to correct his temper.[11] Every creature subdued for the service of man needs his appropriate discipline. The Lord "guides his children with his eye." But let them cultivate a pliable spirit; "not as the horse and the mule, whose mouth must be held in with bit and bridle."[12] *The fool* neither hears the voice, nor sees the directing eye. He will be ruled neither by reason nor persuasion. *A rod therefore is for the fool's back.*[13] Pharaoh provoked this severe chastisement at the hands of God;[14] the men of Succoth and Penuel at Gideon's hands.[15] Many such *fools* are in the Church—self-willed, full of conceit. They need *the rod*, and they have it.[16] Discipline is the most probing test. What is its fruit? In the child submission and tenderness;[17] in *the fool* (except it beat out his folly,[18] which is too often a desperate case[19]) hardness and rebellion.[20] Sad indeed is it, that the child sometimes needs the *rod* intended *for the fool's back*. Yet never does his loving Father use it, till gentle means have been tried in vain. O my God! use

[1] 2 Kings ii. 24.
[2] Jos. vi. 26. 1 Kings xvi. 34. The city of Palms is described by a recent traveller, as an assemblage of huts, 'so low, that at night one might almost ride over them without being aware of the fact.' (Three Weeks in Palestine, p. 89.) Such is the unchangeable truth of God!
[3] Deut. xxviii. 15; xxix. 19, 20. 1 Cor. xvi. 22.
[4] Chap. iii. 33. Zech. v. 3, 4.
[5] Gen. xix. 17.
[6] Rom. viii. 1.
[7] Gal. iii. 10, 13.
[8] Chap. i. 33.
[9] Michaelis was so positive on this point, that he altered his version accordingly, contrary to the authority of all versions and MSS.
[10] Judg. x. 3, 4; xii. 13, 14. 2 Sam. xvii. 23; xix. 26.
[11] Paxton's Natural History of Scripture, p. 221, and Parkhurst.
[12] Ps. xxxii. 8, 9.
[13] Chap. x. 13; xix. 29.
[14] Ex. x. 3.
[15] Jud. viii. 5—7, 16
[16] 2 Cor. x. 6—11; xiii. 2.
[17] Jer. xxxi. 18—20.
[18] 2 Chron. xxxiii. 11—13.
[19] Chap. xvii. 10; xxvii. 22.
[20] 2 Chron. xxviii. 22. Isa. i. 5. Jer. v. 3.

thine own wise means, to save me from my own waywardness, folly and ruin.

4. *Answer not a fool according to his folly, lest thou also be like unto him.*
5. *Answer a fool according to his folly, lest he be wise in his own conceit.*

We are forbidden, yet commanded—to *answer a fool.* The reason however attached to each rule explains the apparent contradiction.[1] Both together are a wise directory for the treatment of *the fool*, according to the difference of character, time, or circumstance. Suppose a free-thinker or scoffer at religion, showing the desperate "*folly* of his heart, by making a mock at sin,"[2] by witty and profane jestings, or specious arguments against the word or ways of God. Generally speaking, it would be better to follow Hezekiah's command against Rabshekah's blasphemy—"*Answer him not.*"[3] Jeremiah thus turned away in silence from the folly of the false prophets.[4] If however we are constrained to reply—*Answer him not according to his folly;* not in his own foolish manner; "not rendering railing for railing."[5] Moses offended here. He *answered* the rebels *according to their folly*—passion for passion, and thus *he became like unto them.*[6] David's answer to Nabal was in the same degradation.[7]

But what may be at one time our duty to restrain, at another time, and under different circumstances, it may be no less our duty to do. Silence may sometimes be mistaken for defeat. Unanswered words may be deemed unanswerable, and *the fool* becomes arrogant, more and more *wise in his own conceit.*[8] An *answer* therefore may be called for; yet not in folly, but to folly; 'not in his foolish manner, but in the manner which his foolishness required;[9] not *according to his folly*, but according to thine own wisdom. Our words should be sharp as rods. The fool's back needs them. Such was Job's answer to his wife—grave, convincing, silencing—"Thou speakest as one of *the foolish* women speaketh. What! shall we receive good at the hand of God, and shall we not receive evil?"[10]

Oh! for wisdom to govern the tongue; to discover "the time to keep silence, and the time to speak;"[11] most of all to suggest the "word fitly spoken"[12] for effective reproof! How instructive is the pattern of our great Master! His silence and his answer were equally worthy of himself. The former always conveyed a dignified rebuke.[13] The latter issued in the confusion of his captious enemies.[14] Will not a prayerful meditative study communicate to us a large measure of his divine wisdom?

[1] Yet the learned Dr. Kennicott was so strangely stumbled by this verbal contradiction, as to propose a rash emendation of the text from the Syriac and Targum, which wholly misses the point of the text. Dissert. ii. on Heb. Text of Old Testament, p. 369.
[2] Chap. xiv. 9. [3] 2 Kings xviii. 36. Comp. Jud. 9. [4] Jer. xxviii. 11.
[5] 1 Pet. iii. 9. [6] Num. xx. 2—10. Ps. cvi. 33. [7] 1 Sam. xxv. 21, 22.
[8] Verse 12. [9] Fuller's Harmony of Scripture. [10] Job ii. 9, 10.
[11] Eccl. iii. 7. [12] Chap. xv. 23; xxv. 11. [13] Matt. xvi. 1—4; xxi. 23—27.
[14] Ib. xxii. 46. Luke xiii. 17.

6. *He that sendeth a message by the hand of a fool cutteth off the feet, and drinketh damage.* 7. *The legs of the lame are not equal: so is a parable in the mouth of fools.* 8. *As he that bindeth a stone in a sling,* (putteth a precious stone in a heap of stones, Marg.) *so is he that giveth honor to a fool.* 9. *As a thorn goeth up into the hand of a drunkard, so is a parable in the mouth of fools.*

Surely this diversified exhibition of the foolishness of folly is an incentive to the study of heavenly wisdom. *The fool is utterly unfit for service. When a message is sent by his hands*, he makes so many mistakes, careless or wilful, that it is like bidding him go, when we have *cut off his legs.* Indeed we can only *drink damage* from his commission.[1] The employment of the unbelieving spies spread *damage* of discontent and rebellion throughout the whole congregation.[2] How careful should we be to entrust important business to trustworthy persons! *Fools* are either unqualified for their mission, or they have their own interests to serve, at whatever cost to their masters. Solomon himself *drank damage* by employing an "industrious" servant, but a *fool* in wickedness—who "lifted up his hand against the king"—and spoiled his son of ten parts of his kingdom.[3] Benhadad *drank damage by sending a message by the hands* of Hazael, who murdered his master, when the way was opened for his own selfish purposes.[4]

See—again—how the fool exposes his shame. Never would *a lame* man show his infirmity so much, as if he were to pretend to feats of agility or strength. Never does *a fool* appear so ridiculous as when making a show of wisdom. It only creates disgust.[5] 'A wise saying doth as ill become a fool, as dancing does a cripple.'[6] *A parable*—'an authoritative weighty saying,'[7]—*in his mouth* becomes a jest. "Is Saul also among the prophets? Why beholdest thou the mote that is in thy brother's eye, and yet considerest not the beam that is in thine own eye? Physician, heal thyself. Thou therefore that teachest another, teachest thou not thyself!"[8]

Place the fool in honor. The sling makes *the stone bound in it* an instrument of death.[9] The *honor given to the fool* makes him a curse to his fellow-creatures.[10] The prime favorite of a despot would have been the murderer of the chosen nation—had not God restrained him.[11] Dangerous indeed is the placing unqualified persons in authority. 'It is like putting a sword or a loaded pistol into a madman's hand.'[12]

But the fool does mischief also unconsciously to himself. 'It

[1] Chap. x. 26. Contrast xiii. 17; xxv. 13.
[2] Num. xiii. 32; xiv. 1—4. [3] 1 Kings xi. 26—40. [4] 2 Kings viii. 8—15.
[5] Chap. xvii. 7. Comp. Ecclus. xx. 20. [6] Bp. Patrick. [7] Parkhurst.
[8] 1 Sam. xix. 24. Matt. vii. 3—5. Luke iv. 23. Rom. ii. 21.
[9] 1 Sam. xvii. 49, 50. [10] Jud. ix. 6. 1 Sam. viii. 1—3. [11] Esth. iii. 1—5.
[12] Scott. Parkhurst, and other critics prefer the Marg. reading—the value of honor upon a fool being lost, like a precious stone covered up in a promiscuous heap. 'He that setteth a foole in hye dignite, that is even as yf a man dyd caste a precious stone upon the galous.' Bp. Coverdale—alluding to the custom of throwing a stone to the heap under which the criminal was buried The reading of the text is however well supported both by the Vulgate and LXX.

is no more fit for a fool to meddle with a wise speech, than for a drunken man to handle a thorn-bush.'[1] When *the thorn goes up into his hand*, his insensibility only makes the wound more deadly. Thus *the fool's parable*—his wise and sharp sayings, gathered he scarcely knows whence—*go up into him like a thorn*—sharply pricking his conscience. Yet he feels no compunction—no alarm.[2] Sad indeed is the sight (should it not make us tremble for ourselves?) of the ungodly prophet, dealing out from the mouth of God—yet with hardened indifference—words enough to "make both his ears to tingle."[3]

Such is *the fool*—a pest to his fellow-creatures—awfully responsible to his God! But in the sacred office how fearfully is this evil and responsibility increased! The great message *sent by the hands* of ungodly servants, brings most serious *damage* to the Church.[4] *The parable*—our Divine Master's wise and holy instruction—*in the mouth of a fool* is perverted and contradicted by his unholy life. "Unto the wicked God saith—What hast thou to do to declare my statutes, or that thou shouldst take my covenant in thy mouth—seeing thou hatest instruction, and castest my words behind thee?"[5] 'Almighty God, who alone worketh great marvels, send down upon all Bishops and Curates the healthful spirit of thy grace;'[6] that "stewards faithful" to their trust,[7] "workmen that need not to be ashamed,"[8]—true and authorized "ambassadors of Christ," may be multiplied in the Church; and that *fools*—unfaithful ministers—may be rebuked and restrained.

10. *The great God, that formed all things, both rewardeth the fool, and rewardeth transgressors.* (A great man grieveth all; and he hireth the fool; he hireth also transgressors, Marg.)

It is difficult to fix with certainty the interpretation of this Proverb.[9] All however expound from it the Divine government—direct or permissive. Suppose *the Great One* to be *God, that formed all things.* He proportions exactly the *reward* of the wicked.[10] *The fool* is responsible for sins of ignorance; not only for the little he knew, but for the much, which—had he not neglected the means—he might have known. *The transgressor* is much more responsible for his sins against knowledge, warning, and conviction. And at "the day of revelation of the righteous judgment of God," he will render to every man according to his deeds. "The servant that knew his Lord's will, and prepared not himself, neither did according to his will, shall be beaten with many stripes. But he that knew not, and did commit things worthy of stripes, shall be beaten with few stripes."[11]

[1] Bishop Hall. [2] Comp. Ecclus. xix. 12. [3] Num. xxiii. xxiv.
[4] 1 Sam. ii. 17. Jer. xxiii. 15. Hence the solemn responsibility of the Ordination Rule. 1 Tim. v. 22.
[5] Ps. l. 16, 17. [6] Liturgy. [7] 1 Cor. iv. 1, 2. [8] 2 Tim. ii. 15.
[9] Our venerable translators have supplied with some doubtfulness an ellipsis of the principal term. The word in the original may mean either *the Great God*, or a great man. Nor does the construction clearly determine either meaning.
[10] Psalm xxxi. 23. Isa. iii. 11. [11] Rom. ii. 5, 6. Luke xii. 47, 48.

Or suppose the Great One to be a mighty Prince—powerful in *forming* the minds, character, and principles of *all* around him. If he be taught to "rule in the fear of God,"[1] will not he *reward the fool and the transgressor*—the ignorant and the presumptuous? For how can his kingdom prosper upon the encouragement of the wicked?[2]

Or if he be a wicked prince, he grieveth all by his countenance of sin; *hiring transgressors* as instruments of his will.[3] Still is it the government of God. The sceptre is in the hands of unlimited power, wisdom, and goodness. "The wicked are his sword—his hand—the rod of his anger, and the staff of his indignation."[4] Shall we then "reply against God?" Reverence, faith, humility, patience, expectation, are graces of the Lord's children. "Clouds and darkness are round about him; righteousness and judgment are the habitations of his throne."[5] There is no sleeping of his Providence; no interruption of his Government. We are living only in a preparatory state. The veil will soon be lifted up, and the grand consummation will explain all. *Fools and transgressors* will receive their just *reward;* and one universal chorus will burst from heaven—"Who shall not fear thee, O Lord, and glorify thy name? For thou only art holy; for thy judgments are made manifest."[6]

11. *As a dog returneth to his vomit, so a fool returneth to his folly.*

And is this the picture of man—"made a little lower than the angels"[7]—yea—"made in the likeness of God?"[8] Who that saw Adam in his universal dominion, sitting as the monarch of creation; summoning all before him; giving to each his name, and receiving in turn his homage[9]—who would have conceived of his children—sunk into such brutish degradation? The tempter's promise was—"Ye shall be as gods."[10] The result of this promise was—'Ye shall be as beasts.' The vilest comparisons are used to show man's loathsomeness in the sight of God. 'Do any feel disgusted at the allusion? Let them remember that the emblem is far less filthy, than the thing denoted by it; and that the whole race of animals does not afford any thing so debasing, as not to be far outdone by the excesses of libertines, drunkards, and gluttons.'[11] We naturally turn away with sickening from this sight. Would that we had the same disgust at the sin, which it so graphically portrays! Would that we might abhor ourselves for that, which God infinitely abhors in us!

The Apostle uses this "true proverb" to describe the awful condition of apostates[12]—temporary conviction, unaccompanied with real conversion of heart, and falling away to desperate hardness. Many reasons may produce disgust in the sinner's mind to his *folly.*

[1] 2 Sam. xxiii. 3. [2] Chap. xxv. 5. 2 Chron. xxviii. 1—8; xxxiii. 1—11.
[3] Jud. ix. 4. 1 Kings xxi. 10. [4] Psalm xvii. 13, 14. Isa. x. 5.
[5] Ps. xcvii. 2. [6] Rev. xv. 4. [7] Ps. viii. 5.
[8] Gen. i. 26. [9] Gen. ii. 20. [10] Ib. iii. 5.
[11] Scott. [12] 2 Pet. ii. 20—22.

He may loathe, and for a while relinquish, it. It has proved so fraught with misery;[1] its very pleasures so impregnated with poison; that no wonder if he make an occasional, or even a strong, effort to be rid of it. But when the sickness has passed away, the sweetness of the forbidden fruit again comes to mind; *and as a dog returneth to his vomit*—to the food which had caused his sickness; *so a fool returneth to his folly*—to that, which had been his hurt and shame.

Thus greedily did Pharaoh *return* from his momentary conviction;[2] Ahab from his feigned repentance;[3] Herod from his partial amendment;[4] the drunkard from his brutish insensibility[5]—all to take a more determinate course of sin—to take their final plunge into ruin. Even a superficial knowledge of Christ is no preservative to an unrenewed heart.[6] The "house may be swept" of outward sin, "and garnished" with external holiness. But if it be "empty;" if the Divine inhabitant be not heartily welcomed, the former possessor will quickly return, and tenant it as his fixed home with sevenfold destruction.[7]

Is not sin then justly termed *folly?* Does not the God of Truth pronounce it to be so now? Will not every *fool* confess it to be so at the end, when its wages shall be fully paid in "shame and everlasting contempt?"[8] Child of God—hearken to thy Father's voice of "peace." But ponder also his solemn warning to "his people and to his saints—*Let them not turn again to folly.*"[9]

12 *Seest thou a man wise in his own conceit? there is more hope of a fool than of him.*

Seest thou the man? God means to point at him.[10] There is something to be learned from him. He castles himself up *in his own conceit.* He is fit to be a standard; for the false persuasion that he has gained wisdom, utterly precludes him from gaining it. He thinks himself wise because he knows not what it is to be wise.[11] His wisdom is "science, falsely so called."[12] For he has yet to learn the first lesson in the school—his own folly—a lesson not to be learned without severe exercise. "Let no man deceive himself. If any man among you seemeth to be wise in this world, let him become a fool, that he may be wise."[13] *There is more hope of the fool,* who knows himself to be one. The natural fool has only one hindrance—his own ignorance. The *conceited fool* has two—ignorance and self-delusion.

It was our Lord's cutting reproof to the *conceited* Pharisees—"The publicans and harlots go into the kingdom of heaven before you."[14] It was his charge against the Laodicean Church—"Because thou sayest—I am rich, and increased in goods, and

[1] Chap. xiii. 15. [2] Ex. viii. 8, 15; ix. 27, 34, 35.
[3] 1 Kings xxi. 27—29; xxii. 6, 37. [4] Mark. vi. 20—27. [5] Chap. xxiii. 35.
[6] 2 Pet. ii. 20, 21. [7] Matt. xii. 43—45. [8] Dan. xii. 2.
[9] Psalm lxxxv. 8. Comp. John v. 14; also Eccl. xxi. 1. [10] Chap. xxii. 29.
[11] 1 Cor. viii. 2. Gal. vi. 3. [12] 1 Tim. vi. 20.
[13] 1 Cor. iii. 18. Comp. Chap. iii. 7. Rom. xii. 3, 16. [14] Matt. xxi. 31.

have need of nothing; and knowest not, that thou art wretched, and miserable, and poor, and blind, and naked."[1] The prodigal *fool*, running into all "the excesses of riot," is more open to conviction, than the man, who prides himself upon his decorous religion.[2] To the profane and ungodly we must go. But to bring a warning to him, he conceives to be knocking at the wrong door—"God! I thank thee, that I am not as other men are"[3]—is his heart's language before God. "Stand by, I am holier than thou"[4]—is his haughty rule with his fellow-sinners. Offer him light. He "walks in the light of his own fire."[5] Offer him life. He is "alive" in his own eyes.[6] Offer him food. His "full soul loatheth the honey-comb!"[7]

Lord! preserve me from this hopeless delusion. Pull down all my pride and fancied wisdom. Take the blind from mine eyes, that I may know what I am in thy sight. "Clothe me with humility" from the soul of the foot to the head.

13. *The slothful man saith, There is a lion in the way; a lion in the streets.*[8] 14. *As the door turneth upon his hinges, so doth the slothful upon his bed.* 15. *The slothful man hideth his hand in his bosom; it grieveth him to bring it again to his mouth.*[9] 16. *The sluggard is wiser in his own conceit than seven men that can render a reason.*[10]

The counterpart to these illustrations may be seen in the man dozing away his life in guilty idleness; without an object, and therefore without a spring for exertion. But let us look at the picture, as it more frequently meets our eye in the Church.

The slothful man is utterly reluctant to his work. When therefore his indolence is disturbed, he is ingenious in inventing excuses, and fancying dangers, which have no real existence. For 'he, who has no mind to labor, never wants pretences for idleness.'[11] Perhaps his insincerity may lull his conscience to sleep in his false excuses. Were it as easy to be spiritual as to wish to be so, who would not be a Christian? If religion were only one great effort, soon to be accomplished, it would be worth the struggle. But to see no end of the toil—duty upon duty—trouble following trouble—no breathing time of peace—is an appalling hindrance. And therefore *a fierce lion in the way*[12]—*a lion in the streets* ('a bugbear rather than a lion'[13]) excuses him from a decided profession.

We wonder not that he shrinks from his work. He loves his bed of ease. Here *he turneth* himself, *as the door upon his hinges*—moving indeed, but making no progress. He works from one excuse to another, but never removes from his place. Difficulties hinder him from going forward. Conscience keeps him from going backward. And therefore, like *the door upon his hinges*, where he was one day, one year, there he is found the next. He moves

[1] Rev. iii. 17. Comp. xxx. 12, 13. [2] Luke xv. 11—18, with John ix. 40, 41.
[3] Luke xviii. 11. See Bunyan's Picture of Ignorance. [4] Isa. lxv. 5.
[5] Isa. l. 11. [6] Rom. vii. 9. [7] Chap. xxvii. 7.
[8] Chap. xxii. 13. [9] Chap. xix. 24.
[10] 'Than seven men that sytt and teach.' Bp. Coverdale. [11] Bp. Patrick.
[12] Scott. [13] Bp. Sanderson's Sermon on Heb. xii. 3.

within a scanty round of duties, always beginning, never finishing, his work; determining nothing; not *quite* at ease; yet with no heart for exertion. Stretched upon his bed of sloth—he cries—O that this were working! O that I could raise my heart to heaven! But is heaven to be gained by complaining and wishing?

Nay—even the most needful exertion is grievous to him. Suppose him to have arisen from his bed, his case is not improved. Ease is still his cry. How to preserve it, his only care. *He hides his hand in his bosom for the cold,* and never makes an effort to *bring it to his mouth* for his necessary food.[1] Thus for the want of the most trifling exercise he starves his soul, though the bread of life is put before him. No marvel—if his life—instead of "a continual feast"—is a constant vexation.

And yet withal—such is the strange union of self-complacency with folly—this worthless being—a mere "cumberer of the ground" —prides himself upon his superior wisdom.[2] Not giving himself the trouble to think, he sees none of the difficulties that are obvious to a considerate mind, and arrives with speed at the most unreasonable conclusions. He will not be beaten out of his sloth. Any *wise man could render a reason* for his conviction. But he *is wiser in his own conceit than them all.*[3]

In how many striking lights is sloth presented in this book! Do I not think too slightly of it? Let me look closely—in what respect am I influenced by it—bodily, mentally or spiritually? Does it never follow me throughout my work—to my knees—to my Bible-reading? Do I not excuse myself from work of painful effort? Or when conscience forces me to it, how is it done? O my God, enable me to resist this paralysis in every shape! If just about to resolve, let me propose my work to myself as to be done with full purpose of heart; not opposing difficulties to necessity; not allowing heartless despondency. What if after all, my faith be a fancy—my hope a delusion? Self-suspicion is the first awakening of the soul—"Search me, O my God."[4]

Well is it, if the slumber be only a little roused; far better, if the eyes are fully opened. Active simple faith carries us onward, in the faces of *the lions in the way,* seeming to stand open-mouthed to devour us. It is a special mercy to realize the holy violence of the conflict. Bunyan puts his pilgrims under the conduct of Greatheart for their encouragement. Heaven never will be won by folded arms. "The violent take it by force."[5]

17. *He that passeth by, and meddleth with strife belonging not to him, is like one that taketh a dog by the ears.*

If we would honor our God in our Christian path, we must take time at every step, for prayer, and for the exercise of a sound judgment. Else we shall often rush on unbidden to our loss. To *take*

[1] Eccl. iv. 5.
[2] Verse 12.
[3] *Seven men*—the number of perfection. Comp. Am. i. 3, 6, 9, 13; ii. 4, 6.
[4] Ps. cxxxix. 23, 24.
[5] Matt. xi. 12.

a dog by the ears will bring good reason to repent of our folly. To *meddle with strife belonging not to us* will surely bring its trouble[1]—its own cross—*not our Master's.* A wide difference is made between "suffering as a busy-body, and suffering as a Christian." The one the Apostle links with "murderers, and thieves, and evil doers." To the other he gives the dignified exhortation—"Let him glorify God on their behalf."[2] If we must not "go forth hastily to strive"[3] in our own cause, still less in our neighbor's. This is "entering into contention"—the wantonness of the fool.[4]

Even with Christian intentions many of us are too fond of *meddling with strife not belonging to us.* We constitute ourselves too readily judges of our neighbor's conduct. Neutrality is often the plain dictate of prudence. Uncalled for interference seldom avails with the contending parties; while the well meaning mediator involves himself in the strife to his own mischief. Our blessed Master reads us a lesson of godly wisdom. He healed the contentions in his own family. But when called to *meddle with strife belonging not to him,* he gave answer—"Who made me a judge or a divider over you?"[5]

Must we then "suffer sin upon our brother?"[6] Certainly not. But we should ponder carefully the most effectual mode of restraining his sin. We do not forget the special "blessing to the peacemakers."[7] But the true peacemaker, while he deplores the *strife,* well knows, that interference in the moment of irritation will kindle, rather than extinguish, the fire. Self-control, however, with him is not indifference. He commits the matter to Him, whose strength and wisdom he so greatly needs. He will seize the first moment for favorable remonstrance; "and a word spoken in due season, how good is it!"[8] Indeed the common intercourse of life much requires that "wisdom, which dwelleth with prudence."[9] "Who is a wise man, and endued with knowledge among you? Let him show out of a good conversation his works with meekness of wisdom."[10]

18. *As a madman who casteth firebrands, arrows and death.* 19. *So is the man that deceiveth his neighbor, and saith, Am not I in sport?*

How little does the thoughtless man consider the misery, which his wantonness occasions to others! He bears no malice—he indulges no revenge. It is the pure love of mischief. He carries on a scheme of imposition as harmless play. His companions compliment him upon his adroitness, and join in the laugh of triumph over the victim of his cruel jest. But "*sporting* with their own *deceivings*"[11]—is a black mark of ungodliness. What the man calls *sport,*[12] the Lord regards as the work of *the madman,* scattering murderous mischief—*firebrands, arrows and death*—'There

[1] See 1 Kings xxii. 4, 32.
[2] 1 Pet. iv. 15, 16.
[3] Chap. xxv. 8.
[4] Chap. xviii. 6; xx. 3.
[5] Matt. xviii. 1—6; xx. 24—28, with Luke xii. 13, 14.
[6] Lev. xix. 17.
[7] Matt. v. 9.
[8] Chap. xv. 23.
[9] Chap. viii. 12.
[10] James iii. 13.
[11] 2 Pet. ii. 13.
[12] Chap. x. 23.

is little difference in this case betwixt fraud and fury. He that purposely deceives his neighbor, under a colour of jest, is no less prejudicial to him than a lunatic, that doth wrong out of frenzy and distemper.'[1] This awful line however is drawn. Whereas the *madman* is irresponsible for his actions, *the deceiver* is accountable to God and his fellow-creatures. 'He that sins in jest, must repent in earnest; or his sin will be his ruin.'[2]

'What hath a Christian'—saith Bernard—'to do with jesting?' Let him practically observe the wholesome caution against it as "not convenient."[3] Let him diligently cultivate the valuable graces of seriousness, consideration, and self-discipline. Let him study the spirit as well as the rules of the Gospel, and honor his Master's image embodied in his rules.

20. *Where no wood is, there the fire goeth out: so where there is no talebearer, the strife ceaseth* (is silent, Marg.) 21. *As coals are to burning coals, and wood to fire: so is a contentious man to kindle strife.* 22. *The words of a talebearer are as wounds, and they go down into the innermost parts* (chambers, Marg.) *of the belly.*[4]

The busy tongue makes work, where it does not find it. Hence the *talebearer's* employment—that despicable trade! So deeply-rooted is the principle of self-love, that 'man is naturally his own grand idol. He would be esteemed and honored by any means; and to magnify that idol self, he kills the name and esteem of others in sacrifice to it.'[5] Real virtue revolts from this base and abominable selfishness.

The fire of holy zeal seizes on things nearest home. This is a wildfire scattering its destruction abroad. The *tale-bearer* should be looked on as an incendiary. His "tongue is a fire, itself set on fire of hell."[6] His raking up old and forgotten tales supplies the fuel, without which *the fire of strife, as where no wood is, goeth out.* To quench the flame we must take away the fuel. We must remove *the talebearer;* stop him in his words; compel him to produce his authority; face him, if possible, with the subject of his tales. This decisive course will prevent a mass of slander, and put him to shame.[7] Near akin is *the contentious man.* His mischief indeed is more open. His determination to have the last word is *as coals to burning coals, and wood to the fire.*[8] It keeps up the flame, kindled perhaps by a mere angry word or a contemptuous look; and which, but for this constant succession of fuel, might quickly have been extinguished. Do we never aim at the wit of a sharp answer, that "stirreth up anger," rather than at the wisdom and grace of "a soft answer, that turneth away wrath?"[9]

The talebearer's wounds are however the most dangerous. They *go down into the chambers*—the vitals of the heart. Only one noiseless word may be the stab of death. But—however he

[1] Bishop Hall. [2] Henry. [3] Eph. v. 4.
[4] Chap. xviii. 8. [5] Leighton on 1 Pet. ii. 17. Comp. Jer. ix. 4.
[6] Jam. iii. 6. Comp. chap. xvi. 27. [7] Chap. xxv. 23. Comp. xxii. 10.
[8] Chap. xv. 18; xvi. 28; xxix. 22. 2 Cor. xii. 20. [9] Chap. xv. 1.

may escape for awhile—all his secret sins shall "be set before his eyes," and his wanton trifling with his brother's character be justly recompensed.[1]

Are we closely watching against these sins? Do we carefully damp the rising flame of *contention?*[2] Do we resist the temptation to speak needlessly of the faults of others? We may feel indignant at the charge of *talebearing*. Yet how many degrees are there of this vice! It requires no ordinary exercise of Christian discipline to maintain the silence of charity, and to regulate both the tongue and the ear within its well-advised limits.[3]

23. *Burning lips and a wicked heart are like a potsherd covered with silver dross.* 24. *He that hateth, dissembleth with his lips, and layeth up deceit within him.* 25. *When he speaketh fair, believe him not: for there are seven abominations in his heart.* 26. *Whose hatred is covered by deceit, his wickedness shall be showed before the whole congregation.* 27. *Whoso diggeth a pit shall fall therein: and he that rolleth a stone, it will return upon him.*

The sin here described is a disgrace to society! Yet is it often *covered* with a flattering garb, as the worthless *potsherd* with a thin coat of *silver*. "The tongue of the just is as choice silver." Here is only *silver dross*—"the heart of the wicked, which is nothing worth;"[4] *lips burning* with warm affection, yet covering a *heart* filled with malice and wickedness.[5] Such were *the lips* of Joseph's brethren, when "they rose up to comfort their father" under the bereavement which they had brought upon him.[6] Such was Absalom's smooth hypocrisy.[7] Such were the traitor's *lips* and heart, uniting with the rest in protestations of faithfulness; yet "betraying the Son of man with a kiss."[8] An open enemy could be much better borne.[9] The cant of hypocrites, the benevolence of infidels, the smooth enticement of the false "angel of light," all answer to this strong figure.

Often also when *the lips* do not *burn*, there is *dissembling of the hatred*. "Cain talked with his brother in the field," while murder was in his heart.[10] Saul pretended to honor David, while he was plotting his ruin.[11] Absalom *dissembled* with his brother, by seeming to let him alone, and for two years *laying up deceit within him.*[12] Joab *covered* his murderous intentions with peaceable profession.[13]

Christian prudence will guard against credulity,[14] which is in fact the "harmlessless of the dove," without "the wisdom of the serpent."[15] This weakness cost Gedaliah his life.[16] A sounder spirit saved Nehemiah from the snare of his malignant adversaries.[17]

[1] Psalm l. 20; lii. 1—5. [2] Chap. xvii. 14. Gen. xiii. 8, 9.

[3] Dr. South recommends '*the tale-bearer* and the tale-hearer both to be hanged up, back to back, only the one by the tongue, the other by the ear.' [4] Chap. x. 20.

[5] Ibid verse 17. Ps. lv. 21. Comp. Ecclus. xix. 26—28. See Bunyan's description of the town of 'Fair-Speech.'

[6] Gen. xxxvii. 25. [7] 2 Sam. xv. 1—9. [8] Matt. xxvi. 35. Luke xxii. 47, 48.

[9] Ps. lv. 12—14. [10] Gen. iv. 8. [11] 1 Sam. xviii. 17, 21. [12] 2 Sam. xiii. 22—28.

[13] Ibid. iii. 27; xx. 9, 10. Comp. Gen. xxxiv. 15—25. Ps. xxviii. 3; lv. 20.

[14] Jer. ix. 8; xii. 6. Mic. vii. 5. Comp. Ecclus. xii. 10—17. [15] Matt. x. 16.

[16] Jer. xl. 14; xli. 6, 7. [17] Neh. vi. 1—4.

The source of this wickedness gives good reason for distrust. *There are seven abominations in his heart*—a great variety[1] of *abominations* closely folded up—only within the ken of that heart-searching eye, "before whom all secret things are naked and open."[2] And here lies the root of the disease. 'A guileful heart makes guileful tongue and lips. It is the workhouse, where is the forge of deceit and slander; and the tongue is only the outer shop, where they are mended; and the lips the door of it; so then such ware as is made within, such and no other can be set out. From evil thoughts, evil speakings; from a deceitful heart, guileful words, well-varnished, but lined with rottenness.'[3] Oh! let this despicable character be a beacon to us to shun all approaches to false dealings. Better to risk giving offence by faithfulness (though let this—so far as conscience allows—be avoided) rather than *cover our hatred* by flattering words.

Dissembling never answers in the end. The Providence of God brings dark deeds to light—"The voice of Abel's blood cried from the ground."[4] "Some men's sin's are open beforehand, going before to judgment; and some men they follow after."[5] The hand strips off the mask, and exposes the flatterer to shame. *His seven abominations* shall be proclaimed—if not more privately—at least *before the whole congregation*, when all shall appear before men and angels as they really are, and when all hypocrites shall receive their just recompense of "everlasting contempt."[6]

Often however does retribution reach the offender in this world—'He will fall into the pits, which he has bestowed pains to dig for his neighbor, and be crushed by the stone which he meant to roll upon him.'[7] Even the place of sinning is sometimes made the place of punishment.[8] Those who plot mischief for others, will be overwhelmed with it themselves.[9] Moab in attempting to curse Israel, fell himself under the curse of God.[10] Haman's gallows for Mordecai was his own "promotion of shame."[11] The enemies of Daniel were devoured in the ruin which they plotted against him.[12] Thus does God "take the wise in his craftiness"[13]—"the wicked in his wickedness."[14] The death of Christ, which was to be the means of warding off national judgment, was the just cause of the deprecated scourge.[15] The malice that meditates the evil, is often the cause of its own overthrow. What an Aceldama would this world be, but for the restraining grace of God! Oh! may my heart, my soul, every member, every principle, not only be restrained from hateful passions; but be imbued with the spirit of the Gospel, and consecrated to the service of God!

1 Bp. Hall. Verse 16; xxiv. 16.
2 Jer. xvii. 10. Heb. iv. 13.
3 Leighton on Pet. iii. 10.
4 Gen. iv. 10. Comp. Acts xxiii. 12—16.
5 1 Tim. v. 24.
6 Luke xii. 1, 2.
7 Scott in loco. Ecclus. xxvii. 25—27.
8 1 Kings xxi. 19, with 2 Kings ix. 26. Comp. Jer. vii. 31, 32.
9 Ps. vii. 15, 16; ix. 15; x. 2; lvii. 6. Eccl. x. 8.
10 Num. xxii. 1—6; xxiv. 17.
11 Chap. iii. 35. Esth. vii. 10.
12 Dan. vi. 25.
13 Job. v. 13.
14 Chap. xi. 5, 6.
15 John xi. 50, with Matt. xxiii. 32, 38.

28. *A lying tongue hateth those that are afflicted by it; and a flattering mouth worketh ruin.*

Rarely do we see a solitary sin. One sin begets another. *Lying* and malice are here linked together. The *lying tongue* against our Lord was the fruit of hateful malice.[1] The slander against Stephen originated from the same source. The tacit reproach of his godly profession was intolerable.[2] If men *afflict* because they hate; much more do they *hate them whom they have afflicted*, and thus made their enemies. Amnon having *afflicted* his sister Tamar, hated her with great hatred than his former love, as the witness against his own shame?[3]

But again and again—watch against *the flatterer*. From some favorable position he presents an attractive face. But a nearer view shows him as a subtle, murderous enemy, *working ruin.*[4] His great advantage is that he has a friend in our own bosom. The sweet song of our own praises lulls us to sleep, and in the moment of security the net is too successfully spread.[5] *The flattering tongue worked the ruin* of the world. The temptation—"Ye shall be as gods"—proved irresistible.[6] And still in the path of sin,[7] in the determinate indulgence of the wayward will,[8] *flattering* is the snare; *ruin* is the end.

What then should be our treatment of *the flatterer?* Homer puts it into his hero's heart to regard him as a fiend of hell.[9] Our safety then is in flight,[10] or at least in frowning resistance.[11] Show plainly that they please us least, who praise us most. Give timely warning, that the repetition of the offence threatens the disruption of friendship. Cherish the deepest views of native corruption, such as will at once belie any fair picture of ourselves that may be presented to us. Pray for wisdom to discover the snare; for gracious principles to raise us above vain praises; for self-denial to be content, and even thankful without them. This will be God's means of Providential deliverance.

All these Scriptures strongly teach, how hateful to a God of truth is the attempt to deceive. All warn us against the common habit of slight deviations from truth, and of any want of sincerity of expression, as totally inconsistent with a Christian profession, a breach of the law of love, and often leading to habitual deceit.[12]

[1] John viii. 44, with 40. [2] Acts vi. 9, 14. [3] 2 Sam. xiii. 5—15
[4] Ps. v. 9; x. 7—10. [5] Chap. xxix. 5. [6] Gen. iii. 5.
[7] Chap. ii. 16; v. 30; vii. 5, 21—23. Ecclus. ix. 3—9.
[8] 1 Kings xxii. 6, 11, 12. Jer. v. 31; xiv. 14—16. [9] Iliad. I. 312, 313.
[10] Chap. xx. 19. [11] Comp. chap. xxv. 23.
[12] See the wise caution, Ecclus. xix. 1.

CHAPTER XXVII.

1. *Boast not thyself of to-morrow; for thou knowest not what a day may bring forth.*

LET the Apostle expound the wise man—"Go to now, ye that say—'To-day or to-morrow we will go into such a city, and continue there a year, and buy and sell, and get gain.'" Both apply the same rebuke to the *boast*;—*Thou knowest not what a day may bring forth*—Whereas "ye know not what shall be on the morrow."[1] *To provide for the morrow* is a scriptural duty.[2] The Christian in his calling, reposing on God's Providence, walks with God. But to *boast of to-morrow*—"all such rejoicing is evil."[3] Indeed it is absurd to *boast* of what is not our own. *To-morrow* is finely described as an unknown birth. It may be in eternity. And yet the sensualist and the worldling[4] *boast*, as if it was their own; and thus virtually put God out of his own world. The ungodly reckon upon being religious *to-morrow*, and therefore put off repentence, forsaking the world, and living for eternity, to some indefinitely future day.[5] Would they do this, if they did not reckon upon *to-morrow* being given to them! Nay, do we not all naturally cherish this looking forward, which the great enemy works up into practical forgetfulness of God! Yet we must not live, as if to-morrow would not come. Else would the world be in a state of stagnation. The present duties of the day would be absorbed in the instant preparation for the coming eternity. We start from death, when he enters our houses, as if we did not expect him. How little do we die daily![6] We can even coolly calculate upon the death of others, for our own benefit. Our intense anxiety about earthly, and apathy about heavenly things, speaks but too plainly. The young look to the middle age; the more advanced to the last stage of life. All, in contradiction to their avowed profession, *boast themselves of to-morrow*.

How awfully has this *boasting* been put to shame! In the days of Noah, "they married wives, and were given in marriage, until the very day, when the flood came, and destroyed them all."[7] Abner promised a kingdom, but could not ensure his life for an hour.[8] Haman plumed himself upon the prospect of the queen's banquet, but was hanged like a dog before night.[9] "The fool's soul was required of him "on the very night" of his worldly projects "for many years" to come.[10] The infidel Gibbon calculated

[1] Jam. iv. 13, 14. 'Quid sit futurum cras, fuge quærere.' Hor. Carm. lib. i. 9.
[2] Chap. vi. 6—8; x. 5; xxiv. 27. Comp. Gen. xli. 35. Acts xi. 28, 29.
[3] Jam. iv. 16.
[4] Isa. lvi. 12. Luke xii. 16—19.
[5] Acts xxiv. 25.
[6] 1 Cor. xv. 31.
[7] Luke xvii. 26—29.
[8] 2 Sam. iii. 9, 10, 27.
[9] Esth. v. 12; vii. 1—10.
[10] Luke xii. 19, 20.

upon fifteen years of life, and died within a few months, at a day's warning. *We know not what a day may bring forth.*

How natural is it for the young to be looking for *to-morrow's* prospect! But have you never seen the lovely flower cropped, and faded in the blossom? Is not the robust as well as the feeble frame cut down in the prime?[1] Have you a lease of your life? If there be a promise of forgiveness to the repenting, where is the promise of *to-morrow* for repentance? Will consideration naturally come with years? Or will not rather long-protracted habits of ungodliness harden into a second nature? What if in the midst of thy *boasting*, flattering thyself that thou shouldest see another and another day—thou shouldest be surprised unprepared, and be left to lament forever thy presumption in the lake of everlasting fire![2] Stop—consider—weep—pray—believe—now—while conscience speaks; while thou art halting between God and the world, between conviction and inclination. Now in this "accepted time" devote thyself to God. Enthrone the Saviour in thine heart.

The universe does not present a more affecting sight than an aged sinner—with one foot in the grave—losing all in the world, infinitely more in eternity. A moment and he is gone. Heaven and hell are no trifles. *To-morrow* presumed upon—to-day neglected—ruins all. Standing on the brink of the precipice—how precious the moment for prayer—ere the door of mercy is closed for ever!

Has the child of God reason to *boast of to-morrow*? What a change may it make in your worldly circumstances,[3] or Christian experience?[4] Never will you feel more secure, than in the consciousness that you have no security for a single hour. Rest all your cares in the bosom of your God.[5] Let disappointment prepare you for your heavenly rest, and bound all your wishes and pleasures by his gracious will.[6] But have you no need of warning? How speaks the too full current of affections towards earthly enjoyment? Did you practically believe that "the time is short, and the fashion of this world passeth away"—would you not "rejoice, as though you rejoiced not?"[7] Would pleasures of earth be so highly prized, if there was no secret dependence on *to-morrow*? Surely this thought may more than sustain in the loss of them—The shadow only is gone—the body of my happiness remains immoveable. To see things temporal, as if we "looked not at them," is the life of spiritual religion.[8] To have "our loins girt about" for our Lord's coming; to live, so as not to be surprised by the call, and in readiness to "open to him *immediately*"—this is our security and our happiness. "Blessed are those servants, whom the Lord, when he cometh, shall find watching."[9]

2. *Let another man praise thee, and not thine own mouth; a stranger, and not thine own lips.*

[1] Job xxi. 23, 24. [2] Matt. xxiv. 48—51. Luke xiii. 25. Comp. Ecclus. v. 7. [3] Job i. [4] Ps. xxx. 5—7. [5] Ibid. xxxvii. 3—7. [6] Jam. iv. 15. [7] 1 Cor. vii. 29—31. Comp. Phil. iv. 5. [8] 2 Cor. iv. 18. [9] Luke xii. 35—40.

'Praise'—says an old expositor—'is a comely garment. Bu though thyself doth wear it, *another* must put it on, or else it will never sit well about thee. Praise is sweet music, but it is never tuneable in *thine own mouth.* If it cometh from the mouth of *another,* it soundeth most tuneably in the ears of all that hear it. Praise is a rich treasure, but it will never make thee rich, unless *another* tell the same.'[1] Indeed—except as the vindication of our character,[2] or our Master's honor connected with it,[3] may require —nothing so degrades a man with his fellow-men, as setting forth his own praise. For though every man is his own flatterer,[4] yet men usually know how to estimate pride in others, while they cherish it in themselves. "The things that are of good report—let us think of them to do them."[5] But "let our works"—not our tongues —"praise us in the gates."[6] And while our works shine, see to it, that ourselves be hid. "Confess our faults one to another."[7] But leave to *another* to speak our *praise.*

Our name will lose nothing by this self-renouncing spirit. If *our own mouth* be silent, *another's* will be opened. John was "unworthy" in his own eyes to "unloose the latchet of his Master's shoes." Yet did his Lord's mouth proclaim him, as "the greatest of all that had been born of women."[8] The centurion spoke of himself, as "not worthy that Christ should come under his roof." Yet did the elders testify, that "he was worthy, for whom he should do this." Yea—the Saviour's own mouth confirmed the testimony—"I have not found so great faith, no not in Israel."[9] Luke mentions nothing in his Records to his own credit. Yet *another praises him* warmly as "the beloved physician," and his sole faithful companion in his trials.[1]

Self-seeking is a shameful blot upon a Christian profession. What! Shall one that has said before God—"Behold, I am vile!" —be ready to say before his fellow-men—"Come see my zeal for the Lord"[11]—Come, see how humble I am? Oh! for the self-abased spirit of our glorious Master—ever ready to endure reproach; but never "receiving honor from men;" never "seeking his own glory."[12] Contrast what God shows us of ourselves in the closet with our "fair show in the flesh." And will this not put self-complacency to shame? Surely that we are so little *really* humble—is matter enough for the deepest humiliation.

3. *A stone is heavy, and the sand weighty; but a fool's wrath is heavier than them both.* 4. *Wrath is cruel,* (cruelty Marg.), *and anger is outrageous* (an overflowing, Marg.); *but who is able to stand before envy?*

[1] Jermin. [2] 1 Sam. xii. 3. Ps. vii. 3—5. 2 Cor. i. 17—19.
[3] 2 Cor. xi. 5—12; xii. 11. [4] Chap. xx. 6. [5] Phil. iv. 8, 9.
[6] Chap. xxxi. 31. Comp. Ruth iii. 11.
[7] Chap. xxv. 27. Matt. v. 16. Jam. v. 16.
[8] Matt. iii. 11. John iii. 30, with Matt. xi, 11. John v. 35.
[9] Matt. viii. 8, with Luke vii. 3, 4, 9.
[10] Col. iv. 14. 2 Tim. iv. 11. It was a fine touch in Sallust's portrait of Cato—'He would rather be, than seem to be, a good man; so that the less he sought glory, the more he obtained it'
[1] Job xl. 4. 2 Kings x. 16. [12] John v. 41; viii. 50.

The wrath even of a wise man in the moment of folly is *cruel* What then must be *a fool's wrath* 'where there is not a drop of heavenly water to quench the fire?'[2] It is indeed like the *weight of a stone or sand*[3]—intolerable, 'being without cause, measure, or end.'[4] Its abiding sullenness marks it from the temporary impulse, to which the child of God may too hastily yield. Absalom kept it in for two years.[5] David's anger melted away under the first conviction of reproof, and "the sun went not down upon his wrath."[6]

And yet *cruel as anger* may be,[7] *overflowing* as the spring-tide, it may be appeased. Esau's wrath was soothed into brotherly love.[8] The *outrageous* despot was subdued in witnessing the presence and power of God.[9] But *envy* is an implacable passion—the native principle,[10] with a fearful train of evils.[11] *Anger* is stirred up by offence; *envy* by godliness,[12] prosperity,[13] or favor.[14] The force of reason is rather the oil to fan the flame, than the water to quench it. The happiness of a neighbor gives pain; his ruin, or at least his injury, would be a source of pleasure. 'Proud men would be admired by all, and preferred above all; and if it be not so, a secret enmity invadeth their spirits, and settleth itself. Men cannot endure the real or reputed excellency of others. The proud creature would shine alone.'[15] The occasion is never wanting for the exercise of this hateful principle. Something is always wrong in a neighbor's conduct; something at least, that, if it does not deserve blame, at least greatly detracted from his praise.

Well then might it be asked—*Who is able to stand before envy?* Even the perfect innocence of paradise fell *before it.* Satan lost his own happiness. Then he *envied* man's, and ceased not to work its destruction.[16] Abel fell a martyr to this malignant passion.[17] Joseph[18] and Daniel[19] were its temporary victims. Nay—even the Saviour in his most benevolent acts was sorely harassed by this evil,[20] and ultimately sunk under its power.[21] His servants, therefore, must not expect to "be above their Master."[22]

But—Christians—remember—Sin is not dead within us. And though the promise is sure, that it "shall not have dominion;"[23] yet the struggle with every corruption is sharp to the end. Let us probe the corruption deeply. Do we love to see a brother's supe-

[1] 1 Sam. xxv. 13, 21.
[2] Cartwright.
'Ira furor brevis est, animum rege; qui, nisi paret
Imperat, hunc frænis; hunc tu compesce catenâ.'
Hor. Ep. i. 61, 62.
[3] Ex. xv. 5. Comp. Ecclus. xxii. 14, 15. [4] Poole. Comp. chap. xvii. 12.
[5] 2 Sam. xiii. 22, 23. [6] 1 Sam. xxv. 32, 33. Eph. iv. 26.
[7] Gen. xlix. 7. Matt. ii. 16. [8] Gen. xxvii. 41; xxxiii. 4. [9] Dan. iii. 13—30.
[10] Mark vii. 22. Gal. v. 20, 21. Tit. iii. 3. Jam. iv. 5.
[11] Rom. i. 29, 30. 2 Cor. xii. 20. Jam. iii. 14, 16. [12] Eccl. iv. 4. Dan. vi. 3—5.
[13] Gen. xxvi. 14. Ps. lxxiii. 3. [14] Gen. iv. 5—6. 1 Sam. xviii. 6—9, 16, 17.
[15] Manton on Psalm cxix. 77. [16] See Wisd. ii. 23, 24. [17] Gen. iv. 8, ut supra.
[18] Gen. xxxvii. 3, 4. Acts vii. 9. [19] Dan. vi. 6—17. [20] John xii. 10, 11.
[21] Matt. xxvii. 18—20. Mark xv. 10.
[22] Acts v. 17, Marg.; xiii. 44, 45; xvii. 4, 5, with Matt. x. 24. [23] Rom. vi. 14.

rior eminence—his larger gifts or graces?[1] Do we take pleasure in his prosperity, in honor paid to him, though to our own disparagement?[2] And are we alive to any risings of content at his success? Is our tone of praise as decided of him, as we should wish that of others to be of us? Can we bear to be past by in favor of others, of those especially, who may seem to be doing our work in opposition to ourselves?[3] Oh! how hateful would be the exhibition of the hidden depths of our deceitful hearts! "Who can understand his errors? Cleanse thou me from secret faults."[4]

5. *Open rebuke is better than secret love.* 6. *Faithful are the wounds of a friend; but the kisses of an enemy are deceitful.*

What is the friend, who will be a real blessing to my soul? Is it one, that will humor my fancies, and flatter my vanity? Is it enough, that he loves my person, and would spend his time and energies in my service? This comes far short of my requirement. I am a poor, straying sinner, with a wayward will and a blinded heart; going wrong at every step. The friend for my case is one, who will watch over me with *open rebuke* (not always public,[5] but with a free and *open* heart); a reprover when needful—not a flatterer. The genuineness of friendship without this mark is more than doubtful; its usefulness utterly paralyzed. That *secret love*, that will not risk *a faithful wound*, and spares *rebuke*, rather than inflict pain—judged by God's standard—is hatred.[6] Far better the wound should be probed than covered. *Rebuke*—kindly, considerately, and prayerfully administered—cements friendship, rather than loosens it.[7] The contrary instances only prove, that the union had never been based upon substantial principle.

Could Paul have answered to God for his *secret love* to a brother apostle, when the compromise of a fundamental principle called *for open rebuke*?[8] Obviously, however, the sin should be brought to view, ere we *rebuke*. Nor should we vehemently reprove involuntary slips;[9] much less forget the exercise of a loving spirit. Leighton's gentleness gave such a power to his reproof, that rare was the repetition of the offence, rather perhaps from shame, than from genuine contrition. The mark of true godliness is an anxiety to have our faults pointed out; and a thankfulness to those, who undertake the self-denying offices.[10] Much more valuable is this *faithfulness*, than the smooth politeness of the world's intercourse. Nay, some defect in this courtesy to be excused for the sake of the sterling quality.

Who would not choose this *faithful wound*—however painful at the moment of infliction—rather than the *deceitful kisses of the*

[1] Num. xi. 28, 29.
[2] John iii. 30.
[3] Phil. i. 15—18.
[4] Ps. xix. 12.
[5] Matt. xviii. 15.
[6] See Lev. xix. 17.
[7] Chap. ix. 8; xxviii 23. Matt. xviii. 15.
[8] Gal. ii. 11—14.
[9] See Ecclus. xix. 16.
[10] Ps. cxli. 5. Even when given most rashly and unkindly—one of the meekest of men could say—'I was thankful to God for admonishing me, and my gratitude to the man was, I think, unfeigned.' In his journal the reprover's name was found specially remembered in prayer. Martyn's Life, chap. iii.

enemy?[1] *The kiss* of the apostate was a bitter ingredient in the Saviour's cup of suffering.[2] His foreknowledge of the treachery[3] in no degree weakened those exquisite sensibilities, which, from their intimate union with the Godhead, rendered him susceptible of suffering beyond all comprehension.

7. *The full soul loatheth* (treadeth under foot, Marg.) *an honeycomb; but to the hungry soul every bitter thing is sweet.*

This is a true figure, as regards the enjoyments of this life. Abundance, instead of increasing the happiness of the possessor, deprives him of the rest, which often belongs to a more scanty portion.[4] The man, whose appetite is cloyed with indulgence, turns with disgust from the sweetest dainties; while *every bitter* and distasteful *thing* is keenly relished by *the hungry soul*, perhaps just saved from starvation.[5] This healthful appetite is one of the many counterbalancing advantages of poverty. The sated epicure might well envy the luxury of a homely meal. The children of Israel, after "eating angels' food to the full," *loathed and trod it under foot* as "light bread."[6]

And is not this so in spiritual things? The Laodicean professor —"rich and increased in goods, and having need of nothing"— *loathes the honeycomb* of the gospel.[7] Christ in his bitter sorrow is nothing "to him, while he passeth by."[8] His love excites no tenderness. His hope no interest. "The consolations of God are small"—of little account—"with him."[9] He can spare them without sensible loss. He reads the Bible only to carp at its most precious truths—offensive, as implying a ruin, of which he has no apprehension, and which he has no heart to contemplate. Thus he nauseates the most nourishing food; having no relish, because he feels no need. Another case presents itself, not less affecting. "Fulness of bread"—richness of spiritual ordinances—does not always bring its corresponding appetite. May not satiety be as great a curse as famine? Upon many a Christian professor it is fearfully written—*The full soul loathed the honeycomb?*

Far more enviable is *the hungry soul*, feeding upon unpalateable truths; yea—welcoming even *bitter* dispensations as medicine for the soul's health[10] *The sweet* of the gospel is known by this *bitterness.* It makes Christ *sweet* to the soul. A sinner in all his guilt—a Saviour in his perfect merit and love.—well does the one answer to the other. Every view of Christ embitters sin. Every view of sin endears Christ. Nor is there any terror in the conviction, that thus endears the Saviour. A sense of want and a

[1] Chap. xxvi. 23—26. Neh. vi. 2. [2] Matt. xxvi. 48, 49, with Ps. xli. 9; lv. 12.
[3] John vi. 70; xiii. 18—26. [4] Comp. Eccl. v. 11.
[5] Job vi. 7. Luke xv. 16, 17.
'Jejunus stomachus raro vulgaria temnit.'
Hor. Lib. ii. Sat. ii. 38.
[6] Ps. lxxviii. 25. Num. xi. 4—20; xxi. 5.
[7] Rev. iii. 17, 18. Comp. Matt. ix. 12. Rom. ix. 30, 31. Lam. i. 12.
[9] Job xv. 11. [10] Ps. cxix. 67, 71.

sense of guilt lay the foundation for solid confidence, and happy privilege.

What then is the genuine pulse of my religion? Am I willing to receive the word in its completeness—the bitter as well as the sweet? Do I love its humbling spirituality, its self-denying requirements, subordinating every desire to a cheerful and unreserved obedience to my God; ready to walk in his narrowest path, to have my most secret corruption exposed, to have my conscience laid open to the "sharp piercing of the two-edged sword?"[1]—Oh! may my soul be preserved in this vigorous devotedness!

8. *As a bird that wandereth from her nest, so is a man that wandereth from his place.*

Instinct teaches *the bird*, that *the nest* is the only place of safety or repose. Here God has provided for her a special cover.[2] Nothing therefore but danger awaits her in her *wanderings*. And seldom does she return from them without some injury to herself or her nestlings. Perhaps *her nest* is cold and inconvenient. But her *wanderings* make her more restless and dissatisfied. She is safe and happy only while she keeps *her nest*.

No less senseless and dangerous is it, lightly to leave the place, society, or calling, which Divine Providence has marked out. Here man is 'in God's precincts, and so under God's protection;'[3] and if he will be content to remain in *his place*, God will bless him with the rich gain of "godly contentment."[4] But *the man wandering from his place* is 'the rolling stone, that gathers no moss.' His want of fixed principles and employment exposes him to perpetual temptation.[5] Always wanting to be something or somewhere different to what and where he is, he only changes imaginary for real troubles. Full of wisdom is it to know and keep our place. The soul, the body, the family, society—all have a claim upon us. This feverish excitement of idleness is the symptom of disease—wholly opposed to religion—the bane both of our comfort and usefulness.

The plain rule cannot ordinarily be broken without sin. "Let every man, wherein he is called, therein abide with God."[6] Would we then abide in fellowship with God? We must "abide in our calling." Every step of departure *without a clear Scriptural warrant* is departure from God. We are safe in following Providence. But to go before it; much more to break away from its guidance[7] —*a man thus wanders from his place* to his own cost. Never can we put our foot out of God's ways, but we shall tread the path back with a cross.

It is often the wayward impulse of pleasure or idleness, but always with the same fruit. Dinah was safe in the bosom of her family, *as the bird in her nest*. But when she "went out to see

[1] Heb. iv. 12.
[2] Deut. xxii. 6, 7.
[3] Swinnock's Christian Man's Calling, i. 346.
[4] 1 Tim. vi. 6.
[5] Chap. xxi. 16. Jer ii. 36.
[6] 1 Cor. vii. 24.
[7] Jon. i. 1—4.

the daughters of the land,"[1] the fowler's snare soon entangled the unsuspecting *wanderer*.

Let us look at this spirit in the Church. *The* "*idler wandereth* about from house to house,"[2] neglecting his own duties, and therefore with plenty of time upon his hands, to "meddle with what doth not belong to him"[3] So busy is the enemy in finding his own work for those, who have no heart to work for God! *The discontented professor* unhappily is shut up in so obscure a corner, that he will die, before the world knows his worth. He wants a larger sphere. The world is scarcely wide enough for him. Thus he *wandereth from his place*, "seeking rest, and finding none." *The gifted professor* is full of zeal for God and his church. His gifts were not intended to run to waste. What he can do, he thinks he ought to do. He sees the minister of God neglecting his flock—Why should not he—as he is well able—step into his room? But is not the *man wandering from his place?* Our Master's charge is—"Give an account of thy"—not of thy neighbor's—"stewardship."[4]

If grace gives the desire for usefulness, Providence must open the path. Our "wisdom is to understand *our own way*;"[5] our duty, to "do *our own business*."[6] Not a single talent need be wasted. Every Christian has his own field, large enough for the exercise of his measure of gifts, without "removing the ancient landmark," that separates the sacred office as the Lord's consecrated service. Many might be found to perform competently the ambassador's office. But who would venture upon it without the accredited authority of his sovereign? *The unsteady professor* has no spiritual home. No church is sound enough for him; none wholly moulded to his taste. Like the *wandering bird*, he is always on the wing. Any one place is too strait for him. The accustomed bread, even though coming down from heaven, is "loathed as light bread."[7] His vitiated appetite leaves him often on the Sabbath morning undecided whom to hear, his own will being his only guide. He is anxious to hear from all; and, as the sure result, he learns from none.[8] In his self-willed delusion the form and substance of the Church is destroyed. It is not a few wandering sheep, but a fold and a shepherd; not a heap of loose scattered stones, but stones cemented, fitted into their several places. "The building, thus fitly framed together, groweth unto an holy temple in the Lord."[9] The Church is "terrible"—not in her single members, but "as an army with banners;"[10] close in rank, where each soldier keeps his own place. The individual profession in the stead of collective unity is a pure schismatical spirit—the essence of pride and selfishness.

And is not this spiritual vagrancy the history of many, who under the pretence of conscience have separated from the Church

[1] Gen. xxxiv. 1, 2. [2] 1 Tim. v. 13.
[3] Chap. xxvi. 17. [4] Luke xvi. 2. [5] Chap. xiv. 8.
[6] 1 Thess. iv. 11. [7] Num. xxi. 5. [8] 2 Tim. iii. 7.
[9] Eph. ii. 21, 22. 1 Pet. ii. 5. [10] Can. vi. 10.

which had "nourished and brought them up as children?" *After their own lusts* "they heap to themselves teachers, having itching ears." The end of this *wandering from their place*, like that of *the bird from her nest*, is the loss of every thing valuable—"*They shall turn away their ears from the truth, and shall be turned unto fables.*"[1]

Christian Professor! Beware of this tampering with simplicity and godly steadfastness. A *wandering* spirit proves—not expansive love, but latitudinarian indifference; freedom—not from prejudices, but from settled principles. Our Lord restrained his disciples from "forbidding" the man, "who was doing a good work," But he did not direct them to *wander from their own place*, and follow him.[2] The rule to "prove all things" is coupled with another —to "hold fast that which is good."[3] Christian establishment is the result of Scriptural balance. "Order and steadfastness"— "Beauty and bands"—are the two staves of the Good Shepherd; —the strength of the Church; the "joy" of her Ministers.[4] If the "order" be broken, "the steadfastness" soon fails. Confusion reigns, instead of peace and unity. The enemy's watchword prevails—'Divide and conquer.' Let every man therefore be in *his own place* in the Church; not weakening his Minister's hands to please his own fancy; but marking carefully "the footsteps of the flock;" and seeking to find "him whom his soul loveth," by "feeding beside the Shepherd's tents."[5]

9. *Ointment and perfume rejoice the heart; so doth the sweetness of a man's friend by hearty counsel* (counsel of the soul, Marg.)

Most refreshing are *ointment and perfume* to the senses.[6] Not less so is the cordial of friendship to the soul.[7] Who does not feel the need of a brother's or sister's bosom—their hand—their heart? Cold indeed is social intercourse without individual sympathy. "Faithful are the wounds of a friend."[8] But his very faithfulness alone would crush. His *sweetness* and tenderness soundly heal the wound. Sympathy is the balm of friendship. "My friend is to me as my own soul,"[9] the sharer of my joys and my sorrows.[10] How could I more than half enjoy my pleasures—how could I bear my sorrows—alone? What *ointment and perfume must have rejoiced the heart* of the two bosom-friends "in the word"— when their *hearty counsel* "strengthened each other's hands in God!"[11]

The heartiness of a friend's counsel constitutes its excellence.

[1] 2 Tim. iv. 3, 4. The principle of separation is shown Rom. xvi. 17, 18; and a black mark is put upon it, Jude 19.
[2] Mark ix. 38—40. [3] 1 Thess. v. 21. [4] Col. ii. 5, with Zech. xi. 7.
[5] Cant. i. 7, 8.
[6] Comp. Ps. cxxxiii. 2. Can. i. 3; iii. 6; iv. 10. John xii. 3. Dan. ii. 46.
[7] Chap. xvii. 17. Comp. Ecclus. vi. 14—16. [8] Verses 5, 6.
[9] Deut. xiii. 6. Philem. 12, 17. Horace calls Virgil—'Animæ dimidium meæ.' Carm. i. 3.
[10] Rom. xii. 15. Job ii. 11, 12; xlii. 11.
[11] 1 Sam. xviii. 1—3; xx. 17. 2 Sam. i. 26, with 1 Sam. xxiii. 16.

It is not official, or merely intelligent. It is *the counsel of his soul.* He puts himself in our case, and counsels, as he would wish to be counselled himself. Moses's *heart was thus rejoiced* by Jethro's *counsel*, relieving him from a heavy and needless burden.[1] Many cases of spiritual perplexity have been thus opened. When unable to see the needful consolation, *a friend's counsel*, like the angel of old, has pointed to the well of water near at hand for our support.[2] Often has the sympathy of a brother's experience cleared our path,[3] and turned the stumbling-block into a way-mark set up for our direction and encouragement. Ought we not then to "comfort" our fellow-sufferers "with the same comfort, wherewith we ourselves have been comforted of God?"[4] The Lord give us, as he did our Divine Master, the gift of "the tongue of the learned!"[5] 'Matchless teacher, that teachest more in one hour than man can do in a whole age! that we may be learned in real living Divinity, we sit down at thy feet! What I know not, teach thou me.'[6]

10. *Thine own friend, and thy father's friend, forsake not; neither go into thy brother's house in the day of thy calamity: for better is a neighbor that is near, than a brother far off.*

Man without principle is the creature of caprice. His friendships have no warranted stability. *The ointment* soon looses its fragrance. *The sweetness of hearty counsel*[7] is forgotten. New friends gain influence; and even *the father's friend*—the long-tried family friend—*is forsaken.* Solomon exemplified his own rule, by cultivating kindly intercourse with Hiram—*his father's friend.*[8] The unprincipled contempt of this rule cost his foolish son his kingdom.[9] If other things are better when new, a friend is better, that it is old and tried.[10] For how can you trust an untried friend? Never forget his rare price. Never be tempted by the lure of advantage to incur the risk of loosing him. His house *not thy brother's*—may be thy shelter *in the day of thy calamity.*[11] For though relationship ought to be the closest bond; yet, without an higher principle, it cannot subdue the energy of selfishness. Joseph found far greater kindness among foreigners than from his own kindred.[12] The affection of Jonathan afforded to David what the jealousy of his brother would never have given him.[13] The Saviour found his most soothing sympathy *in the day of his calamity*—not *in his brethren's house*, but in the persevering attachment of his devoted friends.[14] *One friend and neighbor* closely knit in unity—*near* at hand, and in readiness to assist, is *better than a brother as far off* in affection as in distance.[15]

1 Ex. xviii. 17—24. Comp. Ezra x. 2—4. 2 Gen. xxi. 15—19.
3 Ps. xxxiv. 2; lxvi. 16. 4 2 Cor. i. 4. 5 Isa. l. 4.
6 Leighton's Sermon on Job xxxiv. 31, 32. 7 Verse 9.
8 1 Kings v. 1—10. Even the claims of justice are mitigated. ii. 26. Contrast 2 Chron. xxiv. 22.
9 Ibid. xii. 6—19. 10 See Ecclus. ix. 10. 11 Chap. xviii. 24.
12 Gen. xxxix. 4, 21; xli. 39—45, with xxxvii. 4—18.
13 1 Sam. xx. with xvii. 28. 14 Luke xxii. 28, with John vii. 3, 5.
15 Bishop Patrick.

'But if it be an indecency, and uncomeliness, and a very unfit thing—that is—contrary to the precept of studying "whatsoever is lovely, and thinking of these things"—to forsake *my friend, and my father's friend*, how much more horrid must it be to forsake my God, and my father's God!—"My father's God shall not be my God!"'[1] But was not I given up to this God with great solemnity at my first coming into the world? And was this solemn transaction a trifle at the time, and to be regarded as a trifle to the end of life? Solomon could never forget the injunction of his aged Parent—"Thou, my son, know thou the God of thy father."[2] Exquisitely beautiful is the picture of the venerable Patriarch commending *his friend and his father's friend* to his children for his heavenly blessing—"God, before whom *my fathers, Abraham* and Isaac, did walk—*the God, which fed me* all my life long unto this day—the Angel, which redeemed me from all evil—bless the lads."[3] Here is *a wise friend*, who knows our need;[4] *a sympathizing friend*, who feels our distress;[5] *a mighty friend*, able to cover and provide;[6] *a faithful friend*—true to his word;[7] *a fast friend*—who will never leave.[8] Young people, do you know him as *your father's friend?* Make him *your own* in the hearty receiving of his Gospel. Cleave to him. He will never disappoint you.

11. *My son, be wise, and make my heart glad, that I may answer him that reproacheth me.*

An ungodly child is his parent's *reproach*. Hence the offending damsel was "stoned at the door of her father's house."[9] The graceless children of gracious parents are a special *reproach*, even upon the name of God.[10] The world will charge it (however in many cases most wrongfully) to their parent's example or neglect. *A wise son therefore makes the heart glad.*[11] He is his father's weapon of defence, "when he speaketh with his enemies in the gate."[12] Should not the children of the Church consider carefully the responsibility; to carry such a profession, as may *answer him that reproacheth*, and stop the mouth, ever ready to open with taunts against the Gospel? Specially should this responsibility be felt by children of ministers; to 'adorn' (as Mr. Richmond affectionately inculcated upon his children) 'not only their Christian profession, but their parent's principles; showing, that the principles of their father's house and ministry are the rules of their conduct, and their real delight?'[13]

[1] Howe's Works, vii. 529
[2] 1 Chron. xxviii. 9. Comp. Ex. xv. 2. [3] Gen. xlviii. 15, 16. [4] Col. ii. 3.
[5] Ps. xxxi. 7. [6] Isa. lxiii. 1. Matt. xxviii. 18.
[7] Num. xxiii. 19. Rev. xix. 11. [8] Heb. xiii. 5. [9] Deut. xxii. 21.
[10] Gen. xxxiv. 30. 1 Sam. ii. 17.
[11] Chap. x. 1; xv. 20; xxiii. 15, 16, 24, 25; xxix. 3. [12] Ps. cxxvii. 5.
[13] Life pp. 294, 295. The Mosaic law severely punished the sins of the priest's daughter for the disgrace brought upon the holy office. Lev. xxi. 9. "Faithful children" is a ministerial qualification. 1 Tim. iii. 4, 5. Tit. i. 6. It was a frequent petition in Philip Henry's family worship, that 'Ministers' children might have grace to carry

12. *A prudent man foreseeth the evil, and hideth himself; but the simple pass on, and are punished.*[1]

Even animal instinct is the exercise of *prudence.*[2] Every intelligent man acts upon it. *He foresees coming evil*, and provides himself a shelter. We often see the Christian's patience, security and hope. Here is his *prudence*, securing a refuge. There is frightful evil on every side. But God in Christ is to him "the munition of rocks"—not a cold and barren refuge, safe from enemies, but exposed to hunger; but a storehouse of food, as well as a citadel of defence. "Bread shall be given him, and his water shall be sure."[3] The man who has never realized *the evil* is without an *hiding-place.* The man who stays outside the gate, perishes as if there was no refuge. Only he, who "runneth into the strong tower is safe."[4] A mighty blessing is any dispensation that awakens from slumber, and brings care, *prudence*, confidence.

The Israelites, warned of the destruction of the first-born,[5] and many ages after, of the ruin of their city,[6] *hid themselves.* This prudence combined with faith, rouses us as the man-slayer to flee from impending danger, and to "lay hold of the hope set before us."[7] For him there were six cities[8]—For us there is but one.[9] Nothing short of vital faith brings us into it.

But the simple—the wilfully foolish—leave things to take their course. God is so merciful. All will be well at last. They will not be warned. The fooleries of the world engage their heart. All besides is forgotten; and so they *pass on and are punished.* The *prudent hide* themselves in God. *The simple* rush blindfold into hell. Oh! sinner, does not thy ruin lie at thine own door? What will it be to take the mad pleasures here, and to "lie down in everlasting sorrow?"[10] The tears of the penitent are but for a moment, and end in everlasting joy.[11] Thine will be for eternity—"the weeping" of utter despondency.[12] Wilt thou scorn this warning? The ox is driven to destruction. The sinner plunges into it in despite of every effort to restrain him.

13. *Take his garment that is surety for a stranger, and take a pledge of him for a strange woman.*

This Proverb also we have had before.[13] 'But what conduces to the happiness of life is needful to inculcate again and again, to fix it deep in the mind.'[14] This may be an illustration of the *prudence* just described; *foreseeing evil*, and, instead of rushing into it, avoiding it. For what can be more imprudent, than to trust a man, *that is surety for a stranger*, or *for a strange woman.*

it, that the Ministry might in nothing be blamed.' See the Author's Christian Ministry. Part. iii. chap. ix.

1 Chap. xxii. 3.
2 Job xxxvi. 23. Jer. viii. 7.
3 Isa. xxxiii. 16. Comp. Ps. cxlii. 5.
4 Chap. xviii. 10.
5 Ex. xii. 12, 13, 21—23.
6 Matt. xxiv. 15—21.
7 Heb. vi. 18.
8 Num. xxxv. 11—13.
9 Acts iv. 12.
10 Isa. l. 11.
11 Ps. cxxvi. 5, 6.
12 Matt. viii. 12; xxii. 13. Luke xiii. 28.
13 Chap. xx. 16.
14 Lavater.

Such folly is utterly unworthy of confidence. And therefore *take his garment*—full security for a debt. Rather incur the charge of selfishness, than by imprudence hinder yourself from helping more worthy objects. And yet let not the discipline of prudence chill the glow of active self-denying love. Let every grace be in its order, proportion and combination, "that the man of God may be perfect, thoroughly furnished unto all good works."[1]

14. *He that blesseth his friend with a loud voice, rising early in the morning, it shall be counted a curse to him.*

Is it a sin to *bless our friend?* Often did our Lord openly acknowledge the love of his friends.[2] And yet *a loud voice*, and extravagant praises, bring sincerity into question. When a man exceeds all bounds of truth and decency, affecting pompous words, and hyperbolical expressions, we cannot but suspect some sinister end.[3] Real friendship needs no such assurance. One act of love is more than many *loud blessings.* 'There is no wise man, but had rather have one promise than a thousand fair words, and one performance than ten thousand promises. For what charge is it to spend a little breath, for a man to give one his word who never intends to give him any thing else?'[4] The man may be *rising early in the morning*, lest some one be before him; lest otherwise there would be scarcely time to finish this great business; and yet while harping upon the same string, he may be undermining me all the day. Contrast David's *early rising* for the service of God, with his son's *early rising* for the hypocritical *blessing of his friends.*[5] The Apostle could not endure this exaggerated praise.[6] Indeed every intelligent man must look upon it rather as *a curse to him.* For any supposed encouragement of such fulsome flattery would stamp him as a fool. And *the blessing*—should he be deluded by it—would end in a fearful *curse.*[7]

The Scriptural rule of friendship is—"Let me not love in word, neither in tongue; but in deed and in truth."[8] The rule for ourselves is—"Walk before God"[9]—not before men. Let worldly things and worldly men be little in your eyes. Man's day[10] will soon have passed away. Eternity in all its substance and glory is at hand.

15. *A continual dropping in a very rainy day and a contentious woman are alike.* 16. *Whosoever hideth her hideth the wind, and the ointment of his right hand, which bewrayeth itself.*[11]

The figure of *the dropping* has been given before.[12] The time

[1] 2 Tim. iii. 17. [2] Luke xxii. 28. [3] Chap. xxvi. 23—25.
[4] South's Sermon on Matt. v. 44. Some of Mr. Scott's early friends at the Lock painfully reminded him of this Proverb. Life, pp. 225, 226.
[5] Ps. v. 3; lv. 17; cxix. 147, with 2 Sam. xv. 2—7.
[6] 2 Cor. x. 6. Comp. Rom. xii. 3.
[7] 2 Sam. xvi. 16—19; xvii. 7—13. Acts xii. 22, 23. [8] 1 John iii. 18.
[9] Gen. xvii. 1. [10] 1 Cor. iv. 3, Marg.
[11] 'He that refrayneth her, refrayneth the winde, and holdith oyle fast in hir honde. Bp. Coverdale. [12] Chap. xix. 13.

is here added—*a very rainy day*—shutting us up at home.[1] There is rain without and within—both *alike* troublesome; the one preventing us from going abroad with comfort—the other from staying at home in peace. The storm within is however much the most pitiless. Shelter may be found from the other. None from this. The other wets only to the skin; this even to the bones. *Contention* with a neighbor is a sharp shower, over and gone. This is *a continual dropping*—the bane of a house, even though replete with every luxury.

Whether it be in *the woman* the lust for rule, or the repining discontent under the obligation to submit; either principle breaks the rank, in which God has placed her. Occasions always present themselves for the display of this unhappy temper. After the attempts to soothe and pacify her, the "return of clouds after rain" betokens more showers, and dispels the hope, which a passing sunbeam may have raised. Even under the restraint of Divine grace—much more when wholly unrestrained—she becomes her husband's torment, and her own shame. For as soon might we *hide the wind*, that it should not be known, or the *ointment of our right hand*, that it might not *bewray itself*,[3] as restrain her tongue, or *hide her* turbulence. Nay—as *the wind* pent up howls more frightfully; so the attempt to still her noise, only makes her more clamorous.

Such repeated warnings seem to be needful. "Fleshly lusts" too often rule conscience and judgment in the important choice. "Some shall have trouble in the flesh."[4] Prudence and prayer—not blind affection—give the only security of happiness and peace.

17. *Iron sharpeneth iron; so a man sharpeneth the countenance of his friend.*

Man was framed not for solitude, but for society.[5] It is only as a social being, that his powers and affections are fully expanded. *Iron sharpeneth iron.*[6] Steel, whetted against a knife, sharpens the edge. So the collision of different minds whets each the edge of the other.[7] We owe some of the most valuable discoveries of science to this active reciprocity. Useful hints were thrown out, which have issued in the opening of large fields of hitherto unexplored knowledge. In the sympathies of friendship, when the mind is dull and the countenance overcast, a word from a friend puts an edge upon the blunted energy, and exhilarates the countenance.[8] The commanding word in the field of battle puts a keen edge upon *the iron.*[9] This mutual excitation for evil is a solemn warning against ungodly communication.[10] But most refreshing is it, when as in the dark ages of the Church, "they that feared the Lord

[1] Holden. [2] See Ecclus. xxvi. 6, 7. [3] John xii. 3.
[4] 1 Cor. vii. 28. [5] Gen. ii. 18. [6] 1 Sam. xiii. 20, 21.
[7] . . . . . 'Ergo fungar vice cotis, acutum
Reddere quæ ferrum valet exsors ipsa secandi.'
Hor. Ars. Poet. 304.
[8] Job iv. 3, 4. [9] 2 Sam. x. 11—13.
[10] Chap. i. 10—13. 1 Kings xxi. 25. Isa. xli. 6; with 1 Cor. xv. 33.

spake often one to another."[1] *Sharpening* indeed must have been the intercourse at Emmaus, when "the hearts of the disciples burned within them."[2] The Apostle was often so invigorated by *the countenance of his friends*,[3] that he longed to be "somewhat filled with their company."[4] Upon this principle—"Two are better than one"—our Lord sent his first preachers to their work.[5] And the first Divine ordination in the Christian Church was after this precedent.[6]

'The communion of saints' is an Article in our Creed. But is it practically acknowledged in its high responsibility and Christian privilege? "Am I" not "my brother's keeper?" Gladly take up the bond of brotherhood. If a brother seems to walk alone, *sharpen his iron* by godly communication. Walk together in mutual "consideration" of each other's infirmities, trials, and temptations; and mutual "provocation"[7] of each other's gifts and graces. "If the iron be blunt, the edge will thus be whetted, and more strength put into it."[8] Were this high obligation and privilege more realized; were we walking with God more closely in this holy atmosphere;[9] we should not so often complain of social intercourse, where much might have been communicated, and yet all has ended in barrenness and disappointment.

18. *Whoso keepeth the fig-tree shall eat the fruit thereof: so he that waiteth on his master shall be honored.*

An encouragement to diligence in our calling! *The fig-tree* was a valuable product of Judæa.[10] The cultivation was probably a profitable labor, and therefore illustrated the general reward of faithfulness. The dresser's industry was recompensed by *eating the fruit thereof*.[11] The fidelity of the attached servant will be similarly *honored*.[12]—Eliezer's uprightness,[13] and Deborah's long and faithful services,[14] were suitably *honored*. Elisha's affectionate devotedness to *his master was honored* with a double portion of his spirit.[15] The Centurion's care for his servant was probably an acknowledgment of diligent *waiting upon his master*.[16] The exceptive instances of ingratitude[17] do not invalidate the rule.

There are no exceptions, however, in the service of the Divine *Master*. Our happiness is in receiving his word, and studying his will. Our *honor* is secured by his promises—"If any man serve me, him will my Father *honor*." "Blessed are those servants, whom the Lord, when he cometh, shall find watching. Verily I say unto you, that he shall"—adorable condescension!—"gird himself, and make them to sit down to meat, and will come forth, and

[1] Mal. iii. 16. [2] Luke xxiv. 32. [3] Acts xviii. 5; xxviii. 15. 2 Cor. vii. 16.
[4] Rom. xv. 24. Even a Heathen could say—'Ipse aspectas viri boni delectat.'—Seneca.
[5] Luke x. 1—3, with Eccl. iv. 9—12. [6] Acts xiii. 2—4.
[7] Heb. x. 24, 25; also iii. 13. [8] Eccl. x. 10. [9] See 1 John i. 7.
[10] Jud. ix. 10, 11. Mic. iv. 4. Comp. Joel i. 6. 7. Hab. iii. 17. Luke xiii. 6—9.
[11] 1 Cor. ix. 7. 2 Tim. ii. 6. [12] Chap. xxii. 29. [13] Gen. xxiv.
[14] Ibid. xxxv. 8. [15] 2 Kings ii. 3—15. [16] Luke vii. 7, 8.
[17] Gen. xxxi. 7.

serve them."[1] Their *honor* will be proclaimed to each before the assembled world—"Well done! good and faithful servant; enter thou into the joy of thy Lord."[2] It will seal their overwhelming portion in eternal bliss—"His servants shall serve him; and they shall see his face, and his name shall be in their foreheads."[3]

19. *As in water face answereth to face, so the heart of man to man.*

This proverb does not confound all in one indiscriminate mass, as if all were alike under an endless diversity of condition. We cannot identify infancy with age, or the proper individualities of constitution and education. But under the same circumstances, and on the same level, the coincidence is most remarkable and instructive; and just as *in* the reflection of *the water face answereth to face;* so in another heart we see the reflection of our own.[4] Human nature has suffered no change since the fall. The picture of man's corruption drawn above four thousand years since, is man, as we see and know him now.[5] The Apostle's graphical delineation of the Christian conflict, is as if we had been sitting before his pencil for our own likeness.[6] This identity of Christian experience is most valuable. 'No one'—exclaims a tried child of God—'has ever felt as I do.' Let him open his case to a brother or sister, compare notes with their exercises; and who will hesitate to subscribe their own name to his complaints? Thus, instead of "thinking it strange concerning this fiery trial," he learns that "the same afflictions are accomplished in his brethren that are in the world."[7] The same features and "measure of the stature in Christ," mark the whole family; inasmuch as "all these worketh that one and the self-same Spirit, dividing to every man severally as he will."[8]

Scripture history also illustrates this unity. Ishmael's mocking shows the enmity of the heart in all ages. Who of us does not find something answering to Jonah's evil temper in our own fretfulness, waywardness, or ingratitude.[9] Job shows us our impatience, our mistaken judgments of God's dealings with us, and the special trial of Satan's temptations. David's *heart* in all its varied exercises *answereth to our heart.* Else how could we take up his confession, praises, conflicts, and triumphs, and feel that no words of ours could more entirely and accurately express our own selves? It is these scripture portraits, that make the word of God so "profitable for reproof, correction, and instruction in righteousness."[10]

Hence we learn sympathy with the members of Christ. We share their joys and sorrows, their confidence and temptations. Self-knowledge also instructs us thus to know human nature,[11] and to deal wisely and profitably with our fellow-sinners. The practical lesson of humility and forbearance is also deeply taught. A man observes *a face,* reflected *in the water,* not thinking that it is *his*

[1] John xii. 26. Luke xii. 37.
[2] Matt. xxv. 21, 23.
[3] Rev. xxii. 3, 4.
[4] Ps. xxxiii. 15.
[5] Gen. vi. 5, with Ps. xiv. 2, 3. Rom. iii. 9, 10.
[6] Rom. vii. 14—25.
[7] 1 Pet iv. 12; v. 9.
[8] 1 Cor. xii. 11.
[9] Gal. iv. 29.
[10] 2 Tim. iii. 16.
[11] Ps. xxxvi. 1. P. T.

own face, which is the actual object of disgust. He exclaims with vain self-preference against the ungodliness of the sinner, or the infirmities of the saint. Why! it is thine own nature that thou art reviling. Change then thy language of scorn for self-abhorrence and shame.

20. *Hell and destruction are never full: so the eyes of man are never satisfied.*

A striking picture of the two great devourers—*hell and destruction*[1]—*never full. Hell*—the grave—ever since Adam's sin has been insatiable. It has opened its mouth to receive countless millions; and still it yawns—craving for more.[2] Generations have sunk into *destruction*—doing the work, and earning "the wages of sin." Still the pit is not full. The broad mouth still opens for more.

Thus insatiable are *the eyes*—the desires[3]—*of man*—always requiring new gratification. "He enlargeth his desire as *hell*, and is as death, and *cannot be satisfied*. His eye is *not satisfied* with seeing, nor his ear filled with hearing."[4] Curiosity, love of novelty, covetousness, ambition—all these desires—like thirst in the dropsy, are aggravated in their indulgence.[5] Man is always seeking for what he can never find—satisfaction in earthly things. He toils after his object, and when he has grasped it, he toils still; the possessor of an earthly shadow—not of real happiness.[6] The height of ambition, when reached, is not his resting place—only the point, whence he stretches after something higher. He may fancy his desires to be moderate. He may set bounds to them, and flatter himself, that he shall never overpass them. But give him a world; and, like the far-famed conqueror, he will weep for another.

Nor is this altogether the effect of his depravity. Corruption indeed leads us to seek rest in something short of God. But it is our nature not to find it. How can an immortal being quench his thirst but from an infinite source? Here the gospel meets our case. So often as the eager question starts up—"Who will show us any good?"[7]—listen to the voice—"Ho! every one that thirsteth, come ye to the waters. If any man thirst, let him come unto me, and drink. He that cometh to me shall never thirst."[8] Here our desires are at once increased and *satisfied*. Such is the joyous character of the gospel. God is our satisfying portion—our supreme delight.[9] To delight in any thing else—independent of him[10]—is as if we cast him down from his throne. All is misery

[1] Chap. xv. 11. [2] Chap. xxx. 15, 16. Isa. v. 14. [3] 1 John ii. 16.
[4] Hab. ii. 5. Eccl. i. 8. Comp. ii. 1—11. [5] Eccl. vi. 7.
[6] Ibid. v. 10—12.

'Crescit amor nummi, quantum ipsa pecunia crescit.'
Juv. Sat. xiv. 139.

'Crescentem sequitur cura pecuniam,
Majorumque fames.'
Hor. Carm. iii. 16. Comp. ib. 24.

[7] Ps. iv. 6. [8] Isa. lv. 1, 2. John vii. 37; vi. 35. [9] Ps. xvi. 5. Lam. iii. 24.
[10] Ps. lxxiii. 25.

and delusion. Delighting in him—all ministers to our comfort, as flowing from this great centre. At the grand consummation, the *satisfaction of the eyes* will be complete. "Thine eyes shall see the King in his beauty. As for me, I will behold thy face in righteousness. *I shall be satisfied,* when I awake, with thy likeness."[1]

21. *As the fining-pot for silver, and the furnace for gold; so is a man to his praise.*

The fining-pot and furnace have been before mentioned, as the Lord's "trial of the heart."[2] The most searching *furnace* is here shown. The courting of the *praise* of our fellow-creatures is the world within. *Praise* is a sharper trial of the strength of principle than reproach. 'If a man be vain and light, he will be puffed up with it. If he be wise and solid, we will be no whit moved therewith.'[3] A haughty and supercilious deportment; "loving to have the pre-eminence;[4] forwardness to give our opinion,—and offence, if it be not taken—this is the dross brought out of the furnace. Count the discovery a special mercy. Know thy need of purifying, and let the great Refiner do his perfect work.[5]

But see *a man* humbled by praise, in the consciousness how little he deserves it, and "who maketh him to differ."[6] See him made more careful and diligent, bearing his honor meekly, and the same man as before; here *the furnace* proves the real metal, and brings out "a vessel of honor, meet for the Master's use."[7]

Absalom was tried in *this fining pot,* and found "reprobate silver."[8] Herod, under the shouting praise of his flatterers, "gave not God the glory," and was blasted in shame.[9] Joseph[10] and David[11] maintained their humility; Daniel his consistency;[12] the apostles their singleness for their Master's glory[13]—here was the bright *gold* in the heated *furnace.*

When the Minister of Christ becomes the object of popular applause—his people's idol; when they look at the pole, instead of the brazen serpent; when men of strong impulse and weak judgment put the servant in the Master's place[14]—then he is in *the fining-pot.* He that is but dross consumes. Even if there be true metal, the man of God "is saved, yet so as by fire." Without some painful discipline his usefulness would be withered, his spirituality deadened, his soul lost.[15]

Two rules strongly present themselves—*Be careful in giving*

[1] Isa. xxxiii. 17. Ps. xvii. 15.
[2] Chap. xvii. 3. Comp. Ecclus. ii. 1, 5. [3] Bp. Hall. [4] 3 John 9.
[5] Mal. iii. 2, 3. [6] 1 Cor. iv. 7. [7] 2 Tim. ii 21.
[8] 2 Sam. xiv. 25; xv. 6, with Jer. vi. 30. Ez. xxii. 18. [9] Acts xii. 21—23.
[10] Gen. xli. 41—43; xlv. 5—8. [11] 1 Sam. xviii. 7, 8, 15—18. [12] Dan. vi. 3—5.
[13] Acts iii. 11—16; x. 25, 26; xiv. 11—15.
[14] 'We should feel'—said the venerable Mr. Simeon in his own way—'as if our ears were stung with blasphemy, when we discover any attempt to transfer the crown of glory from the head of the Redeemer to that of any of his servants.' Henry Martyn continually expresses his sensitive conscience upon this besetting temptation. Life, chap. ii. iii. See also Author's Christian Ministry, Part iii. chap. vii.
[15] Comp. 2 Cor. xii. 7.

praise. Is it merciful to expose a weak fellow-sinner to the frown of a jealous God? or to stir up the innate corruption of his heart?[1] For put even the finest *gold into the furnace*—how humbling is the spectacle of the dross, that yet cleaves to it.![2] *Be not less careful in receiving praise.* While our taste revolts from extravagant flattery, yet we are apt to think it kindly meant, and it is very rare not to take unconsciously a drop of the poison. But the praise of the church is by far the most insidious poison—so refined, so luscious. Specially when we feel it to be lawfully obtained, how hard to receive it with self-renouncing consecration to God! 'Christian! thou knowest thou carriest gunpowder about thee. Desire those that carry fire to keep at a distance. It is a dangerous crisis, when a proud heart meets with flattering lips.'[3] May not even the habit of speaking humbly of ourselves be a snare of the devil? Would it not be safer not to speak of ourselves at all? At least to confine our conversation *in strict sincerity* to what we are—not what we appear to be—would be a "wise refraining of our lips."[4] Guard against dwelling even in thought upon any thing, that brings man's approving eye upon us. Delight mainly in those works, that are only under the eye of God. Value alone his approbation. Ever think of the love of human praise as the most deadly bane of a Christian profession,[5] to be resisted with intense energy and perseverance. A steady look into eternity shows its vanity; a glance at the cross its sinfulness.

22. *Though thou shouldest bray a fool in a mortar among wheat with a pestle, yet will not his foolishness depart from him.*

The allusion is to the Eastern mode of beating off the husk from the corn by *braying it in a mortar.* Yet the husk sticks not so close to the grain, as *foolishness to the fool.* The beating of *the mortar* may separate the one. The other *will not depart* by repeated strokes.[6] Much is said of the effectiveness of correction.[7] But of itself it works nothing. What can it do for *the fool* that despises it?[8] "The rod," as an ordinary means, "will drive *foolishness* out of the heart *of a child.*"[9] But the child is here become a man in strength of habit, and stubbornness of will. As soon therefore "can the Ethiopian change his skin, or the leopard his spots," as those can do good, "*who are accustomed to do evil.*"[10]

Examples of this incurable *hardness* abound. The deluge—that besom of Divine vengeance—destroyed the race—not *the foolishness*—of man. Nay—God himself declared its inefficacy for

[1] 'I do not know'—said Neff—'that I ought to thank you so very warmly for what I have too much reason to fear the old man will be ready to take advantage of; his life being, you know, principally supported by praise.' Biography, p. 369.

[2] Isa. xxxix. 2. 2 Chron. xxxii. 31. [3] Flavel. [4] Chap. x. 19.

[5] John v. 44; xii. 42, 43.

[6] Many commentators conceive a reference to this mode of punishment still practiced in the East. See Calmet—Parkhurst. Horne's Introduction, iii. 157. Burder's Oriental customs But perhaps the figurative allusion is more simple.

[7] Chap. xxiii. 13, 14; xxix. 15, 17. [8] Chap. xii. 1; xv. 10.

[9] Chap. xxii. 15. [10] Jer. xiii. 23.

this end.[1] Pharaoh was once and again *brayed in the mortar, yet did not his foolishness depart from* him.[2] Ahaz under the same infliction "trespassed yet more against the Lord," and stands out as a beacon to all ages—"*This is that king Ahaz!*"[3] "Why should ye be stricken any more?"—was the despondent complaint of God concerning his Israel.[4] The deepest affliction of chastisement produces only the fruit of blasphemy and hardened impenitence.[5] If Manasseh's *foolishness when brayed in the mortar—departed from him*;[6] this was not the innate power of affliction, but the super-added power of Sovereign Grace. The belief in the necessary working of affliction for our saving good is a fatal delusion. Never did it *of itself* bring one soul to God. In all cases, it is only what God is pleased to make it. A man may be crushed, yet not humbled. Like the broken pieces of the rock, he may retain all his native hardness. Still will he cling to his *foolishness;* and part with Christ and heaven, rather than with that which is interwoven into every part of his nature. Was it not thus, Christian, with thyself, till Omnipotent love awakened—what chastisement alone could never have stirred—the cry of unreserved submission?—'Lord! spare me not; bruise me; humble me; do any thing with me, but leave me under my sins. Who can deliver me, if thou dost not?' Most welcome is the "bemoaning" of the penitent child to his yearning father—"Thou hast chastised me, and I was chastised, as a bullock unaccustomed to the yoke: turn thou me, and I shall be turned; for thou art the Lord my God. Surely after I was turned, I repented; and after that I was instructed, I smote upon my thigh; I was ashamed, yea, even confounded, because I did bear the reproach of my youth. Is Ephraim my dear son? Is he a pleasant child? For since I spake against him, I do earnestly remember him still; therefore my bowels are troubled for him: I will surely have mercy upon him, saith the Lord."[7]

23. *Be thou diligent to know the state of thy flock, and look well* (set thy heart, Marg.) *to thy herds.* 24. *For riches are not for ever; and doth the crown endure to every generation?* 25. *The hay appeareth, and the tender grass sheweth itself, and herbs of the mountains are gathered.* 26. *The lambs are for thy clothing, and the goats are the price of the field.* 27. *And thou shalt have goats' milk enough for thy food, for the food of thy household, and for the maintenance of thy maidens.*

'This declareth the great goodness of God towards man, and the diligence that he requireth of him for the preservation of his gifts.'[8] It is a lively picture of the occupations, advantages, and responsibilities of rural life in olden days. It is specially appropriate to a nation, whose chief riches were, in its early origin, in *pastures and flocks.* Their father Jacob admirably exemplified this rule. He *knew well the state of his flocks and herds*—probably also their very faces.[9] Even King David—mindful of his ancient interests—

[1] Gen. viii. 21. [2] Ex. ix. 27; x. 16; xii. 29; xiv. 5. [3] 2 Chron. xxvii. 22.
[4] Isa. i. 5. Comp. ix. 13. Jer. v. 3; xliv. 9, 10, 15, 16. Ez. xxiv. 13. Am. iv. 11, 12.
[5] Rev. xvi. 10, 11. [6] 2 Chron. xxxiii. 12, 13.
[7] Jer. xxxi. 18—20. Comp. Hos. xiv. 1—4. Luke xv. 18—24.
[8] Reformer's Notes. [9] Gen. xxx. 32—42; xxxi. 38—40; xxxiii. 13.

kept his *flocks and herds* under constant inspection.[1] Uzziah also deemed a pastoral charge no degradation to his royal dignity.[2] The rule inculcates personal attention. All should not be left to servants. The master's eye—like Boaz[3]—should, as far as possible, overlook the work. *Riches* are a fickle possession. *They would not be for ever.*[4] Even *the crown might not endure to every generation.* Native produce is more permanent wealth. Honest industry secures a more certain maintenance, springing up out of the earth, a more immediate gift of God.

The Bible is thus a directory for all the diversified employments of life. It teaches, that every man ought to have a business, and rebukes the neglect of practical everyday duties. God may be glorified by a single eye and purpose in every station; by the laborer, the farmer, the servant, no less than the master.[5] We must "serve the Lord in fervency of spirit." But a part of this service is, that we be "not slothful in business."[6] Indolence would make the cares of life an excuse for a low standard of religion. But to retire from their burden would be to neglect "serving the will of God in our generation;[7] to "put our light under a bushel, instead of upon a candlestick," to cover it, instead of "letting it shine."[8] Our own calling is the way of God for us; and in this way, let us commit ourselves to God, and be at peace.[9] His Providence extends to little things, as well as to things of greater moment. Thus it becomes a balm for that cankering care, which is the bane of all godliness.

This picture also exhibits the fruits of industry as far preferable to those of ambition. The comparison with those, whose station places them beyond the need of labor, affords no matter for envy; much for thankfulness. The various produce of the field—the *hay and grass* in the pastures; *the herbage on the mountains;*[10] the suitable *clothing from the lambs;*[11] *the goats paying the price of the field;* the sufficiency of wholesome food *for the household and maidens*—all is the overflowing bounty of our gracious God. "How excellent is thy loving-kindness, O God!"[12] Thus "man goeth forth unto his work and unto his labor until the evening," singing his song of praise—"O Lord, how manifold are thy works! in wisdom hast thou made them all: the earth is full of thy riches."[13]

[1] 1 Chron. xxvii. 29—31, with 1 Sam. xvi. 11. Ps. lxxviii. 70, 71
[2] 2 Chron. xxvi. 10. [3] Ruth ii. 4, 5; iii. 7. [4] Chap. xxiii. 5.
[5] Col. iii. 22—24. [6] Rom. xii. 11. [7] Acts xiii. 26.
[8] Matt. v. 14—16. [9] 1 Cor. vii. 20, 24.
[10] Ps. civ. 14. "The word translated *hay* properly means grass. Where vegetation was so abundant, they have seldom occasion to make hay. Holden. Comp. Parkhurst.
[11] Job xxxi. 20. [12] Ps. xxxvi. 7. [13] Ib. civ. 23, 24.

CHAPTER XXVIII.

1. *The wicked flee when no man pursueth: but the righteous are bold as a lion.*

The wicked may appear *bold* in facing danger, so long as they drown reflection, and stupify conscience. But when conscience is roused, guilt is the parent of fear. Adam knew no fear, till he became a guilty creature. *Then*, to the searching question—"Where art thou?"—he replied—"I was afraid, because I heard thy voice in the garden, and I hid myself."[1] But *the wicked flee*—not only when their enemies pursue,[2]—but *when no man pursueth.*[3] Yet is not conscience an invisible *pursuer*, following close—the harbinger of the wrath of God? And there are times, when "the sound of a shaken leaf shall chase them;"[4] when "the shadows upon the mountains" shall make their hearts melt away.[5] Cain was terrified with the apprehension of murder, when there was no man, save his own father, living on the earth.[6] Many a daring infidel has shown himself a coward in a moment of sudden danger. In unwelcome thoughts of judgment to come, conscience has turned pale at the question—"Where shall the ungodly and the sinner appear?"[7]

But if guilt brings fear, the removal of guilt gives confidence.[8] *The wicked flee; the righteous are bold as a lion.* Fearless as the King of the forest,[9] they dare to do any thing but offend their God. The fear of him has drowned every other fear. "Though an host should encamp against me"—saith the man of God—"mine heart shall not fear."[10] Moses "feared not the wrath of the king."[11] Caleb and Joshua stood firm against the current of rebellion.[12] Elijah dared Ahab's anger to his face.[13] Nehemiah in a time of peril exclaimed—"Should such a man as I flee?"[14] The three confessors stood undaunted before the furious autocrat of Babylon.[15] The Apostles' *boldness* astonished their enemies.[16] Paul before the Roman Governor,[17] and even before Nero himself, "witnessed a good confession."[18] Athanasius before the Imperial Council of Heresy; Luther at the Diet of Worms, firmly exem-

[1] Gen. iii. 9, 10. [2] Deut. xxviii. 25. [3] Lev. xxvi. 17, 36. Ps. liii. 5.
[4] Lev. xxvi. 36. Comp. Job xv. 21. [5] Jud. ix. 26. [6] Gen. iv. 13, 14.
[7] 1 Pet. iv. 18. [8] Heb. x. 22. 1 John iii. 21.
[9] Comp. chap. xxx. 30. 2 Sam. xvii. 10. 'This noble animal is the most perfect model of boldness and courage. He never flies from the hunters, nor is frightened by their onset. If their number forces him to yield, he retires slowly, step by step, frequently turning upon his pursuers. He has been known to attack a whole caravan, and when obliged to retire, he always retires fighting, and with his face to the enemy.' Paxton's Illustration of Natural History of Scripture, pp. 295, 296. Pindar refers to the lion as the figure of courage. Isth. iv. Antistr. V.
[10] Ps. xxvii. 1—3. Comp. iii. 5; xlvi. 2, 3; cxii. 7.
[11] Heb. xi. 28. Ex. x. 28, 29. [12] Num. xiv. 6—10.
[13] 1 Kings xviii. 10, 17, 18; xxi. 20. Compare 2 Kings i. 15. 1 Kings xiii. 1—10 2 Chron. xxvi. 17, 18.
[14] Neh. vi. 11. [15] Dan. iii. 16—18. [16] Acts iv. 13.
[17] Ib. xxiv. xxvi. Rom. 1. 15, 16. [18] 2 Tim. iv. 16, 17.

plifie the *lion-like boldness*. Nor is this the character of individuals only. The faithful and constant Christian will be *bold* to walk contrary to the course of this world; outfacing the scorn of men; valiant for despised truth; glorying in a persecuted name. Fearless is he of men. "For if God be for him, who can be against him?"[1] Not less fearless is he of Satan. If he be a "roaring,"[2] he is a chained, "lion." "Resist him," and coward-like, "he will flee from you."[3] If there be a want of *boldness*, is there not a wound of conscience, neglect of prayer, or want of faith? The *boldness* itself is the sense of weakness, and Divine strength made perfect in it."[4] When God intends us to do great things, he makes us feel, that "without him we can do nothing."[5] Thus pride receives its death-blow, and he receives all the glory to himself.[6]

2. *For the transgression of a land many are the princes thereof: but by a man of understanding and knowledge the state thereof shall be prolonged.*

Is God concerned in the falling of a sparrow?[7] Surely then much more in the control of kingdoms.[8] Did we realize more deeply our national dependence, we should see the clouds of anarchy and confusion working his wise, mysterious, or gracious purposes. Rival *princes* desolate the land with the horrors of civil war.[9] A quick succession of *princes* rises by treason, usurpation, or the natural course.[10] Hence a change of laws, spoliation of privileges, imposition of new burdens, or wasteful expenditure of treasure or blood. Many will trace these evils to political causes. But God's voice speaks from the cloud—"This thing is from me."[11] *For the transgression of a land many are the princes thereof.* Nor less must we acknowledge his hand in *the prolongation of the state by men of understanding and knowledge.* The long and prosperous reigns of the kings of Judah are strongly contrasted with the Records of Israel after the revolt.[12] The bloody contentions in our early history, which swept away the flower of our nobility, and those of later date, which overturned for a time our long-established institutions—were they not the scourge of *many princes for the transgression of the land?* And may we not anticipate the bright contrast, in prayer for our beloved Sovereign, that by the choice of

[1] Rom. viii. 31. [2] 1 Pet. v. 8. [3] Jam. iv. 7.
[4] 2 Cor. xii. 9. [5] John xv. 5.
[6] Bishop Hall has finely worked out this contrast—'*The wicked* is a very coward, and is afraid of every thing; of God, because he is his enemy; of Satan, because he is his tormentor; of God's creatures, because they, joining with their Maker, fight against him; of himself, because he bears about with him his own accuser and executioner. The godly man contrarily is afraid of nothing; not of God, because he knows him his best friend, and will not hurt him; not of Satan, because he cannot hurt him; not of afflictions, because he knows they come from a loving God, and end in his good; not of the creatures, since "the very stones in the field are in league with him;" not of himself, since his conscience is at peace.' Medit. and Vows. Cent. ii. lxxiv.
[7] Matt. x. 29. [8] Dan. iv. 25. Comp. Ecclus. x. 4. [9] 1 Kings xii. 16—21
[10] Zech. xi. 8. [11] 1 Kings xii. 24.
[12] Ib. xv. 25—34; xvi. 8—29. 2 Kings xv. 8—31, with 1 Kings xv. 41. 2 Chron. xvii. 1—5; xxxii. 20—26.

men of understanding and knowledge in her council, *the state may be prolonged* "in all godly quietness?"[1]

3. *A poor man that oppresseth the poor is like a sweeping rain which leaveth no food* (without food, Marg.)

Unrestrained power is often an engine of *oppression*;[2] never more so, than when in the grasp of the *poor*. Place an unprincipled spendthrift in power, and he is a destructive flood in his sphere; greedily seizing every advantage by *oppression* to redeem his substance. A *poor man* suddenly raised to power, instead of sympathizing with grievances familiar to his former recollections,[3] is usually pre-eminently distinguished by selfishness. Esther, when raised to a throne from an obscure station, was well reminded to use her power for God; for that some great work was surely intended by the remarkable Providence.[4] But a base mind becomes more corrupt from a hasty elevation. The man's necessities enflame his desires; and, being without a spark of generous humanity, he is only bent upon improving his uncertain opportunities for selfish aggrandizement.[5] Some of the Rulers in the French Revolution were raised from the lowest ranks. And their *oppression* was indeed *a sweeping rain, leaving no food* in fertile districts.

Cheering is the contrast of Him—once *poor* himself by his voluntary abasement—now raised to honor and glory; yet pitying—"not ashamed of his poor brethren."[6] Truly his administration is not the *sweeping rain* of desolation, but "the rain upon the mown grass," rich in mercy. "He shall deliver the needy when he crieth; the poor also, and him that hath no helper. He shall redeem their soul from deceit and violence; and precious shall their blood be in his sight."[7]

4. *They that forsake the law praise the wicked: but such as keep the law contend with them.*

How responsible is the influence of our profession, acting upon all around for evil or for good! Congeniality of taste directs the choice of our companions. Those who love sin, naturally "have pleasure in them that do it."[8] *They praise the wicked*,

[1] 1 Tim. ii. 1, 2.
[2] Gen. xxxi. 29. Comp. Eccl. iv. 1, 2.
[3] Matt. xviii. 28—30.
[4] Esth. iv. 14.
[5] 'It is in matter of power'—as Bp. Sanderson admirably observes—'as it is in matter of learning. They that have but a smattering of scholarship you shall ever observe to be the forwardest to make ostentation of those few ends they have; because they fear there would be little notice taken of their learning, if they should not now show it when they can. It is even so in this case. Men of base spirit and condition, when they have gotten the advantage of a little power, conceive that the world would not know what goodly men they are, if they should not do some act or other, to show forth their power to the world. And then, their minds being too narrow to comprehend any generous way whereby to do it, they cannot frame to do it any other way than by trampling upon those that are below them; and that they do beyond all reason, and without all mercy.' Sermon on Chap. xxiv. 11, 12. Comp. also on 1 Sam. xii. 3.
[6] 2 Cor. viii. 9. Phil. ii. 7—11, with Heb. ii. 11, 12.
[7] Ps. lxxii. 6, 12—14.
[8] Rom. i. 32.

because, like themselves, *they forsake the law*, and "cast it behind them."[1] "The world loveth its own."[2] Each countenances his brother in sin.[3] Each makes the other's conduct—not *the forsaken law*—the standard of action. *The wicked* may possess some praiseworthy qualities.[4] But to *praise them* for their wickedness, identifies us with them. 'It is fearful to sin; more fearful to delight in sin; yet more to defend it.'[5]

The servants of God maintain the same unity of spirit. They cannot call sin by smooth names, and gloss over an ungodly character. If *they keep the law*, they *contend with them that forsake it*. Noah thus *contended* with the ungodly in his day, condemning them not merely in word but in life; and though "a preacher of righteousness," preached more powerfully by his life than by his doctrine.[6] But this *contention* must be aggressive. We must "reprove," as well as separate from, "the unfruitful works of darkness."[7] Our Divine Master's open testimony was the grand offence.[8] So let us plainly show that his enemies are ours;[9] that we hold neutrality in his cause to be treason. For "he that is not with me is against me."[10]

Oh! the appalling recollection of our former influence for evil! the deadly—perhaps the eternal—injury, which all our subsequent labors have never been able to undo! the encouragement, which our *praise of the wicked* gave to sin, hardening our companions in their wickedness! What would Manasseh have given to have undone his sin in all its evil consequence upon his son and his kingdom![11] Intolerable would be the thought of the past, but for the blood which covers the guilt, while it deepens shame and self-abhorrence.[12] But let it ever be present before us, as our constraining obligation to redeem what has been lost, as far as may be, by a holy *contention* against sin, and by the convincing protest of consistent godliness.[13]

5. *Evil men understand not judgment: but they that seek the Lord understand all things.*

Ignorance and knowledge are here contrasted, and each traced to their proper source. The Apostle draws the same contrast. "The natural man receiveth not the things of the Spirit of God. But he that is spiritual judgeth all things."[14] This unity of statement is beautiful and instructive. 'The two Testaments, like our two eyes, mutually enlighten us, and assist each other.'[15]

[1] Comp. 1 Sam. xxiii. 21. Neh. vi. 17—19. Ps. x. 3.
[2] John xv. 18. Comp. Jer. v. 30, 31. [3] Isa. xli. 6. [4] Luke xvi. 8.
[5] Bishop Hall's Works, viii. 36. [6] 2 Pet. ii. 5. Heb. xi. 7.
[7] Eph. v. 11. Elijah, 1 Kings xviii. 18; Elisha, 2 Kings iii. 5; John, Matt. iii. 7; xiv. 3, 4. [8] Matt. xv. 10—12. John. vii. 7.
[9] Ps. cxxxix. 21, 22. See the rebuke given to a godly king, 2 Chron. xix. 2.
[10] Matt. xii. 30.
[11] 2 Chron. xxxiii. 15—17, with 22. 2 Kings xxiii. 26. Mr. Cecil had deep cause to regret his ineffectual labor to reclaim from infidelity more than one, whom in his days of rebellion he had plunged into that gulf of ruin.
[12] Ez. xvi. 63. [13] Phil. ii. 15, 16. 1 Pet. ii. 12; iii. 16. [14] 1 Cor. ii 14, 15.
[15] Serle's Horæ Solitariæ, vol. i. 565.

Evil men understand not judgment.[1] They know not the true standard of right and wrong, the true way to God, or the end of God's dealings with them. Their ignorance is wilful[2]—"Having the understanding darkened, *because of the blindness of the heart.* Men love darkness rather than light, because their deeds are evil. They call darkness light, and light darkness."[3] The most distinguished scholar is a very fool in *understanding judgment;* and except he be humbled in the consciousness of his ignorance, and seek light from above—he will perish in gross darkness.

Nay—sometimes knowledge, no less than ignorance, hinders a right *understanding.* Where the knowledge of the truth goes before or beyond the power of it, the mind is often perplexed with difficulties, which the less intelligent, but more simple, escapes. When knowledge stands in the stead of faith; when the man reasons, instead of submitting to Divine teaching; knowledge abused becomes a positive hindrance to a correct *understanding.*

Pride is indeed a very general cause of ignorance. The source of light is despised.[4] Hence "there is none that *understandeth,*" because "there is none that *seeketh after God.*"[5] *They that seek the Lord*—babes though they may be in intellect, and ignorant in worldly things—shall have an accurate *understanding of all things* profitable, such as no "natural man" can attain.[6] "The words are plain to him that *understandeth,* and right to them that find knowledge."[7] Many things, dark to human reason, are simplified to humility.[8] God's working is the spring of diligence, not of inertion. Man works, but under the Master-worker. He is free, but under the free-making Spirit, giving him a will for the service. Thus while active he is kept dependent.[9] He works with deeper humility, and more assured confidence.[10] This is a mystery to reason. But *they that seek the Lord understand it.* Practical experience shows it to them. Again—how dark are the Lord's ways to man's proud reason! Hard dispensations! a world of sorrow! But the child of God, *seeking* to know "the end," *understands* them "all to be mercy and truth."[11] Is it not the sharp trial, to probe the wound; the bitterness, to wean from the creature comfort; the burden, to prove "the patience and faith of the saints;" the sifting, to separate the chaff from the wheat; the furnace, to purify the gold? Thus does *seeking the Lord* expound the mysteries of Providence and grace! We are neither stumbled by the stones, perplexed by the labyrinths, or "discouraged because

1 Ps. lxxxii. 5. Jer. iv. 22.
2 Job xxi. 14.
3 Eph. iv. 18. John iii. 19. Isa. v. 20.
4 Ps. x. 4.
5 Ibid. xiv. 2. Rom. iii. 11. 'Wickedness'—Bp. Taylor justly observes—'corrupts a man's reasoning, gives him false principles, and evil measuring of things.' Sermon before University of Dublin. 'I regard it as a fundamental error in the study of divinity'—remarks Professor Franke—'for any one to persuade himself, that he can study divinity properly without the Holy Spirit. As long as he remains in this error, all labor is lost on him.' Lect. Parœn. p. 184. 'A grain of true faith is more estimable than a mass of mere historical knowledge.' Ib. Idea studiosi in Theologiæ
6 Ps. xxv. 9, 12; cxix. 98—100, 130. Matt. xi. 25.
7 Chap. viii. 6.
8 Ps. xxv. 14, with Chap. xxiv. 7.
9 Ps. cxix. 4, 5, 8, 10, 32, 173.
10 Phil. ii. 12, 13.
11 James v. 11, with Ps. xxv. 10.

of the length and weariness" of the way. Those who desire the light shall have it.[1] To those who mprove it, more shall be given.[2]

But—'I cannot *seek*—that is—I cannot pray.' Then do as you are taught. Let not inability be indolence, but faith. Carry it to the Lord.[3] Remember the help provided for weakness and ignorance.[4] If you cannot pray as you would, pray as you can. Desire—*sincere and supreme*—is the heart's real prayer—God's own work upon the soul.[5] Is this manifest? Wait in the constant use of the means—Be found in the way.[6] "Light is sown;"[7] and the seed in God's best time will bring the harvest. No one fails to make progress who is really in earnest. It is a grand mistake to suppose that some impression must be felt as *the warrant to seek.* The only true warrant is the free invitation of the gospel. You must come—if at all—as a sinner, not as a saint; as you are, not as you would be; now, not waiting for some better time or preparation; seeking your fitness in Christ, not in yourself. If you think or feel that you cannot seek thus, do not reason or despond about it. Ask for Divine teaching to understand, and Divine grace to follow, the light vouchsafed. No depth of learning, no extraordinary inspiration, is needed. "Ye have an unction from the Holy One, *and ye know all things.*"[8] The heart is given as well as the mind. "The senses are exercised to discern between good and evil."[9] All this light, because the creative word has been given anew—"Let there be light; and there was light."[10] Are Christians then to be despised as fools? They are the most intelligent people in this world. Fixed at wisdom's gate, their religion is Divine wisdom, and "wisdom is justified of her children."[11]

6. *Better is the poor that walketh in his uprightness, than he that is perverse in his ways, though he be rich.*

This proverb is repeated[12] for its valuable instruction. One part of the comparison, which before had been implied, is here expressed—*though he be rich.* Before he was described as *perverse in his lips.* A deeper trait of character is here given—*perverse in his ways*—or his principles. This is one of those paradoxes, that sometimes stumble the feet even of God's children.[13] *A man may walk in his uprightness*, and yet be *poor.* He may be *perverse in his ways* and be *rich.* And yet the *poor man*, with all his external disadvantages, *is* really *better*—more honorable—more happy—more useful *than the rich*, with all his earthly splendor.

[1] John vii. 17. [2] Matt. xiii. 12; xxv. 29.
[3] Luke xi. 2. [4] Rom. viii. 26.
[5] Ps. xxxviii. 9. Isa. xxvi. 8, 9. See Homer's fine description of 'Prayers the daughters of Jove'—perhaps the most remarkable view to be found in Heathen literature as Cowper in his Notes writes—well worthy of observation, considering where it is found. Il. I. 502—514.
[6] Isa. lxiv. 5. [7] Ps xcvii. 11. [8] 1 John ii. 20.
[9] Heb. v. 14. [10] Gen. i. 3. 2 Cor. iv. 6.
[11] Luke vii. 35. Prov. viii. 34. Comp. Wisd. vi. 11—16.
[12] Chap. xix. 1. 'A poor man walking in truth is better than the rich man of a lie. LXX. Chap. xix. 22. [13] Ps. lxxiii. 2—16

And to come to a solid scriptural decision on this point is of great practical moment. For if we are dazzled with the glitter of this world's glory, we shall reverse the golden rule;[1] and "seek" *first* the world as our grand object, and "the kingdom of God"—the interests of the soul—the stake of eternity—will occupy only the second place—that is—virtually will be thrust out.

Calculate—whether this is not a just balance—however counter it may be to common opinion. Dishonesty is the besetting temptation of *the poor.*[2] Yet, in despite of this temptation, does he *walk in his uprightness.* Is there not a glory around his poverty infinitely beyond the vain show of this world? *The rich man is perverse in his ways.* He is "a double-minded man"—endeavoring to walk in two ways;[3]—outwardly following godliness, inwardly deceit; pretending to one way, walking in another—Who can trust him?

So far then as *concerns character*, the comparison holds good, in favor of *the poor.* Now—as regards condition. Who would not prefer the lot of Elijah, subsisting upon his barrel of meal, to Ahab in all the pomp and glory of his throne?[4] Who does not see a dignity in Paul standing at the bar, such as throws the worldly rank of his judges into utter insignificance?[5]

But the truth is of general application. Outward superiority only affects our state before God, as increasing our responsibility, in proportion to our advantages and talents.[6] And how many will wish, that they had lived and died in, obscure poverty, with "a conscience void of offence toward God and toward man"[7]—rather than had riches committed to them—only in *the perverseness of their ways* to embolden them to sin with a high hand against God and their own souls!

7. *Whoso keepeth the law is a wise son: but he that is a companion of riotous men shameth his father.*

Keeping the law is national wisdom and honor.[8] Invaluable is that training, which leads young persons, under the Lord's blessing, to this happy choice. Such are manifestly taught of God, and guided by his Spirit into true *wisdom.*[9] For suppose a son of polished manners and intellectual endowments, yet without right principle; or one of moderate ability—in an humble walk of life, yet deeply imbued with practical godliness—could we hesitate which was the *wise son*[10]—bringing honor to his father's name? Yet how often is *shame* instead of honor, the father's bitter exercise! For how is his name blotted, when the depraved son—bent upon his own gratification—chooses the *companionship* of the ungodly, and shortly becomes one with them![11] Young man! in thy

1 Matt. vi. 33. 2 Chap. xxx. 9.
3 Heb. Jam. i. 8. 4 1 Kings xvii. 13—15, with xxi. 1—4, 19.
5 Acts xxiv. 24—26; xxvi. 27—29. 2 Tim. iv. 16, 17. 6 Luke xii. 48.
7 Acts xxiv. 16. 8 Deut. iv. 6. 9 Isa. lvi. 4—6.
10 Chap. xxvii. 11.
11 Chap. xix. 26; xxiii. 19—22; xxix. 3, 15. Luke xv. 13, 30.

noisy mirth hast thou found solid enduring peace?[1] Let the man of God direct you in the "cleansing thy way, by taking heed thereto according to the word."[2] Let his choice be thine—"I am a *companion*"—*not of riotous persons*—but—"of all them that fear thee, and of them that keep thy precepts."[3] Meet the enticements of thy former *companions* with his decided protest—"depart from me, ye evil doers; I will keep the commandments of my God."[4] Here is honor to thy father—happiness to thyself—usefulness to the Church—meekness for heaven.

Parents! Do we shrink from this overwhelming *shame?* Let us more diligently—more prayerfully, cultivate that wise and holy training of our children, which is God's appointed ordinance; and which—however long or severely he may try our faith—he will not fail to honor in his own best time.[5]

8. *He that by usury and unjust gain increaseth his substance, he shall gather it for him that will pity the poor.*

What a deadly curse is it to be under the spell of covetousness! Every thing that is "honest, just, pure, lovely, and of good report," is sacrificed to this idolatrous principle. No laws can bind it. God had fenced in the rights of his poor people with solemn and plain obligations.[6] And he will not suffer their rights to be lightly regarded. "I know"—saith the man of God—"that the Lord will maintain the cause of the afflicted, and the right of the poor."[7] As a God of equity, often does he make selfishness to punish itself, and even to turn to the advantage of the oppressed.[8] Ill-gotten gains are a dangerous and uncertain possession.[9] A man labors for himself, and his harvest falls into better hands; 'not intending anything of himself; but it is so done through God's secret Providence.'[10] In this, as in every view, godliness "has the promise of the life that now is."[11] It brings "the great gain of contentment,"[12] and restrains those inordinate desires for wealth, which ruin all right principles, and "drown men in destruction and perdition."[13] "A man's life consisteth not in the abundance of the things which he possesseth."[14] Why should we seek to *increase our substance by unjust gain,* when we have our Father's promise —"All things shall be added to you"[15]—yea when his Divine power *hath* given all things pertaining unto life and godliness?[16]

9. *He that turneth away his ear from hearing the law, even his prayer shall be abomination.*

Awful is it, that there should be such a rebel. Yet thus do the ungodly, while they take God's covenant into their mouth, "hate instruction, and cast his words behind them."[17] Nay even in his

[1] Chap. xiv. 13. Ecc. ii. 2; vii. 6. [2] Ps. cxix. 9, 11. [3] Ib. ver. 63.
[4] Ibid. ver. 115. [5] Chap. xxii. 6.
[6] Ex. xxii. 24. Lev. xxv. 36. Deut. xxiii. 19, 20. Ez. xviii. 13.
[7] Ps. cxl. 12. [8] Chap. xiii. 22. Job xxvii. 13, 16, 17.
[9] Chap. x. 2; xiii. 11; xxi. 6. [10] Diodati. Eccl. ii. 26. [11] 1 Tim. iv. 8.
[12] Ibid. vi. 6. [13] Ibid. ver. 9; chap. xxi. 7. [14] Luke xii. 15.
[15] Matt. vi. 33. [16] 2 Pet. i. 3. [17] Ps. l. 16, 17.

church will "they come before him as the people come, and sit before him as his people; *they hear his words but they will not do* them."[1] If the subject thus *turneth away his ear from hearing the law* of his Sovereign, every *prayer* that he may present in time of distress his Lord will regard as an *abomination.*[2] 'Great reason that God shall refuse to hear him, who refuseth to hear God.'[3] And what if his language now—"Depart from me"—should be taken out of his mouth at the great day, as the seal of his everlasting doom![4]

A strange contradiction, that this open rejection of God should be connected with any form or semblance of religion! And yet often would the self-deceiver compensate for the disobedience of a plain command by the performance of some external duty. Israel presented "the multitude of sacrifices" as a price for the neglect of practical obligations. "Vain oblations! Incense that was *abomination!*"[5] *Praying* at home is made an excuse for *turning away from hearing the law* in God's own house. Such *prayer* is solemnly declared to be *abomination.* The law of charity and even of bounden duty is evaded, to maintain a profession of godliness,[6] hateful in His eyes, who will bring to open shame every hypocritical service. Does God trifle with man? Assuredly he will not suffer man thus to trifle with him.

Be it ever remembered—that godliness is God's *whole* worship and service; that "the wisdom from above is without partiality, and without hypocrisy;"[7] that to extol one ordinance at the expence of another—to decry preaching for the sake of commending prayer—is proof alike of a false judgment and an unsound heart. To reject any Divine ordinance is proud will-worship; a plain proof, that the privilege has never been enjoyed. For no beggar would slight the door where he had been used to receive his blessing. O my God! let me lie in thine own bosom, or at thy feet, that my will may be lost in thine, and my happiness found in a whole-hearted devotedness to thyself!

10. *Whoso causeth the righteous to go astray in an evil way, he shall fall himself into his own pit; but the upright shall have good things in possession.*

To delight in the enticing of sinners *in an evil way,* is the very image and character of the tempter. But the chief delight—the main effort—is to *cause the righteous to go astray.* No rejoicing is so great, as when "a standard-bearer fainteth." Because, while it shows the seducer's enmity to the truth, it countenances him in his sin. Yet how transient is his joy! Success is his ruin. By the retributive justice of God, he often *falls into his own pit.*[8] The snare of Balaam for the people of God ended in his own ruin.[9]

The malice of Satan and his emissaries, however, sets out the

1 Ez. xxxiii. 31, 32.
2 Chap. i. 28, 29. Zech. vii 11—13.
3 Bp. Reynolds on Hos. xiv. 8.
4 Job xxi. 14; xxii. 17, with Matt. xxv. 4.
5 Isa. i. 11—15. Comp. Ps. lxvi. 17.
6 Matt xv. 5—9.
7 Jam. iii. 17.
8 Chap. xxvi. 27. Comp. Job xii. 16.
9 Rev. ii. 14. Num. xxxi. 15, 16, with 8.

faithfulness of our Almighty Keeper—"Thou preparest a table for us in the presence of our enemies,"[1] who gnash their teeth at the sight. Even if they succeed for a while *in leading the righteous astray*, recovering mercy is in store for them;[2] and *the upright*, brought out of the snare in deep humiliation—instead of the evil meditated against them—*have good things in possession.* What *good things* they are, "eye hath not seen, nor hath ear heard, neither hath it entered into the heart of man."[3] And if we *have good things in possession*, much more have we in reversion "an inheritance undefiled, unfading," of which none can spoil us.[4] "Who shall separate us from our Father's love? Neither life, nor death; neither earth, nor hell."[5]

11. *The rich man is wise in his own conceit; but the poor that hath understanding searcheth him out.*

To be truly wise, and *wise in our own conceit*, are two things often confounded, but essentially opposite. Riches do not always bring *wisdom*;[6] though *the rich man* often pretends to wisdom, and ascribes his success to his own sagacity. Obviously he has many advantages above *the poor* in leisure and opportunities of instruction. Yet on the other hand, worldly elevation operates unfavorably. He is shut out from many opportunities of Christian instruction. The atmosphere of flattery clouds that faculty of self-knowledge, which is the basis of true wisdom. And how natural is it to think himself as wise, as his flatterers represent him; as much above his neighbors in understanding, as in station! Hence he becomes dogmatical in over-weening *conceit*; fond every way of displaying his fancied superiority. Yet, as in the case of Naaman's servants,[7] the intelligent good *understanding of a poor man may search him out*, and see through this false gloss. Specially, when endued with a measure of spiritual *understanding, the poor man* may expose his superior to just mortification.[8] Indeed the universe possesses not a more dignified character than *the poor wise man.* Did not the Lord incarnate honor this station supremely, by taking it on himself?[9] To walk in his footsteps—in his spirit—is wisdom, honor, and happiness, infinitely beyond what this poor world of vanity can afford.

12. *When righteous men do rejoice, there is great glory: but when the wicked rise, a man is hidden.*

"We are made"—said *a righteous man* "as the filth of the earth, and are the offscouring of all things unto this day."[10] Yet these are the men who "bear up the pillars of the state."[11] *When therefore they rejoice*—when they are raised to honor—*there is great glory.*[12] The whole kingdom feels more or less the influence of this national blessing. Godliness is countenanced. Men are

1 Ps. xxiii. 5. 2 Ib. ver. 3. Luke xxii. 31, 32. 3 1 Cor. ii. 9.
4 1 Pet. i. 4. 5 Rom. viii. 35, 38, 39. 6 Job. xxxii. 9.
7 2 Kings v. 13. 8 John ix. 30—34. 9 2 Cor. viii. 9. Phil. ii. 7.
10 1 Cor iv. 13. 11 Ps. lxxv. 3. 12 Chap. xi. 10, 11; xxix. 2.

protected in the free exercise of their religion. "When Mordecai went out from the presence in the king's royal apparel, the city of Shushan rejoiced, and were glad. "The Jews had light, and gladness, and joy, and honor; in every province a feast, and a good day."[1] The same result is seen in the experience of the Church. When the Churches had rest "from the fiery trial," they were edified, and walked in the fear of the Lord, and in the comfort of the Holy Ghost."[2] And what *glory so great*, as this sunshine of the enjoyment of their God!

But when the wicked rise to honor, how is this *glory* eclipsed! The people of God are "drawn into corners," silenced, *hidden*.[3] The light of upwards of an hundred prophets, and even of Elijah himself, was *hidden* for a while under the tyranny of Ahab.[4] And in every age the power of *the wicked*, especially under a despotic rule, *hides* much valuable influence. Yet it *is hidden* only to the eye of sense. For of those who "wander about in sheep-skins and goat skins, in deserts, and caves of the earth"—what greater *glory* could we give than their Divine inscription—"Of whom the world was not worthy!"[5]

13. *He that covereth his sins shall not prosper: but whoso confesseth and forsaketh them shall have mercy.*

God and man each *cover sin;* God, in free unbounded grace;[6] man, in shame and hypocrisy. The sinners here contrasted are chargeable with the same guilt. But how opposite are the remedies adopted, and their several results! The contrast is not between great sins and small, but between *sins covered*, and *sins confessed and forsaken*. *Who covereth* the smallest *sin*, *shall not prosper*. Who *confesseth and forsaketh* the greatest, *shall find mercy*. "Love *covereth*" our neighbor's sins;[7] pride our own. The proud sinner naturally wishes to be thought better than he is. His sin must have some cover.[8] He must at least give it a good name.[9] He would *cover* it, if possible, from himself; putting it out of mind; banishing all serious thoughts; stifling conviction; and then trying to persuade himself that he is happy. To escape evil consequences, a lie is resorted to.[10] Or if the facts are too plain to be denied; 'the worst part is unfounded. We were not in it so much as our neighbor.' Ignorance; good, or at least not bad, intentions; custom; necessity; strong temptation; sudden surprisal; the first offence; constitutional infirmity; even the decrees of God,[11] one or

[1] Esth. viii. 15—17. [2] Acts ix. 31. [3] Verse 28.
[4] 1 Kings xvii. 2, 3; xviii. 4; xix. 1—6. [5] Heb. xi. 37, 38. Comp. Rev. xii. 6.
[6] Isa. xliii. 25; xliv. 22. [7] Chap. x. 12.
[8] Cicero stamps *confession* of wickedness as disgraceful and dangerous (turpis et periculos.a Contr. Verrem. Lib. iii.) Thus does Heathen morality develope the pride of native depravity. [9] Isa. v. 20.
[10] Cain, Gen. iv. 9; Rachel, xxxi. 34, 35; Joseph's brethren, xxxvii. 31—35; David, 2 Sam. xi. 15, 25: the adulteress, chap. xxx. 20. Comp. Jer. ii. 23; Peter, Matt. xxvi. 69; Ananias and Sapphira, Acts v. 1—8. Is not this a saddening propensity in children? The first offence may be trifling. But the fear of punishment induces a lie. Another lie is necessary to *cover* the first. Every step adds to sin.
[11] Jer. vii. 10. Comp. Calv. Instit. B. iii. c. xxiii. § 12—14.

more are pleaded in palliation. Or to save our honor—rather our pride—the blame must be shifted on another;[1] it may be even upon God himself[2]—more commonly—on the devil.[3] Or some compensation is a *cover*, paying for sin by some supposed good deeds;[4] as if, by balancing good and evil respectively against each other, some preponderance in our favor might be brought out. But all these fig-leaf *coverings*[5] for man's nakedness only show his determination to hold his sin, and his pride of heart, which would rather hide it from God himself, than submit to receive free mercy as a self-condemned sinner.

These attempts, however, to *cover sin shall not prosper.* The voice of an offended God summoned Adam from his hiding-place to receive his sentence.[6] "The voice of Abel's blood cried from the ground;" and the murderer became "a fugitive and a vagabond in the earth."[7] Conscience lashed Joseph's brethren with the sin of bye-gone days.[8] Saul's *covering his sin* cost him his kingdom.[9] "The leprosy of Naaman clave to Gehazi and his seed for ever."[10] The proud accusers of their fellow-sinner were "convicted by their own conscience.[11] "There is no darkness, nor shadow of death, where the workers of iniquity may hide themselves."[12] Their darkest deed is wrought in the open face of an all-seeing God, and "set in the light of his countenance,"[13] to "be proclaimed upon the house-tops" before the assembled world.[14]

This unsuccessful attempt to *cover sin*, while it adds to the guilt,[15] is fraught with misery.[16] The love of sin struggles with the power of conscience. The door of access to God is barred.[17] Christian confidence is clouded;[18] and, unless Sovereign mercy interpose, it must end in the sting of "the never-dying worm." The *covering* of the disease precludes the possibility of the cure. Only the penitent confessor can be the pardoned sinner.

Long indeed is the struggle, ere every false *cover* is cut off; ere the heartless general confession—'We are all sinners,'—is exchanged for the deep-felt personal acknowledgment, "giving glory to God. Thus and thus have I done. Behold! I am vile, What shall I answer thee? I will lay mine hand upon my mouth."[19] But glorious is the Divine victory over pride and sullenness, when this first act of repentance—this first step of return[20] is heartily accomplished. God needs not confession for his own information. But he demands it for our good. It brings no claim on his mercy. But it is a meetness for the reception of it. Christ has fully satisfied the claims of justice. But the claims must be acknowledged

1 Adam and Eve, Gen. iii. 12, 13. Comp. Job xxxi. 33; Aaron, Ex. xxxii. 21—24; Saul, 1 Sam. xv. 20, 21; Pilate, Matt. xxvii. 24—26.
2 Gen. iii. 12, ut supra. Comp. Jam. i. 13, 14.
3 Gen. iii. 13.
4 Mic. vi. 6, 7. Luke xx. 47.
5 Gen. iii. 7.
6 Ib. verses 9—11.
7 Ib. iv. 10—12.
8 Ib. xlii. 21.
9 1 Sam. xv. 21—23.
10 2 Kings v. 27.
11 John viii. 9.
12 Job xxxiv. 22, with xxiv. 14, 15.
13 Ib. xxxiv. 21. Ps. xi. 8.
14 Luke xii. 2, 3. Comp. Eccl. xii. 14. 1 Cor. iv. 5.
15 Isa. xxx. 1.
16 Ib. xxviii. 20.
17 Ps. lxvi. 17.
18 Ib. xxxii. 3, 4.
19 Jos. vii. 19, 20. Job xl. 4. Comp. Jer. viii. 6.
20 Luke xv. 17, 18.

in the humble acceptance of the benefit. The mercy is ready; but the sinner must sue it out—"Only acknowledge thine iniquity."[1] Our yearning Father is "waiting" for this moment, "that he may be gracious."[2] There is no further keeping of anger—*he shall have mercy*—instant reconciliation.[3] Words may be few, while the heart is full. With David it was but a single sentence; but the closest workings of his heart witnessed to the enlargement and ingenuousness of his sorrow.[4] Thus man *confesses* the debt; God crosses it out from his book; and sweet is the penitent's song—"Blessed is he, whose *sin is covered*."[5]

But we must not overlook the distinctive feature of this *confession*. It is not that of Pharaoh, extorted on the rack;[6] or of Saul and Judas,[7] the stinging of remorse; or of the Pharisees and Sadducees,[8] mere formal profession; or of the harlots,[9] a cover for sin. Penitent faith *confesses* in the act of laying the hand upon the great sacrifice;[10] and hence draws strength of purpose to *forsake* all, that has been here *confessed*. For while the hypocrite *confesses* without *forsaking*,[11] the hearty *forsaking* is here the best proof of the sincere *confessing*.

And this first act of the penitent is matured into the daily habit of the saint. The further we advance, the deeper will be the tone of *confession*.[12] The moment sin is seen to be sin, let it be laid on the Surety's Head. Every moment of unconfessed sin adds to its burden and guilt. The thought of a nature estranged from God; a heart full of corruption; sins of youth and age; before and after conversion; against light and conviction, knowledge and love; the sins of our very confessions—their defilement, coldness, and too often self-righteous tendency—all supplies abundant material for abasing acknowledgment. Plead the greatness—not the smallness—of our sin.[13] Never deem any sin so trifling, as not to need the *immediate* application of the blood of atonement. Genuine conviction will give us no rest, until by the believing apprehension of this remedy the peace of God is firmly fixed in the conscience. As Bunyan so accurately pictured—not at the wicket-gate, but at the sight of the cross—did the Christian find the grave of sin.

This evangelical humiliation lays the only solid ground for practical godliness. It is a sorrow full of joy, and not less full of holiness. No Achan will be reserved;[14] no Agag spared;[15] no right hand or right eye favored.[16] It will not be "the unclean spirit going

[1] Jer. iii. 12, 13. [2] Luke xv. 20. Isa. xxx. 18, with Hos. v. 15.

[3] Ps. xxxii. 5. Comp. similar examples, 2 Chron. xxxiii. 12, 13; Jer. xxxi. 18—20; Jon. iii. 5—10; Luke xv. 21—24; xxiii. 40—43. See also the promises, Lev. xxvi. 40—42; 2 Chron. vii. 14; Job xxxiii. 27, 28; Isa. i. 16—18; lv. 7; Ez. xviii. 21, 22; 1 John i. 9.

[4] 2 Sam. xii. 13, with Ps. li. See also his tender dread of *covering sin*. Ps. cxxxix. 1, 23, 24.

[5] Ps. xxxii. 1. [6] Ex. ix. 27, 34.

[7] 1 Sam. xxiv. 16, 17; xxvi. 3, 4. Matt. xxvii. 4, 5. [8] Matt. iii. 6—9.

[9] Chap. vii. 14. [10] Lev. xvi. 21. [11] Pharaoh and Saul, ut supra.

[12] Job xl. 4; xlii. 6. Ez. xvi. 63.

[13] Ps. xxv. 11, with Luke xviii. 11. Comp. Isa. xliii. 24—26. [14] Jos. vii. 1.

[15] 1 Sam. xv. 20. [16] Mark vi. 17—20; ix. 43—48.

out, and returning to his house with sevenfold influence;"[1] or the man who leaves his home, but *forsakes* it not—all his heart and joy being still there. Here the *forsaking* will be without the thought of returning; yea, with the fixed determination never to return.[2] It will not be the exchange of one path in the broad road for another more attractive; but the relinquishment of the whole road with all its bye-paths. The inner principles as well as the outer walk—"the unrighteous thoughts," no less than "the wicked ways" will he *forsake*[3] heartily and for ever.

14. *Happy is the man that feareth alway: but he that hardeneth his heart shall fall into mischief.*

This Proverb fitly follows the last. *Confession* precedes, godly *fear* follows, the reception of mercy, as the end for which it is given,[4] and the proof of its reception. It implies no uncertainty of our safety; but, by guarding us against fresh wounds of conscience, it more firmly maintains our confidence. We may believe and rejoice in the Lord as "our Sun;" and yet we would *fear him alway* as "a consuming fire."[5] And this fear is our security.[6]

We may here profitably glance at some Christian paradoxes. *How is happiness to be found in constant fear?* Is fear to be the atmosphere or the spirit of a child of God? The "fear which hath torment is cast out by love." For where "love makes perfect," there can be no unquiet rollings or doubtings of heart.[7] But godly fear preserves the sunshine, and seals our special acceptance.[8] We walk with our Father in holy watchfulness and peace. Again —*We readily receive of the happiness of trust.*[9] How do we link with it *the happiness of fear?* So far from being contrary to faith, it is a component part of it, or at least its inseparable adjunct;[10] the discipline, that preserves it from presumption. Faith without fear is self-confidence and self-delusion. Nay—the assurance of our "standing by faith" is balanced by an instant and most needful exercise of *fear.*[11] Who grasped a more triumphant confidence than Paul? Yet, without presuming upon a long and consistent profession, self-distrust, watchfulness and diligence established his confidence.[12] 'If there is truth in his assurance, not sin itself can disappoint him, it is true. But it is no less true, that if he do not fear to sin, there is no truth in his assurance.'[13] Instead of being afraid to mix faith and fear, dread their separation. Again—the righteous is bold as a lion;[14] yet *he feareth alway.* But Christian courage, though opposed to slavish, forms the very essence of godly, *fear.* The three confessors, bold before the Babylonish autocrat,

[1] Matt. xii. 43, 44. [2] Job xxxiv. 32. [3] Isa. lv. 7. [4] Ps. cxxx. 4.
[5] Ib. lxxxiv. 11, with Heb. xii. 28, 29. [6] Hab. iii. 16. [7] 1 John iv. 18.
[8] Isa. lxvi. 2. [9] Chap. xvi. 20. [10] Heb. xi. 7.
[11] Rom. xi. 20. [12] Ib. viii. 33—39, with 1 Cor. x. 27.
[13] Leighton on 1 Pet. i. 17. The Romanists—and how many Roman Protestants with them!—have no other idea of fear, than as excluding the certainty of acceptance; whereas its true influence is not fluctuation in doubt, but carefulness in preservation.
[14] Ver. 1.

yet so *feared* to offend against God, that "the burning fiery furnace" was the better alternative in their eyes.[1]

Thus is holy *fear* every way identified with happiness. It is a fear of reverence, not of bondage; of caution, not of distrust; of diligence, not of despondency. In proportion as we are raised above tormenting fear, we cherish a deep reverence of the majesty and holiness of God, a child-like fear of displeasure, a jealousy over our motives, desires, and the risings of our evil propensities, and an abhorrence and shrinking, not only from sin, but from the temptations and occasions of sin. Well does the Christian know the value of this conservative principle—as far removed from legality, as from presumption. One, whose mournful experience gives additional weight to his words, warns us, as "sojourners" in a world of evil, and with hearts so often betraying our steps, to "pass our time *in fear*."[2] If we be surely, we are "scarcely, saved."[3] Though there be no uncertainty in the end, there is appalling difficulty in the way—"Let him that thinketh he standeth, take heed lest he fall."[4] The man who stands in his own security, requires the caution more than any. Suspect a snake in every path—a snare in every creature. "Feed with fear."[5] "Rejoice with trembling." Yea, "work out your whole salvation with fear and trembling."[6] Live in constant dread of yourself.

This godly *fear* proves self-knowledge, preserves from self-confidence, produces self-distrust. In wariness against a fall we are most likely to stand. If weakness be our frailty, the consciousness of it is our strength. "When I am weak, then am I strong."[7]

The importance of this principle will be seen by the contrast with its opposite. *Fear* keeps the heart tender, and the soul safe. Security and presumption *harden* the sinner, and *he falls into mischief.* Pharaoh's *hardness of heart* and its consequence, were but the bravery and ruin of the devil.[8] When David's self-indulgence and carelessness had swept away his tenderness, fearfully did he *fall into mischief.*[9] The latter history of his wise son reads the same awful warning.[10] Peter's fearlessness—though the fruit of ignorance, rather than of wilfulness—brought him to the very brink of destruction.[11]

A deep sensibility of sin is a special mercy. To think what it is —what it may be—that—indulged only in thought—if the Lord restrain not it will end in apostacy—Oh! dare we trifle with it? The man, who presumes upon it, as too harmless for eternal punishment, and promises himself peace in the way of his own heart—a voice from heaven could scarcely describe the tremendous horrors of his case! Every word of God is a thunderbolt levelled at him.[12] Scarcely less pitiable is the man, who makes light of his eternal state; living without prayer; so much better in his own eyes than

[1] Dan. iii. 16—18. Comp. vi. 10. Gen. xxxix. 9. Neh. v. 15.
[2] 1 Pet. i. 17. [3] Ib. iv. 18. [4] Cor. x. 12.
[5] Contrast Jude 12. [6] Ps. ii. 11. Phil. ii. 12. [7] 2 Cor. xii. 9, 10.
[8] Ex. xiv. 5—8, 23. [9] 2 Sam. xi. 2. [10] 1 Kings xi. 1—11.
[11] Matt. xxvi. 33—35, 41, 74. [12] Chap. xxix. 1. Deut. xxix. 19, 20.

his more ungodly neighbors; and fully satisfied with a mere external preparation for eternity. Forget not—Christian Professor—we may be strong in confidence, only because we are sleeping in delusion, or *hardened* in insensibility. 'From' all the *mischief* of self-ignorance and 'hardness of heart, Good Lord, deliver us!'[1]

15. *As a roaring lion, and a ranging bear; so is a wicked ruler over the poor people.* 16. *The prince that wanteth understanding is also a great oppressor; but he that hateth covetousness shall prolong his days.*

A godly ruler is to a land the clear sunshine of an unclouded morning; the fruitfulness of the springing grass after the rain.[2] But such a curse is *a wicked ruler*, that we might as well live among the savage wild beasts of the forest. *The lion roaring* for the prey, and *the bear ranging*[3] in hunger—the terror of their weaker race—are apt emblems of this tyrant *over the poor people.*[4] 'No sentiment of pity softens his bosom. No principle of justice regulates his conduct; complaint only provokes further exactions. Resistance kindles his unfeeling heart into savage fury. *Poor* and miserable indeed are *the people*, whom Divine anger has placed under his misrule.'[5]

His oppression shows *a want of understanding.*[6] His foolish choice of wicked ministers alienates the affections of the people, probably to the shortening of his rule.[7] A considerate ruler—*hating covetousness*,[8] and living only for the good of his people—*shall* usually *prolong his days.* 'He may hope to reign long and happily, having his throne erected in the hearts of his subjects.'[9]

What need then have *rulers* to seek for *understanding*, that they may rule as the fathers of their people![10] And what cause have we to bless God for our mild and happy government, preserved as we are from *wicked* despots,[11] who would not stop at any tyranny that would subserve their selfish purposes![12]

17. *A man that doeth violence to the blood of any person shall flee to the pit; let no man stay him.*

The first law against the murderer must not be broken down. Like the law of the Sabbath—though confirmed by the Levitical code—it was in force from the beginning. The reason given for it

[1] Litany. [2] 2 Sam. xxiii. 3. 4.

[3] The name seems to be given from his growling noise when hungry.
'Nec vespertinus *circumgemit* ursus ovili.'
Hor. Epod. xvi. 51.

[4] Chap. xxix. 2. Ez. xix. 2. Zeph. iii. 3. 2 Tim. iv. 17.

[5] Paxton's Nat. Hist. of Script. p. 333. Comp. 1 Kings xxi. 1—7. Neh. v. 15. Eccl. iv. 1. Amos iv. 1. Mic. iii. 1—3.

[6] Isa. iii. 12. [7] 1 Kings xii. 12—19. [8] Ex. xviii. 21.

[9] Scott. [10] 1 Kings iii. 6—9. [11] 1 Sam. xxii. 17—19. Dan. iii. 6, 19.

[12] Of Tyndal's celebrated work—'The obedience of a Christian Man'—Henry VIII. declared—'This book is for me, and for all kings to read.' He probably only adverted to those parts, that he might turn to accredit his own selfish rapacity. Well would it have been, had he pondered such important instruction as—'The king is but a servant to execute the law of God, and not to rule after his own imagination.' He is brought to the throne—'to minister unto, and to serve his brethren, and must not think that his subjects were made to minister unto his lusts.'

proves its universal obligation.[1] It is therefore miscalled philanthropy, that protests against *all* capital punishments. Shall man pretend to be more pitiful than God? Pity is misplaced here.[2] The heathen judged this awful transgressor to be under the Divine vengeance.[3] God himself deemed the land to be defiled by this guilt.[4] The murderer therefore of his brother is his own murderer. *He shall flee to the pit*, hurried thither by his own horror of conscience,[5] by the sword of justice,[6] or by the certain judgment of God.[7] *Let no man stay him.* Let God's Law take its course.

Yet we must not cast off his soul. Visiting the condemned cell is a special exercise of mercy. While we bow to the stern justice of the great law-giver; joyous indeed it is to bring to the sinner under the sentence of the law, the free forgiveness of the Gospel; not as annulling his sin, but showing the over-abounding of grace beyond the abounding of sin.[8]

18. *Whoso walketh uprightly shall be saved: but he that is perverse in his ways shall fall at once.*

This contrast has been lately drawn.[9] Indeed the Proverb itself in substance has been already given. The "security of the upright," before marked, is here included in his *salvation.* The hypocrite's "known" ruin[10] is here set out as complete—*at once.*[11]

This *upright walk* is Christian perfection—"walking before God."[12] There is no need for Jacob's vision[13] to realize his presence. "Faith seeth him that is invisible."[14] This life may seem to miss much temporal advantage. But what--if the *upright* be not rich, honorable, esteemed? He is *saved.* This one blessing includes all. It is the substance of time and of eternity. All besides is shadow and vanity. To dwell in the presence of God;[15] in the sunshine of his countenance;[16] in the light and gladness of his joy;[17] and at length in his unclouded glory[18]—such is the hope—the *salvation of the upright.*[19] Christian! would you part with this portion—this hope—for kingdoms? What earthly comforts can be a substitute for it? This supplies the place of all. Any want of *uprightness* will bring the child of God under the rod. *But he that is perverse in his way will fall at once.* None of his many shifts shall prosper.[20] His double ways, his vain attempt to "serve two masters,"[21] only bring him to shame—What need have I, in the highest walk of conscious integrity, still to cry—"Redeem me, and be merciful unto me."[22]

19. *He that tilleth his land shall have plenty of bread: but he that followeth after vain persons shall have poverty enough.*

[1] Gen. ix. 6. [2] Deut. xix. 11—13. Comp. Num. xxxv. 31.
[3] Acts xxviii. 4. [4] Num. xxxv. 30—34. [5] Matt. xxvii. 4, 5.
[6] 1 Kings ii. 28—34, with Ex. xxi. 14. 2 Kings xi. 1—16; xv. 10—30.
[7] 1 Kings xxi. 19; xxii. 38. 2 Kings xi. 33—37. [8] Rom. v. 20.
[9] Verse 6. [10] Chap. x. 7. [11] Chap. xxiv. 16; xxix. i. Nah. i. 9.
[12] Gen. xvii. 1. [13] Ib. xxviii. 17. [14] Heb. xi. 1, 27.
[15] Ps. cxl. 13. [16] Ib. xi. 7. [17] Ib. xcvii. 11.
[18] Ib. xv. 1, 2. Rev. xiv. 5. [19] Ib. cxxv. 4. [20] Ib. ver. 5.
[21] Matt. vi. 24. [22] Ps. xxvi. 11.

This Proverb also has been given before.[1] Such memories and hearts as ours need "line upon line"[2] in the enforcement of practical obligation. If labor be a penal ordinance,[3] such a blessing is included in it, that its removal would diminish our most substantial source of happiness. Man was not born to be a stone, without energy; or a machine, to be moved by mere passive force. Our true happiness is active dependence. Habits of diligence are the means of working it out fruitfully. The earth "bringeth forth of itself only thorns and thistles." But *he that tilleth his land shall have plenty of bread.*[4] The blessing comes—not by miracle, to encourage sloth; but in the use of means, to stimulate exertion.

The contrast to this *plenty of bread* is *poverty enough.* The prodigal is a warning beacon. "In his father's house"—doubtless engaged in active exercise—"there was bread enough, and to spare." When in his waywardness he left his *plenty,* and *followed after vain persons*—soon he found *poverty enough*—"I perish with hunger."[5] Idleness is a sin against God, against our neighbor, against ourselves. "Not slothful in business; fervent in spirit; serving the Lord"[6]—is the rule of prosperity in this world's concerns; much more in the momentous concerns of eternity.

20. *A faithful man shall abound with blessings: but he that maketh haste to be rich shall not be innocent* (unpunished, Marg.)

The study of the contrast shows the definite meaning of the terms. *A faithful man* is opposed—not to the rich, but—mark the careful accuracy—to him *that hasteth to be rich.* A man may be rich by the blessing of God.[7] He *hasteth* to be *rich* by his own covetousness.[8] He may be rich, and yet *faithful. He hasteth to be rich* at the expense of *faithfulness.*[9] The *faithful man* makes no loud profession. But he bears to be looked at, even in the veriest trifles.[10] He is true to his word. He fulfils his engagements. He has only one principle—"unto the Lord;" under his eye; in his presence; "to his glory."[11] Try his principle by a worldly bait. He will prefer his conscience to his interest.[12] He would rather be poor by Providence, than rich by sin. This is the man of faithfulness. "Who shall find him."[13] But when you have found him, mark his *abounding blessings;* blessings covering his head;[14] blessings for both worlds.[15] Is there not infinitely more promise in

[1] Chap. xii. 11. [2] Isa. xxviii. 13. [3] Gen. iii. 19.
[4] Ib. ver. 18, with chap. xiv. 4; xxvii. 23—27.
[5] Luke xv. 13—17. Comp. chap. xxiii. 20, 21.
[6] Rom. xii. 11. Comp. Eccl. ix. 10.
[7] Chap. x. 22. Gen. xxiv. 35. 1 Kings iii. 13. [8] 1 Tim. vi. 10.
[9] Verse 22. Chap. xix. 2; xx. 14. Even the Heathen moralists could see this—

'Ουδεις επλύπησε ταχεως δικαιος ων.'

Menander.

. . . . . . 'Nam dives qui fieri vult,
Et cito vult fieri; sed quæ reverentia legum?
Quis metus aut pudor est unquam *properantis avari?*'

Juv. Sat. 14. 176—178.

[10] Luke xvi. 10. [11] Col. iii. 23. 1 Cor. x. 31. [12] Gen. xxxix 9
[13] Heb. Chap. xx. 6. Comp. Matt. xxiv. 45. [14] Chap. x. 6.
[15] Ps. xxxvii. 37; cxii. Isa. xxxiii. 15, 16.

the ways of God, than in the ways of sin? Be the path ever so tried and perplexed, only let it be a strait path,[1] and sunshine will cheer it. But the man who has no faith, can only walk in a crooked path. He leaps over every bound of principle. *He hasteth to be rich.* He cannot wait for God in the path of Christian diligence. The promise does not run fast enough for him. He becomes rich too soon; he scarcely knows or cares by what means; by any means, rather than lose his grasp. Yet all this *haste* is only to his own ruin. Instead of *abounding with blessings, he shall not be innocent.* Jacob, as *a faithful man*, was paid with full wages for his work. Though his master dealt hardly, God dealt bountifully, with him. He *abounded with blessings;* while Laban, *hasting to be rich*, was impoverished.[2] Hard indeed—if not impossible—is it to hold fast *innocency* in such a path of temptation.[3] Even if no criminal means be resorted to, yet the immoderate desire—the perseverance in every track of Mammon—the laboring night and day for the grand object—the delight in the acquisition[4]—all proves the idolatrous heart,[5] and will not go *unpunished.* "They that will be rich—*that haste to be rich*—fall into temptation and a snare, and into many foolish and hurtful lusts, that drown men in destruction and perdition. But thou, O man of God, flee these things."[6]

21. *To have respect of persons is not good: for, for a piece of bread that man will transgress.*

This Proverb has been more than once repeated.[7] The act itself *is not good.* It is positive *transgression.* The principle is worse —sordid selfishness. He is here *a man*—not of slavish or naturally degraded mind—but—such is the debasing influence of lust!—*a man* of weight and influence;[8] and yet abusing his power for his own ends. It is a rich man, or a relation, or he is under some obligation, and therefore he *has respect of judgment.* Now what is right to the rich, is right to the poor. Thus to trample the poor under foot, the Judge of All counts rebellion against his own just standard.[9] Principle once overpowered seldom regains its ascendancy. Each successive trial proves its weakness; till he who once thought himself able to resist a large bribe, for the veriest trifle will break with God and his conscience. *For a piece of bread that man will transgress.*[10]

Is not this, alas! a pulpit sin? Is the minister never drawn away from godly simplicity by some interested motive?—*to transgress* his broadly-marked obligation *for a piece of bread?* In

[1] Chap. iv. 26, 27. Heb. xii. 13. [2] Gen. xxxi. 7—9.
[3] 2 Kings v. 25—27. Comp. chap. xx. 21; xxi. 6.
[4] Job. xxxi. 25. [5] Ib. ver. 24, 28. Col. iii. 5. [6] 1 Tim. vi. 9—11.
[7] Chap. xviii. 5; xxiv. 23, and references. Comp. Jam. ii. 1—4.
[8] The root of the word (*a man*) is wisdom and strength. Chap. xxiv. 5.
[9] *Transgression* in this place is the same word as rebellion. Isa. i. 2. See also 1 Kings xii. 19. 2 Kings i. 1; iii. 5.
[10] Am. ii. 6. Cato used to say of M. Cœlius the Tribune, that 'he might be hired *for a piece of bread* to speak, or to hold his peace.'

olden times this was a besetting temptation of the sacred office. Let the beacon be solemnly regarded.

In ordinary life, a man's bread hanging upon favor, is a strong temptation to *transgress* upright principles. Cowardice and unbelief shelter themselves under the cover of prudence. Christian reproof is neglected from fear of losing custom or advantage. Our interest is preferred to God's. And a plain scriptural obligation[2] is put away *for a piece of bread.* Are Christians wholly guiltless in this matter? Is not conduct sometimes ruled by the fear of man, rather than by "trust in God?"[3] Let the temptation be resisted at the first step—manfully—prayerfully—in the Lord's strength, and the victory is gained.

22. *He that hasteth to be rich hath an evil eye* (He that hath an evil eye hasteth to be rich, Marg.) *and considereth not that poverty shall come upon him.*

Another warning word—"Take heed, and beware of covetousness."[4] "The lust of the eye"[5] is a deadly blast upon the soul. Abraham was rich without *haste*, with God's blessing.[6] Little did Lot *consider*, that his *haste to be rich* was the high road to *poverty.* But, step by step, he "entered into temptation."[7] Every worldly prospect was blasted; and he ends his days, a poor, forlorn, degraded tenant of the desolate cave of Zoar.[8] Thus he who sought the world, lost it; he who was ready to lose it, found it. When Ahab's *evil eye* envied Naboth the enjoyment of his vineyard; when Jehoiakim was grasping by unjust means all that came into his reach; little did they *consider*, how this *haste to be rich* would end in disgrace.[9] But many and loud are the warnings against covetousness, ending in shame, and filled with the curse of an avenging God.[10]

Man of God! Remember—Not he who knows but who loves, most the things of heaven, will be most deadened to the riches of earth. The *evil eye* fixed on earth, can never look above. So much as thou lovest earth, thou losest of heaven. Is it not thy shame, that if heaven be thy possession, thou shouldst have so much interest there, and yet so few thoughts, so little love? Keep down most carefully thine anxiety to rise in the world. For in its highest glory there is nothing worthy of thine heart. Keep the things of earth as thy outer garment, which thou canst "lay aside," when it entangles thee in the heavenly race.[11] But keep heaven next to thine heart—thy treasure—thy love—thy rest—thy crown. Happy to be of the mind of the holy Bishop, who, when he heard of the ruin of all his property by the inroads of the Goths—looked up—'Thou knowest where my treasure has long been.'[12]

23. *He that rebuketh a man, afterwards shall find more favor, than he that flattereth with the tongue.*

Too often *the flatterer* finds *more favor* than the reprover.[13]

[1] Ez. xiii. 18, 19. Hos. iv. 18. Mic. iii. 5. 2 Pet. ii. 3. [2] Lev. xix. 17.
[3] Chap. xxix. 25. [4] Luke xii. 15. [5] 1 John ii. 16.
[6] Gen. xiii. 2. [7] Ib. ver. 10—13; xiv. 12. [8] Gen. xix. 30.
[9] 1 Kings xxi. 2, 18, 19. Jer. xxii. 13—19.
[10] Chap. xxiii. 5, with Job xx. 18—22; xxvii. 16, 17. Jer. xvii. 11. Luke xii. 19, 20.
[11] Heb. xii. 1. [12] Paulinus, Bishop of Nola in the fifth century.
[13] 1 Kings xxi. 6—8, 27. Jer. xxvi. 7, 8.

Few people have the wisdom to like reproofs that would do them good, better than praises that do them hurt.'[1] And yet a candid man, notwithstanding the momentary struggle of wounded pride, will *afterwards* appreciate the purity of the motive, and the value of the discovery. 'He that cries out against his surgeon for hurting him, when he is searching his wound, will yet pay him well, and thank him too, when he has cured it.'[2]

Unbelief, however, palsies Christian *rebuke.* Actual displeasure, or the chilling of friendship, is intolerable. But Paul's public *rebuke* of his brother apostle produced no disruption between them. Many years *afterward* Peter memorialized his "beloved brother Paul" with most affectionate regard.[3] The Apostle's painful *rebuke* of his Corinthian converts eventually increased his *favor* with them, as the friend of their best interests.[4] *The flatterer* is viewed with disgust;[5] the reprover—*afterwards* at least—with acceptance.[6] A less favorable result may often be traced to an unseasonable time,[7] a harsh manner, a neglect of prayer for needful wisdom, or a want of due "consideration" of our own liability to fall.[8] Let us study the spirit of our gracious Master, whose gentleness ever poured balm into the wound, which his faithful love had opened. Such a spirit is more like the support of a friend, than the chastening of a rod.

24. *Whoso robbeth his father or his mother, and saith, It is no transgression; the same is the companion of a destroyer.*

The aggravation of sin is proportioned to the obligation of duty. A murderer is a heinous *transgressor;* how much more a parricide. *To rob* a stranger, a neighbor, a friend is evil; how much more *a father and mother.* The filial obligation of cherishing care is broken. Ingratitude is added to injustice. What length of wickedness will such an hardened sinner stop at! Could we wonder to see him *the companion of a destroyer?* This sin is however often committed without sensibility;[9] as if the children might dispose of their parents' property at their own will. These *robbers* would ill brook the name of thieves. But God, who sees men as they are, and judges of them in sure balances, ranks them among the wicked, "and will deal with them accordingly."[10]

Nor is this guilt confined to the grosser outrage. Surely it is no better, when the young spendthrift wastes *his father's* property,

[1] Dr. South. See his Life. [2] Henry. [3] Gal. ii. 11—14, with 2 Pet. iii. 15.
[4] 1 Cor. v. with 2 Cor. ii. 1—10. [5] Chap. xxvii. 14.
[6] Chap. ix. 8; xxvii. 5, 6. Ps. cxli. 5. Ecclus. vii. 5. Alas! that the example of godly Asa should present an exception to the rule! 2 Chron. xvi. 7—10. When Bernard Gilpin publicly *rebuked* church abuses before his diocesan; instead of incurring his displeasure, the Bishop treated him with marked *favor.* 'Father Gilpin'—said he—'I acknowledge you are fitter to be Bishop of Durham, than I am to be the parson of your church.' Life by Bp. Carleton, p. 58. When the philosopher asked Alexander the reason of his dismissal—'Either'—replied the monarch—'thou hast not marked my errors, which is a proof of thy ignorance; or thou hast held thy peace, which is a proof of thy unfaithfulness.' Plutarch's Life.
[7] Chap. xv. 23. [8] Gal. vi. 1. [9] Gen. xxxi. 19, 34, 35. Jud. xvii. 2.
[10] Chap. xxi. 7.

and counts it *no transgression* to incur debts on his account without his knowledge or consent.[1] Our Lord adverts to another species of *robbery*—the denial of the absolute duty of providing for parents; and this under the pretence of devotedness to God![2] But the gospel admits of no compounding of one duty for another.[3] The upright Christian will place all duties upon the same ground of Christian obedience.[4]

Young people! As you value your soul, your conscience, your happiness—ponder the wide extent of filial obligation; the honor, deference, and consideration included in it; the clear stamp of God's authority upon it; the mark of his reprobation in despising it;[5] the certain seal of his blessing upon its practical and self-denying acknowledgment.

25. *He that is of a proud heart stirreth up strife: but he that putteth his trust in the Lord shall be made fat.*

The contrast between *the proud, and him that trusteth in the Lord* is very remarkable. It shows that pride is the root of unbelief. The man, having cast off God, expects nothing—fears nothing, from him. He lives as if there was no God. His proud heart is *large;* not like the wise man's, in fulness of capacity,[6] but in ambitious grasp, and insatiable appetite.[7] Never is he content within his own bounds. In the world he would be a Haman;[8] in the church a Diotrephes—one "loving to have the pre-eminence."[9] It is his nature *to stir up strife.* Every one that does not accord with his own opinion of himself, is supposed to be wanting in respect. Thus "by pride cometh contention."[10] And always will there be some thorn of mortified ambition,[11] or some fresh craving of unsatisfied desire,[12] wasting him, so that he "fadeth away in his ways."[13] What an empty shadow of fugitive happiness! So contrary to the *fatness* of *him, that putteth his trust in the Lord!*[14] 'He shall be filled with good and solid things.'[15]

Christian! Dread the occasion of *stirring up strife*—the canker of vital godliness. Keep near to thy Lord. It was, when the disciples were talking together by the way, *instead of walking* in *immediate communion with their* Master, that *strife was stirred up.*[16] Does not this point to the grand preservative? Let secret prayer be thine element and thy joy. Here alone we cherish the life of faith. And truly—as Luther says—'Faith is a precious thing.'[17] It rolls away all disquieting care.[18] Our cause is with him, and we are at rest.[19] How much more, when the great burden is removed! 'Smite, Lord, smite; for thou hast pardoned.'

[1] Chap. xix. 26. Comp. Ecclus. iii. 16.
[2] Matt. xv. 3—7. [3] Verse 9. [4] Ps. cxix. 5, 6, 80, 128.
[5] See 1 Sam. ii. 25. [6] 1 Kings iv. 29. [7] Heb. Holden. Dathe.
[8] Esth. iii. 1, 2. [9] 3 John 9. [10] Chap. xiii. 10; xxix. 22.
[11] Esth. v. 11—13. [12] Eccl. v. 10, 11. [13] Jam. i. 11.
[14] Chap. xvi. 20. Ps. lxxxiv. 12. Jer. xvii. 7, 8. [15] Diodati.
[16] Mark ix. 33, 34. [17] Comp. 2 Pet. i. 1. [18] 1 Pet. v. 7.
[19] Ps. xxxvii. 5—7.

"Healed with the beams of the Sun of Righteousness, we shall *be made fat*, as the calves of the stall."[1]

26. *He that trusteth in his own heart is a fool: but whoso walketh wisely, he shall be delivered.*

Contrast the sound and fruitful confidence just mentioned,[2] with man's natural *trust*. Our confidence determines our state.[3] To *trust* an impostor, who has deceived us an hundred times, or a traitor, who has proved himself false to our most important interests, is surely to deserve the name of *fool*. This name therefore, the Scripture—"using great plainness of speech"—gives to him, *that trusteth in his own heart*. Bishop Hall calls it—'The great Impostor.'[4] Has it not been practising a system of deceit upon us from the first moment of consciousness? Yes, verily, the traitor finds his home in our own bosom, prompting, in concert with our deadly enemy, the most elaborate efforts for our destruction.

The wise man awfully illustrates his own Proverb. It must have been some bitter root of self-confidence, that prostrated his wondrous wisdom in the lowest degradation.[5] Peter also—how did he *befool* himself in his *trust!* Presuming upon "the willingness of the spirit," and forgetting his Lord's most needful caution against "the weakness of the flesh,"—though named as a Rock, he fell as a reed before the first breath of temptation.[6] Had not the everlasting arms been underneath, it would have been the fall of Judas into the depths of hell. An instructive lesson to show us, that all dependence upon feelings, impulse, native strength, sincere purpose or conviction—is vain confidence. Sad experience has convinced us of this. Yet in the blindness of our folly, we are ever ready to *trust* again—if the Lord prevent not—to our ruin.

Truly, as good Bishop Wilson remarks—'there is no sin, which a man ought not to fear, or to think himself capable of committing, since we have in our corrupt will the seeds of every sin.' None of us can safely presume that his heart may not hurry him into abominations, which he cannot now contemplate without horror.[7] If Eve in a state of innocence could believe a serpent before her maker;[8] if "the saint of the Lord" could worship the golden calf;[9] if "the man after God's own heart" could wallow in adultery, murder, and deceit;[10] if the wisest of men, and the warm-hearted disciple just referred to, could sink so low—what may not we do? Surely "all men are liars,"—the best of men, when left to themselves, are mournful spectacles of weakness and instability.[11]

Blessed be our God! our standing is not on the uncertainty of man's best purpose; but upon the faithful promise, the unchangeable will, the free grace, and Almighty power of God; not there-

[1] Mal. iv. 2. Comp. Isa. lviii. 11. [2] Verse 25. [3] Matt vii. 24—27.
[4] Title of Sermon on Jer. xvii. 9. See Bunyan's Discourse between Christian and Ignorance.
[5] 1 Kings xi. 1—8. [6] Matt. xxvi. 33, 35, 41, with 69, 70.
[7] 2 Kings viii. 13—15. [8] Gen. iii. 1—6. [9] Ex. xxxii. 2—5, with Ps. cvi. 16.
[10] 2 Sam. xi. 4, 17. [11] 1 Cor. x. 13.

fore on ourselves, but on the Rock, on which the Church is immoveably built. We value then a deep knowledge of our indwelling weakness and corruption. Painful and humbling as it is; it establishes our faith, and grounds us in the gospel far better, than walking over the mere surface. This study of the heart strengthens the principle of that holy fear, which enables us to *walk wisely*, and thus *delivers* us from the evils of a self-confident state. Indeed, in a path, where every step is strewed with snares, and beset with enemies, what need of the caution—"Walk circumspectly,"—looking on all sides—"not as fools, but as wise!"[1] A sound confidence is a proof of wisdom. Let it then be a standing maxim in religion to cultivate self-distrust: never to trust ourselves with our own keeping. We are too weak thus needlessly to expose ourselves to danger. We cannot pray—"Lead us not into temptation"—when we are rushing headlong into it—"Deliver us from evil"—when we seem to invite its approach.[2]

27. *He that giveth unto the poor shall not lack: but he that hideth his eyes shall have many a curse.*

'There is none that desireth want, nor that wisheth to be poor. And therefore the carnally-minded, for to save themselves from it, carefully gather together, and enclose so much wealth as they can by any means possible, and they think that by such means they shall avoid *lack*. And indeed, after man's judgment, it is the best way that a man can take. But the Holy Ghost doth teach us another means—clear contrary to natural reason. *He that giveth unto the poor shall not lack.* This is against reason, which saith, that we must gather and hold fast to avoid poverty. She looketh not to what God can and will do. She is blind in the works of the Lord, and chiefly in those that he worketh according to his free promise.'[3] Here also covetousness combines with reason to contradict the word of God. The promise is given by him, who hath full power to make it good[4]—who has a thousand ways of repaying what is done or sacrificed at his command. The fruit is absolutely certain, 'as the best preventive against poverty, putting money into the bank of heaven which can never forfeit credit. The best securities on earth will not hinder "riches from making to them wings, and flying away."[5] But when have the securities of heaven ever been falsified?[6] Yet after all, with the carnal mind covetousness prevails above faith, and a "trust in uncertain riches makes the living God a liar."[7]

Do we—the professed followers of Christ—lay these truths really to heart—testing our own principles and practice by them—and honestly intending to take them—instead of selfish prudence and expediency—as our rule and measure of conduct. Again and again does God ratify his engagement.[8] Yet many who are "earn-

[1] Eph. v. 15. Comp. chap. iii. 5, 6. [2] Matt. vi. 13, with xxvi. 41.
[3] Cope in loco. [4] Ps. xxiv. 1. [5] Lawson in loco. Chap. xxiii. 5.
[6] Num. xxiii. 19. 2 Cor. i. 20. [7] Comp. 1 Tim. vi. 17. 1 John v. 10.
[8] Chap. iii. 9, 10; xi. 24, 25; xiii. 7; xiv. 22; xix. 17; xxii. 9. Deut. xv. 7—10.

est in contending for the faith" of the Gospel, and who would resist at any cost the invasion of heresy—we fear would be ashamed to expose the scanty limits of their liberality.

Did we really believe the promise annexed to this duty, we should not so often *hide our eyes* from a case of distress. Yet not only do we neglect to look out for objects of compassion, but actually we turn away from them, as the servant of God would turn away from sin;[1] and then justify ourselves on the ground of frequent imposition, and the many worthy objects, which may or may not come before us. *Many a curse* is entailed upon this grudging spirit, both from God and man.[2] And is there no danger here of the everlasting *curse?*[3] Ponder it well—lest prudence and discrimination check the glow of charity, prove a cloak of selfishness, and obscure that light of Christian benevolence and love, which ought to shine before men in the profession of the true servants of God.

28. *When the wicked rise, men hide themselves: but when they perish, the righteous increase.*

This Proverb has in substance been given before.[4] *The rise of the wicked* to power is indeed a national judgment—greatly to be deprecated—as the engine of cruel malice against the Church of God. Thus has it been in all the Pagan and Papal persecutions. And thus it always will be, while she is "in the wilderness."[5] But what a tremendous weight of guilt and punishment is involved in thus fighting against God.[6] Little do *the wicked* know the preciousness of the saints in his sight;[7] their perfect security under his cover;[8] the sovereign restraint which he has placed upon her enemies;[9] and the triumphant issue of all opposition against her.[10]

But the power of the wicked even here is but for a moment; and *when they perish*—as perish they will—*the righteous shall increase.* A great increase was there to the Church in the days of godly Hezekiah, when the doors of his temple, which his wicked father had shut up, were open for a national profession and consecration to God.[11] Thus also after the death of persecuting Herod, "the word of God grew and multiplied."[12] And in our own annals, at the removal of Mary from her ill-used power, the Christian exiles returned from their continental hiding-places, bringing with

Ps. xli. 1—3; cxii. 5—9, with 2 Cor. ix. 6—11. Ecc. xi. 1. Isa. xxxii. 8; lviii. 7—11. Matt. v. 7. Luke vi. 38. Observe the glowing exuberance of this last promise—Not only "shall it be given you"—but *good measure*—justly proportioned to the exercise of love—*pressed down*—to secure it as full measure—*shaken together* as with corn, that it may lie closer in its place—and as if this were not enough—*running over*—without bounds—*given into your bosom*—so that you shall taste the large indulgence of the blessing.

1 Comp. Job xxxi. 1, with Gen. xxxix. 10.
2 Chap. xi. 26. 1 Sam. xxv. 17, 25, 26, 38.
3 Matt. xxv. 41—45. Jam. ii. 13; v. 1—4.
4 Ver. 12. Comp. xxix. 2.
5 Chap. xxix. 27. Gen. iii. 15. Rev. xii. 17.
6 Acts ix. 4.
7 Zech. ii. 8.
8 Isa. xxvi. 20.
9 Ps. lxxvi. 10.
10 Ex. xv. 1. Isa. li. 9—11. Rev. xviii. 20.
11 2 Chron. xxviii. 24; xxix; xxx. 13, 25.
12 Acts xii. 23, 24.

them a large increase of blessing both to the Church and nation. Thus "out of the eater came forth meat, and out of the strong came forth sweetness."[1] The cross is the enriching blessing to the Church, and to every individual member of it.

CHAPTER XXIX.

1. *He, that being often reproved* (a man of reproof, Marg.) *hardeneth his neck, shall suddenly be destroyed, and that without remedy.*

THIS is indeed an awful word. The intractable ox, *hardening his neck* against the yoke,[2] is but too apt a picture of the stubborn sinner, casting off the restraints of God. This was the uniform complaint against Israel,[3] a true picture of the mass of the ungodly before our eyes. Conviction follows upon conviction, chastening upon chastening. Still the rebel *hardens his neck*, stops his ears against the voice of God, and invites his threatened judgments.

Awfully frequent are these instances among the children of godly parents, or the hearers of a faithful minister.[4] Every means of grace is a solemn but despised reproof. Aggravated sin makes the judgment of a righteous God more manifest. The more enlightened the conscience, the more *hardened the neck*. Every beating pulse is rebellion against a God of love.

Sometimes it is the more immediate voice of God. An alarming illness, a dangerous accident, or the death of a companion in wickedness, is "the rod and reproof" intended to "give wisdom."[5] But if the "fool" continue to despise all God's reproof, his *destruction* will be *sudden*[6] *and without remedy.*[7]

Such was the *destruction* of the old world, and of the cities of the plain, long *hardened* against the forbearance of God.[8] Pharaoh grew more stubborn under the rod, and rushed madly upon his *sudden* ruin.[9] Eli's sons "hearkened not unto the voice of their father, and in one day died both of them."[10] Ahab, *often reproved* by the godly prophet, *hardened his neck;* and "the bow, drawn at a venture," received its commission.[11] How must Judas have steeled his heart against his Master's *reproof!*[12] Onward he rushes, "that he might go to his own place."[13] Truly Divine patience has its end. And this fearful moment once arrived, "the

[1] Jud. xiv. 14. [2] Jer. xxxi. 18.
[3] Ex. xxxii. 9. 2 Chron. xxxvi. 13—16. Neh. ix. 29. Isa. xlviii. 8. Jer. xvii. 23. Zech. vii. 11, 12. Acts vii. 51.
[4] Chap. v. 12, 13. 1 Sam. ii. 12. [5] Verse 15. [6] 1 Thess. v. 3.
[7] Chap. i. 22—30; vi. 15; xxviii. 14, 18. 2 Chron. xxxvi. 16. Isa. xxx. 12—14.
[8] Luke xvii. 27—29. [9] Ex. ix. 27, 34; x. 27, 28; xiv. 28.
[10] 1 Sam. ii. 25, 34. [11] 1 Kings xviii. 18; xxi. 20; xxii. 28, 31.
[12] John vi. 70; xiii. 10, 11, 18—27.
[13] Matt. xxvi. 14—16. John xiii. 30. Acts i. 25.

vessels of wrath—endured with much long-suffering"—are now shown more manifestly, as "fitted for destruction."[1] No remedy —not even the Gospel—can remedy the case. As they lived, so they die, so they stand before God—*without remedy*. No blood—no advocate pleads for them. As they sink into the burning lake, every billow of fire, as it rolls over them—seems to sound—*without remedy!*

Sinner! wouldst thou but be wise to consider thy guilt, thy state, thy prospect, while yet "thy judgment and damnation linger!" Is not "the Spirit of grace" pleading with thine heart? Would he not now save thee, wouldst but thou obey his call? Thou art standing upon mercy's ground, betwixt heaven and hell. O thou God of Almighty Sovereign grace, show "the pattern of thy long-suffering."[2] Let the sinner sing thy everlasting praise, as "a brand plucked out of the fire,"[3] a monument of thine over-abounding grace.

2. *When the righteous are in authority, the people rejoice: but when the wicked beareth rule, the people mourn.*

'The robes of honor to *the righteous* are the garments of gladness to *the people*. The sceptre of *authority* to the godly is the staff of comfort to *the people*. On the other hand the vestments of dignity to *the wicked* are the weeds of *mourning to the people*. The throne of command to the one is the dungeon of misery to the other. The titles of honor given to the one are sighs of sorrow wrung from the other.'[4] The contrast of the government of Mordecai and Haman illustrates this *joy and mourning*.[5] The special rejoicings at the accession of Solomon might probably be connected with the confidence, that he would "walk in the ways of David his father."[6] The reigns of *the righteous* kings of Judah were pre-eminently distinguished by national happiness.[7] The glorious era yet in store for the world, is, when "the Lord shall bless" his own kingdom, as "the habitation of justice and mountain of holiness."[8] For what but righteousness can truly bless either an individual, a family, or a nation?[9]

When therefore *the wicked bear rule—the people*—not the godly—*mourn*. According to the depth of *the mourning* will be the joy at the removal of the scourge.[10] Meanwhile it is borne by "the

[1] Rom. ix. 22. [2] 1 Tim. i. 16. [3] Zech. iii. 2.
[4] Jermin. Comp. chap. xxviii. 12, 28. Ecclus. x. 3.
[5] Esth. viii. 15, 16; x. 3, with iii. 15; iv. 1—3.
[6] 1 Kings i. 39, 40, with iii. 3. Comp. iv. 20.
[7] 2 Chron. xv. 12—15; xx. 27—30; xxix. 36; xxx. 21.
[8] Jer. xxxi. 27. Comp. Isa. i. 26.
[9] Ps. lxxii. 1—7. Isa. lxxii. 1. 'It is no peculiar conceit, but a matter of sound consequence, that all duties are by so much the better performed, by how much the men are more religious, from whose abilities the same proceed. For if the course of politic affairs cannot in any good sort go forward without fit instruments, and that which fitteth them be their virtues; let polity acknowledge itself indebted to religion, godliness being the chiefest, top, and well-spring of all true virtue, even as God is of all good things.' Thus admirably does our great Hooker insist, that 'religion unfeignedly loved, perfecteth man's abilities unto all kind of virtuous services in the commonwealth.' Eccles. Pol. Book v. c. I.
[10] 2 Chron. xxi. 19, 20.

faithful in the land" as a national scourge.[1] And 'if tears be their drink, patience will be their bread, till God have mercy on them.'[2] What need have we to thank God, that our guilty country, with so much to humble us in shame—should have been so long spared from the curse of *wicked rulers!* The tyrant rules for his own sinful ends; the Christian Sovereign for the good of the people.

3. *Whoso loveth wisdom rejoiceth his father: but he that keepeth company with harlots spendeth his substance.*

These Proverbs in substance have been given before.[3] Yet the variations are instructive. The wisdom is here more distinctly described as *loving wisdom.* For 'he is wise, not only, who hath arrived at a complete habit of wisdom, but who doth as yet but *love it* or desire it, and listen to it.'[4] Do not we hang off too loosely from its heavenly influence?. Let it be manifestly our great object, not as a good thing, but the best—"the principal thing."[5] The awakened sinner *loves it* from the sense of want; the Christian from its satisfying delight. The taste gives a keen edge to the appetite. What we have grasped of the blessing bears no comparison to what remains.

Young man! consider Wisdom's pleasantness and peace,[6] her light and security,[7] her durable riches,[8] and glorious inheritance[9]—and "wilt thou not from this time cry" to the God of wisdom—"My Father, thou art the guide of my youth?"[10] No worldly honor—no success of talent—will *rejoice a godly father*, as will this choice for eternity.[11]

Folly brings its own shame and sorrow. "*The companion* of the riotous and vain persons" is readily found in fellowship *with harlots*, saddening his father by *spending his substance.*[12] One course of vanity leads to another. All end alike in ruin.[13] He may possess the external endowment. But *the love of wisdom* is the only preservative from besetting snares.[14]

Deep indeed is the anxiety—the joy or the sorrow—connected with children.[15] May it give a deeper tone of simplicity and pleading in dedicating them to God,[16] and training up for his service! Let us early present them as "the children, whom the Lord hath given us;" but as his more than our own—his property—his inheritance.[17] Here are our springs of diligence—of hope—of ultimate reward.

4. *The king by judgment establisheth the land: but he that receiveth gifts* (a man of oblations, Marg.) *overthroweth it.*

[1] Eccl. x. 5, 6. Isa. iii. 4, 5. Mic. iii. 9—12.
[2] Jermin ut supra.
[3] Chap. x. 1; xv. 20; xxiii. 15, 24, 25; xxvii. 11.
[4] Basil quoted by Bp. Patrick. Preface to Proverbs.
[5] Chap. iv. 7. See the beautiful description, Ecclus. vi. 18—31; xxiv. Bp. Lowth' elegant translation. Lect. on Heb. Poetry, xxiv.
[6] Chap. iii. 17.
[7] Chap. viii 20; iv. 11, 12.
[8] Chap. iii. 14, 15; viii. 18, 19.
[9] Chap. iii. 35.
[10] Jer. iii. 4.
[11] Chap. xxiii. 23—25.
[12] Chap. xxviii. 7, 19.
[13] Chap. v. 9; vi. 26. Luke xv. 30.
[14] Chap. iv. 6; vii. 4, 5.
[15] Chap. xvii. 21—25.
[16] Gen. xvii. 7.
[17] Ps. cxxvii. 3.

Of what avail are the best laws, if they be badly administered? Partiality and injustice absolutely make them null and void. And yet it requires great integrity and moral courage to withstand the temptations of worldly policy and self-interest. God's own throne is built and *established by judgment.*[1] This then can be the only *establishment of the land.*[2] The compromise of it to some private ends provokes the anger of God to the chastisement, if not the *overthrow, of the land.* The article in our Magna Charta—'We will sell justice to none'—is but too plain evidence of the recklessness of all social principles, ere the great standard was erected among us.

Under the godly government of Samuel *the land was established by judgment.*[3] "But his sons walked not in his ways." They were *men of oblations. They received gifts;* and the Theocracy —the great Palladium of the land—*was overthrown.*[4] The righteous administration of David "bore up the pillars" of the land, at a time of great national weakness.[5] The same principles in his godly successor were the source of strength and prosperity.[6] The want of uprightness in Saul, shook the kingdom from his grasp;[7] and the covetousness of Jehoiakim[8] destroyed its foundations, and buried him in its ruins. Let the same consistency pervade every grade of official responsibility. Dignity—temporal or spiritual—can convey no solid influence, except it be *established with judgment.* Let men of God be in our high places; and "righteousness will exalt our nation,"[9] and our Church will be "the joy and praise of the whole earth."

5. *A man that flattereth his neighbor spreadeth a net for his feet.*

Most wisely were Bunyan's pilgrims warned—'Beware of *the flatterer.*' Yet 'forgetting to read the note of directions about the way,' they fell into *his net*, and, even though delivered, were justly punished for their folly. The doctrine of man's goodness, strength, or freedom; a general gospel, without close application; its promises and privileges, without the counter-balance of its trials and obligations—All this shows 'the black man clothed in white'—"Satan himself transformed into an angel of light, and his Ministers transformed as Ministers of righteousness."[10] Unwary souls are misled. Even unwatchful Christians fall into *the net.* And while they have to thank their faithful God for deliverance, they cannot forget his sharp and needful chastening of their folly. Where "the root of the matter" is not, heresy,[11] or apostacy,[12] is the baneful fruit of the *flatterer*.

But let us guard against this *net* in our daily path. Too readi-

1 Ps. lxxxix. 14; xcvii. 2. Isa. ix. 7.
2 Ver. 14; xvi. 10—12; xx. 8, 26; xxv. 5. 2 Chron. ix. 8.
3 1 Sam. vii. 3—12, 15—17.
4 Ibid. viii. 2—7.
5 Ps. lxxv. 2—6, 10. 2 Sam. viii. 15.
6 2 Chron. i. 1; xiv. 2—7; xix. 6, 7, with xx. 27—30; xxxi. 20, 21. Isa. xxxii. 1, 2.
7 1 Sam. xiii. 13.
8 Jer. xxii. 13—19.
9 Chap. xiv. 34.
10 2 Cor. xi. 13—15.
11 Rom. xvi. 17, 18.
12 2 Pet. ii. 1—3.

ly do *the flatterer's* words pass current. What else is much of the language of smooth courtesy, or lively interest and affection? Who would venture to act with confidence on this heartless profession? Always is *the net spread* to allure into some devious path; often into the grossest wickedness. Thus *the flattering* woman beguiled her prey.[1] The parasites of Darius deified him for a month, to make him the tool of their malicious plot.[2] The enemies of Christ *spread the flatterer's net for his feet.* But here the wisdom of God was infinitely above them, and "took the wise in their own craftiness."[3]

The feet of many strong men have been entangled in this *net.* Indeed seldom has the frailty of the man of God been more painfully exposed. David honored his God in the endurance of Shimei's curse. But Ziba's smooth words drew him into an act of gross injustice.[4] Usually some want of integrity has predisposed the mind for this poison. David was struggling to discover a plea for leniency to his murderous son, when the woman of Tekoah plied him with her *flattering* lips. The bribery of passion was far more powerful than her arguments.[5] But bitterly did the misguided parent reap the fruit of thus entering into *the net spread for his feet.*[6] Wilful infatuation fully prepared Ahab, by listening to *the flattery* of his lying prophets, to his own ruin.[7]

Does a man thus load us with immoderate commendation? It is *the flatterer's net.* "Ponder the path of thy feet."[8] Exchange confidence for suspicion.[9] Fearful is the snare to those, whose rank or influence dispose them to walk rather before men, than before God. Too often it is *spread for the feet* of the Minister of Christ, whether to gain his good opinions, or from the genuine but imprudent warmth of affection. But oh!—think—"He is a man as thou art"—beset with temptation—perhaps even "besides those that are common to men." His heart, like thine, is fully susceptible of self-exalting imaginations. And to know that he has a reputation for holiness; that he is a man of influence; that his character is looked up to; that his opinion is valued—this is indeed "a fiery trial,"[10] that brings out to view much base dross of vanity. Far better would it be that our Christian intercourse with each other should be moulded by the wise resolution to refrain from "*flattering* titles," as hurtful to the creature, and provoking to God.[11]

[1] Chap. ii. 16; vii. 21; xxvi. 28. [2] Dan. vi. 6—9.
[3] Matt. xxii. 15—23, with 1 Cor. iii. 19. [4] 2 Sam. xvi. 1—12. [5] Ib. xiv. 4—24.
[6] Ib. xv. 1—14. [7] 1 Kings xxii. 11, 12. [8] Chap. iv. 26.
[9] Chap. xxvi. 24, 25; xxvii. 14. [10] Chap. xxvii. 21.
[11] Job xxxii. 21, 22. Comp. LXX. 22, with Acts xii. 22, 23. 'Surely it is enough for us to have foes within and without to contend with, without having snares for our feet laid by our fellow-pilgrims. Oh! it is a cruel thing to *flatter.* The soul is often more exhausted and injured by disentangling itself from these nets, than by the hottest contest with principalities and powers. Those who have once known the torture the believer undergoes, while this poison is pervading his soul, the bitter, lowering medicines he must take as antidotes, the frightful oblivion of lessons of humility which he has been studying for years, will, I think (unless much under the influence of the enemy of souls), not administer the noxious potion a second time.' Helen Plumptre's Letters, pp. 43, 44; a most profitable volume.

6. *In the transgression of an evil man there is a snare: but the righteous doth sing and rejoice.*

There is always *a snare* in the ways of sin; always a song in the ways of God. Which then are "the ways of pleasantness and peace?"[1] The light-hearted sinner goes on in his flowery path. Soon he is "taken captive in *the snare* of the devil;"[2] often in *a snare* of his own toil.[3] *Transgression* is in fact *the snare* of the soul. Sin and ruin are bound together, and who can put them asunder?

The righteous may be in the same outward lot with *the evil man.* But wide indeed is the gulf between their respective states.[4] Joseph's brethren in prison, under the sting of conscience, sank in despondency. Paul and Silas in prison *did sing and rejoice.*[5] Little, however, can be judged by their external state. The ungodly are in prosperity, and the children of God "chastened every morning;"[6] yet rising triumphant in the deepest exercise—"Rejoice not against me, O mine enemy; though I fall, I shall rise again; though I sit in darkness"—my cause apparently forgotten, my light obscured, my character defamed—"the Lord shall be a light unto me."[7] What is it to be possessor of all the promises of God! The wealth of this golden mine no tongue of man can express; no mind of angel comprehend. And how abundant is the solid ground and material of this *rejoicing!* The completeness of the Saviour's work; his constant love; the fulness of his Spirit; the sufficiency of his grace; his faithful promise; his watchful eye; his ready help; his perpetual intercession; and all this joy—not, like that of the world, flowing and ebbing—but heightening and overflowing through all eternity.

But *the righteous also sing*—and only they—Often they have no skill for the song. "Their harp is upon the willows," as if they could not "sing the Lord's song in a strange land."[8] Yet whatever cause of complaint they have, weighing down their spirits, let them not forget to magnify that grace unbounded, which hath been given to them and for them.[9] *Why can they not always sing?* The heart is cold, dead, unbelieving. Oh! for the power from above to quicken it.—'Praised be God,' we are hastening to a world, where the harp will never be unstrung, and the heart never out of tune, and the song will be ever new.[10]

7. *The righteous considereth the cause of the poor: but the wicked regardeth not to know it.*

The original gives to the Proverb a judicial aspect.[11] To "re-

[1] Chap. iii. 17, with xiii. 15.
[2] 2 Tim. ii. 26. Job xviii. 9—11.
[3] Chap. v. 22; xi. 5, 6; xii. 13. Job xviii. 8.
[4] Isa. lxv. 13, 14.
[5] Gen. xlii. 21, with Acts xvi. 25.
[6] Ps. lxxiii. 1—14. Eccl. ix. 2.
[7] Mic. vii. 8—10.
[8] Ps. cxxxvii. 4.
[9] To some Christians of a morbid temperament Bernard's advice may be important—Let us mingle honey with wormwood, that the wholesome bitter may give health, when it is drunk tempered with a mixture of sweetness. While you think humbly of yourselves, think also of the goodness of the Lord.' In Cant. Serm. xi.
[10] Isa. xxxv. 10. Rev. v. 8—10.
[11] Holden, Geier, Bp. Patrick.

spect the person of the poor" is no less unjust, than to "honor the person of the mighty."[1] But *the righteous* judge or advocate will *consider his cause*, judge it as for God, investigate it thoroughly, and take care that it be not lost from his own inability to defend it.[2] This was the *considerate* administration of the great King of righteousness.[3] The man of God will walk after this Divine exemplar.[4] 'Let him have the conscience first'—(says Bishop Sanderson) 'and then the patience too (and yet if he have the conscience, certainly he will have the patience) to make search into the truth of things, and not be dainty of his pains herein, though matters be intricate, and the labor like to be long and irksome.'[5]

Selfishness however—not truth, justice, or mercy, is the standard of *the wicked*. He considers—first *the poor* man's person, then *his cause*. "The unjust judge" would not have "avenged the widow of her adversary," but to save trouble to himself.[6] Felix *regarded not to know* the Apostle's *cause*, but that he might indulge his own covetousness.[7] But fearful is it to sit in the place of God[8] as his representatives, only to pervert his judgment for their own selfish aggrandizement.[9]

The maxim however obviously applies more generally to the *considerate regard of the righteous*—and the cruel disregard of *the wicked*—towards *the poor*. The ordinance that "the poor shall never cease out of the land"—and the inequality of rank that prevails throughout the œconomy of Providence, were doubtless intended as an incitement to Christian sympathy and enlargement.[10] *Consideration of the poor* is the true spirit of Christian sympathy —putting ourselves as far as may be in their place.[11] Oh! how different is this from the impatient—ungracious temper, in which the suit of a poor client is sometimes despatched, as if the advocate grudged his time and pains! Our beloved Lord—not only "went about doing good,"[12] but he did it so tenderly—*considerately*. Always was he ready to yield his own convenience and even necessary comfort to the call of need.[13] The same *considerate regard for the poor* marked the Apostolic administration.[14] Sympathy with the poor is the practical acknowledgment of our own undeserved mercies; specially remembering the Lord's poor—as the representatives of Him,[15]—who is First and Last, and All to us; and who, "though he was rich, yet for our sakes became poor, that we through his poverty might be made rich."[16]

[1] Lev. xix. 15. Ex. xxiii. 3. [2] Ps. lxxxii. 3, 4. [3] Ib. lxxii. 2—4, 12—14.
[4] Job xxix. 11—16; xxxi. 13, 20. Jer. xxii. 16. [5] Serm. on Ex. xxiii. 1—3.
[6] Luke xviii. 2—5. [7] Acts xxiv. 26, 27. [8] Ps. lxxxii. 6. Rom. xiii. 1, 2.
[9] Chap. xxiv. 11, 12. Jer. v. 28, 29. Ez. xxii. 7, 29—31. Mic. iii. 1—4.
[10] Deut. xv. 7—11. 2 Cor. viii. 14, 15.
[11] Ps. xli. 1. A most striking instance of *consideration for the poor*, is recorded of Bp. Ridley, when the dying Martyr at the stake implored the queen in behalf of certain poor men's leases in his bishopric likely to become void by his death. Foxe: vii. 545, 546. In the same noble spirit was the remembrance of the dying Scott to his son, of the arrival of the season when he had been used to plant a root for the supply of the poor.
[12] Acts x. 38. [13] Mark vi. 31—34.
[14] Acts iv. 34, 35; vi. 1—6. 1 Cor. xvi. 2. 2 Cor. ix. 12, 13. Gal. ii. 10.
[15] Matt. x. 42; xxv. 40. [16] 2 Cor. viii. 9.

Well do those, who *regard not to know*, deserve their name—*the wicked*. Like Cain—they acknowledge no interest in their brother.[1] Like Nabal—"It is no concern of mine."[2] If the poor must be fed rather than starve—it is casting food to a dog, rather than holding out an helping hand to a fellow-sinner.[3] This total absence of the image of a God of Love[4]—this utter casting off his royal law[5]—surely he will require it.[6]

8. *Scornful men bring a city into a snare;* (set the city on fire, Marg.) *but wise men turn away wrath.*

The comparison is here between a "proud and haughty *scorner*, and *a wise man*."[7] The one is a public injury; the other a public blessing. The one raises a tumult;[8] the other quells it. The man, who *scorns* to be bound by common restraints, will *bring the city into a snare* by his presumption,[9] or *set it on fire* 'by blowing the fire of Divine wrath upon it.'[10] Happily *wise men* are scattered through the land: their energy and prudence *turn away wrath.*[11] 'Proud and foolish men kindle the fire, which wise and good men must extinguish.'[12]

Another instructive illustration of the Proverb suggests itself. Not the tyrant over his fellow-creatures, but the *scorner* against his God, is the public trouble. Many of the kings of Judah and Israel thus *brought the city into a snare.* Their provocations of Divine wrath did more to further its ruin, than the most powerful foreign enemies. Their influence led the people into deeper aggravations of sin, and ripened them for judgment.[13]

But wise men stand in the gap, and *turn away wrath.*[14] Surely it was *wisdom* in the King and people of Nineveh, instead of *bringing their city into a snare by scornful* rebellion, to avert by timely humiliation the impending destruction.[15] Let the people—let the Ministers of the Lord, gird themselves to their work of weeping and accepted pleaders for the land.[16] Surely "except the Lord of Hosts had left us a very small remnant" of these powerful intercessors, "we should have been as Sodom, and we should have been like unto Gomorrah."[17] Praised be God! The voice is yet heard—"Destroy it not, for a blessing is in it."[18] The salt of the earth preserves it from corruption.[19] Shall not we then honor these *wise men*

[1] Gen. iv. 9. [2] 1 Sam. xxv. 10, 11. [3] Luke xvi. 21. [4] 1 John iii. 17.
[5] Jam. ii. 8. Lev. xix. 18, with Luke x. 31, 32. [6] Chap. xxiv. 12.
[7] Heb. Men of scorn. [8] Chap. xxi. 24.
[9] 1 Sam. xi. 2, 11. 2 Sam. x. 4; xii. 31. [10] LXX. Durell. Comp. chap. i. 11.
[11] 2 Sam. xx. 1. 15—22. Acts xix. 23—41. Comp. Virg. Æn. i. 148—153.
[12] Henry.
[13] 2 Kings xxi. 9—15; xxiii. 26, 27. Isa. xxviii. 14—22. 2 Chron. xxxvi. 16, 17. Jer. xxxvi. 23—32. 1 Thess. ii. 15, 16.
[14] Moses—Ex. xxxii. 10—14. Deut. ix. 8—20. Ps. cvi. 23. Aaron—Num. xvi. 48; Phinehas, xxv. 11. Ps. cvi. 30; Elijah, 1 Kings xviii. 42—45. Jam. v. 16—18. Jeremiah, xviii. 20; Daniel, ix. 3—20; Amos, vii. 1—6. The righteous remnant—Isa. i. 9; vi. 13. Comp. Gen. xviii. 32. Job xxii. 30. Jer. v. 1. Ez. xxii. 30, 31. Contrast xiii. 5.
[15] Jon. iii. 5—10. [16] Joel ii. 15—19. [17] Isa. i. 9.
[18] Ib. lxv. 8. [19] Matt. v. 13.

with reverential gratitude—"My father—my father! the chariots of Israel, and the horsemen thereof!"[1]

9. *If a wise man contendeth with a foolish man, whether he rage or laugh, there is no rest.*

It would generally be far better not to meddle with such *a fool* as is here described. We can only deal with him on very disadvantageous terms, and with little prospect of good.[2] *If a wise man contend* with the wise, he can make himself understood; and there is some hope of bringing the debate to a good issue. But to *contend with a fool, there is no rest*, no peace or quiet. It will go on without end. He will neither listen to reason, nor yield to argument. So intractable is he, that he will either *rage or laugh*—either vent upon us the fury of an ungoverned temper, or *laugh* us to scorn. This *contention* was a point of the poignant trial to our Divine Master. What could be more revolting than sometimes their murderous *rage*[3]—sometimes their scornful *laugh*;[4]—in both "rejecting his counsel against themselves?"[5] And what if *a contention with such fools* should be appointed for me? Let me remember my days of perversity and *folly*. And while this vivid impression brings me back to their level—can I return their unreasonable provocation, save with tenderness and compassion?[6] Yea—when, as the most effectual means for their benefit, I would commend them to the Almighty Sovereign grace of God—can I forget, that, if this grace has healed my deep-rooted stubbornness, it is not less rich—not less free—not less sufficient, for them?

10. *The bloodthirsty hate the upright: but the just seek his soul.*

This bloody hatred is the fulfilment of the first prophecy from the mouth of God.[7] The first history of the fallen world puts the seal to the prophecy—"Cain rose up against Abel his brother, and slew him."[8] Ever since has the same testimony been given.[9] "Which of the prophets have not your fathers persecuted?" (was the indignant remonstrance of Stephen to his countrymen) until they "filled up the measure of their fathers" by being "the betrayers and murderers" of the Son of God.[10] The noble army of martyrs stand before us. Such intensity of malice in the contrivance of the variety of their torture! *The bloodthirsty hate the upright.*[11] Their innocency was the only ground of *hatred*; and on the threatened apprehension of any outbreak of evil—the swelling cry of the *bloodthirsty* multitude was—'The Christians to the lions!' The next picture downward in the annals of the Church is not less illustrative—"I saw the woman"—awful sight!—

[1] 2 Kings ii. 12. This acknowledgment is sometimes forced from the consciences of the ungodly. Chap. xiii. 10—14.
[2] Chap. xvii. 12; xxvi. 4. Ecc. x. 13. Matt. vii. 6.
[3] Luke iv. 29. John vii. 1; viii. 59; xi. 53.
[4] Luke xvi. 14.
[5] Matt. xi. 16, 17.
[6] Tit. iii. 2, 3.
[7] Gen. iii. 15.
[8] Ib. iv. 5—8.
[9] Verse 27. Ps. xxxvii. 12—14, 32. Gal. iv. 29. 2 Tim. iii. 12.
[10] Acts vii. 52. Matt. v. 12; xxiii. 32.
[11] Heb. xi. 36, 37.

"drunken with the blood of the saints, and with the blood of the martyrs of Jesus."[1] We cannot doubt but the fierce elements of the cruelty still lie in slumbering concealment. Nothing but the gospel can kill the principle. Every thing short of this only chains down the violence. In a softer mould it still retains all its substance and power, and waits only for the removal of present restraints to develope the same *bloodthirsty hatred* as ever.

Scripture explains this murderous vindictiveness. "Wherefore slew Cain his brother? Because his own works were evil, and his brother's righteous."[2] Darkness cannot endure the light.[3] The condemning light[4] of godliness excites the enmity of the ungodly. They cannot bear the picture. Thus the *bloodthirsty* Ahab hated *his upright* prophets,[5] and the Jews the holy Saviour.[6] Conformity to him is the great offence still. Such precise fools—contrary to every one beside—"turning the world upside down"—how can they be endured? Their removal would be a rejoicing riddance from the earth.[7]

And yet their God is not unmindful of their threatening troubles. *The bloodthirsty hate the upright: but the just seek his soul.* Saul sought to murder David; Jonathan covered him.[8] Jezebel was thirsting to destroy the prophets of the Lord; Obadiah "hid them in a cave, and fed them with bread and water."[9] The enemies of Jeremiah plotted against him; Ebedmelech saved his life.[10] Herod was proceeding against Peter's life; the Church shielded him with their prayers.[11] *The bloodthirsty* Jews bound themselves to murder Paul; "Priscilla and Aquila" were ready to "lay down their own necks for his life."[12]

What a life of conflict is this world of sin! Need we be dissuaded from loving it? Need we not rather patience to endure it? But while we are in it, let us be found decidedly on the Lord's side,[13] "partakers"—if needs be—"of the afflictions of the gospel."[14] Never let us stand aloof from our brethren's cause.[15] To help them is to be fellow-workers with God Himself. If union is so effective against the Church, surely its influence would not be of less moment on the Church's side—"strengthening her stakes," establishing her foundations, and enlarging her usefulness.

11. *A fool uttereth all his mind: but a wise man keepeth it in till afterwards.*

"There is a time for every thing"—the wise man elsewhere writes—"a time to keep silence, and a time to speak."[16] It is a mark of true wisdom to discern these times.[17] Indeed the discipline—or the want of discipline—upon the "little member" is a sound test of character. The man, who speaks hastily and with conceit,

[1] Rev. xvii. 6. [2] 1 John iii. 12, 13. [3] John iii. 19, 20.
[4] Heb. xi. 7. [5] 1 Kings xxi. 20; xxii. 8. [6] John vii. 7.
[7] Rev. xi. 9, 10. Comp. Acts xxii. 22. [8] 1 Sam. xviii. 11, 25, with xviii. 1—4.
[9] 1 Kings xviii. 4. [10] Jer. xxxviii. 1—13. [11] Acts xii. 1—5.
[12] Ib. xxiii. 12, with Rom. xvi. 4. Comp. ib. ix. 25. 2 Cor. xi. 33.
[13] Matt. xii. 30. [14] 2 Tim. i. 8.
[15] 2 Tim. i. 16, 17. [16] Eccl. iii. 1, 7. [17] Ib. viii. 5. Am. v. 13.

will be put to shame in his folly.[1] He might have been "counted wise in his silence."[2] But silence is beyond his power—*He uttereth all his mind*—tells all he knows, thinks, or intends—runs on, until he has "poured out all his foolishness."[3] It is sometimes thought a proof of honesty to *utter all our mind.* But it is rather a proof of *folly.* For how many things it would be far better never to speak—indeed to suppress in the very thought![4] Much of "foolish talking and jesting"[5]—how many angry—detracting—uncharitable words—do we utter, because we have neglected to watch—or rather to entreat "the Lord to set a watch upon—our lips," as the door of our hearts![6] And what wrong judgments we often pass upon men's actions, because we *utter all our mind* as it were in one breath—without pondering; or perhaps without materials to form a correct judgment!

Indeed the words of the fool—as an old expositor remarks—'are at the very door—so to speak—of his mind, which being always open—they readily fly abroad. But the words of the wise are buried in the inner recess of his mind, whence the coming out is more difficult.'[7] This is the wisdom to be valued and cultivated. Many things we may *keep in till afterward*, which will then be far better spoken than at the present moment.[8] We may find reason afterward to suspect what at the time we were fully persuaded of. There is often a lightness of faith—the fruit of sudden impulse—breaking out in sudden profession. Beware of a loose foundation. Men under the present excitement run through all the sects and parties of the Church—everywhere *uttering their whole mind*—"tossed to and fro, and carried about by every wind of doctrine"[9]—"seeking rest, and finding none." How much better to take time for second thoughts—to weigh and weigh again! Should we not then—instead of exhibiting a changing and doubtful face—seek to gain that "good thing—a heart established with grace?"[10]

This godly prudence holds in common life. Samson fell a victim to the *folly of uttering all his mind.*[11] Samuel was restrained by God from this imprudence, from a regard to his own safety. Never speak against our mind. But it is not necessary to *utter our whole mind.* Take care that we speak nothing but the truth. But the whole truth (as in the instance of Samuel) may sometimes be legitimately restrained.[12] The Apostle was two years at Ephesus, without *uttering all his mind* against the worship of Diana. But was this cowardice shrinking from the truth? His weeping ministry and unceasing efforts proved his faithfulness.[13] His open protest *kept in till afterwards* was self-discipline, consistent with Christian courage and decisiveness.

12. *If a ruler hearken to lies, all his servants are wicked.*

[1] Chap. xviii. 13. [2] Chap. xvii. 28. [3] Chap. xv. 2.
[4] Chap. xxx. 32. Mic. vii. 5. [5] Eph. v. 4. [6] Ps. cxli. 3.
[7] Cartwright. Comp. chap. x 14; xii. 16, 23; xiii. 16; xiv. 33.
[8] 1 Sam xxv. 36, 37. [9] Eph. iv. 14. [10] Heb. xiii. 9.
[11] Jud. xvi. 17. [12] 1 Sam. xvi. 1, 2. [13] Acts xix. 10, 23, with xx. 31.

The influence of the *ruler's* personal character upon his people involves a fearful responsibility.[1] A wicked prince makes a wicked people.[2] In his more immediate sphere, *if he hearken to lies*—contrary to the laws of God and of charity[3]—he will never want those about him ready to minister to his folly. 'Lies will be told to those, that are ready to *hearken to them*.'[4] Envy—ambition—malice—self-interest will always be at hand for prejudice and scandal. The credulous ruler becomes the tool of all manner of wickedness. His corruption pushes away the godly from his presence—and *all his servants are wicked.* Exceptions there are to this maxim (as Obadiah in the court of Ahab[5]—Ebedmelech in the service of Zedekiah[6]—Daniel in Nebuchadnezzar's court[7]). But this is the natural tendency—the general result—to his own disgrace and ruin. If he would therefore rule in uprightness, and in the fear of God; instead of lending himself to detraction or flattery, he must carefully close his ears against doubtful characters, lest he should countenance *wicked servants*; and discourage those that will boldly speak the truth.

How wise was David's determination—both as the sovereign of his people, and the *ruler* of his house—to discountenance lies, and uphold the cause of faithful men![8] Contrast Ahab surrounded with his wicked prophets—all combining in one lie to please their weak and ungodly master. We see how ready he was to *hearken to lies*, and how well the flattery worked; when he punished the only man who was "valiant for the truth," and who persisted in declaring it—"not fearing the wrath of the king."[9]

But all in authority may learn a lesson of responsibility. Let Ministers especially—not only hold the truth in its full integrity, and take heed that their character will bear the strictest scrutiny; but let them turn away from the fawning flattery of those, of whose uprightness there is at best but doubtful proof.

13. *The poor and the deceitful man* (usurer, Marg.) *meet together: the Lord lighteneth both their eyes.*

The doctrine of this proverb—as of one similar to it[10]—seems to be the real equality of the Divine dispensations under apparent inequalities. The rich seem to be intended by *the deceitful*—so called from the deceitfulness of riches,[11] and of the means, by which they are too often obtained.[12] The *usurer*[13] appears to point to the same purport—implying the oppression too often connected with

[1] . . . . componitur orbis
Regis ad exemplum; nec in inflectore sensus.
Humanos edicta valent, quàm vita regentis.
Mobile mutatur semper cum principe vulgus.
Claudian, de Honorii Consul.

[2] 1 Kings xv. 30; xvi. 2. Comp. Ecclus. x. 2.
[3] Ex. xxiii. 1. M. R. Comp. Chap. xiii. 5.
[4] Henry.
[5] 1 Kings xviii. 3
[6] Jer. xxxviii. 7—13.
[7] Dan. ii. 48, 49.
[8] Ps. ci. 2—7.
[9] 1 Kings xxii. 6, 26, 27. Comp. Hos. vii. 3.
[10] Chap. xxii. 2.
[11] Chap. xxiii. 5. Matt. xiii. 22.
[12] 1 Tim. vi. 9.
[13] Comp. chap. xxii. 7.

riches.[1] Both these classes—so distinct in their relative condition —*meet together* on the same level before God. *Men* may differ. One may oppress and despise, and the other envy or hate. *The poor* may be tempted to murmur, because of the oppressions of his richer neighbor. The rich by *usury* or unjust gain may take advantage of the necessities of the poor. But *the Lord enlighteneth both their eyes.* "He is no respecter of persons."[2] Both are partakers of his providential blessings[3]—both are the subjects of his Sovereign grace. *The poor* Lazarus and *the usurer* Zaccheus have long *met together* in one common home[4]—both alike the undeserved monuments of wondrous everlasting mercy—*the eyes of both enlightened*—spiritually—eternally.

Is it not presumption to judge hastily the ways of God; or to judge them at all—by the plummet of our own reason?[5] Let us wait the appointed time, and all will be clear, as all is right. How far beyond our narrow conceptions is every exercise and display of this manifold wisdom, grace, and love!

14. *The king that faithfully judgeth the poor, his throne shall be established for ever.*

This maxim has often been repeated in substance.[6] The writer of this book was a king. He was naturally led to write for his own benefit, while the Divine Spirit guided his pen for the use of rulers to the end of time. May every king—specially may our own beloved Sovereign—place this picture of a godly ruler constantly before her eyes! It is natural for *the king* to desire *the establishment of his throne;* but not natural for him to seek it in God's own way. Jeroboam sought it by wickedness[7]—Rehoboam by worldly policy[8]—Ahaz by worldly alliances.[9] The far more sure mode is the faithful administration of justice; not neglecting the rich; but specially protecting the poor, whose weakness the more needs a covering.[10] David appears to have been a poor man's king. The lowest of his people had familiar access to him for judgment.[11] Solomon[12] and many of his godly successors ordered their kingdom in the same principles of justice, and were abundantly honored of their God.[13] The mal-administration of faithful principle never failed to bring a curse upon the government.[14] "Them that honor me I will honor; and they that despise me shall be lightly esteemed."[15]

When our great Saviour King walked upon earth—his enemies bore testimony—whether in flattery or conviction—to his righteous

[1] Ps. lxii. 9, 10. Jam. v. 1—4. For the same reason our Lord denominates riches generally by the distinctive term of "The mammon of righteousness." Luke xvi. 9.
[2] Acts x. 34. [3] Matt. v. 45. [4] Luke xvi. 22; xix. 9.
[5] Ez. xviii. 25. [6] Ver. 4, 7; xiv. 34; xx. 28; xxv. 4, 5.
[7] 1 Kings xi. 25—30. [8] 2 Chron. xi. 22, 23; xii. 1.
[9] Ib. xxviii. 16—20. [10] Chap. xxxi. 9. Ps. lxxxii. 3, 4.
[11] 2 Sam. xix. 8. [12] 1 Kings iii. 16—28.
[13] Jehoshaphat—2 Chron. xix. 5—11; xx. 30. Josiah—Jer. xxii. 14—16. Comp. Daniel's advice to Nebuchadnezzar, iv. 27.
[14] Isa. iii. 13, 14; x. 1—6. Jer. xxii. 13—19. Zeph. iii. 3. [15] 1 Sam. ii. 30.

character.[1] Not less beautiful than accurate is this description, as applied to the principles of his government, and connected with the promise of the *establishment of his throne.*[2]

15. *The rod and reproof give wisdom: but a child left to himself bringeth his mother to shame.*

Discipline is the order of God's government. Parents are his dispensers of it to their children. The child must be broken in to "bear the yoke in his youth."[3] Let *reproof* be first tried; and if it succeed, let *the rod* be spared.[4] If not, let it do its work. Eli gave the *reproof,* "but spared *the rod.*"[5] Some give *the rod* without *reproof*—without any effort to produce sensibility of conscience. From this tyranny or caprice nothing can be expected. The combined influence not only "drives foolishness far away,"[6] but—as a positive blessing—*gives wisdom.* God's own children grow wiser under correction. They see their folly, and in genuine shame turn from it, blessing him for his rod of faithfulness and love.[7]

But look at the child *left to himself*—without restraint. A more perfect picture of misery and ruin cannot be conceived. His evil tempers are thought to be the accident of childhood. 'They will pass away, as his reason improves. Time only can mend them.' But in fact time of itself mends nothing. It only strengthens and matures the growth of native principles. The poison however does not appear at first. No special anxiety is excited. The child is not nurtured in wickedness, or under the influence of bad example. He is only *left to himself. Left!* The restive horse, with his rein loosened, full of his own spirit, plunges headlong down the precipice. The child, without government, rushes on under the impetuous impulse of his own will;[8] and what but almighty sovereign grace can save him from destruction? Many a hardened villain on the gallows was once perhaps the pleasing, susceptible *child*—only *left to himself*—to his own appetite, pride, self-willed obstinacy.[9]

The sound discipline of heavenly guidance is our Father's best blessing. His most fearful curse is, to be given up to our own ways—"to walk in our own counsels."[10] *A child thus left* is at the furthest point from salvation—in the very jaws of the devouring lion.

Turn we now from the ruined child to the disgraced, broken-hearted parent. *The mother* only is mentioned, as the chief superintendent of the early discipline; perhaps also as the most susceptible of the grievous error. For if the father's stronger character induces him to "provoke his children to wrath;"[11] to rule rather by command than by persuasion; does not *the mother's* softer mould

[1] Matt. xxii. 16. [2] Ps. lxxii. 7, 11—15. Isa. ix. 7; xi. 4, 9.
[3] Lam. iii. 27. Comp. Ecclus. xxx. 12. [4] Chap. xvii. 10.
[5] 1 Sam. ii. 22—25; iii. 13. [6] Chap. xxii. 15.
[7] 2 Chron. xxxiii. 12. Ps. cxix. 67, 71, 75. Luke xv. 13—17. Comp. Mic. vi. 9.
[8] 'Puer, cui frænum laxatum.'—Schultens. Comp. Ecclus. xxx. 8—11.
[9] Comp. 1 Kings i. 6—9 · ii. 23—25. [10] Ps. lxxxi. 12. [11] Col. iii. 21.

tend to the opposite evil? And so far as she yields to mistaken indulgence, she bears the greater share of the punishment. It is not, that she is *brought* to trouble, or even to poverty; but to that, which is the most keenly-felt of all distress—*to shame.*[1] Nowhere is God's retributive justice more strongly marked. The *mother's* sin is visited in the proportioned punishment. What greater neglect of obligation, than *a child left to himself?* What greater affliction, than the *shame, to which he brings her?* Parental influence is lost. The reverence of authority is forgotten,[2] as a bye-gone name. The child rules, instead of being, as a corrected child,[3] in subjection. The parent fears, instead of the child, and thus virtually owns her own degradation. Instead of "the wise son, that maketh a glad father;" it is "the foolish son, that is the heaviness of *his mother.*"[4] The sunshine of bright prospects is clouded. The cup of joy is filled with wormwood. The father's mouth is dumb with the confusion of grief. The dearest object of *the mother's* tenderness, instead of being the staff and comfort of her age, *bringeth her to shame.*

This is not a trial, which, like many others, she might cover in her own bosom. Alas! *the shame* is too public to be concealed. What must have been the open dishonor upon Eli's name, when "the sins of his children made men abhor the offering of the Lord!"[5] When the treason of David's sons *brought him to shame* in the sight of all Israel; surely his own conscience must have brought his own perverted fondness to mind, as the cause of their ruin; both *left to themselves*—one palliated in the most aggravated sin;[6] the other having been not even corrected by a word.[7] And if *the shame* before men be so bitter, what will be the overwhelming confusion at the great consummation; when the evil propensities, cherished with such cruel fondness in the parental bosom, shall produce their harvest "in the day of grief and of desperate sorrow!"[8]

Oh! as our children's happiness or misery, both for time and eternity, is linked with our own responsibilities; shall not we "watch and pray," resisting "the weakness of the flesh," in self-denying firmness? 'Take this for certain,'—says Bishop Hopkins—'that as many deserved stripes as you spare from your children, you do but lay upon your own backs. And those whom you refuse to chastise, God will make severer scourges to chastise you.'[9] At whatever cost, then, establish your authority. Let there be but one will in the house. And let it be felt, that this will is to be the law. The child will readily discover, whether the parent is disposed to yield, or resolved to rule. But however trifling the requirement, let obedience be in small as in great matters, the indispensable point. The awe of parental authority is perfectly consistent with

[1] 'Conturbator matris suæ.'—Schultens. 'Filius confundens, confusione omni arefaciens, et perplexans.' Ib. on Chap. x. 5.
[2] Chap. xix. 26. [3] Heb. xii. 9. [4] Chap. x. 1. Comp. xvii. 21, 25.
[5] 1 Sam. ii. 25. [6] 2 Sam. xiv. 21, 33; xv. 6; xviii. 33. [7] 1 Kings i. 5—9
[8] Isa. xvii. 11. [9] Works, i. 450.

the utmost freedom of childlike confidence; while it operates as a valuable safeguard against a thousand follies of uncontrolled waywardness. But ever let us put the awful alternative vividly before us. Either the child's will, or the parent's heart, must be broken. Without a wise and firm control, the parent is miserable; the child is ruined.

16. *When the wicked are multiplied, transgression increaseth: but the righteous shall see their fall.*

The increase of transgression is obviously proportioned to the increase of transgressors.[1] Nor is it merely a numerical increase, but also in power and daring of sin. "The men, who began to multiply upon the face of the old earth were giants" in wickedness, as in strength; until "the striving of the Spirit of God" could endure no longer.[2] The same was with the Babel-builders,[3] and the cities of the plain.[4] Combination emboldens in sin.[5] Each particle of the mass is corrupt. The mass therefore itself ferments with evil. Hence the prevalence of infidelity in our densely-crowded districts above the more thinly-populated villages. There is the same evil in individual hearts; but not the same fermentation of evil.

But for the prospects of faith the Christian eye could not bear the sight. *But the righteous shall see their fall.*[6] Noah saw the destruction of the old world.[7] Abraham witnessed the ruin of the devoted cities;[8] "Israel saw the Egyptians dead upon the seashore."[9] 'Let not the righteous'—said good Bishop Patrick—'be discouraged; for the wickeder men are, the shorter is their reign.' The faithful minister, conscious of his inability to stem the overflowing torrent of iniquity, would sink in despair, but for the assured confidence, that he is on the conquering side; that his cause, as the cause of his Lord, must eventually prevail. Yes—though now sin seems to triumph, and Satan boasts of his victories; yet "the kingdoms of this world," with all their vast population, shall "become the kingdoms of our Lord and his Christ, and he shall reign for ever and ever."[10] This is indeed the supporting joy of faith; to realize the glory of this day, when *the righteous shall see the fall* of the now triumphing *wicked;* and one universal shout shall swell throughout the earth—"Alleluia, salvation and glory, and honor, and power, unto the Lord our God; for true and righteous are his judgments—Alleluia; for the Lord God Omnipotent reigneth."[11]

17. *Correct thy son, and he shall give thee rest; yea, he shall give delight unto thy soul.*

Once more the wise man returns to the subject of discipline.

1 Hos. iv. 7.
2 Gen. vi. 1—6.
3 Ib. xi. 1—8.
4 Ib. xviii. 20. Ezek. xvi. 49.
5 Ib. xi. 4. Isa. xli. 8.
6 Psalm xxxvii. 34; lviii. 9—11; xci. 8.
7 Gen. vii. 23.
8 Ib. xix. 28.
9 Ex. xiv. 30.
10 Rev. xi. 15.
11 Ib. xix. 1—6, with xv. 4; xviii. 20. Comp. Isa. lxvi. 24.

These repeated inculcations[1] strongly show its importance. The command is positive—*Correct thy son.* How can an upright judgment evade or explain away a plain, literal rule? To try more self-pleasing rules, is to set up our will in opposition to God's; reason or feeling in the stead of faith.

The measure and mode of *correction* must depend upon the age, sex, temper of the child, the character, the aggravation, or the mitigated circumstances, of the fault. Yet let it be, like our gracious Father's discipline, never more than can be borne.[2] Make due allowance for any marks of ingenuous confession. Yet with a wise application of the principle, there must be no exception to the rule. Different tempers, like different soils, require corresponding difference of treatment. But discipline there must be; not relaxed in fondness, not pushed on in harshness; but authority tempered with love.[3] If a gentle hand cannot control, a stronger hand must be applied.

We may take *rest* without *correction;* but such rest will bring trouble in the end. The true *rest* is that, which our *child will give;* and that he may *give it*, the rule is—*Correct.*[4] We may be assured, that God would not have so insisted upon it, if a blessing was not with it. If Eli was rejected, it was, because in this matter, he "honored his sons above God."[5] Those then "that honor him" above their sons "he will honor." Pain is the present exercise both to parent and child;[6] but the *after* blessing is secured.[7] Ground well tilled, trees carefully pruned, "bring forth more fruit."

Observe how the objection of parental weakness is anticipated. 'If I put my son to pain, will he not hate me?' No—when "left to himself," he was a deep and anxious trouble. Now *he shall give thee rest.* Before—he "brought thee to shame."[8] Now *he shall give delight to thy soul.*[9] The momentary feelings of the child under *correction* will give way to the conviction of the parent's wisdom and regard for his profit.[10]

Yet the rule against discouragement would not have been repeated, had there not been some parental evil to be corrected. "Provocation" revolts, transfers confidence to most unworthy associates, and brings into ruinous temptations. Children claim a considerate treatment. They must not be driven by brute force. Authority must be tempered with love. The grounds of extraordinary commands should be explained to them. What is good should be liberally commended. The best construction should be put upon defective efforts. The distinction should be carefully drawn between weakness and wilfulness, between heedlessness and obstinacy. Home should be gladdened with the invigorating joy of spring, and replete with every wholesome indulgence. Every at-

[1] Verse 15. Chap. xiii. 24; xix. 18; xxii. 15; xxiii. 13, 14.
[2] Isa. xxvii. 8; lvii. 16. 1 Cor. x. 13.
[3] See Wisd. vi. 17.
[4] Comp. Ecclus. xxx. 2.
[5] 1 Sam. ii. 29, 30. Contrast Gen. xxii. 12.
[6] Chap. xix. 18; xv. 10.
[7] Heb. xii. 11.
[8] Verse 15.
[9] Chap. xxiii. 13—16, 24, 25.
[10] Heb. xii. 9.

tempt should be made to gain confidence, so that the child, instead of a cold trembling reserve, should run into our arms. But in this glowing atmosphere forget not God's rule. The completeness of discipline is the father's firmness combined with the mother's tenderness; each infusing into the other the quality of each. A wise parent will put his seal to the testimony, that this well-disciplined education is the surest means of securing the children's affection, gratitude and reverence.[1]

18. *Where there is no vision, the people perish;* (is made naked, Marg.) *but he that keepeth the law, happy is he.*

The vision—as appear from the contrast—is Divine instruction.[2] The Ministry is the appointed ordinance to communicate this blessing,[3] and therefore the main instrumentality of conversion,[4] and subsequent Christian perfection.[5] No greater calamity therefore can there be than the removal of the vision. The temporal famine—affecting only the body—is a light judgment, scarcely to be mentioned, compared with that, by which *the people perish*—"the famine of hearing the words of the Lord."[6] For 'when there is none that can edify, and exhort, and comfort the people by the word of God, they must needs *perish.* They become thrall and captives unto Satan. Their heart is bound up. Their eyes are shut up; they can see nothing. Their ears are stopped up; they can hear nothing. They are carried away as a prey into hell, because they have not the knowledge of God."[7]

Often did Israel provoke this most fearful judgment—the removal of the open *vision.*[8] "The candlestick" of the Apocalyptic Churches has from the same cause been long since "removed out of its place;" and for the most part little more remains than the ceremonial of bye-gone days.[9] From the Apostate Church of Rome, *the vision* is well nigh withdrawn, and *the people perish* in ignorance and delusion. And in other bodies—"having a name to live"—the complaint is as real as in days of old—"My people are

[1] Comp. Ex. xxxii. 25. 2 Chron. xxviii. 19. Geier and others give—Dissipantur—scattered. Matt. ix. 36. Evidently however a state of desponding misery is intended.

[2] Comp. 1 Sam. iii. 1. [3] Ibid. ix. 9. Mal. ii. 7. Eph. iv. 8—11.

[4] 1 Cor. i. 21. Jam. i. 18. 1 Pet. i. 23—25.

[5] 1 Cor. xiv. 3. Eph. iv. 11—14. 1 Thess. iii. 10. And yet this most fruitful organ of Divine agency (preaching), which our blessed Lord honored as the grand medium of his own teaching (Ps. xl. 9, 10. Isa. lxi. 1, 2), is now depreciated as the mark of 'a Church only in a weak and a languishing state, and an instrument, which Scripture—*to say the least*—has never much recommended.' (Tracts for the Times, 87, p. 75.) Far more orthodox is the sentiment of one of our venerated reformers. 'Thus we may learn the necessity of preaching, and what inconvenience follows when it is not used. "Where preaching fails"—saith Solomon—"there people perish." Therefore let every one keep himself in God's school-house, and learn his lesson diligently. For as the body is nourished with meat, so is the soul with the word of God.' Bp. Pilkington's Works, p. 112. Parker Society's edition 'The meanest village'—Luther was wont to say—'with a Christian pastor and flock, is a palace of ebony.'

[6] Amos. viii. 11, 12. Comp. Isa. viii. 16; xxx. 20. Jer. vii. 12.

[7] Bp. Jewell on the Scriptures.

[8] 1 Kings xii. 28—32; xiv. 14—16. 2 Chron. xv. 3—5. Ps. lxxiv. 9. Lam. i. 4. ii. 9. Ez. vii. 26. Hos. iii. 4.

[9] Rev. ii. 1—5; iii. 1—3, 15, 16.

destroyed for lack of knowledge."[1] The sun shines not on more wretched objects, than on the awful masses of our fellow-sinners, growing up in habitual estrangement from God.

Take the most awful illustration of this Proverb that can be imagined. If to be without *vision* be the mark of a *perishing* state, what ray of Scriptural hope dawns upon the Heathen world? Being "without Christ," they are described by infallible testimony as "having no hope."[2] Salvation is indeed free to all, "whosoever shall call upon the name of the Lord." But how shall they call without faith; believe without hearing; "hear without a preacher?"[3] If therefore there be *no vision,* how can they but *perish?* "They perish indeed without law"[4] (not condemned under the law of revelation, which they have never known); but still *they perish* "without excuse,"[5] alienated from the life of God through the ignorance that is in them, "because of the blindness of their hearts."[6] Proud reasoning man revolts, and presumes to be more merciful than God. But this false charity is only the cover for selfishness. Men deny the danger, because they are too indolent, too self-indulgent, to stretch out the helping hand, or to make one sacrifice for the rescue. True charity is the fruit of reverential faith. And, while it realizes the tremendous peril, it concentrates all the energy of compassionate tenderness, believing prayer, and self-denying effort upon their salvation.

But the contrast is not between those who have not *the vision,* and those who have it, but between the destitution and the improvement of the blessing. The mere profession of the Gospel may be a nullity. Of what use is light, if we open not our eyes to see it? So far from a blessing, it will only issue in deeper condemnation.[7] If some are enlightened, multitudes are struck blind.[8] But practical godliness—*keeping the law*—brings real abiding *happiness*[9]—no less a privilege than communion with our God and Saviour here and for eternity.[10] Who then can justly cast a cloud of gloom over the ways of God? Let the Pentecostal Christians witness to their gladness.[11] Let every servant of his Lord invite his fellow-sinners to the enjoyment of his privileges, by the manifestation of their holiness and joy.

19. *A servant will not be corrected by words: for though he understand he will not answer.*

Discipline must be carried, not only into the family,[12] but throughout the whole household, in order to preserve God's authority and order. An important hint is here given relative to the management of servants. Though it does not apply to all,[13] it shows a very common temptation to self-will. There is a proud as well as

[1] Hos. iv. 6. [2] Eph. ii. 12. [3] Rom. x. 13, 17.
[4] Ib. ii. 12. [5] Ib. i. 20. [6] Eph. iv. 18.
[7] Matt. xi. 20—24. Luke xii. 47, 48. [8] John xii. 40.
[9] Chap. iii. 21—24; iv. 5—9; viii. 32—35; xix. 16. Luke xi. 28. John xiii. 17.
[10] John xiv. 21—23. Rev. xxii. 12, 14. [11] Acts ii. 46, 47. [12] Verses 15, 17.
[13] The LXX. renders—but without authority from the original—'an obstinate servant.'

an humble silence; as plain a proof of an unsubdued spirit, as a pert and flippant answer. The patience of Job was sorely exercised by this trial, and that under circumstances which made the treatment more aggravated.[1] We must guard against harshness in our spirit.[2] But with servants, as with children, authority must be maintained at any cost. And therefore, if *a servant understand* the command and *will not answer*—if *he will not be corrected by words*, it were better to dismiss him, than to lower our authority, and countenance evil by yielding to his waywardness.

The Scripture fully sets out the duties of servants—"Not answering again. With good-will doing service, as to the Lord, and not to man."[3] Sullen resistance to reproof is most inconsistent with the profession of a Christian; and, if the offender escapes the correction of an earthly master, he will be visited with the rod of his angry Lord, as a self-deceiver, or backslider from his high obligation.[4]

20. *Seest thou a man that is hasty in his words? there is more hope of a fool than of him.*

We have just been warned against sullen silence; here against *hasty words.* When a man flows on in his words, evidently without time for consideration;[5] when he gives his opinion, as if it were a loss of time to take counsel, or regard the judgment of others; when you find him forward in pronouncing judgment before men of acknowledged wisdom and experience; this is the "fool uttering all his mind;"[6] the man lately marked out for our warning,[7] as an *hopeless fool*, "wise in his own conceit."

It is very difficult to deal effectively with him until the strong hold of his own conceit be shaken. Argument and instruction are lost upon him. The man who is conscious of his weakness, who distrusts himself, and is ready to ask and receive counsel, is more likely to be led right, than he, who thinks himself to be right already.

It is a special mercy to be preserved from *hasty* judgments, or expression of judgments. The first stamp upon a perfect mind is infallibly correct. On an imperfect mind it must be subjected to a careful scrutiny. It is sound wisdom to admit, that our judgment may be mistaken. Self-control and self-diffidence give solid consistency. This character of mind is most important in religious disputations. Be careful to defend or contravene nothing, till you have tested it by the true standard. Moses deferred judgment on the sin before his eyes, till he had brought the matter to God.[8] "Be swift to hear; slow to speak."[9]

21. *He that delicately bringeth up his servant from a child shall have him become his son at the length.*

[1] Chap. xix. 16. [2] Lev. xxv. 43. Comp. Ecclus. xxxiii. 28, 29. [3] Tit. ii. 9. Eph. vi. 7. [4] Chap. xix. 29; xxvi. 3. [5] Chap. xviii. 13. [6] Verse 11. [7] Chap. xxvi. 12. [8] Lev. xxiv. 10—23. [9] Jam. i. 19.

We have another[1] valuable rule for domestic discipline, directing masters to a wise treatment of their servants. It is a grievous error to step ourselves, or to induce another to step, out of the path, which a God of order has marked for us. Divine Wisdom has framed the constitution of society, assigning to each their station and their duties. If a servant aspire to be *in the house* any thing but a servant, his character loses its value. A master acts—to say the least—most unseemly, when he forgets his own place and authority, and *delicately bringeth up his servant* by the allowance of undue freedom. It is a great exercise to preserve the true medium between distance and familiarity. An haughty menacing demeanor[2] towards our servants forgets the respect justly due to them. An inconsiderate fondness takes them out of their place, greatly to their own injury. Our Lord's distinction shows, that friends—*not servants*—should be admitted to our familiar intercourse, and entrusted to our confidence.[3] To promote a servant therefore to the rank of a confidant, unfits him for his own condition, and defeats our own end by the natural results of this unnatural treatment. True kindness keeps him in his place. 'Good usage does by no means imply that indulgence, that would ruin a child.'[4] *A servant delicately brought up*—often *from a child*—soon relaxes in respect and attention. Instead of this false kindness stimulating to diligence, and inducing gratitude; he becomes idle, insolent, and ungovernable;[5] assumes the young master—*becomes a son at the length.* This unseemly usurpation is an evil "that the earth cannot bear—a servant, when he reigneth."[6] Ishbosheth must have allowed Abner undue liberty, when he so far forgot the respect due to his sovereign, as to insult him before his face.[7] David also must have loosened the reins of proper authority, when Joab murdered the commander in chief at the head of his army, without being instantly subjected to the penalty of the law.[8] Even the wise man appears to have forgotten his own prudent caution, when he *delicately brought up* Jeroboam in authority; promoted him too suddenly; and lived to regret his error, when with the pretension *of a son* he combined the pride of a rebel.[9] The confusion and anarchy of after years in the kingdom originated in the same false step.[10] The greatest kindness to servants is to "give to them that which is just and equal,"[11]—*but no more.* Any defect in this rule will be sure to bring (as in the case referred to) future trouble, as the unjust chastening for present folly. What need have we of the daily supply of Divine grace, to rule our house well in due subjection. The resolution to "behave ourselves wisely in

[1] Verse 19. [2] Eph. vi. 9.
[3] John xv. 15. [4] Scott. [5] Comp. Ecclus. xxxiii. 25—27.
[6] Chap. xxx. 21, 22. Lord Bacon suggests for the good ordering of servants—1. That we promote them by steps, not by leaps. 2. That we occasionally deny their wishes. 'Sudden elevation'—he adds—'induces insolence. The constant granting of their wishes makes them only more imperative in demand.' Advancement of Learning, Book xii.
[7] 2 Sam. iii. 7—11. [8] Ib. xx. 4—10. Also iii. 27. [9] 1 Kings xi. 26—28.
[10] Ibid. xvi. 9—12. [11] Col. iv. 1.

a perfect way" can only be accomplished in the habitual prayer—"O when wilt thou come unto me?" Then indeed "I will walk within my house with a perfect heart."[1]

22. *An angry man stirreth up strife, and a furious man aboundeth in transgression.*

Anger is not necessarily a sinful passion. Even *furiousness*—the overflowing of the torrent—is a property in God.[2] We can readily conceive of its energy in the unfallen nature of man. Had Satan appeared to Eve in his own hatefulness, her anger against him would have been a holy principle. But in a fallen nature—to preserve its purity is a rare and most difficult matter. It must be confined to points, where God's honor is concerned;[3] and even on these points the rule must be observed—"Let not the sun go down upon your wrath."[4] The short period of the day is abundantly sufficient to express right motives, and to accomplish holy purposes.

The general tendency of anger is however here graphically described. Its active energy *stirreth up strife*[5]—quarrelling even upon trifles,[6] or matters which a forbearing consideration might have satisfactorily explained.[7] And when suppressed, but not laboriously mortified, how often does it become more intense, and break out more *furiously—abounding in transgression!* Indeed it is difficult to take a full view of the mighty power of this mass of sin. It gives the impetus to every besetting propensity. It may be blasphemy![8] It stops at nothing. How many murders do we owe to this paroxysm of the moment![9] But for the Divine restraints the very foundations of society would be torn up.

Parents! Do we feel the responsibility of early checking this ebullition in our children? And do we diligently watch against the first rising in ourselves, incessantly praying for its subjugation? How beautiful are the instances of Almighty grace—such as Henry Martyn[10]—transforming *the furious man* into the likeness of his meek and holy Master!

But let us not be satisfied with the outward restraint upon passion. God condemns the deep-rooted principle that gives it birth. Wretched heart! filled with soul-destroying corruption! Every—even the least—indulgence operates fearfully. So much time spent in excitement! So much more in the unquiet waiting for the desired opportunity! And all given to the Great Murderer! Oh! for the mystery and doctrine of the cross, to mould our temper into its genuine spirit and influence!

23. *A man's pride shall bring him low: but honor shall uphold the humble in spirit.*

This Proverb—Bishop Hall remarks in his own style—'is like

[1] Psalm ci. 2. [2] Nah. i. 2.
[3] Ex. xxxii. 19. John. ii. 15—17. [4] Eph. iv. 26.
[5] Chap. xv. 18; xxvi. 21; xxx. 33. Jam. iii. 16.
[6] 1 Tim. vi. 4. 2 Tim. ii. 23, 24. [7] Acts xv. 39. [8] Lev. xxiv. 10, 11.
[9] 1 Sam. xviii. 9, 10; xxii. 6—19. Matt. ii. 16. Acts vii. 54—59; xii. 19.
[10] Life, p. 8. Pref. to 10th edit.

unto Shushan: in the streets whereof honor is proclaimed to the humble Mordecai; in the palace whereof is erected an engine of death to a proud Haman.'[1] It exhibits the spirit of our Lord's oft-repeated declaration expounded by his daily Providences. "Whosoever shall exalt himself shall be abased; and he that shall humble himself shall be exalted."[2] The real value of man in himself is so small, that the Psalmist is at a loss where to find it.[3] His undue value of himself is utter delusion—having lost all; stripped of all; yet proud, as if he were the possessor of all. He raises himself to heaven in his airy visions; but soon does he meet with his own punishment. *A man's pride shall bring him low.*[4] We see this in the world. The proud conceit of rank, talent, or any superiority, subjects to continual mortification;[5] while on the other hand, humility—at first considered a mean and servile spirit—ultimately comes to its just estimation.

The world counts nothing great without display. But mark the substantial "honor that cometh from God only." "Heaven is my throne, and earth my footstool; yet to this man will I look—to him that is poor, and of a contrite spirit."[6] Yea—"I dwell—saith the high and lofty One that inhabiteth eternity—with him that is of a contrite and humble spirit."[7] Humility is indeed true greatness—'the crown'—as Mr. Howel finely remarks—'of finite beings, made and jewelled by the hand of God himself. Supremacy is the glory of God; humility is the ornament of his child.'[8] "I am but dust and ashes. I am less than the least of all thy mercies. I abhor myself. Sinners—of whom I am chief"[9]—such are the self-abasing confessions of men great in Jehovah's eyes. They shine with the reflection of his glory; but they turn away with genuine humility from their own shining.

Men of this stamp "the king delighteth to honor." Their dignity begins on earth, and is crowned in heaven. "Blessed are the poor in spirit; for theirs is the kingdom of heaven."[10] Poor they may be in station. But they shine forth as mightier conquerors than Alexander. Their real glory eclipses the glare of the pomp and "pride of life."

The elevation of *the proud* is often the step to their downfall. But God's *honor* put upon his own people *upholds them;* as Joseph and Daniel—in their high eminence, as witnesses for his name. And all his chastening discipline is for the great purpose, to "hide pride from man,"[11] and *to bring us low* in our own eyes, that his *honor* may "lift us in due time."[12] It is with us as with our Lord—*honor* comes out of humiliation.[13] 'Thou meanest to

[1] Sermon on text. Works, v. 270.
[2] Matt. xxiii. 12. Luke xiv. 11; xviii. 14.
[3] Psalm viii. 3, 4; cxliv. 3; xxxix. 5.
[4] Job xl. 12. Ps. xviii. 27. Comp. Zeph. ii. 15. Rev. xviii. 7, 8, and references on Chap. xvi. 18, 19.
[5] 1 Kings xxi. 1—4. Esth. v. 13.
[6] Isa. lxvi. 1, 2.
[7] Ib. lvii. 15.
[8] Sermon i. pp. 335, 336.
[9] Gen. xviii. 27; xxxii. 10. Job xl. 4. 1 Tim. i. 15.
[10] Matt. v. 3. Comp. xviii. 4.
[11] Job xxxiii. 17.
[12] 1 Pet. v. 6. Comp. Job xxii. 29.
[13] Chap. xv. 32; xviii. 12

be not our Saviour only, but our pattern too. If we can go down the steps of thine humiliation, we shall rise up the stairs of thy glory.'[1]

24. *Whoso is a partner with a thief hateth his own soul: he heareth cursing and bewrayeth it not.*

This is a warning under the eighth commandment. Do we realize the same solemnity of obligation as under the first? Many professors attach a degree of secularity to a detailed application of the duties of the second table. But both stand on the same authority. The transgressions of both are registered in the same book. The place of the decalogue cannot be of moment, if the word be but there with the imprimatur—"I am the Lord thy God." The law acknowledges no difference between the *thief and his partner.* Consenting to sin—receiving the stolen goods—involves us in the guilt and punishment.[2] The accomplice may be less practised in sin. He may be only commencing his course. But the first step is the way of death—acting as if he *hated his own soul.*[3] One step naturally leads on to another. Supposing him to be called to give evidence upon oath concerning his knowledge or privity of the deed. Would not this be a temptation to perjury, rather than to discover his fellow? Under the perverted obligation of his bond of secrecy *he heareth cursing*—the solemn adjuration to declare the truth on pain of the curse of God—*and he bewrayeth it not.* 'He keeps his wicked counsel, and will not betray.'[4]

Oh! how frightful is the history of thousands, whose fellowship with sinners has drawn them into fellowship with sin, and ultimately to take the lead in sin!—Whose entrance into the path has led them step by step into the very depths of depravity! And of these thousands, how few—it is to be feared—retrace their steps, and become, like Onesimus, true followers of Christ, and faithful servants to man![5]

25. *The fear of man bringeth a snare: but whoso putteth his trust in the Lord shall be safe.* (Marg. set on high.)

A snare brings a man into straits. He is not master of himself. Here Satan spreads *the snare*, and *the fear of man* drives into it. And a fearful *snare* it is, and ever hath been to thousands. Many, once entangled, have never escaped. It besets every step of the pathway to heaven, every sphere of obligation. The King turns aside from the strict integrity.[6] The judge wilfully pronounces an unrighteous sentence.[7] The minister faints under the cross;[8] and to avoid it, compromises the simplicity of the Gospel.[9] There is a timidity in acting out an unpopular doctrine. The people cannot bear the *full* light. The Sun of righteousness is therefore exhibited under a mist; but dimly visible; shorn of his glowing beams.

[1] Bp. Hall ut supra. [2] Chap. i. 10—15. Ps. l. 18—21. Isa. i. 23, 24.
[3] Comp. vi. 32; viii. 36; xvi. 32; xx. 2.
[4] Comp. Lev. v. 1. Num. v. 21. 1 Kings xxii. 16. Matt. xxvi. 63.
[5] Epistle to Philemon. [6] 1 Sam. xv. 24. Matt. xiv. 9. [7] John xix. 8, 13, 14.
[8] 1 Kings xix. 3. Jon. i. 1—3. [9] Gal. ii. 12; vi. 12.

But the strictness of the precepts is unpalatable. It must therefore be softened down, modified, or explained away.[1] Or the same inconstancy of profession must be quietly dealt with, lest the good opinion of some influential man be forfeited. This time-serving shows a man-pleaser, not a true "servant of God,"[2] and brings a blast alike to his work and to his soul.[3]

The same deadly influence operates in families. Sometimes even parents shrink from the open protection of their child.[4] They dare not avow a supreme regard to his primary interests, or profess in opposition to many around them, the Patriarch's godly determination—"As for me and my house"—however evil it may seem to others—"we will serve the Lord."[5]

Every class of society exhibits this corrupt principle. Perhaps the highest are bound in the most abject and hopeless chains. They will set at naught all religion without fear; but, slaves as they are to the omnipotency of fashion, they would "tremble very exceedingly,"[6] at the suspicion of godliness attached to them. Many would be bold to front danger, who would shrink from shame. They would fearlessly face the cannon's mouth, and yet be panic-struck at the ridicule of a puny worm. Or even if some public excitement should have roused an impulse of boldness for religion, in the more quiet atmosphere there is a heart's timidity of silence. They shrink from the bold consistency of a living witness. They are afraid of the stamp of singularity. They are satisfied with a meagre external decorum, with no spiritual character or privilege. All is heartless delusion. What—again, makes so many—specially among the young—ashamed to be found upon their knees—to be known readers of their Bibles—to cast in their lot decidedly among the saints of God? They know the Christian to be on the right side; and oft is there a whisper of conscience—'Would that my soul were in his place.'[7] But they have only half a mind to religion. *The fear of man bringeth a snare.* 'And therefore they ask—not what I ought to do, but what will my friends think of me.' They cannot brave the finger of scorn. And if they seem for a while to be in earnest, 'their slavish fears' (as Bunyan well describes the case) 'overmaster them. They betake themselves to second thoughts—namely—that it is good to be wise, and not to run, for they know not what, the hazard of losing all, or at least bringing themselves into unavoidable and unnecessary troubles.'[8] They would rather writhe under their conviction, till they have worn themselves away, than welcome what Moses "esteemed greater riches than the treasures of Egypt—*the reproach of Christ.*"[9]

But how painful to see the children of God entangled in the *snare!* The father of the faithful twice denied his wife.[10] His son,

[1] Isa. xxx. 9, 10. Jer. v. 31. [2] Gal. i. 10. [3] Zech. xi. 17.
[4] John ix. 22. [5] Jos. xxiv. 15.
[6] Gen. xxvii. 33. The same word in the original.
[7] John vii. 13; xii. 42, 43. Acts xxvi. 11. 2 Tim. i. 15; iv. 16.
[8] Conversation between Hopeful and Christian. [9] Heb. xi. 26.
[10] Gen. xii. 11—13; xx. 2, 11.

following his weak example,[1] "fashions the golden calf."[2] "The man after God's own heart" sinks himself into the lowest degradation.[3] Hezekiah—distinguished for his trust—gives way to his fear.[4] The ardent disciple, even after the most solemn pledges to his Saviour, and after an act of great boldness in his defence, yields up his courage to a servant girl, and solemnly abjures his Lord.[5] Oh! do we not hear the warning voice against "entrance into temptation—against the weakness of the flesh?"[6] Let us run into our hiding-place, and cry—"Hold thou me up, and I shall be safe."[7]

How different is this servile principle from the godly *fear of sin*, which the wise man had lately marked as the substance of happiness![8] *That* is an holy principle; *this* an inlet to sin.[9] *That* is our keeping grace;[10] *this* wounds our conscience, and seduces us from our allegiance.[11] '"By the fear of the Lord men depart from evil;"[12] by *the fear of man* they run themselves into evil.'[13] That one is the pathway to heaven.[14] The other involving the denial of the Saviour—plunges its wretched slave into the lake of fire.[15]

But even apart from this tremendous end—observe its weighty hindrance to Christian integrity. Indeed—as Mr. Scott most truly observes—'it is'—often at least—'the last victory the Christian gains. He will master, by that grace which is given of God, his own lusts and passions, and all manner of inward and outward temptations. He will be dead to the pleasures of the world, long before he has mastered this fear of man. "This kind of spirit goeth not out" but by a very spiritual and devout course of life.'[16] The hindrance meets us at every turn, like a chain upon our wheels; so that, like the Egyptian chariots, they "drive heavily." Oh! for a free deliverance from this principle of bondage;[17] not however to be expected, till we have been made to feel its power.

Thank God—there is a way of deliverance. Faith unbinds the soul from fear. If fear makes the giant tremble before the worm, *trust in the Lord* makes the worm stronger than the giant. The fire, or the den of lions, daunts and hurts not him that "believeth in his God."[18] 'He that fears to flinch, shall never flinch from fear.'[19] Faith gives power to prayer. The strength from prayer makes us cheerful in obedience, and resolute in trial. Here is *safety*, strength, courage, peace. Nothing but faith gives the victory; but the victory of faith is complete.[20] He only, *who putteth his trust in the Lord*, is prepared, when God and man are at contraries—to "obey God rather than man."[21]—A secret union with God is implanted in

1 Ib. xxvi. 7. 2 Ex. xxxii. 22—24.
3 1 Sam. xxi. 10—13. Comp. also xxvii. 1.
4 2 Kings xviii. 13—16. Comp. 2 Chron. xvi. 1—7.
5 Matt. xxvi. 35, 51, 69—74. 6 Ib. ver. 41. 7 Ps. cxix. 117.
8 Chap. xxviii. 14. 9 Gen. xxxix. 9, with Isa. lvii. 11. 10 1 Cor. x. 12. Heb. iv. 1.
11 References notes 3—9 ut supra. 12 Chap. xvi. 6.
13 Flavel's Treatise on Fear, Chap. ii. 14 Chap. xix. 23.
15 Mark viii. 38. Rev. xxi. 8. 16 Life, pp. 116, 117. 17 Ex. xiv. 25.
18 Dan. iii. 28; vi. 23. 19 Hildersham.
20 1 John v. 4, 5. Comp. Heb. xi. 27. 21 Acts iv. 13, 19.

the soul by this faith—an union as mighty as it is secret—a sacred spring of life, the energy of God himself,[1] triumphant therefore in the mightiest conflict with the flesh. The man dependent on the world for happiness is in bondage. The servant of God is in liberty. It matters not to him whether the world smile or frown. *He is safe*—beyond its reach—*set on high.*[2] Faith brings him to his strong tower.[3] There he is "kept by the power of God unto salvation."[4] *Fear brings us to the snare.* Faith brings liberty, *safety, exultation.* Oh! thou God of power and grace, may my soul praise thee for this mighty deliverance—this joyous freedom! May I never be ashamed of my Master! May I be bound to his people, and glory in his cross![5]

26. *Many seek the ruler's favor; but every man's judgment cometh from the Lord.*

Therefore seek God to be your friend. "In his favor is life."[6] Confidence in man is no less sinful[7] and dangerous[8] than *the fear of man.* Yet with what diligence will men seek earthly advantage! *Many seek the ruler's favor*[9] more than God's, and sacrifice their consciences, and hazard their souls, to obtain it. But when they have bought it at such a price, what is it?—as easily lost, as it was hardly gained. The caprice of an hour may destroy the hard-earned object.[10] And then what have they to live upon? All this is forgetting that *every man's judgment cometh from the Lord.* Here then is the solid ground of faith. First, begin with God. All *judgment* is in his hands. "Commit thy way unto the Lord; trust also in him, and he shall bring it to pass."[11] Let him choose and dispose our lot.[12] Ponder every thing that passes as coming from him. In every thing, great and small, deal with him. His favor—unlike the changing *favor of the ruler*—is "without variableness or shadow of turning." And when through the fickleness of man earthly prospects are fading—then rest in quiet—"Surely my judgment is with the Lord."[13] 'As thou wilt—what thou wilt—when thou wilt.'[14] This is the shortest—the surest—way of peace. "Only believe," and doubt nothing.

27. *An unjust man is an abomination to the just: and he that is upright in the way is abomination to the wicked.*

Here is the oldest, the most rooted, the most universal quarrel in the world. It was the first curse of the fall.[15] It has continued ever since, and will last to the end of the world. It is always kept up at the highest point. Each party is an *abomination* to the other. It is not only that they are as contrary in character as light

[1] Gal. ii. 20. Col. iii. 3. [2] Ps. lxix. 29; xci. 14. Isa. xxxiii. 16.
[3] Gal. ii. 20. Col. iii. 3, 4. [4] Chap. xviii 10. [5] 1 Pet. i. 5.
[6] Ps. xxx. 5. [7] Ib. cxlvi. 3. Isa. ii. 22. Jer. xvi. 5, 6.
[8] Isa. xxx. 1—3; xxxi. 1—3. [9] Chap. xix. 6. [10] Gen. xl. 1, 2.
[11] Ps. xxxvii. 5, 6. 'He needeth not to flatter the ruler; for what God hath appointed, that shall come to him.' Reformers' Notes. 'The determination concerning a man is from Jehovah.' Bp. Lowth's Prelim. Dissertation to Isaiah.
[12] Ib. xlvii. 4. Chap. xvi. 33. [13] Isa. xlix. 4. Job xxxiv. 29.
[14] Thomas à Kempis. [15] Gen. iii. 15.

comings the most discerning clear-sighted penitent feels that he can never abase himself as he ought before his God—He would lie low—lower still—infinitely lower—in the dust. Holy Paul, comparing himself with the spirituality of the perfect law—exclaims, "I am carnal, sold under sin."[1] Isaiah in the presence of a holy God—cries out—"Woe is me, for I am undone, because I am a man of unclean lips."[2] Job, in the manifestation of the power of God, sinks into his absolute nothingness and unworthiness[3]—David in the full view of the wisdom of God, is made to see the perverseness of his own folly, and take up the very confession of Agur—"So foolish was I, and ignorant; I was as a beast before thee!"[4] The nearer our contemplation of God—the closer our communion with him—the deeper will be our self-abasement before him—like those "before the throne, who with twain cover their faces, and with twain cover their feet."[5] Well, therefore, may the wisest and holiest of men—though "renewed in knowledge, after the image of him that created him"[6]—take up the humiliating confession—*Surely I am more brutish than any man.* Genuine humility is the only path of wisdom. Unless he stoops, he can never enter the door. He must "become a fool, that he may be wise."[7] And when he is humbled in his shame—then let him measure the house of his God in its breadth and length,[8] enjoying clearer, and panting still for clearer manifestations of the incomprehensible God.

But how reverently should we approach this Divine presence! With what holy hands should we open his revelation, dreading a careless, light, and presumptuous spirit; yet withal cherishing those nobly ambitious desires for deeper and higher knowledge; yea, reiterating them before our God with that repetition, which to a carnal mind would be nauseating tautology; but which he who knows our hearts loves to hear, and will beyond our desires abundantly fulfil.

4. *Who hath ascended up into heaven, or descended? who hath gathered the wind in his fists? who hath bound the waters in a garment? who hath established all the ends of the earth? what is his name, and what is his son's name, if thou canst tell?*

Can we wonder that Agur should have acknowledged his *brutishness*—now that he was contemplating the majesty of God—so wondrous in his work—so incomprehensible in his nature? The eye was blinded by the dazzling blaze of the sun. To behold Jehovah *ascending and descending* in his own glorious person[9]—afterward in the person of his dear Son[10]—(for in his great work

[1] Rom. vii. 14. [2] Isa. vi. 5. [3] Job xl. 1—5; xlii. 1—6.

[4] Psalm lxxiii. 1—22—'a beast.' The original is the plural excellent—conveying an intensiveness not easy to transfer acceptably into our idiom. Bp. Horsley gives it—'I was as a brute before thee.'

[5] Isa. vi. 2. [6] Col. iii. 10.

[7] 1 Cor. iii. 18. There is a fine ray of wisdom in that consciousness of ignorance, that led Socrates to confess—'I only know one thing—that I know nothing.' Comp. 1 Cor. viii. 2.

[8] See Ez. xl. xli. [9] Gen. xi. 7; xvii. 22; xviii. 22. Ex. iii. 8

[10] John i. 51; iii. 13; vi. 62. Eph. iv 9, 10.

was not his Father's name in him?[1])—to see him holding the loose winds as firmly as a man might hold *in his fists*[2]—to see his almighty control of *the waters*[3]—and his *establishment of the ends of the earth*[4]—this is a sight that might make the highest and wisest of men sink into nothingness before him. *Who hath* done this, none can doubt. The challenge is thrown out as a demonstration, that it was God alone. 'Show me the man, that can or dare arrogate this power to himself.'[5]

But when we pass from the works to their great Maker—truly it is an overwhelming view—*What is his name, if thou canst tell?* "Canst thou by searching find out God? Canst thou find out the Almighty unto perfection? He dwelleth in the light, which no man can approach unto; whom no man hath seen, nor can see."[6] How can we express him in words, or conceive of him in thought? Child of God! "Be still, and know that he is God."[7] Restrain thy reason. Humble thy faith. "Lay thine hand upon thy mouth." Lie in the dust before him. "O the depth!"[8] open only to him, whose "understanding is infinite."[9]

But how does the mystery increase! *What is his Son's name, if thou canst tell?* And who *can tell?* "No one knoweth the Son, but the Father."[10] Yet there is a Son in the Eternal Godhead—a Son not begotten in time, but from eternity[11]—his name therefore—not as some would have it—a component part of his humiliation—but the manifestation of his Godhead—co-existent with his father in the same ineffable nature—yet personally distinct.[12] *What is his name? and what is his Son's name?* Sovereignty—Omnipresence—Omnipotence is his. He too controls the winds and waters,[13] and establishes the earth[14] as one, who is the visible "form of God, and thinketh it not robbery to be equal with God."[15]

What is his name? The word even of the secret name is easily spelt.[16] But the mystery is hid. We must not search too curiously;[17] lest we "intrude into those things which we have not seen, vainly puffed up by our fleshly mind."[18] Many, however, think it easy to understand this name. They think far more of their wisdom than Agur did, and are at no loss at all to explain what in their proud ignorance they conceive to be the full meaning of the inscrutable subject. But the genuine disciple acknowledges

[1] John x. 30, 38; xiv. 10.

[2] Job xxviii. 25. Comp. Ps. civ. 3; cxxxv. 7. The Heathens dreamed of a lower Deity, whom Jupiter appointed as store-keeper to still or raise the winds at his pleasure. Hom. Odyss. K. 21, 22. Virg. Æn. i. 69, 70.

[3] Job xxvi. 8; xxxviii. 8—11. Isa. xl. 12. Jer. v. 22.

[4] Job xxvi. 7; xxxviii. 5. Ps. xciii. 1; cxix. 90.

[5] Bp. Hall.

[6] Job xi. 7—9. 1 Tim. vi. 16. Comp. Job xxxviii. 3, 4.

[7] Ps. xlvi. 10.

[8] Rom. xi. 33.

[9] Ps. cxlvii. 5. Isa. xl. 28.

[10] Matt. xi. 27.

[11] Chap. viii. 22—30.

[12] 'We have a full and clear testimony of the distinction of person, and that the Son is equal to the Father, and of the same substance with him.' Lavater. See Scott in loco. Mr. Holden considers this interpretation to be 'natural and unforced, and very suitable to the context.'

[13] Matt. viii. 26; xiv. 32.

[14] Col. i. 17. Heb. i. 3.

[15] Phil. ii. 6.

[16] Rev. xix. 12, 13.

[17] Gen. xxxii. 29. Jud. xiii. 18.

[18] Col. ii. 10.

the nature of the Son to be alike incomprehensible with that of the Father—a mystery to be adored—not understood.

Yet what Revelation hath brought up to us from these untraceable depths are pearls of great price. Let us reverently gather them for the enriching of our souls. So far as our Divine Teacher leads us by the hand, let us diligently follow him. The wholesome dread of being "wise above that which is written," must not damp the holy ardor to be wise and wiser continually in that which is written. 'Curiously to inquire is rashness; to believe is piety; to know indeed is life eternal.'[1] Unsearchable as he is in his greatness; yet so near is he to us, that we can rest in his bosom. Yours—Christian—is the unspeakable privilege to be one with him, who is One with God. And therefore—if you *tell his name*—as you are bound to tell what is revealed—is it not all that is infinitely great, combined with the endearing relations—Husband—Brother—Saviour—King?

5. *Every word of God is pure* (purified, Marg.): *he is a shield unto them that put their trust in him.* 6. *Add thou not unto his words, lest he reprove thee, and thou be found a liar.*

Nothing is learned solidly by abstract speculation. Go to the book. Here all is light and purity. Though "secret things belong to the Lord our God; yet the things that are revealed" are our holy directory. Every thing is intended to influence the heart and conduct.[2] How unlike the sacred books of the heathen, or the sensual religion of Mahomet! Here is no license—no encouragement to sin—no connivance at it. All lurking sins cherished in the dark cavern of pollution, are brought to light, and reproved. *Every word of God is pure.* Of what other book in the world can this be said? Where else is the gold found without alloy? *The word is tried.*[3] It has stood the trial, and no dross has been found in it. 'Having God for its Author, it has truth without any mixture of error for its matter.'[4] "*The words of the Lord are pure words*, as silver tried in a furnace of earth, purified seven times."[5]

But if *every word of God is pure*, take care that no word is slighted. How few range over the whole Revelation of God! To take a whole view of the universe, we should embrace not only its fruitful gardens, bnt its barren deserts, coming equally from the hand of God, and none of them made for nought. To take a similarly comprehensive view of the sacred field, we must study the apparently barren, as well as the more manifestly fruitful portions. Food will be gathered from the detailed code of laws, from the historical annals of the kings, and from the "wars and fightings"—the prolific results of "the lusts of men."[6] The whole Scripture is Scripture, and "all Scripture is profitable."[7]

Favoritism, however, is a besetting snare in the sacred study. A part is too often taken instead of the whole, or as if it were the

[1] Bernard. [2] Deut. xxix. 29. [3] Heb. [4] Locke.
[5] Ps. xii. 6. Comp. Ps. cxix. 140. Chap. viii. 8, 9. [6] James iv. 1.
[7] 2 Tim. iii. 16

whole. One is absorbed in the doctrinal, a second in the practical, a third in the prophetical, a fourth in the experimental, Scriptures; each seeming to forget, that *every word of God is pure.* This want of completeness will show itself in a corresponding defect in the Christian profession. The doctrinist becomes loose in practice; the practical professor self-righteous in principle. The prophetic disciple, absorbed in his imaginative atmosphere, neglects present obligations. The experimental religionist mistakes a religion of feeling, excitement, or fancy, for the sobriety and substantial fruitfulness of the gospel. All remind us of our Lord's rebuke—"Ye do err, not knowing the Scriptures."[1]

The great exercise therefore is—to bring out the whole mass of solid truth in all its bearings and glory. So wisely has God linked together the several parts of his system, that we can receive no portion soundly, except in connection with the whole. The accuracy of any view is more than suspicious, that serves to put a forced construction upon Scripture, to dislocate its connexion, or to throw important truths into the shade. Apparently contradictory statements are in fact only balancing truths; each correcting its opposite, and, like the antagonal muscles, contributing to the strength and completeness of the frame. Every heresy probably stands upon some insulated text, or some exaggerated truth, pressed beyond "the proportion of faith." But none can stand upon the combined view and testimony of Scripture. Nor let it be sufficient, that our system includes no positive error, if some great truths be lacking. Let it be carefully grounded upon the acknowledgment—*every word of God is pure.* Some of us may err in presumptuous familiarity with Scripture; others in unworthy reserve. But if the heart be right, self-knowledge will develope the error, and self-discipline will correct it.

Christian simplicity will teach us to receive every Divine Truth upon this formal ground—that it is the word of God. Though it is not all of equal importance, it will be regarded with equal reverence. We acknowledge implicitly God as the Author of every particle of Scripture, *and that every word of God is pure.* To reject therefore one 'jot or tittle is a sufficient demonstration,'—as Dr. Owen admirably observes—'that *no one jot or tittle of it* is received as it ought. Upon whatsoever this title and inscription is—'The Word cf Jehovah'—there must we stoop, and bow down our souls before it, and captivate our understandings unto the obedience of faith.'[2]

This holy reverence is combined with *trust in God.* Blessed *trust,* which brings *a shield* of special favor over his trembling child![3] Sometimes indeed is Satan permitted to envelope him in darkness, and to picture—as it were—frightful transparencies upon his prison-wall. What would he do in this time of terror, did he not find *a shield*—a covert—in the bosom of his God? Yes—if

[1] Matt. xxii. 29.

[2] Owen on the Perseverance of the Saints, Chap. x. See Life of Mary Jane Graham, Chap. v.

[3] Ps. ii. 11, 12. Isa. lxvi. 2.

the word of God be pure, it must be a sure ground of trust. We may take its dictum with undoubting confidence, that *he is a shield* —as to Abraham of old[1]—so to Abraham's children, *that put their trust* in him.[2] In all consequences from within and from without —when I quake under the terrors of the law—in the hour of death —in the day of judgment—"Thou art my *shield*."[3] Nothing honors God, like this turning to him in every time of need. If there be rest, peaceful confidence, safe keeping—here it is.—And where is it found beside? Despondency meets the poor deluded sinner, who looks for some other stay. And even the child of God traces his frequent want of protection to his feeble uncertain use of his Divine *shield*.

But *the word of God is* not only *pure*, and cannot deceive. It is also sufficient; and therefore, like tried gold, it needs no *addition* for its perfection. Therefore to *add to his words*, stamped as they are with his Divine authority, will expose us to his tremendous *reproof*, and cover us with shame.[4] The Jewish Church virtually *added* their oral law and written traditions.[5] The Church of Rome is not less guilty, and as a church has been *found a liar; adding* to the inspired canon a mass of unwritten Tradition, and Apocryphal Writings, with all their gross errors, and in despite of the clearest proof of their human origin.[6] And is there no approach to this sinful presumption in the attempt in our own day to bring tradition to a near—if not to an equal—level with the Sacred Testimony? A new rule of faith is thus introduced—an addition to the Divine rule—of co-ordinate authority. Never was it so important to clear from all question the momentous controversy— what is—what is not—the Word of God. The Lord has most carefully guarded his *pure word* from all human admixture. May he preserve his ministers from "teaching for doctrines the commandments of men;" "saying, the Lord hath said it, when he hath not spoken!"[7] What a reverential awe—what godly jealousy —should they exercise—to *add not to the pure word* by the glosses of false interpretation; not to expound their own minds in the stead of the mind of God!

7. *Two things have I required of thee; deny me them not before I die:* 8. *Remove far from me vanity and lies: give me neither poverty nor riches; feed me with food convenient* (of my allowance, Marg.) *for me:* 9. *Lest I be full, and deny thee, and say, Who is the Lord? or lest I be poor, and steal, and take the name of my God in vain.*

Though Agur had confessed his *brutishness* before his God; yet his prayers (the most accurate test of a man of God) prove him to have been possessed of deep spiritual understanding. "We ask, and receive not, because we ask amiss, that we may consume it upon

1 Gen. xv. 1.
2 Ps. v. 12. Comp. the same connection, xviii. 30.
3 Ib. cxix. 114.
4 See Deut. iv. 2; xii. 32. Rev. xxii. 18, 19.
5 Mark vii. 7—13.
6 Mr. Horne has conferred an obligation on the Church, by publishing separately his valuable Digest of the Apocryphal question, from the last Edition of his 'Introduction.'
7 Ez. xiii. 7—9, with Matt. xv. 9.

our lusts."[1] How wisely gracious therefore is the teaching of the Divine Comforter, "helping our infirmities" in prayer, and, by moulding our petitions "according to the will of God," ensuring their acceptance![2] Agur's heart must have been under this heavenly teaching; dictating his prayers by a primary regard to his best interests, and by a spiritual discernment of what would probably be beneficial, and what injurious to them.

Two things he especially *required*—not as though he had nothing else to ask—but as being the pressing burden of the present moment. And these he asks—as if he would take no *denial*—with all the intense earnestness of a dying sinner—*Deny me them not before I die.*

His prayers are short, but comprehensive. Though little is said, yet that little is fraught with matter; framed in its proper order. Spiritual blessings occupy the first place; temporal blessings are secondary, and in subserviency to them.

Remove from me vanity and lies. Is not this the atmosphere of the world? *vanity* its character—*lies* its delusion; promising happiness, only to disappoint its weary and restless victims?[3] How can the heaven-born soul breathe in such a world? Every thing deadens the heart, and eclipses the glory of the Saviour. "The soul cleaveth to the dust." "All that is in the world—the lust of the flesh, and the lust of the eyes, and the pride of life—is not of the Father, but is of the world."[4] And therefore "they that observe *lying vanities* forsake their own mercy."[5] A soul that knows its dangers and its besetting temptations, will live in the spirit of this prayer of the godly Agur—*Remove from me—far from me*—as far as possible—*vanity and lies.* "Turn away mine eyes"—prayed a Saint of God in the same watchful jealousy—"from beholding *vanity. Remove from me the way of lying.*"[6]

But how singular—yet how fraught with instruction—is Agur's second prayer! All are ready to pray against *poverty.* But to deprecate *riches*—'Oh! deliver me from this muck-rake'—'that prayer'—as Interpreter remarked to Christiana—'has lain by, till it is almost rusty. 'Give me not riches'—is scarce the prayer of one of ten thousand.[7] Agur, as a wise man, desired the safest and happiest lot—not—as Israel of old—"meat for his lust,"[8] but *food convenient for him,* measured out in daily *allowance*[9]—suitable to his need. This is obviously not a fixed measure. It implies—not a bare sufficiency for natural life, but a provision varying according to the call, in which God has placed us. 'If Agur be the master of a family, then that is his competency, which is sufficient to maintain his wife, children, and household. If Agur be a public person, a Prince or a Ruler of the people, then that is Agur's sufficiency which will conveniently maintain him in that condition.'[10] Jacob,

[1] James iv. 3. [2] Rom. viii. 26, 27. [3] Comp. Gen. xxxii. 26.
[4] 1 John ii. 16. [5] Jon. ii. 8. [6] Ps. cxix. 37, 39.
[7] Pilgrim's Progress. Part. ii. [8] Ps. lxxviii. 18.
[9] Comp. 1 Kings iv. 27. 2 Kings xxv. 30. Jer. xxxvi. 21.
[10] Mede's Sermon on Agur's Choice.

when "he had become two bands," evidently required more, than when in his earlier life "with his staff he had passed over Jordan."[1] What was sufficient for himself alone, would not have been sufficient for the many, that were then dependent upon him. The immense provisions for Solomon's table—considering the vast multitude of his dependents[2]—might be only a competency for the demand. The distribution of the manna was *food convenient*—nothing too much, but no deficiency. "He that gathered much had nothing over; and he that gathered little had no lack."[3] And thus, in the daily dispensation of Providence, a little may be a sufficiency to one; while an overflowing plenty is no superfluity to another. Only let Christian self-denial—not depraved appetite—be the standard of competency. Proud nature never stoops so low.[4] The Apostle distinctly traces to the influence of Divine teaching his Christian moderation in his diversified conditions of abundance and of want.[5] Philosophy may have inculcated the lesson. But Almighty grace alone can command the practice of it.

'It is a question'—says Dr. South—'whether the piety or the prudence of this prayer be greater.'[6] Agur was well persuaded of the temptations incident to these two opposite conditions—*the vanity and lies* belonging to *riches*,[7] the discontent and occasion of sin, which are the snares of *poverty*. Yet he does not pray absolutely against these states—only submissively. It is the prayer of his choice—the desire of his heart. God would graciously exempt him from both, and bless him with a middle condition. Nor does he ask this for the indulgence of the flesh. He deprecates not the trouble, anxieties, and responsibilities of *riches*, which might betoken an indolent self-pleasing spirit; nor the *miseries and sufferings of poverty*. But he cries for deliverance from the snares of each condition—Let me not be *rich, lest I be full and deny thee.* Let me not be poor, *lest I steal, and take the name of my God in vain.*

And alas! the danger of these results is but too evident. Both extremes are the borders of fearful temptation. Strange and irrational as it may appear—such is the depravity of our nature, that mercies induce neglect, and often casting-off, of God.[8] Lust is too strong for conscience. Rarely does "the daughter of Tyre come with her gift, or the rich among the people entreat the favor" of their God.[9] Too often—the more we receive from God, the less he receives from us.[10] The twining thorns choke the heavenly plant.[11] And as we prosper in the flesh, we are impoverished in the spirit.

[1] Gen. xxxii. 10. [2] 1 Kings iv. 22, 23.
[3] Ex. xvi. 18. [4] Comp. Ecc. v. 10. Hab. ii. 5. 1 Tim. vi. 9, 10.
[5] *I have learned—I have been instructed*—expressions taken from the instruction in the Heathen Mysteries. Phil. iv. 11, 12.
[6] Sermon on James iii. 16. [7] Ps. lxii. 9. [8] Job. xxi. 13, 14; xxii. 17, 18
[9] Psalm xlv. 12.
[10] Deut. vi. 11, 12; viii. 10—13; xxxii. 15. Hos. xiii. 6. What a deep knowledge of the heart is implied in that petition of our Litany for deliverance *in all time of wealth* How difficult to realize the *time of wealth* as the time of *special need!*
[11] Matt. xiii. 22.

But not less imminent are the dangers of pinching poverty. And it is not every Christian, that can honorably grapple with them. Dishonesty is a besetting temptation[1]—followed up by perjury to escape punishment.[2] Thus two commandments are broken, and the sinner is in "the snare of the devil, taken captive by him at his will."[3]

The 'golden mean' (for so even a Heathen could describe it)[4] is recommended by patriarchs,[5] prophets,[6] and apostles.[7] Nay, our Lord teaches us to pray for it in terms identical with this petition. For what else is our "daily bread" but *food convenient for us?*[8]

We must however be careful that we use Agur's prayer in his spirit. Perhaps the Gospel rather teaches us to leave the matter entirely with God. Both *riches and poverty* are his appointment.[9] It may please him to place us in a high condition, to entrust us with much *riches*, or to exercise us with the trials of *poverty*. Many of his children are in both these conditions.[10] And shall they wish it otherwise? Let them rather seek for grace to glorify him in either state. Or if it seem lawful to pray for a change of condition, let them not forget to pray for a single eye to his glory—that his will—not ours—may be done in us. 'Whithersoever God gives'—said the pious Bishop Hall—'I am both thankful and indifferent; so as, while I am rich in estate, I may be poor in spirit, and while I am poor in estate, I may be rich in grace.'[11]

10. *Accuse not* (hurt not with thy tongue, Marg.) *a servant unto his master, lest he curse thee, and thou be found guilty.*

Let not this Proverb be a shelter for unfaithfulness. How much evil goes on in a family, because those that are privy to it, and ought to inform, shrink from *accusing a servant to his master!* 'They must not make mischief in the house, or bring themselves into trouble.' But we owe it alike to master[12] and to servant[13] not to wink at sin. We may owe it to ourselves to *accuse a servant to his master* for injury to ourselves.[14] Yet let a fellow servant first observe our Lord's rule of privacy.[15] Let every exercise of faithfulness be in the spirit of love. Beware of the busy wantonness of the talebearer.[16] Never make trouble for trifles; or *accuse the servant,* when he may not have the full liberty and power to

[1] Chap. vi. 30.
[2] Chap xxix. 24. Comp. Lev. vi. 2, 3; xix. 11, 12. Zech. v. 3, 4.
[3] 2 Tim. ii. 26.

[4] '*Auream* quisquis *mediocritatem*
Diligit, tutus caret obsoleti
Sordibus tecti, caret invidendâ
Sobrius aulâ.' Horat. Carm. Lib. ii. 10.

[5] Gen. xxviii. 20. [6] Jer. xlv. 5. [7] Phil. iv. 11, 12. 1 Tim. vi. 6—10.

[8] The learned Mede insists upon this identity. Things fit and sufficient, precisely answers to αρτον επιουσιαν. Matt. xiii. 11—a sufficiency, as it were, επι την ουσιαν, adequate to our being and support—bread sufficient—the bread we have need of.

[9] Ri-hes are his gift, 1 Kings iii. 13. Poverty is his will, Deut. xv. 11. Comp Job i. 21.

[10] Abraham—David—Solomon—with Lazarus and the heirs of his kingdom, Jam. ii. 5.

[11] Works, viii. 195. [12] Matt. vii. 12. [13] Lev. xix. 17.
[14] Gen. xxi. 25, 26. [15] Matt. xviii. 15. [16] Lev. xix. 16.

defend himself. When conscience does not constrain us to speak—the law of love always supplies a reason for silence. The Jewish *servants* were ordinarily slaves, for the most part crushed by their Master's oppression. Cruel therefore would it be without strong cause to heap degradation upon a sinking fellow-creature; for whom the Mosaic law prescribed kindness and protection.[1]

The rule however may be more generally applied. David suffered severely from unkind *accusations to his* royal *Master*.[2] Those who take the most eager pleasure in finding fault are usually those, who can least bear the retort upon themselves. Take heed, lest while thou art exposing "the mote in thy brother's eye," thou be reminded to thy deeper disgrace of "the beam that is in thine own eye."[3] A curse from thy injured brother may not "come causeless to thee."[4] The motive, which plainly actuated the accusation of the adulteress, only retorted shame upon the accusers. "The conviction of their own consciences"[5] brought their own *guilt* to mind. Should not this remembrance constrain us *needlessly* to "speak evil of no man?"[6] Should not the covering of our own infinitely provoking offences, induce us gladly to cast a covering over our offending brother, where the honor of God did not forbid concealment![7]

11. *There is a generation that curseth their father, and doth not bless their mother.* 13. *There is a generation that are pure in their own eyes, and yet is not washed from their filthiness.* 13. *There is a generation, O how lofty are their eyes! and their eyelids are lifted up.* 14. *There is a generation, whose teeth are as swords, and their jaw teeth as knives, to devour the poor from off the earth, and the needy from among men.*

Agur here gives in artificial order (as in some of the Psalms) his observations, probably in answer to his disciples' inquiries. He describes four different masses that came under his eyes—not a few individuals—but *generations*—a race of men—like a large stock—descending from father to son. Truly "the thing that hath been, is that which shall be; and that which is done, is that which shall be done; and there is no new thing under the sun."[8] For these four *generations* belong to every age. They always have been, and always will be, to the end of time.

Take the first *generation*. What a disgrace to human nature! *cursing* their parents! Solon, when asked why he had made no law against parricides, replied, that he could not conceive of any one so impious and cruel. The Divine Law-giver knew his creature better—that his heart was capable of wickedness beyond conception[9]—of this wickedness beyond the imagination of the heathen sage. He has marked it with his most tremendous judgment,[10] The cursing of a parent was visited with the same punishment as

[1] Deut. xxiii. 15. [2] 1 Sam. xxii. 9, 10; xxvi. 19.
[3] Matt. vii. 3—5.
[4] Comp. Chap. xxvi. 2. Deut. xv. 9. 1 Sam. xxvi. 19. Comp. James ii. 13.
[5] John viii. 3—9. Comp. Matt. xii. 2. [6] Tit. iii. 2, 3.
[7] Eph. iv. 31, 32. Col. iii. 12, 13. [8] Eccles. i. 9. [9] Jer. xvii. 9.
[10] Verse 17; xx. 20. Deut. xxi. 18—21; xxvii. 16.

the blaspheming of God[1]—so near does the one in sin approach the other. The rebel against his parent is ready to "stretch out his hand against God" himself, and to "run upon the thick bosses of his buckler."[2] Many are the forms, in which this proud abomination shows itself—resistance of a parent's authority[3]—contempt of his reproof[4]—shamelessly defiling his name[5]—needlessly exposing sin[6]—coveting his substance[7]—denying his obligation.[8] Most fearful is the increase of this *generation* among ourselves. Every village bears sad testimony to this crying sin, that brings down many a parent's grey hairs with sorrow to the grave, and spreads anarchy throughout the whole land. No plea of extenuation can be allowed to justify the sin. The authority of parents, even in the lowest degradation, must be respected, even when we dare not —must not, follow their example. But what can be done to stay the threatened invasion of this devastating flood? Once and again let us remember, ere it be too late—*discipline*—wise—tender—early discipline, *prayer*—pleading—patient—believing prayer; diligence —active—direct—prudently applied. Will not our God in the use of his own means give us yet to praise him? Trust and doubt not.

In what Church do we not find the next *generation?* The Pharisee of the Gospel[9] was the living picture—*pure in his own eyes, yet not washed from his filthiness.* The Laodicean Church was full of such professors.[10] Indeed everywhere it is the great work of Satan to delude the sinner into a good opinion of himself. He estimates himself by some plausible qualities, or some course of external decorum,[11] while a blind infidel as to that depravity of his nature, which—not the gross acts of sin—gives the stamp to the whole character. Sometimes partial obedience maintains this delusion; while he hides from himself the genuine hypocrisy of secret reserves, which mars all.[12] He was once impure; but he has gone through a course of purifying observances. He has *washed* himself *from his filthiness.*

We often see this self-deceiver in the spiritual Church, exhibiting a full and clean profession to his fellow-men; while himself—awful thought!—living at an infinite distance from God.[13] Salvation by free grace is his creed, and he will contend earnestly for the purest simplicity of the Gospel. He can distinguish accurately between sound and unscriptural doctrine. Yet his conscience is sleeping in the "form of godliness," while his heart is wholly uninfluenced by "its power!"[14] There is no mourning for his innate guilt and pollution, no sensibility of sin in his thoughts, objects, motives, or prayers; no perceptible change from a proud, self-

[1] Lev. xx. 9, with xxiv. 11—16. See the same close connection, Isa. xlv. 8, 9. 2 Tim. iii. 2.
[2] Job xv. 25, 26.
[3] 2 Sam. xv. 1—10.
[4] Deut. xxi. 18—20. 1 Sam. ii. 25.
[5] 2 Sam. xvi. 22.
[6] Gen. ix. 22.
[7] Jud. xvii. 2.
[8] Matt. xv. 4—6—showing the identity between *cursing and not blessing* the parent.
[9] Matt. xxiii. 25—27. Luke xvi. 15; xviii. 10. John ix. 40, 41.
[10] Rev. iii. 17, 18.
[11] Matt. xix. 20. Rom. vii. 9. Phil. iii. 6.
[12] 1 Sam. xv. 13, 14.
[13] 1 Cor. xiii. 1.
[14] 2 Tim. iii. 5.

willed, or worldly spirit. He is *pure in his own eyes*—in his own imaginary view, and perverted judgment! Yet until he be disturbed in his complacency, how hopeless his condition![1]

The want of all cheering influence is a plain proof of self-delusion. Vital religion is the sugar in the liquid, which impregnates the whole contents of the cup. The path may be thorny, and our light darkness. But sweetness will be mingled in our sorrow, even till the last drop in the cup of life shall be spent. The formalist's religion is a piece of polished marble in the cup, externally beautiful; but cold and dead; impregnating nothing with an atom of sweetness.

The power of this self-delusion is—that man has no natural conception of the deep stain of sin, such as nothing but the blood of sprinkling can fetch out. The man of God, bathed in the tears of penitence, cries out for this sprinkling alone to "purge him."[2] The tears of the purest repentance in themselves are impure and abominable.[3] It is not the exercise of a day to know the full extent of our corruption. As the Lord leads us into the light of our own hearts, we behold "greater and yet greater abominations."[4] The conscience purged from sin becomes more clear for the discovery of remaining pollution. Those who are most purified will have the deepest sensibility of impurity,[5] and will most deeply value "the fountain opened for sin and uncleanness," with its free invitation—"Wash, and be clean."[6]

Sinner! if thou be found *unwashed from thy filthiness*. must it not be certain exclusion from that "place, into which shall not in any wise enter any thing that defileth?"[7] Awful indeed will be the final sentence—"He that is filthy, let him be filthy still!"[8]

The next *generation* provokes our sorrowful amazement—*O how lofty are their eyes! and their eyelids lifted up*. Such intolerable arrogance! What greater anomaly does the conscience afford than that of a proud sinner! his *eyelids lifted up*, instead of being cast to the ground. Such is his self-confidence even in the presence of his God![9] And before men—all must keep their distance, from these swelling worms! We may see this pride embodied in a system—"the Man of Sin sitting in the temple of God, showing himself that he is God!"[10] We may see it in worldly greatness—in the pride of Moab,[11] and the prince of Tyre;[12] the boasting Antiochus;[13] Haman in all his glory;[14] "Herod arrayed in his royal apparel;"[15] Nebuchadnezzar in his self-pleasing contemplation, before the severe chastening of his God had taught him the wholesome lesson—"Those that walk in pride he is able to abase."[16] In a lower level, it is the pride of birth, rank, wisdom, riches, or ac-

1 Comp. Chap. iii. 7; xii. 15; xvi. 2; xxviii. 11. 2 Psalm li. 7.
3 Job ix. 30, 31. Jer. ii. 22. 4 Ezek. viii. 7—15.
5 Comp. Rom. vii. 9. Phil. iii. 6, with Rom. vii. 14—24. 1 Tim. i. 15.
6 Zech. xiii. 1. 7 Rev. xxi. 27. 8 Ib. xxii. 11.
9 Comp. Luke xviii. 10—13. 10 2 Thess. ii. 3, 4.
11 Isa. xvi. 6. Jer. xlviii. 29. 12 Ez. xxviii. 2—9. 13 Dan. xi. 36, 37.
14 Est. v. 11. 15 Acts xii. 21—23. 16 Dan. iv. 30—37.

complishments. In every circumstance is this high look specially hateful to God;"[1] and the day is appointed in his own purpose for its prostrate humiliation.[2] Meanwhile little is it conceived, how really contemptible this pride makes its deluded votaries appear before their fellow-creatures.[3] One beam of the Divine glory[4] and one sight of the cross of Calvary[5]—must at once dispel their vain splendid illusion.

The last *generation* appears before us as a monster of iniquity. We can scarcely draw the picture in its full colors. Conceive of brutes with iron *teeth*—a wild beast opening his mouth, and displaying—instead of truth—*swords and knives*, sharpened ready for their murderous work.[6] Yet withal, these cruel oppressors are marked by pitiful cowardice. They vent their wantonness only, where there is little or no power of resistance; not the wolf with the wolf, but with the defenceless lamb; *devouring the poor and needy from off the earth*;[7] "eating up my people"—not like an occasional indulgence, but "as they eat bread"[8]—their daily appetite—without intermission. Such cruel oppressors appear from time to time as a chastening curse to the land. Nay, they were found among the rulers of God's own people,[9] even among the teachers of religion,[10] cloaking their covetousness under the garb of special holiness. God thus shows us a picture of man left to himself. When the reins are loosened or given up, is there any length of wickedness, to which he may not proceed?

Indeed the four generations teach us this same lesson—most valuable, yet most humbling, thoroughly to know. Yet so depraved is man, that nothing is so much hidden from him as himself.[11] He keeps a good opinion of himself, by keeping the light out of the heart and conscience. His imagination fancies good, where there is nothing but hateful deformity. Under this self-delusion—we deal so gently and tenderly with sin, that no conflict is maintained with it, no sorrow or burden felt concerning it. How deeply do we need the searching light and convincing power of the Spirit of God, to show us our abominations; to make us tremble at the sight of them; and to let us see, that our remedy must come from God every moment; that no partial change, no external polish—nothing less than the creating power of God—can reach the case for a cure.[12]

Adored indeed be the grace of God, if we be not in one or other of these *generations!* But let us remember "such *were* some of us"—either disobedient to our parents, or self-righteous in the church, proud and contemptuous, or cruel and oppressive. But *we are washed from our filthiness.*[13] Therefore—"who maketh thee to differ?[14] is the grand balancing question, when we are disposed

[1] Chap. vi. 17; xxi. 4. Comp. Ps. cxxxi. 1. [2] Isa. ii. 11—17; iii. 16, 17. [3] Ps. ci. 5. [4] Comp. Job xlii. 5, 6. Isa. vi. 5. [5] Phil. ii. 4—8. [6] Psalm lvii. 4. [7] Ps. x. 8, 9. Eccl. iv. 1. Isa. iii. 15. Am. ii. 6, 7; viii. 4. Mic. ii. 1, 2. Hab. iii. 14. [8] Ps. xiv. 4. [9] Am. iv. 1. Mic. iii. 1—3. Zeph. iii. 3. [10] Matt. xxiii. 14. 2 Pet. ii. 3. [11] 2 Kings viii. 12, 13. [12] Ps. li. 10. [13] 1 Cor. vi. 11. [14] Ib. iv. 7.

to forget from whence we were raised, and to whom we owe all that we have and are for his service.

15. *The horse-leach hath two daughters, crying, Give, give. There are three things that are never satisfied, yea, four things say not, It is enough,* (wealth, Marg.) 16. *The grave; and the barren womb; the earth that is not filled with water: and the fire that saith not, It is enough.*

Agur describes in an artificial mode of expression,[1] but with forcible imagery, the cravings of human lust. If viewed in reference to the last generation, they form an admirably finished picture of the merciless and avaricious tyrant. They are like the *horse-leach, which hath two daughters, crying, Give, give.* They are like the *three and four things, the grave—the womb—the earth, and the fire.*[2] But with a more general reference, the figures are graphically instructive. The *horse-leach* with its two-forked-tongue like *two daughters,* sucked the blood with an insatiable appetite.[3] *The grave* opens the mouth for fresh victims.[4] *The barren womb* eagerly covets the blessing.[5] *The parched earth,* after large supplies, still thirsts for more. *The fire*—when the spark first kindles a coal, or lights upon combustible matter—never ceases to burn, as long as fuel is supplied; and in many a disastrous conflagration, leaves us to cry out in fearful wonder, "Behold! how great a matter a little fire kindleth!"[6] And yet these are scarcely adequate representations of that insatiable thirst within, that *never* says—*It is enough.* The greater the portion, the greater the lust. Every indulgence provokes the appetite.[7] How blessed is that state, to which the gospel brings us. "Having food and raiment, let us be therewith content!" What a merciful deliverance from that "destruction and perdition"—the certain end of lawless lust![8] Happy child of God! weaned from his own indulgence! disciplined under his Father's yoke! satisfied abundantly with his Father's love. Whether "he abound or suffer need"—he can say—"*It is wealth*—I am full, and abound."[9] Has he not found that, which answers every demand, supplies every need, and satisfies every desire? What but God can fill the soul, which God hath made, and made for himself?

17. *The eye that mocketh at his father, and despiseth to obey his mother, the ravens of the valley shall pick it out, and the young eagles shall eat it.*

Agur here returns to the first *generation*—the unnatural *despisers* of their parents.[10] He had before described their character. Now he links it with the punishment. Observe the guilt only of a scornful look—*the mocking eye,* when perhaps not a word is spoke. Certainly if the fifth commandment is "the first with promise,"[1] it

[1] See verses 21, 24, 27; vi. 16. Am. i. 3, 6, 9, 11, 13; ii. 1, 4.
[2] Holden. Comp. Ps. lix. 12, 14, 15.
[3] Reformers' Notes. 'Non missura cutem, nisi plena cruoris hirudo.' Hor. De Arte Poetica, 475.
[4] Chap. xxvii. 20. Hab. ii. 5.
[5] Gen. xxx. 1. 1 Sam. i. 6, 11.
[6] James iii. 6.
[7] See Augustine's Confess. Lib. iii. c. 1
[8] 1 Tim. vi. 6—10.
[9] Phil. iv. 12, 18.
[10] Ver. 11.
[11] Eph. vi. 2.

is also the first with judgment. No commandment in the breach of it is visited with more tremendous threatenings. What a picture is here given of infamy? Perhaps the case of Absalom furnishes the most striking illustration—a self-willed youth and rebel against his father and his sovereign—made a spectacle of shame before his people![1] the vengeance of God inflicting the punishment, which was due at the bar of human justice! But we may observe a more general illustration of the frightful picture. How many confessions on the scaffold have borne testimony, that the first step towards that untimely end was contempt of parental authority and restraint! The bodies of such criminals were deprived of the rites of burial—exposed either on the gallows, or cast out into the valley, as meat for the fowls of the air.[2] Thus *the eye*, that had scornfully *mocked his father*, became the choice morsel of the *eagle or the raven of the valley.*[3]

But even where there is no such literal fulfilment, the curse is not the less sure. Seldom do we see the disobedient rebels prospering, and blessed in their own children. Retributive justice visits them late,—but certain; and the poignant anguish of many a disappointed hope, and many an arrow shot from their own bow, may bear to them the message of their chastising Father—"Thine own iniquities shall correct thee, and thy backslidings shall reprove thee."[4]

18. *There be three things which are too wonderful for me; yea, four which I know not.* 19. *The way of an eagle in the air; the way of a serpent upon a rock: the way of a ship in the midst* (heart, Marg.) *of the sea; and the way of a man with a maid.* 20. *Such is the way of an adulterous woman; she eateth and wipeth her mouth, and saith, I have done no wickedness.*

The kingdom of nature is full of wonders, and these wonders are full of instruction. Where the philosopher cannot give a reason, the humble disciple may learn a lesson. The depths of nature are the figure of the depths of sin—of the unsearchable deceitful heart.[5] *The eagle* soars *in the air* with so lofty and rapid a flight, that the eye cannot follow *her way.* It leaves no scent nor footsteps, by which we might trace it, as the beast on the ground.[6] *The serpent* on the sand would leave its mark. But *the serpent* on the rock, it leaves no slime like the worm—no feathers like the birds—who then can mark *its way? The ship*—like the great monster of the deep—"maketh a path to shine after her."[7] But while she

[1] 2 Sam. xviii. 9—17.

[2] See Gen. xl. 19. I Sam. xvii. 44—46. 2 Sam. xxi. 10.

[3] Bochart conceives the allusion to be to the valley—Jer. xxxi. 40—where probably the dead bodies of the criminals were sent. At all events the denial of the rites of burial was one of the severest marks of Divine chastisement. Comp. Jer. vii. 33; xxii. 18, 19. The Heathens felt this deprivation to be a special affliction. Homer represents the dying Hector as entreating Achilles not to give his body to be torn by his Grecian dogs, but to restore it to his parents for burial. Lib. X. 337—343. Virgil also represents Palinurus as entreating Æneas either to throw the earth himself upon his body, or to carry it with him through the water, rather than expose it to the birds of prey. Æn. VI. 363—371.

[4] Jer. ii. 19. [5] Ib. xvii. 9. [6] Job xxxix. 27.

[7] Ib. xli. 32. Comp. Ps. civ. 26; cvii. 23, 24. This figure, and that of the eagle, as images of the rapid course of life, are finely illustrated. Wisd. v. 11, 12. Witsius ad-

ploughs *in the midst* (*in the heart*) *of the sea*, her furrows are quickly closed up, and *her way* is untraceable. Not less mysterious is *the way of a man with a maid.* Eminently practised is the seducer in "the depths of Satan," and a thousand arts does he practise to allure the affections of his unwary victim. And it is often as difficult to penetrate his designs, and to escape his snares, as to trace *the way of the eagle, the serpent, or the ship.* Let this be a warning to young and inexperienced females, not to trust to their own purity, or to the strength of their own resolutions, or to place themselves in unprotected situations.[1]

Equally unfathomable are the devices of *the adulterous woman* to entangle her prey, and to deceive her unsuspecting husband. Solomon has described the picture with graphical and minute accuracy.[2] Such a course of abomination, wickedness, and hypocrisy, as is scarcely to be conceived! indulging her sin as the sweet morsel under her tongue; feasting greedily upon her "stolen water and secret bread,"[3] yet keeping up the semblance of innocence and purity;[4] *wiping her mouth*, to prevent all suspicion, suffering no sign of the action to remain. A woman must be advanced very far in the way of sin, before she can present so unblushing a front. Yet every fresh indulgence of lust gives rise to new artifices, "hardening" the heart more fully in "the deceitfulness of sin."[5] Its fascinations blind it to its real character. Let then the first step be shunned—the most distant path, that may lead to temptation. Where shame ceases to accompany it, the ruin of the victim is accomplished. Abundant warning is given—solemn instruction —many beacons in the path—to show the certain end of this flowery road.[6]

mirably defends these figures as worthy of inspiration, against the sneers of neological critics. Misc. Sacra. Lib. i. c. xviii. 31—33.

[1] Ambrose has treated fully upon these four figures. Assuming the chapter to be written by Solomon, he explains his ignorance of them—'not that he was not able to know them, but because it was not a time for him to know them.' *The way of the eagle* he understands to be the ascension of Christ, flying back, as an eagle to his Father, carrying man plucked from the jaws of the enemy as his prey with him! And though the ascension was visible, yet what understanding could grasp the apprehension of such Majesty retiring to heaven! *The way of the serpent on the rock* shadowed the assaults of Satan upon Christ—on whom—as *on a rock*—(unlike the first man, who was earth and dust) he could leave no mark—no footsteps of his malice. The pious father seems to be in some doubt upon the third image. *The way of the ship in the sea* is the way of God's church through the sea of persecution. This ship cannot miscarry, because Christ is lifted up on the mast of it—that is—on the cross. The Father sitteth as pilot at the stern of it. The Comforter preserved its prow! Or—Christ is the ship, into which the souls of all true believers do go up; which, that it may be carried more strongly in the midst of the waves, is made of wood, and fixed with iron: this is Christ in the flesh. And who can tell the way of this ship, either in the womb of the Virgin, or the heart of believers *The way of a man in his youth* (LXX. and some other versions) illustrates the ways of our Saviour Christ in his youth upon the earth! Such puerile crudities are calculated to bring ridicule rather than reverence to the sacred book. Yet a combined and powerful effort is now made to palm the Fathers upon the church, as the primary expositors of Scripture, and the standard of faith! Many patristic expositions of the Proverbs equally gross might have been produced. Apart from higher ground—Can we forbear surprise, that men of taste and learning should affix their imprimatur to such undisciplined folly of interpretation?

[2] Chap. vii; v. 6. [3] Chap. ix. 17. [4] Gen. xxxix. 13—19

[5] Heb. iii. 13. [6] Chap. v. 3—5; vii. 24—27; ix. 18.

21. *For three things the earth is disquieted, and for four things it cannot bear.* 22. *For a servant, when he reigneth; and a fool, when he is filled with meat,* 23. *For an odious woman, when she is married: and an handmaid, that is heir to her mistress.*

Next to things which were unsearchable, Agur now mentions some things that were intolerable—*things for which the earth is disquieted*—bringing confusion wherever they are found. Who does not naturally condemn things out of place, as unsuitable and unseemly? Order is the law of the works of God in the world, no less than in the Church;[1] and any breach of order is to be deprecated. *Four* such evils are here mentioned—two connected with men—two with women—the one in the community—the other in the family.

The first evil mentioned is—*a servant when he reigneth.* This is a serious evil in the family, whether it arises from the mismanagement of the master,[2] or from his own intrigue.[3] He is obviously out of place, and ruling, where he ought to serve, must bring disorder.[4] The evil is far greater in a kingdom. Men of low birth may indeed rise honorably by their own merit to a high station. God may call them, as he did Joseph,[5] to *reign.* The evil is the advancement to power of ignorant unprincipled minions.[6] Men of a mean spirit cannot bear to be raised. Intoxicated by the sudden elevation, these upstarts show themselves not only fools but tyrants;[7] swelling with all the insolence of their unseemly honor. Such was the enmity of Tobiah the Ammonite,[8] and the misrule of Haman.[9] What national evils resulted from the elevation of Jeroboam![10] What anarchy from the successful usurpation of Zimri![11] Well therefore might the *reign of servants* be deplored as a component part of the calamity of disconsolate Zion![12] In the ordinary course it can only be viewed as a chastening dispensation.[13] Let us acknowledge with thankfulness our deliverance from it.

Then look at the *fool* (not an idiot, but a wilful sinner) *when he is filled with meat.* Can we wonder that he should be a trouble—a curse; giving the reins to his appetite, and becoming yet more devoid of understanding than before? The history of Nabal, sunk into brutishness by his own sensual lust[14]—Elah murdered by his servant, whilst "drinking himself drunk in his steward's house"[15]—Belshazzar giving himself over to the lust of ungodliness[16]—all these were evils, *for which the earth was disquieted, and* which it *could not bear. Filled with meat*—with "surfeiting and drunkenness"

[1] Ecc. iii. 11. 1 Cor. xiv. 40. [2] Chap. xxix. 21. [3] Verse 23.
[4] Gen. xvi. 4. [5] Ib. xlv. 5. [6] Chap. xix. 10. Eccl. x. 5—7.
[7] Chap. xxviii. 3. This danger is accurately drawn by one of the Classic moralists:—

Asperius nihil est humili; cum surgit in altum:
Cuncta ferit, dum cuncta timet; desævit in omnes,
Ut se posse putet; nec bellua tetrior ulla est,
Quam servi rabius, in libera terga furentis.

Claudian, Lib. I. quoted by Lavater.

[8] Neh. ii. 10. [9] Est. iii. 1. [10] 1 Kings xi. 26—28; xii. 30.
[11] Ib. xvi. 9—20. Comp. 2 Kings viii. 12. [12] Lam. v. 8. [13] Isa. iii. 4, 5.
[14] 1 Sam. xxv. 9, 36, 37. [15] 1 Kings xvi. 9, 10. Comp. Hos. vii. 5—7.
[16] Dan. v. 1—4, 30. Comp. 1 Sam. xxx. 16. 1 Kings xx. 16—18.

—they were set forth as an example in the just punishment of their wicked folly.

Look again into the inner room of the family. What is the origin of discord and palpable misery? *An odious woman* is in rule. She quarrels with all around her. Her ungoverned tongue and temper are an unceasing source of agitation. Had she known herself, much better for her never to have entered into the marriage bond, than to become the inseparable tormentor of her husband and family.[1] Woman is to man either his greatest curse or blessing. If love be not the cement of the sacred union, truly will it be a bond of misery, from which only the special mercy of God can deliver. Let the worldly portion of the wife be the last consideration. Take heed, lest worldly glitter open a door for remediless misery.

The odious woman, when she is married, if she be in authority, becomes a national evil. Jezebel was a scourge to Israel—the spring of all Ahab's wickedness—that brought the heavy judgment of God upon the land.[2] *The earth was disquieted for her,* and at the last cast her out.[3] Herodias brought upon her husband and his nation the guilt of the blood of the murdered prophet "crying from the ground."[4] If marriage be the ordinance of lust—not of godliness; what wonder, if *an odious woman* should be the result—a canker to every domestic comfort?

The last evil noticed is a frequent source of family trouble—*an handmaid that is heir to her mistress.* Want of discipline, simplicity, or integrity leads to waywardness and self-indulgence; and the house, instead of being under wholesome rule—becomes a prey to envy and strife. The ill-regulated connection between Abraham and Hagar, when *the servant became heir to her mistress*—occupying her mistress's place with her husband—became the source of most baneful contention.[5] Our own history presents sad illustration of this intolerable evil. Anne Boleyn and Jane Seymour were *handmaids,* and unhappily *heirs* to their respective *mistresses,* while living in the affections of the sovereign. The royal example of selfishness and lust was a national grievance, in which *the handmaids* were not wholly guiltless.

Nor are such cases unknown in modern society. *An handmaid* treated with that tender familiarity, which breaks down the Divine barriers between the several ranks—has sometimes offensively become *heir to her mistress.* Either she has succeeded to her property—perhaps to the exclusion of more rightful claimants;[6] or risen to her place by marriage with her master—an ill assorted union—like that above-mentioned—usually productive of much family dissension.

How needful is it to preserve consistency in every part of our profession! Oh! let us look carefully to it, that no want of wisdom, godly contentment, or self denial, brings reproach upon that

[1] Chap. xxi. 9, 19; xxvii. 15.
[2] 1 Kings xvi. 31; xxi. 25.
[3] 2 Kings ix. 30—37.
[4] Matt. xiv. 8.
[5] Gen. xvi. 1—6.
[6] Chap. xxix. 21.

worthy name, by which we are called; that there be no spots, that mar that adorning beauty, which might attract those around us to the ways of God.

24. *There be four things, which are little upon the earth, but they are exceeding wise:* (wise, made wise, Marg.) 25. *The ants are a people not strong; yet they prepare their meat in the summer:* 26. *The conies are but a feeble folk; yet make they their houses in the rocks;* 27. *The locusts have no king; yet go they forth all of them by bands;* 28. *The spider taketh hold with her hands, and is in king's palaces.*

God teaches us by his works as well as by his word,[1]—by his works, small as well as great. He instructed Job by Leviathan and Behemoth.[2] Here he instructs us by *the ants and the conies.* And yet in the minute creation his splendor shines as gloriously as in the more majestic. Agur had before mentioned four things that seemed great, but were really despicable. Here he produces *four things little upon the earth, but exceeding wise.* Therefore despise them not for their *littleness:* but admire the wonder-working hand, which hath furnished these little creatures with such sufficient means of provision, defence, and safety. As has been beautifully remarked—'God reigns in a community of ants and ichneumons as visibly, as among living men or mighty seraphim.'[3] Truly nothing was made for nought. The world of insects shows that, which will put to blush our higher world of reason. Yes—these four remarkable instances of Almighty skill—the natures and habits of these four little animals—teach many useful and important lessons; and "he that hath ears to hear may hear" words of suitable wisdom, rebuke, direction, and encouragement for himself.

'Industry is commended to us by all sorts of examples, deserving our regard and imitation. All nature is a copy thereof, and the whole world a glass, wherein we may behold this duty represented to us. Every creature about us is incessantly working toward the ends for which it was designed; indefatigably exercising the powers with which it is endued; diligently observing the laws of its creation.'[4] *The ants* have already been our teachers[5]—*a people not strong;*[6] indeed so weak, that thousands are crushed by one tread of the foot; yet *wise in preparing their meat in the summer.* A quickening sermon do these little insects preach to us! They make *preparation* for the coming winter. What must be the thoughtlessness of making no provision for the coming eternity! whiling away life in inactivity, as if there was no work for God—for the soul—for eternity! Shall not we learn to be wise betimes; to improve the present moment of salvation; not to wait for the winter—the verge of life, when that grace—offered now—shall be

[1] The stupid beasts reprove our ingratitude (Isa. i. 3). The fowls of the air, our inattention (Jer. viii. 7); our unbelieving carefulness (Matt. vi. 26): and anxious fears (Ib. x. 29—31).

[2] Job xl. xli.

[3] McCheyne's Life, p. 34.

[4] Barrow's Sermons on Industry

[5] Chap. vi. 6—8.

[6] The term—nation or *people* is applied to the animal creation, Joel i. 6; xi. 2. This is a frequent classical allusion. Homer spoke of a nation of frogs (Odyss. Σ. l. 73); Virgil, of fishes, Geor. iv. 430.

offered no more? Sinner! if all be lost by thy indolence, wilt not thou be the great loser? What else hast thou to do, but to prepare for eternity? What hope canst thou have of heaven at the last, if thou hast never seriously thought of heaven before? Oh!—ere it be too late—throw thyself at his feet, whose heart overflows with love. If thou art ready, "all things are ready." Exclusion is with thyself, not with thy Saviour.[1]

The ants are a people not strong. Yet what people—beside their wisdom—more diligent—more persevering—more effective? Indeed 'the union of so many noble qualities in so small a corpuscle is one of the most remarkable phenomena in the works of nature.'[2] Weakness, then, is no excuse for indolence—no occasion of despondency. Is it not rather the cheering exercise of faith?[3] "The worm shall thresh the mountains."[4] To the diligent "laborer shall be given the meat, that endureth to everlasting life."[5] In helpless dependence "working out his salvation," his "labor shall not be in vain in the Lord."[6]

As the ants prepare their meat, so *the conies* their refuge. *Feeble folk as they are*, they secure themselves from impending danger, by *making their houses in the* holes of inaccessible *rocks.*[7] Thus what they want in strength they make up in wisdom. Not less *feeble* are we—not less exposed to assault. And is not our refuge—like theirs—"the munition of *rocks*?"[8] Are we then—like them—*making our house*—our home—there? abiding in our shelter in conscious security?

Observe again the instinct of *the locusts.* Some insects—like the bee—are under monarchical government. But *the locusts have no king.* Yet how wonderful is their order—*going forth all of them by bands*—like an army with unbroken ranks, and under the strictest discipline![9] Jerome mentions what he had

1 Luke xiv. 16—24. John vi. 37.

2 Paxton's Natural History of the Scripture, p. 97.

3 2 Cor. xii. 9, 10. 4 Isa. xli. 14—16. 5 John vi. 27.

6 Phil. 4, 12, 13. 1 Cor. xv. 58. Chrysostom ingeniously remarks upon the wonders of Divine wisdom, in inspiring so minute a body with such a perpetual desire for labor; teaching us so strongly the lesson—not to affect softness and delicacy, or to fly from toil and labor.' He adds—that the wise man, sending us to learn of these little creatures—is just as we should in our families put to shame the disobedience of the elder children, by pointing to the little ones—'Behold one much younger and smaller than yourself; yet how pliable and ready he is to do as he is bid!' Hom. xii. ad Pop. Antioch.

7 Ps. civ. 17. There is much difficulty in determining this animal, which was reckoned among the unclean (Lev. xi. 15. Deut. xiv. 7). Dr. Shaw (with whom Parkhurst agrees) considers it to be 'the Daman of Mount Libanus—though common in other parts of Syria and Palestine—of the rabbit size and form. As its usual residence and refuge is in the holes and clefts of the rocks, we have so far a presumptive evidence, that this creature may be the coney of the Scriptures.' Travels, vol. ii. 160, 161. Mr. Bruce strongly confirms this account from his own observation—adding, 'He is above all other animals so much attached to the rock, that I never once saw him on the ground, and from among large stones in the mouth of caves, where is his constant residence. He is in Judæa, Palestine, and Arabia, and consequently must have been known to Solomon.' See his Travels, v. pp. 139—147.

'Gaudet in effossis habitare cuniculus antris.'

Mart. Epig. Lib. xiii Ep. 58.

8 Isa. xxxiii. 16. Comp. Ps. xci. 1, 2. 9 See the picture. Joel ii. 7, 8, 25.

lately seen—'When the swarms of locusts came, and filled the lower region of the air, they flew in such order, by the Divine appointment, and kept their places as exactly, as when several tiles or party-colored stones are skilfully placed in a pavement, so as not to be an hair's breadth out of their several ranks.'[1] Do not these little insects read to us a lesson on the importance of unity and unanimous movement? Here is not an ungoverned disorderly multitude flying in different directions. But all *go forth by bands* All keep their ranks. Many professors—instead of *going by bands*—prefer an individual course. They belong to no cohort. They are under no discipline. This unsettled principle can never issue in a Christian steadfastness. Unity—not diversity—brings "the good thing of the heart established with God."[2] The strength of the Church is—not as an army of irregular soldiers, regiments in loose disorder, unconnected with each other; but when she *goeth forth by bands*—united; concentrated; well disciplined; every officer at his post; every soldier in his ranks; each under rule—helpful to each other and to their great cause![3] "When shall it once be?" Lord, heal our unhappy divisions. Unite our energies 'in one holy bond of Truth and Peace, of Faith and Charity.'[4]

And what lessons does the *spider* teach of ingenuity, patience, and untiring labor and perseverance! 'Its claws or spinning-organs serve both as hands and eyes to the animal.'[5] She forms her web against *the walls*, as if she took hold of *them with her hands*. She frames her fine-spun house with such exactness of proportion, as if conversant with mathematical rule.[6] She steals her way alike into the cottage of the poor, and the *king's palaces;* as if God would instruct even the great ones of the earth by this pattern of diligence. Such assiduity—such "diligence" in the work of our high calling—if it shall not bring us into the *king's palaces*,[7] will ensure the full reward of the man, whom the Great "King delighteth to honor."[8]

How many of us stand condemned by the sermons of these little insects! Are we too proud to learn, or too careless to attend to,

[1] Quoted by Lowth on Joel, ut supra. The mystical locusts have a king. Comp. Rev. ix. 3—11.

[2] See Heb. xiii. 9.

[3] Comp. Numb. ii.

[4] Prayer for Unity in the Service of Accession—a most suitable and spiritual pleading with the God of Peace.

[5] Kirby's Bridgewater Treatise, vol. ii. 186.

[6] 'Who made the spider parallels design,
Sure as Demoivre, without rule or line.'—Pope.

[7] See chap. xxii. 29.

[8] Interpreter expounded this figure to Christiana—'that as the venomous spider hung by her hands by the wall; so—how full of the venom of sin soever we be, yet we may *by the hand* of faith *lay hold* of, and dwell in, the best room that belongs to *the King's house* above.' Pil. Prog. Part ii. Perhaps the lesson is not less true than important, yet our inimitable allegorist we judge to have in this picture pressed his imagination beyond due bounds. Accommodation may admit of far greater latitude than exposition; though even here—as the Writer would remember for himself—a sober discipline must be exercised.

the humbling but most valuable lessons taught in the school of instruction? "A wise man will hear, and will increase learning."[1]

29. *There be three things which go well, yea, four are comely in going;* 30. *A lion, which is strongest among beasts, and turneth not away for any;* 31. *A greyhound:* (a horse—girt in the loins, Marg.) *an he-goat also; and a king, against whom there is no rising up.*

Agur naturally lingers upon this vast field of natural wonders, such a splendid exhibition of the Divine perfections! the source of so much light to the world, before the Book of Revelation was fully opened.[2] After having mentioned some striking instances of wisdom, he now singles out a few objects, which appeared to him remarkable for their *comeliness in going*—the firm and stately walk of *the lion*[3]—fearless and proud—*not turning away for any;* the graceful form and the elegant and swift movements of *the grey-hound;*[4] *the he-goat* at the head of the flock, their guide and protector; and the majesty of *the king*, inspiring all who approach him with reverence for his authority, and not suffering *any rising up against* the exercise of his power.[5] From all these many practical lessons may be learned by the man, "who will be wise and observe these things."

Let us have regard--not only to the various duties of the Christian life, but also to the manner and spirit of their performance. Cultivate not only the integrity, but the *comeliness* of the Christian character—"the beauty" and uniformity of "holiness;" that there be nothing mishapen or distorted; that there be just proportion in all the parts and features. Christians should be attractive and engaging by the courtesy of their general demeanor. It is not enough to observe "whatsoever things are true, whatsoever things are honest, whatsoever things are just, whatsoever things are pure."—But "whatsoever things are *lovely —whatsoever things are of good report*—think on these things."[6] Any manifest want of *comeliness in our going* repels the world from the gospel of Christ. 'If we desire to reign in heaven, we must present ourselves there with this beautiful crown, from whence radiate all kinds of virtue and praise.'[7]

Nor let us forget to imitate the features of this *comeliness* here portrayed; to be fearless as *the lion*, when pursuing the path of duty, *not turning away for any;*[8] to desire the eager spring of *the greyhound* in our heavenly course; to be useful as *the he-goat,*

[1] Chap. i. 5. [2] Job xii. 7—10. [3] See Homer's fine description, Il. M. 299.

[4] This name is—as Mr. Holden remarks—'of doubtful import.' The Hebrew is 'girt in the loins'—a general phrase—admitting of a great variety of conjecture, so that Poole (Synopsis) considers him to be wisest, 'who confesses he knows not what it is.' Our translation is however as well supported as any other. Some conceive it to be a leopard. And perhaps this conjecture, combined with the *lion and the he-goat*, has given rise to the absurd ideality of some Rabbinical and Romanist expositors (not wholly discountenanced by more respectable names), who consider these four creatures to be prophetical of the four great monarchies. Dan. viii. The reader may readily conceive the extent of fancy requisite to maintain this interpretation.

[5] Ecc. viii. 2—4. [6] Phil. iv. 8. [7] Daillè on Phil. iv. 8.

[8] See Neh. vi. 3, 11.

as the leader of a godly band; and to maintain our proper authority in any place of trust—as parents or guardians of families, and not to allow any *rising up against it.*

32. *If thou hast done foolishly in lifting up thyself, or if thou hast thought evil, lay thine hand upon thy mouth.* 33. *Surely the churning of milk bringeth forth butter, and the wringing of the nose bringeth forth blood; so the forcing of wrath bringeth forth strife.*[1]

This evidently applies to the preceding illustration—*a king against whom there is no rising.* But *if thou hast lifted up thyself* in despising his authority;[2] or even *if thou hast but thought evil—lay thine hand upon thy mouth,* restraining the ebullition in silent and humble submission.[3] As a general rule, however, we may be thankful for the caution. If we have *done foolishly* by provoking irritation, *in lifting up ourselves,* at least in some *evil thought,* against a brother; quench the rising spark, ere it kindle into a flame. "*The thought of foolishness* is sin."[4] Yet it is more sinful, when it forces its passage to the mouth. Words increase the sin, show more of its power, and are more hurtful to others. Obviously it is wise to *lay our hand upon our mouth,* and to restrain the expression, when we cannot prevent the thought. Better to keep in the infirmity, than to give it vent. But when, instead of *the hand laid upon the mouth,* there is no discipline, guard, or restraint, "the mouth of the fool poureth out *foolishness;*"[5] overflowing at the lips, and bringing a flood of trouble upon the soul.[6] How much more, when the proud worm *lifts up itself against* the Great King! *The foolishness* even of an *evil thought* against him is such, as no tongue can express. The Lord humble us with a tender sensibility of this sin! "Behold! I am vile: what shall I answer thee? I *will lay mine hand upon my mouth.*"[7]

Towards man however it is often *the forcing of wrath*—not natural irritation. A peaceable man may be goaded to anger;[8] as the violent shaking of the milk in the *churn bringeth forth butter; or the wringing of the nose bringeth forth blood.* The action of force works what would not otherwise have been done. But fearful is *the strife of this forced wrath.* Sihon thus provoked his own ruin[9]—the Ephraimites stirred up a murderous strife[10]—Asahel sharpened Abner's spear by his wilful waywardness[11]—Amaziah plunged into destruction by *the strife of the forced wrath* of Joash, who was disposed to peace and quietness.[12] How multiplied are the sources of misery—the fruit of ungovernable temper and self-will! "Only by pride cometh contention;"[13] and where that contention may end, who can say? 'I am, and profess to be'—said the godly

[1] 'Whoso chyrneth mylck maketh butter; he that rubbeth his nose maketh it blede' and he that causeth wrath bryngeth forth strife.'—Bp. Coverdale.
[2] Rom. xiii. 1, 2. [3] Comp. Chap. xvii. 28. Job xxi. 5. [4] Chap. xxiv. 9.
[5] Chap. xv. 2. [6] Chap. xv. 18; xvi. 28, 29; xvii. 14; xviii. 7.
[7] Job xl. 4, 5. [8] Chap. xv. 1; xxvi. 21; xxix. 22.
[9] Num. xxi. 23, 24. [10] Jud. xii. 1—6. [11] 2 Sam. iii.
[12] 2 Chron. xxv. 17—23. [13] Chap. xiii. 10.

Bishop Hall—'as the terms stand, on neither, and yet on both parts; for the peace of both; for the humor of neither.'

An humble heart would repress the sparks of this unholy fire. A sorrowful spirit for the sins of our thoughts, would be a component part of the cure.[1] We should not readily indulge the sin, for which we had been truly humbled before our God. Whereas in the want of this genuine spirit, how reluctant we are to acknowledge our offence towards each other! We can always find some good reason for *lifting up ourselves, or for thinking evil.* And how hard it goes with our proud tempers to be the first to *lay our hands upon our mouths!* How much more ready are we to open our mouths in self-justification, than in self abasement! Thus instead of quenching, *we force, wrath.* Instead of the "meekness of wisdom," there "is envy and strife, confusion, and every evil work;"[2] enmity between nominal professors of the gospel, and distance even between those, who believe themselves to be members of the same body, heirs of the same inheritance,[3] and bound by the same obligation to love one another.[4] Oh! hasten the blessed time, when the Church shall be fully transformed into the image of the Divine Lord!—when it shall be a Church of perfect love in a world of love!

CHAPTER XXXI.

1. *The words of King Lemuel, the prophecy that his mother taught him.*
2. *What, my son? and what, the son of my womb? and what, the son of my vows?*

Of King Lemuel we know no more than of the prophet Agur in the last chapter.[5] All that we know is, that he was endowed like many of God's people,[6] with the invaluable blessing of a godly mother; who, like Deborah of old,[7] was honored of God, to be the author of a chapter of the Sacred Volume.

What an animating burst from the yearning of a mother's heart! *What! my son—the son of my womb—of my vows!* Happy

[1] Eccl. vii. 4. [2] Jam. iii. 13, 16. [3] Eph. iv. 4—6. [4] John xiii. 34, 35.

[5] Both have been identified with Solomon's though without any historical evidence. It seems unlikely, that Solomon, having given his own name more than once in this book (chap. i. 1; x. 1), should give two mystical names at the close without any distinct personal application. Nor is there any Scriptural testimony in favor of Bathsheba, that would lead us to stamp her with this peculiar honor as one of the writers of God's word. 'The admonitory verses composed for King Lemuel by his mother, when in the flower of youth and high expectation, are an inimitable production, as well in respect to their actual materials, as the delicacy, with which they are selected. Instead of attempting to lay down rules concerning matters of state and political government, the illustrious writer confines herself, with the nicest and most becoming art, to a recommendation of the gentler virtues of temperance, benevolence, and mercy, and a minute and unparalleled delineation of the female character, which might bid fairest to promote the happiness of her son in connubial life.'—Dr. Good.

[6] Ps. cxvi. 16. 2 Tim. i. 6; iii. 15. [7] Judges v.

mother—when *the son of her womb is the son of her vows!*—like Samuel—a dedicated child—a child of many prayers—"asked of the Lord—lent into his service."[1] If there were more Hannahs, would there not be more Samuels? If thou wouldst have, Christian Mother, thy child a Samuel or an Augustine, be thyself a Hannah or a Monica! The child of thy prayers—*of thy vows*—of thy tears—will be in the Lord's best time the child of thy praises, thy rejoicings, thy richest consolation. Yet thy faith will not end with the dedication of thy child. *Lemuel—the son of her vows—his mother taught him.* And such is the practical habit of godliness! Faith in vowing quickens diligence in teaching. The child *truly* consecrated will be "brought up in the nurture and admonition of the Lord."[2]

3. *Give not thy strength unto women, nor thy ways to that which destroyeth kings.* 4. *It is not for kings, O Lemuel, it is not for kings to drink wine: nor for princes strong drink:* 5. *Lest they drink and forget the law, and pervert* (alter, Marg.) *the judgment of any of the afflicted,* (all the sons of affliction, Marg.) 6. *Give strong drink unto him that is ready to perish, and wine unto those that be of heavy hearts.* (bitter of soul, Marg.) 7. *Let him drink, and forget his poverty, and remember his misery no more.*

Solomon has given us his Father's wise counsels.[3] Lemuel gives us his mother's. Both have an equal claim to reverence.[4] Filled with deep anxiety, the impassioned tenderness bursts out in this godly mother; as if some besetting enticements were imminent--perhaps working poison in her beloved son. *What! my son—the son of my womb—of my vows!* My heart is full. I must give it vent. Have I endured all this travail in vain? Beware—*Give not thy strength unto women.* What a beacon had Solomon set up![5] What a beacon had he himself become![6] These forbidden gratifications were *ways that destroyed kings.* Such was the judgment upon David. His kingly authority was shaken.[7] Solomon's sin *destroyed* his kingdom.[8] The fruit of this sin is shame. The end of it—without repentance—is death.

The anxious mother next warns against another cognate sin[9]—of intemperance. The vice that degrades a man into a beast, is shameful to all—specially unseemly *for kings.*—They are "the city set upon a hill." Men look, or ought to look, to them for guidance and example. What a sight for *kings to drink wine and strong drink*—to be given to it! Witness Elah[10]—Benhadad[11]—Belshazzar[12]—"the princes of Israel made sick with bottles of wine!"[13] How was their high office and glory covered with shame! Sometimes it is pleaded as an excuse for sin. But if the drunken king *forgets the law, and perverts the judgment;*[14] will he not be held

[1] 1 Sam. i. 11, 28. [2] Eph. vi. 4.
[3] Chap. iv. 4. [4] Chap. i. 8. [5] Chap. ii. v. vii.
[6] Neh. xiii. 26. [7] 2 Sam. xii. 9, 10.
[8] 1 Kings xii. 11. Comp. chap. v. 9. Job xxxi. 9—12. [9] Hos. iv. 11.
[10] 1 Kings xvi. 8, 9. [11] Ib. xx. 16. [12] Dan. v. 2—4.
[13] Hos. vii. 5. Comp. Ecc. x. 16, 17.
[14] A woman wrongly condemned by Philip of Macedon, when drunk, boldly exclaimed

responsible? Ahasuerus was doubtless responsible for his unseemly conduct to Vashti.[1] Herod murdered the Baptist at an ungodly feast.[2] Priest and prophet "err through *strong drink*."[3] A wise veto therefore is set for the rulers of the Church—"Not given to wine."[4]

And yet the abuse of God's blessings does not destroy their use. "Wine is the gift of God. It maketh glad the heart of man."[5] Yea—by a bold figure of its refreshment—it is said to "cheer God"[6] also. Yet it is *not for kings*—for their indulgences and sinful excitement—but for those that need it. As restoratives and refreshments—cordials are seasonable in the hour of need. *Give strong drink to him that is ready to perish;* as the Samaritan gave it to the wounded traveller;[7] as Paul prescribed it for "the infirmities" of his beloved son in the faith.[8] Many a sinking spirit may be revived, and *forget his misery* under a well-timed restorative. The rule therefore of love and self-denial is—Instead of wasting that upon thyself, in the indulgence of appetite, which will only debase thy nature; see that thou dispense thy luxuries among those, who *really* require them. Seek out cases of penury and wasting misery. Let it be an honor to thee to bring in the poor that is cast out into thine house, *that he may forget his poverty and remember his misery no more.*[9] May not this remind us of the Messenger of love, dealing with those *that are ready to perish*?[10] Their conscience is loaded with guilt. Their *hearts are heavy* with a burden, which they can neither bear nor be rid of. He tells them of God's love to sinners; the ransom found for them; the welcome assured to them. This is a cordial of *strong drink*, and wine such as they need. The *heavy heart* becomes "no more sad."[11] The former *poverty is forgotten*, and his *misery is remembered no more.* Happy minister, gifted, like his Divine Master, with "the tongue of the learned, that he should know how to speak a word in season to him that is weary!"[12]

8. *Open thy mouth for the dumb in the cause of all such as are appointed to destruction.* 9. *Open thy mouth, judge righteously, and plead the cause of the poor and needy.*

Very soundly does the wise mother inculcate mercy upon her royal son. This is one of the pillars of the King's throne.[13] He must be the Father of his people—employing all his authority to

—'I appeal to Philip; but it shall be when he is sober.' Roused by the appeal, the monarch examined the cause, and gave a righteous judgment.

1 Esth. i. 10, 11. 2 Mark vi. 21—28. 3 Isa. xxviii. 7; lvi. 11, 12.
4 1 Tim. iii. 3. Tit. i. 7. 5 Ps. civ. 14, 15. 6 Judges ix. 13.
7 Luke x. 34. 8 1 Tim. v. 23.
9 This was the Classical idea of the power of wine.—'Huic calix mulsi impingendus, *ut plorare desinat.*' Cicero. Tuscal. 3. '*Nunc vino pellite curas.*' Hor. Od. l. i. 7. '*Vinum obliviosum*' (blotting out the remembrance of evil). Ibid. Od. l. ii. 7. 'Tunc dolor et curæ rugaque frontis abit.' Ovid de Arte Amandi. l. i. The mixed wine which Helena gave to Telemachus, called Nepentha, had such an effect, as to remove sorrow, and to bury in forgetfulness past evils. Odyss. iv. 220, 1. Comp. Mark xv. 23.
10 Isa. lxi. 1, 2. Matt. xi 28. 11 Com. 1 Sam. i. 18. 12 Isa. l. 4.
13 Chap. xx. 28.

protect those who cannot protect themselves.[1] No case of distress, when coming to his knowledge, should be below his attention. Thus our law makes the judge the counsel for the prisoner, who is unable to plead for himself—*opening his mouth for the dumb.* Thus should magistrates most carefully consider, that no one should lose his just right from want of ability to defend it.[2] Those who are, or appear to be, *appointed to destruction*, should have their fair and open course to plead and save their lives.[3]

This it was, that made the difference between the prosperity of godly Josiah, and the ruin of his wicked son.[4] How repeatedly did Jonathan *open his mouth* for his friend *appointed for destruction!*[5] How effectively did Esther plead the cause of her helpless and devoted people![6] To descend into lower ranks (for why should we restrict these wise injunctions within the narrow limits of royalty?) what a complete pattern of this mercy does Job exhibit? "Eyes as he was to the blind, and feet to the lame," doubtless he perfected his character as "a father to the poor" by being *a mouth to the dumb.*[7] How was Ebed-melech honored for this merciful advocacy of the condemned![8] How awful is the threatened vengeance for the neglect of his mercies![9] Alas! Jesus, though he had found an advocate in earlier times,[10] yet stood as a sheep before his shearers—*dumb, appointed for destruction.* None was found to *open his mouth* for the Divine afflicted victim.[11] And yet how does he reverse this picture of pitiless neglect, in his powerful effectual pleading *in the cause of those*, whom the voice of justice so loudly —so justly—*appoints for destruction!* Let his representatives on earth study the character of their King in heaven, and be conformed more fully to his image of forgiveness and love.

10. *Who can find a virtuous woman? for her price is above rubies.*

We now come to the principal part of the chapter. The wise mother of Lemuel had warned her royal son against the seduction of evil women, and its attendant temptations, and given him wholesome rules for government. She now sets before him the full length portrait of *a virtuous woman*—that choicest gift, which is emphatically said to be "from the Lord."[12] It is an elegant Poem of twenty-two verses—like the hundred and nineteenth Psalm, artificially constructed; each verse beginning with one of the successive letters of the Hebrew Alphabet.[13] It describes a wife, a mistress, and a mother. 'All mothers and mistresses should teach the female pupils under their care to read and learn it by heart.'[14]

So rare is this treasure, that the challenge is given—"*Who can find a virtuous woman?*"[15] Abraham sent to a distant land for

[1] Ps. lxxii. 12—14.
[2] Deut. xvi. 18—20. Ps. lxxxii. 3, 4.
[3] Contrast 1 Kings xxi. 9—13, with John vii. 51.
[4] Jer. xxii. 15—19.
[5] 1 Sam. xix. 4—7; xx. 32; xxii. 14, 15.
[6] Esth. iii. 9—11; vii.
[7] Job. xxix. 15, 16.
[8] Jer. xxxviii. 8, 9; xxxix. 15—18.
[9] Chap. xxiv. 11, 12. Jer. v. 28. 29.
[10] John vii. 50, 51.
[11] Isa. liii. 7. Matt. xxvi. 59—63.
[12] Chap. xix. 14.
[13] Comp. Ps. cxlv. The Lamentations of Jeremiah.
[14] Bp. Horne's Sermon on the Female Character.
[15] Comp. chap. xx. 6.

this inestimable blessing for his beloved son.[1] Perhaps one reason of the rarity of the gift is—that it is so seldom sought. Too often is the search made for accomplishments—not for *virtues*; for external and adventitious recommendations, rather than for internal godly worth.

The enquiry also implies the value of the gift when found. Even Adam's portion in innocence was not complete, till his bountiful father "made him an helpmate for him."[2] Truly *her price is above rubies.* No treasure is comparable to her.[3] It is not too much to say with the prince of Heathen philosophy—'If women be good, the half of the commonwealth may be happy where they are.'[4]

11. *The heart of her husband doth safely trust in her, so that he shall have no need of spoil.* 12. *She will do him good and not evil all the days of her life.*

The price of the virtuous woman has been told. Her different features will now be given. The first lines of the portrait describe her character as *a wife.* Her fidelity—oneness of heart—affectionate dutifulness—make the *heart of her husband safely to trust in her.*[5] A faithful wife, and a confiding husband mutually bless each other. With such a jewel for his wife, the husband has no misgivings—he feels that his interests are safe in her keeping. There is no need to look into the matters entrusted to her with suspicious eye. He has no reserve—no jealousies. Ruling in his sphere without, he encourages her to rule in her sphere within. All is conducted with such prudence and œconomy, that *he has no need of spoil*—no temptation to unjust gain—*no need* to leave his happy home, in order to enrich himself with the soldier's *spoils.* The attachment of such a wife is as lasting as the time of their union—constant—consistent. Instead of abusing confidence, she only seeks to make herself daily more worthy of it—not fretful—and precarious; caring "how she may please her husband"[6]—*doing him good and not evil, all the days of her life.* Would that it were always so! But look at Eve—the help-meet[7] becoming a tempter: Solomon's wives drawing away his heart[8]—Jezebel stirring up her husband to abominable wickedness[9]—Job's wife calling upon her husband to "curse God and die"[10]—the painful cross of "the brawling woman upon the house-top"[11]—this is a fearful con-

[1] Gen. xxiv. 3, 4. [2] Gen. ii. 18. [3] Comp. Ecclus. vii. 19; xxv. 13—18.
[4] Arist. Rhet. i. 5. Comp. Polit. ii. 9.
[5] Such was Luther's description of his wife—'The greatest gift of God is a pious amiable spouse, who fears God, loves his house, and with *whom one can live in perfect confidence.*' D'Aubigne's Hist. of Reformation, Book x. chap. xiii. Contrast with this picture, Chap. vii. 18—20. Gen. xxxix. 16—19. Ambrose expounds the woman to mean the Church, and explains *the confidence of her husband* as the ground of her perseverance —adding—' that it is not *the heart* of her Lord, who may be deceived, but *of her husband,* which cannot be mistaken. In loc. Would such a conceit with any other name escape severe castigation? Augustine's Exposition is much in the same character—fancy, not judgment.—De Temper. Serm. p. 217. Many Romish commentators apply this description to the Virgin.
[6] 1 Cor. vii. 34. [7] Gen. ii. 18, with iii. 6. [8] 1 Kings xi. 1—5.
[9] Ib. xxi. 25. [10] Job ii. 9. [11] Chap. xxi. 9, 19; xxv. 24.

trast—*evil—not good.* Often again is it a mixture of *evil with the good.* Rebekah caring for her husband in the art of opposition to God; yet wickedly deceiving him[1]—Rachel loving Jacob; yet bringing idolatry into his family[2]—Michal *doing good* to David at first in preserving his life—*evil* afterwards in despising him as a servant of God.[3] Often we hear of prudent management, but not in the fear of God—connected with a teazing temper. But in this picture it is *good, and not evil.* Her husband's character is her interest—her rest. To live for him is her highest happiness. Such a course of conduct upon Christian principles—how does it commend the holy and honorable estate of matrimony! How does it illustrate "the great mystery—Christ and his Church"[4]—the identity of interest between them—her trials his[5]—his cause hers![6]

13. *She seeketh wool, and flax, and worketh willingly with her hands.* 14. *She is like the merchants' ships: she bringeth her food from afar.* 15. *She riseth also while it is yet night, and giveth meat to her household, and a portion to her maidens.* 16. *She considereth a field, and buyeth it; with the fruit of her hands she planteth a vineyard.* 17. *She girdeth her loins with strength, and strengtheneth her arms.* 18. *She perceiveth* (tasteth, Marg.) *that her merchandize is good: her candle goeth not out by night.* 19. *She layeth her hands to the spindle, and her hands hold the distaff.* 20. *She stretcheth out* (spreadeth, Marg.) *her hand to the poor; yea, she reacheth forth her hands to the needy.* 21. *She is not afraid of the snow for her household: for all her household are clothed with scarlet* (double garments, Marg.) 22. *She maketh herself coverings of tapestry; her clothing is silk and purple.* 23. *Her husband is known in the gates, when he sitteth among the elders of the land.* 24. *She maketh fine linen, and selleth it; and delivereth girdles unto the merchant.* 25. *Strength and honor are her clothing; and she shall rejoice in time to come.* 26. *She openeth her mouth with wisdom; and in her tongue is the law of kindness.* 27. *She looketh well to the ways of her household, and eateth not the bread of idleness.*

This lovely character is drawn according to the usage of ancient times; though the general principles are of universal application. It describes not only the wife of a man of rank, but a wise, useful, and goodly matron in her domestic responsibilities. It is "a woman professing godliness," adorned "with good works"[7]—a Mary no less than a Martha. 'It may be necessary to retouch the lines of the picture, that have been obscured by length of years; in plain terms—to explain some parts of the description, which relate to ancient manners and customs, and to show how they may be usefully applied to those of our own age and country.'[8]

One thing however is most remarkable. The standard of godliness here exhibited is not that of a religious recluse, shut up from active obligations under the pretence of greater sanctity and consecration to God. Here are none of those habits of monastic ascetism, that are now extolled as the highest point of Christian perfection. One half at least of the picture of *the virtuous woman* is occupied with her personal and domestic industry. What a rebuke also does this convey to a self-indulgent inactivity! Her several em

[1] Gen. xxvii. [2] Ib. xxxi. 19; xxxv. 1—4.
[3] 1 Sam. xix. 12. 2 Sam. vi. 20—22. [4] Eph. v. 32. [5] Acts ix. 4.
[6] Ps. cxxxix. 22. [7] 1 Tim. ii. 10. [8] Bp. Horne ut supra.

ployments admirably illustrate genuine simplicity of manners, and practical—yet liberal œconomy. *Her personal habits are full of energy.* Manual labor—even menial service—in olden times was the employment of females in the highest ranks.[1] *The virtuous woman* went before her servants in diligence no less than in dignity. She *sought out* her materials for work. She set the pattern of *working willingly with her hands.* Instead of loitering herself, while they were laboring; she counted it no shame to be employed at the *spindle and distaff.*[2] She was early and late at her work, *rising in the night.*[3] The fruit of her work she turned to good account. She exchanged it in commerce for *food brought from far. Her merchandize* was good in quality—*tapestry—fine linen —and girdles delivered to the merchant.*[4] Her whole soul was in her work—*girding her loins with strength, and strengthening her arms;* ready for any work befitting her sex and station. The land had also her due share of attention. Ever careful for her husband's interests, she *considered* the value of *a field;* and, if it were a good purchase, she *bought* it, *and planted the vineyard* for the best produce.

Observe also her conduct as a mistress. And here also her praise is not, that she spends her time in devotional exercises (though these as "a woman that feareth the Lord"[5] she duly prizes); but that according to the Scriptural canon, "she guides her house,"[6] watching carefully over her charge, distributing both her meat and her work in due proportion, and "in due season." This is her responsibility. If "man goeth forth to his work, and to his labor till the evening,[7] the woman finds her work as "a keeper at home."[8] And beautiful indeed is it to see, how her industry, self-denial, and heartiness "buildeth her house."[9] It is not for the sake of being admired and talked of, that she *rises, while it is yet night;* it is to *give meat to her household.* The delicacy also, with which she preserves her own sphere, is remarkable. For

[1] Sarah, Gen. xviii. 6—8; Rebekah, xxiv. 18—20, with 12—14; Rachel, xxix. 9, 10; the daughters of the prince of Midian, Exod. ii. 16; the daughter of a king, 2 Sam. xiii. 5—9.

[2] Compare Paxton's Illustrations, ii. 418—420. Hom. Il. I. 125. Z. 490, 491. X. 440. Odyss. A. 357. E. 62. Ovid advises maidens, if they would have the favor of Minerva, to learn to use the distaff, to card, and spin (Fasti. Lib. iii.) Comp. Metamorph. L. iv. f. l. v. 34. Virg. Georg. iv. 348. Classic readers mention Lucretia found spinning with her maids, when her husband paid her a visit from the camp. The wool spun by Tarquin's wife long remained with a distaff and spindle in the temple. Alexander the Great is said to have shown to the Persian princesses his garments, made by his mother. Augustus—it is said—would wear no clothes, but such as were made by the members of his own family. (Burder's Oriental Customs.) Our English records of female royalty furnish similar proofs of hand-industry. The magnificent far-famed tapestry of Bayeux was the work of William I.'s queen. The messengers of Henry to Katherine of Arragon announcing her divorce, found her with a skein of red silk round her neck, being at work with her maids. Beautiful memorials are still preserved of Queen Katherine Parr's manual skill. See Miss Strickland's Queens of England.

[3] See Parkhurst—Virgil's beautiful picture of the industrious wife. Æn. viii. 407.

[4] See Paxton's Illustr. ii. 420.—Girdles, a rich article of dress both of men (2 Sam. xviii. 11), and women. Isa. iii. 24. *The merchant*—'the Canaanite.' Heb. LXX.

[5] Verse 30. [6] 1 Tim. v. 14. [7] Psalm civ. 23.

[8] Tit. ii. 5. Comp. Gen. xviii. 9. [9] Chap. xiv. 1.

while she provides food for the whole *household*, she *giveth the portion*—that is—of work—not to the man-servants (these with great propriety she leaves to her husband), but *to her maidens.* Their clothing is also provided with every regard to their comfort. While her own *clothing is silk and purple*, suitable to her station, every member of the household is cared for. *She is not afraid of snow for them.* They are *clothed with scarlet*, or rather with *double garments*[2]—well clad for a severe winter. So *well does she look to the ways of her household*—such untiring energy does she show in every department—that none can accuse her of *eating the bread of idleness.* Nothing is neglected, that belongs to order, sobriety, œconomy, or general management.

Need we here advert to the wide exercise of discipline and self-denial involved in this care of our *household?* It implies *looking well* to their moral habits—their religious instruction—attendance on the means of grace—giving them time for secret prayer, and reading the word of God[3]—the daily ordinance of family worship—the careful observance of the Sabbath—anxious watchfulness over their manners, habits, and connexions; in short—considering servants—not as beasts of burden—not as mere mercenaries—but as a solemn and responsible trust for God and for eternity. Who can have the claim to *a virtuous woman* who does not feel this weight of family responsibility?

Nor is her provident care limited to her own dependents. Her *spindle and distaff* are worked—not for herself only, or *for her household*, but for *the poor and needy.* And, having first "drawn out her soul,"[4] *she stretcheth out her hands*,[5] to embrace as it were those at a distance from her with the flow of her love; and thus "the blessing of those that were ready to perish cometh upon her."[6] Her spirit and manner also are of the same character—all in full accordance with her professions. Clever, brisk, and managing minds are often deficient in the softer graces. Their tongues are unrestricted, lawless under provocation. Children, servants, and neighbors, suffer from this revolting hardness, and find "it better to dwell in a corner of the house-top, than with a brawling woman in a wide house."[7] But *the godly matron* has not only the law of love in her heart, but *wisdom in her mouth, and in her tongue the law of kindness.* The same love that binds her heart, governs her tongue, not with the caprice, but with *the law, of kindness*—a law, which she receives from *wisdom*, and which gives the mould to her whole spirit, so that 'she says nothing that is foolish, nothing that is ill-natured.'[8] Richly endued with "the wisdom that is

[1] See Foxe's beautiful picture of Anne Boleyn as the mistress of her household. v. 63.

[2] 'Duplicibus penulis'—such as the wife of Hector made. Il. X. 441. Comp Odyss. Υ. 225, 226, 241. 'All her household folks are double clothed.' Bp. Coverdale

[3] Esther must surely have been in the habit of instructing her maidens; else they could not have been girded for the extraordinary services of the fast. iv. 16.

[4] Isa. lviii. 10.

[5] Comp. Deut. xv. 7, 8.

[6] Job xxix. 13. Comp. Acts ix. 36, 39.

[7] Chap. xxi. 9.

[8] Bp. Horne. Comp. Ecclus. xxxvi. 23. Hooker probably had the portrait before his eyes, when in his exquisite funeral Sermon for his '*virtuous* gentlewoman' he enu

from above," she is "gentle, and easy to be entreated; pitiful, courteous."[1]

Thus indeed "*a virtuous woman* is a crown to her husband."[2] *He is known in the gates, when he sitteth among the elders of the land;* as blessed with no common treasures of happiness; 'as indebted perhaps for his promotion to the wealth acquired by her management at home, and, it may be, for the preservation and establishment of his virtue to the encouragement furnished by her example and conversation.'[3]

For herself—manifest—manifold blessings rest upon her. *Strength is the clothing* of her inner man. Christian courage and resolution lift her up above appalling difficulties. *The clothing of honor* stamps her with the Lord's acceptance, as his faithful servant, the child of his grace, and the heir of his glory. *She rejoices*, not only in her present happiness, but *in time to come.* Having been so wisely provident for the morrow, she is not overburdened with its cares. Having lived in *the fear of God*, and honored her God with the fruits of righteousness; there is sunshine in her hour of trial, "in the valley of the shadow of death," in the unclouded day of eternity. *She shall rejoice in time to come*, when the ministering angels, and with them the blessed recipients of her bounty,[4] shall welcome this daughter of Jerusalem "into the joy of her Lord."

28. *Her children arise up, and call her blessed: her husband also, and he praiseth her.* 29. '*Many daughters have done virtuously, but thou excellest them all.*' 30. *Favor is deceitful, and beauty is vain: but a woman that feareth the Lord, she shall be praised.* 31. *Give her of the fruit of her hands; and let her own works praise her in the gates.*

The virtuous woman is obviously subserving her own interest. For what greater earthly happiness could she know than *her children's* reverence, and her husband's '*blessing?*' We may picture to ourselves her condition—crowned with years; *her children* grown up; perhaps themselves surrounded with families, and endeavoring to train them, as themselves had been trained. Their mother is constantly before their eyes. Her tender guidance, her wise counsels, her loving discipline, her holy example, are vividly kept in remembrance; and they cease not *to call her blessed*, and to bless the Lord for her, as his invaluable gift. No less warmly does *her husband* praise her. His attachment to her was grounded, not on the *deceitful and vain* charms of *beauty*, but on *the fear of the Lord.* She is therefore in his eyes the stay of his declining years, the soother of his cares, the counsellor of his perplexities, the comforter of his sorrows, the sunshine of his earthly joys.[5] Both *children and husband* combine in the grateful acknowledgment—

merates 'among so many virtues hearty devotion towards God; towards poverty tender compassion; motherly affection towards servants; towards friends even serviceable kindness; mild behavior and harmless meaning towards all.' Remedy against Sorrow and Fear.

[1] James iii. 17. 1 Pet. iii. 8. [2] Chap. xii. 4. [3] Bp. Horne.
[4] Luke xvi. 9. [5] Comp. Ecclus. xxxvi. 23, 24.

Many daughters have done virtuously, but thou excellest them all.

But why—it may be asked—do external recommendations form no part of this portrait? All that is described is solid excellence; and *favor is deceitful.* A graceful form and mien often end in disappointment, more bitter than words can tell. Often do they furnish a cover for the vilest corruptions.[1] And then *beauty*—what a fading *vanity* it is![2] One fit of sickness sweeps it away.[3] Sorrow and care wither its charms.[4] And even while it remains, it is little connected with happiness.[5] It proves itself the fruitful occasion of trouble,[6] the source of many hurtful temptations and snares;[7] and, without substantial principle, to a well-judging mind it becomes rather an object of disgust rather than of attraction.[8]

The portrait, pencilled by Divine inspiration, begins with the touch of *a virtuous woman*, and fills up the sketch with the lineaments of *a woman that feareth the Lord.*[9] For the lovely features described—her fidelity to her husband; her active personal habits; her good management and diligence in her family; her consideration for the necessities and comforts of others; her watchfulness of conduct; her tenderness for the poor and afflicted; her kind and courteous behavior to all—this completeness of character and grace could only flow from that *virtue*, which is identified with vital godliness. They are the good fruit, that "prove the tree to be good."[10] They are such fruit, flowing from a right principle, as the natural corrupt stock of man could never produce.

The virtuous woman seeks not the praise of men. Content to be known and loved within her own circle, she never presses herself into notice. But as a public blessing, she cannot be hid.[11] And if she has no herald to sound her praise, all will say—*Give her of the fruit of her hands, and let her own works praise her in the gates.* 'Let every one'—says Bishop Patrick—'extol her virtue. Let her not want the just commendation of her pious labors. But while some are magnified for the nobleness of the stock, from whence they sprung; others for their fortune; others for their beauty; others for other things; let the good deeds, which she herself hath done, be publicly praised in the greatest assemblies; where, if all men should be silent, her own works will declare her excellent worth.'[12] Add to this—as *her works praise her in the gates*, so will they "follow her. The memory of the just is blessed."[13]

If *this picture be viewed as an exhibition of godliness, we observe that religion does not slacken attention to temporal duties.*

[1] 2 Sam. xiv. 25; xv. 6.
[2] Gen. xx. 2, with xxiii. 4. 1 Pet. i. 24. Comp. Virg. Eclog. ii. 17, 18.
[3] Ps. xxxix. 11. [4] Ib. vi. 7. P. T. [5] Gen. xxix. 17; xxx. 1, 2.
[6] Esth. i. 11, 12, 19.
[7] Chap. vi. 25, 26. Gen. xii. 11—19; xx. 1, 2, 11; xxvi. 7; xxxix. 6, 7. 2 Sam. xi. 2; xiii. 1.
[8] Chap. xi. 22. [9] Verses 10, 30. [10] Matt. vii. 17.
[11] Ruth iii. 11. Acts ix. 39. 1 Tim. v. 10, 25. [12] In loco.
[13] Rev. xiv. 3. Chap. x. 7.

It rather renders a woman scrupulously exact in all her household obligations, in every thing within her province; careful not by her negligence to bring reproach upon her holy profession. Why should *she* be careless or slovenly, putting her important duties out of time, out of place? Of her it is specially expected, as the summing up of all her practical exercises, that "she should have diligently followed every good work."[1]

How valuable also is this picture, as a directory for the marriage choice! Let *virtue*—not *beauty*—be the primary object. Set against the *vanity of beauty* the true happiness, connected with *a woman that feareth the Lord.* The external choice was the cause of the destruction of the world.[2] The godly choice is uniformly stamped with the seal of Divine acceptance.

In fine—'if women'—says godly Bishop Pilkington—'would learn what God will plague them for, and how; let them read the third chapter of the prophet Esay. And if they will learn what God willeth them to do, and be occupied withal, though they be of the best sort, let them read the last chapter of the Proverbs. It is enough to note it, and point it out to them that *will* learn.'[3] 'That which is last to be done'—concludes an old Expositor—'is to mark it well, and let every woman strive to make it agree to herself as much as she can. Let every man be ashamed, that any woman shall excel him in virtue and godliness.'[4]

'Thus'—says pious Matthew Henry, in his quaint style—'is shut up this looking-glass for ladies, which they are desired to open and dress themselves by; and if they do so, their adorning will be found to praise, and honor, and glory, at the appearing of Jesus Christ.'[5]

We would conclude with a brief summary of a few prominent points involved in the study of this most instructive Book.

Let us observe the connection between inward principle and outward conduct. Never let it be forgotten, that the exercises, here described or inculcated, suppose an internal source. It is the light within, that shines without. The hidden life is thus manifested. The fountain sendeth forth its wholesome waters. The good tree bringeth forth good fruit. "A good man out of the good treasure of the heart bringeth forth good things."[6] These therefore are the manifestations, not the innate principles. They flow from the cultivation of the source within. Nothing permanent is produced by change of opinion, excitement of feeling, conviction of conscience, but by a new mould of the heart. The "soft answer"[7] is the outward exhibition of the softened and humbled heart. The religion of sincere purposes, however promising, withers away,

[1] 1 Tim. v. 10.
[2] Gen. vi. 2—7.
[3] Works, Parker Society Edit. p. 387.
[4] Jermin in loco.
[5] In loco.
[6] Matt. xii. 33, 34.
[7] Chap. xv. 1.

"having no root in itself."[1] The ways and fashions of the world therefore rule with a far mightier power, than the dictates of God's word, or the voice of conscience. The external apprehensions of the Christian system also are powerless without the internal principle. They exhibit a body of truth indeed, but a body without life, without any spring of influence or consolation. Religion grounded in the heart will regulate the outward conduct, and put every thing in its proper place and proportion.

Let us mark also the flow of true happiness throughout the whole sphere of godliness. Often has the wise man painted this connection in the most glowing interest.[2] Most important is it to leave this impression upon the minds of all—specially of our young—readers—that religion is a joyous thing. With the world it is a matter to be endured, not to be enjoyed. The Pharisaic professor conceives of much to be done, but nothing to be enjoyed. With him it is a serious and most weighty concern. But no gleam of sunshine has he ever found in it. The man of pleasure has no conception of religion, except as the atmosphere of gloom—as absurd as to speak of the darkness of noon-day. But notwithstanding all these misconceptions, no reality is more undoubted than this—Holiness is happiness. It is not indeed the mirth of the fool, or the giddy gaiety of the thoughtless. But it is the only thing, that deserves the name of happiness—the only solid—permanent principle of enjoyment. The unenlightened mind associates it with restraint, never with freedom or confidence. But in fact actions that are valued according to their conformity with the will of God, though they be secular in their character, are a part of his service, and ensure his acceptance. Taking up this right standard, we shall be able to resist our ruling passion. We shall occupy no doubtful position. We shall adopt no questionable course. We shall not lend the influence of our character to the spirit of this world. We shall feel, that we have only one object—only one obligation—to maintain the honor of our God. And yet this yoke of strict discipline is our happiness, not our burden. It is linked with a foretaste of heavenly happiness, of which none of us have an adequate conception. Speculative religion is indeed dry and barren. Practical godliness is rich in its delights.[3] And while the defect of earthly joy is, that it comes to an end; the perfection of this happiness is, that it will endure throughout eternity. Truly we have far more reason for joy than for mourning, and we are hasting onward to the home, where "the days of our mourning will be ended"[4] for ever.

It is of great moment to remark the wise man's estimate of real good. Every particle of the chief good he centres in God. To find him is life.[5] To fear him is wisdom.[6] To trust him is happiness.[7] To love him is substantial treasure.[8] To neglect him

[1] Matt. xiii. 5, 6, 20, 21.
[2] Chap. iii. 13—18; iv. 4—13; viii. 17—21, 32—36.
[3] See Ps. xix. 11; cxix. 14, 127. Isa. xxxii. 17. James i. 25.
[4] Isa. lx. 20.
[5] Chap. viii. 35.
[6] Chap. i. 7.
[7] Chap. xvi. 20.
[8] Chap. viii. 18—21.

is certain ruin.[1] Now man is naturally an idolater. Himself is his centre, his object, his end. Instead of submitting to guidance, he guides himself. He disputes the sovereignty with God. He would amend the laws of the Great Lawgiver. Need we add—"This his way is his folly?"[2] What then is the true good? "Acquaint thyself with God, and be at peace."[3] Not real, but known excellence quickens the desire. Our known God will be our portion.[4] He will claim our entire service.[5] He will show himself to us as our chief good—a privilege worth ten thousand worlds to know—a satisfying portion for eternity.

Let us study Christian completeness and consistency. The elements of this character will be brought out by a diligent and prayerful study of this important Book. Let them be put together in their due connection and proportion; and "the man of God will be perfect, thoroughly furnished unto all good works."[6] We want religion to be to the soul, what the soul is to the body—the animating principle. The soul operates in every member. It sees in the eye, hears in the ear, speaks in the tongue, animates the whole body, with ease and uniformity, without ostentation or effort. Thus should religion direct, and regulate every thought, word, and act. In this day of light and knowledge, ignorance of our duty too often implies neglect of the means of instruction, and therefore is our aggravation, rather than our excuse. The grand object is, that the conscience be intelligently instructed under Divine teaching. Then let the daily course be carefully regulated by it. Never turn aside a single step from its guidance. Never admit the maxims or habits of this world. Guard against every thing, that damps vital spirituality, lowers the high Scriptural standard, or slackens the energy of unremitting Christian watchfulness. Let our path be steadily balanced between compromising concession and needless singularity. Let the Christian only walk with God in the way of the Gospel. He will never be satisfied with appearing to maintain his ground. But he will acknowledge the wisdom of the discipline, which allows him no enjoyment at the present moment, except in grasping at something beyond him.[7] We want not a profession, that will give us a name in the Church, or even a stamp of reproach in the world; but which places the Divine image before our eyes, and animates us to a growing conformity to our standard.[8] The conscience thus enlightened, and the heart readily following its voice—the sins that carry less reproach with the world will be resisted not less, than those which are more revolting. We shall no more indulge an uncharitable spirit than a course of profligacy. An angry tone, lowering look, sharp retort, or disparaging word, will cause grief to the conscience, and will be visited by its rebuke, as severely, as those gross ebullitions, which disgrace our character before men. "Walking thus before God"—not before

[1] Ib. ver. 36.
[2] Ps. xlix. 13.
[3] Job xxii. 21.
[4] Ps. xvi. 5. Lam. iii. 24.
[5] Ps. xlv. 11. Matt. xxii. 37.
[6] 2 Tim. iii. 17.
[7] See Phil iii. 12—14.
[8] Matt. v. 48.

men—is Christian perfection."[1] His eye is our restraint—his judgment our rule—his will our delight.

But "Who is sufficient?" Child of God! let the trembling of insufficiency in thyself be stayed by the recollection of all-sufficiency in thy God.[2] What he demands of thee, that he works in thee. His covenant secures thy holiness, no less than thine acceptance—thine holiness—not as some would have it, as the ground—but as the fruit—of thine acceptance. Let the one then be primarily sought; and the other will assuredly follow.

"I WILL PUT MY LAW IN THEIR INWARD PARTS, AND WRITE IT IN THEIR HEARTS . . . . FOR I WILL FORGIVE THEIR INIQUITY, AND I WILL REMEMBER THEIR SINS NO MORE."[3]

[1] Gen. xvii. 1. [2] Comp. 2 Cor. ii. 16, with iii. 5; also xii. 9.
[3] Jer. xxxi. 33, 34. Comp. Ez. xxxvi. 26, 27.

THE END.

INDEX.